T5-DGQ-034

FOR REFERENCE

Do Not Take From This Room

Waubonsee Community College
Libraries
Aurora · Sugar Grove · Plano

STATE PROFILES

THE POPULATION AND ECONOMY OF EACH U.S. STATE

Fourteenth Edition
2023

Edited by Hannah Anderson Krog

Bernan Press

Lanham • Boulder • New York • London

Published by Bernan Press
An imprint of The Rowman & Littlefield Publishing Group, Inc.
4501 Forbes Boulevard, Suite 200, Lanham, Maryland 20706
www.rowman.com

86-90 Paul Street, London EC2A 4NE

Copyright © 2023 by The Rowman & Littlefield Publishing Group, Inc.

All rights reserved. No part of this book may be reproduced in any form or by any electronic or mechanical means, including information storage and retrieval systems, without written permission from the publisher, except by a reviewer who may quote passages in a review. The Rowman & Littlefield Publishing Group, Inc., does not claim copyright on U.S. government information.

ISBN 978-1-63671-412-7 (cloth) | ISBN 978-1-63671-411-0 (ebook)

CONTENTS

LIST OF TABLES

The following tables are included for each state and the District of Columbia:

PREFACE

Bernan Press is pleased to present the 14th edition of *State Profiles*, a publication that provides a state-by-state view of the United States. Topics covered include population composition by age, sex, race, and ethnicity; marital status; migration, origin, and language; households and housing; income and poverty; health insurance and health indicators; employment; educational indicators; voting; and more.

The publication's primary focus is on the 50 states and the District of Columbia, each of which possesses considerable differences in economic structure and demographics and has experienced various changes over time. Changes at the national level, including the diminished importance of agriculture and manufacturing and the growing influence of global trade, have resulted in today's information-based, service-providing economy. While national trends have laid the broad framework for change, each state has been affected differently. Cyclical fluctuations have also affected states in various ways during the nationwide recessions and the subsequent recovery periods.

Beyond the market forces, local and national government policies and expenditures on items such as education, health care, energy production and conservation, national defense, and homeland security have influenced economic circumstances. This edition includes some data detailing the effects of the global COVID-19 pandemic on U.S. states.

The information provided in *State Profiles* aims to illuminate these trends. As such, the analysis and statistics are of interest not only to researchers and policy analysts but also to businesses seeking a broad basis for investments and expansion or relocation plans. The volume also profiles recent voting patterns, which will be of interest to political scientists.

DATA SELECTION

This edition of *State Profiles* generally continues the broad selection of information from previous editions. All of the data items have been updated through 2020, 2021, and even 2022, as demographic estimates from the U.S. Census Bureau became available.

In prior editions of *State* Profiles, Table 14 looked at state-wide violent and property crime statistics from the FBI. The FBI has changed the way it collects and publishes crime data, and the annual *Crime in the United States* report we used for Table 14 has been discontinued. In this edition of *State Profiles,* we have replaced the crime statistics with CDC estimates for births, deaths, and illnesses at the state level.

Due to the impact of the COVID-19 pandemic on data collection for the American Community Survey (ACS), the U.S. Census Bureau did not release ACS 1-year estimates for the year 2020. Therefore, we have occasionally used ACS 5-year 2020 estimates for some of the tables in this edition, as noted in the footnotes of those tables affected.

As in the past, space constraints have influenced the amount of data presented for each state. The most meaningful and relevant data have thus been selected, analyzed, and highlighted. For most of the subjects addressed in this edition, further data are generally available from the source government agencies. Locations of sources of information are listed in notes and definitions at the end of the volume.

Although the editor has taken care to present accurate data, all statistical data are subject to a degree of error, resulting from sampling variability, erroneous reporting, and other causes. Many of the data are subject to subsequent revision by the source agencies.

The data in this book meet the publication standards of the federal agencies from which they were obtained. The responsibilities of the editor and publisher of this volume are limited to reasonable care in the reproduction and presentation of the data from the established sources.

Hannah Anderson Krog has edited the past eight editions of *State Profiles*. She previously worked as an assistant editor for Bernan Press and is now a freelance writer and editor for several reference titles. She has a B.A. in journalism from the University of Maryland.

STATE PROFILES **2023 PROVIDES:**

- Rankings of states for key demographic, economic, and social indicators

- A chapter for each state, complete with tables and figures that summarize and illustrate demographic, economic, and social characteristics

- Notes and definitions to assist with interpreting the information contained in this volume and to locate related data if desired

THE U.S. OVERVIEW. This short introduction to the demographics of the United States provides commentary on overall trends within the country.

THE STATE RANKINGS. The ranking tables that follow the national overview give state rankings by 32 characteristics, including population, demographic and age composition, income, gross domestic product, homeownership, poverty, health indicators, and educational attainment. These rankings provide the user with a quick analysis of the performance of each state in relation to the other states.

THE STATE CHAPTERS. The state chapters are the focus of this book. Each chapter follows a standard format and contains text highlighting the key features shown in the tables and figures. Some of these tables and figures contain references to the U.S. averages for the same characteristics.

Each of the state chapters is organized as follows:

Population. This table provides data on the state's total population and average annual population growth in comparison with the national average. It also shows the major population groups by sex, age, race, and ethnicity.

Marital status. The table shows the marital status for all men and women age 15 years and over.

Housing. This table showcases data pertaining to housing, such as number of households, types of households, housing characteristics, and median gross rent, mortgage, and monthly owner cost amounts.

Migration, origin, and language. This table provides statistics on residence one year ago, year of entry, place of origin, language spoken at home, and the native-born and foreign-born populations.

Income and poverty. Median household and family income and poverty rates by sex and age are contained in this table.

Health insurance coverage. This table provides information on health insurance, by type and coverage.

Employment. These tables illustrate each state's particular economic configuration. They exhibit employment status by detailed demographic group, labor force, participation rates, employment, unemployment, average wages and salaries by industry, and employment by family type.

Education. These tables provide the user with details on educational attainment, elementary and secondary school enrollment, student/teacher ratios, per student expenditures, and higher education enrollments.

Voter participation. Information is given on voter registration and voter participation in the 2022 midterm election, categorized by sex and race/ethnicity.

Health Indicators. This table include statistics on births, deaths, and common illnesses and compares each state's health indicators to U.S. averages.

Government finance. These tables provide data on revenues and expenditures by source for each state and the District of Columbia. In addition, tax information for each state/district is included.

NOTES AND DEFINITIONS. Each chapter relies on the same standard set of federal data sources. Since the basic data sources are common to all chapters, the main body of the volume contains few footnotes. Basic data and corresponding definitions and sources are identified in the notes and definition section at the end of the volume. It provides brief descriptions, methodologies, data availability, information on calculations made by the editors, and references to additional sources of information.

INTRODUCTION

During the early 2000s, the United States experienced several economic fluctuations that had a great impact on the strength, size, and performance of its economy. The recession that began in March 2001 was concluded in a few months; however, the longer-lasting recession that began in December 2007 left a more serious impact on the country. In March 2020, the global COVID-19 pandemic reached the U.S., upending particular sectors of the economy. The data in this book track the impacts of these changes the United States' economy over the past two decades.

This edition of *State Profiles: The Population and Economy of Each U.S. State* creates a snapshot of the people and economy in each state and the District of Columbia. Each chapter (one per state/district) includes information on topics such as population, employment, marital status, insurance coverage, crime, government finance, housing, education, and language.

SUMMARY

The U.S. population grew 7.9 percent between 2010 and 2022. Idaho experienced the largest population growth during this time period at 23.7 percent. Other states with the largest population growth included Utah (22.3 percent), Texas (19.4 percent), Florida (18.3 percent), Nevada (17.7 percent), Colorado (16.1 percent), North Dakota (15.9 percent), Washington (15.8 percent), Arizona (15.1 percent), and South Carolina (14.2 percent). Three states' populations declined during that time period: West Virginia (-4.2 percent), Illinois (-1.9 percent), and Mississippi (-0.9 percent).

Utah had the highest percentage of population younger than 18 years old in 2022, with 27.6 percent of its population in this age group, followed by Texas at 24.8 percent. Vermont and Maine had the smallest percent of minors (17.7 percent and 17.9 percent, respectively). Maine was also the state with the highest percentage of people 65 years and older (22.5 percent), followed by Florida, which had 21.6 percent of its population in this age group. At 12.0 percent, Utah had the lowest percentage of senior residents, followed by the District of Columbia (13.0 percent) and Texas (13.4 percent).

In 2021, the median household income in the United States was $69,717. Maryland had the highest median household income ($90,203), followed by the District of Columbia ($90,088), Massachusetts ($89,645), New Jersey ($89,296), and New Hampshire ($88,465). The states with the lowest median household incomes were Mississippi ($48,716), West Virginia ($51,248), Louisiana ($52,087), Arkansas ($52,528), and Alabama ($53,913). Some correlation to the percentage of residents with a bachelor's degree or more can be inferred, as the District of Columbia, Massachusetts, Maryland, and New Jersey rank in the top six states in this category. Mississippi, West Virginia, Louisiana, and Arkansas rank as the bottom four states in this category. The unemployment rate for the United States fell from 5.3 percent in 2021 to 3.6 percent in 2022, reflecting some recovery in the U.S. job market from the effects of the COVID-19 pandemic. Nevada had the highest percentage of unemployed residents in 2022 (5.4 percent), followed by the District of Columbia (4.7 percent), Illinois (4.6 percent), and Delaware (4.5 percent). South Dakota (2.1 percent), North Dakota (2.1 percent), Utah (2.3 percent), and Nebraska (2.3 percent) had the lowest percentage of unemployed residents.

In the United States in 2021, 12.8 percent of the population lived below the poverty level. Louisiana, which had the 3rd lowest median household income, had the highest poverty rate, with 19.6 percent of its residents below the poverty level. New Hampshire had the lowest poverty rate (7.2 percent). Mississippi had the highest rate of persons younger than 18 years of age below the poverty level (27.7 percent), followed by Louisiana (26.9 percent), the District of Columbia (23.9 percent), New Mexico (23.9 percent), and Arkansas (22.4 percent). The states with the fewest residents under 18 years of age below the poverty level included Utah (8.1 percent), New Hampshire (9.2 percent), Vermont (10.4 percent), North Dakota (10.5 percent), and Minnesota (10.8 percent).

CONTENTS

UNITED STATES RANKING

Rank	State	Population
	United States....................	333,287,557
1	California.....................	39,029,342
2	Texas...........................	30,029,572
3	Florida.........................	22,244,823
4	New York......................	19,677,151
5	Pennsylvania..................	12,972,008
6	Illinois.........................	12,582,032
7	Ohio............................	11,756,058
8	Georgia	10,912,876
9	North Carolina...............	10,698,973
10	Michigan.......................	10,034,113
11	New Jersey	9,261,699
12	Virginia........................	8,683,619
13	Washington....................	7,785,786
14	Arizona.........................	7,359,197
15	Tennessee.....................	7,051,339
16	Massachusetts................	6,981,974
17	Indiana.........................	6,833,037
18	Missouri........................	6,177,957
19	Maryland.......................	6,164,660
20	Wisconsin	5,892,539
21	Colorado	5,839,926
22	Minnesota......................	5,717,184
23	South Carolina	5,282,634
24	Alabama........................	5,074,296
25	Louisiana	4,590,241
26	Kentucky.......................	4,512,310
27	Oregon	4,240,137
28	Oklahoma......................	4,019,800
29	Connecticut....................	3,626,205
30	Utah.............................	3,380,800
31	Iowa.............................	3,200,517
32	Nevada	3,177,772
33	Arkansas.......................	3,045,637
34	Mississippi.....................	2,940,057
35	Kansas..........................	2,937,150
36	New Mexico	2,113,344
37	Nebraska.......................	1,967,923
38	Idaho............................	1,939,033
39	West Virginia..................	1,775,156
40	Hawaii	1,440,196
41	New Hampshire...............	1,395,231
42	Maine...........................	1,385,340
43	Montana........................	1,122,867
44	Rhode Island..................	1,093,734
45	Delaware.......................	1,018,396
46	South Dakota	909,824
47	North Dakota..................	779,261
48	Alaska..........................	733,583
49	District of Columbia	671,803
50	Vermont........................	647,064
51	Wyoming	581,381

Population, Percent Change, 2010–2022

Rank	State	Percent
	United States....................	7.9
1	Idaho............................	23.7
2	Utah.............................	22.3
3	Texas...........................	19.4
4	Florida.........................	18.3
5	Nevada	17.7
6	Colorado	16.1
7	North Dakota..................	15.9
8	Washington....................	15.8
9	Arizona.........................	15.1
10	South Carolina	14.2
11	Montana........................	13.5
12	Delaware.......................	13.4
13	Georgia	12.6
14	North Carolina...............	12.2
15	South Dakota	11.7
16	District of Columbia	11.6
17	Tennessee	11.1
18	Oregon	10.7
19	Virginia........................	8.5
20	Minnesota......................	7.8
20	Nebraska.......................	7.8
22	Oklahoma......................	7.2
23	Maryland.......................	6.8
24	Massachusetts................	6.6
25	Alabama........................	6.2
26	New Hampshire...............	6.0
27	Hawaii	5.9
28	Indiana.........................	5.4
29	New Jersey	5.3
30	Iowa.............................	5.1
31	California.......................	4.8
32	Arkansas.......................	4.4
33	Maine...........................	4.3
34	Kentucky.......................	4.0
35	Rhode Island..................	3.9
36	Wisconsin	3.6
37	Vermont........................	3.4
38	Alaska..........................	3.3
39	Missouri........................	3.2
39	Wyoming	3.2
41	Kansas..........................	2.9
42	New Mexico	2.6
43	Pennsylvania..................	2.1
44	Ohio............................	1.9
45	New York......................	1.5
45	Michigan.......................	1.5
45	Connecticut....................	1.5
48	Louisiana	1.3
49	Mississippi.....................	-0.9
50	Illinois.........................	-1.9
51	West Virginia..................	-4.2

Percent Population Under 18 Years Old, 2022

Rank	State	Percent
	United States....................	21.7
1	Utah.............................	27.6
2	Texas...........................	24.8
3	Nebraska.......................	24.2
4	South Dakota	24.1
4	Alaska..........................	24.1
6	Idaho............................	23.9
7	Oklahoma......................	23.7
8	Kansas..........................	23.5
8	North Dakota..................	23.5
10	Louisiana	23.1
10	Mississippi.....................	23.1
12	Georgia	23.0
12	Indiana.........................	23.0
14	Arkansas.......................	22.9
15	Iowa.............................	22.6
15	Minnesota......................	22.6
17	Wyoming	22.4
18	Kentucky.......................	22.3
19	Missouri........................	22.1
20	Alabama........................	21.9
21	Maryland.......................	21.8
21	Tennessee	21.8
21	Ohio............................	21.8
21	California.......................	21.8
25	New Mexico	21.7
25	Nevada	21.7
27	Illinois.........................	21.6
27	Arizona.........................	21.6
29	New Jersey	21.5
29	Virginia........................	21.5
31	North Carolina...............	21.4
32	South Carolina	21.2
33	Washington....................	21.1
33	Wisconsin	21.1
35	Michigan.......................	21.0
36	Montana........................	20.8
36	Colorado	20.8
38	Hawaii	20.6
39	Delaware.......................	20.4
40	New York......................	20.3
41	Pennsylvania..................	20.2
41	Connecticut....................	20.2
43	West Virginia..................	19.8
44	Oregon	19.7
45	Florida.........................	19.3
46	Massachusetts................	19.2
47	Rhode Island..................	18.6
48	District of Columbia	18.5
49	New Hampshire...............	18.1
50	Maine...........................	17.9
51	Vermont........................	17.7

4 STATE PROFILES

Percent Population 65 Years and Over, 2022		
Rank	State	Percent
	United States	17.3
1	Maine	22.5
2	Florida	21.6
2	Vermont	21.6
4	West Virginia	21.2
5	Delaware	20.8
6	Hawaii	20.4
7	New Hampshire	20.2
8	Montana	20.0
9	Pennsylvania	19.6
10	Oregon	19.2
11	New Mexico	19.1
11	South Carolina	19.1
13	Rhode Island	18.9
14	Arizona	18.8
15	Michigan	18.7
15	Wisconsin	18.7
17	Wyoming	18.6
18	Ohio	18.4
19	Iowa	18.3
19	Connecticut	18.3
21	New York	18.1
21	Massachusetts	18.1
23	Missouri	18.0
23	Alabama	18.0
23	South Dakota	18.0
26	Arkansas	17.8
27	Kentucky	17.6
28	Minnesota	17.4
28	New Jersey	17.4
28	North Carolina	17.4
31	Tennessee	17.3
31	Mississippi	17.3
33	Illinois	17.2
33	Kansas	17.2
35	Idaho	17.0
35	Louisiana	17.0
37	Maryland	16.9
37	Nebraska	16.9
37	Indiana	16.9
37	Nevada	16.9
37	Virginia	16.9
42	Washington	16.8
43	North Dakota	16.7
44	Oklahoma	16.4
45	California	15.8
46	Colorado	15.7
47	Georgia	15.1
48	Alaska	13.9
49	Texas	13.4
50	District of Columbia	13.0
51	Utah	12.0

Percent White Alone, 2022		
Rank	State	Percent
	United States	75.5
1	Maine	93.9
2	Vermont	93.8
3	West Virginia	92.8
4	Idaho	92.6
4	New Hampshire	92.6
6	Wyoming	92.3
7	Utah	90.0
8	Iowa	89.8
9	Montana	88.7
10	Nebraska	87.5
11	Kentucky	86.9
12	North Dakota	86.6
12	Wisconsin	86.6
14	Colorado	86.2
15	Oregon	85.9
15	Kansas	85.9
17	South Dakota	84.2
18	Indiana	84.0
19	Rhode Island	82.8
20	Minnesota	82.6
21	Missouri	82.5
22	Arizona	81.9
23	New Mexico	81.1
24	Ohio	80.9
25	Pennsylvania	80.8
26	Massachusetts	79.4
27	Michigan	78.8
28	Arkansas	78.5
29	Connecticut	78.4
30	Tennessee	78.3
31	Texas	77.4
32	Washington	76.8
32	Florida	76.8
34	Illinois	76.1
35	Oklahoma	73.0
36	Nevada	72.1
37	California	70.7
37	New Jersey	70.7
39	North Carolina	69.9
40	South Carolina	68.9
40	Alabama	68.9
42	New York	68.6
43	Virginia	68.5
44	Delaware	68.0
45	Alaska	64.1
46	Louisiana	62.5
	Georgia	59.0
48	Mississippi	58.8
49	Maryland	57.3
50	District of Columbia	46.2
51	Hawaii	25.2

Percent Black or African American Alone, 2022		
Rank	State	Percent
	United States	13.6
1	District of Columbia	45.0
2	Mississippi	37.8
3	Georgia	33.1
4	Louisiana	32.8
5	Maryland	31.7
6	Alabama	26.8
7	South Carolina	26.3
8	Delaware	23.8
9	North Carolina	22.2
10	Virginia	20.0
11	New York	17.7
12	Florida	17.0
13	Tennessee	16.7
14	Arkansas	15.6
15	New Jersey	15.4
16	Illinois	14.7
17	Michigan	14.1
18	Texas	13.4
19	Ohio	13.3
20	Connecticut	12.9
21	Pennsylvania	12.2
22	Missouri	11.7
23	Nevada	10.8
24	Indiana	10.3
25	Massachusetts	9.5
26	Rhode Island	9.1
27	Kentucky	8.7
28	Oklahoma	7.9
29	Minnesota	7.6
30	Wisconsin	6.6
31	California	6.5
32	Kansas	6.2
33	Arizona	5.5
34	Nebraska	5.4
35	Colorado	4.7
36	Washington	4.6
37	Iowa	4.4
38	West Virginia	3.7
38	Alaska	3.7
40	North Dakota	3.6
41	New Mexico	2.7
42	South Dakota	2.6
43	Oregon	2.3
44	Hawaii	2.2
45	New Hampshire	2.0
45	Maine	2.0
47	Utah	1.6
48	Vermont	1.5
49	Wyoming	1.2
50	Idaho	1.0
51	Montana	0.6

Percent American Indian and Alaska Native Alone, 2022

Rank	State	Percent
	United States........................	1.3
1	Alaska	15.7
2	New Mexico	11.2
3	Oklahoma.............................	9.5
4	South Dakota	8.5
5	Montana...............................	6.5
6	North Dakota........................	5.3
7	Arizona................................	5.2
8	Wyoming..............................	2.8
9	Washington..........................	2.0
10	Oregon................................	1.9
11	California.............................	1.7
11	Nevada................................	1.7
11	Idaho...................................	1.7
11	Colorado	1.7
15	Nebraska.............................	1.6
15	North Carolina......................	1.6
17	Utah....................................	1.5
18	Minnesota............................	1.4
19	Kansas................................	1.2
19	Rhode Island........................	1.2
19	Wisconsin............................	1.2
22	Arkansas.............................	1.1
22	Texas..................................	1.1
24	New York.............................	1.0
25	Louisiana	0.8
26	Michigan..............................	0.7
26	Connecticut..........................	0.7
26	New Jersey	0.7
26	Alabama..............................	0.7
26	Maine..................................	0.7
26	Delaware.............................	0.7
26	Maryland..............................	0.7
26	District of Columbia	0.7
34	Mississippi...........................	0.6
34	Illinois.................................	0.6
34	Missouri...............................	0.6
34	Iowa....................................	0.6
34	Virginia................................	0.6
34	South Carolina	0.6
34	Georgia	0.6
41	Florida.................................	0.5
41	Massachusetts......................	0.5
41	Tennessee	0.5
44	Pennsylvania........................	0.4
44	Indiana................................	0.4
44	Hawaii.................................	0.4
44	Vermont...............................	0.4
48	Kentucky..............................	0.3
48	New Hampshire.....................	0.3
48	Ohio....................................	0.3
48	West Virginia........................	0.3

Percent Asian Alone, 2022

Rank	State	Percent
	United States........................	6.3
1	Hawaii.................................	37.1
2	California.............................	16.3
3	New Jersey	10.5
3	Washington..........................	10.5
5	New York.............................	9.6
6	Nevada................................	9.4
7	Massachusetts......................	7.7
8	Virginia................................	7.3
9	Maryland..............................	7.1
10	Alaska	6.7
11	Illinois.................................	6.3
12	Texas..................................	5.7
13	Minnesota............................	5.5
14	Connecticut..........................	5.2
15	Oregon................................	5.1
16	Georgia	4.8
17	District of Columbia	4.7
18	Delaware.............................	4.4
19	Pennsylvania........................	4.1
20	Arizona................................	3.9
21	Colorado	3.8
22	Rhode Island........................	3.7
23	North Carolina......................	3.6
24	Michigan..............................	3.5
25	Wisconsin............................	3.2
25	Kansas................................	3.2
25	New Hampshire.....................	3.2
28	Florida.................................	3.1
29	Nebraska.............................	2.8
29	Indiana................................	2.8
29	Utah....................................	2.8
29	Iowa....................................	2.8
33	Ohio....................................	2.7
34	Oklahoma.............................	2.6
35	Missouri...............................	2.3
36	Tennessee	2.1
36	Vermont...............................	2.1
38	South Carolina	2.0
38	New Mexico	2.0
40	Louisiana	1.9
41	Arkansas.............................	1.8
41	South Dakota	1.8
41	Kentucky..............................	1.8
44	North Dakota........................	1.7
44	Idaho...................................	1.7
46	Alabama..............................	1.6
47	Maine..................................	1.4
48	Mississippi...........................	1.2
49	Wyoming..............................	1.1
49	Montana...............................	1.1
51	West Virginia........................	0.9

Percent Native Hawaiian and Other Pacific Islander Alone, 2022

Rank	State	Percent
	United States........................	0.3
1	Hawaii.................................	10.3
2	Alaska	1.7
3	Utah....................................	1.2
4	Nevada................................	0.9
5	Washington..........................	0.8
6	California.............................	0.5
6	Oregon................................	0.5
6	Arkansas.............................	0.5
9	Arizona................................	0.3
9	Oklahoma.............................	0.3
11	Idaho...................................	0.2
11	Iowa....................................	0.2
11	Colorado	0.2
11	Rhode Island........................	0.2
11	Missouri...............................	0.2
11	District of Columbia	0.2
11	New Mexico	0.2
11	Texas..................................	0.2
11	Kansas................................	0.2
20	North Carolina......................	0.1
20	New York.............................	0.1
20	Nebraska.............................	0.1
20	Georgia	0.1
20	New Jersey	0.1
20	South Dakota	0.1
20	Virginia................................	0.1
20	Florida.................................	0.1
20	Maryland..............................	0.1
20	North Dakota........................	0.1
20	Kentucky..............................	0.1
20	Delaware.............................	0.1
20	Connecticut..........................	0.1
20	Massachusetts......................	0.1
20	Tennessee	0.1
20	Alabama..............................	0.1
20	Wyoming..............................	0.1
20	South Carolina	0.1
20	Montana...............................	0.1
20	Pennsylvania........................	0.1
20	Minnesota............................	0.1
20	Indiana................................	0.1
20	Ohio....................................	0.1
20	Illinois.................................	0.1
20	Mississippi...........................	0.1
20	Louisiana	0.1
20	New Hampshire.....................	0.1
20	Wisconsin............................	0.1
48	Michigan..............................	Z
48	Maine..................................	Z
48	Vermont...............................	Z
48	West Virginia........................	Z

Z = Value greater than zero but less than half of the unit shown.

Percent Two or More Races, 2022

Rank	State	Percent
	United States	3.0
1	Hawaii	24.7
2	Alaska	8.2
3	Oklahoma	6.7
4	Washington	5.3
5	Nevada	5.1
6	Oregon	4.3
6	California	4.3
8	Virginia	3.4
8	Colorado	3.4
10	Kansas	3.3
11	Arizona	3.2
11	Maryland	3.2
11	District of Columbia	3.2
14	Rhode Island	3.1
15	Montana	3.0
15	Delaware	3.0
17	Utah	2.9
18	New York	2.8
18	New Mexico	2.8
18	Minnesota	2.8
18	Idaho	2.8
18	Michigan	2.8
18	South Dakota	2.8
24	Massachusetts	2.7
24	Connecticut	2.7
24	Missouri	2.7
24	Ohio	2.7
28	North Carolina	2.6
28	North Dakota	2.6
30	Nebraska	2.5
31	Wyoming	2.4
31	Georgia	2.4
31	New Jersey	2.4
31	Florida	2.4
31	Arkansas	2.4
31	Indiana	2.4
31	Pennsylvania	2.4
38	Kentucky	2.3
38	Texas	2.3
40	Wisconsin	2.2
40	Illinois	2.2
40	Tennessee	2.2
40	South Carolina	2.2
40	West Virginia	2.2
40	Iowa	2.2
46	Vermont	2.1
47	Maine	2.0
47	Alabama	2.0
49	Louisiana	1.9
49	New Hampshire	1.9
51	Mississippi	1.5

Percent Hispanic or Latino,[1] 2022

Rank	State	Percent
	United States	19.1
1	New Mexico	49.8
2	California	40.1
3	Texas	38.7
4	Arizona	31.1
5	Nevada	28.8
6	Florida	25.7
7	Colorado	21.7
8	New Jersey	21.3
9	New York	20.0
10	Illinois	18.1
11	Connecticut	17.2
12	Rhode Island	16.7
13	Utah	14.1
14	Oregon	13.7
15	Washington	13.3
16	Massachusetts	12.6
16	Kansas	12.6
18	Idaho	12.3
19	District of Columbia	11.7
19	Nebraska	11.7
21	Oklahoma	11.3
22	Hawaii	11.1
23	Maryland	10.9
24	Wyoming	10.3
25	Virginia	9.9
26	Georgia	9.8
27	North Carolina	9.7
28	Delaware	9.6
29	Pennsylvania	8.1
30	Arkansas	8.0
31	Indiana	7.4
31	Alaska	7.4
33	Wisconsin	7.3
34	Iowa	6.5
35	South Carolina	5.9
36	Tennessee	5.8
37	Minnesota	5.7
38	Louisiana	5.5
38	Michigan	5.5
40	Alabama	4.6
41	Missouri	4.5
42	North Dakota	4.3
42	South Dakota	4.3
44	Ohio	4.2
45	New Hampshire	4.1
46	Kentucky	4.0
46	Montana	4.0
48	Mississippi	3.4
49	Vermont	2.1
50	West Virginia	1.9
51	Maine	1.8

[1] May be of any race.

Birth Rate, 2021

Rank	State	Rate per 1,000 population
	United States	11.0
1	Utah	14.0
2	North Dakota	13.0
3	District of Columbia	12.9
4	Alaska	12.8
5	South Dakota	12.7
5	Texas	12.7
7	Nebraska	12.5
8	Louisiana	12.4
9	Oklahoma	12.1
10	Arkansas	11.9
10	Mississippi	11.9
12	Idaho	11.8
12	Kansas	11.8
14	Indiana	11.7
14	Tennessee	11.7
16	Kentucky	11.6
17	Alabama	11.5
17	Georgia	11.5
17	Iowa	11.5
20	North Carolina	11.4
21	Minnesota	11.3
21	Missouri	11.3
23	Maryland	11.1
23	Virginia	11.1
25	New Jersey	11.0
25	Ohio	11.0
25	South Carolina	11.0
28	Colorado	10.8
28	Hawaii	10.8
28	Washington	10.8
28	Wyoming	10.8
32	Arizona	10.7
32	California	10.7
32	Nevada	10.7
35	New York	10.6
36	Wisconsin	10.5
37	Delaware	10.4
37	Illinois	10.4
37	Michigan	10.4
40	Montana	10.2
40	Pennsylvania	10.2
42	New Mexico	10.1
43	Connecticut	9.9
43	Florida	9.9
43	Massachusetts	9.9
46	Oregon	9.6
46	Rhode Island	9.6
46	West Virginia	9.6
49	New Hampshire	9.1
50	Maine	8.7
51	Vermont	8.3

Life Expectancy at Birth, 2020

Rank	State	Age-adjusted rate per 100,000 population
	United States............................	77.0
1	Hawaii	80.7
2	Washington	79.2
3	Minnesota	79.1
4	California................................	79.0
5	Massachusetts	79.0
6	New Hampshire........................	79.0
7	Oregon	78.8
8	Vermont	78.8
9	Utah	78.6
10	Connecticut............................	78.4
11	Idaho.....................................	78.4
12	Colorado	78.3
13	Rhode Island...........................	78.2
14	Maine	77.8
15	Nebraska	77.7
16	New York................................	77.7
17	Wisconsin	77.7
18	Virginia..................................	77.6
19	Florida...................................	77.5
20	Iowa	77.5
21	New Jersey	77.5
22	North Dakota	76.9
23	Illinois	76.8
24	Maryland	76.8
25	Montana	76.8
26	Pennsylvania...........................	76.8
27	Delaware	76.7
28	South Dakota	76.7
29	Alaska	76.6
30	Texas	76.5
31	Kansas	76.4
32	Arizona...................................	76.3
33	Nevada	76.3
34	Wyoming	76.3
35	North Carolina.........................	76.1
36	Michigan	76.0
37	Georgia	75.6
38	District of Columbia	75.3
39	Ohio	75.3
40	Missouri	75.1
41	Indiana	75.0
42	South Carolina	74.8
43	New Mexico	74.5
44	Oklahoma	74.1
45	Arkansas	73.8
46	Tennessee	73.8
47	Kentucky	73.5
48	Alabama	73.2
49	Louisiana	73.1
50	West Virginia...........................	72.8
51	Mississippi..............................	71.9

Homicide Mortality Rate, 2021

Rank	State	Percent voted, population 18 years and older
	United States............................	8.2
1	District of Columbia	30.0
2	Mississippi..............................	23.7
3	Louisiana	21.3
4	Alabama	15.9
5	New Mexico	15.3
6	South Carolina	13.4
7	Missouri	12.4
8	Illinois	12.3
9	Maryland	12.2
9	Tennessee	12.2
11	Arkansas	11.7
12	Georgia	11.4
13	Delaware	11.3
14	North Carolina.........................	9.7
15	Indiana	9.6
15	Kentucky	9.6
17	Ohio	9.3
18	Pennsylvania...........................	9.2
19	Oklahoma	8.9
20	Michigan	8.7
21	Nevada	8.5
22	Texas	8.2
23	Arizona...................................	8.1
24	Florida...................................	7.4
25	Virginia..................................	7.2
26	West Virginia...........................	6.9
27	Alaska	6.4
27	California................................	6.4
27	Kansas	6.4
27	Wisconsin	6.4
31	Colorado	6.3
32	South Dakota	5.3
33	Oregon	4.9
34	Connecticut............................	4.8
34	New Jersey	4.8
34	New York................................	4.8
37	Washington	4.5
38	Montana	4.4
39	Minnesota	4.3
40	Nebraska	3.6
40	Rhode Island...........................	3.6
42	North Dakota	3.4
43	Iowa	3.2
44	Hawaii	2.7
44	Utah	2.7
46	Massachusetts	2.3
47	Idaho.....................................	2.2
48	Maine	1.7
49	New Hampshire........................	Z
49	Vermont	Z
49	Wyoming	Z

Drug Overdose Death Rate, 2021

Rank	State	Percent
	United States............................	32.4
1	Washington	90.9
2	South Dakota	56.6
3	Kentucky	55.9
4	Kansas	55.6
5	Delaware	54.0
6	New Jersey	51.6
7	North Dakota	48.1
8	Louisiana	47.1
9	Oregon	43.2
10	Illinois	43.0
11	Maine	42.8
11	Rhode Island...........................	42.8
13	Connecticut............................	42.3
13	Utah	42.3
15	Pennsylvania...........................	41.7
16	New York................................	39.2
17	Arizona...................................	38.7
18	District of Columbia	37.5
19	Maryland	36.8
20	Mississippi..............................	36.5
21	Alaska	35.6
22	New Hampshire........................	32.4
23	Nevada	32.3
24	West Virginia...........................	31.6
25	Massachusetts	31.5
26	Colorado	31.4
27	Vermont	30.5
28	Alabama	30.1
29	Nebraska	29.2
30	Idaho.....................................	29.0
31	New Mexico	28.7
32	Minnesota	28.4
33	Virginia..................................	28.1
34	Oklahoma	26.8
35	California................................	26.6
36	Michigan	24.5
37	Ohio	24.4
38	Iowa	24.3
39	Florida...................................	23.5
40	Arkansas	22.3
41	Texas	21.1
42	Missouri	19.5
43	Hawaii	19.0
44	Wisconsin	18.9
45	Georgia	17.3
46	North Carolina.........................	17.2
47	Tennessee	16.8
48	Indiana	15.3
49	South Carolina	12.6
50	Montana	11.4
51	Wyoming	8.1

Voter Turnout, November 2022

Rank	State	Rate per 100,000 population
	United States	47.7
1	Oregon	65.3
2	Maine	62.7
3	Vermont	61.4
4	Michigan	61.2
4	Minnesota	61.2
6	Wisconsin	59.1
7	Colorado	58.8
8	District of Columbia	58.6
9	Pennsylvania	57.7
10	New Hampshire	57.2
11	Kansas	57.0
12	Montana	56.0
13	Washington	54.7
14	Maryland	53.5
15	Alaska	53.1
16	Rhode Island	52.1
17	Georgia	52.0
17	South Dakota	52.0
19	Missouri	51.9
20	Delaware	51.2
21	Massachusetts	50.3
21	New Mexico	50.3
23	Iowa	50.2
24	North Dakota	50.0
25	Arizona	49.6
26	Kentucky	49.3
27	Utah	49.0
28	Virginia	48.8
29	Wyoming	48.6
30	Illinois	47.7
31	Hawaii	47.2
32	Ohio	46.1
33	Idaho	46.0
34	Louisiana	45.8
34	Nevada	45.8
36	Mississippi	45.7
37	Nebraska	45.1
38	Oklahoma	44.5
39	Connecticut	44.1
40	New Jersey	44.0
41	Alabama	43.8
42	California	43.7
43	New York	43.5
44	Florida	43.2
45	South Carolina	42.9
46	Tennessee	42.5
47	Arkansas	42.2
48	North Carolina	42.1
49	Texas	40.5
50	Indiana	39.5
51	West Virginia	38.2

Percent of Persons 25 Years and Over with a Bachelor's Degree or More, 2021

Rank	State	Rate per 100,000 population
	United States	35.0
1	District of Columbia	63.0
2	Massachusetts	46.6
3	Colorado	44.4
3	Vermont	44.4
5	New Jersey	43.1
6	Maryland	42.5
7	Connecticut	42.1
8	Virginia	41.8
9	New Hampshire	40.2
10	New York	39.9
11	Washington	39.0
12	Minnesota	38.9
13	Illinois	37.1
14	Utah	36.8
15	Rhode Island	36.5
16	Oregon	36.3
17	California	36.2
18	Maine	36.0
19	Delaware	35.6
20	Kansas	35.4
21	Hawaii	35.3
22	North Carolina	34.9
23	Montana	34.8
24	Georgia	34.6
25	Pennsylvania	34.5
26	Nebraska	34.4
27	Florida	33.2
28	Texas	33.1
29	Alaska	32.8
30	Wisconsin	32.5
31	Arizona	32.4
32	Michigan	31.7
32	Missouri	31.7
32	North Dakota	31.7
32	South Dakota	31.7
36	South Carolina	31.5
37	Idaho	30.7
37	Ohio	30.7
39	Iowa	30.5
39	Tennessee	30.5
41	New Mexico	30.1
42	Wyoming	29.2
43	Indiana	28.9
44	Oklahoma	27.9
45	Nevada	27.6
46	Alabama	27.4
47	Kentucky	27.0
48	Louisiana	26.4
49	Arkansas	25.3
50	Mississippi	24.8
51	West Virginia	24.1

State & Local Government Employment, 2022

Rank	State	State & local employees per 1,000 residents
	United States	49.8
1	Wyoming	85.4
2	District of Columbia	74.8
3	Alaska	68.9
4	Kansas	68.2
5	Nebraska	63.5
6	North Dakota	63.4
7	Mississippi	60.9
8	New York	60.2
9	Iowa	59.6
10	Vermont	58.9
11	New Mexico	57.1
12	West Virginia	56.9
13	Alabama	56.0
14	Louisiana	55.5
15	Arkansas	54.9
16	Colorado	53.3
17	Virginia	52.6
18	Kentucky	52.1
18	Maine	52.1
20	South Dakota	52.0
21	North Carolina	51.8
22	Oklahoma	51.6
22	Texas	51.6
24	Minnesota	51.4
25	Montana	51.1
26	Maryland	51.0
27	New Jersey	50.9
28	Washington	50.6
29	South Carolina	50.2
29	Connecticut	50.2
29	Hawaii	50.2
32	Delaware	50.0
33	Missouri	49.7
34	Oregon	49.6
35	Utah	49.3
36	Massachusetts	49.2
36	Illinois	49.2
38	New Hampshire	48.9
38	Ohio	48.9
40	California	48.3
41	Georgia	47.7
42	Wisconsin	47.4
43	Tennessee	47.1
44	Indiana	47.0
45	Idaho	45.2
46	Rhode Island	43.0
47	Michigan	42.6
48	Pennsylvania	41.8
49	Florida	39.7
50	Arizona	38.3
51	Nevada	36.0

[1]Includes offenses reported by the Metro Transit Police and the District of Columbia Fire and Emergency Medical Services: Arson

Unemployment Rate, 2022

Rank	State	Unemployment rate
	United States..........................	3.6
1	Nevada...............................	5.4
2	District of Columbia	4.7
3	Illinois.............................	4.6
4	Delaware.............................	4.5
5	Pennsylvania.........................	4.4
6	New York.............................	4.3
7	California...........................	4.2
7	Connecticut..........................	4.2
7	Michigan.............................	4.2
7	Oregon...............................	4.2
7	Washington...........................	4.2
12	Alaska...............................	4.0
12	New Mexico...........................	4.0
12	Ohio.................................	4.0
15	Kentucky.............................	3.9
15	Mississippi..........................	3.9
15	Texas................................	3.9
15	West Virginia........................	3.9
19	Arizona..............................	3.8
19	Massachusetts........................	3.8
21	Louisiana............................	3.7
21	New Jersey...........................	3.7
21	North Carolina.......................	3.7
24	Wyoming..............................	3.6
25	Hawaii...............................	3.5
26	Tennessee............................	3.4
27	Arkansas.............................	3.3
28	Maryland.............................	3.2
28	Rhode Island.........................	3.2
28	South Carolina.......................	3.2
31	Colorado.............................	3.0
31	Georgia..............................	3.0
31	Indiana..............................	3.0
31	Maine................................	3.0
31	Oklahoma.............................	3.0
36	Florida..............................	2.9
36	Virginia.............................	2.9
36	Wisconsin............................	2.9
39	Idaho................................	2.7
39	Iowa.................................	2.7
39	Kansas...............................	2.7
39	Minnesota............................	2.7
43	Alabama..............................	2.6
43	Montana..............................	2.6
43	Vermont..............................	2.6
46	Missouri.............................	2.5
46	New Hampshire........................	2.5
48	Nebraska.............................	2.3
48	Utah.................................	2.3
50	North Dakota.........................	2.1
50	South Dakota.........................	2.1

Average Hourly Earnings of Employees on Private Nonfarm Payrolls, 2021

Rank	State	Percent
	United States..........................	30.58
1	District of Columbia	51.22
2	Massachusetts........................	36.91
3	California...........................	36.08
4	Washington...........................	35.38
5	New York.............................	35.10
6	Connecticut..........................	33.84
7	Maryland.............................	33.30
8	New Jersey...........................	32.87
9	Minnesota............................	32.81
10	Hawaii...............................	32.57
11	Colorado.............................	31.97
12	Alaska...............................	31.80
13	Illinois.............................	31.43
14	Virginia.............................	31.25
15	New Hampshire........................	31.20
16	Oregon...............................	30.19
17	Rhode Island.........................	29.60
18	Utah.................................	29.57
19	Delaware.............................	28.89
20	Michigan.............................	28.77
21	Texas................................	28.55
21	Vermont..............................	28.55
23	Arizona..............................	28.41
24	Pennsylvania.........................	28.39
25	North Dakota.........................	28.36
26	Wisconsin............................	28.28
27	Florida..............................	28.09
28	Georgia..............................	28.07
29	North Carolina.......................	28.04
30	Nebraska.............................	27.84
31	Missouri.............................	27.61
32	Wyoming..............................	27.53
33	Ohio.................................	27.47
34	Alabama..............................	27.29
35	Kansas...............................	27.27
36	Maine................................	27.16
37	Indiana..............................	27.15
38	South Carolina	26.98
39	Montana..............................	26.87
40	Iowa.................................	26.79
41	Louisiana............................	26.72
42	Nevada...............................	26.56
43	Idaho................................	26.49
44	Tennessee............................	26.40
45	South Dakota.........................	25.90
46	West Virginia........................	25.44
47	Oklahoma.............................	25.33
48	Kentucky.............................	25.20
49	New Mexico...........................	24.68
50	Arkansas.............................	24.14
51	Mississippi..........................	22.90

Per Capita Personal Income, 2022

Rank	State	Dollars
	United States..........................	65,423
1	District of Columbia	96,728
2	Connecticut..........................	84,972
3	Massachusetts........................	84,945
4	New Jersey...........................	78,700
5	New York.............................	78,089
6	California...........................	77,339
7	Washington...........................	75,698
8	New Hampshire........................	74,663
9	Colorado.............................	74,167
10	Wyoming..............................	71,342
11	Maryland.............................	70,730
12	Alaska...............................	68,919
13	Illinois.............................	68,822
14	Virginia.............................	68,211
15	Minnesota............................	68,010
16	North Dakota.........................	66,184
17	South Dakota	65,806
18	Rhode Island.........................	65,377
19	Pennsylvania.........................	65,167
20	Florida..............................	63,597
21	Nebraska.............................	63,321
22	Vermont..............................	63,206
23	Oregon...............................	62,767
24	Texas................................	61,985
25	Delaware.............................	61,387
26	Nevada...............................	61,282
27	Wisconsin............................	61,210
28	Hawaii...............................	61,175
29	Kansas...............................	60,152
30	Maine................................	59,463
31	Iowa.................................	58,905
32	Tennessee............................	58,279
33	Indiana..............................	57,930
34	Utah.................................	57,925
35	Ohio.................................	57,880
36	Montana..............................	57,719
37	North Carolina.......................	57,416
38	Georgia..............................	57,129
39	Michigan.............................	56,813
40	Arizona..............................	56,667
41	Missouri.............................	56,551
42	Oklahoma.............................	54,998
43	Louisiana............................	54,622
44	Idaho................................	54,537
45	South Carolina	53,320
46	Kentucky.............................	52,109
47	Arkansas.............................	51,787
48	New Mexico...........................	51,500
49	Alabama..............................	50,637
50	West Virginia........................	49,169
51	Mississippi..........................	46,248

Real Gross Domestic Product in Chained (2012) Dollars, 2022

Rank	State	Dollars (millions)	Percent of U.S. GDP
	United States....................	20,014,128	100.0
1	California.........................	2,885,627	14.4
2	Texas...............................	1,876,328	9.4
3	New York..........................	1,563,044	7.8
4	Florida.............................	1,070,930	5.4
5	Illinois.............................	797,969	4.0
6	Pennsylvania....................	726,036	3.6
7	Ohio.................................	638,910	3.2
8	Georgia............................	591,257	3.0
9	Washington.......................	582,172	2.9
10	New Jersey.......................	581,704	2.9
11	North Carolina..................	559,510	2.8
12	Massachusetts..................	543,872	2.7
13	Virginia............................	512,946	2.6
14	Michigan...........................	490,318	2.4
15	Colorado..........................	385,835	1.9
16	Maryland..........................	368,680	1.8
17	Tennessee........................	367,776	1.8
18	Arizona............................	356,417	1.8
19	Indiana.............................	352,956	1.8
20	Minnesota.........................	350,315	1.8
21	Wisconsin.........................	311,702	1.6
22	Missouri...........................	300,676	1.5
23	Connecticut.......................	252,533	1.3
24	Oregon.............................	234,806	1.2
25	South Carolina..................	226,420	1.1
26	Louisiana..........................	217,156	1.1
27	Alabama...........................	213,265	1.1
28	Kentucky..........................	201,375	1.0
29	Utah.................................	191,965	1.0
30	Oklahoma.........................	191,388	1.0
31	Iowa.................................	177,090	0.9
32	Nevada.............................	165,455	0.8
33	Kansas.............................	164,939	0.8
34	District of Columbia..........	129,268	0.6
35	Arkansas..........................	126,532	0.6
36	Nebraska..........................	123,540	0.6
37	Mississippi.......................	104,535	0.5
38	New Mexico.......................	94,663	0.5
39	Idaho...............................	84,003	0.4
40	New Hampshire..................	83,004	0.4
41	Hawaii..............................	75,418	0.4
42	West Virginia.....................	71,652	0.4
43	Delaware..........................	65,755	0.3
44	Maine...............................	64,766	0.3
45	Rhode Island.....................	55,413	0.3
46	North Dakota.....................	53,125	0.3
47	South Dakota....................	49,809	0.2
48	Montana...........................	49,752	0.2
49	Alaska.............................	49,634	0.2
50	Wyoming..........................	36,346	0.2
51	Vermont............................	31,395	0.2

Real Gross Domestic Product, Percent Change, 2021–2022

Rank	State	Percent
	United States....................	2.1
1	Idaho...............................	4.9
2	Tennessee........................	4.3
3	Florida.............................	4.0
4	Nevada.............................	3.7
5	Texas...............................	3.4
6	Colorado..........................	3.2
6	New York..........................	3.2
6	North Carolina..................	3.2
9	Oregon.............................	3.0
10	Georgia............................	2.8
10	Vermont............................	2.8
12	Utah.................................	2.7
13	Arkansas..........................	2.6
13	New Jersey.......................	2.6
15	Arizona............................	2.5
16	Connecticut.......................	2.4
16	South Carolina..................	2.4
18	Illinois.............................	2.3
19	Delaware..........................	2.1
19	Pennsylvania....................	2.1
21	Massachusetts..................	2.0
22	Indiana.............................	1.9
23	District of Columbia..........	1.8
23	Kentucky..........................	1.8
23	Maine...............................	1.8
23	Michigan...........................	1.8
27	Missouri...........................	1.7
28	Wisconsin.........................	1.7
29	Alabama...........................	1.6
29	Kansas.............................	1.6
29	Montana...........................	1.6
32	Ohio.................................	1.5
32	Rhode Island.....................	1.5
32	Virginia............................	1.5
35	Hawaii..............................	1.2
35	Minnesota.........................	1.2
35	Washington.......................	1.2
38	Nebraska..........................	1.1
38	New Mexico.......................	1.1
40	South Dakota....................	0.5
41	California.........................	0.4
41	West Virginia.....................	0.4
43	Mississippi.......................	0.2
44	Maryland..........................	Z
44	New Hampshire..................	Z
46	Wyoming..........................	-0.1
47	Oklahoma.........................	-1.0
48	North Dakota.....................	-1.3
49	Iowa.................................	-1.5
50	Louisiana..........................	-1.8
51	Alaska.............................	-2.4

Z = Value greater than zero but less than half of the unit shown.

Median Household Income, 2021

Rank	State	Dollars
	United States....................	69,717
1	Maryland..........................	90,203
2	District of Columbia..........	90,088
3	Massachusetts..................	89,645
4	New Jersey.......................	89,296
5	New Hampshire..................	88,465
6	California.........................	84,907
7	Hawaii..............................	84,857
8	Washington.......................	84,247
9	Connecticut.......................	83,771
10	Colorado..........................	82,254
11	Virginia............................	80,963
12	Utah.................................	79,449
13	Alaska.............................	77,845
14	Minnesota.........................	77,720
15	New York..........................	74,314
16	Rhode Island.....................	74,008
17	Vermont............................	72,431
18	Illinois.............................	72,205
19	Oregon.............................	71,562
20	Delaware..........................	71,091
21	Arizona............................	69,056
22	Pennsylvania....................	68,957
23	Wisconsin.........................	67,125
24	Texas...............................	66,963
25	Nebraska..........................	66,817
26	Georgia............................	66,559
27	North Dakota.....................	66,519
28	Idaho...............................	66,474
29	Nevada.............................	66,274
30	South Dakota....................	66,143
31	Iowa.................................	65,600
32	Wyoming..........................	65,204
33	Maine...............................	64,767
34	Kansas.............................	64,124
35	Michigan...........................	63,498
36	Montana...........................	63,249
37	Florida.............................	63,062
38	Indiana.............................	62,743
39	Ohio.................................	62,262
40	North Carolina..................	61,972
41	Missouri...........................	61,847
42	Tennessee........................	59,695
43	South Carolina..................	59,318
44	Oklahoma.........................	55,826
45	Kentucky..........................	55,573
46	New Mexico.......................	53,992
47	Alabama...........................	53,913
48	Arkansas..........................	52,528
49	Louisiana..........................	52,087
50	West Virginia.....................	51,248
51	Mississippi.......................	48,716

Median Family Income, 2021

Rank	State	Dollars
	United States..........................	85,806
1	District of Columbia	136,184
2	Massachusetts........................	113,822
3	Maryland	110,978
4	New Jersey	110,102
5	New Hampshire......................	108,208
6	Connecticut............................	106,576
7	Washington............................	102,178
8	Colorado	102,073
9	Hawaii	100,890
10	Virginia	100,763
11	Minnesota	99,567
12	California................................	97,388
13	Rhode Island..........................	97,304
14	Alaska	95,344
15	New York................................	92,454
16	Utah	92,192
17	Illinois	90,861
18	Vermont	90,556
19	North Dakota..........................	89,504
20	Nebraska	88,484
21	Oregon	88,085
22	Pennsylvania..........................	87,500
23	Delaware	87,132
24	Wisconsin	85,810
25	Iowa	84,908
26	Wyoming	83,789
27	Maine	82,842
28	Kansas	82,637
29	South Dakota	82,562
30	Arizona...................................	81,622
31	Ohio	80,760
32	Georgia	80,731
33	Michigan	80,523
34	Texas......................................	80,304
35	Idaho......................................	79,993
36	Montana..................................	79,958
37	Indiana	79,243
38	Missouri	79,084
39	Nevada	78,526
40	North Carolina........................	77,601
41	Florida	76,199
42	Tennessee	74,709
43	South Carolina	73,901
44	Alabama	71,006
45	Kentucky	70,060
46	Oklahoma	69,967
47	New Mexico	67,786
48	Louisiana	67,045
49	West Virginia..........................	66,669
50	Arkansas	66,148
51	Mississippi.............................	64,035

Persons Below Poverty Level, 2021

Rank	State	Percent
	United States...........................	12.8
1	Louisiana	19.6
2	Mississippi..............................	19.4
3	New Mexico	18.4
4	West Virginia	16.8
5	District of Columbia	16.5
5	Kentucky	16.5
7	Arkansas	16.3
8	Alabama	16.1
9	Oklahoma	15.6
10	South Carolina	14.6
11	Texas......................................	14.2
12	Nevada	14.1
13	Georgia	14.0
14	New York................................	13.9
15	Tennessee	13.6
16	North Carolina........................	13.4
16	Ohio	13.4
18	Florida	13.1
18	Michigan	13.1
20	Arizona...................................	12.8
21	Missouri	12.7
22	California................................	12.3
22	South Dakota	12.3
24	Indiana	12.2
24	Oregon	12.2
26	Illinois	12.1
26	Pennsylvania..........................	12.1
28	Montana..................................	11.9
29	Kansas	11.7
30	Delaware	11.6
31	Maine	11.5
32	Rhode Island..........................	11.4
32	Wyoming	11.4
34	Hawaii	11.2
35	Iowa	11.1
35	North Dakota..........................	11.1
37	Idaho......................................	11.0
38	Nebraska	10.8
38	Wisconsin	10.8
40	Alaska	10.5
41	Massachusetts........................	10.4
42	Maryland	10.3
42	Vermont	10.3
44	New Jersey	10.2
44	Virginia...................................	10.2
46	Connecticut............................	10.1
47	Washington............................	9.9
48	Colorado	9.7
49	Minnesota	9.3
50	Utah	8.6
51	New Hampshire.......................	7.2

Persons Under 18 Years Old Below Poverty Level, 2021

Rank	State	Percent
	United States...........................	16.9
1	Mississippi..............................	27.7
2	Louisiana	26.9
3	District of Columbia	23.9
3	New Mexico	23.9
5	Arkansas	22.4
6	Alabama	22.2
7	Kentucky	22.1
8	Oklahoma	21.2
9	West Virginia	20.7
10	Georgia	20.2
11	South Carolina	20.1
12	Texas......................................	19.6
13	Nevada	18.8
14	Ohio	18.6
15	New York................................	18.5
16	North Carolina........................	18.1
16	Tennessee	18.1
18	Florida	17.8
18	Michigan	17.8
20	Arizona...................................	17.3
21	Pennsylvania..........................	16.9
22	Delaware	16.8
23	Missouri	16.2
24	Illinois	16.0
24	Indiana	16.0
26	California................................	15.8
27	Maine	15.1
28	Rhode Island..........................	15.0
29	South Dakota	14.6
30	New Jersey	14.2
31	Montana..................................	14.1
32	Maryland	14.0
33	Hawaii	13.6
34	Oregon	13.5
35	Kansas	13.4
35	Wisconsin	13.4
35	Wyoming	13.4
38	Idaho......................................	13.1
38	Virginia...................................	13.1
40	Connecticut............................	12.7
41	Massachusetts........................	12.6
42	Iowa	12.5
42	Nebraska	12.5
44	Alaska	12.4
45	Washington............................	12.0
46	Colorado	11.8
47	Minnesota	10.8
48	North Dakota..........................	10.5
49	Vermont	10.4
50	New Hampshire.......................	9.2
51	Utah	8.1

Per Capita Energy-Related CO2 Emissions, 2021

Rank	State	Metric Tons of CO$_2$
	United States................	14.8
1	Wyoming	94.3
2	North Dakota	72.7
3	Alaska	53.0
4	West Virginia	49.5
5	Louisiana	40.8
6	Montana	25.8
7	Kentucky	24.7
8	Indiana	24.4
9	Nebraska	24.0
10	Iowa	22.9
11	Texas	22.4
12	Oklahoma............	22.0
13	New Mexico	21.7
14	Alabama	21.5
15	Mississippi	21.4
16	Arkansas	20.5
17	Kansas	20.3
18	Missouri	19.0
19	Utah	18.6
20	South Dakota	16.9
21	Ohio	16.5
22	Pennsylvania	16.4
23	Wisconsin	15.7
24	Michigan	14.7
24	Colorado	14.7
26	Minnesota	14.6
27	Illinois	14.5
28	South Carolina	13.4
29	Tennessee	13.3
30	Delaware	12.9
31	Nevada	12.5
32	Hawaii	12.0
33	Georgia	11.5
34	Arizona	11.4
35	Virginia	11.3
36	North Carolina............	10.9
37	Idaho............	10.8
38	Maine	10.5
39	Florida	10.4
40	Connecticut............	10.1
41	Rhode Island	9.7
42	New Jersey	9.6
42	New Hampshire............	9.6
44	Washington	9.5
45	Oregon	9.1
46	Vermont	8.6
47	Maryland	8.5
48	California	8.3
49	Massachusetts	8.0
50	New York............	7.9
51	District of Columbia	3.8

Homeownership Rate, 2022

Rank	State	Percent
	United States................	65.8
1	West Virginia............	78.6
2	Wyoming	75.3
3	Minnesota	75.1
4	Delaware	74.9
4	Maine	74.9
6	South Carolina	74.7
7	New Hampshire............	74.6
8	Michigan	74.0
9	Iowa	73.8
10	Mississippi	73.1
11	Vermont	72.7
12	Indiana	72.6
13	Alabama	72.1
14	Maryland	71.8
15	Kentucky	71.4
16	Idaho............	71.3
17	Utah	71.2
18	New Mexico	71.1
19	South Dakota	70.8
20	Pennsylvania	70.7
21	Missouri	70.6
22	Wisconsin	70.0
23	Louisiana	69.6
24	Kansas	69.0
24	Nebraska	69.0
26	Oklahoma	68.5
27	Montana	68.3
28	Arizona	68.1
29	Colorado	67.4
29	Virginia	67.4
31	Florida	67.3
31	Tennessee	67.3
33	Arkansas	66.8
34	Illinois	66.7
35	Washington	66.6
36	Ohio	66.0
37	North Carolina............	65.9
38	Rhode Island	65.8
39	North Dakota	65.4
40	Alaska	65.1
41	Oregon	64.9
42	Connecticut............	64.8
43	Georgia	64.7
44	New Jersey	64.2
45	Texas............	63.6
46	Massachusetts	61.2
47	Nevada	60.3
48	Hawaii	59.2
49	California	55.3
50	New York............	53.9
51	District of Columbia	42.3

One-Unit Detached or Attached Housing Units, Percent of Total Housing Units, 2021

Rank	State	Percent
	United States................	69.3
1	Indiana	79.1
2	Iowa	78.8
2	Kansas	78.8
4	Idaho	78.1
5	Michigan	77.5
5	Nebraska	77.5
7	Pennsylvania	77.2
8	Oklahoma	77.1
9	Missouri	76.3
10	Utah	76.0
11	Delaware	75.8
12	West Virginia	75.5
13	Ohio	75.3
14	Wyoming	75.2
15	Minnesota	74.9
16	Montana	74.3
16	Tennessee	74.3
18	Arkansas	74.1
19	Maryland	74.0
20	Virginia	73.9
21	Alabama	73.5
22	South Dakota	73.4
23	Georgia	73.0
24	Mississippi............	72.8
25	Kentucky	71.9
26	Alaska	71.6
27	Arizona	71.5
28	Wisconsin	71.4
29	Louisiana	71.3
30	Maine	71.2
30	Vermont	71.2
32	North Carolina	71.1
33	Colorado	71.0
34	South Carolina	70.5
35	New Mexico	69.7
36	New Hampshire............	69.5
37	Oregon	69.3
38	Texas	69.2
39	Nevada	68.0
40	Washington	67.8
41	Connecticut............	67.0
42	Illinois	66.3
43	North Dakota	65.8
44	California	65.6
45	Florida	65.5
46	Hawaii	65.1
47	New Jersey	63.8
48	Rhode Island	60.7
49	Massachusetts	58.1
50	New York............	48.3
51	District of Columbia	34.7

Percent of Population Not Covered by Private or Public Health Insurance, 2021

Rank	State	Percent
	United States	8.6
1	Texas	18.0
2	Oklahoma	13.8
3	Georgia	12.6
4	Wyoming	12.2
5	Florida	12.1
6	Mississippi	11.9
7	Nevada	11.6
8	Alaska	11.4
9	Arizona	10.7
10	North Carolina	10.4
11	New Mexico	10.0
11	South Carolina	10.0
11	Tennessee	10.0
14	Alabama	9.9
15	South Dakota	9.5
16	Missouri	9.4
17	Arkansas	9.2
17	Kansas	9.2
19	Utah	9.0
20	Idaho	8.8
21	Montana	8.2
22	Colorado	8.0
23	North Dakota	7.9
24	Louisiana	7.6
25	Indiana	7.5
26	New Jersey	7.2
27	Nebraska	7.1
28	California	7.0
28	Illinois	7.0
30	Virginia	6.8
31	Ohio	6.5
32	Washington	6.4
33	Maryland	6.1
33	Oregon	6.1
33	West Virginia	6.1
36	Delaware	5.7
36	Kentucky	5.7
36	Maine	5.7
39	Pennsylvania	5.5
40	Wisconsin	5.4
41	Connecticut	5.2
41	New York	5.2
43	New Hampshire	5.1
44	Michigan	5.0
45	Iowa	4.8
46	Minnesota	4.5
47	Rhode Island	4.3
48	Hawaii	3.9
49	District of Columbia	3.7
49	Vermont	3.7
51	Massachusetts	2.5

Traffic Fatalities Per 100,000 Population, 2021

Rank	State	Rate
	United States	12.9
1	Mississippi	26.2
2	South Carolina	23.1
3	Arkansas	22.9
4	New Mexico	22.7
5	Montana	21.6
6	Louisiana	21.0
7	Alabama	19.5
8	Oklahoma	19.1
9	Tennessee	19.0
9	Wyoming	19.0
11	Kentucky	17.9
12	Florida	17.1
13	Georgia	16.7
14	Missouri	16.5
14	South Dakota	16.5
16	Arizona	16.2
17	North Carolina	15.7
17	West Virginia	15.7
19	Texas	15.2
20	Kansas	14.4
21	Idaho	14.2
22	Oregon	14.1
23	Indiana	13.7
24	Delaware	13.5
25	North Dakota	13.0
26	Nevada	12.2
27	Colorado	11.9
28	Ohio	11.5
29	Vermont	11.4
30	Michigan	11.3
30	Nebraska	11.3
32	Virginia	11.2
33	Iowa	11.1
33	Maine	11.1
35	California	10.9
36	Illinois	10.5
36	Wisconsin	10.5
38	Utah	9.8
39	Pennsylvania	9.5
40	Alaska	9.1
40	Maryland	9.1
42	Washington	8.7
43	Minnesota	8.5
43	New Hampshire	8.5
45	Connecticut	8.2
46	New Jersey	7.5
47	Hawaii	6.5
48	District of Columbia	6.1
49	Massachusetts	6.0
50	New York	5.8
51	Rhode Island	5.7

ALABAMA

Facts and Figures

Location: Southeastern United States; bordered on the N by Tennessee, on the E by Georgia, on the S by Florida and the Gulf of Mexico, and on the W by Mississippi

Area: 52,420 sq. mi. (135,765 sq. km.); rank—30th

Population: 5,074,296 (2022 est.); rank—24th

Principal Cities: capital—Montgomery; largest—Birmingham

Statehood: December 14, 1819; 22nd state

U.S. Congress: 2 senators, 7 representatives

State Motto: *Audemus jura nostra defendere* ("We dare defend our rights")

State Song: "Alabama"

State Nicknames: The Yellowhammer State; The Heart of Dixie; The Cotton State

Abbreviations: AL; Ala.

State Symbols: flower—camellia; tree—Southern longleaf pine; bird—yellowhammer

At a Glance

- With an increase in population of 6.2 percent, Alabama ranked 25th among the states in growth from 2010 to 2022.

- Alabama's per capita personal income in 2022 was $50,637, ranking 49th in the nation. The state's median household income of $53,913 ranked 47th in the nation in 2021.

- In 2022, Alabama had 56.0 full-time equivalent state and local government employees per 1,000 residents, a rate that ranked 13th in the nation.

- In 2021, 16.1 percent of Alabama residents lived below the poverty level, a percentage that ranked 8th in the nation.

- Alabama's drug overdose death rate in 2021 was 30.1 per 100,000 residents, compared to 32.4 for the entire nation. The homicide rate in 2021 was 15.9 deaths per 100,000 population, which was the 4th highest in the country.

Table AL-1. Population by Age, Sex, Race, and Hispanic Origin

(Number, percent, except where noted.)

Sex, age, race, and Hispanic origin	2010	2020	2022	Percent change, 2010–2022
Total Population...	4,779,736	5,024,356	5,074,296	6.2
Percent of total U.S. population	1.548	1.516	1.5	X
Sex				
Male...	2,320,188	2,447,300	2,467,360	6.3
Female...	2,459,548	2,577,056	2,606,936	6.0
Age				
Under 5 years...	304,957	293,152	290,299	-4.8
Under 18 years...	1,132,459	1,112,293	1,111,562	-1.8
18 to 64 years...	2,989,485	3,041,563	3,048,001	2.0
65 years and over..	657,792	870,500	914,733	39.1
Median age (years)	37.9	39.3	39.4	4.0
Race and Hispanic Origin				
One race				
White	3,362,877	3,464,538	3,494,189	3.9
Black	1,259,224	1,350,841	1,358,620	7.9
American Indian and Alaska Native	32,903	35,078	36,325	10.4
Asian...	55,240	77,142	80,615	45.9
Native Hawaiian or Other Pacific Islander	5,208	5,386	5,556	6.7
Two or more races	64,284	91,371	98,991	54.0
Hispanic (of any race)..	185,602	231,419	250,253	34.8

NOTE: Population figures for 2022 are July 1 estimates. The 2010 and 2020 estimates are taken from the respective censuses.
X = Not applicable.
- = Zero or rounds to zero.

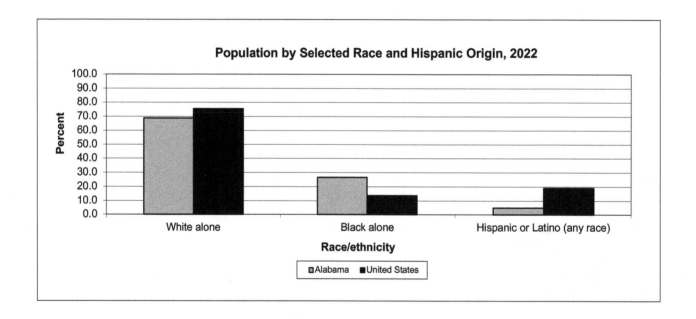

Table AL-2. Marital Status

(Number, percent distribution.)

Sex, age, and marital status	2000	2010	2021
Males, 15 Years and Over	1,666,798	1,844,661	1,973,279
Never married	26.7	32.5	34.4
Now married, except separated..	59.0	50.6	49.3
Separated..	1.8	2.5	1.7
Widowed..	2.8	3.0	3.3
Divorced..	9.8	11.4	11.4
Females, 15 Years and Over	1,847,401	2,004,450	2,140,237
Never married	21.4	26.1	29.3
Now married, except separated..	52.5	45.9	45.1
Separated..	2.5	3.1	2.2
Widowed..	12.4	11.2	10.5
Divorced..	11.2	13.6	12.9

Table AL-3. Households and Housing Characteristics

(Number, percent, dollars.)

Item	2000	2010	2021	Average annual percent change, 2010–2021
Total Households...	1,737,080	1,815,152	1,967,559	0.8
Family households	1,215,968	1,227,884	1,271,383	0.3
Married-couple family	906,916	868,946	904,392	0.4
Other family	309,052	358,938	366,991	0.2
Male householder, no wife present..............	62,586	79,308	90,366	1.3
Female householder, no husband present.......	246,466	279,630	276,625	-0.1
Nonfamily households	521,112	587,268	696,176	1.7
Householder living alone................................	453,898	511,708	607,180	1.7
Householder not living alone...........................	67,214	75,560	88,996	1.6
Housing Characteristics				
Total housing units...	1,963,711	2,174,428	2,313,616	0.6
Occupied housing units	1,737,080	1,815,152	1,967,559	0.8
Owner occupied	1,258,705	1,272,846	1,377,932	0.8
Renter occupied	478,375	542,306	589,627	0.8
Average household size......................................	2.49	2.57	2.50	-0.2
Financial Characteristics				
Median gross rent of renter-occupied housing	447	667	861	2.6
Median monthly owner costs for housing units with a mortgage	816	1,130	1,223	0.7
Median value of owner-occupied housing units........	85,100	123,900	172,800	3.6

Table AL-4. Migration, Origin, and Language

(Number, percent.)

Characteristic	State 2021	U.S. 2021
Residence 1 Year Ago		
Population 1 year and over	4,989,797	328,464,538
Same house	88.0	87.2
Different house in the U.S.	11.7	12.3
Same county	6.6	6.7
Different county	5.1	5.7
Same state	2.8	3.3
Different state	2.3	2.4
Abroad	0.3	0.4
Place of Birth		
Native born	4,863,363	286,623,642
Male	48.5	49.7
Female	51.5	50.3
Foreign born	176,514	45,270,103
Male	49.6	48.7
Female	50.4	51.3
Foreign born; naturalized U.S. citizen..	74,431	24,044,083
Male	45.7	46.4
Female	54.3	53.6
Foreign born; not a U.S. citizen..	102,083	21,226,020
Male	52.5	51.2
Female	47.5	48.8
Entered 2010 or later	34.4	28.1
Entered 2000 to 2009	28.9	23.7
Entered before 2000..	36.7	48.2
World Region of Birth, Foreign		
Foreign-born population, excluding population born at sea	176,514	45,269,644
Europe	13.2	10.7
Asia	29.8	31.0
Africa	4.2	5.7
Oceania	0.3	0.6
Latin America...	49.1	50.1
North America	3.4	1.7
Language Spoken at Home and Ability to Speak English		
Population 5 years and over...	4,749,786	313,232,500
English only	94.9	78.4
Language other than English...	5.1	21.6
Speaks English less than "very well"..	2.1	8.3

Table AL-5. Median Income and Poverty Status, 2021

(Number, percent, except as noted.)

Characteristic	State		U.S.	
	Number	Percent	Number	Percent
Median Income				
Households (dollars)...	53,913	X	69,717	X
Families (dollars)	71,006	X	85,806	X
Below Poverty Level (All People)	794,326	16.1	41,393,176	12.8
Sex				
Male	338,276	14.2	18,518,155	11.6
Female	456,050	17.9	22,875,021	13.9
Age				
Under 18 years..	245,003	22.2	12,243,219	16.9
Related children under 18 years..	242,070	22.0	11,985,424	16.6
18 to 64 years...	450,180	15.3	23,526,341	11.9
65 years and over..	99,143	11.4	5,623,616	10.3

X = Not applicable.

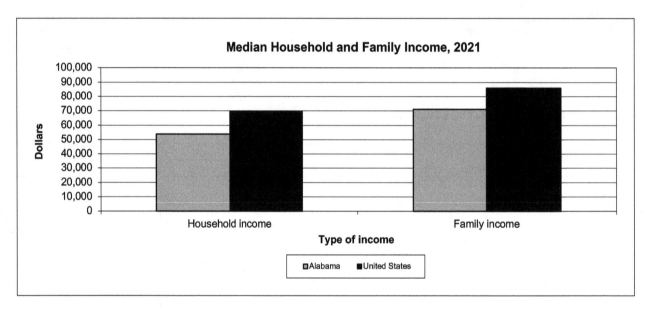

Table AL-6. Health Insurance Coverage Status for the Civilian Noninstitutionalized Population and Children Under 19 Years of Age

(Number; percent.)

Item	2011	2012	2013	2014	2015	2016	2017	2018	2019	2020 [2]	2021
Civilian Noninstitutionalized Population	4,720,067	4,741,698	4,755,381	4,767,383	4,781,070	4,782,529	4,793,512	4,810,094	4,822,514	4,813,429	4,957,633
Covered by Private or Public Insurance											
Number...	4,046,103	4,109,199	4,109,946	4,188,214	4,296,799	4,347,556	4,344,586	4,328,835	4,353,613	4,357,884	4,469,062
Percent..	85.7	86.7	86.4	87.9	89.9	90.9	90.6	90.0	90.3	90.5	90.1
Uninsured											
Number...	673,964	632,499	645,435	579,169	484,271	434,973	448,926	481,259	468,901	455,545	488,571
Percent..	14.3	13.3	13.6	12.1	10.1	9.1	9.4	10.0	9.7	9.5	9.9
Percent in the U.S. not covered..........................	15.1	14.8	14.5	11.7	9.4	8.6	8.7	8.9	9.2	8.7	8.6
Children Under 19 Years of Age[1]	1,122,125	1,123,000	1,107,844	1,106,847	1,106,716	1,098,052	1,169,489	1,162,987	1,154,392	1,160,135	1,190,756
Covered by Private or Public Insurance											
Number...	1,063,064	1,077,390	1,059,663	1,064,425	1,072,948	1,071,320	1,133,440	1,122,269	1,114,232	1,123,421	1,143,511
Percent..	94.7	95.9	95.7	96.2	96.9	97.6	96.9	96.5	96.5	96.8	96.0
Uninsured											
Number...	59,061	45,610	48,181	42,422	33,768	26,732	36,049	40,718	40,160	36,714	47,245
Percent..	5.3	4.1	4.3	3.8	3.1	2.4	3.1	3.5	3.5	3.2	4.0
Percent in the U.S. not covered..........................	7.5	7.2	7.1	6.0	4.8	4.5	5.0	5.2	5.7	5.2	5.4

[1] Data for years prior to 2017 is for individuals under 18 years of age.
[2] 2020 ACS 5-Year estimates. 1-Year estimates were not released for 2020 due to the impact of COVID-19 on data collection that year. Data is not comparable to previous years, which are based on 1-year estimates.

Table AL-7. Employment Status by Demographic Group, 2022

(Numbers in thousands, percent.)

Characteristic	Civilian noninstitutional population	Civilian labor force		Employed		Unemployed	
		Number	Percent of population	Number	Percent of population	Number	Percent of population
Total...	4,004	2,293	57.3	2,235	55.8	59	2.6
Sex							
Male..	1,904	1,217	63.9	1,190	62.5	27	2.2
Female	2,100	1,077	51.3	1,045	49.8	32	3.0
Race, Sex, and Hispanic Origin							
White	2,818	1,610	57.1	1,576	55.9	34	2.1
Male..	1,364	893	65.5	877	64.3	16	1.8
Female	1,454	717	49.3	699	48.0	18	2.5
Black or African American.................	1,042	597	57.3	574	55.1	23	3.9
Male..	464	271	58.5	261	56.4	10	3.7
Female	578	326	56.4	313	54.1	13	4.0
Hispanic or Latino ethnicity[1]	190	132	69.4	127	67.2	4	3.2
Male..	NA	NA	NA	NA	NA	NA	NA
Female	NA	NA	NA	NA	NA	NA	NA
Age							
16 to 19 years................................	NA	NA	NA	NA	NA	NA	NA
20 to 24 years................................	292	199	68.3	190	65.0	9	4.7
25 to 34 years................................	644	509	79.0	494	76.7	15	3.0
35 to 44 years................................	623	492	79.0	482	77.5	10	2.0
45 to 54 years................................	656	500	76.2	490	74.7	10	1.9
55 to 64 years................................	646	375	58.0	369	57.1	6	1.5
65 years and over	871	136	15.6	133	15.2	3	2.2

NOTE: Data in Table 7 are from the Current Population Survey (CPS) and do not match the estimates in Table 8. See notes and definitions for further information.
[1] May be of any race.
NA = Not available.

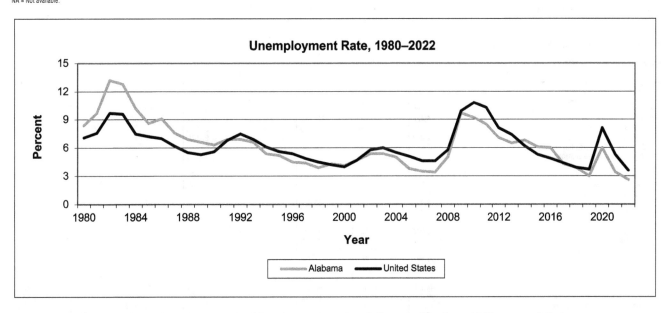

Table AL-8. Employment Status of the Civilian Noninstitutional Population Age 16 Years and Over

(Number, percent.)

Year	Civilian labor force	Civilian participation rate	Employed	Unemployed	Unemployment rate
2010..	301,893	70.1	280,953	20,940	6.9
2011..	302,932	69.3	284,273	18,659	6.2
2012..	303,748	68.4	287,110	16,638	5.5
2013..	302,201	67.4	287,792	14,409	4.8
2014..	302,865	67.3	289,694	13,171	4.3
2015..	301,608	66.8	288,894	12,714	4.2
2016..	300,546	66.6	284,439	16,107	5.4
2017..	293,802	65.9	281,164	12,638	4.3
2018..	292,781	65.7	280,909	11,872	4.1
2019..	294,380	65.8	283,377	11,003	3.7
2020..	293,722	65.3	276,739	16,983	5.8
2021..	290,404	64.1	277,372	13,032	4.5
2022..	2,286,028	57.0	2,226,670	59,358	2.6

Table AL-9. Employment and Average Wages by Industry

(Estimates are based on the 2012 North American Industry Classification System [NAICS].)

Industry	2014	2015	2016	2017	2018	2019	2020	2021
				Number of Jobs				
Wage and Salary Employment by Industry........................	1,996,182	2,024,720	2,049,658	2,072,223	2,098,185	2,127,180	2,044,978	2,096,405
Farm Wage and Salary Employment...............................	5,318	7,451	7,213	9,217	7,242	7,189	6,638	6,370
Nonfarm Wage and Salary Employment..........................	1,990,864	2,017,269	2,042,445	2,063,006	2,090,943	2,119,991	2,038,340	2,090,035
Private wage and salary employment.............................	1,590,896	1,618,569	1,641,038	1,659,832	1,685,234	1,710,870	1,633,159	1,683,008
Forestry, fishing, and related activities........................	8,875	8,938	8,925	8,785	8,900	9,463	8,999	8,604
Mining...	7,549	6,828	5,352	6,031	6,295	6,379	5,863	5,033
Utilities...	14,293	14,437	14,170	13,735	13,774	13,303	13,025	12,907
Construction...	81,857	83,802	86,254	87,258	91,361	95,784	95,115	96,485
Manufacturing...	253,248	258,085	260,646	263,808	266,915	269,159	258,430	264,724
Durable goods manufacturing..................................	165,133	169,191	170,054	171,555	173,814	175,196	168,681	175,221
Nondurable goods manufacturing.............................	88,115	88,894	90,592	92,253	93,101	93,963	89,749	89,503
Wholesale trade...	73,150	73,926	74,025	73,890	74,187	74,680	72,902	73,812
Retail trade...	228,885	232,361	234,301	232,838	232,565	232,380	226,558	233,595
Transportation and warehousing................................	59,202	59,792	59,991	60,738	62,524	65,261	65,330	77,776
Information...	21,962	21,543	20,701	20,818	21,017	21,299	19,297	19,993
Finance and insurance	74,309	74,795	75,063	76,392	75,968	76,698	77,471	77,508
Real estate and rental and leasing..............................	22,039	22,338	22,845	23,258	23,843	24,395	23,851	24,511
Professional, scientific, and technical services	95,325	96,903	98,999	101,786	105,898	108,152	109,340	113,772
Management of companies and enterprises....................	15,130	15,432	16,467	16,116	15,609	16,048	15,807	15,833
Administrative and waste services..............................	113,606	117,874	119,940	123,019	125,484	128,503	119,232	124,682
Educational services...	29,599	29,691	30,392	30,294	29,692	29,759	26,637	27,837
Health care and social assistance..............................	205,157	209,600	214,778	218,050	221,732	226,551	218,492	219,532
Arts, entertainment, and recreation............................	16,990	16,906	19,019	20,062	21,394	21,630	17,867	19,619
Accommodation and food services..............................	168,368	174,090	179,626	183,518	185,807	187,940	161,758	170,055
Other services, except public administration.................	101,352	101,228	99,544	99,436	102,269	103,486	97,185	96,730
Government and government enterprises.......................	399,968	398,700	401,407	403,174	405,709	409,121	405,181	407,027
				Dollars				
Average Wages and Salaries by Industry	42,653	43,632	44,160	45,308	46,718	48,169	51,313	53,558
Average Farm Wages and Salaries	23,427	22,978	19,459	14,836	19,586	14,571	14,507	20,218
Average Nonfarm Wages and Salaries	42,704	43,708	44,248	45,445	46,812	48,283	51,433	53,660
Average private wages and salaries..............................	42,068	43,140	43,659	44,867	46,330	47,816	51,120	53,536
Forestry, fishing, and related activities........................	35,336	36,652	38,235	38,957	39,869	40,933	43,732	45,947
Mining...	80,782	80,450	70,500	76,990	84,615	83,690	83,433	85,901
Utilities...	88,427	95,522	100,657	104,422	108,312	119,165	120,954	121,468
Construction...	47,811	48,728	50,520	52,222	53,941	56,168	59,149	61,468
Manufacturing...	52,849	53,519	54,226	55,171	57,075	58,542	60,401	62,597
Durable goods manufacturing..................................	55,057	55,744	56,609	57,567	59,620	61,210	62,599	64,842
Nondurable goods manufacturing.............................	48,709	49,283	49,755	50,717	52,323	53,569	56,270	58,202
Wholesale trade...	59,953	62,110	62,828	64,485	66,691	68,828	72,027	78,063
Retail trade...	25,873	26,506	27,018	27,569	28,330	29,176	31,545	34,071
Transportation and warehousing................................	46,116	47,341	47,458	48,986	50,947	51,999	53,296	51,356
Information...	53,923	55,771	57,095	58,870	60,029	62,883	69,274	75,016
Finance and insurance	67,934	71,769	71,115	73,915	77,594	79,268	84,516	89,263
Real estate and rental and leasing..............................	40,047	41,559	42,222	43,817	44,602	47,371	49,846	54,080
Professional, scientific, and technical services	71,517	73,321	74,636	76,651	78,854	81,165	87,358	88,141
Management of companies and enterprises....................	85,374	87,533	91,142	102,206	103,433	105,118	102,912	109,065
Administrative and waste services..............................	27,121	27,431	27,784	28,415	29,370	30,737	33,198	36,236
Educational services...	26,112	26,888	27,323	27,378	28,135	29,074	32,843	31,663
Health care and social assistance..............................	44,176	45,495	45,603	46,505	47,304	48,606	51,913	54,938
Arts, entertainment, and recreation............................	20,329	21,420	20,572	20,394	20,998	22,463	23,265	25,588
Accommodation and food services..............................	16,593	17,043	17,542	18,027	19,014	19,794	19,649	23,580
Other services, except public administration.................	30,811	32,033	33,227	34,557	35,565	36,502	40,058	41,538
Government and government enterprises.......................	45,236	46,014	46,654	47,825	48,812	50,237	52,694	54,174

Table AL-10. Employment Characteristics by Family Type

(Number, percent.)

Family type and labor force status	2019 Total	2019 Families with own children under 18 years	2020[1] Total	2020[1] Families with own children under 18 years	2021 Total	2021 Families with own children under 18 years
All Families...	1,237,883	461,753	1,234,552	479,570	1,271,383	490,580
FAMILY TYPE AND LABOR FORCE STATUS						
Opposite-Sex Married-Couple Families...................................	892,050	298,328	888,847	314,225	897,745	313,578
Both husband and wife in labor force...............................	45.4	65.7	46.3	65.8	46.4	65.7
Husband in labor force, wife not in labor force	22.9	26.9	22.9	27.3	22.4	27.8
Wife in labor force, husband not in labor force........................	8.7	4.8	8.6	4.6	8.8	4.4
Both husband and wife not in labor force............................	22.3	2.1	22.2	2.3	22.4	2.1
Other Families	345,833	163,425	340,604	164,286	366,991	175,589
Female householder, no spouse present	76.9	78.0	77.1	80.0	75.4	77.9
In labor force...	49.7	63.3	48.4	63.8	48.1	62.7
Not in labor force	27.2	14.7	28.7	16.2	27.3	15.1
Male householder, no spouse present...............................	23.1	22.0	22.9	20.0	24.6	22.1
In labor force...	16.0	18.9	15.8	17.3	17.2	19.7
Not in labor force	7.1	3.1	7.1	2.7	7.4	2.5

[1] 2020 ACS 5-Year estimates. 1-Year estimates were not released for 2020 due to the impact of COVID-19 on data collection that year. Data is not comparable to previous years, which are based on 1-year estimates.

Table AL-11. School Enrollment and Educational Attainment, 2021

(Number, percent.)

Item	State	U.S.
Enrollment		
Total population 3 years and over, enrolled in school	1,177,441	79,453,524
Enrolled in nursery school or preschool (percent)...	5.4	5.2
Enrolled in kindergarten (percent)...	5.2	5.0
Enrolled in elementary school, grades 1-8 (percent)..	42.3	41.3
Enrolled in high school, grades 9-12 (percent)..	22.3	21.8
Enrolled in college or graduate school (percent)...	24.9	26.7
Attainment		
Total population 25 years and over	3,451,208	228,193,464
Less than ninth grade (percent)..	3.7	4.8
9th to 12th grade, no diploma (percent)...	8.4	5.9
High school graduate, including equivalency (percent)...	31.3	26.3
Some college, no degree (percent)	20.4	19.3
Associate's degree (percent)..	8.8	8.8
Bachelor's degree (percent)	16.6	21.2
Graduate or professional degree (percent)..	10.9	13.8
High school graduate or higher (percent)..	87.9	89.4
Bachelor's degree or higher (percent)...	27.4	35.0

Table AL-12. Public School Characteristics and Educational Indicators

(Number, percent; data derived from National Center of Education Statistics.)

Item	State	U.S.
Public Elementary and Secondary Schools		
Number of regular school districts, 2019-20..	139	13,349
Number of operational schools, 2019-20...	1,533	98,469
Percent charter schools	0.3	7.7
Total public school enrollment, Fall 2021..	748,274	49,433,092
Percent charter school enrollment	0.5	7.5
Student-teacher ratio, Fall 2019	17.7	15.9
Expenditures per student (unadjusted dollars), 2019-20	10,140	13,489
Four-year adjusted cohort graduation rate (ACGR), 2019-20201..	90.6	86.5
Students eligible for free or reduced-price lunch (percent), 2019-20..	55.0	52.1
English language learners (percent), Fall 2020	4.6	10.3
Students age 3 to 21 served under IDEA, part B (percent), 2021-22	12.7	14.7

Public Schools by Type, 2019-20	Number	Percent of state public schools
Total number of schools..	1,533	100.0
Special education..	81	5.3
Vocational education...	68	4.4
Alternative education..	62	4.0

[1] Adjusted Cohort Graduation Rates (ACGR) differ from Averaged Freshmen Graduation Rates (AFGR).
NA = Not available.

Table AL-13. Reported Voting and Registration of the Voting-Age Population, November 2022

(Numbers in thousands, percent.)

Item	Total population	Total citizen population	Registered			Voted		
			Total registered	Percent registered (total population)	Percent registered (total citizen population)	Total voted	Percent voted (total population)	Percent voted (total citizen population)
U.S. Total	255,457	233,546	161,422	63.2	69.1	121,916	47.7	52.2
State Total................	3,857	3,716	2,499	64.8	67.3	1,688	43.8	45.4
Sex								
Male	1,823	1,737	1,143	62.7	65.8	792	43.4	45.6
Female	2,034	1,979	1,357	66.7	68.5	896	44.0	45.3
Race								
White alone................	2,716	2,616	1,817	66.9	69.5	1,184	43.6	45.3
White, non-Hispanic alone ...	2,537	2,520	1,770	69.8	70.2	1,158	45.6	45.9
Black alone................	1,017	1,007	640	62.9	63.6	473	46.5	47.0
Asian alone................	54	35	19	35.2	55.3	14	26.3	41.2
Hispanic (of any race)	195	96	48	24.5	49.7	26	13.5	27.3
White alone or in combination ...	2,763	2,664	1,838	66.5	69.0	1,200	43.4	45.1
Black alone or in combination ...	1,031	1,020	640	62.1	62.7	473	45.9	46.4
Asian alone or in combination ...	65	46	28	42.5	60.8	23	35.0	50.1
Age								
18 to 24 years.............	411	401	179	43.4	44.6	77	18.7	19.2
25 to 34 years.............	617	587	312	50.5	53.1	158	25.6	27.0
35 to 44 years.............	646	604	405	62.7	67.0	270	41.8	44.7
45 to 64 years.............	1,310	1,253	918	70.1	73.3	660	50.4	52.7
65 years and over	873	871	686	78.6	78.8	523	59.9	60.0

- = Zero or rounds to zero.
B = Base is less than 75,000 and therefore too small to show the derived measure.

Table AL-14. Health Indicators

(Number, rate as indicated in footnotes.)

Item	State	U.S.
Births		
Life Expectancy at Birth (years), 2020	73.2	77.0
Fertility Rate by State[1], 2021	59.5	56.3
Percent Home Births, 2021	0.7	1.4
Cesarean Delivery Rate[2], 2021	35.1	32.1
Preterm Birth Rate[3], 2021	13.1	10.5
Teen Birth Rate[4], 2021	22.9	13.9
Percentage of Babies Born Low Birthweight[5], 2021	10.4	8.5
Deaths[6]		
Heart Disease Mortality Rate, 2021	247.5	173.8
Cancer Mortality Rate, 2021	160.2	146.6
Stroke Mortality Rate, 2021	54.9	41.1
Diabetes Mortality Rate, 2021	26.3	25.4
Influenza/Pneumonia Mortality Rate, 2021	16.8	10.5
Suicide Mortality Rate, 2021	15.8	14.1
Drug Overdose Mortality Rate, 2021	30.1	33.6
Firearm Injury Mortality Rate, 2021	26.4	14.6
Homicide Mortality Rate, 2021	15.9	8.2
Disease and Illness		
Lifetime Asthma in Adults, 2020 (percent)	14.7	13.9
Lifetime Asthma in Children, 2020 (percent)[7]	NA	11.3
Diabetes in Adults, 2020 (percent)	12.9	8.2
Self-reported Obesity in Adults, 2021 (percent)	39.9	NA

SOURCE: National Center for Health Statistics, National Vital Statistics System 2020 data; https://wonder.cdc.gov.
[1] General fertility rate per 1,000 women aged 15–44.
[2] This represents the percentage of all live births that were cesarean deliveries.
[3] Babies born prior to 37 weeks of pregnancy (gestation).
[4] Number of births per 1,000 females aged 15–19
[5] Babies born weighing less than 2,500 grams or 5 lbs. 8oz.
[6] Death rates are the number of deaths per 100,000 total population.
[7] U.S. total includes data from 30 states and D.C.
NA = Not available.
- = Zero or rounds to zero.

Table AL-15. State Government Finances, 2021

(Dollar amounts in thousands, percent distribution.)

Item	Dollars	Percent distribution
Total Revenue	42,744,424	100.0
General revenue	38,326,661	89.7
Intergovernmental revenue	15,878,493	37.1
Taxes	14,251,329	33.3
General sales	3,912,037	9.2
Selective sales	3,102,485	7.3
License taxes	606,351	1.4
Individual income tax	4,908,837	11.5
Corporate income tax	1,134,256	2.7
Other taxes	587,363	1.4
Current charges	6,254,758	14.6
Miscellaneous general revenue	1,942,081	4.5
Utility revenue	-	-
Liquor stores revenue	477,392	1.1
Insurance trust revenue[1]	3,940,371	9.2
Total Expenditure	39,430,705	100.0
Intergovernmental expenditure	10,181,590	25.8
Direct expenditure	29,249,115	74.2
Current operation	20,503,369	52.0
Capital outlay	2,228,756	5.7
Insurance benefits and repayments	4,818,736	12.2
Assistance and subsidies	1,334,862	3.4
Interest on debt	363,392	0.9
Exhibit: Salaries and wages	5,598,489	14.2
Total Expenditure	39,430,705	100.0
General expenditure	34,170,937	86.7
Intergovernmental expenditure	10,181,590	25.8
Direct expenditure	23,989,347	60.8
General expenditure, by function:		
Education	14,253,969	36.1
Public welfare	8,442,755	21.4
Hospitals	3,884,472	9.9
Health	614,510	1.6
Highways	1,619,229	4.1
Police protection	174,320	0.4
Correction	756,887	1.9
Natural resources	300,698	0.8
Parks and recreation	31,123	0.1
Governmental administration	795,783	2.0
Interest on general debt	363,392	0.9
Other and unallocable	2,803,799	7.1
Utility expenditure	95	-
Liquor stores expenditure	440,937	1.1
Insurance trust expenditure	4,818,736	12.2
Debt at End of Fiscal Year	9,118,128	X
Cash and Security Holdings	68,405,663	X

X = Not applicable.
- = Zero or rounds to zero.
[1]Within insurance trust revenue, net earnings of state retirement systems is a calculated statistic (the item code in the data file is X08), and thus can be positive or negative. Net earnings is the sum of earnings on investments plus gains on investments minus losses on investments. The change made in 2002 for asset valuation from book to market value in accordance with Statement 34 of the Governmental Accounting Standards Board is reflected in the calculated statistics.

Table AL-16. State Government Tax Collections, 2022

(Dollars in thousands, percent.)

Item	Dollars	Percent distribution
Total Taxes	16,324,900	100.0
Property taxes	495,753	3.0
Sales and gross receipts	7,540,587	46.2
General sales and gross receipts	4,329,546	26.5
Selective sales and gross receipts	3,211,041	19.7
Alcoholic beverages	271,442	1.7
Amusements	0	-
Insurance premiums	513,226	3.1
Motor fuels	949,982	5.8
Pari-mutuels	5,221	-
Public utilities	702,352	4.3
Tobacco products	156,313	1.0
Other selective sales	612,505	3.8
Licenses	596,971	3.7
Alcoholic beverages	4,102	-
Amusements	X	-
Corporations in general	207,653	1.3
Hunting and fishing	26,159	0.2
Motor vehicle	239,930	1.5
Motor vehicle operators	35,999	0.2
Public utilities	12,792	0.1
Occupation and business, NEC	70,335	0.4
Other licenses	1	-
Income taxes	7,552,679	46.3
Individual income	6,089,061	37.3
Corporation net income	1,463,618	9.0
Other taxes	138,910	0.9
Death and gift	X	-
Documentary and stock transfer	78,057	0.5
Severance	60,853	0.4
Taxes, NEC	0	-

- = Zero or rounds to zero.
X = Not applicable.

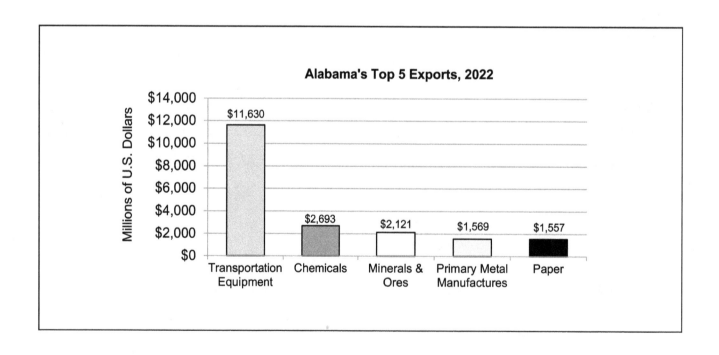

Alabama's Top 5 Exports, 2022

ALASKA

Facts and Figures

Location: Northwestern North America; bordered on the N by the Arctic Ocean, on the E by Canada, on the S by the Pacific Ocean and the Gulf of Alaska, and on the W by the Bering Sea

Area: 665,384 sq. mi. (1,717,854 sq. sq. km.); rank—1st

Population: 733,583 (2022 est.); rank—48th

Principal Cities: capital—Juneau; largest—Anchorage

Statehood: January 3, 1959; 49th state

U.S. Congress: 2 senators, 1 representative

State Motto: North to the Future

State Song: "Alaska's Flag"

State Nicknames: The Last Frontier; The Land of the Midnight Sun

Abbreviations: AK

State Symbols: flower—forget-me-not; tree—Sitka spruce; bird—willow ptarmigan

At a Glance

- With an increase in population of 3.3 percent, Alaska ranked 38th among the states for growth from 2010 to 2022.

- Alaska's drug overdose death rate in 2021 was 35.6 per 100,000 residents, compared to 32.4 for the entire nation. The homicide rate in 2021 was 6.4 deaths per 100,000 population, which ranked 27th in the nation.

- Alaska was the state with the 4rd highest birth rate in 2021, at 12.8 births per 1,000 population.

- In 2021, 10.5 percent of Alaskans lived below the poverty level, a percent that ranked 40th in the nation.

- Of all the states, Alaska had the 4th highest percentage of residents under 18 years old (24.1 percent) and the 4th lowest percentage of residents age 65 and over (13.9 percent) in 2022.

Table AK-1. Population by Age, Sex, Race, and Hispanic Origin

(Number, percent, except where noted.)

Sex, age, race, and Hispanic origin	2010	2020	2022	Percent change, 2010–2022
Total Population..	710,231	733,378	733,583	3.3
Percent of total U.S. population	0.2	0.2	0.2	X
Sex				
Male..	369,628	386,298	385,947	4.4
Female	340,603	347,080	347,636	2.1
Age				
Under 5 years..	53,996	49,333	46,805	-13.3
Under 18 years..	187,378	179,599	176,523	-5.8
18 to 64 years...	467,915	460,808	455,449	-2.7
65 years and over	54,938	92,971	101,611	85.0
Median age (years)	33.8	35.2	35.8	5.9
Race and Hispanic Origin				
One race				
White	483,873	473,223	470,101	-2.8
Black	24,441	26,987	26,837	9.8
American Indian and Alaska Native	106,268	115,019	115,194	8.4
Asian...	38,882	48,654	49,365	27.0
Native Hawaiian or Other Pacific Islander	7,662	11,738	12,269	60.1
Two or more races..	49,105	57,757	59,817	21.8
Hispanic (of any race)..	39,249	54,262	56,495	43.9

NOTE: Population figures for 2022 are July 1 estimates. The 2010 and 2020 estimates are taken from the respective censuses.
- = Zero or rounds to zero.
X = Not applicable.

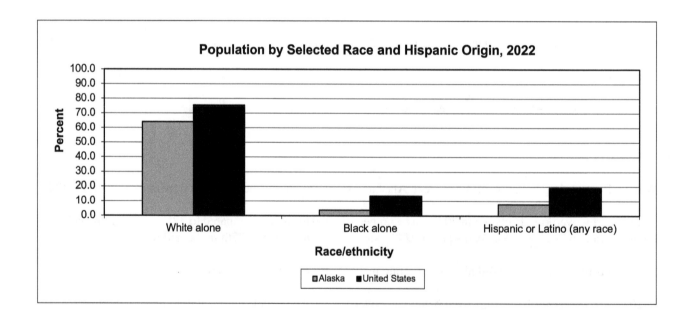

Table AK-2. Marital Status

(Number, percent distribution.)

Sex, age, and marital status	2000	2010	2021
Males, 15 Years and Over	243,024	290,598	305,268
Never married	32.5	35.5	37.8
Now married, except separated...	53.6	49.7	47.8
Separated..	1.7	1.7	1.6
Widowed..	1.4	1.8	2.1
Divorced...	10.8	11.4	10.7
Females, 15 Years and Over	225,837	267,563	276,629
Never married	24.1	27.3	29.0
Now married, except separated...	55.6	50.2	50.3
Separated..	2.3	2.6	2.0
Widowed..	5.6	6.1	6.6
Divorced...	12.5	13.7	12.0

Table AK-3. Households and Housing Characteristics

(Number, percent, dollars.)

Item	2000	2010	2021	Average annual percent change, 2010–2021
Total Households...	221,600	254,610	271,311	0.6
Family households..	152,337	170,859	172,376	0.1
Married-couple family.....................................	116,318	127,969	129,937	0.1
Other family...	36,019	42,890	42,439	-0.1
Male householder, no wife present.................	12,082	14,211	14,924	0.5
Female householder, no husband present........	23,937	28,679	27,515	-0.4
Nonfamily households......................................	69,263	83,751	98,935	1.6
Householder living alone...................................	52,060	63,698	77,681	2.0
Householder not living alone.............................	17,203	20,053	21,254	0.5
Housing Characteristics				
Total housing units..	260,978	307,065	327,889	0.6
Occupied housing units	221,600	254,610	271,311	0.6
Owner occupied..	138,509	162,785	181,145	1.0
Renter occupied...	83,091	91,825	90,166	-0.2
Average household size.....................................	2.74	2.70	2.61	-0.3
Financial Characteristics				
Median gross rent of renter-occupied housing	720	981	1,259	2.6
Median monthly owner costs for housing units with a mortgage	1,315	1,772	1,926	0.8
Median value of owner-occupied housing units.....	144,200	241,400	304,900	2.4

Table AK-4. Migration, Origin, and Language

(Number, percent.)

Characteristic	State 2021	U.S. 2021
Residence 1 Year Ago		
Population 1 year and over	723,949	328,464,538
Same house..	86.3	87.2
Different house in the U.S..................................	13.1	12.3
Same county...	7.0	6.7
Different county	6.1	5.7
Same state..	1.8	3.3
Different state...	4.3	2.4
Abroad...	0.5	0.4
Place of Birth		
Native born	673,612	286,623,642
Male..	52.9	49.7
Female...	47.1	50.3
Foreign born	59,061	45,270,103
Male..	44.9	48.7
Female...	55.1	51.3
Foreign born; naturalized U.S. citizen...................	37,288	24,044,083
Male..	44.0	46.4
Female...	56.0	53.6
Foreign born; not a U.S. citizen...........................	21,773	21,226,020
Male..	46.3	51.2
Female...	53.7	48.8
Entered 2010 or later	30.7	28.1
Entered 2000 to 2009	24.8	23.7
Entered before 2000..	44.5	48.2
World Region of Birth, Foreign		
Foreign-born population, excluding population born at sea	59,061	45,269,644
Europe..	12.7	10.7
Asia..	57.6	31.0
Africa...	4.7	5.7
Oceania..	4.7	0.6
Latin America...	17.1	50.1
North America..	3.2	1.7
Language Spoken at Home and Ability to Speak English		
Population 5 years and over..................................	686,475	313,232,500
English only	84.2	78.4
Language other than English................................	15.8	21.6
Speaks English less than "very well"...................	4.3	8.3

Table AK-5. Median Income and Poverty Status, 2021

(Number, percent, except as noted.)

Characteristic	State Number	State Percent	U.S. Number	U.S. Percent
Median Income				
Households (dollars)..	77,845	X	69,717	X
Families (dollars)	95,344	X	85,806	X
Below Poverty Level (All People)	75,165	10.5	41,393,176	12.8
Sex				
Male	38,028	10.3	18,518,155	11.6
Female	37,137	10.7	22,875,021	13.9
Age				
Under 18 years..	21,833	12.4	12,243,219	16.9
Related children under 18 years............................	20,990	11.9	11,985,424	16.6
18 to 64 years	45,045	10.2	23,526,341	11.9
65 years and over	8,287	8.5	5,623,616	10.3

X = Not applicable.

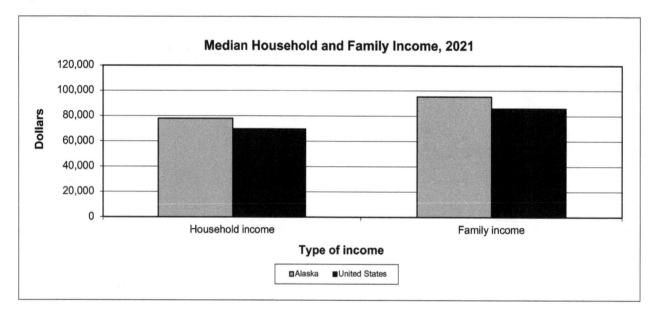

Median Household and Family Income, 2021

Table AK-6. Health Insurance Coverage Status for the Civilian Noninstitutionalized Population and Children Under 19 Years of Age

(Number; percent.)

Item	2011	2012	2013	2014	2015	2016	2017	2018	2019	2020 [2]	2021
Civilian Noninstitutionalized Population	699272	708946	712248	711541	713,082	718,419	716,178	713,033	705,772	711,104	702,154
Covered by Private or Public Insurance											
Number.........................	558,612	563,658	580,262	589,105	607,116	617,791	618,382	622,905	619,585	621,339	622,071
Percent.........................	79.9	79.5	81.5	82.8	85.1	86.0	86.3	87.4	87.8	87.4	88.6
Uninsured											
Number.........................	140,660	145,288	131,986	122,436	105,966	100,628	97,796	90,128	86,187	89,765	80,083
Percent.........................	20.1	20.5	18.5	17.2	14.9	14.0	13.7	12.6	12.2	12.6	11.4
Percent in the U.S. not covered........................	15.1	14.8	14.5	11.7	9.4	8.6	8.7	8.9	9.2	8.7	8.6
Children Under 19 Years of Age[1]	187,708	187,072	187,885	186,245	185,917	186,839	194,383	192,588	190,002	191,841	186,727
Covered by Private or Public Insurance											
Number.........................	165,599	161,115	166,043	164,993	166,252	168,245	175,661	174,413	172,143	173,561	172,028
Percent.........................	88.2	86.1	88.4	88.6	89.4	90.0	90.4	90.6	90.6	90.5	92.1
Uninsured											
Number.........................	22,109	25,957	21,842	21,252	19,665	18,594	18,722	18,175	17,859	18,280	14,699
Percent.........................	11.8	13.9	11.6	11.4	10.6	10.0	9.6	9.4	9.4	9.5	7.9
Percent in the U.S. not covered........................	7.5	7.2	7.1	6.0	4.8	4.5	5.0	5.2	5.7	5.2	5.4

[1] Data for years prior to 2017 are for individuals under 18 years of age.
[2] 2020 ACS 5-Year estimates. 1-Year estimates were not released for 2020 due to the impact of COVID-19 on data collection that year. Data is not comparable to previous years, which are based on 1-year estimates.

Table AK-7. Employment Status by Demographic Group, 2022

(Numbers in thousands, percent.)

Characteristic	Civilian noninstitutional population	Civilian labor force		Employed		Unemployed	
		Number	Percent of population	Number	Percent of population	Number	Percent of population
Total...............................	549	354	64.6	339	61.8	16	4.4
Sex							
Male..................................	281	192	68.2	182	64.8	10	5.0
Female	267	163	60.8	157	58.6	6	3.7
Race, Sex, and Hispanic Origin							
White	359	236	65.8	230	64.0	7	2.7
Male	184	130	70.5	127	68.6	4	2.7
Female	174	106	60.8	103	59.1	3	2.8
Black or African American........................	NA	NA	NA	NA	NA	NA	NA
Male	NA	NA	NA	NA	NA	NA	NA
Female	NA	NA	NA	NA	NA	NA	NA
Hispanic or Latino ethnicity[1]	35	26	74.4	25	72.2	1	3.1
Male	NA	NA	NA	NA	NA	NA	NA
Female	NA	NA	NA	NA	NA	NA	NA
Age							
16 to 19 years	NA	NA	NA	NA	NA	NA	NA
20 to 24 years	48	36	74.2	33	68.2	3	8.1
25 to 34 years	97	76	78.1	73	74.9	3	4.1
35 to 44 years	96	77	80.2	75	77.3	3	3.6
45 to 54 years	86	72	83.4	69	80.6	2	3.2
55 to 64 years	84	56	66.6	54	64.7	2	2.9
65 years and over	100	25	24.4	24	23.5	1	3.7

NOTE: Data in Table 7 are from the Current Population Survey (CPS) and do not match the estimates in Table 8. See notes and definitions for further information.
[1] May be of any race.
NA = Not available.

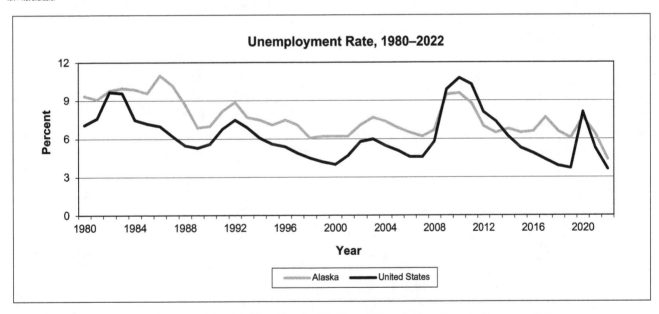

Table AK-8. Employment Status of the Civilian Noninstitutional Population Age 16 Years and Over

(Number, percent.)

Year	Civilian labor force	Civilian participation rate	Employed	Unemployed	Unemployment rate
2010...............................	361,707	69.8	332,185	29,522	8.2
2011...............................	364,599	69.0	336,312	28,287	7.8
2012...............................	364,153	68.1	337,834	26,319	7.2
2013...............................	363,544	67.5	338,104	25,440	7.0
2014...............................	364,281	67.4	339,704	24,577	6.7
2015...............................	362,425	66.8	339,604	22,821	6.3
2016...............................	362,017	66.2	338,193	23,824	6.6
2017...............................	360,589	66.0	337,108	23,481	6.5
2018...............................	355,452	65.1	334,241	21,211	6.0
2019...............................	352,883	64.8	333,541	19,342	5.5
2020...............................	346,883	63.7	318,279	28,604	8.2
2021...............................	354,936	65.0	332,266	22,670	6.4
2022...............................	356,799	65.2	342,400	14,399	4.0

Table AK-9. Employment and Average Wages by Industry

(Estimates are based on the 2012 North American Industry Classification System [NAICS].)

Industry	2014	2015	2016	2017	2018	2019	2020	2021
	Number of Jobs							
Wage and Salary Employment by Industry.........................	366,038	367,546	361,040	356,627	356,145	358,567	332,120	339,994
Farm Wage and Salary Employment.................................	509	465	435	434	722	532	494	597
Nonfarm Wage and Salary Employment...........................	365,529	367,081	360,605	356,193	355,423	358,035	331,626	339,397
Private wage and salary employment...............................	260,470	262,338	256,968	253,093	252,664	255,664	230,671	237,564
Forestry, fishing, and related activities	672	703	651	583	568	621	(D)	509
Mining...	17,602	17,041	14,190	12,790	12,422	13,083	11,025	10,272
Utilities...	2,112	2,138	2,122	2,118	2,197	2,203	2,294	2,465
Construction..	17,546	18,154	16,682	15,550	16,219	16,790	16,222	16,268
Manufacturing...	14,436	14,083	13,609	13,236	12,641	13,077	(D)	12,205
Durable goods manufacturing..................................	2,074	2,143	2,014	1,900	1,858	1,945	(D)	1,855
Nondurable goods manufacturing............................	12,362	11,940	11,595	11,336	10,783	11,132	9,932	10,350
Wholesale trade	6,534	6,570	6,460	6,383	6,479	6,603	6,204	6,188
Retail trade...	37,029	37,684	37,332	36,628	36,095	35,809	33,677	34,554
Transportation and warehousing....................................	19,596	19,855	19,899	19,852	20,113	20,414	17,172	18,217
Information..	6,250	6,320	6,289	5,974	5,612	5,339	4,882	4,780
Finance and insurance	7,323	7,357	7,388	7,312	7,239	7,107	6,888	6,684
Real estate and rental and leasing................................	4,927	4,920	4,827	4,786	4,685	4,807	4,231	4,355
Professional, scientific, and technical services	14,915	14,774	13,631	13,321	13,052	13,208	12,674	12,924
Management of companies and enterprises.....................	3,002	3,139	2,914	2,866	2,819	2,797	2,648	2,857
Administrative and waste services.................................	12,287	12,320	12,144	11,870	11,677	11,856	10,927	10,814
Educational services	3,306	3,345	3,313	3,408	3,292	3,283	2,792	3,051
Health care and social assistance.................................	44,203	44,637	46,076	47,029	47,741	48,214	47,072	47,966
Arts, entertainment, and recreation...............................	4,956	4,816	5,016	5,178	5,160	5,146	3,376	3,837
Accommodation and food services.................................	29,518	30,357	30,546	30,472	30,656	31,317	23,381	26,704
Other services, except public administration...................	14,256	14,125	13,879	13,737	13,997	13,990	12,808	12,914
Government and government enterprises	105,059	104,743	103,637	103,100	102,759	102,371	100,955	101,833
	Dollars							
Average Wages and Salaries by Industry	56,348	57,716	56,711	57,052	59,070	60,840	64,844	66,115
Average Farm Wages and Salaries	32,921	33,882	38,538	38,265	26,378	35,539	37,439	33,263
Average Nonfarm Wages and Salaries	56,381	57,746	56,733	57,074	59,136	60,877	64,885	66,173
Average private wages and salaries................................	55,541	57,074	55,369	55,545	57,829	59,864	64,349	65,768
Forestry, fishing, and related activities	63,138	60,889	60,724	65,909	67,553	73,137	(D)	77,236
Mining...	137,379	141,022	136,045	136,274	147,476	148,663	164,097	167,750
Utilities...	88,411	93,208	91,065	92,863	97,426	99,338	104,163	107,341
Construction..	81,766	83,982	80,225	77,491	81,738	84,016	85,123	84,461
Manufacturing...	45,479	50,904	51,400	53,008	55,390	56,880	(D)	62,517
Durable goods manufacturing..................................	59,770	63,117	59,193	60,685	62,867	61,854	(D)	64,581
Nondurable goods manufacturing............................	43,082	48,711	50,047	51,722	54,102	56,011	59,661	62,147
Wholesale trade	57,680	60,033	59,921	60,143	62,557	64,998	66,146	68,185
Retail trade...	32,446	32,980	32,953	33,527	34,364	35,404	38,146	39,541
Transportation and warehousing....................................	65,986	66,491	66,503	68,266	71,030	73,438	84,508	86,075
Information..	65,864	68,366	66,399	67,627	68,869	71,911	78,686	82,199
Finance and insurance	65,869	68,484	69,305	71,567	72,893	76,117	82,302	90,658
Real estate and rental and leasing................................	44,035	45,346	46,528	46,369	48,703	50,632	54,720	54,111
Professional, scientific, and technical services	77,040	77,669	74,230	73,807	75,392	78,574	80,198	81,406
Management of companies and enterprises.....................	87,345	87,860	88,688	91,782	92,308	100,671	104,932	101,873
Administrative and waste services.................................	46,328	47,849	48,012	48,361	49,311	50,796	54,951	54,412
Educational services	29,120	29,303	29,840	30,899	32,537	34,249	39,944	39,443
Health care and social assistance.................................	50,405	52,809	53,355	54,841	57,320	59,426	62,879	65,982
Arts, entertainment, and recreation...............................	24,264	25,258	25,513	25,739	26,733	27,706	28,541	31,749
Accommodation and food services.................................	26,737	27,572	27,767	28,255	29,583	30,291	28,997	34,229
Other services, except public administration...................	37,296	38,423	39,303	40,625	41,141	41,934	46,248	47,749
Government and government enterprises.............................	58,463	59,431	60,116	60,829	62,350	63,406	66,110	67,118

(D) = Not shown to avoid disclosure of confidential information; estimates are included in higher-level totals.

Table AK-10. Employment Characteristics by Family Type

(Number, percent.)

Family type and labor force status	2019		2020 [1]		2021	
	Total	Families with own children under 18 years	Total	Families with own children under 18 years	Total	Families with own children under 18 years
All Families....................................	163,134	72,677	167,815	77,719	172,376	76,737
FAMILY TYPE AND LABOR FORCE STATUS						
Opposite-Sex Married-Couple Families........................	124,608	51,781	126,464	54,897	128,858	54,015
Both husband and wife in labor force................................	51.1	59.3	54.6	64.1	49.5	61.3
Husband in labor force, wife not in labor force	24.1	32.7	21.9	28.3	24.6	30.8
Wife in labor force, husband not in labor force	8.2	5.3	8.8	5.7	9.0	5.8
Both husband and wife not in labor force............................	15.9	2.1	14.7	1.9	16.9	2.0
Other Families	38,526	20,896	40,503	22,692	42,439	22,697
Female householder, no spouse present	66.9	66.5	64.7	65.6	64.8	71.3
In labor force..	48.3	55.1	47.2	54.2	49.5	60.2
Not in labor force	18.7	11.4	17.5	11.3	15.4	11.0
Male householder, no spouse present........................	33.1	33.5	35.3	34.4	35.2	28.7
In labor force..	25.9	30.9	26.5	30.0	24.9	24.4
Not in labor force	7.2	2.6	8.8	4.5	10.2	4.4

[1] 2020 ACS 5-Year estimates. 1-Year estimates were not released for 2020 due to the impact of COVID-19 on data collection that year. Data is not comparable to previous years, which are based on 1-year estimates.

Table AK-11. School Enrollment and Educational Attainment, 2021

(Number, percent.)

Item	State	U.S.
Enrollment		
Total population 3 years and over, enrolled in school	174,378	79,453,524
Enrolled in nursery school or preschool (percent)	5.8	5.2
Enrolled in kindergarten (percent)..	5.1	5.0
Enrolled in elementary school, grades 1-8 (percent)...................................	45.8	41.3
Enrolled in high school, grades 9-12 (percent)..	21.6	21.8
Enrolled in college or graduate school (percent).......................................	21.7	26.7
Attainment		
Total population 25 years and over	485,779	228,193,464
Less than ninth grade (percent)	2.2	4.8
9th to 12th grade, no diploma (percent)	4.5	5.9
High school graduate, including equivalency (percent)................................	27.9	26.3
Some college, no degree (percent)	24.3	19.3
Associate's degree (percent)...	8.3	8.8
Bachelor's degree (percent)...	20.9	21.2
Graduate or professional degree (percent)...	11.9	13.8
High school graduate or higher (percent)..	93.3	89.4
Bachelor's degree or higher (percent)...	32.8	35.0

Table AK-12. Public School Characteristics and Educational Indicators

(Number, percent; data derived from National Center of Education Statistics.)

Item	State	U.S.
Public Elementary and Secondary Schools		
Number of regular school districts, 2019-20	53	13,349
Number of operational schools, 2019-20...	506	98,469
Percent charter schools	5.7	7.7
Total public school enrollment, Fall 2021...	129,944	49,433,092
Percent charter school enrollment	5.9	7.5
Student-teacher ratio, Fall 2019	17.6	15.9
Expenditures per student (unadjusted dollars), 2019-20	18,313	13,489
Four-year adjusted cohort graduation rate (ACGR), 2019-2020[1]......................	79.1	86.5
Students eligible for free or reduced-price lunch (percent), 2019-20.................	42.9	52.1
English language learners (percent), Fall 2020	11.0	10.3
Students age 3 to 21 served under IDEA, part B (percent), 2021-22	14.6	14.7

Public Schools by Type, 2019-20	Number	Percent of state public schools
Total number of schools..	506	100.0
Special education	4	0.8
Vocational education	3	0.6
Alternative education...	21	4.2

[1] Adjusted Cohort Graduation Rates (ACGR) differ from Averaged Freshmen Graduation Rates (AFGR).

Table AK-13. Reported Voting and Registration of the Voting-Age Population, November 2022

(Numbers in thousands, percent.)

Item	Total population	Total citizen population	Registered			Voted		
			Total registered	Percent registered (total population)	Percent registered (total citizen population)	Total voted	Percent voted (total population)	Percent voted (total citizen population)
U.S. Total	255,457	233,546	161,422	63.2	69.1	121,916	47.7	52.2
State Total	531	516	373	70.2	72.2	282	53.1	54.6
Sex								
Male	273	266	189	69.0	71.0	143	52.3	53.8
Female	258	251	184	71.5	73.5	139	54.0	55.5
Race								
White alone	346	338	269	77.8	79.7	216	62.3	63.9
White, non-Hispanic alone	312	308	249	79.9	80.8	205	65.8	66.6
Black alone	15	14	8	53.8	59.1	5	33.7	37.0
Asian alone	21	16	5	22.4	28.8	2	8.1	10.3
Hispanic (of any race)	44	39	23	53.3	59.3	13	30.1	33.5
White alone or in combination	380	371	291	76.6	78.3	230	60.6	62.0
Black alone or in combination	22	21	11	50.1	53.3	6	26.9	28.6
Asian alone or in combination	30	26	12	38.8	45.7	6	20.1	23.7
Age								
18 to 24 years	65	65	30	45.5	45.9	16	25.0	25.2
25 to 34 years	105	104	65	61.4	62.5	36	33.7	34.3
35 to 44 years	89	88	63	71.0	72.1	46	51.4	52.1
45 to 64 years	170	161	131	77.3	81.7	112	66.2	70.0
65 years and over	101	99	84	82.7	84.4	72	71.0	72.5

B = Base is less than 75,000 and therefore too small to show the derived measure.

Table AK-14. Health Indicators

(Number, rate as indicated in footnotes.)

Item	State	U.S.
Births		
Life Expectancy at Birth (years), 2020	76.6	77.0
Fertility Rate by State[1], 2021	64.9	56.3
Percent Home Births, 2021	2.5	1.4
Cesarean Delivery Rate[2], 2021	24.2	32.1
Preterm Birth Rate[3], 2021	10.2	10.5
Teen Birth Rate[4], 2021	17.5	13.9
Percentage of Babies Born Low Birthweight[5], 2021	6.9	8.5
Deaths[6]		
Heart Disease Mortality Rate, 2021	154.7	173.8
Cancer Mortality Rate, 2021	156.0	146.6
Stroke Mortality Rate, 2021	42.3	41.1
Diabetes Mortality Rate, 2021	27.0	25.4
Influenza/Pneumonia Mortality Rate, 2021	7.2	10.5
Suicide Mortality Rate, 2021	30.8	14.1
Drug Overdose Mortality Rate, 2021	35.6	33.6
Firearm Injury Mortality Rate, 2021	25.2	14.6
Homicide Mortality Rate, 2021	6.4	8.2
Disease and Illness		
Lifetime Asthma in Adults, 2020 (percent)	13.9	13.9
Lifetime Asthma in Children, 2020 (percent)[7]	NA	11.3
Diabetes in Adults, 2020 (percent)	7.4	8.2
Self-reported Obesity in Adults, 2021 (percent)	33.5	NA

SOURCE: National Center for Health Statistics, National Vital Statistics System 2020 data; https://wonder.cdc.gov.
[1] General fertility rate per 1,000 women aged 15–44.
[2] This represents the percentage of all live births that were cesarean deliveries.
[3] Babies born prior to 37 weeks of pregnancy (gestation).
[4] Number of births per 1,000 females aged 15–19
[5] Babies born weighing less than 2,500 grams or 5 lbs. 8oz.
[6] Death rates are the number of deaths per 100,000 total population.
[7] U.S. total includes data from 30 states and D.C.
NA = Not available.
- = Zero or rounds to zero.

Table AK-15. State Government Finances, 2021

(Dollar amounts in thousands, percent distribution.)

Item	Dollars	Percent distribution
Total Revenue	10,389,233	100.0
General revenue	9,178,114	88.3
Intergovernmental revenue	5,260,485	50.6
Taxes	1,053,400	10.1
General sales	-	-
Selective sales	267,842	2.6
License taxes	153,176	1.5
Individual income tax	-	-
Corporate income tax	124,987	1.2
Other taxes	507,395	4.9
Current charges	583,096	5.6
Miscellaneous general revenue	2,281,133	22.0
Utility revenue	22,657	0.2
Liquor stores revenue	-	-
Insurance trust revenue[1]	1,188,462	11.4
Total Expenditure	13,281,202	100.0
Intergovernmental expenditure	2,557,825	19.3
Direct expenditure	10,723,377	80.7
Current operation	7,170,681	54.0
Capital outlay	1,344,675	10.1
Insurance benefits and repayments	1,867,281	14.1
Assistance and subsidies	158,549	1.2
Interest on debt	182,191	1.4
Exhibit: Salaries and wages	1,729,334	13.0
Total Expenditure	13,281,202	100.0
General expenditure	11,260,033	84.8
Intergovernmental expenditure	2,557,825	19.3
Direct expenditure	8,702,208	65.5
General expenditure, by function:		
Education	2,299,005	17.3
Public welfare	2,849,705	21.5
Hospitals	35,256	0.3
Health	548,032	4.1
Highways	1,106,152	8.3
Police protection	191,252	1.4
Correction	407,597	3.1
Natural resources	410,337	3.1
Parks and recreation	13,877	0.1
Governmental administration	782,352	5.9
Interest on general debt	181,032	1.4
Other and unallocable	2,411,074	18.2
Utility expenditure	153,888	1.5
Liquor stores expenditure	-	-
Insurance trust expenditure	1,867,281	14.1
Debt at End of Fiscal Year	5,652,311	X
Cash and Security Holdings	116,520,479	X

X = Not applicable.
- = Zero or rounds to zero.
[1] Within insurance trust revenue, net earnings of state retirement systems is a calculated statistic (the item code in the data file is X08), and thus can be positive or negative. Net earnings is the sum of earnings on investments plus gains on investments minus losses on investments. The change made in 2002 for asset valuation from book to market value in accordance with Statement 34 of the Governmental Accounting Standards Board is reflected in the calculated statistics.

Table AK-16. State Government Tax Collections, 2022

(Dollars in thousands, percent.)

Item	Dollars	Percent distribution
Total Taxes	2,427,795	100.0
Property taxes	125,219	5.2
Sales and gross receipts	270,644	11.1
General sales and gross receipts	X	-
Selective sales and gross receipts	270,644	11.1
Alcoholic beverages	42,032	1.7
Amusements	6805	0.3
Insurance premiums	68,590	2.8
Motor fuels	45,078	1.9
Pari-mutuels	X	-
Public utilities	4,291	0.2
Tobacco products	48,924	2.0
Other selective sales	54,924	2.3
Licenses	139,377	5.7
Alcoholic beverages	1,397	0.1
Amusements	X	-
Corporations in general	X	-
Hunting and fishing	38,378	1.6
Motor vehicle	29,432	1.2
Motor vehicle operators	X	-
Public utilities	8,103	0.3
Occupation and business, NEC	53,084	2.2
Other licenses	8,983	0.4
Income taxes	413,175	17.0
Individual income	X	-
Corporation net income	413,175	17.0
Other taxes	1,479,380	60.9
Death and gift	X	-
Documentary and stock transfer	X	-
Severance	1,479,380	60.9
Taxes, NEC	X	-

X = Not applicable.
- = Zero or rounds to zero.

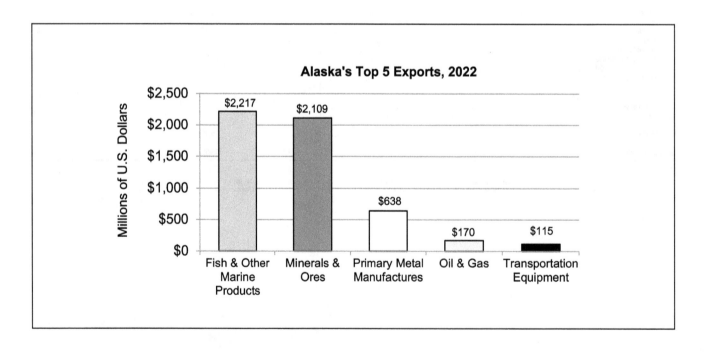

ARIZONA

Facts and Figures

Location: Southwestern United States; bordered on the North by Utah, on the East by New Mexico, on the South by Mexico, and on the West by Nevada and California; Arizona is one of the Four Corner states—at its NE corner it touches Colorado, New Mexico, and Utah

Area: 113,990 sq, mi. (295,254 sq. km.); rank—6th

Population: 7,359,197 (2022 est.); rank—14th

Principal Cities: capital—Phoenix; largest—Phoenix

Statehood: February 14, 1912; 48th state

U.S. Congress: 2 senators, 9 representatives

State Motto: *Ditat Deus* ("God enriches")

State Song: "Arizona"

State Nickname: The Grand Canyon State

Abbreviations: AZ; Ariz.

State Symbols: flower—saguaro cactus blossom; tree—paloverde; bird—cactus wren

At a Glance

- With a 15.1 percent increase in population from 2010 to 2022, Arizona ranked 9th among the states for growth during this time period.

- In 2022, 18.8 percent of Arizonans were age 65 and older, the 14th highest percent in the nation.

- Arizona's median household income in 2021 was $69,056, compared to the national median household income of $69,717.

- In 2021, 12.8 percent of Arizonans lived below the poverty level, a percentage that ranked 20th in the country.

- Arizona had the second fewest government employees per 1,000 residents, with 38.3 full-time equivalent (FTE) state and local government employees per 1,000 residents. This compared to the national average of 49.8 government employees per 1,000 residents.

Table AZ-1. Population by Age, Sex, Race, and Hispanic Origin

(Number, percent, except where noted.)

Sex, age, race, and Hispanic origin	2010	2020	2022	Percent change, 2010–2022
Total Population...	6,392,017	7,151,507	7,359,197	15.1
Percent of total U.S. population	2.1	2.2	2.2	X
Sex				
Male..	3,175,823	3,580,617	3,679,034	15.8
Female	3,216,194	3,570,890	3,680,163	14.4
Age				
Under 5 years..	455,715	404,388	395,006	-13.3
Under 18 years..	1,629,014	1,596,121	1,589,010	-2.5
18 to 64 years...	3,881,172	4,263,826	4,387,801	13.1
65 years and over	881,831	1,291,560	1,382,386	56.8
Median age (years)	35.9	38.3	38.7	7.8
Race and Hispanic Origin				
One race				
White	5,418,483	5,887,641	6,024,591	11.2
Black	280,905	380,220	407,994	45.2
American Indian and Alaska Native	335,278	374,748	379,712	13.3
Asian	188,456	270,493	289,336	53.5
Native Hawaiian or Other Pacific Islander	16,112	20,168	21,465	33.2
Two or more races	152,783	218,237	236,099	54.5
Hispanic (of any race)..	1,895,149	2,287,368	2,388,520	26.0

NOTE: Population figures for 2022 are July 1 estimates. The 2010 and 2020 estimates are taken from the respective censuses.
- = Zero or rounds to zero.
X = Not applicable.

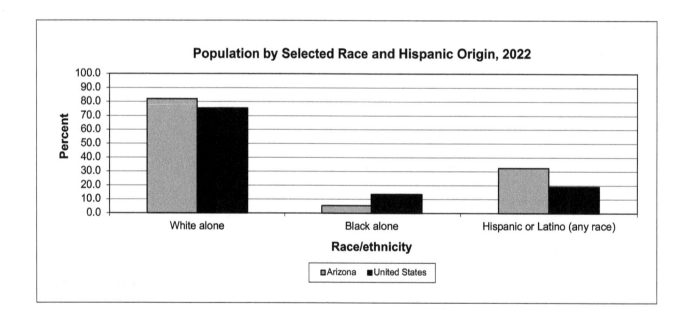

Table AZ-2. Marital Status

(Number, percent distribution.)

Sex, age, race, and Hispanic origin	2000	2010	2021
Males, 15 Years and Over	1,966,032	2,492,590	2,955,484
Never married	29.6	35.3	36.7
Now married, except separated..	56.4	50.1	49.5
Separated...	1.6	1.4	1.4
Widowed...	2.6	2.5	2.5
Divorced...	9.8	10.7	9.9
Females, 15 Years and Over	2,013,304	2,559,409	2,996,023
Never married	22.5	28.0	29.6
Now married, except separated..	53.6	48.0	47.9
Separated...	2.1	2.2	1.6
Widowed...	9.4	8.3	7.8
Divorced...	12.3	13.5	13.3

Table AZ-3. Households and Housing Characteristics

(Number, percent, dollars.)

Item	2000	2010	2021	Average annual percent change, 2010–2021
Total Households	1,901,327	2,334,050	2,817,723	1.9
Family households	1,287,367	1,548,428	1,846,358	1.7
Married-couple family	986,303	1,134,229	1,344,242	1.7
Other family	310,064	414,199	502,116	1.9
Male householder, no wife present	90,283	123,772	163,839	2.9
Female householder, no husband present	210,781	290,427	338,277	1.5
Nonfamily households	613,960	785,622	971,365	2.1
Householder living alone	472,006	621,291	741,675	1.8
Householder not living alone	141,954	164,331	229,690	3.6
Housing Characteristics				
Total housing units	2,189,189	2,846,738	3,138,685	0.9
Occupied housing units	1,901,327	2,334,050	2,817,723	1.9
Owner occupied	1,293,556	1,522,938	1,905,690	2.3
Renter occupied	607,771	811,112	912,033	1.1
Average household size	2.64	2.69	2.53	-0.5
Financial Characteristics				
Median gross rent of renter-occupied housing	619	844	1,253	4.4
Median monthly owner costs for housing units with a mortgage	1,039	1,442	1,544	0.6
Median value of owner-occupied housing units	121,300	168,800	336,300	9.0

Table AZ-4. Migration, Origin, and Language

(Number, percent.)

Characteristic	State 2021	U.S. 2021
Residence 1 Year Ago		
Population 1 year and over	7,202,745	328,464,538
Same house	85.3	87.2
Different house in the U.S.	14.2	12.3
Same county	8.8	6.7
Different county	5.4	5.7
Same state	1.7	3.3
Different state	3.7	2.4
Abroad	0.5	0.4
Place of Birth		
Native born	6,360,382	286,623,642
Male	50.1	49.7
Female	49.9	50.3
Foreign born	915,934	45,270,103
Male	48.5	48.7
Female	51.5	51.3
Foreign born; naturalized U.S. citizen	446,114	24,044,083
Male	46.8	46.4
Female	53.2	53.6
Foreign born; not a U.S. citizen	469,820	21,226,020
Male	50.2	51.2
Female	49.8	48.8
Entered 2010 or later	22.7	28.1
Entered 2000 to 2009	23.7	23.7
Entered before 2000	53.6	48.2
World Region of Birth, Foreign		
Foreign-born population, excluding population born at sea	915,934	45,269,644
Europe	9.1	10.7
Asia	20.4	31.0
Africa	4.2	5.7
Oceania	0.5	0.6
Latin America	61.9	50.1
North America	3.9	1.7
Language Spoken at Home and Ability to Speak English		
Population 5 years and over	6,874,061	313,232,500
English only	70.9	78.4
Language other than English	26.1	21.6
Speaks English less than "very well"	8.1	8.3

Table AZ-5. Median Income and Poverty Status, 2021

(Number, percent, except as noted.)

Characteristic	State Number	State Percent	U.S. Number	U.S. Percent
Median Income				
Households (dollars)...	69,056	X	69,717	X
Families (dollars)	81,622	X	85,806	X
Below Poverty Level (All People)	908,961	12.8	41,393,176	12.8
Sex				
Male	415,649	11.8	18,518,155	11.6
Female	493,312	13.7	22,875,021	13.9
Age				
Under 18 years..	275,064	17.3	12,243,219	16.9
Related children under 18 years............................	267,369	16.9	11,985,424	16.6
18 to 64 years...	506,348	12.0	23,526,341	11.9
65 years and over	127,549	9.6	5,623,616	10.3

X = Not applicable.

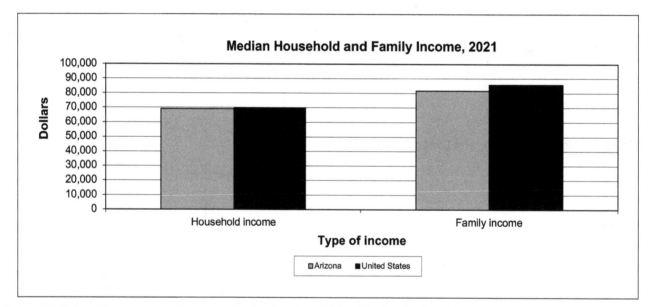

Table AZ-6. Health Insurance Coverage Status for the Civilian Noninstitutionalized Population and Children Under 19 Years of Age

(Number, percent.)

Item	2011	2012	2013	2014	2015	2016	2017	2018	2019	2020 [2]	2021
Civilian Noninstitutionalized Population	6,378,280	6,443,654	6,521,226	6,623,074	6,719,354	6,824,645	6,908,121	7,064,799	7,165,904	7,065,326	7,174,053
Covered by Private or Public Insurance											
Number..	5,283,270	5,312,695	5,403,040	5,719,746	5,991,378	6,143,407	6,213,331	6,314,822	6,357,261	6,317,548	6,407,913
Percent..	82.8	82.4	82.9	86.4	89.2	90.0	89.9	89.4	88.7	89.4	89.3
Uninsured											
Number..	1,095,010	1,130,959	1,118,186	903,328	727,976	681,238	694,790	749,977	808,643	747,778	766,140
Percent..	17.2	17.6	17.1	13.6	10.8	10.0	10.1	10.6	11.3	10.6	10.7
Percent in the U.S. not covered....................	15.1	14.8	14.5	11.7	9.4	8.6	8.7	8.9	9.2	8.7	8.6
Children Under 19 Years of Age [1]	1,621,830	1,617,380	1,613,505	1,620,576	1,619,393	1,629,040	1,729,440	1,745,643	1,744,282	1,739,980	1,715,541
Covered by Private or Public Insurance											
Number..	1,413,411	1,403,418	1,421,745	1,458,722	1,485,146	1,509,594	1,596,296	1,599,359	1,582,952	1,591,384	1,569,610
Percent..	87.1	86.8	88.1	90.0	91.7	92.7	92.3	91.6	90.8	91.5	91.5
Uninsured											
Number..	208,419	213,962	191,760	161,854	134,247	119,446	133,144	146,284	161,330	148,596	145,931
Percent..	12.9	13.2	11.9	10.0	8.3	7.3	7.7	8.4	9.2	8.5	8.5
Percent in the U.S. not covered....................	7.5	7.2	7.1	6.0	4.8	4.5	5.0	5.2	5.7	5.2	5.4

[1] Data for years prior to 2017 are for individuals under 18 years of age.
[2] 2020 ACS 5-Year estimates. 1-Year estimates were not released for 2020 due to the impact of COVID-19 on data collection that year. Data is not comparable to previous years, which are based on 1-year estimates.

Table AZ-7. Employment Status by Demographic Group, 2022

(Numbers in thousands, percent.)

Characteristic	Civilian noninstitutional population	Civilian labor force		Employed		Unemployed	
		Number	Percent of population	Number	Percent of population	Number	Percent of population
Total.................................	5,878	3,625	61.7	3,481	59.2	144	4.0
Sex							
Male..............................	2,893	1,963	67.8	1,888	65.3	75	3.8
Female...........................	2,985	1,662	55.7	1,593	53.4	69	4.2
Race, Sex, and Hispanic Origin							
White.............................	5,045	3,045	60.4	2,925	58.0	120	3.9
Male..............................	2,485	1,653	66.5	1,590	64.0	63	3.8
Female...........................	2,559	1,392	54.4	1,335	52.2	57	4.1
Black or African American.............	303	211	69.8	202	66.7	9	4.3
Male..............................	NA	NA	NA	NA	NA	NA	NA
Female...........................	NA	NA	NA	NA	NA	NA	NA
Hispanic or Latino ethnicity[1]	1,872	1,213	64.8	1,158	61.9	55	4.5
Male..............................	913	677	74.2	650	71.2	28	4.1
Female...........................	960	536	55.9	509	53.0	28	5.1
Age							
16 to 19 years....................	376	133	35.4	111	29.5	22	16.6
20 to 24 years....................	511	376	73.5	353	69.0	23	6.2
25 to 34 years....................	938	784	83.5	752	80.1	32	4.0
35 to 44 years....................	951	787	82.7	763	80.2	24	3.0
45 to 54 years....................	901	743	82.5	728	80.9	15	2.0
55 to 64 years....................	898	586	65.3	570	63.4	17	2.9
65 years and over.................	1,303	216	16.6	205	15.7	12	5.5

NOTE: Data in Table 7 are from the Current Population Survey (CPS) and do not match the estimates in Table 8. See notes and definitions for further information.
[1] May be of any race.
NA = Not available.

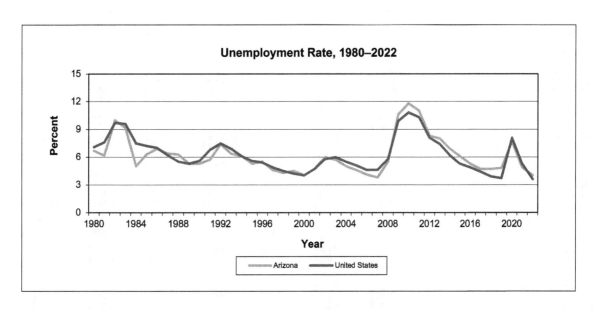

Table AZ-8. Employment Status of the Civilian Noninstitutional Population Age 16 Years and Over

(Number, percent.)

Year	Civilian labor force	Civilian participation rate	Employed	Unemployed	Unemployment rate
2010..........................	3,096,316	63.2	2,777,404	318,912	10.3
2011..........................	3,051,937	62.0	2,763,761	288,176	9.4
2012..........................	3,054,343	61.0	2,799,634	254,709	8.3
2013..........................	3,064,554	60.3	2,825,341	239,213	7.8
2014..........................	3,118,441	60.2	2,906,193	212,248	6.8
2015..........................	3,184,445	60.4	2,990,545	193,900	6.1
2016..........................	3,253,468	60.4	3,075,851	177,617	5.5
2017..........................	3,240,111	60.7	3,079,700	160,411	5.0
2018..........................	3,328,189	61.2	3,168,469	159,720	4.8
2019..........................	3,432,476	62	3,265,925	166,551	4.9
2020..........................	3,456,852	61.2	3,191,100	265,752	7.7
2021..........................	3,518,425	61.1	3,346,319	172,106	4.9
2022..........................	3,615,161	61.7	3,477,033	138,128	3.8

Table AZ-9. Employment and Average Wages by Industry

(Estimates are based on the 2012 North American Industry Classification System [NAICS].)

Industry	2014	2015	2016	2017	2018	2019	2020	2021
	Number of Jobs							
Wage and Salary Employment by Industry	2,669,755	2,745,697	2,816,903	2,881,141	2,962,324	3,048,198	2,967,485	3,076,770
Farm Wage and Salary Employment	12,360	13,584	15,203	13,219	12,815	11,943	12,465	11,453
Nonfarm Wage and Salary Employment	2,657,395	2,732,113	2,801,700	2,867,922	2,949,509	3,036,255	2,955,020	3,065,317
Private wage and salary employment	2,212,261	2,287,470	2,355,879	2,419,272	2,498,275	2,577,461	2,504,186	2,619,075
Forestry, fishing, and related activities	12,121	13,224	12,882	12,039	11,899	11,920	10,518	9,710
Mining	12,303	11,732	11,298	11,723	13,045	13,235	12,139	11,898
Utilities	11,952	12,086	12,369	12,263	12,133	12,270	11,929	11,793
Construction	128,148	130,978	138,537	149,183	162,200	175,209	178,258	182,896
Manufacturing	155,073	156,499	158,462	162,538	168,357	176,131	175,519	179,996
Durable goods manufacturing	121,607	121,099	121,163	123,367	127,221	134,012	134,542	136,528
Nondurable goods manufacturing	33,466	35,400	37,299	39,171	41,136	42,119	40,977	43,468
Wholesale trade	95,608	95,529	96,386	97,539	99,292	100,288	99,962	103,463
Retail trade	314,829	324,208	330,485	334,074	329,685	329,237	322,918	341,204
Transportation and warehousing	75,613	79,808	82,963	86,701	99,677	107,486	119,158	132,078
Information	43,379	45,202	45,360	45,378	47,398	49,088	45,537	48,244
Finance and insurance	140,603	149,899	156,893	166,474	171,875	180,650	186,857	191,189
Real estate and rental and leasing	48,500	49,184	50,665	51,882	55,129	57,432	56,087	57,680
Professional, scientific, and technical services	131,733	134,738	142,187	146,242	154,946	160,480	161,257	171,350
Management of companies and enterprises	29,699	31,356	31,768	31,486	28,942	30,462	32,418	34,049
Administrative and waste services	225,827	235,195	242,520	245,555	250,321	257,243	241,359	245,373
Educational services	57,639	59,936	60,523	61,316	60,591	61,634	61,024	67,456
Health care and social assistance	325,901	340,468	355,341	368,137	381,576	397,103	396,359	404,273
Arts, entertainment, and recreation	38,940	40,121	41,359	43,786	45,318	46,409	34,597	39,349
Accommodation and food services	249,539	260,870	269,978	278,135	283,126	286,001	242,856	267,993
Other services, except public administration	114,854	116,437	115,903	114,821	122,765	125,183	115,434	119,081
Government and government enterprises	445,134	444,643	445,821	448,650	451,234	458,794	450,834	446,242
	Dollars							
Average Wages and Salaries by Industry	47,847	48,814	49,431	51,157	53,004	54,824	59,370	62,792
Average Farm Wages and Salaries	38,593	29,719	30,742	35,559	36,382	27,949	35,670	45,137
Average Nonfarm Wages and Salaries	47,890	48,909	49,533	51,229	53,076	54,929	59,470	62,858
Average private wages and salaries	47,957	48,946	49,567	51,329	53,210	55,155	59,845	63,471
Forestry, fishing, and related activities	25,956	25,729	28,279	30,220	31,799	32,411	37,350	40,381
Mining	79,193	81,501	77,261	80,503	85,963	85,693	88,146	98,280
Utilities	102,398	101,069	104,607	108,747	112,071	112,130	117,008	117,769
Construction	49,560	50,311	51,698	54,383	56,946	59,498	64,040	66,827
Manufacturing	72,639	74,039	74,250	75,498	78,223	80,959	84,545	89,275
Durable goods manufacturing	80,185	82,147	82,699	84,259	87,486	89,693	93,326	99,165
Nondurable goods manufacturing	45,218	46,300	46,804	47,907	49,576	53,171	55,715	58,211
Wholesale trade	72,278	74,866	76,105	78,597	80,777	82,917	87,803	93,859
Retail trade	31,166	31,982	32,412	33,484	34,980	36,176	40,410	43,166
Transportation and warehousing	50,818	52,807	53,029	54,720	53,791	53,662	52,999	53,705
Information	66,659	67,826	71,256	73,319	77,702	79,892	93,485	102,740
Finance and insurance	71,053	73,097	74,341	75,933	79,199	82,961	91,914	95,892
Real estate and rental and leasing	48,586	50,253	51,405	52,749	55,304	57,770	62,509	69,520
Professional, scientific, and technical services	74,841	76,601	76,313	77,800	79,019	81,224	85,085	90,737
Management of companies and enterprises	92,256	89,998	88,594	95,516	93,517	99,682	102,964	123,212
Administrative and waste services	35,935	37,106	37,722	39,262	41,296	42,701	46,103	50,916
Educational services	41,316	41,513	41,371	41,939	43,649	43,767	49,206	46,444
Health care and social assistance	50,265	51,047	51,300	52,877	54,100	55,545	59,256	62,007
Arts, entertainment, and recreation	39,381	39,069	40,522	41,770	43,090	44,736	50,001	49,900
Accommodation and food services	21,953	22,624	22,957	24,399	25,998	26,850	26,697	31,657
Other services, except public administration	31,995	32,893	34,053	36,335	36,813	38,298	41,418	44,310
Government and government enterprises	47,557	48,721	49,354	50,694	52,335	53,660	57,386	59,261

Table AZ-10. Employment Characteristics by Family Type

(Number, percent.)

Family type and labor force status	2019 Total	2019 Families with own children under 18 years	2020[1] Total	2020[1] Families with own children under 18 years	2021 Total	2021 Families with own children under 18 years
All Families.........................	1,740,704	680,442	1,720,736	702,307	1,846,358	727,728
FAMILY TYPE AND LABOR FORCE STATUS						
Opposite-Sex Married-Couple Families...........	1,272,331	453,075	1,242,857	461,475	1,325,466	478,702
Both husband and wife in labor force..........	43.4	61.1	44.0	61.5	44.5	61.6
Husband in labor force, wife not in labor force ...	22.6	32.1	23.0	32.4	22.6	31.4
Wife in labor force, husband not in labor force ...	7.8	4.2	7.8	4.1	8.0	5.1
Both husband and wife not in labor force........	25.0	2.0	25.1	2.0	24.9	2.0
Other Families	468,373	227,367	464,005	238,578	502,116	246,163
Female householder, no spouse present	68.4	68.8	68.9	70.8	67.4	68.1
In labor force..........	48.4	57.3	49.3	59.0	46.8	55.7
Not in labor force	20.0	11.6	19.6	11.8	20.6	12.3
Male householder, no spouse present...........	31.6	31.2	31.1	29.2	32.6	31.9
In labor force..........	24.4	27.3	25.0	26.6	26.8	29.5
Not in labor force	7.2	3.9	6.1	2.6	5.9	2.4

[1] 2020 ACS 5-Year estimates. 1-Year estimates were not released for 2020 due to the impact of COVID-19 on data collection that year. Data is not comparable to previous years, which are based on 1-year estimates.

Table AZ-11. School Enrollment and Educational Attainment, 2021

(Number, percent.)

Item	State	U.S.
Enrollment		
Total population 3 years and over, enrolled in school	1,712,924	79,453,524
Enrolled in nursery school or preschool (percent)......	3.8	5.2
Enrolled in kindergarten (percent)......	4.9	5.0
Enrolled in elementary school, grades 1-8 (percent)......	42.8	41.3
Enrolled in high school, grades 9-12 (percent)......	22.3	21.8
Enrolled in college or graduate school (percent)......	26.2	26.7
Attainment		
Total population 25 years and over	4,980,297	228,193,464
Less than ninth grade (percent)......	4.7	4.8
9th to 12th grade, no diploma (percent)	6.3	5.9
High school graduate, including equivalency (percent)......	23.5	26.3
Some college, no degree (percent)	23.7	19.3
Associate's degree (percent)......	9.4	8.8
Bachelor's degree (percent)	19.8	21.2
Graduate or professional degree (percent)......	12.6	13.8
High school graduate or higher (percent)......	89	89.4
Bachelor's degree or higher (percent)......	32.4	35.0

Table AZ-12. Public School Characteristics and Educational Indicators

(Number, percent; data derived from National Center of Education Statistics.)

Item	State	U.S.
Public Elementary and Secondary Schools		
Number of regular school districts, 2019-20	224	13,349
Number of operational schools, 2019-20......	2,325	98,469
Percent charter schools	24.0	7.7
Total public school enrollment, Fall 2021......	1,133,284	49,433,092
Percent charter school enrollment	20.4	7.5
Student-teacher ratio, Fall 2019	23.6	15.9
Expenditures per student (unadjusted dollars), 2019-20	8,694	13,489
Four-year adjusted cohort graduation rate (ACGR), 2019-2020[1]......	77.3	86.5
Students eligible for free or reduced-price lunch (percent), 2019-20......	51.2	52.1
English language learners (percent), Fall 2020	7.4	10.3
Students age 3 to 21 served under IDEA, part B (percent), 2021-22	12.9	14.7

Public Schools by Type, 2019-20	Number	Percent of state public schools
Total number of schools......	2,325	100.0
Special education......	29	1.2
Vocational education......	271	11.7
Alternative education......	161	6.9

[1] Adjusted Cohort Graduation Rates (ACGR) differ from Averaged Freshmen Graduation Rates (AFGR).

Table AZ-13. Reported Voting and Registration of the Voting-Age Population, November 2022

(Numbers in thousands, percent.)

Item	Total population	Total citizen population	Registered			Voted		
			Total registered	Percent registered (total population)	Percent registered (total citizen population)	Total voted	Percent voted (total population)	Percent voted (total citizen population)
U.S. Total	255,457	233,546	161,422	63.2	69.1	121,916	47.7	52.2
State Total.......................................	5,731	5,093	3,560	62.1	69.9	2,844	49.6	55.8
Sex								
Male	2,820	2,528	1,725	61.2	68.2	1,369	48.5	54.1
Female	2,911	2,565	1,834	63.0	71.5	1,475	50.7	57.5
Race								
White alone......................................	4,995	4,436	3,130	62.7	70.6	2,551	51.1	57.5
White, non-Hispanic alone	3,161	3,105	2,314	73.2	74.5	2,026	64.1	65.3
Black alone......................................	322	311	182	56.6	58.5	132	40.9	42.3
Asian alone	207	138	93	45.2	67.6	62	29.9	44.7
Hispanic (of any race)	1,877	1,374	853	45.4	62.1	550	29.3	40.0
White alone or in combination..............	5,079	4,520	3,207	63.1	71.0	2,599	51.2	57.5
Black alone or in combination.....................	373	362	233	62.5	64.4	152	40.8	42.0
Asian alone or in combination.....................	236	167	122	51.9	73.2	85	36.1	50.9
Age								
18 to 24 years	751	694	322	42.9	46.5	170	22.6	24.5
25 to 34 years	911	782	509	55.9	65.1	300	32.9	38.3
35 to 44 years	937	800	532	56.8	66.5	428	45.7	53.5
45 to 64 years	1,800	1,530	1,148	63.8	75.0	975	54.1	63.7
65 years and over	1,332	1,287	1,047	78.6	81.4	971	72.9	75.5

Table AZ-14. Health Indicators

(Number, rate as indicated in footnotes.)

Item	State	U.S.
Births		
Life Expectancy at Birth (years), 2020	76.3	77.0
Fertility Rate by State[1], 2021...	55.5	56.3
Percent Home Births, 2021...	1.4	1.4
Cesarean Delivery Rate[2], 2021..	28.7	32.1
Preterm Birth Rate[3], 2021...	10.0	10.5
Teen Birth Rate[4], 2021...	15.1	13.9
Percentage of Babies Born Low Birthweight[5], 2021..................................	7.9	8.5
Deaths[6]		
Heart Disease Mortality Rate, 2021...	158.3	173.8
Cancer Mortality Rate, 2021...	134.7	146.6
Stroke Mortality Rate, 2021..	36.1	41.1
Diabetes Mortality Rate, 2021..	27.3	25.4
Influenza/Pneumonia Mortality Rate, 2021	10.2	10.5
Suicide Mortality Rate, 2021...	19.5	14.1
Drug Overdose Mortality Rate, 2021..	38.7	33.6
Firearm Injury Mortality Rate, 2021...	18.3	14.6
Homicide Mortality Rate, 2021..	8.1	8.2
Disease and Illness		
Lifetime Asthma in Adults, 2020 (percent)..	14.5	13.9
Lifetime Asthma in Children, 2020 (percent)[7]..	NA	11.3
Diabetes in Adults, 2020 (percent)..	9.7	8.2
Self-reported Obesity in Adults, 2021 (percent)..	31.3	NA

SOURCE: National Center for Health Statistics, National Vital Statistics System 2020 data; https://wonder.cdc.gov.
[1] General fertility rate per 1,000 women aged 15–44.
[2] This represents the percentage of all live births that were cesarean deliveries.
[3] Babies born prior to 37 weeks of pregnancy (gestation).
[4] Number of births per 1,000 females aged 15–19
[5] Babies born weighing less than 2,500 grams or 5 lbs. 8oz.
[6] Death rates are the number of deaths per 100,000 total population.
[7] U.S. total includes data from 30 states and D.C.
NA = Not available.
- = Zero or rounds to zero.

Table AZ-15. State Government Finances, 2021

(Dollar amounts in thousands, percent distribution.)

Item	Dollars	Percent distribution
Total Revenue	57,705,881	100.0
General revenue	52,047,873	90.2
Intergovernmental revenue	25,561,976	44.3
Taxes	20,817,605	36.1
General sales	9184958	15.9
Selective sales	2,105,939	3.6
License taxes	618,052	1.1
Individual income tax	6532753	11.3
Corporate income tax	905,953	1.6
Other taxes	1,469,950	2.5
Current charges	3,237,036	5.6
Miscellaneous general revenue	2,431,256	4.2
Utility revenue	39,402	0.1
Liquor stores revenue	-	-
Insurance trust revenue[1]	5,618,606	9.7
Total Expenditure	53,245,525	100.0
Intergovernmental expenditure	10,714,256	20.1
Direct expenditure	42,531,269	79.9
Current operation	30,202,223	56.7
Capital outlay	1,765,173	3.3
Insurance benefits and repayments	6,462,980	12.1
Assistance and subsidies	3,720,095	7.0
Interest on debt	380,798	0.7
Exhibit: Salaries and wages	4,571,528	8.6
Total Expenditure	53,245,525	100.0
General expenditure	46,740,828	87.8
Intergovernmental expenditure	10,714,256	20.1
Direct expenditure	36,026,572	67.7
General expenditure, by function:		
Education	15,261,364	28.7
Public welfare	21,136,644	39.7
Hospitals	287	-
Health	994,086	1.9
Highways	2,231,733	4.2
Police protection	427,616	0.8
Correction	1,354,670	2.5
Natural resources	382,942	0.7
Parks and recreation	83,631	0.2
Governmental administration	878,205	1.6
Interest on general debt	379,624	0.7
Other and unallocable	3,551,258	6.7
Utility expenditure	44,447	0.1
Liquor stores expenditure	-	-
Insurance trust expenditure	6,462,980	12.1
Debt at End of Fiscal Year	8,969,733	X
Cash and Security Holdings	83,130,357	X

X = Not applicable.
- = Zero or rounds to zero.
[1] Within insurance trust revenue, net earnings of state retirement systems is a calculated statistic (the item code in the data file is X08), and thus can be positive or negative. Net earnings is the sum of earnings on investments plus gains on investments minus losses on investments. The change made in 2002 for asset valuation from book to market value in accordance with Statement 34 of the Governmental Accounting Standards Board is reflected in the calculated statistics.

Table AZ-16. State Government Tax Collections, 2022

(Dollars in thousands, percent.)

Item	Dollars	Percent distribution
Total Taxes	24,356,760	100.0
Property taxes	1,254,846	5.2
Sales and gross receipts	13,543,177	55.6
General sales and gross receipts	11,169,103	45.9
Selective sales and gross receipts	2,374,074	9.7
Alcoholic beverages	88,925	0.4
Amusements	8,198	-
Insurance premiums	732,224	3.0
Motor fuels	792,145	3.3
Pari-mutuels	186	-
Public utilities	22,149	0.1
Tobacco products	287,427	1.2
Other selective sales	442,820	1.8
Licenses	637,701	2.6
Alcoholic beverages	11,769	-
Amusements	6	-
Corporations in general	20,463	0.1
Hunting and fishing	48,015	0.2
Motor vehicle	319,215	1.3
Motor vehicle operators	37,560	0.2
Public utilities	30	-
Occupation and business, NEC	198,323	0.8
Other licenses	2,320	-
Income taxes	8,693,348	35.7
Individual income	7,529,879	30.9
Corporation net income	1,163,469	4.8
Other taxes	227,688	0.9
Death and gift	0	-
Documentary and stock transfer	20,095	0.1
Severance	37,355	0.2
Taxes, NEC	170,238	0.7

- = Zero or rounds to zero.
X = Not applicable.

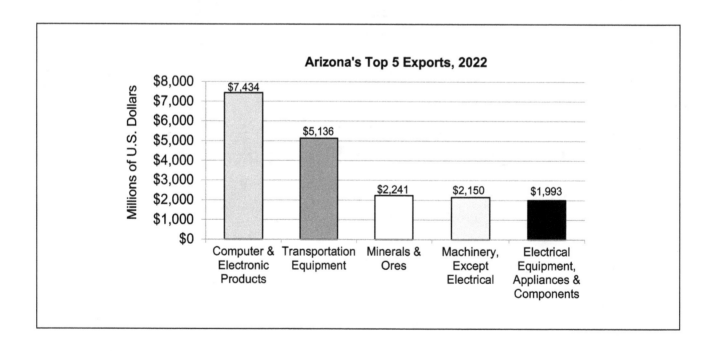

Arizona's Top 5 Exports, 2022

ARKANSAS

Facts and Figures

Location: South central United States; bordered on the N by Missouri, on the E by Tennessee and Mississippi, on the S by Louisiana, and on the W by Oklahoma and Texas

Area: 53,178 sq. mi. (137,733 sq. km.); rank—29th

Population: 3,045,637 (2022 est.); rank—33rd

Principal Cities: capital—Little Rock; largest—Little Rock

Statehood: June 15, 1836; 25th state

U.S. Congress: 2 senators, 4 representatives

State Motto: *Regnat populus* ("The people rule")

State Song: "Arkansas"

State Nicknames: The Natural State; The Land of Opportunity

Abbreviations: AR; Ark.

State Symbols: flower—apple blossom; tree—pine; bird—mockingbird

At a Glance

- With an increase in population of 4.4 percent, Arkansas ranked 32nd among the states in growth from 2010 to 2022.

- In 2021, 25.3 percent of Arkansas residents had a bachelor's degree or higher, the 3rd lowest percent in the nation.

- Arkansas's median household income in 2021 was $52,528, and 16.3 percent of the population lived below the poverty level.

- Arkansas had the 5th lowest voter turnout among the states in the November 2022 election, with just 42.2 percent of the population casting votes.

- Arkansas had the 11th highest homicide rate in the country in 2021, with 11.7 deaths per 100,000 population.

Table AR-1. Population by Age, Sex, Race, and Hispanic Origin

(Number, percent, except where noted.)

Sex, age, race, and Hispanic origin	2010	2020	2022	Percent change, 2010–2022
Total Population...	2,915,918	3,011,555	3,045,637	4.4
Percent of total U.S. population	0.9	0.9	0.9	X
Sex				
Male..	1,431,637	1,489,507	1,505,477	5.2
Female	1,484,281	1,522,048	1,540,160	3.8
Age				
Under 5 years..	197,689	182,788	180,389	-8.8
Under 18 years..	711,475	697,663	697,119	-2.0
18 to 64 years	1,784,462	1,794,030	1,806,162	1.2
65 years and over	419,981	519,862	542,356	29.1
Median age (years)..	37.4	38.4	38.6	3.2
Race and Hispanic Origin				
One race				
White	2,342,403	2,371,077	2,391,860	2.1
Black	454,021	474,927	476,278	4.9
American Indian and Alaska Native	26,134	31,491	33,266	27.3
Asian...	37,537	52,814	56,221	49.8
Native Hawaiian or Other Pacific Islander	6,685	12,814	14,365	114.9
Two or more races	49,138	68,432	73,647	49.9
Hispanic (of any race)...	186,050	242,130	260,536	40.0

NOTE: Population figures for 2022 are July 1 estimates. The 2010 and 2020 estimates are taken from the respective censuses.
- = Zero or rounds to zero.
X = Not applicable.

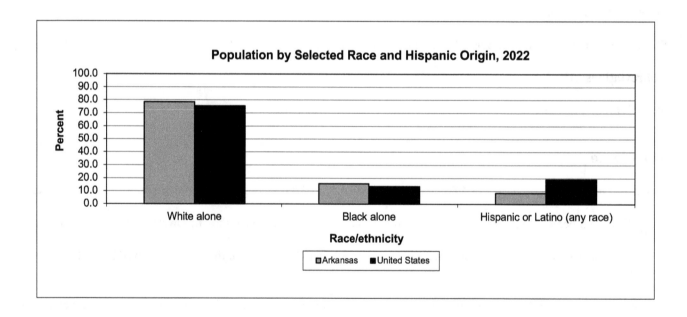

Population by Selected Race and Hispanic Origin, 2022

Table AR-2. Marital Status

(Number, percent distribution.)

Sex, age, race, and Hispanic origin	2000	2010	2021
Males, 15 Years and Over	1,015,594	1,128,804	1,195,066
Never married	24.2	29.5	32.2
Now married, except separated..	61.0	53.3	50.4
Separated...	1.6	2.2	1.8
Widowed..	2.7	3.1	3.1
Divorced..	10.4	12.0	12.4
Females, 15 Years and Over	1,096,069	1,200,974	1,250,140
Never married	18.4	23.5	26.3
Now married, except separated..	55.7	48.8	47.4
Separated...	2.2	2.9	2.3
Widowed..	12.2	11.2	9.8
Divorced..	11.6	13.6	14.1

Table AR-3. Households and Housing Characteristics

(Number, percent, dollars.)

Item	2000	2010	2021	Average annual percent change, 2010–2021
Total Households..	1,042,696	1,114,902	1,183,675	0.6
Family households...	732,261	761,361	777,631	0.2
Married-couple family......................................	566,401	554,946	565,893	0.2
Other family..	165,860	206,415	211,738	0.2
Male householder, no wife present...............	39,299	51,620	59,813	1.4
Female householder, no husband present.....	126,561	154,795	151,925	-0.2
Nonfamily households..	310,435	353,541	406,044	1.4
Householder living alone................................	266,585	302,127	339,397	1.1
Householder not living alone.........................	43,850	51,414	66,647	2.7
Housing Characteristics				
Total housing units...	1,173,043	1,317,818	1,380,768	0.4
Occupied housing units..	1,042,696	1,114,902	1,183,675	0.6
Owner occupied..	723,535	751,568	793,038	0.5
Renter occupied..	319,161	363,334	390,637	0.7
Average household size..	2.49	2.55	2.49	-0.2
Financial Characteristics				
Median gross rent of renter-occupied housing	453	638	820	2.6
Median monthly owner costs for housing units with a mortgage	737	987	1,147	1.5
Median value of owner-occupied housing units.............	72,800	106,300	162,300	4.8

Table AR-4. Migration, Origin, and Language

(Number, percent.)

Characteristic	State 2021	U.S. 2021
Residence 1 Year Ago		
Population 1 year and over	2,990,311	328,464,538
Same house	86.8	87.2
Different house in the U.S.	13.0	12.3
Same county..	7.2	6.7
Different county	5.8	5.7
Same state	3.3	3.3
Different state	2.5	2.4
Abroad	0.2	0.4
Place of Birth		
Native born	2,882,903	286,623,642
Male	49.3	49.7
Female	50.7	50.3
Foreign born	142,988	45,270,103
Male	51.2	48.7
Female	48.8	51.3
Foreign born; naturalized U.S. citizen...........................	50,939	24,044,083
Male	48.0	46.4
Female	52.0	53.6
Foreign born; not a U.S. citizen.................................	92,049	21,226,020
Male	53.0	51.2
Female	47.0	48.8
Entered 2010 or later	28.3	28.1
Entered 2000 to 2009	28.9	23.7
Entered before 2000..	42.8	48.2
World Region of Birth, Foreign		
Foreign-born population, excluding population born at sea	142,988	45,269,644
Europe	7.4	10.7
Asia..	22.5	31.0
Africa	3.1	5.7
Oceania	5.1	0.6
Latin America	60.9	50.1
North America	1.0	1.7
Language Spoken at Home and Ability to Speak English		
Population 5 years and over	2,845,967	313,232,500
English only	92.5	78.4
Language other than English.......................................	7.5	21.6
Speaks English less than "very well"..........................	3.0	8.3

Table AR-5. Median Income and Poverty Status, 2021

(Number, percent, except as noted.)

Characteristic	State		U.S.	
	Number	Percent	Number	Percent
Median Income				
Households (dollars)..	52,528	X	69,717	X
Families (dollars)	66,148	X	85,806	X
Below Poverty Level (All People)	480,153	16.3	41,393,176	12.8
Sex				
Male	213,832	14.8	18,518,155	11.6
Female	266,321	17.8	22,875,021	13.9
Age				
Under 18 years..	154,527	22.4	12,243,219	16.9
Related children under 18 years............................	152,226	22.1	11,985,424	16.6
18 to 64 years...	265,515	15.2	23,526,341	11.9
65 years and over	60,111	11.7	5,623,616	10.3

X = Not applicable.

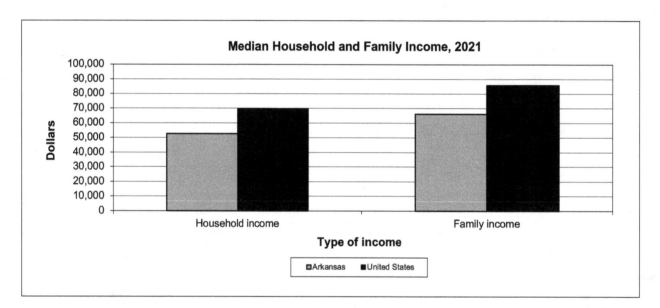

Table AR-6. Health Insurance Coverage Status for the Civilian Noninstitutionalized Population and Children Under 19 Years of Age

(Number, percent.)

Item	2011	2012	2013	2014	2015	2016	2017	2018	2019	2020 [2]	2021
Civilian Noninstitutionalized Population	2,885,212	2,896,297	2,907,014	2,914,376	2,924,307	2,934,272	2,949,305	2,960,503	2,962,596	2,957,271	2,974,701
Covered by Private or Public Insurance											
Number..	2,392,902	2,419,987	2,442,064	2,571,205	2,646,760	2,702,497	2,717,503	2,716,918	2,691,626	2,711,291	2,701,672
Percent..	82.9	83.6	84.0	88.2	90.5	92.1	92.1	91.8	90.9	91.7	90.8
Uninsured											
Number..	492,310	476,310	464,950	343,171	277,547	231,775	231,802	243,585	270,970	245,980	273,029
Percent..	17.1	16.4	16.0	11.8	9.5	7.9	7.9	8.2	9.1	8.3	9.2
Percent in the U.S. not covered................................	15.1	14.8	14.5	11.7	9.4	8.6	8.7	8.9	9.2	8.7	8.6
Children Under 19 Years of Age[1]	708,888	709,407	709,125	703,811	703,701	705,155	751,794	746,754	740,911	742,460	742,925
Covered by Private or Public Insurance											
Number..	668,938	667,257	669,866	669,732	669,147	679,612	718,394	713,039	697,516	707,613	700,001
Percent..	94.4	94.1	94.5	95.2	95.1	96.4	95.6	95.5	94.1	95.3	94.2
Uninsured											
Number..	39,950	42,150	39,259	34,079	34,554	25,543	33,400	33,715	43,395	34,847	42,924
Percent..	5.6	5.9	5.5	4.8	4.9	3.6	4.4	4.5	5.9	4.7	5.8
Percent in the U.S. not covered................................	7.5	7.2	7.1	6.0	4.8	4.5	5.0	5.2	5.7	5.2	5.4

[1] Data for years prior to 2017 are for individuals under 18 years of age.
[2] 2020 ACS 5-Year estimates. 1-Year estimates were not released for 2020 due to the impact of COVID-19 on data collection that year. Data is not comparable to previous years, which are based on 1-year estimates.

Table AR-7. Employment Status by Demographic Group, 2022

(Numbers in thousands, percent.)

Characteristic	Civilian noninstitutional population	Civilian labor force		Employed		Unemployed	
		Number	Percent of population	Number	Percent of population	Number	Percent of population
Total...............................	2,380	1,366	57.4	1,316	55.3	51	3.7
Sex							
Male..............................	1,153	714	62.0	688	59.7	26	3.6
Female...........................	1,227	652	53.1	627	51.1	25	3.8
Race, Sex, and Hispanic Origin							
White.............................	1,913	1,085	56.7	1,049	54.8	37	3.4
Male..............................	940	583	62.0	565	60.1	18	3.1
Female...........................	974	503	51.6	484	49.7	19	3.7
Black or African American..........	351	206	58.7	195	55.7	10	5.0
Male..............................	160	96	60.3	90	56.4	6	6.5
Female...........................	191	109	57.3	105	55.2	4	3.8
Hispanic or Latino ethnicity[1]	171	119	69.7	115	67.3	4	3.4
Male..............................	89	74	83.4	72	81.4	2	2.4
Female...........................	NA	NA	NA	NA	NA	NA	NA
Age							
16 to 19 years.....................	167	66	39.4	59	35.6	6	9.6
20 to 24 years.....................	184	142	77.1	133	72.1	9	6.5
25 to 34 years.....................	400	323	80.9	310	77.5	14	4.2
35 to 44 years.....................	364	295	81.1	286	78.5	10	3.2
45 to 54 years.....................	335	245	73.0	239	71.4	6	2.2
55 to 64 years.....................	390	214	55.0	210	53.8	5	2.1
65 years and over	541	82	15.1	79	14.6	2	2.9

NOTE: Data in Table 7 are from the Current Population Survey (CPS) and do not match the estimates in Table 8. See notes and definitions for further information.
[1] May be of any race.

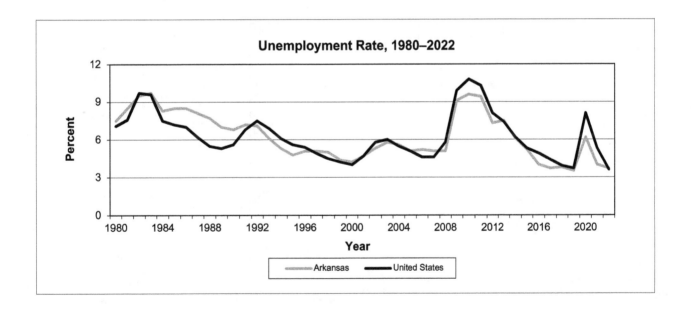

Table AR-8. Employment Status of the Civilian Noninstitutional Population Age 16 Years and Over

(Number, percent.)

Year	Civilian labor force	Civilian participation rate	Employed	Unemployed	Unemployment rate
2010..............................	1,353,635	60.6	1,247,059	106,576	7.9
2011..............................	1,357,819	60.2	1,250,431	107,388	7.9
2012..............................	1,349,888	59.5	1,251,883	98,005	7.3
2013..............................	1,331,609	58.5	1,237,609	94,000	7.1
2014..............................	1,327,959	58.1	1,249,766	78,193	5.9
2015..............................	1,339,301	58.3	1,272,785	66,516	5.0
2016..............................	1,343,891	58.1	1,290,430	53,461	4.0
2017..............................	1,348,088	58.3	1,297,854	50,234	3.7
2018..............................	1,351,686	58.2	1,302,629	49,057	3.6
2019..............................	1,365,790	58.6	1,318,465	47,325	3.5
2020..............................	1,356,579	57.9	1,274,070	82,509	6.1
2021..............................	1,332,620	56.5	1,278,984	53,636	4.0
2022..............................	1,369,367	57.5	1,323,949	45,418	3.3

Table AR-9. Employment and Average Wages by Industry

(Estimates are based on the 2012 North American Industry Classification System [NAICS].)

Industry	2014	2015	2016	2017	2018	2019	2020	2021
	Number of Jobs							
Wage and Salary Employment by Industry	1,243,481	1,264,491	1,279,315	1,286,301	1,296,707	1,304,362	1,263,189	1,287,757
Farm Wage and Salary Employment	11,319	12,578	15,485	15,067	13,815	14,156	18,686	15,784
Nonfarm Wage and Salary Employment	1,232,162	1,251,913	1,263,830	1,271,234	1,282,892	1,290,206	1,244,503	1,271,973
Private wage and salary employment	999,839	1,021,012	1,035,525	1,044,980	1,056,345	1,064,676	1,022,447	1,051,294
Forestry, fishing, and related activities	8,138	8,120	8,195	8,196	8,140	8,297	8,063	7,617
Mining	6,714	5,858	4,135	3,789	3,808	3,782	3,465	3,305
Utilities	7,903	7,950	7,706	7,707	7,802	7,818	7,871	7,513
Construction	47,269	50,481	51,554	52,333	52,061	53,780	54,455	56,421
Manufacturing	153,246	155,035	154,876	157,462	160,671	162,316	155,046	157,357
Durable goods manufacturing	76,254	75,951	74,259	74,645	76,214	77,289	72,491	74,992
Nondurable goods manufacturing	76,992	79,084	80,617	82,817	84,457	85,027	82,555	82,365
Wholesale trade	46,707	47,396	46,424	47,076	47,460	47,650	46,413	47,828
Retail trade	136,980	141,322	143,065	141,373	140,050	137,531	135,937	140,842
Transportation and warehousing	54,971	56,785	56,652	56,385	58,102	60,292	58,059	60,520
Information	14,848	13,342	13,244	12,778	10,911	10,964	11,498	11,673
Finance and insurance	37,058	37,458	38,441	38,804	39,731	41,078	41,691	41,626
Real estate and rental and leasing	13,133	13,346	13,520	13,616	13,971	14,350	14,004	14,528
Professional, scientific, and technical services	40,942	41,710	42,877	43,163	44,429	45,345	43,053	45,020
Management of companies and enterprises	32,432	33,440	35,078	35,131	34,814	33,781	33,605	34,017
Administrative and waste services	61,160	64,396	65,246	66,703	68,362	67,546	63,434	67,320
Educational services	16,627	16,465	16,776	16,946	16,737	16,799	15,876	17,411
Health care and social assistance	160,455	163,297	169,383	174,015	176,721	177,956	171,687	170,714
Arts, entertainment, and recreation	10,772	10,774	11,237	11,418	11,633	11,932	10,378	11,619
Accommodation and food services	97,670	101,521	104,760	106,011	107,493	109,390	96,738	104,966
Other services, except public administration	52,814	52,316	52,356	52,074	53,449	54,069	51,174	50,997
Government and government enterprises	232,323	230,901	228,305	226,254	226,547	225,530	222,056	220,679
	Dollars							
Average Wages and Salaries by Industry	40,580	41,444	42,102	43,490	44,593	46,071	49,011	51,996
Average Farm Wages and Salaries	21,544	22,574	19,813	16,662	18,506	21,241	12,278	15,195
Average Nonfarm Wages and Salaries	40,755	41,634	42,375	43,807	44,874	46,343	49,562	52,453
Average private wages and salaries	40,952	41,856	42,561	44,064	45,146	46,706	50,169	53,235
Forestry, fishing, and related activities	34,564	36,158	38,048	38,546	39,967	41,576	43,522	45,814
Mining	71,749	70,983	66,626	65,906	67,654	66,901	68,326	69,616
Utilities	82,651	83,731	86,407	89,436	92,725	94,963	101,275	105,117
Construction	43,247	45,023	46,673	48,195	48,937	50,493	53,201	55,452
Manufacturing	45,927	46,431	47,187	48,695	49,961	51,173	53,699	56,374
Durable goods manufacturing	48,254	48,503	49,290	51,779	53,008	54,334	56,226	59,634
Nondurable goods manufacturing	43,622	44,441	45,251	45,915	47,213	48,299	51,479	53,406
Wholesale trade	63,998	66,635	67,785	69,617	70,482	72,934	77,213	82,277
Retail trade	25,794	26,288	27,250	28,023	28,608	29,489	31,839	34,419
Transportation and warehousing	47,698	48,328	47,359	49,090	50,769	51,837	54,296	58,908
Information	53,498	55,713	56,971	58,904	56,034	60,116	72,117	77,196
Finance and insurance	59,968	61,981	63,509	64,980	67,493	69,536	74,839	77,615
Real estate and rental and leasing	35,968	37,085	37,755	39,084	40,398	41,721	44,615	47,278
Professional, scientific, and technical services	58,294	59,877	60,534	62,596	64,678	65,102	68,648	72,283
Management of companies and enterprises	105,737	107,812	106,958	117,489	118,485	129,802	135,728	146,317
Administrative and waste services	27,610	28,070	29,188	30,142	31,734	32,884	36,119	40,618
Educational services	27,896	28,608	29,578	29,619	30,988	31,315	35,101	33,625
Health care and social assistance	40,340	41,522	42,367	43,305	44,298	45,862	49,595	52,555
Arts, entertainment, and recreation	21,391	22,325	22,977	23,611	24,247	24,974	28,031	31,542
Accommodation and food services	16,294	16,769	17,406	18,145	18,879	19,652	19,722	23,391
Other services, except public administration	29,357	30,718	31,793	32,971	34,110	35,163	38,515	40,890
Government and government enterprises	39,907	40,652	41,533	42,625	43,604	44,630	46,766	48,730

Table AR-10. Employment Characteristics by Family Type

(Number, percent.)

Family type and labor force status	2019 Total	2019 Families with own children under 18 years	2020[1] Total	2020[1] Families with own children under 18 years	2021 Total	2021 Families with own children under 18 years
All Families....................	755,305	306,648	770,111	321,021	777,631	323,039
FAMILY TYPE AND LABOR FORCE STATUS						
Opposite-Sex Married-Couple Families....................	553,179	199,570	560,691	210,523	561,856	209,700
Both husband and wife in labor force....................	47.5	64.0	47.8	65.9	49.4	68.1
Husband in labor force, wife not in labor force....................	21.0	27.3	21.3	26.4	19.9	25.3
Wife in labor force, husband not in labor force....................	9.2	5.8	9.2	5.5	8.3	4.7
Both husband and wife not in labor force....................	21.6	2.4	21.7	2.2	22.3	1.9
Other Families....................	202,126	107,078	205,812	109,895	211,738	112,838
Female householder, no spouse present....................	74.4	76.0	74.5	76.8	71.8	74.4
In labor force....................	49.7	62.6	49.4	61.9	47.8	59.2
Not in labor force....................	24.7	13.5	25.1	14.9	24.0	15.2
Male householder, no spouse present....................	25.6	24.0	25.5	23.2	28.2	25.6
In labor force....................	18.4	20.8	18.2	20.2	21.8	23.8
Not in labor force....................	7.1	3.2	7.3	3.0	6.5	1.8

[1] 2020 ACS 5-Year estimates. 1-Year estimates were not released for 2020 due to the impact of COVID-19 on data collection that year. Data is not comparable to previous years, which are based on 1-year estimates.

Table AR-11. School Enrollment and Educational Attainment, 2021

(Number, percent.)

Item	State	U.S.
Enrollment		
Total population 3 years and over, enrolled in school....................	700,877	79,453,524
Enrolled in nursery school or preschool (percent)....................	5.5	5.2
Enrolled in kindergarten (percent)....................	5.1	5.0
Enrolled in elementary school, grades 1-8 (percent)....................	44.9	41.3
Enrolled in high school, grades 9-12 (percent)....................	22.3	21.8
Enrolled in college or graduate school (percent)....................	22.2	26.7
Attainment		
Total population 25 years and over....................	2,037,763	228,193,464
Less than ninth grade (percent)....................	4.4	4.8
9th to 12th grade, no diploma (percent)....................	6.9	5.9
High school graduate, including equivalency (percent)....................	34.1	26.3
Some college, no degree (percent)....................	21.4	19.3
Associate's degree (percent)....................	7.9	8.8
Bachelor's degree (percent)....................	15.9	21.2
Graduate or professional degree (percent)....................	9.4	13.8
High school graduate or higher (percent)....................	88.7	89.4
Bachelor's degree or higher (percent)....................	25.3	35.0

Table AR-12. Public School Characteristics and Educational Indicators

(Number, percent; data derived from National Center of Education Statistics.)

Item	State	U.S.
Public Elementary and Secondary Schools		
Number of regular school districts, 2019-20....................	234	13,349
Number of operational schools, 2019-20....................	1,075	98,469
Percent charter schools....................	7.7	7.7
Total public school enrollment, Fall 2021....................	489,565	49,433,092
Percent charter school enrollment....................	8.6	7.5
Student-teacher ratio, Fall 2019....................	12.9	15.9
Expenditures per student (unadjusted dollars), 2019-20....................	10,369	13,489
Four-year adjusted cohort graduation rate (ACGR), 2019-20201....................	88.8	86.5
Students eligible for free or reduced-price lunch (percent), 2019-20....................	65.5	52.1
English language learners (percent), Fall 2020....................	8.3	10.3
Students age 3 to 21 served under IDEA, part B (percent), 2021-22....................	15.9	14.7

Public Schools by Type, 2019-20	Number	Percent of state public schools
Total number of schools....................	1,075	100.0
Special education....................	2	0.2
Vocational education....................	22	2.0
Alternative education....................	3	0.3

[1] Adjusted Cohort Graduation Rates (ACGR) differ from Averaged Freshmen Graduation Rates (AFGR).

Table AR-13. Reported Voting and Registration of the Voting-Age Population, November 2022

(Numbers in thousands, percent.)

Item	Total population	Total citizen population	Registered			Voted		
			Total registered	Percent registered (total population)	Percent registered (total citizen population)	Total voted	Percent voted (total population)	Percent voted (total citizen population)
U.S. Total	255,457	233,546	161,422	63.2	69.1	121,916	47.7	52.2
State Total..........................	2,277	2,188	1,360	59.8	62.2	961	42.2	43.9
Sex								
Male	1,089	1,043	673	61.8	64.5	457	42.0	43.8
Female	1,188	1,145	688	57.9	60.1	504	42.4	44.0
Race								
White alone............................	1,841	1,783	1,133	61.5	63.5	823	44.7	46.1
White, non-Hispanic alone	1,692	1,686	1,106	65.4	65.6	810	47.9	48.0
Black alone.................................	337	326	191	56.6	58.6	117	34.9	36.1
Asian alone	56	36	17	29.7	46.2	10	18.8	29.3
Hispanic (of any race)	156	102	27	17.2	26.2	13	8.3	12.6
White alone or in combination	1,872	1,815	1,145	61.2	63.1	831	44.4	45.8
Black alone or in combination.....	342	330	194	56.8	58.8	119	34.8	36.0
Asian alone or in combination.....	62	42	19	30.4	44.8	10	16.9	24.9
Age								
18 to 24 years	261	250	107	40.9	42.6	57	21.8	22.7
25 to 34 years	366	348	193	52.8	55.5	100	27.5	28.9
35 to 44 years	382	361	224	58.7	62.1	144	37.8	40.0
45 to 64 years	726	691	481	66.2	69.6	368	50.6	53.2
65 years and over	542	539	356	65.7	66.1	292	53.8	54.2

B = Base is less than 75,000 and therefore too small to show the derived measure.

Table AR-14. Health Indicators

(Number, rate as indicated in footnotes.)

Item	State	U.S.
Births		
Life Expectancy at Birth (years), 2020	73.8	77.0
Fertility Rate by State[1], 2021	61.7	56.3
Percent Home Births, 2021	1.2	1.4
Cesarean Delivery Rate[2], 2021	34.3	32.1
Preterm Birth Rate[3], 2021	12.0	10.5
Teen Birth Rate[4], 2021	26.5	13.9
Percentage of Babies Born Low Birthweight[5], 2021	9.5	8.5
Deaths[6]		
Heart Disease Mortality Rate, 2021..	231.0	173.8
Cancer Mortality Rate, 2021...	168.2	146.6
Stroke Mortality Rate, 2021	49.9	41.1
Diabetes Mortality Rate, 2021	39.3	25.4
Influenza/Pneumonia Mortality Rate, 2021	14.7	10.5
Suicide Mortality Rate, 2021	20.6	14.1
Drug Overdose Mortality Rate, 2021	22.3	33.6
Firearm Injury Mortality Rate, 2021	23.3	14.6
Homicide Mortality Rate, 2021...	11.7	8.2
Disease and Illness		
Lifetime Asthma in Adults, 2020 (percent).............................	12.5	13.9
Lifetime Asthma in Children, 2020 (percent)[7]	NA	11.3
Diabetes in Adults, 2020 (percent)..	11.7	8.2
Self-reported Obesity in Adults, 2021 (percent).....................	38.7	NA

SOURCE: National Center for Health Statistics, National Vital Statistics System 2020 data; https://wonder.cdc.gov.
[1] General fertility rate per 1,000 women aged 15–44.
[2] This represents the percentage of all live births that were cesarean deliveries.
[3] Babies born prior to 37 weeks of pregnancy (gestation).
[4] Number of births per 1,000 females aged 15–19
[5] Babies born weighing less than 2,500 grams or 5 lbs. 8oz.
[6] Death rates are the number of deaths per 100,000 total population.
[7] U.S. total includes data from 30 states and D.C.
NA = Not available.
- = Zero or rounds to zero.

Table AR-15. State Government Finances, 2021

(Dollar amounts in thousands, percent distribution.)

Item	Dollars	Percent distribution
Total Revenue	28,213,820	100.0
General revenue	26,644,503	94.4
Intergovernmental revenue	10,746,792	38.1
Taxes	11,726,678	41.6
General sales	4,187,473	14.8
Selective sales	1,565,355	5.5
License taxes	423,851	1.5
Individual income tax	3,467,141	12.3
Corporate income tax	618,457	2.2
Other taxes	1,464,401	5.2
Current charges	2,993,199	10.6
Miscellaneous general revenue	1,177,834	4.2
Utility revenue	-	-
Liquor stores revenue	-	-
Insurance trust revenue[1]	1,569,317	5.6
Total Expenditure	27,542,132	100.0
Intergovernmental expenditure	7,143,191	25.9
Direct expenditure	20,398,941	74.1
Current operation	14,680,969	53.3
Capital outlay	1,577,430	5.7
Insurance benefits and repayments	3,367,560	12.2
Assistance and subsidies	577,140	2.1
Interest on debt	195,842	0.7
Exhibit: Salaries and wages	3,338,769	12.1
Total Expenditure	27,542,132	100.0
General expenditure	24,174,572	87.8
Intergovernmental expenditure	7,143,191	25.9
Direct expenditure	17,031,381	61.8
General expenditure, by function:		
Education	9,347,291	33.9
Public welfare	7,912,728	28.7
Hospitals	1,396,482	5.1
Health	311,709	1.1
Highways	1,949,806	7.1
Police protection	108,896	0.4
Correction	338,275	1.2
Natural resources	282,436	1.0
Parks and recreation	75,222	0.3
Governmental administration	898,561	3.3
Interest on general debt	195,842	0.7
Other and unallocable	1,331,376	4.8
Utility expenditure	4,493	-
Liquor stores expenditure	-	-
Insurance trust expenditure	3,367,560	12.2
Debt at End of Fiscal Year	7,868,953	X
Cash and Security Holdings	53,525,293	X

X = Not applicable.
- = Zero or rounds to zero.
[1] Within insurance trust revenue, net earnings of state retirement systems is a calculated statistic (the item code in the data file is X08), and thus can be positive or negative. Net earnings is the sum of earnings on investments plus gains on investments minus losses on investments. The change made in 2002 for asset valuation from book to market value in accordance with Statement 34 of the Governmental Accounting Standards Board is reflected in the calculated statistics.

Table AR-16. State Government Tax Collections, 2022

(Dollars in thousands, percent.)

Item	Dollars	Percent distribution
Total Taxes	12,768,129	100.0
Property taxes	1,318,147	10.3
Sales and gross receipts	6,216,131	48.7
General sales and gross receipts	4,587,956	35.9
Selective sales and gross receipts	1,628,175	12.8
Alcoholic beverages	75,051	0.6
Amusements	85,468	0.7
Insurance premiums	345,234	2.7
Motor fuels	606,201	4.7
Pari-mutuels	1,858	-
Public utilities	X	-
Tobacco products	223,936	1.8
Other selective sales	290,427	2.3
Licenses	447,288	3.5
Alcoholic beverages	7,146	0.1
Amusements	1,058	-
Corporations in general	42,395	0.3
Hunting and fishing	30,397	0.2
Motor vehicle	189,242	1.5
Motor vehicle operators	19,158	0.2
Public utilities	8,940	0.1
Occupation and business, NEC	147,819	1.2
Other licenses	1,133	-
Income taxes	4,544,583	35.6
Individual income	3,717,880	29.1
Corporation net income	826,703	6.5
Other taxes	241,980	1.9
Death and gift	0	-
Documentary and stock transfer	87,752	0.7
Severance	84,054	0.7
Taxes, NEC	70,174	0.5

- = Zero or rounds to zero.
X = Not applicable.

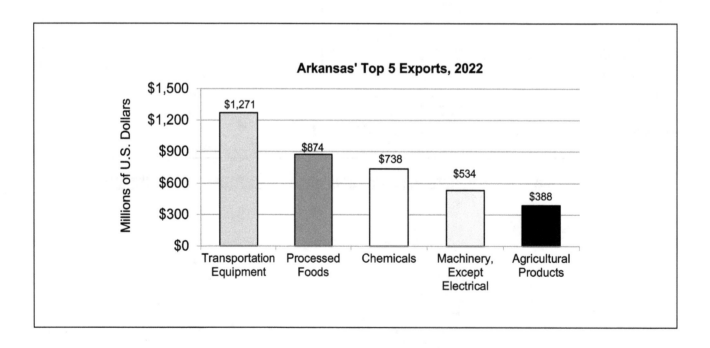

Arkansas' Top 5 Exports, 2022

CALIFORNIA

Facts and Figures

Location: Western United States; bordered on the N by Oregon, on the E by Nevada and Arizona, on the S by Mexico, and on the W by the Pacific Ocean

Area: 163,694 sq. mi. (423,970 sq. km.); rank—3rd

Population: 39,029,342 (2022 est.); rank—1st

Principal Cities: capital—Sacramento; largest—Los Angeles

Statehood: September 9, 1850; 31st state

U.S. Congress: 2 senators, 53 representatives

State Motto: *Eureka* ("I have found it")

State Song: "I Love You, California"

State Nickname: The Golden State

Abbreviations: CA; Calif.

State Symbols: flower—California poppy; tree—redwood; bird—California valley quail

At a Glance

- With an increase in population of 4.8 percent, California ranked 31st among the states in growth from 2010 to 2022.

- In 2021, California's median household income was $84,907, and 12.3 percent of the population lived below the poverty level.

- California's drug overdose death rate in 2021 was 26.6 deaths per 100,000 population, compared to 32.4 for the entire nation. The state had the 8th lowest rate of deaths caused by firearms (9.0 per 100,000 population).

- California's GDP ($2.9 trillion in chained 2012 dollars) comprised 14.4 percent of the nation's total GDP in 2022.

- Approximately 16.3 percent of Californians self-identified their race as "Asian Alone" in 2022, which was the 2nd highest percent in the country.

Table CA-1. Population by Age, Sex, Race, and Hispanic Origin

(Number, percent, except where noted.)

Sex, age, race, and Hispanic origin	2010	2020	2022	Percent change, 2010–2022
Total population	37,253,956	39,538,245	39,029,342	4.8
Percent of total U.S. population	12.1	11.9	11.7	X
Sex				
Male..	18,517,830	19,824,312	19,535,016	5.5
Female	18,736,126	19,713,933	19,494,326	4.0
Age				
Under 5 years..	2,531,333	2,289,033	2,127,764	-15.9
Under 18 years..	9,295,040	8,854,839	8,506,027	-8.5
18 to 64 years...	23,712,402	24,847,878	24,367,568	2.8
65 years and over	4,246,514	5,835,528	6,155,747	45.0
Median age (years)	35.2	37.1	37.8	7.4
Race and Hispanic origin				
One race				
White	27,636,403	28,217,478	27,607,325	-0.1
Black	2,486,549	2,573,288	2,531,957	1.8
American Indian and Alaska Native	622,107	670,281	672,768	8.1
Asian..	5,038,123	6,236,943	6,347,727	26.0
Native Hawaiian or Other Pacific Islander	181,431	203,787	203,788	12.3
Two or more races	1,289,343	1,636,468	1,665,777	29.2
Hispanic (of any race)	14,013,719	15,637,488	15,732,180	12.3

NOTE: Population figures for 2022 are July 1 estimates. The 2010 and 2020 estimates are taken from the respective censuses.
- = Zero or rounds to zero.
X = Not applicable.

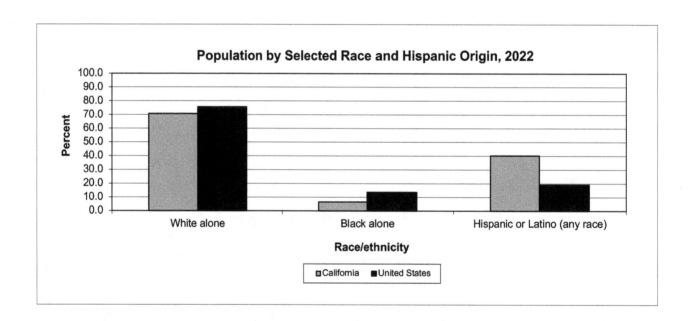

Table CA-2. Marital Status

(Number, percent distribution.)

Sex, age, race, and Hispanic origin	2000	2010	2021
Males, 15 Years and Over	12,844,669	14,662,335	15,922,331
Never married	33.8	39.8	41.4
Now married, except separated...	54.1	48.2	47.9
Separated...	2.0	1.9	1.6
Widowed..	2.2	2.1	2.0
Divorced..	7.9	8.0	7.1
Females, 15 Years and Over	13,231,494	15,043,190	16,098,910
Never married	26.5	32.3	35.1
Now married, except separated...	50.7	45.7	45.0
Separated...	2.9	2.7	2.2
Widowed..	8.9	8.1	7.2
Divorced..	11.0	11.2	10.5

Table CA-3. Households and Housing Characteristics

(Number, percent, dollars.)

Item	2000	2010	2021	Average annual percent change, 2010–2021
Total Households	11,502,870	12,406,475	13,429,063	0.7
Family households	7,920,049	8,507,856	9,146,618	0.7
Married-couple family	5,877,084	6,082,566	6,517,082	0.6
Other family	2,042,965	2,425,290	2,629,536	0.8
Male householder, no wife present	594,455	736,626	864,894	1.6
Female householder, no husband present	1,448,510	1,688,664	1,764,642	0.4
Nonfamily households	3,582,821	3,898,619	4,282,445	0.9
Householder living alone	2,708,308	3,001,307	3,218,519	0.7
Householder not living alone	874,513	897,312	1,063,926	1.7
Housing Characteristics				
Total housing units	12,214,549	13,682,976	14,512,149	0.6
Occupied housing units	11,502,870	12,406,475	13,429,063	0.7
Owner occupied	6,546,334	6,903,175	7,502,706	0.8
Renter occupied	4,956,536	5,503,300	5,926,357	0.7
Average household size	2.87	2.94	2.86	-0.2
Financial Characteristics				
Median gross rent of renter-occupied housing	747	1,163	1,750	4.6
Median monthly owner costs for housing units with a mortgage	1,478	2,242	2,523	1.1
Median value of owner-occupied housing units	211,500	370,900	648,100	6.8

Table CA-4. Migration, Origin, and Language

(Number, percent.)

Characteristic	State 2021	U.S. 2021
Residence 1 Year Ago		
Population 1 year and over	38,833,197	328,464,538
Same house	88.7	87.2
Different house in the U.S.	10.8	12.3
Same county	6.7	6.7
Different county	4.1	5.7
Same state	2.9	3.3
Different state	1.1	2.4
Abroad	0.5	0.4
Place of Birth		
Native born	28,786,026	286,623,642
Male	50.6	49.7
Female	49.4	50.3
Foreign born	10,451,810	45,270,103
Male	48.4	48.7
Female	51.6	51.3
Foreign born; naturalized U.S. citizen	5,713,304	24,044,083
Male	46.1	46.4
Female	53.9	53.6
Foreign born; not a U.S. citizen	4,738,506	21,226,020
Male	51.1	51.2
Female	48.9	48.8
Entered 2010 or later	20.3	28.1
Entered 2000 to 2009	21.4	23.7
Entered before 2000	58.2	48.2
World Region of Birth, Foreign		
Foreign-born population, excluding population born at sea	10,451,777	45,269,644
Europe	6.4	10.7
Asia	40.3	31.0
Africa	2.1	5.7
Oceania	0.9	0.6
Latin America	49.3	50.1
North America	1.2	1.7
Language Spoken at Home and Ability to Speak English		
Population 5 years and over	37,027,601	313,232,500
English only	56.1	78.4
Language other than English	43.9	21.6
Speaks English less than "very well"	17.4	8.3

Table CA-5. Median Income and Poverty Status, 2021

(Number, percent, except as noted.)

Characteristic	State		U.S.	
	Number	Percent	Number	Percent
Median Income				
Households (dollars)..	84,907	X	69,717	X
Families (dollars)	97,388	X	85,806	X
Below Poverty Level (All People)	4,733,036	12.3	41,393,176	12.8
Sex				
Male	2,157,533	11.3	18,518,155	11.6
Female	2,575,503	13.3	22,875,021	13.9
Age				
Under 18 years...	1,362,975	15.8	12,243,219	16.9
Related children under 18 years...	1,334,099	15.5	11,985,424	16.6
18 to 64 years..	2,715,140	11.3	23,526,341	11.9
65 years and over	654,921	11.1	5,623,616	10.3

X = Not applicable.

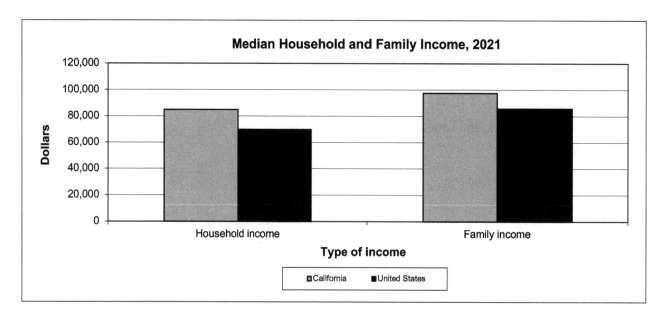

Median Household and Family Income, 2021

Table CA-6. Health Insurance Coverage Status for the Civilian Noninstitutionalized Population and Children Under 19 Years of Age

(Number, percent.)

Item	2011	2012	2013	2014	2015	2016	2017	2018	2019	2020 [2]	2021
Civilian Noninstitutionalized Population	37,161,789	37,524,274	37,831,553	38,297,457	38,649,621	38,763,815	39,046,835	39,062,465	38,997,581	38,838,726	38,724,294
Covered by Private or Public Insurance											
Number...	30,436,185	30,814,688	31,331,374	33,530,746	35,332,356	35,919,912	36,250,246	36,236,845	35,995,584	36,032,553	36,011,754
Percent..	81.9	82.1	82.8	87.6	91.4	92.7	92.8	92.8	92.3	92.8	93.0
Uninsured											
Number...	6,725,604	6,709,586	6,500,179	4,766,711	3,317,265	2,843,903	2,796,589	2,825,620	3,001,997	2,806,173	2,712,540
Percent..	18.1	17.9	17.2	12.4	8.6	7.3	7.2	7.2	7.7	7.2	7.0
Percent in the U.S. not covered.................................	15.1	14.8	14.5	11.7	9.4	8.6	8.7	8.9	9.2	8.7	8.6
Children Under 19 Years of Age [1]	9,252,466	9,223,488	9,157,955	9,135,133	9,103,139	9,079,778	9,567,473	9,514,348	9,405,057	9,465,391	9,274,768
Covered by Private or Public Insurance											
Number...	8,507,669	8,493,396	8,484,747	8,638,043	8,800,771	8,811,963	9,266,841	9,215,649	9,071,023	9,157,036	8,953,440
Percent..	92.0	92.1	92.6	94.6	96.7	97.1	96.9	96.9	96.4	96.7	96.5
Uninsured											
Number...	744,797	730,092	673,208	497,090	302,368	267,815	300,632	298,699	334,034	308,355	321,328
Percent..	8.0	7.9	7.4	5.4	3.3	2.9	3.1	3.1	3.6	3.3	3.5
Percent in the U.S. not covered.................................	7.5	7.2	7.1	6.0	4.8	4.5	5.0	5.2	5.7	5.2	5.4

[1] Data for years prior to 2017 are for individuals under 18 years of age.
[2] 2020 ACS 5-Year estimates. 1-Year estimates were not released for 2020 due to the impact of COVID-19 on data collection that year. Data is not comparable to previous years, which are based on 1-year estimates.

Table CA-7. Employment Status by Demographic Group, 2022

(Numbers in thousands, percent.)

Characteristic	Civilian noninstitutional population	Civilian labor force		Employed		Unemployed	
		Number	Percent of population	Number	Percent of population	Number	Percent of population
Total...	30,969	19,178	61.9	18,377	59.3	802	4.2
Sex							
Male	15,245	10,477	68.7	10,033	65.8	445	4.2
Female	15,725	8,701	55.3	8,344	53.1	357	4.1
Race, Sex, and Hispanic Origin							
White	21,924	13,586	62.0	13,045	59.5	541	4.0
Male	10,968	7,609	69.4	7,309	66.6	300	3.9
Female	10,957	5,977	54.5	5,736	52.4	241	4.0
Black or African American.....................	1,972	1,200	60.8	1,111	56.3	89	7.4
Male	953	618	64.9	567	59.5	52	8.3
Female	1,020	582	57.1	544	53.3	38	6.5
Hispanic or Latino ethnicity[1]	11,559	7,577	65.6	7,241	62.6	336	4.4
Male	5,829	4,330	74.3	4,147	71.1	183	4.2
Female	5,730	3,247	56.7	3,094	54.0	153	4.7
Age							
16 to 19 years.................................	2,003	587	29.3	519	25.9	67	11.5
20 to 24 years.................................	2,494	1,630	65.4	1,509	60.5	121	7.4
25 to 34 years.................................	5,532	4,481	81.0	4,286	77.5	196	4.4
35 to 44 years.................................	5,349	4,356	81.4	4,199	78.5	156	3.6
45 to 54 years.................................	4,798	3,868	80.6	3,755	78.3	113	2.9
55 to 64 years.................................	4,716	3,079	65.3	2,974	63.1	105	3.4
65 years and over	6,079	1,178	19.4	1,135	18.7	43	3.7

NOTE: Data in Table 7 are from the Current Population Survey (CPS) and do not match the estimates in Table 8. See notes and definitions for further information.
[1] May be of any race.

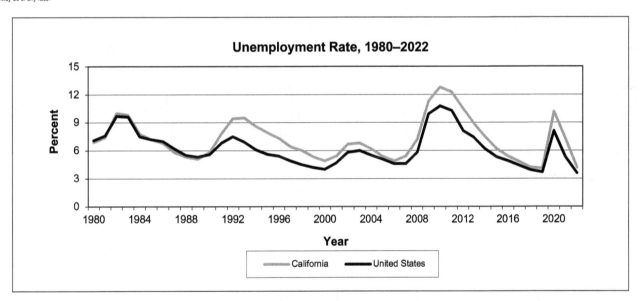

Unemployment Rate, 1980–2022

Table CA-8. Employment Status of the Civilian Noninstitutional Population Age 16 Years and Over

(Number, percent.)

Year	Civilian labor force	Civilian participation rate	Employed	Unemployed	Unemployment rate
2010..	18,370,536	64.4	16,078,454	2,292,082	12.5
2011..	18,406,756	63.6	16,220,602	2,186,154	11.9
2012..	18,484,881	63.1	16,541,039	1,943,842	10.5
2013..	18,565,408	62.7	16,887,864	1,677,544	9.0
2014..	18,676,692	62.3	17,264,518	1,412,174	7.6
2015..	18,824,141	62.2	17,647,409	1,176,732	6.3
2016..	19,012,017	62.2	17,965,407	1,046,610	5.5
2017..	19,185,366	62.3	18,258,064	927,302	4.8
2018..	19,289,507	62.3	18,468,143	821,364	4.3
2019..	19,409,413	62.5	18,612,607	796,806	4.1
2020..	18,901,110	60.9	16,996,660	1,904,450	10.2
2021..	18,923,194	61.0	17,541,944	1,381,250	7.3
2022..	19,251,974	61.9	18,440,895	811,079	4.2

Table CA-9. Employment and Average Wages by Industry

(Estimates are based on the 2012 North American Industry Classification System [NAICS].)

Industry	2014	2015	2016	2017	2018	2019	2020	2021
	Number of Jobs							
Wage and Salary Employment by Industry...............	16,693,308	17,184,799	17,601,469	17,908,517	18,295,976	18,598,619	17,291,678	17,891,462
Farm Wage and Salary Employment.......................	180,221	179,440	176,653	172,128	177,621	180,956	174,153	172,529
Nonfarm Wage and Salary Employment.....................	16,513,087	17,005,359	17,424,816	17,736,389	18,118,355	18,417,663	17,117,525	17,718,933
Private wage and salary employment.......................	13,874,518	14,311,872	14,675,233	14,955,488	15,306,818	15,580,053	14,381,887	14,994,238
Forestry, fishing, and related activities................	216,078	221,675	227,847	229,704	232,947	237,462	223,852	227,688
Mining...	28,616	26,194	22,024	19,497	20,207	20,261	17,404	16,585
Utilities..	57,870	57,551	58,632	58,396	56,510	56,399	58,477	59,476
Construction...	689,301	749,682	794,232	828,950	881,131	906,056	876,730	901,930
Manufacturing..	1,271,835	1,294,100	1,304,558	1,313,515	1,321,645	1,323,833	1,264,613	1,279,135
Durable goods manufacturing...........................	793,945	811,294	817,927	824,782	844,834	848,865	819,188	823,244
Nondurable goods manufacturing........................	477,890	482,806	486,631	488,733	476,811	474,968	445,425	455,891
Wholesale trade..	714,838	722,323	723,793	726,800	703,551	696,584	647,455	649,766
Retail trade...	1,640,400	1,672,856	1,689,860	1,701,741	1,698,297	1,670,585	1,537,355	1,611,946
Transportation and warehousing.........................	466,636	499,896	531,662	572,178	608,153	650,546	676,643	734,521
Information..	460,552	488,581	523,574	530,963	526,707	551,184	527,740	561,565
Finance and insurance..................................	556,165	566,857	580,509	587,953	583,215	585,265	584,424	581,212
Real estate and rental and leasing.....................	269,110	277,188	283,083	289,013	302,571	311,961	290,955	297,757
Professional, scientific, and technical services.......	1,184,133	1,217,060	1,229,180	1,239,785	1,297,540	1,343,604	1,313,870	1,360,761
Management of companies and enterprises................	221,154	225,551	227,375	232,202	253,366	255,536	243,862	243,121
Administrative and waste services......................	1,033,800	1,066,852	1,094,415	1,110,782	1,137,078	1,141,532	1,059,665	1,125,119
Educational services...................................	382,035	389,083	396,083	404,030	420,236	430,484	397,621	440,395
Health care and social assistance......................	2,043,669	2,128,175	2,216,053	2,294,651	2,364,338	2,441,279	2,390,694	2,456,569
Arts, entertainment, and recreation....................	286,999	292,053	304,940	312,929	322,060	334,905	212,296	242,096
Accommodation and food services........................	1,484,742	1,546,596	1,605,211	1,648,514	1,681,785	1,712,688	1,284,315	1,410,230
Other services, except public administration...........	866,585	869,599	862,202	853,885	895,481	909,889	773,916	794,366
Government and government enterprises..................	2,638,569	2,693,487	2,749,583	2,780,901	2,811,537	2,837,610	2,735,638	2,724,695
	Dollars							
Average Wages and Salaries by Industry..............	59,412	62,099	63,389	66,308	68,790	71,678	79,368	85,739
Average Farm Wages and Salaries.....................	28,480	28,742	28,763	36,215	29,971	37,078	36,857	35,559
Average Nonfarm Wages and Salaries..................	59,750	62,451	63,740	66,600	69,171	72,018	79,800	86,227
Average private wages and salaries.....................	59,607	62,447	63,668	66,744	69,382	72,319	80,754	87,631
Forestry, fishing, and related activities.............	26,635	28,554	30,769	31,560	32,752	34,567	37,777	38,919
Mining...	138,799	138,043	135,635	123,937	125,358	125,791	119,877	118,834
Utilities..	118,239	127,775	127,185	134,138	135,776	142,746	149,568	151,222
Construction...	60,303	63,126	65,313	68,477	70,965	74,239	77,756	80,343
Manufacturing..	83,083	85,683	88,883	94,066	97,447	100,059	111,862	121,389
Durable goods manufacturing...........................	95,085	97,536	102,554	109,955	114,098	116,527	130,897	145,212
Nondurable goods manufacturing........................	63,144	65,766	65,906	67,253	67,945	70,627	76,853	78,369
Wholesale trade..	73,481	77,371	77,302	80,533	80,221	83,058	88,618	94,625
Retail trade...	34,297	35,809	35,632	36,627	37,774	39,281	43,418	47,252
Transportation and warehousing.........................	52,784	54,206	56,792	58,508	62,099	69,451	66,272	73,451
Information..	138,154	147,503	149,199	170,295	190,366	193,382	220,711	253,343
Finance and insurance..................................	109,870	114,562	117,344	124,158	128,440	134,918	147,726	173,529
Real estate and rental and leasing.....................	60,432	63,881	65,138	68,984	70,206	74,262	78,998	85,525
Professional, scientific, and technical services.......	105,281	113,039	113,017	118,157	123,628	129,037	143,107	156,134
Management of companies and enterprises................	121,048	126,291	130,292	131,384	138,046	138,887	154,395	169,205
Administrative and waste services......................	40,736	42,688	43,755	46,016	46,732	49,338	54,004	58,391
Educational services...................................	45,536	46,688	47,300	47,979	49,230	49,749	56,243	53,112
Health care and social assistance......................	47,956	49,614	50,456	51,587	52,957	54,683	58,383	62,011
Arts, entertainment, and recreation....................	57,359	58,589	59,729	61,765	63,981	66,146	81,649	84,018
Accommodation and food services........................	23,712	24,922	26,344	27,335	29,119	30,910	32,543	38,761
Other services, except public administration...........	32,521	34,052	35,424	37,965	38,069	39,158	43,591	45,547
Government and government enterprises..................	60,498	62,471	64,124	65,824	68,018	70,365	74,787	78,501

Table CA-10. Employment Characteristics by Family Type

(Number, percent.)

Family type and labor force status	2019 Total	2019 Families with own children under 18 years	2020 [1] Total	2020 [1] Families with own children under 18 years	2021 Total	2021 Families with own children under 18 years
All Families..	8,972,643	3,807,571	8,986,666	3,894,122	9,146,618	3,823,351
FAMILY TYPE AND LABOR FORCE STATUS						
Opposite-Sex Married-Couple Families..	6,490,186	2,713,223	6,427,608	2,768,180	6,414,495	2,656,451
Both husband and wife in labor force...	49.6	62.0	50.5	62.1	49.9	62.6
Husband in labor force, wife not in labor force...................................	24.8	32.2	25.2	32.1	24.5	31.0
Wife in labor force, husband not in labor force...................................	7.3	3.8	7.6	4.0	7.7	4.3
Both husband and wife not in labor force..	16.9	1.6	16.6	1.8	17.9	2.2
Other Families	2,482,457	1,094,348	2,476,086	1,112,876	2,629,536	1,150,360
Female householder, no spouse present	68.0	70.8	68.4	70.5	67.1	69.8
In labor force..	47.5	58.6	47.3	57.2	46.7	57.0
Not in labor force...	20.5	12.3	21.1	13.3	20.4	12.8
Male householder, no spouse present..	32.0	29.2	31.6	29.5	32.9	30.2
In labor force..	25.7	26.8	25.3	27.1	26.3	27.7
Not in labor force...	6.4	2.4	6.3	2.4	6.6	2.5

[1] 2020 ACS 5-Year estimates. 1-Year estimates were not released for 2020 due to the impact of COVID-19 on data collection that year. Data is not comparable to previous years, which are based on 1-year estimates.

Table CA-11. School Enrollment and Educational Attainment, 2021

(Number, percent.)

Item	State	U.S.
Enrollment		
Total population 3 years and over, enrolled in school	9,874,004	79,453,524
Enrolled in nursery school or preschool (percent)..	4.4	5.2
Enrolled in kindergarten (percent)...	4.9	5.0
Enrolled in elementary school, grades 1-8 (percent)..	39.0	41.3
Enrolled in high school, grades 9-12 (percent)	21.7	21.8
Enrolled in college or graduate school (percent)...	29.9	26.7
Attainment		
Total population 25 years and over	26,909,869	228,193,464
Less than ninth grade (percent)	8.8	4.8
9th to 12th grade, no diploma (percent)	6.7	5.9
High school graduate, including equivalency (percent)...	20.7	26.3
Some college, no degree (percent)	19.7	19.3
Associate's degree (percent)...	7.9	8.8
Bachelor's degree (percent)	22.1	21.2
Graduate or professional degree (percent)..	14.0	13.8
High school graduate or higher (percent)	84.4	89.4
Bachelor's degree or higher (percent)...	36.2	35.0

Table CA-12. Public School Characteristics and Educational Indicators

(Number, percent; data derived from National Center of Education Statistics.)

Item	State	U.S.
Public Elementary and Secondary Schools		
Number of regular school districts, 2019-20	994	13,349
Number of operational schools, 2019-20..	10,374	98,469
Percent charter schools	12.7	7.7
Total public school enrollment, Fall 2021...	5,959,858	49,433,092
Percent charter school enrollment	11.5	7.5
Student-teacher ratio, Fall 2019...	23.0	15.9
Expenditures per student (unadjusted dollars), 2019-20	13,841	13,489
Four-year adjusted cohort graduation rate (ACGR), 2019-2020[1].......................................	84.3	86.5
Students eligible for free or reduced-price lunch (percent), 2019-20...................................	59.4	52.1
English language learners (percent), Fall 2020	17.7	10.3
Students age 3 to 21 served under IDEA, part B (percent), 2021-22	13.1	14.7

Public Schools by Type, 2019-20	Number	Percent of state public schools
Total number of schools...	10,374	100.0
Special education	156	1.5
Vocational education	66	0.6
Alternative education..	1053	10.2

[1] Adjusted Cohort Graduation Rates (ACGR) differ from Averaged Freshmen Graduation Rates (AFGR).

Table CA-13. Reported Voting and Registration of the Voting-Age Population, November 2022

(Numbers in thousands, percent.)

Item	Total population	Total citizen population	Registered			Voted		
			Total registered	Percent registered (total population)	Percent registered (total citizen population)	Total voted	Percent voted (total population)	Percent voted (total citizen population)
U.S. Total	255,457	233,546	161,422	63.2	69.1	121,916	47.7	52.2
State Total	29,870	25,315	17,032	57.0	67.3	13,044	43.7	51.5
Sex								
Male	14,693	12,323	8,140	55.4	66.1	6,185	42.1	50.2
Female	15,176	12,992	8,892	58.6	68.4	6,860	45.2	52.8
Race								
White alone	20,845	17,698	12,334	59.2	69.7	9,731	46.7	55.0
White, non-Hispanic alone	11,368	10,917	8,194	72.1	75.1	6,851	60.3	62.8
Black alone	1,843	1,735	1,121	60.8	64.6	751	40.8	43.3
Asian alone	5,559	4,458	2,628	47.3	59.0	1,888	34.0	42.3
Hispanic (of any race)	10,562	7,705	4,674	44.3	60.7	3,242	30.7	42.1
White alone or in combination..............	21,651	18,422	12,875	59.5	69.9	10,136	46.8	55.0
Black alone or in combination.............	2,046	1,921	1,266	61.9	65.9	835	40.8	43.5
Asian alone or in combination............	5,965	4,840	2,918	48.9	60.3	2,129	35.7	44.0
Age								
18 to 24 years	3,460	3,110	1,502	43.4	48.3	900	26.0	29.0
25 to 34 years	5,457	4,591	2,920	53.5	63.6	1,970	36.1	42.9
35 to 44 years	5,325	4,164	2,904	54.5	69.7	2,132	40.0	51.2
45 to 64 years	9,476	7,815	5,535	58.4	70.8	4,343	45.8	55.6
65 years and over	6,151	5,635	4,170	67.8	74.0	3,699	60.1	65.6

Table CA-14. Health Indicators

(Number, rate as indicated in footnotes.)

Item	State	U.S.
Births		
Life Expectancy at Birth (years), 2020	79.0	77.0
Fertility Rate by State[1], 2021	52.8	56.3
Percent Home Births, 2021	1.0	1.4
Cesarean Delivery Rate[2], 2021	30.8	32.1
Preterm Birth Rate[3], 2021	9.1	10.5
Teen Birth Rate[4], 2021	9.9	13.9
Percentage of Babies Born Low Birthweight[5], 2021	7.3	8.5
Deaths[6]		
Heart Disease Mortality Rate, 2021	147.8	173.8
Cancer Mortality Rate, 2021	132.4	146.6
Stroke Mortality Rate, 2021	42.1	41.1
Diabetes Mortality Rate, 2021	25.5	25.4
Influenza/Pneumonia Mortality Rate, 2021	10.5	10.5
Suicide Mortality Rate, 2021	10.1	14.1
Drug Overdose Mortality Rate, 2021	26.6	33.6
Firearm Injury Mortality Rate, 2021	9.0	14.6
Homicide Mortality Rate, 2021	6.4	8.2
Disease and Illness		
Lifetime Asthma in Adults, 2020 (percent)..	15.1	13.9
Lifetime Asthma in Children, 2020 (percent)[7]	10.0	11.3
Diabetes in Adults, 2020 (percent)..	9.2	8.2
Self-reported Obesity in Adults, 2021 (percent)	27.6	NA

SOURCE: National Center for Health Statistics, National Vital Statistics System 2020 data; https://wonder.cdc.gov.
[1] General fertility rate per 1,000 women aged 15–44.
[2] This represents the percentage of all live births that were cesarean deliveries.
[3] Babies born prior to 37 weeks of pregnancy (gestation).
[4] Number of births per 1,000 females aged 15–19
[5] Babies born weighing less than 2,500 grams or 5 lbs. 8oz.
[6] Death rates are the number of deaths per 100,000 total population.
[7] U.S. total includes data from 30 states and D.C.
NA = Not available.
- = Zero or rounds to zero.

Table CA-15. State Government Finances, 2021

(Dollar amounts in thousands, percent distribution.)

Item	Dollars	Percent distribution
Total Revenue	504,381,850	100.0
General revenue	410,636,676	81.4
Intergovernmental revenue	116,803,579	23.2
Taxes	248,188,154	49.2
General sales	41,973,959	8.3
Selective sales	19,217,894	3.8
License taxes	11,292,132	2.2
Individual income tax	146,324,579	29.0
Corporate income tax	26,097,277	5.2
Other taxes	3,282,313	0.7
Current charges	30,989,671	6.1
Miscellaneous general revenue	14,655,272	2.9
Utility revenue	334,929	0.1
Liquor stores revenue	-	-
Insurance trust revenue[1]	93,410,245	18.5
Total Expenditure	468,457,717	100.0
Intergovernmental expenditure	123,802,864	26.4
Direct expenditure	344,654,853	73.6
Current operation	224,443,272	47.9
Capital outlay	14,687,185	3.1
Insurance benefits and repayments	93,284,353	19.9
Assistance and subsidies	6,993,222	1.5
Interest on debt	5,246,821	1.1
Exhibit: Salaries and wages	39,459,594	8.4
Total Expenditure	468,457,717	100.0
General expenditure	372,024,133	79.4
Intergovernmental expenditure	123,802,864	26.4
Direct expenditure	248,221,269	53.0
General expenditure, by function:		
Education	113,385,225	24.2
Public welfare	165,107,693	35.2
Hospitals	17,644,292	3.8
Health	8,739,904	1.9
Highways	17,123,175	3.7
Police protection	2,354,536	0.5
Correction	11,364,231	2.4
Natural resources	6,642,773	1.4
Parks and recreation	1,256,086	0.3
Governmental administration	8,014,655	1.7
Interest on general debt	5,204,821	1.1
Other and unallocable	13,487,894	2.9
Utility expenditure	4,129,684	0.8
Liquor stores expenditure	-	-
Insurance trust expenditure	93,284,353	19.9
Debt at End of Fiscal Year	144,313,743	X
Cash and Security Holdings	1,054,946,557	X

X = Not applicable.
- = Zero or rounds to zero.
[1] Within insurance trust revenue, net earnings of state retirement systems is a calculated statistic (the item code in the data file is X08), and thus can be positive or negative. Net earnings is the sum of earnings on investments plus gains on investments minus losses on investments. The change made in 2002 for asset valuation from book to market value in accordance with Statement 34 of the Governmental Accounting Standards Board is reflected in the calculated statistics.

Table CA-16. State Government Tax Collections, 2022

(Dollars in thousands, percent.)

Item	Dollars	Percent distribution
Total Taxes	280,828,418	100.0
Property taxes	2,986,154	1.1
Sales and gross receipts	72,026,518	25.6
General sales and gross receipts	52,228,035	18.6
Selective sales and gross receipts	19,798,483	7.1
Alcoholic beverages	432,629	0.2
Amusements	X	-
Insurance premiums	3,319,048	1.2
Motor fuels	8,638,712	3.1
Pari-mutuels	18,244	-
Public utilities	741,713	0.3
Tobacco products	1,853,535	0.7
Other selective sales	4,794,602	1.7
Licenses	10,974,064	3.9
Alcoholic beverages	88,240	-
Amusements	20,273	-
Corporations in general	91,871	-
Hunting and fishing	115,196	-
Motor vehicle	5,141,552	1.8
Motor vehicle operators	384,578	0.1
Public utilities	569,181	0.2
Occupation and business, NEC	4,500,750	1.6
Other licenses	62,423	-
Income taxes	192,195,516	68.4
Individual income	146,190,014	52.1
Corporation net income	46,005,502	16.4
Other taxes	2,646,166	0.9
Death and gift	64	-
Documentary and stock transfer	X	-
Severance	128,600	0.0
Taxes, NEC	2,517,502	0.9

- = Zero or rounds to zero.
X = Not applicable.

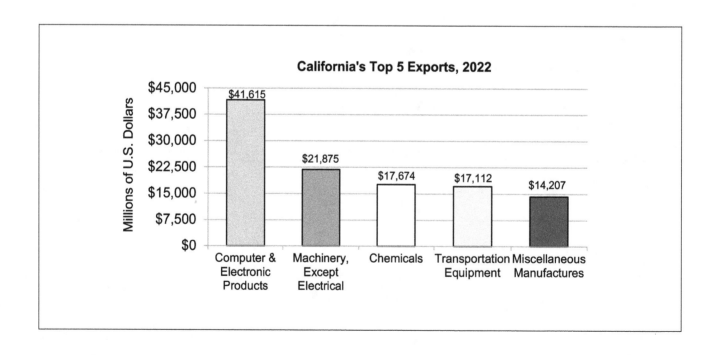

California's Top 5 Exports, 2022

COLORADO

Facts and Figures

Location: Western United States; bordered on the N by Wyoming and Nebraska, on the E by Nebraska and Kansas, on the S by Oklahoma and New Mexico, and on the W by Utah; Colorado is one of the Four Corner states—at its SW corner it touches Arizona, New Mexico, and Utah

Area: 104,093 sq. mi. (269,601 sq. km.); rank—8th

Population: 5,839,926 (2022 est.); rank—21st

Principal Cities: capital—Denver; largest—Denver

Statehood: August 1, 1876; 38th state

U.S. Congress: 2 senators, 7 representatives

State Motto: *Nil sine numine* ("Nothing without providence")

State Songs: "Where the Columbines Grow"; "Rocky Mountain High"

State Nicknames: The Centennial State; Colorful Colorado

Abbreviations: CO; Colo.

State Symbols: flower—Rocky Mountain columbine; tree—Colorado blue spruce; bird—lark bunting

At a Glance

- With an increase in population of 16.1 percent, Colorado ranked 6th among the states in growth from 2010 to 2022.

- In 2021, 8.0 percent of Coloradans did not have health insurance, compared to 8.6 percent of the total U.S. population.

- At a rate of 31.4 per 100,000 residents, the 2021 drug overdose death rate in Colorado was lower than the national average of 32.4 deaths per 100,000 ranking, 26th in the nation.

- In Colorado, 9.7 percent of the total population lived below the poverty level in 2021, which was the 4th lowest percent among the states. Colorado's childhood poverty rate of 11.8 percent ranked 46th in the nation.

Table CO-1. Population by Age, Sex, Race, and Hispanic Origin

(Number, percent, except where noted.)

Sex, age, race, and Hispanic origin	2010	2020	2022	Percent change, 2010–2022
Total Population..	5,029,196	5,773,733	5,839,926	16.1
Percent of total U.S. population	1.6	1.7	1.8	X
Sex				
Male...	2,520,662	2,931,768	2,964,544	17.6
Female	2,508,534	2,841,965	2,875,382	14.6
Age				
Under 5 years...	343,960	318,593	309,020	-10.2
Under 18 years...	1,225,609	1,249,475	1,215,575	-0.8
18 to 64 years...	3,253,962	3,675,361	3,710,313	14.0
65 years and over...	549,625	848,897	914,038	66.3
Median age (years)...	36.1	37.2	37.6	4.2
Race and Hispanic Origin				
One race				
White	4,450,623	5,005,923	5,032,844	13.1
Black..	214,919	266,851	276,966	28.9
American Indian and Alaska Native	78,144	95,239	97,828	25.2
Asian..	144,819	205,558	219,273	51.4
Native Hawaiian or Other Pacific Islander	8,420	12,179	13,003	54.4
Two or more races	132,271	187,983	200,012	51.2
Hispanic (of any race)..	1,038,687	1,268,135	1,314,965	26.6

NOTE: Population figures for 2022 are July 1 estimates. The 2010 and 2020 estimates are taken from the respective censuses.
- = Zero or rounds to zero.
X = Not applicable.

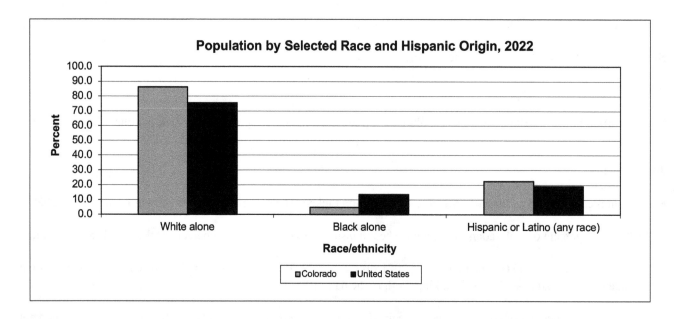

Population by Selected Race and Hispanic Origin, 2022

(Colorado / United States; Percent by Race/ethnicity: White alone, Black alone, Hispanic or Latino (any race))

Table CO-2. Marital Status

(Number, percent distribution.)

Sex, age, race, and Hispanic origin	2000	2010	2021
Males, 15 Years and Over	1,694,635	2,004,303	2,418,698
Never married	30.5	34.4	36.7
Now married, except separated.......................................	56.6	51.7	50.4
Separated..	1.4	1.6	1.0
Widowed..	1.9	2.0	2.1
Divorced..	9.6	10.3	9.7
Females, 15 Years and Over	1,690,734	2,017,425	2,374,996
Never married	23.4	26.9	29.7
Now married, except separated.......................................	54.7	50.8	50.0
Separated..	1.8	2.0	1.5
Widowed..	7.6	7.0	6.2
Divorced..	12.5	13.3	12.5

Table CO-3. Households and Housing Characteristics

(Number, percent, dollars.)

Item	2000	2010	2021	Average annual percent change, 2010–2021
Total Households	1,658,238	1,960,585	2,313,042	1.6
Family households	1,084,461	1,258,885	1,448,655	1.4
Married-couple family	858,671	959,624	1,124,072	1.6
Other family	225,790	299,261	324,583	0.8
Male householder, no wife present	66,811	90,518	107,081	1.7
Female householder, no husband present	158,979	208,743	217,502	0.4
Nonfamily households	573,777	701,700	864,387	2.1
Householder living alone	435,778	555,080	644,981	1.5
Householder not living alone	137,999	146,620	219,406	4.5
Housing Characteristics				
Total housing units	1,808,037	2,214,262	2,540,783	1.3
Occupied housing units	1,658,238	1,960,585	2,313,042	1.6
Owner occupied	1,116,173	1,292,792	1,546,233	1.8
Renter occupied	542,101	667,793	766,809	1.3
Average household size	2.53	2.52	2.46	-0.2
Financial Characteristics				
Median gross rent of renter-occupied housing	671	863	1,491	6.6
Median monthly owner costs for housing units with a mortgage	1,197	1,590	1,962	2.1
Median value of owner-occupied housing units	166,600	236,600	466,200	8.8

Table CO-4. Migration, Origin, and Language

(Number, percent.)

Characteristic	State 2021	U.S. 2021
Residence 1 Year Ago		
Population 1 year and over	5,757,628	328,464,538
Same house	83.3	87.2
Different house in the U.S.	16.3	12.3
Same county	6.9	6.7
Different county	9.4	5.7
Same state	5.0	3.3
Different state	4.3	2.4
Abroad	0.5	0.4
Place of Birth		
Native born	5,241,796	286,623,642
Male	50.8	49.7
Female	49.2	50.3
Foreign born	570,273	45,270,103
Male	49.4	48.7
Female	50.6	51.3
Foreign born; naturalized U.S. citizen	279,215	24,044,083
Male	47.2	46.4
Female	52.8	53.6
Foreign born; not a U.S. citizen	291,058	21,226,020
Male	51.5	51.2
Female	48.5	48.8
Entered 2010 or later	29.1	28.1
Entered 2000 to 2009	27.7	23.7
Entered before 2000	43.3	48.2
World Region of Birth, Foreign		
Foreign-born population, excluding population born at sea	570,273	45,269,644
Europe	14.4	10.7
Asia	23.7	31.0
Africa	7.4	5.7
Oceania	0.8	0.6
Latin America	51.0	50.1
North America	2.7	1.7
Language Spoken at Home and Ability to Speak English		
Population 5 years and over	5,504,232	313,232,500
English only	83.8	78.4
Language other than English	16.2	21.6
Speaks English less than "very well"	5.7	8.3

Table CO-5. Median Income and Poverty Status, 2021

(Number, percent, except as noted.)

Characteristic	State		U.S.	
	Number	Percent	Number	Percent
Median Income				
Households (dollars)...	82,254	X	69,717	X
Families (dollars)	102,073	X	85,806	X
Below Poverty Level (All People)	553,272	9.7	41,393,176	12.8
Sex				
Male	252,334	8.8	18,518,155	11.6
Female	300,938	10.6	22,875,021	13.9
Age				
Under 18 years..	144,882	11.8	12,243,219	16.9
Related children under 18 years............................	139,663	11.5	11,985,424	16.6
18 to 64 years...	341,510	9.5	23,526,341	11.9
65 years and over	66,880	7.7	5,623,616	10.3

X = Not applicable.

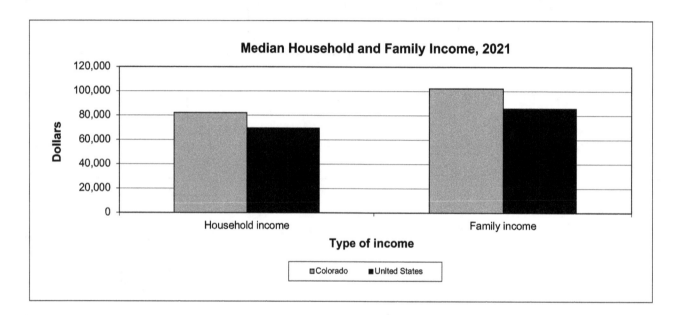

Table CO-6. Health Insurance Coverage Status for the Civilian Noninstitutionalized Population and Children Under 19 Years of Age

(Number, percent.)

Item	2011	2012	2013	2014	2015	2016	2017	2018	2019	2020 [2]	2021
Civilian Noninstitutionalized Population	5,024,885	5,094,766	5,173,272	5,266,022	5,367,335	5,447,760	5,514,070	5,604,105	5,664,199	5,588,760	5,715,497
Covered by Private or Public Insurance											
Number..	4,265,266	4,343,522	4,444,084	4,723,411	4,934,713	5,038,017	5,099,993	5,182,461	5,210,724	5,152,499	5,260,137
Percent...	84.9	85.3	85.9	89.7	91.9	92.5	92.5	92.5	92.0	92.2	92.0
Uninsured											
Number..	759,619	751,244	729,188	542,611	432,622	409,743	414,077	421,644	453,475	436,261	455,360
Percent...	15.1	14.7	14.1	10.3	8.1	7.5	7.5	7.5	8.0	7.8	8.0
Percent in the U.S. not covered................	15.1	14.8	14.5	11.7	9.4	8.6	8.7	8.9	9.2	8.7	8.6
Children Under 19 Years of Age[1]	1,226,828	1,229,008	1,239,191	1,245,432	1,254,800	1,258,167	1,334,235	1,345,058	1,331,001	1,331,681	1,317,605
Covered by Private or Public Insurance											
Number..	1,111,102	1,120,313	1,137,042	1,175,348	1,202,377	1,207,518	1,276,752	1,282,826	1,258,445	1,267,329	1,256,505
Percent...	90.6	91.2	91.8	94.4	95.8	96.0	95.7	95.4	94.5	95.2	95.4
Uninsured											
Number..	115,726	108,695	102,149	70,084	52,423	50,649	57,483	62,232	72,556	64,352	61,100
Percent...	9.4	8.8	8.2	5.6	4.2	4.0	4.3	4.6	5.5	4.8	4.6
Percent in the U.S. not covered................	7.5	7.2	7.1	6.0	4.8	4.5	5.0	5.2	5.7	5.2	5.4

[1] Data for years prior to 2017 are for individuals under 18 years of age.
[2] 2020 ACS 5-Year estimates. 1-Year estimates were not released for 2020 due to the impact of COVID-19 on data collection that year. Data is not comparable to previous years, which are based on 1-year estimates.

Table CO-7. Employment Status by Demographic Group, 2022

(Numbers in thousands, percent.)

Characteristic	Civilian noninstitutional population	Civilian labor force		Employed		Unemployed	
		Number	Percent of population	Number	Percent of population	Number	Percent of population
Total.........................	4,677	3,210	68.6	3,110	66.5	100	3.1
Sex							
Male............................	2,342	1,733	74.0	1,677	71.6	56	3.2
Female	2,335	1,476	63.2	1,433	61.4	44	3.0
Race, Sex, and Hispanic Origin							
White	4,103	2,801	68.3	2,720	66.3	81	2.9
Male........................	2,040	1,503	73.7	1,459	71.5	45	3.0
Female	2,063	1,297	62.9	1,261	61.1	36	2.8
Black or African American............	NA	NA	NA	NA	NA	NA	NA
Male........................	NA	NA	NA	NA	NA	NA	NA
Female	NA	NA	NA	NA	NA	NA	NA
Hispanic or Latino ethnicity[1]	801	559	69.7	543	67.7	16	2.9
Male........................	417	324	77.7	315	75.5	9	2.7
Female	385	235	61.1	228	59.2	7	3.1
Age							
16 to 19 years.................	NA	NA	NA	NA	NA	NA	NA
20 to 24 years.................	383	295	77.1	272	71.1	23	7.7
25 to 34 years.................	893	775	86.7	751	84.1	23	3.0
35 to 44 years.................	813	698	85.9	678	83.3	21	3.0
45 to 54 years.................	728	627	86.1	615	84.5	12	1.9
55 to 64 years.................	705	501	71.1	494	70.0	8	1.6
65 years and over	860	196	22.8	192	22.3	4	2.1

NOTE: Data in Table 7 are from the Current Population Survey (CPS) and do not match the estimates in Table 8. See notes and definitions for further information.
[1] May be of any race.
NA = Not available.

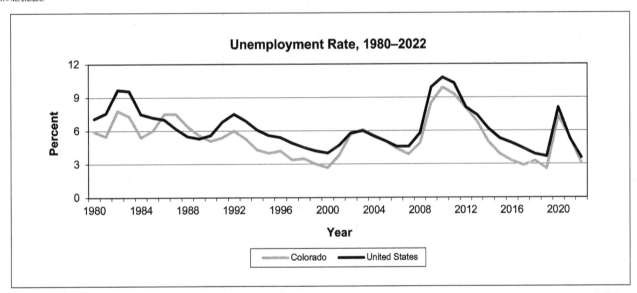

Unemployment Rate, 1980–2022

Table CO-8. Employment Status of the Civilian Noninstitutional Population Age 16 Years and Over

(Number, percent.)

Year	Civilian labor force	Civilian participation rate	Employed	Unemployed	Unemployment rate
2010...............................	2,715,723	70.2	2,466,996	248,727	9.2
2011...............................	2,730,262	69.6	2,493,472	236,790	8.7
2012...............................	2,749,192	68.8	2,529,785	219,407	8.0
2013...............................	2,766,140	68.0	2,579,568	186,572	6.7
2014...............................	2,800,666	67.6	2,661,070	139,596	5.0
2015...............................	2,825,761	66.7	2,719,997	105,764	3.7
2016...............................	2,894,157	67.0	2,803,504	90,653	3.1
2017...............................	2,963,790	67.7	2,885,980	77,810	2.6
2018...............................	3,049,640	68.5	2,957,690	91,950	3.0
2019...............................	3,100,598	68.6	3,019,934	80,664	2.6
2020...............................	3,087,271	67.4	2,874,857	212,414	6.0
2021...............................	3,156,110	68.2	2,986,711	169,399	5.4
2022...............................	3,200,625	68.4	3,103,531	97,094	3.0

Table CO-9. Employment and Average Wages by Industry

(Estimates are based on the 2012 North American Industry Classification System [NAICS].)

Industry	2014	2015	2016	2017	2018	2019	2020	2021
	Dollars							
Wage and Salary Employment by Industry......	2,593,887	2,670,453	2,726,685	2,784,085	2,852,274	2,916,438	2,781,124	2,881,642
Farm Wage and Salary Employment...........	11,976	11,633	12,285	14,783	12,934	12,965	13,700	12,471
Nonfarm Wage and Salary Employment.........	2,581,911	2,658,820	2,714,400	2,769,302	2,839,340	2,903,473	2,767,424	2,869,171
Private wage and salary employment.........	2,111,086	2,180,679	2,227,860	2,276,555	2,339,140	2,392,647	2,262,877	2,360,069
Forestry, fishing, and related activities......	6,409	6,495	6,562	6,819	6,898	7,174	6,817	6,162
Mining..............	33,706	30,394	23,467	25,450	28,067	28,583	21,487	19,604
Utilities............	8,148	8,209	8,235	8,078	8,042	8,172	8,308	8,465
Construction........	145,844	152,503	159,077	167,337	177,343	183,371	179,203	181,217
Manufacturing......	136,558	141,021	142,505	144,217	147,446	150,378	146,685	148,819
Durable goods manufacturing........	88,226	90,250	89,998	90,372	92,253	94,243	91,653	91,819
Nondurable goods manufacturing......	48,332	50,771	52,507	53,845	55,193	56,135	55,032	57,000
Wholesale trade......	100,328	103,721	105,320	107,159	108,744	110,688	108,267	110,130
Retail trade........	256,824	264,890	270,865	272,508	275,075	274,370	264,149	274,130
Transportation and warehousing......	69,499	71,547	71,747	76,057	80,841	87,081	89,994	96,161
Information........	70,263	70,896	71,819	71,692	75,111	76,388	74,924	76,322
Finance and insurance......	108,816	111,546	114,229	117,228	118,922	120,090	121,413	123,084
Real estate and rental and leasing......	45,165	47,843	49,637	51,414	53,541	56,156	53,858	56,514
Professional, scientific, and technical services......	198,200	206,260	211,670	217,294	226,649	237,425	241,258	256,642
Management of companies and enterprises......	35,483	36,532	36,902	39,048	40,861	42,406	42,010	43,403
Administrative and waste services......	155,233	158,618	159,784	159,123	159,790	163,153	150,648	156,208
Educational services......	47,937	49,513	51,541	52,255	53,536	54,714	50,489	57,203
Health care and social assistance......	264,876	278,667	290,427	296,680	302,528	307,992	301,847	308,456
Arts, entertainment, and recreation......	50,692	51,295	53,627	56,534	57,917	60,020	45,342	50,958
Accommodation and food services......	252,399	263,057	272,071	278,945	284,078	287,685	229,038	256,404
Other services, except public administration......	124,706	127,672	128,375	128,717	133,751	136,801	127,140	130,187
Government and government enterprises......	470,825	478,141	486,540	492,747	500,200	510,826	504,547	509,102
	Dollars							
Average Wages and Salaries by Industry......	53,428	54,855	55,370	57,603	59,715	62,435	67,285	71,234
Average Farm Wages and Salaries......	40,852	35,594	39,020	32,613	38,974	27,836	35,088	44,817
Average Nonfarm Wages and Salaries......	53,486	54,939	55,444	57,736	59,809	62,589	67,444	71,349
Average private wages and salaries......	54,236	55,709	56,096	58,590	60,662	63,662	68,941	73,219
Forestry, fishing, and related activities......	27,564	29,364	30,278	31,656	32,594	35,467	37,267	39,847
Mining..............	113,727	115,767	115,853	118,670	122,675	126,428	141,280	139,646
Utilities............	93,431	96,785	99,390	103,508	108,570	114,540	120,028	124,452
Construction........	54,558	56,260	58,235	60,346	63,339	65,481	69,319	72,473
Manufacturing......	67,036	68,409	68,151	71,315	72,610	75,852	79,466	83,118
Durable goods manufacturing........	73,717	76,079	76,279	81,167	82,053	85,845	89,547	92,814
Nondurable goods manufacturing......	54,841	54,776	54,218	54,778	56,828	59,075	62,675	67,499
Wholesale trade......	78,930	80,926	81,393	84,954	87,431	92,256	97,197	104,836
Retail trade........	30,248	31,248	31,739	32,732	33,600	34,955	38,495	41,217
Transportation and warehousing......	54,509	55,752	56,478	59,225	59,834	61,773	61,985	64,670
Information........	97,812	96,212	97,571	102,935	102,862	111,470	126,091	134,116
Finance and insurance......	84,937	89,862	91,805	94,354	98,129	103,625	113,525	120,729
Real estate and rental and leasing......	51,946	54,434	56,279	58,544	60,835	62,674	67,267	74,816
Professional, scientific, and technical services......	88,599	90,251	91,729	94,929	99,166	104,471	107,739	118,103
Management of companies and enterprises......	136,932	145,522	131,163	151,767	139,317	151,858	156,070	166,849
Administrative and waste services......	37,137	38,891	40,050	42,401	45,374	47,161	50,224	54,536
Educational services......	35,525	36,042	36,304	36,687	38,453	38,807	45,416	43,273
Health care and social assistance......	48,225	49,540	50,098	51,116	52,600	54,093	57,810	60,511
Arts, entertainment, and recreation......	36,906	39,520	40,065	40,151	42,245	42,758	47,602	50,068
Accommodation and food services......	22,479	23,385	24,106	25,429	27,365	28,802	28,424	33,532
Other services, except public administration......	35,861	37,392	38,704	40,419	41,612	42,906	47,108	50,041
Government and government enterprises......	50,124	51,429	52,460	53,795	55,822	57,562	60,733	62,679

Table CO-10. Employment Characteristics by Family Type

(Number, percent.)

Family type and labor force status	2019 Total	2019 Families with own children under 18 years	2020 [1] Total	2020 [1] Families with own children under 18 years	2021 Total	2021 Families with own children under 18 years
All Families..	1,421,844	595,144	1,358,903	589,228	1,448,655	599,496
FAMILY TYPE AND LABOR FORCE STATUS						
Opposite-Sex Married-Couple Families..	1,116,767	443,303	1,058,010	434,625	1,109,088	433,391
Both husband and wife in labor force...........................	53.9	66.8	54.7	67.0	54.8	69.1
Husband in labor force, wife not in labor force	21.7	27.9	22.0	28.0	20.9	26.1
Wife in labor force, husband not in labor force	7.2	3.6	7.2	3.7	7.1	3.7
Both husband and wife not in labor force............	16.0	1.1	16.1	1.3	17.2	1.1
Other Families	305,077	151,841	289,237	152,275	324,583	162,953
Female householder, no spouse present	66.0	67.8	66.9	68.1	67.0	69.4
In labor force..	49.3	59.1	50.7	59.5	49.8	60.0
Not in labor force	16.6	8.7	16.3	8.6	17.2	9.4
Male householder, no spouse present	34.0	32.2	33.1	31.9	33.0	30.6
In labor force..	28.7	30.5	27.5	29.8	26.8	27.8
Not in labor force	5.3	1.7	5.5	2.0	6.2	2.8

[1] 2020 ACS 5-Year estimates. 1-Year estimates were not released for 2020 due to the impact of COVID-19 on data collection that year. Data is not comparable to previous years, which are based on 1-year estimates.

Table CO-11. School Enrollment and Educational Attainment, 2021

(Number, percent.)

Item	State	U.S.
Enrollment		
Total population 3 years and over, enrolled in school	1,383,214	79,453,524
Enrolled in nursery school or preschool (percent)	5.5	5.2
Enrolled in kindergarten (percent)	4.7	5.0
Enrolled in elementary school, grades 1-8 (percent)...........	41.1	41.3
Enrolled in high school, grades 9-12 (percent)	21.7	21.8
Enrolled in college or graduate school (percent)	27	26.7
Attainment		
Total population 25 years and over	4,044,182	228,193,464
Less than ninth grade (percent)	3.3	4.8
9th to 12th grade, no diploma (percent)	4.2	5.9
High school graduate, including equivalency (percent).........	20.1	26.3
Some college, no degree (percent)	19.6	19.3
Associate's degree (percent)	8.3	8.8
Bachelor's degree (percent)	27.4	21.2
Graduate or professional degree (percent)	17.0	13.8
High school graduate or higher (percent)	92.4	89.4
Bachelor's degree or higher (percent).........................	44.4	35.0

Table CO-12. Public School Characteristics and Educational Indicators

(Number, percent; data derived from National Center of Education Statistics.)

Item	State	U.S.
Public Elementary and Secondary Schools		
Number of regular school districts, 2019-20	178	13,349
Number of operational schools, 2019-20....................	1,920	98,469
Percent charter schools	13.6	7.7
Total public school enrollment, Fall 2021	880,597	49,433,092
Percent charter school enrollment	14.8	7.5
Student-teacher ratio, Fall 2019	16.9	15.9
Expenditures per student (unadjusted dollars), 2019-20	11,583	13,489
Four-year adjusted cohort graduation rate (ACGR), 2019-2020[1].........	81.9	86.5
Students eligible for free or reduced-price lunch (percent), 2019-20........	40.7	52.1
English language learners (percent), Fall 2020	10.5	10.3
Students age 3 to 21 served under IDEA, part B (percent), 2021-22	12.4	14.7

Public Schools by Type, 2019-20	Number	Percent of state public schools
Total number of schools....................................	1,920	100.0
Special education	5	0.3
Vocational education	7	0.4
Alternative education..	113	5.9

[1] Adjusted Cohort Graduation Rates (ACGR) differ from Averaged Freshmen Graduation Rates (AFGR).

Table CO-13. Reported Voting and Registration of the Voting-Age Population, November 2022

(Numbers in thousands, percent.)

Item	Total population	Total citizen population	Registered			Voted		
			Total registered	Percent registered (total population)	Percent registered (total citizen population)	Total voted	Percent voted (total population)	Percent voted (total citizen population)
U.S. Total	255,457	233,546	161,422	63.2	69.1	121,916	47.7	52.2
State Total	4,571	4,384	3,162	69.2	72.1	2,687	58.8	61.3
Sex								
Male	2,282	2,190	1,510	66.2	68.9	1,283	56.2	58.6
Female	2,290	2,194	1,653	72.2	75.3	1,404	61.3	64.0
Race								
White alone	4,083	3,925	2,897	71.0	73.8	2,504	61.3	63.8
White, non-Hispanic alone	3,438	3,396	2,558	74.4	75.3	2,273	66.1	66.9
Black alone	197	197	108	55.0	55.0	56	28.3	28.3
Asian alone	109	89	62	57.4	70.0	52	47.8	58.2
Hispanic (of any race)	748	623	391	52.3	62.8	269	35.9	43.1
White alone or in combination	4,203	4,035	2,957	70.4	73.3	2,553	60.8	63.3
Black alone or in combination	219	219	121	55.5	55.5	69	31.5	31.5
Asian alone or in combination	161	141	99	61.5	70.0	81	50.4	57.4
Age								
18 to 24 years	471	458	227	48.2	49.6	158	33.6	34.5
25 to 34 years	918	875	577	62.8	65.9	437	47.6	50.0
35 to 44 years	873	825	608	69.7	73.7	490	56.2	59.4
45 to 64 years	1,465	1,419	1,110	75.8	78.2	1,001	68.3	70.5
65 years and over	845	808	640	75.8	79.3	601	71.1	74.4

Table CO-14. Health Indicators

(Number, rate as indicated in footnotes.)

Item	State	U.S.
Births		
Life Expectancy at Birth (years), 2020	78.3	77.0
Fertility Rate by State[1], 2021	52.5	56.3
Percent Home Births, 2021	2.0	1.4
Cesarean Delivery Rate[2], 2021	27.3	32.1
Preterm Birth Rate[3], 2021	9.8	10.5
Teen Birth Rate[4], 2021	11.4	13.9
Percentage of Babies Born Low Birthweight[5], 2021	9.5	8.5
Deaths[6]		
Heart Disease Mortality Rate, 2021	135.1	173.8
Cancer Mortality Rate, 2021	126.5	146.6
Stroke Mortality Rate, 2021	35.5	41.1
Diabetes Mortality Rate, 2021	19.0	25.4
Influenza/Pneumonia Mortality Rate, 2021	4.8	10.5
Suicide Mortality Rate, 2021	22.8	14.1
Drug Overdose Mortality Rate, 2021	31.4	33.6
Firearm Injury Mortality Rate, 2021	17.8	14.6
Homicide Mortality Rate, 2021	6.3	8.2
Disease and Illness		
Lifetime Asthma in Adults, 2020 (percent)	14.1	13.9
Lifetime Asthma in Children, 2020 (percent)[7]	NA	11.3
Diabetes in Adults, 2020 (percent)	7.1	8.2
Self-reported Obesity in Adults, 2021 (percent)	25.1	NA

SOURCE: National Center for Health Statistics, National Vital Statistics System 2020 data; https://wonder.cdc.gov.
[1] General fertility rate per 1,000 women aged 15–44.
[2] This represents the percentage of all live births that were cesarean deliveries.
[3] Babies born prior to 37 weeks of pregnancy (gestation).
[4] Number of births per 1,000 females aged 15–19
[5] Babies born weighing less than 2,500 grams or 5 lbs. 8oz.
[6] Death rates are the number of deaths per 100,000 total population.
[7] U.S. total includes data from 30 states and D.C.
NA = Not available.
- = Zero or rounds to zero.

Table CO-15. State Government Finances, 2021

(Dollar amounts in thousands, percent distribution.)

Item	Dollars	Percent distribution
Total Revenue	46,751,819	100.0
General revenue	40,076,190	85.7
Intergovernmental revenue	14,384,700	30.8
Taxes	18,817,848	40.3
General sales	3,660,590	7.8
Selective sales	2,912,346	6.2
License taxes	720,335	1.5
Individual income tax	10,246,531	21.9
Corporate income tax	1,278,046	2.7
Other taxes	-	-
Current charges	4,517,774	9.7
Miscellaneous general revenue	2,355,868	5.0
Utility revenue	-	-
Liquor stores revenue	-	-
Insurance trust revenue[1]	6,675,629	14.3
Total Expenditure	46,270,243	100.0
Intergovernmental expenditure	9,067,544	19.6
Direct expenditure	37,202,699	80.4
Current operation	23,748,203	51.3
Capital outlay	1,886,935	4.1
Insurance benefits and repayments	9,753,962	21.1
Assistance and subsidies	929,630	2.0
Interest on debt	883,969	1.9
Exhibit: Salaries and wages	6,522,600	14.1
Total Expenditure	46,270,243	100.0
General expenditure	36,505,227	78.9
Intergovernmental expenditure	9,067,544	19.6
Direct expenditure	27,437,683	59.3
General expenditure, by function:		
Education	13,138,558	28.4
Public welfare	11,915,017	25.8
Hospitals	1,444,119	3.1
Health	1,094,763	2.4
Highways	2,144,872	4.6
Police protection	304,303	0.7
Correction	1,179,230	2.5
Natural resources	420,936	0.9
Parks and recreation	114,954	0.2
Governmental administration	1,615,908	3.5
Interest on general debt	875,822	1.9
Other and unallocable	2,174,762	4.7
Utility expenditure	11,347	-
Liquor stores expenditure	-	-
Insurance trust expenditure	9,753,962	21.1
Debt at End of Fiscal Year	22,328,511	X
Cash and Security Holdings	107,921,745	X

X = Not applicable.
- = Zero or rounds to zero.
[1] Within insurance trust revenue, net earnings of state retirement systems is a calculated statistic (the item code in the data file is X08), and thus can be positive or negative. Net earnings is the sum of earnings on investments plus gains on investments minus losses on investments. The change made in 2002 for asset valuation from book to market value in accordance with Statement 34 of the Governmental Accounting Standards Board is reflected in the calculated statistics.

Table CO-16. State Government Tax Collections, 2022

(Dollars in thousands, percent.)

Item	Dollars	Percent distribution
Total Taxes	21,711,093	100.0
Property taxes	X	-
Sales and gross receipts	7,491,009	34.5
General sales and gross receipts	4,286,196	19.7
Selective sales and gross receipts	3,204,813	14.8
Alcoholic beverages	55,555	0.3
Amusements	153,595	0.7
Insurance premiums	338,355	1.6
Motor fuels	665,944	3.1
Pari-mutuels	373	-
Public utilities	X	-
Tobacco products	352,438	1.6
Other selective sales	1,638,553	7.5
Licenses	718,795	3.3
Alcoholic beverages	6,263	-
Amusements	978	-
Corporations in general	24,014	0.1
Hunting and fishing	119,501	0.6
Motor vehicle	436,209	2.0
Motor vehicle operators	47,673	0.2
Public utilities	16,545	0.1
Occupation and business, NEC	67,582	0.3
Other licenses	30	-
Income taxes	13,194,479	60.8
Individual income	11,685,999	53.8
Corporation net income	1,508,480	6.9
Other taxes	306,810	-
Death and gift	X	-
Documentary and stock transfer	X	-
Severance	306,810	1.4
Taxes, NEC	X	-

X = Not applicable.
- = Zero or rounds to zero.

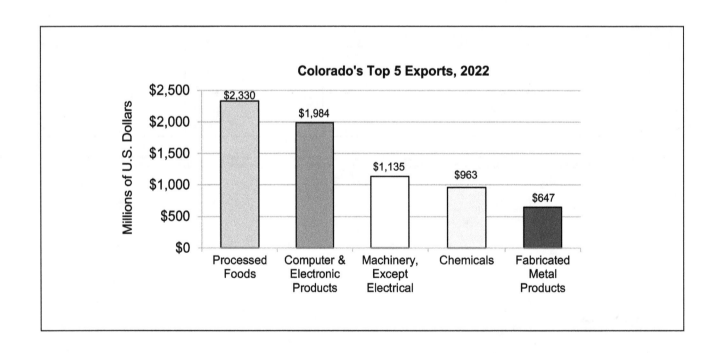

CONNECTICUT

Facts and Figures

Location: Northeastern United States; bordered on the N by Massachusetts, on the E by Rhode Island, on the S by Long Island Sound, and on the W by New York

Area: 5,543 sq. mi. (14,357); rank—48th

Population: 3,626,205 (2022 est.); rank—29th

Principal Cities: capital—Hartford; largest—Bridgeport

Statehood: January 9, 1788; 5th state

U.S. Congress: 2 senators, 5 representatives

State Motto: *Qui transtulit sustinet* ("He who transplanted still sustains")

State Song: "Yankee Doodle"

State Nicknames: The Constitution State; The Nutmeg State

Abbreviations: CT; Conn.

State Symbols: flower—mountain laurel; tree—white oak; bird—American robin

At a Glance

- Connecticut experienced a 1.5 percent increase in population between 2010 and 2022, which ranked 45th in the country.

- Connecticut's median household income in 2021 was $83,771, compared to the national median household income of $69,717.

- In 2021, 42.1 percent of Connecticut residents age 25 and older had a bachelor's degree or higher, which was the 7th highest percent in the country.

- Connecticut's per capita personal income in 2022 was $84,972, ranking 2nd in the nation.

- Connecticut's drug overdose death rate in 2021 was 42.3 deaths per 100,000 population, compared to the national rate of 32.4 deaths. The state's homicide rate was 4.8 deaths per 100,000 population, which ranked 34th in the nation.

Table CT-1. Population by Age, Sex, Race, and Hispanic Origin

(Number, percent, except where noted.)

Sex, age, race, and Hispanic origin	2010	2020	2022	Percent change, 2010–2022
Total Population...	3,574,097	3,605,942	3,626,205	1.5
Percent of total U.S. population	1.2	1.1	1.1	X
Sex				
Male	1,739,614	1,768,524	1,776,254	2.1
Female	1,834,483	1,837,418	1,849,951	0.8
Age				
Under 5 years..	202,106	182,947	181,607	-10.1
Under 18 years..	817,015	746,267	731,030	-10.5
18 to 64 years...	2,250,523	2,233,294	2,231,857	-0.8
65 years and over..	506,559	626,381	663,318	30.9
Median age (years)	40.0	40.9	40.9	2.2
Race and Hispanic Origin				
One race				
White	2,950,820	2,855,341	2,841,487	-3.7
Black	392,131	449,309	467,161	19.1
American Indian and Alaska Native	16,734	23,088	26,709	59.6
Asian...	140,516	181,288	187,571	33.5
Native Hawaiian or Other Pacific Islander	3,491	4,062	4,154	19.0
Two or more races	70,405	92,854	99,123	40.8
Hispanic (of any race)..	479,087	623,511	658,979	37.5

NOTE: Population figures for 2022 are July 1 estimates. The 2010 and 2020 estimates are taken from the respective censuses.
- = Zero or rounds to zero.
X = Not applicable.

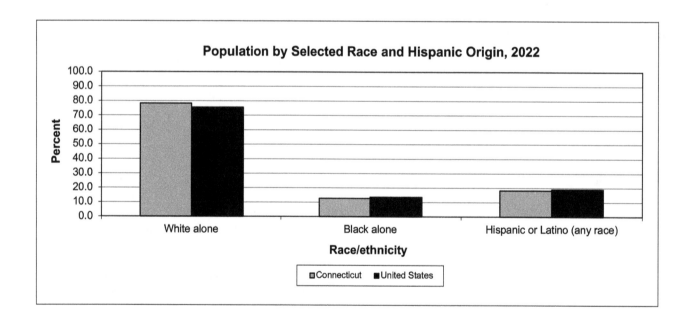

Table CT-2. Marital Status

(Number, percent distribution.)

Sex, age, race, and Hispanic origin	2000	2010	2021
Males, 15 Years and Over	1,284,881	1,399,329	1,468,595
Never married	30.0	36.3	38.7
Now married, except separated...	58.0	50.6	49.5
Separated...	1.3	1.1	1.2
Widowed...	2.7	2.7	2.5
Divorced...	7.9	9.3	8.1
Females, 15 Years and Over	1,411,369	1,512,492	1,549,940
Never married	24.5	29.9	33.2
Now married, except separated...	52.3	46.5	44.5
Separated...	1.8	1.8	1.6
Widowed...	10.8	9.3	8.1
Divorced...	10.5	12.5	12.5

Table CT-3. Households and Housing Characteristics

(Number, percent, dollars.)

Item	2000	2010	2021	Average annual percent change, 2010–2021
Total Households	1,301,670	1,358,809	1,428,313	0.5
Family households	881,170	890,770	916,362	0.3
Married-couple family	676,467	656,629	664,848	0.1
Other family	204,703	234,141	251,514	0.7
Male householder, no wife present	47,292	58,325	64,625	1.0
Female householder, no husband present	157,411	175,816	186,889	0.6
Nonfamily households	420,500	468,039	511,951	0.9
Householder living alone	334,224	384,382	411,766	0.6
Householder not living alone	76,276	83,657	100,185	1.8
Housing Characteristics				
Total housing units	1,385,975	1,488,215	1,536,327	0.3
Occupied housing units	1,301,670	1,358,809	1,428,313	0.5
Owner occupied	869,729	923,617	951,516	0.3
Renter occupied	431,941	435,192	476,797	0.9
Average household size	2.53	2.55	2.45	-0.4
Financial Characteristics				
Median gross rent of renter-occupied housing	681	992	1,277	2.6
Median monthly owner costs for housing units with a mortgage	1,426	2,068	2,083	0.1
Median value of owner-occupied housing units	166,900	288,800	311,500	0.7

Table CT-4. Migration, Origin, and Language

(Number, percent.)

Characteristic	State 2021	U.S. 2021
Residence 1 Year Ago		
Population 1 year and over	3,571,470	328,464,538
Same house	88.7	87.2
Different house in the U.S.	10.8	12.3
Same county	5.9	6.7
Different county	4.9	5.7
Same state	1.9	3.3
Different state	3.0	2.4
Abroad	0.5	0.4
Place of Birth		
Native born	3,056,156	286,623,642
Male	49.3	49.7
Female	50.7	50.3
Foreign born	549,441	45,270,103
Male	47.8	48.7
Female	52.2	51.3
Foreign born; naturalized U.S. citizen	309,158	24,044,083
Male	45.2	46.4
Female	54.8	53.6
Foreign born; not a U.S. citizen	240,283	21,226,020
Male	51.2	51.2
Female	48.8	48.8
Entered 2010 or later	27.9	28.1
Entered 2000 to 2009	25.7	23.7
Entered before 2000	46.4	48.2
World Region of Birth, Foreign		
Foreign-born population, excluding population born at sea	549,441	45,269,644
Europe	22.3	10.7
Asia	23.7	31.0
Africa	5.2	5.7
Oceania	0.4	0.6
Latin America	46.1	50.1
North America	2.3	1.7
Language Spoken at Home and Ability to Speak English		
Population 5 years and over	3,428,020	313,232,500
English only	77.2	78.4
Language other than English	22.8	21.6
Speaks English less than "very well"	8.9	8.3

Table CT-5. Median Income and Poverty Status, 2021

(Number, percent, except as noted.)

Characteristic	State Number	State Percent	U.S. Number	U.S. Percent
Median Income				
Households (dollars)..	83,771	X	69,717	X
Families (dollars)	106,576	X	85,806	X
Below Poverty Level (All People)	354,166	10.1	41,393,176	12.8
Sex				
Male	160,723	9.4	18,518,155	11.6
Female	193,443	10.8	22,875,021	13.9
Age				
Under 18 years...	91,767	12.7	12,243,219	16.9
Related children under 18 years...............................	88,900	12.4	11,985,424	16.6
18 to 64 years..	208,425	9.7	23,526,341	11.9
65 years and over	53,974	8.6	5,623,616	10.3

X = Not applicable.

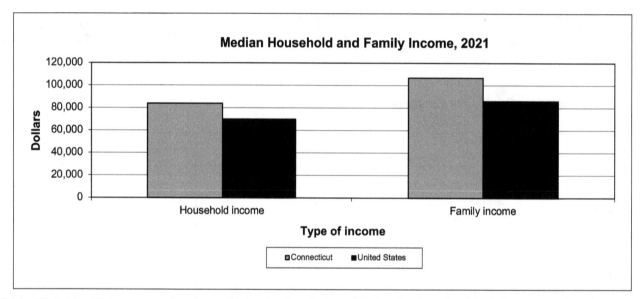

Table CT-6. Health Insurance Coverage Status for the Civilian Noninstitutionalized Population and Children Under 19 Years of Age

(Number, percent.)

Item	2011	2012	2013	2014	2015	2016	2017	2018	2019	2020 [2]	2021
Civilian Noninstitutionalized Population	3,522,709	3,534,619	3,541,409	3,541,282	3,537,983	3,525,154	3,536,522	3,523,842	3,514,562	3,520,172	3,557,526
Covered by Private or Public Insurance											
Number..	3,213,764	3,212,647	3,208,906	3,295,883	3,327,461	3,352,940	3,342,726	3,336,919	3,307,378	3,341,106	3,373,995
Percent..	91.2	90.9	90.6	93.1	94.0	95.1	94.5	94.7	94.1	94.9	94.8
Uninsured											
Number..	308,945	321,972	332,503	245,399	210,522	172,214	193,796	186,923	207,184	179,066	183,531
Percent..	8.8	9.1	9.4	6.9	6.0	4.9	5.5	5.3	5.9	5.1	5.2
Percent in the U.S. not covered................................	15.1	14.8	14.5	11.7	9.4	8.6	8.7	8.9	9.2	8.7	8.6
Children Under 19 Years of Age[1]	802,350	791,825	784,159	774,021	761,921	751,459	792,881	788,981	773,214	786,563	775,396
Covered by Private or Public Insurance											
Number..	778,973	761,897	750,504	745,151	736,821	730,592	768,525	768,609	746,313	764,094	756,774
Percent..	97.1	96.2	95.7	96.3	96.7	97.2	96.9	97.4	96.5	97.1	97.6
Uninsured											
Number..	23,377	29,928	33,655	28,870	25,100	20,867	24,356	20,372	26,901	22,469	18,622
Percent..	2.9	3.8	4.3	3.7	3.3	2.8	3.1	2.6	3.5	2.9	2.4
Percent in the U.S. not covered	7.5	7.2	7.1	6.0	4.8	4.5	5.0	5.2	5.7	5.2	5.4

[1] Data for years prior to 2017 are for individuals under 18 years of age.
[2] 2020 ACS 5-Year estimates. 1-Year estimates were not released for 2020 due to the impact of COVID-19 on data collection that year. Data is not comparable to previous years, which are based on 1-year estimates.

Table CT-7. Employment Status by Demographic Group, 2022

(Numbers in thousands, percent.)

Characteristic	Civilian noninstitutional population	Civilian labor force		Employed		Unemployed	
		Number	Percent of population	Number	Percent of population	Number	Percent of population
Total.................................	2,944	1,923	65.3	1,843	62.6	80	4.2
Sex							
Male.................................	1,429	1,005	70.3	955	66.9	50	4.9
Female..............................	1,515	918	60.6	888	58.6	31	3.3
Race, Sex, and Hispanic Origin							
White	2,360	1,524	64.6	1,466	62.1	58	3.8
Male..............................	1,148	800	69.7	765	66.6	35	4.4
Female	1,212	724	59.8	701	57.9	23	3.2
Black or African American.................	354	246	69.6	232	65.5	15	5.9
Male..............................	165	119	72.3	109	65.9	11	8.8
Female	189	127	67.3	123	65.1	4	3.3
Hispanic or Latino ethnicity[1]	457	324	70.8	305	66.8	18	5.6
Male..............................	223	169	75.7	159	71.3	10	5.8
Female	234	155	66.1	147	62.5	8	5.4
Age							
16 to 19 years...................	NA	NA	NA	NA	NA	NA	NA
20 to 24 years...................	199	133	67.1	121	60.8	13	9.5
25 to 34 years...................	488	430	88.0	408	83.6	22	5.0
35 to 44 years...................	466	391	83.9	379	81.3	12	3.2
45 to 54 years...................	434	360	82.9	350	80.6	10	2.8
55 to 64 years...................	544	408	75.0	396	72.8	12	2.9
65 years and over	630	133	21.1	130	20.6	3	2.2

NOTE: Data in Table 7 are from the Current Population Survey (CPS) and do not match the estimates in Table 8. See notes and definitions for further information.
[1] May be of any race.

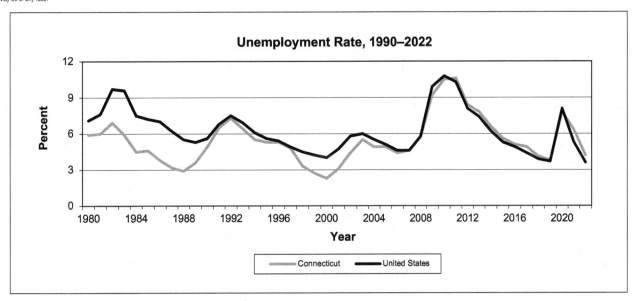

Unemployment Rate, 1990–2022

Table CT-8. Employment Status of the Civilian Noninstitutional Population Age 16 Years and Over

(Number, percent.)

Year	Civilian labor force	Civilian participation rate	Employed	Unemployed	Unemployment rate
2010...............................	1,911,289	68.3	1,728,121	183,168	9.6
2011...............................	1,914,449	67.7	1,741,971	172,478	9.0
2012...............................	1,887,545	66.3	1,729,687	157,858	8.4
2013...............................	1,867,378	65.4	1,718,834	148,544	8.0
2014...............................	1,889,102	65.9	1,764,118	124,984	6.6
2015...............................	1,892,087	65.9	1,785,788	106,299	5.6
2016...............................	1,893,200	65.9	1,801,390	91,810	4.8
2017...............................	1,923,711	66.3	1,838,833	84,878	4.4
2018...............................	1,931,495	66.4	1,855,969	75,526	3.9
2019...............................	1,950,349	66.9	1,881,688	68,661	3.5
2020...............................	1,897,782	65.1	1,749,954	147,828	7.8
2021...............................	1,855,923	63.4	1,739,815	116,108	6.3
2022...............................	1,932,463	65.6	1,851,993	80,470	4.2

Table CT-9. Employment and Average Wages by Industry

(Estimates are based on the 2012 North American Industry Classification System [NAICS].)

Industry	2014	2015	2016	2017	2018	2019	2020	2021
	Dollars							
Wage and Salary Employment by Industry	1,730,733	1,740,318	1,744,009	1,745,197	1,752,016	1,750,171	1,628,139	1,674,998
Farm Wage and Salary Employment	5,478	5,457	5,093	5,082	4,554	4,588	4,382	4,492
Nonfarm Wage and Salary Employment	1,725,255	1,734,861	1,738,916	1,740,115	1,747,462	1,745,583	1,623,757	1,670,506
Private wage and salary employment	1,464,155	1,474,568	1,480,847	1,485,960	1,494,933	1,492,909	1,385,842	1,432,614
Forestry, fishing, and related activities	701	699	665	640	625	638	(D)	604
Mining	547	553	556	539	525	518	(D)	481
Utilities	5,943	5,613	5,624	5,333	5,177	5,161	5,095	4,978
Construction	57,247	59,404	60,582	59,702	60,165	61,097	58,325	60,629
Manufacturing	159,808	159,090	156,561	158,977	160,594	162,030	153,961	153,175
Durable goods manufacturing	124,431	123,740	122,910	124,503	126,263	127,367	121,575	119,994
Nondurable goods manufacturing	35,377	35,350	33,651	34,474	34,331	34,663	32,386	33,181
Wholesale trade	63,318	62,765	62,774	62,813	61,792	59,912	56,166	57,509
Retail trade	186,160	186,038	185,905	184,782	182,205	176,859	161,782	168,685
Transportation and warehousing	43,729	45,324	46,057	47,477	50,153	52,906	56,409	61,604
Information	32,073	32,462	32,412	31,604	31,752	31,514	29,255	29,967
Finance and insurance	111,566	112,247	111,681	110,578	108,108	106,772	104,831	102,208
Real estate and rental and leasing	19,550	20,255	20,355	20,197	20,499	20,675	19,321	19,180
Professional, scientific, and technical services	95,986	96,505	97,601	97,079	97,199	96,642	93,521	96,057
Management of companies and enterprises	31,893	32,936	32,956	32,344	33,663	33,031	31,705	30,477
Administrative and waste services	86,270	88,780	88,997	90,347	91,722	90,541	82,815	88,337
Educational services	69,227	69,664	70,996	72,567	74,318	75,773	73,668	77,815
Health care and social assistance	263,880	265,909	268,872	270,919	272,427	274,854	267,352	271,981
Arts, entertainment, and recreation	27,197	27,025	27,802	28,861	28,993	29,056	20,300	23,464
Accommodation and food services	124,573	125,095	127,212	128,884	129,890	129,688	98,212	111,818
Other services, except public administration	84,487	84,204	83,239	82,317	85,126	85,242	72,026	73,645
Government and government enterprises	261,100	260,293	258,069	254,155	252,529	252,674	237,915	237,892
	Dollars							
Average Wages and Salaries by Industry	62,975	64,569	64,903	65,748	66,798	68,768	73,783	76,221
Average Farm Wages and Salaries	28,804	23,619	29,043	26,415	25,216	19,874	20,209	19,805
Average Nonfarm Wages and Salaries	63,084	64,698	65,008	65,863	66,906	68,896	73,927	76,373
Average private wages and salaries	64,319	65,835	66,145	66,938	67,949	70,154	75,271	77,804
Forestry, fishing, and related activities	26,502	28,070	30,146	29,830	31,029	31,201	(D)	34,028
Mining	70,247	71,329	71,847	76,534	75,309	77,736	(D)	66,177
Utilities	111,297	116,881	112,092	124,289	131,257	135,157	138,584	137,221
Construction	61,080	64,270	66,586	68,656	69,762	72,364	75,609	77,184
Manufacturing	81,393	80,712	79,460	81,880	82,441	85,031	87,747	89,665
Durable goods manufacturing	82,095	81,069	81,468	83,623	84,963	87,708	89,773	91,696
Nondurable goods manufacturing	78,927	79,465	72,127	75,585	73,169	75,191	80,141	82,317
Wholesale trade	87,743	92,686	93,605	94,572	95,480	97,718	103,255	111,287
Retail trade	32,092	33,016	33,264	33,529	34,622	35,876	39,188	41,698
Transportation and warehousing	47,790	48,688	48,832	48,587	48,974	49,833	49,439	51,446
Information	92,966	99,237	102,355	103,193	110,701	120,452	138,941	150,422
Finance and insurance	159,068	163,498	163,344	166,847	169,581	171,827	180,808	192,018
Real estate and rental and leasing	65,776	69,524	70,679	66,303	70,319	72,627	76,503	79,237
Professional, scientific, and technical services	95,867	99,005	101,154	103,410	105,266	110,903	114,903	122,205
Management of companies and enterprises	163,472	162,487	163,349	154,205	151,398	159,995	153,877	157,493
Administrative and waste services	43,014	44,072	44,064	45,640	46,153	47,486	51,473	54,193
Educational services	52,516	53,340	52,998	54,359	54,566	56,871	59,712	59,339
Health care and social assistance	49,835	50,277	50,890	51,493	52,733	54,660	58,210	60,666
Arts, entertainment, and recreation	30,081	31,216	31,386	31,777	32,957	33,659	39,751	40,640
Accommodation and food services	22,063	23,102	23,922	24,574	25,680	26,413	26,027	30,879
Other services, except public administration	33,578	34,657	35,312	36,517	37,307	38,224	41,639	43,552
Government and government enterprises	56,160	58,257	58,482	59,577	60,734	61,468	66,098	67,756

(D) = Not shown to avoid disclosure of confidential information; estimates are included in higher-level totals.

Table CT-10. Employment Characteristics by Family Type

(Number, percent.)

Family type and labor force status	2019 Total	2019 Families with own children under 18 years	2020[1] Total	2020[1] Families with own children under 18 years	2021 Total	2021 Families with own children under 18 years
All Families	885,911	346,517	902,996	372,439	916,362	368,451
FAMILY TYPE AND LABOR FORCE STATUS						
Opposite-Sex Married-Couple Families	649,536	237,151	657,447	254,720	655,536	247,213
Both husband and wife in labor force	56.0	72.8	56.7	72.6	56.2	72.8
Husband in labor force, wife not in labor force	19.1	21.8	19.5	22.7	19.7	22.3
Wife in labor force, husband not in labor force	7.4	3.6	7.7	3.6	7.5	4.0
Both husband and wife not in labor force	16.5	1.3	16.1	1.2	16.5	1.0
Other Families	236,375	109,366	238,567	116,424	251,514	119,623
Female householder, no spouse present	72.1	74.8	72.7	76.2	74.3	76.5
In labor force	52.5	65.4	53.5	65.6	54.4	67.3
Not in labor force	19.7	9.3	19.2	10.6	19.9	9.2
Male householder, no spouse present	27.9	25.2	27.3	23.8	25.7	23.5
In labor force	21.9	23.4	22.0	22.1	19.4	21.0
Not in labor force	5.9	1.9	5.4	1.7	6.3	2.5

[1] 2020 ACS 5-Year estimates. 1-Year estimates were not released for 2020 due to the impact of COVID-19 on data collection that year. Data is not comparable to previous years, which are based on 1-year estimates.

Table CT-11. School Enrollment and Educational Attainment, 2021

(Number, percent.)

Item	State	U.S.
Enrollment		
Total population 3 years and over, enrolled in school	874,560	79,453,524
Enrolled in nursery school or preschool (percent)	5.4	5.2
Enrolled in kindergarten (percent)	4.3	5.0
Enrolled in elementary school, grades 1-8 (percent)	37.2	41.3
Enrolled in high school, grades 9-12 (percent)	22.1	21.8
Enrolled in college or graduate school (percent)	30.9	26.7
Attainment		
Total population 25 years and over	2,534,376	228,193,464
Less than ninth grade (percent)	4.3	4.8
9th to 12th grade, no diploma (percent)	4.6	5.9
High school graduate, including equivalency (percent)	25.5	26.3
Some college, no degree (percent)	16	19.3
Associate's degree (percent)	7.4	8.8
Bachelor's degree (percent)	23.2	21.2
Graduate or professional degree (percent)	18.9	13.8
High school graduate or higher (percent)	91.1	89.4
Bachelor's degree or higher (percent)	42.1	35.0

Table CT-12. Public School Characteristics and Educational Indicators

(Number, percent; data derived from National Center of Education Statistics.)

Item	State	U.S.
Public Elementary and Secondary Schools		
Number of regular school districts, 2019-20	169	13,349
Number of operational schools, 2019-20	1,004	98,469
Percent charter schools	2.2	7.7
Total public school enrollment, Fall 2021	509,748	49,433,092
Percent charter school enrollment	2.2	7.5
Student-teacher ratio, Fall 2019	12.4	15.9
Expenditures per student (unadjusted dollars), 2019-20	20,889	13,489
Four-year adjusted cohort graduation rate (ACGR), 2019-2020[1]	88.3	86.5
Students eligible for free or reduced-price lunch (percent), 2019-20	42.7	52.1
English language learners (percent), Fall 2020	8.0	10.3
Students age 3 to 21 served under IDEA, part B (percent), 2021-22	16.9	14.7

Public Schools by Type, 2019-20	Number	Percent of state public schools
Total number of schools	1,004	100.0
Special education	2	0.2
Vocational education	17	1.7
Alternative education	3	0.3

[1] Adjusted Cohort Graduation Rates (ACGR) differ from Averaged Freshmen Graduation Rates (AFGR).

Table CT-13. Reported Voting and Registration of the Voting-Age Population, November 2022

(Numbers in thousands, percent.)

Item	Total population	Total citizen population	Registered			Voted		
			Total registered	Percent registered (total population)	Percent registered (total citizen population)	Total voted	Percent voted (total population)	Percent voted (total citizen population)
U.S. Total	255,457	233,546	161,422	63.2	69.1	121,916	47.7	52.2
State Total..	2,839	2,527	1,778	62.6	70.4	1,253	44.1	49.6
Sex								
Male	1,388	1,201	839	60.4	69.8	604	43.5	50.3
Female	1,451	1,325	939	64.7	70.9	649	44.7	49.0
Race								
White alone..	2,247	2,086	1,489	66.2	71.3	1,107	49.3	53.0
White, non-Hispanic alone	1,824	1,763	1,305	71.6	74.0	993	54.5	56.3
Black alone	355	282	204	57.5	72.4	107	30.1	37.9
Asian alone	203	128	64	31.7	50.2	30	15.0	23.8
Hispanic (of any race)	488	356	201	41.1	56.4	126	25.8	35.3
White alone or in combination	2,267	2,104	1,497	66.0	71.2	1,107	48.8	52.6
Black alone or in combination	358	285	207	57.9	72.8	107	29.8	37.5
Asian alone or in combination	220	142	69	31.4	48.7	30	13.8	21.4
Age								
18 to 24 years......................................	298	289	126	42.1	43.5	70	23.4	24.2
25 to 34 years......................................	458	388	287	62.5	74.0	146	31.8	37.6
35 to 44 years......................................	465	355	220	47.3	62.0	123	26.4	34.6
45 to 64 years......................................	1,031	939	713	69.2	76.0	556	53.9	59.2
65 years and over	585	556	432	73.9	77.7	359	61.3	64.6

Table CT-14. Health Indicators

(Number, rate as indicated in footnotes.)

Item	State	U.S.
Births		
Life Expectancy at Birth (years), 2020	78.4	77.0
Fertility Rate by State[1], 2021	52.1	56.3
Percent Home Births, 2021..	0.7	1.4
Cesarean Delivery Rate[2], 2021	35.4	32.1
Preterm Birth Rate[3], 2021	9.6	10.5
Teen Birth Rate[4], 2021	7.1	13.9
Percentage of Babies Born Low Birthweight[5], 2021	8.2	8.5
Deaths[6]		
Heart Disease Mortality Rate, 2021...	136.7	173.8
Cancer Mortality Rate, 2021..	133.5	146.6
Stroke Mortality Rate, 2021...	29.5	41.1
Diabetes Mortality Rate, 2021..	15.9	25.4
Influenza/Pneumonia Mortality Rate, 2021	8.3	10.5
Suicide Mortality Rate, 2021..	10.0	14.1
Drug Overdose Mortality Rate, 2021..	42.3	33.6
Firearm Injury Mortality Rate, 2021...	6.7	14.6
Homicide Mortality Rate, 2021...	4.8	8.2
Disease and Illness		
Lifetime Asthma in Adults, 2020 (percent)...	15.2	13.9
Lifetime Asthma in Children, 2020 (percent)[7]	18.0	11.3
Diabetes in Adults, 2020 (percent)..	8.2	8.2
Self-reported Obesity in Adults, 2021 (percent)..	30.4	NA

SOURCE: National Center for Health Statistics, National Vital Statistics System 2020 data; https://wonder.cdc.gov.
[1] General fertility rate per 1,000 women aged 15–44.
[2] This represents the percentage of all live births that were cesarean deliveries.
[3] Babies born prior to 37 weeks of pregnancy (gestation).
[4] Number of births per 1,000 females aged 15–19
[5] Babies born weighing less than 2,500 grams or 5 lbs. 8oz.
[6] Death rates are the number of deaths per 100,000 total population.
[7] U.S. total includes data from 30 states and D.C.
NA = Not available.
- = Zero or rounds to zero.

Table CT-15. State Government Finances, 2021

(Dollar amounts in thousands, percent distribution.)

Item	Dollars	Percent distribution
Total Revenue	47,470,892	100.0
General revenue	40,117,376	84.5
Intergovernmental revenue	12,777,730	26.9
Taxes	22,066,648	46.5
General sales	5,252,683	11.1
Selective sales	2,895,587	6.1
License taxes	387,836	0.8
Individual income tax	10,259,183	21.6
Corporate income tax	2,607,064	5.5
Other taxes	664,295	1.4
Current charges	2,435,821	5.1
Miscellaneous general revenue	2,837,177	6.0
Utility revenue	38,925	0.1
Liquor stores revenue	-	-
Insurance trust revenue[1]	7,314,591	15.4
Total Expenditure	36,900,207	100.0
Intergovernmental expenditure	7,389,642	20.0
Direct expenditure	29,510,565	80.0
Current operation	19,194,690	52.0
Capital outlay	1,557,101	4.2
Insurance benefits and repayments	6,476,902	17.6
Assistance and subsidies	552,203	1.5
Interest on debt	1,729,669	4.7
Exhibit: Salaries and wages	4,672,762	12.7
Total Expenditure	36,900,207	100.0
General expenditure	29,572,187	80.1
Intergovernmental expenditure	7,389,642	20.0
Direct expenditure	22,182,545	60.1
General expenditure, by function:		
Education	8,194,812	22.2
Public welfare	4,844,467	13.1
Hospitals	1,697,534	4.6
Health	1,484,517	4.0
Highways	1,674,628	4.5
Police protection	284,884	0.8
Correction	879,406	2.4
Natural resources	190,558	0.5
Parks and recreation	47,562	0.1
Governmental administration	1,786,202	4.8
Interest on general debt	1,729,669	4.7
Other and unallocable	6,710,432	18.2
Utility expenditure	855,372	1.8
Liquor stores expenditure	-	-
Insurance trust expenditure	6,476,902	17.6
Debt at End of Fiscal Year	41,965,429	X
Cash and Security Holdings	63,834,586	X

X = Not applicable.
- = Zero or rounds to zero.
[1] Within insurance trust revenue, net earnings of state retirement systems is a calculated statistic (the item code in the data file is X08), and thus can be positive or negative. Net earnings is the sum of earnings on investments plus gains on investments minus losses on investments. The change made in 2002 for asset valuation from book to market value in accordance with Statement 34 of the Governmental Accounting Standards Board is reflected in the calculated statistics.

Table CT-16. State Government Tax Collections, 2022

(Dollars in thousands, percent.)

Item	Dollars	Percent distribution
Total Taxes	22,477,477	100.0
Property taxes	X	-
Sales and gross receipts	8,198,701	36.5
General sales and gross receipts	5,193,413	23.1
Selective sales and gross receipts	3,005,288	13.4
Alcoholic beverages	71,123	0.3
Amusements	260,239	1.2
Insurance premiums	191,176	0.9
Motor fuels	373,779	1.7
Pari-mutuels	5,708	-
Public utilities	246,437	1.1
Tobacco products	303,664	1.4
Other selective sales	1,553,162	6.9
Licenses	400,119	1.8
Alcoholic beverages	9,924	-
Amusements	161	-
Corporations in general	36,591	0.2
Hunting and fishing	5,333	-
Motor vehicle	249,106	1.1
Motor vehicle operators	59,890	0.3
Public utilities	578	-
Occupation and business, NEC	33,872	0.2
Other licenses	4,664	-
Income taxes	13,348,748	59.4
Individual income	9,861,264	43.9
Corporation net income	3,487,484	15.5
Other taxes	529,909	2.4
Death and gift	199,409	0.9
Documentary and stock transfer	328,938	1.5
Severance	X	-
Taxes, NEC	1,562	-

- = Zero or rounds to zero.
X = Not applicable.

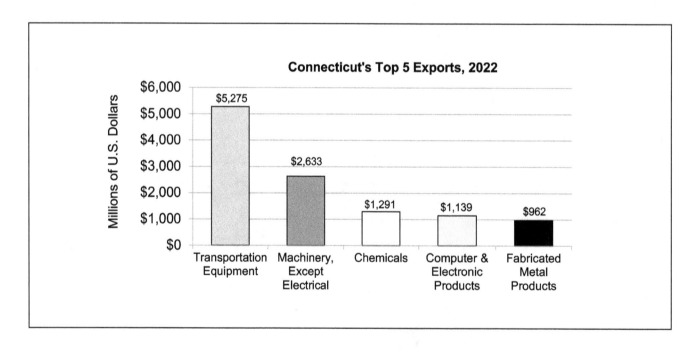

Connecticut's Top 5 Exports, 2022

DELAWARE

Facts and Figures

Location: Northeastern United States; bordered on the N by Pennsylvania, on the E by New Jersey, and on the S and W by Maryland

Area: 2,488 sq. mi. (6,447 sq. km.); rank—49th

Population: 1,018,396 (2022 est.); rank—45th

Principal Cities: capital—Dover; largest—Wilmington

Statehood: December 7, 1787; 1st state

U.S. Congress: 2 senators, 1 representative

State Motto: Liberty and Independence

State Song: "Our Delaware"

State Nickname: The First State

Abbreviations: DE; Del.

State Symbols: flower—peach blossom; tree—American holly; bird—blue hen chicken

At a Glance

- With an increase in population of 13.4 percent, Delaware ranked 12th among the states in growth from 2010 to 2022.

- In 2021, 5.7 percent of Delawareans did not have health insurance, compared to 8.6 percent of the total U.S. population.

- Delaware had the 5th highest drug overdose death rate in the country in 2021, with 54.0 deaths per 100,000 population.

- Delaware's homeownership rate ranked 4th in the nation in 2022, with 74.9 percent of homes being occupied by the owner.

- In 2021, 11.6 percent of Delawareans lived below the poverty level, compared to 12.8 percent of the total U.S. population.

Table DE-1. Population by Age, Sex, Race, and Hispanic Origin

(Number, percent, except where noted.)

Sex, age, race, and Hispanic origin	2010	2020	2022	Percent change, 2010–2022
Total Population..	897,934	989,957	1,018,396	13.4
Percent of total U.S. population	0.3	0.3	0.3	X
Sex				
Male..	434,939	481,499	494,520	13.7
Female	462,995	508,458	523,876	13.1
Age				
Under 5 years...	55,886	54,072	53,766	-3.8
Under 18 years..	205,765	206,848	208,127	1.1
18 to 64 years...	562,892	590,216	598,425	6.3
65 years and over	129,277	192,893	211,844	63.9
Median age (years)..	38.8	41.1	41.8	7.7
Race and Hispanic Origin				
One race				
White	645,770	680,226	692,506	7.2
Black	196,281	230,899	242,210	23.4
American Indian and Alaska Native	5,929	6,909	7,176	21.0
Asian	29,342	42,001	44,490	51.6
Native Hawaiian or Other Pacific Islander	690	1,129	1,173	70.0
Two or more races	19,922	28,793	30,841	54.8
Hispanic (of any race)...	73,221	97,878	105,299	43.8

NOTE: Population figures for 2022 are July 1 estimates. The 2010 and 2020 estimates are taken from the respective censuses.
- = Zero or rounds to zero.
X = Not applicable.

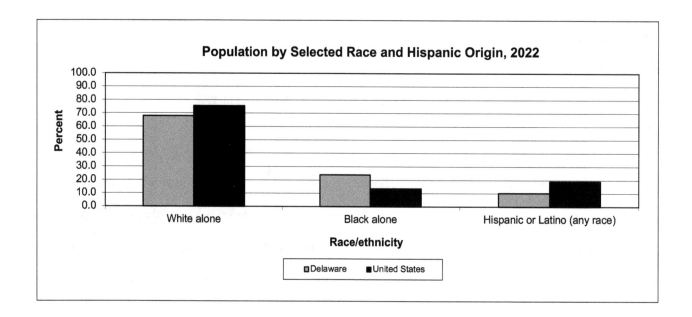

Table DE-2. Marital Status

(Number, percent distribution.)

Sex, age, race, and Hispanic origin	2000	2010	2021
Males, 15 Years and Over	296,619	350,025	398,809
Never married	29.4	35.3	36.7
Now married, except separated...	57.4	50.4	50.2
Separated..	1.8	1.9	1.5
Widowed..	2.8	2.9	3.4
Divorced..	8.7	9.4	8.3
Females, 15 Years and Over	324,042	380,618	433,218
Never married	25.3	30.8	31.7
Now married, except separated...	50.9	45.3	46.1
Separated..	2.2	2.0	1.7
Widowed..	10.7	9.8	9.1
Divorced..	10.9	12.1	11.3

Table DE-3. Households and Housing Characteristics

(Number, percent, dollars.)

Item	2000	2010	2021	Average annual percent change, 2010–2021
Total Households..	298,736	328,765	395,656	1.8
Family households...	204,590	221,233	256,408	1.4
Married-couple family..	153,136	161,575	186,477	1.4
Other family...	51,454	59,658	69,931	1.6
Male householder, no wife present..	12,468	14,124	18,932	3.1
Female householder, no husband present..	38,986	45,534	50,999	1.1
Nonfamily households...	94,146	107,532	139,248	2.7
Householder living alone...	74,639	86,990	114,678	2.9
Householder not living alone...	19,507	20,542	24,570	1.8
Housing Characteristics				
Total housing units...	343,072	406,489	457,978	1.2
Occupied housing units	298,736	328,765	395,656	1.8
Owner occupied...	216,038	239,884	287,111	1.8
Renter occupied..	86,698	88,881	108,545	2.0
Average household size..	2.54	2.66	2.47	-0.6
Financial Characteristics				
Median gross rent of renter-occupied housing	639	952	1,208	2.4
Median monthly owner costs for housing units with a mortgage	1,101	1,569	1,585	0.1
Median value of owner-occupied housing units...	130,400	243,600	300,500	2.1

Table DE-4. Migration, Origin, and Language

(Number, percent.)

Characteristic	State 2021	U.S. 2021
Residence 1 Year Ago		
Population 1 year and over	994,669	328,464,538
Same house	89.4	87.2
Different house in the U.S.	10.1	12.3
Same county	4.9	6.7
Different county	5.2	5.7
Same state	1.0	3.3
Different state	4.3	2.4
Abroad	0.5	0.4
Place of Birth		
Native born	902,124	286,623,642
Male	48.3	49.7
Female	51.7	50.3
Foreign born	101,260	45,270,103
Male	49.7	48.7
Female	50.3	51.3
Foreign born; naturalized U.S. citizen...	56,831	24,044,083
Male	48.3	46.4
Female	51.7	53.6
Foreign born; not a U.S. citizen...	44,429	21,226,020
Male	51.5	51.2
Female	48.5	48.8
Entered 2010 or later	32.4	28.1
Entered 2000 to 2009	27.2	23.7
Entered before 2000...	40.3	48.2
World Region of Birth, Foreign		
Foreign-born population, excluding population born at sea	101,260	45,269,644
Europe	9.2	10.7
Asia	31.9	31.0
Africa	13.7	5.7
Oceania	0.1	0.6
Latin America..	43.4	50.1
North America...	1.7	1.7
Language Spoken at Home and Ability to Speak English		
Population 5 years and over...	950,345	313,232,500
English only	85.3	78.4
Language other than English...	14.7	21.6
Speaks English less than "very well"...	5.4	8.3

Table DE-5. Median Income and Poverty Status, 2021

(Number, percent, except as noted.)

Characteristic	State		U.S.	
	Number	Percent	Number	Percent
Median Income				
Households (dollars)...	71,091	X	69,717	X
Families (dollars)	87,132	X	85,806	X
Below Poverty Level (All People)	113,450	11.6	41,393,176	12.8
Sex				
Male	47,571	10.1	18,518,155	11.6
Female	65,879	13.0	22,875,021	13.9
Age				
Under 18 years...	34,539	16.8	12,243,219	16.9
Related children under 18 years.............................	34,297	16.7	11,985,424	16.6
18 to 64 years	65,198	11.3	23,526,341	11.9
65 years and over	13,713	6.9	5,623,616	10.3

X = Not applicable.

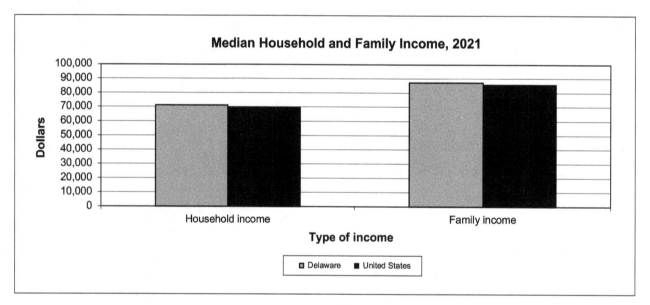

Table DE-6. Health Insurance Coverage Status for the Civilian Noninstitutionalized Population and Children Under 19 Years of Age

(Number, percent.)

Item	2011	2012	2013	2014	2015	2016	2017	2018	2019	2020 [2]	2021
Civilian Noninstitutionalized Population	892132	902,915	911,502	920,930	931,203	937,935	947,259	952,211	956,378	951,930	987,964
Covered by Private or Public Insurance											
Number..	808,137	823,021	828,218	849,333	876,705	884,796	896,016	898,249	893,608	896,359	931,238
Percent..	90.6	91.2	90.9	92.2	94.1	94.3	94.6	94.3	93.4	94.2	94.3
Uninsured											
Number..	83,995	79,894	83,284	71,597	54,498	53,139	51,243	53,962	62,770	55,571	56,726
Percent..	9.4	8.8	9.1	7.8	5.9	5.7	5.4	5.7	6.6	5.8	5.7
Percent in the U.S. not covered.............................	15.1	14.8	14.5	11.7	9.4	8.6	8.7	8.9	9.2	8.7	8.6
Children Under 19 Years of Age[1]	204,295	204,494	203,339	203,414	203,771	203,704	218,473	215,130	215,399	217,221	221,810
Covered by Private or Public Insurance											
Number..	194,916	197,329	194,251	191,762	197,686	197,461	210,828	207,292	205,017	208,934	213,559
Percent..	95.4	96.5	95.5	94.3	97.0	96.9	96.5	96.4	95.2	96.2	96.3
Uninsured											
Number..	9,379	7,165	9,088	11,652	6,085	6,243	7,645	7,838	10,382	8,287	8,251
Percent..	4.6	3.5	4.5	5.7	3.0	3.1	3.5	3.6	4.8	3.8	3.7
Percent in the U.S. not covered.............................	7.5	7.2	7.1	6.0	4.8	4.5	5.0	5.2	5.7	5.2	5.4

[1] Data for years prior to 2017 are for individuals under 18 years of age.
[2] 2020 ACS 5-Year estimates. 1-Year estimates were not released for 2020 due to the impact of COVID-19 on data collection that year. Data is not comparable to previous years, which are based on 1-year estimates.

Table DE-7. Employment Status by Demographic Group, 2022

(Numbers in thousands, percent.)

Characteristic	Civilian noninstitutional population	Civilian labor force		Employed		Unemployed	
		Number	Percent of population	Number	Percent of population	Number	Percent of population
Total.............................	819	490	59.8	468	57.1	22	4.4
Sex							
Male.............................	390	245	62.8	233	59.9	12	4.7
Female...........................	429	245	57.0	234	54.6	10	4.1
Race, Sex, and Hispanic Origin							
White............................	572	332	58.1	320	56.0	12	3.5
Male.............................	276	169	61.1	162	58.7	7	3.9
Female...........................	296	163	55.3	158	53.6	5	3.1
Black or African American.......	184	118	64.2	110	59.6	8	7.2
Male.............................	83	53	64.2	49	59.1	4	7.9
Female...........................	100	65	64.3	60	60.1	4	6.6
Hispanic or Latino ethnicity[1]..	79	55	69.8	53	66.5	3	4.8
Male.............................	39	29	75.5	28	70.9	2	6.3
Female...........................	41	26	64.4	25	62.5	1	3.1
Age							
16 to 19 years..................	NA	NA	NA	NA	NA	NA	NA
20 to 24 years..................	56	42	75.2	38	68.0	4	9.5
25 to 34 years..................	127	109	85.5	103	80.9	6	5.4
35 to 44 years..................	122	103	84.0	100	81.9	3	2.5
45 to 54 years..................	107	87	81.3	85	79.0	2	2.8
55 to 64 years..................	141	90	64.1	88	62.3	2	2.5
65 years and over...............	216	39	17.8	37	17.2	1	3.6

NOTE: Data in Table 7 are from the Current Population Survey (CPS) and do not match the estimates in Table 8. See notes and definitions for further information.
[1] May be of any race.
NA = Not Available

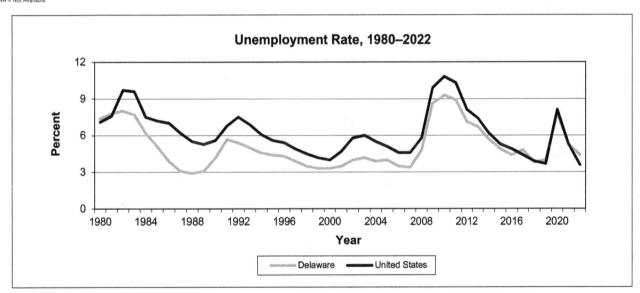

Unemployment Rate, 1980–2022

Table DE-8. Employment Status of the Civilian Noninstitutional Population Age 16 Years and Over

(Number, percent.)

Year	Civilian labor force	Civilian participation rate	Employed	Unemployed	Unemployment rate
2010............................	436,196	62.2	398,388	37,808	8.7
2011............................	443,971	62.4	410,229	33,742	7.6
2012............................	445,962	62.0	414,489	31,473	7.1
2013............................	443,551	61.0	414,215	29,336	6.6
2014............................	452,712	61.4	427,400	25,312	5.6
2015............................	462,752	62.0	440,555	22,197	4.8
2016............................	468,808	62.1	447,640	21,168	4.5
2017............................	475,214	62.2	453,949	21,265	4.5
2018............................	480,154	62.1	462,143	18,011	3.8
2019............................	484,845	61.9	466,856	17,989	3.7
2020............................	485,813	61.2	449,114	36,699	7.6
2021............................	496,430	61.7	469,875	26,555	5.3
2022............................	496,688	60.5	474,258	22,430	4.5

Table DE-9. Employment and Average Wages by Industry

(Estimates are based on the 2012 North American Industry Classification System [NAICS].)

Industry	2014	2015	2016	2017	2018	2019	2020	2021
	Number of Jobs							
Wage and Salary Employment by Industry.........................	450,681	459,075	464,150	466,853	472,585	478,205	452,189	463,995
Farm Wage and Salary Employment..............................	1,797	1,740	2,100	2,022	1,549	1,423	1,198	1,484
Nonfarm Wage and Salary Employment..........................	448,884	457,335	462,050	464,831	471,036	476,782	450,991	462,511
Private wage and salary employment............................	374,768	384,132	388,238	390,629	396,869	401,749	376,787	386,939
Forestry, fishing, and related activities	(D)	(D)	(D)	(D)	(D)	(D)	526	423
Mining...	(D)	(D)	(D)	(D)	(D)	(D)	70	71
Utilities...	2,148	2,158	2,156	2,194	2,124	2,073	2,058	2,060
Construction..	20,893	21,283	21,484	22,274	22,717	23,450	22,955	23,676
Manufacturing..	25,713	27,070	25,749	25,777	27,090	27,313	25,582	24,976
Durable goods manufacturing............................	9,198	9,370	9,325	9,321	9,557	9,838	9,312	9,051
Nondurable goods manufacturing......................	16,515	17,700	16,424	16,456	17,533	17,475	16,270	15,925
Wholesale trade	12,028	11,850	11,915	10,901	10,770	11,023	10,873	11,259
Retail trade...	52,732	53,335	54,029	53,774	53,581	52,164	48,177	50,290
Transportation and warehousing.............................	12,910	14,433	14,703	14,371	14,460	15,788	16,692	18,500
Information	4,893	4,724	4,614	4,557	4,064	3,907	3,617	3,572
Finance and insurance	40,628	42,034	42,412	43,259	43,170	43,639	43,119	42,830
Real estate and rental and leasing..........................	5,359	5,455	5,581	5,552	5,549	5,763	5,716	5,893
Professional, scientific, and technical services	29,138	28,700	25,828	25,930	27,002	26,298	25,566	25,959
Management of companies and enterprises.................	5,498	4,888	8,654	8,305	7,652	8,038	8,429	8,515
Administrative and waste services	25,469	26,699	27,155	28,027	29,188	29,754	28,353	29,187
Educational services	6,951	6,807	6,814	6,850	6,809	6,928	6,096	6,531
Health care and social assistance...........................	64,096	66,848	68,691	69,809	71,586	72,969	70,615	70,145
Arts, entertainment, and recreation.........................	10,261	10,202	10,020	10,247	9,307	10,047	7,656	7,970
Accommodation and food services	37,252	38,776	39,780	40,191	42,746	43,334	33,938	37,839
Other services, except public administration................	18,132	18,171	17,968	17,987	18,380	18,631	16,749	17,243
Government and government enterprises	74,116	73,203	73,812	74,202	74,167	75,033	74,204	75,572
	Dollars							
Average Wages and Salaries by Industry	52,400	53,319	53,090	55,134	56,270	57,944	61,689	64,115
Average Farm Wages and Salaries	24,949	21,048	20,014	18,864	23,626	20,421	23,558	19,106
Average Nonfarm Wages and Salaries	52,510	53,442	53,241	55,292	56,378	58,056	61,791	64,259
Average private wages and salaries............................	53,225	54,024	53,664	55,837	56,828	58,566	62,538	65,369
Forestry, fishing, and related activities	(D)	(D)	(D)	(D)	(D)	(D)	37,561	39,678
Mining...	(D)	(D)	(D)	(D)	(D)	(D)	58,886	63,056
Utilities...	104,323	106,632	108,019	112,877	114,365	120,205	124,236	122,209
Construction..	53,826	55,137	56,708	59,142	59,809	62,496	64,953	67,560
Manufacturing..	59,590	64,072	59,925	62,019	64,163	66,193	67,968	70,449
Durable goods manufacturing............................	70,859	71,350	69,125	71,670	73,423	74,171	74,586	75,497
Nondurable goods manufacturing......................	53,313	60,219	54,702	56,552	59,116	61,702	64,180	67,580
Wholesale trade	83,268	79,874	80,225	72,552	74,382	76,004	80,608	84,060
Retail trade...	27,181	28,290	28,453	28,844	29,597	30,784	33,732	36,437
Transportation and warehousing.............................	46,350	46,374	45,770	47,972	50,251	50,656	50,513	52,924
Information	62,356	63,640	64,959	64,658	65,758	69,948	78,944	85,083
Finance and insurance	91,004	91,800	92,870	97,349	100,827	102,625	108,659	113,217
Real estate and rental and leasing..........................	44,534	46,197	47,648	49,847	52,304	55,445	59,119	62,817
Professional, scientific, and technical services	100,162	107,091	93,242	101,410	100,675	106,895	112,065	117,758
Management of companies and enterprises.................	143,788	115,525	128,572	154,953	152,781	153,030	140,371	146,065
Administrative and waste services	35,343	36,623	37,228	39,067	41,829	42,491	45,790	49,039
Educational services	41,294	41,321	40,943	40,990	41,766	41,780	47,574	44,678
Health care and social assistance...........................	50,998	51,986	52,299	53,505	54,174	55,679	57,711	61,298
Arts, entertainment, and recreation.........................	27,057	27,177	27,852	27,891	27,011	26,877	29,274	32,647
Accommodation and food services	19,488	20,220	20,872	21,212	22,574	23,694	22,892	27,730
Other services, except public administration................	33,288	34,261	35,257	35,979	36,870	38,227	41,081	43,355
Government and government enterprises	48,890	50,389	51,015	52,421	53,968	55,326	57,993	58,578

(D) = Not shown to avoid disclosure of confidential information; estimates are included in higher-level totals.

Table DE-10. Employment Characteristics by Family Type

(Number, percent.)

Family type and labor force status	2019 Total	2019 Families with own children under 18 years	2020[1] Total	2020[1] Families with own children under 18 years	2021 Total	2021 Families with own children under 18 years
All Families.........	242,584	86,583	243,012	90,822	256,408	91,640
FAMILY TYPE AND LABOR FORCE STATUS						
Opposite-Sex Married-Couple Families........	177,794	54,679	175,257	57,394	182,713	59,069
Both husband and wife in labor force....	47.2	71.9	49.2	70.4	46.2	69.1
Husband in labor force, wife not in labor force....	18.8	23.2	19.6	25.0	18.9	24.6
Wife in labor force, husband not in labor force....	8.3	3.4	8.0	3.1	9.1	5.1
Both husband and wife not in labor force....	23.9	1.2	23.2	1.4	25.8	1.2
Other Families........	64,790	31,904	64,982	33,166	69,931	32,258
Female householder, no spouse present....	69.4	69.7	72.7	74.0	72.9	75.1
In labor force....	50.2	58.8	53.2	64.9	50.4	62.4
Not in labor force....	19.2	10.9	19.5	9.1	22.5	12.8
Male householder, no spouse present....	30.6	30.3	27.3	26.0	27.1	24.9
In labor force....	24.7	28.2	21.5	24.2	21.1	22.1
Not in labor force....	5.9	2.1	5.8	1.8	6.0	2.8

[1] 2020 ACS 5-Year estimates. 1-Year estimates were not released for 2020 due to the impact of COVID-19 on data collection that year. Data is not comparable to previous years, which are based on 1-year estimates.

Table DE-11. School Enrollment and Educational Attainment, 2021

(Number, percent.)

Item	State	U.S.
Enrollment		
Total population 3 years and over, enrolled in school....	234,867	79,453,524
Enrolled in nursery school or preschool (percent)....	5.6	5.2
Enrolled in kindergarten (percent)....	4.9	5.0
Enrolled in elementary school, grades 1-8 (percent)....	37.9	41.3
Enrolled in high school, grades 9-12 (percent)....	21.8	21.8
Enrolled in college or graduate school (percent)....	29.8	26.7
Attainment		
Total population 25 years and over....	711,104	228,193,464
Less than ninth grade (percent)....	3.3	4.8
9th to 12th grade, no diploma (percent)....	5.4	5.9
High school graduate, including equivalency (percent)....	28.3	26.3
Some college, no degree (percent)....	18.1	19.3
Associate's degree (percent)....	9.3	8.8
Bachelor's degree (percent)....	20.6	21.2
Graduate or professional degree (percent)....	15.0	13.8
High school graduate or higher (percent)....	91.4	89.4
Bachelor's degree or higher (percent)....	35.6	35.0

Table DE-12. Public School Characteristics and Educational Indicators

(Number, percent; data derived from National Center of Education Statistics.)

Item	State	U.S.
Public Elementary and Secondary Schools		
Number of regular school districts, 2019-20....	19	13,349
Number of operational schools, 2019-20....	222	98,469
Percent charter schools....	9.9	7.7
Total public school enrollment, Fall 2021....	139,935	49,433,092
Percent charter school enrollment....	12.3	7.5
Student-teacher ratio, Fall 2019....	14.4	15.9
Expenditures per student (unadjusted dollars), 2019-20....	14,114	13,489
Four-year adjusted cohort graduation rate (ACGR), 2019-2020[1]....	89.0	86.5
Students eligible for free or reduced-price lunch (percent), 2019-20....	28.3	52.1
English language learners (percent), Fall 2020....	10.7	10.3
Students age 3 to 21 served under IDEA, part B (percent), 2021-22....	18.8	14.7

Public Schools by Type, 2019-20	Number	Percent of state public schools
Total number of schools....	222	100.0
Special education....	19	8.6
Vocational education....	6	2.7
Alternative education....	5	2.3

[1] Adjusted Cohort Graduation Rates (ACGR) differ from Averaged Freshmen Graduation Rates (AFGR).

Table DE-13. Reported Voting and Registration of the Voting-Age Population, November 2022

(Numbers in thousands, percent.)

Item	Total population	Total citizen population	Registered			Voted		
			Total registered	Percent registered (total population)	Percent registered (total citizen population)	Total voted	Percent voted (total population)	Percent voted (total citizen population)
U.S. Total	255,457	233,546	161,422	63.2	69.1	121,916	47.7	52.2
State Total	798	754	578	72.4	76.6	409	51.2	54.2
Sex								
Male	381	357	266	69.8	74.5	188	49.3	52.6
Female	418	397	312	74.7	78.6	221	52.9	55.6
Race								
White alone.............................	561	541	431	76.7	79.5	318	56.7	58.8
White, non-Hispanic alone	520	518	416	80.0	80.4	312	59.9	60.2
Black alone	176	168	111	63.1	66.3	67	38.1	40.1
Asian alone	26	17	13	49.4	75.4	8	31.2	47.5
Hispanic (of any race)	71	47	32	45.3	68.8	18	24.9	37.8
White alone or in combination...........	581	561	447	77.0	79.8	331	57.0	59.0
Black alone or in combination.........	190	181	122	64.2	67.2	74	39.1	41.0
Asian alone or in combination.........	28	19	15	52.7	77.7	8	29.2	43.0
Age								
18 to 24 years	96	88	49	51.0	55.6	25	25.6	27.9
25 to 34 years	124	110	76	61.6	69.7	39	31.2	35.3
35 to 44 years	108	97	77	71.7	79.4	44	41.1	45.5
45 to 64 years	219	211	167	76.5	79.5	122	55.5	57.7
65 years and over	252	249	208	82.5	83.6	180	71.3	72.2

B = Base is less than 75,000 and therefore too small to show the derived measure.

Table DE-14. Health Indicators

(Number, rate as indicated in footnotes.)

Item	State	U.S.
Births		
Life Expectancy at Birth (years), 2020	76.7	77.0
Fertility Rate by State[1], 2021...	56.5	56.3
Percent Home Births, 2021...	1.0	1.4
Cesarean Delivery Rate[2], 2021...	31.9	32.1
Preterm Birth Rate[3], 2021..	11.0	10.5
Teen Birth Rate[4], 2021..	13.5	13.9
Percentage of Babies Born Low Birthweight[5], 2021..............	9.1	8.5
Deaths[6]		
Heart Disease Mortality Rate, 2021....................................	162.7	173.8
Cancer Mortality Rate, 2021..	153.2	146.6
Stroke Mortality Rate, 2021...	56.8	41.1
Diabetes Mortality Rate, 2021..	23.9	25.4
Influenza/Pneumonia Mortality Rate, 2021	8.6	10.5
Suicide Mortality Rate, 2021..	13.6	14.1
Drug Overdose Mortality Rate, 2021...................................	54.0	33.6
Firearm Injury Mortality Rate, 2021....................................	16.6	14.6
Homicide Mortality Rate, 2021...	11.3	8.2
Disease and Illness		
Lifetime Asthma in Adults, 2020 (percent)............................	14.5	13.9
Lifetime Asthma in Children, 2020 (percent)[7]......................	NA	11.3
Diabetes in Adults, 2020 (percent)......................................	10.5	8.2
Self-reported Obesity in Adults, 2021 (percent).....................	33.9	NA

SOURCE: National Center for Health Statistics, National Vital Statistics System 2020 data; https://wonder.cdc.gov.
[1] General fertility rate per 1,000 women aged 15–44.
[2] This represents the percentage of all live births that were cesarean deliveries.
[3] Babies born prior to 37 weeks of pregnancy (gestation).
[4] Number of births per 1,000 females aged 15–19
[5] Babies born weighing less than 2,500 grams or 5 lbs. 8oz.
[6] Death rates are the number of deaths per 100,000 total population.
[7] U.S. total includes data from 30 states and D.C.
NA = Not available.
- = Zero or rounds to zero.

Table DE-15. State Government Finances, 2021

(Dollar amounts in thousands, percent distribution.)

Item	Dollars	Percent distribution
Total Revenue	13,932,880	100.0
General revenue	13,045,792	93.6
Intergovernmental revenue	5,315,164	38.1
Taxes	5,395,712	38.7
General sales	-	-
Selective sales	587,923	4.2
License taxes	2,076,828	14.9
Individual income tax	2,148,289	15.4
Corporate income tax	334,805	2.4
Other taxes	247,867	1.8
Current charges	1,014,797	7.3
Miscellaneous general revenue	1,320,119	9.5
Utility revenue	11,772	0.1
Liquor stores revenue	-	-
Insurance trust revenue[1]	875,316	6.3
Total Expenditure	12,839,920	100.0
Intergovernmental expenditure	2,274,071	17.7
Direct expenditure	10,565,849	82.3
Current operation	7,731,489	60.2
Capital outlay	1,055,635	8.2
Insurance benefits and repayments	1,096,081	8.5
Assistance and subsidies	433,983	3.4
Interest on debt	248,661	1.9
Exhibit: Salaries and wages	1,595,099	12.4
Total Expenditure	12,839,920	100.0
General expenditure	11,555,188	90.0
Intergovernmental expenditure	2,274,071	17.7
Direct expenditure	9,281,117	72.3
General expenditure, by function:		
Education	4,093,072	31.9
Public welfare	3,171,154	24.7
Hospitals	84,943	0.7
Health	609,231	4.7
Highways	684,976	5.3
Police protection	183,528	1.4
Correction	414,403	3.2
Natural resources	83,646	0.7
Parks and recreation	58,590	0.5
Governmental administration	688,644	5.4
Interest on general debt	248,661	1.9
Other and unallocable	1,207,398	9.4
Utility expenditure	188,750	1.4
Liquor stores expenditure	-	-
Insurance trust expenditure	1,096,081	8.5
Debt at End of Fiscal Year	5,370,040	X
Cash and Security Holdings	24,975,615	X

X = Not applicable.
- = Zero or rounds to zero.
[1] Within insurance trust revenue, net earnings of state retirement systems is a calculated statistic (the item code in the data file is X08), and thus can be positive or negative. Net earnings is the sum of earnings on investments plus gains on investments minus losses on investments. The change made in 2002 for asset valuation from book to market value in accordance with Statement 34 of the Governmental Accounting Standards Board is reflected in the calculated statistics.

Table DE-16. State Government Tax Collections, 2022

(Dollars in thousands, percent.)

Item	Dollars	Percent distribution
Total Taxes	6,310,891	100.0
Property taxes	X	-
Sales and gross receipts	644,552	10.2
General sales and gross receipts	X	-
Selective sales and gross receipts	644,552	10.2
Alcoholic beverages	30,911	0.5
Amusements	X	-
Insurance premiums	146,051	2.3
Motor fuels	134,474	2.1
Pari-mutuels	62	-
Public utilities	43,826	0.7
Tobacco products	115,332	1.8
Other selective sales	173,896	2.8
Licenses	2,437,040	38.6
Alcoholic beverages	2,566	-
Amusements	434	-
Corporations in general	2,210,216	35.0
Hunting and fishing	4,766	0.1
Motor vehicle	59,629	0.9
Motor vehicle operators	5,902	0.1
Public utilities	700	-
Occupation and business, NEC	140,463	2.2
Other licenses	12,364	0.2
Income taxes	2,903,928	46.0
Individual income	2,405,043	38.1
Corporation net income	498,885	7.9
Other taxes	325,371	5.2
Death and gift	4	-
Documentary and stock transfer	324,273	5.1
Severance	X	-
Taxes, NEC	1,094	-

X = Not applicable.
- = Zero or rounds to zero.

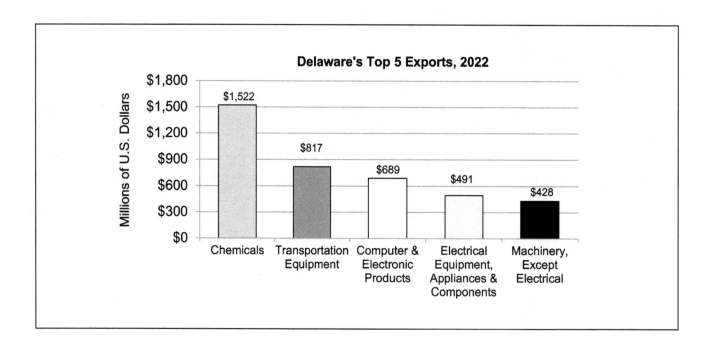

Delaware's Top 5 Exports, 2022

DISTRICT OF COLUMBIA

Facts and Figures:

Location: South Atlantic United States; bordered on the SE, NE, and NW by Maryland and on the SW by Virginia

Area: 68 sq. mi.

Population: 671,803 (2022 est.); rank—49th

Official Motto: Justitia omnibus ("Justice for All")

U.S. Congress: 1 delegate

Abbreviation: D.C.

Symbols: flower—American beauty rose; tree—scarlet oak; bird—wood thrush

At a Glance

- The District of Columbia saw an increase in population of 11.6 percent from 2010 to 2022.

- In 2022, the District of Columbia had the 4th lowest percentage of people under 18 years of age (18.5 percent). It also had the 2nd lowest percentage of people 65 years and older (13.0 percent).

- The homicide rate in the District of Columbia was the highest in the nation, at 30.0 deaths per 100,000 population in 2021.

- The District of Columbia had the 2nd highest median household income in the United States ($90,088), and it ranked 5th for the percent of residents below the poverty level (16.5 percent) in 2021. It ranked 3rd for percent of children under 18 years of age in poverty (23.9 percent).

Table DC-1. Population by Age, Sex, Race, and Hispanic Origin

(Number, percent, except where noted.)

Sex, age, race, and Hispanic origin	2010	2020	2022	Percent change, 2010–2022
Total Population...	601,723	689,546	671,803	11.6
Percent of total U.S. population	0.2	0.2	0.2	X
Sex				
Male..	284,222	330,006	319,682	12.5
Female	317,501	359,540	352,121	10.9
Age				
Under 5 years...	32,613	42,395	39,099	19.9
Under 18 years..	100,815	125,157	124,475	23.5
18 to 64 years...	432,099	479,608	460,068	6.5
65 years and over..	68,809	84,781	87,260	26.8
Median age (years)	33.8	34.4	34.8	3.0
Race and Hispanic Origin				
One race				
White	251,265	317,370	310,692	23.7
Black..	310,379	315,230	302,568	-2.5
American Indian and Alaska Native	3,264	4,139	4,688	43.6
Asian	21,705	31,203	31,360	44.5
Native Hawaiian or Other Pacific Islander	770	1,149	1,127	46.4
Two or more races..	14,340	20,455	21,368	49.0
Hispanic (of any race).......................................	54,749	78,492	78,911	44.1

NOTE: Population figures for 2022 are July 1 estimates. The 2010 and 2020 estimates are taken from the respective censuses.
- = Zero or rounds to zero.
X = Not applicable.

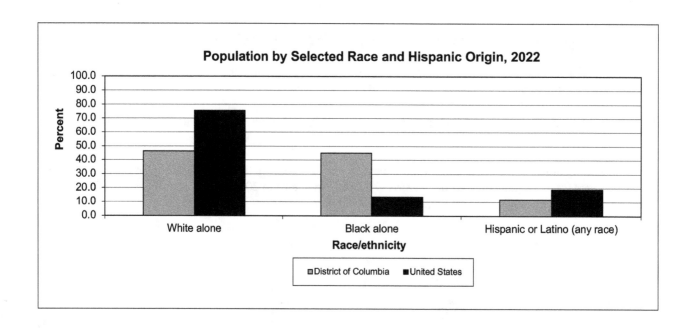

Table DC-2. Marital Status

(Number, percent distribution.)

Sex, age, race, and Hispanic origin	2000	2010	2021
Males, 15 Years and Over	219,706	243,152	263,114
Never married	51.2	58.9	54.6
Now married, except separated...	32.8	28.2	34.4
Separated..	3.9	2.4	1.3
Widowed..	3.4	2.1	1.7
Divorced..	8.7	8.4	8.0
Females, 15 Years and Over	254,711	277,203	296,559
Never married	46.0	55.8	56.0
Now married, except separated...	27.5	22.8	26.4
Separated..	4.4	3.1	1.3
Widowed..	11.6	7.5	5.7
Divorced..	10.6	10.8	10.5

Table DC-3. Households and Housing Characteristics

(Number, percent, dollars.)

Item	2000	2010	2021	Average annual percent change, 2010–2021
Total Households.	248,338	252,388	319,565	2.4
Family households	114,166	101,519	128,733	2.4
Married-couple family	56,631	57,275	77,478	3.2
Other family	57,535	44,244	51,255	1.4
Male householder, no wife present	10,503	8,740	9,856	1.2
Female householder, no husband present	47,032	35,504	41,399	1.5
Nonfamily households	134,172	150,869	190,832	2.4
Householder living alone	108,744	121,036	154,140	2.5
Householder not living alone	25,428	29,833	36,692	2.1
Housing Characteristics				
Total housing units	274,845	296,836	357,482	1.9
Occupied housing units	248,338	252,388	319,565	2.4
Owner occupied	101,214	107,193	132,936	2.2
Renter occupied	147,124	145,195	186,629	2.6
Average household size	2.16	2.24	1.98	-1.1
Financial Characteristics				
Median gross rent of renter-occupied housing	618	1,198	1,668	3.6
Median monthly owner costs for housing units with a mortgage	1,291	2,297	2,639	1.4
Median value of owner-occupied housing units	157,200	426,900	669,900	5.2

Table DC-4. Migration, Origin, and Language

(Number, percent.)

Characteristic	State 2021	U.S. 2021
Residence 1 Year Ago		
Population 1 year and over	661,026	328,464,538
Same house	79.7	87.2
Different house in the U.S.	19.1	12.3
Same county	10.4	6.7
Different county	8.7	5.7
Same state	-	3.3
Different state	8.7	2.4
Abroad	1.1	0.4
Place of Birth		
Native born	580,824	286,623,642
Male	47.9	49.7
Female	52.1	50.3
Foreign born	89,226	45,270,103
Male	46.0	48.7
Female	54.0	51.3
Foreign born; naturalized U.S. citizen	44,900	24,044,083
Male	42.7	46.4
Female	57.3	53.6
Foreign born; not a U.S. citizen	44,326	21,226,020
Male	49.3	51.2
Female	50.7	48.8
Entered 2010 or later	33.5	28.1
Entered 2000 to 2009	24.2	23.7
Entered before 2000	42.4	48.2
World Region of Birth, Foreign		
Foreign-born population, excluding population born at sea	89,226	45,269,644
Europe	15.6	10.7
Asia	23.2	31.0
Africa	17.3	5.7
Oceania	0.7	0.6
Latin America	41.5	50.1
North America	1.7	1.7
Language Spoken at Home and Ability to Speak English		
Population 5 years and over	629,241	313,232,500
English only	82.6	78.4
Language other than English	17.4	21.0
Speaks English less than "very well"	5.0	8.3

- = Zero or rounds to zero.

Table DC-5. Median Income and Poverty Status, 2021

(Number, percent, except as noted.)

Characteristic	State		U.S.	
	Number	Percent	Number	Percent
Median Income				
Households (dollars)..	90,088	X	69,717	X
Families (dollars)	136,184	X	85,806	X
Below Poverty Level (All People)	105,007	16.5	41,393,176	12.8
Sex				
Male	44,023	14.5	18,518,155	11.6
Female	60,984	18.3	22,875,021	13.9
Age				
Under 18 years..	29,258	23.9	12,243,219	16.9
Related children under 18 years.......................................	28,958	23.7	11,985,424	16.6
18 to 64 years...	64,219	14.9	23,526,341	11.9
65 years and over	11,530	13.8	5,623,616	10.3

X = Not applicable.

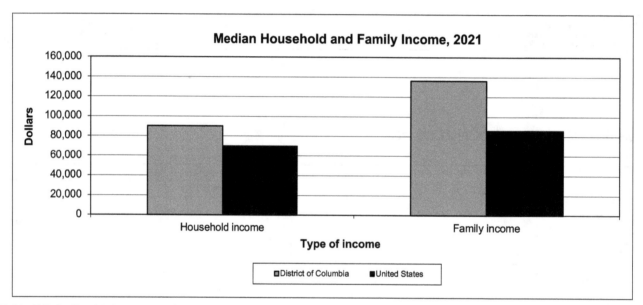

Table DC-6. Health Insurance Coverage Status for the Civilian Noninstitutionalized Population and Children Under 19 Years of Age

(Number, percent.)

Item	2011	2012	2013	2014	2015	2016	2017	2018	2019	2020 [2]	2021
Civilian Noninstitutionalized Population	608,165	621,380	635,833	647,966	660,682	670,985	683,808	692,817	696,599	692,059	659,979
Covered by Private or Public Insurance											
Number...	566,158	584,526	593,538	613,778	635,702	644,639	657,797	670,920	672,093	666,771	635,752
Percent...	93.1	94.1	93.3	94.7	96.2	96.1	96.2	96.8	96.5	96.3	96.3
Uninsured											
Number...	42,007	36,854	42,295	34,188	24,980	26,346	26,011	21,897	24,506	25,288	24,227
Percent...	6.9	5.9	6.7	5.3	3.8	3.9	3.8	3.2	3.5	3.7	3.7
Percent in the U.S. not covered....................................	15.1	14.8	14.5	11.7	9.4	8.6	8.7	8.9	9.2	8.7	8.6
Children Under 19 Years of Age[1]	105,312	109,182	111,287	114,834	117,415	120,313	133,635	137,437	138,489	136,567	133,787
Covered by Private or Public Insurance											
Number...	101,179	107,312	108,657	112,449	115,609	116,572	132,060	135,008	135,665	133,898	128,871
Percent...	96.1	98.3	97.6	97.9	98.5	96.9	98.8	98.2	98.0	98.0	96.3
Uninsured											
Number...	4,133	1,870	2,630	2,385	1,806	3,741	1,575	2,429	2,824	2,669	4,916
Percent...	3.9	1.7	2.4	2.1	1.5	3.1	1.2	1.8	2.0	2.0	3.7
Percent in the U.S. not covered....................................	7.5	7.2	7.1	6.0	4.8	4.5	5.0	5.2	5.7	5.2	5.4

[1] Data for years prior to 2017 are for individuals under 18 years of age.
[2] 2020 ACS 5-Year estimates. 1-Year estimates were not released for 2020 due to the impact of COVID-19 on data collection that year. Data is not comparable to previous years, which are based on 1-year estimates.

Table DC-7. Employment Status by Demographic Group, 2022

(Numbers in thousands, percent.)

Characteristic	Civilian noninstitutional population	Civilian labor force		Employed		Unemployed	
		Number	Percent of population	Number	Percent of population	Number	Percent of population
Total..	530	371	70.1	354	66.9	17	4.6
Sex							
Male..	246	183	74.3	175	71.1	8	4.3
Female.......................................	283	188	66.5	179	63.2	9	4.9
Race, Sex, and Hispanic Origin							
White..	251	200	79.5	197	78.2	3	1.6
Male.......................................	127	104	81.7	102	80.2	2	1.8
Female....................................	125	96	77.3	95	76.1	1	1.5
Black or African American..............	235	141	59.9	127	54.2	13	9.4
Male.......................................	102	66	64.1	60	58.6	6	8.6
Female....................................	132	75	56.6	67	50.9	8	10.1
Hispanic or Latino ethnicity[1]...........	45	34	75.3	33	73.4	1	2.7
Male.......................................	23	19	82.9	19	81.0	1	2.4
Female....................................	22	15	67.1	14	65.3	*	3.0
Age							
16 to 19 years............................	NA	NA	NA	NA	NA	NA	NA
20 to 24 years............................	42	28	68.4	26	63.1	2	7.7
25 to 34 years............................	144	128	88.8	122	84.9	6	4.5
35 to 44 years............................	107	96	89.5	92	86.0	4	3.8
45 to 54 years............................	65	53	82.1	51	79.0	2	3.8
55 to 64 years............................	65	42	64.5	40	61.2	2	5.0
65 years and over........................	87	21	23.6	20	22.8	1	2.9

NOTE: Data in Table 7 are from the Current Population Survey (CPS) and do not match the estimates in Table 8. See notes and definitions for further information.
[1] May be of any race.
NA = Not available.
* = Fewer than 500 people.

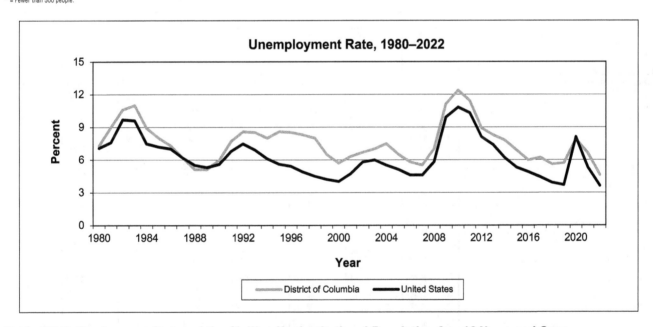

Unemployment Rate, 1980–2022

Table DC-8. Employment Status of the Civilian Noninstitutional Population Age 16 Years and Over

(Number, percent.)

Year	Civilian labor force	Civilian participation rate	Employed	Unemployed	Unemployment rate
2010..	346,707	68.9	312,132	34,575	10.0
2011..	352,193	68.1	316,372	35,821	10.2
2012..	365,176	69.1	332,412	32,764	9.0
2013..	374,199	69.4	342,609	31,590	8.4
2014..	379,678	69.3	350,415	29,263	7.7
2015..	388,446	69.7	361,556	26,890	6.9
2016..	395,124	69.9	370,553	24,571	6.2
2017..	393,326	70.5	369,388	23,938	6.1
2018..	396,039	70.5	373,772	22,267	5.6
2019..	400,577	71.1	379,016	21,561	5.4
2020..	389,384	69.2	358,370	31,014	8.0
2021..	381,673	69.8	356,578	25,095	6.6
2022..	388,403	70.7	370,229	18,174	4.7

Table DC-9. Employment and Average Wages by Industry

(Estimates are based on the 2012 North American Industry Classification System [NAICS].)

Industry	2014	2015	2016	2017	2018	2019	2020	2021
	Number of Jobs							
Wage and Salary Employment by Industry	767,130	775,658	788,013	793,524	801,650	806,196	754,454	754,495
Farm Wage and Salary Employment	0	0	0	0	0	0	0	0
Nonfarm Wage and Salary Employment	767,130	775,658	788,013	793,524	801,650	806,196	754,454	754,495
Private wage and salary employment	515,390	527,234	537,330	543,372	552,662	557,885	503,967	502,337
Forestry, fishing, and related activities	0	0	0	0	0	0	0	(D)
Mining	0	0	0	0	0	0	0	0
Utilities	1,920	2,004	1,998	2,028	2,037	1,988	(D)	1,979
Construction	14,679	15,019	15,762	(D)	15,981	15,187	15,377	15,384
Manufacturing	1,031	1,104	1,218	(D)	1,337	1,331	(D)	(D)
Durable goods manufacturing	418	456	542	(D)	512	487	(D)	(D)
Nondurable goods manufacturing	613	648	676	(D)	825	844	648	655
Wholesale trade	4,934	4,874	5,035	4,948	4,866	5,136	4,942	4,983
Retail trade	21,465	22,636	23,084	23,489	23,243	23,237	20,167	20,133
Transportation and warehousing	3,938	4,435	4,397	4,643	4,775	4,361	3,415	3,486
Information	17,245	17,190	17,058	17,853	19,204	20,009	19,802	19,738
Finance and insurance	15,137	15,157	14,986	15,142	15,295	15,309	15,024	14,533
Real estate and rental and leasing	11,988	12,280	12,609	12,708	12,846	13,245	12,961	12,615
Professional, scientific, and technical services	109,564	113,169	115,828	117,328	119,770	121,879	122,476	121,808
Management of companies and enterprises	2,157	2,148	2,434	2,770	2,619	2,739	2,865	2,867
Administrative and waste services	46,928	48,013	48,184	47,528	46,808	47,437	42,660	43,133
Educational services	56,763	56,811	57,552	56,729	55,484	55,016	51,586	51,109
Health care and social assistance	65,113	66,150	68,204	68,973	70,230	70,349	67,874	66,834
Arts, entertainment, and recreation	7,501	7,757	8,397	9,156	9,579	10,072	6,400	6,489
Accommodation and food services	62,993	65,735	66,657	68,005	70,567	71,969	41,219	43,688
Other services, except public administration	72,034	72,752	73,927	75,133	78,021	78,621	74,203	72,474
Government and government enterprises	251,740	248,424	250,683	250,152	248,988	248,311	250,487	252,158
	Dollars							
Average Wages and Salaries by Industry	84,301	87,230	88,771	91,720	95,266	97,321	106,107	111,259
Average Farm Wages and Salaries	0	0	0	0	0	0	0	0
Average Nonfarm Wages and Salaries	84,301	87,230	88,771	91,720	95,266	97,321	106,107	111,259
Average private wages and salaries	78,350	81,005	82,164	85,094	88,336	90,973	101,744	107,813
Forestry, fishing, and related activities	0	0	0	0	0	0	0	(D)
Mining	0	0	0	0	0	0	0	0
Utilities	98,384	103,130	107,138	112,671	130,476	121,342	(D)	131,471
Construction	65,118	63,558	63,956	(D)	71,819	73,546	77,243	80,218
Manufacturing	95,381	95,827	93,412	(D)	93,049	89,545	(D)	(D)
Durable goods manufacturing	82,557	91,037	96,915	(D)	120,020	116,008	(D)	(D)
Nondurable goods manufacturing	104,126	99,198	90,604	(D)	76,312	74,276	88,514	106,420
Wholesale trade	120,472	121,059	117,984	123,920	124,883	138,833	154,289	163,902
Retail trade	33,259	33,784	35,894	36,001	37,909	38,660	42,685	43,203
Transportation and warehousing	76,131	75,677	78,164	75,769	74,468	78,546	94,768	92,886
Information	120,673	121,514	126,473	131,082	133,919	139,011	166,723	190,725
Finance and insurance	156,450	167,244	171,256	179,061	185,860	189,697	195,835	219,604
Real estate and rental and leasing	94,266	94,226	94,846	104,188	107,756	110,924	112,653	114,770
Professional, scientific, and technical services	126,655	128,788	131,857	135,788	141,229	144,522	152,415	162,740
Management of companies and enterprises	232,866	297,382	222,637	215,427	248,596	253,012	280,397	274,468
Administrative and waste services	49,074	51,283	50,649	52,521	53,081	54,872	61,316	64,016
Educational services	48,006	50,042	50,840	52,272	55,282	56,746	62,452	61,024
Health care and social assistance	60,404	62,661	62,653	63,999	65,385	67,561	72,246	76,992
Arts, entertainment, and recreation	57,353	82,527	76,579	86,288	89,625	87,546	89,616	108,188
Accommodation and food services	34,457	35,685	36,833	37,848	39,425	41,008	37,521	44,850
Other services, except public administration	83,422	86,877	88,936	90,897	93,416	96,012	104,495	107,840
Government and government enterprises	96,486	100,441	102,932	106,114	110,648	111,583	114,885	118,123

(D) = Not shown to avoid disclosure of confidential information; estimates are included in higher-level totals.

Table DC-10. Employment Characteristics by Family Type

(Number, percent.)

Family type and labor force status	2019 Total	2019 Families with own children under 18 years	2020 [1] Total	2020 [1] Families with own children under 18 years	2021 Total	2021 Families with own children under 18 years
All Families...............................	124,978	47,438	123,496	50,882	128,733	51,202
FAMILY TYPE AND LABOR FORCE STATUS						
Opposite-Sex Married-Couple Families................	78,331	25,730	70,719	27,992	72,830	28,958
Both husband and wife in labor force............	63.1	76.7	66.8	79.4	66.9	75.9
Husband in labor force, wife not in labor force ...	13.6	15.7	14.0	17.0	14.9	17.0
Wife in labor force, husband not in labor force....	7.2	3.9	7.8	2.2	7.4	4.4
Both husband and wife not in labor force.........	10.6	1.3	11.5	1.3	10.7	2.6
Other Families	46,647	21,708	48,191	22,389	51,255	21,476
Female householder, no spouse present...........	81.7	82.5	79.6	82.7	80.8	88.1
In labor force................................	54.4	74.8	51.6	67.4	49.6	62.5
Not in labor force	27.3	7.7	28.1	15.3	31.2	25.5
Male householder, no spouse present.............	18.3	17.5	20.4	17.3	19.2	11.9
In labor force...............................	13.3	14.9	16.3	14.9	14.4	10.0
Not in labor force	4.9	2.6	4.1	2.4	4.9	1.9

[1] 2020 ACS 5-Year estimates. 1-Year estimates were not released for 2020 due to the impact of COVID-19 on data collection that year. Data is not comparable to previous years, which are based on 1-year estimates.

Table DC-11. School Enrollment and Educational Attainment, 2021

(Number, percent.)

Item	District	U.S.
Enrollment		
Total population 3 years and over, enrolled in school	158,721	79,453,524
Enrolled in nursery school or preschool (percent)....	8.5	5.2
Enrolled in kindergarten (percent).................	6.1	5.0
Enrolled in elementary school, grades 1-8 (percent)....	32.0	41.3
Enrolled in high school, grades 9-12 (percent)	13.6	21.8
Enrolled in college or graduate school (percent)....	39.8	26.7
Attainment		
Total population 25 years and over	478,774	228,193,464
Less than ninth grade (percent)...................	3.4	4.8
9th to 12th grade, no diploma (percent)...........	3.8	5.9
High school graduate, including equivalency (percent)....	14.8	26.3
Some college, no degree (percent).................	11.7	19.3
Associate's degree (percent)......................	3.2	8.8
Bachelor's degree (percent).......................	25.2	21.2
Graduate or professional degree (percent).........	37.8	13.8
High school graduate or higher (percent)	92.8	89.4
Bachelor's degree or higher (percent).............	63	35.0

Table DC-12. Public School Characteristics and Educational Indicators

(Number, percent; data derived from National Center of Education Statistics.)

Item	State	U.S.
Public Elementary and Secondary Schools		
Number of regular school districts, 2019-20..........	1	13,349
Number of operational schools, 2019-20..............	230	98,469
Percent charter schools	49.6	7.7
Total public school enrollment, Fall 2021...........	88,908	49,433,092
Percent charter school enrollment..................	44.8	7.5
Student-teacher ratio, Fall 2019...................	12.1	15.9
Expenditures per student (unadjusted dollars), 2019-20	23,754	13,489
Four-year adjusted cohort graduation rate (ACGR), 2019-2020[1]....	73.0	86.5
Students eligible for free or reduced-price lunch (percent), 2019-20....	76.4	52.1
English language learners (percent), Fall 2020.....	12.0	10.3
Students age 3 to 21 served under IDEA, part B (percent), 2021-22	16.1	14.7

Public Schools by Type, 2019-20	Number	Percent of district public schools
Total number of schools............................	230	100.0
Special education..................................	2	0.9
Vocational education...............................	n	-
Alternative education..............................	6	2.6

[1] Adjusted Cohort Graduation Rates (ACGR) differ from Averaged Freshmen Graduation Rates (AFGR).
- = Zero or rounds to zero.

Table DC-13. Reported Voting and Registration of the Voting-Age Population, November 2022

(Numbers in thousands, percent.)

Item	Total population	Total citizen population	Registered			Voted		
			Total registered	Percent registered (total population)	Percent registered (total citizen population)	Total voted	Percent voted (total population)	Percent voted (total citizen population)
U.S. Total	255,457	233,546	161,422	63.2	69.1	121,916	47.7	52.2
State Total	512	476	393	76.7	82.4	300	58.6	62.9
Sex								
Male	241	223	179	74.4	80.5	135	56.2	60.8
Female	271	254	213	78.8	84.1	164	60.7	64.8
Race								
White alone............................	241	224	196	81.2	87.6	156	64.6	69.7
White, non-Hispanic alone	212	203	180	85.1	88.9	145	68.6	71.7
Black alone............................	225	217	168	74.8	77.6	124	55.1	57.1
Asian alone	27	19	15	53.7	75.1	9	34.5	48.2
Hispanic (of any race)	44	31	22	50.3	70.6	14	32.1	45.1
White alone or in combination..............	251	233	204	80.9	87.2	162	64.5	69.5
Black alone or in combination....................	230	222	173	74.9	77.8	127	55.4	57.5
Asian alone or in combination..................	33	25	20	59.2	77.3	13	38.8	50.7
Age								
18 to 24 years	53	51	32	60.0	63.4	23	43.7	46.1
25 to 34 years	146	138	109	74.9	79.3	77	52.8	55.9
35 to 44 years	97	82	73	75.0	88.1	52	53.5	62.8
45 to 64 years	125	117	106	84.4	89.9	81	64.6	68.9
65 years and over	91	88	73	80.7	83.0	67	73.5	75.6

B = Base is less than 75,000 and therefore too small to show the derived measure.

Table DC-14. Health Indicators

(Number, rate as indicated in footnotes.)

Item	District	U.S.
Births		
Life Expectancy at Birth (years), 2020	75.3	77.0
Fertility Rate by State[1], 2021	48.7	56.3
Percent Home Births, 2021	1.0	1.4
Cesarean Delivery Rate[2], 2021	31.1	32.1
Preterm Birth Rate[3], 2021	10.1	10.5
Teen Birth Rate[4], 2021	13.9	13.9
Percentage of Babies Born Low Birthweight[5], 2021	9.6	8.5
Deaths[6]		
Heart Disease Mortality Rate, 2021...	192.8	173.8
Cancer Mortality Rate, 2021..	147.1	146.6
Stroke Mortality Rate, 2021...	43.6	41.1
Diabetes Mortality Rate, 2021..	24.4	25.4
Influenza/Pneumonia Mortality Rate, 2021	10.0	10.5
Suicide Mortality Rate, 2021..	6.2	14.1
Drug Overdose Mortality Rate, 2021..	32.4	33.6
Firearm Injury Mortality Rate, 2021	24.4	14.6
Homicide Mortality Rate, 2021..	30.0	8.2
Disease and Illness		
Lifetime Asthma in Adults, 2020 (percent)...	16.0	13.9
Lifetime Asthma in Children, 2020 (percent)[7]	12.8	11.3
Diabetes in Adults, 2020 (percent)...	8.3	8.2
Self-reported Obesity in Adults, 2021 (percent)...	24.7	NA

SOURCE: National Center for Health Statistics, National Vital Statistics System 2020 data; https://wonder.cdc.gov.
[1] General fertility rate per 1,000 women aged 15–44.
[2] This represents the percentage of all live births that were cesarean deliveries.
[3] Babies born prior to 37 weeks of pregnancy (gestation).
[4] Number of births per 1,000 females aged 15–19
[5] Babies born weighing less than 2,500 grams or 5 lbs. 8oz.
[6] Death rates are the number of deaths per 100,000 total population.
[7] U.S. total includes data from 30 states and D.C.
NA = Not available.
- = Zero or rounds to zero.

Table DC-15. Local Government Finances, 2021

(Dollar amounts in thousands, percent distribution.)

Item	Dollars	Percent distribution
Total Revenue	19,736,037	100.0
General revenue	16,991,638	86.1
Intergovernmental revenue	6,451,061	32.7
Taxes	8,894,003	45.1
Property	3,007,722	15.2
Sales and gross receipts	1,591,327	8.1
Individual income tax	2,643,213	13.4
Corporate income tax	863,057	4.4
Motor vehicle license	55,085	0.3
Other taxes	733,599	3.7
Current charges	800,897	4.1
Miscellaneous general revenue	845,677	4.3
Utility revenue	390,742	2.0
Liquor stores revenue	0	-
Insurance trust revenue[1]	2,353,657	11.9
Total Expenditure	22,552,255	100.0
Intergovernmental expenditure	0	-
Direct expenditure	22,552,255	100.0
Current operation	15,677,868	69.5
Capital outlay	3,350,716	14.9
Assistance and subsidies	707,175	3.1
Interest on debt	779,994	3.5
Insurance benefits and repayments	2,036,502	9.0
Exhibit: Salaries and wages	4,583,928	20.3
Direct Expenditure	22,552,255	100.0
Direct expenditure by function:		
Direct general expenditure	16,760,701	74.3
Education	3,479,917	15.4
Public welfare	4,711,332	20.9
Hospitals	302,614	1.3
Health	1,335,426	5.9
Highways	671,219	3.0
Police protection	668,928	3.0
Correction	275,847	1.2
Natural resources	111,503	0.5
Parks and recreation	345,910	1.5
Governmental administration	1,118,570	5.0
Interest on general debt	663,008	2.9
Other and unallocable	1,208,418	5.4
Utility expenditure	3,755,052	16.7
Liquor stores expenditure	0	-
Insurance trust expenditure	2,036,502	9.0
Debt at End of Fiscal Year	19,908,084	X
Cash and Security Holdings	24,318,173	X

X = Not applicable.
- = Zero or rounds to zero.
[1] Within insurance trust revenue, net earnings of state retirement systems is a calculated statistic (the item code in the data file is X08), and thus can be positive or negative. Net earnings is the sum of earnings on investments plus gains on investments minus losses on investments. The change made in 2002 for asset valuation from book to market value in accordance with Statement 34 of the Governmental Accounting Standards Board is reflected in the calculated statistics.

Table DC-16. District Government Tax Collections, 2022

(Dollars in thousands, percent.)

Item	Dollars	Percent distribution
Total Taxes	10,208,679	100.0
Property taxes	2,897,418	28.4
Sales and gross receipts	2,177,472	21.3
General sales and gross receipts	1,695,175	16.6
Selective sales and gross receipts	482,297	4.7
Alcoholic beverages	6,919	0.1
Amusements	3,963	-
Insurance premiums	148,438	1.5
Motor fuels	28,290	0.3
Pari-mutuels	X	-
Public utilities	176,078	1.7
Tobacco products	22,465	0.2
Other selective sales	96,144	0.9
Licenses	224,380	2.2
Alcoholic beverages	9,522	0.1
Amusements	603	-
Corporations in general	41,975	0.4
Hunting and fishing	89	-
Motor vehicle	31,553	0.3
Motor vehicle operators	5,033	-
Public utilities	X	-
Occupation and business, NEC	82,641	0.8
Other licenses	52,964	0.5
Income taxes	4,108,314	40.2
Individual income	3,116,991	30.5
Corporation net income	991,323	9.7
Other taxes	801,095	7.8
Death and gift	48,202	0.5
Documentary and stock transfer	689,983	6.8
Severance	X	-
Taxes, NEC	62,910	0.6

X = Not applicable.
- = Zero or rounds to zero.

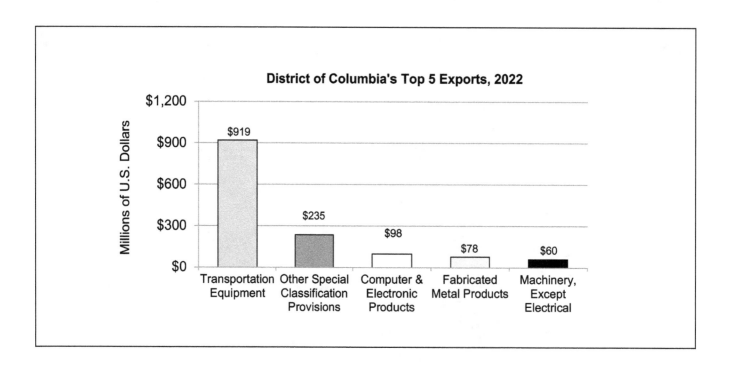

District of Columbia's Top 5 Exports, 2022

FLORIDA

Facts and Figures

Location: Southeastern United States; bordered on the N by Georgia and Alabama, on the E by the Atlantic Ocean, on the S by the Straits of Florida, and on the W by Alabama and the Gulf of Mexico

Area: 65,757 sq. mi. (170,304 sq. km.); rank—22nd

Population: 22,244,823 (2022 est.); rank—3rd

Principal Cities: capital—Tallahassee; largest—Jacksonville

Statehood: March 3, 1845; 27th state

U.S. Congress: 2 senators, 27 representatives

State Motto: In God We Trust

State Song: "The Swanee River (Old Folks at Home)"

State Nickname: The Sunshine State

Abbreviations: FL; Fla.

State Symbols: flower—orange blossom; tree—Sabal palm (cabbage palm); bird—mockingbird

At a Glance

- With an increase in population of 18.3 percent, Florida ranked 4th among the states in growth from 2010 to 2022.

- Florida's homicide rate in 2021 was 7.4 deaths per 100,000 population, compared to 8.2 per 100,000 for the entire nation.

- In 2022, Florida was the state with the 2nd largest percentage of its population in the 65 and older age group (21.6 percent).

- Florida ranked 6th among the states for the highest percent of Hispanic or Latino residents (25.7 percent) in 2022. Hispanic or Latino residents may be of any race.

- In 2021, 12.1 percent of all Florida residents were uninsured, the 5th highest percent in the nation.

Table FL-1. Population by Age, Sex, Race, and Hispanic Origin

(Number, percent, except where noted.)

Sex, age, race, and Hispanic origin	2010	2020	2022	Percent change, 2010–2022
Total Population...	18,801,310	21,538,226	22,244,823	18.3
Percent of total U.S. population	6.1	6.5	6.7	X
Sex				
Male..	9,189,355	10,603,302	10,945,426	19.1
Female	9,611,955	10,934,924	11,299,397	17.6
Age				
Under 5 years...	1,073,506	1,110,188	1,106,804	3.1
Under 18 years...	4,002,091	4,233,142	4,296,354	7.4
18 to 64 years..	11,539,617	12,818,133	13,154,273	14.0
65 years and over	3,259,602	4,486,951	4,794,196	47.1
Median age (years)	40.7	42.4	42.7	4.9
Race and Hispanic Origin				
One race				
White	14,808,867	16,585,502	17,084,651	15.4
Black	3,078,067	3,674,189	3,773,336	22.6
American Indian and Alaska Native	89,119	112,490	122,012	36.9
Asian	474,199	647,695	697,294	47.0
Native Hawaiian or Other Pacific Islander	18,790	25,782	28,081	49.4
Two or more races	332,268	492,568	539,449	62.4
Hispanic (of any race)...	4,223,806	5,716,478	6,025,030	42.6

NOTE: Population figures for 2022 are July 1 estimates. The 2010 and 2020 estimates are taken from the respective censuses.
- = Zero or rounds to zero.
X = Not applicable.

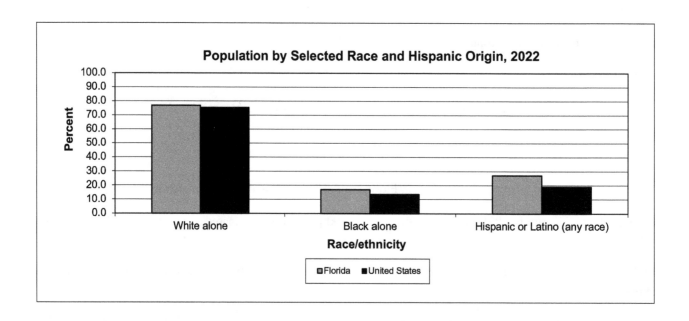

Table FL-2. Marital Status

(Number, percent distribution.)

Sex, age, race, and Hispanic origin	2000	2010	2021
Males, 15 Years and Over	6,232,987	7,534,535	8,907,701
Never married	27.3	33.9	34.8
Now married, except separated...	56.9	49.3	49.7
Separated...	2.1	2.2	1.7
Widowed...	3.2	3.2	3.0
Divorced...	10.5	11.5	10.7
Females, 15 Years and Over	6,714,003	8,021,290	9,343,870
Never married	20.5	26.6	28.6
Now married, except separated...	51.9	45.1	45.3
Separated...	2.7	3.0	2.1
Widowed...	12.3	10.8	9.7
Divorced...	12.7	14.5	14.3

Table FL-3. Households and Housing Characteristics

(Number, percent, dollars.)

Item	2000	2010	2021	Average annual percent change, 2010–2021
Total Households..	6,337,929	7,035,068	8,565,329	2.0
Family households	4,210,760	4,556,930	5,510,665	1.9
Married-couple family	3,192,266	3,307,884	3,975,785	1.8
Other family	1,018,494	1,249,046	1,534,880	2.1
Male householder, no wife present.........................	259,924	313,305	430,783	3.4
Female householder, no husband present.................	759,000	935,741	1,104,097	1.6
Nonfamily households	2,127,169	2,478,138	3,054,664	2.1
Householder living alone......................................	1,687,303	2,013,028	2,435,836	1.9
Householder not living alone.................................	439,886	465,110	618,828	3.0
Housing Characteristics				
Total housing units...	7,302,947	8,994,091	10,054,509	1.1
Occupied housing units	6,337,929	7,035,068	8,565,329	2.0
Owner occupied	4,441,799	4,794,130	5,772,329	1.9
Renter occupied	1,896,130	2,240,938	2,793,000	2.2
Average household size..	2.46	2.62	2.49	-0.5
Financial Characteristics				
Median gross rent of renter-occupied housing	641	947	1,348	3.8
Median monthly owner costs for housing units with a mortgage ...	1,004	1,505	1,616	0.7
Median value of owner-occupied housing units..........	105,500	164,200	290,700	7.0

Table FL-4. Migration, Origin, and Language

(Number, percent.)

Characteristic	State 2021	U.S. 2021
Residence 1 Year Ago		
Population 1 year and over	21,590,684	328,464,538
Same house	86.0	87.2
Different house in the U.S.	13.3	12.3
Same county	7.1	6.7
Different county	6.3	5.7
Same state	3.1	3.3
Different state	3.1	2.4
Abroad	0.6	0.4
Place of Birth		
Native born	17,172,475	286,623,642
Male	49.6	49.7
Female	50.4	50.3
Foreign born	4,608,653	45,270,103
Male	47.5	48.7
Female	52.5	51.3
Foreign born; naturalized U.S. citizen.................................	2,774,478	24,044,083
Male	45.2	46.4
Female	54.8	53.6
Foreign born; not a U.S. citizen...	1,834,175	21,226,020
Male	51.1	51.2
Female	48.9	48.8
Entered 2010 or later	31.5	28.1
Entered 2000 to 2009	23.8	23.7
Entered before 2000..	44.7	48.2
World Region of Birth, Foreign		
Foreign-born population, excluding population born at sea	4,608,601	45,269,644
Europe	9.8	10.7
Asia	10.8	31.0
Africa	1.6	5.7
Oceania	0.2	0.6
Latin America	75.6	50.1
North America	2.1	1.7
Language Spoken at Home and Ability to Speak English		
Population 5 years and over..	20,689,174	313,232,500
English only	70.0	78.4
Language other than English..	30.0	21.6
Speaks English less than "very well"................................	11.9	8.3

Table FL-5. Median Income and Poverty Status, 2021

(Number, percent, except as noted.)

Characteristic	State		U.S.	
	Number	Percent	Number	Percent
Median Income				
Households (dollars)..	63,062	X	69,717	X
Families (dollars)	76,199	X	85,806	X
Below Poverty Level (All People)	2,805,433	13.1	41,393,176	12.8
Sex				
Male	1,259,820	12.0	18,518,155	11.6
Female	1,545,613	14.2	22,875,021	13.9
Age				
Under 18 years..	752,966	17.8	12,243,219	16.9
Related children under 18 years...	734,224	17.5	11,985,424	16.6
18 to 64 years...	1,553,606	12.3	23,526,341	11.9
65 years and over	498,861	11.0	5,623,616	10.3

X = Not applicable.

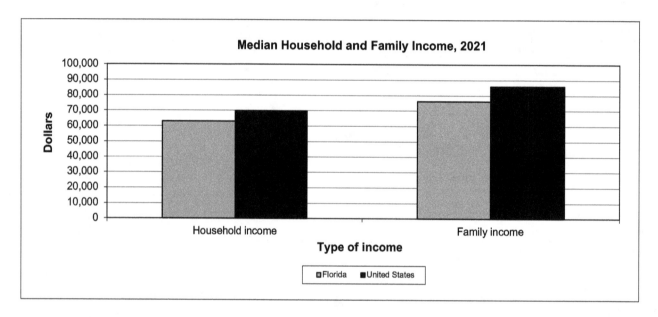

Table FL-6. Health Insurance Coverage Status for the Civilian Noninstitutionalized Population and Children Under 19 Years of Age

(Number, percent.)

Item	2011	2012	2013	2014	2015	2016	2017	2018	2019	2020 [2]	2021
Civilian Noninstitutionalized Population	18,752,294	19,011,070	19,245,127	19,583,357	19,960,169	20,294,479	20,678,704	20,996,007	21,156,770	20,897,188	21,465,883
Covered by Private or Public Insurance											
Number..	14,840,913	15,195,230	15,392,164	16,338,196	17,298,620	17,750,232	18,002,557	18,267,522	18,372,422	18,250,257	18,867,416
Percent..	79.1	79.9	80.0	83.4	86.7	87.5	87.1	87.0	86.8	87.3	87.9
Uninsured											
Number..	3,911,381	3,815,840	3,852,963	3,245,161	2,661,549	2,544,247	2,676,147	2,728,485	2,784,348	2,646,931	2,598,467
Percent..	20.9	20.1	20.0	16.6	13.3	12.5	12.9	13.0	13.2	12.7	12.1
Percent in the U.S. not covered................................	15.1	14.8	14.5	11.7	9.4	8.6	8.7	8.9	9.2	8.7	8.6
Children Under 19 Years of Age[1]	3,986,946	3,991,143	4,019,835	4,046,150	4,093,401	4,136,345	4,450,443	4,488,358	4,479,868	4,455,752	4,533,799
Covered by Private or Public Insurance											
Number..	3,511,834	3,554,977	3,574,800	3,668,163	3,809,595	3,879,598	4,125,583	4,149,314	4,137,189	4,134,956	4,202,071
Percent..	88.1	89.1	88.9	90.7	93.1	93.8	92.7	92.4	92.4	92.8	92.7
Uninsured											
Number..	475,112	436,166	445,035	377,987	283,806	256,747	324,860	339,044	342,679	320,796	331,728
Percent..	11.9	10.9	11.1	9.3	6.9	6.2	7.3	7.6	7.6	7.2	7.3
Percent in the U.S. not covered................................	7.5	7.2	7.1	6.0	4.8	4.5	5.0	5.2	5.7	5.2	5.4

[1] Data for years prior to 2017 are for individuals under 18 years of age.
[2] 2020 ACS 5-Year estimates. 1-Year estimates were not released for 2020 due to the impact of COVID-19 on data collection that year. Data is not comparable to previous years, which are based on 1-year estimates.

Table FL-7. Employment Status by Demographic Group, 2022

(Numbers in thousands, percent.)

Characteristic	Civilian noninstitutional population	Civilian labor force		Employed		Unemployed	
		Number	Percent of population	Number	Percent of population	Number	Percent of population
Total...........................	17,962	10,677	59.4	10,374	57.8	304	2.8
Sex							
Male..................................	8,695	5,627	64.7	5,464	62.8	164	2.9
Female	9,267	5,050	54.5	4,910	53.0	140	2.8
Race, Sex, and Hispanic Origin							
White	14,283	8,361	58.5	8,154	57.1	207	2.5
Male..............................	6,984	4,490	64.3	4,377	62.7	114	2.5
Female	7,299	3,871	53.0	3,777	51.7	94	2.4
Black or African American........	2,820	1,782	63.2	1,705	60.5	77	4.3
Male..............................	1,312	872	66.5	832	63.4	41	4.7
Female	1,508	910	60.3	874	57.9	36	4.0
Hispanic or Latino ethnicity[1]	4,967	3,220	64.8	3,124	62.9	97	3.0
Male..............................	2,417	1,744	72.2	1,699	70.3	45	2.6
Female	2,550	1,476	57.9	1,425	55.9	51	3.5
Age							
16 to 19 years	939	295	31.5	259	27.6	36	12.2
20 to 24 years	1,247	882	70.7	838	67.2	44	4.9
25 to 34 years	2,694	2,190	81.3	2,115	78.5	75	3.4
35 to 44 years	2,739	2,235	81.6	2,185	79.8	49	2.2
45 to 54 years	2,838	2,284	80.5	2,241	79.0	42	1.9
55 to 64 years	3,040	1,969	64.7	1,928	63.4	41	2.1
65 years and over	4,466	824	18.5	808	18.1	16	2.0

NOTE: Data in Table 7 are from the Current Population Survey (CPS) and do not match the estimates in Table 8. See notes and definitions for further information.
[1] May be of any race.

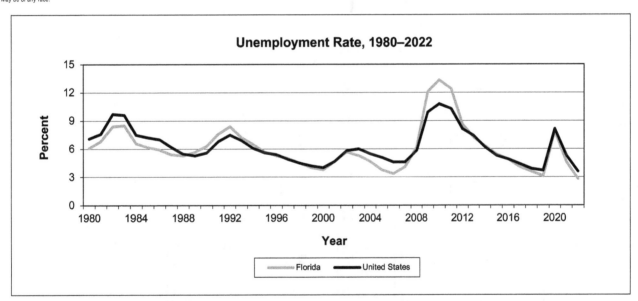

Unemployment Rate, 1980–2022

Table FL-8. Employment Status of the Civilian Noninstitutional Population Age 16 Years and Over

(Number, percent.)

Year	Civilian labor force	Civilian participation rate	Employed	Unemployed	Unemployment rate
2010.................................	9,147,107	61.2	8,155,401	991,706	10.8
2011.................................	9,260,348	60.9	8,334,119	926,229	10.0
2012.................................	9,335,727	60.5	8,529,063	806,664	8.6
2013.................................	9,414,664	60.1	8,706,060	708,604	7.5
2014.................................	9,546,407	59.9	8,931,440	614,967	6.4
2015.................................	9,639,737	59.3	9,106,772	532,965	5.5
2016.................................	9,841,301	59.2	9,360,237	481,064	4.9
2017.................................	9,972,990	59.3	9,544,892	428,098	4.3
2018.................................	10,107,191	59.2	9,734,029	373,162	3.7
2019.................................	10,259,198	59.4	9,928,235	330,963	3.2
2020.................................	10,094,878	57.7	9,267,151	827,727	8.2
2021.................................	10,312,768	58.3	9,843,057	469,711	4.6
2022.................................	10,762,307	59.3	10,449,041	313,266	2.9

Table FL-9. Employment and Average Wages by Industry

(Estimates are based on the 2012 North American Industry Classification System [NAICS].)

Industry	2014	2015	2016	2017	2018	2019	2020	2021
	Number of Jobs							
Wage and Salary Employment by Industry	8,192,310	8,472,417	8,736,178	8,917,106	9,147,156	9,338,828	8,901,285	9,300,736
Farm Wage and Salary Employment	48,772	42,091	40,153	41,185	39,342	39,774	42,061	32,937
Nonfarm Wage and Salary Employment	8,143,538	8,430,326	8,696,025	8,875,921	9,107,814	9,299,054	8,859,224	9,267,799
Private wage and salary employment	6,985,325	7,264,806	7,518,605	7,689,525	7,912,192	8,094,459	7,661,648	8,072,794
Forestry, fishing, and related activities	45,168	45,084	44,502	44,302	44,463	44,615	42,578	38,325
Mining	4,101	4,086	4,168	4,072	4,135	4,045	3,720	3,768
Utilities	21,994	22,482	22,870	23,027	23,305	22,581	22,821	22,871
Construction	406,888	442,777	486,257	516,274	554,468	577,952	576,307	588,944
Manufacturing	331,796	342,989	355,287	363,807	372,181	384,440	377,185	388,989
Durable goods manufacturing	222,982	233,236	240,649	246,969	254,171	262,761	258,893	267,021
Nondurable goods manufacturing	108,814	109,753	114,638	116,838	118,010	121,679	118,292	121,968
Wholesale trade	329,238	336,379	341,302	345,243	347,116	354,252	345,192	357,423
Retail trade	1,048,918	1,089,637	1,109,347	1,122,391	1,138,600	1,118,374	1,063,850	1,105,229
Transportation and warehousing	236,636	247,659	258,231	267,916	282,822	326,492	328,246	371,653
Information	136,999	136,522	137,186	138,289	139,102	139,040	130,504	139,110
Finance and insurance	362,719	373,924	382,421	398,315	409,407	420,619	434,018	450,839
Real estate and rental and leasing	173,664	181,370	184,489	186,498	193,336	201,926	193,550	202,100
Professional, scientific, and technical services	490,220	512,240	533,897	550,970	577,093	600,412	607,907	659,709
Management of companies and enterprises	94,208	96,989	100,512	103,655	108,063	115,441	111,698	114,494
Administrative and waste services	589,521	623,558	659,953	678,097	691,590	686,516	649,709	695,629
Educational services	157,364	160,664	163,712	168,159	172,397	176,363	164,313	182,496
Health care and social assistance	1,012,894	1,050,710	1,089,556	1,113,358	1,139,554	1,170,050	1,147,720	1,172,214
Arts, entertainment, and recreation	214,735	218,786	226,725	232,269	237,128	244,864	190,449	207,871
Accommodation and food services	880,179	921,201	955,848	975,798	999,692	1,021,751	827,270	921,674
Other services, except public administration	448,083	457,749	462,342	457,085	477,740	484,726	444,611	449,456
Government and government enterprises	1,158,213	1,165,520	1,177,420	1,186,396	1,195,622	1,204,595	1,197,576	1,195,005
	Dollars							
Average Wages and Salaries by Industry	46,225	47,674	48,463	49,906	51,674	53,292	57,360	61,988
Average Farm Wages and Salaries	23,125	23,223	28,468	25,060	28,199	30,986	32,381	52,041
Average Nonfarm Wages and Salaries	46,363	47,796	48,555	50,021	51,775	53,387	57,479	62,024
Average private wages and salaries	45,764	47,262	48,007	49,506	51,319	52,990	57,253	62,178
Forestry, fishing, and related activities	25,086	26,977	28,353	29,273	30,518	32,006	34,803	38,200
Mining	66,302	67,422	68,235	71,827	73,848	73,663	77,419	84,459
Utilities	92,404	95,342	100,224	104,623	106,348	103,449	111,784	113,160
Construction	44,725	46,835	48,240	50,231	52,368	53,988	57,079	60,440
Manufacturing	57,716	59,611	59,927	61,537	64,029	66,165	69,099	72,356
Durable goods manufacturing	60,813	62,234	62,727	65,002	67,710	69,654	72,679	76,063
Nondurable goods manufacturing	51,370	54,036	54,050	54,214	56,099	58,630	61,262	64,241
Wholesale trade	70,252	72,746	73,188	75,809	79,280	81,956	85,836	94,164
Retail trade	29,809	30,765	31,067	31,819	32,833	33,947	37,189	41,322
Transportation and warehousing	52,104	53,956	54,211	55,791	57,004	56,034	57,002	58,070
Information	72,998	76,092	79,632	82,763	83,685	88,808	96,389	106,938
Finance and insurance	79,152	81,777	83,081	86,374	89,740	91,914	99,491	110,877
Real estate and rental and leasing	46,655	48,658	49,090	50,948	52,785	53,525	57,307	62,827
Professional, scientific, and technical services	71,547	73,655	75,571	77,110	79,999	82,706	87,326	94,203
Management of companies and enterprises	104,365	107,054	106,511	114,612	115,661	118,479	123,660	137,442
Administrative and waste services	35,356	36,550	37,422	38,271	39,898	41,491	44,678	50,268
Educational services	38,711	39,170	39,757	39,045	39,812	40,327	45,290	43,365
Health care and social assistance	49,229	50,874	51,147	52,237	53,815	55,076	58,386	62,696
Arts, entertainment, and recreation	38,860	40,840	41,769	42,900	44,423	45,328	50,347	52,600
Accommodation and food services	23,595	24,264	24,726	25,245	26,689	27,442	26,626	32,770
Other services, except public administration	32,436	33,747	34,762	36,175	37,182	38,375	41,893	44,436
Government and government enterprises	49,977	51,123	52,059	53,362	54,798	56,060	58,921	60,981

Table FL-10. Employment Characteristics by Family Type

(Number, percent.)

Family type and labor force status	2019 Total	2019 Families with own children under 18 years	2020 [1] Total	2020 [1] Families with own children under 18 years	2021 Total	2021 Families with own children under 18 years
All Families..	5,083,272	1,772,760	5,118,059	1,863,076	5,510,665	1,957,238
FAMILY TYPE AND LABOR FORCE STATUS						
Opposite-Sex Married-Couple Families...	3,670,205	1,132,833	3,674,806	1,202,544	3,912,658	1,246,772
Both husband and wife in labor force..............................	45.1	67.7	45.1	66.1	45.0	65.9
Husband in labor force, wife not in labor force	19.3	25.6	20.4	27.1	20.3	26.9
Wife in labor force, husband not in labor force	8.0	4.6	8.3	4.6	8.4	4.9
Both husband and wife not in labor force........................	26.3	1.7	26.2	2.2	26.2	2.2
Other Families	1,413,067	639,927	1,396,701	654,262	1,534,880	701,253
Female householder, no spouse present	71.3	73.8	71.9	74.1	71.9	74.7
In labor force..	49.7	63.1	50.4	63.1	50.1	62.5
Not in labor force	21.7	10.7	21.5	11.0	21.9	12.2
Male householder, no spouse present...	28.7	26.2	28.1	25.9	28.1	25.3
In labor force..	21.9	24.3	21.5	23.7	21.4	22.6
Not in labor force	6.7	1.9	6.5	2.2	6.6	2.8

[1] 2020 ACS 5-Year estimates. 1-Year estimates were not released for 2020 due to the impact of COVID-19 on data collection that year. Data is not comparable to previous years, which are based on 1-year estimates.

Table FL-11. School Enrollment and Educational Attainment, 2021

(Number, percent.)

Item	State	U.S.
Enrollment		
Total population 3 years and over, enrolled in school	4,730,466	79,453,524
Enrolled in nursery school or preschool (percent)	5.3	5.2
Enrolled in kindergarten (percent)...	5.1	5.0
Enrolled in elementary school, grades 1-8 (percent)...	40.9	41.3
Enrolled in high school, grades 9-12 (percent)...	21.5	21.8
Enrolled in college or graduate school (percent)..	27.2	26.7
Attainment		
Total population 25 years and over	15,762,122	228,193,464
Less than ninth grade (percent)..	4.4	4.8
9th to 12th grade, no diploma (percent)	5.8	5.9
High school graduate, including equivalency (percent)...	27.7	26.3
Some college, no degree (percent)...	18.9	19.3
Associate's degree (percent)	10.0	8.8
Bachelor's degree (percent)	20.6	21.2
Graduate or professional degree (percent)...	12.6	13.8
High school graduate or higher (percent)	89.8	89.4
Bachelor's degree or higher (percent)...	33.2	35.0

Table FL-12. Public School Characteristics and Educational Indicators

(Number, percent; data derived from National Center of Education Statistics.)

Item	State	U.S.
Public Elementary and Secondary Schools		
Number of regular school districts, 2019-20	67	13,349
Number of operational schools, 2019-20...	4,192	98,469
Percent charter schools	16.1	7.7
Total public school enrollment, Fall 2021	2,833,186	49,433,092
Percent charter school enrollment	12.8	7.5
Student-teacher ratio, Fall 2019	17.2	15.9
Expenditures per student (unadjusted dollars), 2019-20	10,305	13,489
Four-year adjusted cohort graduation rate (ACGR), 2019-2020[1]....................................	90.2	86.5
Students eligible for free or reduced-price lunch (percent), 2019-20................................	53.9	52.1
English language learners (percent), Fall 2020	9.7	10.3
Students age 3 to 21 served under IDEA, part B (percent), 2021-22	14.8	14.7

Public Schools by Type, 2019-20	Number	Percent of state public schools
Total number of schools..	4,192	100.0
Special education...	158	3.8
Vocational education..	36	0.9
Alternative education...	387	9.2

[1] Adjusted Cohort Graduation Rates (ACGR) differ from Averaged Freshmen Graduation Rates (AFGR).

Table FL-13. Reported Voting and Registration of the Voting-Age Population, November 2022

(Numbers in thousands, percent.)

Item	Total population	Total citizen population	Registered			Voted		
			Total registered	Percent registered (total population)	Percent registered (total citizen population)	Total voted	Percent voted (total population)	Percent voted (total citizen population)
U.S. Total	255,457	233,546	161,422	63.2	69.1	121,916	47.7	52.2
State Total	17,520	15,449	9,770	55.8	63.2	7,575	43.2	49.0
Sex								
Male	8,414	7,373	4,548	54.0	61.7	3,550	42.2	48.1
Female	9,105	8,077	5,223	57.4	64.7	4,025	44.2	49.8
Race								
White alone.................................	13,941	12,340	7,925	56.8	64.2	6,274	45.0	50.8
White, non-Hispanic alone	9,505	9,193	6,113	64.3	66.5	5,007	52.7	54.5
Black alone.................................	2,703	2,419	1,450	53.6	59.9	1,007	37.3	41.6
Asian alone	504	380	216	42.9	57.0	151	30.0	39.8
Hispanic (of any race)	4,885	3,506	2,024	41.4	57.7	1,408	28.8	40.2
White alone or in combination...............	14,121	12,477	8,027	56.8	64.3	6,349	45.0	50.9
Black alone or in combination......................	2,817	2,513	1,512	53.7	60.2	1,046	37.1	41.6
Asian alone or in combination......................	541	400	234	43.2	58.5	163	30.2	40.8
Age								
18 to 24 years	1,630	1,450	596	36.5	41.1	346	21.2	23.9
25 to 34 years	2,637	2,211	1,237	46.9	55.9	744	28.2	33.7
35 to 44 years	2,809	2,266	1,349	48.0	59.5	950	33.8	41.9
45 to 64 years	5,898	5,172	3,466	58.8	67.0	2,790	47.3	53.9
65 years and over	4,546	4,350	3,123	68.7	71.8	2,744	60.4	63.1

Table FL-14. Health Indicators

(Number, rate as indicated in footnotes.)

Item	State	U.S.
Births		
Life Expectancy at Birth (years), 2020	77.5	77.0
Fertility Rate by State[1], 2021	54.9	56.3
Percent Home Births, 2021	1.3	1.4
Cesarean Delivery Rate[2], 2021	35.8	32.1
Preterm Birth Rate[3], 2021	10.9	10.5
Teen Birth Rate[4], 2021	13.5	13.9
Percentage of Babies Born Low Birthweight[5], 2021	9.0	8.5
Deaths[6]		
Heart Disease Mortality Rate, 2021...	151.3	173.8
Cancer Mortality Rate, 2021...	141.6	146.6
Stroke Mortality Rate, 2021	46.5	41.1
Diabetes Mortality Rate, 2021	24.8	25.4
Influenza/Pneumonia Mortality Rate, 2021	8.8	10.5
Suicide Mortality Rate, 2021	14.0	14.1
Drug Overdose Mortality Rate, 2021	37.5	33.6
Firearm Injury Mortality Rate, 2021	14.1	14.6
Homicide Mortality Rate, 2021...	7.4	8.2
Disease and Illness		
Lifetime Asthma in Adults, 2020 (percent)...	11.7	13.9
Lifetime Asthma in Children, 2020 (percent)[7]	10.1	11.3
Diabetes in Adults, 2020 (percent)...	9.5	8.2
Self-reported Obesity in Adults, 2021 (percent)	NA	NA

SOURCE: National Center for Health Statistics, National Vital Statistics System 2020 data; https://wonder.cdc.gov.
[1] General fertility rate per 1,000 women aged 15–44.
[2] This represents the percentage of all live births that were cesarean deliveries.
[3] Babies born prior to 37 weeks of pregnancy (gestation).
[4] Number of births per 1,000 females aged 15–19
[5] Babies born weighing less than 2,500 grams or 5 lbs. 8oz.
[6] Death rates are the number of deaths per 100,000 total population.
[7] U.S. total includes data from 30 states and D.C.
NA = Not available.
- = Zero or rounds to zero.

Table FL-15. State Government Finances, 2021

(Dollar amounts in thousands, percent distribution.)

Item	Dollars	Percent distribution
Total Revenue	126,292,984	100.0
General revenue	114,029,559	90.3
Intergovernmental revenue	42,721,773	33.8
Taxes	49,314,384	39.0
General sales	29,873,668	23.7
Selective sales	8,648,445	6.8
License taxes	2,509,455	2.0
Individual income tax	-	-
Corporate income tax	3,407,190	2.7
Other taxes	4,875,626	3.9
Current charges	8,992,428	7.1
Miscellaneous general revenue	13,000,974	10.3
Utility revenue	20,519	-
Liquor stores revenue	-	-
Insurance trust revenue[1]	12,242,906	9.7
Total Expenditure	121,129,290	100.0
Intergovernmental expenditure	21,387,014	17.7
Direct expenditure	99,742,276	82.3
Current operation	70,110,832	57.9
Capital outlay	7,404,819	6.1
Insurance benefits and repayments	18,206,988	15.0
Assistance and subsidies	3,346,908	2.8
Interest on debt	672,729	0.6
Exhibit: Salaries and wages	10,258,220	8.5
Total Expenditure	121,129,290	100.0
General expenditure	102,660,242	84.8
Intergovernmental expenditure	21,387,014	17.7
Direct expenditure	81,273,228	67.1
General expenditure, by function:		
Education	33,026,652	27.3
Public welfare	31,713,307	26.2
Hospitals	1,654,926	1.4
Health	6,245,187	5.2
Highways	8,763,391	7.2
Police protection	703,361	0.6
Correction	3,109,361	2.6
Natural resources	1,882,320	1.6
Parks and recreation	163,418	0.1
Governmental administration	3,309,428	2.7
Interest on general debt	672,729	0.6
Other and unallocable	10,979,473	9.1
Utility expenditure	330,181	0.3
Liquor stores expenditure	-	-
Insurance trust expenditure	18,206,988	15.0
Debt at End of Fiscal Year	21,437,107	X
Cash and Security Holdings	308,722,720	X

X = Not applicable.
- = Zero or rounds to zero.
[1] Within insurance trust revenue, net earnings of state retirement systems is a calculated statistic (the item code in the data file is X08), and thus can be positive or negative. Net earnings is the sum of earnings on investments plus gains on investments minus losses on investments. The change made in 2002 for asset valuation from book to market value in accordance with Statement 34 of the Governmental Accounting Standards Board is reflected in the calculated statistics.

Table FL-16. State Government Tax Collections, 2022

(Dollars in thousands, percent.)

Item	Dollars	Percent distribution
Total Taxes	59,236,859	100.0
Property taxes	0	-
Sales and gross receipts	47,015,449	79.4
General sales and gross receipts	37,841,294	63.9
Selective sales and gross receipts	9,174,155	15.5
Alcoholic beverages	359,022	0.6
Amusements	178,210	0.3
Insurance premiums	1,571,412	2.7
Motor fuels	3,111,445	5.3
Pari-mutuels	12,311	-
Public utilities	1,799,972	3.0
Tobacco products	1,048,913	1.8
Other selective sales	1,092,870	1.8
Licenses	2,245,168	3.8
Alcoholic beverages	10,677	-
Amusements	3,460	-
Corporations in general	278,526	0.5
Hunting and fishing	19,374	-
Motor vehicle	1,510,808	2.6
Motor vehicle operators	182,189	0.3
Public utilities	24,180	-
Occupation and business, NEC	202,755	0.3
Other licenses	13,199	-
Income taxes	3,780,770	6.4
Individual income	X	-
Corporation net income	3,780,770	6.4
Other taxes	6,195,472	10.5
Death and gift	X	-
Documentary and stock transfer	6,166,778	10.4
Severance	28,694	-
Taxes, NEC	0	-

X = Not applicable.
- = Zero or rounds to zero.

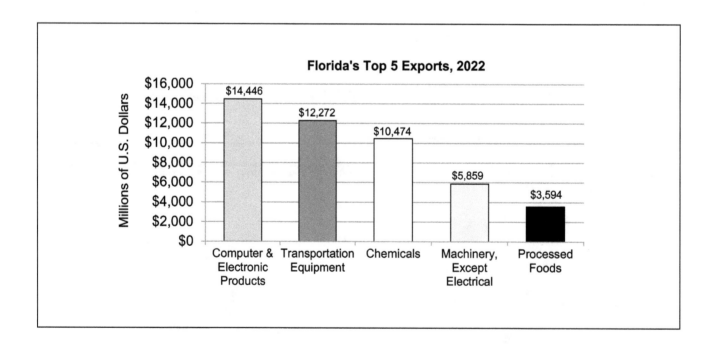

Florida's Top 5 Exports, 2022

GEORGIA

Facts and Figures

Location: Southeastern United States; bordered on the N by Tennessee and North Carolina, on the E by South Carolina and the Atlantic Ocean, on the S by Florida, and on the W by Florida and Alabama

Area: 59,425 sq. mi. (153,909 sq. km.); rank—21st

Population: 10,912,876 (2022 est.); rank—8th

Principal Cities: capital—Atlanta; largest—Atlanta

Statehood: January 2, 1788; 4th state

U.S. Congress: 2 senators, 14 representatives

State Motto: Wisdom, Justice, and Moderation

State Song: "Georgia on My Mind"

State Nicknames: The Empire State of the South; The Peach State

Abbreviations: GA; Ga.

State Symbols: flower—Cherokee rose; tree—live oak; bird—brown thrasher

At a Glance

- With an increase in population of 12.6 percent, Georgia ranked 13th among the states in growth from 2010 to 2022.

- Georgia's median household income in 2021 was $66,559, and 14.0 percent of the state's population lived below the poverty level.

- In 2021, 12.6 percent of Georgians did not have health insurance, which was the 3rd highest percent among the states.

- Georgia had the 7th lowest drug overdose death rate in 2021, with 17.3 deaths per 100,000 population. The national rate was 32.4 deaths per 100,000 population.

- Georgia was the state with the 3rd highest percent of people who identified as "Black or African American Alone," with 33.1 percent of its population in this demographic.

Table GA-1. Population by Age, Sex, Race, and Hispanic Origin

(Number, percent, except where noted.)

Sex, age, race, and Hispanic origin	2010	2020	2022	Percent change, 2010–2022
Total Population...	9,687,653	10,711,937	10,912,876	12.6
Percent of total U.S. population	3.1	3.2	3.3	X
Sex				
Male...	4,729,171	5,241,709	5,330,652	12.7
Female...	4,958,482	5,470,228	5,582,224	12.6
Age				
Under 5 years..	686,785	640,239	631,545	-8.0
Under 18 years..	2,491,552	2,519,224	2,510,123	0.7
18 to 64 years...	6,164,066	6,657,839	6,757,726	9.6
65 years and over..	1,032,035	1,534,874	1,645,027	59.4
Median age (years)..	35.3	37.2	37.5	6.2
Race and Hispanic Origin				
One race				
White	6,144,931	6,398,580	6,436,683	4.7
Black..	2,993,927	3,512,372	3,613,543	20.7
American Indian and Alaska Native	48,599	57,635	60,396	24.3
Asian..	323,459	482,994	520,964	61.1
Native Hawaiian or Other Pacific Islander	10,454	14,432	14,944	43.0
Two or more races..	166,283	245,924	266,346	60.2
Hispanic (of any race)...	853,689	1,073,745	1,140,548	33.6

NOTE: Population figures for 2022 are July 1 estimates. The 2010 and 2020 estimates are taken from the respective censuses.
- = Zero or rounds to zero.
X = Not applicable.

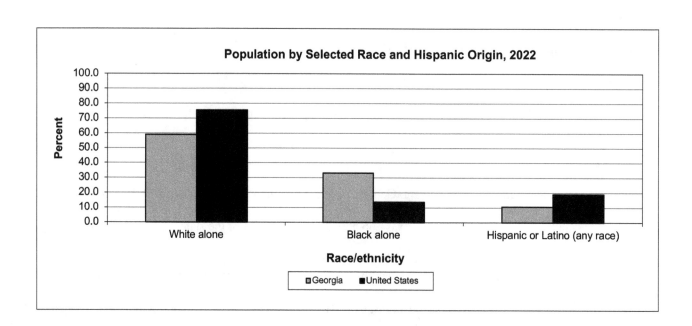

Table GA-2. Marital Status

(Number, percent distribution.)

Sex, age, race, and Hispanic origin	2000	2010	2021
Males, 15 Years and Over	3,092,736	3,683,258	4,207,788
Never married	30.4	35.4	37.9
Now married, except separated..	56.5	50.5	48.6
Separated..	2.0	2.1	1.6
Widowed..	2.1	2.2	2.4
Divorced..	9.0	9.9	9.5
Females, 15 Years and Over	3,273,889	3,954,542	4,523,622
Never married	24.4	29.7	32.7
Now married, except separated..	51.5	46.1	44.5
Separated..	2.7	2.9	2.0
Widowed..	9.8	8.6	7.8
Divorced..	11.6	12.7	13.0

Table GA-3. Households and Housing Characteristics

(Number, percent, dollars.)

Item	2000	2010	2021	Average annual percent change, 2010–2021
Total Households	3,006,369	3,482,420	4,001,109	1.4
Family households	2,111,647	2,385,969	2,675,262	1.1
Married-couple family	1,548,800	1,688,896	1,881,572	1.0
Other family	562,847	697,073	793,690	1.3
Male householder, no wife present	127,437	161,001	192,141	1.8
Female householder, no husband present	435,410	536,072	601,549	1.1
Nonfamily households	894,722	1,096,451	1,325,847	1.9
Householder living alone	710,523	921,005	1,073,419	1.5
Householder not living alone	184,199	175,446	252,428	4.0
Housing Characteristics				
Total housing units	3,281,737	4,091,482	4,475,242	0.9
Occupied housing units	3,006,369	3,482,420	4,001,109	1.4
Owner occupied	2,029,154	2,304,165	2,642,126	1.3
Renter occupied	977,215	1,178,255	1,358,983	1.4
Average household size	2.65	2.72	2.64	-0.3
Financial Characteristics				
Median gross rent of renter-occupied housing	613	819	1,153	3.7
Median monthly owner costs for housing units with a mortgage	1,039	1,390	1,501	0.7
Median value of owner-occupied housing units	111,200	156,200	249,700	5.4

Table GA-4. Migration, Origin, and Language

(Number, percent.)

Characteristic	State 2021	U.S. 2021
Residence 1 Year Ago		
Population 1 year and over	10,688,429	328,464,538
Same house	86.5	87.2
Different house in the U.S.	13.2	12.3
Same county	5.9	6.7
Different county	7.3	5.7
Same state	4.5	3.3
Different state	2.8	2.4
Abroad	0.3	0.4
Place of Birth		
Native born	9,716,601	286,623,642
Male	48.9	49.7
Female	51.1	50.3
Foreign born	1,082,965	45,270,103
Male	47.6	48.7
Female	52.4	51.3
Foreign born; naturalized U.S. citizen	541,613	24,044,083
Male	44.0	46.4
Female	56.0	53.6
Foreign born; not a U.S. citizen	541,352	21,226,020
Male	51.3	51.2
Female	48.7	48.8
Entered 2010 or later	29.6	28.1
Entered 2000 to 2009	26.9	23.7
Entered before 2000	43.5	48.2
World Region of Birth, Foreign		
Foreign-born population, excluding population born at sea	1,082,965	45,269,644
Europe	9.2	10.7
Asia	31.5	31.0
Africa	10.7	5.7
Oceania	0.3	0.6
Latin America	46.8	50.1
North America	1.4	1.7
Language Spoken at Home and Ability to Speak English		
Population 5 years and over	10,173,597	313,232,500
English only	85.0	78.4
Language other than English	14.4	21.6
Speaks English less than "very well"	5.2	8.3

Table GA-5. Median Income and Poverty Status, 2021

(Number, percent, except as noted.)

Characteristic	State		U.S.	
	Number	Percent	Number	Percent
Median Income				
Households (dollars)...	66,559	X	69,717	X
Families (dollars)	80,731	X	85,806	X
Below Poverty Level (All People)	1,476,348	14.0	41,393,176	12.8
Sex				
Male	651,305	12.8	18,518,155	11.6
Female	825,043	15.2	22,875,021	13.9
Age				
Under 18 years..	501,818	20.2	12,243,219	16.9
Related children under 18 years................................	493,398	19.9	11,985,424	16.6
18 to 64 years...	819,300	12.6	23,526,341	11.9
65 years and over	155,230	10.0	5,623,616	10.3

X = Not applicable.

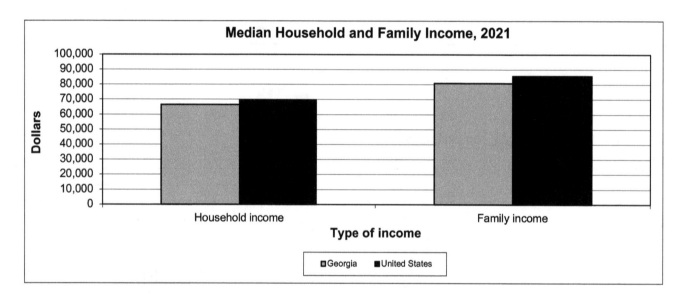

Table GA-6. Health Insurance Coverage Status for the Civilian Noninstitutionalized Population and Children Under 19 Years of Age

(Number, percent.)

Item	2011	2012	2013	2014	2015	2016	2017	2018	2019	2020 [2]	2021
Civilian Noninstitutionalized Population	9,619,740	9,719,411	9,800,887	9,906,878	10,024,056	10,120,788	10,241,594	10,334,958	10,420,412	10,321,846	10,600,385
Covered by Private or Public Insurance											
Number...	7,736,982	7,927,092	7,954,582	8,338,497	8,635,656	8,811,215	8,866,418	8,923,775	9,022,589	8,976,552	9,261,463
Percent..	80.4	81.6	81.2	84.2	86.1	87.1	86.6	86.3	86.6	87.0	87.4
Uninsured											
Number...	1,882,758	1,792,319	1,846,305	1,568,381	1,388,400	1,309,573	1,375,176	1,411,183	1,397,823	1,345,294	1,338,922
Percent..	19.6	18.4	18.8	15.8	13.9	12.9	13.4	13.7	13.4	13.0	12.6
Percent in the U.S. not covered................................	15.1	14.8	14.5	11.7	9.4	8.6	8.7	8.9	9.2	8.7	8.6
Children Under 19 Years of Age[1]............................	2,484,715	2,492,161	2,487,079	2,488,247	2,499,334	2,506,326	2,670,877	2,670,578	2,661,991	2,658,741	2,684,219
Covered by Private or Public Insurance											
Number...	2,248,147	2,272,200	2,249,028	2,299,212	2,333,101	2,343,554	2,471,248	2,453,288	2,464,855	2,462,470	2,508,118
Percent..	90.5	91.2	90.4	92.4	93.3	93.5	92.5	91.9	92.6	92.6	93.4
Uninsured											
Number...	236,568	219,961	238,051	189,035	166,233	162,772	199,629	217,290	197,136	196,271	176,101
Percent..	9.5	8.8	9.6	7.6	6.7	6.5	7.5	8.1	7.4	7.4	6.6
Percent in the U.S. not covered................................	7.5	7.2	7.1	6.0	4.8	4.5	5.0	5.2	5.7	5.2	5.4

[1] Data for years prior to 2017 are for individuals under 18 years of age.
[2] 2020 ACS 5-Year estimates. 1-Year estimates were not released for 2020 due to the impact of COVID-19 on data collection that year. Data is not comparable to previous years, which are based on 1-year estimates.

Table GA-7. Employment Status by Demographic Group, 2022

(Numbers in thousands, percent.)

Characteristic	Civilian noninstitutional population	Civilian labor force Number	Civilian labor force Percent of population	Employed Number	Employed Percent of population	Unemployed Number	Unemployed Percent of population
Total..	8,491	5,240	61.7	5,077	59.8	163	3.1
Sex							
Male..	4,026	2,750	68.3	2,677	66.5	73	2.7
Female..	4,465	2,490	55.8	2,400	53.8	90	3.6
Race, Sex, and Hispanic Origin							
White	5,173	3,161	61.1	3,094	59.8	67	2.1
Male..	2,533	1,769	69.8	1,734	68.4	35	2.0
Female..	2,640	1,393	52.7	1,360	51.5	32	2.3
Black or African American............	2,732	1,690	61.8	1,603	58.7	86	5.1
Male..	1,217	761	62.6	727	59.7	35	4.6
Female..	1,515	928	61.3	877	57.9	52	5.6
Hispanic or Latino ethnicity[1]	868	616	71.0	609	70.1	8	1.2
Male..	438	373	85.0	368	84.0	5	1.2
Female..	430	244	56.7	241	56.0	3	1.2
Age							
16 to 19 years................................	NA	NA	NA	NA	NA	NA	NA
20 to 24 years................................	686	447	65.2	410	59.7	37	8.4
25 to 34 years................................	1,522	1,261	82.9	1,219	80.1	42	3.4
35 to 44 years................................	1,407	1,156	82.1	1,133	80.5	23	2.0
45 to 54 years................................	1,338	1,061	79.3	1,040	77.7	21	2.0
55 to 64 years................................	1,319	852	64.6	836	63.4	15	1.8
65 years and over	1,686	311	18.4	301	17.9	10	3.1

NOTE: Data in Table 7 are from the Current Population Survey (CPS) and do not match the estimates in Table 8. See notes and definitions for further information.
[1] May be of any race.

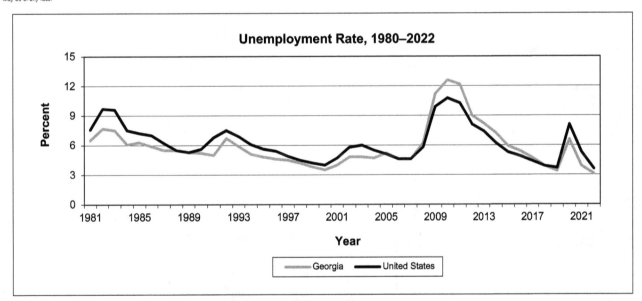

Unemployment Rate, 1980–2022

Table GA-8. Employment Status of the Civilian Noninstitutional Population Age 16 Years and Over

(Number, percent.)

Year	Civilian labor force	Civilian participation rate	Employed	Unemployed	Unemployment rate
2010..	4,709,781	64.3	4,207,266	502,515	10.7
2011..	4,739,281	64.2	4,258,833	480,448	10.1
2012..	4,770,618	63.8	4,339,369	431,249	9.0
2013..	4,750,046	62.8	4,363,292	386,754	8.1
2014..	4,745,859	62.0	4,407,067	338,792	7.1
2015..	4,734,088	61.0	4,446,515	287,573	6.1
2016..	4,921,814	62.4	4,653,740	268,074	5.4
2017..	5,107,889	63.9	4,864,813	243,076	4.8
2018..	5,121,172	63.2	4,915,713	205,459	4.0
2019..	5,152,944	62.8	4,967,503	185,441	3.6
2020..	5,079,555	61.2	4,751,105	328,450	6.5
2021..	5,186,969	61.9	4,983,732	203,237	3.9
2022..	5,234,275	61.5	5,075,093	159,182	3.0

Table GA-9. Employment and Average Wages by Industry

(Estimates are based on the 2012 North American Industry Classification System [NAICS].)

Industry	2014	2015	2016	2017	2018	2019	2020	2021
	Number of Jobs							
Wage and Salary Employment by Industry	4,319,374	4,438,480	4,551,906	4,641,076	4,722,305	4,804,775	4,609,427	4,776,500
Farm Wage and Salary Employment	16,194	15,830	19,165	22,342	16,454	16,331	21,110	21,794
Nonfarm Wage and Salary Employment	4,303,180	4,422,650	4,532,741	4,618,734	4,705,851	4,788,444	4,588,317	4,754,706
Private wage and salary employment	3,538,369	3,655,461	3,762,412	3,842,545	3,926,305	4,003,960	3,810,531	3,983,926
Forestry, fishing, and related activities	15,296	15,945	16,024	15,497	15,528	15,591	15,141	14,545
Mining	4,851	4,839	5,056	5,175	5,226	5,318	5,239	5,404
Utilities	19,784	20,081	20,117	19,628	19,124	19,396	19,702	19,731
Construction	160,672	170,197	181,116	187,242	200,754	209,453	206,897	210,471
Manufacturing	367,979	377,861	388,287	398,346	408,690	405,694	385,322	395,700
Durable goods manufacturing	177,266	182,689	187,999	193,741	201,501	202,826	192,596	200,186
Nondurable goods manufacturing	190,713	195,172	200,288	204,605	207,189	202,868	192,726	195,514
Wholesale trade	211,049	218,267	220,140	221,978	216,205	218,646	209,389	212,074
Retail trade	470,363	487,904	495,594	500,521	499,093	497,879	482,226	503,623
Transportation and warehousing	177,721	186,180	195,626	204,878	215,522	214,453	218,592	235,351
Information	107,159	106,459	111,825	116,656	114,633	116,238	109,348	124,035
Finance and insurance	171,889	175,162	178,824	182,621	184,691	188,488	192,434	197,507
Real estate and rental and leasing	60,375	63,838	65,293	67,025	70,859	74,348	71,802	74,803
Professional, scientific, and technical services	253,845	262,918	263,526	272,074	279,367	285,638	285,087	301,983
Management of companies and enterprises	62,511	66,017	68,431	68,370	73,717	91,058	88,631	88,899
Administrative and waste services	306,243	314,679	326,336	334,688	342,532	348,454	327,069	351,027
Educational services	83,138	83,652	86,476	88,034	88,754	90,646	86,093	91,657
Health care and social assistance	436,674	452,427	470,611	478,321	491,239	506,906	491,769	504,742
Arts, entertainment, and recreation	45,308	47,015	50,133	52,343	54,879	57,223	44,342	51,229
Accommodation and food services	386,845	402,836	418,930	428,991	437,586	446,117	374,762	401,858
Other services, except public administration	196,667	199,184	200,067	200,157	207,906	212,414	196,686	199,287
Government and government enterprises	764,811	767,189	770,329	776,189	779,546	784,484	777,786	770,780
	Dollars							
Average Wages and Salaries by Industry	49,111	50,474	51,557	53,035	54,611	56,292	59,735	63,005
Average Farm Wages and Salaries	23,633	22,913	19,254	14,500	19,603	19,654	15,005	19,166
Average Nonfarm Wages and Salaries	49,207	50,572	51,694	53,221	54,733	56,417	59,941	63,206
Average private wages and salaries	50,085	51,472	52,661	54,193	55,702	57,459	61,333	64,654
Forestry, fishing, and related activities	34,282	35,229	37,054	37,234	38,221	39,926	43,473	45,778
Mining	63,247	66,017	70,118	71,195	71,780	72,077	72,187	74,526
Utilities	86,958	92,943	98,948	100,514	105,143	110,117	114,944	116,492
Construction	51,770	53,933	56,808	59,240	62,038	64,716	67,313	70,156
Manufacturing	57,070	57,906	58,598	59,861	61,534	60,416	62,521	65,256
Durable goods manufacturing	59,990	60,915	61,134	62,112	64,117	65,542	66,631	69,402
Nondurable goods manufacturing	54,356	55,089	56,217	57,729	59,021	55,291	58,415	61,011
Wholesale trade	73,984	75,963	77,316	78,791	78,805	81,638	84,571	90,462
Retail trade	28,843	30,268	30,699	31,407	32,358	33,288	35,964	38,759
Transportation and warehousing	58,889	59,733	62,536	62,881	63,125	59,622	60,002	59,861
Information	89,003	88,600	92,509	98,349	98,984	103,280	111,752	121,395
Finance and insurance	84,165	87,955	89,532	93,267	96,986	99,955	106,766	111,825
Real estate and rental and leasing	53,684	55,099	57,553	58,964	62,518	63,253	66,816	72,301
Professional, scientific, and technical services	79,297	82,387	85,929	86,474	88,676	91,924	96,576	101,132
Management of companies and enterprises	106,149	110,283	107,215	115,838	122,329	133,180	138,863	138,312
Administrative and waste services	36,367	37,775	38,479	39,730	40,742	42,581	45,564	49,277
Educational services	44,515	45,027	45,784	46,431	48,737	50,055	55,157	55,217
Health care and social assistance	48,411	49,960	50,823	51,945	53,419	55,166	58,601	62,113
Arts, entertainment, and recreation	36,602	36,978	36,253	38,858	38,760	39,708	45,303	46,787
Accommodation and food services	20,197	19,876	20,332	21,041	22,096	22,770	21,996	26,535
Other services, except public administration	31,744	33,016	34,093	35,444	36,216	37,404	41,196	43,506
Government and government enterprises	45,143	46,287	46,969	48,411	49,854	51,101	53,119	55,721

Table GA-10. Employment Characteristics by Family Type

(Number, percent.)

Family type and labor force status	2019		2020 [1]		2021	
	Total	Families with own children under 18 years	Total	Families with own children under 18 years	Total	Families with own children under 18 years
All Families..	2,555,440	1,072,198	2,565,233	1,114,023	2,675,262	1,116,678
FAMILY TYPE AND LABOR FORCE STATUS						
Opposite-Sex Married-Couple Families..	1,802,484	704,892	1,796,279	729,626	1,860,616	719,397
Both husband and wife in labor force	50.6	66.0	51.6	65.9	50.6	66.8
Husband in labor force, wife not in labor force	22.7	27.4	23.1	28.1	22.7	26.5
Wife in labor force, husband not in labor force	8.1	4.5	7.9	4.3	7.8	4.7
Both husband and wife not in labor force	17.7	1.6	17.5	1.6	18.9	2.0
Other Families	752,956	367,306	751,440	380,718	793,690	393,613
Female householder, no spouse present	75.4	79.5	76.0	79.1	75.8	78.2
In labor force..	53.5	68.4	54.0	67.3	53.6	64.5
Not in labor force	22.0	11.2	22.0	11.7	22.2	13.7
Male householder, no spouse present...	24.6	20.5	24.0	20.9	24.2	21.8
In labor force..	18.8	19.0	18.1	18.9	18.1	19.1
Not in labor force	5.8	1.5	5.8	2.0	6.1	2.7

[1] 2020 ACS 5-Year estimates. 1-Year estimates were not released for 2020 due to the impact of COVID-19 on data collection that year. Data is not comparable to previous years, which are based on 1-year estimates.

Table GA-11. School Enrollment and Educational Attainment, 2021

(Number, percent.)

Item	State	U.S.
Enrollment		
Total population 3 years and over, enrolled in school	2,746,549	79,453,524
Enrolled in nursery school or preschool (percent)..	5.5	5.2
Enrolled in kindergarten (percent)...	5.1	5.0
Enrolled in elementary school, grades 1-8 (percent)...	41.9	41.3
Enrolled in high school, grades 9-12 (percent)..	22.0	21.8
Enrolled in college or graduate school (percent)..	25.5	26.7
Attainment		
Total population 25 years and over	7,234,271	228,193,464
Less than ninth grade (percent)...	4.2	4.8
9th to 12th grade, no diploma (percent)	6.8	5.9
High school graduate, including equivalency (percent)...	26.7	26.3
Some college, no degree (percent)...	19.2	19.3
Associate's degree (percent)..	8.4	8.8
Bachelor's degree (percent)...	20.9	21.2
Graduate or professional degree (percent)...	13.7	13.8
High school graduate or higher (percent)	89	89.4
Bachelor's degree or higher (percent)..	34.6	35.0

[1] 2020 ACS 5-Year estimates. 1-Year estimates were not released for 2020 due to the impact of COVID-19 on data collection that year.

Table GA-12. Public School Characteristics and Educational Indicators

(Number, percent; data derived from National Center of Education Statistics.)

Item	State	U.S.
Public Elementary and Secondary Schools		
Number of regular school districts, 2019-20	180	13,349
Number of operational schools, 2019-20..	2,304	98,469
Percent charter schools	3.9	7.7
Total public school enrollment, Fall 2021	1,740,875	49,433,092
Percent charter school enrollment	4.0	7.5
Student-teacher ratio, Fall 2019	15.0	15.9
Expenditures per student (unadjusted dollars), 2019-20	11,686	13,489
Four-year adjusted cohort graduation rate (ACGR), 2019-2020[1]...	83.8	86.5
Students eligible for free or reduced-price lunch (percent), 2019-20..	59.7	52.1
English language learners (percent), Fall 2020	7.5	10.3
Students age 3 to 21 served under IDEA, part B (percent), 2021-22	12.9	14.7

Public Schools by Type, 2019-20	Number	Percent of state public schools
Total number of schools...	2,304	100.0
Special education	12	0.5
Vocational education..	0	0.0
Alternative education..	31	1.3

[1] Adjusted Cohort Graduation Rates (ACGR) differ from Averaged Freshmen Graduation Rates (AFGR).
- = Zero or rounds to zero.

Table GA-13. Reported Voting and Registration of the Voting-Age Population, November 2022

(Numbers in thousands, percent.)

Item	Total population	Total citizen population	Registered Total registered	Registered Percent registered (total population)	Registered Percent registered (total citizen population)	Voted Total voted	Voted Percent voted (total population)	Voted Percent voted (total citizen population)
U.S. Total	255,457	233,546	161,422	63.2	69.1	121,916	47.7	52.2
State Total	8,314	7,601	5,275	63.4	69.4	4,323	52.0	56.9
Sex								
Male	3,955	3,521	2,434	61.6	69.1	1,994	50.4	56.6
Female	4,359	4,080	2,840	65.2	69.6	2,329	53.4	57.1
Race								
White alone	4,935	4,591	3,256	66.0	70.9	2,729	55.3	59.5
White, non-Hispanic alone	4,328	4,280	3,090	71.4	72.2	2,598	60.0	60.7
Black alone	2,648	2,584	1,766	66.7	68.3	1,397	52.7	54.0
Asian alone	517	250	152	29.4	60.9	127	24.6	51.0
Hispanic (of any race)	815	429	234	28.7	54.6	186	22.8	43.3
White alone or in combination	5,067	4,723	3,342	65.9	70.8	2,784	54.9	58.9
Black alone or in combination	2,723	2,660	1,804	66.2	67.8	1,423	52.3	53.5
Asian alone or in combination	553	286	168	30.4	58.8	136	24.6	47.6
Age								
18 to 24 years	924	859	466	50.4	54.2	322	34.9	37.5
25 to 34 years	1,620	1,395	918	56.7	65.8	640	39.5	45.9
35 to 44 years	1,400	1,176	812	58.0	69.0	628	44.9	53.4
45 to 64 years	2,610	2,451	1,695	64.9	69.1	1,457	55.8	59.5
65 years and over	1,760	1,720	1,384	78.6	80.5	1,276	72.5	74.2

Table GA-14. Health Indicators

(Number, rate as indicated in footnotes.)

Item	State	U.S.
Births		
Life Expectancy at Birth (years), 2020	75.6	77.0
Fertility Rate by State[1], 2021	55.9	56.3
Percent Home Births, 2021	1.0	1.4
Cesarean Delivery Rate[2], 2021	35.1	32.1
Preterm Birth Rate[3], 2021	11.9	10.5
Teen Birth Rate[4], 2021	16.6	13.9
Percentage of Babies Born Low Birthweight[5], 2021	10.6	8.5
Deaths[6]		
Heart Disease Mortality Rate, 2021	195.2	173.8
Cancer Mortality Rate, 2021	151.5	146.6
Stroke Mortality Rate, 2021	47.9	41.1
Diabetes Mortality Rate, 2021	25.1	25.4
Influenza/Pneumonia Mortality Rate, 2021	11.3	10.5
Suicide Mortality Rate, 2021	15.3	14.1
Drug Overdose Mortality Rate, 2021	23.5	33.6
Firearm Injury Mortality Rate, 2021	20.3	14.6
Homicide Mortality Rate, 2021	11.4	8.2
Disease and Illness		
Lifetime Asthma in Adults, 2020 (percent)	13.2	13.9
Lifetime Asthma in Children, 2020 (percent)[7]	16.6	11.3
Diabetes in Adults, 2020 (percent)	10.7	8.2
Self-reported Obesity in Adults, 2021 (percent)	33.9	NA

SOURCE: National Center for Health Statistics, National Vital Statistics System 2020 data; https://wonder.cdc.gov.
[1] General fertility rate per 1,000 women aged 15–44.
[2] This represents the percentage of all live births that were cesarean deliveries.
[3] Babies born prior to 37 weeks of pregnancy (gestation).
[4] Number of births per 1,000 females aged 15–19
[5] Babies born weighing less than 2,500 grams or 5 lbs. 8oz.
[6] Death rates are the number of deaths per 100,000 total population.
[7] U.S. total includes data from 30 states and D.C.
NA = Not available.
- = Zero or rounds to zero.

Table GA-15. State Government Finances, 2021

(Dollar amounts in thousands, percent distribution.)

Item	Dollars	Percent distribution
Total Revenue	68,300,546	100.0
General revenue	60,932,942	89.2
Intergovernmental revenue	26,262,760	38.5
Taxes	27,850,996	40.8
General sales	6,948,296	10.2
Selective sales	3,309,634	4.8
License taxes	750,136	1.1
Individual income tax	14,220,906	20.8
Corporate income tax	1,750,735	2.6
Other taxes	871,289	1.3
Current charges	4,006,188	5.9
Miscellaneous general revenue	2,812,998	4.1
Utility revenue	1,112	-
Liquor stores revenue	-	-
Insurance trust revenue[1]	7,366,492	10.8
Total Expenditure	71,193,683	100.0
Intergovernmental expenditure	18,559,916	26.1
Direct expenditure	52,633,767	73.9
Current operation	32,687,566	45.9
Capital outlay	3,726,856	5.2
Insurance benefits and repayments	13,995,850	19.7
Assistance and subsidies	1,659,083	2.3
Interest on debt	564,412	0.8
Exhibit: Salaries and wages	7,376,922	10.4
Total Expenditure	71,193,683	100.0
General expenditure	57,120,072	80.2
Intergovernmental expenditure	18,559,916	26.1
Direct expenditure	38,560,156	54.2
General expenditure, by function:		
Education	25,938,436	36.4
Public welfare	14,934,312	21.0
Hospitals	1,617,303	2.3
Health	2,156,881	3.0
Highways	3,575,409	5.0
Police protection	580,617	0.8
Correction	1,432,195	2.0
Natural resources	721,540	1.0
Parks and recreation	163,700	0.2
Governmental administration	1,171,893	1.6
Interest on general debt	564,412	0.8
Other and unallocable	4,219,740	5.9
Utility expenditure	78,104	0.1
Liquor stores expenditure	-	-
Insurance trust expenditure	13,995,850	19.7
Debt at End of Fiscal Year	14,627,512	X
Cash and Security Holdings	150,078,884	X

X = Not applicable.
- = Zero or rounds to zero.
[1] Within insurance trust revenue, net earnings of state retirement systems is a calculated statistic (the item code in the data file is X08), and thus can be positive or negative. Net earnings is the sum of earnings on investments plus gains on investments minus losses on investments. The change made in 2002 for asset valuation from book to market value in accordance with Statement 34 of the Governmental Accounting Standards Board is reflected in the calculated statistics.

Table GA-16. State Government Tax Collections, 2022

(Dollars in thousands, percent.)

Item	Dollars	Percent distribution
Total Taxes	33,933,816	100.0
Property taxes	799,564	2.4
Sales and gross receipts	11,405,066	33.6
General sales and gross receipts	8,320,361	24.5
Selective sales and gross receipts	3,084,705	9.1
Alcoholic beverages	228,617	0.7
Amusements	X	-
Insurance premiums	482,092	1.4
Motor fuels	1,602,054	4.7
Pari-mutuels	X	-
Public utilities	0	-
Tobacco products	238,574	0.7
Other selective sales	533,368	1.6
Licenses	743,492	2.2
Alcoholic beverages	4,717	-
Amusements	0	-
Corporations in general	55,673	0.2
Hunting and fishing	28,735	0.1
Motor vehicle	413,341	1.2
Motor vehicle operators	123,174	0.4
Public utilities	X	-
Occupation and business, NEC	85,652	0.3
Other licenses	32,200	0.1
Income taxes	20,796,528	61.3
Individual income	18,286,845	53.9
Corporation net income	2,509,683	7.4
Other taxes	189,166	0.6
Death and gift	0	-
Documentary and stock transfer	0	-
Severance	X	-
Taxes, NEC	189,166	0.6

X = Not applicable.
- = Zero or rounds to zero.

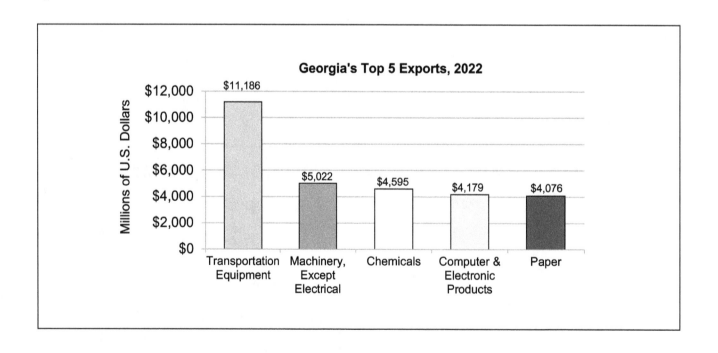

Georgia's Top 5 Exports, 2022

- Transportation Equipment: $11,186
- Machinery, Except Electrical: $5,022
- Chemicals: $4,595
- Computer & Electronic Products: $4,179
- Paper: $4,076

(Millions of U.S. Dollars)

HAWAII

Location: North Pacific Ocean

Area: 10,931 sq. mi. (28,311 sq. km.); rank—43rd

Population: 1,440,196 (2022 est.); rank—40th

Principal Cities: capital—Honolulu; largest—Honolulu

Statehood: August 21, 1959; 50th state

U.S. Congress: 2 senators, 2 representatives

State Motto: *Ua mau ke ea o ka'ina i ka pono* ("The life of the land is perpetuated in righteousness")

State Song: "Hawai'i Pono' (Hawaii's Own)"

State Nickname: The Aloha State

Abbreviations: HI

State Symbols: flower—native yellow hibiscus; tree—kukui (candlenut tree); bird—nene (Hawaiian goose)

At a Glance

- With an increase in population of 5.9 percent, Hawaii ranked 27th among the states in growth from 2010 to 2022.

- In 2021, 3.9 percent of Hawaiians did not have health insurance, compared to 8.6 percent of the total U.S. population, a rate that was the 4th lowest in the country.

- Hawaii had 19.0 drug overdose deaths per 100,000 population in 2021, which ranked 43rd in the country. The national rate was 32.4 deaths per 100,000 population.

- Hawaii was the state with the longest life expectancy at birth in 2020 (80.7 years) compared to the national life expectancy of 77.0 years.

- Hawaii had the largest percent of residents who identified with two or more races in 2022, with 24.7 percent of its residents in this demographic.

Table HI-1. Population by Age, Sex, Race, and Hispanic Origin

(Number, percent, except where noted.)

Sex, age, race, and Hispanic origin	2010	2020	2022	Percent change, 2010–2022
Total Population...	1,360,301	1,455,273	1,440,196	5.9
Percent of total U.S. population	0.4	0.4	0.4	X
Sex				
Male..	681,243	735,038	724,711	6.4
Female	679,058	720,235	715,485	5.4
Age				
Under 5 years..	87,407	86,179	79,600	-8.9
Under 18 years...	303,818	308,076	297,326	-2.1
18 to 64 years	861,345	870,340	848,505	-1.5
65 years and over	195,138	276,857	294,365	50.8
Median age (years)	38.6	39.8	40.7	5.4
Race and Hispanic Origin				
One race				
White	349,051	366,032	363,260	4.1
Black	22,473	32,155	31,516	40.2
American Indian and Alaska Native	4,960	5,635	5,730	15.5
Asian	531,633	541,773	534,794	0.6
Native Hawaiian or Other Pacific Islander	138,292	151,393	148,844	7.6
Two or more races	313,892	358,285	356,052	13.4
Hispanic (of any race).................................	120,842	159,400	160,103	32.5

NOTE: Population figures for 2022 are July 1 estimates. The 2010 and 2020 estimates are taken from the respective censuses.
- = Zero or rounds to zero.
X = Not applicable.

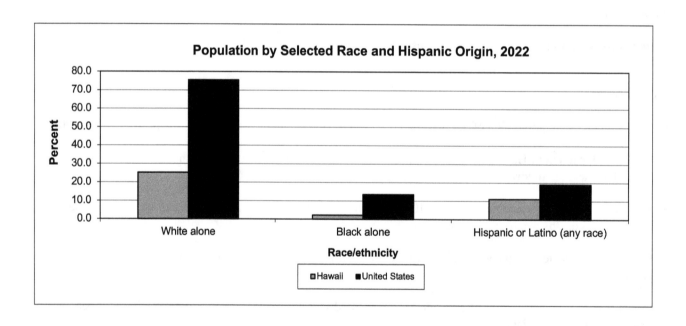

Table HI-2. Marital Status

(Number, percent distribution.)

Sex, age, race, and Hispanic origin	2000	2010	2021
Males, 15 Years and Over	481,768	554,154	592,582
Never married	34.6	37.8	38.5
Now married, except separated............................	53.7	49.1	50.9
Separated..	1.4	1.2	0.7
Widowed..	2.2	2.7	2.2
Divorced...	8.1	9.2	7.6
Females, 15 Years and Over	484,107	556,915	592,219
Never married	25.9	28.7	29.5
Now married, except separated............................	52.5	48.5	49.0
Separated..	1.7	1.8	1.1
Widowed..	9.8	10.1	9.1
Divorced...	10.0	11.0	11.3

Table HI-3. Households and Housing Characteristics

(Number, percent, dollars.)

Item	2000	2010	2021	Average annual percent change, 2010–2021
Total Households..	403,240	445,812	490,080	0.9
Family households...	287,068	303,075	334,899	1.0
Married-couple family	216,077	224,402	248,069	1.0
Other family	70,991	78,673	86,830	0.9
Male householder, no wife present............................	21,068	24,247	26,631	0.9
Female householder, no husband present...................	49,923	54,426	60,199	1.0
Nonfamily households	116,172	142,737	155,181	0.8
Householder living alone	88,153	108,872	120,635	1.0
Householder not living alone	28,019	33,865	34,546	0.2
Housing Characteristics				
Total housing units..	460,542	519,992	564,878	0.8
Occupied housing units	403,240	445,812	490,080	0.9
Owner occupied	227,888	258,533	306,653	1.7
Renter occupied	175,352	187,279	183,427	-0.2
Average household size..	2.92	2.96	2.86	-0.3
Financial Characteristics				
Median gross rent of renter-occupied housing	779	1,291	1,774	3.4
Median monthly owner costs for housing units with a mortgage	1,636	2,240	2,584	1.4
Median value of owner-occupied housing units	272,700	525,400	722,500	3.4

Table HI-4. Migration, Origin, and Language

(Number, percent.)

Characteristic	State 2021	U.S. 2021
Residence 1 Year Ago		
Population 1 year and over	1,426,298	328,464,538
Same house	86.3	87.2
Different house in the U.S.	12.8	12.3
Same county	7.3	6.7
Different county	5.5	5.7
Same state	0.5	3.3
Different state	5.0	2.4
Abroad	0.9	0.4
Place of Birth		
Native born	1,171,208	286,623,642
Male	51.8	49.7
Female	48.2	50.3
Foreign born	270,345	45,270,103
Male	43.8	48.7
Female	56.2	51.3
Foreign born; naturalized U.S. citizen..	166,389	24,044,083
Male	43.0	46.4
Female	57.0	53.6
Foreign born; not a U.S. citizen...	103,956	21,226,020
Male	45.3	51.2
Female	54.7	48.8
Entered 2010 or later	25.5	28.1
Entered 2000 to 2009	20.3	23.7
Entered before 2000...	54.2	48.2
World Region of Birth, Foreign		
Foreign-born population, excluding population born at sea	270,345	45,269,644
Europe	4.1	10.7
Asia	77.8	31.0
Africa	1.0	5.7
Oceania	10.5	0.6
Latin America	4.6	50.1
North America	1.9	1.7
Language Spoken at Home and Ability to Speak English		
Population 5 years and over...	1,360,333	313,232,500
English only	74.2	78.4
Language other than English..	25.8	21.6
Speaks English less than "very well"..	11.1	8.3

Table HI-5. Median Income and Poverty Status, 2021

(Number, percent, except as noted.)

Characteristic	State Number	State Percent	U.S. Number	U.S. Percent
Median Income				
Households (dollars)...............	84,857	X	69,717	X
Families (dollars)	100,890	X	85,806	X
Below Poverty Level (All People)	156,735	11.2	41,393,176	12.8
Sex				
Male	75,384	10.8	18,518,155	11.6
Female	81,351	11.6	22,875,021	13.9
Age				
Under 18 years...............	40,502	13.6	12,243,219	16.9
Related children under 18 years...............	38,878	13.2	11,985,424	16.6
18 to 64 years	90,154	10.9	23,526,341	11.9
65 years and over	26,079	9.4	5,623,616	10.3

X = Not applicable.

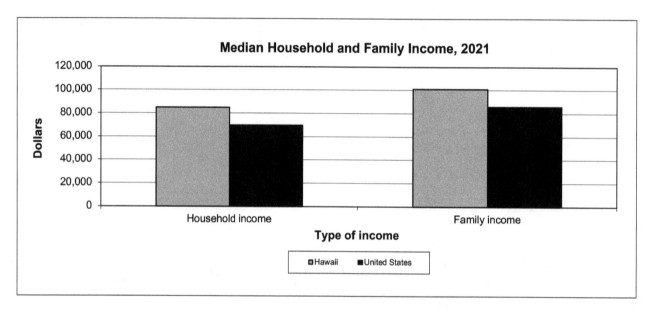

Table HI-6. Health Insurance Coverage Status for the Civilian Noninstitutionalized Population and Children Under 19 Years of Age

(Number, percent.)

Item	2011	2012	2013	2014	2015	2016	2017	2018	2019	2020 [2]	2021
Civilian Noninstitutionalized Population	1,326,065	1,341,708	1,345,168	1,367,770	1,375,062	1,378,730	1,373,202	1,368,549	1,358,715	1,365,172	1,381,713
Covered by Private or Public Insurance											
Number...............	1,231,666	1,249,370	1,254,413	1,295,659	1,320,531	1,330,057	1,320,375	1,312,750	1,302,236	1,312,365	1,327,251
Percent...............	92.9	93.1	93.3	94.7	96.0	96.5	96.2	95.9	95.8	96.1	96.1
Uninsured											
Number...............	94,399	92,338	90,755	72,111	54,531	48,673	52,827	55,799	56,479	52,807	54,462
Percent...............	7.1	6.9	6.7	5.3	4.0	3.5	3.8	4.1	4.2	3.9	3.9
Percent in the U.S. not covered...............	15.1	14.8	14.5	11.7	9.4	8.6	8.7	8.9	9.2	8.7	8.6
Children Under 19 Years of Age[1]	304,077	302,565	306,848	308,018	310,995	307,561	320,949	318,909	315,053	317,280	318,134
Covered by Private or Public Insurance											
Number...............	293,097	292,102	297,513	298,466	305,950	300,664	313,911	310,599	306,230	308,771	309,179
Percent...............	96.4	96.5	97.0	96.9	98.4	97.8	97.8	97.4	97.2	97.3	97.2
Uninsured											
Number...............	10,980	10,463	9,335	9,552	5,045	6,897	7,038	8,310	8,823	8,509	8,955
Percent...............	3.6	3.5	3.0	3.1	1.6	2.2	2.2	2.6	2.8	2.7	2.8
Percent in the U.S. not covered...............	7.5	7.2	7.1	6.0	4.8	4.5	5.0	5.2	5.7	5.2	5.4

[1] Data for years prior to 2017 are for individuals under 18 years of age.
[2] 2020 ACS 5-Year estimates. 1-Year estimates were not released for 2020 due to the impact of COVID-19 on data collection that year. Data is not comparable to previous years, which are based on 1-year estimates.

Table HI-7. Employment Status by Demographic Group, 2022

(Numbers in thousands, percent.)

Characteristic	Civilian noninstitutional population	Civilian labor force		Employed		Unemployed	
		Number	Percent of population	Number	Percent of population	Number	Percent of population
Total..	1,114	666	59.8	642	57.7	24	3.7
Sex							
Male..	542	349	64.3	336	62.1	12	3.5
Female	572	318	55.6	306	53.5	12	3.8
Race, Sex, and Hispanic Origin							
White	249	147	58.8	141	56.4	6	4.1
Male....................................	130	84	64.4	81	62.5	3	2.9
Female	120	63	52.7	59	49.7	4	5.6
Black or African American................	NA	NA	NA	NA	NA	NA	NA
Male....................................	NA	NA	NA	NA	NA	NA	NA
Female	NA	NA	NA	NA	NA	NA	NA
Hispanic or Latino ethnicity[1]	94	63	67.1	60	64.1	3	4.3
Male....................................	49	37	75	36	73	1	3
Female	NA	NA	NA	NA	NA	NA	NA
Age							
16 to 19 years.........................	NA	NA	NA	NA	NA	NA	NA
20 to 24 years.........................	65	45	68.8	40	62.1	5	10.0
25 to 34 years.........................	166	134	80.4	128	77.1	6	4.1
35 to 44 years.........................	183	150	82.0	146	79.9	4	2.7
45 to 54 years.........................	168	135	80.0	132	78.1	3	2.4
55 to 64 years.........................	174	117	67.0	114	65.6	3	2.2
65 years and over	287	65	22.5	64	22.1	1	1.7

NOTE: Data in Table 7 are from the Current Population Survey (CPS) and do not match the estimates in Table 8. See notes and definitions for further information.
[1] May be of any race.
NA = Not available.

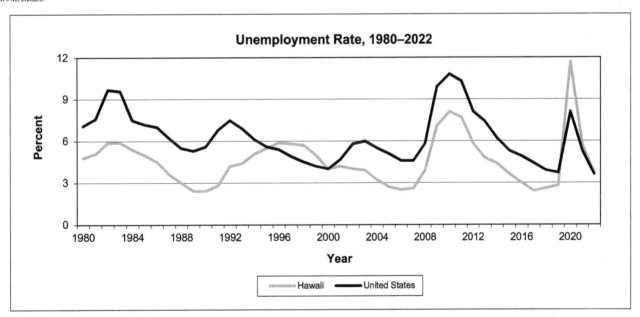

Table HI-8. Employment Status of the Civilian Noninstitutional Population Age 16 Years and Over

(Number, percent.)

Year	Civilian labor force	Civilian participation rate	Employed	Unemployed	Unemployment rate
2010..	648,549	63.0	604,210	44,339	6.8
2011..	660,634	62.6	615,470	45,164	6.8
2012..	650,415	61.0	611,985	38,430	5.9
2013..	650,978	60.6	620,005	30,973	4.8
2014..	664,014	61.5	635,913	28,101	4.2
2015..	670,594	61.7	647,616	22,978	3.4
2016..	679,121	62.1	659,557	19,564	2.9
2017..	695,303	62.0	679,865	15,438	2.2
2018..	691,982	61.6	675,681	16,001	2.4
2019..	684,690	60.9	667,914	16,776	2.5
2020..	662,491	59	582,979	79,512	12.0
2021..	668,413	59.8	630,187	38,226	5.7
2022..	676,299	60.2	652,677	23,622	3.5

Table HI-9. Employment and Average Wages by Industry

(Estimates are based on the 2012 North American Industry Classification System [NAICS].)

Industry	2014	2015	2016	2017	2018	2019	2020	2021
					Number of Jobs			
Wage and Salary Employment by Industry.........................	702,977	715,201	722,186	727,610	732,550	730,842	626,110	655,084
Farm Wage and Salary Employment...............................	7,376	6,734	6,294	6,281	6,568	4,843	4,489	5,435
Nonfarm Wage and Salary Employment..........................	695,601	708,467	715,892	721,329	725,982	725,999	621,621	649,649
Private wage and salary employment...........................	512,575	522,855	532,367	538,955	544,437	543,150	450,068	477,422
Forestry, fishing, and related activities..........................	1,532	1,574	1,534	1,517	1,490	1,545	1,467	(D)
Mining..	252	279	232	237	220	231	238	233
Utilities...	3,808	3,827	3,772	3,785	3,800	3,714	3,673	3,587
Construction..	32,592	35,572	38,592	36,747	36,833	37,868	37,008	37,535
Manufacturing..	13,934	14,097	14,130	14,281	14,210	14,013	11,978	(D)
Durable goods manufacturing..................................	3,600	3,699	3,728	3,853	3,783	3,773	3,415	(D)
Nondurable goods manufacturing.............................	10,334	10,398	10,402	10,428	10,427	10,240	8,563	8,795
Wholesale trade	17,778	18,085	17,902	18,001	17,887	18,367	16,501	16,563
Retail trade..	70,323	71,285	71,115	71,669	72,365	71,774	61,829	63,818
Transportation and warehousing................................	26,659	27,442	28,075	29,333	29,907	30,702	23,992	26,289
Information..	8,482	8,724	8,829	9,039	9,144	8,688	7,273	7,896
Finance and insurance	15,671	15,962	16,168	16,344	16,342	17,032	16,990	16,682
Real estate and rental and leasing.............................	12,197	12,213	12,542	12,691	13,092	13,659	11,157	11,431
Professional, scientific, and technical services...........	24,554	24,763	24,638	24,549	25,034	25,088	24,112	25,423
Management of companies and enterprises.................	8,377	8,507	8,720	8,886	8,968	9,185	8,297	8,367
Administrative and waste services.............................	49,794	50,888	50,865	49,380	49,449	40,528	34,481	34,922
Educational services	15,805	15,566	15,791	16,051	16,509	16,555	13,679	15,321
Health care and social assistance..............................	65,709	67,839	69,307	70,974	72,271	73,955	71,619	72,795
Arts, entertainment, and recreation............................	12,398	11,860	12,243	12,882	13,257	14,029	8,285	9,562
Accommodation and food services.............................	101,678	103,306	106,668	110,982	111,324	113,276	69,876	85,563
Other services, except public administration...............	31,032	31,066	31,244	31,607	32,335	32,941	27,613	27,953
Government and government enterprises.....................	183,026	185,612	183,525	182,374	181,545	182,849	171,553	172,227
					Dollars			
Average Wages and Salaries by Industry	46,681	48,332	49,584	50,968	52,274	54,143	58,281	60,548
Average Farm Wages and Salaries	32,882	33,869	38,552	38,271	26,393	35,534	37,502	33,259
Average Nonfarm Wages and Salaries	46,828	48,470	49,681	51,078	52,508	54,267	58,431	60,776
Average private wages and salaries............................	43,490	45,347	46,621	48,169	49,615	51,431	55,667	58,271
Forestry, fishing, and related activities......................	24,690	26,890	29,399	29,452	30,386	32,248	33,373	(D)
Mining..	93,694	96,878	94,345	86,181	93,150	100,905	99,660	99,326
Utilities...	94,486	99,620	97,875	102,023	106,175	107,839	106,568	109,345
Construction	66,496	70,603	72,552	73,834	75,674	77,018	80,491	80,490
Manufacturing..	41,272	42,871	44,634	45,428	46,924	46,559	49,122	(D)
Durable goods manufacturing..................................	53,247	55,157	57,387	57,994	60,160	61,170	64,718	(D)
Nondurable goods manufacturing.............................	37,101	38,500	40,064	40,785	42,123	41,176	42,903	43,479
Wholesale trade	54,246	55,790	57,552	60,247	59,738	61,865	63,720	68,820
Retail trade..	29,668	30,302	31,310	32,202	33,215	34,092	36,564	39,049
Transportation and warehousing................................	48,239	50,711	52,924	56,569	56,529	57,571	63,298	63,075
Information..	61,975	63,566	62,027	62,255	69,510	67,470	73,321	87,082
Finance and insurance	65,693	69,119	71,270	74,809	76,093	79,718	87,999	95,886
Real estate and rental and leasing.............................	46,937	49,914	51,520	55,526	56,240	56,858	62,825	67,006
Professional, scientific, and technical services...........	68,333	69,889	71,154	74,432	75,894	78,331	84,638	89,054
Management of companies and enterprises.................	84,358	86,738	87,986	88,437	90,474	94,274	95,827	95,957
Administrative and waste services.............................	31,586	32,928	34,415	35,500	36,652	38,091	41,752	42,731
Educational services	34,911	35,627	35,237	36,045	36,259	37,358	44,482	43,742
Health care and social assistance..............................	49,759	51,504	52,256	54,016	55,775	58,186	62,435	65,100
Arts, entertainment, and recreation............................	30,001	30,141	29,660	32,452	34,407	35,448	39,151	43,162
Accommodation and food services.............................	33,759	35,234	36,416	37,749	39,578	41,192	36,356	43,118
Other services, except public administration...............	34,818	36,223	37,368	38,602	40,065	41,322	44,992	46,959
Government and government enterprises.....................	56,176	57,266	58,557	59,676	61,183	62,691	65,682	67,721

Table HI-10. Employment Characteristics by Family Type

(Number, percent.)

Family type and labor force status	2019 Total	2019 Families with own children under 18 years	2020 [1] Total	2020 [1] Families with own children under 18 years	2021 Total	2021 Families with own children under 18 years
All Families..	316,206	110,403	324,482	118,089	334,899	120,549
FAMILY TYPE AND LABOR FORCE STATUS						
Opposite-Sex Married-Couple Families..	232,024	80,229	236,910	85,444	244,547	89,108
Both husband and wife in labor force....................................	50.9	67.3	52.7	68.1	50.8	65.5
Husband in labor force, wife not in labor force	19.4	25.4	19.2	25.1	18.8	25.9
Wife in labor force, husband not in labor force	9.6	4.8	9.5	4.9	10.3	6.2
Both husband and wife not in labor force.................................	19.3	1.9	18.6	1.9	20.1	2.4
Other Families	84,182	30,174	84,934	32,250	86,830	30,986
Female householder, no spouse present	69.2	71.8	68.2	69.0	69.3	67.5
In labor force...	44.1	59.1	43.0	58.0	42.2	54.3
Not in labor force	25.1	12.7	25.2	11.1	27.2	13.2
Male householder, no spouse present...............................	30.8	28.2	31.8	31.0	30.7	32.5
In labor force...	22.8	24.8	22.9	27.3	21.8	28.9
Not in labor force	7.9	3.4	8.9	3.7	8.9	3.6

[1] 2020 ACS 5-Year estimates. 1-Year estimates were not released for 2020 due to the impact of COVID-19 on data collection that year. Data is not comparable to previous years, which are based on 1-year estimates.

Table HI-11. School Enrollment and Educational Attainment, 2021

(Number, percent.)

Item	State	U.S.
Enrollment		
Total population 3 years and over, enrolled in school	333,721	79,453,524
Enrolled in nursery school or preschool (percent)	5.1	5.2
Enrolled in kindergarten (percent)..	5.0	5.0
Enrolled in elementary school, grades 1-8 (percent)	40.8	41.3
Enrolled in high school, grades 9-12 (percent)	20.0	21.8
Enrolled in college or graduate school (percent)..............................	29.1	26.7
Attainment		
Total population 25 years and over	1,021,687	228,193,464
Less than ninth grade (percent)	3.3	4.8
9th to 12th grade, no diploma (percent)	3.7	5.9
High school graduate, including equivalency (percent)........................	26.3	26.3
Some college, no degree (percent)	20.2	19.3
Associate's degree (percent)..	11.0	8.8
Bachelor's degree (percent)	22.2	21.2
Graduate or professional degree (percent).................................	13.1	13.8
High school graduate or higher (percent)...................................	92.9	89.4
Bachelor's degree or higher (percent).....................................	35.3	35.0

Table HI-12. Public School Characteristics and Educational Indicators

(Number, percent; data derived from National Center of Education Statistics.)

Item	State	U.S.
Public Elementary and Secondary Schools		
Number of regular school districts, 2019-20	1	13,349
Number of operational schools, 2019-20.....................................	293	98,469
Percent charter schools	12.6	7.7
Total public school enrollment, Fall 2021	173,178	49,433,092
Percent charter school enrollment	7.0	7.5
Student-teacher ratio, Fall 2019	14.8	15.9
Expenditures per student (unadjusted dollars), 2019-20	16,564	13,489
Four-year adjusted cohort graduation rate (ACGR), 2019-2020[1]................	86.3	86.5
Students eligible for free or reduced-price lunch (percent), 2019-20.............	45.5	52.1
English language learners (percent), Fall 2020...............................	9.6	10.3
Students age 3 to 21 served under IDEA, part B (percent), 2021-22	11.3	14.7

Public Schools by Type, 2019-20	Number	Percent of state public schools
Total number of schools...	293	100.0
Special education...	1	0.3
Vocational education..	0	-
Alternative education..	1	0.3

[1] Adjusted Cohort Graduation Rates (ACGR) differ from Averaged Freshmen Graduation Rates (AFGR).
- = Zero or rounds to zero.

Table HI-13. Reported Voting and Registration of the Voting-Age Population, November 2022

(Numbers in thousands, percent.)

Item	Total population	Total citizen population	Registered			Voted		
			Total registered	Percent registered (total population)	Percent registered (total citizen population)	Total voted	Percent voted (total population)	Percent voted (total citizen population)
U.S. Total	255,457	233,546	161,422	63.2	69.1	121,916	47.7	52.2
State Total..	1,079	1,019	651	60.3	63.9	509	47.2	50.0
Sex								
Male	520	497	321	61.7	64.5	245	47.1	49.2
Female	560	522	331	59.1	63.3	265	47.3	50.7
Race								
White alone....................................	259	247	169	65.1	68.5	137	52.7	55.4
White, non-Hispanic alone	233	222	158	67.7	71.1	130	55.9	58.6
Black alone....................................	17	17	12	70.5	70.5	9	53.4	53.4
Asian alone	377	343	211	56.0	61.7	179	47.5	52.2
Hispanic (of any race)	96	92	54	56.8	58.9	33	34.5	35.8
White alone or in combination..............	437	423	277	63.3	65.4	218	49.7	51.4
Black alone or in combination	46	46	26	55.9	55.9	19	40.8	40.8
Asian alone or in combination	563	529	343	60.9	64.9	281	49.9	53.1
Age								
18 to 24 years	94	91	39	41.9	43.4	27	29.0	30.1
25 to 34 years	167	158	99	59.2	62.9	56	33.6	35.6
35 to 44 years	187	176	120	64.3	68.3	81	43.4	46.2
45 to 64 years	320	294	185	57.9	62.9	156	49.0	53.2
65 years and over	311	301	207	66.5	68.9	188	60.4	62.6

B = Base is less than 75,000 and therefore too small to show the derived measure.

Table HI-14. Health Indicators

(Number, rate as indicated in footnotes.)

Item	State	U.S.
Births		
Life Expectancy at Birth (years), 2020	80.7	77.0
Fertility Rate by State[1], 2021	59.2	56.3
Percent Home Births, 2021	3.3	1.4
Cesarean Delivery Rate[2], 2021	27.7	32.1
Preterm Birth Rate[3], 2021	10.2	10.5
Teen Birth Rate[4], 2021	12.3	13.9
Percentage of Babies Born Low Birthweight[5], 2021	8.9	8.5
Deaths[6]		
Heart Disease Mortality Rate, 2021..	126.5	173.8
Cancer Mortality Rate, 2021..	125.4	146.6
Stroke Mortality Rate, 2021	43.8	41.1
Diabetes Mortality Rate, 2021	17.7	25.4
Influenza/Pneumonia Mortality Rate, 2021	9.8	10.5
Suicide Mortality Rate, 2021	13.7	14.1
Drug Overdose Mortality Rate, 2021...	17.3	33.6
Firearm Injury Mortality Rate, 2021..	4.8	14.6
Homicide Mortality Rate, 2021...	2.7	8.2
Disease and Illness		
Lifetime Asthma in Adults, 2020 (percent)...	14.5	13.9
Lifetime Asthma in Children, 2020 (percent)[7]	13.6	11.3
Diabetes in Adults, 2020 (percent)...	9.5	8.2
Self-reported Obesity in Adults, 2021 (percent)..	25.0	NA

SOURCE: National Center for Health Statistics, National Vital Statistics System 2020 data; https://wonder.cdc.gov.
[1] General fertility rate per 1,000 women aged 15–44.
[2] This represents the percentage of all live births that were cesarean deliveries.
[3] Babies born prior to 37 weeks of pregnancy (gestation).
[4] Number of births per 1,000 females aged 15–19
[5] Babies born weighing less than 2,500 grams or 5 lbs. 8oz.
[6] Death rates are the number of deaths per 100,000 total population.
[7] U.S. total includes data from 30 states and D.C.
NA = Not available.
- = Zero or rounds to zero.

Table HI-15. State Government Finances, 2021

(Dollar amounts in thousands, percent distribution.)

Item	Dollars	Percent distribution
Total Revenue	23,277,323	100.0
General revenue	20,506,030	88.1
Intergovernmental revenue	9,018,177	38.7
Taxes	8,046,691	34.6
General sales	3,296,268	14.2
Selective sales	851,356	3.7
License taxes	258,953	1.1
Individual income tax	3,354,690	14.4
Corporate income tax	191,426	0.8
Other taxes	93,998	0.4
Current charges	1,469,071	6.3
Miscellaneous general revenue	1,972,091	8.5
Utility revenue	-	-
Liquor stores revenue	-	-
Insurance trust revenue[1]	2,771,293	11.9
Total Expenditure	17,817,850	100.0
Intergovernmental expenditure	207,067	1.2
Direct expenditure	17,610,783	98.8
Current operation	13,397,429	75.2
Capital outlay	1,098,065	6.2
Insurance benefits and repayments	2,839,737	15.9
Assistance and subsidies	140,879	0.8
Interest on debt	134,673	0.8
Exhibit: Salaries and wages	3,519,350	19.8
Total Expenditure	17,817,850	100.0
General expenditure	14,978,113	84.1
Intergovernmental expenditure	207,067	1.2
Direct expenditure	14,771,046	82.9
General expenditure, by function:		
Education	3,616,893	20.3
Public welfare	3,542,444	19.9
Hospitals	506,009	2.8
Health	746,970	4.2
Highways	687,431	3.9
Police protection	62,513	0.4
Correction	221,229	1.2
Natural resources	152,714	0.9
Parks and recreation	63,210	0.4
Governmental administration	710,523	4.0
Interest on general debt	134,673	0.8
Other and unallocable	4,517,479	25.4
Utility expenditure	-	-
Liquor stores expenditure	-	-
Insurance trust expenditure	2,839,737	15.9
Debt at End of Fiscal Year	11,521,014	X
Cash and Security Holdings	34,652,790	X

X = Not applicable.
- = Zero or rounds to zero.
[1] Within insurance trust revenue, net earnings of state retirement systems is a calculated statistic (the item code in the data file is X08), and thus can be positive or negative. Net earnings is the sum of earnings on investments plus gains on investments minus losses on investments. The change made in 2002 for asset valuation from book to market value in accordance with Statement 34 of the Governmental Accounting Standards Board is reflected in the calculated statistics.

Table HI-16. State Government Tax Collections, 2022

(Dollars in thousands, percent.)

Item	Dollars	Percent distribution
Total Taxes	10,279,504	100.0
Property taxes	X	-
Sales and gross receipts	5,647,969	54.9
General sales and gross receipts	4,265,799	41.5
Selective sales and gross receipts	1,382,170	13.4
Alcoholic beverages	53,981	0.5
Amusements	X	-
Insurance premiums	201,859	2.0
Motor fuels	81,845	0.8
Pari-mutuels	X	-
Public utilities	122,068	1.2
Tobacco products	91,658	0.9
Other selective sales	830,759	8.1
Licenses	310,983	3.0
Alcoholic beverages	X	-
Amusements	X	-
Corporations in general	2,415	-
Hunting and fishing	878	-
Motor vehicle	219,306	2.1
Motor vehicle operators	369	-
Public utilities	15,153	0.1
Occupation and business, NEC	57,933	0.6
Other licenses	14,929	0.1
Income taxes	4,074,729	39.6
Individual income	3,759,856	36.6
Corporation net income	314,873	3.1
Other taxes	245,823	2.4
Death and gift	57,405	0.6
Documentary and stock transfer	188,418	1.8
Severance	X	-
Taxes, NEC	0	-

X = Not applicable.
- = Zero or rounds to zero.

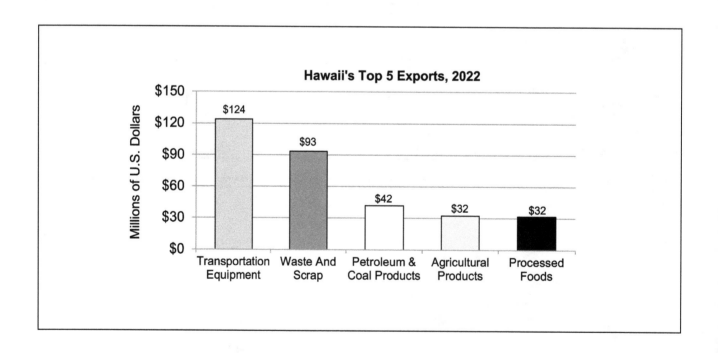

Hawaii's Top 5 Exports, 2022

IDAHO

Facts and Figures

Location: Northwestern United States; bordered on the N by Canada, on the E by Montana and Wyoming, on the S by Nevada and Utah, and on the W by Washington and Oregon

Area: 83,568 sq. mi. (216,446 sq. km.); rank—14th

Population: 1,939,033 (2022 est.); rank—38th

Principal Cities: capital—Boise; largest—Boise

Statehood: July 3, 1890; 43rd state

U.S. Congress: 2 senators, 2 representatives

State Motto: *Esto perpetua* ("Let it be perpetual")

State Song: "Here We Have Idaho"

State Nickname: The Gem State

Abbreviations: ID

State Symbols: flower—syringa (mock orange); tree—Western white pine; bird—mountain bluebird

At a Glance

- With an increase in population of 23.7 percent, Idaho ranked 1st among the states in growth from 2010 to 2022.

- With 2.2 deaths per 100,000 population, Idaho had the 5th lowest homicide rate in the country in 2021.

- Idaho's per capita personal income in 2022 was $54,537, compared to the national average of $65,423.

- With 23.9 percent of its population under age 18, Idaho ranked 6th among the states for the highest percent of minors in 2022.

- Idaho's unemployment rate ranked 39th in the nation in 2022, with 2.7 percent of the population unemployed, compared to 3.6 percent of the entire country.

Table ID-1. Population by Age, Sex, Race, and Hispanic Origin

(Number, percent, except where noted.)

Sex, age, race, and Hispanic origin	2010	2020	2022	Percent change, 2010–2022
Total Population..	1,567,582	1,839,092	1,939,033	23.7
Percent of total U.S. population	0.5	0.6	0.6	X
Sex				
Male..	785,324	925,695	977,139	24.4
Female	782,258	913,397	961,894	23.0
Age				
Under 5 years...	121,772	112,358	113,283	-7.0
Under 18 years...	429,072	452,546	463,404	8.0
18 to 64 years	943,842	1,086,374	1,145,177	21.3
65 years and over	194,668	300,172	330,452	69.8
Median age (years)	34.6	36.8	37.3	7.8
Race and Hispanic Origin				
One race				
White	1,476,097	1,708,551	1,795,997	21.7
Black	10,950	16,881	18,882	72.4
American Indian and Alaska Native	25,782	31,809	33,188	28.7
Asian..	20,034	29,296	32,203	60.7
Native Hawaiian or Other Pacific Islander	2,786	4,184	4,540	63.0
Two or more races	31,933	48,371	54,223	69.8
Hispanic (of any race)	175,901	238,628	261,920	48.9

NOTE: Population figures for 2022 are July 1 estimates. The 2010 and 2020 estimates are taken from the respective censuses.
- = Zero or rounds to zero.
X = Not applicable.

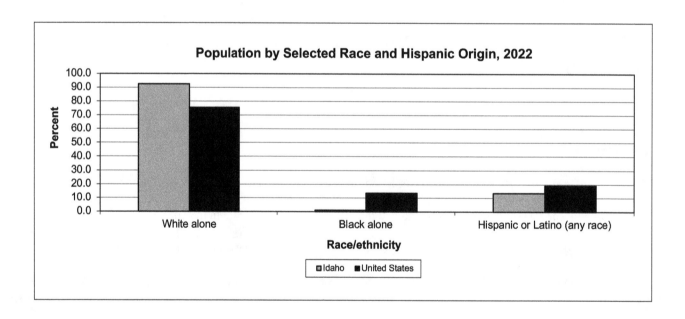

Table ID-2. Marital Status

(Number, percent distribution.)

Sex, age, race, and Hispanic origin	2000	2010	2021
Males, 15 Years and Over	493,045	602,308	757,497
Never married	26.1	28.3	30.4
Now married, except separated...	61.0	57.0	55.7
Separated...	1.0	1.4	0.9
Widowed...	2.1	2.4	2.2
Divorced...	9.9	10.9	10.8
Females, 15 Years and Over	498,579	608,900	758,348
Never married	19.6	22.4	24.4
Now married, except separated...	59.0	55.3	54.0
Separated...	1.3	1.6	1.2
Widowed...	8.6	7.6	7.3
Divorced...	11.4	13.1	13.1

Table ID-3. Households and Housing Characteristics

(Number, percent, dollars.)

Item	2000	2010	2021	Average annual percent change, 2010–2021
Total Households...	469,645	576,709	693,882	1.8
Family households	333,588	401,806	476,470	1.7
Married-couple family	276,511	322,129	385,704	1.8
Other family	59,077	79,677	90,766	1.3
Male householder, no wife present..................................	18,228	23,583	30,931	2.8
Female householder, no husband present........................	40,849	56,094	59,835	0.6
Nonfamily households	134,057	174,903	217,412	2.2
Householder living alone...	105,175	139,909	168,018	1.8
Householder not living alone..	28,882	34,994	49,394	3.7
Housing Characteristics				
Total housing units	527,824	668,634	775,330	1.5
Occupied housing units	469,645	576,709	693,882	1.8
Owner occupied	339,960	401,532	498,872	2.2
Renter occupied	129,685	175,177	195,010	1.0
Average household size...	2.69	2.67	2.70	0.1
Financial Characteristics				
Median gross rent of renter-occupied housing	515	683	1035	4.7
Median monthly owner costs for housing units with a mortgage ...	887	1,187	1,425	1.8
Median value of owner-occupied housing units......................	106,300	165,100	369,300	11.2

Table ID-4. Migration, Origin, and Language

(Number, percent.)

Characteristic	State 2021	U.S. 2021
Residence 1 Year Ago		
Population 1 year and over	1,879,719	328,464,538
Same house	85.2	87.2
Different house in the U.S.	14.5	12.3
Same county	6.4	6.7
Different county	8.1	5.7
Same state	3.0	3.3
Different state	5.1	2.4
Abroad	0.3	0.4
Place of Birth		
Native born	1,785,531	286,623,642
Male	50.3	49.7
Female	49.7	50.3
Foreign born	115,392	45,270,103
Male	48.4	48.7
Female	51.6	51.3
Foreign born; naturalized U.S. citizen..	51,854	24,044,083
Male	43.7	46.4
Female	56.3	53.6
Foreign born; not a U.S. citizen	63,538	21,226,020
Male	52.2	51.2
Female	47.8	48.8
Entered 2010 or later	29.4	28.1
Entered 2000 to 2009	25.4	23.7
Entered before 2000..	45.3	48.2
World Region of Birth, Foreign		
Foreign-born population, excluding population born at sea	115,392	45,269,644
Europe	15.4	10.7
Asia..	17.1	31.0
Africa..	3.3	5.7
Oceania..	0.7	0.6
Latin America...	59.7	50.1
North America..	4.0	1.7
Language Spoken at Home and Ability to Speak English		
Population 5 years and over...	1,787,872	313,232,500
English only	88.9	78.4
Language other than English..	11.1	21.6
Speaks English less than "very well"..	4.0	8.3

Table ID-5. Median Income and Poverty Status, 2021

(Number, percent, except as noted.)

Characteristic	State		U.S.	
	Number	Percent	Number	Percent
Median Income				
Households (dollars)..	66,474	X	69,717	X
Families (dollars)	79,993	X	85,806	X
Below Poverty Level (All People)	205,702	11.0	41,393,176	12.8
Sex				
Male	92,866	9.9	18,518,155	11.6
Female	112,836	12.1	22,875,021	13.9
Age				
Under 18 years..	60,418	13.1	12,243,219	16.9
Related children under 18 years........................	58,057	12.6	11,985,424	16.6
18 to 64 years	115,740	10.6	23,526,341	11.9
65 years and over	29,544	9.5	5,623,616	10.3

X = Not applicable.

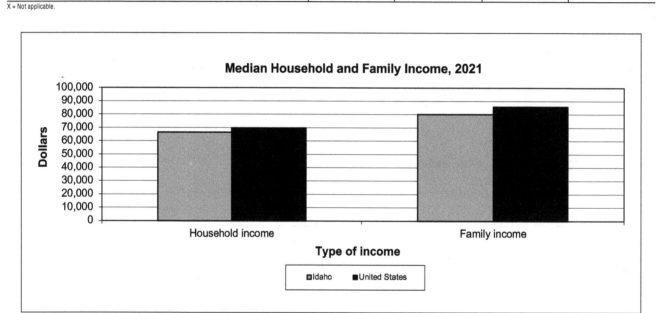

Table ID-6. Health Insurance Coverage Status for the Civilian Noninstitutionalized Population and Children Under 19 Years of Age

(Number, percent.)

Item	2011	2012	2013	2014	2015	2016	2017	2018	2019	2020 [2]	2021
Civilian Noninstitutionalized Population	1,565,645	1,575,682	1,592,172	1,612,889	1,632,247	1,662,867	1,695,273	1,733,484	1,764,911	1,732,106	1,879,248
Covered by Private or Public Insurance											
Number..	1,306,551	1,320,939	1,334,697	1,394,182	1,451,902	1,494,757	1,523,260	1,540,864	1,573,716	1,552,616	1,713,319
Percent...	83.5	83.8	83.8	86.4	89.0	89.9	89.9	88.9	89.2	89.6	91.2
Uninsured											
Number..	259,094	254,743	257,475	218,707	180,345	168,110	172,013	192,620	191,195	179,490	165,929
Percent...	16.5	16.2	16.2	13.6	11.0	10.1	10.1	11.1	10.8	10.4	8.8
Percent in the U.S. not covered..............................	15.1	14.8	14.5	11.7	9.4	8.6	8.7	8.9	9.2	8.7	8.6
Children Under 19 Years of Age[1]	427,064	423,926	425,948	430,662	431,339	435,630	471,739	471,103	474,852	469,258	498,286
Covered by Private or Public Insurance											
Number..	388,096	387,897	387,931	396,885	406,497	415,147	450,102	442,305	451,283	444,561	463,174
Percent...	90.9	91.5	91.1	92.2	94.2	95.3	95.4	93.9	95.0	94.7	93.0
Uninsured											
Number..	38,968	36,029	38,017	33,777	24,842	20,483	21,637	28,798	23,569	24,697	35,112
Percent...	9.1	8.5	8.9	7.8	5.8	4.7	4.6	6.1	5.0	5.3	7.0
Percent in the U.S. not covered..............................	7.5	7.2	7.1	6.0	4.8	4.5	5.0	5.2	5.7	5.2	5.4

[1] Data for years prior to 2017 are for individuals under 18 years of age.
[2] 2020 ACS 5-Year estimates. 1-Year estimates were not released for 2020 due to the impact of COVID-19 on data collection that year. Data is not comparable to previous years, which are based on 1-year estimates.

Table ID-7. Employment Status by Demographic Group, 2022

(Numbers in thousands, percent.)

Characteristic	Civilian noninstitutional population	Civilian labor force		Employed		Unemployed	
		Number	Percent of population	Number	Percent of population	Number	Percent of population
Total.........................	1,520	970	63.8	943	62.0	27	2.8
Sex							
Male..........................	758	533	70.3	517	68.2	16	3.0
Female........................	761	437	57.4	426	55.9	11	2.6
Race, Sex, and Hispanic Origin							
White.........................	1,427	910	63.7	885	62.0	24	2.7
Male........................	709	499	70.3	484	68.3	14	2.8
Female......................	718	411	57.2	401	55.8	10	2.4
Black or African American..............	NA	NA	NA	NA	NA	NA	NA
Male........................	NA	NA	NA	NA	NA	NA	NA
Female......................	NA	NA	NA	NA	NA	NA	NA
Hispanic or Latino ethnicity[1].............	193	141	73.1	136	70.6	5	3.4
Male........................	104	86	82.9	83	80.5	3	2.9
Female......................	89	55	61.7	53	59.2	2	4.1
Age							
16 to 19 years..................	107	56	52	52	48	4	7
20 to 24 years..................	140	113	81.0	108	77.5	5	4.4
25 to 34 years..................	265	220	83.0	214	80.5	7	3.0
35 to 44 years..................	228	191	83.6	187	82.1	4	1.9
45 to 54 years..................	220	183	83.4	180	82.0	3	1.7
55 to 64 years..................	227	150	66.0	146	64.4	4	2.3
65 years and over................	334	57	17.2	56	16.8	1	2.3

NOTE: Data in Table 7 are from the Current Population Survey (CPS) and do not match the estimates in Table 8. See notes and definitions for further information.
[1] May be of any race.
NA = Not available.

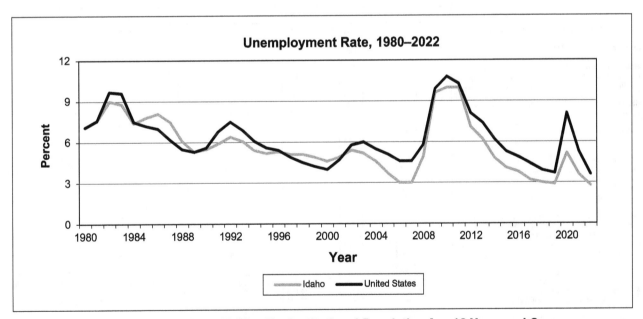

Unemployment Rate, 1980–2022

Table ID-8. Employment Status of the Civilian Noninstitutional Population Age 16 Years and Over

(Number, percent.)

Year	Civilian labor force	Civilian participation rate	Employed	Unemployed	Unemployment rate
2010....................	762,147	65.4	695,265	66,882	8.8
2011....................	764,205	64.8	701,660	62,545	8.2
2012....................	772,112	64.7	714,969	57,143	7.4
2013....................	777,606	64.3	724,545	53,061	6.8
2014....................	776,937	63.3	742,805	34,132	4.4
2015....................	795,014	63.8	764,121	30,893	3.9
2016....................	812,921	63.8	783,180	29,741	3.7
2017....................	830,776	63.9	812,875	26,901	3.2
2018....................	862,513	64.1	837,514	24,999	2.9
2019....................	889,194	64.4	862,864	26,330	3.0
2020....................	897,739	63.2	848,741	48,998	5.5
2021....................	917,056	62.5	884,328	32,728	3.6
2022....................	950,672	63.1	925,358	25,314	2.7

Table ID-9. Employment and Average Wages by Industry

(Estimates are based on the 2012 North American Industry Classification System [NAICS].)

Industry	2014	2015	2016	2017	2018	2019	2020	2021
	Number of Jobs							
Wage and Salary Employment by Industry........................	685,278	703,568	726,463	748,265	772,994	796,965	792,781	831,903
Farm Wage and Salary Employment................................	17,623	17,001	17,215	19,927	18,627	19,608	18,283	16,350
Nonfarm Wage and Salary Employment...........................	667,655	686,567	709,248	728,338	754,367	777,357	774,498	815,553
Private wage and salary employment...............................	540,229	557,474	578,017	595,200	619,224	640,325	639,878	680,680
Forestry, fishing, and related activities..........................	8,381	8,669	8,502	8,412	8,504	8,631	8,605	8,191
Mining..	2,417	2,322	2,364	2,178	2,217	2,290	2,488	2,786
Utilities..	2,912	3,013	3,010	2,983	3,012	2,944	2,966	3,047
Construction..	34,682	37,071	40,444	43,723	47,934	51,904	54,754	59,194
Manufacturing..	59,928	61,656	63,840	66,166	67,819	68,448	67,736	70,292
Durable goods manufacturing..............................	34,482	35,615	36,847	37,811	39,325	39,315	38,508	40,114
Nondurable goods manufacturing.........................	25,446	26,041	26,993	28,355	28,494	29,133	29,228	30,178
Wholesale trade...	28,721	28,728	28,476	28,783	29,442	30,669	30,955	32,748
Retail trade...	80,215	83,374	85,021	86,158	87,041	87,547	87,642	92,774
Transportation and warehousing...............................	19,520	20,481	20,570	21,109	22,248	23,254	23,932	29,068
Information..	9,221	9,187	9,001	8,960	8,797	8,809	7,355	7,970
Finance and insurance..	22,246	22,870	23,766	24,698	25,836	26,368	27,445	28,517
Real estate and rental and leasing............................	6,925	7,281	7,390	7,819	8,277	8,814	9,006	10,029
Professional, scientific, and technical services............	32,732	34,369	35,433	36,228	38,193	40,452	42,231	45,569
Management of companies and enterprises.................	5,479	5,538	5,302	5,832	6,793	7,106	7,246	7,804
Administrative and waste services............................	40,258	39,886	44,552	46,743	47,334	47,354	48,346	49,038
Educational services	11,482	11,994	12,077	12,150	13,571	14,009	15,761	17,478
Health care and social assistance............................	83,485	86,519	89,123	90,422	94,124	98,774	99,873	103,116
Arts, entertainment, and recreation..........................	9,990	9,684	10,373	11,113	12,349	12,867	11,488	12,988
Accommodation and food services............................	56,054	58,519	61,884	64,414	67,090	70,199	63,815	70,772
Other services, except public administration................	25,581	26,313	26,889	27,309	28,643	29,886	28,234	29,299
Government and government enterprises......................	127,426	129,093	131,231	133,138	135,143	137,032	134,620	134,873
	Dollars							
Average Wages and Salaries by Industry	38,886	39,610	40,488	42,022	43,700	44,731	48,224	51,679
Average Farm Wages and Salaries	36,986	30,600	34,986	30,398	36,423	24,772	35,388	46,010
Average Nonfarm Wages and Salaries	38,936	39,833	40,621	42,341	43,879	45,234	48,527	51,792
Average private wages and salaries.............................	39,248	40,072	40,897	42,708	44,286	45,652	49,090	52,618
Forestry, fishing, and related activities......................	30,530	31,918	33,602	34,944	36,384	36,983	39,583	43,252
Mining..	76,496	71,394	72,985	72,739	71,729	74,831	75,061	81,299
Utilities..	81,030	83,034	83,414	87,769	90,700	92,477	98,019	96,551
Construction..	40,059	40,859	42,485	43,691	45,202	47,099	49,554	53,176
Manufacturing..	60,062	57,217	56,983	63,310	65,822	64,366	67,565	68,946
Durable goods manufacturing..............................	69,867	63,801	63,429	73,275	76,071	72,941	76,430	77,854
Nondurable goods manufacturing.........................	46,776	48,214	48,184	50,023	51,677	52,793	55,884	57,105
Wholesale trade	53,289	56,868	58,131	60,051	62,558	65,835	70,046	76,663
Retail trade...	28,755	29,828	30,673	31,508	31,855	32,535	35,480	38,655
Transportation and warehousing...............................	42,278	43,129	43,367	45,122	46,566	48,462	49,871	49,447
Information..	48,206	48,946	51,110	53,068	54,879	58,310	67,150	77,891
Finance and insurance..	55,761	58,075	60,895	62,298	64,747	68,803	79,181	85,350
Real estate and rental and leasing............................	33,981	34,640	34,647	36,383	38,630	40,681	45,101	49,749
Professional, scientific, and technical services............	59,336	61,457	60,824	63,902	65,989	69,389	74,854	82,019
Management of companies and enterprises.................	78,953	78,142	81,546	85,748	93,754	102,049	109,852	110,704
Administrative and waste services............................	27,832	29,584	32,197	34,791	36,954	38,541	42,034	47,091
Educational services	27,426	28,293	27,745	28,234	27,800	29,465	29,260	29,777
Health care and social assistance............................	39,640	41,028	42,382	42,486	43,706	45,000	47,149	50,485
Arts, entertainment, and recreation..........................	19,864	20,702	21,393	21,799	23,287	24,551	25,941	28,544
Accommodation and food services............................	16,618	17,175	17,809	18,494	19,614	20,121	20,012	24,112
Other services, except public administration................	27,565	28,517	29,643	31,227	32,260	33,284	36,283	39,097
Government and government enterprises......................	37,617	38,804	39,407	40,696	42,015	43,284	45,854	47,623

Table ID-10. Employment Characteristics by Family Type

(Number, percent.)

Family type and labor force status	2019		2020 [1]		2021	
	Total	Families with own children under 18 years	Total	Families with own children under 18 years	Total	Families with own children under 18 years
All Families..	448,979	189,358	441,391	190,133	476,470	206,006
FAMILY TYPE AND LABOR FORCE STATUS						
Opposite-Sex Married-Couple Families.............................	357,453	144,669	354,311	142,579	383,612	154,517
Both husband and wife in labor force............................	48.9	63.0	48.8	62.1	48.8	62.9
Husband in labor force, wife not in labor force	23.3	31.6	23.9	32.4	23.0	31.1
Wife in labor force, husband not in labor force	7.7	3.6	7.1	3.6	8.3	4.3
Both husband and wife not in labor force.........................	19.7	1.5	20.2	1.8	19.9	1.7
Other Families	91,526	44,689	85,223	47,132	90,766	50,925
Female householder, no spouse present	66.3	68.6	66.1	67.3	65.9	63.3
In labor force...	47.4	61.0	48.4	57.7	49.1	57.3
Not in labor force..	19.0	7.6	17.7	9.6	16.9	6.0
Male householder, no spouse present...........................	33.7	31.4	33.9	32.7	34.1	36.7
In labor force...	25.4	29.0	27.1	30.0	28.0	33.5
Not in labor force..	8.3	2.4	6.8	2.7	6.0	3.2

[1] 2020 ACS 5-Year estimates. 1-Year estimates were not released for 2020 due to the impact of COVID-19 on data collection that year. Data is not comparable to previous years, which are based on 1-year estimates.

Table ID-11. School Enrollment and Educational Attainment, 2021

(Number, percent.)

Item	State	U.S.
Enrollment		
Total population 3 years and over, enrolled in school	481,832	79,453,524
Enrolled in nursery school or preschool (percent)	5.0	5.2
Enrolled in kindergarten (percent)........................	5.1	5.0
Enrolled in elementary school, grades 1-8 (percent)........................	44.6	41.3
Enrolled in high school, grades 9-12 (percent)	22.9	21.8
Enrolled in college or graduate school (percent)........................	22.4	26.7
Attainment		
Total population 25 years and over	1,257,566	228,193,464
Less than ninth grade (percent)	3.2	4.8
9th to 12th grade, no diploma (percent)	5.6	5.9
High school graduate, including equivalency (percent)	26.9	26.3
Some college, no degree (percent)	23.6	19.3
Associate's degree (percent)	10.1	8.8
Bachelor's degree (percent)	20.2	21.2
Graduate or professional degree (percent)........................	10.5	13.8
High school graduate or higher (percent)	91.3	89.4
Bachelor's degree or higher (percent)........................	30.7	35.0

Table ID-12. Public School Characteristics and Educational Indicators

(Number, percent; data derived from National Center of Education Statistics.)

Item	State	U.S.
Public Elementary and Secondary Schools		
Number of regular school districts, 2019-20	115	13,349
Number of operational schools, 2019-20..	751	98,469
Percent charter schools	9.1	7.7
Total public school enrollment, Fall 2021..	314,258	49,433,092
Percent charter school enrollment	8.9	7.5
Student-teacher ratio, Fall 2019	18.1	15.9
Expenditures per student (unadjusted dollars), 2019-20	8,337	13,489
Four-year adjusted cohort graduation rate (ACGR), 2019-2020[1]........................	82.2	86.5
Students eligible for free or reduced-price lunch (percent), 2019-20........................	37.1	52.1
English language learners (percent), Fall 2020	6.1	10.3
Students age 3 to 21 served under IDEA, part B (percent), 2021-22	11.7	14.7

Public Schools by Type, 2019-20	Number	Percent of state public schools
Total number of schools..	751	100.0
Special education..	10	1.3
Vocational education..	13	1.7
Alternative education..	74	9.9

[1] Adjusted Cohort Graduation Rates (ACGR) differ from Averaged Freshmen Graduation Rates (AFGR).

Table ID-13. Reported Voting and Registration of the Voting-Age Population, November 2022

(Numbers in thousands, percent.)

Item	Total population	Total citizen population	Registered			Voted		
			Total registered	Percent registered (total population)	Percent registered (total citizen population)	Total voted	Percent voted (total population)	Percent voted (total citizen population)
U.S. Total	255,457	233,546	161,422	63.2	69.1	121,916	47.7	52.2
State Total...........................	1,489	1,417	917	61.6	64.7	685	46.0	48.3
Sex								
Male	742	706	437	58.8	61.9	332	44.7	47.0
Female	746	711	480	64.4	67.6	353	47.3	49.6
Race								
White alone................................	1,397	1,337	888	63.6	66.4	668	47.8	50.0
White, non-Hispanic alone	1,245	1,235	849	68.2	68.8	643	51.7	52.1
Black alone.............................	6	-	-	-	-	-	-	-
Asian alone	22	18	2	9.0	11.2	1	4.3	5.4
Hispanic (of any race)	165	113	40	24.4	35.5	25	15.0	21.9
White alone or in combination	1,425	1,363	896	62.9	65.7	675	47.3	49.5
Black alone or in combination	11	6	2	18.3	37.1	-	-	-
Asian alone or in combination.....................	29	25	6	19.8	23.2	3	9.0	10.6
Age								
18 to 24 years	176	168	78	44.2	46.3	39	22.1	23.2
25 to 34 years	302	284	140	46.4	49.5	83	27.4	29.2
35 to 44 years	217	196	125	57.7	63.9	89	40.8	45.1
45 to 64 years	447	426	303	67.8	71.0	233	52.1	54.6
65 years and over	346	343	271	78.3	79.1	241	69.7	70.4

B = Base is less than 75,000 and therefore too small to show the derived measure.
- = Zero or rounds to zero.

Table ID-14. Health Indicators

(Number, rate as indicated in footnotes.)

Item	State	U.S.
Births		
Life Expectancy at Birth (years), 2020	78.4	77.0
Fertility Rate by State[1], 2021	60.7	56.3
Percent Home Births, 2021	3.6	1.4
Cesarean Delivery Rate[2], 2021	24.1	32.1
Preterm Birth Rate[3], 2021	9.0	10.5
Teen Birth Rate[4], 2021	12.0	13.9
Percentage of Babies Born Low Birthweight[5], 2021	6.7	8.5
Deaths[6]		
Heart Disease Mortality Rate, 2021..	166.4	173.8
Cancer Mortality Rate, 2021..	140.4	146.6
Stroke Mortality Rate, 2021..	36.8	41.1
Diabetes Mortality Rate, 2021..	24.4	25.4
Influenza/Pneumonia Mortality Rate, 2021	7.8	10.5
Suicide Mortality Rate, 2021..	20.5	14.1
Drug Overdose Mortality Rate, 2021..	19.0	33.6
Firearm Injury Mortality Rate, 2021..	16.3	14.6
Homicide Mortality Rate, 2021..	2.2	8.2
Disease and Illness		
Lifetime Asthma in Adults, 2020 (percent)..	13.0	13.9
Lifetime Asthma in Children, 2020 (percent)[7]	NA	11.3
Diabetes in Adults, 2020 (percent)..	7.9	8.2
Self-reported Obesity in Adults, 2021 (percent)..	31.6	NA

SOURCE: National Center for Health Statistics, National Vital Statistics System 2020 data; https://wonder.cdc.gov.
[1] General fertility rate per 1,000 women aged 15–44.
[2] This represents the percentage of all live births that were cesarean deliveries.
[3] Babies born prior to 37 weeks of pregnancy (gestation).
[4] Number of births per 1,000 females aged 15–19
[5] Babies born weighing less than 2,500 grams or 5 lbs. 8oz.
[6] Death rates are the number of deaths per 100,000 total population.
[7] U.S. total includes data from 30 states and D.C.
NA = Not available.
- = Zero or rounds to zero.

Table ID-15. State Government Finances, 2021

(Dollar amounts in thousands, percent distribution.)

Item	Dollars	Percent distribution
Total Revenue	15,246,700	100.0
General revenue	13,265,103	87.0
Intergovernmental revenue	5,152,842	33.8
Taxes	6,472,467	42.5
General sales	2,516,997	16.5
Selective sales	663,229	4.3
License taxes	473,872	3.1
Individual income tax	2,457,943	16.1
Corporate income tax	351,479	2.3
Other taxes	8,947	0.1
Current charges	1,030,841	6.8
Miscellaneous general revenue	608,953	4.0
Utility revenue	-	-
Liquor stores revenue	233639	1.5
Insurance trust revenue[1]	1,747,958	11.5
Total Expenditure	13,394,246	100.0
Intergovernmental expenditure	3,377,431	25.2
Direct expenditure	10,016,815	74.8
Current operation	7,206,284	53.8
Capital outlay	876,364	6.5
Insurance benefits and repayments	1,562,087	11.7
Assistance and subsidies	231,160	1.7
Interest on debt	140,920	1.1
Exhibit: Salaries and wages	1,612,436	12.0
Total Expenditure	13,394,246	100.0
General expenditure	11,650,159	87.0
Intergovernmental expenditure	3,377,431	25.2
Direct expenditure	8,272,728	61.8
General expenditure, by function:		
Education	3,903,751	29.1
Public welfare	3,754,602	28.0
Hospitals	59,247	0.4
Health	183,562	1.4
Highways	997,892	7.5
Police protection	78,415	0.6
Correction	350,318	2.6
Natural resources	257,490	1.9
Parks and recreation	52,181	0.4
Governmental administration	592,228	4.4
Interest on general debt	140,920	1.1
Other and unallocable	1,231,826	9.2
Utility expenditure	2,537	-
Liquor stores expenditure	182,000	1.4
Insurance trust expenditure	1,562,087	11.7
Debt at End of Fiscal Year	3,422,989	X
Cash and Security Holdings	37,659,369	X

X = Not applicable.
- = Zero or rounds to zero.
[1] Within insurance trust revenue, net earnings of state retirement systems is a calculated statistic (the item code in the data file is X08), and thus can be positive or negative. Net earnings is the sum of earnings on investments plus gains on investments minus losses on investments. The change made in 2002 for asset valuation from book to market value in accordance with Statement 34 of the Governmental Accounting Standards Board is reflected in the calculated statistics.

Table ID-16. State Government Tax Collections, 2022

(Dollars in thousands, percent.)

Item	Dollars	Percent distribution
Total Taxes	7,710,289	100.0
Property taxes	X	-
Sales and gross receipts	3,594,947	46.6
General sales and gross receipts	2,904,133	37.7
Selective sales and gross receipts	690,814	9.0
Alcoholic beverages	10,557	0.1
Amusements	X	-
Insurance premiums	137,183	1.8
Motor fuels	412,051	5.3
Pari-mutuels	1,447	-
Public utilities	1,619	-
Tobacco products	45,499	0.6
Other selective sales	82,458	1.1
Licenses	471,370	6.1
Alcoholic beverages	2,279	-
Amusements	179	-
Corporations in general	6,128	0.1
Hunting and fishing	56,329	0.7
Motor vehicle	229,108	3.0
Motor vehicle operators	10,526	0.1
Public utilities	64,442	0.8
Occupation and business, NEC	97,555	1.3
Other licenses	4,824	0.1
Income taxes	3,635,505	47.2
Individual income	2,594,552	33.7
Corporation net income	1,040,953	13.5
Other taxes	8,467	0.1
Death and gift	X	-
Documentary and stock transfer	X	-
Severance	5,828	0.1
Taxes, NEC	2,639	-

X = Not applicable.
- = Zero or rounds to zero.

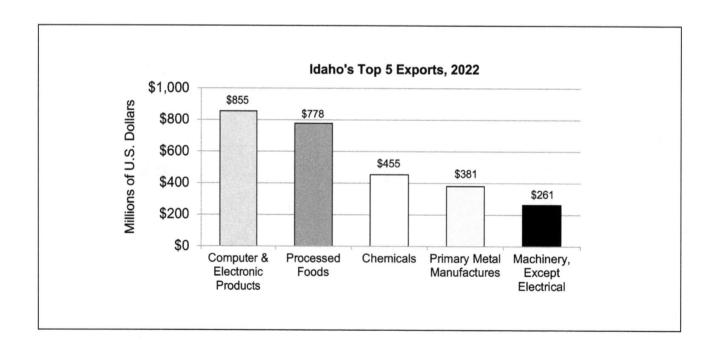

Idaho's Top 5 Exports, 2022

Computer & Electronic Products: $855
Processed Foods: $778
Chemicals: $455
Primary Metal Manufactures: $381
Machinery, Except Electrical: $261

Facts and Figures

Location: North central United States; bordered on the N by Wisconsin, on the E by Lake Michigan and Indiana, on the S by Kentucky, and on the W by Iowa and Missouri

Area: 57,913 sq. mi. (149,998 sq. km.); rank—25th

Population: 12,582,032 (2022 est.); rank—6th

Principal Cities: capital—Springfield; largest—Chicago

Statehood: December 3, 1818; 21st state

U.S. Congress: 2 senators, 18 representatives

State Motto: State Sovereignty, National Union

State Song: "Illinois"

State Nicknames: The Prairie State; The Land of Lincoln

Abbreviations: IL; Ill.

State Symbols: flower—native violet; tree—white oak; bird—cardinal

At a Glance

- Illinois was one of three states that experienced a population decline between 2010 and 2022, with a decrease in population of 1.9 percent.

- In 2022, Illinois employed 49.2 state and local government employees per 1,000 residents, which ranked 36th in the country.

- Illinois had the 5th highest real GDP among the states in 2022 at $798 billion (in chained 2012 dollars). This equated to 4.0 percent of the nation's total GDP.

- Illinois ranked 18th for median household income in 2021, with an income of $72,205.

- In 2021, 7.0 percent of Illinois residents did not have health insurance, compared to 8.6 percent of the entire U.S. population.

Table IL-1. Population by Age, Sex, Race, and Hispanic Origin

(Number, percent, except where noted.)

Sex, age, race, and Hispanic origin	2010	2020	2022	Percent change, 2010–2022
Total Population..........	12,830,632	12,812,545	12,582,032	-1.9
Percent of total U.S. population	4.2	3.9	3.8	X
Sex				
Male.........	6,292,276	6,346,057	6,228,734	-1.0
Female	6,538,356	6,466,488	6,353,298	-2.8
Age				
Under 5 years.........	835,577	732,133	680,341	-18.6
Under 18 years.........	3,129,179	2,845,249	2,720,131	-13.1
18 to 64 years.........	8,092,240	7,900,885	7,698,604	-4.9
65 years and over.........	1,609,213	2,066,411	2,163,297	34.4
Median age (years)	36.6	38.6	39.2	7.1
Race and Hispanic Origin				
One race				
White.........	10,030,587	9,786,710	9,572,606	-4.6
Black.........	1,903,458	1,889,403	1,851,472	-2.7
American Indian and Alaska Native.........	73,846	78,984	79,326	7.4
Asian.........	604,399	776,319	787,633	30.3
Native Hawaiian or Other Pacific Islander.........	7,436	8,604	8,599	15.6
Two or more races.........	210,906	272,525	282,396	33.9
Hispanic (of any race).........	2,027,578	2,279,728	2,303,725	13.6

NOTE: Population figures for 2022 are July 1 estimates. The 2010 and 2020 estimates are taken from the respective censuses.
- = Zero or rounds to zero.
X = Not applicable.

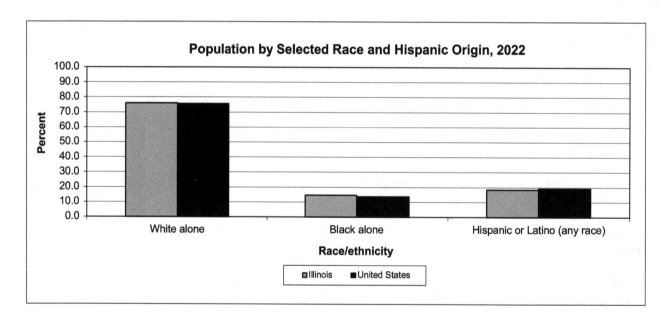

Table IL-2. Marital Status

(Number, percent distribution.)

Sex, age, race, and Hispanic origin	2000	2010	2021
Males, 15 Years and Over.........	4,685,982	4,977,964	5,092,734
Never married.........	31.9	37.2	38.7
Now married, except separated.........	56.1	50.0	49.0
Separated.........	1.6	1.4	1.4
Widowed.........	2.5	2.6	2.5
Divorced.........	7.9	8.8	8.4
Females, 15 Years and Over.........	5,021,855	5,289,803	5,283,987
Never married.........	26.1	31.1	33.5
Now married, except separated.........	51.3	46.3	45.8
Separated.........	2.0	2.1	1.6
Widowed.........	10.7	9.5	8.3
Divorced.........	9.9	11.0	10.8

Table IL-3. Households and Housing Characteristics

(Number, percent, dollars.)

Item	2000	2010	2021	Average annual percent change, 2010–2021
Total Households	4,591,779	4,752,857	4,991,641	0.5
Family households	3,105,513	3,133,813	3,135,600	-
Married-couple family	2,353,892	2,301,009	2,300,396	-
Other family	751,621	832,804	835,204	-
Male householder, no wife present	187,903	220,197	240,515	0.8
Female householder, no husband present	563,718	612,607	594,689	-0.3
Nonfamily households	1,486,266	1,619,044	1,856,041	1.3
Householder living alone	1,229,807	1,340,394	1,528,037	1.3
Householder not living alone	256,459	278,650	328,004	1.6
Housing Characteristics				
Total housing units	4,885,615	5,297,077	5,440,294	0.2
Occupied housing units	4,591,779	4,752,857	4,991,641	0.5
Owner occupied	3,088,884	3,219,338	3,370,654	0.4
Renter occupied	1,502,895	1,533,519	1,620,987	0.5
Average household size	2.63	2.64	2.48	-0.6
Financial Characteristics				
Median gross rent of renter-occupied housing	605	848	1,106	2.8
Median monthly owner costs for housing units with a mortgage	1,198	1,655	1,717	0.3
Median value of owner-occupied housing units	130,800	191,800	231,500	1.9

- = Zero or rounds to zero.

Table IL-4. Migration, Origin, and Language

(Number, percent.)

Characteristic	State 2021	U.S. 2021
Residence 1 Year Ago		
Population 1 year and over	12,544,435	328,464,538
Same house	88.5	87.2
Different house in the U.S.	11.1	12.3
Same county	7.0	6.7
Different county	4.1	5.7
Same state	2.5	3.3
Different state	1.6	2.4
Abroad	0.4	0.4
Place of Birth		
Native born	10,866,907	286,623,642
Male	49.3	49.7
Female	50.7	50.3
Foreign born	1,804,562	45,270,103
Male	50.0	48.7
Female	50.0	51.3
Foreign born; naturalized U.S. citizen	965,352	24,044,083
Male	48.5	46.4
Female	51.5	53.6
Foreign born; not a U.S. citizen	839,210	21,226,020
Male	51.7	51.2
Female	48.3	48.8
Entered 2010 or later	22.5	28.1
Entered 2000 to 2009	23.1	23.7
Entered before 2000	54.5	48.2
World Region of Birth, Foreign		
Foreign-born population, excluding population born at sea	1,804,562	45,269,644
Europe	20.6	10.7
Asia	29.9	31.0
Africa	4.5	5.7
Oceania	0.3	0.6
Latin America	43.8	50.1
North America	1.0	1.7
Language Spoken at Home and Ability to Speak English		
Population 5 years and over	11,967,918	313,232,500
English only	76.7	78.4
Language other than English	23.3	21.6
Speaks English less than "very well"	8.7	8.3

Table IL-5. Median Income and Poverty Status, 2021

(Number, percent, except as noted.)

Characteristic	State		U.S.	
	Number	Percent	Number	Percent
Median Income				
Households (dollars)...	72,205	X	69,717	X
Families (dollars)	90,861	X	85,806	X
Below Poverty Level (All People)	1,498,523	12.1	41,393,176	12.8
Sex				
Male	672,435	11.0	18,518,155	11.6
Female	826,088	13.1	22,875,021	13.9
Age				
Under 18 years..	442,261	16.0	12,243,219	16.9
Related children under 18 years...	434,684	15.8	11,985,424	16.6
18 to 64 years...	851,062	11.2	23,526,341	11.9
65 years and over	205,200	10.0	5,623,616	10.3

X = Not applicable.

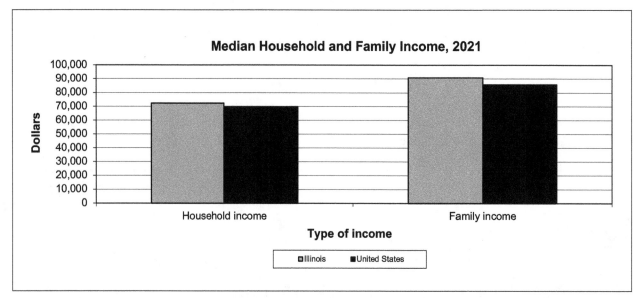

Table IL-6. Health Insurance Coverage Status for the Civilian Noninstitutionalized Population and Children Under 19 Years of Age

(Number, percent.)

Item	2011	2012	2013	2014	2015	2016	2017	2018	2019	2020 [2]	2021
Civilian Noninstitutionalized Population	12,688,006	12,698,371	12,704,616	12,702,393	12,679,860	12,620,388	12,620,126	12,563,908	12,488,377	12,536,614	12,495,329
Covered by Private or Public Insurance											
Number.........................	11,028,731	11,075,906	11,086,412	11,464,467	11,779,571	11,803,786	11,760,869	11,689,300	11,565,086	11,682,181	11,620,230
Percent..........................	86.9	87.2	87.3	90.3	92.9	93.5	93.2	93.0	92.6	93.2	93.0
Uninsured											
Number.........................	1,659,275	1,622,465	1,618,204	1,237,926	900,289	816,602	859,257	874,608	923,291	854,433	875,099
Percent..........................	13.1	12.8	12.7	9.7	7.1	6.5	6.8	7.0	7.4	6.8	7.0
Percent in the U.S. not covered................................	15.1	14.8	14.5	11.7	9.4	8.6	8.7	8.9	9.2	8.7	8.6
Children Under 19 Years of Age[1]	3,091,887	3,059,055	3,017,960	2,980,902	2,956,262	2,919,863	3,069,418	3,027,744	2,981,525	3,023,805	2,968,090
Covered by Private or Public Insurance											
Number.........................	2,978,576	2,957,589	2,892,609	2,881,400	2,880,990	2,848,544	2,980,069	2,925,278	2,861,486	2,929,145	2,872,877
Percent..........................	96.3	96.7	95.8	96.7	97.5	97.6	97.1	96.6	96.0	96.9	96.8
Uninsured											
Number.........................	113,311	101,466	125,351	99,502	75,272	71,319	89,349	102,466	120,039	94,660	95,213
Percent..........................	3.7	3.3	4.2	3.3	2.5	2.4	2.9	3.4	4.0	3.1	3.2
Percent in the U.S. not covered	7.5	7.2	7.1	6.0	4.8	4.5	5.0	5.2	5.7	5.2	5.4

[1] Data for years prior to 2017 are for individuals under 18 years of age.
[2] 2020 ACS 5-Year estimates. 1-Year estimates were not released for 2020 due to the impact of COVID-19 on data collection that year. Data is not comparable to previous years, which are based on 1-year estimates.

Table IL-7. Employment Status by Demographic Group, 2022

(Numbers in thousands, percent.)

Characteristic	Civilian noninstitutional population	Civilian labor force		Employed		Unemployed	
		Number	Percent of population	Number	Percent of population	Number	Percent of population
Total...	9,998	6,460	64.6	6,177	61.8	283	4.4
Sex							
Male...	4,877	3,384	69.4	3,231	66.3	152	4.5
Female	5,122	3,076	60.1	2,945	57.5	131	4.2
Race, Sex, and Hispanic Origin							
White..	7,735	5,013	64.8	4,837	62.5	176	3.5
Male......................................	3,811	2,675	70.2	2,576	67.6	100	3.7
Female...................................	3,923	2,338	59.6	2,261	57.6	77	3.3
Black or African American...........	1,402	826	58.9	736	52.5	90	10.9
Male......................................	628	381	60.7	336	53.5	45	11.9
Female...................................	774	445	57.5	400	51.7	45	10.1
Hispanic or Latino ethnicity[1]	1,733	1,217	70.2	1,158	66.8	59	4.8
Male......................................	899	707	78.7	673	74.9	35	4.9
Female...................................	834	509	61.0	485	58.1	24	4.8
Age							
16 to 19 years...........................	625	239	38.2	211	33.7	28	11.8
20 to 24 years...........................	853	596	69.9	555	65.1	41	6.9
25 to 34 years...........................	1,642	1,402	85.4	1,344	81.8	58	4.1
35 to 44 years...........................	1,627	1,420	87.3	1,368	84.1	52	3.6
45 to 54 years...........................	1,538	1,264	82.2	1,219	79.3	45	3.6
55 to 64 years...........................	1,638	1,136	69.4	1,095	66.8	42	3.7
65 years and over	2,076	403	19.4	386	18.6	17	4.2

NOTE: Data in Table 7 are from the Current Population Survey (CPS) and do not match the estimates in Table 8. See notes and definitions for further information.
[1] May be of any race.

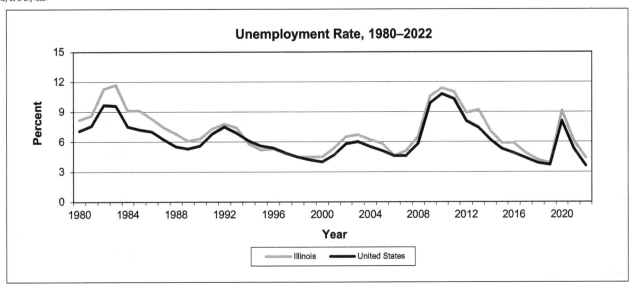

Table IL-8. Employment Status of the Civilian Noninstitutional Population Age 16 Years and Over

(Number, percent.)

Year	Civilian labor force	Civilian participation rate	Employed	Unemployed	Unemployment rate
2010...	6,612,433	66.8	5,918,202	694,231	10.5
2011...	6,567,531	66.0	5,925,787	641,744	9.8
2012...	6,583,689	65.9	5,989,454	594,235	9.0
2013...	6,556,593	65.4	5,961,201	595,392	9.1
2014...	6,516,372	64.8	6,049,059	467,313	7.2
2015...	6,511,797	64.8	6,119,934	391,863	6.0
2016...	6,559,038	65.3	6,172,672	386,366	5.9
2017...	6,562,291	64.7	6,237,933	324,358	4.9
2018...	6,568,208	64.8	6,281,764	286,444	4.4
2019...	6,568,815	64.9	6,308,535	260,280	4.0
2020...	6,366,716	63.0	5,781,084	585,632	9.2
2021...	6,318,915	62.9	5,935,974	382,941	6.1
2022...	6,472,663	64.5	6,176,876	295,787	4.6

Table IL-9. Employment and Average Wages by Industry

(Estimates are based on the 2012 North American Industry Classification System [NAICS].)

Industry	2014	2015	2016	2017	2018	2019	2020	2021
	Number of Jobs							
Wage and Salary Employment by Industry.........................	6,044,058	6,139,569	6,176,576	6,210,786	6,253,799	6,280,415	5,848,155	5,968,913
Farm Wage and Salary Employment................................	11,710	14,743	14,215	13,744	14,744	12,981	13,142	16,537
Nonfarm Wage and Salary Employment..........................	6,032,348	6,124,826	6,162,361	6,197,042	6,239,055	6,267,434	5,835,013	5,952,376
Private wage and salary employment.........................	5,157,446	5,248,161	5,289,354	5,325,125	5,370,287	5,392,079	4,997,414	5,116,486
Forestry, fishing, and related activities	5,916	5,539	5,506	5,545	5,421	5,351	5,155	4,776
Mining..	9,862	9,281	7,991	7,767	7,797	8,191	6,745	6,558
Utilities..	24,015	24,175	24,342	24,498	24,641	24,494	23,813	23,307
Construction	206,988	219,298	224,264	225,044	231,364	233,367	221,949	227,109
Manufacturing...	580,285	581,803	575,079	577,022	586,446	586,569	555,273	555,099
Durable goods manufacturing...................................	349,987	348,363	338,173	337,375	345,359	344,430	321,779	317,925
Nondurable goods manufacturing.............................	230,298	233,440	236,906	239,647	241,087	242,139	233,494	237,174
Wholesale trade	301,268	302,974	303,421	307,063	295,398	295,891	282,552	282,826
Retail trade...	608,907	619,278	621,993	616,295	605,535	591,070	559,034	577,718
Transportation and warehousing..................................	250,953	260,188	263,092	267,560	289,241	299,376	296,690	302,428
Information	99,409	101,208	99,945	96,901	94,355	95,003	87,577	89,490
Finance and insurance	292,392	301,046	300,797	303,359	306,556	315,110	316,319	313,042
Real estate and rental and leasing..............................	76,273	78,867	80,978	83,064	84,356	86,138	80,693	81,273
Professional, scientific, and technical services..............	390,558	405,693	413,069	414,877	421,084	425,811	415,114	428,695
Management of companies and enterprises....................	103,279	94,810	94,766	97,166	92,884	87,035	83,633	82,860
Administrative and waste services...............................	428,116	429,444	431,272	437,045	441,746	441,695	399,707	420,587
Educational services	167,562	167,399	171,459	172,250	169,081	167,768	157,405	165,401
Health care and social assistance...............................	739,200	756,950	767,222	773,274	783,569	790,579	759,858	768,328
Arts, entertainment, and recreation.............................	84,554	85,565	89,245	92,370	94,104	95,974	65,226	73,877
Accommodation and food services	477,469	495,937	511,854	521,878	527,246	531,167	400,813	431,922
Other services, except public administration.................	310,440	308,706	303,059	302,147	309,463	311,490	279,858	281,190
Government and government enterprises	874,902	876,665	873,007	871,917	868,768	875,355	837,599	835,890
	Dollars							
Average Wages and Salaries by Industry	55,135	57,019	57,568	59,191	61,225	62,877	67,399	71,331
Average Farm Wages and Salaries	35,797	31,985	33,559	28,697	28,950	31,220	32,827	31,068
Average Nonfarm Wages and Salaries	55,173	57,080	57,623	59,258	61,301	62,943	67,477	71,442
Average private wages and salaries............................	55,691	57,765	58,368	60,081	62,138	63,838	68,547	72,829
Forestry, fishing, and related activities	30,293	32,704	34,104	36,287	38,363	40,081	43,239	47,205
Mining..	74,133	75,785	77,109	76,964	79,016	81,085	79,743	82,827
Utilities..	112,947	115,566	119,109	121,534	121,579	128,755	131,329	133,022
Construction	65,709	68,753	70,235	71,990	73,042	74,875	77,759	79,892
Manufacturing...	67,867	70,429	70,689	72,453	74,183	75,089	77,174	81,844
Durable goods manufacturing...................................	67,130	68,518	70,030	71,696	73,417	74,616	74,802	78,003
Nondurable goods manufacturing.............................	68,987	73,281	71,508	73,518	75,279	75,762	80,444	86,993
Wholesale trade	77,996	80,382	80,954	82,827	86,594	89,269	92,063	99,140
Retail trade...	29,240	30,427	30,769	31,820	32,851	34,396	37,434	40,688
Transportation and warehousing..................................	54,647	56,069	56,608	58,339	58,586	59,517	58,829	62,424
Information	79,721	82,940	84,910	87,456	93,689	99,227	112,905	125,712
Finance and insurance	105,553	110,729	112,954	117,580	122,748	125,929	134,844	147,396
Real estate and rental and leasing..............................	60,964	64,986	66,051	67,422	71,181	74,201	76,912	84,963
Professional, scientific, and technical services..............	91,935	95,726	96,237	98,477	102,516	104,071	109,643	116,282
Management of companies and enterprises....................	124,603	129,845	127,623	130,002	135,520	137,584	141,982	147,213
Administrative and waste services...............................	36,660	38,853	39,585	41,630	43,316	45,473	49,267	54,317
Educational services	45,434	46,491	46,500	47,462	49,382	50,990	54,753	54,415
Health care and social assistance...............................	47,377	48,431	49,375	50,726	52,370	53,287	56,900	59,489
Arts, entertainment, and recreation.............................	36,316	38,594	39,220	39,405	40,560	41,421	46,793	49,247
Accommodation and food services	21,616	22,573	23,148	23,865	25,204	26,161	24,773	30,152
Other services, except public administration.................	37,582	38,926	40,012	41,637	42,665	43,916	48,234	50,510
Government and government enterprises.................................	52,120	52,979	53,109	54,235	56,126	57,429	61,095	62,953

Table IL-10. Employment Characteristics by Family Type

(Number, percent.)

Family type and labor force status	2019 Total	2019 Families with own children under 18 years	2020 [1] Total	2020 [1] Families with own children under 18 years	2021 Total	2021 Families with own children under 18 years
All Families..	3,059,067	1,272,523	3,116,415	1,323,108	3,135,600	1,302,481
FAMILY TYPE AND LABOR FORCE STATUS						
Opposite-Sex Married-Couple Families...............................	2,251,401	873,220	2,281,604	910,040	2,275,266	893,563
Both husband and wife in labor force..........................	53.6	69.8	54.5	69.8	53.0	69.6
Husband in labor force, wife not in labor force	20.5	25.9	20.7	25.7	20.5	25.0
Wife in labor force, husband not in labor force	7.7	3.0	7.6	3.4	8.2	3.9
Both husband and wife not in labor force..........................	17.3	0.9	17.1	1.1	18.3	1.5
Other Families	807,666	399,303	815,301	409,602	835,204	404,323
Female householder, no spouse present	71.7	75.2	72.5	75.6	71.2	73.4
In labor force................................	51.9	65.0	52.9	65.5	51.5	62.2
Not in labor force........................	19.8	10.2	19.6	10.1	19.7	11.1
Male householder, no spouse present.....................	28.3	24.8	27.5	24.4	28.8	26.6
In labor force................................	22.4	23.0	21.9	22.5	23.0	24.5
Not in labor force........................	6.0	1.9	5.6	1.9	5.8	2.1

[1] 2020 ACS 5-Year estimates. 1-Year estimates were not released for 2020 due to the impact of COVID-19 on data collection that year. Data is not comparable to previous years, which are based on 1-year estimates.

Table IL-11. School Enrollment and Educational Attainment, 2021

(Number, percent.)

Item	State	U.S.
Enrollment		
Total population 3 years and over, enrolled in school	3,049,269	79,453,524
Enrolled in nursery school or preschool (percent)..................................	5.9	5.2
Enrolled in kindergarten (percent)..	5.1	5.0
Enrolled in elementary school, grades 1-8 (percent)................................	40.8	41.3
Enrolled in high school, grades 9-12 (percent)................................	22.0	21.8
Enrolled in college or graduate school (percent)................................	26.2	26.7
Attainment		
Total population 25 years and over	8,730,697	228,193,464
Less than ninth grade (percent)..	4.6	4.8
9th to 12th grade, no diploma (percent)..	5.3	5.9
High school graduate, including equivalency (percent)............................	25.1	26.3
Some college, no degree (percent)..	19.6	19.3
Associate's degree (percent)..	8.3	8.8
Bachelor's degree (percent)	22.1	21.2
Graduate or professional degree (percent)................................	15.0	13.8
High school graduate or higher (percent)..	90.2	89.4
Bachelor's degree or higher (percent)..	37.1	35.0

Table IL-12. Public School Characteristics and Educational Indicators

(Number, percent; data derived from National Center of Education Statistics.)

Item	State	U.S.
Public Elementary and Secondary Schools		
Number of regular school districts, 2019-20	853	13,349
Number of operational schools, 2019-20...................................	4,351	98,469
Percent charter schools	3.2	7.7
Total public school enrollment, Fall 2021...................................	1,868,482	49,433,092
Percent charter school enrollment	3.2	7.5
Student-teacher ratio, Fall 2019..	14.6	15.9
Expenditures per student (unadjusted dollars), 2019-20	17,483	13,489
Four-year adjusted cohort graduation rate (ACGR), 2019-2020[1]................	*	86.5
Students eligible for free or reduced-price lunch (percent), 2019-20...........	48.4	52.1
English language learners (percent), Fall 2020	12.0	10.3
Students age 3 to 21 served under IDEA, part B (percent), 2021-22	15.5	14.7

Public Schools by Type, 2019-20	Number	Percent of state public schools
Total number of schools...	4,351	100.0
Special education...	217	5.0
Vocational education..	0	-
Alternative education...	141	3.2

[1] Adjusted Cohort Graduation Rates (ACGR) differ from Averaged Freshmen Graduation Rates (AFGR).
- = Zero or rounds to zero.
* = Reporting standards not met.

Table IL-13. Reported Voting and Registration of the Voting-Age Population, November 2022

(Numbers in thousands, percent.)

Item	Total population	Total citizen population	Registered Total registered	Registered Percent registered (total population)	Registered Percent registered (total citizen population)	Voted Total voted	Voted Percent voted (total population)	Voted Percent voted (total citizen population)
U.S. Total	255,457	233,546	161,422	63.2	69.1	121,916	47.7	52.2
State Total	9,648	8,824	6,110	63.3	69.2	4,600	47.7	52.1
Sex								
Male	4,738	4,251	2,912	61.5	68.5	2,210	46.6	52.0
Female	4,909	4,573	3,197	65.1	69.9	2,390	48.7	52.3
Race								
White alone	7,638	7,022	4,983	65.2	71.0	3,811	49.9	54.3
White, non-Hispanic alone	5,881	5,800	4,357	74.1	75.1	3,437	58.4	59.2
Black alone	1,360	1,238	760	55.9	61.4	567	41.7	45.8
Asian alone	480	394	229	47.7	58.1	157	32.8	39.9
Hispanic (of any race)	1,896	1,336	666	35.1	49.9	391	20.6	29.3
White alone or in combination	7,759	7,144	5,086	65.6	71.2	3,860	49.8	54.0
Black alone or in combination	1,416	1,294	811	57.3	62.7	582	41.1	44.9
Asian alone or in combination	536	450	272	50.7	60.3	189	35.2	42.0
Age								
18 to 24 years	1,154	1,057	552	47.8	52.2	263	22.8	24.8
25 to 34 years	1,421	1,255	837	58.9	66.7	618	43.5	49.3
35 to 44 years	1,816	1,624	1,144	63.0	70.5	885	48.7	54.5
45 to 64 years	3,208	2,892	2,098	65.4	72.5	1,599	49.8	55.3
65 years and over	2,048	1,997	1,479	72.2	74.0	1,236	60.3	61.9

Table IL-14. Health Indicators

(Number, rate as indicated in footnotes.)

Item	State	U.S.
Births		
Life Expectancy at Birth (years), 2020[1]	76.8	77.0
Fertility Rate by State[1], 2021	53.0	56.3
Percent Home Births, 2021	0.9	1.4
Cesarean Delivery Rate[2], 2021	31.2	32.1
Preterm Birth Rate[3], 2021	10.7	10.5
Teen Birth Rate[4], 2021	11.1	13.9
Percentage of Babies Born Low Birthweight[5], 2021	8.5	8.5
Deaths[6]		
Heart Disease Mortality Rate, 2021	169.8	173.8
Cancer Mortality Rate, 2021	150.0	146.6
Stroke Mortality Rate, 2021	44.1	41.1
Diabetes Mortality Rate, 2021	21.8	25.4
Influenza/Pneumonia Mortality Rate, 2021	11.0	10.5
Suicide Mortality Rate, 2021	11.1	14.1
Drug Overdose Mortality Rate, 2021	29.0	33.6
Firearm Injury Mortality Rate, 2021	16.1	14.6
Homicide Mortality Rate, 2021	12.3	8.2
Disease and Illness		
Lifetime Asthma in Adults, 2020 (percent)	12.3	13.9
Lifetime Asthma in Children, 2020 (percent)[7]	NA	11.3
Diabetes in Adults, 2020 (percent)	9.3	8.2
Self-reported Obesity in Adults, 2021 (percent)	34.2	NA

SOURCE: National Center for Health Statistics, National Vital Statistics System 2020 data; https://wonder.cdc.gov.
[1] General fertility rate per 1,000 women aged 15–44.
[2] This represents the percentage of all live births that were cesarean deliveries.
[3] Babies born prior to 37 weeks of pregnancy (gestation).
[4] Number of births per 1,000 females aged 15–19
[5] Babies born weighing less than 2,500 grams or 5 lbs. 8oz.
[6] Death rates are the number of deaths per 100,000 total population.
[7] U.S. total includes data from 30 states and D.C.
NA = Not available.
- = Zero or rounds to zero.

Table IL-15. State Government Finances, 2021

(Dollar amounts in thousands, percent distribution.)

Item	Dollars	Percent distribution
Total Revenue	118,117,046	100.0
General revenue	97,479,077	82.5
Intergovernmental revenue	31,262,939	26.5
Taxes	55,531,962	47.0
General sales	13,429,355	11.4
Selective sales	10,056,980	8.5
License taxes	3,818,851	3.2
Individual income tax	21,870,696	18.5
Corporate income tax	5,729,501	4.9
Other taxes	626,579	0.5
Current charges	5,019,070	4.2
Miscellaneous general revenue	5,665,106	4.8
Utility revenue	-	-
Liquor stores revenue	-	-
Insurance trust revenue[1]	20,637,969	17.5
Total Expenditure	123,261,594	100.0
Intergovernmental expenditure	27,562,599	22.4
Direct expenditure	95,698,995	77.6
Current operation	61,794,529	50.1
Capital outlay	5,215,328	4.2
Insurance benefits and repayments	23,317,944	18.9
Assistance and subsidies	1,649,794	1.3
Interest on debt	3,721,400	3.0
Exhibit: Salaries and wages	9,484,082	7.7
Total Expenditure	123,261,594	100.0
General expenditure	99,921,379	81.1
Intergovernmental expenditure	27,562,599	22.4
Direct expenditure	72,358,780	58.7
General expenditure, by function:		
Education	26,759,895	21.7
Public welfare	34,728,688	28.2
Hospitals	1,173,930	1.0
Health	1,994,909	1.6
Highways	7,441,863	6.0
Police protection	589,916	0.5
Correction	1,699,079	1.4
Natural resources	306,347	0.2
Parks and recreation	258,147	0.2
Governmental administration	2,606,262	2.1
Interest on general debt	3,721,400	3.0
Other and unallocable	17,539,266	14.2
Utility expenditure	1,020,870	0.8
Liquor stores expenditure	-	-
Insurance trust expenditure	23,317,944	18.9
Debt at End of Fiscal Year	64,743,158	X
Cash and Security Holdings	212,626,421	X

X = Not applicable.
- = Zero or rounds to zero.
[1] Within insurance trust revenue, net earnings of state retirement systems is a calculated statistic (the item code in the data file is X08), and thus can be positive or negative. Net earnings is the sum of earnings on investments plus gains on investments minus losses on investments. The change made in 2002 for asset valuation from book to market value in accordance with Statement 34 of the Governmental Accounting Standards Board is reflected in the calculated statistics.

Table IL-16. State Government Tax Collections, 2022

(Dollars in thousands, percent.)

Item	Dollars	Percent distribution
Total Taxes	62,571,178	100.0
Property taxes	68,795	0.1
Sales and gross receipts	25,865,408	41.3
General sales and gross receipts	15,289,031	24.4
Selective sales and gross receipts	10,576,377	16.9
Alcoholic beverages	320,000	0.5
Amusements	1,258,697	2.0
Insurance premiums	491,053	0.8
Motor fuels	2,527,365	4.0
Pari-mutuels	7,668	-
Public utilities	1,257,528	2.0
Tobacco products	841,366	1.3
Other selective sales	3,872,700	6.2
Licenses	3,546,164	5.7
Alcoholic beverages	20,395	-
Amusements	28,868	-
Corporations in general	342,853	0.5
Hunting and fishing	43,522	0.1
Motor vehicle	2,268,984	3.6
Motor vehicle operators	191,480	0.3
Public utilities	23,302	-
Occupation and business, NEC	604,295	1.0
Other licenses	22,465	-
Income taxes	32,327,125	51.7
Individual income	22,697,437	36.3
Corporation net income	9,629,688	15.4
Other taxes	763,686	1.2
Death and gift	641,815	1.0
Documentary and stock transfer	121,871	0.2
Severance	X	-
Taxes, NEC	0	-

X = Not applicable.
- = Zero or rounds to zero.

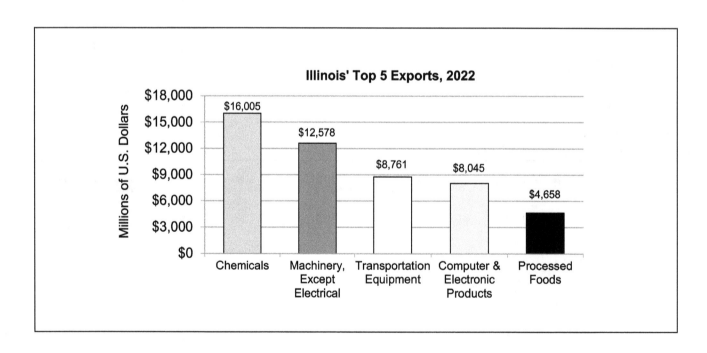

INDIANA

Facts and Figures

Location: East north central United States; bordered on the N by Michigan and Lake Michigan, on the E by Ohio, on the S by Kentucky, and on the W by Illinois

Area: 36,418 sq. mi. (94,321 sq. km.); rank—38th

Population: 6,833,037 (2022 est.); rank—17th

Principal Cities: capital—Indianapolis; largest—Indianapolis

Statehood: December 11, 1816; 19th state

U.S. Congress: 2 senators, 9 representatives

State Motto: The Crossroads of America

State Song: "On the Banks of the Wabash, Far Away"

State Nickname: The Hoosier State

Abbreviations: IN; Ind.

State Symbols: flower—peony; tree—tulip tree; bird—cardinal

At a Glance

- With an increase in population of 5.4 percent, Indiana ranked 28th among the states in growth from 2010 to 2022.

- Indiana had the 4th lowest drug overdose death rate in 2021, with 15.3 deaths per 100,000 population.

- Indiana had the 2nd lowest voter turnout in the nation for the midterm election in November 2022 (39.5 percent). Nationwide, 47.7 percent of the population voted in the election.

- The median household income in Indiana in 2021 was $62,743, compared to the nationwide median of $69,717.

- Approximately 12.2 percent of all Indianans and 16.0 percent of children under 18 years of age in Indiana lived in poverty in 2021, percentages that both ranked 24th in the nation.

Table IN-1. Population by Age, Sex, Race, and Hispanic Origin

(Number, percent, except where noted.)

Sex, age, race, and Hispanic origin	2010	2020	2022	Percent change, 2010–2022
Total Population..	6,483,802	6,785,668	6,833,037	5.4
Percent of total U.S. population	2.1	2.0	2.1	X
Sex				
Male...	3,189,737	3,371,167	3,395,488	6.5
Female...	3,294,065	3,414,501	3,437,549	4.4
Age				
Under 5 years..	434,075	412,163	404,946	-6.7
Under 18 years..	1,608,298	1,582,207	1,569,923	-2.4
18 to 64 years...	4,034,396	4,107,290	4,107,436	1.8
65 years and over..	841,108	1,096,171	1,155,678	37.4
Median age (years)	37.0	38.0	38.2	3.2
Race and Hispanic Origin				
One race				
White	5,638,833	5,735,828	5,736,944	1.7
Black	603,797	685,041	704,235	16.6
American Indian and Alaska Native	24,487	29,307	30,332	23.9
Asian..	105,535	178,581	192,821	82.7
Native Hawaiian or Other Pacific Islander	3,532	4,782	5,162	46.1
Two or more races	107,618	152,129	163,543	52.0
Hispanic (of any race)..	389,707	507,764	541,749	39.0

NOTE: Population figures for 2022 are July 1 estimates. The 2010 and 2020 estimates are taken from the respective censuses.
- = Zero or rounds to zero.
X = Not applicable.

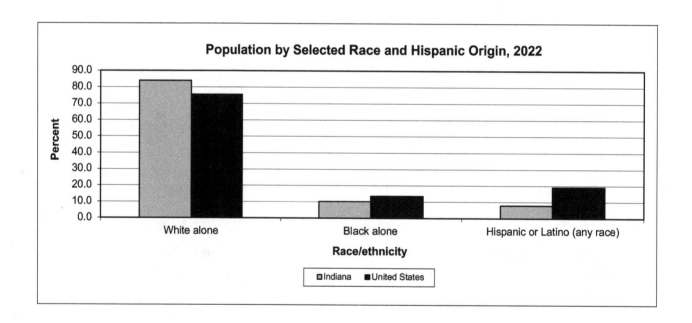

Table IN-2. Marital Status

(Number, percent distribution.)

Sex, age, race, and Hispanic origin	2000	2010	2021
Males, 15 Years and Over	2,308,917	2,513,953	2,705,168
Never married	27.9	32.6	34.1
Now married, except separated.....................................	58.5	52.3	50.8
Separated..	1.3	1.1	0.9
Widowed..	2.4	2.5	2.7
Divorced..	10.0	11.4	11.5
Females, 15 Years and Over	2,462,123	2,644,068	2,795,508
Never married	22.0	26.7	28.8
Now married, except separated.....................................	54.3	49.1	47.8
Separated..	1.5	1.8	1.4
Widowed..	10.6	9.2	8.5
Divorced..	11.6	13.2	13.6

Table IN-3. Households and Housing Characteristics

(Number, percent, dollars.)

Item	2000	2010	2021	Average annual percent change, 2010–2021
Total Households	2,336,306	2,470,905	2,680,694	0.8
Family households	1,602,501	1,656,386	1,717,448	0.3
Married-couple family	1,251,458	1,236,518	1,285,451	0.4
Other family	351,043	419,868	431,997	0.3
Male householder, no wife present	91,671	110,663	130,454	1.6
Female householder, no husband present	259,372	309,205	301,543	-0.2
Nonfamily households	733,805	814,519	963,246	1.7
Householder living alone	605,428	678,460	779,671	1.4
Householder not living alone	128,377	136,059	183,575	3.2
Housing Characteristics				
Total housing units	2,532,319	2,797,172	2,950,121	0.5
Occupied housing units	2,336,306	2,470,905	2,680,694	0.8
Owner occupied	1,669,192	1,736,751	1,905,849	0.9
Renter occupied	667,144	734,154	774,845	0.5
Average household size	2.53	2.55	2.47	-0.3
Financial Characteristics				
Median gross rent of renter-occupied housing	521	683	905	3.0
Median monthly owner costs for housing units with a mortgage	869	1,090	1,195	0.9
Median value of owner-occupied housing units	94,300	123,300	182,400	4.4

Table IN-4. Migration, Origin, and Language

(Number, percent.)

Characteristic	State 2021	U.S. 2021
Residence 1 Year Ago		
Population 1 year and over	6,729,771	328,464,538
Same house	86.7	87.2
Different house in the U.S.	12.9	12.3
Same county	6.8	6.7
Different county	6.1	5.7
Same state	3.8	3.3
Different state	2.3	2.4
Abroad	0.3	0.4
Place of Birth		
Native born	6,426,578	286,623,642
Male	49.5	49.7
Female	50.5	50.3
Foreign born	379,407	45,270,103
Male	50.8	48.7
Female	49.2	51.3
Foreign born; naturalized U.S. citizen	164,232	24,044,083
Male	47.4	46.4
Female	52.6	53.6
Foreign born; not a U.S. citizen	215,175	21,226,020
Male	53.4	51.2
Female	46.6	48.8
Entered 2010 or later	38.8	28.1
Entered 2000 to 2009	28.8	23.7
Entered before 2000	32.4	48.2
World Region of Birth, Foreign		
Foreign-born population, excluding population born at sea	379,407	45,269,644
Europe	10.5	10.7
Asia	33.3	31.0
Africa	11.3	5.7
Oceania	0.4	0.6
Latin America	42.4	50.1
North America	2.1	1.7
Language Spoken at Home and Ability to Speak English		
Population 5 years and over	6,397,955	313,232,500
English only	90.7	70.4
Language other than English	9.3	21.6
Speaks English less than "very well"	3.2	8.3

Table IN-5. Median Income and Poverty Status, 2021

(Number, percent, except as noted.)

Characteristic	State		U.S.	
	Number	Percent	Number	Percent
Median Income				
Households (dollars)...	62,743	X	69,717	X
Families (dollars)	79,243	X	85,806	X
Below Poverty Level (All People)	803,021	12.2	41,393,176	12.8
Sex				
Male	351,437	10.8	18,518,155	11.6
Female	451,584	13.5	22,875,021	13.9
Age				
Under 18 years...	248,513	16.0	12,243,219	16.9
Related children under 18 years..	241,746	15.7	11,985,424	16.6
18 to 64 years..	461,738	11.6	23,526,341	11.9
65 years and over	92,770	8.6	5,623,616	10.3

X = Not applicable.

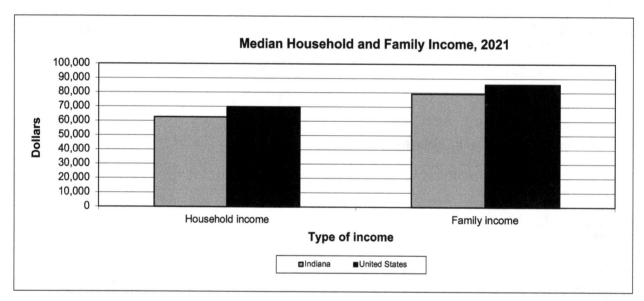

Table IN-6. Health Insurance Coverage Status for the Civilian Noninstitutionalized Population and Children Under 19 Years of Age

(Number, percent.)

Item	2011	2012	2013	2014	2015	2016	2017	2018	2019	2020 [2]	2021
Civilian Noninstitutionalized Population	6,417,644	6,437,142	6,471,551	6,498,029	6,520,267	6,534,914	6,568,434	6,592,504	6,631,529	6,597,701	6,707,875
Covered by Private or Public Insurance											
Number..	5,486,815	5,517,276	5,568,640	5,722,145	5,892,506	6,004,551	6,032,035	6,047,381	6,053,093	6,069,525	6,203,479
Percent..	85.5	85.7	86.0	88.1	90.4	91.9	91.8	91.7	91.3	92.0	92.5
Uninsured											
Number..	930,829	919,866	902,911	775,884	627,761	530,363	536,399	545,123	578,436	528,176	504,396
Percent..	14.5	14.3	14.0	11.9	9.6	8.1	8.2	8.3	8.7	8.0	7.5
Percent in the U.S. not covered...................	15.1	14.8	14.5	11.7	9.4	8.6	8.7	8.9	9.2	8.7	8.6
Children Under 19 Years of Age[1]	1,593,636	1,585,435	1,584,015	1,579,992	1,576,006	1,573,925	1,670,417	1,660,376	1,663,849	1,664,343	1,679,745
Covered by Private or Public Insurance											
Number..	1,464,911	1,451,515	1,454,011	1,466,497	1,469,681	1,481,775	1,564,632	1,551,382	1,545,066	1,559,331	1,579,612
Percent..	91.9	91.6	91.8	92.8	93.3	94.1	93.7	93.4	92.9	93.7	94.0
Uninsured											
Number..	128,725	133,920	130,004	113,495	106,325	92,150	105,785	108,994	118,783	105,012	100,133
Percent..	8.1	8.4	8.2	7.2	6.7	5.9	6.3	6.6	7.1	6.3	6.0
Percent in the U.S. not covered...................	7.5	7.2	7.1	6.0	4.8	4.5	5.0	5.2	5.7	5.2	5.4

[1] Data for years prior to 2017 are for individuals under 18 years of age.
[2] 2020 ACS 5-Year estimates. 1-Year estimates were not released for 2020 due to the impact of COVID-19 on data collection that year. Data is not comparable to previous years, which are based on 1-year estimates.

Table IN-7. Employment Status by Demographic Group, 2022

(Numbers in thousands, percent.)

Characteristic	Civilian noninstitutional population	Civilian labor force		Employed		Unemployed	
		Number	Percent of population	Number	Percent of population	Number	Percent of population
Total...	5,356	3,415	63.7	3,305	61.7	110	3.2
Sex							
Male...	2,618	1,838	70.2	1,783	68.1	55	3.0
Female	2,738	1,576	57.6	1,522	55.6	55	3.5
Race, Sex, and Hispanic Origin							
White	4,530	2,857	63.1	2,777	61.3	81	2.8
Male.....................................	2,218	1,543	69.6	1,500	67.6	43	2.8
Female	2,311	1,314	56.9	1,277	55.2	37	2.8
Black or African American...........	507	352	69.3	332	65.4	20	5.6
Male.....................................	243	179	73.7	171	70.5	8	4.4
Female	264	173	65.3	161	60.9	12	6.9
Hispanic or Latino ethnicity[1]	401	275	68.5	264	65.8	11	4.0
Male.....................................	207	166	80.4	160	77.4	6	3.7
Female	NA	NA	NA	NA	NA	NA	NA
Age							
16 to 19 years	NA	NA	NA	NA	NA	NA	NA
20 to 24 years	471	361	76.6	338	71.8	23	6.3
25 to 34 years	893	761	85.1	733	82.0	28	3.6
35 to 44 years	875	741	84.6	726	83.0	14	1.9
45 to 54 years	787	633	80.4	618	78.5	15	2.4
55 to 64 years	857	557	65.0	545	63.6	12	2.1
65 years and over	1,148	219	19.1	215	18.7	4	1.7

NOTE: Data in Table 7 are from the Current Population Survey (CPS) and do not match the estimates in Table 8. See notes and definitions for further information.
[1] May be of any race.

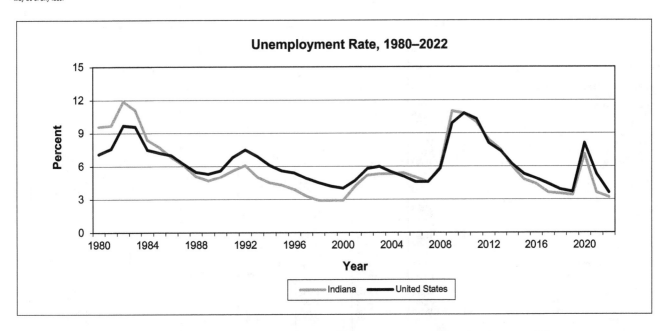

Unemployment Rate, 1980–2022

Table IN-8. Employment Status of the Civilian Noninstitutional Population Age 16 Years and Over

(Number, percent.)

Year	Civilian labor force	Civilian participation rate	Employed	Unemployed	Unemployment rate
2010......................................	3,175,885	64.0	2,854,843	321,042	10.1
2011......................................	3,189,011	63.7	2,904,397	284,614	8.9
2012......................................	3,172,556	63.0	2,911,925	260,631	8.2
2013......................................	3,193,683	63.1	2,953,672	240,011	7.5
2014......................................	3,228,524	63.4	3,036,685	191,839	5.9
2015......................................	3,266,392	63.8	3,109,791	156,601	4.8
2016......................................	3,331,821	64.7	3,186,420	145,401	4.4
2017......................................	3,333,693	64.2	3,217,049	116,644	3.5
2018......................................	3,385,707	64.8	3,270,727	114,980	3.4
2019......................................	3,393,763	64.5	3,282,443	111,320	3.3
2020......................................	3,322,829	62.8	3,083,159	239,670	7.2
2021......................................	3,321,548	62.5	3,203,166	118,382	3.6
2022......................................	3,404,443	63.5	3,302,632	101,811	3.0

Table IN-9. Employment and Average Wages by Industry

(Estimates are based on the 2012 North American Industry Classification System [NAICS].)

Industry	2014	2015	2016	2017	2018	2019	2020	2021
	Number of Jobs							
Wage and Salary Employment by Industry	3,054,388	3,104,469	3,150,896	3,185,079	3,226,669	3,250,655	3,089,435	3,172,200
Farm Wage and Salary Employment	11,533	10,443	10,556	12,285	14,713	12,954	11,675	10,815
Nonfarm Wage and Salary Employment	3,042,855	3,094,026	3,140,340	3,172,794	3,211,956	3,237,701	3,077,760	3,161,385
Private wage and salary employment	2,599,475	2,650,738	2,694,913	2,728,126	2,763,464	2,789,547	2,636,045	2,727,841
Forestry, fishing, and related activities	4,115	3,997	4,124	4,082	4,099	4,438	(D)	3,999
Mining	6,876	6,511	5,900	5,749	5,946	5,780	(D)	4,726
Utilities	14,131	13,984	13,782	13,796	13,940	13,805	13,844	13,559
Construction	126,078	130,349	135,007	141,283	144,386	149,318	147,538	152,760
Manufacturing	507,857	519,217	522,988	534,745	542,076	541,085	504,843	525,093
Durable goods manufacturing	363,607	373,274	375,482	384,838	392,110	389,033	358,087	372,525
Nondurable goods manufacturing	144,250	145,943	147,506	149,907	149,966	152,052	146,756	152,568
Wholesale trade	118,184	119,785	118,612	119,705	121,125	123,632	119,491	122,335
Retail trade	320,938	326,942	334,474	335,031	323,554	319,098	307,639	316,001
Transportation and warehousing	124,819	125,909	129,155	129,575	142,219	146,783	151,017	159,579
Information	35,616	33,673	32,752	31,528	29,365	28,647	26,060	26,141
Finance and insurance	99,242	101,191	102,928	103,924	104,887	106,928	107,622	108,492
Real estate and rental and leasing	33,324	33,986	35,123	35,450	36,754	37,824	35,932	36,422
Professional, scientific, and technical services	105,982	110,404	113,407	115,596	120,231	123,473	124,560	131,760
Management of companies and enterprises	32,149	33,353	34,601	34,425	34,370	34,873	34,065	34,077
Administrative and waste services	185,014	188,620	187,984	189,081	190,591	189,623	171,096	183,837
Educational services	66,540	67,741	68,557	68,623	71,331	72,349	63,732	67,889
Health care and social assistance	374,814	383,901	397,702	406,602	413,532	421,303	409,988	412,873
Arts, entertainment, and recreation	41,968	41,120	42,036	42,842	43,329	43,922	33,956	36,671
Accommodation and food services	254,236	261,550	266,700	267,348	269,167	272,104	232,069	248,307
Other services, except public administration	147,592	148,505	149,081	148,741	152,562	154,562	143,243	143,320
Government and government enterprises	443,380	443,288	445,427	444,668	448,492	448,154	441,715	433,544
	Dollars							
Average Wages and Salaries by Industry	43,306	44,675	45,264	46,897	48,293	49,525	52,635	55,770
Average Farm Wages and Salaries	35,447	32,159	32,835	29,055	29,777	27,763	28,930	29,514
Average Nonfarm Wages and Salaries	43,336	44,717	45,306	46,966	48,378	49,612	52,725	55,860
Average private wages and salaries	43,969	45,426	45,968	47,720	49,208	50,399	53,745	56,989
Forestry, fishing, and related activities	29,100	30,843	33,179	33,525	35,114	37,448	(D)	44,153
Mining	70,368	69,950	68,931	72,557	72,360	78,262	(D)	79,293
Utilities	90,448	94,778	94,861	96,836	100,913	104,486	105,911	109,709
Construction	53,371	54,650	55,692	57,983	59,342	60,957	63,727	66,412
Manufacturing	59,489	60,997	61,016	63,016	64,695	65,424	67,383	71,061
Durable goods manufacturing	58,775	60,495	60,308	62,335	64,294	64,799	65,860	70,102
Nondurable goods manufacturing	61,289	62,282	62,817	64,763	65,744	67,025	71,100	73,402
Wholesale trade	62,019	64,345	65,951	67,765	70,433	71,254	74,856	79,708
Retail trade	26,193	27,217	27,645	28,542	29,160	30,126	32,890	35,533
Transportation and warehousing	45,507	47,211	47,009	48,645	49,633	50,695	52,092	55,366
Information	56,579	58,084	58,733	61,370	62,542	64,655	70,040	74,690
Finance and insurance	65,697	68,542	68,568	71,403	74,665	77,284	81,904	86,216
Real estate and rental and leasing	41,596	42,902	43,488	45,251	47,112	48,308	52,731	56,809
Professional, scientific, and technical services	62,616	64,875	66,661	68,955	71,045	72,119	76,731	81,348
Management of companies and enterprises	90,730	94,601	97,003	101,034	103,320	104,492	108,909	118,058
Administrative and waste services	29,571	30,392	31,466	33,129	34,363	35,678	38,985	42,183
Educational services	32,192	32,735	32,878	33,646	33,313	34,177	38,258	37,880
Health care and social assistance	44,893	46,549	47,232	49,008	50,056	51,537	55,250	58,695
Arts, entertainment, and recreation	33,707	35,054	35,368	36,379	37,887	39,380	42,544	43,060
Accommodation and food services	16,536	17,214	17,695	18,404	19,539	20,051	19,980	23,895
Other services, except public administration	30,655	31,865	32,698	33,895	34,888	35,817	39,407	41,553
Government and government enterprises	39,624	40,482	41,302	42,339	43,263	44,712	46,633	48,757

(D) = Not shown to avoid disclosure of confidential information; estimates are included in higher-level totals.

Table IN-10. Employment Characteristics by Family Type

(Number, percent.)

Family type and labor force status	2019		2020 [1]		2021	
	Total	Families with own children under 18 years	Total	Families with own children under 18 years	Total	Families with own children under 18 years
All Families...	1,639,230	683,069	1,679,392	716,930	1,717,448	714,835
FAMILY TYPE AND LABOR FORCE STATUS						
Opposite-Sex Married-Couple Families...	1,221,373	449,915	1,242,485	473,369	1,273,314	482,080
Both husband and wife in labor force.................................	53.1	70.4	53.4	69.4	52.2	67.8
Husband in labor force, wife not in labor force	20.4	24.8	20.8	25.6	21.2	26.6
Wife in labor force, husband not in labor force	7.3	3.1	7.6	3.6	7.8	4.2
Both husband and wife not in labor force............................	18.3	1.2	18.3	1.5	18.9	1.4
Other Families	417,857	233,154	427,242	241,496	431,997	230,193
Female householder, no spouse present	68.6	70.7	70.2	72.0	69.8	72.7
In labor force...	49.6	60.6	50.2	60.5	48.9	60.1
Not in labor force	19.0	10.1	20.0	11.4	20.9	12.5
Male householder, no spouse present...............................	31.4	29.3	29.8	28.0	30.2	27.3
In labor force...	24.4	26.5	23.4	25.3	24.1	25.1
Not in labor force	7.0	2.8	6.4	2.7	6.1	2.2

[1] 2020 ACS 5-Year estimates. 1-Year estimates were not released for 2020 due to the impact of COVID-19 on data collection that year. Data is not comparable to previous years, which are based on 1-year estimates.

Table IN-11. School Enrollment and Educational Attainment, 2021

(Number, percent.)

Item	State	U.S.
Enrollment		
Total population 3 years and over, enrolled in school	1,645,886	79,453,524
Enrolled in nursery school or preschool (percent)...	5.6	5.2
Enrolled in kindergarten (percent)...	4.9	5.0
Enrolled in elementary school, grades 1-8 (percent)...	42.9	41.3
Enrolled in high school, grades 9-12 (percent)...	21.9	21.8
Enrolled in college or graduate school (percent)...	24.7	26.7
Attainment		
Total population 25 years and over	4,559,631	228,193,464
Less than ninth grade (percent)	3.6	4.8
9th to 12th grade, no diploma (percent)	5.7	5.9
High school graduate, including equivalency (percent)...	33.3	26.3
Some college, no degree (percent)...	19.4	19.3
Associate's degree (percent)..	9.1	8.8
Bachelor's degree (percent)..	18.5	21.2
Graduate or professional degree (percent)..	10.4	13.8
High school graduate or higher (percent)	90.6	89.4
Bachelor's degree or higher (percent)..	28.9	35.0

Table IN-12. Public School Characteristics and Educational Indicators

(Number, percent; data derived from National Center of Education Statistics.)

Item	State	U.S.
Public Elementary and Secondary Schools		
Number of regular school districts, 2019-20	295	13,349
Number of operational schools, 2019-20..	1,912	98,469
Percent charter schools	5.3	7.7
Total public school enrollment, Fall 2021	1,036,625	49,433,092
Percent charter school enrollment	4.8	7.5
Student-teacher ratio, Fall 2019	17.0	15.9
Expenditures per student (unadjusted dollars), 2019-20	10,798	13,489
Four-year adjusted cohort graduation rate (ACGR), 2019-2020[1]..................................	90.9	86.5
Students eligible for free or reduced-price lunch (percent), 2019-20................................	48.4	52.1
English language learners (percent), Fall 2020	6.7	10.3
Students age 3 to 21 served under IDEA, part B (percent), 2021-22	17.6	14.7

Public Schools by Type, 2019-20	Number	Percent of state public schools
Total number of schools...	1,912	100.0
Special education	21	1.1
Vocational education...	30	1.6
Alternative education...	7	0.4

[1] Adjusted Cohort Graduation Rates (ACGR) differ from Averaged Freshmen Graduation Rates (AFGR).

Table IN-13. Reported Voting and Registration of the Voting-Age Population, November 2022

(Numbers in thousands, percent.)

Item	Total population	Total citizen population	Registered			Voted		
			Total registered	Percent registered (total population)	Percent registered (total citizen population)	Total voted	Percent voted (total population)	Percent voted (total citizen population)
U.S. Total	255,457	233,546	161,422	63.2	69.1	121,916	47.7	52.2
State Total......................	5,199	4,903	3,259	62.7	66.5	2,056	39.5	41.9
Sex								
Male	2,525	2,349	1,544	61.1	65.7	1,009	39.9	42.9
Female	2,674	2,554	1,715	64.1	67.2	1,047	39.2	41.0
Race								
White alone........................	4,406	4,259	2,898	65.8	68.1	1,865	42.3	43.8
White, non-Hispanic alone	3,984	3,939	2,711	68.0	68.8	1,801	45.2	45.7
Black alone........................	477	456	256	53.6	56.0	147	30.8	32.2
Asian alone	86	61	31	35.8	50.7	18	20.5	29.0
Hispanic (of any race)...................	590	386	221	37.5	57.4	71	12.0	18.4
White alone or in combination	4,617	4,380	2,966	64.2	67.7	1,888	40.9	43.1
Black alone or in combination...................	545	506	278	51.0	55.0	156	28.5	30.8
Asian alone or in combination...................	188	91	61	32.5	67.2	21	11.4	23.6
Age								
18 to 24 years	588	541	245	41.7	45.3	89	15.1	16.4
25 to 34 years	906	838	431	47.5	51.4	200	22.1	23.9
35 to 44 years	909	828	582	64.0	70.2	304	33.4	36.7
45 to 64 years	1,636	1,547	1,103	67.4	71.3	762	46.6	49.3
65 years and over	1,160	1,148	899	77.5	78.2	700	60.4	61.0

B = Base is less than 75,000 and therefore too small to show the derived measure.

Table IN-14. Health Indicators

(Number, rate as indicated in footnotes.)

Item	State	U.S.
Births		
Life Expectancy at Birth (years), 2020	75.0	77.0
Fertility Rate by State[1], 2021..	60.2	56.3
Percent Home Births, 2021..	2.0	1.4
Cesarean Delivery Rate[2], 2021..	30.4	32.1
Preterm Birth Rate[3], 2021...	10.9	10.5
Teen Birth Rate[4], 2021..	17.0	13.9
Percentage of Babies Born Low Birthweight[5], 2021......................	8.4	8.5
Deaths[6]		
Heart Disease Mortality Rate, 2021......................................	191.2	173.8
Cancer Mortality Rate, 2021..	169.7	146.6
Stroke Mortality Rate, 2021..	43.9	41.1
Diabetes Mortality Rate, 2021..	31.3	25.4
Influenza/Pneumonia Mortality Rate, 2021................................	9.2	10.5
Suicide Mortality Rate, 2021...	16.4	14.1
Drug Overdose Mortality Rate, 2021......................................	43.0	33.6
Firearm Injury Mortality Rate, 2021.....................................	18.4	14.6
Homicide Mortality Rate, 2021..	9.6	8.2
Disease and Illness		
Lifetime Asthma in Adults, 2020 (percent)...............................	14.0	13.9
Lifetime Asthma in Children, 2020 (percent)[7]	8.6	11.3
Diabetes in Adults, 2020 (percent).....................................	10.5	8.2
Self-reported Obesity in Adults, 2021 (percent).........................	36.3	NA

SOURCE: National Center for Health Statistics, National Vital Statistics System 2020 data; https://wonder.cdc.gov.
[1] General fertility rate per 1,000 women aged 15–44.
[2] This represents the percentage of all live births that were cesarean deliveries.
[3] Babies born prior to 37 weeks of pregnancy (gestation).
[4] Number of births per 1,000 females aged 15–19
[5] Babies born weighing less than 2,500 grams or 5 lbs. 8oz.
[6] Death rates are the number of deaths per 100,000 total population.
[7] U.S. total includes data from 30 states and D.C.
NA = Not available.
- = Zero or rounds to zero.

Table IN-15. State Government Finances, 2021

(Dollar amounts in thousands, percent distribution.)

Item	Dollars	Percent distribution
Total Revenue	70,059,871	100.0
General revenue	66,391,645	94.8
Intergovernmental revenue	31,122,742	44.4
Taxes	26,645,852	38.0
General sales	9,282,907	13.2
Selective sales	4,564,816	6.5
License taxes	819,109	1.2
Individual income tax	10,578,929	15.1
Corporate income tax	1,385,158	2.0
Other taxes	14,933	-
Current charges	3,560,968	5.1
Miscellaneous general revenue	5,062,083	7.2
Utility revenue	-	-
Liquor stores revenue	-	-
Insurance trust revenue[1]	3,668,226	5.2
Total Expenditure	52,188,949	100.0
Intergovernmental expenditure	11,196,135	21.5
Direct expenditure	40,992,814	78.5
Current operation	30,552,252	58.5
Capital outlay	3,269,289	6.3
Insurance benefits and repayments	4,869,862	9.3
Assistance and subsidies	1,345,838	2.6
Interest on debt	955,573	1.8
Exhibit: Salaries and wages	5,170,376	9.9
Total Expenditure	52,188,949	100.0
General expenditure	47,319,087	90.7
Intergovernmental expenditure	11,196,135	21.5
Direct expenditure	36,122,952	69.2
General expenditure, by function:		
Education	17,013,044	32.6
Public welfare	18,237,702	34.9
Hospitals	155,070	0.3
Health	1,008,134	1.9
Highways	3,815,677	7.3
Police protection	362,963	0.7
Correction	784,488	1.5
Natural resources	419,009	0.8
Parks and recreation	63,442	0.1
Governmental administration	944,517	1.8
Interest on general debt	955,573	1.8
Other and unallocable	3,404,503	6.5
Utility expenditure	71,707	0.1
Liquor stores expenditure	-	-
Insurance trust expenditure	4,869,862	9.3
Debt at End of Fiscal Year	21,781,589	X
Cash and Security Holdings	79,838,698	X

X = Not applicable.
- = Zero or rounds to zero.
[1] Within insurance trust revenue, net earnings of state retirement systems is a calculated statistic (the item code in the data file is X08), and thus can be positive or negative. Net earnings is the sum of earnings on investments plus gains on investments minus losses on investments. The change made in 2002 for asset valuation from book to market value in accordance with Statement 34 of the Governmental Accounting Standards Board is reflected in the calculated statistics.

Table IN-16. State Government Tax Collections, 2022

(Dollars in thousands, percent.)

Item	Dollars	Percent distribution
Total Taxes	29,258,967	100.0
Property taxes	15,898	0.1
Sales and gross receipts	15,081,598	51.5
General sales and gross receipts	10,388,976	35.5
Selective sales and gross receipts	4,692,622	16.0
Alcoholic beverages	53,718	0.2
Amusements	722,972	2.5
Insurance premiums	257,529	0.9
Motor fuels	1,658,104	5.7
Pari-mutuels	1,696	-
Public utilities	218,703	0.7
Tobacco products	387,364	1.3
Other selective sales	1,392,536	4.8
Licenses	871,383	3.0
Alcoholic beverages	32,131	0.1
Amusements	8,140	-
Corporations in general	11,747	-
Hunting and fishing	21,961	0.1
Motor vehicle	356,767	1.2
Motor vehicle operators	270,819	0.9
Public utilities	X	-
Occupation and business, NEC	62,918	0.2
Other licenses	106,900	0.4
Income taxes	13,288,580	45.4
Individual income	11,749,037	40.2
Corporation net income	1,539,543	5.3
Other taxes	1,508	-
Death and gift	25	-
Documentary and stock transfer	X	-
Severance	1,483	-
Taxes, NEC	0	-

- = Zero or rounds to zero.
X = Not applicable.

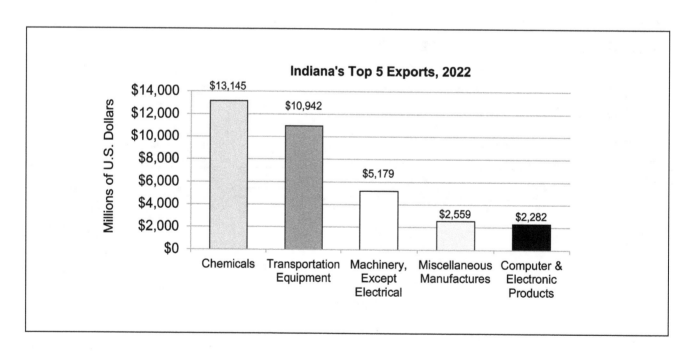

Indiana's Top 5 Exports, 2022

IOWA

Facts and Figures

Location: North central United States; bordered on the N by Minnesota, on the E by Wisconsin and Illinois, on the S by Missouri, and on the W by Nebraska and South Dakota

Area: 56,272 sq. mi. (145,743 sq. km.); rank—26th

Population: 3,200,517 (2022 est.); rank—31st

Principal Cities: capital—Des Moines; largest—Des Moines

Statehood: December 28, 1846; 29th state

U.S. Congress: 2 senators, 4 representatives

State Motto: Our Liberties We Prize and Our Rights We Will Maintain

State Song: "The Song of Iowa"

State Nickname: The Hawkeye State

Abbreviations: IA; Ia.

State Symbols: flower—wild prairie rose; tree—oak; bird—Eastern goldfinch

At a Glance

- With an increase in population of 5.1 percent, Iowa ranked 30th among the states in growth from 2010 to 2022.

- In 2021, Iowa's median household income was $65,600, and 11.1 percent of the population lived below the poverty level.

- Compared to 8.6 percent of the total U.S. population, 4.8 percent of Iowans did not have health insurance in 2021, which was the 7th lowest percent in the country.

- Iowa's homicide rate in 2021 was 3.2 deaths per 100,000 population, compared to the rate of 8.2 per 100,000 for the U.S. as a whole.

- Iowa had the 2nd highest percent of single-family homes in 2021, with 78.8 percent of housing units being one-unit attached or detached homes.

Table IA-1. Population by Age, Sex, Race, and Hispanic Origin

(Number, percent, except where noted.)

Sex, age, race, and Hispanic origin	2010	2020	2022	Percent change, 2010–2022
Total Population..	3,046,355	3,190,372	3,200,517	5.1
Percent of total U.S. population	1.0	1.0	1.0	X
Sex				
Male...	1,508,319	1,600,224	1,606,737	6.5
Female..	1,538,036	1,590,148	1,593,780	3.6
Age				
Under 5 years..	202,123	191,709	186,200	-7.9
Under 18 years..	727,993	733,631	724,489	-0.5
18 to 64 years...	1,865,474	1,898,070	1,889,998	1.3
65 years and over..	452,888	558,671	586,030	29.4
Median age (years)	38.1	38.4	38.8	1.8
Race and Hispanic Origin				
One race				
White	2,839,615	2,882,888	2,874,863	1.2
Black...	91,695	132,240	141,178	54.0
American Indian and Alaska Native	13,563	17,632	18,984	40.0
Asian..	54,232	87,116	88,649	63.5
Native Hawaiian or Other Pacific Islander	2,419	5,417	7,382	205.2
Two or more races..	44,831	65,079	69,461	54.9
Hispanic (of any race)...	151,544	207,821	221,805	46.4

NOTE: Population figures for 2022 are July 1 estimates. The 2010 and 2020 estimates are taken from the respective censuses.
- = Zero or rounds to zero.
X = Not applicable.

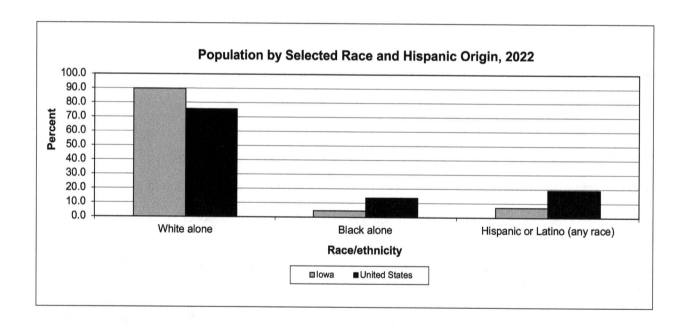

Table IA-2. Marital Status

(Number, percent distribution.)

Sex, age, race, and Hispanic origin	2000	2010	2021
Males, 15 Years and Over	1,126,566	1,199,509	1,291,356
Never married	28.2	31.3	35.3
Now married, except separated..	59.8	55.2	51.9
Separated..	0.9	1.1	0.9
Widowed..	2.5	2.6	2.4
Divorced..	8.5	9.7	9.4
Females, 15 Years and Over	1,198,297	1,250,612	1,296,684
Never married	21.8	24.7	28.1
Now married, except separated..	55.8	52.4	50.5
Separated..	1.1	1.5	1.2
Widowed..	11.6	10.2	8.5
Divorced..	9.6	11.2	11.6

Table IA-3. Households and Housing Characteristics

(Number, percent, dollars.)

Item	2000	2010	2021	Average annual percent change, 2010–2021
Total Households..	1,149,276	1,223,439	1,300,467	0.6
Family households	769,684	793,768	807,506	0.2
Married-couple family	633,254	633,602	638,989	0.1
Other family	136,430	160,166	168,517	0.5
Male householder, no wife present...............	38,160	46,829	54,496	1.5
Female householder, no husband present.......	98,270	113,337	114,021	0.1
Nonfamily households	379,592	429,671	492,961	1.3
Householder living alone............................	313,083	349,736	392,932	1.1
Householder not living alone.......................	66,509	79,935	100,029	2.3
Housing Characteristics				
Total housing units	1,232,511	1,337,563	1,426,039	0.6
Occupied housing units	1,149,276	1,223,439	1,300,467	0.6
Owner occupied	831,419	885,284	935,111	0.5
Renter occupied	317,857	338,155	365,356	0.7
Average household size................................	2.46	2.41	2.38	-0.1
Financial Characteristics				
Median gross rent of renter-occupied housing	470	629	847	3.2
Median monthly owner costs for housing units with a mortgage ...	829	1,140	1,328	1.5
Median value of owner-occupied housing units........	82,500	123,400	174,400	3.8

Table IA-4. Migration, Origin, and Language

(Number, percent.)

Characteristic	State 2021	U.S. 2021
Residence 1 Year Ago		
Population 1 year and over	3,159,672	328,464,538
Same house	86.3	87.2
Different house in the U.S.	13.4	12.3
Same county	7.2	6.7
Different county	6.2	5.7
Same state	3.8	3.3
Different state	2.4	2.4
Abroad	0.3	0.4
Place of Birth		
Native born	3,020,058	286,623,642
Male	50.1	49.7
Female	49.9	50.3
Foreign born	173,021	45,270,103
Male	51.5	48.7
Female	48.5	51.3
Foreign born; naturalized U.S. citizen....................	84,614	24,044,083
Male	46.3	46.4
Female	53.7	53.6
Foreign born; not a U.S. citizen...........................	88,407	21,226,020
Male	56.5	51.2
Female	43.5	48.8
Entered 2010 or later	37.8	28.1
Entered 2000 to 2009	26.8	23.7
Entered before 2000..	35.3	48.2
World Region of Birth, Foreign		
Foreign-born population, excluding population born at sea	173,021	45,269,644
Europe..	11.2	10.7
Asia..	31.8	31.0
Africa..	17.0	5.7
Oceania..	2.1	0.6
Latin America..	36.3	50.1
North America...	1.6	1.7
Language Spoken at Home and Ability to Speak English		
Population 5 years and over.....................................	3,005,822	313,232,500
English only	91.4	78.4
Language other than English..............................	8.6	21.6
Speaks English less than "very well"..................	3.2	8.3

Table IA-5. Median Income and Poverty Status, 2021

(Number, percent, except as noted.)

Characteristic	State		U.S.	
	Number	Percent	Number	Percent
Median Income				
Households (dollars)...	65,600	X	69,717	X
Families (dollars)	84,908	X	85,806	X
Below Poverty Level (All People)	344,696	11.1	41,393,176	12.8
Sex				
Male	153,072	9.9	18,518,155	11.6
Female	191,624	12.4	22,875,021	13.9
Age				
Under 18 years..	90,715	12.5	12,243,219	16.9
Related children under 18 years...	87,933	12.2	11,985,424	16.6
18 to 64 years..	207,646	11.4	23,526,341	11.9
65 years and over	46,335	8.4	5,623,616	10.3

X = Not applicable.

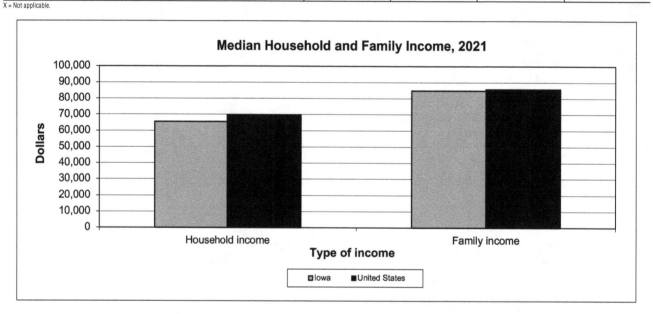

Median Household and Family Income, 2021

Table IA-6. Health Insurance Coverage Status for the Civilian Noninstitutionalized Population and Children Under 19 Years of Age

(Number, percent.)

Item	2011	2012	2013	2014	2015	2016	2017	2018	2019	2020 [2]	2021
Civilian Noninstitutionalized Population	3,017,465	3,028,864	3,045,284	3,062,900	3,080,411	3,091,437	3,102,179	3,113,029	3,111,914	3,106,492	3,151,182
Covered by Private or Public Insurance											
Number..	2,747,975	2,774,589	2,797,567	2,874,015	2,925,441	2,959,825	2,956,162	2,965,990	2,955,852	2,960,859	2,999,897
Percent..	91.1	91.6	91.9	93.8	95.0	95.7	95.3	95.3	95.0	95.3	95.2
Uninsured											
Number..	269,490	254,275	247,717	188,885	154,970	131,612	146,017	147,039	156,062	145,633	151,285
Percent..	8.9	8.4	8.1	6.2	5.0	4.3	4.7	4.7	5.0	4.7	4.8
Percent in the U.S. not covered...............................	15.1	14.8	14.5	11.7	9.4	8.6	8.7	8.9	9.2	8.7	8.6
Children Under 19 Years of Age[1]	721,561	720,427	721,264	723,351	726,495	724,997	775,929	780,762	765,322	770,491	781,749
Covered by Private or Public Insurance											
Number..	689,820	691,735	691,509	700,117	700,899	706,555	751,885	759,740	742,971	749,201	755,543
Percent..	95.6	96.0	95.9	96.8	96.5	97.5	96.9	97.3	97.1	97.2	96.6
Uninsured											
Number..	31,741	28,692	29,755	23,234	25,596	18,442	24,044	21,022	22,351	21,290	26,206
Percent..	4.4	4.0	4.1	3.2	3.5	2.5	3.1	2.7	2.9	2.8	3.4
Percent in the U.S. not covered...............................	7.5	7.2	7.1	6.0	4.8	4.5	5.0	5.2	5.7	5.2	5.4

[1] Data for years prior to 2017 are for individuals under 18 years of age.
[2] 2020 ACS 5-Year estimates. 1-Year estimates were not released for 2020 due to the impact of COVID-19 on data collection that year. Data is not comparable to previous years, which are based on 1-year estimates.

Table IA-7. Employment Status by Demographic Group, 2022

(Numbers in thousands, percent.)

Characteristic	Civilian noninstitutional population	Civilian labor force		Employed		Unemployed	
		Number	Percent of population	Number	Percent of population	Number	Percent of population
Total..	2,522	1,724	68.4	1,680	66.6	44	2.6
Sex							
Male...	1,258	926	73.6	899	71.5	26	2.8
Female..	1,264	799	63.2	780	61.7	18	2.3
Race, Sex, and Hispanic Origin							
White	2,352	1,602	68.1	1,564	66.5	38	2.3
Male..	1,167	858	73.5	836	71.6	22	2.5
Female..	1,185	744	62.8	729	61.5	16	2.1
Black or African American...........................	NA	NA	NA	NA	NA	NA	NA
Male..	NA	NA	NA	NA	NA	NA	NA
Female..	NA	NA	NA	NA	NA	NA	NA
Hispanic or Latino ethnicity[1]	NA	NA	NA	NA	NA	NA	NA
Male..	NA	NA	NA	NA	NA	NA	NA
Female..	NA	NA	NA	NA	NA	NA	NA
Age							
16 to 19 years	NA	NA	NA	NA	NA	NA	NA
20 to 24 years	204	156	76.5	148	72.4	8	5.3
25 to 34 years	396	352	89.1	345	87.3	7	2.0
35 to 44 years	428	382	89.3	374	87.2	9	2.3
45 to 54 years	336	293	87.2	289	86.0	4	1.4
55 to 64 years	406	293	72.2	286	70.5	7	2.4
65 years and over	580	149	25.6	145	25.1	3	2.1

NOTE: Data in Table 7 are from the Current Population Survey (CPS) and do not match the estimates in Table 8. See notes and definitions for further information.
[1] May be of any race.
NA = Not available

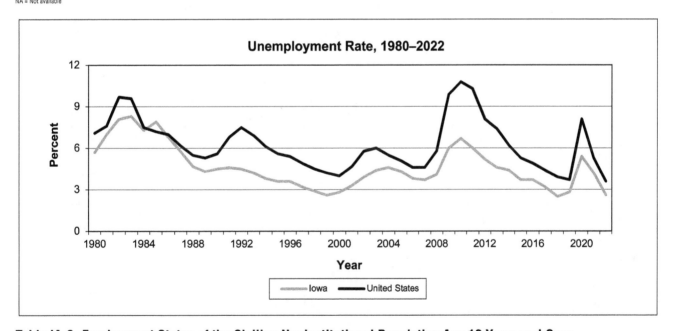

Unemployment Rate, 1980–2022

Table IA-8. Employment Status of the Civilian Noninstitutional Population Age 16 Years and Over

(Number, percent.)

Year	Civilian labor force	Civilian participation rate	Employed	Unemployed	Unemployment rate
2010..	1,674,411	71.0	1,571,960	102,451	6.1
2011..	1,670,056	70.3	1,575,767	94,289	5.6
2012..	1,660,180	69.5	1,576,236	83,944	5.1
2013..	1,676,565	69.7	1,597,139	79,426	4.7
2014..	1,698,718	70.2	1,626,676	72,042	4.2
2015..	1,700,549	69.9	1,637,467	63,082	3.7
2016..	1,703,164	69.7	1,642,152	61,012	3.6
2017..	1,697,495	68.9	1,645,660	51,835	3.1
2018..	1,714,951	69.3	1,671,631	43,320	2.5
2019..	1,749,620	70.3	1,704,063	45,557	2.6
2020..	1,682,257	67.4	1,595,824	86,433	5.1
2021..	1,676,075	66.9	1,605,206	70,869	4.2
2022..	1,716,894	68.1	1,669,933	46,961	2.7

Table IA-9. Employment and Average Wages by Industry

(Estimates are based on the 2012 North American Industry Classification System [NAICS].)

Industry	2014	2015	2016	2017	2018	2019	2020	2021
	Number of Jobs							
Wage and Salary Employment by Industry........................	1,607,246	1,626,375	1,632,862	1,630,848	1,638,255	1,644,686	1,569,147	1,595,083
Farm Wage and Salary Employment.................................	14,833	19,160	18,686	16,838	16,937	19,397	19,861	19,888
Nonfarm Wage and Salary Employment...........................	1,592,413	1,607,215	1,614,176	1,614,010	1,621,318	1,625,289	1,549,286	1,575,195
Private wage and salary employment.................................	1,324,779	1,339,726	1,345,784	1,344,056	1,350,506	1,353,331	1,284,713	1,307,464
Forestry, fishing, and related activities..........................	7,618	7,516	7,536	7,560	7,597	7,640	7,429	6,845
Mining..	2,166	2,218	2,185	2,319	2,434	2,394	2,231	2,223
Utilities..	6,483	6,576	6,467	6,424	6,397	6,205	6,048	5,860
Construction	76,100	80,228	82,845	77,897	79,063	79,966	78,436	79,915
Manufacturing..	217,229	216,587	214,043	216,231	222,841	226,358	216,894	218,347
Durable goods manufacturing..................................	130,959	129,087	124,756	123,658	128,010	130,431	122,032	121,753
Nondurable goods manufacturing.............................	86,270	87,500	89,287	92,573	94,831	95,927	94,862	96,594
Wholesale trade	69,307	67,995	67,051	66,789	66,363	66,470	65,092	64,869
Retail trade..	178,004	181,529	183,744	182,861	180,115	176,283	169,434	174,495
Transportation and warehousing..................................	60,184	61,221	60,391	60,944	61,988	63,866	62,682	65,185
Information	25,715	24,997	22,635	21,916	22,016	21,329	19,152	18,886
Finance and insurance	94,402	95,725	98,235	99,336	99,312	100,858	101,191	99,951
Real estate and rental and leasing...............................	14,192	14,529	14,629	14,835	15,161	15,320	14,791	15,011
Professional, scientific, and technical services	48,713	49,874	52,159	52,940	54,082	53,227	52,842	53,812
Management of companies and enterprises.......................	18,215	19,227	19,069	19,177	19,602	20,670	21,024	22,176
Administrative and waste services	70,349	70,442	68,255	67,838	67,825	66,320	61,886	65,338
Educational services	40,632	40,515	41,968	42,206	38,399	37,906	34,930	36,417
Health care and social assistance................................	187,465	189,647	192,604	193,817	194,415	194,458	186,920	186,177
Arts, entertainment, and recreation..............................	19,168	18,999	20,958	20,780	21,238	21,874	16,728	18,404
Accommodation and food services	119,711	121,618	122,631	123,249	123,423	123,259	102,734	110,571
Other services, except public administration...................	69,126	70,283	68,379	66,937	68,235	68,928	64,269	62,982
Government and government enterprises	267,634	267,489	268,392	269,954	270,812	271,958	264,573	267,731
	Dollars							
Average Wages and Salaries by Industry	41,763	43,053	43,898	45,186	46,636	47,711	50,963	53,118
Average Farm Wages and Salaries	46,445	30,060	30,621	42,389	37,398	33,538	27,375	34,143
Average Nonfarm Wages and Salaries	41,720	43,208	44,052	45,215	46,732	47,880	51,265	53,358
Average private wages and salaries.................................	41,730	43,269	44,086	45,292	46,937	48,147	51,666	53,998
Forestry, fishing, and related activities..........................	29,698	30,753	31,868	32,863	34,447	35,845	38,347	41,623
Mining..	51,767	54,337	57,509	58,119	58,483	60,698	60,731	62,537
Utilities..	86,365	86,924	88,081	91,440	94,397	96,968	102,697	101,061
Construction	51,967	54,959	58,064	55,428	57,442	58,954	61,809	62,966
Manufacturing..	54,389	55,915	56,038	58,605	60,248	60,176	63,083	65,470
Durable goods manufacturing..................................	57,375	58,761	58,312	61,859	63,755	62,760	65,174	68,488
Nondurable goods manufacturing.............................	49,854	51,717	52,861	54,258	55,514	56,662	60,394	61,665
Wholesale trade	58,796	60,250	61,105	63,237	65,782	66,985	69,803	74,403
Retail trade..	24,595	25,212	25,820	26,526	27,266	27,929	30,361	31,992
Transportation and warehousing..................................	44,646	45,973	45,679	47,242	49,149	49,193	51,537	53,683
Information	50,756	52,858	53,842	55,937	58,539	60,526	66,810	71,998
Finance and insurance	68,254	71,512	72,359	75,272	77,801	80,261	84,995	88,583
Real estate and rental and leasing...............................	42,772	44,782	44,589	45,680	46,763	48,181	51,829	54,833
Professional, scientific, and technical services	60,423	62,962	64,378	66,684	68,212	70,871	75,301	79,493
Management of companies and enterprises.......................	77,926	81,841	82,341	83,123	84,202	87,713	95,779	103,819
Administrative and waste services	28,546	29,634	30,970	32,308	34,031	35,649	38,647	42,305
Educational services	24,755	24,740	26,212	26,242	28,871	29,398	31,512	31,084
Health care and social assistance................................	39,437	41,349	41,944	42,701	43,644	45,018	47,789	50,198
Arts, entertainment, and recreation..............................	19,642	20,242	19,494	19,791	20,324	20,898	22,514	24,328
Accommodation and food services	16,179	16,755	17,547	18,113	19,018	19,449	19,025	22,433
Other services, except public administration...................	29,461	30,625	32,619	33,421	34,369	36,097	38,750	40,690
Government and government enterprises.............................	41,667	42,903	43,878	44,830	45,712	46,552	49,316	50,229

Table IA-10. Employment Characteristics by Family Type

(Number, percent.)

Family type and labor force status	2019 Total	2019 Families with own children under 18 years	2020 [1] Total	2020 [1] Families with own children under 18 years	2021 Total	2021 Families with own children under 18 years
All Families...	808,802	343,739	800,738	349,346	807,506	348,971
FAMILY TYPE AND LABOR FORCE STATUS						
Opposite-Sex Married-Couple Families...	628,853	237,254	627,590	241,897	634,732	244,298
Both husband and wife in labor force...	57.7	78.9	58.4	78.4	56.6	77.4
Husband in labor force, wife not in labor force...	15.7	16.8	16.6	17.8	16.5	18.3
Wife in labor force, husband not in labor force...	7.1	2.9	7.0	2.7	7.3	3.4
Both husband and wife not in labor force...	19.0	1.1	18.1	1.1	19.6	1.0
Other Families...	179,949	106,485	169,480	106,733	168,517	103,933
Female householder, no spouse present...	68.4	71.0	68.2	70.0	67.7	69.8
In labor force...	52.8	62.0	53.1	60.9	51.5	59.6
Not in labor force...	15.6	9.0	15.0	9.1	16.1	10.2
Male householder, no spouse present...	31.6	29.0	31.8	30.0	32.3	30.2
In labor force...	26.2	27.2	26.8	28.0	26.9	28.6
Not in labor force...	5.4	1.8	5.0	2.0	5.4	1.7

[1] 2020 ACS 5-Year estimates. 1-Year estimates were not released for 2020 due to the impact of COVID-19 on data collection that year. Data is not comparable to previous years, which are based on 1-year estimates.

Table IA-11. School Enrollment and Educational Attainment, 2021

(Number, percent.)

Item	State	U.S.
Enrollment		
Total population 3 years and over, enrolled in school...	789,863	79,453,524
Enrolled in nursery school or preschool (percent)...	5.9	5.2
Enrolled in kindergarten (percent)...	5.5	5.0
Enrolled in elementary school, grades 1-8 (percent)...	41.4	41.3
Enrolled in high school, grades 9-12 (percent)...	21.9	21.8
Enrolled in college or graduate school (percent)...	25.3	26.7
Attainment		
Total population 25 years and over...	2,137,261	228,193,464
Less than ninth grade (percent)...	2.7	4.8
9th to 12th grade, no diploma (percent)...	3.9	5.9
High school graduate, including equivalency (percent)...	30.3	26.3
Some college, no degree (percent)...	20.6	19.3
Associate's degree (percent)...	12.0	8.8
Bachelor's degree (percent)...	20.7	21.2
Graduate or professional degree (percent)...	9.9	13.8
High school graduate or higher (percent)...	93.3	89.4
Bachelor's degree or higher (percent)...	30.5	35.0

Table IA-12. Public School Characteristics and Educational Indicators

(Number, percent; data derived from National Center of Education Statistics.)

Item	State	U.S.
Public Elementary and Secondary Schools		
Number of regular school districts, 2019-20...	327	13,349
Number of operational schools, 2019-20...	1,310	98,469
Percent charter schools...	0.2	7.7
Total public school enrollment, Fall 2021...	510,661	49,433,092
Percent charter school enrollment...	0.0	7.5
Student-teacher ratio, Fall 2019...	14.5	15.9
Expenditures per student (unadjusted dollars), 2019-20...	11,986	13,489
Four-year adjusted cohort graduation rate (ACGR), 2019-2020[1]...	91.8	86.5
Students eligible for free or reduced-price lunch (percent), 2019-20...	42.0	52.1
English language learners (percent), Fall 2020...	6.3	10.3
Students age 3 to 21 served under IDEA, part B (percent), 2021-22...	13.7	14.7

Public Schools by Type, 2019-20	Number	Percent of state public schools
Total number of schools...	1,310	100.0
Special education...	2	0.2
Vocational education...	0	-
Alternative education...	17	1.3

[1] Adjusted Cohort Graduation Rates (ACGR) differ from Averaged Freshmen Graduation Rates (AFGR).
- = Zero or rounds to zero.

Table IA-13. Reported Voting and Registration of the Voting-Age Population, November 2022

(Numbers in thousands, percent.)

Item	Total population	Total citizen population	Registered			Voted		
			Total registered	Percent registered (total population)	Percent registered (total citizen population)	Total voted	Percent voted (total population)	Percent voted (total citizen population)
U.S. Total	255,457	233,546	161,422	63.2	69.1	121,916	47.7	52.2
State Total.............................	2,422	2,345	1,732	71.5	73.9	1,215	50.2	51.8
Sex								
Male	1,219	1,186	882	72.4	74.4	603	49.5	50.9
Female	1,203	1,160	850	70.6	73.3	612	50.9	52.8
Race								
White alone..............................	2,241	2,202	1,667	74.4	75.7	1,184	52.8	53.8
White, non-Hispanic alone	2,145	2,136	1,627	75.9	76.2	1,167	54.4	54.6
Black alone..............................	87	84	34	38.9	40.5	24	27.9	29.1
Asian alone	64	31	14	21.4	44.7	3	4.3	9.0
Hispanic (of any race)	100	70	40	40.3	57.9	18	17.7	25.5
White alone or in combination	2,254	2,215	1,678	74.4	75.8	1,188	52.7	53.7
Black alone or in combination	93	90	37	39.9	41.5	24	26.1	27.1
Asian alone or in combination.....................	64	31	14	21.4	44.7	3	4.3	9.0
Age								
18 to 24 years................................	302	302	155	51.3	51.3	69	22.8	22.8
25 to 34 years................................	396	358	266	67.2	74.3	141	35.7	39.5
35 to 44 years................................	395	377	282	71.3	74.7	162	41.0	43.0
45 to 64 years................................	747	728	582	78.0	79.9	447	59.8	61.3
65 years and over.............................	582	580	448	76.9	77.2	397	68.1	68.4

B = Base is less than 75,000 and therefore too small to show the derived measure.

Table IA-14. Health Indicators

(Number, rate as indicated in footnotes.)

Item	State	U.S.
Births		
Life Expectancy at Birth (years), 2020	77.5	77.0
Fertility Rate by State[1], 2021..	60.8	56.3
Percent Home Births, 2021...	1.9	1.4
Cesarean Delivery Rate[2], 2021..	29.7	32.1
Preterm Birth Rate[3], 2021...	10.0	10.5
Teen Birth Rate[4], 2021...	12.7	13.9
Percentage of Babies Born Low Birthweight[5], 2021..	6.8	8.5
Deaths[6]		
Heart Disease Mortality Rate, 2021..	184.9	173.8
Cancer Mortality Rate, 2021..	150.9	146.6
Stroke Mortality Rate, 2021..	33.8	41.1
Diabetes Mortality Rate, 2021...	25.0	25.4
Influenza/Pneumonia Mortality Rate, 2021	8.7	10.5
Suicide Mortality Rate, 2021...	17.5	14.1
Drug Overdose Mortality Rate, 2021..	15.3	33.6
Firearm Injury Mortality Rate, 2021	11.2	14.6
Homicide Mortality Rate, 2021..	3.2	8.2
Disease and Illness		
Lifetime Asthma in Adults, 2020 (percent)...	11.9	13.9
Lifetime Asthma in Children, 2020 (percent)[7]	NA	11.3
Diabetes in Adults, 2020 (percent)..	9.0	8.2
Self-reported Obesity in Adults, 2021 (percent)...	36.4	NA

SOURCE: National Center for Health Statistics, National Vital Statistics System 2020 data; https://wonder.cdc.gov.
[1] General fertility rate per 1,000 women aged 15–44.
[2] This represents the percentage of all live births that were cesarean deliveries.
[3] Babies born prior to 37 weeks of pregnancy (gestation).
[4] Number of births per 1,000 females aged 15–19
[5] Babies born weighing less than 2,500 grams or 5 lbs. 8oz.
[6] Death rates are the number of deaths per 100,000 total population.
[7] U.S. total includes data from 30 states and D.C.
NA = Not available.
- = Zero or rounds to zero.

Table IA-15. State Government Finances, 2021

(Dollar amounts in thousands, percent distribution.)

Item	Dollars	Percent distribution
Total Revenue	29,114,357	100.0
General revenue	26,132,201	89.8
Intergovernmental revenue	8,452,676	29.0
Taxes	11,816,502	40.6
General sales	4,002,493	13.7
Selective sales	1,519,624	5.2
License taxes	1,101,447	3.8
Individual income tax	4,266,534	14.7
Corporate income tax	793,641	2.7
Other taxes	132,763	0.5
Current charges	4,273,537	14.7
Miscellaneous general revenue	1,589,486	5.5
Utility revenue	-	-
Liquor stores revenue	416015	1.4
Insurance trust revenue[1]	2,566,141	8.8
Total Expenditure	28,838,245	100.0
Intergovernmental expenditure	6,388,257	22.2
Direct expenditure	22,449,988	77.8
Current operation	15,571,210	54.0
Capital outlay	1,795,871	6.2
Insurance benefits and repayments	4,166,826	14.4
Assistance and subsidies	724,505	2.5
Interest on debt	191,576	0.7
Exhibit: Salaries and wages	3,717,130	12.9
Total Expenditure	28,838,245	100.0
General expenditure	24,373,422	84.5
Intergovernmental expenditure	6,388,257	22.2
Direct expenditure	17,985,165	62.4
General expenditure, by function:		
Education	7,858,964	27.3
Public welfare	7,710,531	26.7
Hospitals	2,701,584	9.4
Health	295,801	1.0
Highways	2,425,739	8.4
Police protection	136,674	0.5
Correction	325,883	1.1
Natural resources	443,317	1.5
Parks and recreation	37,304	0.1
Governmental administration	757,618	2.6
Interest on general debt	191,576	0.7
Other and unallocable	1,402,452	4.9
Utility expenditure	67,805	0.2
Liquor stores expenditure	297,161	1.0
Insurance trust expenditure	4,166,826	14.4
Debt at End of Fiscal Year	6,379,930	X
Cash and Security Holdings	64,711,673	X

X = Not applicable.
- = Zero or rounds to zero.
[1] Within insurance trust revenue, net earnings of state retirement systems is a calculated statistic (the item code in the data file is X08), and thus can be positive or negative. Net earnings is the sum of earnings on investments plus gains on investments minus losses on investments. The change made in 2002 for asset valuation from book to market value in accordance with Statement 34 of the Governmental Accounting Standards Board is reflected in the calculated statistics.

Table IA-16. State Government Tax Collections, 2022

(Dollars in thousands, percent.)

Item	Dollars	Percent distribution
Total Taxes	12,908,955	100.0
Property taxes	2,110	-
Sales and gross receipts	5,807,099	45.0
General sales and gross receipts	4,235,827	32.8
Selective sales and gross receipts	1,571,272	12.2
Alcoholic beverages	22,218	0.2
Amusements	373,500	2.9
Insurance premiums	152,546	1.2
Motor fuels	701,213	5.4
Pari-mutuels	3,947	-
Public utilities	71,453	0.6
Tobacco products	190,402	1.5
Other selective sales	55,993	0.4
Licenses	1,135,112	8.8
Alcoholic beverages	22,017	0.2
Amusements	28,780	0.2
Corporations in general	79,982	0.6
Hunting and fishing	35,356	0.3
Motor vehicle	770,930	6.0
Motor vehicle operators	17,039	0.1
Public utilities	11,841	0.1
Occupation and business, NEC	162,295	1.3
Other licenses	6,872	0.1
Income taxes	5,834,787	45.2
Individual income	4,974,623	38.5
Corporation net income	860,164	6.7
Other taxes	129,847	1.0
Death and gift	91,826	0.7
Documentary and stock transfer	38,021	0.3
Severance	X	-
Taxes, NEC	0	-

X = Not applicable.
- = Zero or rounds to zero.

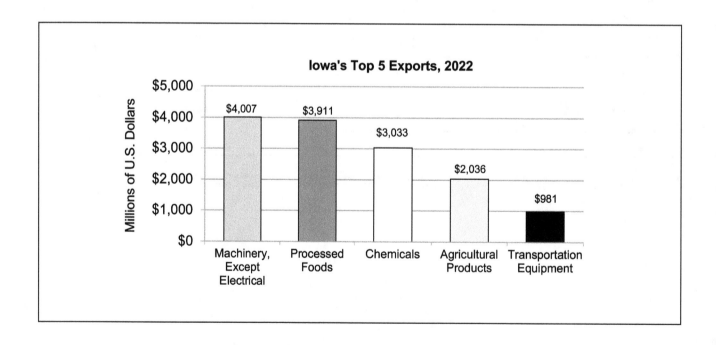

Iowa's Top 5 Exports, 2022

KANSAS

Facts and Figures

Location: Central United States; bordered on the N by Nebraska, on the E by Missouri, on the S by Oklahoma, and on the W by Colorado

Area: 82,277 sq. mi. (213,096 sq. km.); rank—15th

Population: 2,937,150 (2022 est.); rank—35th

Principal Cities: capital—Topeka; largest—Wichita

Statehood: January 29, 1861; 34th state

U.S. Congress: 2 senators, 4 representatives

State Motto: *Ad astra per aspera* ("To the stars through difficulties")

State Song: "Home on the Range"

State Nicknames: The Sunflower State; The Jayhawk State

Abbreviations: KS; Kan.; Kans.

State Symbols: flower—wild native sunflower; tree—cottonwood; bird—Western meadowlark

At a Glance

- With an increase in population of 2.9 percent, Kansas ranked 41st among the states in growth from 2010 to 2022.

- In 2021, 9.2 percent of Kansans did not have health insurance, compared to the national rate of 8.6 percent.

- Kansans younger than 18 years old comprised 23.5 percent of the state's population in 2022, which was the 8th highest percentage in the United States.

- Kansas's unemployment rate was 2.7 percent in 2022, which ranked 39th in the country.

- In 2021, Kansas had the 3rd highest drug overdose death rate in the country, with 55.6 deaths per 100,000 population.

Table KS-1. Population by Age, Sex, Race, and Hispanic Origin

(Number, percent, except where noted.)

Sex, age, race, and Hispanic origin	2010	2020	2022	Percent change, 2010–2022
Total Population...	2,853,118	2,937,847	2,937,150	2.9
Percent of total U.S. population	0.9	0.9	0.9	X
Sex				
Male...	1,415,408	1,476,399	1,475,455	4.2
Female...	1,437,710	1,461,448	1,461,695	1.7
Age				
Under 5 years...	205,492	182,282	175,442	-14.6
Under 18 years...	726,939	704,869	690,832	-5.0
18 to 64 years..	1,750,063	1,755,270	1,742,301	-0.4
65 years and over...	376,116	477,708	504,017	34.0
Median age (years)	36.0	37.1	37.5	4.2
Race and Hispanic Origin				
One race				
White	2,501,057	2,527,422	2,521,658	0.8
Black...	173,298	182,835	182,656	5.4
American Indian and Alaska Native	33,044	35,587	36,176	9.5
Asian	69,628	94,123	94,616	35.9
Native Hawaiian or Other Pacific Islander	2,864	4,019	4,446	55.2
Two or more races..	73,227	93,861	97,598	33.3
Hispanic (of any race)..	300,042	368,613	383,035	27.7

NOTE: Population figures for 2022 are July 1 estimates. The 2010 and 2020 estimates are taken from the respective censuses.
- = Zero or rounds to zero.
X = Not applicable.

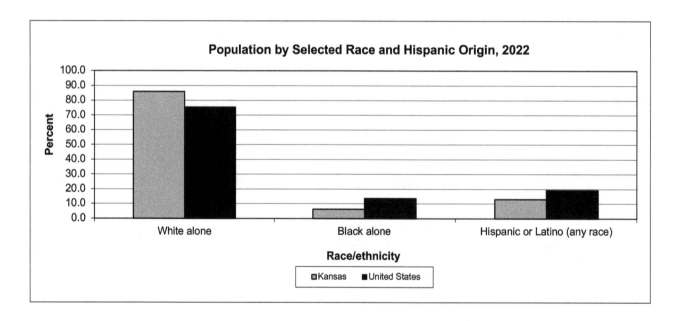

Table KS-2. Marital Status

(Number, percent distribution.)

Sex, age, race, and Hispanic origin	2000	2010	2021
Males, 15 Years and Over	1,025,114	1,106,102	1,174,169
Never married	27.4	31.6	34.1
Now married, except separated..	59.9	53.9	52.3
Separated...	1.1	1.4	1.1
Widowed..	2.3	2.6	2.7
Divorced..	9.2	10.5	9.8
Females, 15 Years and Over	1,075,542	1,145,453	1,180,769
Never married	20.8	25.1	27.2
Now married, except separated..	56.4	51.4	50.5
Separated...	1.3	1.7	1.4
Widowed..	10.6	9.2	8.6
Divorced..	10.9	12.6	12.3

Table KS-3. Households and Housing Characteristics

(Number, percent, dollars.)

Item	2000	2010	2021	Average annual percent change, 2010–2021
Total Households..	1,037,891	1,101,658	1,159,026	0.5
Family households..	701,547	721,592	741,029	0.2
Married-couple family...	567,924	559,199	574,260	0.2
Other family...	133,623	162,393	166,769	0.2
Male householder, no wife present........................	36,962	46,692	53,926	1.4
Female householder, no husband present.................	96,661	115,701	112,843	-0.2
Nonfamily households...	336,344	380,066	417,997	0.9
Householder living alone.....................................	280,387	313,390	347,598	1.0
Householder not living alone................................	55,957	66,676	70,399	0.5
Housing Characteristics				
Total housing units...	1,131,200	1,234,037	1,284,353	0.4
Occupied housing units	1,037,891	1,101,658	1,159,026	0.5
Owner occupied...	718,703	749,907	776,740	0.3
Renter occupied..	319,188	351,751	382,286	0.8
Average household size...	2.51	2.52	2.47	-0.2
Financial Characteristics				
Median gross rent of renter-occupied housing	498	682	904	3.0
Median monthly owner costs for housing units with a mortgage ...	888	1,239	1,446	1.5
Median value of owner-occupied housing units...........	83,500	127,300	183,800	4.0

Table KS-4. Migration, Origin, and Language

(Number, percent.)

Characteristic	State 2021	U.S. 2021
Residence 1 Year Ago		
Population 1 year and over	2,900,594	328,464,538
Same house	84.9	87.2
Different house in the U.S.......................................	14.7	12.3
Same county	7.9	6.7
Different county	6.8	5.7
Same state	3.3	3.3
Different state	3.5	2.4
Abroad..	0.5	0.4
Place of Birth		
Native born	2,732,671	286,623,642
Male..	50.2	49.7
Female...	49.8	50.3
Foreign born	201,911	45,270,103
Male..	51.1	48.7
Female...	48.9	51.3
Foreign born; naturalized U.S. citizen........................	89,402	24,044,083
Male..	47.5	46.4
Female...	52.5	53.6
Foreign born; not a U.S. citizen	112,509	21,226,020
Male..	54.1	51.2
Female...	45.9	48.8
Entered 2010 or later	30.5	28.1
Entered 2000 to 2009	28.2	23.7
Entered before 2000..	41.3	48.2
World Region of Birth, Foreign		
Foreign-born population, excluding population born at sea ...	201,911	45,269,644
Europe...	7.6	10.7
Asia..	29.0	31.0
Africa..	6.8	5.7
Oceania..	0.8	0.6
Latin America..	54.3	50.1
North America...	1.6	1.7
Language Spoken at Home and Ability to Speak English		
Population 5 years and over.....................................	2,757,015	313,232,500
English only	00.4	70.4
Language other than English....................................	11.6	21.6
Speaks English less than "very well"........................	4.6	8.3

Table KS-5. Median Income and Poverty Status, 2021

(Number, percent, except as noted.)

Characteristic	State		U.S.	
	Number	Percent	Number	Percent
Median Income				
Households (dollars)	64,124	X	69,717	X
Families (dollars)	82,637	X	85,806	X
Below Poverty Level (All People)	333,518	11.7	41,393,176	12.8
Sex				
Male	151,137	10.6	18,518,155	11.6
Female	182,381	12.8	22,875,021	13.9
Age				
Under 18 years	92,213	13.4	12,243,219	16.9
Related children under 18 years	88,633	12.9	11,985,424	16.6
18 to 64 years	198,383	11.7	23,526,341	11.9
65 years and over	42,922	9.1	5,623,616	10.3

X = Not applicable.

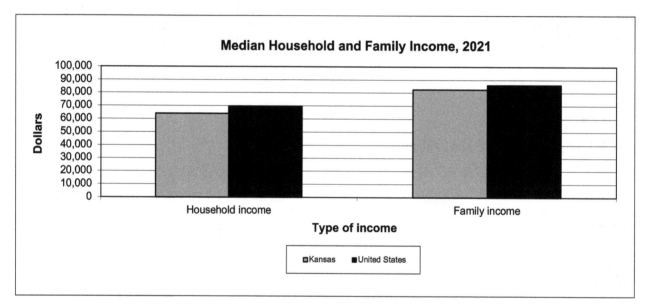

Median Household and Family Income, 2021

Legend: Kansas, United States

Table KS-6. Health Insurance Coverage Status for the Civilian Noninstitutionalized Population and Children Under 19 Years of Age

(Number, percent.)

Item	2011	2012	2013	2014	2015	2016	2017	2018	2019	2020 [2]	2021
Civilian Noninstitutionalized Population	2,813,530	2,825,416	2,836,733	2,845,414	2,850,159	2,850,862	2,855,454	2,854,774	2,851,831	2,853,649	2,878,792
Covered by Private or Public Insurance											
Number	2,458,900	2,469,852	2,488,636	2,553,940	2,589,651	2,601,888	2,606,062	2,604,419	2,589,439	2,604,426	2,615,062
Percent	87.4	87.4	87.7	89.8	90.9	91.3	91.3	91.2	90.8	91.3	90.8
Uninsured											
Number	354,630	355,564	348,097	291,474	260,508	248,974	249,392	250,355	262,392	249,223	263,730
Percent	12.6	12.6	12.3	10.2	9.1	8.7	8.7	8.8	9.2	8.7	9.2
Percent in the U.S. not covered	15.1	14.8	14.5	11.7	9.4	8.6	8.7	8.9	9.2	8.7	8.6
Children Under 19 Years of Age [1]	721,211	719,917	718,934	720,908	718,994	713,102	755,441	746,787	739,651	745,240	745,739
Covered by Private or Public Insurance											
Number	674,866	672,059	674,804	681,497	682,459	682,190	715,965	708,650	696,615	706,959	708,174
Percent	93.6	93.4	93.9	94.5	94.9	95.7	94.8	94.9	94.2	94.9	95.0
Uninsured											
Number	46,345	47,858	44,130	39,411	36,535	30,912	39,476	38,137	43,036	38,281	37,565
Percent	6.4	6.6	6.1	5.5	5.1	4.3	5.2	5.1	5.8	5.1	5.0
Percent in the U.S. not covered	7.5	7.2	7.1	6.0	4.8	4.5	5.0	5.2	5.7	5.2	5.4

[1] Data for years prior to 2017 are for individuals under 18 years of age.
[2] 2020 ACS 5-Year estimates. 1-Year estimates were not released for 2020 due to the impact of COVID-19 on data collection that year. Data is not comparable to previous years, which are based on 1-year estimates.

Table KS-7. Employment Status by Demographic Group, 2022

(Numbers in thousands, percent.)

Characteristic	Civilian noninstitutional population	Civilian labor force		Employed		Unemployed	
		Number	Percent of population	Number	Percent of population	Number	Percent of population
Total...	2,267	1,505	66.4	1,464	64.6	41	2.7
Sex							
Male..	1,116	799	71.6	778	69.8	21	2.6
Female.......................................	1,151	706	61.3	685	59.6	20	2.9
Race, Sex, and Hispanic Origin							
White..	1,964	1,292	65.8	1,259	64.1	34	2.6
Male......................................	964	683	70.9	666	69.1	17	2.5
Female...................................	1,000	609	60.9	593	59.3	17	2.7
Black or African American..............	NA	NA	NA	NA	NA	NA	NA
Male......................................	NA	NA	NA	NA	NA	NA	NA
Female...................................	NA	NA	NA	NA	NA	NA	NA
Hispanic or Latino ethnicity[1]	228	168	73.7	162	71.2	6	3.4
Male......................................	NA	NA	NA	NA	NA	NA	NA
Female...................................	NA	NA	NA	NA	NA	NA	NA
Age							
16 to 19 years...........................	NA	NA	NA	NA	NA	NA	NA
20 to 24 years...........................	181	143	79.1	138	76.2	5	3.7
25 to 34 years...........................	401	347	86.5	337	84.0	10	2.9
35 to 44 years...........................	358	306	85.6	301	84.0	6	1.8
45 to 54 years...........................	318	273	85.7	267	83.9	6	2.2
55 to 64 years...........................	362	261	71.9	257	71.0	3	1.3
65 years and over.......................	NA	NA	NA	NA	NA	NA	NA

NOTE: Data in Table 7 are from the Current Population Survey (CPS) and do not match the estimates in Table 8. See notes and definitions for further information.
[1] May be of any race.

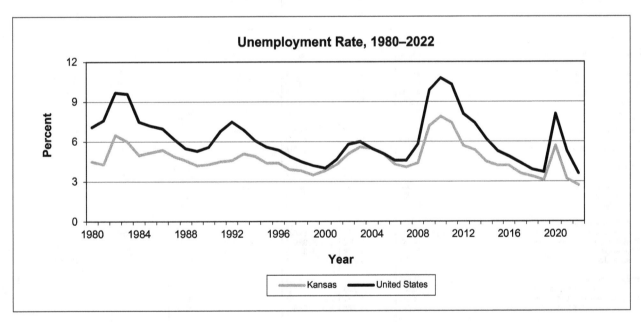

Table KS-8. Employment Status of the Civilian Noninstitutional Population Age 16 Years and Over

(Number, percent.)

Year	Civilian labor force	Civilian participation rate	Employed	Unemployed	Unemployment rate
2010..............................	1,500,463	69.8	1,396,172	104,291	7.0
2011..............................	1,498,000	69.3	1,402,198	95,802	6.4
2012..............................	1,490,808	68.6	1,405,638	85,170	5.7
2013..............................	1,489,395	68.2	1,410,470	78,925	5.3
2014..............................	1,494,203	68.1	1,426,892	67,311	4.5
2015..............................	1,493,782	67.8	1,431,533	62,249	4.2
2016..............................	1,491,961	67.4	1,431,920	60,041	4.0
2017..............................	1,488,346	66.8	1,434,516	53,830	3.6
2018..............................	1,488,027	66.6	1,439,329	48,698	3.3
2019..............................	1,497,517	66.8	1,450,705	46,812	3.1
2020..............................	1,493,706	66.4	1,408,965	84,741	5.7
2021..............................	1,495,665	66.3	1,447,323	48,342	3.2
2022..............................	1,504,932	66.4	1,464,834	40,098	2.7

Table KS-9. Employment and Average Wages by Industry

(Estimates are based on the 2012 North American Industry Classification System [NAICS].)

Industry	2014	2015	2016	2017	2018	2019	2020	2021
	Number of Jobs							
Wage and Salary Employment by Industry.........................	1,471,209	1,481,464	1,480,741	1,479,026	1,497,980	1,509,013	1,445,399	1,468,863
Farm Wage and Salary Employment.................................	11,907	12,622	13,057	12,209	12,664	12,696	14,273	15,140
Nonfarm Wage and Salary Employment............................	1,459,302	1,468,842	1,467,684	1,466,817	1,485,316	1,496,317	1,431,126	1,453,723
Private wage and salary employment.................................	1,162,817	1,173,655	1,176,547	1,176,479	1,187,744	1,196,770	1,138,543	1,159,654
Forestry, fishing, and related activities...........................	4,873	4,946	4,972	4,844	5,016	5,124	4,934	4,507
Mining..	10,397	8,453	6,803	6,703	6,723	6,729	5,805	5,871
Utilities..	7,779	6,751	6,677	6,557	6,363	6,221	6,263	6,083
Construction...	61,255	62,557	62,853	61,666	62,662	65,229	64,711	65,295
Manufacturing...	162,639	161,550	160,402	161,240	164,708	166,848	158,814	160,847
Durable goods manufacturing....................................	98,917	98,142	95,852	94,849	97,762	99,771	92,078	91,728
Nondurable goods manufacturing................................	63,722	63,408	64,550	66,391	66,946	67,077	66,736	69,119
Wholesale trade	61,612	60,459	60,006	60,251	59,748	58,602	56,220	56,091
Retail trade...	147,386	149,623	151,142	148,429	146,802	143,161	137,658	140,398
Transportation and warehousing....................................	49,893	50,656	52,515	55,652	58,631	62,114	62,425	66,955
Information...	27,822	21,004	20,589	19,304	18,658	18,258	16,725	16,907
Finance and insurance	62,461	63,930	63,287	64,110	62,801	64,174	64,391	63,508
Real estate and rental and leasing.................................	14,708	15,414	15,638	15,578	16,251	16,401	15,663	15,704
Professional, scientific, and technical services	67,723	70,277	73,532	73,923	74,885	74,898	73,767	72,980
Management of companies and enterprises........................	18,627	27,605	24,459	25,001	25,610	27,520	22,661	21,484
Administrative and waste services	83,957	82,181	81,524	79,596	80,140	77,950	73,546	78,028
Educational services	21,013	21,120	20,862	21,170	21,263	21,382	19,461	21,139
Health care and social assistance...................................	172,158	177,433	180,201	180,522	183,142	185,958	183,893	183,106
Arts, entertainment, and recreation.................................	16,638	16,432	17,015	17,241	17,519	17,310	13,407	15,145
Accommodation and food services..................................	107,159	110,080	111,220	112,067	112,698	113,431	98,139	105,857
Other services, except public administration......................	64,717	63,184	62,850	62,625	64,124	65,460	60,060	59,749
Government and government enterprises	296,485	295,187	291,137	290,338	297,572	299,547	292,583	294,069
	Dollars							
Average Wages and Salaries by Industry	43,805	45,013	45,361	46,413	47,756	49,218	52,441	54,444
Average Farm Wages and Salaries	40,727	35,122	39,385	36,632	36,446	40,872	30,248	33,194
Average Nonfarm Wages and Salaries	43,830	45,097	45,414	46,494	47,852	49,289	52,662	54,666
Average private wages and salaries.................................	44,747	46,113	46,215	47,413	48,983	50,479	54,515	56,657
Forestry, fishing, and related activities...........................	25,900	27,664	29,592	29,970	31,012	33,104	35,507	38,429
Mining..	59,869	56,546	56,131	55,936	59,427	59,929	58,882	62,623
Utilities..	89,266	91,013	93,697	95,824	102,435	103,040	109,642	108,711
Construction...	50,537	51,819	52,538	53,775	55,739	58,022	60,235	62,024
Manufacturing...	55,328	56,996	57,782	59,548	61,311	61,750	65,308	66,908
Durable goods manufacturing....................................	59,423	60,941	61,125	62,178	63,869	64,477	66,700	68,626
Nondurable goods manufacturing................................	48,971	50,890	52,817	55,791	57,576	57,694	63,388	64,628
Wholesale trade	65,377	66,424	67,079	69,026	72,211	74,781	77,669	82,013
Retail trade...	26,073	27,013	27,461	27,880	28,512	29,284	31,615	33,511
Transportation and warehousing....................................	49,923	50,841	49,755	50,404	51,711	52,802	54,793	54,682
Information...	73,230	62,757	63,733	63,392	65,711	68,919	76,646	83,588
Finance and insurance	69,665	71,941	74,125	75,414	77,463	78,899	86,213	93,182
Real estate and rental and leasing.................................	38,449	40,661	41,516	42,101	43,205	44,941	48,545	51,069
Professional, scientific, and technical services	65,809	68,735	69,406	70,123	71,579	73,515	78,093	83,745
Management of companies and enterprises........................	94,652	105,172	99,034	103,795	107,480	114,219	137,799	128,350
Administrative and waste services	36,741	36,928	37,215	38,426	40,820	42,195	44,663	48,886
Educational services	29,754	30,428	29,731	30,055	31,101	31,549	34,836	33,515
Health care and social assistance...................................	41,531	42,671	42,265	43,473	44,728	46,055	50,986	53,633
Arts, entertainment, and recreation.................................	20,862	21,623	21,620	21,948	23,202	24,044	25,877	27,733
Accommodation and food services..................................	16,695	17,271	17,783	18,388	19,231	19,760	19,560	23,228
Other services, except public administration......................	30,345	32,065	32,862	34,125	35,017	36,087	39,508	41,793
Government and government enterprises............................	40,232	41,060	42,181	42,771	43,339	44,533	45,454	46,814

Table KS-10. Employment Characteristics by Family Type

(Number, percent.)

Family type and labor force status	2019 Total	2019 Families with own children under 18 years	2020 [1] Total	2020 [1] Families with own children under 18 years	2021 Total	2021 Families with own children under 18 years
All Families...	733,489	317,647	737,611	324,122	741,029	323,032
FAMILY TYPE AND LABOR FORCE STATUS						
Opposite-Sex Married-Couple Families...	571,620	223,616	572,332	228,772	571,635	227,414
Both husband and wife in labor force..	55.8	72.7	56.1	71.4	54.9	71.1
Husband in labor force, wife not in labor force	19.9	23.0	20.4	24.5	19.4	23.8
Wife in labor force, husband not in labor force	7.3	2.9	7.2	3.0	8.0	4.1
Both husband and wife not in labor force..................................	16.4	1.1	16.3	1.1	17.7	1.1
Other Families	161,869	94,031	161,461	94,512	166,769	95,113
Female householder, no spouse present.....................................	68.3	70.7	69.2	71.2	67.7	69.8
In labor force..	50.9	60.5	52.7	62.3	52.0	59.6
Not in labor force..	17.4	10.2	16.5	8.9	15.7	10.2
Male householder, no spouse present..	31.7	29.3	30.8	28.8	32.3	30.2
In labor force..	25.6	27.5	25.5	26.9	26.4	28.3
Not in labor force..	6.1	1.9	5.3	1.9	6.0	1.9

[1] 2020 ACS 5-Year estimates. 1-Year estimates were not released for 2020 due to the impact of COVID-19 on data collection that year. Data is not comparable to previous years, which are based on 1-year estimates.

Table KS-11. School Enrollment and Educational Attainment, 2021

(Number, percent.)

Item	State	U.S.
Enrollment		
Total population 3 years and over, enrolled in school	753,828	79,453,524
Enrolled in nursery school or preschool (percent)	6.0	5.2
Enrolled in kindergarten (percent)..	4.9	5.0
Enrolled in elementary school, grades 1-8 (percent)...	42.7	41.3
Enrolled in high school, grades 9-12 (percent)...	21.9	21.8
Enrolled in college or graduate school (percent)...	24.6	26.7
Attainment		
Total population 25 years and over	1,942,133	228,193,464
Less than ninth grade (percent)	3.5	4.8
9th to 12th grade, no diploma (percent)	4.6	5.9
High school graduate, including equivalency (percent)..	25.4	26.3
Some college, no degree (percent)	22.5	19.3
Associate's degree (percent)...	8.6	8.8
Bachelor's degree (percent)	22.0	21.2
Graduate or professional degree (percent)...	13.4	13.8
High school graduate or higher (percent)	91.9	89.4
Bachelor's degree or higher (percent)...	35.4	35.0

Table KS-12. Public School Characteristics and Educational Indicators

(Number, percent; data derived from National Center of Education Statistics.)

Item	State	U.S.
Public Elementary and Secondary Schools		
Number of regular school districts, 2019-20	286	13,349
Number of operational schools, 2019-20...	1,311	98,469
Percent charter schools	0.7	7.7
Total public school enrollment, Fall 2021..	485,424	49,433,092
Percent charter school enrollment	0.6	7.5
Student-teacher ratio, Fall 2019...	13.6	15.9
Expenditures per student (unadjusted dollars), 2019-20	11,960	13,489
Four-year adjusted cohort graduation rate (ACGR), 2019-2020[1]..	88.2	86.5
Students eligible for free or reduced-price lunch (percent), 2019-20..	46.6	52.1
English language learners (percent), Fall 2020	9.2	10.3
Students age 3 to 21 served under IDEA, part B (percent), 2021-22...	16.1	14.7

Public Schools by Type, 2019-20	Number	Percent of state public schools
Total number of schools...	1,311	100.0
Special education..	4	0.3
Vocational education	0	-
Alternative education..	1	0.1

[1] Adjusted Cohort Graduation Rates (ACGR) differ from Averaged Freshmen Graduation Rates (AFGR).
- = Zero or rounds to zero.

Table KS-13. Reported Voting and Registration of the Voting-Age Population, November 2022

(Numbers in thousands, percent.)

Item	Total population	Total citizen population	Registered			Voted		
			Total registered	Percent registered (total population)	Percent registered (total citizen population)	Total voted	Percent voted (total population)	Percent voted (total citizen population)
U.S. Total	255,457	233,546	161,422	63.2	69.1	121,916	47.7	52.2
State Total	2,173	2,087	1,587	73.0	76.1	1,239	57.0	59.4
Sex								
Male	1,081	1,034	762	70.5	73.7	595	55.0	57.5
Female	1,092	1,052	825	75.5	78.4	644	59.0	61.2
Race								
White alone..............................	1,922	1,856	1,412	73.5	76.1	1,097	57.1	59.1
White, non-Hispanic alone	1,775	1,757	1,361	76.7	77.5	1,067	60.1	60.7
Black alone..............................	130	126	89	68.3	70.8	76	58.4	60.5
Asian alone	47	32	28	59.5	87.6	24	50.4	74.3
Hispanic (of any race)...................	179	130	73	40.8	56.3	53	29.5	40.6
White alone or in combination	1,972	1,906	1,454	73.7	76.3	1,123	56.9	58.9
Black alone or in combination....................	153	148	106	69.3	71.5	88	57.6	59.4
Asian alone or in combination....................	49	34	30	61.5	88.5	24	47.9	68.9
Age								
18 to 24 years...........................	268	253	136	50.7	53.6	74	27.7	29.3
25 to 34 years...........................	397	372	255	64.3	68.6	161	40.6	43.3
35 to 44 years...........................	335	321	231	68.9	71.7	177	53.0	55.2
45 to 64 years...........................	687	660	546	79.6	82.7	445	64.9	67.4
65 years and over	487	479	419	86.1	87.4	381	78.3	79.5

B = Base is less than 75,000 and therefore too small to show the derived measure.

Table KS-14. Health Indicators

(Number, rate as indicated in footnotes.)

Item	State	U.S.
Births		
Life Expectancy at Birth (years), 2020	76.4	77.0
Fertility Rate by State[1], 2021..................................	61.0	56.3
Percent Home Births, 2021	1.9	1.4
Cesarean Delivery Rate[2], 2021	29.6	32.1
Preterm Birth Rate[3], 2021	9.8	10.5
Teen Birth Rate[4], 2021	16.3	13.9
Percentage of Babies Born Low Birthweight[5], 2021	7.4	8.5
Deaths[6]		
Heart Disease Mortality Rate, 2021	176.1	173.8
Cancer Mortality Rate, 2021......................................	150.8	146.6
Stroke Mortality Rate, 2021......................................	38.4	41.1
Diabetes Mortality Rate, 2021....................................	25.6	25.4
Influenza/Pneumonia Mortality Rate, 2021	11.1	10.5
Suicide Mortality Rate, 2021.....................................	19.4	14.1
Drug Overdose Mortality Rate, 2021...............................	24.3	33.6
Firearm Injury Mortality Rate, 2021	17.3	14.6
Homicide Mortality Rate, 2021....................................	6.4	8.2
Disease and Illness		
Lifetime Asthma in Adults, 2020 (percent).......................	14.2	13.9
Lifetime Asthma in Children, 2020 (percent)[7]...................	10.7	11.3
Diabetes in Adults, 2020 (percent)..............................	10.0	8.2
Self-reported Obesity in Adults, 2021 (percent).................	36.0	NA

SOURCE: National Center for Health Statistics, National Vital Statistics System 2020 data; https://wonder.cdc.gov.
[1] General fertility rate per 1,000 women aged 15–44.
[2] This represents the percentage of all live births that were cesarean deliveries.
[3] Babies born prior to 37 weeks of pregnancy (gestation).
[4] Number of births per 1,000 females aged 15–19
[5] Babies born weighing less than 2,500 grams or 5 lbs. 8oz.
[6] Death rates are the number of deaths per 100,000 total population.
[7] U.S. total includes data from 30 states and D.C.
NA = Not available.
- = Zero or rounds to zero.

Table KS-15. State Government Finances, 2021

(Dollar amounts in thousands, percent distribution.)

Item	Dollars	Percent distribution
Total Revenue	26,575,714	100.0
General revenue	24,485,238	92.1
Intergovernmental revenue	6,617,130	24.9
Taxes	11,615,757	43.7
General sales	3,767,434	14.2
Selective sales	1,202,695	4.5
License taxes	457,796	1.7
Individual income tax	4,617,143	17.4
Corporate income tax	727,435	2.7
Other taxes	843,254	3.2
Current charges	4,925,592	18.5
Miscellaneous general revenue	1,326,759	5.0
Utility revenue	-	-
Liquor stores revenue	-	-
Insurance trust revenue[1]	2,090,476	7.9
Total Expenditure	24,713,773	100.0
Intergovernmental expenditure	6,105,039	24.7
Direct expenditure	18,608,734	75.3
Current operation	14,137,557	57.2
Capital outlay	1,127,407	4.6
Insurance benefits and repayments	2,953,526	12.0
Assistance and subsidies	258,182	1.0
Interest on debt	132,062	0.5
Exhibit: Salaries and wages	3,369,777	13.6
Total Expenditure	24,713,773	100.0
General expenditure	21,760,247	88.0
Intergovernmental expenditure	6,105,039	24.7
Direct expenditure	15,655,208	63.3
General expenditure, by function:		
Education	8,054,179	32.6
Public welfare	5,419,392	21.9
Hospitals	3,306,026	13.4
Health	606,000	2.5
Highways	1,368,271	5.5
Police protection	138,316	0.6
Correction	431,633	1.7
Natural resources	228,852	0.9
Parks and recreation	45,186	0.2
Governmental administration	701,494	2.8
Interest on general debt	132,062	0.5
Other and unallocable	1,310,652	5.3
Utility expenditure	-	-
Liquor stores expenditure	-	-
Insurance trust expenditure	2,953,526	12.0
Debt at End of Fiscal Year	6,706,015	X
Cash and Security Holdings	34,386,347	X

X = Not applicable.
- = Zero or rounds to zero.
[1] Within insurance trust revenue, net earnings of state retirement systems is a calculated statistic (the item code in the data file is X08), and thus can be positive or negative. Net earnings is the sum of earnings on investments plus gains on investments minus losses on investments. The change made in 2002 for asset valuation from book to market value in accordance with Statement 34 of the Governmental Accounting Standards Board is reflected in the calculated statistics.

Table KS-16. State Government Tax Collections, 2022

(Dollars in thousands, percent.)

Item	Dollars	Percent distribution
Total Taxes	12,592,576	100.0
Property taxes	841,790	6.7
Sales and gross receipts	5,539,663	44.0
General sales and gross receipts	4,269,472	33.9
Selective sales and gross receipts	1,270,191	10.1
Alcoholic beverages	163,962	1.3
Amusements	291	-
Insurance premiums	466,396	3.7
Motor fuels	466,589	3.7
Pari-mutuels	X	-
Public utilities	349	-
Tobacco products	119,585	0.9
Other selective sales	53,019	0.4
Licenses	436,528	3.5
Alcoholic beverages	3,951	-
Amusements	7,704	0.1
Corporations in general	14,870	0.1
Hunting and fishing	34,658	0.3
Motor vehicle	243,464	1.9
Motor vehicle operators	29,748	0.2
Public utilities	6,522	0.1
Occupation and business, NEC	92,717	0.7
Other licenses	2,894	-
Income taxes	5,704,392	45.3
Individual income	4,836,130	38.4
Corporation net income	868,262	6.9
Other taxes	70,203	0.6
Death and gift	X	-
Documentary and stock transfer	X	-
Severance	70,203	0.6
Taxes, NEC	X	-

- = Zero or rounds to zero.

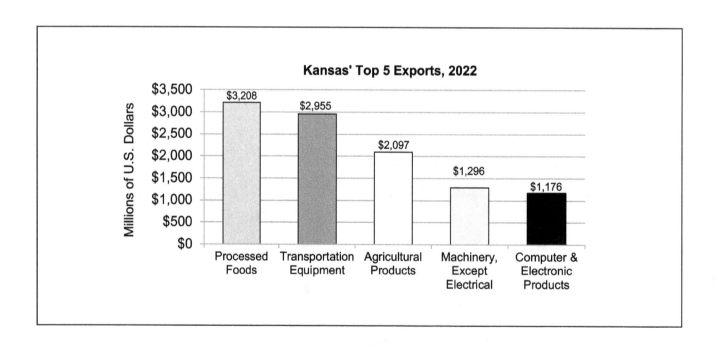

KENTUCKY

Facts and Figures

Location: East central United States; bordered on the N by Illinois, Indiana, and Ohio, on the E by West Virginia and Virginia, on the S by Tennessee, and on the W by Missouri and Illinois

Area: 40,409 sq. mi. (104,659 sq. km.); rank—37th

Population: 4,512,310 (2022 est.); rank—26th

Principal Cities: capital—Frankfort; largest—Lexington

Statehood: June 1, 1792; 15th state

U.S. Congress: 2 senators, 6 representatives

State Motto: United We Stand, Divided We Fall

State Song: "My Old Kentucky Home"

State Nickname: The Bluegrass State

Abbreviations: KY; Ky.

State Symbols: flower—goldenrod; tree—tulip poplar; bird—cardinal

At a Glance

- With an increase in population of 4.0 percent, Kentucky ranked 34th among the states in growth from 2010 to 2022.

- Kentucky ranked 3rd in the nation for drug overdose deaths in 2021, with 55.9 deaths per 100,000 population.

- In 2021, Kentucky's median household income was $55,573, the 7th lowest in the country. The state's poverty level was 16.5 percent, the 5th highest in the country.

- The life expectancy at birth in 2020 in Kentucky was 73.5 years, compared to the national life expectancy of 77.0 years.

- In 2021, 5.7 percent of Kentucky residents did not have health insurance, compared to 8.6 percent of all U.S. residents.

Table KY-1. Population by Age, Sex, Race, and Hispanic Origin

(Number, percent, except where noted.)

Sex, age, race, and Hispanic origin	2010	2020	2022	Percent change, 2010–2022
Total Population...	4,339,367	4,505,893	4,512,310	4.0
Percent of total U.S. population	1.4	1.4	1.4	X
Sex				
Male..	2,134,952	2,238,186	2,240,509	4.9
Female..	2,204,415	2,267,707	2,271,801	3.1
Age				
Under 5 years..	282,367	268,550	262,713	-7.0
Under 18 years..	1,023,371	1,012,760	1,004,575	-1.8
18 to 64 years...	2,737,769	2,736,845	2,714,728	-0.8
65 years and over..	578,227	756,288	793,007	37.1
Median age (years)	38.1	39.1	39.4	3.4
Race and Hispanic Origin				
One race				
White	3,864,193	3,933,939	3,920,114	1.4
Black...	342,804	383,522	391,006	14.1
American Indian and Alaska Native	12,105	13,616	14,509	19.9
Asian...	50,177	75,105	79,374	58.2
Native Hawaiian or Other Pacific Islander	3,199	4,615	5,260	64.4
Two or more races..	66,889	95,096	102,047	52.6
Hispanic (of any race).......................................	132,836	180,589	194,987	46.8

NOTE: Population figures for 2022 are July 1 estimates. The 2010 and 2020 estimates are taken from the respective censuses.
- = Zero or rounds to zero.
X = Not applicable.

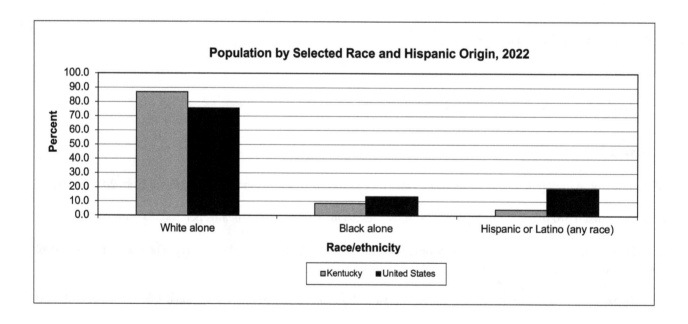

Population by Selected Race and Hispanic Origin, 2022

Table KY-2. Marital Status

(Number, percent distribution.)

Sex, age, race, and Hispanic origin	2000	2010	2021
Males, 15 Years and Over	1,551,174	1,702,020	1,799,395
Never married	25.9	30.8	33.7
Now married, except separated...........................	59.9	52.0	50.1
Separated..	1.5	2.1	1.5
Widowed..	2.6	2.8	3.2
Divorced..	10.2	12.3	11.5
Females, 15 Years and Over	1,665,993	1,794,164	1,873,510
Never married	19.7	24.2	26.3
Now married, except separated...........................	55.0	48.9	48.0
Separated..	2.1	2.6	2.2
Widowed..	11.5	10.6	9.8
Divorced..	11.8	13.7	13.6

Table KY-3. Households and Housing Characteristics

(Number, percent, dollars.)

Item	2000	2010	2021	Average annual percent change, 2010–2021
Total Households.........	1,590,647	1,684,348	1,785,682	0.5
Family households	1,104,398	1,126,685	1,159,532	0.3
Married-couple family	857,944	833,872	850,400	0.2
Other family	246,454	292,813	309,132	0.5
Male householder, no wife present	58,497	76,832	91,550	1.7
Female householder, no husband present	187,957	215,981	217,582	0.1
Nonfamily households	486,249	557,663	626,150	1.1
Householder living alone	414,095	470,103	509,745	0.8
Householder not living alone	72,154	87,560	116,405	3.0
Housing Characteristics				
Total housing units	1,750,927	1,928,617	2,008,227	0.4
Occupied housing units	1,590,647	1,684,348	1,785,682	0.5
Owner occupied	1,125,397	1,156,292	1,225,996	0.5
Renter occupied	465,250	528,056	559,686	0.5
Average household size	2.47	2.51	2.46	-0.2
Financial Characteristics				
Median gross rent of renter-occupied housing	445	613	830	3.2
Median monthly owner costs for housing units with a mortgage	816	1,072	1,227	1.3
Median value of owner-occupied housing units	86,700	121,600	173,300	3.9

Table KY-4. Migration, Origin, and Language

(Number, percent.)

Characteristic	State 2021	U.S. 2021
Residence 1 Year Ago		
Population 1 year and over	4,460,646	328,464,538
Same house	86.9	87.2
Different house in the U.S.	12.8	12.3
Same county	6.8	6.7
Different county	6.0	5.7
Same state	3.6	3.3
Different state	2.4	2.4
Abroad	0.3	0.4
Place of Birth		
Native born	4,327,383	286,623,642
Male	49.4	49.7
Female	50.6	50.3
Foreign born	182,011	45,270,103
Male	50.3	48.7
Female	49.7	51.3
Foreign born; naturalized U.S. citizen	77,493	24,044,083
Male	47.3	46.4
Female	52.7	53.6
Foreign born; not a U.S. citizen	104,518	21,226,020
Male	52.6	51.2
Female	47.4	48.8
Entered 2010 or later	47.3	28.1
Entered 2000 to 2009	25.1	23.7
Entered before 2000	27.6	48.2
World Region of Birth, Foreign		
Foreign-born population, excluding population born at sea	182,011	45,269,644
Europe	14.1	10.7
Asia	31.1	31.0
Africa	14.1	5.7
Oceania	1.6	0.6
Latin America	37.0	50.1
North America	2.1	1.7
Language Spoken at Home and Ability to Speak English		
Population 5 years and over	4,250,116	313,232,500
English only	94.1	78.4
Language other than English	5.9	21.6
Speaks English less than "very well"	2.5	8.3

Table KY-5. Median Income and Poverty Status, 2021

(Number, percent, except as noted.)

Characteristic	State		U.S.	
	Number	Percent	Number	Percent
Median Income				
Households (dollars)..	55,573	X	69,717	X
Families (dollars)	70,060	X	85,806	X
Below Poverty Level (All People)	721,878	16.5	41,393,176	12.8
Sex				
Male	320,389	14.9	18,518,155	11.6
Female	401,489	18.0	22,875,021	13.9
Age				
Under 18 years..	219,560	22.1	12,243,219	16.9
Related children under 18 years..	213,626	21.6	11,985,424	16.6
18 to 64 years...	414,815	15.7	23,526,341	11.9
65 years and over	87,503	11.7	5,623,616	10.3

X = Not applicable.

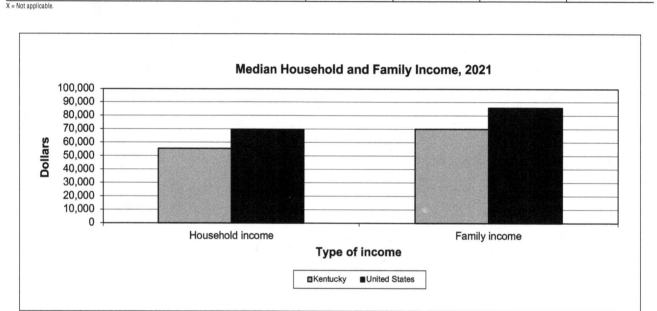

Median Household and Family Income, 2021

Kentucky / United States

Table KY-6. Health Insurance Coverage Status for the Civilian Noninstitutionalized Population and Children Under 19 Years of Age

(Number, percent.)

Item	2011	2012	2013	2014	2015	2016	2017	2018	2019	2020 [2]	2021
Civilian Noninstitutionalized Population	4,284,357	4,292,718	4,312,100	4,328,524	4,342,711	4,354,380	4,370,940	4,388,204	4,384,896	4,379,339	4,428,392
Covered by Private or Public Insurance											
Number..	3,665,899	3,697,258	3,695,652	3,962,462	4,081,243	4,131,030	4,135,713	4,140,563	4,102,333	4,133,261	4,177,605
Percent..	85.6	86.1	85.7	91.5	94.0	94.9	94.6	94.4	93.6	94.4	94.3
Uninsured											
Number..	618,458	595,460	616,448	366,062	261,468	223,350	235,227	247,641	282,563	246,078	250,787
Percent..	14.4	13.9	14.3	8.5	6.0	5.1	5.4	5.6	6.4	5.6	5.7
Percent in the U.S. not covered................	15.1	14.8	14.5	11.7	9.4	8.6	8.7	8.9	9.2	8.7	8.6
Children Under 19 Years of Age[1]	1,022,948	1,016,026	1,012,120	1,012,771	1,008,187	1,009,986	1,078,842	1,066,094	1,058,586	1,065,464	1,072,962
Covered by Private or Public Insurance											
Number..	960,504	959,668	952,590	969,473	965,380	977,991	1,037,936	1,026,070	1,013,495	1,024,009	1,030,272
Percent..	93.9	94.5	94.1	95.7	95.8	96.8	96.2	96.2	95.7	96.1	96.0
Uninsured											
Number..	62,444	56,358	59,530	43,298	42,807	31,995	40,906	40,024	45,091	41,455	42,690
Percent..	6.1	5.5	5.9	4.3	4.2	3.2	3.8	3.8	4.3	3.9	4.0
Percent in the U.S. not covered................	7.5	7.2	7.1	6.0	4.8	4.5	5.0	5.2	5.7	5.2	5.4

[1] Data for years prior to 2017 are for individuals under 18 years of age.
[2] 2020 ACS 5-Year estimates. 1-Year estimates were not released for 2020 due to the impact of COVID-19 on data collection that year. Data is not comparable to previous years, which are based on 1-year estimates.

Table KY-7. Employment Status by Demographic Group, 2022

(Numbers in thousands, percent.)

Characteristic	Civilian noninstitutional population	Civilian labor force		Employed		Unemployed	
		Number	Percent of population	Number	Percent of population	Number	Percent of population
Total...	3,553	2,042	57.5	1,964	55.3	78	3.8
Sex							
Male..	1,728	1,081	62.5	1,048	60.6	33	3.1
Female...	1,825	961	52.6	916	50.2	45	4.6
Race, Sex, and Hispanic Origin							
White...	3,140	1,808	57.6	1,745	55.6	62	3.5
Male..	1,529	955	62.5	928	60.7	27	2.8
Female...	1,611	853	52.9	817	50.7	36	4.2
Black or African American....................	290	170	58.5	160	55.2	10	5.6
Male..	NA	NA	NA	NA	NA	NA	NA
Female...	NA	NA	NA	NA	NA	NA	NA
Hispanic or Latino ethnicity[1]	179	124	69.7	120	67.2	4	3.5
Male..	NA	NA	NA	NA	NA	NA	NA
Female...	NA	NA	NA	NA	NA	NA	NA
Age							
16 to 19 years.................................	262	107	41.0	99	37.7	9	8.0
20 to 24 years.................................	265	193	72.9	181	68.1	13	6.5
25 to 34 years.................................	555	436	78.7	417	75.2	19	4.4
35 to 44 years.................................	562	456	81.2	442	78.5	15	3.2
45 to 54 years.................................	479	366	76.4	356	74.4	10	2.6
55 to 64 years.................................	624	346	55.4	337	54.1	8	2.3
65 years and over.............................	806	137	16.9	132	16.4	5	3.4

NOTE: Data in Table 7 are from the Current Population Survey (CPS) and do not match the estimates in Table 8. See notes and definitions for further information.
[1] May be of any race.
NA = Not available.

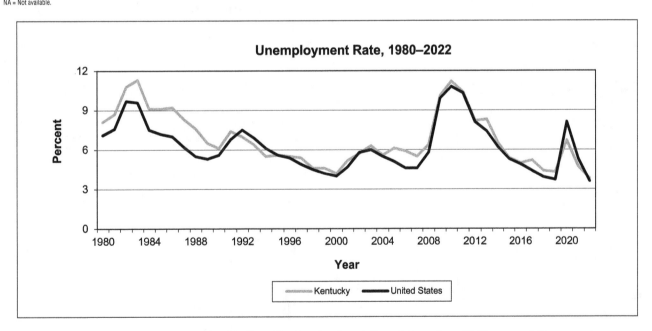

Unemployment Rate, 1980–2022

Table KY-8. Employment Status of the Civilian Noninstitutional Population Age 16 Years and Over

(Number, percent.)

Year	Civilian labor force	Civilian participation rate	Employed	Unemployed	Unemployment rate
2010...................................	2,065,023	61.6	1,852,302	212,721	10.3
2011...................................	2,061,500	61.1	1,868,168	193,332	9.4
2012...................................	2,060,084	60.8	1,891,109	168,975	8.2
2013...................................	2,055,895	60.3	1,892,777	163,118	7.9
2014...................................	2,006,518	58.5	1,877,551	128,967	6.4
2015...................................	1,979,641	57.5	1,876,009	103,632	5.2
2016...................................	2,015,645	58.3	1,914,479	101,166	5.0
2017...................................	2,053,398	58.8	1,955,234	98,164	4.8
2018...................................	2,054,913	58.7	1,968,398	86,515	4.2
2019...................................	2,070,409	58.9	1,986,171	84,238	4.1
2020...................................	2,016,802	57.2	1,886,999	129,803	6.4
2021...................................	2,036,942	57.6	1,941,737	95,205	4.7
2022...................................	2,048,066	57.8	1,968,121	79,945	3.9

Table KY-9. Employment and Average Wages by Industry

(Estimates are based on the 2012 North American Industry Classification System [NAICS].)

Industry	2014	2015	2016	2017	2018	2019	2020	2021
				Number of Jobs				
Wage and Salary Employment by Industry	1,948,724	1,978,345	1,996,627	2,011,592	2,024,711	2,039,331	1,934,420	1,995,684
Farm Wage and Salary Employment	14,615	16,632	13,699	15,865	15,398	15,100	15,098	15,386
Nonfarm Wage and Salary Employment	1,934,109	1,961,713	1,982,928	1,995,727	2,009,313	2,024,231	1,919,322	1,980,298
Private wage and salary employment	1,571,828	1,604,398	1,629,710	1,642,284	1,655,129	1,670,245	1,576,247	1,640,048
Forestry, fishing, and related activities	7,494	7,642	7,676	7,522	7,659	7,952	7,779	7,299
Mining	16,239	13,697	10,269	9,970	10,036	9,794	7,213	7,332
Utilities	6,624	6,569	6,630	6,689	6,782	6,764	6,730	6,817
Construction	74,634	77,693	78,754	79,214	79,817	82,385	79,719	81,196
Manufacturing	235,105	241,530	247,875	250,363	251,511	252,812	236,054	243,335
Durable goods manufacturing	149,467	155,815	161,255	162,396	163,632	164,081	150,667	156,952
Nondurable goods manufacturing	85,638	85,715	86,620	87,967	87,879	88,731	85,387	86,383
Wholesale trade	74,692	74,963	76,045	76,620	75,193	76,175	72,837	74,300
Retail trade	206,292	211,056	215,557	216,755	215,550	211,666	203,439	208,825
Transportation and warehousing	91,110	96,076	100,709	103,806	108,015	112,499	115,553	124,163
Information	26,348	25,234	22,753	22,723	21,980	21,676	20,178	20,760
Finance and insurance	74,966	76,865	77,606	78,109	77,644	77,985	77,932	79,422
Real estate and rental and leasing	18,477	18,904	19,521	19,817	20,091	21,123	20,042	20,713
Professional, scientific, and technical services	72,136	73,925	75,209	74,403	76,922	77,634	77,441	80,840
Management of companies and enterprises	20,674	19,975	20,917	20,127	20,135	20,011	20,150	20,657
Administrative and waste services	119,005	122,984	122,011	120,656	121,679	119,797	111,750	119,136
Educational services	32,688	32,355	31,982	32,246	30,799	31,320	28,247	30,384
Health care and social assistance	231,575	236,804	242,165	246,350	251,536	256,361	248,840	256,466
Arts, entertainment, and recreation	20,657	21,259	22,144	23,239	23,596	24,399	18,801	21,480
Accommodation and food services	162,843	167,682	172,860	175,063	175,632	178,719	148,416	161,134
Other services, except public administration	80,269	79,185	79,027	78,612	80,552	81,173	75,126	75,789
Government and government enterprises	362,281	357,315	353,218	353,443	354,184	353,986	343,075	340,250
				Dollars				
Average Wages and Salaries by Industry	41,801	43,129	43,894	44,855	46,049	47,371	50,235	52,432
Average Farm Wages and Salaries	22,251	16,509	23,002	18,025	19,390	15,202	15,152	14,937
Average Nonfarm Wages and Salaries	41,948	43,355	44,038	45,068	46,253	47,611	50,511	52,723
Average private wages and salaries	41,710	43,154	43,888	44,971	46,226	47,718	50,786	52,943
Forestry, fishing, and related activities	28,264	29,557	31,139	32,106	33,059	35,072	37,909	39,938
Mining	68,621	68,432	66,123	70,065	71,299	71,493	69,301	72,925
Utilities	79,771	82,316	82,806	84,902	88,371	90,299	93,857	96,253
Construction	49,895	51,655	51,748	53,167	53,964	55,599	58,544	59,595
Manufacturing	55,076	56,727	57,098	58,153	59,256	61,176	62,863	64,124
Durable goods manufacturing	56,307	58,260	58,546	59,528	59,859	62,354	62,956	63,602
Nondurable goods manufacturing	52,927	53,940	54,404	55,615	58,134	58,997	62,700	65,071
Wholesale trade	57,413	60,114	60,932	62,489	64,977	66,938	69,944	73,155
Retail trade	25,140	26,006	26,702	27,199	27,829	28,890	31,284	33,266
Transportation and warehousing	50,633	52,110	51,977	53,637	55,120	56,149	58,175	60,253
Information	48,989	48,963	52,807	54,778	54,652	58,579	63,164	66,506
Finance and insurance	63,905	66,598	68,434	71,541	74,641	76,775	82,204	84,755
Real estate and rental and leasing	37,190	38,383	39,440	40,079	41,684	44,619	47,628	50,076
Professional, scientific, and technical services	57,921	60,464	61,523	62,967	64,403	66,765	70,564	72,976
Management of companies and enterprises	91,845	97,259	100,861	102,759	103,048	109,604	108,043	111,969
Administrative and waste services	27,252	28,340	29,978	31,059	32,286	33,743	36,439	39,187
Educational services	24,816	25,708	25,813	26,209	28,719	29,119	32,656	31,058
Health care and social assistance	44,570	46,584	47,347	48,077	49,073	49,991	52,862	56,465
Arts, entertainment, and recreation	23,848	23,492	23,118	23,447	24,686	25,505	30,561	31,093
Accommodation and food services	16,848	17,412	17,968	18,617	19,519	20,095	19,694	23,424
Other services, except public administration	30,997	32,279	33,146	34,407	35,546	36,634	40,116	41,471
Government and government enterprises	42,985	44,256	44,728	45,520	46,377	47,109	49,248	51,664

Table KY-10. Employment Characteristics by Family Type

(Number, percent.)

Family type and labor force status	2019 Total	2019 Families with own children under 18 years	2020 [1] Total	2020 [1] Families with own children under 18 years	2021 Total	2021 Families with own children under 18 years
All Families..........	1,129,276	458,870	1,139,116	467,621	1,159,532	462,946
FAMILY TYPE AND LABOR FORCE STATUS						
Married-Couple Families..........	830,268	300,337	832,608	309,219	842,382	308,491
Both husband and wife in labor force..........	47.6	68.1	49.0	68.6	47.8	68.0
Husband in labor force, wife not in labor force	19.8	23.4	19.8	23.4	20.1	24.3
Wife in labor force, husband not in labor force	9.7	5.1	9.2	4.9	9.2	5.2
Both husband and wife not in labor force..........	22.2	3.2	22.1	3.1	22.9	2.6
Other Families	299,008	158,533	299,896	156,848	309,132	151,964
Female householder, no husband present..........	69.7	69.6	71.1	72.1	70.4	72.6
In labor force..........	43.2	54.7	45.4	57.4	43.4	57.0
Not in labor force..........	26.6	14.9	25.8	14.7	27.0	15.6
Male householder, no wife present..........	30.3	30.4	28.9	27.9	29.6	27.4
In labor force..........	21.7	26.2	20.8	24.3	19.4	22.3
Not in labor force..........	8.5	4.2	8.0	3.6	10.2	5.1

[1] 2020 ACS 5-Year estimates. 1-Year estimates were not released for 2020 due to the impact of COVID-19 on data collection that year. Data is not comparable to previous years, which are based on 1-year estimates.

Table KY-11. School Enrollment and Educational Attainment, 2021

(Number, percent.)

Item	State	U.S.
Enrollment		
Total population 3 years and over, enrolled in school	1,033,023	79,453,524
Enrolled in nursery school or preschool (percent)..........	5.3	5.2
Enrolled in kindergarten (percent)..........	5.4	5.0
Enrolled in elementary school, grades 1-8 (percent)..........	43.1	41.3
Enrolled in high school, grades 9-12 (percent)..........	22.2	21.8
Enrolled in college or graduate school (percent)..........	24	26.7
Attainment		
Total population 25 years and over	3,077,867	228,193,464
Less than ninth grade (percent)..........	4.7	4.8
9th to 12th grade, no diploma (percent)..........	7.4	5.9
High school graduate, including equivalency (percent)..........	32.7	26.3
Some college, no degree (percent)..........	19.3	19.3
Associate's degree (percent)..........	9.0	8.8
Bachelor's degree (percent)	15.9	21.2
Graduate or professional degree (percent)..........	11.1	13.8
High school graduate or higher (percent)	88	89.4
Bachelor's degree or higher (percent)..........	27	35.0

Table KY-12. Public School Characteristics and Educational Indicators

(Number, percent; data derived from National Center of Education Statistics.)

Item	State	U.S.
Public Elementary and Secondary Schools		
Number of regular school districts, 2019-20	172	13,349
Number of operational schools, 2019-20..........	1,535	98,469
Percent charter schools	0.0	7.7
Total public school enrollment, Fall 2021..........	654,239	49,433,092
Percent charter school enrollment	NA	7.5
Student-teacher ratio, Fall 2019	16.4	15.9
Expenditures per student (unadjusted dollars), 2019-20	11,370	13,489
Four-year adjusted cohort graduation rate (ACGR), 2019-2020[1]..........	91.1	86.5
Students eligible for free or reduced-price lunch (percent), 2019-20..........	55.7	52.1
English language learners (percent), Fall 2020	5.0	10.3
Students age 3 to 21 served under IDEA, part B (percent), 2021-22	16.0	14.7

Public Schools by Type, 2019-20	Number	Percent of state public schools
Total number of schools..........	1,535	100.0
Special education..........	10	0.7
Vocational education..........	126	8.2
Alternative education..........	188	12.2

[1] Adjusted Cohort Graduation Rates (ACGR) differ from Averaged Freshmen Graduation Rates (AFGR).
- = Zero or rounds to zero.

Table KY-13. Reported Voting and Registration of the Voting-Age Population, November 2022

(Numbers in thousands, percent.)

Item	Total population	Total citizen population	Registered			Voted		
			Total registered	Percent registered (total population)	Percent registered (total citizen population)	Total voted	Percent voted (total population)	Percent voted (total citizen population)
U.S. Total	255,457	233,546	161,422	63.2	69.1	121,916	47.7	52.2
State Total....................................	3,431	3,233	2,321	67.6	71.8	1,690	49.3	52.3
Sex								
Male	1,670	1,573	1,131	67.7	71.9	834	50.0	53.0
Female	1,761	1,660	1,190	67.6	71.7	856	48.6	51.6
Race								
White alone....................................	3,066	2,912	2,110	68.8	72.4	1,559	50.8	53.5
White, non-Hispanic alone	2,860	2,851	2,083	72.8	73.1	1,547	54.1	54.3
Black alone....................................	286	261	174	60.9	66.6	99	34.7	37.9
Asian alone	42	23	6	15.4	28.5	6	15.4	28.5
Hispanic (of any race)...........................	220	70	36	16.2	51.1	12	5.6	17.7
White alone or in combination	3,104	2,949	2,140	69.0	72.6	1,585	51.1	53.7
Black alone or in combination	299	275	188	62.7	68.3	113	37.7	41.0
Asian alone or in combination..................	52	33	17	32.3	51.3	12	22.6	35.9
Age								
18 to 24 years....................................	376	354	187	49.7	52.8	123	32.7	34.8
25 to 34 years....................................	587	532	322	54.8	60.4	168	28.6	31.6
35 to 44 years....................................	553	475	332	60.1	70.0	221	40.0	46.6
45 to 64 years....................................	1,150	1,112	869	75.5	78.1	683	59.4	61.5
65 years and over	765	761	612	80.0	80.4	494	64.6	65.0

B = Base is less than 75,000 and therefore too small to show the derived measure.

Table KY-14. Health Indicators

(Number, rate as indicated in footnotes.)

Item	State	U.S.
Births		
Life Expectancy at Birth (years), 2020	73.5	77.0
Fertility Rate by State[1], 2021	60.8	56.3
Percent Home Births, 2021	1.9	1.4
Cesarean Delivery Rate[2], 2021	34.7	32.1
Preterm Birth Rate[3], 2021	12.0	10.5
Teen Birth Rate[4], 2021	22.3	13.9
Percentage of Babies Born Low Birthweight[5], 2021	9.1	8.5
Deaths[6]		
Heart Disease Mortality Rate, 2021..	217.5	173.8
Cancer Mortality Rate, 2021...	181.1	146.6
Stroke Mortality Rate, 2021	45.8	41.1
Diabetes Mortality Rate, 2021	32.5	25.4
Influenza/Pneumonia Mortality Rate, 2021	13.8	10.5
Suicide Mortality Rate, 2021	17.9	14.1
Drug Overdose Mortality Rate, 2021..	55.6	33.6
Firearm Injury Mortality Rate, 2021	21.1	14.6
Homicide Mortality Rate, 2021..	9.6	8.2
Disease and Illness		
Lifetime Asthma in Adults, 2020 (percent)..	16.1	13.9
Lifetime Asthma in Children, 2020 (percent)[7]	9.9	11.3
Diabetes in Adults, 2020 (percent)...	11.4	8.2
Self-reported Obesity in Adults, 2021 (percent)..	40.3	NA

SOURCE: National Center for Health Statistics, National Vital Statistics System 2020 data; https://wonder.cdc.gov.
[1] General fertility rate per 1,000 women aged 15–44.
[2] This represents the percentage of all live births that were cesarean deliveries.
[3] Babies born prior to 37 weeks of pregnancy (gestation).
[4] Number of births per 1,000 females aged 15–19
[5] Babies born weighing less than 2,500 grams or 5 lbs. 8oz.
[6] Death rates are the number of deaths per 100,000 total population.
[7] U.S. total includes data from 30 states and D.C.
NA = Not available.
- = Zero or rounds to zero.

Table KY-15. State Government Finances, 2021

(Dollar amounts in thousands, percent distribution.)

Item	Dollars	Percent distribution
Total Revenue	44,566,408	100.0
General revenue	39,004,301	87.5
Intergovernmental revenue	18,058,670	40.5
Taxes	14,617,202	32.8
General sales	4,558,439	10.2
Selective sales	2,529,699	5.7
License taxes	533,047	1.2
Individual income tax	5,212,818	11.7
Corporate income tax	926,075	2.1
Other taxes	857,124	1.9
Current charges	4,819,601	10.8
Miscellaneous general revenue	1,508,828	3.4
Utility revenue	-	-
Liquor stores revenue	-	-
Insurance trust revenue[1]	5,562,107	12.5
Total Expenditure	43,747,754	100.0
Intergovernmental expenditure	5,665,213	12.9
Direct expenditure	38,082,541	87.1
Current operation	28,030,715	64.1
Capital outlay	1,774,538	4.1
Insurance benefits and repayments	6,518,907	14.9
Assistance and subsidies	1,172,605	2.7
Interest on debt	585,776	1.3
Exhibit: Salaries and wages	4,436,244	10.1
Total Expenditure	43,747,754	100.0
General expenditure	37,197,688	85.0
Intergovernmental expenditure	5,665,213	12.9
Direct expenditure	31,532,475	72.1
General expenditure, by function:		
Education	9,971,071	22.8
Public welfare	16,194,371	37.0
Hospitals	2,547,272	5.8
Health	778,249	1.8
Highways	2,100,778	4.8
Police protection	375,960	0.9
Correction	686,497	1.6
Natural resources	471,413	1.1
Parks and recreation	116,809	0.3
Governmental administration	1,466,064	3.4
Interest on general debt	585,776	1.3
Other and unallocable	1,769,335	4.0
Utility expenditure	71,123	0.2
Liquor stores expenditure	-	-
Insurance trust expenditure	6,518,907	14.9
Debt at End of Fiscal Year	15,362,300	X
Cash and Security Holdings	64,191,410	X

X = Not applicable.
- = Zero or rounds to zero.
[1] Within insurance trust revenue, net earnings of state retirement systems is a calculated statistic (the item code in the data file is X08), and thus can be positive or negative. Net earnings is the sum of earnings on investments plus gains on investments minus losses on investments. The change made in 2002 for asset valuation from book to market value in accordance with Statement 34 of the Governmental Accounting Standards Board is reflected in the calculated statistics.

Table KY-16. State Government Tax Collections, 2022

(Dollars in thousands, percent.)

Item	Dollars	Percent distribution
Total Taxes	16,546,544	100.0
Property taxes	725,415	4.4
Sales and gross receipts	7,718,476	46.6
General sales and gross receipts	5,162,018	31.2
Selective sales and gross receipts	2,556,458	15.5
Alcoholic beverages	186,487	1.1
Amusements	136	-
Insurance premiums	179,015	1.1
Motor fuels	728,190	4.4
Pari-mutuels	47,733	0.3
Public utilities	77,310	0.5
Tobacco products	374,873	2.3
Other selective sales	962,714	5.8
Licenses	551,706	3.3
Alcoholic beverages	8,027	-
Amusements	300	-
Corporations in general	121,266	0.7
Hunting and fishing	31,953	0.2
Motor vehicle	224,860	1.4
Motor vehicle operators	28,500	0.2
Public utilities	X	-
Occupation and business, NEC	134,556	0.8
Other licenses	2,244	-
Income taxes	7,349,096	44.4
Individual income	6,180,726	37.4
Corporation net income	1,168,370	7.1
Other taxes	201,851	1.2
Death and gift	82,953	0.5
Documentary and stock transfer	9,879	0.1
Severance	109,019	0.7
Taxes, NEC	0	-

- = Zero or rounds to zero.
X = Not applicable.

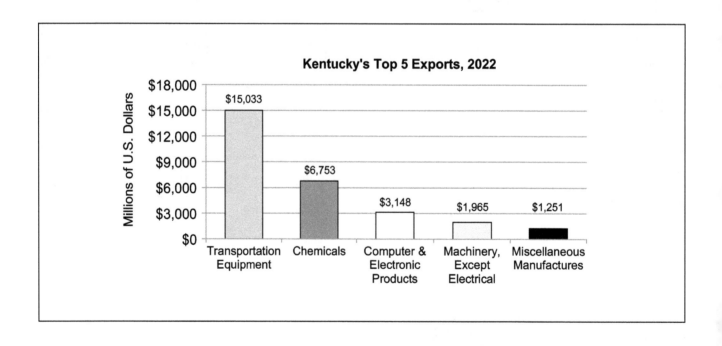

Kentucky's Top 5 Exports, 2022

LOUISIANA

Location: South central United States; bordered on the N by Arkansas, on the E by Mississippi, on the S by the Gulf of Mexico, and on the W by Texas

Area: 51,840 sq. mi. (134,264 sq. km.); rank—31st

Population: 4,590,241 (2022 est.); rank—25th

Principal Cities: capital—Baton Rouge; largest—New Orleans

Statehood: April 30, 1812; 18th state

U.S. Congress: 2 senators, 6 representatives

State Motto: Union, Justice, Confidence

State Song: "Give Me Louisiana"

State Nicknames: The Pelican State; The Bayou State

Abbreviations: LA; La.

State Symbols: flower—magnolia; tree—bald cypress; bird—Eastern brown pelican

At a Glance

- With an increase in population of 1.3 percent, Louisiana ranked 48th in population growth from 2010 to 2022.

- Louisiana's median household income in 2021 was $52,087, the 3rd lowest in the country. Louisiana had the highest poverty rate in the country in 2021, with 19.6 percent of the population living below the poverty level.

- In 2022, Louisiana had the 4th highest percent of residents who self-identified as "Black or African-American Alone," with 32.8 percent of residents in this demographic.

- In 2021, 7.6 percent of Louisiana's population did not have health insurance, which was less than the national rate of 8.6 percent uninsured.

- Louisiana ranked 5th among the states for per capita energy-related CO_2 emissions in 2021, releasing 40.8 metric tons of CO_2 per person, compared to the national average of 14.8 metric tons per capita.

Table LA-1. Population by Age, Sex, Race, and Hispanic Origin

(Number, percent, except where noted.)

Sex, age, race, and Hispanic origin	2010	2020	2022	Percent change, 2010–2022
Total Population..	4,533,372	4,657,749	4,590,241	1.3
Percent of total U.S. population	1.5	1.4	1.4	X
Sex				
Male..	2,219,292	2,284,699	2,247,370	1.3
Female..	2,314,080	2,373,050	2,342,871	1.2
Age				
Under 5 years..	314,260	293,387	280,020	-10.9
Under 18 years..	1,118,015	1,089,507	1,061,693	-5.0
18 to 64 years...	2,857,500	2,823,941	2,748,487	-3.8
65 years and over..	557,857	744,301	780,061	39.8
Median age (years)	35.8	37.6	38.1	6.4
Race and Hispanic Origin				
One race				
White...	2,902,875	2,917,750	2,868,945	-1.2
Black..	1,462,969	1,529,129	1,504,750	2.9
American Indian and Alaska Native	33,037	37,102	38,096	15.3
Asian...	71,829	87,803	88,314	23.0
Native Hawaiian or Other Pacific Islander	2,588	2,946	3,020	16.7
Two or more races...	60,074	83,019	87,116	45.0
Hispanic (of any race)...	192,560	254,689	266,237	38.3

NOTE: Population figures for 2022 are July 1 estimates. The 2010 and 2020 estimates are taken from the respective censuses.
- = Zero or rounds to zero.
X = Not applicable.

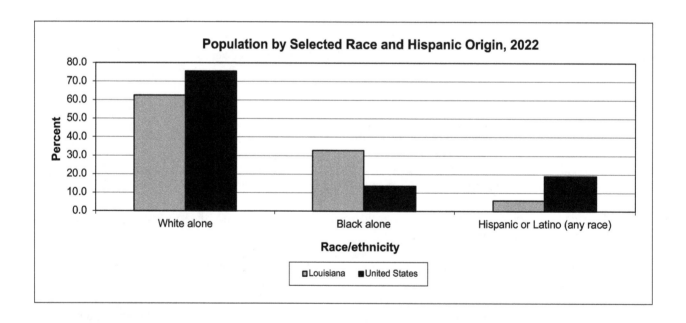

Table LA-2. Marital Status

(Number, percent distribution.)

Sex, age, race, and Hispanic origin	2000	2010	2021
Males, 15 Years and Over	1,648,133	1,751,556	1,804,755
Never married	31.2	37.0	39.2
Now married, except separated..	54.5	47.2	45.2
Separated..	2.2	2.2	1.9
Widowed..	2.8	2.8	3.0
Divorced..	9.2	10.8	10.7
Females, 15 Years and Over	1,828,247	1,861,490	1,921,052
Never married	26.3	30.8	33.7
Now married, except separated..	48.2	42.6	41.9
Separated..	2.9	3.2	2.5
Widowed..	11.5	10.1	9.3
Divorced..	11.1	13.3	12.6

Table LA-3. Households and Housing Characteristics

(Number, percent, dollars.)

Item	2000	2010	2021	Average annual percent change, 2010–2021
Total Households...	1,656,053	1,689,822	1,783,924	0.5
Family households	1,156,438	1,129,117	1,138,131	0.1
Married-couple family	809,498	753,423	756,880	-
Other family	346,940	375,694	381,251	0.1
Male householder, no wife present............................	71,865	79,560	96,044	1.9
Female householder, no husband present...................	275,075	296,134	285,207	-0.3
Nonfamily households	499,615	560,705	645,793	1.4
Householder living alone	419,200	468,853	547,033	1.5
Householder not living alone	80,415	91,852	98,760	0.7
Housing Characteristics				
Total housing units	1,847,181	1,967,947	2,093,387	0.6
Occupied housing units	1,656,053	1,689,822	1,783,924	0.5
Owner occupied	1,125,135	1,141,504	1,200,910	0.5
Renter occupied	530,918	548,318	583,014	0.6
Average household size...	2.62	2.61	2.52	-0.3
Financial Characteristics				
Median gross rent of renter-occupied housing	466	736	924	2.3
Median monthly owner costs for housing units with a mortgage	816	1,163	1,349	1.5
Median value of owner-occupied housing units...................	85,000	137,500	192,800	3.7

- = Zero or rounds to zero.

Table LA-4. Migration, Origin, and Language

(Number, percent.)

Characteristic	State 2021	U.S. 2021
Residence 1 Year Ago		
Population 1 year and over	4,571,302	328,464,538
Same house	87.2	87.2
Different house in the U.S.	12.4	12.3
Same county	7.2	6.7
Different county	5.2	5.7
Same state	3.4	3.3
Different state	1.8	2.4
Abroad	0.4	0.4
Place of Birth		
Native born	4,424,132	286,623,642
Male	48.8	49.7
Female	51.2	50.3
Foreign born	199,915	45,270,103
Male	50.1	48.7
Female	49.9	51.3
Foreign born; naturalized U.S. citizen......................................	82,738	24,044,083
Male...	46.2	46.4
Female	53.8	53.6
Foreign born; not a U.S. citizen	117,177	21,226,020
Male...	52.9	51.2
Female	47.1	48.8
Entered 2010 or later	42.5	28.1
Entered 2000 to 2009	22.7	23.7
Entered before 2000...	34.8	48.2
World Region of Birth, Foreign		
Foreign-born population, excluding population born at sea	199,915	45,269,644
Europe	7.7	10.7
Asia	32.1	31.0
Africa	4.7	5.7
Oceania	0.1	0.6
Latin America	53.8	50.1
North America	1.5	1.7
Language Spoken at Home and Ability to Speak English		
Population 5 years and over..	4,342,089	313,232,500
English only	92.0	70.4
Language other than English..	7.4	21.6
Speaks English less than "very well".....................................	2.7	8.3

Table LA-5. Median Income and Poverty Status, 2021

(Number, percent, except as noted.)

Characteristic	State Number	State Percent	U.S. Number	U.S. Percent
Median Income				
Households (dollars)...	52,087	X	69,717	X
Families (dollars)	67,045	X	85,806	X
Below Poverty Level (All People)	883,236	19.6	41,393,176	12.8
Sex				
Male	383,684	17.6	18,518,155	11.6
Female	499,552	21.5	22,875,021	13.9
Age				
Under 18 years..	287,337	26.9	12,243,219	16.9
Related children under 18 years.........................	285,150	26.7	11,985,424	16.6
18 to 64 years...	490,652	18.3	23,526,341	11.9
65 years and over	105,247	14.1	5,623,616	10.3

X = Not applicable.

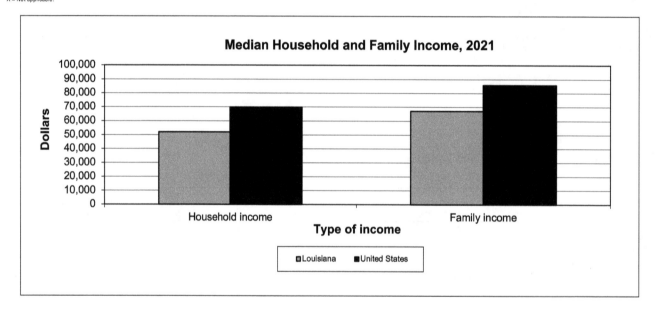

Table LA-6. Health Insurance Coverage Status for the Civilian Noninstitutionalized Population and Children Under 19 Years of Age

(Number, percent.)

Item	2011	2012	2013	2014	2015	2016	2017	2018	2019	2020 [2]	2021
Civilian Noninstitutionalized Population	4,473,068	4,498,884	4,522,910	4,547,572	4,567,431	4,577,182	4,580,258	4,556,078	4,539,690	4,556,953	4,518,319
Covered by Private or Public Insurance											
Number..	3,689,053	3,739,257	3,771,587	3,875,819	4,021,800	4,107,350	4,197,609	4,192,716	4,135,437	4,161,694	4,172,820
Percent..	82.5	83.1	83.4	85.2	88.1	89.7	91.6	92.0	91.1	91.3	92.4
Uninsured											
Number..	784,015	759,627	751,323	671,753	545,631	469,832	382,649	363,362	404,253	395,259	345,499
Percent..	17.5	16.9	16.6	14.8	11.9	10.3	8.4	8.0	8.9	8.7	7.6
Percent in the U.S. not covered...............................	15.1	14.8	14.5	11.7	9.4	8.6	8.7	8.9	9.2	8.7	8.6
Children Under 19 Years of Age[1]	1,117,293	1,117,427	1,110,977	1,112,618	1,114,678	1,115,457	1,175,200	1,160,494	1,148,751	1,154,339	1,138,144
Covered by Private or Public Insurance											
Number..	1,052,658	1,058,356	1,047,665	1,055,087	1,074,755	1,081,831	1,139,133	1,121,290	1,098,713	1,111,075	1,092,673
Percent..	94.2	94.7	94.3	94.8	96.4	97.0	96.9	96.6	95.6	96.3	96.0
Uninsured											
Number..	64,635	59,071	63,312	57,531	39,923	33,626	36,067	39,204	50,038	43,264	45,471
Percent..	5.8	5.3	5.7	5.2	3.6	3.0	3.1	3.4	4.4	3.7	4.0
Percent in the U.S. not covered...............................	7.5	7.2	7.1	6.0	4.8	4.5	5.0	5.2	5.7	5.2	5.4

[1] Data for years prior to 2017 are for individuals under 18 years of age.
[2] 2020 ACS 5-Year estimates. 1-Year estimates were not released for 2020 due to the impact of COVID-19 on data collection that year. Data is not comparable to previous years, which are based on 1-year estimates.

Table LA-7. Employment Status by Demographic Group, 2022

(Numbers in thousands, percent.)

Characteristic	Civilian noninstitutional population	Civilian labor force		Employed		Unemployed	
		Number	Percent of population	Number	Percent of population	Number	Percent of population
Total..	3,571	2,088	58.5	2,013	56.4	75	3.6
Sex							
Male..	1,701	1,079	63.4	1,037	61.0	42	3.8
Female....................................	1,870	1,010	54.0	976	52.2	34	3.3
Race, Sex, and Hispanic Origin							
White......................................	2,291	1,358	59.2	1,322	57.7	36	2.7
Male....................................	1,124	738	65.6	717	63.8	20	2.7
Female................................	1,168	620	53.1	604	51.7	16	2.5
Black or African American.........	1,127	638	56.6	601	53.3	37	5.8
Male....................................	506	291	57.5	271	53.5	20	6.9
Female................................	621	347	55.9	330	53.2	17	4.8
Hispanic or Latino ethnicity[1]...	210	140	66.6	134	63.7	6	4.3
Male....................................	110	88	80.5	84	76.7	4	4.6
Female................................	NA	NA	NA	NA	NA	NA	NA
Age							
16 to 19 years.........................	234	82	35.3	74	31.7	8	10.1
20 to 24 years.........................	267	176	66.1	167	62.8	9	5.1
25 to 34 years.........................	632	503	79.5	483	76.5	19	3.8
35 to 44 years.........................	574	457	79.6	439	76.6	17	3.8
45 to 54 years.........................	528	385	72.8	375	71.0	10	2.5
55 to 64 years.........................	572	324	56.7	319	55.7	6	1.7
65 years and over....................	765	162	21.1	156	20.4	6	3.5

NOTE: Data in Table 7 are from the Current Population Survey (CPS) and do not match the estimates in Table 8. See notes and definitions for further information.
[1] May be of any race.

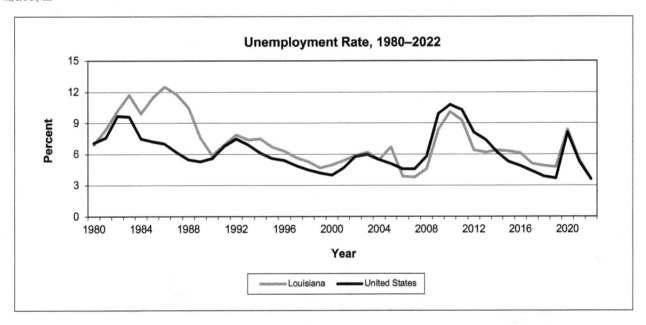

Table LA-8. Employment Status of the Civilian Noninstitutional Population Age 16 Years and Over

(Number, percent.)

Year	Civilian labor force	Civilian participation rate	Employed	Unemployed	Unemployment rate
2010..	2,084,462	60.6	1,927,720	156,742	7.5
2011..	2,080,525	59.8	1,926,038	154,487	7.4
2012..	2,089,644	59.7	1,948,630	141,014	6.7
2013..	2,101,974	59.6	1,966,755	135,219	6.4
2014..	2,141,519	60.4	2,007,668	133,851	6.3
2015..	2,150,050	60.3	2,015,081	134,969	6.3
2016..	2,123,690	59.3	1,994,639	129,051	6.1
2017..	2,108,485	58.8	2,000,487	107,998	5.1
2018..	2,112,495	58.9	2,010,719	101,776	4.8
2019..	2,108,410	58.8	2,010,405	98,005	4.6
2020..	2,062,175	57.6	1,882,665	179,510	8.7
2021..	2,062,492	57.8	1,949,403	113,089	5.5
2022..	2,088,217	58.7	2,011,867	76,350	3.7

Table LA-9. Employment and Average Wages by Industry

(Estimates are based on the 2012 North American Industry Classification System [NAICS].)

Industry	2014	2015	2016	2017	2018	2019	2020	2021
	Number of Jobs							
Wage and Salary Employment by Industry	2,066,426	2,074,947	2,048,289	2,044,106	2,063,260	2,062,866	1,912,917	1,949,233
Farm Wage and Salary Employment	6,186	8,839	7,889	8,873	8,844	9,063	7,213	9,611
Nonfarm Wage and Salary Employment	2,060,240	2,066,108	2,040,400	2,035,233	2,054,416	2,053,803	1,905,704	1,939,622
Private wage and salary employment	1,694,081	1,703,916	1,680,979	1,677,702	1,694,401	1,694,786	1,556,485	1,594,838
Forestry, fishing, and related activities	7,301	7,323	7,371	7,079	7,166	7,365	7,050	6,565
Mining	50,921	44,887	35,578	32,369	34,137	34,740	28,769	27,464
Utilities	8,838	8,606	8,442	8,487	8,692	8,605	8,677	8,576
Construction	142,781	144,369	143,671	150,707	155,783	145,480	124,582	129,763
Manufacturing	147,286	143,922	135,936	134,813	135,589	137,786	131,541	129,087
Durable goods manufacturing	77,252	73,206	65,135	63,599	63,603	65,419	60,815	59,291
Nondurable goods manufacturing	70,034	70,716	70,801	71,214	71,986	72,367	70,726	69,796
Wholesale trade	73,774	72,620	70,785	69,877	69,792	69,308	65,603	65,226
Retail trade	228,572	234,486	236,483	233,064	228,940	224,611	214,958	220,665
Transportation and warehousing	80,813	80,318	74,609	73,039	75,994	78,915	74,392	74,411
Information	26,099	26,756	23,668	22,917	22,865	22,454	18,705	20,899
Finance and insurance	61,150	60,897	61,030	61,345	60,319	60,174	59,609	58,601
Real estate and rental and leasing	32,488	31,900	30,773	30,020	30,677	31,304	28,626	28,967
Professional, scientific, and technical services	89,156	89,874	87,375	87,347	88,764	90,506	87,266	90,281
Management of companies and enterprises	25,220	23,716	23,372	23,543	22,468	22,305	20,903	21,272
Administrative and waste services	100,015	101,498	100,804	100,190	103,574	104,629	97,711	102,809
Educational services	43,269	44,070	44,700	44,975	44,030	45,291	42,420	49,487
Health care and social assistance	256,461	261,494	267,282	269,971	271,972	275,917	268,049	272,493
Arts, entertainment, and recreation	31,221	30,565	29,819	30,004	29,371	29,693	22,200	22,537
Accommodation and food services	191,715	199,015	203,324	204,593	208,453	208,820	167,513	178,011
Other services, except public administration	97,001	97,600	95,957	93,362	95,815	96,883	87,911	87,724
Government and government enterprises	366,159	362,192	359,421	357,531	360,015	359,017	349,219	344,784
	Dollars							
Average Wages and Salaries by Industry	46,186	46,833	46,684	47,645	49,294	50,427	53,218	54,833
Average Farm Wages and Salaries	20,814	21,564	19,807	17,157	18,455	13,103	15,363	15,419
Average Nonfarm Wages and Salaries	46,262	46,941	46,788	47,778	49,426	50,592	53,361	55,029
Average private wages and salaries	46,801	47,441	47,117	48,140	49,847	51,047	53,882	55,630
Forestry, fishing, and related activities	36,254	36,193	38,268	39,337	42,069	42,208	44,619	46,448
Mining	95,698	95,943	94,793	93,516	97,341	101,280	102,098	101,838
Utilities	84,563	87,825	88,130	91,684	94,704	97,217	105,912	107,019
Construction	56,620	58,684	60,537	62,713	64,860	66,009	66,612	68,135
Manufacturing	69,388	71,444	72,816	74,772	78,083	79,805	80,647	83,177
Durable goods manufacturing	60,885	60,902	60,435	62,618	64,798	65,801	65,357	67,806
Nondurable goods manufacturing	78,768	82,357	84,207	85,627	89,821	92,464	93,795	96,235
Wholesale trade	63,252	64,206	63,641	65,421	67,820	70,352	73,259	76,628
Retail trade	27,388	27,991	28,197	28,823	29,400	30,140	32,516	34,744
Transportation and warehousing	64,640	63,532	60,855	60,990	61,391	62,589	65,116	66,332
Information	52,546	53,560	55,040	57,467	60,621	63,098	68,913	71,290
Finance and insurance	65,880	66,183	67,369	69,275	72,864	73,622	81,155	83,045
Real estate and rental and leasing	50,114	49,381	47,632	48,999	51,241	52,623	53,747	55,347
Professional, scientific, and technical services	68,199	69,956	68,919	70,296	72,344	73,798	75,814	76,198
Management of companies and enterprises	78,501	81,133	83,247	86,760	87,023	87,651	93,238	98,641
Administrative and waste services	36,807	38,452	37,464	38,200	39,848	40,827	43,272	46,312
Educational services	34,902	35,099	36,045	36,065	38,837	39,217	45,104	40,378
Health care and social assistance	41,189	42,843	43,304	43,977	45,020	46,531	50,304	53,125
Arts, entertainment, and recreation	34,571	36,219	37,456	38,079	41,238	42,821	47,713	51,065
Accommodation and food services	20,380	20,944	21,063	21,532	22,390	22,697	21,752	25,165
Other services, except public administration	32,111	33,273	34,236	35,510	36,562	37,552	40,838	42,392
Government and government enterprises	43,770	44,586	45,249	46,079	47,446	48,442	51,039	52,247

Table LA-10. Employment Characteristics by Family Type

(Number, percent.)

Family type and labor force status	2019 Total	2019 Families with own children under 18 years	2020 [1] Total	2020 [1] Families with own children under 18 years	2021 Total	2021 Families with own children under 18 years
All Families..	1,113,831	457,978	1,116,752	469,595	1,138,131	469,336
FAMILY TYPE AND LABOR FORCE STATUS						
Opposite-Sex Married-Couple Families...........................	737,222	263,834	753,924	280,608	749,638	272,640
Both husband and wife in labor force........................	47.3	68.5	48.0	67.5	47.8	67.9
Husband in labor force, wife not in labor force	23.0	25.6	22.9	25.9	22.3	24.2
Wife in labor force, husband not in labor force	8.2	3.8	8.4	4.5	8.7	5.5
Both husband and wife not in labor force.....................	20.8	1.7	20.6	2.1	21.2	2.4
Other Families	376,609	194,144	356,813	187,494	381,251	195,645
Female householder, no spouse present.....................	75.7	78.6	76.0	77.7	74.8	76.4
In labor force...	48.9	62.0	49.9	62.4	47.9	61.2
Not in labor force	26.8	16.6	26.0	15.3	26.9	15.2
Male householder, no spouse present...........................	24.3	21.4	24.0	22.3	25.2	23.6
In labor force...	16.5	18.7	16.9	18.7	17.5	20.3
Not in labor force	7.8	2.7	7.2	3.6	7.7	3.2

[1] 2020 ACS 5-Year estimates. 1-Year estimates were not released for 2020 due to the impact of COVID-19 on data collection that year. Data is not comparable to previous years, which are based on 1-year estimates.

Table LA-11. School Enrollment and Educational Attainment, 2021

(Number, percent.)

Item	State	U.S.
Enrollment		
Total population 3 years and over, enrolled in school	1,119,445	79,453,524
Enrolled in nursery school or preschool (percent)..	6.1	5.2
Enrolled in kindergarten (percent)..	5.1	5.0
Enrolled in elementary school, grades 1-8 (percent)...	43.9	41.3
Enrolled in high school, grades 9-12 (percent)...	21.5	21.8
Enrolled in college or graduate school (percent)...	23.5	26.7
Attainment		
Total population 25 years and over	3,117,186	228,193,464
Less than ninth grade (percent)...	4.3	4.8
9th to 12th grade, no diploma (percent)	9.0	5.9
High school graduate, including equivalency (percent)...	32.8	26.3
Some college, no degree (percent)...	20.6	19.3
Associate's degree (percent)..	6.8	8.8
Bachelor's degree (percent)...	16.8	21.2
Graduate or professional degree (percent)...	9.7	13.8
High school graduate or higher (percent)..	86.7	89.4
Bachelor's degree or higher (percent)...	26.4	35.0

Table LA-12. Public School Characteristics and Educational Indicators

(Number, percent; data derived from National Center of Education Statistics.)

Item	State	U.S.
Public Elementary and Secondary Schools		
Number of regular school districts, 2019-20	72	13,349
Number of operational schools, 2019-20...	1,363	98,469
Percent charter schools	10.7	7.7
Total public school enrollment, Fall 2021..	683,216	49,433,092
Percent charter school enrollment	12.7	7.5
Student-teacher ratio, Fall 2019	18.4	15.9
Expenditures per student (unadjusted dollars), 2019-20	12,009	13,489
Four-year adjusted cohort graduation rate (ACGR), 2019-2020[1].......................................	82.9	86.5
Students eligible for free or reduced-price lunch (percent), 2019-20................................	56.8	52.1
English language learners (percent), Fall 2020	4.1	10.3
Students age 3 to 21 served under IDEA, part B (percent), 2021-22	12.6	14.7

Public Schools by Type, 2019-20	Number	Percent of state public schools
Total number of schools...	1,363	100.0
Special education	29	2.1
Vocational education	10	0.7
Alternative education..	6	0.4

[1] Adjusted Cohort Graduation Rates (ACGR) differ from Averaged Freshmen Graduation Rates (AFGR).

Table LA-13. Reported Voting and Registration of the Voting-Age Population, November 2022

(Numbers in thousands, percent.)

Item	Total population	Total citizen population	Registered			Voted		
			Total registered	Percent registered (total population)	Percent registered (total citizen population)	Total voted	Percent voted (total population)	Percent voted (total citizen population)
U.S. Total	255,457	233,546	161,422	63.2	69.1	121,916	47.7	52.2
State Total	3,437	3,263	2,215	64.4	67.9	1,574	45.8	48.2
Sex								
Male	1,629	1,535	1,012	62.1	65.9	726	44.6	47.3
Female	1,808	1,729	1,203	66.5	69.6	848	46.9	49.0
Race								
White alone........................	2,222	2,086	1,471	66.2	70.5	1,021	46.0	49.0
White, non-Hispanic alone........................	2,012	1,990	1,420	70.6	71.4	994	49.4	50.0
Black alone........................	1,065	1,044	659	61.9	63.1	515	48.4	49.4
Asian alone........................	55	48	16	28.9	33.3	8	14.9	17.1
Hispanic (of any race)	250	112	58	23.4	52.1	30	12.0	26.6
White alone or in combination	2,272	2,129	1,506	66.3	70.7	1,034	45.5	48.6
Black alone or in combination........................	1,093	1,071	685	62.7	63.9	526	48.2	49.1
Asian alone or in combination........................	68	60	28	42.1	47.2	8	12.1	13.6
Age								
18 to 24 years........................	349	333	144	41.3	43.2	80	23.1	24.2
25 to 34 years........................	607	564	352	58.0	62.4	195	32.0	34.5
35 to 44 years........................	608	558	375	61.6	67.1	244	40.2	43.8
45 to 64 years........................	1,138	1,082	801	70.4	74.1	601	52.8	55.5
65 years and over	736	727	543	73.7	74.7	454	61.6	62.4

B = Base is less than 75,000 and therefore too small to show the derived measure.

Table LA-14. Health Indicators

(Number, rate as indicated in footnotes.)

Item	State	U.S.
Births		
Life Expectancy at Birth (years), 2020	73.1	77.0
Fertility Rate by State[1], 2021........................	62.7	56.3
Percent Home Births, 2021........................	0.3	1.4
Cesarean Delivery Rate[2], 2021........................	37.1	32.1
Preterm Birth Rate[3], 2021........................	13.5	10.5
Teen Birth Rate[4], 2021........................	24.5	13.9
Percentage of Babies Born Low Birthweight[5], 2021........................	11.3	8.5
Deaths[6]		
Heart Disease Mortality Rate, 2021........................	235.5	173.8
Cancer Mortality Rate, 2021........................	163.9	146.6
Stroke Mortality Rate, 2021........................	52.0	41.1
Diabetes Mortality Rate, 2021........................	35.7	25.4
Influenza/Pneumonia Mortality Rate, 2021	12.2	10.5
Suicide Mortality Rate, 2021........................	14.8	14.1
Drug Overdose Mortality Rate, 2021........................	55.9	33.6
Firearm Injury Mortality Rate, 2021........................	29.1	14.6
Homicide Mortality Rate, 2021........................	21.3	8.2
Disease and Illness		
Lifetime Asthma in Adults, 2020 (percent)........................	14.1	13.9
Lifetime Asthma in Children, 2020 (percent)[7]	NA	11.3
Diabetes in Adults, 2020 (percent)........................	12.7	8.2
Self-reported Obesity in Adults, 2021 (percent)........................	38.6	NA

SOURCE: National Center for Health Statistics, National Vital Statistics System 2020 data; https://wonder.cdc.gov.
[1] General fertility rate per 1,000 women aged 15–44.
[2] This represents the percentage of all live births that were cesarean deliveries.
[3] Babies born prior to 37 weeks of pregnancy (gestation).
[4] Number of births per 1,000 females aged 15–19
[5] Babies born weighing less than 2,500 grams or 5 lbs. 8oz.
[6] Death rates are the number of deaths per 100,000 total population.
[7] U.S. total includes data from 30 states and D.C.
NA = Not available.
- = Zero or rounds to zero.

Table LA-15. State Government Finances, 2021

(Dollar amounts in thousands, percent distribution.)

Item	Dollars	Percent distribution
Total Revenue	43,362,871	100.0
General revenue	37,907,510	87.4
Intergovernmental revenue	20,913,908	48.2
Taxes	12,257,234	28.3
General sales	4,048,616	9.3
Selective sales	2,804,897	6.5
License taxes	477,174	1.1
Individual income tax	3,933,108	9.1
Corporate income tax	587,747	1.4
Other taxes	405,692	0.9
Current charges	2,296,339	5.3
Miscellaneous general revenue	2,440,029	5.6
Utility revenue	14,824	-
Liquor stores revenue	-	-
Insurance trust revenue[1]	5,440,537	12.5
Total Expenditure	44,147,286	100.0
Intergovernmental expenditure	8,117,842	18.4
Direct expenditure	36,029,444	81.6
Current operation	25,196,233	57.1
Capital outlay	2,403,444	5.4
Insurance benefits and repayments	6,687,124	15.1
Assistance and subsidies	939,192	2.1
Interest on debt	803,451	1.8
Exhibit: Salaries and wages	4,429,653	10.0
Total Expenditure	44,147,286	100.0
General expenditure	37,448,880	84.8
Intergovernmental expenditure	8,117,842	18.4
Direct expenditure	29,331,038	66.4
General expenditure, by function:		
Education	10,802,383	24.5
Public welfare	14,650,317	33.2
Hospitals	468,374	1.1
Health	761,841	1.7
Highways	1,748,523	4.0
Police protection	501,318	1.1
Correction	823,107	1.9
Natural resources	951,684	2.2
Parks and recreation	373,512	0.8
Governmental administration	1,007,937	2.3
Interest on general debt	803,451	1.8
Other and unallocable	4,449,190	10.1
Utility expenditure	11,282	-
Liquor stores expenditure	-	-
Insurance trust expenditure	6,687,124	15.1
Debt at End of Fiscal Year	16,982,504	X
Cash and Security Holdings	91,147,404	X

X = Not applicable.
- = Zero or rounds to zero.
[1] Within insurance trust revenue, net earnings of state retirement systems is a calculated statistic (the item code in the data file is X08), and thus can be positive or negative. Net earnings is the sum of earnings on investments plus gains on investments minus losses on investments. The change made in 2002 for asset valuation from book to market value in accordance with Statement 34 of the Governmental Accounting Standards Board is reflected in the calculated statistics.

Table LA-16. State Government Tax Collections, 2022

(Dollars in thousands, percent.)

Item	Dollars	Percent distribution
Total Taxes	14,484,028	100.0
Property taxes	94,860	0.7
Sales and gross receipts	7,741,107	53.4
General sales and gross receipts	4,748,279	32.8
Selective sales and gross receipts	2,992,828	20.7
Alcoholic beverages	79,331	0.5
Amusements	760,972	5.3
Insurance premiums	1,080,293	7.5
Motor fuels	650,966	4.5
Pari-mutuels	5,727	-
Public utilities	11,299	0.1
Tobacco products	258,537	1.8
Other selective sales	145,703	1.0
Licenses	638,392	4.4
Alcoholic beverages	0	-
Amusements	X	-
Corporations in general	389,642	2.7
Hunting and fishing	34,505	0.2
Motor vehicle	80,086	0.6
Motor vehicle operators	11,775	0.1
Public utilities	7,406	0.1
Occupation and business, NEC	109,448	0.8
Other licenses	5,530	-
Income taxes	5,518,637	38.1
Individual income	4,478,708	30.9
Corporation net income	1,039,929	7.2
Other taxes	491,032	3.4
Death and gift	0	-
Documentary and stock transfer	X	-
Severance	491,032	3.4
Taxes, NEC	X	-

- = Zero or rounds to zero.
X = Not applicable.

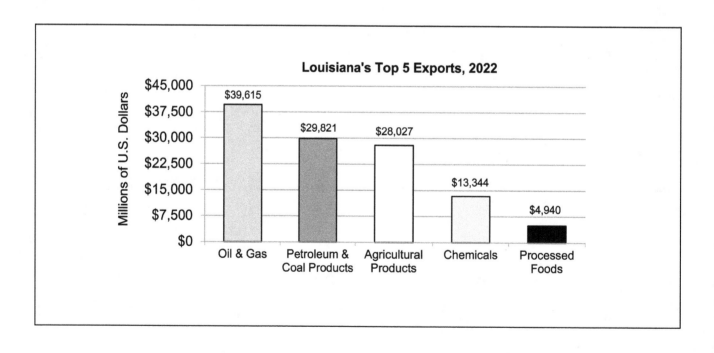

MAINE

Facts and Figures

Location: Northeast corner of the United States; bordered on the N and E by New Brunswick, Canada; on the S by the Atlantic Ocean; on the W by New Hampshire; and on the NW by Quebec, Canada

Area: 35,385 sq. mi. (91,646 sq. km.); rank—39th

Population: 1,385,340 (2022 est.); rank—42nd

Principal Cities: capital—Augusta; largest—Portland

Statehood: March 15, 1820; 23rd state

U.S. Congress: 2 senators, 2 representatives

State Motto: *Dirigo* ("I lead")

State Song: "State of Maine Song"

State Nickname: The Pine Tree State

Abbreviations: ME; Me.

State Symbols: flower—white pinecone and tassel; tree—Eastern white pine; bird—chickadee

At a Glance

- With a population that grew 4.3 percent, Maine ranked 33rd among the states in growth from 2010 to 2022.

- Maine had the highest percent of residents who self-identified as "White alone" in 2022, with 93.9 percent of its residents in this demographic.

- Maine was the state with the lowest percent of its population who identified as "Hispanic or Latino" in 2022, with just 1.8 percent of residents in this demographic.

- In 2022, Maine was the state with the highest percent of its population in the 65 years and over age group (22.5 percent).

- Maine's drug overdose rate of 42.8 per 100,000 population ranked 11th among the states in 2021.

Table ME-1. Population by Age, Sex, Race, and Hispanic Origin

(Number, percent, except where noted.)

Sex, age, race, and Hispanic origin	2010	2020	2022	Percent change, 2010–2022
Total Population..	1,328,361	1,362,341	1,385,340	4.3
Percent of total U.S. population	0.4	0.4	0.4	X
Sex				
Male...	650,056	672,648	683,232	5.1
Female...	678,305	689,693	702,108	3.5
Age				
Under 5 years..	69,520	63,145	61,744	-11.2
Under 18 years...	274,533	251,612	247,898	-9.7
18 to 64 years..	842,748	820,235	825,218	-2.1
65 years and over..	211,080	290,494	312,224	47.9
Median age (years)	42.7	44.9	44.8	4.9
Race and Hispanic Origin				
One race				
White	1,269,764	1,285,049	1,301,207	2.5
Black...	16,269	23,876	27,405	68.4
American Indian and Alaska Native...............................	8,771	9,601	9,786	11.6
Asian...	13,783	18,010	19,143	38.9
Native Hawaiian or Other Pacific Islander	377	512	561	48.8
Two or more races..	19,397	25,293	27,238	40.4
Hispanic (of any race)...	16,935	25,414	28,986	71.2

NOTE: Population figures for 2022 are July 1 estimates. The 2010 and 2020 estimates are taken from the respective censuses.
- = Zero or rounds to zero.
X = Not applicable.

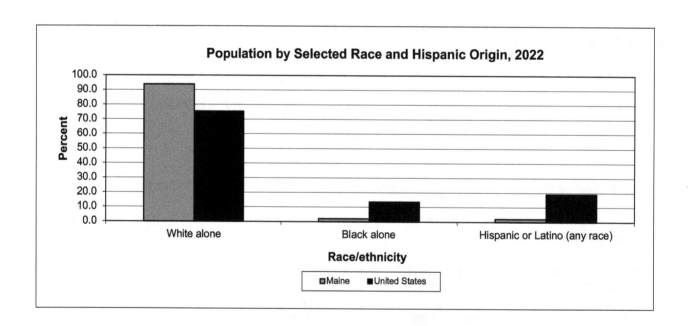

Table ME-2. Marital Status

(Number, percent distribution.)

Sex, age, race, and Hispanic origin	2000	2010	2021
Males, 15 Years and Over	494,217	534,474	569,783
Never married	26.8	31.0	31.0
Now married, except separated...	58.8	52.5	53.3
Separated..	1.1	1.2	0.8
Widowed..	2.8	2.9	2.8
Divorced...	10.5	12.5	12.0
Females, 15 Years and Over	534,606	570,281	599,100
Never married	21.2	24.2	26.3
Now married, except separated...	54.1	49.3	50.0
Separated..	1.3	1.6	0.9
Widowed..	11.0	9.9	8.6
Divorced...	12.4	15.0	14.2

Table ME-3. Households and Housing Characteristics

(Number, percent, dollars.)

Item	2000	2010	2021	Average annual percent change, 2010–2021
Total Households..	518,200	545,417	593,626	0.8
Family households	340,685	345,328	365,226	0.5
Married-couple family	272,152	266,670	288,115	0.7
Other family	68,533	78,658	77,111	-0.2
Male householder, no wife present..	19,511	23,620	23,378	-0.1
Female householder, no husband present................................	49,022	55,038	53,733	-0.2
Nonfamily households	177,515	200,089	228,400	1.3
Householder living alone..	139,969	155,623	177,419	1.3
Householder not living alone...	37,546	44,466	50,981	1.3
Housing Characteristics				
Total housing units..	651,901	722,217	744,620	0.3
Occupied housing units	518,200	545,417	593,626	0.8
Owner occupied	370,905	396,395	444,231	1.1
Renter occupied	147,295	149,022	149,395	-
Average household size..	2.39	2.37	2.25	-0.5
Financial Characteristics				
Median gross rent of renter-occupied housing	497	707	945	3.1
Median monthly owner costs for housing units with a mortgage	923	1,289	1,464	1.2
Median value of owner-occupied housing units................................	98,700	179,100	252,100	3.7

- = Zero or rounds to zero.

Table ME-4. Migration, Origin, and Language

(Number, percent.)

Characteristic	State	U.S.
	2021	2021
Residence 1 Year Ago		
Population 1 year and over	1,360,264	328,464,538
Same house	88.5	87.2
Different house in the U.S.	11.4	12.3
Same county	5.6	6.7
Different county	5.8	5.7
Same state	2.6	3.3
Different state	3.2	2.4
Abroad	0.2	0.4
Place of Birth		
Native born	1,316,179	286,623,642
Male	49.4	49.7
Female	50.6	50.3
Foreign born	56,068	45,270,103
Male	40.4	48.7
Female	59.6	51.3
Foreign born; naturalized U.S. citizen..	31,514	24,044,083
Male	39.3	46.4
Female	60.7	53.6
Foreign born; not a U.S. citizen	24,554	21,226,020
Male	41.8	51.2
Female	58.2	48.8
Entered 2010 or later	36.8	28.1
Entered 2000 to 2009	16.7	23.7
Entered before 2000...	46.5	48.2
World Region of Birth, Foreign		
Foreign-born population, excluding population born at sea	56,068	45,269,644
Europe	25.3	10.7
Asia...	24.9	31.0
Africa..	17.2	5.7
Oceania...	1.1	0.6
Latin America..	11.0	50.1
North America	20.5	1.7
Language Spoken at Home and Ability to Speak English		
Population 5 years and over..	1,311,213	313,232,500
English only	94.2	78.4
Language other than English..	5.8	21.6
Speaks English less than "very well"...	1.5	8.3

Table ME-5. Median Income and Poverty Status, 2021

(Number, percent, except as noted.)

Characteristic	State		U.S.	
	Number	Percent	Number	Percent
Median Income				
Households (dollars)...	64,767	X	69,717	X
Families (dollars)	82,842	X	85,806	X
Below Poverty Level (All People)	154,117	11.5	41,393,176	12.8
Sex				
Male	67,502	10.3	18,518,155	11.6
Female	86,615	12.7	22,875,021	13.9
Age				
Under 18 years..	36,926	15.1	12,243,219	16.9
Related children under 18 years............................	35,626	14.7	11,985,424	16.6
18 to 64 years...	90,666	11.3	23,526,341	11.9
65 years and over	26,525	9.2	5,623,616	10.3

X = Not applicable.

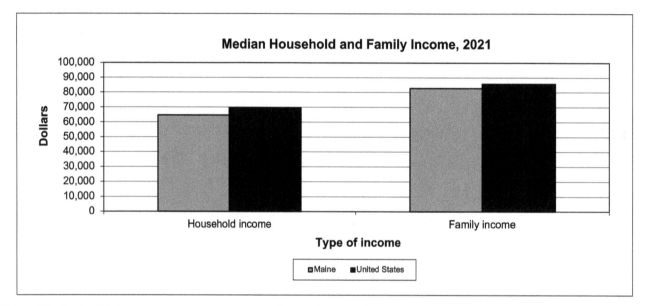

Table ME-6. Health Insurance Coverage Status for the Civilian Noninstitutionalized Population and Children Under 19 Years of Age

(Number, percent.)

Item	2011	2012	2013	2014	2015	2016	2017	2018	2019	2020 [2]	2021
Civilian Noninstitutionalized Population	1,314,121	1,315,703	1,314,191	1,315,996	1,314,849	1,317,148	1,321,649	1,323,289	1,327,623	1,325,025	1,357,120
Covered by Private or Public Insurance											
Number...	1,173,956	1,180,994	1,167,176	1,182,465	1,204,341	1,211,175	1,214,582	1,217,102	1,221,086	1,223,980	1,279,481
Percent..	89.3	89.8	88.8	89.9	91.6	92.0	91.9	92.0	92.0	92.4	94.3
Uninsured											
Number...	140,165	134,709	147,015	133,531	110,508	105,973	107,067	106,187	106,537	101,045	77,639
Percent..	10.7	10.2	11.2	10.1	8.4	8.0	8.1	8.0	8.0	7.6	5.7
Percent in the U.S. not covered................................	15.1	14.8	14.5	11.7	9.4	8.6	8.7	8.9	9.2	8.7	8.6
Children Under 19 Years of Age[1]	269,901	265,495	259,827	257,390	255,319	254,723	271,746	264,131	261,737	266,859	263,488
Covered by Private or Public Insurance											
Number...	255,736	253,255	244,441	241,098	240,871	243,104	258,321	249,619	247,074	253,589	252,204
Percent..	94.8	95.4	94.1	93.7	94.3	95.4	95.1	94.5	94.4	95.0	95.7
Uninsured											
Number...	14,165	12,240	15,386	16,292	14,448	11,619	13,425	14,512	14,663	13,270	11,284
Percent..	5.2	4.6	5.9	6.3	5.7	4.6	4.9	5.5	5.6	5.0	4.3
Percent in the U.S. not covered................................	7.5	7.2	7.1	6.0	4.8	4.5	5.0	5.2	5.7	5.2	5.4

[1] Data for years prior to 2017 are for individuals under 18 years of age.
[2] 2020 ACS 5-Year estimates. 1-Year estimates were not released for 2020 due to the impact of COVID-19 on data collection that year. Data is not comparable to previous years, which are based on 1-year estimates.

Table ME-7. Employment Status by Demographic Group, 2022

(Numbers in thousands, percent.)

Characteristic	Civilian noninstitutional population	Civilian labor force		Employed		Unemployed	
		Number	Percent of population	Number	Percent of population	Number	Percent of population
Total...	1,153	673	58.4	649	56.3	24	3.5
Sex							
Male...	563	349	61.9	335	59.5	14	3.9
Female..	590	324	54.9	314	53.3	10	3.0
Race, Sex, and Hispanic Origin							
White..	1,092	639	58.5	617	56.5	22	3.4
Male..	534	331	61.9	318	59.5	13	3.9
Female.....................................	558	308	55.2	299	53.7	9	2.8
Black or African American................	NA	NA	NA	NA	NA	NA	NA
Male..	NA	NA	NA	NA	NA	NA	NA
Female.....................................	NA	NA	NA	NA	NA	NA	NA
Hispanic or Latino ethnicity[1]...........	NA	NA	NA	NA	NA	NA	NA
Male..	NA	NA	NA	NA	NA	NA	NA
Female.....................................	NA	NA	NA	NA	NA	NA	NA
Age							
16 to 19 years..............................	NA	NA	NA	NA	NA	NA	NA
20 to 24 years..............................	NA	NA	NA	NA	NA	NA	NA
25 to 34 years..............................	159	129	81.1	125	78.3	4	3.4
35 to 44 years..............................	184	151	82.2	148	80.3	4	2.3
45 to 54 years..............................	156	124	79.7	121	77.6	3	2.6
55 to 64 years..............................	198	125	63.2	123	62.2	2	1.7
65 years and over..........................	329	63	19.1	60	18.4	3	4.0

NOTE: Data in Table 7 are from the Current Population Survey (CPS) and do not match the estimates in Table 8. See notes and definitions for further information.
[1] May be of any race.
NA = Not available.

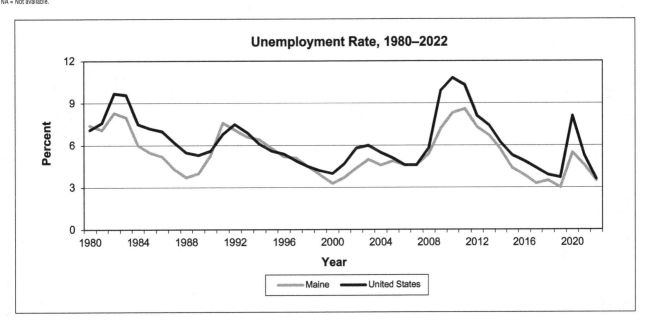

Table ME-8. Employment Status of the Civilian Noninstitutional Population Age 16 Years and Over

(Number, percent.)

Year	Civilian labor force	Civilian participation rate	Employed	Unemployed	Unemployment rate
2010..	697,832	65.0	638,984	58,848	8.4
2011..	698,979	64.8	644,967	54,012	7.7
2012..	700,730	64.7	650,315	50,415	7.2
2013..	704,240	64.9	657,058	47,182	6.7
2014..	698,035	64.1	659,008	39,027	5.6
2015..	687,859	63.0	657,550	30,309	4.4
2016..	693,917	63.4	667,723	26,194	3.8
2017..	703,871	63.6	680,164	23,707	3.4
2018..	703,130	63.2	681,304	21,804	3.1
2019..	701,631	62.7	682,271	19,360	2.8
2020..	675,231	59.9	641,262	33,969	5.0
2021..	681,884	59.9	650,334	31,550	4.6
2022..	674,875	58.6	654,965	19,910	3.0

Table ME-9. Employment and Average Wages by Industry

(Estimates are based on the 2012 North American Industry Classification System [NAICS].)

Industry	2014	2015	2016	2017	2018	2019	2020	2021
	Number of Jobs							
Wage and Salary Employment by Industry	619,376	624,837	632,306	637,895	645,481	651,621	612,484	637,018
Farm Wage and Salary Employment	4,166	4,151	3,875	3,867	3,563	3,589	3,429	3,514
Nonfarm Wage and Salary Employment	615,210	620,686	628,431	634,028	641,918	648,032	609,055	633,504
Private wage and salary employment	508,479	514,553	521,322	526,706	534,164	539,265	504,329	528,806
Forestry, fishing, and related activities	4,150	4,240	4,080	4,173	4,221	4,227	4,087	3,940
Mining	190	191	211	209	230	214	228	242
Utilities	1,551	1,630	1,647	1,669	1,632	1,628	1,612	1,674
Construction	26,613	27,220	28,095	28,994	30,070	30,757	31,075	32,649
Manufacturing	50,253	50,700	50,744	51,059	52,013	53,284	50,326	53,972
Durable goods manufacturing	27,769	28,159	28,490	28,695	29,447	30,146	28,390	30,409
Nondurable goods manufacturing	22,484	22,541	22,254	22,364	22,566	23,138	21,936	23,563
Wholesale trade	19,815	20,120	20,027	19,693	19,576	19,727	18,876	19,178
Retail trade	82,192	82,224	82,522	82,039	81,746	80,993	76,460	80,220
Transportation and warehousing	16,578	16,584	16,987	17,579	17,026	17,222	16,163	16,930
Information	7,453	7,595	7,710	7,366	7,417	7,163	6,403	6,678
Finance and insurance	23,683	23,984	24,024	24,270	24,539	25,258	25,343	25,017
Real estate and rental and leasing	6,550	6,517	6,736	6,756	7,088	7,213	6,924	7,156
Professional, scientific, and technical services	25,004	25,341	25,527	26,019	27,609	28,416	28,446	30,291
Management of companies and enterprises	9,091	9,124	9,984	10,484	11,191	12,129	12,035	14,690
Administrative and waste services	29,666	30,492	30,824	30,685	31,173	29,734	28,802	28,404
Educational services	15,339	15,703	16,406	16,750	17,614	17,915	17,169	18,402
Health care and social assistance	102,230	103,776	104,899	106,554	106,444	107,747	104,789	105,136
Arts, entertainment, and recreation	8,594	8,747	9,148	9,384	9,685	10,037	7,450	8,382
Accommodation and food services	55,013	55,712	56,993	58,499	59,368	60,004	44,865	52,328
Other services, except public administration	24,514	24,653	24,758	24,524	25,522	25,597	23,276	23,517
Government and government enterprises	106,731	106,133	107,109	107,322	107,754	108,767	104,726	104,698
	Dollars							
Average Wages and Salaries by Industry	41,622	42,896	43,715	45,053	46,514	48,315	52,718	55,756
Average Farm Wages and Salaries	28,810	23,619	29,036	26,405	25,219	19,879	20,208	19,810
Average Nonfarm Wages and Salaries	41,709	43,025	43,806	45,167	46,632	48,472	52,901	55,955
Average private wages and salaries	41,481	42,792	43,586	44,989	46,469	48,347	53,197	56,421
Forestry, fishing, and related activities	42,281	44,051	44,496	47,475	49,575	50,123	49,790	52,453
Mining	58,853	59,550	58,867	61,407	58,635	61,696	63,434	63,864
Utilities	87,721	82,707	83,565	91,798	91,738	92,041	101,532	98,983
Construction	45,895	46,668	47,453	48,840	50,578	52,626	56,665	59,391
Manufacturing	54,619	55,913	55,856	57,467	57,941	59,194	63,876	64,263
Durable goods manufacturing	54,578	56,096	56,135	57,058	57,790	58,474	61,176	62,545
Nondurable goods manufacturing	54,669	55,684	55,500	57,992	58,138	60,133	67,370	66,480
Wholesale trade	59,646	62,620	63,598	65,400	68,414	70,235	75,082	82,883
Retail trade	26,691	27,567	28,042	28,984	29,987	31,341	34,963	37,070
Transportation and warehousing	42,107	43,350	43,183	43,805	45,068	46,474	50,313	53,293
Information	47,964	49,867	53,244	54,814	56,727	59,621	66,759	72,820
Finance and insurance	68,723	70,446	71,553	75,841	78,593	80,556	86,357	94,343
Real estate and rental and leasing	39,041	40,832	41,897	43,063	44,293	45,566	50,023	53,630
Professional, scientific, and technical services	63,727	66,422	68,131	70,484	72,671	75,644	81,843	86,986
Management of companies and enterprises	74,508	76,518	79,648	79,996	83,176	87,272	92,136	100,097
Administrative and waste services	34,423	35,872	36,926	37,732	38,356	39,985	43,864	47,106
Educational services	36,647	37,438	37,335	38,057	37,530	38,631	40,499	39,841
Health care and social assistance	44,540	45,798	46,556	47,676	49,372	51,469	55,763	58,784
Arts, entertainment, and recreation	26,737	27,027	28,177	28,616	29,393	30,116	34,724	36,262
Accommodation and food services	20,553	21,471	22,489	23,731	25,276	26,396	26,994	32,986
Other services, except public administration	29,414	30,528	31,576	32,844	33,676	34,710	38,522	40,742
Government and government enterprises	42,794	44,153	44,875	46,041	47,440	49,094	51,476	53,601

Table ME-10. Employment Characteristics by Family Type

(Number, percent.)

Family type and labor force status	2019 Total	2019 Families with own children under 18 years	2020 [1] Total	2020 [1] Families with own children under 18 years	2021 Total	2021 Families with own children under 18 years
All Families..	342,894	124,352	349,955	129,627	365,226	129,912
FAMILY TYPE AND LABOR FORCE STATUS						
Opposite-Sex Married-Couple Families...........................	268,258	82,161	271,707	86,932	284,406	89,711
Both husband and wife in labor force............................	51.5	74.8	52.6	74.9	50.5	72.4
Husband in labor force, wife not in labor force	16.9	19.5	16.9	19.0	16.9	20.6
Wife in labor force, husband not in labor force	8.7	3.1	9.1	4.3	9.3	5.3
Both husband and wife not in labor force	21.4	1.3	21.5	1.8	23.3	1.7
Other Families	74,636	42,191	74,809	41,929	77,111	39,906
Female householder, no spouse present	69.1	68.7	68.1	68.0	69.7	71.5
In labor force..	47.0	55.8	47.2	55.5	49.2	58.3
Not in labor force..	22.0	12.8	20.9	12.5	20.5	13.2
Male householder, no spouse present...........................	30.9	31.3	31.9	32.0	30.3	28.5
In labor force..	24.2	28.7	24.8	28.3	23.0	24.8
Not in labor force..	6.8	2.7	7.1	3.7	7.3	3.6

[1] 2020 ACS 5-Year estimates. 1-Year estimates were not released for 2020 due to the impact of COVID-19 on data collection that year. Data is not comparable to previous years, which are based on 1-year estimates.

Table ME-11. School Enrollment and Educational Attainment, 2021

(Number, percent.)

Item	State	U.S.
Enrollment		
Total population 3 years and over, enrolled in school	274,439	79,453,524
Enrolled in nursery school or preschool (percent)	4.4	5.2
Enrolled in kindergarten (percent)..	4.4	5.0
Enrolled in elementary school, grades 1-8 (percent)...	41.9	41.3
Enrolled in high school, grades 9-12 (percent)	21.8	21.8
Enrolled in college or graduate school (percent)...	27.5	26.7
Attainment		
Total population 25 years and over	1,015,078	228,193,464
Less than ninth grade (percent)..	1.9	4.8
9th to 12th grade, no diploma (percent)	3.6	5.9
High school graduate, including equivalency (percent)...	29.6	26.3
Some college, no degree (percent)..	18.4	19.3
Associate's degree (percent)...	10.6	8.8
Bachelor's degree (percent)	22.2	21.2
Graduate or professional degree (percent)...	13.8	13.8
High school graduate or higher (percent)	94.5	89.4
Bachelor's degree or higher (percent)...	36	35.0

Table ME-12. Public School Characteristics and Educational Indicators

(Number, percent; data derived from National Center of Education Statistics.)

Item	State	U.S.
Public Elementary and Secondary Schools		
Number of regular school districts, 2019-20	255	13,349
Number of operational schools, 2019-20..	594	98,469
Percent charter schools	2.0	7.7
Total public school enrollment, Fall 2021	173,215	49,433,092
Percent charter school enrollment	1.6	7.5
Student-teacher ratio, Fall 2019	12.2	15.9
Expenditures per student (unadjusted dollars), 2019-20	16,067	13,489
Four-year adjusted cohort graduation rate (ACGR), 2019-2020[1]...	87.4	86.5
Students eligible for free or reduced-price lunch (percent), 2019-20..	42.0	52.1
English language learners (percent), Fall 2020	3.1	10.3
Students age 3 to 21 served under IDEA, part B (percent), 2021-22	20.1	14.7

Public Schools by Type, 2019-20	Number	Percent of state public schools
Total number of schools..	594	100.0
Special education..	1	0.2
Vocational education..	27	4.5
Alternative education..	0	-

[1] Adjusted Cohort Graduation Rates (ACGR) differ from Averaged Freshmen Graduation Rates (AFGR).
- = Zero or rounds to zero.

Table ME-13. Reported Voting and Registration of the Voting-Age Population, November 2022

(Numbers in thousands, percent.)

Item	Total population	Total citizen population	Registered			Voted		
			Total registered	Percent registered (total population)	Percent registered (total citizen population)	Total voted	Percent voted (total population)	Percent voted (total citizen population)
U.S. Total	255,457	233,546	161,422	63.2	69.1	121,916	47.7	52.2
State Total......................	1,150	1,131	856	74.4	75.6	722	62.7	63.8
Sex								
Male	562	552	404	71.9	73.2	350	62.2	63.3
Female	588	579	451	76.7	77.9	372	63.2	64.2
Race								
White alone......................	1,083	1,074	815	75.2	75.8	695	64.2	64.7
White, non-Hispanic alone	1,072	1,063	810	75.6	76.2	690	64.4	64.9
Black alone......................	13	7	3	22.0	43.6	3	22.0	43.6
Asian alone	19	15	9	45.6	57.0	9	45.6	57.0
Hispanic (of any race)	11	11	5	42.5	42.5	5	42.5	42.5
White alone or in combination	1,118	1,109	844	75.5	76.1	710	63.5	64.0
Black alone or in combination	21	14	8	40.3	59.3	8	40.3	59.3
Asian alone or in combination......................	24	20	14	56.7	67.4	14	56.7	67.4
Age								
18 to 24 years	96	96	48	49.7	49.7	31	32.6	32.6
25 to 34 years......................	166	161	111	67.2	69.3	91	55.0	56.7
35 to 44 years	206	200	137	66.5	68.6	110	53.4	55.1
45 to 64 years	352	348	283	80.3	81.2	231	65.8	66.5
65 years and over	331	326	277	83.7	84.8	258	77.9	78.9

B = Base is less than 75,000 and therefore too small to show the derived measure.

Table ME-14. Health Indicators

(Number, rate as indicated in footnotes.)

Item	State	U.S.
Births		
Life Expectancy at Birth (years), 2020	77.8	77.0
Fertility Rate by State[1], 2021	49.9	56.3
Percent Home Births, 2021	2.6	1.4
Cesarean Delivery Rate[2], 2021	30.9	32.1
Preterm Birth Rate[3], 2021	9.4	10.5
Teen Birth Rate[4], 2021	7.8	13.9
Percentage of Babies Born Low Birthweight[5], 2021	7.3	8.5
Deaths[6]		
Heart Disease Mortality Rate, 2021..	168.4	173.8
Cancer Mortality Rate, 2021...	161.3	146.6
Stroke Mortality Rate, 2021..	32.5	41.1
Diabetes Mortality Rate, 2021..	27.0	25.4
Influenza/Pneumonia Mortality Rate, 2021	10.6	10.5
Suicide Mortality Rate, 2021..	19.5	14.1
Drug Overdose Mortality Rate, 2021..	47.1	33.6
Firearm Injury Mortality Rate, 2021...	12.6	14.6
Homicide Mortality Rate, 2021...	1.7	8.2
Disease and Illness		
Lifetime Asthma in Adults, 2020 (percent)..	14.8	13.9
Lifetime Asthma in Children, 2020 (percent)[7]	12.2	11.3
Diabetes in Adults, 2020 (percent)..	8.3	8.2
Self-reported Obesity in Adults, 2021 (percent)...	31.9	NA

SOURCE: National Center for Health Statistics, National Vital Statistics System 2020 data; https://wonder.cdc.gov.
[1] General fertility rate per 1,000 women aged 15–44.
[2] This represents the percentage of all live births that were cesarean deliveries.
[3] Babies born prior to 37 weeks of pregnancy (gestation).
[4] Number of births per 1,000 females aged 15–19
[5] Babies born weighing less than 2,500 grams or 5 lbs. 8oz.
[6] Death rates are the number of deaths per 100,000 total population.
[7] U.S. total includes data from 30 states and D.C.
NA = Not available.
- = Zero or rounds to zero.

Table ME-15. State Government Finances, 2021

(Dollar amounts in thousands, percent distribution.)

Item	Dollars	Percent distribution
Total Revenue	12,826,585	100.0
General revenue	11,776,444	91.8
Intergovernmental revenue	4,914,655	38.3
Taxes	5,452,250	42.5
General sales	1,909,696	14.9
Selective sales	719,821	5.6
License taxes	325,922	2.5
Individual income tax	2,075,273	16.2
Corporate income tax	284,317	2.2
Other taxes	137,221	1.1
Current charges	884,698	6.9
Miscellaneous general revenue	524,841	4.1
Utility revenue	1,815	-
Liquor stores revenue	236999	1.8
Insurance trust revenue[1]	811,327	6.3
Total Expenditure	12,584,585	100.0
Intergovernmental expenditure	1,948,226	15.5
Direct expenditure	10,636,359	84.5
Current operation	8,210,298	65.2
Capital outlay	448,852	3.6
Insurance benefits and repayments	1,563,370	12.4
Assistance and subsidies	228,042	1.8
Interest on debt	185,797	1.5
Exhibit: Salaries and wages	1,239,886	9.9
Total Expenditure	12,584,585	100.0
General expenditure	10,840,390	86.1
Intergovernmental expenditure	1,948,226	15.5
Direct expenditure	8,892,164	70.7
General expenditure, by function:		
Education	2,791,156	22.2
Public welfare	4,350,025	34.6
Hospitals	128,373	1.0
Health	306,072	2.4
Highways	760,476	6.0
Police protection	113,920	0.9
Correction	201,591	1.6
Natural resources	204,037	1.6
Parks and recreation	11,744	0.1
Governmental administration	618,430	4.9
Interest on general debt	185,797	1.5
Other and unallocable	1,110,953	8.8
Utility expenditure	20,022	0.2
Liquor stores expenditure	160,803	1.3
Insurance trust expenditure	1,563,370	12.4
Debt at End of Fiscal Year	5,627,663	X
Cash and Security Holdings	28,390,087	X

X = Not applicable.
- = Zero or rounds to zero.
[1] Within insurance trust revenue, net earnings of state retirement systems is a calculated statistic (the item code in the data file is X08), and thus can be positive or negative. Net earnings is the sum of earnings on investments plus gains on investments minus losses on investments. The change made in 2002 for asset valuation from book to market value in accordance with Statement 34 of the Governmental Accounting Standards Board is reflected in the calculated statistics.

Table ME-16. State Government Tax Collections, 2022

(Dollars in thousands, percent.)

Item	Dollars	Percent distribution
Total Taxes	6,439,268	100.0
Property taxes	45,023	0.7
Sales and gross receipts	2,974,225	46.2
General sales and gross receipts	2,171,258	33.7
Selective sales and gross receipts	802,967	12.5
Alcoholic beverages	18,464	0.3
Amusements	68,073	1.1
Insurance premiums	136,120	2.1
Motor fuels	246,951	3.8
Pari-mutuels	1,911	-
Public utilities	21,784	0.3
Tobacco products	141,941	2.2
Other selective sales	167,723	2.6
Licenses	317,257	4.9
Alcoholic beverages	7,465	0.1
Amusements	901	-
Corporations in general	13,011	0.2
Hunting and fishing	19,167	0.3
Motor vehicle	121,049	1.9
Motor vehicle operators	13,598	0.2
Public utilities	X	-
Occupation and business, NEC	128,544	2.0
Other licenses	13,522	0.2
Income taxes	3,006,721	46.7
Individual income	2,590,903	40.2
Corporation net income	415,818	6.5
Other taxes	96,042	1.5
Death and gift	34,183	0.5
Documentary and stock transfer	61,859	1.0
Severance	X	-
Taxes, NEC	0	-

X = Not applicable.
- = Zero or rounds to zero.

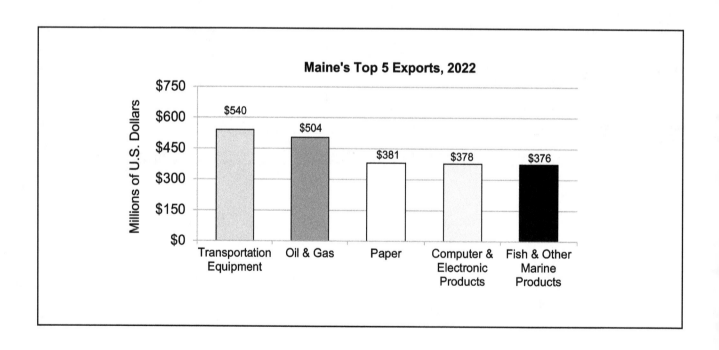

Maine's Top 5 Exports, 2022

Export	Millions of U.S. Dollars
Transportation Equipment	$540
Oil & Gas	$504
Paper	$381
Computer & Electronic Products	$378
Fish & Other Marine Products	$376

MARYLAND

Facts and Figures

Location: Eastern United States; bordered on the N by Pennsylvania, on the E by Delaware and the Atlantic Ocean, and on the S and W by Virginia and West Virginia

Area: 12,407 sq. mi. (32,133 sq. km.); rank—42nd

Population: 6,164,660 (2022 est.); rank—19th

Principal Cities: capital—Annapolis; largest—Baltimore

Statehood: April 28, 1788; 7th state

U.S. Congress: 2 senators, 8 representatives

State Motto: *Fatti maschii parole femine* ("Manly deeds, womanly words")

State Song: "Maryland, My Maryland"

State Nicknames: The Old Line State; The Free State

Abbreviations: MD; Md.

State Symbols: flower—black-eyed susan; tree—white oak; bird—Baltimore oriole

At a Glance

- With an increase in population of 6.8 percent, Maryland ranked 23rd among the states in growth from 2010 to 2022.

- Maryland's 2021 median household income of $90,203 was the highest in the country, and its poverty rate of 10.3 percent ranked 42nd among the states.

- Approximately 31.7 percent of Marylanders self-identified their race as "Black or African American alone" in 2022, which was the 5th highest percentage in the country.

- Maryland's homicide rate in 2021 was 12.2 deaths per 100,000 population, compared to 8.2 for the entire nation.

- In 2022, Maryland had the 3rd lowest percent of residents who self-identified as "white alone" (57.3 percent).

Table MD-1. Population by Age, Sex, Race, and Hispanic Origin

(Number, percent, except where noted.)

Sex, age, race, and Hispanic origin	2010	2020	2022	Percent change, 2010–2022
Total Population..	5,773,552	6,177,213	6,164,660	6.8
Percent of total U.S. population	1.9	1.9	1.8	X
Sex				
Male...	2,791,762	3,011,869	3,001,909	7.5
Female	2,981,790	3,165,344	3,162,751	6.1
Age				
Under 5 years..	364,488	362,028	349,844	-4.0
Under 18 years..	1,352,964	1,369,149	1,346,589	-0.5
18 to 64 years...	3,712,946	3,825,341	3,773,862	1.6
65 years and over..	707,642	982,723	1,044,209	47.6
Median age (years)	38.0	39.1	39.6	4.2
Race and Hispanic Origin				
One race				
White	3,541,379	3,576,750	3,530,719	-0.3
Black..	1,731,513	1,942,558	1,951,658	12.7
American Indian and Alaska Native	30,885	39,426	43,339	40.3
Asian..	326,655	423,464	435,183	33.2
Native Hawaiian or Other Pacific Islander	5,391	7,513	7,647	41.8
Two or more races	137,729	187,502	196,114	42.4
Hispanic (of any race)...	470,632	672,653	706,816	50.2

NOTE: Population figures for 2022 are July 1 estimates. The 2010 and 2020 estimates are taken from the respective censuses.
- = Zero or rounds to zero.
X = Not applicable.

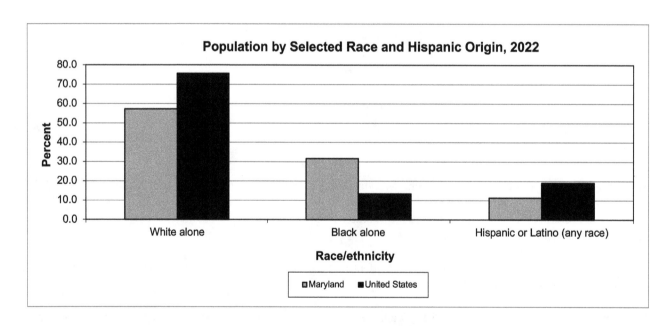

Table MD-2. Marital Status

(Number, percent distribution.)

Sex, age, race, and Hispanic origin	2000	2010	2021
Males, 15 Years and Over	1,972,921	2,232,162	2,428,942
Never married	31.0	36.8	38.0
Now married, except separated..	56.3	50.2	50.0
Separated...	2.8	2.3	1.7
Widowed..	2.5	2.7	2.4
Divorced...	7.4	8.0	7.9
Females, 15 Years and Over	2,186,715	2,442,021	2,613,355
Never married	26.8	32.2	33.4
Now married, except separated..	49.7	45.3	45.1
Separated...	3.4	2.9	1.9
Widowed..	10.1	9.0	8.1
Divorced...	10.1	10.7	11.5

Table MD-3. Households and Housing Characteristics

(Number, percent, dollars.)

Item	2000	2010	2021	Average annual percent change, 2010–2021
Total Households...	1,980,859	2,127,439	2,355,652	1.0
Family households	1,359,318	1,431,958	1,549,154	0.7
Married-couple family	994,549	1,022,613	1,108,456	0.8
Other family	364,789	409,345	440,698	0.7
Male householder, no wife present................................	84,893	104,112	115,941	1.0
Female householder, no husband present	279,876	305,233	324,757	0.6
Nonfamily households	621,541	695,481	806,498	1.5
Householder living alone...	495,459	570,388	658,306	1.4
Householder not living alone..	126,082	125,093	148,192	1.7
Housing Characteristics				
Total housing units...	2,145,283	2,380,605	2,546,364	0.6
Occupied housing units	1,980,859	2,127,439	2,355,652	1.0
Owner occupied	1,341,751	1,426,267	1,597,663	1.1
Renter occupied	639,108	701,172	757,989	0.7
Average household size...	2.61	2.65	2.56	-0.3
Financial Characteristics				
Median gross rent of renter-occupied housing	689	1,131	1,473	2.7
Median monthly owner costs for housing units with a mortgage	1,296	2,016	2,013	-
Median value of owner-occupied housing units...........................	146,000	301,400	370,800	2.1

- = Zero or rounds to zero.

Table MD-4. Migration, Origin, and Language

(Number, percent.)

Characteristic	State 2021	U.S. 2021
Residence 1 Year Ago		
Population 1 year and over	6,099,715	328,464,538
Same house	88.3	87.2
Different house in the U.S.	11.1	12.3
Same county	5.5	6.7
Different county	5.6	5.7
Same state	3.0	3.3
Different state	2.6	2.4
Abroad..	0.5	0.4
Place of Birth		
Native born	5,186,078	286,623,642
Male	48.8	49.7
Female	51.2	50.3
Foreign born	979,051	45,270,103
Male	48.5	48.7
Female	51.5	51.3
Foreign born; naturalized U.S. citizen...	543,222	24,044,083
Male	46.6	46.4
Female	53.4	53.6
Foreign born; not a U.S. citizen...	435,829	21,226,020
Male	50.8	51.2
Female	49.2	48.8
Entered 2010 or later	31.6	28.1
Entered 2000 to 2009	28.4	23.7
Entered before 2000..	40.0	48.2
World Region of Birth, Foreign		
Foreign-born population, excluding population born at sea	979,051	45,269,644
Europe	8.7	10.7
Asia..	32.2	31.0
Africa...	19.7	5.7
Oceania..	0.2	0.6
Latin America...	38.2	50.1
North America..	0.9	1.7
Language Spoken at Home and Ability to Speak English		
Population 5 years and over...	5,814,479	313,232,500
English only	79.6	78.4
Language other than English...	20.4	21.6
Speaks English less than "very well"..	7.5	8.3

Table MD-5. Median Income and Poverty Status, 2021

(Number, percent, except as noted.)

Characteristic	State		U.S.	
	Number	Percent	Number	Percent
Median Income				
Households (dollars)...	90,203	X	69,717	X
Families (dollars)	110,978	X	85,806	X
Below Poverty Level (All People)	618,372	10.3	41,393,176	12.8
Sex				
Male	269,123	9.2	18,518,155	11.6
Female	349,249	11.2	22,875,021	13.9
Age				
Under 18 years..	187,386	14.0	12,243,219	16.9
Related children under 18 years...........................	183,212	13.7	11,985,424	16.6
18 to 64 years...	341,700	9.2	23,526,341	11.9
65 years and over	89,286	9.1	5,623,616	10.3

X = Not applicable.

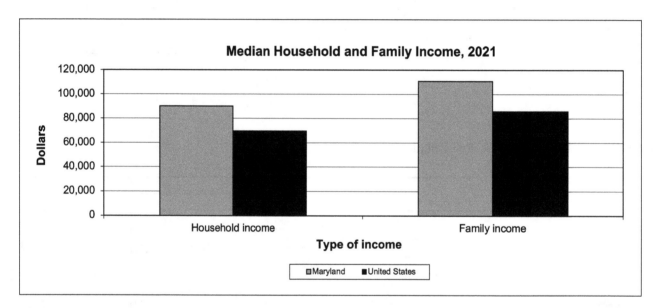

Median Household and Family Income, 2021

Table MD-6. Health Insurance Coverage Status for the Civilian Noninstitutionalized Population and Children Under 19 Years of Age

(Number, percent.)

Item	2011	2012	2013	2014	2015	2016	2017	2018	2019	2020 [2]	2021
Civilian Noninstitutionalized Population	5,736,588	5,788,196	5,834,039	5,885,847	5,908,522	5,918,535	5,957,871	5,943,064	5,945,846	5,938,200	6,059,298
Covered by Private or Public Insurance											
Number..	5,138,144	5,190,642	5,240,861	5,422,579	5,519,323	5,555,356	5,592,274	5,586,356	5,589,015	5,586,014	5,690,029
Percent...	89.6	89.7	89.8	92.1	93.4	93.9	93.9	94.0	94.0	94.1	93.9
Uninsured											
Number..	598,444	597,554	593,178	463,268	389,199	363,179	365,597	356,708	356,831	352,186	369,269
Percent...	10.4	10.3	10.2	7.9	6.6	6.1	6.1	6.0	6.0	5.9	6.1
Percent in the U.S. not covered..........................	15.1	14.8	14.5	11.7	9.4	8.6	8.7	8.9	9.2	8.7	8.6
Children Under 19 Years of Age[1]	1,344,498	1,341,118	1,343,118	1,349,767	1,346,154	1,344,588	1,419,540	1,420,111	1,410,735	1,417,908	1,437,990
Covered by Private or Public Insurance											
Number..	1,283,012	1,289,667	1,283,833	1,307,172	1,293,887	1,299,633	1,365,464	1,373,341	1,362,953	1,368,443	1,375,603
Percent...	95.4	96.2	95.6	96.8	96.1	96.7	96.2	96.7	96.6	96.5	95.7
Uninsured											
Number..	61,486	51,451	59,285	42,595	52,267	44,955	54,076	46,770	47,782	49,465	62,387
Percent...	4.6	3.8	4.4	3.2	3.9	3.3	3.8	3.3	3.4	3.5	4.3
Percent in the U.S. not covered..........................	7.5	7.2	7.1	6.0	4.8	4.5	5.0	5.2	5.7	5.2	5.4

[1] Data for years prior to 2017 are for individuals under 18 years of age.
[2] 2020 ACS 5-Year estimates. 1-Year estimates were not released for 2020 due to the impact of COVID-19 on data collection that year. Data is not comparable to previous years, which are based on 1-year estimates.

Table MD-7. Employment Status by Demographic Group, 2022

(Numbers in thousands, percent.)

Characteristic	Civilian noninstitutional population	Civilian labor force		Employed		Unemployed	
		Number	Percent of population	Number	Percent of population	Number	Percent of population
Total..	4,882	3,181	65.2	3,079	63.1	102	3.2
Sex							
Male..	2,329	1,667	71.6	1,620	69.6	47	2.8
Female.......................................	2,553	1,514	59.3	1,459	57.2	55	3.6
Race, Sex, and Hispanic Origin							
White..	2,925	1,910	65.3	1,856	63.4	54	2.8
Male.....................................	1,432	1,037	72.4	1,008	70.4	29	2.8
Female...................................	1,493	873	58.5	848	56.8	25	2.8
Black or African American..................	1,507	987	65.5	942	62.5	45	4.5
Male.....................................	681	480	70.4	462	67.8	18	3.7
Female...................................	825	507	61.4	480	58.2	27	5.3
Hispanic or Latino ethnicity[1]	416	296	71.2	285	68.6	11	3.8
Male.....................................	NA	NA	NA	NA	NA	NA	NA
Female...................................	NA	NA	NA	NA	NA	NA	NA
Age							
16 to 19 years.............................	NA	NA	NA	NA	NA	NA	NA
20 to 24 years.............................	408	279	68.3	264	64.7	15	5.3
25 to 34 years.............................	763	648	84.9	621	81.4	27	4.1
35 to 44 years.............................	807	686	85.0	672	83.2	14	2.1
45 to 54 years.............................	721	607	84.2	595	82.6	12	2.0
55 to 64 years.............................	886	635	71.7	620	70.0	16	2.4
65 years and over	991	219	22.1	216	21.8	3	1.5

NOTE: Data in Table 7 are from the Current Population Survey (CPS) and do not match the estimates in Table 8. See notes and definitions for further information.
[1] May be of any race.

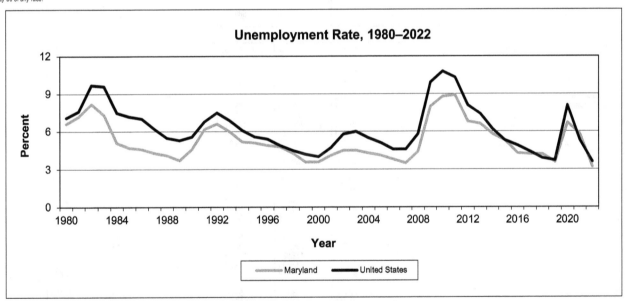

Unemployment Rate, 1980–2022

Table MD-8. Employment Status of the Civilian Noninstitutional Population Age 16 Years and Over

(Number, percent.)

Year	Civilian labor force	Civilian participation rate	Employed	Unemployed	Unemployment rate
2010..	3,078,368	68.6	2,836,945	241,423	7.8
2011..	3,097,300	68.0	2,870,857	226,443	7.3
2012..	3,120,947	67.8	2,906,518	214,429	6.9
2013..	3,128,908	67.4	2,924,626	204,282	6.5
2014..	3,125,017	66.9	2,945,911	179,106	5.7
2015..	3,139,988	66.8	2,983,083	156,905	5.0
2016..	3,155,918	66.9	3,020,827	135,091	4.3
2017..	3,243,896	67.6	3,114,580	129,316	4.0
2018..	3,261,068	67.6	3,142,323	118,745	3.6
2019..	3,326,497	68.6	3,212,155	114,342	3.4
2020..	3,227,527	66.4	3,012,106	215,421	6.7
2021..	3,175,550	65.3	2,992,228	183,322	5.8
2022..	3,171,513	64.9	3,068,700	102,813	3.2

Table MD-9. Employment and Average Wages by Industry

(Estimates are based on the 2012 North American Industry Classification System [NAICS].)

Industry	2014	2015	2016	2017	2018	2019	2020	2021
	Number of Jobs							
Wage and Salary Employment by Industry	2,727,672	2,767,425	2,804,311	2,828,811	2,859,504	2,880,591	2,689,103	2,756,430
Farm Wage and Salary Employment	6,416	6,214	7,499	7,224	7,046	6,467	5,450	6,747
Nonfarm Wage and Salary Employment	2,721,256	2,761,211	2,796,812	2,821,587	2,852,458	2,874,124	2,683,653	2,749,683
Private wage and salary employment	2,154,238	2,194,027	2,229,746	2,252,674	2,280,274	2,301,259	2,122,910	2,183,361
Forestry, fishing, and related activities	2,049	2,148	2,180	2,143	2,099	2,193	1,935	1,856
Mining	1,260	1,297	1,165	1,147	1,115	1,128	1,114	1,145
Utilities	9,738	9,579	9,836	9,760	9,729	9,633	9,669	9,534
Construction	153,215	158,344	165,045	165,951	167,025	169,933	164,284	163,723
Manufacturing	103,372	103,588	103,395	106,654	109,795	112,356	108,662	108,799
Durable goods manufacturing	53,737	54,416	53,950	55,618	57,992	58,413	56,650	56,093
Nondurable goods manufacturing	49,635	49,172	49,445	51,036	51,803	53,943	52,012	52,706
Wholesale trade	85,221	86,291	86,195	86,660	85,555	86,778	81,735	81,320
Retail trade	288,620	291,328	291,889	289,803	286,043	280,400	257,358	268,286
Transportation and warehousing	71,829	77,313	78,919	81,963	87,154	92,841	99,112	106,298
Information	38,977	38,457	38,667	37,633	36,233	35,689	33,049	33,445
Finance and insurance	98,448	99,469	100,123	98,738	98,129	96,011	94,413	93,198
Real estate and rental and leasing	44,236	45,492	45,800	48,103	47,675	47,319	43,697	42,523
Professional, scientific, and technical services	241,058	243,808	248,333	248,745	254,090	260,349	258,310	266,880
Management of companies and enterprises	25,570	25,198	26,278	26,043	27,429	28,666	27,640	27,481
Administrative and waste services	159,631	164,658	171,021	171,937	174,381	175,998	159,609	167,808
Educational services	73,895	74,754	77,105	79,593	83,226	84,123	77,452	85,032
Health care and social assistance	349,793	359,018	366,468	373,141	380,290	385,588	362,440	362,832
Arts, entertainment, and recreation	45,412	45,917	46,235	47,084	48,202	45,850	30,977	34,951
Accommodation and food services	217,225	223,139	228,047	235,163	235,748	238,666	181,742	197,206
Other services, except public administration	144,689	144,229	143,045	142,413	146,356	147,738	129,712	131,044
Government and government enterprises	567,018	567,184	567,066	568,913	572,184	572,865	560,743	566,322
	Dollars							
Average Wages and Salaries by Industry	56,911	58,701	59,587	61,133	62,831	64,626	70,446	73,080
Average Farm Wages and Salaries	24,960	21,052	20,019	18,860	23,620	20,434	23,549	19,110
Average Nonfarm Wages and Salaries	56,987	58,786	59,693	61,242	62,928	64,726	70,541	73,212
Average private wages and salaries	54,484	56,173	57,088	58,632	60,248	61,942	67,853	70,667
Forestry, fishing, and related activities	29,364	30,863	32,305	33,701	34,323	35,944	38,153	40,173
Mining	62,669	61,487	68,482	71,257	70,505	72,529	71,979	73,161
Utilities	114,555	122,170	123,671	129,820	130,278	134,708	133,563	136,267
Construction	59,213	61,090	63,514	66,103	67,092	68,921	71,894	73,850
Manufacturing	72,408	75,452	75,788	79,280	80,629	81,286	87,904	89,486
Durable goods manufacturing	78,132	80,302	82,117	84,914	85,464	88,342	93,505	95,126
Nondurable goods manufacturing	66,210	70,084	68,883	73,140	75,217	73,644	81,803	83,484
Wholesale trade	77,533	79,704	79,625	80,876	83,508	84,582	89,759	95,915
Retail trade	30,137	31,544	31,935	32,526	33,523	34,597	38,097	40,287
Transportation and warehousing	53,256	54,576	54,904	54,494	54,809	52,736	53,480	52,844
Information	85,334	86,578	90,327	90,499	95,389	101,228	113,754	151,906
Finance and insurance	96,713	100,457	103,524	106,609	110,903	116,411	129,924	136,504
Real estate and rental and leasing	60,650	62,817	63,249	65,219	66,813	67,479	73,715	75,960
Professional, scientific, and technical services	92,647	94,261	95,588	97,803	100,999	105,131	110,775	114,714
Management of companies and enterprises	111,217	116,537	112,929	123,799	126,010	128,106	126,604	134,074
Administrative and waste services	40,229	42,003	42,838	44,869	45,440	46,282	51,061	55,143
Educational services	49,286	50,578	50,678	51,205	52,500	52,807	57,846	55,543
Health care and social assistance	51,012	52,786	53,166	54,291	55,420	56,701	61,165	63,800
Arts, entertainment, and recreation	33,114	34,714	36,461	37,046	36,477	36,391	44,052	43,989
Accommodation and food services	21,879	22,668	23,458	24,789	26,183	27,203	26,979	31,076
Other services, except public administration	38,414	39,904	41,073	42,745	44,080	45,128	49,102	50,817
Government and government enterprises	66,494	68,891	69,937	71,575	73,608	75,909	80,719	83,024

Table MD-10. Employment Characteristics by Family Type

(Number, percent.)

Family type and labor force status	2019		2020 [1]		2021	
	Total	Families with own children under 18 years	Total	Families with own children under 18 years	Total	Families with own children under 18 years
All Families...	1,462,070	608,132	1,479,378	626,188	1,549,154	639,813
FAMILY TYPE AND LABOR FORCE STATUS						
Opposite-Sex Married-Couple Families..........................	1,051,319	418,663	1,051,014	425,831	1,094,674	433,435
Both husband and wife in labor force............................	57.9	74.7	58.7	74.4	57.5	73.9
Husband in labor force, wife not in labor force	18.0	20.5	19.0	21.5	18.7	21.3
Wife in labor force, husband not in labor force	7.9	3.1	7.5	3.2	7.5	3.4
Both husband and wife not in labor force.......................	15.2	0.9	14.8	0.9	16.3	1.4
Other Families	410,751	189,469	416,987	197,563	440,698	203,082
Female householder, no spouse present.........................	74.0	74.8	74.8	75.2	73.7	75.8
In labor force...	54.8	65.4	55.8	66.1	54.8	64.3
Not in labor force	19.2	9.4	19.0	9.1	18.9	11.5
Male householder, no spouse present...........................	26.0	25.2	25.2	24.8	26.3	24.2
In labor force...	21.4	24.4	20.8	23.6	21.4	22.2
Not in labor force	4.6	0.8	4.4	1.2	4.9	2.0

[1] 2020 ACS 5-Year estimates. 1-Year estimates were not released for 2020 due to the impact of COVID-19 on data collection that year. Data is not comparable to previous years, which are based on 1-year estimates.

Table MD-11. School Enrollment and Educational Attainment, 2021

(Number, percent.)

Item	State	U.S.
Enrollment		
Total population 3 years and over, enrolled in school	1,516,189	79,453,524
Enrolled in nursery school or preschool (percent)...	4.8	5.2
Enrolled in kindergarten (percent)...	5.1	5.0
Enrolled in elementary school, grades 1-8 (percent)..	39.5	41.3
Enrolled in high school, grades 9-12 (percent)...	21.1	21.8
Enrolled in college or graduate school (percent)..	29.6	26.7
Attainment		
Total population 25 years and over	4,273,260	228,193,464
Less than ninth grade (percent)..	3.7	4.8
9th to 12th grade, no diploma (percent)	5.2	5.9
High school graduate, including equivalency (percent)..	23.8	26.3
Some college, no degree (percent)...	17.8	19.3
Associate's degree (percent)...	6.9	8.8
Bachelor's degree (percent)..	22.4	21.2
Graduate or professional degree (percent)...	20.2	13.8
High school graduate or higher (percent)..	91.1	89.4
Bachelor's degree or higher (percent)..	42.5	35.0

Table MD-12. Public School Characteristics and Educational Indicators

(Number, percent; data derived from National Center of Education Statistics.)

Item	State	U.S.
Public Elementary and Secondary Schools		
Number of regular school districts, 2019-20	24	13,349
Number of operational schools, 2019-20..	1,420	98,469
Percent charter schools	3.2	7.7
Total public school enrollment, Fall 2021	881,461	49,433,092
Percent charter school enrollment	2.7	7.5
Student-teacher ratio, Fall 2019	14.8	15.9
Expenditures per student (unadjusted dollars), 2019-20	15,926	13,489
Four-year adjusted cohort graduation rate (ACGR), 2019-2020[1]..................................	86.8	86.5
Students eligible for free or reduced-price lunch (percent), 2019-20...........................	42.0	52.1
English language learners (percent), Fall 2020	10.3	10.3
Students age 3 to 21 served under IDEA, part B (percent), 2021-22	12.4	14.7

Public Schools by Type, 2019-20	Number	Percent of state public schools
Total number of schools..	1,420	100.0
Special education..	36	2.5
Vocational education...	26	1.8
Alternative education..	46	3.2

[1] Adjusted Cohort Graduation Rates (ACGR) differ from Averaged Freshmen Graduation Rates (AFGR).

Table MD-13. Reported Voting and Registration of the Voting-Age Population, November 2022

(Numbers in thousands, percent.)

Item	Total population	Total citizen population	Registered			Voted		
			Total registered	Percent registered (total population)	Percent registered (total citizen population)	Total voted	Percent voted (total population)	Percent voted (total citizen population)
U.S. Total	255,457	233,546	161,422	63.2	69.1	121,916	47.7	52.2
State Total...........................	4,716	4,364	3,301	70.0	75.6	2,525	53.5	57.9
Sex								
Male	2,234	2,064	1,540	68.9	74.6	1,146	51.3	55.5
Female	2,482	2,300	1,761	71.0	76.6	1,379	55.5	59.9
Race								
White alone	2,852	2,639	2,017	70.7	76.4	1,626	57.0	61.6
White, non-Hispanic alone	2,553	2,480	1,946	76.2	78.5	1,577	61.8	63.6
Black alone	1,476	1,425	1,058	71.7	74.3	769	52.1	54.0
Asian alone	249	188	156	62.4	82.6	74	29.8	39.5
Hispanic (of any race)	406	224	125	30.8	55.7	91	22.4	40.5
White alone or in combination	2,954	2,728	2,069	70.1	75.9	1,663	56.3	61.0
Black alone or in combination......	1,559	1,495	1,091	70.0	73.0	794	51.0	53.1
Asian alone or in combination......	249	188	156	62.4	82.6	74	29.8	39.5
Age								
18 to 24 years	522	506	291	55.7	57.4	123	23.5	24.2
25 to 34 years	697	602	434	62.4	72.2	273	39.2	45.4
35 to 44 years	888	758	570	64.2	75.1	409	46.0	53.9
45 to 64 years	1,574	1,488	1,141	72.5	76.7	969	61.6	65.1
65 years and over	1,036	1,010	866	83.5	85.7	752	72.6	74.5

Table MD-14. Health Indicators

(Number, rate as indicated in footnotes.)

Item	State	U.S.
Births		
Life Expectancy at Birth (years), 2020	76.8	77.0
Fertility Rate by State[1], 2021	56.4	56.3
Percent Home Births, 2021	1.3	1.4
Cesarean Delivery Rate[2], 2021	34.3	32.1
Preterm Birth Rate[3], 2021	10.7	10.5
Teen Birth Rate[4], 2021	11.3	13.9
Percentage of Babies Born Low Birthweight[5], 2021	8.9	8.5
Deaths[6]		
Heart Disease Mortality Rate, 2021	165.2	173.8
Cancer Mortality Rate, 2021	139.2	146.6
Stroke Mortality Rate, 2021	47.3	41.1
Diabetes Mortality Rate, 2021	23.2	25.4
Influenza/Pneumonia Mortality Rate, 2021	8.7	10.5
Suicide Mortality Rate, 2021	9.7	14.1
Drug Overdose Mortality Rate, 2021	42.8	33.6
Firearm Injury Mortality Rate, 2021	15.2	14.6
Homicide Mortality Rate, 2021	12.2	8.2
Disease and Illness		
Lifetime Asthma in Adults, 2020 (percent)........................	13.1	13.9
Lifetime Asthma in Children, 2020 (percent)[7]	NA	11.3
Diabetes in Adults, 2020 (percent)........................	9.1	8.2
Self-reported Obesity in Adults, 2021 (percent)........................	34.3	NA

SOURCE: National Center for Health Statistics, National Vital Statistics System 2020 data; https://wonder.cdc.gov.
[1] General fertility rate per 1,000 women aged 15–44.
[2] This represents the percentage of all live births that were cesarean deliveries.
[3] Babies born prior to 37 weeks of pregnancy (gestation).
[4] Number of births per 1,000 females aged 15–19
[5] Babies born weighing less than 2,500 grams or 5 lbs. 8oz.
[6] Death rates are the number of deaths per 100,000 total population.
[7] U.S. total includes data from 30 states and D.C.
NA = Not available.
- = Zero or rounds to zero.

Table MD-15. State Government Finances, 2021

(Dollar amounts in thousands, percent distribution.)

Item	Dollars	Percent distribution
Total Revenue	58,049,343	100.0
General revenue	51,031,162	87.9
Intergovernmental revenue	19,392,050	33.4
Taxes	25,220,541	43.4
General sales	5,458,909	9.4
Selective sales	5,128,294	8.8
License taxes	969,440	1.7
Individual income tax	10,186,240	17.5
Corporate income tax	1,840,705	3.2
Other taxes	1,636,953	2.8
Current charges	3,675,833	6.3
Miscellaneous general revenue	2,742,738	4.7
Utility revenue	46,551	0.1
Liquor stores revenue	-	-
Insurance trust revenue[1]	6,971,630	12.0
Total Expenditure	59,400,461	100.0
Intergovernmental expenditure	11,267,430	19.0
Direct expenditure	48,133,031	81.0
Current operation	33,779,975	56.9
Capital outlay	3,122,824	5.3
Insurance benefits and repayments	6,587,703	11.1
Assistance and subsidies	3,298,127	5.6
Interest on debt	1,344,402	2.3
Exhibit: Salaries and wages	6,174,988	10.4
Total Expenditure	59,400,461	100.0
General expenditure	50,644,053	85.3
Intergovernmental expenditure	11,267,430	19.0
Direct expenditure	39,376,623	66.3
General expenditure, by function:		
Education	15,826,653	26.6
Public welfare	16,822,942	28.3
Hospitals	492,860	0.8
Health	3,801,475	6.4
Highways	2,286,272	3.8
Police protection	926,798	1.6
Correction	1,605,817	2.7
Natural resources	743,920	1.3
Parks and recreation	153,454	0.3
Governmental administration	2,268,160	3.8
Interest on general debt	1,344,402	2.3
Other and unallocable	4,171,347	7.0
Utility expenditure	2,284,195	3.9
Liquor stores expenditure	-	-
Insurance trust expenditure	6,587,703	11.1
Debt at End of Fiscal Year	30,652,002	X
Cash and Security Holdings	99,715,152	X

X = Not applicable.

- = Zero or rounds to zero.

[1] Within insurance trust revenue, net earnings of state retirement systems is a calculated statistic (the item code in the data file is X08), and thus can be positive or negative. Net earnings is the sum of earnings on investments plus gains on investments minus losses on investments. The change made in 2002 for asset valuation from book to market value in accordance with Statement 34 of the Governmental Accounting Standards Board is reflected in the calculated statistics.

Table MD-16. State Government Tax Collections, 2022

(Dollars in thousands, percent.)

Item	Dollars	Percent distribution
Total Taxes	29,361,279	100.0
Property taxes	930,810	3.2
Sales and gross receipts	12,139,837	41.3
General sales and gross receipts	6,638,205	22.6
Selective sales and gross receipts	5,501,632	18.7
Alcoholic beverages	36,930	0.1
Amusements	1,194,074	4.1
Insurance premiums	791,320	2.7
Motor fuels	1,113,264	3.8
Pari-mutuels	1,124	-
Public utilities	141,835	0.5
Tobacco products	479,132	1.6
Other selective sales	1,743,953	5.9
Licenses	1,008,665	3.4
Alcoholic beverages	1,174	-
Amusements	1,964	-
Corporations in general	140,820	0.5
Hunting and fishing	18,175	0.1
Motor vehicle	503,958	1.7
Motor vehicle operators	33,538	0.1
Public utilities	X	-
Occupation and business, NEC	307,187	1.0
Other licenses	1,849	-
Income taxes	14,370,565	48.9
Individual income	12,228,623	41.6
Corporation net income	2,141,942	7.3
Other taxes	911,402	3.1
Death and gift	265,493	0.9
Documentary and stock transfer	357,373	1.2
Severance	X	-
Taxes, NEC	288,536	1.0

X = Not applicable.
- = Zero or rounds to zero.

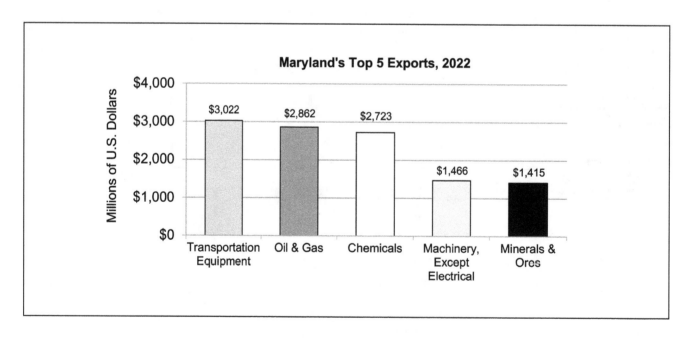

Maryland's Top 5 Exports, 2022

MASSACHUSETTS

Facts and Figures

Location: Northeastern United States; bordered on the N by Vermont and New Hampshire, on the E by the Atlantic Ocean, on the S by Connecticut and Rhode Island, and on the W by New York

Area: 10,555 sq. mi. (27,336 sq. km.); rank—44th

Population: 6,981,974 (2022 est.); rank—16th

Principal Cities: capital—Boston; largest—Boston

Statehood: February 6, 1788; 6th state

U.S. Congress: 2 senators, 9 representatives

State Motto: *Ense petit placidam sub libertate quietem* ("By the sword we seek peace, but peace only under liberty")

State Song: "All Hail to Massachusetts"

State Nickname: The Bay State

Abbreviations: MA; Mass.

State Symbols: flower—mayflower; tree—American elm; bird—chickadee

At a Glance

- With an increase in population of 6.6 percent, Massachusetts ranked 24th among the states in growth from 2010 to 2022.

- Massachusetts's median household income in 2021 was $89,645, the 3rd highest in the country.

- Approximately 10.4 percent of Massachusetts' population lived below the poverty level in 2021, compared to 12.8 percent of the entire U.S. population.

- Massachusetts had the 6th lowest homicide rate in 2021, with 2.3 deaths per 100,000 population, compared to 8.2 deaths per 100,000 population for the entire nation.

- Massachusetts had the 2nd highest percent of people age 25 years and older with a bachelor's degree or more in 2021 (46.6 percent).

Table MA-1. Population by Age, Sex, Race, and Hispanic Origin

(Number, percent, except where noted.)

Sex, age, race, and Hispanic origin	2010	2020	2022	Percent change, 2010–2022
Total Population..	6,547,629	7,029,949	6,981,974	6.6
Percent of total U.S. population	2.1	2.1	2.1	X
Sex				
Male...	3,166,628	3,443,345	3,417,950	7.9
Female	3,381,001	3,586,604	3,564,024	5.4
Age				
Under 5 years..	367,087	354,127	343,596	-6.4
Under 18 years...	1,418,923	1,378,143	1,337,434	-5.7
18 to 64 years	4,225,982	4,457,151	4,384,002	3.7
65 years and over	902,724	1,194,655	1,260,538	39.6
Median age (years)	39.1	39.6	40.1	2.6
Race and Hispanic Origin				
One race				
White	5,524,937	5,641,969	5,546,349	0.4
Black	504,365	642,642	660,810	31.0
American Indian and Alaska Native	29,944	36,302	36,928	23.3
Asian	359,673	518,330	538,245	49.6
Native Hawaiian or Other Pacific Islander	5,971	7,618	7,789	30.4
Two or more races	122,739	183,088	191,853	56.3
Hispanic (of any race)..	627,654	880,949	913,626	45.6

NOTE: Population figures for 2022 are July 1 estimates. The 2010 and 2020 estimates are taken from the respective censuses.
- = Zero or rounds to zero.
X = Not applicable.

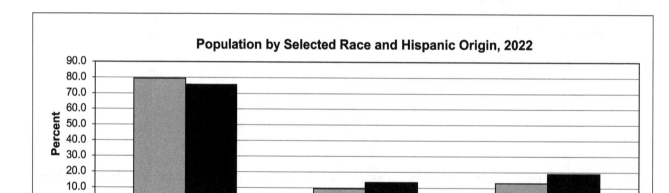

Table MA-2. Marital Status

(Number, percent distribution.)

Sex, age, race, and Hispanic origin	2000	2010	2021
Males, 15 Years and Over	2,412,349	2,579,221	2,840,285
Never married	33.9	38.7	39.8
Now married, except separated...............................	54.7	49.1	49.1
Separated..	1.6	1.6	1.2
Widowed..	2.7	2.7	2.3
Divorced..	7.0	8.0	7.6
Females, 15 Years and Over	2,679,020	2,819,768	3,031,022
Never married	28.5	33.2	35.4
Now married, except separated...............................	48.9	44.1	44.3
Separated..	2.3	2.4	1.8
Widowed..	10.8	9.1	7.8
Divorced..	9.5	11.1	10.8

Table MA-3. Households and Housing Characteristics

(Number, percent, dollars.)

Item	2000	2010	2021	Average annual percent change, 2010–2021
Total Households	2,443,580	2,520,419	2,759,018	0.9
Family households	1,576,696	1,590,257	1,719,532	0.7
Married-couple family	1,197,917	1,166,204	1,268,347	0.8
Other family	378,779	424,053	451,185	0.6
Male householder, no wife present	88,835	100,400	123,694	2.1
Female householder, no husband present	289,944	323,653	327,491	0.1
Nonfamily households	866,884	930,162	1,039,486	1.1
Householder living alone	684,345	736,320	787,526	0.6
Householder not living alone	182,539	193,842	251,960	2.7
Housing Characteristics				
Total housing units	2,621,989	2,808,727	3,017,772	0.7
Occupied housing units	2,443,580	2,520,419	2,759,018	0.9
Owner occupied	1,508,052	1,568,382	1,742,436	1.0
Renter occupied	935,528	952,037	1,016,582	0.6
Average household size	2.51	2.51	2.44	-0.3
Financial Characteristics				
Median gross rent of renter-occupied housing	684	1,009	1,487	4.3
Median monthly owner costs for housing units with a mortgage	1,353	2,036	2,323	1.3
Median value of owner-occupied housing units	185,700	334,100	480,600	4.0

Table MA-4. Migration, Origin, and Language

(Number, percent.)

Characteristic	State 2021	U.S. 2021
Residence 1 Year Ago		
Population 1 year and over	6,916,314	328,464,538
Same house	87.4	87.2
Different house in the U.S.	11.9	12.3
Same county	6.3	6.7
Different county	5.6	5.7
Same state	3.3	3.3
Different state	2.3	2.4
Abroad	0.7	0.4
Place of Birth		
Native born	5,757,235	286,623,642
Male	48.9	49.7
Female	51.1	50.3
Foreign born	1,227,488	45,270,103
Male	48.2	48.7
Female	51.8	51.3
Foreign born; naturalized U.S. citizen	669,636	24,044,083
Male	46.5	46.4
Female	53.5	53.6
Foreign born; not a U.S. citizen	557,852	21,226,020
Male	50.4	51.2
Female	49.6	48.8
Entered 2010 or later	36.0	28.1
Entered 2000 to 2009	22.7	23.7
Entered before 2000	41.3	48.2
World Region of Birth, Foreign		
Foreign-born population, excluding population born at sea	1,227,488	45,269,644
Europe	18.5	10.7
Asia	30.7	31.0
Africa	9.6	5.7
Oceania	0.3	0.6
Latin America	38.8	50.1
North America	2.2	1.7
Language Spoken at Home and Ability to Speak English		
Population 5 years and over	6,638,548	313,232,500
English only	75.5	70.4
Language other than English	24.5	21.6
Speaks English less than "very well"	10.0	8.3

Table MA-5. Median Income and Poverty Status, 2021

(Number, percent, except as noted.)

Characteristic	State		U.S.	
	Number	Percent	Number	Percent
Median Income				
Households (dollars)..	89,645	X	69,717	X
Families (dollars)	113,822	X	85,806	X
Below Poverty Level (All People)	700,138	10.4	41,393,176	12.8
Sex				
Male	303,094	9.2	18,518,155	11.6
Female	397,044	11.5	22,875,021	13.9
Age				
Under 18 years...	169,324	12.6	12,243,219	16.9
Related children under 18 years...	164,803	12.3	11,985,424	16.6
18 to 64 years...	405,109	9.6	23,526,341	11.9
65 years and over	125,705	10.6	5,623,616	10.3

X = Not applicable.

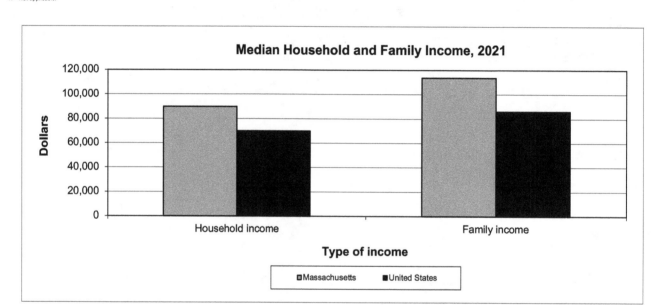

Median Household and Family Income, 2021

Table MA-6. Health Insurance Coverage Status for the Civilian Noninstitutionalized Population and Children Under 19 Years of Age

(Number, percent.)

Item	2011	2012	2013	2014	2015	2016	2017	2018	2019	2020 [2]	2021
Civilian Noninstitutionalized Population	6,507,596	6,566,851	6,613,654	6,668,348	6,718,090	6,736,017	6,785,622	6,830,796	6,820,969	6,800,682	6,916,106
Covered by Private or Public Insurance											
Number.........................	6,230,656	6,312,556	6,366,988	6,449,626	6,528,817	6,564,958	6,595,821	6,641,889	6,616,890	6,614,995	6,743,451
Percent..........................	95.7	96.1	96.3	96.7	97.2	97.5	97.2	97.2	97.0	97.3	97.5
Uninsured											
Number.........................	276,940	254,295	246,666	218,722	189,273	171,059	189,801	188,907	204,079	185,687	172,655
Percent..........................	4.3	3.9	3.7	3.3	2.8	2.5	2.8	2.8	3.0	2.7	2.5
Percent in the U.S. not covered..................	15.1	14.8	14.5	11.7	9.4	8.6	8.7	8.9	9.2	8.7	8.6
Children Under 19 Years of Age [1]	1,401,873	1,397,972	1,389,165	1,387,398	1,383,924	1,375,244	1,478,961	1,470,670	1,446,247	1,464,881	1,468,672
Covered by Private or Public Insurance											
Number.........................	1,377,774	1,377,766	1,368,086	1,366,087	1,368,039	1,362,535	1,457,076	1,452,714	1,424,224	1,443,612	1,450,206
Percent..........................	98.3	98.6	98.5	98.5	98.9	99.1	98.5	98.8	98.5	98.5	98.7
Uninsured											
Number.........................	24,099	20,206	21,079	21,311	15,885	12,709	21,885	17,956	22,023	21,269	18,466
Percent..........................	1.7	1.4	1.5	1.5	1.1	0.9	1.5	1.2	1.5	1.5	1.3
Percent in the U.S. not covered..................	7.5	7.2	7.1	6.0	4.8	4.5	5.0	5.2	5.7	5.2	5.4

[1] Data for years prior to 2017 are for individuals under 18 years of age.
[2] 2020 ACS 5-Year estimates. 1-Year estimates were not released for 2020 due to the impact of COVID-19 on data collection that year. Data is not comparable to previous years, which are based on 1-year estimates.

Table MA-7. Employment Status by Demographic Group, 2022

(Numbers in thousands, percent.)

Characteristic	Civilian noninstitutional population	Civilian labor force		Employed		Unemployed	
		Number	Percent of population	Number	Percent of population	Number	Percent of population
Total.................................	5,720	3,711	64.9	3,585	62.7	126	3.4
Sex							
Male.................................	2,762	1,910	69.2	1,837	66.5	74	3.9
Female..............................	2,958	1,800	60.9	1,748	59.1	52	2.9
Race, Sex, and Hispanic Origin							
White...............................	4,565	2,969	65.0	2,870	62.9	99	3.3
Male...............................	2,206	1,527	69.2	1,467	66.5	60	3.9
Female.............................	2,359	1,443	61.2	1,404	59.5	39	2.7
Black or African American.........	502	323	64.4	311	61.9	12	3.8
Male...............................	240	163	67.9	156	65.0	7	4.4
Female.............................	262	160	61.1	155	59.2	5	3.1
Hispanic or Latino ethnicity[1]	716	457	63.8	432	60.3	25	5.5
Male...............................	339	242	71.3	229	67.7	12	5.1
Female.............................	377	215	57.0	202	53.6	13	5.9
Age							
16 to 19 years.....................	381	142	37.2	127	33.4	14	10.2
20 to 24 years.....................	417	267	64.0	246	59.1	20	7.7
25 to 34 years.....................	1,010	855	84.7	826	81.8	30	3.5
35 to 44 years.....................	889	758	85.2	737	82.9	21	2.7
45 to 54 years.....................	849	726	85.4	708	83.3	18	2.5
55 to 64 years.....................	950	674	70.9	660	69.4	14	2.1
65 years and over	1,223	290	23.7	281	22.9	9	3.2

NOTE: Data in Table 7 are from the Current Population Survey (CPS) and do not match the estimates in Table 8. See notes and definitions for further information.
[1] May be of any race.

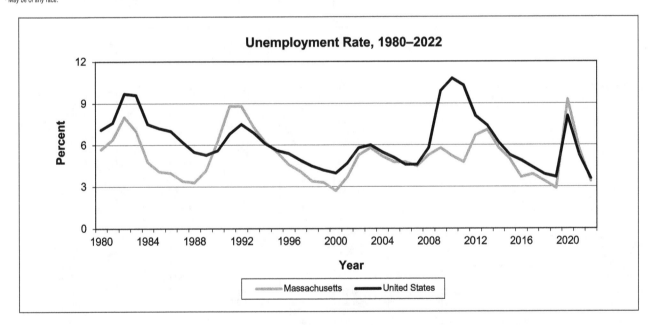

Table MA-8. Employment Status of the Civilian Noninstitutional Population Age 16 Years and Over

(Number, percent.)

Year	Civilian labor force	Civilian participation rate	Employed	Unemployed	Unemployment rate
2010..	3,479,304	66.2	3,198,617	280,687	8.1
2011..	3,484,135	65.8	3,232,458	251,677	7.2
2012..	3,506,457	65.5	3,271,256	235,201	6.7
2013..	3,516,689	65.0	3,283,144	233,545	6.6
2014..	3,569,557	65.4	3,364,853	204,704	5.7
2015..	3,589,409	65.2	3,417,296	172,113	4.8
2016..	3,617,498	65.3	3,472,327	145,171	4.0
2017..	3,724,520	65.9	3,582,389	142,131	3.8
2018..	3,809,873	66.9	3,678,445	131,428	3.4
2019..	3,831,947	66.9	3,714,547	117,400	3.1
2020..	3,741,684	65.2	3,390,249	351,435	9.4
2021..	3,750,870	65.5	3,535,478	215,392	5.7
2022..	3,743,924	65.1	3,603,172	140,752	3.8

Table MA-9. Employment and Average Wages by Industry

(Estimates are based on the 2012 North American Industry Classification System [NAICS].)

Industry	2014	2015	2016	2017	2018	2019	2020	2021
	Number of Jobs							
Wage and Salary Employment by Industry..............................	3,541,525	3,610,422	3,674,544	3,719,842	3,777,588	3,822,709	3,509,394	3,646,171
Farm Wage and Salary Employment......................................	5,086	5,067	4,729	4,718	4,205	4,237	4,046	4,147
Nonfarm Wage and Salary Employment.................................	3,536,439	3,605,355	3,669,815	3,715,124	3,773,383	3,818,472	3,505,348	3,642,024
Private wage and salary employment.................................	3,074,997	3,144,958	3,206,294	3,252,372	3,307,550	3,350,193	3,053,905	3,188,195
Forestry, fishing, and related activities	3,804	4,241	4,283	4,411	4,165	4,300	4,160	3,951
Mining..	931	984	995	998	985	968	910	876
Utilities...	10,683	10,478	10,750	11,345	10,949	11,496	11,615	12,122
Construction	132,057	142,509	150,148	155,526	162,367	166,697	156,137	167,884
Manufacturing..	250,705	249,312	245,917	244,876	245,219	244,379	230,060	233,081
Durable goods manufacturing....................	162,504	161,249	158,703	157,566	157,912	158,025	150,742	151,242
Nondurable goods manufacturing...............	88,201	88,063	87,214	87,310	87,307	86,354	79,318	81,839
Wholesale trade	124,461	124,366	125,948	126,080	124,786	124,156	116,544	119,112
Retail trade..	351,989	355,737	357,947	357,605	356,956	354,322	320,742	335,203
Transportation and warehousing.....................	80,756	83,769	86,032	89,712	92,247	94,553	84,678	91,050
Information	86,286	88,393	89,427	91,898	91,844	92,985	89,354	93,379
Finance and insurance	171,493	173,584	175,885	176,642	176,477	177,614	175,505	174,360
Real estate and rental and leasing.................	43,688	44,862	46,241	47,264	48,751	50,225	46,201	46,895
Professional, scientific, and technical services.....	285,445	296,561	307,409	316,886	330,228	347,078	349,038	360,817
Management of companies and enterprises...........	63,553	65,262	65,663	67,545	74,210	74,188	69,797	68,870
Administrative and waste services	173,016	178,042	181,947	184,767	186,805	187,467	168,659	180,623
Educational services	196,028	200,043	202,199	205,229	215,866	217,298	209,891	223,384
Health care and social assistance...................	587,124	606,592	625,701	634,959	636,246	648,054	609,963	626,467
Arts, entertainment, and recreation.................	56,126	57,355	60,112	61,901	64,225	64,271	40,945	48,696
Accommodation and food services	289,644	295,598	304,429	309,789	314,140	317,429	223,660	250,794
Other services, except public administration............	167,208	167,270	165,261	164,939	171,084	172,713	146,046	150,631
Government and government enterprises.................	461,442	460,397	463,521	462,752	465,833	468,279	451,443	453,829
	Dollars							
Average Wages and Salaries by Industry	62,668	65,208	65,995	68,455	70,935	73,694	81,315	85,260
Average Farm Wages and Salaries	28,801	23,615	29,038	26,415	25,215	19,870	20,209	19,808
Average Nonfarm Wages and Salaries	62,717	65,267	66,043	68,508	70,986	73,754	81,385	85,334
Average private wages and salaries..................	63,557	66,096	66,932	69,487	72,037	74,912	83,175	87,358
Forestry, fishing, and related activities	51,466	50,127	52,105	54,212	57,207	58,856	57,556	76,636
Mining..	62,006	65,063	68,340	68,096	69,002	76,028	82,134	79,013
Utilities...	110,017	111,654	111,359	125,368	131,119	137,228	139,365	140,064
Construction	68,657	71,081	72,698	75,377	78,838	81,480	84,946	87,490
Manufacturing..	83,375	86,138	86,358	88,088	88,594	89,701	96,071	99,340
Durable goods manufacturing....................	91,978	92,882	96,440	98,467	97,879	100,471	105,430	109,325
Nondurable goods manufacturing...............	67,525	73,790	68,013	69,358	71,799	69,992	78,285	80,888
Wholesale trade	88,341	91,561	93,483	97,610	98,742	102,177	110,336	123,211
Retail trade..	30,072	31,369	32,368	33,531	34,947	36,993	40,870	43,835
Transportation and warehousing.....................	48,371	50,048	50,924	51,593	53,419	55,219	60,565	60,972
Information	103,276	107,910	110,437	114,193	123,204	128,183	146,754	157,287
Finance and insurance	136,261	144,057	143,052	150,147	160,379	163,478	173,848	181,117
Real estate and rental and leasing.................	72,759	73,244	74,656	76,834	79,672	83,285	92,048	97,981
Professional, scientific, and technical services...........	113,987	118,817	121,441	128,560	134,807	141,224	152,958	168,279
Management of companies and enterprises...........	126,648	140,155	130,775	131,718	135,075	139,077	145,743	149,317
Administrative and waste services	42,262	44,277	45,426	47,122	49,181	53,011	56,529	60,393
Educational services	48,623	49,361	50,544	51,947	50,959	52,283	55,852	54,354
Health care and social assistance...................	52,548	53,537	54,033	55,205	55,780	57,218	61,661	64,162
Arts, entertainment, and recreation.................	38,551	39,923	40,817	42,075	43,852	45,590	50,147	53,391
Accommodation and food services	23,978	25,130	26,266	27,426	28,787	30,694	29,572	35,123
Other services, except public administration............	34,127	35,356	36,731	37,845	39,121	40,673	45,478	47,550
Government and government enterprises.................	57,114	59,603	59,895	61,634	63,523	65,463	69,277	71,120

Table MA-10. Employment Characteristics by Family Type

(Number, percent.)

Family type and labor force status	2019 Total	2019 Families with own children under 18 years	2020 [1] Total	2020 [1] Families with own children under 18 years	2021 Total	2021 Families with own children under 18 years
All Families.........................	1,665,005	668,195	1,673,992	690,194	1,719,532	701,666
FAMILY TYPE AND LABOR FORCE STATUS						
Opposite-Sex Married-Couple Families...................	1,238,203	468,989	1,221,968	479,354	1,246,346	483,811
Both husband and wife in labor force....................	58.3	75.2	59.1	75.3	58.6	75.7
Husband in labor force, wife not in labor force	17.0	19.8	17.4	19.9	17.1	19.1
Wife in labor force, husband not in labor force	7.9	3.1	7.9	3.4	8.2	4.0
Both husband and wife not in labor force	15.3	1.1	15.6	1.4	16.1	1.2
Other Families	426,802	199,206	433,278	206,681	451,185	213,627
Female householder, no spouse present	71.3	76.0	73.5	77.4	72.6	76.1
In labor force.........................	49.4	63.6	52.4	64.3	51.8	62.0
Not in labor force.....................	21.8	12.5	21.1	13.1	20.7	14.1
Male householder, no spouse present.................	28.7	24.0	26.5	22.6	27.4	23.9
In labor force.........................	23.2	22.2	20.8	20.7	21.6	21.6
Not in labor force.....................	5.5	1.8	5.7	1.9	5.8	2.3

[1] 2020 ACS 5-Year estimates. 1-Year estimates were not released for 2020 due to the impact of COVID-19 on data collection that year. Data is not comparable to previous years, which are based on 1-year estimates.

Table MA-11. School Enrollment and Educational Attainment, 2021

(Number, percent.)

Item	State	U.S.
Enrollment		
Total population 3 years and over, enrolled in school	1,669,642	79,453,524
Enrolled in nursery school or preschool (percent).................................	5.2	5.2
Enrolled in kindergarten (percent)...	4.4	5.0
Enrolled in elementary school, grades 1-8 (percent)...............................	36.4	41.3
Enrolled in high school, grades 9-12 (percent).....................................	20.4	21.8
Enrolled in college or graduate school (percent)..................................	33.5	26.7
Attainment		
Total population 25 years and over	4,934,755	228,193,464
Less than ninth grade (percent)..	4.5	4.8
9th to 12th grade, no diploma (percent)...	4.4	5.9
High school graduate, including equivalency (percent)............................	22.8	26.3
Some college, no degree (percent)..	14.1	19.3
Associate's degree (percent)...	7.6	8.8
Bachelor's degree (percent)	25.3	21.2
Graduate or professional degree (percent)...	21.3	13.8
High school graduate or higher (percent)...	91.1	89.4
Bachelor's degree or higher (percent)...	46.6	35.0

Table MA-12. Public School Characteristics and Educational Indicators

(Number, percent; data derived from National Center of Education Statistics.)

Item	State	U.S.
Public Elementary and Secondary Schools		
Number of regular school districts, 2019-20	322	13,349
Number of operational schools, 2019-20..	1,847	98,469
Percent charter schools	4.4	7.7
Total public school enrollment, Fall 2021...	921,180	49,433,092
Percent charter school enrollment	5.3	7.5
Student-teacher ratio, Fall 2019...	12.8	15.9
Expenditures per student (unadjusted dollars), 2019-20	19,747	13,489
Four-year adjusted cohort graduation rate (ACGR), 2019-2020[1]............	89.0	86.5
Students eligible for free or reduced-price lunch (percent), 2019-20...........	32.8	52.1
English language learners (percent), Fall 2020	10.2	10.3
Students age 3 to 21 served under IDEA, part B (percent), 2021-22...........	19.3	14.7

Public Schools by Type, 2019-20	Number	Percent of state public schools
Total number of schools..	1,847	100.0
Special education..	11	0.6
Vocational education...	36	1.9
Alternative education..	24	1.3

[1] Adjusted Cohort Graduation Rates (ACGR) differ from Averaged Freshmen Graduation Rates (AFGR).

Table MA-13. Reported Voting and Registration of the Voting-Age Population, November 2022

(Numbers in thousands, percent.)

Item	Total population	Total citizen population	Registered			Voted		
			Total registered	Percent registered (total population)	Percent registered (total citizen population)	Total voted	Percent voted (total population)	Percent voted (total citizen population)
U.S. Total	255,457	233,546	161,422	63.2	69.1	121,916	47.7	52.2
State Total.................................	5,518	4,892	3,618	65.6	74.0	2,776	50.3	56.7
Sex								
Male	2,668	2,349	1,717	64.4	73.1	1,260	47.2	53.6
Female	2,850	2,543	1,901	66.7	74.8	1,516	53.2	59.6
Race								
White alone...........................	4,532	4,173	3,158	69.7	75.7	2,479	54.7	59.4
White, non-Hispanic alone	3,924	3,728	2,921	74.4	78.4	2,336	59.5	62.7
Black alone...........................	466	364	263	56.6	72.4	168	36.1	46.2
Asian alone...........................	331	222	128	38.7	57.5	73	22.2	32.9
Hispanic (of any race)......................	787	561	299	37.9	53.2	186	23.6	33.1
White alone or in combination	4,693	4,277	3,221	68.6	75.3	2,532	53.9	59.2
Black alone or in combination......................	579	421	289	49.9	68.7	189	32.6	44.8
Asian alone or in combination......................	371	263	159	42.7	60.3	101	27.2	38.4
Age								
18 to 24 years	591	510	286	48.3	56.0	164	27.8	32.2
25 to 34 years............................	1,001	843	570	57.0	67.7	363	36.2	43.0
35 to 44 years............................	896	742	545	60.8	73.5	412	45.9	55.5
45 to 64 years............................	1,867	1,680	1,300	69.6	77.4	1,007	53.9	60.0
65 years and over............................	1,163	1,118	917	78.9	82.0	830	71.4	74.3

Table MA-14. Health Indicators

(Number, rate as indicated in footnotes.)

Item	State	U.S.
Births		
Life Expectancy at Birth (years), 2020	79.0	77.0
Fertility Rate by State[1], 2021...	49.0	56.3
Percent Home Births, 2021..	0.8	1.4
Cesarean Delivery Rate[2], 2021..	31.8	32.1
Preterm Birth Rate[3], 2021...	9.0	10.5
Teen Birth Rate[4], 2021..	5.7	13.9
Percentage of Babies Born Low Birthweight[5], 2021..	7.5	8.5
Deaths[6]		
Heart Disease Mortality Rate, 2021..	134.0	173.8
Cancer Mortality Rate, 2021...	137.4	146.6
Stroke Mortality Rate, 2021..	25.6	41.1
Diabetes Mortality Rate, 2021..	17.3	25.4
Influenza/Pneumonia Mortality Rate, 2021	9.1	10.5
Suicide Mortality Rate, 2021...	8.0	14.1
Drug Overdose Mortality Rate, 2021...	36.8	33.6
Firearm Injury Mortality Rate, 2021	3.4	14.6
Homicide Mortality Rate, 2021..	2.3	8.2
Disease and Illness		
Lifetime Asthma in Adults, 2020 (percent)...	15.6	13.9
Lifetime Asthma in Children, 2020 (percent)[7]	NA	11.3
Diabetes in Adults, 2020 (percent)...	7.7	8.2
Self-reported Obesity in Adults, 2021 (percent)...	27.4	NA

SOURCE: National Center for Health Statistics, National Vital Statistics System 2020 data; https://wonder.cdc.gov.
[1] General fertility rate per 1,000 women aged 15–44.
[2] This represents the percentage of all live births that were cesarean deliveries.
[3] Babies born prior to 37 weeks of pregnancy (gestation).
[4] Number of births per 1,000 females aged 15–19
[5] Babies born weighing less than 2,500 grams or 5 lbs. 8oz.
[6] Death rates are the number of deaths per 100,000 total population.
[7] U.S. total includes data from 30 states and D.C.
NA = Not available.
- = Zero or rounds to zero.

Table MA-15. State Government Finances, 2021

(Dollar amounts in thousands, percent distribution.)

Item	Dollars	Percent distribution
Total Revenue	86,120,499	100.0
General revenue	74,528,984	86.5
Intergovernmental revenue	27,578,584	32.0
Taxes	36,336,125	42.2
General sales	7,785,108	9.0
Selective sales	2,642,763	3.1
License taxes	1,274,252	1.5
Individual income tax	19,683,486	22.9
Corporate income tax	3,672,995	4.3
Other taxes	1,277,521	1.5
Current charges	5,374,248	6.2
Miscellaneous general revenue	5,240,027	6.1
Utility revenue	466,553	0.5
Liquor stores revenue	-	-
Insurance trust revenue[1]	11,124,962	12.9
Total Expenditure	85,007,834	100.0
Intergovernmental expenditure	11,540,754	13.6
Direct expenditure	73,467,080	86.4
Current operation	48,133,376	56.6
Capital outlay	5,571,344	6.6
Insurance benefits and repayments	15,627,836	18.4
Assistance and subsidies	1,268,639	1.5
Interest on debt	2,865,885	3.4
Exhibit: Salaries and wages	8,111,195	9.5
Total Expenditure	85,007,834	100.0
General expenditure	65,081,460	76.6
Intergovernmental expenditure	11,540,754	13.6
Direct expenditure	53,540,706	63.0
General expenditure, by function:		
Education	14,506,460	17.1
Public welfare	27,361,985	32.2
Hospitals	742,265	0.9
Health	2,115,004	2.5
Highways	2,672,805	3.1
Police protection	678,593	0.8
Correction	1,635,211	1.9
Natural resources	344,834	0.4
Parks and recreation	153,551	0.2
Governmental administration	2,686,192	3.2
Interest on general debt	2,588,913	3.0
Other and unallocable	9,338,827	11.0
Utility expenditure	4,322,008	5.0
Liquor stores expenditure	-	-
Insurance trust expenditure	15,627,836	18.4
Debt at End of Fiscal Year	79,692,181	X
Cash and Security Holdings	133,351,794	X

X = Not applicable.
- = Zero or rounds to zero.
[1] Within insurance trust revenue, net earnings of state retirement systems is a calculated statistic (the item code in the data file is X08), and thus can be positive or negative. Net earnings is the sum of earnings on investments plus gains on investments minus losses on investments. The change made in 2002 for asset valuation from book to market value in accordance with Statement 34 of the Governmental Accounting Standards Board is reflected in the calculated statistics.

Table MA-16. State Government Tax Collections, 2022

(Dollars in thousands, percent.)

Item	Dollars	Percent distribution
Total Taxes	43,492,334	100.0
Property taxes	12,996	-
Sales and gross receipts	11,767,883	27.1
General sales and gross receipts	8,716,276	20.0
Selective sales and gross receipts	3,051,607	7.0
Alcoholic beverages	97,643	0.2
Amusements	301,510	0.7
Insurance premiums	587,997	1.4
Motor fuels	722,788	1.7
Pari-mutuels	1,080	-
Public utilities	X	-
Tobacco products	390,686	0.9
Other selective sales	949,903	2.2
Licenses	1,299,106	3.0
Alcoholic beverages	4,313	-
Amusements	13,153	-
Corporations in general	28,332	0.1
Hunting and fishing	6,330	-
Motor vehicle	452,807	1.0
Motor vehicle operators	84,265	0.2
Public utilities	X	-
Occupation and business, NEC	418,163	1.0
Other licenses	291,743	0.7
Income taxes	29,000,910	66.7
Individual income	24,399,902	56.1
Corporation net income	4,601,008	10.6
Other taxes	1,411,439	3.2
Death and gift	868,444	2.0
Documentary and stock transfer	542,995	1.2
Severance	X	-
Taxes, NEC	0	-

X = Not applicable.
- = Zero or rounds to zero.

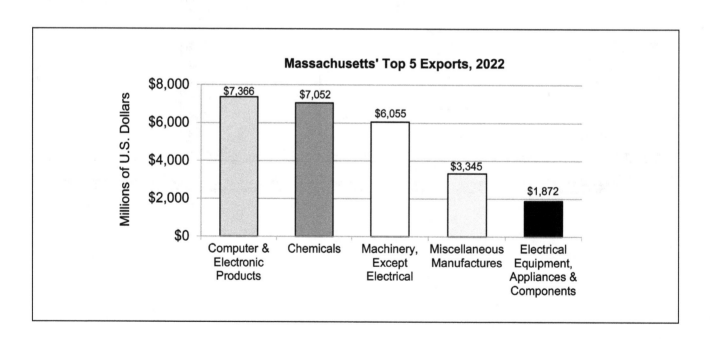

MICHIGAN

Facts and Figures

Location: East north central United States; bordered on the N by Lake Superior, on the E by Ontario, Canada, and Lakes Huron and Erie, on the S by Indiana and Ohio, and on the W by Wisconsin and Lake Michigan

Area: 96,716 sq. mi. (250,494 sq. km.); rank—11th

Population: 10,034,113 (2022 est.); rank—10th

Principal Cities: capital—Lansing; largest—Detroit

Statehood: January 26, 1837; 26th state

U.S. Congress: 2 senators, 14 representatives

State Motto: *Si quaeris peninsulam amoenam, circumspice* ("If you seek a pleasant peninsula, look about you")

State Song: "Michigan, My Michigan"

State Nicknames: The Wolverine State; The Great Lakes State

Abbreviations: MI; Mich.

State Symbols: flower—apple blossom; tree—Eastern white pine; bird—robin

At a Glance

- With an increase in population of 1.5 percent, Michigan ranked 45th among the states in growth from 2010 to 2022.

- In 2021, 5.0 percent of Michiganders did not have health insurance, compared to 8.6 percent of the total U.S. population.

- Michigan had the 4th highest voter turnout in November 2022, with 61.2 percent of population 18 years and over placing votes.

- Approximately 13.1 percent of Michigan residents lived below the poverty level in 2021, compared to the national poverty rate of 12.8 percent.

- Michigan's unemployment rate of 4.2 percent ranked 7th in the nation in 2022.

Table MI-1. Population by Age, Sex, Race, and Hispanic Origin

(Number, percent, except where noted.)

Sex, age, race, and Hispanic origin	2010	2020	2022	Percent change, 2010–2022
Total Population................................	9,883,640	10,077,325	10,034,113	1.5
Percent of total U.S. population	3.2	3.0	3.0	X
Sex				
Male....................................	4,848,114	5,005,664	4,982,544	2.8
Female	5,035,526	5,071,661	5,051,569	0.3
Age				
Under 5 years....................................	596,286	557,127	536,425	-10.0
Under 18 years....................................	2,344,068	2,160,020	2,109,695	-10.0
18 to 64 years....................................	6,178,042	6,135,565	6,044,083	-2.2
65 years and over	1,361,530	1,781,740	1,880,335	38.1
Median age (years)	38.9	39.9	40.2	3.3
Race and Hispanic Origin				
One race				
White	7,949,497	7,957,150	7,906,333	-0.5
Black	1,416,067	1,433,468	1,418,343	0.2
American Indian and Alaska Native	68,396	73,638	74,397	8.8
Asian....................................	243,062	343,180	352,444	45.0
Native Hawaiian or Other Pacific Islander	3,442	4,410	4,702	36.6
Two or more races	203,176	265,479	277,894	36.8
Hispanic (of any race)....................................	436,358	548,697	573,514	31.4

NOTE: Population figures for 2022 are July 1 estimates. The 2010 and 2020 estimates are taken from the respective censuses.
- = Zero or rounds to zero.
X = Not applicable.

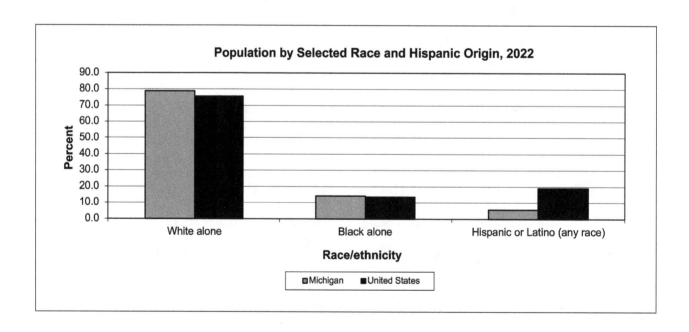

Table MI-2. Marital Status

(Number, percent distribution.)

Sex, age, race, and Hispanic origin	2000	2010	2021
Males, 15 Years and Over	3,761,881	3,875,107	4,074,070
Never married	30.8	34.9	36.9
Now married, except separated................................	56.1	50.5	49.1
Separated................................	1.3	1.3	1.1
Widowed................................	2.5	2.7	2.8
Divorced................................	9.3	10.6	10.2
Females, 15 Years and Over	4,013,722	4,099,384	4,213,117
Never married	25.0	29.0	31.0
Now married, except separated................................	51.8	47.2	46.4
Separated................................	1.6	1.6	1.3
Widowed................................	10.4	9.7	8.5
Divorced................................	11.2	12.5	12.8

Table MI-3. Households and Housing Characteristics

(Number, percent, dollars.)

Item	2000	2010	2021	Average annual percent change, 2010–2021
Total Households...	3,785,661	3,806,621	4,051,798	0.6
Family households...	2,575,699	2,508,780	2,549,542	0.1
Married-couple family.......................................	1,947,610	1,845,094	1,875,558	0.2
Other family..	627,989	663,686	673,984	0.1
Male householder, no wife present...................	154,187	168,337	202,365	1.8
Female householder, no husband present...........	473,802	495,349	471,619	-0.4
Nonfamily households...	1,209,962	1,297,841	1,502,256	1.4
Householder living alone...................................	993,607	1,090,126	1,221,831	1.1
Householder not living alone..............................	216,335	207,715	280,425	3.2
Housing Characteristics				
Total housing units...	4,234,279	4,531,231	4,590,384	0.1
Occupied housing units..	3,785,661	3,806,621	4,051,798	0.6
Owner occupied..	2,793,124	2,769,474	2,966,347	0.6
Renter occupied...	992,537	1,037,147	1,085,451	0.4
Average household size...	2.56	2.53	2.43	-0.4
Financial Characteristics				
Median gross rent of renter-occupied housing	546	730	969	3.0
Median monthly owner costs for housing units with a mortgage ...	972	1,288	1,348	0.4
Median value of owner-occupied housing units...........	115,600	123,300	199,100	5.6

Table MI-4. Migration, Origin, and Language

(Number, percent.)

Characteristic	State 2021	U.S. 2021
Residence 1 Year Ago		
Population 1 year and over	9,950,336	328,464,538
Same house	88.7	87.2
Different house in the U.S.	11.0	12.3
Same county	5.9	6.7
Different county	5.1	5.7
Same state	3.7	3.3
Different state	1.4	2.4
Abroad	0.3	0.4
Place of Birth		
Native born	9,367,518	286,623,642
Male	49.5	49.7
Female	50.5	50.3
Foreign born	683,293	45,270,103
Male	49.6	48.7
Female	50.4	51.3
Foreign born; naturalized U.S. citizen.............................	398,991	24,044,083
Male..	48.0	46.4
Female..	52.0	53.6
Foreign born; not a U.S. citizen.....................................	284,302	21,226,020
Male..	51.9	51.2
Female..	48.1	48.8
Entered 2010 or later	33.4	28.1
Entered 2000 to 2009	22.9	23.7
Entered before 2000..	43.7	48.2
World Region of Birth, Foreign		
Foreign-born population, excluding population born at sea	683,293	45,269,644
Europe	17.5	10.7
Asia	53.2	31.0
Africa	5.2	5.7
Oceania	0.4	0.6
Latin America..	18.9	50.1
North America	4.9	1.7
Language Spoken at Home and Ability to Speak English		
Population 5 years and over..	9,504,832	313,232,500
English only	90.1	78.4
Language other than English...	9.9	21.6
Speaks English less than "very well"..............................	3.4	8.3

Table MI-5. Median Income and Poverty Status, 2021

(Number, percent, except as noted.)

Characteristic	State		U.S.	
	Number	Percent	Number	Percent
Median Income				
Households (dollars)..	63,498	X	69,717	X
Families (dollars)	80,523	X	85,806	X
Below Poverty Level (All People)	1,286,329	13.1	41,393,176	12.8
Sex				
Male	582,730	12.0	18,518,155	11.6
Female	703,599	14.1	22,875,021	13.9
Age				
Under 18 years..	376,831	17.8	12,243,219	16.9
Related children under 18 years.........................	368,435	17.5	11,985,424	16.6
18 to 64 years...	743,893	12.5	23,526,341	11.9
65 years and over	165,605	9.3	5,623,616	10.3

X = Not applicable.

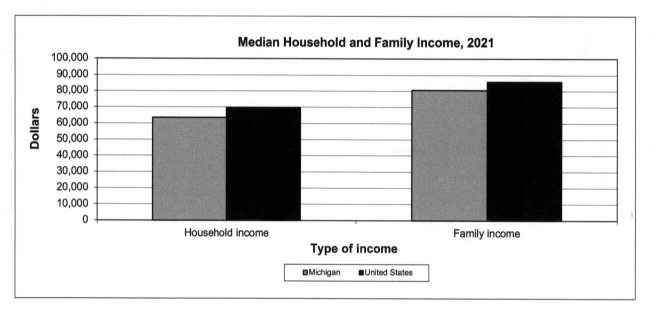

Median Household and Family Income, 2021

☐ Michigan   ■ United States

Table MI-6. Health Insurance Coverage Status for the Civilian Noninstitutionalized Population and Children Under 19 Years of Age

(Number, percent.)

Item	2011	2012	2013	2014	2015	2016	2017	2018	2019	2020 [2]	2021
Civilian Noninstitutionalized Population	9,762,306	9,772,550	9,784,451	9,798,621	9,810,800	9,818,099	9,853,156	9,888,529	9,879,486	9,866,076	9,949,959
Covered by Private or Public Insurance											
Number...	8,612,395	8,658,229	8,712,930	8,961,893	9,214,158	9,291,109	9,343,617	9,353,978	9,308,346	9,337,676	9,454,555
Percent..	88.2	88.6	89.0	91.5	93.9	94.6	94.8	94.6	94.2	94.6	95.0
Uninsured											
Number...	1,149,911	1,114,321	1,071,521	836,728	596,642	526,990	509,539	534,551	571,140	528,400	495,404
Percent..	11.8	11.4	11.0	8.5	6.1	5.4	5.2	5.4	5.8	5.4	5.0
Percent in the U.S. not covered................	15.1	14.8	14.5	11.7	9.4	8.6	8.7	8.9	9.2	8.7	8.6
Children Under 19 Years of Age[1]	2,289,531	2,263,671	2,240,003	2,219,940	2,204,443	2,187,554	2,312,692	2,295,104	2,280,491	2,293,655	2,276,805
Covered by Private or Public Insurance											
Number...	2,195,721	2,173,626	2,150,062	2,136,686	2,136,367	2,124,318	2,243,515	2,217,245	2,202,527	2,222,672	2,207,440
Percent..	95.9	96.0	96.0	96.2	96.9	97.1	97.0	96.6	96.6	96.9	97.0
Uninsured											
Number...	93,810	90,045	89,941	83,254	68,076	63,236	69,177	77,859	77,964	70,983	69,365
Percent..	4.1	4.0	4.0	3.8	3.1	2.9	3.0	3.4	3.4	3.1	3.0
Percent in the U.S. not covered................	7.5	7.2	7.1	6.0	4.8	4.5	5.0	5.2	5.7	5.2	5.4

[1] Data for years prior to 2017 are for individuals under 18 years of age.
[2] 2020 ACS 5-Year estimates. 1-Year estimates were not released for 2020 due to the impact of COVID-19 on data collection that year. Data is not comparable to previous years, which are based on 1-year estimates.

Table MI-7. Employment Status by Demographic Group, 2022

(Numbers in thousands, percent.)

Characteristic	Civilian noninstitutional population	Civilian labor force		Employed		Unemployed	
		Number	Percent of population	Number	Percent of population	Number	Percent of population
Total..	8,087	4,842	59.9	4,643	57.4	199	4.1
Sex							
Male..	3,957	2,580	65.2	2,476	62.6	104	4.0
Female...	4,130	2,262	54.8	2,168	52.5	95	4.2
Race, Sex, and Hispanic Origin							
White...	6,499	3,886	59.8	3,748	57.7	139	3.6
Male...	3,212	2,088	65.0	2,012	62.6	76	3.6
Female..	3,288	1,798	54.7	1,736	52.8	63	3.5
Black or African American...................	1,070	621	58.1	576	53.8	46	7.4
Male...	485	305	62.8	287	59.1	18	5.9
Female..	586	317	54.1	289	49.4	28	8.8
Hispanic or Latino ethnicity[1]...............	424	290	68.5	276	65.2	14	4.8
Male...	219	164	74.9	154	70.2	10	6.1
Female..	205	127	61.7	123	59.8	4	3.1
Age							
16 to 19 years..................................	510	210	41.2	184	36.1	26	12.4
20 to 24 years..................................	637	479	75.2	435	68.3	44	9.1
25 to 34 years..................................	1,316	1,062	80.7	1,017	77.3	45	4.2
35 to 44 years..................................	1,212	990	81.7	954	78.8	36	3.7
45 to 54 years..................................	1,194	940	78.7	918	76.9	22	2.4
55 to 64 years..................................	1,309	800	61.1	783	59.8	17	2.2
65 years and over..............................	1,909	360	18.9	352	18.4	8	2.2

NOTE: Data in Table 7 are from the Current Population Survey (CPS) and do not match the estimates in Table 8. See notes and definitions for further information.
[1] May be of any race.

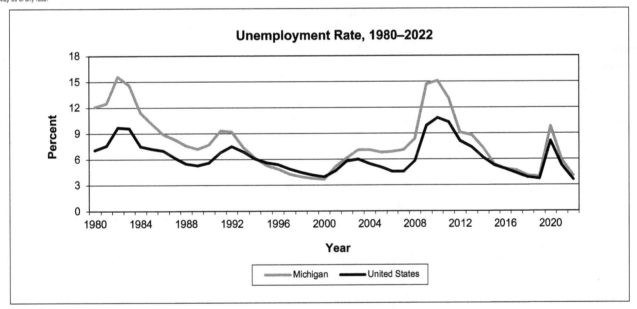

Table MI-8. Employment Status of the Civilian Noninstitutional Population Age 16 Years and Over

(Number, percent.)

Year	Civilian labor force	Civilian participation rate	Employed	Unemployed	Unemployment rate
2010......................................	4,754,799	61.4	4,173,946	580,853	12.2
2011......................................	4,668,979	60.2	4,201,785	467,194	10.0
2012......................................	4,685,462	60.1	4,261,963	423,499	9.0
2013......................................	4,736,919	60.5	4,323,410	413,509	8.7
2014......................................	4,759,720	60.6	4,416,017	343,703	7.2
2015......................................	4,760,207	60.4	4,501,816	258,391	5.4
2016......................................	4,848,638	61.2	4,606,948	241,690	5.0
2017......................................	4,911,247	61.4	4,685,853	225,394	4.6
2018......................................	4,940,313	61.5	4,734,158	206,155	4.2
2019......................................	4,969,294	61.7	4,766,050	203,244	4.1
2020......................................	4,846,013	60.1	4,361,873	484,140	10.0
2021......................................	4,776,110	59.2	4,495,651	280,459	5.9
2022......................................	4,835,966	59.9	4,632,539	203,427	4.2

Table MI-9. Employment and Average Wages by Industry

(Estimates are based on the 2012 North American Industry Classification System [NAICS].)

Industry	2014	2015	2016	2017	2018	2019	2020	2021
	Number of Jobs							
Wage and Salary Employment by Industry.........................	4,254,464	4,326,978	4,403,195	4,450,757	4,498,209	4,521,246	4,129,357	4,279,524
Farm Wage and Salary Employment................................	22,981	25,200	23,888	19,689	22,033	23,806	20,933	19,831
Nonfarm Wage and Salary Employment..........................	4,231,483	4,301,778	4,379,307	4,431,068	4,476,176	4,497,440	4,108,424	4,259,693
Private wage and salary employment..........................	3,625,384	3,697,754	3,770,111	3,817,777	3,861,690	3,878,971	3,517,406	3,673,327
Forestry, fishing, and related activities.....................	8,841	8,733	8,844	8,774	8,770	8,918	8,594	8,456
Mining...	6,647	6,001	5,442	5,440	5,543	5,539	4,893	4,911
Utilities..	19,771	19,886	20,128	20,221	20,340	20,633	20,468	20,746
Construction...	145,189	151,927	158,918	165,982	173,005	177,608	168,814	180,352
Manufacturing..	569,317	587,225	601,514	616,940	629,372	627,651	556,876	588,135
Durable goods manufacturing............................	429,988	444,244	453,043	465,504	476,156	473,943	416,250	442,411
Nondurable goods manufacturing......................	139,329	142,981	148,471	151,436	153,216	153,708	140,626	145,724
Wholesale trade...	168,267	170,394	172,668	173,444	172,294	172,243	161,720	165,673
Retail trade..	463,520	470,246	475,776	477,144	473,605	467,660	432,489	453,016
Transportation and warehousing............................	111,706	116,778	118,748	123,588	130,262	140,253	140,742	147,080
Information..	60,548	59,398	59,691	56,720	56,371	55,491	50,725	52,002
Finance and insurance..	148,015	149,836	153,793	157,815	158,255	163,827	167,971	172,624
Real estate and rental and leasing.........................	51,416	52,223	53,548	55,161	56,269	57,771	53,025	54,773
Professional, scientific, and technical services.........	278,920	289,045	297,902	295,285	301,141	303,083	291,288	302,455
Management of companies and enterprises..............	55,222	56,447	58,820	66,206	68,545	70,613	70,772	71,051
Administrative and waste services.........................	290,280	294,446	293,249	290,334	294,671	287,917	244,237	261,607
Educational services...	80,199	79,975	77,807	78,560	74,562	74,779	65,438	69,110
Health care and social assistance.........................	564,568	575,466	590,800	597,455	603,606	605,688	573,696	580,268
Arts, entertainment, and recreation.......................	50,633	50,767	52,477	54,146	54,218	54,537	36,604	43,344
Accommodation and food services........................	358,738	364,933	375,190	380,854	381,785	383,594	290,892	315,780
Other services, except public administration............	193,587	194,028	194,796	193,708	199,076	201,166	178,162	181,944
Government and government enterprises....................	606,099	604,024	609,196	613,291	614,486	618,469	591,018	586,366
	Dollars							
Average Wages and Salaries by Industry	47,998	49,580	50,526	52,069	53,474	54,594	58,761	61,178
Average Farm Wages and Salaries	35,035	31,790	38,290	37,907	36,137	33,770	29,903	32,723
Average Nonfarm Wages and Salaries	48,069	49,684	50,592	52,132	53,559	54,704	58,908	61,310
Average private wages and salaries..........................	48,099	49,830	50,794	52,421	53,838	54,977	59,417	61,874
Forestry, fishing, and related activities.....................	27,683	29,663	31,352	32,479	33,679	35,011	37,662	39,711
Mining...	77,103	75,619	73,910	75,506	81,515	82,033	81,370	88,345
Utilities..	109,025	112,220	112,552	117,090	120,606	122,994	130,248	133,142
Construction...	55,588	57,317	59,088	61,529	62,382	63,563	67,559	70,158
Manufacturing..	63,557	65,106	65,174	66,205	67,543	68,450	70,875	71,675
Durable goods manufacturing............................	65,872	67,441	67,389	68,333	69,651	70,662	72,505	73,063
Nondurable goods manufacturing......................	56,412	57,851	58,417	59,662	60,992	61,627	66,052	67,461
Wholesale trade...	69,917	71,148	72,291	73,923	76,263	77,361	80,911	85,964
Retail trade..	27,351	28,511	29,225	30,108	31,122	32,083	35,361	37,864
Transportation and warehousing............................	52,009	53,215	54,242	55,121	56,744	57,072	58,480	60,355
Information..	65,440	67,887	69,531	70,832	73,578	77,470	88,679	94,495
Finance and insurance..	70,864	73,988	75,787	77,812	80,011	82,354	89,762	92,427
Real estate and rental and leasing.........................	39,689	42,286	43,734	45,355	48,000	49,116	55,306	58,999
Professional, scientific, and technical services.........	77,809	80,717	82,247	86,365	87,805	89,077	92,611	97,060
Management of companies and enterprises..............	119,947	122,438	124,357	132,243	128,099	126,525	127,527	131,448
Administrative and waste services.........................	32,443	33,934	34,730	35,934	36,776	37,753	42,043	45,895
Educational services...	30,854	31,474	32,628	33,123	35,195	35,171	39,114	39,266
Health care and social assistance.........................	46,451	48,168	48,775	49,479	50,779	51,984	55,230	57,621
Arts, entertainment, and recreation.......................	32,998	33,896	35,378	36,358	36,438	36,980	42,972	42,006
Accommodation and food services........................	17,584	18,576	19,244	20,117	21,438	21,954	21,503	25,816
Other services, except public administration............	31,225	32,649	33,645	34,729	35,808	36,689	40,808	42,585
Government and government enterprises....................	47,887	48,791	49,343	50,335	51,804	52,990	55,880	57,777

Table MI-10. Employment Characteristics by Family Type

(Number, percent.)

Family type and labor force status	2019		2020 [1]		2021	
	Total	Families with own children under 18 years	Total	Families with own children under 18 years	Total	Families with own children under 18 years
All Families...	2,496,550	977,424	2,526,437	1,017,313	2,549,542	996,119
FAMILY TYPE AND LABOR FORCE STATUS						
Opposite-Sex Married-Couple Families..	1,825,191	643,620	1,852,632	674,027	1,860,369	658,093
Both husband and wife in labor force.................................	48.8	68.5	49.3	67.5	48.4	67.6
Husband in labor force, wife not in labor force	20.3	25.5	20.4	26.2	20.3	26.4
Wife in labor force, husband not in labor force	8.0	4.0	8.6	4.5	8.3	4.2
Both husband and wife not in labor force..........................	22.3	1.7	21.8	1.8	23.0	1.8
Other Families	671,359	333,804	661,274	341,132	673,984	335,203
Female householder, no spouse present..........................	70.0	71.6	71.2	73.2	70.0	71.6
In labor force.......................................	47.8	60.7	48.9	60.6	46.4	57.4
Not in labor force	22.2	10.9	22.3	12.7	23.6	14.2
Male householder, no spouse present...........................	30.0	28.4	28.8	26.8	30.0	28.4
In labor force.......................................	22.5	25.5	21.4	23.8	22.4	24.8
Not in labor force	7.5	2.9	7.4	3.0	7.6	3.6

[1] 2020 ACS 5-Year estimates. 1-Year estimates were not released for 2020 due to the impact of COVID-19 on data collection that year. Data is not comparable to previous years, which are based on 1-year estimates.

Table MI-11. School Enrollment and Educational Attainment, 2021

(Number, percent.)

Item	State	U.S.
Enrollment		
Total population 3 years and over, enrolled in school	2,313,566	79,453,524
Enrolled in nursery school or preschool (percent)..	5.1	5.2
Enrolled in kindergarten (percent)..	4.9	5.0
Enrolled in elementary school, grades 1-8 (percent)..	41.2	41.3
Enrolled in high school, grades 9-12 (percent)..	22.1	21.8
Enrolled in college or graduate school (percent)..	26.7	26.7
Attainment		
Total population 25 years and over	6,971,895	228,193,464
Less than ninth grade (percent)..	2.5	4.8
9th to 12th grade, no diploma (percent)	5.5	5.9
High school graduate, including equivalency (percent)..	28.7	26.3
Some college, no degree (percent)..	21.8	19.3
Associate's degree (percent)..	9.8	8.8
Bachelor's degree (percent)	19.2	21.2
Graduate or professional degree (percent)..	12.5	13.8
High school graduate or higher (percent)..	92.0	89.4
Bachelor's degree or higher (percent)..	31.7	35.0

Table MI-12. Public School Characteristics and Educational Indicators

(Number, percent; data derived from National Center of Education Statistics.)

Item	State	U.S.
Public Elementary and Secondary Schools		
Number of regular school districts, 2019-20	537	13,349
Number of operational schools, 2019-20..	3,550	98,469
Percent charter schools	10.4	7.7
Total public school enrollment, Fall 2021	1,440,090	49,433,092
Percent charter school enrollment	10.7	7.5
Student-teacher ratio, Fall 2019..	17.6	15.9
Expenditures per student (unadjusted dollars), 2019-20	12,323	13,489
Four-year adjusted cohort graduation rate (ACGR), 2019-2020[1]..	82.1	86.5
Students eligible for free or reduced-price lunch (percent), 2019-20..	50.5	52.1
English language learners (percent), Fall 2020	6.4	10.3
Students age 3 to 21 served under IDEA, part B (percent), 2021-22	13.5	14.7

Public Schools by Type, 2019-20	Number	Percent of state public schools
Total number of schools..	3,550	100.0
Special education..	188	5.3
Vocational education..	46	1.3
Alternative education..	360	10.1

[1] Adjusted Cohort Graduation Rates (ACGR) differ from Averaged Freshmen Graduation Rates (AFGR).

Table MI-13. Reported Voting and Registration of the Voting-Age Population, November 2022

(Numbers in thousands, percent.)

Item	Total population	Total citizen population	Registered			Voted		
			Total registered	Percent registered (total population)	Percent registered (total citizen population)	Total voted	Percent voted (total population)	Percent voted (total citizen population)
U.S. Total	255,457	233,546	161,422	63.2	69.1	121,916	47.7	52.2
State Total..	7,777	7,517	5,797	74.5	77.1	4,757	61.2	63.3
Sex								
Male	3,788	3,643	2,787	73.6	76.5	2,197	58.0	60.3
Female	3,989	3,874	3,009	75.4	77.7	2,560	64.2	66.1
Race								
White alone..	6,330	6,167	4,802	75.9	77.9	3,941	62.3	63.9
White, non-Hispanic alone	5,900	5,810	4,568	77.4	78.6	3,776	64.0	65.0
Black alone..	1,015	1,015	797	78.5	78.5	659	64.9	64.9
Asian alone..	294	196	95	32.3	48.3	76	25.8	38.6
Hispanic (of any race)	443	370	247	55.8	66.7	177	40.1	47.9
White alone or in combination	6,433	6,270	4,893	76.1	78.0	4,010	62.3	63.9
Black alone or in combination	1,054	1,054	831	78.9	78.9	680	64.5	64.5
Asian alone or in combination..................	303	206	104	34.3	50.6	85	28.1	41.4
Age								
18 to 24 years......................................	826	799	532	64.3	66.5	371	44.9	46.5
25 to 34 years......................................	1,304	1,223	852	65.3	69.7	622	47.7	50.8
35 to 44 years......................................	1,228	1,183	894	72.7	75.5	689	56.1	58.2
45 to 64 years......................................	2,639	2,545	2,025	76.7	79.6	1,710	64.8	67.2
65 years and over	1,779	1,767	1,494	84.0	84.6	1,365	76.7	77.2

Table MI-14. Health Indicators

(Number, rate as indicated in footnotes.)

Item	State	U.S.
Births		
Life Expectancy at Birth (years), 2020	76.0	77.0
Fertility Rate by State[1], 2021	55.4	56.3
Percent Home Births, 2021	2.1	1.4
Cesarean Delivery Rate[2], 2021	33.2	32.1
Preterm Birth Rate[3], 2021	10.6	10.5
Teen Birth Rate[4], 2021	12.2	13.9
Percentage of Babies Born Low Birthweight[5], 2021	9.2	8.5
Deaths[6]		
Heart Disease Mortality Rate, 2021..	209.6	173.8
Cancer Mortality Rate, 2021...	160.1	146.6
Stroke Mortality Rate, 2021..	46.2	41.1
Diabetes Mortality Rate, 2021...	26.7	25.4
Influenza/Pneumonia Mortality Rate, 2021	10.4	10.5
Suicide Mortality Rate, 2021...	14.3	14.1
Drug Overdose Mortality Rate, 2021...	31.5	33.6
Firearm Injury Mortality Rate, 2021	15.4	14.6
Homicide Mortality Rate, 2021..	8.7	8.2
Disease and Illness		
Lifetime Asthma in Adults, 2020 (percent)...	15.4	13.9
Lifetime Asthma in Children, 2020 (percent)[7]	12.4	11.3
Diabetes in Adults, 2020 (percent)...	10.6	8.2
Self-reported Obesity in Adults, 2021 (percent)..	34.4	NA

SOURCE: National Center for Health Statistics, National Vital Statistics System 2020 data; https://wonder.cdc.gov.
[1] General fertility rate per 1,000 women aged 15–44.
[2] This represents the percentage of all live births that were cesarean deliveries.
[3] Babies born prior to 37 weeks of pregnancy (gestation).
[4] Number of births per 1,000 females aged 15–19
[5] Babies born weighing less than 2,500 grams or 5 lbs. 8oz.
[6] Death rates are the number of deaths per 100,000 total population.
[7] U.S. total includes data from 30 states and D.C.
NA = Not available.
- = Zero or rounds to zero.

Table MI-15. State Government Finances, 2021

(Dollar amounts in thousands, percent distribution.)

Item	Dollars	Percent distribution
Total Revenue	88,194,407	100.0
General revenue	78,992,870	89.6
Intergovernmental revenue	29,459,635	33.4
Taxes	34,431,625	39.0
General sales	11,190,298	12.7
Selective sales	4,735,465	5.4
License taxes	2,178,822	2.5
Individual income tax	11,999,165	13.6
Corporate income tax	1,496,498	1.7
Other taxes	2,831,377	3.2
Current charges	10,377,079	11.8
Miscellaneous general revenue	4,724,531	5.4
Utility revenue	32	-
Liquor stores revenue	1459225	1.7
Insurance trust revenue[1]	7,742,280	8.8
Total Expenditure	89,748,230	100.0
Intergovernmental expenditure	26,336,101	29.3
Direct expenditure	63,412,129	70.7
Current operation	44,233,985	49.3
Capital outlay	2,419,102	2.7
Insurance benefits and repayments	13,644,957	15.2
Assistance and subsidies	1,866,879	2.1
Interest on debt	1,247,206	1.4
Exhibit: Salaries and wages	10,744,790	12.0
Total Expenditure	89,748,230	100.0
General expenditure	74,922,656	83.5
Intergovernmental expenditure	26,336,101	29.3
Direct expenditure	48,586,555	54.1
General expenditure, by function:		
Education	26,567,497	29.6
Public welfare	23,518,423	26.2
Hospitals	5,364,321	6.0
Health	2,418,289	2.7
Highways	4,332,680	4.8
Police protection	601,200	0.7
Correction	1,877,849	2.1
Natural resources	436,817	0.5
Parks and recreation	174,909	0.2
Governmental administration	2,129,997	2.4
Interest on general debt	1,247,206	1.4
Other and unallocable	5,437,922	6.1
Utility expenditure	350,772	0.4
Liquor stores expenditure	1,180,521	1.3
Insurance trust expenditure	13,644,957	15.2
Debt at End of Fiscal Year	33,621,791	X
Cash and Security Holdings	143,557,744	X

X = Not applicable.
- = Zero or rounds to zero.
[1] Within insurance trust revenue, net earnings of state retirement systems is a calculated statistic (the item code in the data file is X08), and thus can be positive or negative. Net earnings is the sum of earnings on investments plus gains on investments minus losses on investments. The change made in 2002 for asset valuation from book to market value in accordance with Statement 34 of the Governmental Accounting Standards Board is reflected in the calculated statistics.

Table MI-16. State Government Tax Collections, 2022

(Dollars in thousands, percent.)

Item	Dollars	Percent distribution
Total Taxes	37,056,989	100.0
Property taxes	2,535,211	6.8
Sales and gross receipts	17,017,985	45.9
General sales and gross receipts	12,204,862	32.9
Selective sales and gross receipts	4,813,123	13.0
Alcoholic beverages	219,449	0.6
Amusements	285,629	0.8
Insurance premiums	398,371	1.1
Motor fuels	1,416,157	3.8
Pari-mutuels	2,924	-
Public utilities	42,928	0.1
Tobacco products	805,030	2.2
Other selective sales	1,642,635	4.4
Licenses	2,240,237	6.0
Alcoholic beverages	18,643	0.1
Amusements	X	-
Corporations in general	34,998	0.1
Hunting and fishing	66,902	0.2
Motor vehicle	1,498,851	4.0
Motor vehicle operators	66,444	0.2
Public utilities	32,696	0.1
Occupation and business, NEC	292,138	0.8
Other licenses	229,565	0.6
Income taxes	14,674,116	39.6
Individual income	12,879,815	34.8
Corporation net income	1,794,301	4.8
Other taxes	589,440	1.6
Death and gift	6	-
Documentary and stock transfer	542,386	1.5
Severance	46,951	0.1
Taxes, NEC	97	-

- = Zero or rounds to zero.
X = Not applicable.

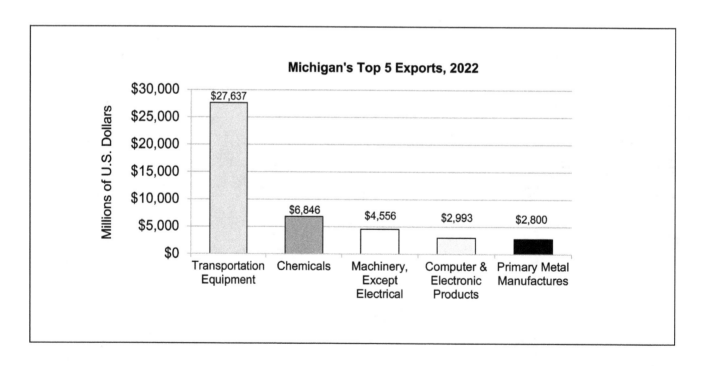

MINNESOTA

Facts and Figures

Location: North central United States; bordered on the N by Canada (Manitoba and Ontario), on the E by Lake Superior and Wisconsin, on the S by Iowa, and on the W by North Dakota and South Dakota

Area: 86,939 sq. mi. (225,171 sq. km.); rank—12th

Population: 5,717,184 (2022 est.); rank—22nd

Principal Cities: capital—St. Paul; largest—Minneapolis

Statehood: May 11, 1858; 32nd state

U.S. Congress: 2 senators, 8 representatives

State Motto: *L'Etoile du Nord* ("The Star of the North")

State Song: "Hail! Minnesota"

State Nicknames: The North Star State; The Land of 10,000 Lakes; The Gopher State

Abbreviations: MN; Minn.

State Symbols: flower—showy (pink and white) lady's slipper; tree—red (Norway) pine; bird—loon

At a Glance

- With an increase in population of 7.8 percent, Minnesota ranked 20th among the states in growth from 2010 to 2022.

- Minnesota had the 4th highest voter turnout in the November 2022 midterm election, with 61.2 percent of the voting-age population casting votes.

- The unemployment rate in Minnesota in 2022 was 2.7 percent, compared to the national unemployment rate of 3.6 percent.

- Minnesota's median household income was $77,720 in 2021, which ranked 14th among the states.

- In 2021, 9.3 percent of all Minnesotans and 10.8 percent of children in Minnesota lived below the poverty level, compared to 12.8 percent of the entire U.S. population and 16.9 percent of all U.S. children.

Table MN-1. Population by Age, Sex, Race, and Hispanic Origin

(Number, percent, except where noted.)

Sex, age, race, and Hispanic origin	2010	2020	2022	Percent change, 2010–2022
Total Population..	5,303,925	5,706,504	5,717,184	7.8
Percent of total U.S. population	1.7	1.7	1.7	X
Sex				
Male...	2,632,132	2,865,847	2,871,216	9.1
Female	2,671,793	2,840,657	2,845,968	6.5
Age				
Under 5 years..	355,504	344,112	330,126	-7.1
Under 18 years..	1,284,063	1,315,808	1,294,162	0.8
18 to 64 years...	3,336,741	3,456,676	3,425,490	2.7
65 years and over	683,121	934,020	997,532	46.0
Median age (years)	37.4	38.4	38.9	4.0
Race and Hispanic Origin				
One race				
White	4,623,461	4,756,562	4,722,046	2.1
Black	280,949	411,429	437,333	55.7
American Indian and Alaska Native	67,325	77,452	78,885	17.2
Asian...	217,792	302,890	313,223	43.8
Native Hawaiian or Other Pacific Islander	2,958	4,630	5,025	69.9
Two or more races	111,440	153,541	160,672	44.2
Hispanic (of any race)...................................	250,258	325,521	341,414	36.4

NOTE: Population figures for 2022 are July 1 estimates. The 2010 and 2020 estimates are taken from the respective censuses.
- = Zero or rounds to zero.
X = Not applicable.

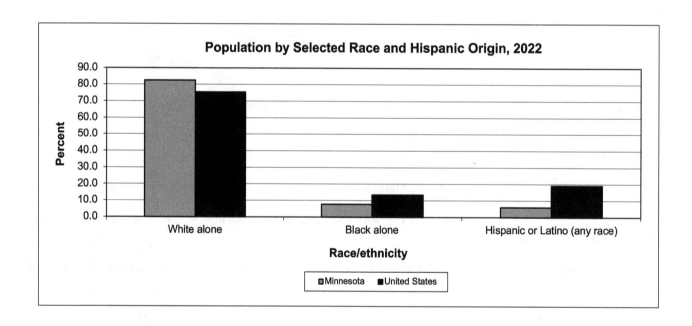

Table MN-2. Marital Status

(Number, percent distribution.)

Sex, age, race, and Hispanic origin	2000	2010	2021
Males, 15 Years and Over	1,889,936	2,090,940	2,307,887
Never married	31.3	34.6	36.2
Now married, except separated..	57.7	53.5	51.7
Separated...	0.9	0.9	0.8
Widowed...	2.1	2.2	2.4
Divorced...	8.0	8.7	8.9
Females, 15 Years and Over	1,967,819	2,155,042	2,320,971
Never married	25.0	28.2	30.4
Now married, except separated..	55.0	51.5	50.0
Separated...	1.2	1.2	1.0
Widowed...	9.4	8.4	7.3
Divorced...	9.5	10.7	11.4

Table MN-3. Households and Housing Characteristics

(Number, percent, dollars.)

Item	2000	2010	2021	Average annual percent change, 2010–2021
Total Households..	1,895,127	2,091,548	2,281,033	0.8
Family households.......................................	1,255,141	1,353,758	1,427,221	0.5
Married-couple family..................................	1,018,245	1,069,000	1,122,121	0.5
Other family..	236,986	284,758	305,100	0.6
Male householder, no wife present................	68,114	87,757	101,601	1.4
Female householder, no husband present.......	168,782	197,001	203,499	0.3
Nonfamily households..	639,986	737,790	853,812	1.4
Householder living alone..............................	509,468	591,124	663,548	1.1
Householder not living alone........................	130,518	146,666	190,264	2.7
Housing Characteristics				
Total housing units.....................................	2,065,946	2,348,242	2,517,173	0.7
Occupied housing units...............................	1,895,127	2,091,548	2,281,033	0.8
Owner occupied..	1,412,865	1,527,328	1,665,101	0.8
Renter occupied...	482,262	564,220	615,932	0.8
Average household size................................	2.52	2.47	2.45	-0.1
Financial Characteristics				
Median gross rent of renter-occupied housing	566	764	1,113	4.2
Median monthly owner costs for housing units with a mortgage	1,044	1,503	1,667	1.0
Median value of owner-occupied housing units...........	122,400	194,300	285,400	4.3

Table MN-4. Migration, Origin, and Language

(Number, percent.)

Characteristic	State 2021	U.S. 2021
Residence 1 Year Ago		
Population 1 year and over...	5,645,866	328,464,538
Same house...	87.3	87.2
Different house in the U.S..	12.4	12.3
Same county..	6.2	6.7
Different county..	6.2	5.7
Same state..	4.6	3.3
Different state..	1.7	2.4
Abroad...	0.3	0.4
Place of Birth		
Native born...	5,219,945	286,623,642
Male..	50.2	49.7
Female...	49.8	50.3
Foreign born...	487,445	45,270,103
Male..	49.3	48.7
Female...	50.7	51.3
Foreign born; naturalized U.S. citizen...............................	284,613	24,044,083
Male..	47.6	46.4
Female...	52.4	53.6
Foreign born; not a U.S. citizen.......................................	202,832	21,226,020
Male..	51.7	51.2
Female...	48.3	48.8
Entered 2010 or later..	35.0	28.1
Entered 2000 to 2009...	27.8	23.7
Entered before 2000..	37.2	48.2
World Region of Birth, Foreign		
Foreign-born population, excluding population born at sea	487,445	45,269,644
Europe...	9.1	10.7
Asia...	37.0	31.0
Africa...	28.7	5.7
Oceania..	0.3	0.6
Latin America...	22.5	50.1
North America..	2.5	1.7
Language Spoken at Home and Ability to Speak English		
Population 5 years and over...	5,376,656	313,232,500
English only...	00.0	78.4
Language other than English..	12.0	21.6
Speaks English less than "very well"................................	4.5	8.3

Table MN-5. Median Income and Poverty Status, 2021

(Number, percent, except as noted.)

Characteristic	State		U.S.	
	Number	Percent	Number	Percent
Median Income				
Households (dollars)...	77,720	X	69,717	X
Families (dollars)...	99,567	X	85,806	X
Below Poverty Level (All People)	519,731	9.3	41,393,176	12.8
Sex				
Male	236,324	8.4	18,518,155	11.6
Female	283,407	10.2	22,875,021	13.9
Age				
Under 18 years..	138,621	10.8	12,243,219	16.9
Related children under 18 years........................	132,285	10.4	11,985,424	16.6
18 to 64 years...	301,878	9.0	23,526,341	11.9
65 years and over	79,232	8.5	5,623,616	10.3

X = Not applicable.

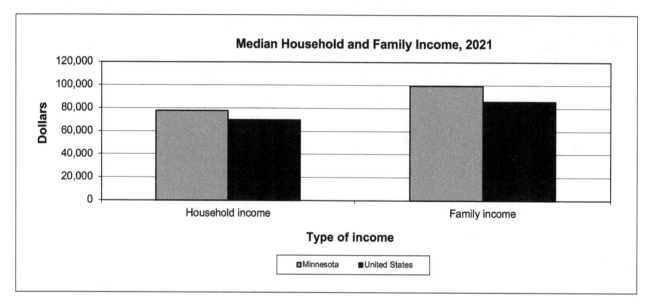

Median Household and Family Income, 2021

Table MN-6. Health Insurance Coverage Status for the Civilian Noninstitutionalized Population and Children Under 19 Years of Age

(Number, percent.)

Item	2011	2012	2013	2014	2015	2016	2017	2018	2019	2020 [2]	2021
Civilian Noninstitutionalized Population	5,286,728	5,319,783	5,362,681	5,398,211	5,431,894	5,462,438	5,519,199	5,553,564	5,580,828	5,541,421	5,651,958
Covered by Private or Public Insurance											
Number...	4,819,295	4,895,121	4,922,902	5,080,954	5,186,786	5,237,492	5,276,690	5,309,185	5,308,216	5,289,521	5,400,134
Percent..	91.2	92.0	91.8	94.1	95.5	95.9	95.6	95.6	95.1	95.5	95.5
Uninsured											
Number...	467,433	424,662	439,779	317,257	245,108	224,946	242,509	244,379	272,612	251,900	251,824
Percent..	8.8	8.0	8.2	5.9	4.5	4.1	4.4	4.4	4.9	4.5	4.5
Percent in the U.S. not covered................................	15.1	14.8	14.5	11.7	9.4	8.6	8.7	8.9	9.2	8.7	8.6
Children Under 19 Years of Age[1]	1,276,035	1,275,509	1,280,236	1,280,791	1,280,978	1,286,323	1,372,988	1,376,114	1,378,383	1,374,076	1,382,530
Covered by Private or Public Insurance											
Number...	1,196,211	1,207,024	1,208,254	1,231,774	1,241,570	1,243,038	1,325,783	1,330,920	1,335,996	1,328,225	1,338,685
Percent..	93.7	94.6	94.4	96.2	96.9	96.6	96.6	96.7	96.9	96.7	96.8
Uninsured											
Number...	79,824	68,485	71,982	49,017	39,408	43,285	47,205	45,194	42,387	45,851	43,845
Percent..	6.3	5.4	5.6	3.8	3.1	3.4	3.4	3.3	3.1	3.3	3.2
Percent in the U.S. not covered................................	7.5	7.2	7.1	6.0	4.8	4.5	5.0	5.2	5.7	5.2	5.4

[1] Data for years prior to 2017 are for individuals under 18 years of age.
[2] 2020 ACS 5-Year estimates. 1-Year estimates were not released for 2020 due to the impact of COVID-19 on data collection that year. Data is not comparable to previous years, which are based on 1-year estimates.

Table MN-7. Employment Status by Demographic Group, 2022

(Numbers in thousands, percent.)

Characteristic	Civilian noninstitutional population	Civilian labor force		Employed		Unemployed	
		Number	Percent of population	Number	Percent of population	Number	Percent of population
Total...	4,514	3,081	68.3	3,000	66.5	81	2.6
Sex							
Male..	2,249	1,634	72.6	1,583	70.4	51	3.1
Female.......................................	2,265	1,447	63.9	1,417	62.6	31	2.1
Race, Sex, and Hispanic Origin							
White...	3,818	2,589	67.8	2,531	66.3	58	2.3
Male......................................	1,909	1,364	71.5	1,327	69.5	37	2.7
Female...................................	1,909	1,225	64.2	1,204	63.0	21	1.7
Black or African American................	295	208	70.7	200	67.9	8	3.9
Male......................................	NA	NA	NA	NA	NA	NA	NA
Female...................................	NA	NA	NA	NA	NA	NA	NA
Hispanic or Latino ethnicity[1]............	NA	NA	NA	NA	NA	NA	NA
Male......................................	NA	NA	NA	NA	NA	NA	NA
Female...................................	NA	NA	NA	NA	NA	NA	NA
Age							
16 to 19 years.............................	NA	NA	NA	NA	NA	NA	NA
20 to 24 years.............................	348	262	75.3	247	70.9	15	5.9
25 to 34 years.............................	715	650	90.9	633	88.6	17	2.5
35 to 44 years.............................	769	666	86.6	654	85.0	12	1.8
45 to 54 years.............................	698	594	85.0	584	83.6	10	1.7
55 to 64 years.............................	709	514	72.5	507	71.6	6	1.2
65 years and over.........................	951	227	23.9	220	23.1	7	3.2

NOTE: Data in Table 7 are from the Current Population Survey (CPS) and do not match the estimates in Table 8. See notes and definitions for further information.
[1] May be of any race.
NA = Not available.

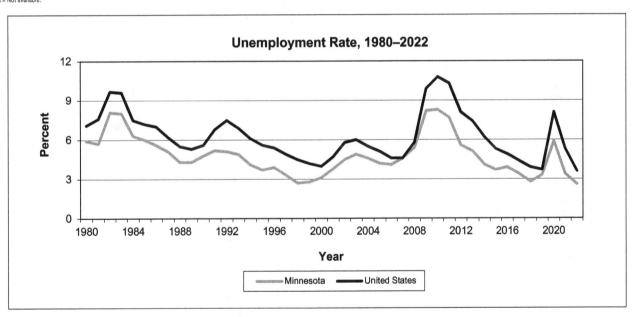

Unemployment Rate, 1980–2022

Table MN-8. Employment Status of the Civilian Noninstitutional Population Age 16 Years and Over

(Number, percent.)

Year	Civilian labor force	Civilian participation rate	Employed	Unemployed	Unemployment rate
2010...	2,940,696	71.5	2,722,623	218,073	7.4
2011...	2,952,527	71.1	2,760,400	192,127	6.5
2012...	2,949,770	70.5	2,783,181	166,589	5.6
2013...	2,961,729	70.2	2,812,453	149,276	5.0
2014...	2,979,798	70.1	2,852,488	127,310	4.3
2015...	3,005,414	70.2	2,891,673	113,741	3.8
2016...	3,023,110	70.0	2,906,348	116,762	3.9
2017...	3,071,006	70.1	2,963,830	107,176	3.5
2018...	3,085,627	69.8	2,989,055	96,572	3.1
2019...	3,129,844	70.3	3,021,984	107,860	3.4
2020...	3,122,981	69.7	2,925,515	197,466	6.3
2021...	3,021,360	67.2	2,918,393	102,967	3.4
2022...	3,077,500	68.1	2,994,920	82,580	2.7

Table MN-9. Employment and Average Wages by Industry

(Estimates are based on the 2012 North American Industry Classification System [NAICS].)

Industry	2014	2015	2016	2017	2018	2019	2020	2021
	Number of Jobs							
Wage and Salary Employment by Industry.....................	2,873,671	2,923,387	2,956,259	2,993,016	3,019,075	3,038,946	2,841,249	2,908,034
Farm Wage and Salary Employment..............................	14,250	17,516	15,629	14,372	14,899	16,097	17,463	19,409
Nonfarm Wage and Salary Employment........................	2,859,421	2,905,871	2,940,630	2,978,644	3,004,176	3,022,849	2,823,786	2,888,625
Private wage and salary employment...................	2,439,900	2,484,119	2,517,643	2,549,805	2,576,194	2,593,210	2,413,080	2,478,476
Forestry, fishing, and related activities................	6,024	6,349	6,319	6,394	6,296	6,452	6,311	5,869
Mining...	6,370	6,164	5,364	5,735	5,887	5,825	5,462	5,805
Utilities...	12,863	12,787	12,506	12,365	12,302	12,053	11,890	11,965
Construction..	110,288	118,035	118,934	122,517	124,553	130,104	126,858	133,158
Manufacturing..	312,306	317,562	317,743	319,342	322,096	324,247	309,365	313,378
Durable goods manufacturing........................	198,796	202,763	201,568	201,543	204,715	208,254	198,913	200,463
Nondurable goods manufacturing..................	113,510	114,799	116,175	117,799	117,381	115,993	110,452	112,915
Wholesale trade...	132,434	133,441	132,365	132,904	131,331	128,820	125,208	126,871
Retail trade..	290,302	295,140	300,057	300,353	300,447	294,975	277,871	283,681
Transportation and warehousing.........................	84,145	86,677	89,201	93,829	95,511	97,465	91,781	93,827
Information..	52,715	51,801	50,471	50,343	49,178	46,989	43,188	42,612
Finance and insurance	142,018	145,230	144,212	148,179	150,236	155,402	154,557	152,159
Real estate and rental and leasing....................	39,814	40,067	35,163	35,368	36,111	36,526	34,939	35,084
Professional, scientific, and technical services........	142,057	146,753	159,537	160,647	164,258	160,961	155,489	159,403
Management of companies and enterprises...........	78,753	78,193	78,539	80,109	81,307	89,205	87,020	87,450
Administrative and waste services.....................	134,589	135,137	136,995	134,942	135,367	135,633	121,051	128,728
Educational services	71,779	73,374	73,845	74,390	73,882	73,699	66,893	71,278
Health care and social assistance.....................	428,762	437,733	451,246	462,523	473,365	477,388	464,973	470,918
Arts, entertainment, and recreation...................	41,508	42,073	43,559	45,825	46,854	48,374	32,908	38,005
Accommodation and food services....................	215,110	218,979	223,638	226,752	227,871	228,975	173,620	192,046
Other services, except public administration............	138,063	138,624	137,949	137,288	139,342	140,117	123,696	126,239
Government and government enterprises....................	419,521	421,752	422,987	428,839	427,982	429,639	410,706	410,149
	Dollars							
Average Wages and Salaries by Industry	50,759	52,611	53,460	55,310	57,238	58,857	63,051	65,933
Average Farm Wages and Salaries	35,874	32,212	39,843	38,819	36,808	41,997	33,627	32,903
Average Nonfarm Wages and Salaries	50,833	52,734	53,533	55,389	57,339	58,947	63,233	66,155
Average private wages and salaries...................	51,602	53,601	54,303	56,365	58,202	59,847	64,265	67,430
Forestry, fishing, and related activities................	29,394	30,746	32,471	33,376	34,507	35,419	37,874	41,168
Mining...	85,443	79,646	78,727	84,829	92,388	92,372	86,741	112,626
Utilities...	99,314	102,120	104,112	107,561	112,602	117,417	122,667	123,986
Construction..	58,950	61,519	63,271	65,467	67,256	69,733	72,848	77,732
Manufacturing..	61,096	63,256	63,760	65,731	67,115	68,085	70,890	74,601
Durable goods manufacturing........................	65,804	67,881	68,161	70,303	71,744	72,215	74,404	78,957
Nondurable goods manufacturing..................	52,850	55,087	56,125	57,908	59,041	60,668	64,561	66,869
Wholesale trade...	76,985	79,117	78,961	83,308	84,437	85,073	89,404	95,874
Retail trade..	27,215	28,235	28,815	29,513	30,757	31,512	34,008	36,175
Transportation and warehousing.........................	50,238	51,247	52,538	53,053	54,819	56,415	58,535	59,547
Information..	69,447	72,050	72,019	75,483	78,945	83,810	92,290	98,817
Finance and insurance	92,787	96,809	95,689	100,079	105,596	107,379	114,894	119,534
Real estate and rental and leasing....................	55,046	58,217	50,221	51,800	52,619	54,738	58,186	62,756
Professional, scientific, and technical services........	83,875	85,984	90,119	91,695	94,630	97,647	102,560	108,233
Management of companies and enterprises...........	115,301	120,493	119,059	125,055	127,264	129,420	131,752	140,480
Administrative and waste services.....................	33,895	35,996	38,245	41,339	40,780	42,605	46,631	49,808
Educational services	30,746	30,931	31,215	31,695	33,221	33,945	37,718	36,298
Health care and social assistance.....................	45,851	48,030	49,005	50,481	52,318	53,453	55,797	58,894
Arts, entertainment, and recreation...................	32,425	34,035	34,692	35,635	38,862	39,439	46,788	46,172
Accommodation and food services....................	18,240	19,426	20,382	21,342	22,551	23,257	21,922	26,071
Other services, except public administration............	30,973	32,240	33,063	34,938	35,844	37,073	41,000	42,532
Government and government enterprises....................	46,364	47,629	48,950	49,589	52,149	53,514	57,168	58,450

Table MN-10. Employment Characteristics by Family Type

(Number, percent.)

Family type and labor force status	2019		2020 [1]		2021	
	Total	Families with own children under 18 years	Total	Families with own children under 18 years	Total	Families with own children under 18 years
All Families..	1,401,623	601,811	1,404,798	619,373	1,427,221	609,156
FAMILY TYPE AND LABOR FORCE STATUS						
Opposite-Sex Married-Couple Families..	1,100,581	427,830	1,100,940	441,327	1,111,555	438,460
Both husband and wife in labor force.............................	59.7	78.8	60.2	78.3	58.6	79.0
Husband in labor force, wife not in labor force	15.0	17.5	15.4	17.6	14.8	16.1
Wife in labor force, husband not in labor force	7.1	2.8	7.2	3.2	7.5	3.7
Both husband and wife not in labor force.............................	17.4	0.6	17.2	0.9	19.0	1.3
Other Families	301,042	173,981	294,248	175,827	305,100	168,624
Female householder, no spouse present	65.2	67.2	67.6	69.9	66.7	68.4
In labor force...	51.1	59.6	53.4	61.7	51.1	59.1
Not in labor force	14.1	7.6	14.1	8.1	15.6	9.3
Male householder, no spouse present...........................	34.8	32.8	32.4	30.1	33.3	31.6
In labor force...	29.5	30.1	27.9	28.3	28.1	29.4
Not in labor force	5.2	2.7	4.6	1.9	5.2	2.2

[1] 2020 ACS 5-Year estimates. 1-Year estimates were not released for 2020 due to the impact of COVID-19 on data collection that year. Data is not comparable to previous years, which are based on 1-year estimates.

Table MN-11. School Enrollment and Educational Attainment, 2021

(Number, percent.)

Item	State	U.S.
Enrollment		
Total population 3 years and over, enrolled in school	1,385,795	79,453,524
Enrolled in nursery school or preschool (percent)	5.9	5.2
Enrolled in kindergarten (percent)..	5.4	5.0
Enrolled in elementary school, grades 1-8 (percent)	42.1	41.3
Enrolled in high school, grades 9-12 (percent)	21.9	21.8
Enrolled in college or graduate school (percent)..	24.7	26.7
Attainment		
Total population 25 years and over	3,898,742	228,193,464
Less than ninth grade (percent)	2.6	4.8
9th to 12th grade, no diploma (percent)	3.2	5.9
High school graduate, including equivalency (percent)..	23.3	26.3
Some college, no degree (percent)	20.1	19.3
Associate's degree (percent)	11.8	8.8
Bachelor's degree (percent)	25.5	21.2
Graduate or professional degree (percent)..	13.4	13.8
High school graduate or higher (percent)	94.1	89.4
Bachelor's degree or higher (percent)..	38.9	35.0

Table MN-12. Public School Characteristics and Educational Indicators

(Number, percent; data derived from National Center of Education Statistics.)

Item	State	U.S.
Public Elementary and Secondary Schools		
Number of regular school districts, 2019-20..	331	13,349
Number of operational schools, 2019-20..	2,545	98,469
Percent charter schools	9.6	7.7
Total public school enrollment, Fall 2021..	870,506	49,433,092
Percent charter school enrollment	7.7	7.5
Student-teacher ratio, Fall 2019	16.1	15.9
Expenditures per student (unadjusted dollars), 2019-20	13,502	13,489
Four-year adjusted cohort graduation rate (ACGR), 2019-2020[1]..	83.8	86.5
Students eligible for free or reduced-price lunch (percent), 2019-20..	35.8	52.1
English language learners (percent), Fall 2020	8.6	10.3
Students age 3 to 21 served under IDEA, part B (percent), 2021-22	16.8	14.7

Public Schools by Type, 2019-20	Number	Percent of state public schools
Total number of schools..	2,545	100.0
Special education..	331	13.0
Vocational education..	/	0.3
Alternative education..	471	18.5

[1] Adjusted Cohort Graduation Rates (ACGR) differ from Averaged Freshmen Graduation Rates (AFGR).

Table MN-13. Reported Voting and Registration of the Voting-Age Population, November 2022

(Numbers in thousands, percent.)

Item	Total population	Total citizen population	Registered			Voted		
			Total registered	Percent registered (total population)	Percent registered (total citizen population)	Total voted	Percent voted (total population)	Percent voted (total citizen population)
U.S. Total	255,457	233,546	161,422	63.2	69.1	121,916	47.7	52.2
State Total	4,380	4,210	3,255	74.3	77.3	2,680	61.2	63.7
Sex								
Male	2,174	2,094	1,595	73.4	76.2	1,290	59.3	61.6
Female	2,205	2,116	1,660	75.3	78.4	1,390	63.0	65.7
Race								
White alone................................	3,752	3,689	2,905	77.4	78.7	2,419	64.5	65.6
White, non-Hispanic alone	3,551	3,529	2,797	78.8	79.3	2,357	66.4	66.8
Black alone................................	302	302	202	67.0	67.0	147	48.6	48.6
Asian alone	242	135	81	33.2	59.8	54	22.3	40.1
Hispanic (of any race)	254	214	162	63.5	75.4	87	34.2	40.6
White alone or in combination	3,820	3,758	2,957	77.4	78.7	2,468	64.6	65.7
Black alone or in combination	309	309	202	65.5	65.5	147	47.5	47.5
Asian alone or in combination	254	147	92	36.3	63.0	66	25.9	44.9
Age								
18 to 24 years............................	565	526	295	52.3	56.1	194	34.4	36.9
25 to 34 years............................	718	657	449	62.5	68.4	368	51.3	56.1
35 to 44 years............................	728	698	578	79.4	82.7	487	67.0	69.8
45 to 64 years............................	1,426	1,389	1,141	80.0	82.1	952	66.7	68.5
65 years and over	943	939	793	84.0	84.4	678	71.9	72.2

B = Base is less than 75,000 and therefore too small to show the derived measure.

Table MN-14. Health Indicators

(Number, rate as indicated in footnotes.)

Item	State	U.S.
Births		
Life Expectancy at Birth (years), 2020	79.1	77.0
Fertility Rate by State[1], 2021	58.6	56.3
Percent Home Births, 2021	1.6	1.4
Cesarean Delivery Rate[2], 2021	28.9	32.1
Preterm Birth Rate[3], 2021	9.6	10.5
Teen Birth Rate[4], 2021	8.5	13.9
Percentage of Babies Born Low Birthweight[5], 2021	7.3	8.5
Deaths[6]		
Heart Disease Mortality Rate, 2021	123.9	173.8
Cancer Mortality Rate, 2021	143.2	146.6
Stroke Mortality Rate, 2021	34.5	41.1
Diabetes Mortality Rate, 2021	22.6	25.4
Influenza/Pneumonia Mortality Rate, 2021	5.7	10.5
Suicide Mortality Rate, 2021	13.9	14.1
Drug Overdose Mortality Rate, 2021	24.5	33.6
Firearm Injury Mortality Rate, 2021	10.0	14.6
Homicide Mortality Rate, 2021	4.3	8.2
Disease and Illness		
Lifetime Asthma in Adults, 2020 (percent)...	12.0	13.9
Lifetime Asthma in Children, 2020 (percent)[7]	6.6	11.3
Diabetes in Adults, 2020 (percent)...	7.8	8.2
Self-reported Obesity in Adults, 2021 (percent)..	32.4	NA

SOURCE: National Center for Health Statistics, National Vital Statistics System 2020 data; https://wonder.cdc.gov.
[1] General fertility rate per 1,000 women aged 15–44.
[2] This represents the percentage of all live births that were cesarean deliveries.
[3] Babies born prior to 37 weeks of pregnancy (gestation).
[4] Number of births per 1,000 females aged 15–19
[5] Babies born weighing less than 2,500 grams or 5 lbs. 8oz.
[6] Death rates are the number of deaths per 100,000 total population.
[7] U.S. total includes data from 30 states and D.C.
NA = Not available.
- = Zero or rounds to zero.

Table MN-15. State Government Finances, 2021

(Dollar amounts in thousands, percent distribution.)

Item	Dollars	Percent distribution
Total Revenue	61,465,272	100.0
General revenue	53,128,580	86.4
Intergovernmental revenue	15,732,974	25.6
Taxes	31,793,412	51.7
General sales	6,698,560	10.9
Selective sales	4,505,898	7.3
License taxes	1,505,670	2.4
Individual income tax	15,170,613	24.7
Corporate income tax	2,423,383	3.9
Other taxes	1,489,288	2.4
Current charges	2,770,639	4.5
Miscellaneous general revenue	2,831,555	4.6
Utility revenue	45,036	0.1
Liquor stores revenue	-	-
Insurance trust revenue[1]	8,291,656	13.5
Total Expenditure	59,990,344	100.0
Intergovernmental expenditure	17,289,345	28.8
Direct expenditure	42,700,999	71.2
Current operation	29,629,147	49.4
Capital outlay	1,840,865	3.1
Insurance benefits and repayments	9,385,876	15.6
Assistance and subsidies	1,471,788	2.5
Interest on debt	373,323	0.6
Exhibit: Salaries and wages	6,420,193	10.7
Total Expenditure	59,990,344	100.0
General expenditure	50,011,495	83.4
Intergovernmental expenditure	17,289,345	28.8
Direct expenditure	32,722,150	54.5
General expenditure, by function:		
Education	17,752,188	29.6
Public welfare	17,904,724	29.8
Hospitals	332,416	0.6
Health	1,170,451	2.0
Highways	3,146,785	5.2
Police protection	637,990	1.1
Correction	628,518	1.0
Natural resources	756,609	1.3
Parks and recreation	307,313	0.5
Governmental administration	2,304,144	3.8
Interest on general debt	373,323	0.6
Other and unallocable	4,387,309	7.3
Utility expenditure	715,954	1.2
Liquor stores expenditure	-	-
Insurance trust expenditure	9,385,876	15.6
Debt at End of Fiscal Year	16,497,365	X
Cash and Security Holdings	122,640,879	X

X = Not applicable.
- = Zero or rounds to zero.
[1] Within insurance trust revenue, net earnings of state retirement systems is a calculated statistic (the item code in the data file is X08), and thus can be positive or negative. Net earnings is the sum of earnings on investments plus gains on investments minus losses on investments. The change made in 2002 for asset valuation from book to market value in accordance with Statement 34 of the Governmental Accounting Standards Board is reflected in the calculated statistics.

Table MN-16. State Government Tax Collections, 2022

(Dollars in thousands, percent.)

Item	Dollars	Percent distribution
Total Taxes	34,911,881	100.0
Property taxes	773,877	2.2
Sales and gross receipts	12,092,155	34.6
General sales and gross receipts	7,287,411	20.9
Selective sales and gross receipts	4,804,744	13.8
Alcoholic beverages	105,074	0.3
Amusements	201,832	0.6
Insurance premiums	718,431	2.1
Motor fuels	900,563	2.6
Pari-mutuels	1,906	-
Public utilities	87,276	0.2
Tobacco products	610,055	1.7
Other selective sales	2,179,607	6.2
Licenses	1,474,333	4.2
Alcoholic beverages	3,336	-
Amusements	8,213	-
Corporations in general	16,259	-
Hunting and fishing	103,313	0.3
Motor vehicle	926,172	2.7
Motor vehicle operators	51,328	0.1
Public utilities	7,297	-
Occupation and business, NEC	273,841	0.8
Other licenses	84,574	0.2
Income taxes	19,860,533	56.9
Individual income	15,130,683	43.3
Corporation net income	4,729,850	13.5
Other taxes	710,983	2.0
Death and gift	212,421	0.6
Documentary and stock transfer	393,946	1.1
Severance	104,616	0.3
Taxes, NEC	X	-

- = Zero or rounds to zero.

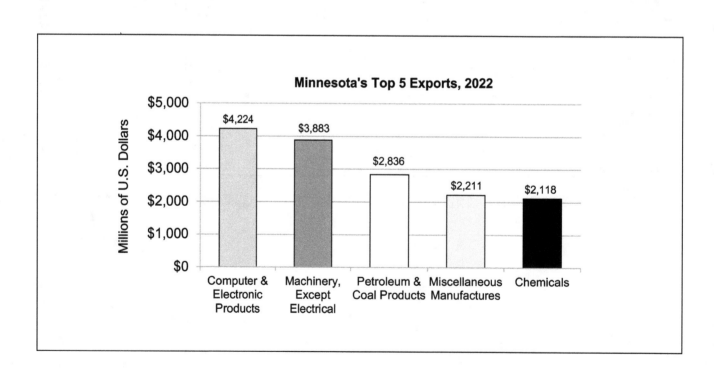

Minnesota's Top 5 Exports, 2022

MISSISSIPPI

Facts and Figures

Location: South central United States; bordered on the N by Tennessee, on the E by Alabama, on the S by Louisiana and the Gulf of Mexico, and on the W by Arkansas and Louisiana

Area: 48,430 sq. mi. (125,434 sq. km.); rank—32nd

Population: 2,940,057 (2022 est.); rank—34th

Principal Cities: capital—Jackson; largest—Jackson

Statehood: December 10, 1817; 20th state

U.S. Congress: 2 senators, 4 representatives

State Motto: *Virtute et armis* ("By valor and arms")

State Song: "Go, Mississippi"

State Nicknames: The Magnolia State; The Hospitality State

Abbreviations: MS; Miss.

State Symbols: flower—magnolia blossom; tree—Southern magnolia; bird—mockingbird

At a Glance

- With a 0.9 percent decrease in population, Mississippi was one of three states that experienced a population decline from 2010 to 2022.

- In 2021, Mississippi had the lowest median household income in the country ($48,716) and the 2nd highest percent of population living the below the poverty level (19.4 percent).

- In 2021, 11.9 percent of Mississippians did not have health insurance, compared to 8.6 percent of the total U.S. population.

- Mississippi had the highest traffic fatality rate in 2021, with 26.2 deaths per 100,000 population.

- In 2021, 24.8 percent of Mississippians age 25 years and older had a bachelor's degree or higher, which was the 2nd lowest percentage among the states.

Table MS-1. Population by Age, Sex, Race, and Hispanic Origin

(Number, percent, except where noted.)

Sex, age, race, and Hispanic origin	2010	2020	2022	Percent change, 2010–2022
Total Population..	2,967,297	2,961,288	2,940,057	-0.9
Percent of total U.S. population	1.0	0.9	0.9	X
Sex				
Male...	1,441,240	1,441,742	1,428,776	-0.9
Female	1,526,057	1,519,546	1,511,281	-1.0
Age				
Under 5 years...	210,956	178,500	174,518	-17.3
Under 18 years..	755,555	692,898	678,061	-10.3
18 to 64 years	1,831,335	1,780,588	1,754,456	-4.2
65 years and over	380,407	487,802	507,540	33.4
Median age (years)	36.0	38.1	38.5	6.9
Race and Hispanic Origin				
One race				
White	1,789,391	1,743,888	1,729,691	-3.3
Black	1,103,101	1,121,870	1,110,533	0.7
American Indian and Alaska Native	16,837	18,618	18,894	12.2
Asian...	26,477	33,143	34,179	29.1
Native Hawaiian or Other Pacific Islander	1,700	1,939	2,007	18.1
Two or more races	29,791	41,830	44,753	50.2
Hispanic (of any race)...	81,481	99,445	104,879	28.7

NOTE: Population figures for 2022 are July 1 estimates. The 2010 and 2020 estimates are taken from the respective censuses.
- = Zero or rounds to zero.
X = Not applicable.

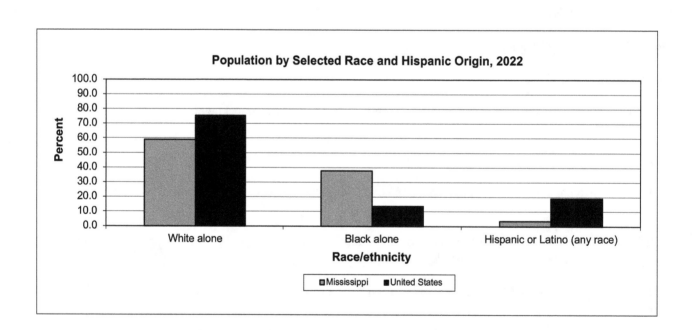

Table MS-2. Marital Status

(Number, percent distribution.)

Sex, age, race, and Hispanic origin	2000	2010	2021
Males, 15 Years and Over	1,046,252	1,121,265	1,143,948
Never married	30.6	34.9	37.4
Now married, except separated..	54.6	48.3	46.6
Separated..	2.4	2.5	2.2
Widowed..	2.9	2.7	3.5
Divorced..	9.5	11.7	10.3
Females, 15 Years and Over	1,157,363	1,224,423	1,238,570
Never married	25.1	29.8	31.9
Now married, except separated..	48.6	43.8	42.5
Separated..	3.2	3.4	2.8
Widowed..	12.5	10.8	10.1
Divorced..	10.6	12.3	12.7

Table MS-3. Households and Housing Characteristics

(Number, percent, dollars.)

Item	2000	2010	2021	Average annual percent change, 2010–2021
Total Households	1,046,434	1,079,999	1,129,611	0.4
Family households	747,159	746,115	742,851	-
Married-couple family	520,884	501,571	498,803	-0.1
Other family	226,315	244,544	244,048	-
Male householder, no wife present	45,610	51,400	52,635	0.2
Female householder, no husband present	180,705	193,144	191,413	-0.1
Nonfamily households	299,275	333,884	386,760	1.4
Householder living alone	257,708	293,185	334,983	1.3
Householder not living alone	41,567	40,699	51,777	2.5
Housing Characteristics				
Total housing units	1,161,953	1,276,441	1,332,041	0.4
Occupied housing units	1,046,434	1,079,999	1,129,611	0.4
Owner occupied	756,967	753,374	787,068	0.4
Renter occupied	289,467	326,625	342,543	0.4
Average household size	2.63	2.66	2.54	-0.4
Financial Characteristics				
Median gross rent of renter-occupied housing	439	672	831	2.2
Median monthly owner costs for housing units with a mortgage	762	1,043	1,200	1.4
Median value of owner-occupied housing units	71,400	100,100	145,600	4.1

- = Zero or rounds to zero.

Table MS-4. Migration, Origin, and Language

(Number, percent.)

Characteristic	State 2021	U.S. 2021
Residence 1 Year Ago		
Population 1 year and over	2,919,574	328,464,538
Same house	89.3	87.2
Different house in the U.S.	10.3	12.3
Same county	5.4	6.7
Different county	4.9	5.7
Same state	2.9	3.3
Different state	2.0	2.4
Abroad	0.3	0.4
Place of Birth		
Native born	2,887,106	286,623,642
Male	48.6	49.7
Female	51.4	50.3
Foreign born	62,859	45,270,103
Male	49.1	48.7
Female	50.9	51.3
Foreign born; naturalized U.S. citizen	29,125	24,044,083
Male	44.0	46.4
Female	56.0	53.6
Foreign born; not a U.S. citizen	33,734	21,226,020
Male	53.6	51.2
Female	46.4	48.8
Entered 2010 or later	37.2	28.1
Entered 2000 to 2009	22.6	23.7
Entered before 2000	40.3	48.2
World Region of Birth, Foreign		
Foreign-born population, excluding population born at sea	62,859	45,269,644
Europe	9.5	10.7
Asia	32.0	31.0
Africa	5.6	5.7
Oceania	1.1	0.6
Latin America	48.9	50.1
North America	2.9	1.7
Language Spoken at Home and Ability to Speak English		
Population 5 years and over	2,776,683	313,232,500
English only	96.2	70.4
Language other than English	3.8	21.6
Speaks English less than "very well"	1.5	8.3

Table MS-5. Median Income and Poverty Status, 2021

(Number, percent, except as noted.)

Characteristic	State Number	State Percent	U.S. Number	U.S. Percent
Median Income				
Households (dollars)...	48,716	X	69,717	X
Families (dollars)	64,035	X	85,806	X
Below Poverty Level (All People)	554,152	19.4	41,393,176	12.8
Sex				
Male	240,788	17.5	18,518,155	11.6
Female	313,364	21.1	22,875,021	13.9
Age				
Under 18 years..	188,567	27.7	12,243,219	16.9
Related children under 18 years...............................	187,075	27.6	11,985,424	16.6
18 to 64 years..	298,673	17.6	23,526,341	11.9
65 years and over	66,912	13.8	5,623,616	10.3

X = Not applicable.

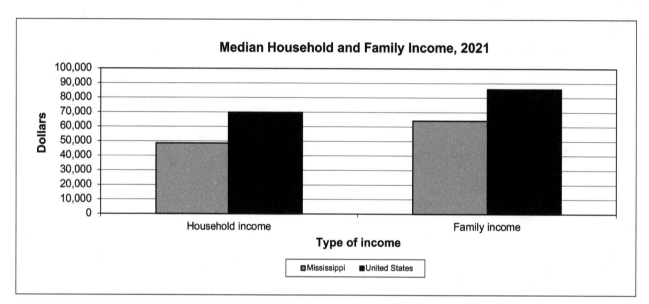

Table MS-6. Health Insurance Coverage Status for the Civilian Noninstitutionalized Population and Children Under 19 Years of Age

(Number, percent.)

Item	2011	2012	2013	2014	2015	2016	2017	2018	2019	2020 [2]	2021
Civilian Noninstitutionalized Population	2,911,811	2,918,405	2,925,211	2,927,088	2,927,568	2,924,168	2,920,808	2,919,673	2,904,609	2,912,057	2,885,936
Covered by Private or Public Insurance											
Number...	2,395,398	2,420,895	2,425,362	2,502,958	2,555,983	2,577,987	2,569,054	2,565,522	2,527,737	2,562,055	2,542,934
Percent..	82.3	83.0	82.9	85.5	87.3	88.2	88.0	87.9	87.0	88.0	88.1
Uninsured											
Number...	516,413	497,510	499,849	424,130	371,585	346,181	351,754	354,151	376,872	350,002	343,002
Percent..	17.7	17.0	17.1	14.5	12.7	11.8	12.0	12.1	13.0	12.0	11.9
Percent in the U.S. not covered................................	15.1	14.8	14.5	11.7	9.4	8.6	8.7	8.9	9.2	8.7	8.6
Children Under 19 Years of Age[1]	749,572	745,603	734,075	729,802	725,664	721,108	763,456	756,077	744,641	749,257	735,542
Covered by Private or Public Insurance											
Number...	688,589	690,862	677,926	690,970	696,297	688,518	726,463	720,648	698,928	710,968	689,666
Percent..	91.9	92.7	92.4	94.7	96.0	95.5	95.2	95.3	93.9	94.9	93.8
Uninsured											
Number...	60,983	54,741	56,149	38,832	29,367	32,590	36,993	35,429	45,713	38,289	45,876
Percent..	8.1	7.3	7.6	5.3	4.0	4.5	4.8	4.7	6.1	5.1	6.2
Percent in the U.S. not covered................................	7.5	7.2	7.1	6.0	4.8	4.5	5.0	5.2	5.7	5.2	5.4

[1] Data for years prior to 2017 are for individuals under 18 years of age.
[2] 2020 ACS 5-Year estimates. 1-Year estimates were not released for 2020 due to the impact of COVID-19 on data collection that year. Data is not comparable to previous years, which are based on 1-year estimates.

Table MS-7. Employment Status by Demographic Group, 2022

(Numbers in thousands, percent.)

Characteristic	Civilian noninstitutional population	Civilian labor force		Employed		Unemployed	
		Number	Percent of population	Number	Percent of population	Number	Percent of population
Total..	2,286	1,260	55.1	1,211	53.0	50	3.9
Sex							
Male..	1,081	645	59.6	617	57.0	29	4.4
Female.......................................	1,205	615	51.1	594	49.3	21	3.5
Race, Sex, and Hispanic Origin							
White...	1,386	764	55.1	744	53.7	20	2.6
Male..	674	412	61.0	401	59.5	10	2.5
Female.....................................	712	352	49.4	343	48.1	9	2.7
Black or African American..................	843	466	55.3	438	51.9	28	6.0
Male..	378	212	56.2	195	51.7	17	8.0
Female.....................................	465	253	54.5	242	52.1	11	4.4
Hispanic or Latino ethnicity[1]	NA	NA	NA	NA	NA	NA	NA
Male..	NA	NA	NA	NA	NA	NA	NA
Female.....................................	NA	NA	NA	NA	NA	NA	NA
Age							
16 to 19 years...............................	NA	NA	NA	NA	NA	NA	NA
20 to 24 years...............................	176	119	67.2	111	62.9	8	6.4
25 to 34 years...............................	373	292	78.4	278	74.6	14	4.7
35 to 44 years...............................	368	284	77.2	273	74.0	12	4.1
45 to 54 years...............................	328	240	73.2	234	71.4	6	2.5
55 to 64 years...............................	395	209	52.9	205	51.8	5	2.2
65 years and over	493	76	15.3	73	14.8	3	3.7

NOTE: Data in Table 7 are from the Current Population Survey (CPS) and do not match the estimates in Table 8. See notes and definitions for further information.
[1] May be of any race.
NA = Not available.

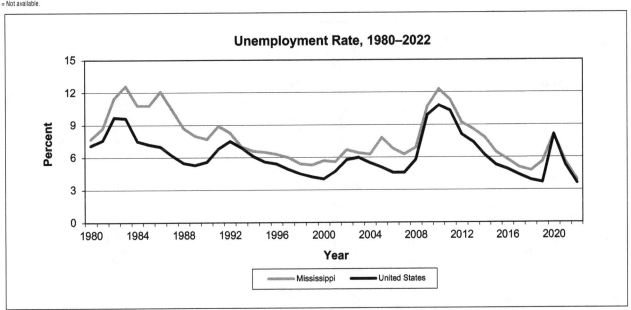

Unemployment Rate, 1980–2022

Table MS-8. Employment Status of the Civilian Noninstitutional Population Age 16 Years and Over

(Number, percent.)

Year	Civilian labor force	Civilian participation rate	Employed	Unemployed	Unemployment rate
2010...................................	1,309,128	58.8	1,176,938	132,190	10.1
2011...................................	1,345,990	60.0	1,214,638	131,352	9.8
2012...................................	1,330,450	59.0	1,213,245	117,205	8.8
2013...................................	1,273,057	56.2	1,164,832	108,225	8.5
2014...................................	1,243,934	54.7	1,149,277	94,657	7.6
2015...................................	1,260,015	55.3	1,178,018	81,997	6.5
2016...................................	1,271,836	55.7	1,196,241	75,595	5.9
2017...................................	1,272,685	55.7	1,206,102	66,583	5.2
2018...................................	1,268,435	55.6	1,205,737	62,698	4.9
2019...................................	1,277,143	56	1,207,543	69,600	5.4
2020...................................	1,243,515	54.6	1,145,211	98,304	7.9
2021...................................	1,254,239	55.0	1,184,401	69,838	5.6
2022...................................	1,251,022	54.9	1,201,880	49,142	3.9

Table MS-9. Employment and Average Wages by Industry

(Estimates are based on the 2012 North American Industry Classification System [NAICS].)

Industry	2014	2015	2016	2017	2018	2019	2020	2021
	Number of Jobs							
Wage and Salary Employment by Industry........................	1,194,211	1,202,135	1,209,425	1,214,455	1,217,171	1,223,735	1,174,858	1,201,273
Farm Wage and Salary Employment.................................	12,119	9,375	8,367	9,411	9,162	9,388	7,471	9,955
Nonfarm Wage and Salary Employment...........................	1,182,092	1,192,760	1,201,058	1,205,044	1,208,009	1,214,347	1,167,387	1,191,318
Private wage and salary employment...............................	906,128	918,425	927,828	933,189	938,213	943,012	899,342	927,199
Forestry, fishing, and related activities............................	7,883	7,956	8,133	7,925	8,217	8,298	7,826	7,743
Mining...	6,254	5,053	3,840	4,062	3,975	3,838	3,078	3,068
Utilities..	7,826	7,870	7,942	8,058	7,896	7,748	7,727	7,819
Construction..	50,321	47,193	45,577	44,493	44,985	45,622	44,988	45,867
Manufacturing...	139,717	141,925	143,245	144,164	144,907	146,919	139,607	143,998
Durable goods manufacturing.......................................	93,638	94,756	94,960	95,211	95,437	96,879	90,687	94,820
Nondurable goods manufacturing.................................	46,079	47,169	48,285	48,953	49,470	50,040	48,920	49,178
Wholesale trade..	34,202	34,673	34,443	34,920	34,260	34,570	33,584	33,995
Retail trade...	136,557	139,036	141,604	141,263	139,303	136,665	133,911	137,605
Transportation and warehousing.....................................	42,729	44,834	46,905	48,292	50,525	52,758	53,952	56,944
Information..	13,246	13,622	12,143	11,579	10,968	10,690	9,625	9,600
Finance and insurance..	33,162	33,233	33,380	33,517	33,489	33,873	33,542	33,350
Real estate and rental and leasing..................................	11,679	11,756	11,781	11,823	11,896	12,011	11,415	11,516
Professional, scientific, and technical services................	31,226	31,088	30,949	31,390	31,657	31,668	32,402	34,393
Management of companies and enterprises......................	10,658	10,611	11,055	11,017	11,493	11,237	11,073	11,182
Administrative and waste services...................................	60,368	63,962	66,616	66,079	67,481	66,276	65,063	70,533
Educational services	19,651	19,368	18,769	19,094	18,423	18,355	16,018	17,308
Health care and social assistance..................................	124,814	127,523	129,870	132,735	134,585	136,796	130,396	130,023
Arts, entertainment, and recreation................................	11,562	11,413	11,572	9,780	9,742	9,932	8,269	8,878
Accommodation and food services..................................	115,149	118,393	122,156	125,560	125,755	127,032	110,762	117,825
Other services, except public administration....................	49,124	48,916	47,848	47,438	48,656	48,724	46,104	45,552
Government and government enterprises.......................	275,964	274,335	273,230	271,855	269,796	271,335	268,045	264,119
	Dollars							
Average Wages and Salaries by Industry	37,993	38,553	39,118	39,825	40,904	41,800	44,448	46,263
Average Farm Wages and Salaries	20,815	21,563	19,807	17,156	18,454	13,300	15,364	15,420
Average Nonfarm Wages and Salaries	38,169	38,687	39,252	40,002	41,074	42,020	44,634	46,521
Average private wages and salaries................................	37,953	38,369	38,778	39,557	40,623	41,534	44,366	46,286
Forestry, fishing, and related activities............................	33,883	35,655	36,681	37,378	39,368	41,157	43,874	45,620
Mining...	78,592	78,763	76,571	75,657	76,448	80,940	86,281	85,103
Utilities..	73,931	77,768	79,649	81,758	84,902	86,149	93,230	91,631
Construction..	47,288	47,198	48,655	49,772	51,302	51,898	54,901	56,836
Manufacturing...	47,644	48,334	49,256	50,376	51,382	52,171	54,328	56,276
Durable goods manufacturing.......................................	49,077	49,515	50,790	52,063	52,712	53,243	55,214	56,824
Nondurable goods manufacturing.................................	44,732	45,963	46,239	47,095	48,818	50,096	52,685	55,219
Wholesale trade..	54,638	56,191	57,121	59,080	61,180	62,767	65,678	69,288
Retail trade...	25,352	25,866	26,212	26,539	27,076	27,764	30,202	32,082
Transportation and warehousing.....................................	44,378	45,444	44,486	45,661	46,979	48,190	50,625	52,261
Information..	47,748	46,180	49,525	50,490	51,491	51,820	57,279	59,345
Finance and insurance..	55,916	57,529	58,760	60,371	62,741	64,225	68,953	71,275
Real estate and rental and leasing..................................	34,837	35,615	35,607	36,758	37,755	39,090	42,570	44,557
Professional, scientific, and technical services................	55,970	57,826	59,015	59,463	60,708	61,153	63,439	64,895
Management of companies and enterprises......................	82,985	84,889	83,167	87,488	88,719	89,495	98,721	98,858
Administrative and waste services...................................	27,745	27,822	27,891	28,005	28,234	29,353	30,771	33,786
Educational services	28,893	28,131	29,306	29,244	29,997	30,266	35,162	32,943
Health care and social assistance..................................	41,006	41,532	41,904	42,486	43,712	44,644	48,014	50,374
Arts, entertainment, and recreation................................	23,540	24,256	24,112	21,757	22,556	22,776	24,590	25,443
Accommodation and food services..................................	18,920	18,869	19,190	19,671	20,535	20,855	20,509	23,840
Other services, except public administration....................	29,567	30,401	31,647	32,748	33,311	34,562	37,629	39,380
Government and government enterprises.........................	38,877	39,748	40,862	41,532	42,645	43,707	45,533	47,345

Table MS-10. Employment Characteristics by Family Type

(Number, percent.)

Family type and labor force status	2019 Total	2019 Families with own children under 18 years	2020[1] Total	2020[1] Families with own children under 18 years	2021 Total	2021 Families with own children under 18 years
All Families...	718,382	281,962	740,489	302,379	742,851	292,636
FAMILY TYPE AND LABOR FORCE STATUS						
Opposite-Sex Married-Couple Families....................................	481,478	166,838	496,679	181,657	494,887	174,933
Both husband and wife in labor force............................	46.9	66.9	48.6	68.9	47.9	68.6
Husband in labor force, wife not in labor force	21.7	26.9	21.1	24.6	20.8	23.4
Wife in labor force, husband not in labor force	8.7	4.2	9.1	4.7	9.4	6.3
Both husband and wife not in labor force..........................	22.1	1.8	21.2	1.9	21.8	1.6
Other Families	236,904	115,124	240,854	120,355	244,048	117,021
Female householder, no spouse present..........................	78.2	83.3	79.0	82.0	78.4	81.9
In labor force...	49.8	66.5	50.9	65.7	48.5	63.4
Not in labor force..	28.4	16.8	28.0	16.3	30.0	18.5
Male householder, no spouse present...........................	21.8	16.7	21.0	18.0	21.6	18.1
In labor force...	14.1	14.8	14.2	15.8	14.4	16.1
Not in labor force..	7.8	1.9	6.8	2.2	7.1	2.0

[1] 2020 ACS 5-Year estimates. 1-Year estimates were not released for 2020 due to the impact of COVID-19 on data collection that year. Data is not comparable to previous years, which are based on 1-year estimates.

Table MS-11. School Enrollment and Educational Attainment, 2021

(Number, percent.)

Item	State	U.S.
Enrollment		
Total population 3 years and over, enrolled in school	728,376	79,453,524
Enrolled in nursery school or preschool (percent)...............................	4.9	5.2
Enrolled in kindergarten (percent)..	4.8	5.0
Enrolled in elementary school, grades 1-8 (percent)............................	43.4	41.3
Enrolled in high school, grades 9-12 (percent)	22.5	21.8
Enrolled in college or graduate school (percent)...............................	24.3	26.7
Attainment		
Total population 25 years and over	1,968,167	228,193,464
Less than ninth grade (percent)..	4.8	4.8
9th to 12th grade, no diploma (percent)	8.8	5.9
High school graduate, including equivalency (percent).........................	29.8	26.3
Some college, no degree (percent)..	21.8	19.3
Associate's degree (percent)...	10.2	8.8
Bachelor's degree (percent)..	15.4	21.2
Graduate or professional degree (percent).....................................	9.3	13.8
High school graduate or higher (percent)......................................	86.5	89.4
Bachelor's degree or higher (percent)...	24.8	35.0

Table MS-12. Public School Characteristics and Educational Indicators

(Number, percent; data derived from National Center of Education Statistics.)

Item	State	U.S.
Public Elementary and Secondary Schools		
Number of regular school districts, 2019-20	140	13,349
Number of operational schools, 2019-20.......................................	1,047	98,469
Percent charter schools	0.6	7.7
Total public school enrollment, Fall 2021......................................	442,000	49,433,092
Percent charter school enrollment	0.7	7.5
Student-teacher ratio, Fall 2019...	14.8	15.9
Expenditures per student (unadjusted dollars), 2019-20	9,614	13,489
Four-year adjusted cohort graduation rate (ACGR), 2019-2020[1].................	87.7	86.5
Students eligible for free or reduced-price lunch (percent), 2019-20...............	74.8	52.1
English language learners (percent), Fall 2020	3.0	10.3
Students age 3 to 21 served under IDEA, part B (percent), 2021-22	15.3	14.7

Public Schools by Type, 2019-20	Number	Percent of state public schools
Total number of schools...	1,047	100.0
Special education..	2	0.2
Vocational education..	92	8.8
Alternative education...	68	6.5

[1] Adjusted Cohort Graduation Rates (ACGR) differ from Averaged Freshmen Graduation Rates (AFGR).

Table MS-13. Reported Voting and Registration of the Voting-Age Population, November 2022

(Numbers in thousands, percent.)

Item	Total population	Total citizen population	Registered			Voted		
			Total registered	Percent registered (total population)	Percent registered (total citizen population)	Total voted	Percent voted (total population)	Percent voted (total citizen population)
U.S. Total...	255,457	233,546	161,422	63.2	69.1	121,916	47.7	52.2
State Total...	2,198	2,166	1,572	71.5	72.6	1,005	45.7	46.4
Sex								
Male	1,036	1,017	703	67.8	69.1	440	42.5	43.2
Female	1,162	1,149	869	74.8	75.7	565	48.6	49.2
Race								
White alone..	1,334	1,313	963	72.2	73.3	612	45.9	46.6
White, non-Hispanic alone	1,288	1,284	955	74.1	74.3	612	47.5	47.6
Black alone..	808	806	583	72.2	72.4	379	46.9	47.0
Asian alone	29	26	10	33.4	36.6	3	10.5	11.5
Hispanic (of any race)	64	41	10	15.0	23.3	2	2.9	4.5
White alone or in combination	1,352	1,325	972	71.9	73.4	617	45.6	46.5
Black alone or in combination	812	809	584	72.0	72.2	380	46.8	47.0
Asian alone or in combination..................	29	26	10	33.4	36.6	3	10.5	11.5
Age								
18 to 24 years....................................	256	241	115	45.0	47.8	61	23.9	25.5
25 to 34 years....................................	327	323	218	66.7	67.6	108	33.0	33.4
35 to 44 years....................................	392	388	287	73.1	74.0	158	40.3	40.8
45 to 64 years....................................	702	695	518	73.8	74.6	346	49.3	49.8
65 years and over	520	519	433	83.1	83.3	331	63.6	63.8

B = Base is less than 75,000 and therefore too small to show the derived measure.
- = Zero or rounds to zero.

Table MS-14. Health Indicators

(Number, rate as indicated in footnotes.)

Item	State	U.S.
Births		
Life Expectancy at Birth (years), 2020	71.9	77.0
Fertility Rate by State[1], 2021..	60.7	56.3
Percent Home Births, 2021..	0.6	1.4
Cesarean Delivery Rate[2], 2021..	38.5	32.1
Preterm Birth Rate[3], 2021...	15.0	10.5
Teen Birth Rate[4], 2021...	25.6	13.9
Percentage of Babies Born Low Birthweight[5], 2021...	12.4	8.5
Deaths[6]		
Heart Disease Mortality Rate, 2021...	255.2	173.8
Cancer Mortality Rate, 2021...	181.8	146.6
Stroke Mortality Rate, 2021..	57.8	41.1
Diabetes Mortality Rate, 2021...	42.1	25.4
Influenza/Pneumonia Mortality Rate, 2021..	20.0	10.5
Suicide Mortality Rate, 2021...	16.2	14.1
Drug Overdose Mortality Rate, 2021...	28.4	33.6
Firearm Injury Mortality Rate, 2021...	33.9	14.6
Homicide Mortality Rate, 2021..	23.7	8.2
Disease and Illness		
Lifetime Asthma in Adults, 2020 (percent)..	14.2	13.9
Lifetime Asthma in Children, 2020 (percent)[7]..	13.9	11.3
Diabetes in Adults, 2020 (percent)..	13.1	8.2
Self-reported Obesity in Adults, 2021 (percent)...	39.1	NA

SOURCE: National Center for Health Statistics, National Vital Statistics System 2020 data; https://wonder.cdc.gov.
[1] General fertility rate per 1,000 women aged 15–44.
[2] This represents the percentage of all live births that were cesarean deliveries.
[3] Babies born prior to 37 weeks of pregnancy (gestation).
[4] Number of births per 1,000 females aged 15–19
[5] Babies born weighing less than 2,500 grams or 5 lbs. 8oz.
[6] Death rates are the number of deaths per 100,000 total population.
[7] U.S. total includes data from 30 states and D.C.
NA = Not available.
- = Zero or rounds to zero.

Table MS-15. State Government Finances, 2021

(Dollar amounts in thousands, percent distribution.)

Item	Dollars	Percent distribution
Total Revenue	26,705,382	100.0
General revenue	23,358,365	87.5
Intergovernmental revenue	10,601,280	39.7
Taxes	9,353,158	35.0
General sales	4,230,391	15.8
Selective sales	1,426,971	5.3
License taxes	570,447	2.1
Individual income tax	2,515,630	9.4
Corporate income tax	550,199	2.1
Other taxes	59,520	0.2
Current charges	2,484,755	9.3
Miscellaneous general revenue	919,172	3.4
Utility revenue	-	-
Liquor stores revenue	508,466	1.9
Insurance trust revenue[1]	2,838,551	10.6
Total Expenditure	25,271,477	100.0
Intergovernmental expenditure	6,305,224	24.9
Direct expenditure	18,966,253	75.1
Current operation	13,502,536	53.4
Capital outlay	967,797	3.8
Insurance benefits and repayments	3,722,846	14.7
Assistance and subsidies	482,370	1.9
Interest on debt	290,704	1.2
Exhibit: Salaries and wages	2,795,098	11.1
Total Expenditure	25,271,477	100.0
General expenditure	21,040,165	83.3
Intergovernmental expenditure	6,305,224	24.9
Direct expenditure	14,734,941	58.3
General expenditure, by function:		
Education	6,248,285	24.7
Public welfare	7,061,869	27.9
Hospitals	1,633,354	6.5
Health	536,726	2.1
Highways	1,202,197	4.8
Police protection	162,665	0.6
Correction	356,624	1.4
Natural resources	308,929	1.2
Parks and recreation	37,377	0.1
Governmental administration	583,322	2.3
Interest on general debt	290,704	1.2
Other and unallocable	2,493,823	9.9
Utility expenditure	-	-
Liquor stores expenditure	508,466	2.0
Insurance trust expenditure	3,722,846	14.7
Debt at End of Fiscal Year	7,465,082	X
Cash and Security Holdings	49,566,145	X

X = Not applicable.
- = Zero or rounds to zero.
[1] Within insurance trust revenue, net earnings of state retirement systems is a calculated statistic (the item code in the data file is X08), and thus can be positive or negative. Net earnings is the sum of earnings on investments plus gains on investments minus losses on investments. The change made in 2002 for asset valuation from book to market value in accordance with Statement 34 of the Governmental Accounting Standards Board is reflected in the calculated statistics.

Table MS-16. State Government Tax Collections, 2022

(Dollars in thousands, percent.)

Item	Dollars	Percent distribution
Total Taxes	10,182,769	100.0
Property taxes	29,025	0.3
Sales and gross receipts	6,244,106	61.3
General sales and gross receipts	4,770,468	46.8
Selective sales and gross receipts	1,473,638	14.5
Alcoholic beverages	42,938	0.4
Amusements	169,119	1.7
Insurance premiums	383,652	3.8
Motor fuels	449,230	4.4
Pari-mutuels	184	-
Public utilities	1,786	-
Tobacco products	136,113	1.3
Other selective sales	290,616	2.9
Licenses	609,768	6.0
Alcoholic beverages	1,425	-
Amusements	18,549	0.2
Corporations in general	220,789	2.2
Hunting and fishing	3,186	-
Motor vehicle	179,589	1.8
Motor vehicle operators	17,527	0.2
Public utilities	6,579	0.1
Occupation and business, NEC	98,567	1.0
Other licenses	63,557	0.6
Income taxes	3,248,506	31.9
Individual income	2,537,787	24.9
Corporation net income	710,719	7.0
Other taxes	51,364	0.5
Death and gift	X	
Documentary and stock transfer	X	-
Severance	51,364	0.5
Taxes, NEC	0	-

- = Zero or rounds to zero.
X = Not applicable.

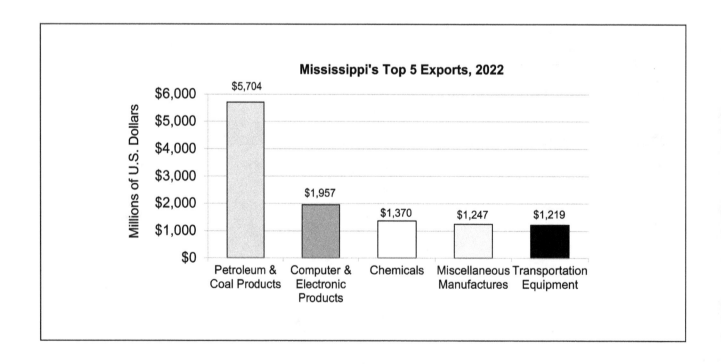

MISSOURI

Facts and Figures

Location: Central United States; bordered on the N by Iowa, on the E by Illinois, Kentucky, and Tennessee, on the S by Arkansas, and on the W by Oklahoma, Kansas, and Nebraska

Area: 69,704 sq. mi. (180,533 sq. km.); rank—21st

Population: 6,177,957 (2022 est.); rank—18th

Principal Cities: capital—Jefferson City; largest—Kansas City

Statehood: August 10, 1821; 24th state

U.S. Congress: 2 senators, 8 representatives

State Motto: *Salus populi suprema lex esto* ("The welfare of the people shall be the supreme law")

State Song: "Missouri Waltz"

State Nickname: The Show Me State

Abbreviations: MO; Mo

State Symbols: flower—hawthorn; tree—flowering dogwood; bird—Eastern bluebird

At a Glance

- With an increase in population of 3.2 percent, Missouri ranked 39th among the states in growth from 2010 to 2022.

- In 2021, 9.4 percent of Missourians did not have health insurance, compared to the national average of 8.6 percent.

- Missouri's homicide rate was 12.4 deaths per 100,000 population in 2021, compared to the U.S. rate of 8.2 deaths per 100,000 population.

- Missouri's median household income of $61,847 ranked 41st in the country in 2021.

- Missouri had the 6th lowest unemployment rate in the country in 2022, with 2.5 percent of the population unemployed.

Table MO-1. Population by Age, Sex, Race, and Hispanic Origin

(Number, percent, except where noted.)

Sex, age, race, and Hispanic origin	2010	2020	2022	Percent change, 2010–2022
Total Population..	5,988,927	6,154,920	6,177,957	3.2
Percent of total U.S. population	1.9	1.9	1.9	X
Sex				
Male..	2,933,477	3,045,043	3,054,821	4.1
Female	3,055,450	3,109,877	3,123,136	2.2
Age				
Under 5 years..	390,237	362,573	353,605	-9.4
Under 18 years..	1,425,436	1,377,266	1,364,908	-4.2
18 to 64 years	3,725,197	3,718,913	3,698,694	-0.7
65 years and over	838,294	1,058,741	1,114,355	32.9
Median age (years)	37.9	38.8	39.2	3.4
Race and Hispanic Origin				
One race				
White	5,038,407	5,084,432	5,095,625	1.1
Black	700,178	731,985	725,317	3.6
American Indian and Alaska Native	30,595	36,455	37,863	23.8
Asian...	100,213	137,841	142,623	42.3
Native Hawaiian or Other Pacific Islander	7,178	10,432	11,788	64.2
Two or more races	112,356	153,775	164,741	46.6
Hispanic (of any race)......................................	212,470	278,190	298,485	40.5

NOTE: Population figures for 2022 are July 1 estimates. The 2010 and 2020 estimates are taken from the respective censuses.
- = Zero or rounds to zero.
X = Not applicable.

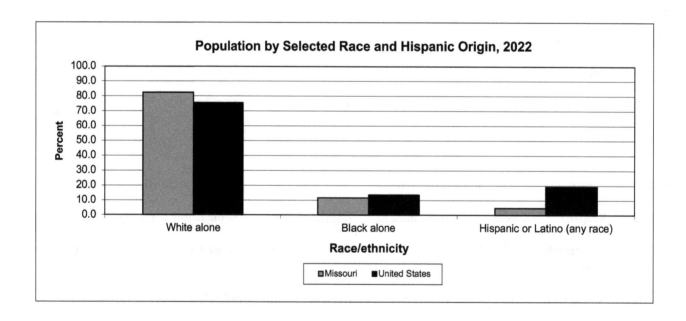

Table MO-2. Marital Status

(Number, percent distribution.)

Sex, age, race, and Hispanic origin	2000	2010	2021
Males, 15 Years and Over	2,114,280	2,332,888	2,458,376
Never married	27.8	32.1	33.9
Now married, except separated..	58.0	52.5	50.9
Separated..	1.6	1.7	1.5
Widowed..	2.6	2.6	2.8
Divorced..	10.0	11.0	10.8
Females, 15 Years and Over	2,300,111	2,492,198	2,568,323
Never married	22.1	26.8	28.3
Now married, except separated..	53.1	48.2	48.0
Separated..	2.0	2.2	1.9
Widowed..	11.3	10.0	9.0
Divorced..	11.5	12.8	12.8

Table MO-3. Households and Housing Characteristics

(Number, percent, dollars.)

Item	2000	2010	2021	Average annual percent change, 2010–2021
Total Households..	2,194,594	2,350,628	2,468,726	0.5
Family households	1,476,516	1,524,078	1,555,743	0.2
Married-couple family	1,140,866	1,146,501	1,176,418	0.2
Other family	335,650	377,577	379,325	-
Male householder, no wife present...	81,890	99,807	108,954	0.8
Female householder, no husband present..	253,760	277,770	270,371	-0.2
Nonfamily households	718,078	826,550	912,983	1.0
Householder living alone..	599,808	689,361	743,280	0.7
Householder not living alone..	118,270	137,189	169,703	2.2
Housing Characteristics				
Total housing units...	2,442,017	2,714,017	2,807,632	0.3
Occupied housing units	2,194,594	2,350,628	2,468,726	0.5
Owner occupied	1,542,149	1,621,371	1,698,595	0.4
Renter occupied	652,445	729,257	770,131	0.5
Average household size...	2.48	2.48	2.43	-0.2
Financial Characteristics				
Median gross rent of renter-occupied housing	484	682	882	2.7
Median monthly owner costs for housing units with a mortgage	861	1,182	1,316	1.0
Median value of owner-occupied housing units...	89,900	139,000	198,300	3.9

- = Zero or rounds to zero

Table MO-4. Migration, Origin, and Language

(Number, percent.)

Characteristic	State 2021	U.S. 2021
Residence 1 Year Ago		
Population 1 year and over	6,102,443	328,464,538
Same house	86.6	87.2
Different house in the U.S.	13.1	12.3
Same county	6.5	6.7
Different county	6.6	5.7
Same state	3.9	3.3
Different state	2.7	2.4
Abroad	0.3	0.4
Place of Birth		
Native born	5,916,949	286,623,642
Male	49.4	49.7
Female	50.6	50.3
Foreign born	251,238	45,270,103
Male	48.3	48.7
Female	51.7	51.3
Foreign born; naturalized U.S. citizen..	132,154	24,044,083
Male	45.7	46.4
Female	54.3	53.6
Foreign born; not a U.S. citizen	119,084	21,226,020
Male	51.1	51.2
Female	48.9	48.8
Entered 2010 or later	33.7	28.1
Entered 2000 to 2009	25.4	23.7
Entered before 2000...	40.9	48.2
World Region of Birth, Foreign		
Foreign-born population, excluding population born at sea	251,238	45,269,644
Europe	17.3	10.7
Asia	38.4	31.0
Africa	9.7	5.7
Oceania	1.9	0.6
Latin America	31.2	50.1
North America	1.6	1.7
Language Spoken at Home and Ability to Speak English		
Population 5 years and over...	5,814,241	313,232,500
English only	94.0	78.4
Language other than English..	6.0	21.6
Speaks English less than "very well"..	2.0	8.3

Table MO-5. Median Income and Poverty Status, 2021

(Number, percent, except as noted.)

Characteristic	State		U.S.	
	Number	Percent	Number	Percent
Median Income				
Households (dollars)..	61,847	X	69,717	X
Families (dollars)	79,084	X	85,806	X
Below Poverty Level (All People)	761,311	12.7	41,393,176	12.8
Sex				
Male	336,091	11.4	18,518,155	11.6
Female	425,220	13.9	22,875,021	13.9
Age				
Under 18 years..	218,688	16.2	12,243,219	16.9
Related children under 18 years........................	212,579	15.8	11,985,424	16.6
18 to 64 years	443,053	12.3	23,526,341	11.9
65 years and over	99,570	9.5	5,623,616	10.3

X = Not applicable.

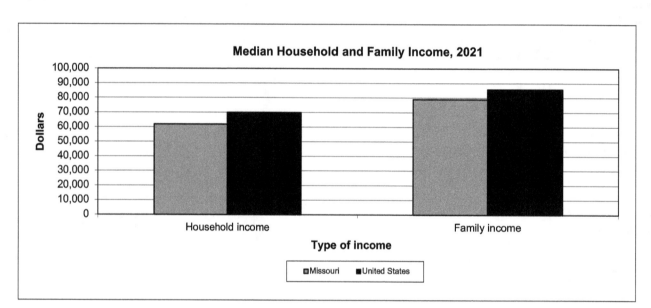

Table MO-6. Health Insurance Coverage Status for the Civilian Noninstitutionalized Population and Children Under 19 Years of Age

(Number, percent.)

Item	2011	2012	2013	2014	2015	2016	2017	2018	2019	2020 [2]	2021
Civilian Noninstitutionalized Population	5,898,968	5,908,769	5,930,677	5,950,606	5,969,392	5,977,199	6,000,326	6,014,742	6,020,665	6,011,968	6,063,301
Covered by Private or Public Insurance											
Number..	5,091,554	5,107,389	5,157,844	5,256,728	5,386,284	5,445,276	5,452,055	5,448,415	5,416,963	5,446,869	5,492,403
Percent..	86.3	86.4	87.0	88.3	90.2	91.1	90.9	90.6	90.0	90.6	90.6
Uninsured											
Number..	807,414	801,380	772,833	693,878	583,108	531,923	548,271	566,327	603,702	565,099	570,898
Percent..	13.7	13.6	13.0	11.7	9.8	8.9	9.1	9.4	10.0	9.4	9.4
Percent in the U.S. not covered............................	15.1	14.8	14.5	11.7	9.4	8.6	8.7	8.9	9.2	8.7	8.6
Children Under 19 Years of Age[1]	1,409,255	1,399,674	1,394,588	1,387,561	1,387,714	1,386,471	1,464,725	1,453,042	1,446,554	1,454,835	1,462,172
Covered by Private or Public Insurance											
Number..	1,314,321	1,301,641	1,297,042	1,287,589	1,308,016	1,324,598	1,390,219	1,370,509	1,351,868	1,370,412	1,376,551
Percent..	93.3	93.0	93.0	92.8	94.3	95.5	94.9	94.3	93.5	94.2	94.1
Uninsured											
Number..	94,934	98,033	97,546	99,972	79,698	61,873	74,506	82,533	94,686	84,423	85,621
Percent..	6.7	7.0	7.0	7.2	5.7	4.5	5.1	5.7	6.5	5.8	5.9
Percent in the U.S. not covered............................	7.5	7.2	7.1	6.0	4.8	4.5	5.0	5.2	5.7	5.2	5.4

[1] Data for years prior to 2017 are for individuals under 18 years of age.
[2] 2020 ACS 5-Year estimates. 1-Year estimates were not released for 2020 due to the impact of COVID-19 on data collection that year. Data is not comparable to previous years, which are based on 1-year estimates.

Table MO-7. Employment Status by Demographic Group, 2022

(Numbers in thousands, percent.)

Characteristic	Civilian noninstitutional population	Civilian labor force		Employed		Unemployed	
		Number	Percent of population	Number	Percent of population	Number	Percent of population
Total..	4,886	3,047	62.4	2,965	60.7	81	2.7
Sex							
Male..	2,373	1,605	67.6	1,562	65.8	43	2.7
Female...	2,513	1,442	57.4	1,403	55.8	39	2.7
Race, Sex, and Hispanic Origin							
White	4,146	2,565	61.9	2,501	60.3	64	2.5
Male.......................................	2,037	1,382	67.9	1,347	66.1	35	2.6
Female....................................	2,108	1,183	56.1	1,154	54.7	29	2.4
Black or African American...................	538	342	63.5	328	61.0	14	4.0
Male.......................................	NA	NA	NA	NA	NA	NA	NA
Female....................................	295	182	61.7	174	58.9	8	4.6
Hispanic or Latino ethnicity[1]	NA	NA	NA	NA	NA	NA	NA
Male.......................................	NA	NA	NA	NA	NA	NA	NA
Female....................................	NA	NA	NA	NA	NA	NA	NA
Age							
16 to 19 years................................	NA	NA	NA	NA	NA	NA	NA
20 to 24 years................................	391	276	70.4	262	66.8	14	5.0
25 to 34 years................................	762	645	84.7	632	83.0	14	2.1
35 to 44 years................................	813	694	85.3	677	83.2	17	2.5
45 to 54 years................................	722	608	84.1	600	83.1	7	1.2
55 to 64 years................................	801	499	62.3	488	61.0	10	2.1
65 years and over	1,084	196	18.0	192	17.7	4	2.0

NOTE: Data in Table 7 are from the Current Population Survey (CPS) and do not match the estimates in Table 8. See notes and definitions for further information.
[1] May be of any race.

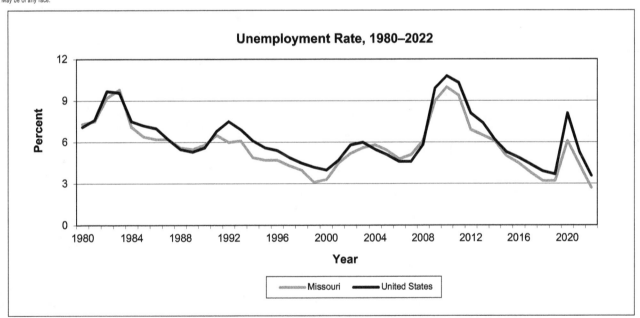

Unemployment Rate, 1980–2022

Table MO-8. Employment Status of the Civilian Noninstitutional Population Age 16 Years and Over

(Number, percent.)

Year	Civilian labor force	Civilian participation rate	Employed	Unemployed	Unemployment rate
2010..	3,043,249	65.7	2,753,910	289,339	9.5
2011..	3,032,960	65.2	2,770,662	262,298	8.6
2012..	3,004,347	64.3	2,789,025	215,322	7.2
2013..	3,011,198	64.2	2,807,115	204,083	6.8
2014..	3,035,599	64.4	2,848,571	187,028	6.2
2015..	3,057,859	64.6	2,901,467	156,392	5.1
2016..	3,072,904	64.6	2,933,457	139,447	4.5
2017..	3,053,526	63.9	2,939,306	114,220	3.7
2018..	3,045,865	63.6	2,949,910	95,955	3.2
2019..	3,072,073	63.8	2,976,643	95,430	3.1
2020..	3,037,162	62.9	2,853,353	183,809	6.1
2021..	3,062,449	63.1	2,928,368	134,081	4.4
2022..	3,061,279	62.7	2,984,340	76,939	2.5

Table MO-9. Employment and Average Wages by Industry

(Estimates are based on the 2012 North American Industry Classification System [NAICS].)

Industry	2014	2015	2016	2017	2018	2019	2020	2021
	Number of Jobs							
Wage and Salary Employment by Industry.........................	2,834,816	2,886,985	2,925,546	2,948,639	2,971,173	2,993,332	2,856,984	2,916,729
Farm Wage and Salary Employment.................................	7,131	9,971	10,251	7,000	7,363	8,433	9,106	7,861
Nonfarm Wage and Salary Employment............................	2,827,685	2,877,014	2,915,295	2,941,639	2,963,810	2,984,899	2,847,878	2,908,868
Private wage and salary employment.............................	2,355,073	2,406,070	2,444,246	2,470,258	2,491,968	2,512,272	2,387,134	2,453,102
Forestry, fishing, and related activities.........................	5,511	5,563	5,548	5,555	5,775	6,059	5,912	5,624
Mining..	3,896	3,924	3,874	4,045	4,143	4,156	4,101	4,141
Utilities..	11,960	11,859	11,696	11,721	11,761	11,847	11,671	11,621
Construction	112,846	117,327	123,585	125,925	125,564	129,527	129,490	134,671
Manufacturing..	256,197	261,529	263,424	266,025	273,273	277,301	266,647	271,079
Durable goods manufacturing...................................	152,374	157,248	158,166	158,627	164,214	167,575	159,695	162,174
Nondurable goods manufacturing..............................	103,823	104,281	105,258	107,398	109,059	109,726	106,952	108,905
Wholesale trade	121,339	120,887	120,876	121,688	121,566	124,031	120,484	121,888
Retail trade..	307,128	313,852	317,778	315,670	313,444	306,455	293,447	303,070
Transportation and warehousing..................................	93,645	97,436	97,739	99,446	100,736	104,668	103,800	110,967
Information..	52,327	50,237	49,421	48,280	47,637	46,729	43,666	45,376
Finance and insurance	127,945	128,619	130,039	134,287	133,889	136,704	139,198	139,952
Real estate and rental and leasing................................	35,433	36,487	37,286	37,875	38,109	39,884	38,080	39,254
Professional, scientific, and technical services	137,240	147,236	154,149	160,098	163,591	163,611	162,584	168,232
Management of companies and enterprises....................	66,114	65,571	65,139	65,320	65,541	65,284	62,053	59,613
Administrative and waste services................................	155,217	159,788	161,260	158,683	159,185	156,050	143,464	147,667
Educational services..	66,661	67,075	67,722	68,420	71,943	72,174	71,881	77,458
Health care and social assistance...............................	382,244	392,708	401,488	411,141	415,593	423,366	411,550	411,151
Arts, entertainment, and recreation.............................	44,674	41,793	42,888	41,938	42,590	43,548	32,836	38,149
Accommodation and food services..............................	243,763	252,424	258,390	263,189	264,819	267,112	222,601	238,707
Other services, except public administration.................	130,933	131,755	131,944	130,952	132,809	133,766	123,669	124,482
Government and government enterprises...................	472,612	470,944	471,049	471,381	471,842	472,627	460,744	455,766
	Dollars							
Average Wages and Salaries by Industry	45,342	46,609	47,193	48,525	50,203	51,644	55,076	57,449
Average Farm Wages and Salaries	48,171	28,872	30,824	41,151	38,446	36,160	31,186	34,516
Average Nonfarm Wages and Salaries	45,334	46,671	47,250	48,543	50,232	51,688	55,152	57,511
Average private wages and salaries.............................	46,008	47,384	47,959	49,290	51,089	52,629	56,329	58,814
Forestry, fishing, and related activities.........................	27,280	28,299	30,393	32,143	32,924	34,200	36,958	39,951
Mining..	69,599	69,625	66,847	69,193	68,581	73,091	73,570	75,884
Utilities..	89,324	91,273	94,222	98,147	98,479	103,602	107,857	108,003
Construction	53,441	55,396	57,009	58,802	60,496	62,778	65,853	68,652
Manufacturing..	56,945	58,403	58,309	59,247	60,567	61,941	64,312	65,706
Durable goods manufacturing...................................	59,918	60,666	60,625	61,818	63,544	65,039	66,006	67,640
Nondurable goods manufacturing..............................	52,580	54,990	54,828	55,450	56,084	57,211	61,781	62,826
Wholesale trade	64,575	66,392	67,400	69,105	72,340	73,007	76,999	81,847
Retail trade..	26,916	27,918	28,370	29,096	29,784	30,640	33,540	35,794
Transportation and warehousing..................................	48,232	49,109	49,582	50,545	51,695	52,276	53,845	54,774
Information..	71,213	74,871	75,881	76,091	84,311	88,453	92,351	94,891
Finance and insurance	71,785	75,164	77,124	79,329	83,838	86,604	93,624	96,405
Real estate and rental and leasing................................	40,598	42,984	43,107	44,272	46,442	48,569	52,294	55,090
Professional, scientific, and technical services	72,691	76,146	76,178	78,016	79,273	82,791	86,698	91,803
Management of companies and enterprises....................	102,956	101,218	100,100	104,518	112,963	112,088	114,084	118,100
Administrative and waste services................................	33,927	34,429	35,530	37,246	38,617	40,383	44,411	48,667
Educational services..	36,057	36,151	36,371	36,764	36,333	36,962	38,440	37,535
Health care and social assistance...............................	43,102	44,536	45,155	46,096	47,591	49,015	52,224	54,846
Arts, entertainment, and recreation.............................	39,973	42,390	41,782	40,560	40,599	41,437	43,213	45,555
Accommodation and food services..............................	18,114	18,959	19,477	20,339	21,536	22,201	21,982	26,227
Other services, except public administration.................	31,653	32,865	33,987	35,224	36,453	37,584	41,489	43,670
Government and government enterprises...................	41,980	43,028	43,572	44,626	45,702	46,685	49,055	50,499

Table MO-10. Employment Characteristics by Family Type

(Number, percent.)

Family type and labor force status	2019 Total	2019 Families with own children under 18 years	2020 [1] Total	2020 [1] Families with own children under 18 years	2021 Total	2021 Families with own children under 18 years
All Families...	1,546,045	627,679	1,551,056	640,224	1,555,743	627,394
FAMILY TYPE AND LABOR FORCE STATUS						
Opposite-Sex Married-Couple Families..	1,160,554	420,287	1,155,339	429,636	1,166,516	421,631
Both husband and wife in labor force..............................	52.3	72.5	52.5	71.9	51.9	71.5
Husband in labor force, wife not in labor force	18.2	21.7	19.1	22.8	19.1	22.9
Wife in labor force, husband not in labor force	8.2	4.1	8.2	3.6	8.7	4.1
Both husband and wife not in labor force..........................	20.4	1.3	20.2	1.6	20.3	1.5
Other Families	385,491	207,392	385,838	208,153	379,325	203,587
Female householder, no spouse present............................	71.1	70.6	71.9	72.5	71.3	73.9
In labor force..	51.0	60.3	51.4	62.0	51.0	63.0
Not in labor force	20.1	10.2	20.4	10.5	20.3	10.9
Male householder, no spouse present...........................	28.9	29.4	28.1	27.5	28.7	26.1
In labor force..	21.9	26.4	21.9	25.2	22.1	24.2
Not in labor force	7.0	3.0	6.3	2.4	6.6	2.0

[1] 2020 ACS 5-Year estimates. 1-Year estimates were not released for 2020 due to the impact of COVID-19 on data collection that year. Data is not comparable to previous years, which are based on 1-year estimates.

Table MO-11. School Enrollment and Educational Attainment, 2021

(Number, percent.)

Item	State	U.S.
Enrollment		
Total population 3 years and over, enrolled in school	1,456,311	79,453,524
Enrolled in nursery school or preschool (percent)..........................	6.0	5.2
Enrolled in kindergarten (percent)............................	5.0	5.0
Enrolled in elementary school, grades 1-8 (percent)..........................	43.0	41.3
Enrolled in high school, grades 9-12 (percent)............................	21.6	21.8
Enrolled in college or graduate school (percent)............................	24.5	26.7
Attainment		
Total population 25 years and over	4,226,634	228,193,464
Less than ninth grade (percent)............................	2.6	4.8
9th to 12th grade, no diploma (percent)............................	5.9	5.9
High school graduate, including equivalency (percent)............................	30.8	26.3
Some college, no degree (percent)............................	20.7	19.3
Associate's degree (percent)............................	8.3	8.8
Bachelor's degree (percent)............................	19.5	21.2
Graduate or professional degree (percent)............................	12.2	13.8
High school graduate or higher (percent)	91.6	89.4
Bachelor's degree or higher (percent)............................	31.7	35.0

Table MO-12. Public School Characteristics and Educational Indicators

(Number, percent; data derived from National Center of Education Statistics.)

Item	State	U.S.
Public Elementary and Secondary Schools		
Number of regular school districts, 2019-20	518	13,349
Number of operational schools, 2019-20.............................	2,431	98,469
Percent charter schools	2.9	7.7
Total public school enrollment, Fall 2021.............................	888,823	49,433,092
Percent charter school enrollment	2.7	7.5
Student-teacher ratio, Fall 2019.............................	13.2	15.9
Expenditures per student (unadjusted dollars), 2019-20	11,397	13,489
Four-year adjusted cohort graduation rate (ACGR), 2019-2020[1].............................	89.5	86.5
Students eligible for free or reduced-price lunch (percent), 2019-20..........................	50.0	52.1
English language learners (percent), Fall 2020	3.8	10.3
Students age 3 to 21 served under IDEA, part B (percent), 2021-22	14.1	14.7

Public Schools by Type, 2019-20	Number	Percent of state public schools
Total number of schools.............................	2,431	100.0
Special education.............................	48	2.0
Vocational education.............................	62	2.6
Alternative education.............................	60	2.5

[1] Adjusted Cohort Graduation Rates (ACGR) differ from Averaged Freshmen Graduation Rates (AFGR).

Table MO-13. Reported Voting and Registration of the Voting-Age Population, November 2022

(Numbers in thousands, percent.)

Item	Total population	Total citizen population	Registered			Voted		
			Total registered	Percent registered (total population)	Percent registered (total citizen population)	Total voted	Percent voted (total population)	Percent voted (total citizen population)
U.S. Total	255,457	233,546	161,422	63.2	69.1	121,916	47.7	52.2
State Total	4,744	4,655	3,532	74.5	75.9	2,460	51.9	52.9
Sex								
Male	2,313	2,271	1,686	72.9	74.2	1,156	50.0	50.9
Female	2,430	2,384	1,846	76.0	77.4	1,304	53.7	54.7
Race								
White alone....................................	4,105	4,025	3,092	75.3	76.8	2,158	52.6	53.6
White, non-Hispanic alone	3,935	3,902	3,016	76.7	77.3	2,110	53.6	54.1
Black alone....................................	505	497	334	66.3	67.3	254	50.4	51.2
Asian alone	26	26	8	30.9	30.9	4	16.0	16.0
Hispanic (of any race)	176	129	83	46.8	63.9	48	27.5	37.5
White alone or in combination	4,180	4,100	3,160	75.6	77.1	2,191	52.4	53.5
Black alone or in combination	534	526	356	66.8	67.8	258	48.3	49.1
Asian alone or in combination	52	52	34	65.0	65.0	22	43.2	43.2
Age								
18 to 24 years	536	525	322	60.1	61.4	143	26.7	27.2
25 to 34 years	736	713	466	63.4	65.4	255	34.6	35.7
35 to 44 years	861	838	648	75.2	77.3	434	50.4	51.8
45 to 64 years	1,511	1,497	1,179	78.0	78.8	880	58.3	58.8
65 years and over	1,100	1,083	917	83.4	84.6	749	68.1	69.1

B = Base is less than 75,000 and therefore too small to show the derived measure.

Table MO-14. Health Indicators

(Number, rate as indicated in footnotes.)

Item	State	U.S.
Births		
Life Expectancy at Birth (years), 2020	75.1	77.0
Fertility Rate by State[1], 2021	58.4	56.3
Percent Home Births, 2021	2.0	1.4
Cesarean Delivery Rate[2], 2021	30.2	32.1
Preterm Birth Rate[3], 2021	11.3	10.5
Teen Birth Rate[4], 2021	17.1	13.9
Percentage of Babies Born Low Birthweight[5], 2021	8.9	8.5
Deaths[6]		
Heart Disease Mortality Rate, 2021..	202.4	173.8
Cancer Mortality Rate, 2021..	164.2	146.6
Stroke Mortality Rate, 2021	41.0	41.1
Diabetes Mortality Rate, 2021..	24.0	25.4
Influenza/Pneumonia Mortality Rate, 2021...	11.5	10.5
Suicide Mortality Rate, 2021..	18.7	14.1
Drug Overdose Mortality Rate, 2021..	36.5	33.6
Firearm Injury Mortality Rate, 2021...	23.2	14.6
Homicide Mortality Rate, 2021..	12.4	8.2
Disease and Illness		
Lifetime Asthma in Adults, 2020 (percent)...	13.4	13.9
Lifetime Asthma in Children, 2020 (percent)[7]	12.2	11.3
Diabetes in Adults, 2020 (percent)..	9.4	8.2
Self-reported Obesity in Adults, 2021 (percent)..	37.3	NA

SOURCE: National Center for Health Statistics, National Vital Statistics System 2020 data; https://wonder.cdc.gov.
[1] General fertility rate per 1,000 women aged 15–44.
[2] This represents the percentage of all live births that were cesarean deliveries.
[3] Babies born prior to 37 weeks of pregnancy (gestation).
[4] Number of births per 1,000 females aged 15–19
[5] Babies born weighing less than 2,500 grams or 5 lbs. 8oz.
[6] Death rates are the number of deaths per 100,000 total population.
[7] U.S. total includes data from 30 states and D.C.
NA = Not available.
- = Zero or rounds to zero.

Table MO-15. State Government Finances, 2021

(Dollar amounts in thousands, percent distribution.)

Item	Dollars	Percent distribution
Total Revenue	42,145,677	100.0
General revenue	37,442,085	88.8
Intergovernmental revenue	15,389,965	36.5
Taxes	15,091,423	35.8
General sales	4,119,671	9.8
Selective sales	1,825,622	4.3
License taxes	691,696	1.6
Individual income tax	7,715,511	18.3
Corporate income tax	686,857	1.6
Other taxes	52,066	0.1
Current charges	3,279,780	7.8
Miscellaneous general revenue	3,680,917	8.7
Utility revenue	-	-
Liquor stores revenue	-	-
Insurance trust revenue[1]	4,703,592	11.2
Total Expenditure	41,341,575	100.0
Intergovernmental expenditure	6,940,011	16.8
Direct expenditure	34,401,564	83.2
Current operation	24,757,046	59.9
Capital outlay	1,502,945	3.6
Insurance benefits and repayments	6,463,226	15.6
Assistance and subsidies	810,607	2.0
Interest on debt	867,740	2.1
Exhibit: Salaries and wages	4,100,792	9.9
Total Expenditure	41,341,575	100.0
General expenditure	34,872,053	84.4
Intergovernmental expenditure	6,940,011	16.8
Direct expenditure	27,932,042	67.6
General expenditure, by function:		
Education	10,600,115	25.6
Public welfare	10,890,277	26.3
Hospitals	2,706,192	6.5
Health	2,418,408	5.8
Highways	1,758,135	4.3
Police protection	277,615	0.7
Correction	709,840	1.7
Natural resources	369,975	0.9
Parks and recreation	36,897	0.1
Governmental administration	909,103	2.2
Interest on general debt	867,740	2.1
Other and unallocable	3,240,384	7.8
Utility expenditure	42,522	0.1
Liquor stores expenditure	-	-
Insurance trust expenditure	6,463,226	15.6
Debt at End of Fiscal Year	19,143,395	X
Cash and Security Holdings	122,752,696	X

X = Not applicable.
- = Zero or rounds to zero.
[1] Within insurance trust revenue, net earnings of state retirement systems is a calculated statistic (the item code in the data file is X08), and thus can be positive or negative. Net earnings is the sum of earnings on investments plus gains on investments minus losses on investments. The change made in 2002 for asset valuation from book to market value in accordance with Statement 34 of the Governmental Accounting Standards Board is reflected in the calculated statistics.

Table MO-16. State Government Tax Collections, 2022

(Dollars in thousands, percent.)

Item	Dollars	Percent distribution
Total Taxes	16,887,389	100.0
Property taxes	39,591	0.2
Sales and gross receipts	6,462,312	38.3
General sales and gross receipts	4,553,244	27.0
Selective sales and gross receipts	1,909,068	11.3
Alcoholic beverages	47,193	0.3
Amusements	390,854	2.3
Insurance premiums	465,920	2.8
Motor fuels	803,261	4.8
Pari-mutuels	X	-
Public utilities	X	-
Tobacco products	96,111	0.6
Other selective sales	105,729	0.6
Licenses	675,239	4.0
Alcoholic beverages	6,126	-
Amusements	22	-
Corporations in general	0	-
Hunting and fishing	40,878	0.2
Motor vehicle	317,073	1.9
Motor vehicle operators	15,922	0.1
Public utilities	18,442	0.1
Occupation and business, NEC	182,212	1.1
Other licenses	94,564	0.6
Income taxes	9,694,630	57.4
Individual income	8,942,661	53.0
Corporation net income	751,969	4.5
Other taxes	15,617	0.1
Death and gift	49	-
Documentary and stock transfer	15,496	0.1
Severance	0	-
Taxes, NEC	72	-

- = Zero or rounds to zero.
X = Not applicable.

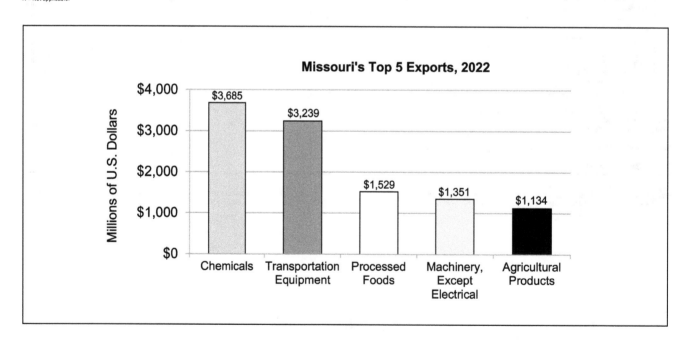

MONTANA

Facts and Figures

Location: Northwestern United States; bordered on the N by Canada (British Columbia, Alberta, and Saskatchewan), on the E by North Dakota and South Dakota, on the S by Idaho and Wyoming, and on the W by Idaho

Area: 147,042 sq. mi. (380,838 sq. km.); rank—4th

Population: 1,122,867 (2022 est.); rank—43rd

Principal Cities: capital—Helena; largest—Billings

Statehood: November 8, 1889; 41st state

U.S. Congress: 2 senators, 1 representative

State Motto: *Oro y plata* ("Gold and silver")

State Song: "Montana"

State Nicknames: The Treasure State; Big Sky Country

Abbreviations: MT; Mont.

State Symbols: flower—bitterroot; tree—ponderosa pine; bird—Western meadowlark

At a Glance

- With an increase in population of 13.5 percent, Montana ranked 11th among the states in growth from 2010 to 2022.

- The median household income in Montana in 2021 was $63,249 compared to the national median household income of $69,717.

- In 2022, 20.0 percent of Montana residents were in the 65 and older age group, a percentage that ranked 8th in the country.

- Montana had the 2nd lowest drug overdose death rate among the states in 2021, with 11.4 drug overdose deaths per 100,000 population. The national rate was 32.4 deaths per 100,000 population.

Table MT-1. Population by Age, Sex, Race, and Hispanic Origin

(Number, percent, except where noted.)

Sex, age, race, and Hispanic origin	2010	2020	2022	Percent change, 2010–2022
Total Population...	989,415	1,084,197	1,122,867	13.5
Percent of total U.S. population	0.3	0.3	0.3	X
Sex				
Male...	496,667	550,595	569,846	14.7
Female..	492,748	533,602	553,021	12.2
Age				
Under 5 years...	62,423	59,512	57,646	-7.7
Under 18 years..	223,563	231,175	233,753	4.6
18 to 64 years...	619,110	643,801	663,988	7.2
65 years and over..	146,742	209,221	225,126	53.4
Median age (years)	39.8	40	40.2	1.0
Race and Hispanic Origin				
One race				
White	891,529	963,257	996,179	11.7
Black	4,215	6,505	6,993	65.9
American Indian and Alaska Native	63,495	71,355	72,451	14.1
Asian..	6,379	10,694	12,084	89.4
Native Hawaiian or Other Pacific Islander	734	937	1,108	51.0
Two or more races	23,063	31,449	34,052	47.6
Hispanic (of any race)...	28,565	44,932	50,719	77.6

NOTE: Population figures for 2022 are July 1 estimates. The 2010 and 2020 estimates are taken from the respective censuses.
- = Zero or rounds to zero.
X = Not applicable.

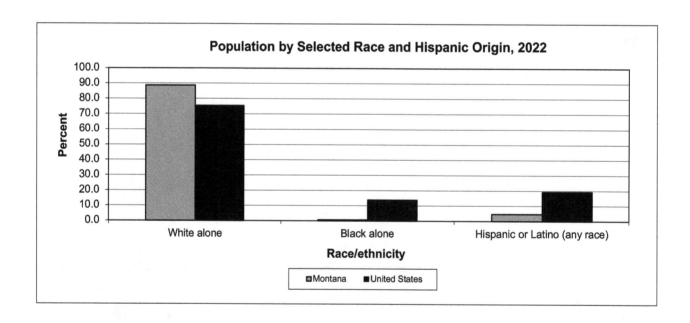

Table MT-2. Marital Status

(Number, percent distribution.)

Sex, age, race, and Hispanic origin	2000	2010	2021
Males, 15 Years and Over	353,801	404,179	459,769
Never married	27.7	30.5	34.3
Now married, except separated...	58.3	53.4	50.4
Separated...	1.2	1.5	1.1
Widowed...	2.6	2.3	2.9
Divorced...	10.2	12.4	11.3
Females, 15 Years and Over	362,114	403,766	450,830
Never married	20.4	23.5	26.8
Now married, except separated...	56.3	52.9	51.4
Separated...	1.3	1.6	1.4
Widowed...	10.4	9.7	7.9
Divorced...	11.6	12.3	12.5

Table MT-3. Households and Housing Characteristics

(Number, percent, dollars.)

Item	2000	2010	2021	Average annual percent change, 2010–2021
Total Households..	358,667	402,747	448,949	1.0
Family households	237,407	255,199	275,623	0.7
Married-couple family	192,067	203,500	219,056	0.7
Other family	45,340	51,699	56,567	0.9
Male householder, no wife present..	13,324	16,926	20,003	1.7
Female householder, no husband present.................................	32,016	34,773	36,564	0.5
Nonfamily households	121,260	147,548	173,326	1.6
Householder living alone..	98,422	119,762	131,040	0.9
Householder not living alone..	22,838	27,786	42,286	4.7
Housing Characteristics				
Total housing units..	412,633	483,006	521,916	0.7
Occupied housing units	358,667	402,747	448,949	1.0
Owner occupied	247,723	280,633	311,861	1.0
Renter occupied	110,944	122,114	137,088	1.1
Average household size..	2.45	2.39	2.40	-
Financial Characteristics				
Median gross rent of renter-occupied housing	447	642	883	3.4
Median monthly owner costs for housing units with a mortgage	863	1,217	1,558	2.5
Median value of owner-occupied housing units.............................	99,500	181,200	322,800	7.1

- = Zero or rounds to zero.

Table MT-4. Migration, Origin, and Language

(Number, percent.)

Characteristic	State 2021	U.S. 2021
Residence 1 Year Ago		
Population 1 year and over	1,093,888	328,464,538
Same house	86.3	87.2
Different house in the U.S.	13.2	12.3
Same county	6.3	6.7
Different county	6.9	5.7
Same state	2.8	3.3
Different state	4.1	2.4
Abroad	0.4	0.4
Place of Birth		
Native born	1,079,814	286,623,642
Male	51.0	49.7
Female	49.0	50.3
Foreign born	24,457	45,270,103
Male	41.6	48.7
Female	58.4	51.3
Foreign born; naturalized U.S. citizen...	12,167	24,044,083
Male	38.5	46.4
Female	61.5	53.6
Foreign born; not a U.S. citizen	12,290	21,226,020
Male	44.7	51.2
Female	55.3	48.8
Entered 2010 or later	35.8	28.1
Entered 2000 to 2009	20.6	23.7
Entered before 2000...	43.6	48.2
World Region of Birth, Foreign		
Foreign-born population, excluding population born at sea	24,457	45,269,644
Europe	36.7	10.7
Asia	27.2	31.0
Africa	0.9	5.7
Oceania	4.0	0.6
Latin America...	20.2	50.1
North America	11.0	1.7
Language Spoken at Home and Ability to Speak English		
Population 5 years and over..	1,048,180	313,232,500
English only	96.1	78.4
Language other than English...	3.9	21.6
Speaks English less than "very well"...	0.8	8.3

Table MT-5. Median Income and Poverty Status, 2021

(Number, percent, except as noted.)

Characteristic	State Number	State Percent	U.S. Number	U.S. Percent
Median Income				
Households (dollars)..	63,249	X	69,717	X
Families (dollars)	79,958	X	85,806	X
Below Poverty Level (All People)	128,123	11.9	41,393,176	12.8
Sex				
Male	60,981	11.1	18,518,155	11.6
Female	67,142	12.6	22,875,021	13.9
Age				
Under 18 years...	32,436	14.1	12,243,219	16.9
Related children under 18 years................................	31,547	13.8	11,985,424	16.6
18 to 64 years	76,915	12.1	23,526,341	11.9
65 years and over	18,772	8.8	5,623,616	10.3

X = Not applicable.

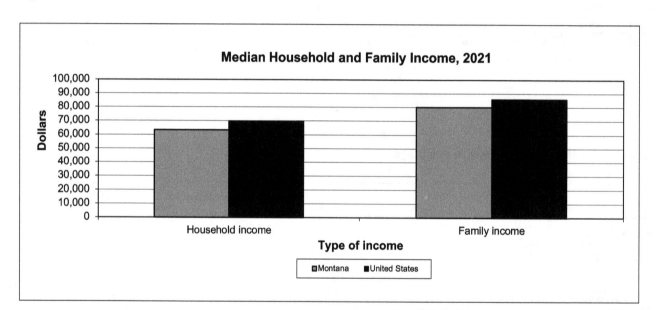

Median Household and Family Income, 2021

Table MT-6. Health Insurance Coverage Status for the Civilian Noninstitutionalized Population and Children Under 19 Years of Age

(Number, percent.)

Item	2011	2012	2013	2014	2015	2016	2017	2018	2019	2020 [2]	2021
Civilian Noninstitutionalized Population	983,214	989,823	999,390	1,008,116	1,017,458	1,027,510	1,036,245	1,047,075	1,053,646	1,046,670	1,088,496
Covered by Private or Public Insurance											
Number..	803,639	811,411	834,842	864,795	898,949	944,094	948,536	961,046	966,505	958,813	999,064
Percent...	81.7	82.0	83.5	85.8	88.4	91.9	91.5	91.8	91.7	91.6	91.8
Uninsured											
Number..	179,575	178,412	164,548	143,321	118,509	83,416	87,709	86,029	87,141	87,857	89,432
Percent...	18.3	18.0	16.5	14.2	11.6	8.1	8.5	8.2	8.3	8.4	8.2
Percent in the U.S. not covered.............................	15.1	14.8	14.5	11.7	9.4	8.6	8.7	8.9	9.2	8.7	8.6
Children Under 19 Years of Age[1]	222,102	219,198	223,043	224,051	225,169	227,631	240,764	244,049	241,743	240,362	248,375
Covered by Private or Public Insurance											
Number..	196,540	194,796	200,548	205,630	208,050	217,003	226,900	229,132	226,709	226,050	231,000
Percent...	88.5	88.9	89.9	91.8	92.4	95.3	94.2	93.9	93.8	94.0	93.0
Uninsured											
Number..	25,562	24,402	22,495	18,421	17,119	10,628	13,864	14,917	15,034	14,312	17,375
Percent...	11.5	11.1	10.1	8.2	7.6	4.7	5.8	6.1	6.2	6.0	7.0
Percent in the U.S. not covered.............................	7.5	7.2	7.1	6.0	4.8	4.5	5.0	5.2	5.7	5.2	5.4

[1] Data for years prior to 2017 are for individuals under 18 years of age.
[2] 2020 ACS 5-Year estimates. 1-Year estimates were not released for 2020 due to the impact of COVID-19 on data collection that year. Data is not comparable to previous years, which are based on 1-year estimates.

Table MT-7. Employment Status by Demographic Group, 2022

(Numbers in thousands, percent.)

Characteristic	Civilian noninstitutional population	Civilian labor force		Employed		Unemployed	
		Number	Percent of population	Number	Percent of population	Number	Percent of population
Total...	903	577	63.9	561	62.2	16	2.7
Sex							
Male..	453	304	67.0	294	64.9	9	3.0
Female..	449	273	60.8	267	59.3	7	2.4
Race, Sex, and Hispanic Origin							
White..	840	535	63.7	521	62.0	14	2.6
Male..	419	281	67.0	272	65.0	8	3.0
Female..	421	254	60.4	249	59.1	6	2.2
Black or African American...................	NA	NA	NA	NA	NA	NA	NA
Male..	NA	NA	NA	NA	NA	NA	NA
Female..	NA	NA	NA	NA	NA	NA	NA
Hispanic or Latino ethnicity[1]	NA	NA	NA	NA	NA	NA	NA
Male..	NA	NA	NA	NA	NA	NA	NA
Female..	NA	NA	NA	NA	NA	NA	NA
Age							
16 to 19 years..................................	NA	NA	NA	NA	NA	NA	NA
20 to 24 years..................................	71	56	78.6	52	73.9	3	5.7
25 to 34 years..................................	142	126	88.5	122	86.1	3	2.7
35 to 44 years..................................	146	126	86.4	124	84.8	2	1.9
45 to 54 years..................................	126	105	83.7	104	82.4	2	1.5
55 to 64 years..................................	134	87	65.3	86	64.1	2	2.1
65 years and over.............................	229	48	20.8	47	20.4	1	2.1

NOTE: Data in Table 7 are from the Current Population Survey (CPS) and do not match the estimates in Table 8. See notes and definitions for further information.
[1] May be of any race.
NA = Not available.

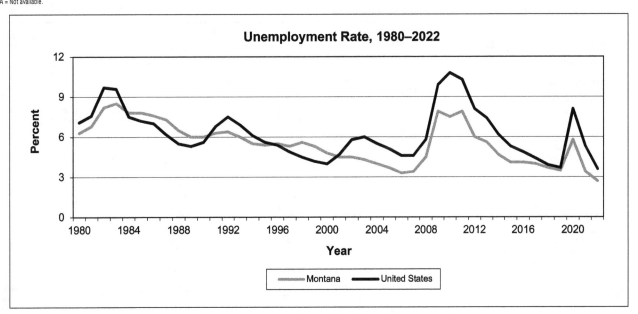

Unemployment Rate, 1980–2022

Table MT-8. Employment Status of the Civilian Noninstitutional Population Age 16 Years and Over

(Number, percent.)

Year	Civilian labor force	Civilian participation rate	Employed	Unemployed	Unemployment rate
2010..	500,895	64.4	464,808	36,087	7.2
2011..	501,065	63.9	467,786	33,279	6.6
2012..	506,441	64.0	477,056	29,385	5.8
2013..	511,199	64.0	483,798	27,401	5.4
2014..	512,613	63.5	488,738	23,875	4.7
2015..	517,901	63.6	495,725	22,176	4.3
2016..	521,736	63.3	499,266	22,470	4.3
2017..	528,441	63.2	506,871	21,570	4.1
2018..	533,821	63.1	513,858	19,963	3.7
2019..	542,279	63.5	522,898	19,381	3.6
2020..	542,917	62.7	511,616	31,301	5.8
2021..	549,743	62.3	531,202	18,541	3.4
2022..	567,787	63.1	552,842	14,945	2.6

Table MT-9. Employment and Average Wages by Industry

(Estimates are based on the 2012 North American Industry Classification System [NAICS].)

Industry	2014	2015	2016	2017	2018	2019	2020	2021
	Number of Jobs							
Wage and Salary Employment by Industry.......................	470,408	479,194	484,003	489,276	494,412	501,103	486,849	507,125
Farm Wage and Salary Employment................................	6,407	6,867	6,954	8,049	6,741	7,096	6,617	5,918
Nonfarm Wage and Salary Employment...........................	464,001	472,327	477,049	481,227	487,671	494,007	480,232	501,207
Private wage and salary employment...............................	368,689	376,987	380,970	385,073	392,247	397,872	384,777	405,393
Forestry, fishing, and related activities..........................	3,663	3,809	3,850	3,882	3,921	4,025	3,973	3,936
Mining..	8,527	7,560	6,377	6,322	6,655	6,725	6,232	6,199
Utilities...	3,157	3,080	3,029	2,874	2,826	2,823	2,793	2,789
Construction..	25,585	27,160	27,736	28,405	29,809	30,672	31,639	33,782
Manufacturing...	18,909	19,131	19,513	19,921	20,581	20,991	20,454	21,365
Durable goods manufacturing..................................	11,567	11,714	11,778	11,925	11,958	12,238	11,995	12,678
Nondurable goods manufacturing.............................	7,342	7,417	7,735	7,996	8,623	8,753	8,459	8,687
Wholesale trade..	17,000	17,621	17,378	17,268	17,252	17,260	16,973	17,522
Retail trade...	57,657	59,101	59,697	59,453	59,488	58,721	57,721	60,740
Transportation and warehousing..................................	15,491	15,610	15,252	15,218	15,644	15,883	15,360	16,009
Information..	6,420	6,377	6,334	6,408	6,351	6,219	5,807	5,619
Finance and insurance..	16,059	16,196	16,209	16,324	16,496	17,504	17,584	17,751
Real estate and rental and leasing..............................	5,375	5,699	5,685	6,007	6,188	6,372	6,227	6,664
Professional, scientific, and technical services	20,296	21,004	21,774	22,127	22,747	23,384	23,749	25,444
Management of companies and enterprises......................	1,962	2,067	2,074	2,079	2,068	2,071	2,046	2,274
Administrative and waste services..............................	17,304	17,545	16,943	17,124	17,966	18,361	18,161	19,579
Educational services	6,064	6,066	6,004	6,138	6,525	6,699	5,838	6,832
Health care and social assistance................................	63,958	65,115	67,420	69,089	69,492	70,563	69,698	71,128
Arts, entertainment, and recreation.............................	11,535	11,596	11,876	11,941	12,324	12,627	11,027	12,269
Accommodation and food services..............................	49,326	51,399	52,932	53,548	54,228	54,899	48,425	54,249
Other services, except public administration..................	20,401	20,851	20,887	20,945	21,686	22,073	21,070	21,242
Government and government enterprises.....................	95,312	95,340	96,079	96,154	95,424	96,135	95,455	95,814
	Dollars							
Average Wages and Salaries by Industry	39,059	40,143	40,885	42,133	43,643	44,905	48,342	51,440
Average Farm Wages and Salaries	38,757	30,604	34,987	30,401	36,426	24,774	35,388	46,005
Average Nonfarm Wages and Salaries	39,063	40,282	40,971	42,329	43,743	45,194	48,520	51,505
Average private wages and salaries..............................	38,558	39,768	40,303	41,712	43,193	44,753	48,242	51,632
Forestry, fishing, and related activities..........................	31,018	33,383	35,761	37,654	38,378	38,776	43,885	48,255
Mining..	88,252	87,576	88,061	87,727	90,951	92,178	89,613	96,255
Utilities...	81,114	87,486	86,271	88,971	87,855	92,876	100,346	97,886
Construction..	46,108	47,823	48,673	50,355	52,981	53,970	55,890	59,184
Manufacturing...	45,742	47,243	47,751	48,811	50,262	51,743	54,292	57,300
Durable goods manufacturing..................................	44,078	45,719	46,455	47,771	49,478	50,292	53,685	56,422
Nondurable goods manufacturing.............................	48,363	49,649	49,724	50,362	51,349	53,770	55,153	58,581
Wholesale trade..	53,237	54,828	55,004	56,941	59,147	61,435	65,398	71,575
Retail trade...	26,867	27,695	28,327	29,254	29,991	31,339	33,923	36,553
Transportation and warehousing..................................	51,891	51,640	51,166	52,802	55,181	56,964	59,722	59,041
Information..	45,667	48,405	50,183	51,874	54,524	56,601	65,700	81,205
Finance and insurance..	57,632	60,144	61,507	64,932	67,673	69,269	76,184	83,628
Real estate and rental and leasing..............................	32,246	34,492	34,976	35,784	38,318	39,563	43,506	52,046
Professional, scientific, and technical services	57,893	59,350	59,324	61,327	63,219	66,667	73,076	78,960
Management of companies and enterprises......................	71,993	75,761	75,235	76,186	78,471	81,898	89,043	98,992
Administrative and waste services..............................	30,153	32,095	33,560	34,415	35,431	35,989	39,116	44,822
Educational services	22,756	23,552	24,347	24,793	24,803	25,097	29,763	28,411
Health care and social assistance................................	42,133	44,380	45,445	47,345	48,711	50,497	53,832	56,317
Arts, entertainment, and recreation.............................	22,631	23,280	23,988	25,163	25,685	25,923	28,936	31,327
Accommodation and food services..............................	18,179	18,862	19,437	20,211	21,284	22,115	21,753	26,362
Other services, except public administration..................	27,976	28,968	30,204	31,470	32,389	33,628	36,393	38,368
Government and government enterprises.....................	41,016	42,311	43,616	44,801	46,005	47,019	49,643	50,964

Table MT-10. Employment Characteristics by Family Type

(Number, percent.)

Family type and labor force status	2019 Total	2019 Families with own children under 18 years	2020 [1] Total	2020 [1] Families with own children under 18 years	2021 Total	2021 Families with own children under 18 years
All Families	269,009	99,398	267,258	103,839	275,623	102,466
FAMILY TYPE AND LABOR FORCE STATUS						
Opposite-Sex Married-Couple Families	213,679	67,092	213,825	74,254	218,114	72,779
Both husband and wife in labor force	48.9	68.4	51.5	70.4	48.5	70.9
Husband in labor force, wife not in labor force	19.2	25.1	18.6	23.9	18.0	21.9
Wife in labor force, husband not in labor force	8.2	4.7	8.4	4.1	8.9	5.6
Both husband and wife not in labor force	23.2	1.6	21.5	1.6	24.7	1.6
Other Families	55,330	32,306	52,173	29,249	56,567	29,452
Female householder, no spouse present	64.2	66.5	64.4	65.3	64.6	63.1
In labor force	48.5	58.6	45.9	55.5	44.1	54.3
Not in labor force	15.8	7.8	18.6	9.7	20.6	8.8
Male householder, no spouse present	35.8	33.5	35.6	34.7	35.4	36.9
In labor force	27.2	30.1	27.6	30.8	27.1	34.8
Not in labor force	8.6	3.5	8.0	3.9	8.3	2.1

[1] 2020 ACS 5-Year estimates. 1-Year estimates were not released for 2020 due to the impact of COVID-19 on data collection that year. Data is not comparable to previous years, which are based on 1-year estimates.

Table MT-11. School Enrollment and Educational Attainment, 2021

(Number, percent.)

Item	State	U.S.
Enrollment		
Total population 3 years and over, enrolled in school	247,237	79,453,524
Enrolled in nursery school or preschool (percent)	5.8	5.2
Enrolled in kindergarten (percent)	5.9	5.0
Enrolled in elementary school, grades 1-8 (percent)	42.3	41.3
Enrolled in high school, grades 9-12 (percent)	21.8	21.8
Enrolled in college or graduate school (percent)	24.2	26.7
Attainment		
Total population 25 years and over	766,758	228,193,464
Less than ninth grade (percent)	1.4	4.8
9th to 12th grade, no diploma (percent)	4.2	5.9
High school graduate, including equivalency (percent)	26.8	26.3
Some college, no degree (percent)	23.7	19.3
Associate's degree (percent)	9.1	8.8
Bachelor's degree (percent)	22.4	21.2
Graduate or professional degree (percent)	12.4	13.8
High school graduate or higher (percent)	94.4	89.4
Bachelor's degree or higher (percent)	34.8	35.0

Table MT-12. Public School Characteristics and Educational Indicators

(Number, percent; data derived from National Center of Education Statistics.)

Item	State	U.S.
Public Elementary and Secondary Schools		
Number of regular school districts, 2019-20	400	13,349
Number of operational schools, 2019-20	826	98,469
Percent charter schools	-	7.7
Total public school enrollment, Fall 2021	150,195	49,433,092
Percent charter school enrollment	NA	7.5
Student-teacher ratio, Fall 2019	14.0	15.9
Expenditures per student (unadjusted dollars), 2019-20	12,065	13,489
Four-year adjusted cohort graduation rate (ACGR), 2019-2020[1]	85.9	86.5
Students eligible for free or reduced-price lunch (percent), 2019-20	40.2	52.1
English language learners (percent), Fall 2020	2.5	10.3
Students age 3 to 21 served under IDEA, part B (percent), 2021-22	13.3	14.7

Public Schools by Type, 2019-20	Number	Percent of state public schools
Total number of schools	826	100.0
Special education	2	0.2
Vocational education	-	-
Alternative education	2	0.2

[1] Adjusted Cohort Graduation Rates (ACGR) differ from Averaged Freshmen Graduation Rates (AFGR).
- = Zero or rounds to zero.
NA = Not available.

Table MT-13. Reported Voting and Registration of the Voting-Age Population, November 2022

(Numbers in thousands, percent.)

Item	Total population	Total citizen population	Registered			Voted		
			Total registered	Percent registered (total population)	Percent registered (total citizen population)	Total voted	Percent voted (total population)	Percent voted (total citizen population)
U.S. Total	255,457	233,546	161,422	63.2	69.1	121,916	47.7	52.2
State Total...............................	886	878	613	69.1	69.8	496	56.0	56.5
Sex								
Male	446	443	304	68.3	68.8	249	55.8	56.2
Female	441	435	308	70.0	70.8	247	56.2	56.9
Race								
White alone............................	837	831	583	69.7	70.2	476	56.9	57.3
White, non-Hispanic alone	816	813	570	69.8	70.1	466	57.1	57.4
Black alone.............................	4	2	1	34.3	52.2	1	34.3	52.2
Asian alone	5	4	3	48.7	67.3	2	36.6	50.7
Hispanic (of any race)	24	21	14	57.9	64.9	10	42.0	47.1
White alone or in combination	851	844	593	69.7	70.2	483	56.7	57.1
Black alone or in combination....................	6	5	3	49.9	62.6	1	20.3	25.4
Asian alone or in combination....................	10	8	6	59.3	70.5	5	52.4	62.3
Age								
18 to 24 years	110	109	55	49.9	50.5	34	31.3	31.6
25 to 34 years	125	123	81	65.3	66.1	52	41.4	41.9
35 to 44 years	159	155	107	67.3	68.8	77	48.7	49.8
45 to 64 years	259	258	190	73.2	73.7	158	60.9	61.3
65 years and over	234	233	180	76.9	77.2	175	74.8	75.1

- = Zero or rounds to zero.
B = Base is less than 75,000 and therefore too small to show the derived measure.

Table MT-14. Health Indicators

(Number, rate as indicated in footnotes.)

Item	State	U.S.
Births		
Life Expectancy at Birth (years), 2020	76.8	77.0
Fertility Rate by State[1], 2021	54.8	56.3
Percent Home Births, 2021	2.9	1.4
Cesarean Delivery Rate[2], 2021	27.8	32.1
Preterm Birth Rate[3], 2021	9.7	10.5
Teen Birth Rate[4], 2021	13.6	13.9
Percentage of Babies Born Low Birthweight[5], 2021	7.6	8.5
Deaths[6]		
Heart Disease Mortality Rate, 2021	175.2	173.8
Cancer Mortality Rate, 2021	142.2	146.6
Stroke Mortality Rate, 2021	31.2	41.1
Diabetes Mortality Rate, 2021	21.6	25.4
Influenza/Pneumonia Mortality Rate, 2021	7.5	10.5
Suicide Mortality Rate, 2021	32.0	14.1
Drug Overdose Mortality Rate, 2021	19.5	33.6
Firearm Injury Mortality Rate, 2021	25.1	14.6
Homicide Mortality Rate, 2021	4.4	8.2
Disease and Illness		
Lifetime Asthma in Adults, 2020 (percent)...	15.1	13.9
Lifetime Asthma in Children, 2020 (percent)[7]	9.4	11.3
Diabetes in Adults, 2020 (percent)...	7.8	8.2
Self-reported Obesity in Adults, 2021 (percent)...	31.8	NA

SOURCE: National Center for Health Statistics, National Vital Statistics System 2020 data; https://wonder.cdc.gov.
[1] General fertility rate per 1,000 women aged 15–44.
[2] This represents the percentage of all live births that were cesarean deliveries.
[3] Babies born prior to 37 weeks of pregnancy (gestation).
[4] Number of births per 1,000 females aged 15–19
[5] Babies born weighing less than 2,500 grams or 5 lbs. 8oz.
[6] Death rates are the number of deaths per 100,000 total population.
[7] U.S. total includes data from 30 states and D.C.
NA = Not available.
- = Zero or rounds to zero.

Table MT-15. State Government Finances, 2021

(Dollar amounts in thousands, percent distribution.)

Item	Dollars	Percent distribution
Total Revenue	11,032,106	100.0
General revenue	9,977,337	90.4
Intergovernmental revenue	5,140,433	46.6
Taxes	3,880,366	35.2
General sales	-	-
Selective sales	768,499	7.0
License taxes	481,678	4.4
Individual income tax	1,889,444	17.1
Corporate income tax	268,444	2.4
Other taxes	472,301	4.3
Current charges	532,956	4.8
Miscellaneous general revenue	423,582	3.8
Utility revenue	-	-
Liquor stores revenue	135420	1.2
Insurance trust revenue[1]	919,349	8.3
Total Expenditure	9,307,013	100.0
Intergovernmental expenditure	1,274,789	13.7
Direct expenditure	8,032,224	86.3
Current operation	5,844,337	62.8
Capital outlay	550,656	5.9
Insurance benefits and repayments	1,399,113	15.0
Assistance and subsidies	131,957	1.4
Interest on debt	106,161	1.1
Exhibit: Salaries and wages	1,272,067	13.7
Total Expenditure	9,307,013	100.0
General expenditure	7,770,611	83.5
Intergovernmental expenditure	1,274,789	13.7
Direct expenditure	6,495,822	69.8
General expenditure, by function:		
Education	2,046,276	22.0
Public welfare	2,723,012	29.3
Hospitals	56,249	0.6
Health	211,063	2.3
Highways	793,913	8.5
Police protection	73,222	0.8
Correction	245,187	2.6
Natural resources	351,178	3.8
Parks and recreation	18,157	0.2
Governmental administration	529,471	5.7
Interest on general debt	106,161	1.1
Other and unallocable	544,583	5.9
Utility expenditure	18,675	0.2
Liquor stores expenditure	120,913	1.3
Insurance trust expenditure	1,399,113	15.0
Debt at End of Fiscal Year	2,622,550	X
Cash and Security Holdings	26,345,505	X

X = Not applicable.
- = Zero or rounds to zero.
[1] Within insurance trust revenue, net earnings of state retirement systems is a calculated statistic (the item code in the data file is X08), and thus can be positive or negative. Net earnings is the sum of earnings on investments plus gains on investments minus losses on investments. The change made in 2002 for asset valuation from book to market value in accordance with Statement 34 of the Governmental Accounting Standards Board is reflected in the calculated statistics.

Table MT-16. State Government Tax Collections, 2022

(Dollars in thousands, percent.)

Item	Dollars	Percent distribution
Total Taxes	4,622,866	100.0
Property taxes	359,844	7.8
Sales and gross receipts	851,812	18.4
General sales and gross receipts	X	-
Selective sales and gross receipts	851,812	18.4
Alcoholic beverages	48,267	1.0
Amusements	123,282	2.7
Insurance premiums	153,056	3.3
Motor fuels	292,452	6.3
Pari-mutuels	169	-
Public utilities	39,067	0.8
Tobacco products	74,249	1.6
Other selective sales	121,270	2.6
Licenses	499,840	10.8
Alcoholic beverages	5,571	0.1
Amusements	4,628	0.1
Corporations in general	7,694	0.2
Hunting and fishing	77,246	1.7
Motor vehicle	195,703	4.2
Motor vehicle operators	9,732	0.2
Public utilities	5	-
Occupation and business, NEC	183,629	4.0
Other licenses	15,632	0.3
Income taxes	2,678,206	57.9
Individual income	2,387,008	51.6
Corporation net income	291,198	6.3
Other taxes	233,164	5.0
Death and gift	X	-
Documentary and stock transfer	X	-
Severance	227,029	4.9
Taxes, NEC	6,135	0.1

X = Not applicable.
- = Zero or rounds to zero.

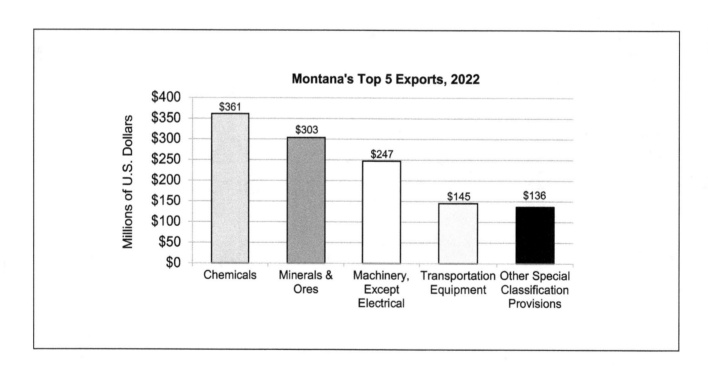

Montana's Top 5 Exports, 2022

NEBRASKA

Facts and Figures

Location: Central United States; bordered on the N by South Dakota, on the E by Iowa and Missouri, on the S by Kansas and Colorado, and on the W by Wyoming

Area: 77,354 sq. mi. (200,345 sq. km.); rank—16th

Population: 1,967,923 (2022 est.); rank—37th

Principal Cities: capital—Lincoln; largest—Omaha

Statehood: March 1, 1867; 37th state

U.S. Congress: 2 senators, 3 representatives

State Motto: Equality Before the Law

State Song: "Beautiful Nebraska"

State Nickname: The Cornhusker State

Abbreviations: NE; Nebr.; Neb.

State Symbols: flower—goldenrod; tree—cottonwood; bird—Western meadowlark

At a Glance

- With an increase in population of 7.8 percent, Nebraska ranked 20th among the states in growth from 2010 to 2022.

- In 2021, 7.1 percent of Nebraskans did not have health insurance, which was lower than the national average of 8.6 percent.

- The birth rate in Nebraska in 2021 was 12.5 births per 1,000 population, ranking 7th in the country.

- Nebraska ranked 42nd for the percent of children in poverty, with 10.8 percent of persons under 18 years old below the poverty level.

- The state's homicide rate in 2021 was 3.6 deaths per 100,000 population, compared to the national rate of 8.2 deaths per 100,000 population.

Table NE-1. Population by Age, Sex, Race, and Hispanic Origin

(Number, percent, except where noted.)

Sex, age, race, and Hispanic origin	2010	2020	2022	Percent change, 2010–2022
Total Population....................................	1,826,341	1,961,489	1,967,923	7.8
Percent of total U.S. population	0.6	0.6	0.6	X
Sex				
Male....................................	906,296	987,371	990,672	9.3
Female	920,045	974,118	977,251	6.2
Age				
Under 5 years....................................	131,908	128,846	123,837	-6.1
Under 18 years....................................	459,221	482,790	476,677	3.8
18 to 64 years....................................	1,120,443	1,163,253	1,158,190	3.4
65 years and over	246,677	315,446	333,056	35.0
Median age (years)	36.2	36.8	37.3	3.0
Race and Hispanic Origin				
One race				
White	1,649,264	1,723,909	1,721,883	4.4
Black....................................	85,971	103,750	105,601	22.8
American Indian and Alaska Native	23,418	30,800	32,344	38.1
Asian....................................	33,322	53,981	55,591	66.8
Native Hawaiian or Other Pacific Islander	2,061	2,527	2,757	33.8
Two or more races	32,305	46,522	49,747	54.0
Hispanic (of any race)	167,405	229,650	242,517	44.9

NOTE: Population figures for 2022 are July 1 estimates. The 2010 and 2020 estimates are taken from the respective censuses.
- = Zero or rounds to zero.
X = Not applicable.

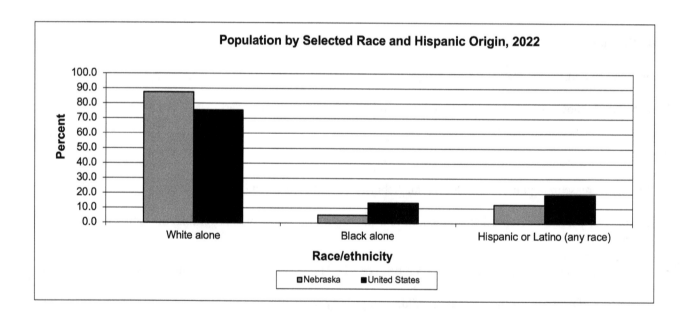

Table NE-2. Marital Status

(Number, percent distribution.)

Sex, age, race, and Hispanic origin	2000	2010	2021
Males, 15 Years and Over	654,559	708,783	780,043
Never married	29.2	32.4	33.9
Now married, except separated....................................	59.1	54.0	53.8
Separated....................................	1.0	1.4	0.8
Widowed....................................	2.4	2.3	2.5
Divorced....................................	8.3	9.9	9.1
Females, 15 Years and Over	687,863	735,744	783,771
Never married	22.5	25.3	28.5
Now married, except separated....................................	55.7	52.7	50.7
Separated....................................	1.3	1.5	1.1
Widowed....................................	10.8	9.5	7.9
Divorced....................................	9.7	10.9	11.8

Table NE-3. Households and Housing Characteristics

(Number, percent, dollars.)

Item	2000	2010	2021	Average annual percent change, 2010–2021
Total Households..	666,184	719,304	785,982	0.8
Family households	443,411	468,407	495,142	0.5
Married-couple family	360,996	368,023	391,102	0.6
Other family	82,415	100,384	104,040	0.3
Male householder, no wife present...........................	22,072	31,177	34,063	0.8
Female householder, no husband present..................	60,343	69,207	69,977	0.1
Nonfamily households	222,773	250,897	290,840	1.4
Householder living alone...	183,550	205,263	238,923	1.5
Householder not living alone....................................	39,223	45,634	51,917	1.3
Housing Characteristics				
Total housing units	722,668	797,677	854,298	0.6
Occupied housing units	666,184	719,304	785,982	0.8
Owner occupied	449,317	484,649	532,582	0.9
Renter occupied	216,867	234,655	253,400	0.7
Average household size...	2.49	2.47	2.44	-0.1
Financial Characteristics				
Median gross rent of renter-occupied housing	491	669	912	3.3
Median monthly owner costs for housing units with a mortgage ...	895	1,218	1,491	2.0
Median value of owner-occupied housing units............	88,000	127,600	204,900	5.5

Table NE-4. Migration, Origin, and Language

(Number, percent.)

Characteristic	State 2021	U.S. 2021
Residence 1 Year Ago		
Population 1 year and over	1,939,700	328,464,538
Same house	86.5	87.2
Different house in the U.S..	13.0	12.3
Same county	7.5	6.7
Different county	5.5	5.7
Same state	3.3	3.3
Different state	2.2	2.4
Abroad	0.5	0.4
Place of Birth		
Native born	1,819,248	286,623,642
Male	50.1	49.7
Female	49.9	50.3
Foreign born	144,444	45,270,103
Male	51.2	48.7
Female	48.8	51.3
Foreign born; naturalized U.S. citizen........................	62,571	24,044,083
Male	49.4	46.4
Female	50.6	53.6
Foreign born; not a U.S. citizen................................	81,873	21,226,020
Male	52.5	51.2
Female	47.5	48.8
Entered 2010 or later	44.3	28.1
Entered 2000 to 2009	22.8	23.7
Entered before 2000..	32.9	48.2
World Region of Birth, Foreign		
Foreign-born population, excluding population born at sea ...	144,444	45,269,644
Europe	6.0	10.7
Asia...	29.2	31.0
Africa...	9.7	5.7
Oceania..	0.2	0.6
Latin America..	53.5	50.1
North America...	1.3	1.7
Language Spoken at Home and Ability to Speak English		
Population 5 years and over......................................	1,839,096	313,232,500
English only	00.4	78.4
Language other than English....................................	11.6	21.6
Speaks English less than "very well"..........................	5.3	8.3

Table NE-5. Median Income and Poverty Status, 2021

(Number, percent, except as noted.)

Characteristic	State		U.S.	
	Number	Percent	Number	Percent
Median Income				
Households (dollars)..	66,817	X	69,717	X
Families (dollars)	88,484	X	85,806	X
Below Poverty Level (All People)	205,852	10.8	41,393,176	12.8
Sex				
Male	91,468	9.5	18,518,155	11.6
Female	114,384	12.0	22,875,021	13.9
Age				
Under 18 years..	59,447	12.5	12,243,219	16.9
Related children under 18 years..	56,887	12.1	11,985,424	16.6
18 to 64 years	118,987	10.6	23,526,341	11.9
65 years and over	27,418	8.7	5,623,616	10.3

X = Not applicable.

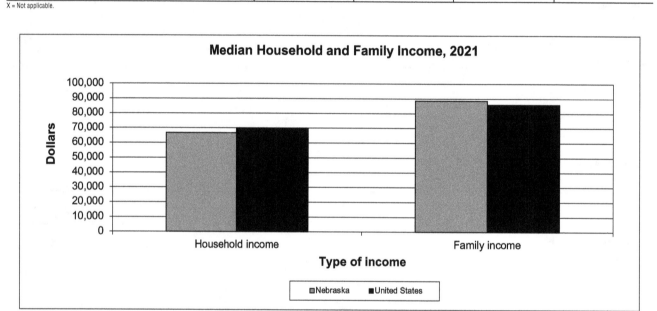

Table NE-6. Health Insurance Coverage Status for the Civilian Noninstitutionalized Population and Children Under 19 Years of Age

(Number, percent.)

Item	2011	2012	2013	2014	2015	2016	2017	2018	2019	2020 [2]	2021
Civilian Noninstitutionalized Population	1,814,388	1,826,832	1,840,659	1,853,684	1,866,488	1,877,654	1,891,453	1,900,165	1,904,211	1,894,327	1,936,190
Covered by Private or Public Insurance											
Number...	1,607,294	1,621,225	1,632,081	1,674,478	1,712,699	1,717,091	1,734,669	1,742,553	1,746,288	1,740,040	1,798,586
Percent...	88.6	88.7	88.7	90.3	91.8	91.4	91.7	91.7	91.7	91.9	92.9
Uninsured											
Number...	207,094	205,607	208,578	179,206	153,789	160,563	156,784	157,612	157,923	154,287	137,604
Percent...	11.4	11.3	11.3	9.7	8.2	8.6	8.3	8.3	8.3	8.1	7.1
Percent in the U.S. not covered............................	15.1	14.8	14.5	11.7	9.4	8.6	8.7	8.9	9.2	8.7	8.6
Children Under 19 Years of Age[1]	459,191	461,309	462,637	466,590	469,243	472,689	500,004	501,129	502,094	500,238	509,295
Covered by Private or Public Insurance											
Number...	432,299	433,503	437,258	441,795	444,513	448,982	474,289	474,901	473,700	474,029	485,317
Percent...	94.1	94.0	94.5	94.7	94.7	95.0	94.9	94.8	94.3	94.8	95.3
Uninsured											
Number...	26,892	27,806	25,379	24,795	24,730	23,707	25,715	26,228	28,394	26,209	23,978
Percent...	5.9	6.0	5.5	5.3	5.3	5.0	5.1	5.2	5.7	5.2	4.7
Percent in the U.S. not covered............................	7.5	7.2	7.1	6.0	4.8	4.5	5.0	5.2	5.7	5.2	5.4

[1] Data for years prior to 2017 are for individuals under 18 years of age.
[2] 2020 ACS 5-Year estimates. 1-Year estimates were not released for 2020 due to the impact of COVID-19 on data collection that year. Data is not comparable to previous years, which are based on 1-year estimates.

Table NE-7. Employment Status by Demographic Group, 2022

(Numbers in thousands, percent.)

Characteristic	Civilian noninstitutional population	Civilian labor force		Employed		Unemployed	
		Number	Percent of population	Number	Percent of population	Number	Percent of population
Total..	1,519	1,065	70.1	1,038	68.3	26	2.5
Sex							
Male...	755	564	74.7	551	72.9	13	2.3
Female..	764	501	65.5	487	63.8	13	2.7
Race, Sex, and Hispanic Origin							
White..	1,367	957	70.0	937	68.5	20	2.1
Male...	677	504	74.5	493	72.9	11	2.2
Female..	690	453	65.6	444	64.3	9	2.1
Black or African American...............	NA	NA	NA	NA	NA	NA	NA
Male...	NA	NA	NA	NA	NA	NA	NA
Female..	NA	NA	NA	NA	NA	NA	NA
Hispanic or Latino ethnicity[1]...........	150	111	74.4	106	70.9	5	4.8
Male...	80	65	81.2	62	77.6	3	4.4
Female..	NA	NA	NA	NA	NA	NA	NA
Age							
16 to 19 years.................................	NA	NA	NA	NA	NA	NA	NA
20 to 24 years.................................	108	86	79.7	83	76.4	4	4.1
25 to 34 years.................................	268	235	87.4	230	85.7	5	2.0
35 to 44 years.................................	269	240	89.2	234	87.2	5	2.2
45 to 54 years.................................	202	178	88.4	174	86.6	4	2.0
55 to 64 years.................................	252	189	75.2	186	73.7	4	1.9
65 years and over............................	319	82	25.8	81	25.4	2	1.8

NOTE: Data in Table 7 are from the Current Population Survey (CPS) and do not match the estimates in Table 8. See notes and definitions for further information.
[1] May be of any race.
NA = Not available.

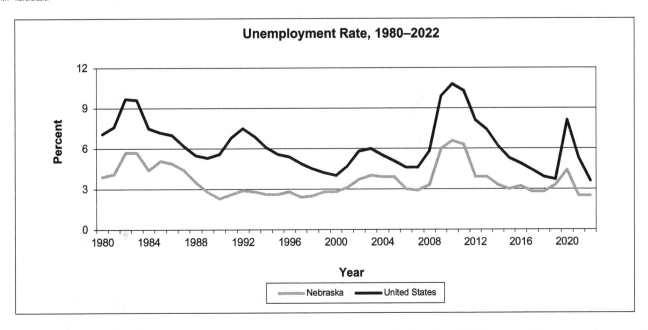

Unemployment Rate, 1980–2022

Nebraska — United States

Table NE-8. Employment Status of the Civilian Noninstitutional Population Age 16 Years and Over

(Number, percent.)

Year	Civilian labor force	Civilian participation rate	Employed	Unemployed	Unemployment rate
2010..	992,009	71.6	945,195	46,814	4.7
2011..	1,003,635	71.7	959,325	44,310	4.4
2012..	1,012,807	71.8	973,448	39,359	3.9
2013..	1,014,830	71.4	977,464	37,366	3.7
2014..	1,012,727	70.8	979,728	32,999	3.3
2015..	1,011,666	70.2	981,326	30,340	3.0
2016..	1,016,062	70.0	984,966	31,096	3.1
2017..	1,023,163	69.4	992,740	30,423	3.0
2018..	1,034,214	69.7	1,004,261	29,953	2.9
2019..	1,048,820	70.2	1,016,904	31,916	3.0
2020..	1,044,541	69.5	1,001,426	43,115	4.1
2021..	1,049,033	69.5	1,022,662	26,371	2.5
2022..	1,058,927	69.7	1,034,091	24,836	2.3

Table NE-9. Employment and Average Wages by Industry

(Estimates are based on the 2012 North American Industry Classification System [NAICS].)

Industry	2014	2015	2016	2017	2018	2019	2020	2021
	Number of Jobs							
Wage and Salary Employment by Industry..........	1,013,641	1,030,768	1,036,447	1,040,572	1,048,136	1,052,893	1,015,211	1,031,336
Farm Wage and Salary Employment..........	12,168	16,089	14,485	15,416	16,600	16,644	16,226	16,365
Nonfarm Wage and Salary Employment..........	1,001,473	1,014,679	1,021,962	1,025,156	1,031,536	1,036,249	998,985	1,014,971
Private wage and salary employment..........	827,481	840,079	846,330	849,342	855,798	860,545	826,027	841,763
Forestry, fishing, and related activities..........	6,009	5,629	5,935	5,895	5,893	5,794	5,542	5,102
Mining..........	1,133	1,066	982	1,044	1,081	1,025	970	1,009
Utilities..........	1,264	1,081	1,072	1,090	1,070	1,082	1,014	1,005
Construction..........	47,336	50,140	51,812	52,402	53,557	55,054	56,530	57,053
Manufacturing..........	97,553	97,417	96,952	98,181	99,859	100,022	97,508	99,613
Durable goods manufacturing..........	45,916	45,416	44,055	43,982	44,748	45,202	43,195	44,167
Nondurable goods manufacturing..........	51,637	52,001	52,897	54,199	55,111	54,820	54,313	55,446
Wholesale trade..........	43,089	42,490	42,021	41,258	40,345	40,251	40,049	39,584
Retail trade..........	108,732	110,649	111,143	109,938	108,667	106,055	102,104	105,276
Transportation and warehousing..........	52,871	53,998	51,282	50,974	51,896	52,980	50,315	50,432
Information..........	17,068	17,581	18,515	18,224	17,652	17,188	16,169	17,721
Finance and insurance..........	56,626	57,200	58,296	59,214	59,152	60,444	60,173	57,646
Real estate and rental and leasing..........	9,269	9,605	9,828	10,059	10,408	10,769	10,586	10,854
Professional, scientific, and technical services..........	44,353	44,885	44,306	45,234	45,956	46,390	47,238	48,353
Management of companies and enterprises..........	20,410	22,127	21,451	21,638	21,812	21,672	21,261	19,987
Administrative and waste services..........	48,908	50,543	52,286	51,371	52,208	52,770	49,521	50,290
Educational services..........	18,393	18,736	18,806	18,916	18,953	19,295	17,962	19,200
Health care and social assistance..........	122,955	123,890	127,301	128,331	129,829	130,720	126,752	129,239
Arts, entertainment, and recreation..........	13,996	14,280	14,418	14,951	15,172	15,545	12,021	13,730
Accommodation and food services..........	73,748	74,629	76,602	77,491	78,028	78,931	68,122	73,192
Other services, except public administration..........	43,768	44,133	43,322	43,131	44,260	44,558	42,190	42,477
Government and government enterprises..........	173,992	174,600	175,632	175,814	175,738	175,704	172,958	173,208
	Dollars							
Average Wages and Salaries by Industry..........	42,842	44,387	45,205	46,540	48,102	49,701	53,256	55,635
Average Farm Wages and Salaries..........	41,575	35,024	37,944	36,458	36,743	35,439	29,270	32,573
Average Nonfarm Wages and Salaries..........	42,857	44,535	45,308	46,692	48,285	49,930	53,646	56,007
Average private wages and salaries..........	42,463	44,215	44,963	46,406	48,082	49,794	53,800	56,349
Forestry, fishing, and related activities..........	26,665	28,705	29,078	29,900	30,590	33,448	37,804	40,167
Mining..........	53,190	54,466	56,775	55,635	58,622	60,506	63,949	65,110
Utilities..........	111,415	108,917	97,390	100,708	116,661	137,373	134,714	302,850
Construction..........	46,649	48,319	49,264	50,577	52,776	54,857	57,784	59,756
Manufacturing..........	47,428	48,627	49,341	51,502	53,840	55,001	59,010	62,325
Durable goods manufacturing..........	50,525	51,226	51,690	54,307	56,070	56,616	59,290	62,886
Nondurable goods manufacturing..........	44,674	46,357	47,385	49,226	52,030	53,669	58,787	61,879
Wholesale trade..........	58,760	60,528	61,600	63,149	65,648	68,409	71,097	75,323
Retail trade..........	25,664	26,526	27,528	28,349	29,164	30,313	32,811	34,477
Transportation and warehousing..........	55,065	56,732	56,582	58,875	60,366	61,414	64,204	65,564
Information..........	57,571	60,021	62,532	63,741	67,027	69,608	79,504	80,304
Finance and insurance..........	62,849	65,635	67,233	70,110	74,312	76,768	83,395	87,052
Real estate and rental and leasing..........	39,145	40,540	42,149	42,300	43,838	45,255	48,023	50,097
Professional, scientific, and technical services..........	62,021	64,690	66,513	68,473	70,800	73,272	76,778	80,044
Management of companies and enterprises..........	95,500	100,137	96,435	97,150	89,540	91,255	100,556	107,206
Administrative and waste services..........	34,211	36,077	37,227	39,015	40,142	42,199	44,571	49,350
Educational services..........	29,690	30,322	31,358	31,732	32,934	33,553	35,746	34,432
Health care and social assistance..........	41,594	44,045	45,098	46,216	48,642	50,804	54,201	57,144
Arts, entertainment, and recreation..........	19,227	19,496	20,154	20,578	21,115	21,809	25,044	25,472
Accommodation and food services..........	16,169	17,072	17,899	18,437	19,420	19,869	19,670	23,066
Other services, except public administration..........	29,881	30,758	32,064	33,175	34,199	35,430	39,023	41,380
Government and government enterprises..........	44,733	46,075	46,971	48,071	49,276	50,596	52,912	54,347

Table NE-10. Employment Characteristics by Family Type

(Number, percent.)

Family type and labor force status	2019 Total	2019 Families with own children under 18 years	2020 [1] Total	2020 [1] Families with own children under 18 years	2021 Total	2021 Families with own children under 18 years
All Families...	493,013	221,206	488,849	222,321	495,142	216,267
FAMILY TYPE AND LABOR FORCE STATUS						
Opposite-Sex Married-Couple Families..	388,538	161,340	380,736	157,958	388,340	154,585
Both husband and wife in labor force............................	61.5	80.0	60.6	76.4	59.6	75.6
Husband in labor force, wife not in labor force	16.3	17.1	17.6	19.9	17.2	19.4
Wife in labor force, husband not in labor force	6.3	2.3	6.6	3.1	7.5	3.7
Both husband and wife not in labor force........................	15.3	0.4	15.2	0.7	15.7	1.3
Other Families	104,475	59,866	105,661	63,905	104,040	61,022
Female householder, no spouse present	67.4	70.7	67.8	70.3	67.3	68.2
In labor force...	52.0	61.9	53.7	63.0	52.0	59.8
Not in labor force	15.3	8.8	14.2	7.3	15.3	8.4
Male householder, no spouse present.............................	32.6	29.3	32.2	29.7	32.7	31.8
In labor force...	28.7	28.6	27.2	27.5	28.7	30.2
Not in labor force	4.0	0.8	4.9	2.2	4.0	1.6

[1] 2020 ACS 5-Year estimates. 1-Year estimates were not released for 2020 due to the impact of COVID-19 on data collection that year. Data is not comparable to previous years, which are based on 1-year estimates.

Table NE-11. School Enrollment and Educational Attainment, 2021

(Number, percent.)

Item	State	U.S.
Enrollment		
Total population 3 years and over, enrolled in school	514,905	79,453,524
Enrolled in nursery school or preschool (percent)	7.0	5.2
Enrolled in kindergarten (percent)...	5.1	5.0
Enrolled in elementary school, grades 1-8 (percent).............................	41.6	41.3
Enrolled in high school, grades 9-12 (percent)	21.4	21.8
Enrolled in college or graduate school (percent)................................	24.9	26.7
Attainment		
Total population 25 years and over	1,292,536	228,193,464
Less than ninth grade (percent)	3.7	4.8
9th to 12th grade, no diploma (percent)	4.1	5.9
High school graduate, including equivalency (percent)............................	25.2	26.3
Some college, no degree (percent)	21.7	19.3
Associate's degree (percent)...	10.8	8.8
Bachelor's degree (percent)	22.2	21.2
Graduate or professional degree (percent).......................................	12.3	13.8
High school graduate or higher (percent).................................	92.2	89.4
Bachelor's degree or higher (percent)...	34.4	35.0

Table NE-12. Public School Characteristics and Educational Indicators

(Number, percent; data derived from National Center of Education Statistics.)

Item	State	U.S.
Public Elementary and Secondary Schools		
Number of regular school districts, 2019-20	244	13,349
Number of operational schools, 2019-20...	1,082	98,469
Percent charter schools	-	7.7
Total public school enrollment, Fall 2021	327,564	49,433,092
Percent charter school enrollment	NA	7.5
Student-teacher ratio, Fall 2019	13.7	15.9
Expenditures per student (unadjusted dollars), 2019-20	12,829	13,489
Four-year adjusted cohort graduation rate (ACGR), 2019-2020 [1]..........................	87.5	86.5
Students eligible for free or reduced-price lunch (percent), 2019-20.......................	45.6	52.1
English language learners (percent), Fall 2020	7.2	10.3
Students age 3 to 21 served under IDEA, part B (percent), 2021-22	16.2	14.7

Public Schools by Type, 2019-20	Number	Percent of state public schools
Total number of schools...	1,082	100.0
Special education	27	2.5
Vocational education	-	-
Alternative education..	51	4.7

[1] Adjusted Cohort Graduation Rates (ACGR) differ from Averaged Freshmen Graduation Rates (AFGR).
- = Zero or rounds to zero.
NA = Not available.

Table NE-13. Reported Voting and Registration of the Voting-Age Population, November 2022

(Numbers in thousands, percent.)

Item	Total population	Total citizen population	Registered			Voted		
			Total registered	Percent registered (total population)	Percent registered (total citizen population)	Total voted	Percent voted (total population)	Percent voted (total citizen population)
U.S. Total	255,457	233,546	161,422	63.2	69.1	121,916	47.7	52.2
State Total...........................	1,460	1,351	933	63.9	69.1	659	45.1	48.8
Sex								
Male	721	656	441	61.2	67.3	312	43.2	47.5
Female	739	695	492	66.5	70.8	347	46.9	49.9
Race								
White alone..............................	1,314	1,235	880	67.0	71.2	628	47.8	50.9
White, non-Hispanic alone	1,161	1,159	843	72.6	72.8	615	53.0	53.1
Black alone..............................	37	34	19	50.8	55.3	9	24.7	26.8
Asian alone	41	18	9	22.0	50.4	5	11.2	25.6
Hispanic (of any race)	162	81	37	22.7	45.1	14	8.4	16.7
White alone or in combination	1,322	1,244	885	66.9	71.1	633	47.9	50.9
Black alone or in combination	45	42	19	41.8	44.7	9	20.3	21.7
Asian alone or in combination	51	29	14	26.9	48.4	9	18.3	33.0
Age								
18 to 24 years	145	131	49	34.0	37.6	19	12.9	14.3
25 to 34 years	270	244	161	59.6	66.0	89	32.9	36.5
35 to 44 years	267	239	178	66.5	74.2	112	42.0	46.8
45 to 64 years	489	449	336	68.8	74.9	259	53.0	57.7
65 years and over	289	288	209	72.2	72.6	180	62.2	62.5

B = Base is less than 75,000 and therefore too small to show the derived measure.

Table NE-14. Health Indicators

(Number, rate as indicated in footnotes.)

Item	State	U.S.
Births		
Life Expectancy at Birth (years), 2020	77.7	77.0
Fertility Rate by State[1], 2021	64.4	56.3
Percent Home Births, 2021	0.4	1.4
Cesarean Delivery Rate[2], 2021	28.6	32.1
Preterm Birth Rate[3], 2021	10.8	10.5
Teen Birth Rate[4], 2021	14.0	13.9
Percentage of Babies Born Low Birthweight[5], 2021	7.6	8.5
Deaths[6]		
Heart Disease Mortality Rate, 2021..	160.8	173.8
Cancer Mortality Rate, 2021..	150.9	146.6
Stroke Mortality Rate, 2021	36.5	41.1
Diabetes Mortality Rate, 2021..	24.6	25.4
Influenza/Pneumonia Mortality Rate, 2021	10.1	10.5
Suicide Mortality Rate, 2021..	15.0	14.1
Drug Overdose Mortality Rate, 2021..	11.4	33.6
Firearm Injury Mortality Rate, 2021	10.3	14.6
Homicide Mortality Rate, 2021..	3.6	8.2
Disease and Illness		
Lifetime Asthma in Adults, 2020 (percent)..	10.7	13.9
Lifetime Asthma in Children, 2020 (percent)[7]	7.3	11.3
Diabetes in Adults, 2020 (percent)..	8.9	8.2
Self-reported Obesity in Adults, 2021 (percent)..	35.9	NA

SOURCE: National Center for Health Statistics, National Vital Statistics System 2020 data; https://wonder.cdc.gov.
[1] General fertility rate per 1,000 women aged 15–44.
[2] This represents the percentage of all live births that were cesarean deliveries.
[3] Babies born prior to 37 weeks of pregnancy (gestation).
[4] Number of births per 1,000 females aged 15–19
[5] Babies born weighing less than 2,500 grams or 5 lbs. 8oz.
[6] Death rates are the number of deaths per 100,000 total population.
[7] U.S. total includes data from 30 states and D.C.
NA = Not available.
- = Zero or rounds to zero.

Table NE-15. State Government Finances, 2021

(Dollar amounts in thousands, percent distribution.)

Item	Dollars	Percent distribution
Total Revenue	15,206,074	100.0
General revenue	14,524,893	95.5
Intergovernmental revenue	5,527,373	36.3
Taxes	6,960,988	45.8
General sales	2,382,381	15.7
Selective sales	658,241	4.3
License taxes	194,771	1.3
Individual income tax	3,130,599	20.6
Corporate income tax	571,220	3.8
Other taxes	23,776	0.2
Current charges	1,002,647	6.6
Miscellaneous general revenue	1,033,885	6.8
Utility revenue	-	-
Liquor stores revenue	-	-
Insurance trust revenue[1]	681,181	4.5
Total Expenditure	14,350,526	100.0
Intergovernmental expenditure	3,271,480	22.8
Direct expenditure	11,079,046	77.2
Current operation	8,797,831	61.3
Capital outlay	823,853	5.7
Insurance benefits and repayments	1,150,040	8.0
Assistance and subsidies	252,585	1.8
Interest on debt	54,737	0.4
Exhibit: Salaries and wages	1,987,924	13.9
Total Expenditure	14,350,526	100.0
General expenditure	13,200,486	92.0
Intergovernmental expenditure	3,271,480	22.8
Direct expenditure	9,929,006	69.2
General expenditure, by function:		
Education	4,221,163	29.4
Public welfare	3,641,438	25.4
Hospitals	201,347	1.4
Health	352,887	2.5
Highways	967,129	6.7
Police protection	97,628	0.7
Correction	438,463	3.1
Natural resources	207,867	1.4
Parks and recreation	61,005	0.4
Governmental administration	604,958	4.2
Interest on general debt	54,737	0.4
Other and unallocable	2,323,226	16.2
Utility expenditure	-	-
Liquor stores expenditure	-	-
Insurance trust expenditure	1,150,040	8.0
Debt at End of Fiscal Year	2,578,278	X
Cash and Security Holdings	34,230,833	X

X = Not applicable.
- = Zero or rounds to zero.
[1] Within insurance trust revenue, net earnings of state retirement systems is a calculated statistic (the item code in the data file is X08), and thus can be positive or negative. Net earnings is the sum of earnings on investments plus gains on investments minus losses on investments. The change made in 2002 for asset valuation from book to market value in accordance with Statement 34 of the Governmental Accounting Standards Board is reflected in the calculated statistics.

Table NE-16. State Government Tax Collections, 2022

(Dollars in thousands, percent.)

Item	Dollars	Percent distribution
Total Taxes	7,475,982	100.0
Property taxes	122	-
Sales and gross receipts	3,285,152	43.9
General sales and gross receipts	2,635,775	35.3
Selective sales and gross receipts	649,377	8.7
Alcoholic beverages	34,574	0.5
Amusements	7,613	0.1
Insurance premiums	78,815	1.1
Motor fuels	384,474	5.1
Pari-mutuels	175	-
Public utilities	59,836	0.8
Tobacco products	52,147	0.7
Other selective sales	31,743	0.4
Licenses	204,270	2.7
Alcoholic beverages	1,344	-
Amusements	554	-
Corporations in general	14,009	0.2
Hunting and fishing	19,498	0.3
Motor vehicle	118,247	1.6
Motor vehicle operators	11,357	0.2
Public utilities	X	-
Occupation and business, NEC	38,055	0.5
Other licenses	1,206	-
Income taxes	3,954,644	52.9
Individual income	3,239,491	43.3
Corporation net income	715,153	9.6
Other taxes	31,794	0.4
Death and gift	X	-
Documentary and stock transfer	27,151	0.4
Severance	4,643	-
Taxes, NEC	0	-

- = Zero or rounds to zero.
X = Not applicable.

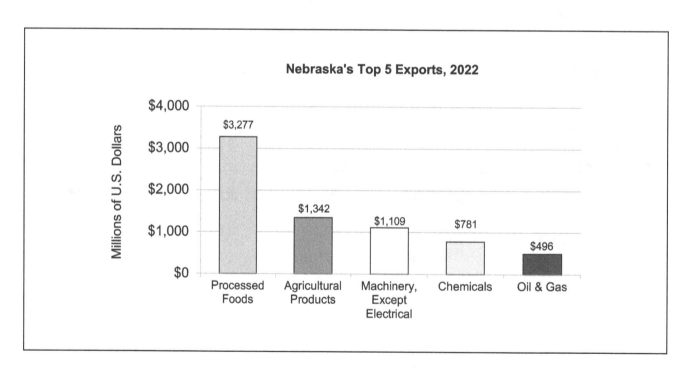

Nebraska's Top 5 Exports, 2022

NEVADA

Location: Western United States; bordered on the N by Oregon and Idaho, on the E by Utah and Arizona, on the S by Arizona and California, and on the W by California

Area: 110,561 sq. mi. (286,351 sq. km.); rank—7th

Population: 3,177,772 (2022 est.); rank—32nd

Principal Cities: capital—Carson City; largest—Las Vegas

Statehood: October 31, 1864; 36th state

U.S. Congress: 2 senators, 4 representatives

State Motto: All for Our Country

State Song: "Home Means Nevada"

State Nicknames: The Silver State; The Sagebrush State

Abbreviations: NV; Nev.

State Symbols: flower—sagebrush; tree—single-leaf piñon and bristlecone pine; bird—mountain bluebird

At a Glance

- With an increase in population of 17.7 percent, Nevada ranked 5th among the states in growth from 2010 to 2022.

- Approximately 28.8 percent of Nevadans self-identified their ethnicity as "Hispanic or Latino" in 2022, the 5th highest percentage in the country.

- In 2022, Nevada had the highest unemployment rate in the country, with 5.4 percent of residents unemployed, compared to 3.6 percent of the whole nation.

- Nevada had the fewest government employees per capita in 2022, with 36.0 full-time equivalent state and local government employees per 1,000 residents.

Table NV-1. Population by Age, Sex, Race, and Hispanic Origin

(Number, percent, except where noted.)

Sex, age, race, and Hispanic origin	2010	2020	2022	Percent change, 2010–2022
Total Population..	2,700,551	3,104,624	3,177,772	17.7
Percent of total U.S. population	0.9	0.9	1.0	X
Sex				
Male..	1,363,616	1,569,209	1,603,852	17.6
Female...	1,336,935	1,535,415	1,573,920	17.7
Age				
Under 5 years...	187,478	180,262	174,244	-7.1
Under 18 years..	665,008	693,479	689,778	3.7
18 to 64 years...	1,711,184	1,910,740	1,950,990	14.0
65 years and over..	324,359	500,405	537,004	65.6
Median age (years)..	36.3	38.4	38.9	7.2
Race and Hispanic Origin				
One race				
White..	2,106,494	2,279,588	2,290,214	8.7
Black..	231,224	321,893	344,357	48.9
American Indian and Alaska Native	42,965	52,806	54,495	26.8
Asian..	203,478	275,821	299,940	47.4
Native Hawaiian or Other Pacific Islander	19,307	26,058	28,000	45.0
Two or more races..	97,083	148,458	160,766	65.6
Hispanic (of any race)...	716,501	915,169	961,354	34.2

NOTE: Population figures for 2022 are July 1 estimates. The 2010 and 2020 estimates are taken from the respective censuses.
- = Zero or rounds to zero.
X = Not applicable.

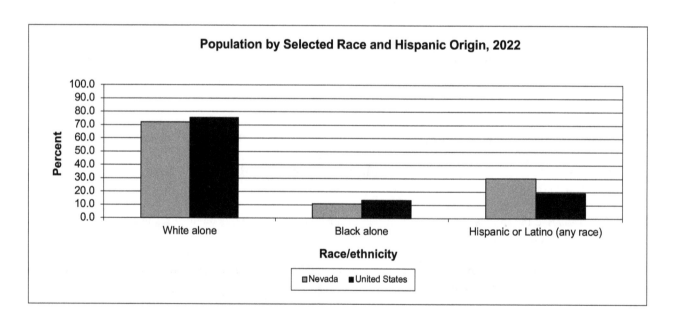

Table NV-2. Marital Status

(Number, percent distribution.)

Sex, age, race, and Hispanic origin	2000	2010	2021
Males, 15 Years and Over..	792,317	1,081,514	1,290,165
Never married	28.8	35.0	38.3
Now married, except separated..	53.8	47.6	45.6
Separated..	2.0	2.0	1.6
Widowed..	2.5	2.9	2.8
Divorced..	12.9	12.5	11.7
Females, 15 Years and Over..	771,263	1,069,123	1,277,376
Never married	20.9	27.2	31.6
Now married, except separated..	53.1	47.2	44.5
Separated..	2.7	2.8	2.0
Widowed..	8.6	8.0	8.0
Divorced..	14.7	14.8	13.9

Table NV-3. Households and Housing Characteristics

(Number, percent, dollars.)

Item	2000	2010	2021	Average annual percent change, 2010–2021
Total Households..	751,165	989,811	1,191,380	1.9
Family households	498,333	639,686	753,696	1.6
Married-couple family	373,201	452,361	522,193	1.4
Other family	125,132	187,325	231,503	2.1
Male householder, no wife present............................	41,650	63,327	79,604	2.3
Female householder, no husband present...................	83,482	123,998	151,899	2.0
Nonfamily households	252,832	350,125	437,684	2.3
Householder living alone..	186,745	266,232	333,295	2.3
Householder not living alone..	66,087	83,893	104,389	2.2
Housing Characteristics				
Total housing units	827,457	1,175,070	1,305,534	1.0
Occupied housing units	751,165	989,811	1,191,380	1.9
Owner occupied	457,247	565,869	704,548	2.2
Renter occupied	293,918	423,942	486,832	1.3
Average household size..	2.62	2.7	2.61	-0.3
Financial Characteristics				
Median gross rent of renter-occupied housing	699	952	1,311	3.4
Median monthly owner costs for housing units with a mortgage	1,190	1,638	1,625	-0.1
Median value of owner-occupied housing units....................	142,000	174,800	373,000	10.3

Table NV-4. Migration, Origin, and Language

(Number, percent.)

Characteristic	State 2021	U.S. 2021
Residence 1 Year Ago		
Population 1 year and over	3,111,722	328,464,538
Same house	85.5	87.2
Different house in the U.S.	14.1	12.3
Same county	9.1	6.7
Different county	5.0	5.7
Same state	0.7	3.3
Different state	4.3	2.4
Abroad	0.4	0.4
Place of Birth		
Native born	2,564,299	286,623,642
Male	50.9	49.7
Female	49.1	50.3
Foreign born	579,692	45,270,103
Male	48.1	48.7
Female	51.9	51.3
Foreign born; naturalized U.S. citizen...	314,224	24,044,083
Male..	46.2	46.4
Female	53.8	53.6
Foreign born; not a U.S. citizen	265,468	21,226,020
Male	50.4	51.2
Female	49.6	48.8
Entered 2010 or later	20.1	28.1
Entered 2000 to 2009	25.1	23.7
Entered before 2000..	54.8	48.2
World Region of Birth, Foreign		
Foreign-born population, excluding population born at sea	579,692	45,269,644
Europe	6.9	10.7
Asia..	33.1	31.0
Africa..	3.4	5.7
Oceania...	1.0	0.6
Latin America...	53.4	50.1
North America..	2.2	1.7
Language Spoken at Home and Ability to Speak English		
Population 5 years and over..	2,966,914	313,232,500
English only	71.7	78.4
Language other than English..	28.3	21.6
Speaks English less than "very well"...	10.7	8.3

Table NV-5. Median Income and Poverty Status, 2021

(Number, percent, except as noted.)

Characteristic	State		U.S.	
	Number	Percent	Number	Percent
Median Income				
Households (dollars)...	66,274	X	69,717	X
Families (dollars)	78,526	X	85,806	X
Below Poverty Level (All People)	437,385	14.1	41,393,176	12.8
Sex				
Male	205,033	13.2	18,518,155	11.6
Female	232,352	15.0	22,875,021	13.9
Age				
Under 18 years...	128,531	18.8	12,243,219	16.9
Related children under 18 years..	125,421	18.4	11,985,424	16.6
18 to 64 years	250,400	13.2	23,526,341	11.9
65 years and over	58,454	11.3	5,623,616	10.3

X = Not applicable.

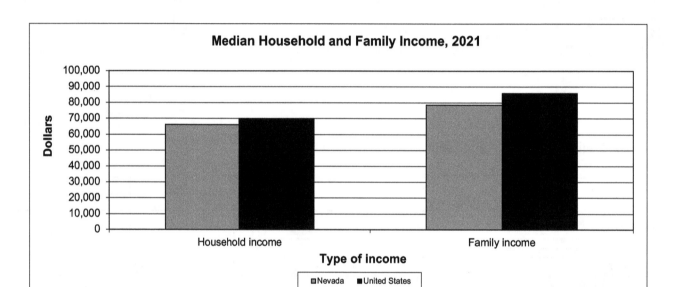

Table NV-6. Health Insurance Coverage Status for the Civilian Noninstitutionalized Population and Children Under 19 Years of Age

(Number, percent.)

Item	2011	2012	2013	2014	2015	2016	2017	2018	2019	2020 [2]	2021
Civilian Noninstitutionalized Population	2,686,989	2,723,965	2,757,207	2,805,532	2,855,974	2,905,767	2,962,236	2,998,585	3,043,419	2,993,632	3,105,760
Covered by Private or Public Insurance											
Number..	2,098,195	2,120,540	2,187,128	2,378,879	2,505,290	2,575,349	2,629,612	2,662,394	2,695,788	2,659,502	2,744,096
Percent..	78.1	77.8	79.3	84.8	87.7	88.6	88.8	88.8	88.6	88.8	88.4
Uninsured											
Number..	588,794	603,425	570,079	426,653	350,684	330,418	332,624	336,191	347,631	334,130	361,664
Percent..	21.9	22.2	20.7	15.2	12.3	11.4	11.2	11.2	11.4	11.2	11.6
Percent in the U.S. not covered................................	15.1	14.8	14.5	11.7	9.4	8.6	8.7	8.9	9.2	8.7	8.6
Children Under 19 Years of Age[1]	662,359	663,481	661,097	661,634	667,602	676,435	718,836	721,982	724,678	720,745	731,892
Covered by Private or Public Insurance											
Number..	554,955	553,334	562,588	597,902	617,152	630,576	661,283	664,442	666,692	665,384	668,660
Percent..	83.8	83.4	85.1	90.4	92.4	93.2	92.0	92.0	92.0	92.3	91.4
Uninsured											
Number..	107,404	110,147	98,509	63,732	50,450	45,859	57,553	57,540	57,986	55,361	63,232
Percent..	16.2	16.6	14.9	9.6	7.6	6.8	8.0	8.0	8.0	7.7	8.6
Percent in the U.S. not covered................................	7.5	7.2	7.1	6.0	4.8	4.5	5.0	5.2	5.7	5.2	5.4

[1] Data for years prior to 2017 are for individuals under 18 years of age.
[2] 2020 ACS 5-Year estimates. 1-Year estimates were not released for 2020 due to the impact of COVID-19 on data collection that year. Data is not comparable to previous years, which are based on 1-year estimates.

Table NV-7. Employment Status by Demographic Group, 2022

(Numbers in thousands, percent.)

Characteristic	Civilian noninstitutional population	Civilian labor force		Employed		Unemployed	
		Number	Percent of population	Number	Percent of population	Number	Percent of population
Total..	2,528	1,543	61.0	1,459	57.7	84	5.4
Sex							
Male..	1,258	835	66.4	790	62.8	45	5.4
Female.....................................	1,270	708	55.7	669	52.7	38	5.4
Race, Sex, and Hispanic Origin							
White.......................................	1,855	1,120	60.4	1,069	57.6	51	4.5
Male.....................................	936	621	66.4	594	63.4	28	4.5
Female..................................	919	498	54.2	475	51.7	23	4.6
Black or African American.............	261	168	64.6	151	58.0	17	10.3
Male.....................................	126	84	66.7	76	60.4	8	9.4
Female..................................	134	84	62.7	75	55.7	9	11.1
Hispanic or Latino ethnicity[1].........	670	456	68.1	436	65.0	20	4.4
Male.....................................	322	243	75.6	235	72.9	8	3.5
Female..................................	349	213	61.1	201	57.7	12	5.6
Age							
16 to 19 years............................	176	60	34.2	53	30.1	7	11.9
20 to 24 years............................	193	150	77.7	138	71.7	12	7.8
25 to 34 years............................	411	334	81.2	317	77.2	17	5.0
35 to 44 years............................	423	345	81.5	329	77.7	16	4.6
45 to 54 years............................	393	315	80.2	302	76.8	13	4.2
55 to 64 years............................	375	235	62.8	222	59.1	14	5.8
65 years and over........................	558	104	18.7	99	17.7	5	5.1

NOTE: Data in Table 7 are from the Current Population Survey (CPS) and do not match the estimates in Table 8. See notes and definitions for further information.
[1] May be of any race.

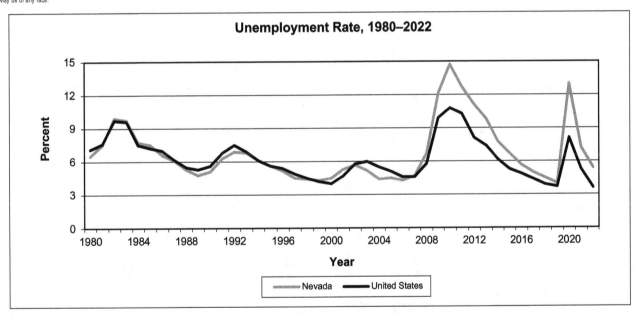

Table NV-8. Employment Status of the Civilian Noninstitutional Population Age 16 Years and Over

(Number, percent.)

Year	Civilian labor force	Civilian participation rate	Employed	Unemployed	Unemployment rate
2010..	1,358,860	65.9	1,171,879	186,981	13.8
2011..	1,360,791	65.0	1,179,653	181,138	13.3
2012..	1,366,208	64.4	1,207,733	158,475	11.6
2013..	1,370,727	63.6	1,234,021	136,706	10.0
2014..	1,380,084	63.0	1,267,424	112,660	8.2
2015..	1,396,761	62.5	1,301,094	95,667	6.8
2016..	1,414,233	62.0	1,332,390	81,843	5.8
2017..	1,444,262	62.6	1,372,022	72,240	5.0
2018..	1,492,831	63.3	1,427,371	65,460	4.4
2019..	1,541,772	64	1,479,777	61,995	4.0
2020..	1,502,848	61.2	1,299,640	203,208	13.5
2021..	1,504,761	60.5	1,395,939	108,822	7.2
2022..	1,549,859	61.2	1,466,213	83,646	5.4

Table NV-9. Employment and Average Wages by Industry

(Estimates are based on the 2012 North American Industry Classification System [NAICS].)

Industry	2014	2015	2016	2017	2018	2019	2020	2021
	Number of Jobs							
Wage and Salary Employment by Industry........................	1,251,274	1,292,456	1,329,421	1,371,359	1,419,789	1,458,453	1,317,100	1,409,465
Farm Wage and Salary Employment................................	2,109	2,049	2,164	2,603	2,121	2,126	2,247	2,046
Nonfarm Wage and Salary Employment............................	1,249,165	1,290,407	1,327,257	1,368,756	1,417,668	1,456,327	1,314,853	1,407,419
Private wage and salary employment................................	1,081,124	1,121,731	1,156,181	1,193,494	1,239,981	1,276,146	1,137,861	1,230,278
Forestry, fishing, and related activities	707	719	700	701	740	719	705	687
Mining...	14,382	14,174	13,681	14,208	14,576	14,708	14,855	14,932
Utilities...	3,884	3,962	4,068	4,094	4,089	4,088	4,091	4,029
Construction...	64,752	71,996	77,697	85,110	91,358	98,298	96,620	100,243
Manufacturing...	41,555	42,157	43,570	47,829	55,505	59,475	56,237	60,905
Durable goods manufacturing..................................	25,800	26,121	26,827	30,175	36,804	40,177	37,754	40,900
Nondurable goods manufacturing............................	15,755	16,036	16,743	17,654	18,701	19,298	18,483	20,005
Wholesale trade..	34,105	34,600	34,727	36,305	37,398	38,778	36,575	38,365
Retail trade...	140,762	144,244	145,018	146,844	149,099	149,608	141,751	150,427
Transportation and warehousing..................................	53,705	57,727	60,242	63,774	66,867	71,631	75,054	85,882
Information	13,727	13,934	14,801	14,805	15,674	15,924	13,433	15,403
Finance and insurance	33,420	34,592	35,972	37,272	38,253	39,781	40,769	42,937
Real estate and rental and leasing..............................	23,939	25,681	26,386	26,800	28,094	28,669	25,744	26,957
Professional, scientific, and technical services............	50,786	52,762	54,782	56,657	60,235	62,315	61,449	64,455
Management of companies and enterprises....................	20,909	22,638	24,016	25,319	26,868	27,459	24,528	26,045
Administrative and waste services...............................	85,369	92,745	98,446	101,020	105,349	108,130	95,763	101,392
Educational services	10,509	10,642	11,015	11,429	12,312	13,433	12,791	16,087
Health care and social assistance................................	104,345	109,657	115,611	120,868	127,337	132,538	131,452	136,907
Arts, entertainment, and recreation.............................	28,927	28,979	30,571	31,876	33,661	34,968	26,178	31,021
Accommodation and food services...............................	308,993	313,804	316,293	319,533	320,676	322,762	233,157	264,972
Other services, except public administration..................	46,348	46,718	48,585	49,050	51,890	52,862	46,709	48,632
Government and government enterprises	168,041	168,676	171,076	175,262	177,687	180,181	176,992	177,141
	Dollars							
Average Wages and Salaries by Industry	46,109	47,113	48,331	49,316	51,222	52,473	56,368	60,302
Average Farm Wages and Salaries	40,856	35,590	39,012	32,620	38,983	27,843	35,090	44,808
Average Nonfarm Wages and Salaries	46,118	47,131	48,346	49,348	51,240	52,509	56,404	60,324
Average private wages and salaries...............................	45,206	46,204	47,459	48,439	50,393	51,613	55,509	59,851
Forestry, fishing, and related activities	35,950	34,978	34,819	35,665	37,828	38,961	38,702	40,038
Mining...	88,539	92,025	93,753	94,809	97,406	102,277	102,954	105,829
Utilities...	103,117	106,040	106,302	108,021	111,328	113,703	116,986	120,880
Construction	52,620	53,287	55,375	58,144	61,211	64,582	68,217	70,005
Manufacturing...	54,809	55,581	54,849	56,591	58,650	59,570	67,148	70,670
Durable goods manufacturing..................................	61,833	62,200	60,834	63,007	64,471	64,732	74,477	78,807
Nondurable goods manufacturing............................	43,307	44,799	45,260	45,625	47,196	48,824	52,178	54,032
Wholesale trade..	67,763	70,536	71,324	75,419	77,627	77,431	82,462	87,527
Retail trade...	29,575	29,951	30,484	31,317	32,174	33,345	36,498	39,589
Transportation and warehousing..................................	52,110	53,037	50,946	51,427	51,908	51,722	51,709	55,653
Information	59,454	61,440	62,446	65,834	70,383	73,286	88,614	113,833
Finance and insurance	67,013	71,723	72,278	74,901	78,542	82,905	94,190	102,920
Real estate and rental and leasing..............................	43,620	46,815	47,385	48,945	50,618	52,672	55,488	61,570
Professional, scientific, and technical services	71,397	72,256	73,481	74,571	75,644	78,721	82,770	93,164
Management of companies and enterprises....................	120,702	114,037	130,468	123,383	138,029	126,520	140,219	167,257
Administrative and waste services...............................	30,274	31,341	31,766	32,851	34,468	36,039	38,567	41,514
Educational services	37,533	38,453	39,003	39,420	42,419	40,778	49,091	44,410
Health care and social assistance................................	51,255	52,504	53,106	54,111	55,031	55,785	58,823	61,374
Arts, entertainment, and recreation.............................	35,955	37,027	50,390	38,694	39,503	40,685	51,598	52,386
Accommodation and food services...............................	35,906	36,402	36,775	37,563	38,587	39,311	36,146	40,962
Other services, except public administration..................	32,461	33,688	34,388	35,731	36,727	37,418	40,073	43,713
Government and government enterprises.....................	51,989	53,295	54,345	55,537	57,150	58,854	62,158	63,610

Table NV-10. Employment Characteristics by Family Type

(Number, percent.)

Family type and labor force status	2019 Total	2019 Families with own children under 18 years	2020[1] Total	2020[1] Families with own children under 18 years	2021 Total	2021 Families with own children under 18 years
All Families	723,755	293,612	720,213	302,429	753,696	315,044
FAMILY TYPE AND LABOR FORCE STATUS						
Opposite-Sex Married-Couple Families	506,470	188,766	495,482	191,193	513,584	196,630
Both husband and wife in labor force	47.7	63.2	48.2	63.0	47.5	62.7
Husband in labor force, wife not in labor force	22.3	30.5	22.9	30.8	21.8	28.7
Wife in labor force, husband not in labor force	7.4	3.8	8.2	4.2	9.3	5.6
Both husband and wife not in labor force	21.3	2.0	20.7	2.1	21.4	3.1
Other Families	217,285	104,846	218,385	109,916	231,503	116,038
Female householder, no spouse present	67.5	70.1	67.2	70.1	65.6	68.0
In labor force	49.1	59.5	49.4	59.7	49.5	58.7
Not in labor force	18.5	10.7	17.8	10.3	16.1	9.4
Male householder, no spouse present	32.5	29.9	32.8	29.9	34.4	32.0
In labor force	26.1	27.6	26.7	27.7	26.6	28.1
Not in labor force	6.3	2.3	6.1	2.2	7.8	3.9

[1] 2020 ACS 5-Year estimates. 1-Year estimates were not released for 2020 due to the impact of COVID-19 on data collection that year. Data is not comparable to previous years, which are based on 1-year estimates.

Table NV-11. School Enrollment and Educational Attainment, 2021

(Number, percent.)

Item	State	U.S.
Enrollment		
Total population 3 years and over, enrolled in school	709,413	79,453,524
Enrolled in nursery school or preschool (percent)	3.6	5.2
Enrolled in kindergarten (percent)	5.0	5.0
Enrolled in elementary school, grades 1-8 (percent)	43.7	41.3
Enrolled in high school, grades 9-12 (percent)	23.2	21.8
Enrolled in college or graduate school (percent)	24.5	26.7
Attainment		
Total population 25 years and over	2,192,826	228,193,464
Less than ninth grade (percent)	5.9	4.8
9th to 12th grade, no diploma (percent)	7.0	5.9
High school graduate, including equivalency (percent)	27.2	26.3
Some college, no degree (percent)	23.4	19.3
Associate's degree (percent)	9.0	8.8
Bachelor's degree (percent)	17.9	21.2
Graduate or professional degree (percent)	9.6	13.8
High school graduate or higher (percent)	87.2	89.4
Bachelor's degree or higher (percent)	27.6	35.0

Table NV-12. Public School Characteristics and Educational Indicators

(Number, percent; data derived from National Center of Education Statistics.)

Item	State	U.S.
Public Elementary and Secondary Schools		
Number of regular school districts, 2019-20	19	13,349
Number of operational schools, 2019-20	708	98,469
Percent charter schools	11.0	7.7
Total public school enrollment, Fall 2021	486,648	49,433,092
Percent charter school enrollment	13.2	7.5
Student-teacher ratio, Fall 2019	19.5	15.9
Expenditures per student (unadjusted dollars), 2019-20	9,548	13,489
Four-year adjusted cohort graduation rate (ACGR), 2019-2020[1]	82.6	86.5
Students eligible for free or reduced-price lunch (percent), 2019-20	64.6	52.1
English language learners (percent), Fall 2020	13.7	10.3
Students age 3 to 21 served under IDEA, part B (percent), 2021-22	12.7	14.7

Public Schools by Type, 2019-20	Number	Percent of state public schools
Total number of schools	708	100.0
Special education	13	1.8
Vocational education	-	-
Alternative education	32	4.5

[1] Adjusted Cohort Graduation Rates (ACGR) differ from Averaged Freshmen Graduation Rates (AFGR).
- = Zero or rounds to zero.

Table NV-13. Reported Voting and Registration of the Voting-Age Population, November 2022

(Numbers in thousands, percent.)

Item	Total population	Total citizen population	Registered			Voted		
			Total registered	Percent registered (total population)	Percent registered (total citizen population)	Total voted	Percent voted (total population)	Percent voted (total citizen population)
U.S. Total	255,457	233,546	161,422	63.2	69.1	121,916	47.7	52.2
State Total....................................	2,451	2,206	1,436	58.6	65.1	1,123	45.8	50.9
Sex								
Male	1,212	1,093	703	58.0	64.3	553	45.7	50.7
Female	1,238	1,113	734	59.3	65.9	569	46.0	51.1
Race								
White alone................................	1,787	1,598	1,049	58.7	65.6	845	47.3	52.9
White, non-Hispanic alone	1,249	1,223	853	68.3	69.7	731	58.5	59.8
Black alone................................	240	228	149	62.1	65.4	120	50.1	52.7
Asian alone................................	218	177	105	48.1	59.2	62	28.6	35.2
Hispanic (of any race)................................	636	470	252	39.6	53.6	151	23.7	32.1
White alone or in combination	1,879	1,687	1,096	58.3	65.0	879	46.8	52.1
Black alone or in combination....................	294	279	166	56.5	59.6	128	43.7	46.1
Asian alone or in combination......................	243	202	120	49.2	59.1	77	31.7	38.1
Age								
18 to 24 years............................	297	287	122	41.0	42.4	63	21.2	21.9
25 to 34 years............................	414	355	222	53.6	62.6	153	37.0	43.2
35 to 44 years............................	406	358	229	56.4	63.9	170	41.9	47.5
45 to 64 years............................	789	694	458	58.0	66.0	378	47.9	54.5
65 years and over	544	511	405	74.5	79.3	358	65.9	70.1

Table NV-14. Health Indicators

(Number, rate as indicated in footnotes.)

Item	State	U.S.
Births		
Life Expectancy at Birth (years), 2020	76.3	77.0
Fertility Rate by State[1], 2021	54.8	56.3
Percent Home Births, 2021..	1.9	1.4
Cesarean Delivery Rate[2], 2021	32.9	32.1
Preterm Birth Rate[3], 2021	11.2	10.5
Teen Birth Rate[4], 2021	15.1	13.9
Percentage of Babies Born Low Birthweight[5], 2021	9.7	8.5
Deaths[6]		
Heart Disease Mortality Rate, 2021...	208.1	173.8
Cancer Mortality Rate, 2021..	143.2	146.6
Stroke Mortality Rate, 2021...	41.7	41.1
Diabetes Mortality Rate, 2021...	23.5	25.4
Influenza/Pneumonia Mortality Rate, 2021	12.8	10.5
Suicide Mortality Rate, 2021..	21.5	14.1
Drug Overdose Mortality Rate, 2021..	29.2	33.6
Firearm Injury Mortality Rate, 2021...	19.8	14.6
Homicide Mortality Rate, 2021...	8.5	8.2
Disease and Illness		
Lifetime Asthma in Adults, 2020 (percent)...	13.3	13.9
Lifetime Asthma in Children, 2020 (percent)[7]	8.6	11.3
Diabetes in Adults, 2020 (percent)...	9.7	8.2
Self-reported Obesity in Adults, 2021 (percent)..	31.3	NA

SOURCE: National Center for Health Statistics, National Vital Statistics System 2020 data; https://wonder.cdc.gov.
[1] General fertility rate per 1,000 women aged 15–44.
[2] This represents the percentage of all live births that were cesarean deliveries.
[3] Babies born prior to 37 weeks of pregnancy (gestation).
[4] Number of births per 1,000 females aged 15–19
[5] Babies born weighing less than 2,500 grams or 5 lbs. 8oz.
[6] Death rates are the number of deaths per 100,000 total population.
[7] U.S. total includes data from 30 states and D.C.
NA = Not available.
- = Zero or rounds to zero.

Table NV-15. State Government Finances, 2021

(Dollar amounts in thousands, percent distribution.)

Item	Dollars	Percent distribution
Total Revenue	21,876,113	100.0
General revenue	18,677,128	85.4
Intergovernmental revenue	6,589,132	30.1
Taxes	10,416,344	47.6
General sales	6,179,597	28.2
Selective sales	2,213,033	10.1
License taxes	623,260	2.8
Individual income tax	-	-
Corporate income tax	-	-
Other taxes	1,400,454	6.4
Current charges	854,345	3.9
Miscellaneous general revenue	817,307	3.7
Utility revenue	40,046	0.2
Liquor stores revenue	-	-
Insurance trust revenue[1]	3,158,939	14.4
Total Expenditure	22,844,761	100.0
Intergovernmental expenditure	5,478,715	24.0
Direct expenditure	17,366,046	76.0
Current operation	9,293,032	40.7
Capital outlay	787,613	3.4
Insurance benefits and repayments	6,360,825	27.8
Assistance and subsidies	771,765	3.4
Interest on debt	152,811	0.7
Exhibit: Salaries and wages	2,003,396	8.8
Total Expenditure	22,844,761	100.0
General expenditure	16,448,149	72.0
Intergovernmental expenditure	5,478,715	24.0
Direct expenditure	10,969,434	48.0
General expenditure, by function:		
Education	6,069,691	26.6
Public welfare	4,504,613	19.7
Hospitals	340,928	1.5
Health	349,636	1.5
Highways	894,371	3.9
Police protection	128,303	0.6
Correction	423,621	1.9
Natural resources	152,249	0.7
Parks and recreation	34,423	0.2
Governmental administration	613,715	2.7
Interest on general debt	152,811	0.7
Other and unallocable	2,746,388	12.0
Utility expenditure	38,606	0.2
Liquor stores expenditure	-	-
Insurance trust expenditure	6,360,825	27.8
Debt at End of Fiscal Year	3,593,979	X
Cash and Security Holdings	67,526,639	X

X = Not applicable.
- = Zero or rounds to zero.
[1] Within insurance trust revenue, net earnings of state retirement systems is a calculated statistic (the item code in the data file is X08), and thus can be positive or negative. Net earnings is the sum of earnings on investments plus gains on investments minus losses on investments. The change made in 2002 for asset valuation from book to market value in accordance with Statement 34 of the Governmental Accounting Standards Board is reflected in the calculated statistics.

Table NV-16. State Government Tax Collections, 2022

(Dollars in thousands, percent.)

Item	Dollars	Percent distribution
Total Taxes	12,072,213	100.0
Property taxes	1,399,442	11.6
Sales and gross receipts	8,842,212	73.2
General sales and gross receipts	5,506,268	45.6
Selective sales and gross receipts	3,335,944	27.6
Alcoholic beverages	51,794	0.4
Amusements	1,689,128	14.0
Insurance premiums	518,019	4.3
Motor fuels	377,553	3.1
Pari-mutuels	3	-
Public utilities	49,872	0.4
Tobacco products	179,824	1.5
Other selective sales	469,751	3.9
Licenses	664,675	5.5
Alcoholic beverages	X	-
Amusements	56,090	0.5
Corporations in general	92,114	0.8
Hunting and fishing	13,137	0.1
Motor vehicle	223,192	1.8
Motor vehicle operators	26,613	0.2
Public utilities	X	-
Occupation and business, NEC	244,478	2.0
Other licenses	9,051	0.1
Income taxes	X	-
Individual income	X	-
Corporation net income	X	-
Other taxes	1,165,884	9.7
Death and gift	X	-
Documentary and stock transfer	191,497	1.6
Severance	218,715	1.8
Taxes, NEC	755,672	6.3

X = Not applicable.
- = Zero or rounds to zero.

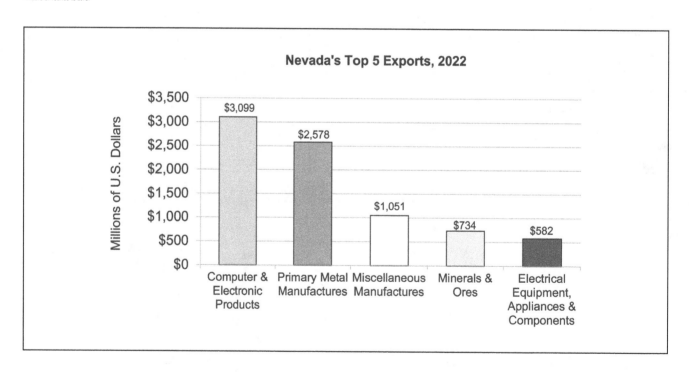

Nevada's Top 5 Exports, 2022

Export	Millions of U.S. Dollars
Computer & Electronic Products	$3,099
Primary Metal Manufactures	$2,578
Miscellaneous Manufactures	$1,051
Minerals & Ores	$734
Electrical Equipment, Appliances & Components	$582

NEW HAMPSHIRE

Facts and Figures

Location: Northeastern United States; bordered on the N by Canada (Quebec), on the E by Maine, on the SE by the Atlantic Ocean, on the S by Massachusetts, and on the W by Vermont

Area: 9,350 sq. mi. (24,216 sq. km.); rank—46th

Population: 1,395,231 (2022 est.); rank—41st

Principal Cities: capital—Concord; largest—Manchester

Statehood: June 21, 1788; 9th state

U.S. Congress: 2 senators, 2 representatives

State Motto: Live Free or Die

State Song: "Old New Hampshire"

State Nickname: The Granite State

Abbreviations: NH; N.H.

State Symbols: flower—purple lilac; tree—white birch; bird—purple finch

At a Glance

- With an increase in population of 6.0 percent, New Hampshire ranked 26th among the states in growth from 2010 to 2022.

- New Hampshire's homicide rate of less than half a percent was the 3rd lowest in the country in 2021.

- New Hampshire had the 7th highest homeownership rate in 2022, with 74.6 percent of homes being owner-occupied.

- New Hampshire had the 3rd lowest birth rate in the country in 2021, with 9.1 births per 1,000 population.

Table NH-1. Population by Age, Sex, Race, and Hispanic Origin

(Number, percent, except where noted.)

Sex, age, race, and Hispanic origin	2010	2020	2022	Percent change, 2010–2022
Total Population..	1,316,470	1,377,518	1,395,231	6.0
Percent of total U.S. population	0.4	0.4	0.4	X
Sex				
Male...	649,394	688,202	697,809	7.5
Female	667,076	689,316	697,422	4.5
Age				
Under 5 years..	69,806	62,757	62,944	-9.8
Under 18 years...	287,234	257,106	252,924	-11.9
18 to 64 years...	850,968	861,837	860,801	1.2
65 years and over..	178,268	258,575	281,506	57.9
Median age (years)	41.1	43	43.3	5.4
Race and Hispanic Origin				
One race				
White	1,248,321	1,280,148	1,291,413	3.5
Black	16,365	25,685	27,993	71.1
American Indian and Alaska Native	3,530	4,211	4,426	25.4
Asian	28,933	41,935	44,265	53.0
Native Hawaiian or Other Pacific Islander	532	728	875	64.5
Two or more races	18,789	24,811	26,259	39.8
Hispanic (of any race)	36,704	57,807	64,192	74.9

NOTE: Population figures for 2022 are July 1 estimates. The 2010 and 2020 estimates are taken from the respective censuses.
- = Zero or rounds to zero.
X = Not applicable.

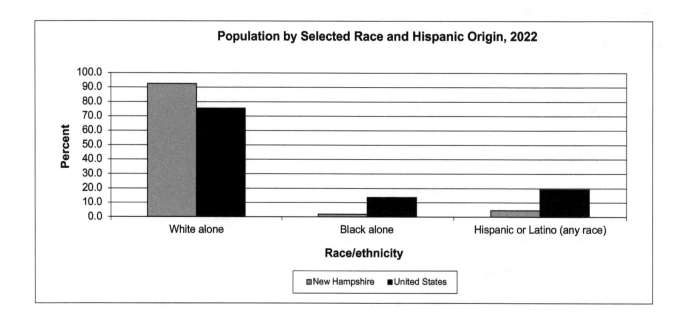

Table NH-2. Marital Status

(Number, percent distribution.)

Sex, age, race, and Hispanic origin	2000	2010	2021
Males, 15 Years and Over	476,409	529,439	585,971
Never married	27.7	30.5	33.7
Now married, except separated....................................	59.1	54.7	52.1
Separated...	1.2	1.3	1.0
Widowed...	2.4	2.6	2.4
Divorced..	9.6	10.9	10.8
Females, 15 Years and Over	502,232	555,698	594,502
Never married	22.3	25.4	27.6
Now married, except separated....................................	55.7	51.4	50.7
Separated...	1.5	1.3	1.3
Widowed...	9.2	8.6	7.8
Divorced..	11.3	13.4	12.5

Table NH-3. Households and Housing Characteristics

(Number, percent, dollars.)

Item	2000	2010	2021	Average annual percent change, 2010–2021
Total Households...	474,606	515,431	548,026	0.6
Family households	323,651	344,057	361,209	0.5
Married-couple family	262,438	274,195	286,604	0.4
Other family	61,213	69,862	74,605	0.6
Male householder, no wife present........................	18,261	22,205	25,947	1.5
Female householder, no husband present...............	42,952	47,657	48,658	0.2
Nonfamily households	150,955	171,374	186,817	0.8
Householder living alone.....................................	116,014	130,327	142,107	0.8
Householder not living alone................................	34,941	41,047	44,710	0.8
Housing Characteristics				
Total housing units..	547,024	614,996	643,979	0.4
Occupied housing units	474,606	515,431	548,026	0.6
Owner occupied	330,700	369,448	397,225	0.7
Renter occupied	143,906	145,983	150,801	0.3
Average household size..	2.53	2.48	2.46	-0.1
Financial Characteristics				
Median gross rent of renter-occupied housing	646	951	1,263	3.0
Median monthly owner costs for housing units with a mortgage ...	1,226	1,853	2,004	0.7
Median value of owner-occupied housing units.........	133,300	243,000	345,200	3.8

Table NH-4. Migration, Origin, and Language

(Number, percent.)

Characteristic	State 2021	U.S. 2021
Residence 1 Year Ago		
Population 1 year and over	1,377,638	328,464,538
Same house	88.8	87.2
Different house in the U.S.	10.9	12.3
Same county	4.9	6.7
Different county	6.0	5.7
Same state	2.1	3.3
Different state	3.9	2.4
Abroad	0.2	0.4
Place of Birth		
Native born	1,306,865	286,623,642
Male	50.0	49.7
Female	50.0	50.3
Foreign born	82,127	45,270,103
Male	49.1	48.7
Female	50.9	51.3
Foreign born; naturalized U.S. citizen...................................	50,166	24,044,083
Male	49.1	46.4
Female	50.9	53.6
Foreign born; not a U.S. citizen	31,961	21,226,020
Male	49.2	51.2
Female	50.8	48.8
Entered 2010 or later	34.5	28.1
Entered 2000 to 2009	22.4	23.7
Entered before 2000...	43.1	48.2
World Region of Birth, Foreign		
Foreign-born population, excluding population born at sea	82,127	45,269,644
Europe	26.0	10.7
Asia...	34.1	31.0
Africa...	6.9	5.7
Oceania	1.0	0.6
Latin America..	22.3	50.1
North America...	9.7	1.7
Language Spoken at Home and Ability to Speak English		
Population 5 years and over..	1,326,772	313,232,500
English only	92.3	70.4
Language other than English..	7.7	21.6
Speaks English less than "very well"....................................	2.1	8.3

Table NH-5. Median Income and Poverty Status, 2021

(Number, percent, except as noted.)

Characteristic	State Number	State Percent	U.S. Number	U.S. Percent
Median Income				
Households (dollars)...	88,465	X	69,717	X
Families (dollars)	108,208	X	85,806	X
Below Poverty Level (All People)	97,403	7.2	41,393,176	12.8
Sex				
Male	40,193	6.0	18,518,155	11.6
Female	57,210	8.5	22,875,021	13.9
Age				
Under 18 years...	23,089	9.2	12,243,219	16.9
Related children under 18 years............................	22,084	8.8	11,985,424	16.6
18 to 64 years..	56,405	6.7	23,526,341	11.9
65 years and over	17,909	6.9	5,623,616	10.3

X = Not applicable.

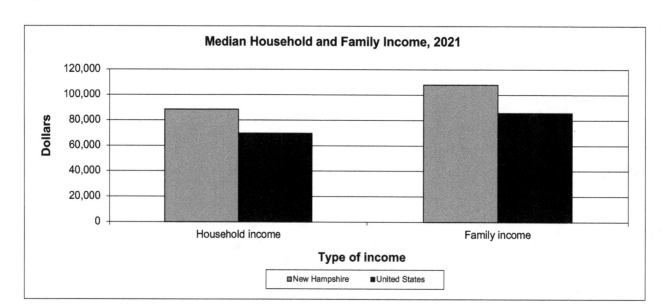

Median Household and Family Income, 2021

Table NH-6. Health Insurance Coverage Status for the Civilian Noninstitutionalized Population and Children Under 19 Years of Age

(Number, percent.)

Item	2011	2012	2013	2014	2015	2016	2017	2018	2019	2020 [2]	2021
Civilian Noninstitutionalized Population	1,303,868	1,306,026	1,308,658	1,311,921	1,314,249	1,316,467	1,325,016	1,339,549	1,343,337	1,338,372	1,372,918
Covered by Private or Public Insurance											
Number..	1,166,946	1,167,184	1,168,406	1,191,465	1,230,861	1,238,790	1,247,957	1,262,538	1,259,313	1,258,301	1,302,407
Percent..	89.5	89.4	89.3	90.8	93.7	94.1	94.2	94.3	93.7	94.0	94.9
Uninsured											
Number..	136,922	138,842	140,252	120,456	83,388	77,677	77,059	77,011	84,024	80,071	70,511
Percent..	10.5	10.6	10.7	9.2	6.3	5.9	5.8	5.7	6.3	6.0	5.1
Percent in the U.S. not covered..............................	15.1	14.8	14.5	11.7	9.4	8.6	8.7	8.9	9.2	8.7	8.6
Children Under 19 Years of Age[1]	279,210	274,563	270,642	266,833	262,932	259,410	275,977	279,907	276,888	276,273	273,429
Covered by Private or Public Insurance											
Number..	269,018	263,665	260,381	255,132	255,940	252,563	269,639	272,651	266,712	268,397	262,610
Percent..	96.3	96.0	96.2	95.6	97.3	97.4	97.7	97.4	96.3	97.1	96.0
Uninsured											
Number..	10,192	10,898	10,261	11,701	6,992	6,847	6,338	7,256	10,176	7,876	10,819
Percent..	3.7	4.0	3.8	4.4	2.7	2.6	2.3	2.6	3.7	2.9	4.0
Percent in the U.S. not covered..............................	7.5	7.2	7.1	6.0	4.8	4.5	5.0	5.2	5.7	5.2	5.4

[1] Data for years prior to 2017 are for individuals under 18 years of age.
[2] 2020 ACS 5-Year estimates. 1-Year estimates were not released for 2020 due to the impact of COVID-19 on data collection that year. Data is not comparable to previous years, which are based on 1-year estimates.

Table NH-7. Employment Status by Demographic Group, 2022

(Numbers in thousands, percent.)

Characteristic	Civilian noninstitutional population	Civilian labor force		Employed		Unemployed	
		Number	Percent of population	Number	Percent of population	Number	Percent of population
Total...	1,167	769	65.9	747	64.1	22	2.8
Sex							
Male...	579	412	71.1	399	68.8	13	3.2
Female...	587	357	60.7	349	59.4	8	2.3
Race, Sex, and Hispanic Origin							
White...	1,092	716	65.6	697	63.9	19	2.6
Male...	547	387	70.8	376	68.8	11	2.8
Female.......................................	545	329	60.4	321	58.9	8	2.4
Black or African American...................	NA	NA	NA	NA	NA	NA	NA
Male...	NA	NA	NA	NA	NA	NA	NA
Female.......................................	NA	NA	NA	NA	NA	NA	NA
Hispanic or Latino ethnicity[1].............	NA	NA	NA	NA	NA	NA	NA
Male...	NA	NA	NA	NA	NA	NA	NA
Female.......................................	NA	NA	NA	NA	NA	NA	NA
Age							
16 to 19 years...............................	NA	NA	NA	NA	NA	NA	NA
20 to 24 years...............................	72	54	74.1	52	71.2	2	3.7
25 to 34 years...............................	186	156	84.1	151	81.4	5	3.3
35 to 44 years...............................	176	152	86.3	147	83.5	5	3.3
45 to 54 years...............................	152	130	85.5	128	84.4	2	1.4
55 to 64 years...............................	222	167	75.1	164	74.0	2	1.4
65 years and over...........................	286	70	24.4	68	23.6	2	3.3

NOTE: Data in Table 7 are from the Current Population Survey (CPS) and do not match the estimates in Table 8. See notes and definitions for further information.
[1] May be of any race.
NA = Not available.

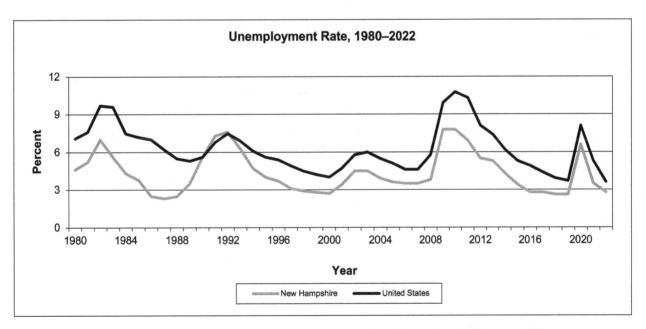

Unemployment Rate, 1980–2022

Table NH-8. Employment Status of the Civilian Noninstitutional Population Age 16 Years and Over

(Number, percent.)

Year	Civilian labor force	Civilian participation rate	Employed	Unemployed	Unemployment rate
2010...	739,340	70.0	694,132	45,208	6.1
2011...	736,785	69.5	696,591	40,194	5.5
2012...	740,796	69.3	700,448	40,348	5.4
2013...	743,036	69.1	704,023	39,013	5.3
2014...	743,756	68.6	711,740	32,016	4.3
2015...	746,317	68.5	720,832	25,485	3.4
2016...	752,478	68.5	731,002	21,476	2.9
2017...	758,133	68.1	736,918	21,215	2.8
2018...	767,629	68.5	747,415	20,214	2.6
2019...	776,471	68.7	756,267	20,204	2.6
2020...	759,770	66.7	708,566	51,204	6.7
2021...	755,422	65.6	728,940	26,482	3.5
2022...	766,672	66.1	747,339	19,333	2.5

Table NH-9. Employment and Average Wages by Industry

(Estimates are based on the 2012 North American Industry Classification System [NAICS].)

Industry	2014	2015	2016	2017	2018	2019	2020	2021
	Number of Jobs							
Wage and Salary Employment by Industry.........................	655,565	666,446	676,434	682,227	688,974	695,650	653,928	679,137
Farm Wage and Salary Employment................................	1,664	1,658	1,548	1,544	1,311	1,320	1,261	1,292
Nonfarm Wage and Salary Employment..........................	653,901	664,788	674,886	680,683	687,663	694,330	652,667	677,845
Private wage and salary employment.................................	558,847	569,930	580,407	586,304	593,359	599,865	561,837	587,921
Forestry, fishing, and related activities............................	825	820	803	769	783	805	775	720
Mining..	532	526	556	548	565	549	579	579
Utilities..	2,320	2,182	2,129	2,090	2,032	2,002	2,002	2,008
Construction...	23,787	24,864	26,118	27,100	27,554	28,515	28,618	29,693
Manufacturing..	66,598	67,273	68,179	69,179	70,685	71,574	67,415	67,951
Durable goods manufacturing.......................................	49,950	50,169	50,801	51,455	52,679	53,488	50,586	50,798
Nondurable goods manufacturing..................................	16,648	17,104	17,378	17,724	18,006	18,086	16,829	17,153
Wholesale trade...	27,214	27,681	27,896	28,127	28,168	28,288	27,524	29,343
Retail trade..	95,065	95,615	96,650	96,216	95,321	94,823	89,603	91,746
Transportation and warehousing.....................................	13,008	13,483	14,322	14,617	14,921	15,374	15,347	16,284
Information...	12,044	12,285	12,532	12,579	12,365	12,349	11,753	11,686
Finance and insurance...	29,418	30,159	30,841	28,467	27,983	28,207	28,406	28,913
Real estate and rental and leasing................................	6,932	6,809	7,021	7,164	7,317	7,249	6,784	6,957
Professional, scientific, and technical services...............	32,687	33,719	34,252	37,797	38,230	39,123	39,420	42,987
Management of companies and enterprises......................	8,191	8,646	8,906	8,956	9,163	9,270	9,005	9,451
Administrative and waste services..................................	33,191	34,843	35,172	35,585	36,097	35,736	33,892	35,908
Educational services	23,362	24,540	25,391	25,666	27,007	27,164	25,854	28,753
Health care and social assistance..................................	87,429	89,129	91,116	92,308	93,656	95,319	90,753	92,607
Arts, entertainment, and recreation................................	11,389	11,450	11,797	12,012	12,524	13,077	9,558	11,353
Accommodation and food services.................................	56,218	57,446	58,473	59,259	60,024	60,691	48,182	54,056
Other services, except public administration....................	28,637	28,460	28,253	27,865	28,964	29,750	26,367	26,926
Government and government enterprises....................	95,054	94,858	94,479	94,379	94,304	94,465	90,830	89,924
	Dollars							
Average Wages and Salaries by Industry	50,382	51,727	52,767	54,319	55,941	57,787	63,653	70,743
Average Farm Wages and Salaries	28,806	23,616	29,029	26,413	25,207	19,877	20,210	19,816
Average Nonfarm Wages and Salaries	50,437	51,797	52,821	54,383	55,999	57,859	63,737	70,840
Average private wages and salaries................................	51,549	52,890	53,957	55,589	57,217	59,203	65,421	73,382
Forestry, fishing, and related activities............................	45,013	47,511	44,724	47,568	45,442	46,884	48,665	56,265
Mining..	54,147	57,757	58,453	63,111	63,193	66,811	72,570	70,941
Utilities..	102,353	103,231	103,327	111,422	116,766	110,781	123,795	121,585
Construction	54,208	57,292	58,909	61,595	62,715	64,838	68,922	71,246
Manufacturing..	66,253	66,915	68,346	70,454	71,795	73,412	77,894	80,774
Durable goods manufacturing.......................................	69,827	70,096	71,524	73,725	75,441	77,453	82,123	85,131
Nondurable goods manufacturing..................................	55,530	57,585	59,056	60,958	61,129	61,462	65,184	67,870
Wholesale trade...	84,863	90,571	89,896	91,618	93,917	97,218	105,764	117,664
Retail trade..	29,670	30,752	31,013	31,676	32,874	34,029	37,885	41,143
Transportation and warehousing.....................................	40,888	43,020	43,336	44,760	46,847	48,640	50,168	52,784
Information	91,493	82,669	85,312	88,097	93,685	97,288	107,338	116,983
Finance and insurance	94,523	94,655	100,186	100,414	104,989	110,077	119,710	133,119
Real estate and rental and leasing................................	47,654	50,873	52,139	53,369	55,082	59,383	64,375	72,503
Professional, scientific, and technical services	84,859	86,971	88,698	93,886	97,735	100,730	108,935	117,083
Management of companies and enterprises......................	106,453	106,548	103,648	109,439	102,285	106,391	111,176	361,960
Administrative and waste services..................................	43,547	45,242	46,226	47,577	49,753	51,821	57,880	62,537
Educational services	44,025	45,157	45,049	44,804	44,778	46,116	51,358	49,073
Health care and social assistance..................................	50,368	51,841	52,995	54,534	56,248	58,251	63,781	65,475
Arts, entertainment, and recreation................................	24,347	24,508	24,324	25,126	26,261	26,787	30,559	31,735
Accommodation and food services.................................	20,897	21,783	22,693	23,517	24,909	25,814	26,107	30,784
Other services, except public administration....................	33,261	34,714	35,607	36,457	37,654	38,718	41,998	44,843
Government and government enterprises.............................	43,902	45,227	45,843	46,890	48,336	49,326	53,317	54,223

Table NH-10. Employment Characteristics by Family Type

(Number, percent.)

Family type and labor force status	2019		2020 [1]		2021	
	Total	Families with own children under 18 years	Total	Families with own children under 18 years	Total	Families with own children under 18 years
All Families..	346,413	126,375	351,445	133,128	361,209	131,361
FAMILY TYPE AND LABOR FORCE STATUS						
Opposite-Sex Married-Couple Families..	273,682	90,194	278,389	94,874	283,203	94,849
Both husband and wife in labor force................................	54.9	75.7	56.3	75.2	55.3	74.8
Husband in labor force, wife not in labor force	17.1	18.2	17.8	20.1	17.4	20.3
Wife in labor force, husband not in labor force	7.9	3.9	8.1	3.6	7.9	3.7
Both husband and wife not in labor force..........................	18.7	1.1	17.8	1.1	19.4	1.3
Other Families	72,731	36,181	69,838	37,469	74,605	36,231
Female householder, no spouse present	65.6	67.5	66.1	67.2	65.2	66.9
In labor force	48.6	56.9	48.1	55.7	47.3	53.5
Not in labor force	17.0	10.6	18.0	11.5	17.9	13.3
Male householder, no spouse present.............................	34.4	32.5	33.9	32.8	34.8	33.1
In labor force..	27.6	30.5	27.7	30.1	27.7	30.2
Not in labor force	6.8	2.0	6.2	2.7	7.1	3.0

[1] 2020 ACS 5-Year estimates. 1-Year estimates were not released for 2020 due to the impact of COVID-19 on data collection that year. Data is not comparable to previous years, which are based on 1-year estimates.

Table NH-11. School Enrollment and Educational Attainment, 2021

(Number, percent.)

Item	State	U.S.
Enrollment		
Total population 3 years and over, enrolled in school	293,741	79,453,524
Enrolled in nursery school or preschool (percent)	4.8	5.2
Enrolled in kindergarten (percent)...	4.3	5.0
Enrolled in elementary school, grades 1-8 (percent)...	39.5	41.3
Enrolled in high school, grades 9-12 (percent)	21.9	21.8
Enrolled in college or graduate school (percent)...	29.6	26.7
Attainment		
Total population 25 years and over	1,008,318	228,193,464
Less than ninth grade (percent)	2.1	4.8
9th to 12th grade, no diploma (percent)	3.5	5.9
High school graduate, including equivalency (percent)...	26.6	26.3
Some college, no degree (percent)	17.8	19.3
Associate's degree (percent)..	9.8	8.8
Bachelor's degree (percent)...	24.5	21.2
Graduate or professional degree (percent)...	15.7	13.8
High school graduate or higher (percent)	94.4	89.4
Bachelor's degree or higher (percent)..	40.2	35.0

Table NH-12. Public School Characteristics and Educational Indicators

(Number, percent; data derived from National Center of Education Statistics.)

Item	State	U.S.
Public Elementary and Secondary Schools		
Number of regular school districts, 2019-20	180	13,349
Number of operational schools, 2019-20..	496	98,469
Percent charter schools	8.1	7.7
Total public school enrollment, Fall 2021	170,005	49,433,092
Percent charter school enrollment..	2.9	7.5
Student-teacher ratio, Fall 2019..	12.1	15.9
Expenditures per student (unadjusted dollars), 2019-20	17,825	13,489
Four-year adjusted cohort graduation rate (ACGR), 2019-2020[1].......................................	88.1	86.5
Students eligible for free or reduced-price lunch (percent), 2019-20..................................	24.7	52.1
English language learners (percent), Fall 2020	2.9	10.3
Students age 3 to 21 served under IDEA, part B (percent), 2021-22	17.8	14.7

Public Schools by Type, 2019-20	Number	Percent of state public schools
Total number of schools...	496	100.0
Special education...	-	-
Vocational education..	-	-
Alternative education..	-	-

[1] Adjusted Cohort Graduation Rates (ACGR) differ from Averaged Freshmen Graduation Rates (AFGR).
- = Zero or rounds to zero.

Table NH-13. Reported Voting and Registration of the Voting-Age Population, November 2022

(Numbers in thousands, percent.)

Item	Total population	Total citizen population	Registered			Voted		
			Total registered	Percent registered (total population)	Percent registered (total citizen population)	Total voted	Percent voted (total population)	Percent voted (total citizen population)
U.S. Total	255,457	233,546	161,422	63.2	69.1	121,916	47.7	52.2
State Total............................	1,143	1,106	804	70.3	72.6	654	57.2	59.1
Sex								
Male	567	552	398	70.2	72.1	316	55.7	57.3
Female	577	554	406	70.4	73.2	338	58.6	61.0
Race								
White alone..................................	1,053	1,042	762	72.4	73.2	627	59.6	60.2
White, non-Hispanic alone	1,026	1,016	752	73.3	74.0	620	60.4	61.0
Black alone..................................	22	19	15	68.3	79.4	8	35.2	40.9
Asian alone	56	33	19	34.8	59.2	15	27.2	46.3
Hispanic (of any race)	33	32	11	34.4	36.1	7	21.5	22.6
White alone or in combination	1,064	1,053	769	72.3	73.1	631	59.3	60.0
Black alone or in combination	23	20	17	70.7	81.2	8	32.5	37.3
Asian alone or in combination.....................	60	37	23	37.9	61.5	17	28.6	46.3
Age								
18 to 24 years	120	119	52	43.5	44.0	35	29.5	29.8
25 to 34 years	199	186	111	55.6	59.5	74	37.2	39.8
35 to 44 years	160	151	109	68.4	72.6	82	51.5	54.6
45 to 64 years	366	355	277	75.6	78.0	236	64.4	66.5
65 years and over	298	296	254	85.3	86.0	226	75.9	76.5

B = Base is less than 75,000 and therefore too small to show the derived measure.

Table NH-14. Health Indicators

(Number, rate as indicated in footnotes.)

Item	State	U.S.
Births		
Life Expectancy at Birth (years), 2020	79.0	77.0
Fertility Rate by State[1], 2021	49.9	56.3
Percent Home Births, 2021	1.9	1.4
Cesarean Delivery Rate[2], 2021	32.7	32.1
Preterm Birth Rate[3], 2021	8.5	10.5
Teen Birth Rate[4], 2021	5.4	13.9
Percentage of Babies Born Low Birthweight[5], 2021	7.0	8.5
Deaths[6]		
Heart Disease Mortality Rate, 2021..	154.1	173.8
Cancer Mortality Rate, 2021..	145.7	146.6
Stroke Mortality Rate, 2021	30.3	41.1
Diabetes Mortality Rate, 2021...	20.8	25.4
Influenza/Pneumonia Mortality Rate, 2021	6.5	10.5
Suicide Mortality Rate, 2021...	15.1	14.1
Drug Overdose Mortality Rate, 2021...	32.3	33.6
Firearm Injury Mortality Rate, 2021..	8.3	14.6
Homicide Mortality Rate, 2021..	-	8.2
Disease and Illness		
Lifetime Asthma in Adults, 2020 (percent)...	15.4	13.9
Lifetime Asthma in Children, 2020 (percent)[7]	12.2	11.3
Diabetes in Adults, 2020 (percent)..	7.5	8.2
Self-reported Obesity in Adults, 2021 (percent)...	30.6	NA

SOURCE: National Center for Health Statistics, National Vital Statistics System 2020 data; https://wonder.cdc.gov.
[1] General fertility rate per 1,000 women aged 15–44.
[2] This represents the percentage of all live births that were cesarean deliveries.
[3] Babies born prior to 37 weeks of pregnancy (gestation).
[4] Number of births per 1,000 females aged 15–19
[5] Babies born weighing less than 2,500 grams or 5 lbs. 8oz.
[6] Death rates are the number of deaths per 100,000 total population.
[7] U.S. total includes data from 30 states and D.C.
NA = Not available.
- = Zero or rounds to zero.

Table NH-15. State Government Finances, 2021

(Dollar amounts in thousands, percent distribution.)

Item	Dollars	Percent distribution
Total Revenue	10,904,056	100.0
General revenue	9,087,504	83.3
Intergovernmental revenue	4,100,526	37.6
Taxes	3,213,039	29.5
General sales	-	-
Selective sales	977,640	9.0
License taxes	472,669	4.3
Individual income tax	148,648	1.4
Corporate income tax	1,009,975	9.3
Other taxes	604,107	5.5
Current charges	843,314	7.7
Miscellaneous general revenue	930,625	8.5
Utility revenue	-	-
Liquor stores revenue	788,621	7.2
Insurance trust revenue[1]	1,027,931	9.4
Total Expenditure	10,919,342	100.0
Intergovernmental expenditure	2,104,779	19.3
Direct expenditure	8,814,563	80.7
Current operation	6,794,260	62.2
Capital outlay	376,506	3.4
Insurance benefits and repayments	1,060,296	9.7
Assistance and subsidies	291,991	2.7
Interest on debt	291,510	2.7
Exhibit: Salaries and wages	1,199,666	11.0
Total Expenditure	10,919,342	100.0
General expenditure	9,219,967	84.4
Intergovernmental expenditure	2,104,779	19.3
Direct expenditure	7,115,188	65.2
General expenditure, by function:		
Education	2,637,701	24.2
Public welfare	3,210,944	29.4
Hospitals	77,881	0.7
Health	199,402	1.8
Highways	512,034	4.7
Police protection	84,611	0.8
Correction	155,945	1.4
Natural resources	48,351	0.4
Parks and recreation	26,512	0.2
Governmental administration	761,824	7.0
Interest on general debt	291,510	2.7
Other and unallocable	1,205,983	11.0
Utility expenditure	18,629	0.2
Liquor stores expenditure	620,459	5.7
Insurance trust expenditure	1,060,296	9.7
Debt at End of Fiscal Year	7,225,623	X
Cash and Security Holdings	20,025,923	X

X = Not applicable.
- = Zero or rounds to zero.
[1] Within insurance trust revenue, net earnings of state retirement systems is a calculated statistic (the item code in the data file is X08), and thus can be positive or negative. Net earnings is the sum of earnings on investments plus gains on investments minus losses on investments. The change made in 2002 for asset valuation from book to market value in accordance with Statement 34 of the Governmental Accounting Standards Board is reflected in the calculated statistics.

Table NH-16. State Government Tax Collections, 2022

(Dollars in thousands, percent.)

Item	Dollars	Percent distribution
Total Taxes	3,497,660	100.0
Property taxes	406,541	11.6
Sales and gross receipts	943,410	27.0
General sales and gross receipts	X	-
Selective sales and gross receipts	943,410	27.0
Alcoholic beverages	-	-
Amusements	24,323	0.7
Insurance premiums	136,733	3.9
Motor fuels	180,010	5.1
Pari-mutuels	497	-
Public utilities	29,079	0.8
Tobacco products	182,626	5.2
Other selective sales	390,142	11.2
Licenses	545,704	15.6
Alcoholic beverages	5,613	0.2
Amusements	328	-
Corporations in general	84,348	2.4
Hunting and fishing	12,726	0.4
Motor vehicle	116,455	3.3
Motor vehicle operators	15,201	0.4
Public utilities	20,912	0.6
Occupation and business, NEC	250,192	7.2
Other licenses	39,929	1.1
Income taxes	1,366,620	39.1
Individual income	153,620	4.4
Corporation net income	1,213,000	34.7
Other taxes	235,385	6.7
Death and gift	-	-
Documentary and stock transfer	235,385	6.7
Severance	X	-
Taxes, NEC	-	-

X = Not applicable.
- = Zero or rounds to zero.

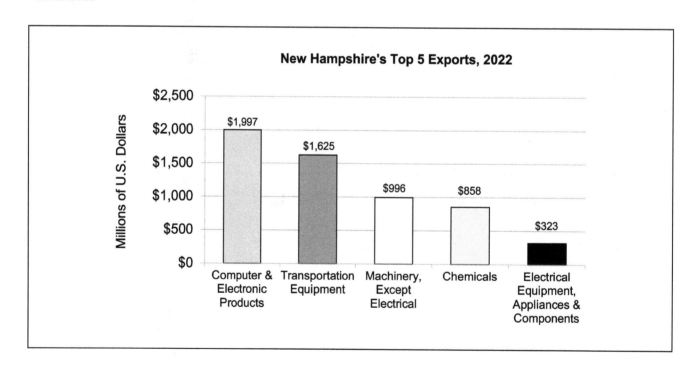

New Hampshire's Top 5 Exports, 2022

Export	Millions of U.S. Dollars
Computer & Electronic Products	$1,997
Transportation Equipment	$1,625
Machinery, Except Electrical	$996
Chemicals	$858
Electrical Equipment, Appliances & Components	$323

Facts and Figures

Location: Middle Atlantic region of the United States; bordered on the N and NE by New York, on the E by the Atlantic Ocean, on the S by Delaware Bay, and on the W by Delaware and Pennsylvania

Area: 8,721 sq. mi. (22,588 sq. km.); rank—47th

Population: 9,261,699 (2022 est.); rank—11th

Principal Cities: capital—Trenton; largest—Newark

Statehood: December 18, 1787; 3rd state

U.S. Congress: 2 senators, 12 representatives

State Motto: Liberty and Prosperity

State Song: None

State Nickname: The Garden State

Abbreviations: NJ; N.J.

State Symbols: flower—common meadow violet; tree—red oak; bird—Eastern goldfinch

At a Glance

- With an increase in population of 5.3 percent, New Jersey ranked 29th among the states in growth from 2010 to 2022.

- New Jersey's median household income was $89,296 in 2021, the 4th highest in the country.

- In 2021, 10.2 percent of the New Jersey's population lived below the poverty level, compared to 12.8 percent of the entire U.S. population.

- New Jersey's drug overdose death rate of 51.6 deaths per 100,000 population ranked 6th in the nation in 2021.

- Approximately 43.1 percent of New Jersey residents had a bachelor's degree or more in 2021, the 5th highest percentage in the country.

Table NJ-1. Population by Age, Sex, Race, and Hispanic Origin

(Number, percent, except where noted.)

Sex, age, race, and Hispanic origin	2010	2020	2022	Percent change, 2010–2022
Total Population..	8,791,894	9,289,031	9,261,699	5.3
Percent of total U.S. population	2.8	2.8	2.8	X
Sex				
Male..	4,279,600	4,579,070	4,565,014	6.7
Female	4,512,294	4,709,961	4,696,685	4.1
Age				
Under 5 years..	541,020	529,546	516,455	-4.5
Under 18 years..	2,065,214	2,031,444	1,994,109	-3.4
18 to 64 years...	5,540,687	5,724,747	5,655,823	2.1
65 years and over	1,185,993	1,532,840	1,611,767	35.9
Median age (years)	39.0	40.0	40.3	3.3
Race and Hispanic Origin				
One race				
White	6,546,498	6,632,907	6,549,769	-
Black...	1,282,005	1,414,448	1,429,864	11.5
American Indian and Alaska Native	49,907	62,871	67,366	35.0
Asian..	746,212	952,060	976,812	30.9
Native Hawaiian or Other Pacific Islander	7,731	11,206	12,286	58.9
Two or more races	159,541	215,539	225,602	41.4
Hispanic (of any race)...	1,555,144	1,968,291	2,028,471	30.4

NOTE: Population figures for 2022 are July 1 estimates. The 2010 and 2020 estimates are taken from the respective censuses.
- = Zero or rounds to zero.
X = Not applicable.

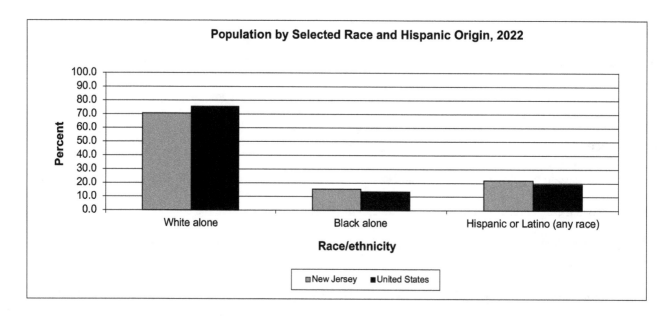

Table NJ-2. Marital Status

(Number, percent distribution.)

Sex, age, race, and Hispanic origin	2000	2010	2021
Males, 15 Years and Over	3,176,413	3,419,050	3,714,614
Never married	31.1	36.4	37.1
Now married, except separated...	57.7	52.1	52.1
Separated...	2.0	1.8	1.4
Widowed..	2.9	2.6	2.5
Divorced..	6.2	7.1	6.9
Females, 15 Years and Over	3,478,920	3,690,673	3,891,754
Never married	25.3	30.2	31.8
Now married, except separated...	51.8	47.6	47.8
Separated...	2.7	2.2	1.9
Widowed..	11.5	10.2	8.4
Divorced..	8.7	9.8	10.1

Table NJ-3. Households and Housing Characteristics

(Number, percent, dollars.)

Item	2000	2010	2021	Average annual percent change, 2010–2021
Total Households..	3,064,645	3,172,421	3,497,945	0.9
Family households..	2,154,539	2,185,732	2,379,328	0.8
Married-couple family..	1,638,322	1,614,230	1,763,645	0.8
Other family..	516,217	571,502	615,683	0.7
Male householder, no wife present......................................	129,205	154,036	173,007	1.1
Female householder, no husband present.............................	387,012	417,466	442,676	0.5
Nonfamily households..	910,106	986,689	1,118,617	1.2
Householder living alone...	751,287	827,294	915,841	1.0
Householder not living alone..	158,819	159,395	202,776	2.5
Housing Characteristics				
Total housing units..	3,310,275	3,554,909	3,779,591	0.6
Occupied housing units	3,064,645	3,172,421	3,497,945	0.9
Owner occupied..	2,012,473	2,106,728	2,252,974	0.6
Renter occupied...	1,053,172	1,065,693	1,244,971	1.5
Average household size...	2.68	2.72	2.60	-0.4
Financial Characteristics				
Median gross rent of renter-occupied housing	751	1,114	1,457	2.8
Median monthly owner costs for housing units with a mortgage ..	1,560	2,370	2,458	0.3
Median value of owner-occupied housing units.......................	170,800	339,200	389,800	1.4

Table NJ-4. Migration, Origin, and Language

(Number, percent.)

Characteristic	State 2021	U.S. 2021
Residence 1 Year Ago		
Population 1 year and over	9,174,117	328,464,538
Same house..	89.4	87.2
Different house in the U.S.	10.0	12.3
Same county..	5.0	6.7
Different county	5.1	5.7
Same state..	2.9	3.3
Different state	2.1	2.4
Abroad..	0.6	0.4
Place of Birth		
Native born	7,132,149	286,623,642
Male...	49.4	49.7
Female..	50.6	50.3
Foreign born	2,134,981	45,270,103
Male...	48.7	48.7
Female..	51.3	51.3
Foreign born; naturalized U.S. citizen...................................	1,222,873	24,044,083
Male...	47.6	46.4
Female..	52.4	53.6
Foreign born; not a U.S. citizen...	912,108	21,226,020
Male...	50.3	51.2
Female..	49.7	48.8
Entered 2010 or later	29.4	28.1
Entered 2000 to 2009	23.7	23.7
Entered before 2000...	46.9	48.2
World Region of Birth, Foreign		
Foreign-born population, excluding population born at sea	2,134,981	45,269,644
Europe..	13.5	10.7
Asia..	32.3	31.0
Africa..	6.3	5.7
Oceania...	0.2	0.6
Latin America...	46.9	50.1
North America...	0.8	1.7
Language Spoken at Home and Ability to Speak English		
Population 5 years and over...	8,750,930	313,232,500
English only	68.3	78.4
Language other than English..	31.7	21.6
Speaks English less than "very well"..................................	12.1	8.3

Table NJ-5. Median Income and Poverty Status, 2021

(Number, percent, except as noted.)

Characteristic	State		U.S.	
	Number	Percent	Number	Percent
Median Income				
Households (dollars)..	89,296	X	69,717	X
Families (dollars)	110,102	X	85,806	X
Below Poverty Level (All People)	930,602	10.2	41,393,176	12.8
Sex				
Male	405,131	9.1	18,518,155	11.6
Female	525,471	11.3	22,875,021	13.9
Age				
Under 18 years..	284,150	14.2	12,243,219	16.9
Related children under 18 years.........................	277,497	14.0	11,985,424	16.6
18 to 64 years...	503,348	9.0	23,526,341	11.9
65 years and over	143,104	9.4	5,623,616	10.3

X = Not applicable.

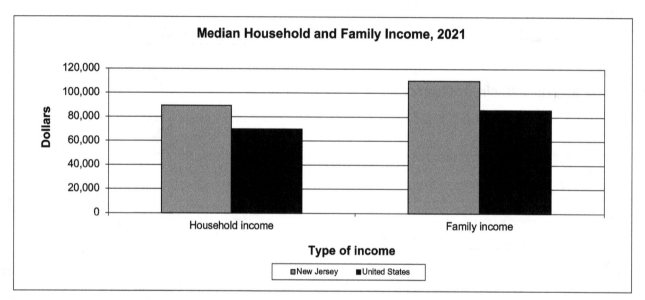

Table NJ-6. Health Insurance Coverage Status for the Civilian Noninstitutionalized Population and Children Under 19 Years of Age

(Number, percent.)

Item	2011	2012	2013	2014	2015	2016	2017	2018	2019	2020 [2]	2021
Civilian Noninstitutionalized Population	8,712,982	8,756,542	8,791,652	8,830,969	8,850,415	8,837,578	8,902,432	8,803,988	8,775,976	8,780,160	9,163,640
Covered by Private or Public Insurance											
Number..	7,573,878	7,643,733	7,631,358	7,865,558	8,079,219	8,132,608	8,214,364	8,148,988	8,083,635	8,117,243	8,506,912
Percent..	86.9	87.3	86.8	89.1	91.3	92.0	92.3	92.6	92.1	92.4	92.8
Uninsured											
Number..	1,139,104	1,112,809	1,160,294	965,411	771,196	704,970	688,068	655,000	692,341	662,917	656,728
Percent..	13.1	12.7	13.2	10.9	8.7	8.0	7.7	7.4	7.9	7.6	7.2
Percent in the U.S. not covered..............................	15.1	14.8	14.5	11.7	9.4	8.6	8.7	8.9	9.2	8.7	8.6
Children Under 19 Years of Age[1]	2,038,167	2,024,150	2,017,712	2,007,362	1,993,774	1,979,948	2,093,669	2,059,124	2,041,577	2,059,449	2,128,602
Covered by Private or Public Insurance											
Number..	1,933,002	1,921,334	1,905,595	1,915,520	1,919,180	1,909,909	2,015,469	1,979,363	1,953,456	1,978,171	2,052,837
Percent..	94.8	94.9	94.4	95.4	96.3	96.5	96.3	96.1	95.7	96.1	96.4
Uninsured											
Number..	105,165	102,816	112,117	91,842	74,594	70,039	78,200	79,761	88,121	81,278	75,765
Percent..	5.2	5.1	5.6	4.6	3.7	3.5	3.7	3.9	4.3	3.9	3.6
Percent in the U.S. not covered..............................	7.5	7.2	7.1	6.0	4.8	4.5	5.0	5.2	5.7	5.2	5.4

[1] 2017 data is for individuals under 19 years of age.
[2] 2020 ACS 5-Year estimates. 1-Year estimates were not released for 2020 due to the impact of COVID-19 on data collection that year. Data is not comparable to previous years, which are based on 1-year estimates.

Table NJ-7. Employment Status by Demographic Group, 2022

(Numbers in thousands, percent.)

Characteristic	Civilian noninstitutional population	Civilian labor force		Employed		Unemployed	
		Number	Percent of population	Number	Percent of population	Number	Percent of population
Total...	7,411	4,734	63.9	4,552	61.4	182	3.8
Sex							
Male...	3,597	2,541	70.6	2,437	67.8	104	4.1
Female...	3,814	2,193	57.5	2,115	55.5	78	3.6
Race, Sex, and Hispanic Origin							
White...	5,370	3,376	62.9	3,263	60.8	113	3.3
Male...	2,630	1,833	69.7	1,769	67.3	64	3.5
Female.....................................	2,740	1,543	56.3	1,493	54.5	49	3.2
Black or African American.................	1,084	723	66.6	676	62.4	46	6.4
Male...	500	352	70.4	326	65.2	26	7.3
Female.....................................	584	370	63.4	350	59.9	21	5.6
Hispanic or Latino ethnicity[1]............	1,510	1,056	69.9	1,016	67.3	40	3.8
Male...	750	594	79.2	571	76.2	23	3.8
Female.....................................	760	462	60.8	445	58.5	17	3.7
Age							
16 to 19 years..............................	505	172	33.9	157	31.0	15	8.6
20 to 24 years..............................	529	356	67.3	317	60.0	38	10.8
25 to 34 years..............................	1,142	979	85.8	940	82.3	39	4.0
35 to 44 years..............................	1,204	1,014	84.2	986	81.8	28	2.8
45 to 54 years..............................	1,136	979	86.2	951	83.7	28	2.8
55 to 64 years..............................	1,252	875	69.9	849	67.8	26	3.0
65 years and over.........................	1,642	359	21.9	352	21.4	7	2.0

NOTE: Data in Table 7 are from the Current Population Survey (CPS) and do not match the estimates in Table 8. See notes and definitions for further information.
[1] May be of any race.

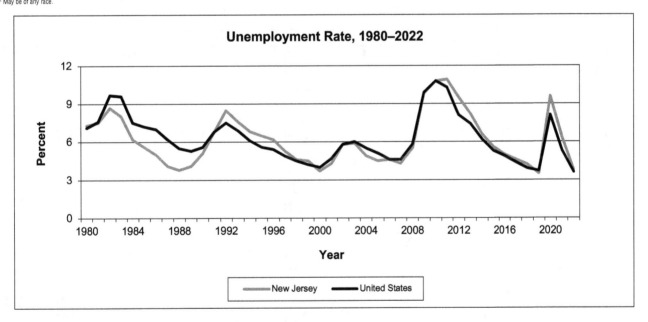

Unemployment Rate, 1980–2022

Table NJ-8. Employment Status of the Civilian Noninstitutional Population Age 16 Years and Over

(Number, percent.)

Year	Civilian labor force	Civilian participation rate	Employed	Unemployed	Unemployment rate
2010...	4,559,778	66.5	4,118,982	440,796	9.7
2011...	4,561,786	66.0	4,134,708	427,078	9.4
2012...	4,576,286	65.9	4,147,221	429,065	9.4
2013...	4,528,019	64.9	4,147,661	380,358	8.4
2014...	4,493,894	64.2	4,191,318	302,576	6.7
2015...	4,494,606	64.1	4,237,876	256,730	5.7
2016...	4,492,821	63.9	4,271,201	221,620	4.9
2017...	4,614,953	63.5	4,406,151	208,802	4.5
2018...	4,609,773	63	4,426,617	183,156	4.0
2019...	4,686,701	63.8	4,528,168	158,533	3.4
2020...	4,642,945	62.9	4,203,278	439,667	9.5
2021...	4,661,087	63.1	4,365,397	295,690	6.3
2022...	4,739,804	63.9	4,564,113	175,691	3.7

Table NJ-9. Employment and Average Wages by Industry

(Estimates are based on the 2012 North American Industry Classification System [NAICS].)

Industry	2014	2015	2016	2017	2018	2019	2020	2021
	Number of Jobs							
Wage and Salary Employment by Industry	4,010,203	4,061,862	4,123,132	4,174,996	4,221,213	4,261,715	3,920,973	4,100,453
Farm Wage and Salary Employment	9,552	9,252	11,166	10,756	8,865	8,136	6,858	8,489
Nonfarm Wage and Salary Employment	4,000,651	4,052,610	4,111,966	4,164,240	4,212,348	4,253,579	3,914,115	4,091,964
Private wage and salary employment	3,383,679	3,439,130	3,501,160	3,553,573	3,600,236	3,640,015	3,325,678	3,505,865
Forestry, fishing, and related activities	3,522	3,785	4,251	4,089	3,998	3,968	3,703	3,530
Mining	1,412	1,388	1,323	1,290	1,339	1,375	1,366	1,287
Utilities	13,659	14,208	14,174	14,180	15,273	14,707	13,955	14,186
Construction	144,904	151,919	157,215	159,593	161,771	164,232	155,785	161,441
Manufacturing	242,371	238,039	242,349	244,530	247,076	251,399	237,941	241,239
Durable goods manufacturing	108,906	109,329	110,017	111,336	115,301	116,705	109,608	111,129
Nondurable goods manufacturing	133,465	128,710	132,332	133,194	131,775	134,694	128,333	130,110
Wholesale trade	215,024	217,519	217,139	218,755	216,669	215,659	202,471	205,869
Retail trade	457,378	464,351	464,953	466,095	460,592	453,438	411,624	432,780
Transportation and warehousing	153,622	161,009	172,195	187,858	196,745	206,332	205,626	220,499
Information	75,507	74,437	73,264	70,987	69,894	67,979	68,241	70,822
Finance and insurance	184,597	189,520	191,194	196,766	197,633	198,746	196,938	201,087
Real estate and rental and leasing	55,509	56,949	58,483	59,759	61,267	63,335	57,779	59,366
Professional, scientific, and technical services	289,737	297,578	303,202	301,219	305,236	308,129	301,684	316,639
Management of companies and enterprises	79,003	79,991	80,733	83,389	84,378	86,624	84,694	83,660
Administrative and waste services	268,683	274,765	282,029	287,238	290,126	291,910	265,249	289,774
Educational services	97,744	99,396	101,924	103,260	103,689	105,743	94,964	106,260
Health care and social assistance	540,275	551,789	563,699	576,097	587,851	600,776	558,923	578,336
Arts, entertainment, and recreation	61,268	62,579	65,376	67,672	69,602	71,006	46,139	57,323
Accommodation and food services	298,823	299,157	306,793	310,914	320,871	325,669	240,082	275,390
Other services, except public administration	200,641	200,751	200,864	199,882	206,226	208,988	178,514	186,377
Government and government enterprises	616,972	613,480	610,806	610,667	612,112	613,564	588,437	586,099
	Dollars							
Average Wages and Salaries by Industry	59,968	61,775	62,270	63,563	65,241	66,868	73,234	75,614
Average Farm Wages and Salaries	24,962	21,052	20,018	18,860	23,621	20,436	23,546	19,110
Average Nonfarm Wages and Salaries	60,052	61,868	62,385	63,679	65,329	66,956	73,321	75,731
Average private wages and salaries	59,820	61,751	62,261	63,578	65,211	66,896	73,758	76,324
Forestry, fishing, and related activities	27,435	28,011	31,280	32,914	35,199	37,204	40,096	45,703
Mining	71,305	77,421	76,745	81,604	81,420	87,079	88,197	91,895
Utilities	113,032	116,156	118,690	120,284	123,274	122,246	130,481	128,167
Construction	64,990	67,612	68,730	71,115	72,667	74,653	78,020	80,236
Manufacturing	79,949	77,057	78,574	78,771	80,105	81,634	86,252	89,003
Durable goods manufacturing	72,136	73,705	75,390	77,739	80,331	79,752	82,808	85,567
Nondurable goods manufacturing	86,323	79,904	81,221	79,635	79,907	83,264	89,194	91,938
Wholesale trade	85,235	87,506	87,065	87,457	88,736	90,458	94,679	100,484
Retail trade	31,707	32,929	33,262	33,914	34,646	36,312	39,875	42,895
Transportation and warehousing	52,541	54,213	54,506	53,957	54,862	55,568	56,288	59,491
Information	98,928	102,954	105,041	108,470	114,617	117,566	130,535	145,659
Finance and insurance	115,946	120,813	122,880	127,795	131,150	134,595	145,190	152,651
Real estate and rental and leasing	60,365	63,656	62,872	64,042	67,046	67,407	74,053	76,268
Professional, scientific, and technical services	100,182	106,531	106,327	108,951	111,912	115,701	124,930	128,473
Management of companies and enterprises	151,816	159,410	160,244	167,189	170,595	174,833	183,214	184,388
Administrative and waste services	39,740	40,821	41,479	43,688	45,134	46,729	51,305	53,761
Educational services	41,313	42,341	42,787	42,811	44,493	44,870	50,693	47,616
Health care and social assistance	49,511	50,971	51,576	52,245	53,516	55,269	60,265	62,783
Arts, entertainment, and recreation	36,288	37,064	37,444	37,360	40,570	41,312	51,784	51,970
Accommodation and food services	24,517	24,651	25,262	25,681	27,469	27,201	26,845	32,432
Other services, except public administration	33,480	34,653	35,317	36,433	37,440	38,408	41,700	43,935
Government and government enterprises	61,322	62,526	63,094	64,267	66,020	67,313	70,855	72,184

Table NJ-10. Employment Characteristics by Family Type

(Number, percent.)

Family type and labor force status	2019		2020 [1]		2021	
	Total	Families with own children under 18 years	Total	Families with own children under 18 years	Total	Families with own children under 18 years
All Families...	2,241,555	931,496	2,247,306	959,366	2,379,328	997,844
FAMILY TYPE AND LABOR FORCE STATUS						
Opposite-Sex Married-Couple Families...........................	1,667,463	680,701	1,655,629	696,311	1,743,992	725,061
Both husband and wife in labor force	54.7	69.6	55.7	69.5	55.3	68.9
Husband in labor force, wife not in labor force	21.4	25.6	21.7	25.7	20.9	25.0
Wife in labor force, husband not in labor force	7.7	3.5	7.6	3.7	8.4	4.7
Both husband and wife not in labor force......................	15.3	1.0	15.0	1.0	15.4	1.4
Other Families	574,092	250,795	577,869	260,423	615,683	268,776
Female householder, no spouse present	71.3	74.6	72.6	75.4	71.9	74.5
In labor force...	52.3	65.0	52.8	64.6	50.8	62.0
Not in labor force	19.0	9.5	19.8	10.8	21.1	12.5
Male householder, no spouse present...........................	28.7	25.4	27.4	24.6	28.1	25.5
In labor force...	23.2	23.9	21.9	23.0	22.7	23.8
Not in labor force	5.5	1.5	5.5	1.6	5.4	1.8

[1] 2020 ACS 5-Year estimates. 1-Year estimates were not released for 2020 due to the impact of COVID-19 on data collection that year. Data is not comparable to previous years, which are based on 1-year estimates.

Table NJ-11. School Enrollment and Educational Attainment, 2021

(Number, percent.)

Item	State	U.S.
Enrollment		
Total population 3 years and over, enrolled in school	2,240,670	79,453,524
Enrolled in nursery school or preschool (percent)	6.3	5.2
Enrolled in kindergarten (percent)...	5.4	5.0
Enrolled in elementary school, grades 1-8 (percent)...	40.1	41.3
Enrolled in high school, grades 9-12 (percent)...	21.5	21.8
Enrolled in college or graduate school (percent)	26.8	26.7
Attainment		
Total population 25 years and over	6,474,427	228,193,464
Less than ninth grade (percent)	4.5	4.8
9th to 12th grade, no diploma (percent)	4.5	5.9
High school graduate, including equivalency (percent)...	25.5	26.3
Some college, no degree (percent)	15.4	19.3
Associate's degree (percent)	7.0	8.8
Bachelor's degree (percent)	25.7	21.2
Graduate or professional degree (percent)...	17.4	13.8
High school graduate or higher (percent)	91.0	89.4
Bachelor's degree or higher (percent)...	43.1	35.0

Table NJ-12. Public School Characteristics and Educational Indicators

(Number, percent; data derived from National Center of Education Statistics.)

Item	State	U.S.
Public Elementary and Secondary Schools		
Number of regular school districts, 2019-20	563	13,349
Number of operational schools, 2019-20...	2,565	98,469
Percent charter schools	3.4	7.7
Total public school enrollment, Fall 2021	1,372,381	49,433,092
Percent charter school enrollment	4.4	7.5
Student-teacher ratio, Fall 2019...	12.1	15.9
Expenditures per student (unadjusted dollars), 2019-20	21,385	13,489
Four-year adjusted cohort graduation rate (ACGR), 2019-2020[1]...	91.0	86.5
Students eligible for free or reduced-price lunch (percent), 2019-20...	38.2	52.1
English language learners (percent), Fall 2020	7.2	10.3
Students age 3 to 21 served under IDEA, part B (percent), 2021-22	17.4	14.7

Public Schools by Type, 2019-20	Number	Percent of state public schools
Total number of schools...	2,565	100.0
Special education...	61	2.4
Vocational education	70	2.7
Alternative education...	70	2.7

[1] Adjusted Cohort Graduation Rates (ACGR) differ from Averaged Freshmen Graduation Rates (AFGR).

Table NJ-13. Reported Voting and Registration of the Voting-Age Population, November 2022

(Numbers in thousands, percent.)

Item	Total population	Total citizen population	Registered			Voted		
			Total registered	Percent registered (total population)	Percent registered (total citizen population)	Total voted	Percent voted (total population)	Percent voted (total citizen population)
U.S. Total	255,457	233,546	161,422	63.2	69.1	121,916	47.7	52.2
State Total............................	7,163	6,241	4,402	61.5	70.5	3,151	44.0	50.5
Sex								
Male	3,487	3,029	2,081	59.7	68.7	1,482	42.5	48.9
Female	3,676	3,212	2,321	63.1	72.3	1,669	45.4	52.0
Race								
White alone............................	5,160	4,574	3,311	64.2	72.4	2,462	47.7	53.8
White, non-Hispanic alone	3,912	3,803	2,830	72.3	74.4	2,158	55.2	56.7
Black alone............................	1,047	931	617	58.9	66.3	388	37.1	41.7
Asian alone	799	615	400	50.0	65.0	258	32.3	42.0
Hispanic (of any race)	1,486	934	547	36.8	58.6	346	23.3	37.0
White alone or in combination..............	5,250	4,646	3,349	63.8	72.1	2,478	47.2	53.3
Black alone or in combination......................	1,100	973	640	58.2	65.8	398	36.2	40.9
Asian alone or in combination......................	822	631	416	50.6	65.9	264	32.2	41.9
Age								
18 to 24 years	740	654	411	55.4	62.8	200	27.0	30.5
25 to 34 years	1,139	847	500	43.9	59.0	247	21.7	29.2
35 to 44 years	1,244	973	640	51.4	65.8	409	32.9	42.1
45 to 64 years	2,519	2,281	1,676	66.6	73.5	1,319	52.4	57.8
65 years and over	1,521	1,487	1,175	77.3	79.1	976	64.2	65.7

Table NJ-14. Health Indicators

(Number, rate as indicated in footnotes.)

Item	State	U.S.
Births		
Life Expectancy at Birth (years), 2020	77.5	77.0
Fertility Rate by State[1], 2021...	58.0	56.3
Percent Home Births, 2021	0.6	1.4
Cesarean Delivery Rate[2], 2021	32.5	32.1
Preterm Birth Rate[3], 2021	9.2	10.5
Teen Birth Rate[4], 2021	7.9	13.9
Percentage of Babies Born Low Birthweight[5], 2021	7.7	8.5
Deaths[6]		
Heart Disease Mortality Rate, 2021...	157.5	173.8
Cancer Mortality Rate, 2021...	130.6	146.6
Stroke Mortality Rate, 2021..	32.3	41.1
Diabetes Mortality Rate, 2021...	17.6	25.4
Influenza/Pneumonia Mortality Rate, 2021	9.9	10.5
Suicide Mortality Rate, 2021...	7.1	14.1
Drug Overdose Mortality Rate, 2021...	32.4	33.6
Firearm Injury Mortality Rate, 2021..	5.2	14.6
Homicide Mortality Rate, 2021...	4.8	8.2
Disease and Illness		
Lifetime Asthma in Adults, 2020 (percent)...	12.6	13.9
Lifetime Asthma in Children, 2020 (percent)[7]	12.0	11.3
Diabetes in Adults, 2020 (percent)...	8.6	8.2
Self-reported Obesity in Adults, 2021 (percent)..	28.2	NA

SOURCE: National Center for Health Statistics, National Vital Statistics System 2020 data; https://wonder.cdc.gov.
[1] General fertility rate per 1,000 women aged 15–44.
[2] This represents the percentage of all live births that were cesarean deliveries.
[3] Babies born prior to 37 weeks of pregnancy (gestation).
[4] Number of births per 1,000 females aged 15–19
[5] Babies born weighing less than 2,500 grams or 5 lbs. 8oz.
[6] Death rates are the number of deaths per 100,000 total population.
[7] U.S. total includes data from 30 states and D.C.
NA = Not available.
- = Zero or rounds to zero.

Table NJ-15. State Government Finances, 2021

(Dollar amounts in thousands, percent distribution.)

Item	Dollars	Percent distribution
Total Revenue	95,472,433	100.0
General revenue	81,223,527	85.1
Intergovernmental revenue	24,884,158	26.1
Taxes	43,683,029	45.8
General sales	12,803,267	13.4
Selective sales	5,068,719	5.3
License taxes	1,986,338	2.1
Individual income tax	16,833,495	17.6
Corporate income tax	5,959,760	6.2
Other taxes	1,031,450	1.1
Current charges	6,691,812	7.0
Miscellaneous general revenue	5,964,528	6.2
Utility revenue	388,969	0.4
Liquor stores revenue	-	-
Insurance trust revenue[1]	13,859,937	14.5
Total Expenditure	88,176,004	100.0
Intergovernmental expenditure	17,321,885	19.6
Direct expenditure	70,854,119	80.4
Current operation	50,253,897	57.0
Capital outlay	4,247,241	4.8
Insurance benefits and repayments	12,272,129	13.9
Assistance and subsidies	1,717,952	1.9
Interest on debt	2,362,900	2.7
Exhibit: Salaries and wages	10,124,386	11.5
Total Expenditure	88,176,004	100.0
General expenditure	72,030,242	81.7
Intergovernmental expenditure	17,321,885	19.6
Direct expenditure	54,708,357	62.0
General expenditure, by function:		
Education	25,064,602	28.4
Public welfare	22,809,970	25.9
Hospitals	2,768,268	3.1
Health	1,887,939	2.1
Highways	3,242,927	3.7
Police protection	1,301,612	1.5
Correction	1,493,438	1.7
Natural resources	700,692	0.8
Parks and recreation	161,433	0.2
Governmental administration	2,277,477	2.6
Interest on general debt	2,362,457	2.7
Other and unallocable	7,797,481	8.8
Utility expenditure	3,873,633	4.1
Liquor stores expenditure	-	-
Insurance trust expenditure	12,272,129	13.9
Debt at End of Fiscal Year	70,952,710	X
Cash and Security Holdings	150,550,653	X

X = Not applicable.
- = Zero or rounds to zero.
[1] Within insurance trust revenue, net earnings of state retirement systems is a calculated statistic (the item code in the data file is X08), and thus can be positive or negative. Net earnings is the sum of earnings on investments plus gains on investments minus losses on investments. The change made in 2002 for asset valuation from book to market value in accordance with Statement 34 of the Governmental Accounting Standards Board is reflected in the calculated statistics.

Table NJ-16. State Government Tax Collections, 2022

(Dollars in thousands, percent.)

Item	Dollars	Percent distribution
Total Taxes	52,771,929	100.0
Property taxes	5,068	-
Sales and gross receipts	19,740,884	37.4
General sales and gross receipts	14,178,031	26.9
Selective sales and gross receipts	5,562,853	10.5
Alcoholic beverages	175,890	0.3
Amusements	386,996	0.7
Insurance premiums	747,723	1.4
Motor fuels	414,269	0.8
Pari-mutuels	X	-
Public utilities	949,949	1.8
Tobacco products	566,185	1.1
Other selective sales	2,321,841	4.4
Licenses	2,187,730	4.1
Alcoholic beverages	4,515	-
Amusements	54,590	0.1
Corporations in general	719,362	1.4
Hunting and fishing	14,272	-
Motor vehicle	662,194	1.3
Motor vehicle operators	58,724	0.1
Public utilities	20,961	-
Occupation and business, NEC	651,094	1.2
Other licenses	2,018	-
Income taxes	29,290,446	55.5
Individual income	20,630,297	39.1
Corporation net income	8,660,149	16.4
Other taxes	1,547,801	2.9
Death and gift	599,428	1.1
Documentary and stock transfer	948,373	1.8
Severance	X	-
Taxes, NEC	0	-

X = Not applicable.
- = Zero or rounds to zero.

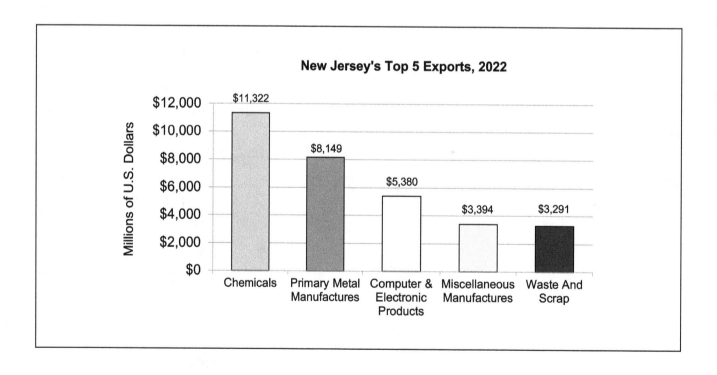

New Jersey's Top 5 Exports, 2022

NEW MEXICO

Facts and Figures

Location: Southwestern United States; bordered on the N by Colorado, on the E by Oklahoma and Texas, on the S by Texas and Mexico, and on the W by Arizona; New Mexico is one of the Four Corner states—at its NW corner it touches Arizona, Colorado, and Utah

Area: 121,590 sq. mi. (314,915 sq. km.); rank—5th

Population: 2,113,344 (2022 est.); rank—36th

Principal Cities: capital—Santa Fe; largest—Albuquerque

Statehood: January 6, 1912; 47th state

U.S. Congress: 2 senators, 3 representatives

State Motto: *Crescit eundo* ("It grows as it goes")

State Song: "O, Fair New Mexico"

State Nickname: The Land of Enchantment

Abbreviations: NM; N. Mex.

State Symbols: flower—yucca; tree—piñon; bird—roadrunner

At a Glance

- With an increase in population of 2.6 percent, New Mexico ranked 42nd among the states in growth from 2010 to 2022.

- In 2021, New Mexico's homicide rate of 15.3 deaths per 100,000 population ranked 5th in the nation.

- New Mexico had the 3rd highest percentage of residents living below the poverty level in 2021 (18.4 percent).

- In 2021, New Mexico's median household income was $53,992, which ranked 46th among the states. The national median was $69,717.

- With approximately 49.8 percent of its residents self-identifying as "Hispanic or Latino," New Mexico was the state with the highest percentage of this demographic in 2022.

Table NM-1. Population by Age, Sex, Race, and Hispanic Origin

(Number, percent, except where noted.)

Sex, age, race, and Hispanic origin	2010	2020	2022	Percent change, 2010–2022
Total Population..	2,059,179	2,117,527	2,113,344	2.6
Percent of total U.S. population	0.7	0.6	0.6	X
Sex				
Male..	1,017,421	1,055,364	1,053,151	3.5
Female	1,041,758	1,062,163	1,060,193	1.8
Age				
Under 5 years..	144,981	118,075	110,028	-24.1
Under 18 years..	518,672	478,287	459,513	-11.4
18 to 64 years...	1,268,252	1,257,314	1,250,428	-1.4
65 years and over..	272,255	381,926	403,403	48.2
Median age (years)	36.7	38.4	39.0	6.3
Race and Hispanic origin				
One race				
White	1,720,992	1,726,412	1,714,851	-0.4
Black	49,006	56,531	58,095	18.5
American Indian and Alaska Native	208,890	234,658	236,149	13.0
Asian..	31,253	39,232	41,247	32.0
Native Hawaiian or Other Pacific Islander	3,132	3,488	3,515	12.2
Two or more races	45,906	57,206	59,487	29.6
Hispanic (of any race)	953,403	1,053,350	1,059,865	11.2

NOTE: Population figures for 2022 are July 1 estimates. The 2010 and 2020 estimates are taken from the respective censuses.
- = Zero or rounds to zero.
X = Not applicable.

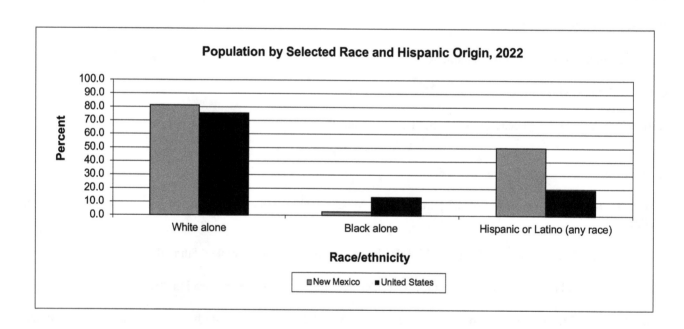

Population by Selected Race and Hispanic Origin, 2022

Table NM-2. Marital Status

(Number, percent distribution.)

Sex, age, race, and Hispanic origin	2000	2010	2021
Males, 15 Years and Over..	677,967	801,901	853,853
Never married	30.5	35.4	38.8
Now married, except separated..	55.0	48.4	46.0
Separated...	1.6	1.6	1.3
Widowed...	2.6	2.6	3.1
Divorced...	10.4	11.9	10.7
Females, 15 Years and Over..	720,529	833,357	874,360
Never married	24.7	29.9	31.6
Now married, except separated..	51.2	45.0	43.5
Separated...	2.0	2.6	1.9
Widowed...	9.4	8.5	8.2
Divorced...	12.8	14.1	14.8

Table NM-3. Households and Housing Characteristics

(Number, percent, dollars.)

Item	2000	2010	2021	Average annual percent change, 2010–2021
Total Households..	677,971	765,183	834,007	0.8
Family households	466,515	501,092	522,651	0.4
Married-couple family	341,818	349,344	357,938	0.2
Other family	124,697	151,748	164,713	0.8
Male householder, no wife present...	35,075	49,041	50,975	0.4
Female householder, no husband present...	89,622	102,707	113,738	1.0
Nonfamily households	211,456	264,091	311,356	1.6
Householder living alone...	172,181	216,704	257,954	1.7
Householder not living alone...	39,275	47,387	53,402	1.2
Housing Characteristics				
Total housing units	780,579	902,242	948,042	0.5
Occupied housing units	677,971	765,183	834,007	0.8
Owner occupied	474,445	519,864	579,708	1.0
Renter occupied	203,526	245,319	254,299	0.3
Average household size...	2.63	2.64	2.49	-0.5
Financial Characteristics				
Median gross rent of renter-occupied housing	503	699	906	2.7
Median monthly owner costs for housing units with a mortgage	929	1,202	1,354	1.1
Median value of owner-occupied housing units.......................................	108,100	161,200	214,000	3.0

Table NM-4. Migration, Origin, and Language

(Number, percent.)

Characteristic	State 2021	U.S. 2021
Residence 1 Year Ago		
Population 1 year and over	2,092,251	328,464,538
Same house	87.4	87.2
Different house in the U.S.	12.3	12.3
Same county	6.6	6.7
Different county	5.7	5.7
Same state	2.4	3.3
Different state	3.3	2.4
Abroad	0.3	0.4
Place of Birth		
Native born	1,923,243	286,623,642
Male	49.9	49.7
Female	50.1	50.3
Foreign born	192,634	45,270,103
Male	48.1	48.7
Female	51.9	51.3
Foreign born; naturalized U.S. citizen...	87,364	24,044,083
Male	46.5	46.4
Female	53.5	53.6
Foreign born; not a U.S. citizen	105,270	21,226,020
Male	49.4	51.2
Female	50.6	48.8
Entered 2010 or later	21.5	28.1
Entered 2000 to 2009	26.3	23.7
Entered before 2000..	52.2	48.2
World Region of Birth, Foreign		
Foreign-born population, excluding population born at sea	192,634	45,269,644
Europe	7.7	10.7
Asia...	12.8	31.0
Africa...	2.2	5.7
Oceania...	0.5	0.6
Latin America	75.2	50.1
North America	1.6	1.7
Language Spoken at Home and Ability to Speak English		
Population 5 years and over...	2,000,775	313,232,500
English only	68.8	78.4
Language other than English..	31.2	21.6
Speaks English less than "very well"...	8.5	8.3

Table NM-5. Median Income and Poverty Status, 2021

(Number, percent, except as noted.)

Characteristic	State		U.S.	
	Number	Percent	Number	Percent
Median Income				
Households (dollars)..	53,992	X	69,717	X
Families (dollars)	67,786	X	85,806	X
Below Poverty Level (All People)	382,798	18.4	41,393,176	12.8
Sex				
Male	174,749	17.1	18,518,155	11.6
Female	208,049	19.8	22,875,021	13.9
Age				
Under 18 years..	111,324	23.9	12,243,219	16.9
Related children under 18 years..................................	110,211	23.7	11,985,424	16.6
18 to 64 years...	221,954	18.2	23,526,341	11.9
65 years and over	49,520	12.8	5,623,616	10.3

X = Not applicable.

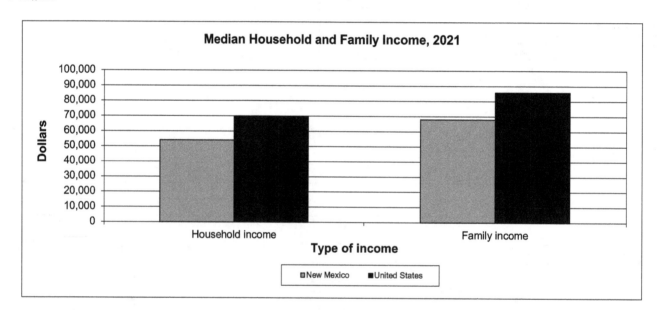

Table NM-6. Health Insurance Coverage Status for the Civilian Noninstitutionalized Population and Children Under 19 Years of Age

(Number, percent.)

Item	2011	2012	2013	2014	2015	2016	2017	2018	2019	2020 [2]	2021
Civilian Noninstitutionalized Population	2,047,242	2,051,805	2,051,900	2,050,369	2,050,178	2,046,001	2,054,301	2,060,718	2,058,918	2,060,539	2,077,326
Covered by Private or Public Insurance											
Number..	1,641,058	1,673,819	1,669,460	1,752,620	1,826,147	1,858,312	1,867,305	1,864,468	1,853,762	1,865,643	1,870,201
Percent...	80.2	81.6	81.4	85.5	89.1	90.8	90.9	90.5	90.0	90.5	90.0
Uninsured											
Number..	406,184	377,986	382,440	297,749	224,031	187,689	186,996	196,250	205,156	194,896	207,125
Percent...	19.8	18.4	18.6	14.5	10.9	9.2	9.1	9.5	10.0	9.5	10.0
Percent in the U.S. not covered.................................	15.1	14.8	14.5	11.7	9.4	8.6	8.7	8.9	9.2	8.7	8.6
Children Under 19 Years of Age[1]	516,787	515,341	506,951	498,680	498,415	488,598	522,820	510,645	501,566	510,571	503,467
Covered by Private or Public Insurance											
Number..	469,318	473,906	463,846	462,278	475,997	462,513	496,366	483,836	472,729	481,630	471,359
Percent...	90.8	92.0	91.5	92.7	95.5	94.7	94.9	94.7	94.3	94.3	93.6
Uninsured											
Number..	47,469	41,435	43,105	36,402	22,418	26,085	26,454	26,809	28,837	28,941	32,108
Percent...	9.2	8.0	8.5	7.3	4.5	5.3	5.1	5.3	5.7	5.7	6.4
Percent in the U.S. not covered.................................	7.5	7.2	7.1	6.0	4.8	4.5	5.0	5.2	5.7	5.2	5.4

[1] Data for years prior to 2017 are for individuals under 18 years of age.
[2] 2020 ACS 5-Year estimates. 1-Year estimates were not released for 2020 due to the impact of COVID-19 on data collection that year. Data is not comparable to previous years, which are based on 1-year estimates.

Table NM-7. Employment Status by Demographic Group, 2022

(Numbers in thousands, percent.)

Characteristic	Civilian noninstitutional population	Civilian labor force		Employed		Unemployed	
		Number	Percent of population	Number	Percent of population	Number	Percent of population
Total..	1,675	927	55.3	890	53.1	37	4.0
Sex							
Male..	818	493	60.4	472	57.8	21	4.3
Female...	857	433	50.5	418	48.7	16	3.6
Race, Sex, and Hispanic Origin							
White...	1,332	736	55.3	712	53.4	24	3.3
Male..	654	396	60.6	382	58.4	14	3.5
Female...	678	340	50.2	330	48.6	10	3.1
Black or African American.........................	NA	NA	NA	NA	NA	NA	NA
Male..	NA	NA	NA	NA	NA	NA	NA
Female...	NA	NA	NA	NA	NA	NA	NA
Hispanic or Latino ethnicity[1]	724	411	56.8	395	54.5	16	4.0
Male..	350	218	62.2	208	59.4	10	4.5
Female...	374	193	51.7	187	50.0	7	3.3
Age							
16 to 19 years.....................................	NA	NA	NA	NA	NA	NA	NA
20 to 24 years.....................................	132	93	70.5	87	65.8	6	6.7
25 to 34 years.....................................	256	197	77.2	190	74.4	7	3.6
35 to 44 years.....................................	269	212	78.8	206	76.6	6	2.9
45 to 54 years.....................................	231	174	75.5	169	73.1	5	3.1
55 to 64 years.....................................	258	153	59.1	149	57.5	4	2.7
65 years and over.................................	406	63	15.5	61	14.9	2	3.5

NOTE: Data in Table 7 are from the Current Population Survey (CPS) and do not match the estimates in Table 8. See notes and definitions for further information.
[1] May be of any race.
NA = Not available.

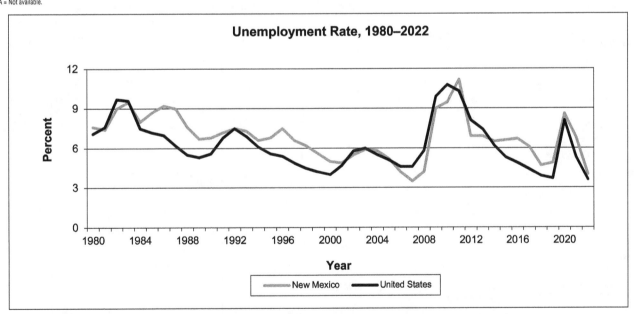

Unemployment Rate, 1980–2022

Table NM-8. Employment Status of the Civilian Noninstitutional Population Age 16 Years and Over

(Number, percent.)

Year	Civilian labor force	Civilian participation rate	Employed	Unemployed	Unemployment rate
2010..	928,862	59.5	856,602	72,260	7.8
2011..	925,108	58.4	858,165	66,943	7.2
2012..	928,762	58.3	863,937	64,825	7.0
2013..	929,410	58.1	865,207	64,203	6.9
2014..	931,950	58.1	870,570	61,380	6.6
2015..	938,300	58.3	876,206	62,094	6.6
2016..	944,245	58.4	880,515	63,730	6.7
2017..	948,581	58.3	890,988	57,593	6.1
2018..	950,366	58.1	903,757	46,609	4.9
2019..	963,804	58.6	916,149	47,655	4.9
2020..	935,706	56.5	860,105	75,601	8.1
2021..	943,356	56.7	879,329	64,027	6.8
2022..	947,025	56.5	908,870	38,155	4.0

Table NM-9. Employment and Average Wages by Industry

(Estimates are based on the 2012 North American Industry Classification System [NAICS].)

Industry	2014	2015	2016	2017	2018	2019	2020	2021
	Number of Jobs							
Wage and Salary Employment by Industry........................	852,348	860,023	861,222	862,272	876,083	889,967	834,033	846,784
Farm Wage and Salary Employment...............................	6,789	7,461	8,350	7,261	7,435	6,929	7,233	6,644
Nonfarm Wage and Salary Employment..........................	845,559	852,562	852,872	855,011	868,648	883,038	826,800	840,140
Private wage and salary employment.............................	636,207	643,993	644,350	648,726	662,478	675,090	625,136	641,337
Forestry, fishing, and related activities	3,369	3,534	3,617	3,549	3,491	3,447	3,228	2,947
Mining..	27,679	25,328	19,693	20,925	24,446	25,824	19,860	18,451
Utilities..	4,418	4,384	4,441	4,353	4,316	4,215	4,155	4,241
Construction...	43,838	44,627	44,365	46,562	48,374	51,257	49,745	48,799
Manufacturing...	28,019	27,818	26,847	26,412	27,159	28,502	27,243	27,699
Durable goods manufacturing................................	17,293	16,880	15,621	15,040	15,325	15,840	14,987	15,060
Nondurable goods manufacturing..........................	10,726	10,938	11,226	11,372	11,834	12,662	12,256	12,639
Wholesale trade...	21,716	21,544	21,516	21,174	21,082	21,449	20,266	19,776
Retail trade..	93,371	94,387	93,999	91,813	92,021	90,296	87,133	90,882
Transportation and warehousing................................	19,851	20,275	19,509	19,754	21,106	21,517	20,944	22,264
Information...	12,564	12,735	13,063	12,421	12,012	11,171	9,082	10,315
Finance and insurance	22,870	23,173	23,476	23,978	24,089	24,648	24,271	23,650
Real estate and rental and leasing.............................	10,159	10,267	10,224	10,145	10,506	10,961	10,340	10,134
Professional, scientific, and technical services.................	53,006	53,958	54,674	56,148	57,747	60,274	60,603	61,834
Management of companies and enterprises......................	5,055	5,177	5,312	5,383	5,649	5,821	5,565	5,447
Administrative and waste services..............................	41,799	41,424	41,813	43,432	44,273	45,914	42,138	44,428
Educational services	10,253	10,138	10,081	10,065	9,582	9,841	8,707	9,750
Health care and social assistance..............................	109,707	114,570	119,340	119,784	120,863	122,135	119,181	120,807
Arts, entertainment, and recreation............................	9,169	9,521	9,563	10,010	10,204	10,976	7,218	8,774
Accommodation and food services.............................	82,358	84,357	86,510	86,874	88,158	88,944	72,030	77,549
Other services, except public administration...................	37,006	36,776	36,307	35,944	37,400	37,898	33,427	33,590
Government and government enterprises......................	209,352	208,569	208,522	206,285	206,170	207,948	201,664	198,803
	Dollars							
Average Wages and Salaries by Industry	42,950	43,538	43,653	44,725	46,371	48,095	51,426	53,867
Average Farm Wages and Salaries	38,591	29,719	30,742	35,556	36,383	27,950	35,665	45,144
Average Nonfarm Wages and Salaries	42,985	43,659	43,779	44,803	46,456	48,253	51,564	53,936
Average private wages and salaries.............................	41,997	42,577	42,447	43,539	45,299	47,149	50,169	52,611
Forestry, fishing, and related activities	23,532	24,613	26,570	27,785	30,333	32,850	35,248	37,528
Mining..	77,569	76,469	75,594	77,618	81,149	85,289	84,314	90,888
Utilities..	79,459	81,273	82,243	82,452	84,434	88,230	92,308	94,721
Construction...	43,427	44,347	45,205	47,223	50,195	52,893	54,389	56,473
Manufacturing...	58,810	59,086	57,418	55,153	54,955	57,506	60,599	60,779
Durable goods manufacturing................................	66,134	65,449	65,920	61,552	61,758	65,247	68,682	69,424
Nondurable goods manufacturing..........................	47,000	49,267	45,588	46,691	46,145	47,822	50,714	50,479
Wholesale trade...	53,311	54,299	53,913	55,373	57,262	60,449	62,425	66,359
Retail trade..	27,909	28,790	29,056	29,748	30,583	30,903	32,853	35,446
Transportation and warehousing................................	52,104	52,244	50,140	52,760	56,039	57,489	57,993	58,501
Information...	49,723	52,678	53,210	53,172	55,207	59,797	64,966	74,193
Finance and insurance	59,661	61,931	61,721	62,793	65,289	67,009	72,142	76,275
Real estate and rental and leasing.............................	37,863	38,619	38,090	39,900	41,420	43,172	45,484	48,271
Professional, scientific, and technical services.................	75,202	76,772	78,775	80,140	82,073	84,244	89,565	92,744
Management of companies and enterprises......................	69,820	70,353	67,972	70,062	71,853	76,079	85,918	91,265
Administrative and waste services..............................	34,620	35,212	35,218	36,290	37,606	39,571	43,301	47,059
Educational services	32,897	33,245	34,494	34,873	37,043	37,487	42,842	40,288
Health care and social assistance..............................	40,641	41,234	41,353	42,132	43,150	44,307	46,608	48,285
Arts, entertainment, and recreation............................	24,008	24,311	23,914	24,675	26,168	28,029	32,072	34,154
Accommodation and food services.............................	18,880	19,255	19,726	20,185	21,318	22,148	21,296	26,077
Other services, except public administration...................	28,672	29,503	30,087	31,700	32,961	33,777	37,596	40,131
Government and government enterprises......................	45,989	47,001	47,894	48,779	50,175	51,838	55,887	58,208

Table NM-10. Employment Characteristics by Family Type

(Number, percent.)

Family type and labor force status	2019 Total	2019 Families with own children under 18 years	2020 [1] Total	2020 [1] Families with own children under 18 years	2021 Total	2021 Families with own children under 18 years
All Families...	496,961	198,891	496,734	199,483	522,651	208,332
FAMILY TYPE AND LABOR FORCE STATUS						
Opposite-Sex Married-Couple Families...	331,505	114,145	336,492	117,177	352,696	121,335
Both husband and wife in labor force................................	41.3	60.0	42.5	59.7	42.2	59.9
Husband in labor force, wife not in labor force	23.5	30.2	23.3	30.9	21.5	31.4
Wife in labor force, husband not in labor force	9.1	6.9	9.7	6.4	10.3	6.6
Both husband and wife not in labor force.........................	24.7	2.6	24.5	3.0	26.0	2.1
Other Families	165,456	84,746	155,998	81,426	164,713	86,136
Female householder, no spouse present	70.5	71.7	69.5	70.4	69.1	70.2
In labor force...	49.2	59.4	47.0	56.6	47.2	58.5
Not in labor force...	21.3	12.3	22.5	13.8	21.9	11.6
Male householder, no spouse present...........................	29.5	28.3	30.5	29.6	30.9	29.8
In labor force...	22.2	25.2	22.8	25.9	23.0	26.5
Not in labor force...	7.3	3.1	7.7	3.7	7.9	3.4

[1] 2020 ACS 5-Year estimates. 1-Year estimates were not released for 2020 due to the impact of COVID-19 on data collection that year. Data is not comparable to previous years, which are based on 1-year estimates.

Table NM-11. School Enrollment and Educational Attainment, 2021

(Number, percent.)

Item	State	U.S.
Enrollment		
Total population 3 years and over, enrolled in school	495,428	79,453,524
Enrolled in nursery school or preschool (percent)	3.7	5.2
Enrolled in kindergarten (percent)...	5.1	5.0
Enrolled in elementary school, grades 1-8 (percent).........................	42.7	41.3
Enrolled in high school, grades 9-12 (percent).........................	23.1	21.8
Enrolled in college or graduate school (percent).........................	25.4	26.7
Attainment		
Total population 25 years and over	1,450,549	228,193,464
Less than ninth grade (percent)..	5.1	4.8
9th to 12th grade, no diploma (percent)...................................	7.4	5.9
High school graduate, including equivalency (percent)..................	25.7	26.3
Some college, no degree (percent)	22.7	19.3
Associate's degree (percent)...	9.1	8.8
Bachelor's degree (percent)..	16.0	21.2
Graduate or professional degree (percent)................................	14.1	13.8
High school graduate or higher (percent)..................................	87.5	89.4
Bachelor's degree or higher (percent)......................................	30.1	35.0

Table NM-12. Public School Characteristics and Educational Indicators

(Number, percent; data derived from National Center of Education Statistics.)

Item	State	U.S.
Public Elementary and Secondary Schools		
Number of regular school districts, 2019-20	89	13,349
Number of operational schools, 2019-20...	884	98,469
Percent charter schools	11.0	7.7
Total public school enrollment, Fall 2021	316,785	49,433,092
Percent charter school enrollment	9.5	7.5
Student-teacher ratio, Fall 2019	15.2	15.9
Expenditures per student (unadjusted dollars), 2019-20	11,617	13,489
Four-year adjusted cohort graduation rate (ACGR), 2019-2020[1].............	76.9	86.5
Students eligible for free or reduced-price lunch (percent), 2019-20..........	71.9	52.1
English language learners (percent), Fall 2020	16.0	10.3
Students age 3 to 21 served under IDEA, part B (percent), 2021-22	17.1	14.7

Public Schools by Type, 2019-20	Number	Percent of state public schools
Total number of schools...	884	100.0
Special education...	9	1.0
Vocational education...	-	-
Alternative education...	45	5.1

[1] Adjusted Cohort Graduation Rates (ACGR) differ from Averaged Freshmen Graduation Rates (AFGR).
- = Zero or rounds to zero.

Table NM-13. Reported Voting and Registration of the Voting-Age Population, November 2022

(Numbers in thousands, percent.)

Item	Total population	Total citizen population	Registered			Voted		
			Total registered	Percent registered (total population)	Percent registered (total citizen population)	Total voted	Percent voted (total population)	Percent voted (total citizen population)
U.S. Total	255,457	233,546	161,422	63.2	69.1	121,916	47.7	52.2
State Total	1,625	1,511	1,026	63.1	67.9	818	50.3	54.1
Sex								
Male	783	721	478	61.0	66.3	376	48.0	52.2
Female	842	790	548	65.1	69.4	442	52.4	55.9
Race								
White alone................................	1,275	1,177	822	64.5	69.9	667	52.3	56.7
White, non-Hispanic alone..................	641	634	510	79.5	80.4	440	68.6	69.4
Black alone................................	46	46	33	72.6	72.6	25	54.1	54.1
Asian alone................................	32	26	17	53.5	66.1	14	43.1	53.2
Hispanic (of any race)................	701	602	345	49.2	57.3	254	36.3	42.2
White alone or in combination..........	1,311	1,213	849	64.7	70.0	684	52.2	56.4
Black alone or in combination..........	59	59	44	75.2	75.2	32	54.4	54.4
Asian alone or in combination..........	36	30	19	51.5	61.8	14	37.5	44.9
Age								
18 to 24 years................................	175	171	78	44.8	45.8	56	32.0	32.7
25 to 34 years................................	300	275	150	50.1	54.6	93	31.0	33.8
35 to 44 years................................	251	231	157	62.5	68.0	107	42.5	46.3
45 to 64 years................................	486	436	333	68.6	76.5	285	58.6	65.4
65 years and over	413	398	307	74.3	77.2	277	67.0	69.6

B = Base is less than 75,000 and therefore too small to show the derived measure.

Table NM-14. Health Indicators

(Number, rate as indicated in footnotes.)

Item	State	U.S.
Births		
Life Expectancy at Birth (years), 2020	74.5	77.0
Fertility Rate by State[1], 2021	52.9	56.3
Percent Home Births, 2021	1.9	1.4
Cesarean Delivery Rate[2], 2021	27.3	32.1
Preterm Birth Rate[3], 2021	10.0	10.5
Teen Birth Rate[4], 2021	19.0	13.9
Percentage of Babies Born Low Birthweight[5], 2021	9.4	8.5
Deaths[6]		
Heart Disease Mortality Rate, 2021................................	156.5	173.8
Cancer Mortality Rate, 2021................................	137.3	146.6
Stroke Mortality Rate, 2021................................	37.2	41.1
Diabetes Mortality Rate, 2021................................	31.0	25.4
Influenza/Pneumonia Mortality Rate, 2021	11.5	10.5
Suicide Mortality Rate, 2021................................	25.0	14.1
Drug Overdose Mortality Rate, 2021................	51.6	33.6
Firearm Injury Mortality Rate, 2021................	27.8	14.6
Homicide Mortality Rate, 2021................................	15.3	8.2
Disease and Illness		
Lifetime Asthma in Adults, 2020 (percent)................	14.2	13.9
Lifetime Asthma in Children, 2020 (percent)[7]	10.7	11.3
Diabetes in Adults, 2020 (percent)................	11.0	8.2
Self-reported Obesity in Adults, 2021 (percent)................	34.6	NA

SOURCE: National Center for Health Statistics, National Vital Statistics System 2020 data; https://wonder.cdc.gov.
[1] General fertility rate per 1,000 women aged 15–44.
[2] This represents the percentage of all live births that were cesarean deliveries.
[3] Babies born prior to 37 weeks of pregnancy (gestation).
[4] Number of births per 1,000 females aged 15–19
[5] Babies born weighing less than 2,500 grams or 5 lbs. 8oz.
[6] Death rates are the number of deaths per 100,000 total population.
[7] U.S. total includes data from 30 states and D.C.
NA = Not available.
- = Zero or rounds to zero.

Table NM-15. State Government Finances, 2021

(Dollar amounts in thousands, percent distribution.)

Item	Dollars	Percent distribution
Total Revenue	28,013,443	100.0
General revenue	25,398,916	90.7
Intergovernmental revenue	12,146,268	43.4
Taxes	7,471,575	26.7
General sales	2,971,970	10.6
Selective sales	850,605	3.0
License taxes	343,487	1.2
Individual income tax	1,198,906	4.3
Corporate income tax	152,728	0.5
Other taxes	1,953,879	7.0
Current charges	2,165,462	7.7
Miscellaneous general revenue	3,615,611	12.9
Utility revenue	-	-
Liquor stores revenue	-	-
Insurance trust revenue[1]	2,614,527	9.3
Total Expenditure	27,742,123	100.0
Intergovernmental expenditure	6,233,442	22.5
Direct expenditure	21,508,681	77.5
Current operation	15,887,787	57.3
Capital outlay	988,215	3.6
Insurance benefits and repayments	3,789,787	13.7
Assistance and subsidies	320,704	1.2
Interest on debt	522,188	1.9
Exhibit: Salaries and wages	2,806,134	10.1
Total Expenditure	27,742,123	100.0
General expenditure	23,949,330	86.3
Intergovernmental expenditure	6,233,442	22.5
Direct expenditure	17,715,888	63.9
General expenditure, by function:		
Education	6,521,748	23.5
Public welfare	8,228,629	29.7
Hospitals	1,617,017	5.8
Health	472,632	1.7
Highways	966,928	3.5
Police protection	184,120	0.7
Correction	538,858	1.9
Natural resources	254,164	0.9
Parks and recreation	72,010	0.3
Governmental administration	789,592	2.8
Interest on general debt	522,188	1.9
Other and unallocable	3,664,972	13.2
Utility expenditure	25,321	0.1
Liquor stores expenditure	-	-
Insurance trust expenditure	3,789,787	13.7
Debt at End of Fiscal Year	7,434,683	X
Cash and Security Holdings	82,063,216	X

X = Not applicable.
- = Zero or rounds to zero.
[1] Within insurance trust revenue, net earnings of state retirement systems is a calculated statistic (the item code in the data file is X08), and thus can be positive or negative. Net earnings is the sum of earnings on investments plus gains on investments minus losses on investments. The change made in 2002 for asset valuation from book to market value in accordance with Statement 34 of the Governmental Accounting Standards Board is reflected in the calculated statistics.

Table NM-16. State Government Tax Collections, 2022

(Dollars in thousands, percent.)

Item	Dollars	Percent distribution
Total Taxes	8,601,717	100.0
Property taxes	116,584	1.4
Sales and gross receipts	4,187,126	48.7
General sales and gross receipts	3,291,197	38.3
Selective sales and gross receipts	895,929	10.4
Alcoholic beverages	21,719	0.3
Amusements	69,276	0.8
Insurance premiums	235,866	2.7
Motor fuels	266,949	3.1
Pari-mutuels	1,184	-
Public utilities	35,695	0.4
Tobacco products	101,968	1.2
Other selective sales	163,272	1.9
Licenses	372,541	4.3
Alcoholic beverages	-	-
Amusements	2,175	-
Corporations in general	50,255	0.6
Hunting and fishing	29,415	0.3
Motor vehicle	223,076	2.6
Motor vehicle operators	13,550	0.2
Public utilities	1,856	-
Occupation and business, NEC	52,214	0.6
Other licenses	-	-
Income taxes	1,611,166	18.7
Individual income	1,301,085	15.1
Corporation net income	310,081	3.6
Other taxes	2,314,300	26.9
Death and gift	X	-
Documentary and stock transfer	X	-
Severance	2,250,072	26.2
Taxes, NEC	64,228	

- = Zero or rounds to zero.

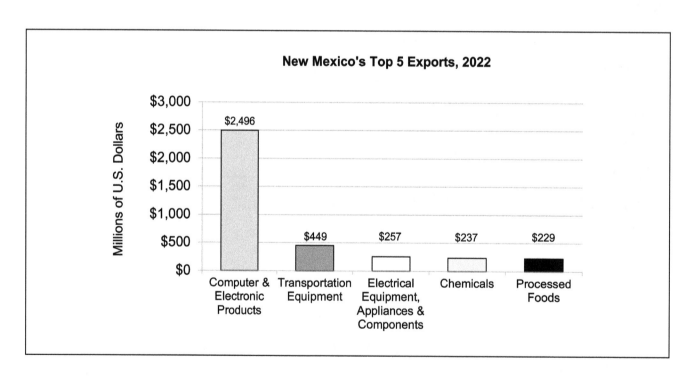

New Mexico's Top 5 Exports, 2022

NEW YORK

Facts and Figures

Location: Northeastern United States; bordered on the N by Canada (Ontario and Quebec) and Lake Ontario; on the E by Vermont, Massachusetts, and Connecticut; on the S by New Jersey and Pennsylvania; and on the W by Pennsylvania, Lake Erie, Canada (Ontario), and Lake Ontario

Area: 54,556 sq. mi. (141,299 sq. km.); rank—27th

Population: 19,677,151 (2022 est.); rank—4th

Principal Cities: capital—Albany; largest—New York City

Statehood: July 26, 1788; 11th state

U.S. Congress: 2 senators, 27 representatives

State Motto: *Excelsior* ("Ever upward")

State Song: "I Love New York"

State Nickname: The Empire State

Abbreviations: NY; N.Y.

State Symbols: flower—rose; tree—sugar maple; bird—bluebird

At a Glance

- With an increase in population of 1.5 percent, New York ranked 45th for population growth from 2010 to 2022.

- In 2021, 5.2 percent of New Yorkers did not have health insurance, compared to 8.6 percent of the total U.S. population.

- New York had the 2nd lowest homeownership rate in 2022, with 53.9 percent of homes being owner-occupied.

- New York's homicide rate was 4.8 deaths per 100,000 population in 2021, compared to the national rate of 8.2 deaths per 100,000 population.

- New York's GDP of $1.6 trillion (in chained 2012 dollars) comprised 7.8 percent of the nation's total GDP in 2022.

Table NY-1. Population by Age, Sex, Race, and Hispanic Origin

(Number, percent, except where noted.)

Sex, age, race, and Hispanic origin	2010	2020	2022	Percent change, 2010–2022
Total Population...	19,378,102	20,201,230	19,677,151	1.5
Percent of total U.S. population	6.3	6.1	5.9	X
Sex				
Male..	9,377,147	9,888,029	9,626,210	2.7
Female	10,000,955	10,313,201	10,050,941	0.5
Age				
Under 5 years..	1,155,822	1,146,450	1,059,217	-8.4
Under 18 years...	4,324,929	4,187,251	3,989,288	-7.8
18 to 64 years...	12,435,230	12,599,630	12,124,287	-2.5
65 years and over	2,617,943	3,414,349	3,563,576	36.1
Median age (years)	38.0	39.2	39.9	5.0
Race and Hispanic Origin				
One race				
White	13,901,661	13,927,282	13,501,459	-2.9
Black	3,378,047	3,606,651	3,491,532	3.4
American Indian and Alaska Native	183,046	205,884	205,972	12.5
Asian	1,481,555	1,888,277	1,894,327	27.9
Native Hawaiian or Other Pacific Islander	24,000	29,096	28,627	19.3
Two or more races	409,793	544,040	555,234	35.5
Hispanic (of any race)......................................	3,416,922	3,942,705	3,867,076	13.2

NOTE: Population figures for 2022 are July 1 estimates. The 2010 and 2020 estimates are taken from the respective censuses.
- = Zero or rounds to zero.
X = Not applicable.

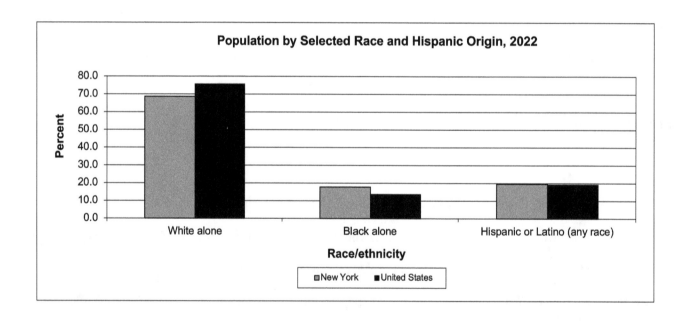

Table NY-2. Marital Status

(Number, percent distribution.)

Sex, age, race, and Hispanic origin	2000	2010	2021
Males, 15 Years and Over	7,125,715	7,586,733	7,957,806
Never married	34.7	40.5	41.3
Now married, except separated......................................	53.3	47.6	46.9
Separated..	2.7	2.2	1.8
Widowed..	2.8	2.6	2.5
Divorced..	6.5	7.2	7.4
Females, 15 Years and Over	7,932,161	8,283,542	8,485,443
Never married	29.0	34.8	36.2
Now married, except separated......................................	47.1	42.8	42.0
Separated..	3.7	3.1	2.5
Widowed..	11.2	9.6	8.5
Divorced..	8.9	9.7	10.8

Table NY-3. Households and Housing Characteristics

(Number, percent, dollars.)

Item	2000	2010	2021	Average annual percent change, 2010–2021
Total Households..	7,056,860	7,196,427	7,652,666	0.6
Family households	4,639,387	4,632,676	4,715,750	0.2
Married-couple family	3,289,514	3,210,895	3,268,729	0.2
Other family	1,349,873	1,421,781	1,447,021	0.2
Male householder, no wife present...................................	311,697	355,236	395,689	1.0
Female householder, no husband present..........................	1,038,176	1,066,545	1,051,332	-0.1
Nonfamily households	2,417,473	2,563,751	2,936,916	1.3
Householder living alone	1,982,742	2,089,816	2,365,770	1.2
Householder not living alone	434,731	473,935	571,146	1.9
Housing Characteristics				
Total housing units...	7,679,301	8,108,211	8,530,561	0.5
Occupied housing units	7,056,860	7,196,427	7,652,666	0.6
Owner occupied	3,739,166	3,904,123	4,239,037	0.8
Renter occupied	3,317,694	3,292,304	3,413,629	0.3
Average household size..	2.61	2.61	2.52	-0.3
Financial Characteristics				
Median gross rent of renter-occupied housing	627	1,020	1,409	3.5
Median monthly owner costs for housing units with a mortgage	1,357	1,963	2,199	1.1
Median value of owner-occupied housing units...................	148,700	296,500	368,800	2.2

Table NY-4. Migration, Origin, and Language

(Number, percent.)

Characteristic	State 2021	U.S. 2021
Residence 1 Year Ago		
Population 1 year and over	19,626,300	328,464,538
Same house	89.6	87.2
Different house in the U.S...	10.0	12.3
Same county	5.7	6.7
Different county	4.3	5.7
Same state	2.8	3.3
Different state	1.5	2.4
Abroad	0.5	0.4
Place of Birth		
Native born	15,408,557	286,623,642
Male	49.4	49.7
Female	50.6	50.3
Foreign born	4,427,356	45,270,103
Male	47.2	48.7
Female	52.8	51.3
Foreign born; naturalized U.S. citizen................................	2,671,070	24,044,083
Male	45.1	46.4
Female	54.9	53.6
Foreign born; not a U.S. citizen..	1,756,286	21,226,020
Male	50.3	51.2
Female	49.7	48.8
Entered 2010 or later	25.7	28.1
Entered 2000 to 2009	22.2	23.7
Entered before 2000..	52.1	48.2
World Region of Birth, Foreign		
Foreign-born population, excluding population born at sea	4,427,154	45,269,644
Europe	15.8	10.7
Asia...	29.1	31.0
Africa	4.6	5.7
Oceania	0.3	0.6
Latin America	48.8	50.1
North America	1.2	1.7
Language Spoken at Home and Ability to Speak English		
Population 5 years and over..	18,743,215	313,232,500
English only	70.0	78.4
Language other than English..	30.0	21.6
Speaks English less than "very well"..............................	13.0	8.3

Table NY-5. Median Income and Poverty Status, 2021

(Number, percent, except as noted.)

Characteristic	State Number	State Percent	U.S. Number	U.S. Percent
Median Income				
Households (dollars)..	74,314	X	69,717	X
Families (dollars)	92,454	X	85,806	X
Below Poverty Level (All People)	2,688,587	13.9	41,393,176	12.8
Sex				
Male	1,209,895	12.9	18,518,155	11.6
Female	1,478,692	14.9	22,875,021	13.9
Age				
Under 18 years..	746,684	18.5	12,243,219	16.9
Related children under 18 years........................	734,406	18.3	11,985,424	16.6
18 to 64 years...	1,527,562	12.8	23,526,341	11.9
65 years and over	414,341	12.2	5,623,616	10.3

X = Not applicable.

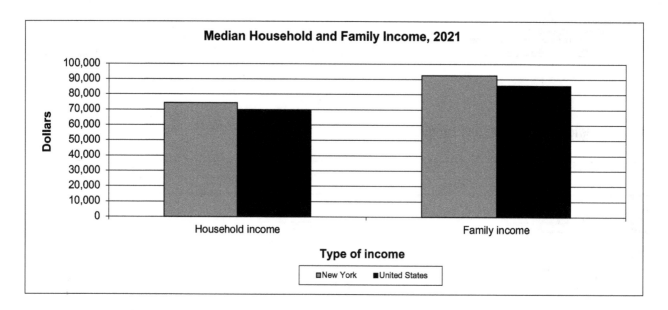

Table NY-6. Health Insurance Coverage Status for the Civilian Noninstitutionalized Population and Children Under 19 Years of Age

(Number, percent.)

Item	2011	2012	2013	2014	2015	2016	2017	2018	2019	2020 [2]	2021
Civilian Noninstitutionalized Population	19,208,419	19,316,728	19,400,069	19,499,548	19,556,452	19,505,596	19,608,066	19,302,636	19,212,803	19,276,809	19,599,048
Covered by Private or Public Insurance											
Number..	17,013,070	17,213,819	17,330,548	17,802,989	18,175,904	18,322,902	18,495,124	18,261,403	18,206,275	18,239,538	18,579,761
Percent...	88.6	89.1	89.3	91.3	92.9	93.9	94.3	94.6	94.8	94.6	94.8
Uninsured											
Number..	2,195,349	2,102,909	2,069,521	1,696,559	1,380,548	1,182,694	1,112,942	1,041,233	1,006,528	1,037,271	1,019,287
Percent...	11.4	10.9	10.7	8.7	7.1	6.1	5.7	5.4	5.2	5.4	5.2
Percent in the U.S. not covered...............................	15.1	14.8	14.5	11.7	9.4	8.6	8.7	8.9	9.2	8.7	8.6
Children Under 19 Years of Age [1]	4,270,110	4,252,821	4,230,975	4,217,078	4,204,378	4,170,786	4,403,144	4,306,394	4,264,419	4,310,934	4,357,303
Covered by Private or Public Insurance											
Number..	4,089,276	4,085,154	4,060,192	4,079,553	4,100,735	4,069,720	4,285,641	4,199,013	4,163,624	4,202,562	4,241,922
Percent...	95.8	96.1	96.0	96.7	97.5	97.6	97.3	97.5	97.6	97.5	97.4
Uninsured											
Number..	180,834	167,667	170,783	137,525	103,643	101,066	117,503	107,381	100,795	108,372	115,381
Percent...	4.2	3.9	4.0	3.3	2.5	2.4	2.7	2.5	2.4	2.5	2.6
Percent in the U.S. not covered...............................	7.5	7.2	7.1	6.0	4.8	4.5	5.0	5.2	5.7	5.2	5.4

[1] Data for years prior to 2017 are for individuals under 18 years of age.
[2] 2020 ACS 5-Year estimates. 1-Year estimates were not released for 2020 due to the impact of COVID-19 on data collection that year. Data is not comparable to previous years, which are based on 1-year estimates.

Table NY-7. Employment Status by Demographic Group, 2022

(Numbers in thousands, percent.)

Characteristic	Civilian noninstitutional population	Civilian labor force		Employed		Unemployed	
		Number	Percent of population	Number	Percent of population	Number	Percent of population
Total..	15,796	9,531	60.3	9,109	57.7	422	4.4
Sex							
Male...	7,609	4,998	65.7	4,773	62.7	225	4.5
Female..	8,187	4,533	55.4	4,336	53.0	197	4.3
Race, Sex, and Hispanic Origin							
White	10,980	6,651	60.6	6,418	58.5	233	3.5
Male...	5,366	3,545	66.1	3,415	63.6	129	3.6
Female......................................	5,614	3,106	55.3	3,003	53.5	103	3.3
Black or African American..................	2,684	1,584	59.0	1,446	53.9	138	8.7
Male...	1,215	776	63.9	706	58.1	70	9.1
Female......................................	1,468	808	55.0	740	50.4	68	8.4
Hispanic or Latino ethnicity[1]	2,709	1,646	60.8	1,548	57.1	98	6.0
Male...	1,332	882	66.2	827	62.1	56	6.3
Female......................................	1,377	764	55.5	721	52.4	42	5.5
Age							
16 to 19 years...............................	936	270	28.9	234	25.0	36	13.4
20 to 24 years...............................	1,234	774	62.7	686	55.6	88	11.3
25 to 34 years...............................	2,668	2,225	83.4	2,121	79.5	104	4.7
35 to 44 years...............................	2,471	2,036	82.4	1,973	79.8	63	3.1
45 to 54 years...............................	2,375	1,896	79.8	1,832	77.1	64	3.4
55 to 64 years...............................	2,611	1,646	63.0	1,599	61.2	48	2.9
65 years and over	3,501	684	19.5	664	19.0	21	3.0

NOTE: Data in Table 7 are from the Current Population Survey (CPS) and do not match the estimates in Table 8. See notes and definitions for further information.
[1] May be of any race.

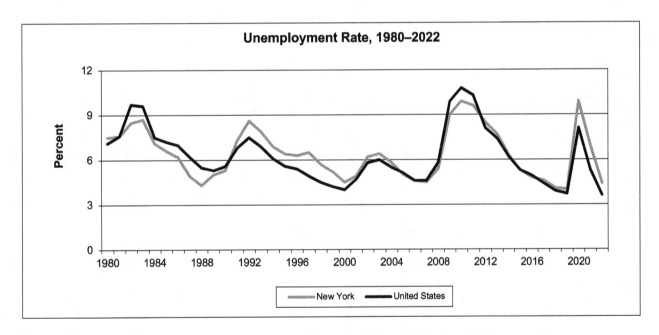

Unemployment Rate, 1980–2022

Table NY-8. Employment Status of the Civilian Noninstitutional Population Age 16 Years and Over

(Number, percent.)

Year	Civilian labor force	Civilian participation rate	Employed	Unemployed	Unemployment rate
2010..	9,630,297	62.6	8,790,607	839,690	8.7
2011..	9,537,752	61.6	8,741,662	796,090	8.3
2012..	9,602,599	61.7	8,775,083	827,516	8.6
2013..	9,632,949	61.6	8,880,792	752,157	7.8
2014..	9,523,567	60.7	8,925,328	598,239	6.3
2015..	9,536,519	60.7	9,035,989	500,530	5.2
2016..	9,527,021	60.6	9,062,866	464,155	4.9
2017..	9,838,170	60.8	9,382,750	455,420	4.6
2018..	9,842,263	60.7	9,440,487	401,776	4.1
2019..	9,880,211	60.8	9,502,625	377,586	3.8
2020..	9,575,032	59.1	8,631,276	943,756	9.9
2021..	9,441,458	59.0	8,786,280	655,178	6.9
2022..	9,616,989	60.2	9,205,821	411,168	4.3

Table NY-9. Employment and Average Wages by Industry

(Estimates are based on the 2012 North American Industry Classification System [NAICS].)

Industry	2014	2015	2016	2017	2018	2019	2020	2021
	Number of Jobs							
Wage and Salary Employment by Industry	9,221,011	9,385,967	9,510,338	9,623,705	9,794,133	9,914,379	8,934,657	9,165,392
Farm Wage and Salary Employment	22,608	22,524	21,022	20,976	21,562	21,723	20,749	21,268
Nonfarm Wage and Salary Employment	9,198,403	9,363,443	9,489,316	9,602,729	9,772,571	9,892,656	8,913,908	9,144,124
Private wage and salary employment	7,744,644	7,910,686	8,034,010	8,143,784	8,273,806	8,388,177	7,450,235	7,703,526
Forestry, fishing, and related activities	5,545	5,743	5,671	5,756	5,814	5,889	5,640	5,375
Mining	4,621	4,655	4,437	4,400	4,729	4,706	4,514	4,699
Utilities	37,697	38,330	37,643	38,082	37,718	37,132	36,301	35,505
Construction	351,440	370,582	386,441	395,718	409,981	416,147	371,865	384,235
Manufacturing	453,410	455,253	451,155	446,646	442,898	439,018	401,447	409,524
Durable goods manufacturing	265,267	266,133	262,446	257,245	256,394	254,315	232,196	233,627
Nondurable goods manufacturing	188,143	189,120	188,709	189,401	186,504	184,703	169,251	175,897
Wholesale trade	339,723	342,648	340,359	340,199	331,662	328,292	296,571	297,558
Retail trade	948,836	952,897	951,509	945,365	939,712	923,136	809,211	836,683
Transportation and warehousing	240,732	250,266	253,715	259,523	266,297	277,126	245,093	266,805
Information	265,665	267,490	268,216	271,047	276,659	279,065	269,156	280,497
Finance and insurance	520,750	528,371	530,540	533,040	536,169	544,593	538,711	531,345
Real estate and rental and leasing	189,128	195,425	199,673	203,192	207,406	209,490	196,273	195,331
Professional, scientific, and technical services	634,744	656,986	669,050	680,032	684,215	693,668	670,005	678,354
Management of companies and enterprises	142,417	143,255	142,857	144,343	144,831	145,877	132,061	134,464
Administrative and waste services	461,331	475,662	490,507	502,584	523,618	544,106	453,747	473,904
Educational services	390,058	406,604	413,045	416,976	416,079	420,824	383,042	405,198
Health care and social assistance	1,396,266	1,426,030	1,479,629	1,524,164	1,585,007	1,651,157	1,571,103	1,600,772
Arts, entertainment, and recreation	165,446	165,806	170,018	174,218	181,199	182,509	114,004	127,742
Accommodation and food services	714,197	737,033	754,615	778,692	785,232	785,487	527,677	601,889
Other services, except public administration	482,638	487,650	484,930	479,807	494,580	499,955	423,814	433,646
Government and government enterprises	1,453,759	1,452,757	1,455,306	1,458,945	1,498,765	1,504,479	1,463,673	1,440,598
	Dollars							
Average Wages and Salaries by Industry	65,173	66,820	67,348	69,947	72,320	74,667	82,070	86,878
Average Farm Wages and Salaries	28,804	23,616	29,039	26,412	25,548	19,415	20,209	19,806
Average Nonfarm Wages and Salaries	65,262	66,924	67,433	70,043	72,423	74,789	82,214	87,034
Average private wages and salaries	66,683	68,318	68,716	71,491	73,155	75,634	84,027	88,736
Forestry, fishing, and related activities	30,350	32,417	33,621	34,478	35,522	36,487	38,882	41,320
Mining	65,188	64,937	63,561	65,455	68,331	70,528	71,632	75,369
Utilities	107,817	110,484	114,262	120,084	123,702	126,527	132,948	141,292
Construction	65,249	67,511	70,104	71,465	73,251	75,611	78,189	80,051
Manufacturing	62,072	65,497	64,161	65,874	67,612	69,123	73,053	74,978
Durable goods manufacturing	66,870	70,323	69,343	71,240	73,533	75,526	78,660	80,697
Nondurable goods manufacturing	55,309	58,706	56,953	58,586	59,472	60,308	65,361	67,382
Wholesale trade	79,573	82,993	82,573	84,342	86,380	88,565	94,392	100,574
Retail trade	32,476	33,432	33,865	35,141	36,560	38,490	41,886	44,674
Transportation and warehousing	49,219	50,011	51,322	52,371	53,685	54,435	56,389	58,679
Information	110,359	115,022	120,004	119,384	129,862	135,908	154,344	169,849
Finance and insurance	216,989	213,880	211,239	231,098	226,449	230,884	247,356	280,064
Real estate and rental and leasing	63,839	66,736	69,376	71,824	74,278	76,724	81,817	85,495
Professional, scientific, and technical services	102,994	106,116	108,546	111,438	114,712	119,934	129,420	140,578
Management of companies and enterprises	143,631	149,070	140,474	147,583	151,249	155,389	164,490	177,601
Administrative and waste services	44,937	48,456	47,720	50,535	53,700	58,526	63,562	60,967
Educational services	46,228	49,656	51,080	52,438	54,779	55,328	62,229	61,594
Health care and social assistance	47,473	48,117	48,508	49,679	51,236	52,444	56,400	58,398
Arts, entertainment, and recreation	51,339	54,150	55,126	56,447	57,984	61,069	72,285	74,859
Accommodation and food services	27,726	28,247	29,729	31,109	33,212	34,995	32,356	37,866
Other services, except public administration	36,408	37,993	39,222	41,018	42,352	43,466	48,720	49,542
Government and government enterprises	57,690	59,338	60,346	61,955	68,383	70,074	72,987	77,930

Table NY-10. Employment Characteristics by Family Type

(Number, percent.)

Family type and labor force status	2019 Total	2019 Families with own children under 18 years	2020 [1] Total	2020 [1] Families with own children under 18 years	2021 Total	2021 Families with own children under 18 years
All Families....................	4,636,356	1,839,198	4,670,153	1,899,744	4,715,750	1,835,492
FAMILY TYPE AND LABOR FORCE STATUS						
Opposite-Sex Married-Couple Families........................	3,222,615	1,236,787	3,218,990	1,275,301	3,216,979	1,222,538
Both husband and wife in labor force....................	52.6	68.8	52.8	67.9	52.2	68.6
Husband in labor force, wife not in labor force	19.7	24.5	20.5	25.4	19.4	24.2
Wife in labor force, husband not in labor force	8.8	4.6	8.7	4.8	9.1	5.1
Both husband and wife not in labor force..............	17.7	1.5	18.0	1.9	19.2	2.1
Other Families	1,413,741	602,411	1,410,255	616,846	1,447,021	605,981
Female householder, no spouse present...................	73.0	76.9	73.7	77.2	72.7	74.9
In labor force..........................	49.1	62.1	49.3	62.2	48.2	59.7
Not in labor force	23.9	14.8	24.5	15.1	24.5	15.2
Male householder, no spouse present.................	27.0	23.1	26.3	22.8	27.3	25.1
In labor force.......................	20.2	20.7	20.0	20.3	20.9	22.6
Not in labor force	6.8	2.4	6.3	2.4	6.5	2.5

[1] 2020 ACS 5-Year estimates. 1-Year estimates were not released for 2020 due to the impact of COVID-19 on data collection that year. Data is not comparable to previous years, which are based on 1-year estimates.

Table NY-11. School Enrollment and Educational Attainment, 2021

(Number, percent.)

Item	State	U.S.
Enrollment		
Total population 3 years and over, enrolled in school	4,624,625	79,453,524
Enrolled in nursery school or preschool (percent)........................	5.7	5.2
Enrolled in kindergarten (percent)........................	4.8	5.0
Enrolled in elementary school, grades 1-8 (percent)....................	39.4	41.3
Enrolled in high school, grades 9-12 (percent).....................	20.4	21.8
Enrolled in college or graduate school (percent)......................	29.7	26.7
Attainment		
Total population 25 years and over	13,987,094	228,193,464
Less than ninth grade (percent)	5.9	4.8
9th to 12th grade, no diploma (percent)	6.1	5.9
High school graduate, including equivalency (percent)...................	24.4	26.3
Some college, no degree (percent)	14.9	19.3
Associate's degree (percent)........................	8.9	8.8
Bachelor's degree (percent)	22.2	21.2
Graduate or professional degree (percent)......................	17.7	13.8
High school graduate or higher (percent)........................	88.0	89.4
Bachelor's degree or higher (percent)........................	39.9	35.0

Table NY-12. Public School Characteristics and Educational Indicators

(Number, percent; data derived from National Center of Education Statistics.)

Item	State	U.S.
Public Elementary and Secondary Schools		
Number of regular school districts, 2019-20............................	687	13,349
Number of operational schools, 2019-20............................	4,819	98,469
Percent charter schools	6.6	7.7
Total public school enrollment, Fall 2021............................	2,548,490	49,433,092
Percent charter school enrollment	6.9	7.5
Student-teacher ratio, Fall 2019........................	12.4	15.9
Expenditures per student (unadjusted dollars), 2019-20	25,273	13,489
Four-year adjusted cohort graduation rate (ACGR), 2019-2020[1]....................	83.5	86.5
Students eligible for free or reduced-price lunch (percent), 2019-20....................	56.1	52.1
English language learners (percent), Fall 2020	9.4	10.3
Students age 3 to 21 served under IDEA, part B (percent), 2021-22	20.5	14.7

Public Schools by Type, 2019-20	Number	Percent of state public schools
Total number of schools........................	4,819	100.0
Special education........................	135	2.8
Vocational education........................	49	1.0
Alternative education........................	39	0.8

[1] Adjusted Cohort Graduation Rates (ACGR) differ from Averaged Freshmen Graduation Rates (AFGR).

Table NY-13. Reported Voting and Registration of the Voting-Age Population, November 2022

(Numbers in thousands, percent.)

Item	Total population	Total citizen population	Registered			Voted		
			Total registered	Percent registered (total population)	Percent registered (total citizen population)	Total voted	Percent voted (total population)	Percent voted (total citizen population)
U.S. Total	255,457	233,546	161,422	63.2	69.1	121,916	47.7	52.2
State Total..	15,238	13,516	8,897	58.4	65.8	6,631	43.5	49.1
Sex								
Male	7,353	6,527	4,201	57.1	64.4	3,159	43.0	48.4
Female	7,885	6,988	4,696	59.6	67.2	3,472	44.0	49.7
Race								
White alone..	10,512	9,578	6,548	62.3	68.4	5,146	49.0	53.7
White, non-Hispanic alone	8,714	8,380	5,864	67.3	70.0	4,690	53.8	56.0
Black alone..	2,591	2,283	1,408	54.3	61.7	947	36.5	41.5
Asian alone	1,712	1,277	680	39.7	53.3	375	21.9	29.4
Hispanic (of any race)	2,446	1,682	992	40.5	59.0	639	26.1	38.0
White alone or in combination	10,780	9,839	6,728	62.4	68.4	5,268	48.9	53.5
Black alone or in combination....................	2,808	2,492	1,564	55.7	62.8	1,046	37.2	42.0
Asian alone or in combination..................	1,788	1,353	750	41.9	55.4	426	23.8	31.5
Age								
18 to 24 years	1,679	1,516	669	39.8	44.1	348	20.7	22.9
25 to 34 years	2,809	2,369	1,303	46.4	55.0	811	28.9	34.2
35 to 44 years	2,264	1,913	1,290	57.0	67.4	926	40.9	48.4
45 to 64 years	4,903	4,324	3,092	63.1	71.5	2,442	49.8	56.5
65 years and over	3,583	3,394	2,543	71.0	74.9	2,104	58.7	62.0

Table NY-14. Health Indicators

(Number, rate as indicated in footnotes.)

Item	State	U.S.
Births		
Life Expectancy at Birth (years), 2020	77.7	77.0
Fertility Rate by State[1], 2021	54.1	56.3
Percent Home Births, 2021	1.4	1.4
Cesarean Delivery Rate[2], 2021	34.1	32.1
Preterm Birth Rate[3], 2021	9.7	10.5
Teen Birth Rate[4], 2021	9.1	13.9
Percentage of Babies Born Low Birthweight[5], 2021	8.4	8.5
Deaths[6]		
Heart Disease Mortality Rate, 2021...	162.3	173.8
Cancer Mortality Rate, 2021..	125.3	146.6
Stroke Mortality Rate, 2021...	25.7	41.1
Diabetes Mortality Rate, 2021...	18.8	25.4
Influenza/Pneumonia Mortality Rate, 2021	14.4	10.5
Suicide Mortality Rate, 2021...	7.9	14.1
Drug Overdose Mortality Rate, 2021...	28.7	33.6
Firearm Injury Mortality Rate, 2021..	5.4	14.6
Homicide Mortality Rate, 2021...	4.8	8.2
Disease and Illness		
Lifetime Asthma in Adults, 2020 (percent)..	13.6	13.9
Lifetime Asthma in Children, 2020 (percent)[7]	12.4	11.3
Diabetes in Adults, 2020 (percent)...	9.1	8.2
Self-reported Obesity in Adults, 2021 (percent)...	29.1	NA

SOURCE: National Center for Health Statistics, National Vital Statistics System 2020 data; https://wonder.cdc.gov.
[1] General fertility rate per 1,000 women aged 15–44.
[2] This represents the percentage of all live births that were cesarean deliveries.
[3] Babies born prior to 37 weeks of pregnancy (gestation).
[4] Number of births per 1,000 females aged 15–19
[5] Babies born weighing less than 2,500 grams or 5 lbs. 8oz.
[6] Death rates are the number of deaths per 100,000 total population.
[7] U.S. total includes data from 30 states and D.C.
NA = Not available.
- = Zero or rounds to zero.

Table NY-15. State Government Finances, 2021

(Dollar amounts in thousands, percent distribution.)

Item	Dollars	Percent distribution
Total Revenue	233,384,146	100.0
General revenue	200,232,890	85.8
Intergovernmental revenue	83,883,457	35.9
Taxes	93,503,736	40.1
General sales	15,612,861	6.7
Selective sales	11,551,492	4.9
License taxes	1,793,375	0.8
Individual income tax	54,996,670	23.6
Corporate income tax	4,954,149	2.1
Other taxes	4,595,189	2.0
Current charges	11,274,240	4.8
Miscellaneous general revenue	11,571,457	5.0
Utility revenue	7,149,485	3.1
Liquor stores revenue	-	-
Insurance trust revenue[1]	26,001,771	11.1
Total Expenditure	241,779,293	100.0
Intergovernmental expenditure	62,218,474	25.7
Direct expenditure	179,560,819	74.3
Current operation	123,457,151	51.1
Capital outlay	13,246,253	5.5
Insurance benefits and repayments	34,566,640	14.3
Assistance and subsidies	2,016,577	0.8
Interest on debt	6,274,198	2.6
Exhibit: Salaries and wages	19,428,801	8.0
Total Expenditure	241,779,293	100.0
General expenditure	188,984,017	78.2
Intergovernmental expenditure	62,218,474	25.7
Direct expenditure	126,765,543	52.4
General expenditure, by function:		
Education	47,100,508	19.5
Public welfare	78,463,127	32.5
Hospitals	6,643,822	2.7
Health	10,551,698	4.4
Highways	6,273,221	2.6
Police protection	1,028,657	0.4
Correction	3,091,821	1.3
Natural resources	588,929	0.2
Parks and recreation	728,807	0.3
Governmental administration	6,969,689	2.9
Interest on general debt	4,344,824	1.8
Other and unallocable	19,457,111	8.0
Utility expenditure	21,780,064	9.3
Liquor stores expenditure	-	-
Insurance trust expenditure	34,566,640	14.3
Debt at End of Fiscal Year	170,355,214	X
Cash and Security Holdings	540,688,124	X

X = Not applicable.
- = Zero or rounds to zero.
[1] Within insurance trust revenue, net earnings of state retirement systems is a calculated statistic (the item code in the data file is X08), and thus can be positive or negative. Net earnings is the sum of earnings on investments plus gains on investments minus losses on investments. The change made in 2002 for asset valuation from book to market value in accordance with Statement 34 of the Governmental Accounting Standards Board is reflected in the calculated statistics.

Table NY-16. State Government Tax Collections, 2022

(Dollars in thousands, percent.)

Item	Dollars	Percent distribution
Total Taxes	117,983,717	100.0
Property taxes	X	-
Sales and gross receipts	31,223,289	26.5
General sales and gross receipts	18,034,495	15.3
Selective sales and gross receipts	13,188,794	11.2
Alcoholic beverages	307,900	0.3
Amusements	1,710	-
Insurance premiums	2,409,677	2.0
Motor fuels	1,511,214	1.3
Pari-mutuels	13,899	-
Public utilities	776,052	0.7
Tobacco products	929,109	0.8
Other selective sales	7,239,233	6.1
Licenses	1,893,522	1.6
Alcoholic beverages	83,800	0.1
Amusements	0	-
Corporations in general	219	-
Hunting and fishing	55,100	-
Motor vehicle	1,419,966	1.2
Motor vehicle operators	176,100	0.1
Public utilities	11,458	-
Occupation and business, NEC	145,200	0.1
Other licenses	1,679	-
Income taxes	77,977,711	66.1
Individual income	70,196,866	59.5
Corporation net income	7,780,845	6.6
Other taxes	6,889,195	5.8
Death and gift	1,417,294	1.2
Documentary and stock transfer	3,657,497	3.1
Severance	X	-
Taxes, NEC	1,814,404	1.5

X = Not applicable.
- = Zero or rounds to zero.

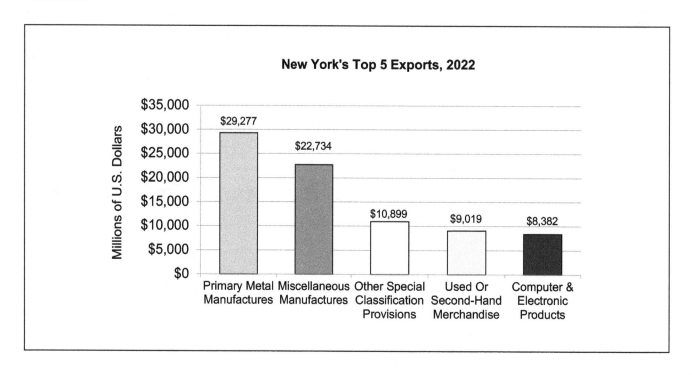

New York's Top 5 Exports, 2022

NORTH CAROLINA

Facts and Figures

Location: Southeastern United States; bordered on the N by Virginia, on the E by the Atlantic Ocean, on the S by South Carolina and Georgia, and on the W by Tennessee

Area: 53,819 sq. mi. (139,389 sq. km.); rank—28th

Population: 10,698,973 (2022 est.); rank—9th

Principal Cities: capital—Raleigh; largest—Charlotte

Statehood: November 21, 1789; 12th state

U.S. Congress: 2 senators, 13 representatives

State Motto: *Esse quam videri* ("To be rather than to seem")

State Song: "The Old North State"

State Nicknames: The Tar Heel State; The Old North State

Abbreviations: NC; N.C.

State Symbols: flower—flowering dogwood; tree—pine; bird—cardinal

At a Glance

- With an increase in population of 12.2 percent, North Carolina ranked 14th among the states in growth from 2010 to 2022.

- North Carolina's median household income of $61,972 ranked 40th among all states in 2021, and 13.4 percent of the population lived below the poverty level, a percent which ranked 16th in the country.

- In 2021, 10.4 percent of North Carolinians did not have health insurance, compared to 8.6 percent of the entire U.S. population.

- North Carolina had the 4th lowest voter turnout in the midterm election of November 2022, with 42.1 percent of the voting age population casting votes.

- North Carolina's unemployment rate of 3.7 percent ranked 21st in the nation in 2022 and was lower than the national unemployment rate of 3.6 percent.

Table NC-1. Population by Age, Sex, Race, and Hispanic Origin

(Number, percent, except where noted.)

Sex, age, race, and Hispanic origin	2010	2020	2022	Percent change, 2010–2022
Total Population..	9,535,483	10,439,414	10,698,973	12.2
Percent of total U.S. population	3.1	3.1	3.2	X
Sex				
Male..	4,645,492	5,120,421	5,239,829	12.8
Female	4,889,991	5,318,993	5,459,144	11.6
Age				
Under 5 years..	632,040	589,096	596,490	-5.6
Under 18 years...	2,281,635	2,282,578	2,294,879	0.6
18 to 64 years	6,019,769	6,420,705	6,542,215	8.7
65 years and over	1,234,079	1,736,131	1,861,879	50.9
Median age (years)	37.4	39	39.2	4.8
Race and Hispanic Origin				
One race				
White	6,898,296	7,341,412	7,480,293	8.4
Black	2,088,362	2,318,816	2,373,876	13.7
American Indian and Alaska Native	147,566	159,555	166,226	12.6
Asian..	215,952	349,168	383,271	77.5
Native Hawaiian or Other Pacific Islander	10,309	14,852	15,878	54.0
Two or more races...	174,998	255,611	279,429	59.7
Hispanic (of any race).......................................	800,120	1,040,521	1,122,009	40.2

NOTE: Population figures for 2022 are July 1 estimates. The 2010 and 2020 estimates are taken from the respective censuses.
- = Zero or rounds to zero.
X = Not applicable.

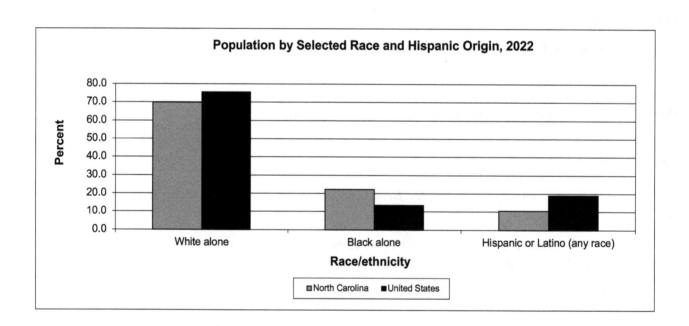

Table NC-2. Marital Status

(Number, percent distribution.)

Sex, age, race, and Hispanic origin	2000	2010	2021
Males, 15 Years and Over	3,092,380	3,678,950	4,184,722
Never married	28.2	33.3	35.8
Now married, except separated...	58.7	51.8	50.4
Separated..	2.7	2.9	1.9
Widowed..	2.4	2.5	2.7
Divorced..	8.1	9.6	9.2
Females, 15 Years and Over	3,301,327	3,975,748	4,476,152
Never married	22.0	27.3	30.2
Now married, except separated...	53.9	47.3	46.6
Separated..	3.3	3.5	2.5
Widowed..	10.9	9.8	8.6
Divorced..	9.9	12.1	12.0

Table NC-3. Households and Housing Characteristics

(Number, percent, dollars.)

Item	2000	2010	2021	Average annual percent change, 2010–2021
Total Households....................................	3,132,012	3,670,859	4,179,632	1.3
Family households..................................	2,158,869	2,441,916	2,685,695	0.9
Married-couple family............................	1,645,346	1,770,863	1,976,957	1.1
Other family......................................	513,523	671,053	708,738	0.5
Male householder, no wife present.........	123,526	159,752	181,424	1.2
Female householder, no husband present...	389,997	511,301	527,314	0.3
Nonfamily households.............................	973,144	1,228,943	1,493,937	2.0
Householder living alone........................	795,271	1,022,017	1,228,467	1.8
Householder not living alone...................	177,873	206,926	265,470	2.6
Housing Characteristics				
Total housing units...............................	3,523,944	4,333,479	4,801,698	1.0
Occupied housing units..........................	3,132,012	3,670,859	4,179,632	1.3
Owner occupied..................................	2,172,355	2,465,551	2,794,211	1.2
Renter occupied..................................	959,658	1,205,308	1,385,421	1.4
Average household size...........................	2.49	2.53	2.46	-0.3
Financial Characteristics				
Median gross rent of renter-occupied housing...	548	731	1026	3.7
Median monthly owner costs for housing units with a mortgage...	985	1,250	1,387	1.0
Median value of owner-occupied housing units...	108,300	154,200	236,900	4.9

Table NC-4. Migration, Origin, and Language

(Number, percent.)

Characteristic	State 2021	U.S. 2021
Residence 1 Year Ago		
Population 1 year and over...............	10,446,881	328,464,538
Same house......................	86.5	87.2
Different house in the U.S.........	13.1	12.3
Same county....................	6.1	6.7
Different county................	7.0	5.7
Same state...................	3.8	3.3
Different state...............	3.2	2.4
Abroad...........................	0.4	0.4
Place of Birth		
Native born........................	9,681,376	286,623,642
Male..........................	48.7	49.7
Female........................	51.3	50.3
Foreign born......................	869,786	45,270,103
Male..........................	49.9	48.7
Female........................	50.1	51.3
Foreign born; naturalized U.S. citizen...	377,929	24,044,083
Male..........................	47.6	46.4
Female........................	52.4	53.6
Foreign born; not a U.S. citizen...	491,857	21,226,020
Male..........................	51.6	51.2
Female........................	48.4	48.8
Entered 2010 or later...............	32.2	28.1
Entered 2000 to 2009...............	29.2	23.7
Entered before 2000...............	38.6	48.2
World Region of Birth, Foreign		
Foreign-born population, excluding population born at sea...	869,786	45,269,644
Europe........................	10.7	10.7
Asia..........................	28.4	31.0
Africa........................	8.1	5.7
Oceania.......................	0.4	0.6
Latin America..................	50.6	50.1
North America..................	2.0	1.7
Language Spoken at Home and Ability to Speak English		
Population 5 years and over...............	9,968,361	313,232,500
English only...................	87.6	78.4
Language other than English........	12.4	21.6
Speaks English less than "very well"...	4.8	8.3

Table NC-5. Median Income and Poverty Status, 2021

(Number, percent, except as noted.)

Characteristic	State		U.S.	
	Number	Percent	Number	Percent
Median Income				
Households (dollars)..	61,972	X	69,717	X
Families (dollars)	77,601	X	85,806	X
Below Poverty Level (All People)	1,378,621	13.4	41,393,176	12.8
Sex				
Male	605,925	12.1	18,518,155	11.6
Female	772,696	14.6	22,875,021	13.9
Age				
Under 18 years..	410,555	18.1	12,243,219	16.9
Related children under 18 years.......................................	402,621	17.8	11,985,424	16.6
18 to 64 years	787,589	12.6	23,526,341	11.9
65 years and over	180,477	10.2	5,623,616	10.3

X = Not applicable.

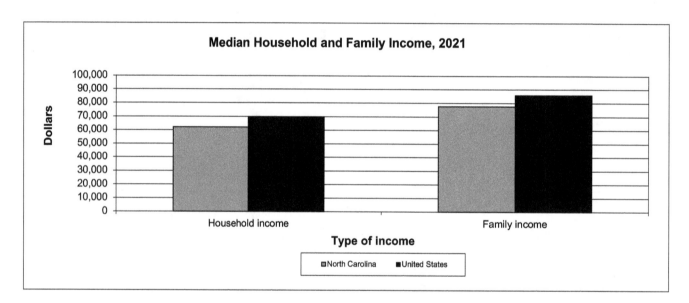

Median Household and Family Income, 2021

Legend: ■ North Carolina   ■ United States

Table NC-6. Health Insurance Coverage Status for the Civilian Noninstitutionalized Population and Children Under 19 Years of Age

(Number, percent.)

Item	2011	2012	2013	2014	2015	2016	2017	2018	2019	2020 [2]	2021
Civilian Noninstitutionalized Population	9,461,018	9,552,529	9,645,320	9,752,148	9,855,612	9,957,830	10,070,781	10,183,721	10,281,062	10,178,084	10,345,935
Covered by Private or Public Insurance											
Number..	7,916,111	7,970,289	8,136,322	8,476,094	8,752,825	8,919,431	8,994,798	9,091,675	9,123,782	9,093,981	9,267,826
Percent...	83.7	83.4	84.4	86.9	88.8	89.6	89.3	89.3	88.7	89.3	89.6
Uninsured											
Number..	1,544,907	1,582,240	1,508,998	1,276,054	1,102,787	1,038,399	1,075,983	1,092,046	1,157,280	1,084,103	1,078,109
Percent...	16.3	16.6	15.6	13.1	11.2	10.4	10.7	10.7	11.3	10.7	10.4
Percent in the U.S. not covered.........................	15.1	14.8	14.5	11.7	9.4	8.6	8.7	8.9	9.2	8.7	8.6
Children Under 19 Years of Age [1]	2,286,872	2,281,544	2,280,549	2,286,665	2,283,011	2,292,483	2,450,911	2,446,320	2,454,735	2,446,253	2,451,472
Covered by Private or Public Insurance											
Number..	2,112,300	2,108,583	2,136,355	2,167,587	2,183,693	2,190,251	2,332,345	2,316,258	2,313,207	2,316,476	2,316,816
Percent...	92.4	92.4	93.7	94.8	95.6	95.5	95.2	94.7	94.2	94.7	94.5
Uninsured											
Number..	174,572	172,961	144,194	119,078	99,318	102,232	118,566	130,062	141,528	129,777	134,656
Percent...	7.6	7.6	6.3	5.2	4.4	4.5	4.8	5.3	5.8	5.3	5.5
Percent in the U.S. not covered.........................	7.5	7.2	7.1	6.0	4.8	4.5	5.0	5.2	5.7	5.2	5.4

[1] Data for years prior to 2017 are for individuals under 18 years of age.
[2] 2020 ACS 5-Year estimates. 1-Year estimates were not released for 2020 due to the impact of COVID-19 on data collection that year. Data is not comparable to previous years, which are based on 1-year estimates.

Table NC-7. Employment Status by Demographic Group, 2022

(Numbers in thousands, percent.)

Characteristic	Civilian noninstitutional population	Civilian labor force		Employed		Unemployed	
		Number	Percent of population	Number	Percent of population	Number	Percent of population
Total...............................	8,442	5,129	60.7	4,941	58.5	188	3.7
Sex							
Male.................................	4,022	2,651	65.9	2,562	63.7	89	3.4
Female.............................	4,421	2,478	56.1	2,380	53.8	98	4.0
Race, Sex, and Hispanic Origin							
White...............................	5,890	3,527	59.9	3,426	58.2	101	2.9
Male.............................	2,867	1,899	66.2	1,846	64.4	53	2.8
Female.........................	3,024	1,628	53.8	1,580	52.2	48	2.9
Black or African American............	1,829	1,131	61.8	1,058	57.8	73	6.5
Male.............................	824	515	62.5	485	58.9	30	5.8
Female.........................	1,006	616	61.2	572	56.9	44	7.1
Hispanic or Latino ethnicity[1]...........	818	545	66.7	529	64.6	17	3.0
Male.............................	397	314	79.1	304	76.7	10	3.1
Female.........................	422	232	54.9	225	53.3	7	3.0
Age							
16 to 19 years....................	559	199	35.5	180	32.2	18	9.3
20 to 24 years....................	707	491	69.5	441	62.3	51	10.3
25 to 34 years....................	1,347	1,118	83.0	1,065	79.1	53	4.7
35 to 44 years....................	1,295	1,057	81.6	1,032	79.7	25	2.3
45 to 54 years....................	1,311	1,045	79.7	1,027	78.3	18	1.7
55 to 64 years....................	1,407	900	64.0	882	62.7	18	2.0
65 years and over................	1,816	320	17.6	315	17.3	5	1.6

NOTE: Data in Table 7 are from the Current Population Survey (CPS) and do not match the estimates in Table 8. See notes and definitions for further information.
[1] May be of any race.

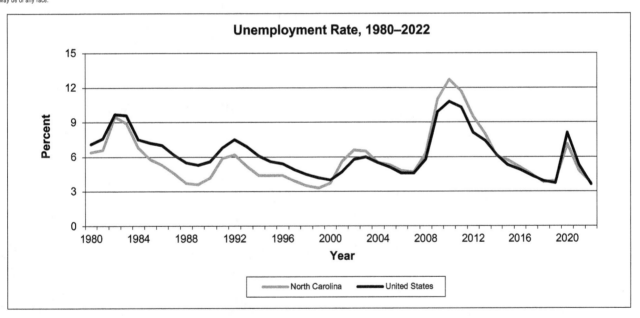

Unemployment Rate, 1980–2022

Table NC-8. Employment Status of the Civilian Noninstitutional Population Age 16 Years and Over

(Number, percent.)

Year	Civilian labor force	Civilian participation rate	Employed	Unemployed	Unemployment rate
2010.............................	4,633,695	63.5	4,135,783	497,912	10.7
2011.............................	4,657,873	62.8	4,180,071	477,802	10.3
2012.............................	4,720,203	62.9	4,271,383	448,820	9.5
2013.............................	4,701,391	61.9	4,336,379	365,012	7.8
2014.............................	4,698,287	61.1	4,410,647	287,640	6.1
2015.............................	4,763,821	61.1	4,493,882	269,939	5.7
2016.............................	4,844,851	61.2	4,598,456	246,395	5.1
2017.............................	4,865,900	61.3	4,646,212	219,688	4.5
2018.............................	4,915,963	61.2	4,719,018	196,945	4.0
2019.............................	4,999,810	61.5	4,808,270	191,540	3.8
2020.............................	4,848,893	59.0	4,505,462	343,431	7.1
2021.............................	4,959,672	59.6	4,721,198	238,474	4.8
2022.............................	5,159,329	60.9	4,970,998	188,331	3.7

Table NC-9. Employment and Average Wages by Industry

(Estimates are based on the 2012 North American Industry Classification System [NAICS].)

Industry	2014	2015	2016	2017	2018	2019	2020	2021
	Number of Jobs							
Wage and Salary Employment by Industry......................	4,380,948	4,494,854	4,588,883	4,657,504	4,735,868	4,826,288	4,643,484	4,831,200
Farm Wage and Salary Employment................................	24,334	27,259	27,288	24,799	22,325	24,197	25,175	27,665
Nonfarm Wage and Salary Employment..........................	4,356,614	4,467,595	4,561,595	4,632,705	4,713,543	4,802,091	4,618,309	4,803,535
Private wage and salary employment............................	3,504,358	3,615,821	3,706,737	3,772,330	3,852,963	3,936,723	3,770,160	3,964,045
Forestry, fishing, and related activities	14,797	15,007	14,982	14,941	15,115	15,134	14,402	13,333
Mining...	2,812	2,769	2,759	2,927	3,123	3,111	3,137	3,123
Utilities..	13,645	14,045	13,947	13,908	14,518	14,243	14,287	14,369
Construction	183,470	194,223	205,634	213,525	225,986	237,270	234,963	243,547
Manufacturing...	450,002	461,737	464,990	468,299	474,813	477,526	452,825	464,721
Durable goods manufacturing................................	240,409	248,749	251,268	253,040	258,753	260,601	244,111	250,939
Nondurable goods manufacturing...........................	209,593	212,988	213,722	215,259	216,060	216,925	208,714	213,782
Wholesale trade	177,372	179,489	183,563	185,843	182,885	187,957	183,148	191,053
Retail trade..	474,567	487,154	498,286	501,478	503,496	504,709	492,334	514,206
Transportation and warehousing..............................	115,817	121,641	124,544	131,328	137,339	146,232	162,387	180,050
Information	72,592	76,099	78,813	78,879	80,071	75,991	73,430	77,317
Finance and insurance	161,047	166,284	171,484	177,742	183,622	196,677	205,743	218,899
Real estate and rental and leasing...........................	53,022	55,797	57,884	59,438	61,556	63,290	61,624	65,328
Professional, scientific, and technical services	209,216	220,955	230,394	240,886	256,916	266,365	269,324	291,790
Management of companies and enterprises.................	80,496	81,975	83,966	82,884	83,890	84,917	82,585	76,686
Administrative and waste services	284,228	290,402	295,206	295,877	298,872	302,393	289,773	313,616
Educational services	94,565	106,701	108,158	108,113	107,269	109,422	101,245	108,824
Health care and social assistance............................	476,081	483,927	493,711	504,272	515,733	525,329	509,578	526,515
Arts, entertainment, and recreation..........................	63,327	63,774	69,711	71,940	73,598	75,744	56,235	63,421
Accommodation and food services...........................	383,833	398,078	413,711	424,934	432,020	442,594	367,422	397,822
Other services, except public administration...............	193,469	195,764	194,994	195,116	202,141	207,819	195,718	199,425
Government and government enterprises......................	852,256	851,774	854,858	860,375	860,580	865,368	848,149	839,490
	Dollars							
Average Wages and Salaries by Industry	45,865	47,351	48,252	49,867	51,835	53,438	57,014	60,618
Average Farm Wages and Salaries	22,765	20,045	24,658	27,103	23,164	26,996	25,643	25,556
Average Nonfarm Wages and Salaries	45,994	47,518	48,393	49,989	51,971	53,572	57,185	60,820
Average private wages and salaries............................	46,075	47,572	48,405	50,176	52,167	53,811	57,858	61,662
Forestry, fishing, and related activities	31,408	32,608	34,004	34,706	35,458	37,054	39,306	42,437
Mining...	50,326	56,308	60,957	65,152	63,321	67,833	67,236	74,047
Utilities..	91,011	91,068	96,026	96,315	99,403	101,541	103,494	102,892
Construction	46,445	48,536	50,959	53,273	55,488	57,884	60,174	62,624
Manufacturing...	57,017	58,344	58,478	60,219	61,781	63,076	65,414	68,095
Durable goods manufacturing................................	61,058	62,228	62,627	64,650	66,599	68,151	69,551	73,052
Nondurable goods manufacturing...........................	52,383	53,808	53,600	55,011	56,010	56,978	60,575	62,276
Wholesale trade	68,455	70,456	70,933	74,187	76,064	78,455	83,593	89,104
Retail trade..	27,342	27,921	28,399	28,954	29,788	30,985	33,646	36,911
Transportation and warehousing..............................	47,291	48,211	48,331	49,747	51,556	51,748	50,758	51,833
Information	76,075	78,498	80,443	82,712	86,533	89,340	98,728	108,495
Finance and insurance	86,739	90,658	91,746	96,770	101,530	103,801	110,988	116,786
Real estate and rental and leasing...........................	45,190	47,057	48,371	49,963	52,255	54,037	57,431	61,936
Professional, scientific, and technical services	73,882	76,181	78,250	80,836	86,101	86,653	91,275	99,526
Management of companies and enterprises.................	102,849	108,409	106,492	111,064	111,853	116,531	122,601	131,404
Administrative and waste services	33,621	34,362	35,691	37,419	38,462	40,668	43,557	47,760
Educational services	38,039	41,100	41,409	40,792	44,241	45,254	50,283	49,923
Health care and social assistance............................	44,129	45,329	46,263	48,072	49,444	51,223	54,389	58,411
Arts, entertainment, and recreation..........................	33,031	34,239	33,160	33,543	34,459	34,938	39,797	42,290
Accommodation and food services...........................	18,068	18,565	19,138	19,828	20,936	21,652	21,377	25,816
Other services, except public administration...............	31,167	32,386	33,945	35,277	36,321	37,656	41,641	43,569
Government and government enterprises......................	45,657	47,291	48,341	49,167	51,093	52,482	54,191	56,845

Table NC-10. Employment Characteristics by Family Type

(Number, percent.)

Family type and labor force status	2019 Total	2019 Families with own children under 18 years	2020 [1] Total	2020 [1] Families with own children under 18 years	2021 Total	2021 Families with own children under 18 years
All Families...	2,630,365	1,073,988	2,625,055	1,084,168	2,685,695	1,061,167
FAMILY TYPE AND LABOR FORCE STATUS						
Opposite-Sex Married-Couple Families.......................................	1,926,079	701,522	1,915,378	719,449	1,960,000	706,521
Both husband and wife in labor force......................................	49.8	67.5	50.1	66.7	49.1	67.3
Husband in labor force, wife not in labor force	21.2	26.5	21.7	27.6	21.9	26.8
Wife in labor force, husband not in labor force	7.9	4.0	8.3	4.2	7.9	4.2
Both husband and wife not in labor force.................................	20.2	1.5	19.9	1.5	21.1	1.7
Other Families	704,286	372,466	694,016	361,595	708,738	352,523
Female householder, no spouse present	74.0	75.6	74.1	76.0	74.4	77.1
In labor force...	51.7	63.5	51.2	63.5	51.6	63.4
Not in labor force...	22.3	12.1	22.9	12.5	22.8	13.7
Male householder, no spouse present......................................	26.0	24.4	25.9	24.0	25.6	22.9
In labor force...	19.9	22.2	19.8	22.0	19.6	21.1
Not in labor force...	6.1	2.2	6.1	2.1	6.0	1.8

[1] 2020 ACS 5-Year estimates. 1-Year estimates were not released for 2020 due to the impact of COVID-19 on data collection that year. Data is not comparable to previous years, which are based on 1-year estimates.

Table NC-11. School Enrollment and Educational Attainment, 2021

(Number, percent.)

Item	State	U.S.
Enrollment		
Total population 3 years and over, enrolled in school	2,522,354	79,453,524
Enrolled in nursery school or preschool (percent)..........................	4.9	5.2
Enrolled in kindergarten (percent)...	5.2	5.0
Enrolled in elementary school, grades 1-8 (percent).......................	41.2	41.3
Enrolled in high school, grades 9-12 (percent)............................	21.1	21.8
Enrolled in college or graduate school (percent)..........................	27.6	26.7
Attainment		
Total population 25 years and over	7,245,632	228,193,464
Less than ninth grade (percent)..	4	4.8
9th to 12th grade, no diploma (percent)....................................	6.3	5.9
High school graduate, including equivalency (percent)......................	24.9	26.3
Some college, no degree (percent)..	19.8	19.3
Associate's degree (percent)...	10.1	8.8
Bachelor's degree (percent)..	21.7	21.2
Graduate or professional degree (percent)..................................	13.2	13.8
High school graduate or higher (percent)...................................	89.7	89.4
Bachelor's degree or higher (percent)......................................	34.9	35.0

Table NC-12. Public School Characteristics and Educational Indicators

(Number, percent; data derived from National Center of Education Statistics.)

Item	State	U.S.
Public Elementary and Secondary Schools		
Number of regular school districts, 2019-20	121	13,349
Number of operational schools, 2019-20....................................	2,664	98,469
Percent charter schools	7.4	7.7
Total public school enrollment, Fall 2021	1,525,223	49,433,092
Percent charter school enrollment	8.6	7.5
Student-teacher ratio, Fall 2019...	15.5	15.9
Expenditures per student (unadjusted dollars), 2019-20	9,903	13,489
Four-year adjusted cohort graduation rate (ACGR), 2019-2020[1]............	87.6	86.5
Students eligible for free or reduced-price lunch (percent), 2019-20......	57.8	52.1
English language learners (percent), Fall 2020	7.7	10.3
Students age 3 to 21 served under IDEA, part B (percent), 2021-22	12.8	14.7

Public Schools by Type, 2019-20	Number	Percent of state public schools
Total number of schools..	2,664	100.0
Special education..	25	0.9
Vocational education...	8	0.3
Alternative education..	76	2.9

[1] Adjusted Cohort Graduation Rates (ACGR) differ from Averaged Freshmen Graduation Rates (AFGR).

Table NC-13. Reported Voting and Registration of the Voting-Age Population, November 2022

(Numbers in thousands, percent.)

Item	Total population	Total citizen population	Registered			Voted		
			Total registered	Percent registered (total population)	Percent registered (total citizen population)	Total voted	Percent voted (total population)	Percent voted (total citizen population)
U.S. Total	255,457	233,546	161,422	63.2	69.1	121,916	47.7	52.2
State Total................................	8,175	7,533	4,583	56.1	60.8	3,439	42.1	45.7
Sex								
Male	3,893	3,576	2,184	56.1	61.1	1,635	42.0	45.7
Female	4,282	3,957	2,399	56.0	60.6	1,804	42.1	45.6
Race								
White alone................................	5,631	5,245	3,325	59.1	63.4	2,587	45.9	49.3
White, non-Hispanic alone	4,932	4,867	3,133	63.5	64.4	2,469	50.1	50.7
Black alone................................	1,760	1,714	999	56.7	58.3	706	40.1	41.2
Asian alone	436	231	126	28.8	54.4	72	16.5	31.2
Hispanic (of any race)	765	413	215	28.1	52.2	128	16.8	31.1
White alone or in combination	5,776	5,391	3,408	59.0	63.2	2,632	45.6	48.8
Black alone or in combination	1,869	1,817	1,032	55.2	56.8	711	38.1	39.2
Asian alone or in combination	483	273	167	34.7	61.3	99	20.5	36.3
Age								
18 to 24 years	921	866	372	40.3	42.9	202	21.9	23.3
25 to 34 years	1,395	1,236	652	46.7	52.7	386	27.7	31.2
35 to 44 years	1,290	1,069	675	52.3	63.1	460	35.7	43.0
45 to 64 years	2,687	2,523	1,581	58.9	62.7	1,280	47.6	50.7
65 years and over	1,881	1,838	1,303	69.3	70.9	1,111	59.1	60.4

Table NC-14. Health Indicators

(Number, rate as indicated in footnotes.)

Item	State	U.S.
Births		
Life Expectancy at Birth (years), 2020	76.1	77.0
Fertility Rate by State[1], 2021................................	58.1	56.3
Percent Home Births, 2021	0.8	1.4
Cesarean Delivery Rate[2], 2021................................	30.3	32.1
Preterm Birth Rate[3], 2021................................	10.8	10.5
Teen Birth Rate[4], 2021................................	16.0	13.9
Percentage of Babies Born Low Birthweight[5], 2021	9.4	8.5
Deaths[6]		
Heart Disease Mortality Rate, 2021................................	170.9	173.8
Cancer Mortality Rate, 2021................................	153.6	146.6
Stroke Mortality Rate, 2021	46.5	41.1
Diabetes Mortality Rate, 2021................................	30.4	25.4
Influenza/Pneumonia Mortality Rate, 2021	12.4	10.5
Suicide Mortality Rate, 2021................................	13.2	14.1
Drug Overdose Mortality Rate, 2021................................	39.2	33.6
Firearm Injury Mortality Rate, 2021	17.3	14.6
Homicide Mortality Rate, 2021................................	9.7	8.2
Disease and Illness		
Lifetime Asthma in Adults, 2020 (percent)................................	12.3	13.9
Lifetime Asthma in Children, 2020 (percent)[7]	NA	11.3
Diabetes in Adults, 2020 (percent)................................	11.0	8.2
Self-reported Obesity in Adults, 2021 (percent)	36.0	NA

SOURCE: National Center for Health Statistics, National Vital Statistics System 2020 data; https://wonder.cdc.gov.
[1] General fertility rate per 1,000 women aged 15–44.
[2] This represents the percentage of all live births that were cesarean deliveries.
[3] Babies born prior to 37 weeks of pregnancy (gestation).
[4] Number of births per 1,000 females aged 15–19
[5] Babies born weighing less than 2,500 grams or 5 lbs. 8oz.
[6] Death rates are the number of deaths per 100,000 total population.
[7] U.S. total includes data from 30 states and D.C.
NA = Not available.
- = Zero or rounds to zero.

Table NC-15. State Government Finances, 2021

(Dollar amounts in thousands, percent distribution.)

Item	Dollars	Percent distribution
Total Revenue	98,872,610	100.0
General revenue	73,865,856	74.7
Intergovernmental revenue	28,099,181	28.4
Taxes	34,711,694	35.1
General sales	9,717,598	9.8
Selective sales	4,850,582	4.9
License taxes	2,596,969	2.6
Individual income tax	15,908,051	16.1
Corporate income tax	1,515,650	1.5
Other taxes	122,844	0.1
Current charges	6,854,034	6.9
Miscellaneous general revenue	4,200,947	4.2
Utility revenue	1,044	-
Liquor stores revenue	-	-
Insurance trust revenue[1]	25,005,710	25.3
Total Expenditure	76,023,189	100.0
Intergovernmental expenditure	19,029,254	25.0
Direct expenditure	56,993,935	75.0
Current operation	40,553,594	53.3
Capital outlay	4,637,168	6.1
Insurance benefits and repayments	9,295,215	12.2
Assistance and subsidies	1,867,649	2.5
Interest on debt	640,309	0.8
Exhibit: Salaries and wages	9,444,367	12.4
Total Expenditure	76,023,189	100.0
General expenditure	66,652,195	87.7
Intergovernmental expenditure	19,029,254	25.0
Direct expenditure	47,622,941	62.6
General expenditure, by function:		
Education	24,309,949	32.0
Public welfare	19,932,563	26.2
Hospitals	3,015,264	4.0
Health	2,018,889	2.7
Highways	4,874,260	6.4
Police protection	732,503	1.0
Correction	1,771,835	2.3
Natural resources	716,680	0.9
Parks and recreation	277,422	0.4
Governmental administration	3,325,613	4.4
Interest on general debt	640,309	0.8
Other and unallocable	4,647,077	6.1
Utility expenditure	232,038	0.2
Liquor stores expenditure	-	-
Insurance trust expenditure	9,295,215	12.2
Debt at End of Fiscal Year	15,073,723	X
Cash and Security Holdings	167,195,902	X

X = Not applicable.
- = Zero or rounds to zero.
[1] Within insurance trust revenue, net earnings of state retirement systems is a calculated statistic (the item code in the data file is X08), and thus can be positive or negative. Net earnings is the sum of earnings on investments plus gains on investments minus losses on investments. The change made in 2002 for asset valuation from book to market value in accordance with Statement 34 of the Governmental Accounting Standards Board is reflected in the calculated statistics.

Table NC-16. State Government Tax Collections, 2022

(Dollars in thousands, percent.)

Item	Dollars	Percent distribution
Total Taxes	38,453,594	100.0
Property taxes	X	-
Sales and gross receipts	16,328,599	42.5
General sales and gross receipts	11,039,816	28.7
Selective sales and gross receipts	5,288,783	13.8
Alcoholic beverages	561,333	1.5
Amusements	6	-
Insurance premiums	1,003,553	2.6
Motor fuels	2,193,373	5.7
Pari-mutuels	X	-
Public utilities	295	-
Tobacco products	295,188	0.8
Other selective sales	1,235,035	3.2
Licenses	2,657,879	6.9
Alcoholic beverages	31,434	-
Amusements	117	-
Corporations in general	1,012,322	2.6
Hunting and fishing	41,449	0.1
Motor vehicle	987,146	2.6
Motor vehicle operators	118,066	0.3
Public utilities	18,876	-
Occupation and business, NEC	397,873	1.0
Other licenses	50,596	0.1
Income taxes	19,303,124	50.2
Individual income	17,672,005	46.0
Corporation net income	1,631,119	4.2
Other taxes	163,992	0.4
Death and gift	213	-
Documentary and stock transfer	162,055	0.4
Severance	1,724	-
Taxes, NEC	0	-

X = Not applicable.
- = Zero or rounds to zero.

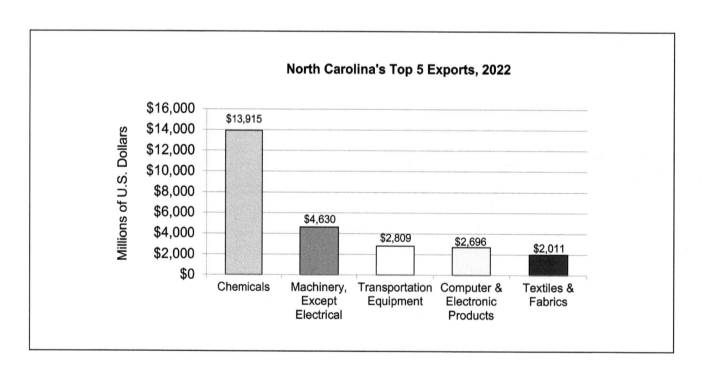

North Carolina's Top 5 Exports, 2022

Facts and Figures

Location: North central United States; bordered on the N by Canada (Manitoba and Saskatchewan), on the E by Minnesota, on the S by South Dakota, and on the W by Montana

Area: 70,700 sq. mi. (183,112 sq. km.); rank—19th

Population: 779,261 (2022 est.); rank—47th

Principal Cities: capital—Bismarck; largest—Fargo

Statehood: November 2, 1889; 39th state

U.S. Congress: 2 senators, 1 representative

State Motto: Liberty and Union, Now and Forever, One and Inseparable

State Song: "North Dakota Hymn"

State Nicknames: The Peace Garden State; The Flickertail State; The Rough Rider State

Abbreviations: ND; N.D.; N. Dak.

State Symbols: flower—wild prairie rose; tree—American elm; bird—Western meadowlark

At a Glance

- With an increase in population of 15.9 percent, North Dakota ranked 7th for population growth between 2010 and 2022.

- In 2021, 7.9 percent of North Dakotans did not have health insurance, compared to 8.6 percent of the total U.S. population.

- North Dakota had the 2nd highest birth rate in the country in 2021 (13.0 births per 1,000 population).

- In 2021, North Dakota had the 7th highest drug overdose death rate of 48.1 deaths per 100,000 population.

- North Dakota had the 4th lowest childhood poverty rate in 2021, with 10.5 percent of children under 18 years old living in poverty. The national childhood poverty rate was 16.9 percent.

Table ND-1. Population by Age, Sex, Race, and Hispanic Origin

(Number, percent, except where noted.)

Sex, age, race, and Hispanic origin	2010	2020	2022	Percent change, 2010–2022
Total Population................................	672,591	779,091	779,261	15.9
Percent of total U.S. population	0.2	0.2	0.2	X
Sex				
Male..	339,864	401,242	400,463	17.8
Female	332,727	377,849	378,798	13.8
Age				
Under 5 years..	44,595	53,276	49,929	12.0
Under 18 years...	149,871	184,326	182,775	22.0
18 to 64 years	425,243	471,723	466,558	9.7
65 years and over	97,477	123,042	129,928	33.3
Median age (years)	37	35.4	35.8	-3.2
Race and Hispanic Origin				
One race				
White	609,136	678,494	675,085	10.8
Black	8,248	26,914	28,128	241.0
American Indian and Alaska Native	36,948	40,965	41,435	12.1
Asian	7,032	13,431	13,611	93.6
Native Hawaiian or Other Pacific Islander	334	665	919	175.1
Two or more races	10,893	18,622	20,083	84.4
Hispanic (of any race)	13,467	33,851	36,075	167.9

NOTE: Population figures for 2022 are July 1 estimates. The 2010 and 2020 estimates are taken from the respective censuses.
- = Zero or rounds to zero.
X = Not applicable.

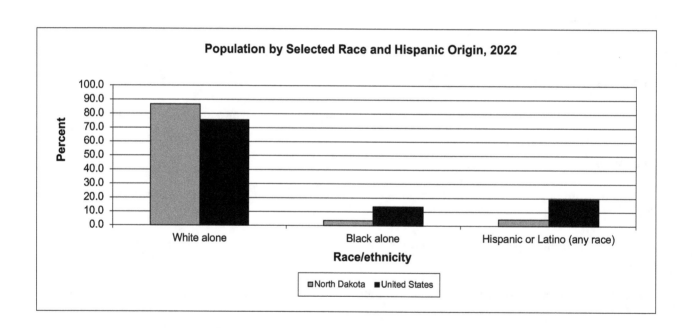

Table ND-2. Marital Status

(Number, percent distribution.)

Sex, age, race, and Hispanic origin	2000	2010	2021
Males, 15 Years and Over	253,900	278,276	319,166
Never married	32.0	35.8	38.5
Now married, except separated..............................	57.5	53.1	49.4
Separated...	0.6	0.6	1.1
Widowed..	2.5	2.1	2.4
Divorced..	7.3	8.4	8.6
Females, 15 Years and Over	258,381	271,462	300,961
Never married	23.2	26.6	28.9
Now married, except separated..............................	56.0	52.5	51.1
Separated...	0.8	0.7	0.8
Widowed..	11.7	10.1	8.2
Divorced..	8.2	10.2	11.0

Table ND-3. Households and Housing Characteristics

(Number, percent, dollars.)

Item	2000	2010	2021	Average annual percent change, 2010–2021
Total Households	257,252	280,412	322,511	1.4
Family households	166,150	171,945	190,518	1.0
Married-couple family	137,433	140,277	148,550	0.5
Other family	28,717	31,668	41,968	3.0
Male householder, no wife present	8,569	8,846	17,460	8.9
Female householder, no husband present	20,148	22,822	24,508	0.7
Nonfamily households	91,002	108,467	131,993	2.0
Householder living alone	75,420	87,883	107,095	2.0
Householder not living alone	15,582	20,584	24,898	1.9
Housing Characteristics				
Total housing units	289,677	318,099	374,435	1.6
Occupied housing units	257,252	280,412	322,511	1.4
Owner occupied	171,299	187,673	203,549	0.8
Renter occupied	85,853	92,739	118,962	2.6
Average household size	2.41	2.32	2.33	-
Financial Characteristics				
Median gross rent of renter-occupied housing	412	583	839	4.0
Median monthly owner costs for housing units with a mortgage	818	1,133	1,488	2.8
Median value of owner-occupied housing units	74,400	123,000	224,400	7.5

Table ND-4. Migration, Origin, and Language

(Number, percent.)

Characteristic	State 2021	U.S. 2021
Residence 1 Year Ago		
Population 1 year and over	764,638	328,464,538
Same house	83.8	87.2
Different house in the U.S.	15.9	12.3
Same county	7.7	6.7
Different county	8.2	5.7
Same state	3.2	3.3
Different state	4.9	2.4
Abroad	0.3	0.4
Place of Birth		
Native born	741,124	286,623,642
Male	51.6	49.7
Female	48.4	50.3
Foreign born	33,824	45,270,103
Male	50.8	48.7
Female	49.2	51.3
Foreign born; naturalized U.S. citizen	16,337	24,044,083
Male	48.8	46.4
Female	51.2	53.6
Foreign born; not a U.S. citizen	17,487	21,226,020
Male	52.6	51.2
Female	47.4	48.8
Entered 2010 or later	54.1	28.1
Entered 2000 to 2009	24.0	23.7
Entered before 2000	21.9	48.2
World Region of Birth, Foreign		
Foreign-born population, excluding population born at sea	33,824	45,269,644
Europe	12.1	10.7
Asia	29.1	31.0
Africa	28.8	5.7
Oceania	0.7	0.6
Latin America	21.0	50.1
North America	8.3	1.7
Language Spoken at Home and Ability to Speak English		
Population 5 years and over	723,798	313,232,500
English only	93.0	78.4
Language other than English	7.0	21.6
Speaks English less than "very well"	2.1	8.3

Table ND-5. Median Income and Poverty Status, 2021

(Number, percent, except as noted.)

Characteristic	State Number	State Percent	U.S. Number	U.S. Percent
Median Income				
Households (dollars)............	66,519	X	69,717	X
Families (dollars)	89,504	X	85,806	X
Below Poverty Level (All People)	83,350	11.1	41,393,176	12.8
Sex				
Male	37,084	9.6	18,518,155	11.6
Female	46,266	12.7	22,875,021	13.9
Age				
Under 18 years............	18,884	10.5	12,243,219	16.9
Related children under 18 years............	18,089	10.1	11,985,424	16.6
18 to 64 years............	53,307	11.8	23,526,341	11.9
65 years and over	11,159	9.4	5,623,616	10.3

X = Not applicable.

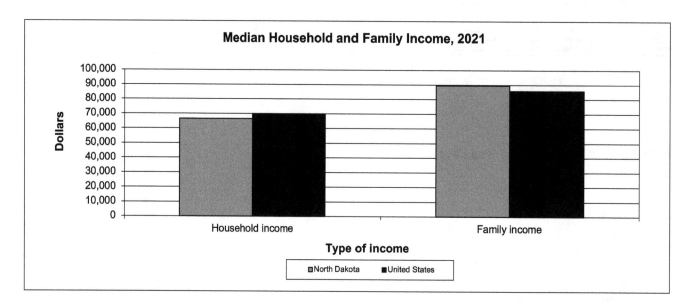

Table ND-6. Health Insurance Coverage Status for the Civilian Noninstitutionalized Population and Children Under 19 Years of Age

(Number, percent.)

Item	2011	2012	2013	2014	2015	2016	2017	2018	2019	2020[2]	2021
Civilian Noninstitutionalized Population	669425	684776	708,181	724,451	740,547	741,486	738,177	743,793	744,172	743,105	756,440
Covered by Private or Public Insurance											
Number............	603,977	616,252	634,882	667,553	683,096	689,348	682,595	689,858	692,848	689,270	697,043
Percent............	90.2	90.0	89.6	92.1	92.2	93.0	92.5	92.7	93.1	92.8	92.1
Uninsured											
Number............	65,448	68,524	73,299	56,898	57,451	52,138	55,582	53,935	51,324	53,835	59,397
Percent............	9.8	10.0	10.4	7.9	7.8	7.0	7.5	7.3	6.9	7.2	7.9
Percent in the U.S. not covered............	15.1	14.8	14.5	11.7	9.4	8.6	8.7	8.9	9.2	8.7	8.6
Children Under 19 Years of Age[1]	150853	153705	160,430	167,191	170,994	174,130	183,593	185,726	187,129	188,147	194,529
Covered by Private or Public Insurance											
Number............	141,238	143,156	147,705	155,649	157,564	160,506	169,775	174,551	172,595	174,405	180,242
Percent............	93.6	93.1	92.1	93.1	92.1	92.2	92.5	94.0	92.2	92.7	92.7
Uninsured											
Number............	9,615	10,549	12,725	11,542	13,430	13,624	13,818	11,175	14,534	13,742	14,287
Percent............	6.4	6.9	7.9	6.9	7.9	7.8	7.5	6.0	7.8	7.3	7.3
Percent in the U.S. not covered............	7.5	7.2	7.1	6.0	4.8	4.5	5.0	5.2	5.7	5.2	5.4

[1] Data for years prior to 2017 are for individuals under 18 years of age.
[2] 2020 ACS 5-Year estimates. 1-Year estimates were not released for 2020 due to the impact of COVID-19 on data collection that year. Data is not comparable to previous years, which are based on 1-year estimates.

Table ND-7. Employment Status by Demographic Group, 2022

(Numbers in thousands, percent.)

Characteristic	Civilian noninstitutional population	Civilian labor force		Employed		Unemployed	
		Number	Percent of population	Number	Percent of population	Number	Percent of population
Total..	593	409	68.9	401	67.7	7	1.8
Sex							
Male..	303	223	73.8	219	72.5	4	1.8
Female..	290	185	63.8	182	62.6	3	1.8
Race, Sex, and Hispanic Origin							
White..	529	367	69.3	361	68.2	6	1.6
Male..	272	201	74.1	198	72.8	3	1.7
Female......................................	257	165	64.3	163	63.3	3	1.6
Black or African American............	NA	NA	NA	NA	NA	NA	NA
Male..	NA	NA	NA	NA	NA	NA	NA
Female......................................	NA	NA	NA	NA	NA	NA	NA
Hispanic or Latino ethnicity[1]........	NA	NA	NA	NA	NA	NA	NA
Male..	NA	NA	NA	NA	NA	NA	NA
Female......................................	NA	NA	NA	NA	NA	NA	NA
Age							
16 to 19 years............................	NA	NA	NA	NA	NA	NA	NA
20 to 24 years............................	51	42	82.2	40	79.1	2	3.6
25 to 34 years............................	112	99	88.8	98	87.5	1	1.3
35 to 44 years............................	103	91	88.3	90	87.3	1	1.1
45 to 54 years............................	79	69	87.3	68	85.6	1	1.7
55 to 64 years............................	87	65	74.4	64	73.7	1	0.9
65 years and over........................	NA	NA	NA	NA	NA	NA	NA

NOTE: Data in Table 7 are from the Current Population Survey (CPS) and do not match the estimates in Table 8. See notes and definitions for further information.
[1] May be of any race.
NA = Not available.

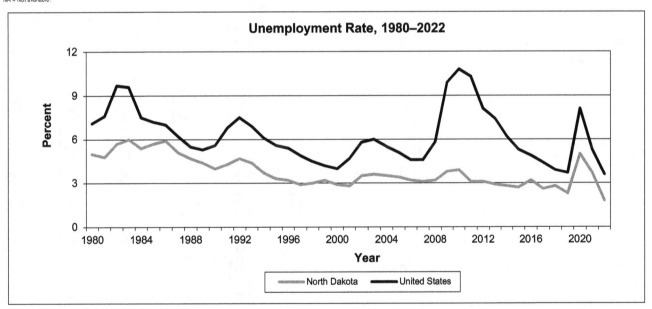

Unemployment Rate, 1980–2022

Table ND-8. Employment Status of the Civilian Noninstitutional Population Age 16 Years and Over

(Number, percent.)

Year	Civilian labor force	Civilian participation rate	Employed	Unemployed	Unemployment rate
2010..................................	379,062	72.8	365,041	14,021	3.7
2011..................................	387,383	72.6	374,434	12,949	3.3
2012..................................	395,490	72.6	383,888	11,602	2.9
2013..................................	401,518	71.9	389,928	11,590	2.9
2014..................................	409,503	71.8	398,783	10,720	2.6
2015..................................	410,764	70.8	399,296	11,468	2.8
2016..................................	411,778	70.9	399,001	12,777	3.1
2017..................................	415,765	70.7	404,901	10,864	2.6
2018..................................	412,764	70	403,002	9,762	2.4
2019..................................	415,169	70	406,304	8,865	2.1
2020..................................	411,550	69.2	390,504	21,046	5.1
2021..................................	406,187	68.5	391,255	14,932	3.7
2022..................................	414,311	69.2	405,580	8,731	2.1

Table ND-9. Employment and Average Wages by Industry

(Estimates are based on the 2012 North American Industry Classification System [NAICS].)

Industry	2014	2015	2016	2017	2018	2019	2020	2021
	Number of Jobs							
Wage and Salary Employment by Industry......................	480,665	471,312	450,659	447,667	451,269	456,960	430,442	434,811
Farm Wage and Salary Employment................................	7,292	5,149	4,849	5,223	5,393	5,407	6,632	6,438
Nonfarm Wage and Salary Employment..........................	473,373	466,163	445,810	442,444	445,876	451,553	423,810	428,373
Private wage and salary employment................................	387,500	378,606	356,734	353,855	357,448	362,543	336,497	338,863
Forestry, fishing, and related activities............................	2,612	2,598	2,632	2,626	2,666	2,734	2,684	2,489
Mining...	29,598	23,038	15,189	17,705	20,660	21,272	15,049	13,706
Utilities...	3,702	3,831	3,843	3,781	3,669	3,446	3,325	3,236
Construction...	35,617	34,940	31,876	27,381	26,637	28,646	26,001	25,260
Manufacturing...	25,968	25,449	24,574	24,704	25,923	26,490	25,279	26,167
Durable goods manufacturing..................................	17,655	17,089	16,197	16,273	17,392	17,803	16,557	17,026
Nondurable goods manufacturing.............................	8,313	8,360	8,377	8,431	8,531	8,687	8,722	9,141
Wholesale trade...	27,406	26,773	24,524	24,034	23,966	24,342	23,171	22,714
Retail trade...	50,890	51,048	49,465	48,024	47,205	45,936	44,074	45,095
Transportation and warehousing.................................	24,662	22,747	18,326	18,506	19,047	19,795	18,041	17,761
Information..	6,844	6,622	6,638	6,510	6,219	6,097	5,780	5,727
Finance and insurance..	18,521	18,843	18,880	18,863	18,809	18,918	18,734	18,264
Real estate and rental and leasing..............................	5,821	5,732	5,194	5,296	5,430	5,568	5,117	5,014
Professional, scientific, and technical services....................	16,841	17,192	16,484	16,029	16,103	16,400	16,061	16,209
Management of companies and enterprises.....................	5,291	5,338	5,258	5,318	5,287	3,581	3,821	4,023
Administrative and waste services................................	14,311	13,816	12,921	13,170	13,418	13,108	11,990	12,900
Educational services..	4,129	4,303	4,451	4,540	4,331	4,507	4,001	4,833
Health care and social assistance...............................	56,098	57,435	59,200	59,940	60,300	63,801	62,515	62,583
Arts, entertainment, and recreation..............................	4,399	4,354	4,545	4,651	5,793	5,711	4,860	5,504
Accommodation and food services..............................	36,365	36,292	34,988	34,913	34,840	34,969	29,647	31,634
Other services, except public administration..................	18,425	18,255	17,746	17,864	17,145	17,222	16,347	15,744
Government and government enterprises.................................	85,873	87,557	89,076	88,589	88,428	89,010	87,313	89,510
	Dollars							
Average Wages and Salaries by Industry	49,904	49,718	48,041	49,441	51,448	53,246	54,327	55,761
Average Farm Wages and Salaries	40,004	33,785	38,597	38,163	36,002	45,309	33,614	34,119
Average Nonfarm Wages and Salaries	50,057	49,894	48,144	49,574	51,635	53,341	54,651	56,086
Average private wages and salaries................................	51,953	51,522	49,258	50,780	53,154	55,036	56,022	57,655
Forestry, fishing, and related activities............................	28,243	29,958	31,852	32,727	32,967	34,762	38,386	40,377
Mining...	103,875	100,835	95,404	100,871	106,477	108,669	106,709	105,965
Utilities...	90,554	95,223	96,277	100,355	106,186	110,372	112,378	118,622
Construction...	64,853	64,917	64,240	63,000	64,549	68,106	66,695	66,687
Manufacturing...	49,760	51,187	51,039	52,601	53,886	55,179	57,696	62,822
Durable goods manufacturing..................................	49,960	50,765	50,302	51,550	53,266	54,339	56,087	62,560
Nondurable goods manufacturing.............................	49,335	52,050	52,463	54,631	55,148	56,901	60,751	63,311
Wholesale trade...	68,068	66,617	62,722	65,070	68,066	70,280	71,145	74,697
Retail trade...	29,706	30,809	30,288	30,633	31,134	32,075	34,140	35,970
Transportation and warehousing.................................	68,577	66,695	61,650	64,608	66,830	69,692	67,548	66,467
Information..	58,339	59,769	63,207	65,083	70,251	71,521	79,637	82,917
Finance and insurance..	56,343	59,359	60,735	63,069	66,354	69,208	73,818	78,127
Real estate and rental and leasing..............................	59,749	56,583	48,343	50,454	53,095	54,575	53,174	54,121
Professional, scientific, and technical services....................	71,693	69,698	67,564	69,903	72,892	75,592	76,888	74,572
Management of companies and enterprises.....................	76,662	81,419	77,015	80,856	85,712	102,504	99,830	108,397
Administrative and waste services................................	34,061	34,947	36,590	37,986	38,948	38,611	40,199	42,926
Educational services..	23,699	23,625	22,600	22,835	24,755	25,753	29,275	26,152
Health care and social assistance...............................	46,553	49,318	49,461	50,531	51,928	53,067	55,732	59,133
Arts, entertainment, and recreation..............................	17,591	18,437	18,079	18,366	18,679	20,120	20,766	21,236
Accommodation and food services..............................	19,564	19,773	19,660	19,801	20,799	21,355	20,818	24,217
Other services, except public administration..................	31,954	33,434	33,443	34,799	37,227	38,554	41,059	43,881
Government and government enterprises.............................	41,498	42,850	43,683	44,759	45,496	46,439	49,370	50,150

Table ND-10. Employment Characteristics by Family Type

(Number, percent.)

Family type and labor force status	2019		2020 [1]		2021	
	Total	Families with own children under 18 years	Total	Families with own children under 18 years	Total	Families with own children under 18 years
All Families...	189,509	86,211	189,465	84,213	190,518	79,604
FAMILY TYPE AND LABOR FORCE STATUS						
Opposite-Sex Married-Couple Families..	151,995	63,023	151,905	60,266	147,445	56,087
Both husband and wife in labor force................................	61.3	78.7	60.7	77.7	57.8	74.4
Husband in labor force, wife not in labor force	16.2	17.3	16.8	18.9	17.1	21.3
Wife in labor force, husband not in labor force	5.7	2.1	6.6	2.4	7.0	3.1
Both husband and wife not in labor force...........................	16.4	1.9	15.9	1.0	18.0	1.2
Other Families	37,514	23,188	36,814	23,683	41,968	23,474
Female householder, no spouse present	65.1	65.6	65.2	66.5	58.4	61.6
In labor force	50.3	55.5	51.8	57.7	41.2	50.5
Not in labor force	14.7	10.1	13.4	8.8	17.2	11.1
Male householder, no spouse present...........................	34.9	34.4	34.8	33.5	41.6	38.4
In labor force	29.8	31.8	30.3	31.1	37.0	37.4
Not in labor force	5.1	2.6	4.5	2.4	4.6	1.0

[1] 2020 ACS 5-Year estimates. 1-Year estimates were not released for 2020 due to the impact of COVID-19 on data collection that year. Data is not comparable to previous years, which are based on 1-year estimates.

Table ND-11. School Enrollment and Educational Attainment, 2021

(Number, percent.)

Item	State	U.S.
Enrollment		
Total population 3 years and over, enrolled in school	190,174	79,453,524
Enrolled in nursery school or preschool (percent)	5.4	5.2
Enrolled in kindergarten (percent)..	5.0	5.0
Enrolled in elementary school, grades 1-8 (percent)..	42.6	41.3
Enrolled in high school, grades 9-12 (percent)	18.6	21.8
Enrolled in college or graduate school (percent)...	28.4	26.7
Attainment		
Total population 25 years and over	506,739	228,193,464
Less than ninth grade (percent)	2.8	4.8
9th to 12th grade, no diploma (percent)	3.5	5.9
High school graduate, including equivalency (percent)..	26.3	26.3
Some college, no degree (percent)	21.1	19.3
Associate's degree (percent)	14.5	8.8
Bachelor's degree (percent)	22.4	21.2
Graduate or professional degree (percent)..	9.4	13.8
High school graduate or higher (percent)	93.6	89.4
Bachelor's degree or higher (percent)...	31.7	35.0

Table ND-12. Public School Characteristics and Educational Indicators

(Number, percent; data derived from National Center of Education Statistics.)

Item	State	U.S.
Public Elementary and Secondary Schools		
Number of regular school districts, 2019-20	174	13,349
Number of operational schools, 2019-20...	477	98,469
Percent charter schools	0.0	7.7
Total public school enrollment, Fall 2021	116,864	49,433,092
Percent charter school enrollment	NA	7.5
Student-teacher ratio, Fall 2019	12.5	15.9
Expenditures per student (unadjusted dollars), 2019-20	14,252	13,489
Four-year adjusted cohort graduation rate (ACGR), 2019-2020[1]................................	89.0	86.5
Students eligible for free or reduced-price lunch (percent), 2019-20..............................	30.2	52.1
English language learners (percent), Fall 2020	3.6	10.3
Students age 3 to 21 served under IDEA, part B (percent), 2021-22	14.6	14.7

Public Schools by Type, 2019-20	Number	Percent of state public schools
Total number of schools...	477	100.0
Special education	-	-
Vocational education	-	-
Alternative education..	-	-

[1] Adjusted Cohort Graduation Rates (ACGR) differ from Averaged Freshmen Graduation Rates (AFGR).
NA = Not available.
- = Zero or rounds to zero.

Table ND-13. Reported Voting and Registration of the Voting-Age Population, November 2022

(Numbers in thousands, percent.)

Item	Total population	Total citizen population	Registered			Voted		
			Total registered	Percent registered (total population)	Percent registered (total citizen population)	Total voted	Percent voted (total population)	Percent voted (total citizen population)
U.S. Total	255,457	233,546	161,422	63.2	69.1	121,916	47.7	52.2
State Total................................	575	554	418	72.8	75.6	288	50.0	52.0
Sex								
Male	296	283	209	70.7	74.0	144	48.4	50.7
Female	279	271	209	75.0	77.2	144	51.7	53.3
Race								
White alone..............................	518	509	396	76.5	77.8	278	53.7	54.7
White, non-Hispanic alone	501	497	387	77.3	77.9	275	55.0	55.4
Black alone..............................	15	13	9	58.5	67.4	1	8.6	9.9
Asian alone	8	3	2	23.1	68.1	1	16.7	49.0
Hispanic (of any race).............	18	13	10	52.5	74.4	3	17.7	25.2
White alone or in combination ..	524	515	400	76.4	77.7	280	53.5	54.4
Black alone or in combination...	19	17	10	54.0	62.6	1	6.8	7.9
Asian alone or in combination...	9	4	3	30.4	75.6	1	15.1	37.5
Age								
18 to 24 years...........................	72	69	38	52.2	54.8	18	24.8	26.0
25 to 34 years...........................	112	100	68	61.0	67.9	39	34.8	38.7
35 to 44 years...........................	101	96	76	75.7	79.2	45	44.7	46.8
45 to 64 years...........................	149	148	123	82.8	83.5	88	59.3	59.8
65 years and over	142	141	113	79.9	80.4	98	69.0	69.4

- = Zero or rounds to zero.
B = Base is less than 75,000 and therefore too small to show the derived measure.

Table ND-14. Health Indicators

(Number, rate as indicated in footnotes.)

Item	State	U.S.
Births		
Life Expectancy at Birth (years), 2020	76.9	77.0
Fertility Rate by State[1], 2021	66.7	56.3
Percent Home Births, 2021	1.4	1.4
Cesarean Delivery Rate[2], 2021	26.3	32.1
Preterm Birth Rate[3], 2021	9.6	10.5
Teen Birth Rate[4], 2021	12.9	13.9
Percentage of Babies Born Low Birthweight[5], 2021	6.7	8.5
Deaths[6]		
Heart Disease Mortality Rate, 2021..	152.8	173.8
Cancer Mortality Rate, 2021...	137.8	146.6
Stroke Mortality Rate, 2021	29.4	41.1
Diabetes Mortality Rate, 2021..	25.2	25.4
Influenza/Pneumonia Mortality Rate, 2021...	13.1	10.5
Suicide Mortality Rate, 2021...	20.8	14.1
Drug Overdose Mortality Rate, 2021...	17.2	33.6
Firearm Injury Mortality Rate, 2021..	16.8	14.6
Homicide Mortality Rate, 2021..	3.4	8.2
Disease and Illness		
Lifetime Asthma in Adults, 2020 (percent)..	11.9	13.9
Lifetime Asthma in Children, 2020 (percent)[7]	NA	11.3
Diabetes in Adults, 2020 (percent)...	9.3	8.2
Self-reported Obesity in Adults, 2021 (percent)..	35.2	NA

SOURCE: National Center for Health Statistics, National Vital Statistics System 2020 data; https://wonder.cdc.gov.
[1] General fertility rate per 1,000 women aged 15–44.
[2] This represents the percentage of all live births that were cesarean deliveries.
[3] Babies born prior to 37 weeks of pregnancy (gestation).
[4] Number of births per 1,000 females aged 15–19
[5] Babies born weighing less than 2,500 grams or 5 lbs. 8oz.
[6] Death rates are the number of deaths per 100,000 total population.
[7] U.S. total includes data from 30 states and D.C.
NA = Not available.
- = Zero or rounds to zero.

Table ND-15. State Government Finances, 2021

(Dollar amounts in thousands, percent distribution.)

Item	Dollars	Percent distribution
Total Revenue	10,419,472	100.0
General revenue	9,331,669	89.6
Intergovernmental revenue	3,750,161	36.0
Taxes	3,908,672	37.5
General sales	919,915	8.8
Selective sales	506,973	4.9
License taxes	210,333	2.0
Individual income tax	448,704	4.3
Corporate income tax	155,458	1.5
Other taxes	1,667,289	16.0
Current charges	827,616	7.9
Miscellaneous general revenue	845,220	8.1
Utility revenue	-	-
Liquor stores revenue	-	-
Insurance trust revenue[1]	1,087,803	10.4
Total Expenditure	9,295,476	100.0
Intergovernmental expenditure	2,381,658	25.6
Direct expenditure	6,913,818	74.4
Current operation	4,932,289	53.1
Capital outlay	758,111	8.2
Insurance benefits and repayments	963,967	10.4
Assistance and subsidies	145,925	1.6
Interest on debt	113,526	1.2
Exhibit: Salaries and wages	1,152,418	12.4
Total Expenditure	9,295,476	100.0
General expenditure	8,288,136	89.2
Intergovernmental expenditure	2,381,658	25.6
Direct expenditure	5,906,478	63.5
General expenditure, by function:		
Education	2,762,598	29.7
Public welfare	1,786,618	19.2
Hospitals	84,125	0.9
Health	306,925	3.3
Highways	818,612	8.8
Police protection	49,481	0.5
Correction	128,843	1.4
Natural resources	331,022	3.6
Parks and recreation	30,661	0.3
Governmental administration	361,919	3.9
Interest on general debt	113,526	1.2
Other and unallocable	1,321,706	14.2
Utility expenditure	216,584	2.1
Liquor stores expenditure	-	-
Insurance trust expenditure	963,967	10.4
Debt at End of Fiscal Year	2,683,267	X
Cash and Security Holdings	41,513,723	X

X = Not applicable.
- = Zero or rounds to zero.
[1] Within insurance trust revenue, net earnings of state retirement systems is a calculated statistic (the item code in the data file is X08), and thus can be positive or negative. Net earnings is the sum of earnings on investments plus gains on investments minus losses on investments. The change made in 2002 for asset valuation from book to market value in accordance with Statement 34 of the Governmental Accounting Standards Board is reflected in the calculated statistics.

Table ND-16. State Government Tax Collections, 2022

(Dollars in thousands, percent.)

Item	Dollars	Percent distribution
Total Taxes	5,350,784	100.0
Property taxes	5,322	0.1
Sales and gross receipts	1,586,316	29.6
General sales and gross receipts	1,074,703	20.1
Selective sales and gross receipts	511,613	9.6
Alcoholic beverages	9,800	0.2
Amusements	23,928	0.4
Insurance premiums	75,216	1.4
Motor fuels	179,821	3.4
Pari-mutuels	1,579	-
Public utilities	35,122	0.7
Tobacco products	24,677	0.5
Other selective sales	161,470	3.0
Licenses	198,784	3.7
Alcoholic beverages	410	-
Amusements	2,533	-
Corporations in general	X	-
Hunting and fishing	18,191	0.3
Motor vehicle	116,140	2.2
Motor vehicle operators	3,905	0.1
Public utilities	2	-
Occupation and business, NEC	57,603	1.1
Other licenses	-	-
Income taxes	702,126	13.1
Individual income	472,925	8.8
Corporation net income	229,201	4.3
Other taxes	2,858,236	53.4
Death and gift	X	-
Documentary and stock transfer	X	-
Severance	2,858,236	53.4
Taxes, NEC	-	-

- = Zero or rounds to zero.
X = Not applicable.

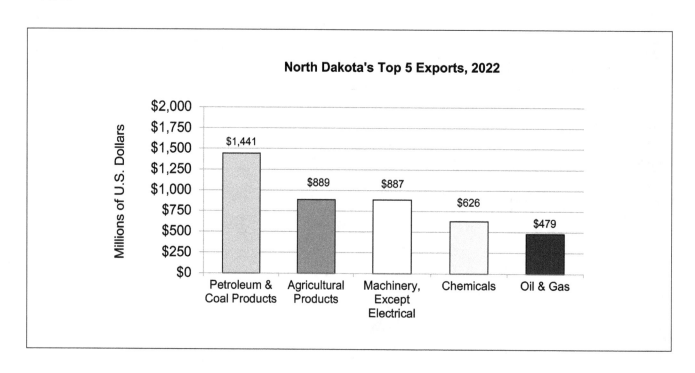

North Dakota's Top 5 Exports, 2022

Facts and Figures

Location: East north central United States; bordered on the N by Michigan and Lake Erie, on the E by Pennsylvania and West Virginia, on the S by West Virginia and Kentucky, and on the W by Indiana

Area: 44,825 sq. mi. (116,096 sq. km.); rank—34th

Population: 11,756,058 (2022 est.); rank—7th

Principal Cities: capital—Columbus; largest—Columbus

Statehood: March 1, 1803; 17th state

U.S. Congress: 2 senators, 16 representatives

State Motto: With God, All Things Are Possible

State Song: "Beautiful Ohio"

State Nickname: The Buckeye State

Abbreviations: OH

State Symbols: flower—scarlet carnation; tree—Ohio buckeye; bird—cardinal

At a Glance

- With an increase in population of 1.9 percent, Ohio ranked 44th among the states in growth from 2010 to 2022.

- Ohio's median household income in 2021 was $62,262, compared to the U.S. median of $69,717.

- In 2021, 6.5 percent of Ohioans did not have health insurance, compared to 8.6 percent of the entire U.S. population.

- Ohio's real GDP of $639 billion ranked 7th in the nation in 2022 and comprised 3.2 percent of the nation's total GDP.

- Ohio had 48.9 full-time equivalent state and local government employees per 1,000 residents in 2022, compared to the national average of 49.8 employees per 1,000 residents.

Table OH-1. Population by Age, Sex, Race, and Hispanic Origin

(Number, percent, except where noted.)

Sex, age, race, and Hispanic origin	2010	2020	2022	Percent change, 2010–2022
Total Population...	11,536,504	11,799,374	11,756,058	1.9
Percent of total U.S. population	3.7	3.6	3.5	X
Sex				
Male..	5,632,156	5,831,241	5,809,684	3.2
Female	5,904,348	5,968,133	5,946,374	0.7
Age				
Under 5 years..	720,856	681,096	661,421	-8.2
Under 18 years...	2,730,751	2,604,419	2,562,550	-6.2
18 to 64 years	7,183,738	7,131,593	7,031,310	-2.1
65 years and over	1,622,015	2,063,362	2,162,198	33.3
Median age (years)	38.8	39.5	39.7	2.3
Race and Hispanic Origin				
One race				
White	9,664,524	9,604,940	9,509,945	-1.6
Black	1,426,861	1,551,898	1,565,976	9.7
American Indian and Alaska Native	29,674	34,542	35,841	20.8
Asian...	196,693	306,701	323,165	64.3
Native Hawaiian or Other Pacific Islander	5,336	7,803	8,420	57.8
Two or more races	213,416	293,490	312,711	46.5
Hispanic (of any race)	354,674	491,866	524,999	48.0

NOTE: Population figures for 2022 are July 1 estimates. The 2010 and 2020 estimates are taken from the respective censuses.
- = Zero or rounds to zero.
X = Not applicable.

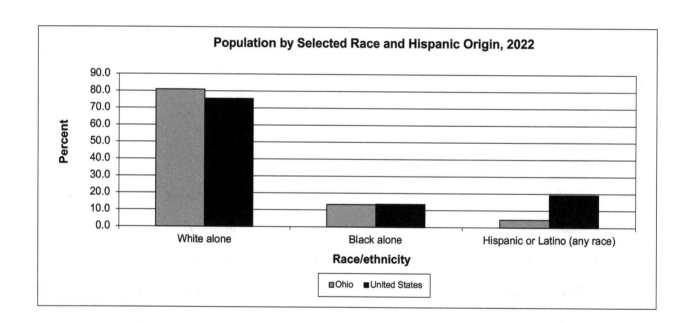

Table OH-2. Marital Status

(Number, percent distribution.)

Sex, age, race, and Hispanic origin	2000	2010	2021
Males, 15 Years and Over	4,281,736	4,487,900	4,709,124
Never married	29.2	33.5	36.4
Now married, except separated..	57.0	51.2	48.4
Separated...	1.4	1.7	1.4
Widowed...	2.7	2.9	3.1
Divorced...	9.7	10.8	10.7
Females, 15 Years and Over	4,670,985	4,809,613	4,927,624
Never married	23.5	27.9	30.5
Now married, except separated..	52.1	46.9	46.0
Separated...	1.7	2.1	1.7
Widowed...	11.1	10.1	8.9
Divorced...	11.5	12.9	13.1

Table OH-3. Households and Housing Characteristics

(Number, percent, dollars.)

Item	2000	2010	2021	Average annual percent change, 2010–2021
Total Households...	4,445,773	4,525,066	4,832,922	0.6
Family households...	2,993,023	2,960,107	2,986,455	0.1
Married-couple family.......................................	2,285,798	2,169,003	2,162,168	-
Other family..	707,225	791,104	824,287	0.4
Male householder, no wife present...................	170,347	196,130	230,594	1.6
Female householder, no husband present..........	536,878	594,974	593,693	-
Nonfamily households...	1,452,750	1,564,959	1,846,467	1.6
Householder living alone..................................	1,215,614	1,315,321	1,504,931	1.3
Householder not living alone............................	237,136	249,638	341,536	3.3
Housing Characteristics				
Total housing units...	4,783,051	5,128,113	5,269,498	0.3
Occupied housing units......................................	4,445,773	4,525,066	4,832,922	0.6
Owner occupied...	3,072,522	3,095,197	3,246,486	0.4
Renter occupied..	1,373,251	1,429,869	1,586,436	1.0
Average household size......................................	2.49	2.48	2.38	-0.4
Financial Characteristics				
Median gross rent of renter-occupied housing	515	685	870	2.5
Median monthly owner costs for housing units with a mortgage ...	983	1,246	1,293	0.3
Median value of owner-occupied housing units........	103,700	134,400	180,200	3.1

- = Zero or rounds to zero.

Table OH-4. Migration, Origin, and Language

(Number, percent.)

Characteristic	State 2021	U.S. 2021
Residence 1 Year Ago		
Population 1 year and over	11,660,200	328,464,538
Same house	87.6	87.2
Different house in the U.S.	12.1	12.3
Same county	7.3	6.7
Different county	4.8	5.7
Same state	3.2	3.3
Different state	1.6	2.4
Abroad	0.3	0.4
Place of Birth		
Native born	11,195,178	286,623,642
Male	49.2	49.7
Female	50.8	50.3
Foreign born	584,839	45,270,103
Male	50.5	48.7
Female	49.5	51.3
Foreign born; naturalized U.S. citizen................................	315,144	24,044,083
Male...	47.8	46.4
Female	52.2	53.6
Foreign born; not a U.S. citizen.......................................	269,695	21,226,020
Male...	53.6	51.2
Female	46.4	48.8
Entered 2010 or later	39.0	28.1
Entered 2000 to 2009	25.3	23.7
Entered before 2000..	35.8	48.2
World Region of Birth, Foreign		
Foreign-born population, excluding population born at sea	584,667	45,269,644
Europe..	17.8	10.7
Asia..	41.4	31.0
Africa..	18.1	5.7
Oceania...	0.6	0.6
Latin America..	19.2	50.1
North America...	2.9	1.7
Language Spoken at Home and Ability to Speak English		
Population 5 years and over	11,111,082	313,232,500
English only	92.4	78.4
Language other than English..	7.6	21.6
Speaks English less than "very well"	2.7	8.3

Table OH-5. Median Income and Poverty Status, 2021

(Number, percent, except as noted.)

Characteristic	State		U.S.	
	Number	Percent	Number	Percent
Median Income				
Households (dollars)...	62,262	X	69,717	X
Families (dollars)	80,760	X	85,806	X
Below Poverty Level (All People)	1,536,524	13.4	41,393,176	12.8
Sex				
Male	681,383	12.1	18,518,155	11.6
Female	855,141	14.6	22,875,021	13.9
Age				
Under 18 years..	474,953	18.6	12,243,219	16.9
Related children under 18 years..........................	463,841	18.2	11,985,424	16.6
18 to 64 years	867,786	12.6	23,526,341	11.9
65 years and over	193,785	9.5	5,623,616	10.3

X = Not applicable.

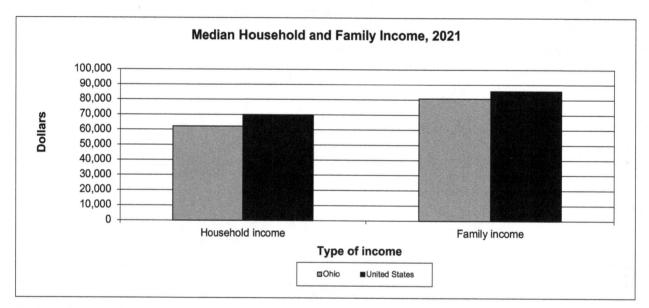

Median Household and Family Income, 2021

Table OH-6. Health Insurance Coverage Status for the Civilian Noninstitutionalized Population and Children Under 19 Years of Age

(Number, percent.)

Item	2011	2012	2013	2014	2015	2016	2017	2018	2019	2020 [2]	2021
Civilian Noninstitutionalized Population	11,369,102	11,371,766	11,398,298	11,420,809	11,442,029	11,439,848	11,485,078	11,517,226	11,514,951	11,501,751	11,611,229
Covered by Private or Public Insurance											
Number...	10,014,671	10,067,519	10,140,742	10,465,604	10,695,753	10,796,120	10,799,064	10,773,321	10,757,189	10,793,219	10,853,520
Percent...	88.1	88.5	89.0	91.6	93.5	94.4	94.0	93.5	93.4	93.8	93.5
Uninsured											
Number...	1,354,431	1,304,247	1,257,556	955,205	746,276	643,728	686,014	743,905	757,762	708,532	757,709
Percent...	11.9	11.5	11.0	8.4	6.5	5.6	6.0	6.5	6.6	6.2	6.5
Percent in the U.S. not covered................................	15.1	14.8	14.5	11.7	9.4	8.6	8.7	8.9	9.2	8.7	8.6
Children Under 19 Years of Age [1]	2,688,340	2,656,700	2,644,952	2,631,481	2,626,771	2,605,997	2,759,296	2,748,263	2,736,050	2,747,909	2,756,774
Covered by Private or Public Insurance											
Number...	2,531,138	2,516,034	2,503,584	2,505,342	2,511,790	2,511,444	2,633,901	2,615,696	2,605,021	2,625,949	2,617,225
Percent...	94.2	94.7	94.7	95.2	95.6	96.4	95.5	95.2	95.2	95.6	94.9
Uninsured											
Number...	157,202	140,666	141,368	126,139	114,981	94,553	125,395	132,567	131,029	121,960	139,549
Percent...	5.8	5.3	5.3	4.8	4.4	3.6	4.5	4.8	4.8	4.4	5.1
Percent in the U.S. not covered................................	7.5	7.2	7.1	6.0	4.8	4.5	5.0	5.2	5.7	5.2	5.4

[1] Data for years prior to 2017 are for individuals under 18 years of age.
[2] 2020 ACS 5-Year estimates. 1-Year estimates were not released for 2020 due to the impact of COVID-19 on data collection that year. Data is not comparable to previous years, which are based on 1-year estimates.

Table OH-7. Employment Status by Demographic Group, 2022

(Numbers in thousands, percent.)

Characteristic	Civilian noninstitutional population	Civilian labor force		Employed		Unemployed	
		Number	Percent of population	Number	Percent of population	Number	Percent of population
Total..........................	9,354	5,732	61.3	5,507	58.9	225	3.9
Sex							
Male..........................	4,542	3,036	66.8	2,917	64.2	120	3.9
Female........................	4,812	2,696	56.0	2,591	53.8	105	3.9
Race, Sex, and Hispanic Origin							
White..........................	7,747	4,701	60.7	4,541	58.6	160	3.4
Male..........................	3,793	2,523	66.5	2,430	64.1	93	3.7
Female........................	3,954	2,178	55.1	2,111	53.4	67	3.1
Black or African American....	1,151	732	63.6	680	59.1	52	7.1
Male..........................	532	360	67.7	341	64.1	19	5.3
Female........................	619	372	60.0	339	54.7	33	8.8
Hispanic or Latino ethnicity[1]	386	243	63.0	232	60.2	11	4.4
Male..........................	NA	NA	NA	NA	NA	NA	NA
Female........................	NA	NA	NA	NA	NA	NA	NA
Age							
16 to 19 years................	626	305	48.7	273	43.6	32	10.5
20 to 24 years................	822	635	77.2	583	70.9	52	8.2
25 to 34 years................	1,491	1,247	83.6	1,192	80.0	54	4.3
35 to 44 years................	1,356	1,132	83.5	1,104	81.4	28	2.5
45 to 54 years................	1,308	1,055	80.7	1,031	78.8	24	2.3
55 to 64 years................	1,570	993	63.2	972	61.9	21	2.1
65 years and over............	2,181	366	16.8	351	16.1	14	3.9

NOTE: Data in Table 7 are from the Current Population Survey (CPS) and do not match the estimates in Table 8. See notes and definitions for further information.
[1] May be of any race.

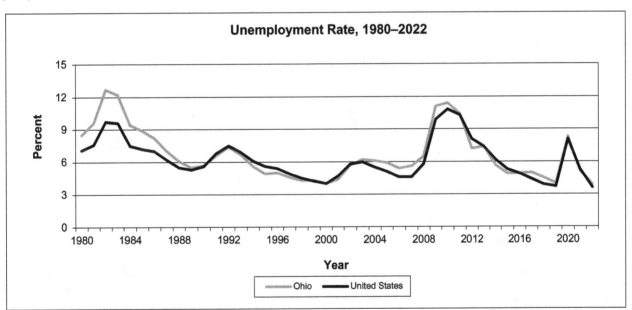

Table OH-8. Employment Status of the Civilian Noninstitutional Population Age 16 Years and Over

(Number, percent.)

Year	Civilian labor force	Civilian participation rate	Employed	Unemployed	Unemployment rate
2010..........................	5,871,473	65.5	5,267,304	604,169	10.3
2011..........................	5,773,480	64.2	5,263,728	509,752	8.8
2012..........................	5,712,475	63.3	5,290,392	422,083	7.4
2013..........................	5,706,777	63.0	5,281,459	425,318	7.5
2014..........................	5,713,176	62.8	5,381,787	331,389	5.8
2015..........................	5,710,776	62.6	5,427,850	282,926	5.0
2016..........................	5,754,480	62.8	5,464,097	290,383	5.0
2017..........................	5,818,975	63.0	5,529,479	289,496	5.0
2018..........................	5,815,510	62.7	5,553,767	261,782	4.5
2019..........................	5,871,248	63.1	5,626,326	244,922	4.2
2020..........................	5,734,179	61.5	5,263,034	471,145	8.2
2021..........................	5,736,882	61.5	5,441,879	295,003	5.1
2022..........................	5,741,277	61.5	5,510,327	230,950	4.0

Table OH-9. Employment and Average Wages by Industry

(Estimates are based on the 2012 North American Industry Classification System [NAICS].)

Industry	2014	2015	2016	2017	2018	2019	2020	2021
	Number of Jobs							
Wage and Salary Employment by Industry.........................	5,442,337	5,521,571	5,583,348	5,625,472	5,666,700	5,701,013	5,374,037	5,484,487
Farm Wage and Salary Employment.................................	12,576	18,013	20,092	17,618	17,754	15,631	17,244	14,272
Nonfarm Wage and Salary Employment...........................	5,429,761	5,503,558	5,563,256	5,607,854	5,648,946	5,685,382	5,356,793	5,470,215
Private wage and salary employment...............................	4,635,030	4,709,574	4,762,380	4,801,924	4,841,846	4,871,552	4,569,543	4,691,210
Forestry, fishing, and related activities............................	5,236	5,411	5,425	5,394	5,551	5,665	5,449	5,268
Mining..	14,398	13,722	11,019	11,100	11,806	11,531	8,972	8,284
Utilities...	18,217	19,208	19,228	19,112	19,126	18,681	18,425	18,183
Construction...	200,442	205,508	211,088	222,156	225,978	231,878	224,229	228,734
Manufacturing...	675,230	686,582	685,684	687,099	699,221	701,252	653,656	666,501
Durable goods manufacturing...............................	459,947	467,557	462,738	462,182	471,607	473,264	433,853	440,453
Nondurable goods manufacturing..........................	215,283	219,025	222,946	224,917	227,614	227,988	219,803	226,048
Wholesale trade...	233,781	237,114	236,645	237,338	235,786	238,166	226,445	229,734
Retail trade...	569,189	574,164	579,110	580,148	568,134	558,974	535,158	545,714
Transportation and warehousing...................................	181,930	191,299	193,718	196,132	208,200	219,442	230,854	246,678
Information..	72,722	71,803	71,809	71,652	70,931	69,364	63,901	65,050
Finance and insurance	220,267	224,716	230,399	237,204	242,032	240,841	240,858	243,867
Real estate and rental and leasing................................	61,905	63,623	64,309	64,798	65,741	67,711	64,259	65,394
Professional, scientific, and technical services................	250,318	252,930	259,046	260,183	265,252	270,535	264,319	272,593
Management of companies and enterprises.....................	137,524	138,957	138,015	141,689	140,553	141,245	138,232	137,924
Administrative and waste services................................	324,531	328,336	330,050	326,695	328,093	327,607	299,399	313,790
Educational services	114,519	115,911	117,368	119,075	113,646	114,455	101,949	110,109
Health care and social assistance................................	775,945	790,032	806,728	812,228	820,479	827,863	794,552	793,526
Arts, entertainment, and recreation..............................	77,706	78,010	79,434	81,053	83,232	84,703	63,098	72,843
Accommodation and food services................................	453,318	464,355	475,727	482,971	487,308	489,346	407,180	436,534
Other services, except public administration....................	247,852	247,893	247,578	245,897	250,777	252,293	228,608	230,484
Government and government enterprises	794,731	793,984	800,876	805,930	807,100	813,830	787,250	779,005
	Dollars							
Average Wages and Salaries by Industry	46,865	47,936	48,494	49,988	51,570	53,122	56,657	59,430
Average Farm Wages and Salaries	34,633	31,486	32,229	27,750	28,775	32,989	23,552	29,175
Average Nonfarm Wages and Salaries	46,893	47,990	48,553	50,058	51,642	53,177	56,764	59,509
Average private wages and salaries...............................	46,849	47,895	48,437	49,971	51,548	53,126	56,783	59,617
Forestry, fishing, and related activities............................	29,101	29,728	31,554	33,020	33,817	34,963	37,922	40,112
Mining..	71,149	69,419	69,963	72,797	74,963	76,176	75,936	78,134
Utilities...	93,300	96,641	96,947	100,997	105,544	106,965	110,914	112,347
Construction...	54,960	56,790	57,951	61,761	62,189	63,365	66,046	68,307
Manufacturing...	59,483	60,150	60,692	61,994	63,622	65,019	67,054	69,152
Durable goods manufacturing...............................	60,535	60,776	61,260	62,760	64,302	65,194	66,114	68,190
Nondurable goods manufacturing..........................	57,237	58,813	59,514	60,420	62,211	64,656	68,908	71,024
Wholesale trade...	66,543	68,357	68,783	71,094	73,808	75,584	78,676	83,701
Retail trade...	27,348	28,094	28,287	29,061	29,895	30,949	33,577	36,432
Transportation and warehousing...................................	49,270	50,337	50,348	52,012	53,574	53,991	54,584	57,504
Information..	64,904	66,919	68,299	70,192	72,324	74,985	82,493	88,461
Finance and insurance	72,291	74,433	75,574	78,797	82,021	85,461	92,170	95,666
Real estate and rental and leasing................................	44,426	45,920	46,855	48,418	50,032	51,887	54,825	58,453
Professional, scientific, and technical services................	70,598	72,618	73,905	74,954	77,061	79,528	83,737	88,694
Management of companies and enterprises.....................	108,850	106,428	108,894	109,831	112,698	118,227	124,945	129,330
Administrative and waste services................................	33,125	34,287	34,111	35,617	36,663	38,088	41,156	45,238
Educational services	31,175	31,544	31,868	32,054	33,690	34,626	38,301	37,228
Health care and social assistance................................	44,722	45,995	46,520	47,825	49,058	50,483	53,956	56,940
Arts, entertainment, and recreation..............................	34,110	35,066	35,583	37,444	38,206	39,027	43,991	44,102
Accommodation and food services................................	17,289	17,867	18,351	18,844	19,868	20,563	20,060	24,046
Other services, except public administration....................	30,080	31,320	32,394	34,299	35,465	36,392	39,692	41,888
Government and government enterprises.............................	47,153	48,553	49,242	50,576	52,206	53,482	56,654	58,862

Table OH-10. Employment Characteristics by Family Type

(Number, percent.)

Family type and labor force status	2019 Total	2019 Families with own children under 18 years	2020[1] Total	2020[1] Families with own children under 18 years	2021 Total	2021 Families with own children under 18 years
All Families..	2,942,581	1,191,572	2,952,151	1,221,667	2,986,455	1,218,706
FAMILY TYPE AND LABOR FORCE STATUS						
Opposite-Sex Married-Couple Families...	2,126,672	755,544	2,129,907	777,751	2,142,972	776,173
Both husband and wife in labor force........................	51.6	70.3	52.4	70.7	52.5	71.8
Husband in labor force, wife not in labor force	19.9	23.8	19.7	23.8	19.2	22.7
Wife in labor force, husband not in labor force........................	8.3	4.3	8.3	4.1	8.1	4.1
Both husband and wife not in labor force........................	19.5	1.1	19.6	1.4	20.1	1.4
Other Families	815,909	436,028	806,546	440,429	824,287	439,137
Female householder, no spouse present	71.6	74.2	72.0	73.6	72.0	74.0
In labor force........................	50.1	62.1	50.5	61.5	49.2	60.5
Not in labor force........................	21.5	12.1	21.5	12.1	22.8	13.5
Male householder, no spouse present........................	28.4	25.8	28.0	26.4	28.0	26.0
In labor force........................	21.4	23.0	21.7	23.7	21.3	23.3
Not in labor force........................	7.0	2.8	6.3	2.6	6.7	2.7

[1] 2020 ACS 5-Year estimates. 1-Year estimates were not released for 2020 due to the impact of COVID-19 on data collection that year. Data is not comparable to previous years, which are based on 1-year estimates.

Table OH-11. School Enrollment and Educational Attainment, 2021

(Number, percent.)

Item	State	U.S.
Enrollment		
Total population 3 years and over, enrolled in school	2,724,429	79,453,524
Enrolled in nursery school or preschool (percent)	5.7	5.2
Enrolled in kindergarten (percent)	5.1	5.0
Enrolled in elementary school, grades 1-8 (percent)...........................	42.7	41.3
Enrolled in high school, grades 9-12 (percent)...........................	21.8	21.8
Enrolled in college or graduate school (percent)...........................	24.7	26.7
Attainment		
Total population 25 years and over	8,117,973	228,193,464
Less than ninth grade (percent)	2.7	4.8
9th to 12th grade, no diploma (percent)	5.5	5.9
High school graduate, including equivalency (percent)...........................	32.8	26.3
Some college, no degree (percent)...........................	19.2	19.3
Associate's degree (percent)...........................	9.0	8.8
Bachelor's degree (percent)	18.9	21.2
Graduate or professional degree (percent)...........................	11.8	13.8
High school graduate or higher (percent)	91.7	89.4
Bachelor's degree or higher (percent)...........................	30.7	35.0

Table OH-12. Public School Characteristics and Educational Indicators

(Number, percent; data derived from National Center of Education Statistics.)

Item	State	U.S.
Public Elementary and Secondary Schools		
Number of regular school districts, 2019-20	619	13,349
Number of operational schools, 2019-20...	3,536	98,469
Percent charter schools	8.9	7.7
Total public school enrollment, Fall 2021...	1,683,612	49,433,092
Percent charter school enrollment	6.8	7.5
Student-teacher ratio, Fall 2019	15.9	15.9
Expenditures per student (unadjusted dollars), 2019-20	13,729	13,489
Four-year adjusted cohort graduation rate (ACGR), 2019-2020[1]...	84.4	86.5
Students eligible for free or reduced-price lunch (percent), 2019-20...	45.5	52.1
English language learners (percent), Fall 2020	3.7	10.3
Students age 3 to 21 served under IDEA, part B (percent), 2021-22	16.2	14.7

Public Schools by Type, 2019-20	Number	Percent of state public schools
Total number of schools...	3,536	100.0
Special education...	13	0.4
Vocational education...	73	2.1
Alternative education...	-	-

[1] Adjusted Cohort Graduation Rates (ACGR) differ from Averaged Freshmen Graduation Rates (AFGR).
- = Zero or rounds to zero.

Table OH-13. Reported Voting and Registration of the Voting-Age Population, November 2022

(Numbers in thousands, percent.)

Item	Total population	Total citizen population	Registered			Voted		
			Total registered	Percent registered (total population)	Percent registered (total citizen population)	Total voted	Percent voted (total population)	Percent voted (total citizen population)
U.S. Total	255,457	233,546	161,422	63.2	69.1	121,916	47.7	52.2
State Total	9,024	8,708	5,890	65.3	67.6	4,162	46.1	47.8
Sex								
Male	4,371	4,216	2,842	65.0	67.4	1,994	45.6	47.3
Female	4,653	4,492	3,048	65.5	67.9	2,169	46.6	48.3
Race								
White alone	7,395	7,284	5,115	69.2	70.2	3,689	49.9	50.6
White, non-Hispanic alone	7,098	7,073	4,978	70.1	70.4	3,607	50.8	51.0
Black alone	1,111	1,045	550	49.5	52.6	344	30.9	32.9
Asian alone	264	140	96	36.3	68.7	75	28.5	53.9
Hispanic (of any race)	380	267	162	42.6	60.5	89	23.3	33.1
White alone or in combination	7,629	7,504	5,240	68.7	69.8	3,739	49.0	49.8
Black alone or in combination	1,263	1,183	628	49.7	53.1	383	30.3	32.4
Asian alone or in combination	307	182	123	40.2	67.8	75	24.6	41.4
Age								
18 to 24 years	1,114	1,094	486	43.6	44.5	209	18.7	19.1
25 to 34 years	1,547	1,438	911	58.9	63.4	518	33.5	36.1
35 to 44 years	1,314	1,203	864	65.7	71.8	559	42.5	46.5
45 to 64 years	2,855	2,798	2,004	70.2	71.6	1,499	52.5	53.6
65 years and over	2,195	2,175	1,625	74.0	74.7	1,378	62.8	63.3

Table OH-14. Health Indicators

(Number, rate as indicated in footnotes.)

Item	State	U.S.
Births		
Life Expectancy at Birth (years), 2020	75.3	77.0
Fertility Rate by State[1], 2021	57.9	56.3
Percent Home Births, 2021	1.6	1.4
Cesarean Delivery Rate[2], 2021	31.5	32.1
Preterm Birth Rate[3], 2021	10.6	10.5
Teen Birth Rate[4], 2021	15.5	13.9
Percentage of Babies Born Low Birthweight[5], 2021	8.7	8.5
Deaths[6]		
Heart Disease Mortality Rate, 2021	204.7	173.8
Cancer Mortality Rate, 2021	163.0	146.6
Stroke Mortality Rate, 2021	49.0	41.1
Diabetes Mortality Rate, 2021	29.5	25.4
Influenza/Pneumonia Mortality Rate, 2021	11.4	10.5
Suicide Mortality Rate, 2021	14.6	14.1
Drug Overdose Mortality Rate, 2021	48.1	33.6
Firearm Injury Mortality Rate, 2021	16.5	14.6
Homicide Mortality Rate, 2021	9.3	8.2
Disease and Illness		
Lifetime Asthma in Adults, 2020 (percent)	14.4	13.9
Lifetime Asthma in Children, 2020 (percent)[7]	10.2	11.3
Diabetes in Adults, 2020 (percent)	10.9	8.2
Self-reported Obesity in Adults, 2021 (percent)	37.8	NA

SOURCE: National Center for Health Statistics, National Vital Statistics System 2020 data; https://wonder.cdc.gov.
[1] General fertility rate per 1,000 women aged 15–44.
[2] This represents the percentage of all live births that were cesarean deliveries.
[3] Babies born prior to 37 weeks of pregnancy (gestation).
[4] Number of births per 1,000 females aged 15–19
[5] Babies born weighing less than 2,500 grams or 5 lbs. 8oz.
[6] Death rates are the number of deaths per 100,000 total population.
[7] U.S. total includes data from 30 states and D.C.
NA = Not available.
- = Zero or rounds to zero.

Table OH-15. State Government Finances, 2021

(Dollar amounts in thousands, percent distribution.)

Item	Dollars	Percent distribution
Total Revenue	105,906,603	100.0
General revenue	87,270,553	82.4
Intergovernmental revenue	35,943,796	33.9
Taxes	34,909,388	33.0
General sales	14,393,197	13.6
Selective sales	7,755,321	7.3
License taxes	2,029,060	1.9
Individual income tax	10,662,810	10.1
Corporate income tax	5,955	-
Other taxes	63,045	0.1
Current charges	9,880,455	9.3
Miscellaneous general revenue	6,536,914	6.2
Utility revenue	-	-
Liquor stores revenue	1672571	1.6
Insurance trust revenue[1]	16,963,479	16.0
Total Expenditure	104,296,674	100.0
Intergovernmental expenditure	22,420,190	21.5
Direct expenditure	81,876,484	78.5
Current operation	52,775,675	50.6
Capital outlay	4,284,877	4.1
Insurance benefits and repayments	20,970,514	20.1
Assistance and subsidies	2,535,352	2.4
Interest on debt	1,310,066	1.3
Exhibit: Salaries and wages	8,663,486	8.3
Total Expenditure	104,296,674	100.0
General expenditure	81,958,719	78.6
Intergovernmental expenditure	22,420,190	21.5
Direct expenditure	59,538,529	57.1
General expenditure, by function:		
Education	23,340,114	22.4
Public welfare	34,080,335	32.7
Hospitals	5,017,599	4.8
Health	2,747,411	2.6
Highways	4,498,450	4.3
Police protection	606,362	0.6
Correction	2,072,333	2.0
Natural resources	469,363	0.5
Parks and recreation	163,985	0.2
Governmental administration	2,178,003	2.1
Interest on general debt	1,310,066	1.3
Other and unallocable	5,270,399	5.1
Utility expenditure	62,052	0.1
Liquor stores expenditure	1,367,441	1.3
Insurance trust expenditure	20,970,514	20.1
Debt at End of Fiscal Year	34,849,903	X
Cash and Security Holdings	307,076,393	X

X = Not applicable.
- = Zero or rounds to zero.
[1] Within insurance trust revenue, net earnings of state retirement systems is a calculated statistic (the item code in the data file is X08), and thus can be positive or negative. Net earnings is the sum of earnings on investments plus gains on investments minus losses on investments. The change made in 2002 for asset valuation from book to market value in accordance with Statement 34 of the Governmental Accounting Standards Board is reflected in the calculated statistics.

Table OH-16. State Government Tax Collections, 2022

(Dollars in thousands, percent.)

Item	Dollars	Percent distribution
Total Taxes	37,388,627	100.0
Property taxes	X	-
Sales and gross receipts	24,014,162	64.2
General sales and gross receipts	15,640,329	41.8
Selective sales and gross receipts	8,373,833	22.4
Alcoholic beverages	120,832	0.3
Amusements	334,176	0.9
Insurance premiums	675,158	1.8
Motor fuels	2,710,980	7.3
Pari-mutuels	3,987	-
Public utilities	1,017,791	2.7
Tobacco products	885,881	2.4
Other selective sales	2,625,028	7.0
Licenses	2,065,666	5.5
Alcoholic beverages	49,013	0.1
Amusements	39,699	0.1
Corporations in general	234,925	0.6
Hunting and fishing	45,413	0.1
Motor vehicle	508,070	1.4
Motor vehicle operators	92,224	0.2
Public utilities	2,801	-
Occupation and business, NEC	957,708	2.6
Other licenses	135,813	0.4
Income taxes	11,247,715	30.1
Individual income	11,246,994	30.1
Corporation net income	721	-
Other taxes	61,084	0.2
Death and gift	58	-
Documentary and stock transfer	X	-
Severance	61,026	0.2
Taxes, NEC	0	-

X = Not applicable.
- = Zero or rounds to zero.

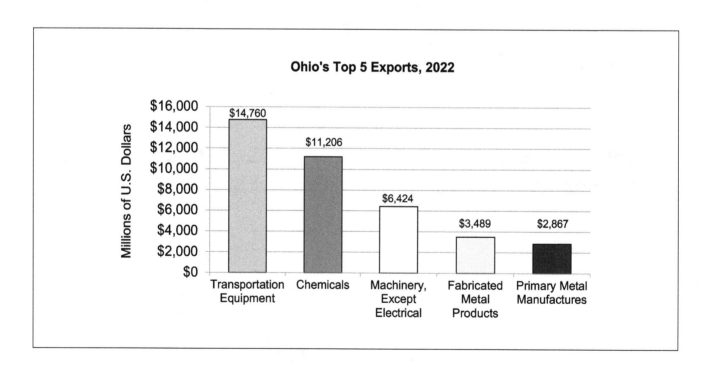

Ohio's Top 5 Exports, 2022

Category	Millions of U.S. Dollars
Transportation Equipment	$14,760
Chemicals	$11,206
Machinery, Except Electrical	$6,424
Fabricated Metal Products	$3,489
Primary Metal Manufactures	$2,867

OKLAHOMA

Facts and Figures

Location: West south central United States; bordered on the N by Colorado and Kansas, on the E by Missouri and Arkansas, on the S by Texas, and on the W by Texas and New Mexico

Area: 69,898 sq. mi. (181,036 sq. km.); rank—20th

Population: 4,019,800 (2022 est.); rank—28th

Principal Cities: capital—Oklahoma City; largest—Oklahoma City

Statehood: November 16, 1907; 46th state

U.S. Congress: 2 senators, 5 representatives

State Motto: *Labor omnia vincit* ("Labor conquers all things")

State Song: "Oklahoma!"

State Nickname: The Sooner State

Abbreviations: OK; Okla.

State Symbols: flower—mistletoe; tree—redbud; bird—scissor-tailed flycatcher

At a Glance

- With an increase in population of 7.2 percent, Oklahoma ranked 22nd among the states in growth from 2010 to 2022.

- Oklahoma's median household income in 2021 was $55,826, and 15.6 percent of the population lived below the poverty level.

- In 2021, 13.8 percent of Oklahomans did not have health insurance, making it the state with the 2nd highest percent of uninsured residents.

- Oklahoma's drug overdose death rate was 26.8 deaths per 100,000 population in 2021, compared to the national rate of 32.4 deaths per 100,000 population.

- Oklahoma was the state with the 3rd highest percent of people who self-identified as "American Indian or Alaska Native alone," with 9.5 percent of its population in this demographic.

Table OK-1. Population by Age, Sex, Race, and Hispanic Origin

(Number, percent, except where noted.)

Sex, age, race, and Hispanic origin	2010	2020	2022	Percent change, 2010–2022
Total Population..	3,751,351	3,959,346	4,019,800	7.2
Percent of total U.S. population	1.2	1.2	1.2	X
Sex				
Male...	1,856,977	1,976,840	2,004,482	7.9
Female..	1,894,374	1,982,506	2,015,318	6.4
Age				
Under 5 years..	264,126	248,454	243,671	-7.7
Under 18 years...	929,666	950,342	953,146	2.5
18 to 64 years...	2,314,971	2,377,375	2,405,759	3.9
65 years and over...	506,714	631,629	660,895	30.4
Median age (years)	36.2	36.9	37.1	2.5
Race and Hispanic Origin				
One race				
White	2,851,510	2,914,212	2,936,122	3.0
Black	284,332	310,305	318,339	12.0
American Indian and Alaska Native	335,664	373,920	382,638	14.0
Asian..	67,126	96,522	103,765	54.6
Native Hawaiian or Other Pacific Islander	5,354	9,190	10,079	88.3
Two or more races...	207,365	255,197	268,857	29.7
Hispanic (of any race)....................................	332,007	453,373	486,693	46.6

NOTE: Population figures for 2022 are July 1 estimates. The 2010 and 2020 estimates are taken from the respective censuses.
- = Zero or rounds to zero.
X = Not applicable.

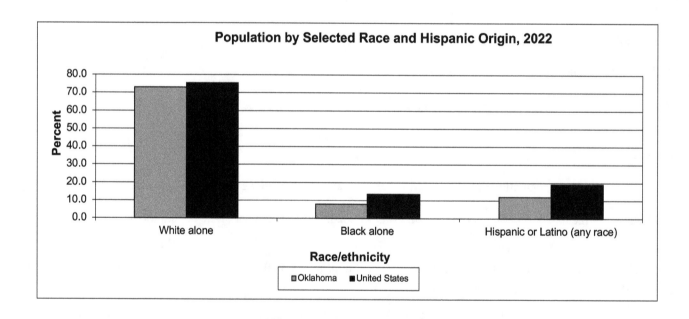

Table OK-2. Marital Status

(Number, percent distribution.)

Sex, age, race, and Hispanic origin	2000	2010	2021
Males, 15 Years and Over	1,318,729	1,457,860	1,575,096
Never married	25.8	30.7	33.9
Now married, except separated......................................	59.5	52.2	50.0
Separated...	1.6	1.8	1.6
Widowed..	2.5	3.0	3.1
Divorced..	10.6	12.3	11.3
Females, 15 Years and Over	1,398,823	1,521,546	1,620,614
Never married	19.1	23.8	26.9
Now married, except separated......................................	55.3	49.7	47.8
Separated...	1.9	2.7	2.0
Widowed..	11.1	10.1	9.3
Divorced..	12.5	13.7	13.9

Table OK-3. Households and Housing Characteristics

(Number, percent, dollars.)

Item	2000	2010	2021	Average annual percent change, 2010–2021
Total Households	1,342,293	1,432,959	1,547,967	0.7
Family households	921,750	954,622	999,852	0.4
Married-couple family	717,611	709,256	731,871	0.3
Other family	204,139	245,366	267,981	0.8
Male householder, no wife present	51,564	62,855	80,753	2.6
Female householder, no husband present	152,575	182,511	187,228	0.2
Nonfamily households	420,543	478,337	548,115	1.3
Householder living alone	358,560	400,840	454,073	1.2
Householder not living alone	61,983	77,497	94,042	1.9
Housing Characteristics				
Total housing units	1,514,400	1,666,205	1,762,113	0.5
Occupied housing units	1,342,293	1,432,959	1,547,967	0.7
Owner occupied	918,259	971,378	1,013,837	0.4
Renter occupied	424,034	461,581	534,130	1.4
Average household size	2.49	2.55	2.51	-0.1
Financial Characteristics				
Median gross rent of renter-occupied housing	456	659	855	2.7
Median monthly owner costs for housing units with a mortgage	764	1,089	1,295	1.7
Median value of owner-occupied housing units	70,700	111,400	168,500	4.7

Table OK-4. Migration, Origin, and Language

(Number, percent.)

Characteristic	State 2021	U.S. 2021
Residence 1 Year Ago		
Population 1 year and over	3,943,443	328,464,538
Same house	84.9	87.2
Different house in the U.S.	14.8	12.3
Same county	8.0	6.7
Different county	6.8	5.7
Same state	4.0	3.3
Different state	2.7	2.4
Abroad	0.3	0.4
Place of Birth		
Native born	3,756,019	286,623,642
Male	49.7	49.7
Female	50.3	50.3
Foreign born	230,620	45,270,103
Male	50.7	48.7
Female	49.3	51.3
Foreign born; naturalized U.S. citizen	95,114	24,044,083
Male	46.5	46.4
Female	53.5	53.6
Foreign born; not a U.S. citizen	135,506	21,226,020
Male	53.7	51.2
Female	46.3	48.8
Entered 2010 or later	30.2	28.1
Entered 2000 to 2009	28.2	23.7
Entered before 2000	41.6	48.2
World Region of Birth, Foreign		
Foreign-born population, excluding population born at sea	230,620	45,269,644
Europe	7.2	10.7
Asia	27.4	31.0
Africa	5.4	5.7
Oceania	1.2	0.6
Latin America	56.8	50.1
North America	2.0	1.7
Language Spoken at Home and Ability to Speak English		
Population 5 years and over	3,745,034	313,232,500
English only	89.4	78.4
Language other than English	10.6	21.6
Speaks English less than "very well"	3.0	8.0

Table OK-5. Median Income and Poverty Status, 2021

(Number, percent, except as noted.)

Characteristic	State		U.S.	
	Number	Percent	Number	Percent
Median Income				
Households (dollars)...	55,826	X	69,717	X
Families (dollars)	69,967	X	85,806	X
Below Poverty Level (All People)	606,782	15.6	41,393,176	12.8
Sex				
Male	274,906	14.3	18,518,155	11.6
Female	331,876	16.9	22,875,021	13.9
Age				
Under 18 years..	198,923	21.2	12,243,219	16.9
Related children under 18 years...	195,400	20.9	11,985,424	16.6
18 to 64 years...	340,921	14.8	23,526,341	11.9
65 years and over	66,938	10.6	5,623,616	10.3

X = Not applicable.

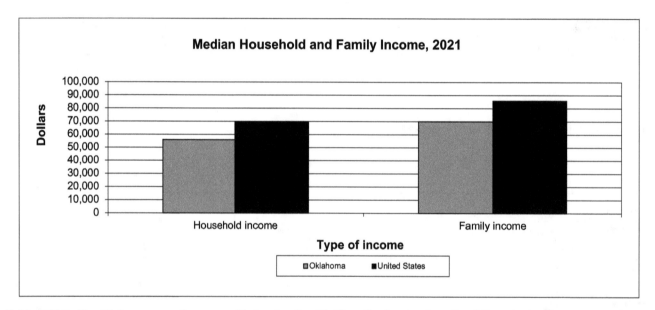

Median Household and Family Income, 2021

Table OK-6. Health Insurance Coverage Status for the Civilian Noninstitutionalized Population and Children Under 19 Years of Age

(Number, percent.)

Item	2011	2012	2013	2014	2015	2016	2017	2018	2019	2020 [2]	2021
Civilian Noninstitutionalized Population	3,710,368	3,733,058	3,770,254	3,797,966	3,830,329	3,845,697	3,851,302	3,861,581	3,871,658	3,867,023	3,905,272
Covered by Private or Public Insurance											
Number..	3,016,823	3,047,982	3,104,481	3,214,454	3,297,820	3,316,039	3,305,819	3,313,265	3,318,823	3,310,379	3,367,447
Percent..	81.3	81.6	82.3	84.6	86.1	86.2	85.8	85.8	85.7	85.6	86.2
Uninsured											
Number..	693,545	685,076	665,773	583,512	532,509	529,658	545,483	548,316	552,835	556,644	537,825
Percent..	18.7	18.4	17.7	15.4	13.9	13.8	14.2	14.2	14.3	14.4	13.8
Percent in the U.S. not covered.................................	15.1	14.8	14.5	11.7	9.4	8.6	8.7	8.9	9.2	8.7	8.6
Children Under 19 Years of Age[1]	933,893	934,617	946,133	950,123	958,418	959,850	1,018,753	1,011,428	1,005,168	1,007,665	1,011,261
Covered by Private or Public Insurance											
Number..	834,509	840,408	851,091	867,872	887,310	889,761	936,357	928,012	918,889	921,784	935,965
Percent..	89.4	89.9	90.0	91.3	92.6	92.7	91.9	91.8	91.4	91.5	92.6
Uninsured											
Number..	99,384	94,209	95,042	82,251	71,108	70,089	82,396	83,416	86,279	85,881	75,296
Percent..	10.6	10.1	10.0	8.7	7.4	7.3	8.1	8.2	8.6	8.5	7.4
Percent in the U.S. not covered.................................	7.5	7.2	7.1	6.0	4.8	4.5	5.0	5.2	5.7	5.2	5.4

[1] Data for years prior to 2017 are for individuals under 18 years of age.
[2] 2020 ACS 5-Year estimates. 1-Year estimates were not released for 2020 due to the impact of COVID-19 on data collection that year. Data is not comparable to previous years, which are based on 1-year estimates.

Table OK-7. Employment Status by Demographic Group, 2022

(Numbers in thousands, percent.)

Characteristic	Civilian noninstitutional population	Civilian labor force		Employed		Unemployed	
		Number	Percent of population	Number	Percent of population	Number	Percent of population
Total.........................	3,094	1,891	61.1	1,821	58.9	70	3.7
Sex							
Male	1,507	1,003	66.5	970	64.3	34	3.3
Female	1,587	888	55.9	851	53.6	36	4.1
Race, Sex, and Hispanic Origin							
White	2,309	1,413	61.2	1,369	59.3	44	3.1
Male	1,148	767	66.9	744	64.8	23	3.0
Female	1,161	646	55.6	625	53.8	21	3.2
Black or African American.......	221	132	59.6	124	55.9	8	6.2
Male	NA	NA	NA	NA	NA	NA	NA
Female	NA	NA	NA	NA	NA	NA	NA
Hispanic or Latino ethnicity[1]	360	236	65.5	226	62.9	9	4.0
Male	192	145	75.7	141	73.4	4	3.0
Female	168	91	53.9	86	50.8	5	5.6
Age							
16 to 19 years	223	95	42.5	83	37.4	11	11.9
20 to 24 years	251	185	73.9	176	70.1	9	5.1
25 to 34 years	557	442	79.4	423	75.9	19	4.4
35 to 44 years	485	395	81.4	383	79.1	11	2.8
45 to 54 years	466	361	77.4	351	75.3	10	2.8
55 to 64 years	450	283	62.8	276	61.4	6	2.1
65 years and over	663	131	19.7	129	19.4	3	1.9

NOTE: Data in Table 7 are from the Current Population Survey (CPS) and do not match the estimates in Table 8. See notes and definitions for further information.
[1] May be of any race.

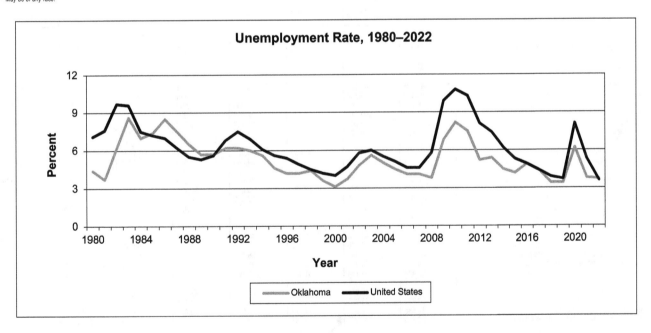

Table OK-8. Employment Status of the Civilian Noninstitutional Population Age 16 Years and Over

(Number, percent.)

Year	Civilian labor force	Civilian participation rate	Employed	Unemployed	Unemployment rate
2010..............................	1,765,708	62.3	1,650,502	115,206	6.5
2011..............................	1,767,056	61.6	1,668,235	98,821	5.6
2012..............................	1,794,901	62.0	1,703,624	91,277	5.1
2013..............................	1,799,525	61.6	1,707,220	92,305	5.1
2014..............................	1,797,769	61.0	1,719,826	77,943	4.3
2015..............................	1,829,046	61.5	1,750,501	78,545	4.3
2016..............................	1,828,055	61.1	1,743,225	84,830	4.6
2017..............................	1,826,272	61.1	1,752,733	73,539	4.0
2018..............................	1,833,020	61.2	1,773,125	59,895	3.3
2019..............................	1,840,199	61.0	1,782,686	57,513	3.1
2020..............................	1,835,861	60.5	1,721,525	114,336	6.2
2021..............................	1,854,234	60.6	1,783,080	71,154	3.8
2022..............................	1,887,040	61.0	1,830,061	56,979	3.0

Table OK-9. Employment and Average Wages by Industry

(Estimates are based on the 2012 North American Industry Classification System [NAICS].)

Industry	2014	2015	2016	2017	2018	2019	2020	2021
	Number of Jobs							
Wage and Salary Employment by Industry	1,699,657	1,705,980	1,688,995	1,693,826	1,719,591	1,736,582	1,667,511	1,677,934
Farm Wage and Salary Employment	9,773	5,799	7,400	6,980	6,274	5,742	10,688	7,504
Nonfarm Wage and Salary Employment	1,689,884	1,700,181	1,681,595	1,686,846	1,713,317	1,730,840	1,656,823	1,670,430
Private wage and salary employment	1,320,453	1,328,465	1,310,569	1,317,325	1,345,938	1,357,061	1,287,279	1,305,190
Forestry, fishing, and related activities	4,451	4,554	4,675	4,688	4,842	4,805	4,836	4,823
Mining	61,379	53,544	43,902	47,518	52,667	47,982	31,183	27,267
Utilities	12,021	12,094	11,495	10,717	10,750	10,892	9,534	9,551
Construction	77,541	79,330	79,335	79,109	82,237	84,754	80,716	79,752
Manufacturing	142,097	139,486	131,205	130,697	140,266	140,993	131,456	128,761
Durable goods manufacturing	98,877	96,557	87,858	87,629	96,768	97,215	88,284	84,896
Nondurable goods manufacturing	43,220	42,929	43,347	43,068	43,498	43,778	43,172	43,865
Wholesale trade	63,623	60,478	58,589	58,546	57,909	58,270	55,289	54,336
Retail trade	179,677	184,473	184,893	180,201	179,331	177,708	177,420	183,078
Transportation and warehousing	47,723	52,146	52,916	55,285	53,410	56,920	63,030	67,808
Information	21,733	21,142	21,130	20,449	19,848	19,612	18,245	17,810
Finance and insurance	59,776	60,256	60,074	60,371	60,155	60,708	59,846	59,720
Real estate and rental and leasing	20,971	21,015	20,693	20,899	21,681	22,112	20,507	20,922
Professional, scientific, and technical services	68,275	69,874	69,739	70,392	73,503	75,709	74,005	75,839
Management of companies and enterprises	18,678	18,689	18,096	18,744	19,158	20,101	20,543	21,393
Administrative and waste services	98,508	98,290	94,569	97,596	100,015	100,095	92,017	95,461
Educational services	21,887	22,086	22,581	22,122	22,900	22,908	21,185	23,605
Health care and social assistance	188,083	191,840	194,774	195,501	196,243	199,131	195,801	196,347
Arts, entertainment, and recreation	15,353	16,159	17,216	17,517	17,728	18,502	16,043	17,006
Accommodation and food services	141,445	146,142	148,705	151,052	154,890	156,722	141,472	149,392
Other services, except public administration	77,232	76,867	75,982	75,921	78,405	79,137	74,151	72,319
Government and government enterprises	369,431	371,716	371,026	369,521	367,379	373,779	369,544	365,240
	Dollars							
Average Wages and Salaries by Industry	44,454	45,083	44,716	45,997	47,679	48,982	50,533	52,477
Average Farm Wages and Salaries	32,314	33,121	28,820	32,319	30,607	42,197	20,629	28,931
Average Nonfarm Wages and Salaries	44,524	45,124	44,785	46,054	47,741	49,004	50,726	52,583
Average private wages and salaries	45,118	45,652	45,026	46,476	48,114	49,236	50,762	52,555
Forestry, fishing, and related activities	26,285	27,597	29,672	31,600	32,802	32,350	34,327	36,228
Mining	96,610	103,110	97,233	102,268	103,908	102,921	109,738	110,127
Utilities	114,337	99,909	98,566	101,112	100,643	115,355	103,648	100,902
Construction	47,990	49,707	50,617	51,569	53,811	55,475	56,313	57,867
Manufacturing	55,245	55,690	55,496	57,433	60,734	62,156	63,361	64,858
Durable goods manufacturing	57,406	57,313	57,033	59,098	62,871	64,174	65,150	67,176
Nondurable goods manufacturing	50,301	52,041	52,381	54,045	55,978	57,675	59,702	60,371
Wholesale trade	58,056	59,204	58,784	60,973	63,899	65,259	66,597	70,849
Retail trade	27,905	28,383	28,633	29,245	30,174	31,050	33,010	35,178
Transportation and warehousing	57,678	56,858	54,282	57,628	54,658	54,541	53,233	52,632
Information	56,547	57,110	58,111	60,274	61,421	62,845	66,634	71,279
Finance and insurance	60,089	60,659	61,995	64,273	66,485	68,568	73,171	76,351
Real estate and rental and leasing	42,818	43,248	42,238	43,685	45,145	46,158	47,910	49,822
Professional, scientific, and technical services	62,141	63,030	63,172	64,447	66,362	68,260	70,780	73,602
Management of companies and enterprises	82,009	88,985	86,988	86,885	87,303	97,730	104,823	107,386
Administrative and waste services	34,634	35,925	35,762	36,986	38,511	39,508	42,405	45,194
Educational services	32,413	31,178	31,981	32,160	32,462	32,795	38,928	36,941
Health care and social assistance	43,465	45,045	45,546	46,175	47,733	48,946	51,342	54,077
Arts, entertainment, and recreation	33,707	35,225	36,303	35,955	37,115	36,754	37,226	38,219
Accommodation and food services	17,538	17,873	18,173	18,558	19,403	19,796	19,729	23,122
Other services, except public administration	30,243	31,461	32,294	33,563	34,403	35,297	38,627	41,054
Government and government enterprises	42,402	43,236	43,934	44,552	46,376	48,162	50,600	52,684

Table OK-10. Employment Characteristics by Family Type

(Number, percent.)

Family type and labor force status	2019		2020[1]		2021	
	Total	Families with own children under 18 years	Total	Families with own children under 18 years	Total	Families with own children under 18 years
All Families	975,754	414,106	975,207	422,118	999,852	425,645
FAMILY TYPE AND LABOR FORCE STATUS						
Opposite-Sex Married-Couple Families	713,636	273,587	712,079	279,925	725,942	280,304
Both husband and wife in labor force	49.1	64.4	48.9	64.3	48.7	64.3
Husband in labor force, wife not in labor force	23.3	28.9	23.4	28.7	23.1	28.8
Wife in labor force, husband not in labor force	7.9	4.1	8.1	4.4	9.0	4.8
Both husband and wife not in labor force	19.0	2.0	19.6	2.6	19.3	2.1
Other Families	262,118	140,519	257,327	140,573	267,981	144,055
Female householder, no spouse present	69.7	70.7	70.8	71.8	69.9	71.9
In labor force	46.9	58.4	47.5	58.1	47.5	58.5
Not in labor force	22.8	12.4	23.3	13.7	22.4	13.4
Male householder, no spouse present	30.3	29.3	29.2	28.2	30.1	28.1
In labor force	23.6	26.8	22.3	25.1	22.7	25.1
Not in labor force	6.8	2.5	6.9	3.1	7.4	3.1

[1] 2020 ACS 5-Year estimates. 1-Year estimates were not released for 2020 due to the impact of COVID-19 on data collection that year. Data is not comparable to previous years, which are based on 1-year estimates.

Table OK-11. School Enrollment and Educational Attainment, 2021

(Number, percent.)

Item	State	U.S.
Enrollment		
Total population 3 years and over, enrolled in school	985,616	79,453,524
Enrolled in nursery school or preschool (percent)	5.8	5.2
Enrolled in kindergarten (percent)	5.8	5.0
Enrolled in elementary school, grades 1-8 (percent)	44.4	41.3
Enrolled in high school, grades 9-12 (percent)	21.8	21.8
Enrolled in college or graduate school (percent)	22.2	26.7
Attainment		
Total population 25 years and over	2,639,889	228,193,464
Less than ninth grade (percent)	3.9	4.8
9th to 12th grade, no diploma (percent)	7.4	5.9
High school graduate, including equivalency (percent)	30.7	26.3
Some college, no degree (percent)	21.9	19.3
Associate's degree (percent)	8.1	8.8
Bachelor's degree (percent)	18.3	21.2
Graduate or professional degree (percent)	9.6	13.8
High school graduate or higher (percent)	88.7	89.4
Bachelor's degree or higher (percent)	27.9	35.0

Table OK-12. Public School Characteristics and Educational Indicators

(Number, percent; data derived from National Center of Education Statistics.)

Item	State	U.S.
Public Elementary and Secondary Schools		
Number of regular school districts, 2019-20	511	13,349
Number of operational schools, 2019-20	1,794	98,469
Percent charter schools	3.6	7.7
Total public school enrollment, Fall 2021	698,696	49,433,092
Percent charter school enrollment	8.6	7.5
Student-teacher ratio, Fall 2019	16.2	15.9
Expenditures per student (unadjusted dollars), 2019-20	9,395	13,489
Four-year adjusted cohort graduation rate (ACGR), 2019-2020[1]	80.8	86.5
Students eligible for free or reduced-price lunch (percent), 2019-20	59.1	52.1
English language learners (percent), Fall 2020	9.2	10.3
Students age 3 to 21 served under IDEA, part B (percent), 2021-22	16.8	14.7

Public Schools by Type, 2019-20	Number	Percent of state public schools
Total number of schools	1,794	100.0
Special education	4	0.2
Vocational education	-	-
Alternative education	5	0.3

[1] Adjusted Cohort Graduation Rates (ACGR) differ from Averaged Freshmen Graduation Rates (AFGR).
- = Zero or rounds to zero.

Table OK-13. Reported Voting and Registration of the Voting-Age Population, November 2022

(Numbers in thousands, percent.)

Item	Total population	Total citizen population	Registered			Voted		
			Total registered	Percent registered (total population)	Percent registered (total citizen population)	Total voted	Percent voted (total population)	Percent voted (total citizen population)
U.S. Total	255,457	233,546	161,422	63.2	69.1	121,916	47.7	52.2
State Total......................	2,999	2,841	1,936	64.6	68.1	1,335	44.5	47.0
Sex								
Male	1,460	1,360	922	63.1	67.8	643	44.1	47.3
Female	1,539	1,481	1,014	65.9	68.5	691	44.9	46.7
Race								
White alone........................	2,223	2,128	1,535	69.0	72.1	1,091	49.0	51.3
White, non-Hispanic alone	1,907	1,905	1,435	75.3	75.4	1,037	54.4	54.5
Black alone........................	208	172	79	38.1	45.9	47	22.7	27.3
Asian alone	89	72	34	37.9	46.7	23	26.0	32.1
Hispanic (of any race)	341	244	108	31.6	44.2	57	16.6	23.2
White alone or in combination	2,344	2,248	1,605	68.5	71.4	1,131	48.3	50.3
Black alone or in combination.....................	238	203	91	38.4	45.0	53	22.2	26.1
Asian alone or in combination.....................	103	86	37	36.4	43.5	23	22.5	27.0
Age								
18 to 24 years	364	335	167	45.8	49.8	70	19.3	21.0
25 to 34 years	590	535	296	50.1	55.3	157	26.7	29.4
35 to 44 years	461	441	308	66.8	69.8	203	43.9	45.9
45 to 64 years	938	892	672	71.6	75.3	503	53.6	56.4
65 years and over	645	638	493	76.5	77.4	401	62.2	62.9

B = Base is less than 75,000 and therefore too small to show the derived measure.

Table OK-14. Health Indicators

(Number, rate as indicated in footnotes.)

Item	State	U.S.
Births		
Life Expectancy at Birth (years), 2020	74.1	77.0
Fertility Rate by State[1], 2021	61.5	56.3
Percent Home Births, 2021	1.3	1.4
Cesarean Delivery Rate[2], 2021	32.5	32.1
Preterm Birth Rate[3], 2021	11.9	10.5
Teen Birth Rate[4], 2021	24.1	13.9
Percentage of Babies Born Low Birthweight[5], 2021	8.8	8.5
Deaths[6]		
Heart Disease Mortality Rate, 2021...	264.2	173.8
Cancer Mortality Rate, 2021...	175.1	146.6
Stroke Mortality Rate, 2021..	42.5	41.1
Diabetes Mortality Rate, 2021...	35.1	25.4
Influenza/Pneumonia Mortality Rate, 2021..	12.3	10.5
Suicide Mortality Rate, 2021...	22.1	14.1
Drug Overdose Mortality Rate, 2021...	24.4	33.6
Firearm Injury Mortality Rate, 2021...	21.2	14.6
Homicide Mortality Rate, 2021...	8.9	8.2
Disease and Illness		
Lifetime Asthma in Adults, 2020 (percent)..	15.4	13.9
Lifetime Asthma in Children, 2020 (percent)[7]	NA	11.3
Diabetes in Adults, 2020 (percent)...	11.9	8.2
Self-reported Obesity in Adults, 2021 (percent)..	39.4	NA

SOURCE: National Center for Health Statistics, National Vital Statistics System 2020 data; https://wonder.cdc.gov.
[1] General fertility rate per 1,000 women aged 15–44.
[2] This represents the percentage of all live births that were cesarean deliveries.
[3] Babies born prior to 37 weeks of pregnancy (gestation).
[4] Number of births per 1,000 females aged 15–19
[5] Babies born weighing less than 2,500 grams or 5 lbs. 8oz.
[6] Death rates are the number of deaths per 100,000 total population.
[7] U.S. total includes data from 30 states and D.C.
NA = Not available.
- = Zero or rounds to zero.

Table OK-15. State Government Finances, 2021

(Dollar amounts in thousands, percent distribution.)

Item	Dollars	Percent distribution
Total Revenue	30,978,736	100.0
General revenue	27,683,745	89.4
Intergovernmental revenue	10,355,355	33.4
Taxes	11,299,244	36.5
General sales	3,116,195	10.1
Selective sales	1,859,475	6.0
License taxes	1,085,111	3.5
Individual income tax	3,767,669	12.2
Corporate income tax	601,224	1.9
Other taxes	869,570	2.8
Current charges	3,095,086	10.0
Miscellaneous general revenue	2,934,060	9.5
Utility revenue	591,523	1.9
Liquor stores revenue	-	-
Insurance trust revenue[1]	2,703,468	8.7
Total Expenditure	30,002,030	100.0
Intergovernmental expenditure	5,675,541	18.9
Direct expenditure	24,326,489	81.1
Current operation	16,337,129	54.5
Capital outlay	2,479,637	8.3
Insurance benefits and repayments	4,437,423	14.8
Assistance and subsidies	779,900	2.6
Interest on debt	292,400	1.0
Exhibit: Salaries and wages	3,505,471	11.7
Total Expenditure	30,002,030	100.0
General expenditure	24,926,432	83.1
Intergovernmental expenditure	5,675,541	18.9
Direct expenditure	19,250,891	64.2
General expenditure, by function:		
Education	9,040,237	30.1
Public welfare	7,487,550	25.0
Hospitals	283,507	0.9
Health	1,231,594	4.1
Highways	2,609,453	8.7
Police protection	210,392	0.7
Correction	624,921	2.1
Natural resources	244,980	0.8
Parks and recreation	88,037	0.3
Governmental administration	1,065,800	3.6
Interest on general debt	217,069	0.7
Other and unallocable	1,702,645	5.7
Utility expenditure	682,002	2.2
Liquor stores expenditure	-	-
Insurance trust expenditure	4,437,423	14.8
Debt at End of Fiscal Year	8,151,947	X
Cash and Security Holdings	65,879,554	X

X = Not applicable.
- = Zero or rounds to zero.
[1] Within insurance trust revenue, net earnings of state retirement systems is a calculated statistic (the item code in the data file is X08), and thus can be positive or negative. Net earnings is the sum of earnings on investments plus gains on investments minus losses on investments. The change made in 2002 for asset valuation from book to market value in accordance with Statement 34 of the Governmental Accounting Standards Board is reflected in the calculated statistics.

Table OK-16. State Government Tax Collections, 2022

(Dollars in thousands, percent.)

Item	Dollars	Percent distribution
Total Taxes	13,188,031	100.0
Property taxes	X	-
Sales and gross receipts	5,348,189	40.6
General sales and gross receipts	3,546,080	26.9
Selective sales and gross receipts	1,802,109	13.7
Alcoholic beverages	171,393	1.3
Amusements	30,878	0.2
Insurance premiums	349,723	2.7
Motor fuels	600,189	4.6
Pari-mutuels	1,105	-
Public utilities	55,280	0.4
Tobacco products	441,544	3.3
Other selective sales	151,997	1.2
Licenses	1,173,638	8.9
Alcoholic beverages	158	-
Amusements	193,315	1.5
Corporations in general	62,716	0.5
Hunting and fishing	26,106	0.2
Motor vehicle	863,147	6.5
Motor vehicle operators	26,434	0.2
Public utilities	5	-
Occupation and business, NEC	909	-
Other licenses	848	-
Income taxes	4,969,501	37.7
Individual income	4,157,808	31.5
Corporation net income	811,693	6.2
Other taxes	1,696,703	12.9
Death and gift	1	-
Documentary and stock transfer	37,756	0.3
Severance	1,529,945	11.6
Taxes, NEC	129,001	1.0

X = Not applicable.
- = Zero or rounds to zero.

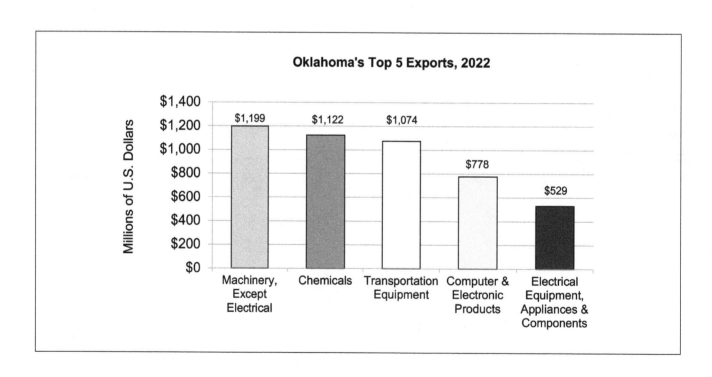

Oklahoma's Top 5 Exports, 2022

OREGON

Facts and Figures

Location: Northwestern United States; bordered on the N by Washington, on the E by Idaho, on the S by Nevada and California, and on the W by the Pacific Ocean

Area: 98,381 sq. mi. (254,805 sq. km.); rank—9th

Population: 4,240,137 (2022 est.); rank—27th

Principal Cities: capital—Salem; largest—Portland

Statehood: February 14, 1859; 33rd state

U.S. Congress: 2 senators, 5 representatives

State Motto: She Flies With Her Own Wings

State Song: "Oregon, My Oregon"

State Nickname: The Beaver State

Abbreviations: OR; Oreg.

State Symbols: flower—Oregon grape; tree—Douglas fir; bird—Western meadowlark

At a Glance

- With an increase in population of 10.7 percent, Oregon ranked 18th among the states in growth from 2010 to 2022.

- In 2021, 6.1 percent of Oregonians did not have health insurance, compared to 8.6 percent of the total U.S. population.

- Oregon's drug overdose death rate of 43.2 deaths per 100,000 population ranked 9th in the nation in 2021.

- The homeownership rate in Oregon in 2022 was 64.9 percent, compared to the national homeownership rate of 65.8 percent.

- The median household income in Oregon was $71,562 in 2021, compared to the national median of $69,717. Oregon's poverty rate was 12.2 percent, which ranked 24th in the nation.

Table OR-1. Population by Age, Sex, Race, and Hispanic Origin

(Number, percent, except where noted.)

Sex, age, race, and Hispanic origin	2010	2020	2022	Percent change, 2010–2022
Total Population..	3,831,074	4,237,291	4,240,137	10.7
Percent of total U.S. population	1.2	1.3	1.3	X
Sex				
Male	1,896,002	2,117,979	2,117,172	11.7
Female	1,935,072	2,119,312	2,122,965	9.7
Age				
Under 5 years..	237,556	218,342	206,074	-13.3
Under 18 years..	866,453	863,636	836,988	-3.4
18 to 64 years	2,431,088	2,603,059	2,587,471	6.4
65 years and over	533,533	770,596	815,678	52.9
Median age (years)	38.4	39.7	40.3	4.9
Race and Hispanic Origin				
One race				
White	3,403,252	3,662,859	3,640,385	7.0
Black	74,414	94,551	99,222	33.3
American Indian and Alaska Native	66,784	78,495	80,145	20.0
Asian	145,009	207,587	217,147	49.7
Native Hawaiian or Other Pacific Islander	14,649	19,937	20,692	41.3
Two or more races	126,966	173,862	182,546	43.8
Hispanic (of any race)	450,062	579,292	609,534	35.4

NOTE: Population figures for 2022 are July 1 estimates. The 2010 and 2020 estimates are taken from the respective censuses.
- = Zero or rounds to zero.
X = Not applicable.

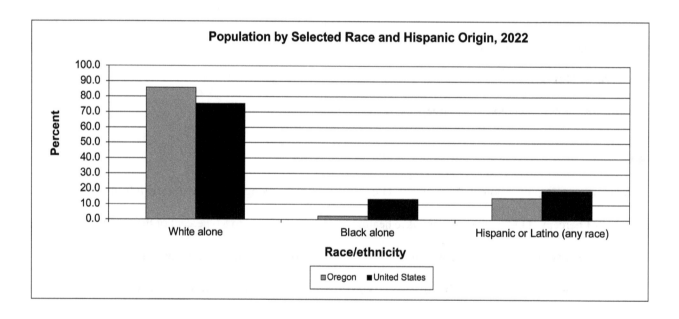

Table OR-2. Marital Status

(Number, percent distribution.)

Sex, age, race, and Hispanic origin	2000	2010	2021
Males, 15 Years and Over	1,336,805	1,533,177	1,758,576
Never married	28.5	32.6	36.1
Now married, except separated...........................	57.1	51.4	49.7
Separated..	1.5	1.6	1.1
Widowed..	2.4	2.7	2.3
Divorced..	10.6	11.8	10.8
Females, 15 Years and Over	1,385,329	1,588,428	1,781,970
Never married	21.9	25.8	28.9
Now married, except separated...........................	53.9	48.9	47.8
Separated..	1.9	1.9	1.4
Widowed..	9.6	8.5	7.4
Divorced..	12.7	14.9	14.5

Table OR-3. Households and Housing Characteristics

(Number, percent, dollars.)

Item	2000	2010	2021	Average annual percent change, 2010–2021
Total Households...	1,333,723	1,507,137	1,702,599	1.2
Family households	877,671	963,362	1,054,032	0.9
Married-couple family	692,532	733,095	806,612	0.9
Other family	185,139	230,267	247,420	0.7
Male householder, no wife present.............................	54,357	65,972	82,016	2.2
Female householder, no husband present....................	130,782	164,295	165,404	0.1
Nonfamily households	456,032	543,775	648,567	1.8
Householder living alone...	347,624	416,500	479,248	1.4
Householder not living alone..	108,428	127,275	169,319	3.0
Housing Characteristics				
Total housing units..	1,452,709	1,676,476	1,837,009	0.9
Occupied housing units	1,333,723	1,507,137	1,702,599	1.2
Owner occupied	856,951	942,674	1,086,030	1.4
Renter occupied	476,772	564,463	616,569	0.8
Average household size...	2.51	2.49	2.44	-0.2
Financial Characteristics				
Median gross rent of renter-occupied housing	620	816	1,282	5.2
Median monthly owner costs for housing units with a mortgage	1,125	1,577	1,835	1.5
Median value of owner-occupied housing units.................	152,100	244,500	422,700	6.6

Table OR-4. Migration, Origin, and Language

(Number, percent.)

Characteristic	State 2021	U.S. 2021
Residence 1 Year Ago		
Population 1 year and over	4,207,387	328,464,538
Same house	85.6	87.2
Different house in the U.S.	14.1	12.3
Same county	7.3	6.7
Different county	6.8	5.7
Same state	3.6	3.3
Different state	3.2	2.4
Abroad	0.3	0.4
Place of Birth		
Native born	3,833,759	286,623,642
Male	49.9	49.7
Female	50.1	50.3
Foreign born	412,396	45,270,103
Male	50.2	48.7
Female	49.8	51.3
Foreign born; naturalized U.S. citizen............................	213,662	24,044,083
Male	47.9	46.4
Female	52.1	53.6
Foreign born; not a U.S. citizen.....................................	198,734	21,226,020
Male	52.7	51.2
Female	47.3	48.8
Entered 2010 or later	25.5	28.1
Entered 2000 to 2009	22.3	23.7
Entered before 2000...	52.2	48.2
World Region of Birth, Foreign		
Foreign-born population, excluding population born at sea ...	412,396	45,269,644
Europe	15.0	10.7
Asia..	33.8	31.0
Africa..	4.3	5.7
Oceania	2.3	0.6
Latin America...	40.9	50.1
North America	3.7	1.7
Language Spoken at Home and Ability to Speak English		
Population 5 years and over..	4,035,825	313,232,500
English only	84.8	78.4
Language other than English...	15.2	21.6
Speaks English less than "very well"...........................	5.4	0.0

Table OR-5. Median Income and Poverty Status, 2021

(Number, percent, except as noted.)

Characteristic	State		U.S.	
	Number	Percent	Number	Percent
Median Income				
Households (dollars)...............................	71,562	X	69,717	X
Families (dollars)	88,085	X	85,806	X
Below Poverty Level (All People)	507,829	12.2	41,393,176	12.8
Sex				
Male	238,704	11.5	18,518,155	11.6
Female	269,125	12.9	22,875,021	13.9
Age				
Under 18 years....................................	113,211	13.5	12,243,219	16.9
Related children under 18 years.............	108,412	13.0	11,985,424	16.6
18 to 64 years....................................	321,754	12.6	23,526,341	11.9
65 years and over	72,864	9.3	5,623,616	10.3

X = Not applicable.

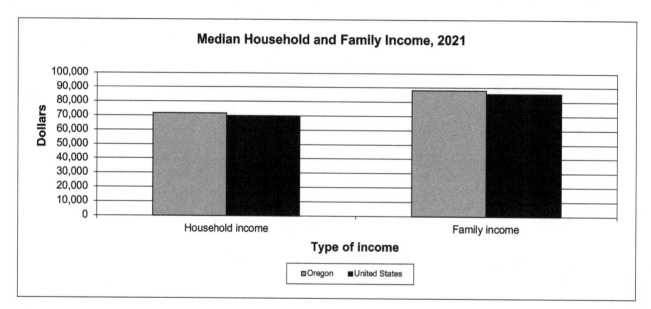

Median Household and Family Income, 2021

Table OR-6. Health Insurance Coverage Status for the Civilian Noninstitutionalized Population and Children Under 19 Years of Age

(Number, percent.)

Item	2011	2012	2013	2014	2015	2016	2017	2018	2019	2020 [2]	2021
Civilian Noninstitutionalized Population	3,832,640	3,860,452	3,893,092	3,931,306	3,991,133	4,054,353	4,102,901	4,151,076	4,175,002	4,135,531	4,206,414
Covered by Private or Public Insurance											
Number..	3,230,263	3,284,443	3,322,210	3,548,645	3,710,870	3,801,587	3,822,085	3,857,969	3,875,582	3,861,117	3,950,976
Percent...	84.3	85.1	85.3	90.3	93.0	93.8	93.2	92.9	92.8	93.4	93.9
Uninsured											
Number..	602,377	576,009	570,882	382,661	280,263	252,766	280,816	293,107	299,420	274,414	255,438
Percent...	15.7	14.9	14.7	9.7	7.0	6.2	6.8	7.1	7.2	6.6	6.1
Percent in the U.S. not covered	15.1	14.8	14.5	11.7	9.4	8.6	8.7	8.9	9.2	8.7	8.6
Children Under 19 Years of Age[1]	861,059	859,846	858,259	857,084	859,408	866,585	928,115	924,284	914,386	918,429	911,427
Covered by Private or Public Insurance											
Number..	798,172	805,216	808,087	818,051	828,340	837,985	895,141	891,393	876,871	886,179	880,064
Percent...	92.7	93.6	94.2	95.4	96.4	96.7	96.4	96.4	95.9	96.5	96.6
Uninsured											
Number..	62,887	54,630	50,172	39,033	31,068	28,600	32,974	32,891	37,515	32,250	31,363
Percent...	7.3	6.4	5.8	4.6	3.6	3.3	3.6	3.6	4.1	3.5	3.4
Percent in the U.S. not covered................	7.5	7.2	7.1	6.0	4.8	4.5	5.0	5.2	5.7	5.2	5.4

[1] Data for years prior to 2017 are for individuals under 18 years of age.
[2] 2020 ACS 5-Year estimates. 1-Year estimates were not released for 2020 due to the impact of COVID-19 on data collection that year. Data is not comparable to previous years, which are based on 1-year estimates.

Table OR-7. Employment Status by Demographic Group, 2022

(Numbers in thousands, percent.)

Characteristic	Civilian noninstitutional population	Civilian labor force		Employed		Unemployed	
		Number	Percent of population	Number	Percent of population	Number	Percent of population
Total...	3,474	2,182	62.8	2,090	60.2	92	4.2
Sex							
Male...	1,712	1,152	67.3	1,097	64.1	55	4.8
Female...	1,762	1,030	58.5	993	56.4	37	3.6
Race, Sex, and Hispanic Origin							
White...	3,081	1,908	61.9	1,829	59.4	79	4.1
Male...	1,511	1,004	66.4	956	63.3	48	4.8
Female..	1,571	904	57.6	873	55.6	31	3.4
Black or African American........................	NA	NA	NA	NA	NA	NA	NA
Male...	NA	NA	NA	NA	NA	NA	NA
Female..	NA	NA	NA	NA	NA	NA	NA
Hispanic or Latino ethnicity[1]	399	283	71.0	263	66.0	20	7.0
Male...	213	167	78.2	155	72.8	12	6.9
Female..	186	117	62.8	108	58.2	8	7.2
Age							
16 to 19 years...	224	87	38.7	74	33.0	13	14.9
20 to 24 years...	206	151	73.1	136	66.0	15	9.8
25 to 34 years...	583	501	85.9	475	81.4	26	5.3
35 to 44 years...	617	516	83.6	503	81.4	14	2.6
45 to 54 years...	563	470	83.6	458	81.4	12	2.6
55 to 64 years...	477	315	66.0	308	64.6	7	2.1
65 years and over	804	143	17.8	137	17.1	6	4.0

NOTE: Data in Table 7 are from the Current Population Survey (CPS) and do not match the estimates in Table 8. See notes and definitions for further information.
[1] May be of any race.
NA = Not available.

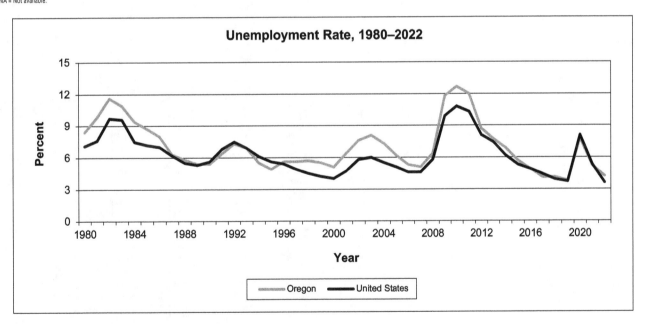

Table OR-8. Employment Status of the Civilian Noninstitutional Population Age 16 Years and Over

(Number, percent.)

Year	Civilian labor force	Civilian participation rate	Employed	Unemployed	Unemployment rate
2010...	1,991,749	65.6	1,778,034	213,715	10.7
2011...	1,995,931	65.1	1,804,257	191,674	9.6
2012...	1,964,662	63.4	1,791,248	173,414	8.8
2013...	1,924,692	61.6	1,775,139	149,553	7.8
2014...	1,950,128	61.6	1,820,202	129,926	6.7
2015...	1,979,475	61.6	1,871,286	108,189	5.5
2016...	2,042,929	62.3	1,946,233	96,696	4.7
2017...	2,075,682	62.4	1,991,503	84,179	4.1
2018...	2,080,199	61.8	1,996,790	83,409	4.0
2019...	2,094,977	61.6	2,017,379	77,598	3.7
2020...	2,104,558	61.3	1,944,845	159,713	7.6
2021...	2,148,333	62.3	2,036,138	112,195	5.2
2022...	2,176,734	62.8	2,085,939	90,795	4.2

Table OR-9. Employment and Average Wages by Industry

(Estimates are based on the 2012 North American Industry Classification System [NAICS].)

Industry	2014	2015	2016	2017	2018	2019	2020	2021
	Number of Jobs							
Wage and Salary Employment by Industry........................	1,799,533	1,851,480	1,901,515	1,945,586	1,990,185	2,021,591	1,900,653	1,952,352
Farm Wage and Salary Employment...............................	29,615	24,152	24,674	30,223	33,263	33,557	25,029	34,890
Nonfarm Wage and Salary Employment.........................	1,769,918	1,827,328	1,876,841	1,915,363	1,956,922	1,988,034	1,875,624	1,917,462
Private wage and salary employment............................	1,492,363	1,544,909	1,590,073	1,627,274	1,663,944	1,691,720	1,589,777	1,629,494
Forestry, fishing, and related activities............................	22,400	22,938	22,334	22,169	23,188	22,934	22,289	21,795
Mining..	1,546	1,701	1,748	1,832	1,935	1,836	1,773	1,815
Utilities...	4,512	4,485	4,563	4,666	4,802	4,827	4,785	4,745
Construction	81,274	84,610	91,724	99,193	107,117	111,341	110,357	112,784
Manufacturing...	179,225	185,655	187,821	189,475	194,880	197,773	185,352	186,986
Durable goods manufacturing....................................	125,982	130,082	131,012	131,309	135,420	136,816	128,294	128,969
Nondurable goods manufacturing...............................	53,243	55,573	56,809	58,166	59,460	60,957	57,058	58,017
Wholesale trade	72,583	73,997	75,611	76,785	75,538	76,546	74,376	74,737
Retail trade..	197,116	203,335	206,266	211,664	212,858	210,987	201,975	210,254
Transportation and warehousing..................................	53,195	55,346	56,580	59,008	61,379	66,436	70,350	73,055
Information	32,179	33,224	33,370	34,258	34,323	35,063	33,228	35,059
Finance and insurance	59,178	59,596	59,574	61,115	61,194	61,115	61,497	60,215
Real estate and rental and leasing...............................	24,584	25,558	26,266	27,099	28,635	29,798	28,352	29,225
Professional, scientific, and technical services	84,603	88,052	92,517	94,974	98,136	100,582	99,409	104,374
Management of companies and enterprises........................	40,220	42,951	45,352	47,108	48,620	50,542	48,994	48,092
Administrative and waste services	95,308	98,635	101,534	101,967	103,757	104,154	95,581	99,400
Educational services	45,548	45,784	45,379	45,952	43,189	43,456	36,427	37,516
Health care and social assistance................................	229,829	240,739	250,851	256,215	261,888	268,122	269,101	270,516
Arts, entertainment, and recreation...............................	23,993	24,055	25,974	27,322	27,988	28,327	19,609	20,748
Accommodation and food services................................	159,980	168,344	174,556	179,765	184,285	186,386	143,590	154,712
Other services, except public administration.....................	85,090	85,904	88,053	86,707	90,232	91,495	82,732	83,466
Government and government enterprises	277,555	282,419	286,768	288,089	292,978	296,314	285,847	287,968
	Dollars							
Average Wages and Salaries by Industry	47,258	49,154	50,383	51,951	53,839	55,634	60,649	64,687
Average Farm Wages and Salaries	29,294	30,400	34,450	28,287	27,939	20,006	29,662	29,534
Average Nonfarm Wages and Salaries	47,559	49,402	50,592	52,325	54,280	56,236	61,063	65,326
Average private wages and salaries	47,068	48,985	50,101	51,776	53,770	55,679	60,628	65,032
Forestry, fishing, and related activities............................	36,363	38,506	38,901	39,760	41,842	40,823	46,175	51,084
Mining..	51,229	53,831	57,496	59,248	61,306	63,581	65,261	68,929
Utilities...	93,693	96,245	98,575	103,211	105,180	110,942	119,292	123,197
Construction	54,158	54,434	56,667	58,795	61,341	63,953	67,810	71,147
Manufacturing...	65,742	67,445	69,136	69,853	72,368	73,146	76,856	80,473
Durable goods manufacturing....................................	74,781	76,524	79,015	79,361	82,783	83,677	87,038	91,276
Nondurable goods manufacturing...............................	44,355	46,192	46,354	48,386	48,648	49,509	53,963	56,459
Wholesale trade	65,118	67,518	68,925	72,026	74,732	77,401	82,032	90,442
Retail trade..	29,054	29,890	30,671	31,533	32,494	33,662	36,934	39,910
Transportation and warehousing..................................	47,122	47,990	48,429	50,192	52,077	51,915	53,322	56,712
Information	72,606	75,381	77,148	82,084	89,657	91,580	104,100	116,010
Finance and insurance	71,420	76,212	79,047	80,609	83,198	87,514	95,950	103,254
Real estate and rental and leasing...............................	38,275	40,309	42,517	44,844	46,951	50,173	53,369	56,937
Professional, scientific, and technical services	70,558	73,715	75,580	78,992	80,903	84,051	89,855	94,660
Management of companies and enterprises........................	112,297	121,932	117,284	119,523	121,528	126,571	141,879	165,019
Administrative and waste services	33,351	34,852	35,780	37,070	38,596	41,002	45,348	50,156
Educational services	26,176	26,726	27,866	28,259	30,366	31,214	36,620	36,383
Health care and social assistance................................	47,043	49,070	49,986	51,529	52,750	54,433	56,718	60,435
Arts, entertainment, and recreation...............................	27,511	28,905	29,038	31,107	32,811	34,104	38,642	41,390
Accommodation and food services................................	20,551	21,364	22,123	23,373	25,349	26,391	25,354	30,349
Other services, except public administration.....................	31,283	33,102	34,297	36,085	37,271	38,571	42,812	45,091
Government and government enterprises	50,195	51,679	53,316	55,425	57,173	59,415	63,484	66,991

Table OR-10. Employment Characteristics by Family Type

(Number, percent.)

Family type and labor force status	2019		2020 [1]		2021	
	Total	Families with own children under 18 years	Total	Families with own children under 18 years	Total	Families with own children under 18 years
All Families..........................	1,021,588	400,064	1,034,877	420,914	1,054,032	420,391
FAMILY TYPE AND LABOR FORCE STATUS						
Opposite-Sex Married-Couple Families..........................	780,807	276,756	783,066	291,116	793,984	290,450
Both husband and wife in labor force..........................	48.8	67.0	49.6	66.5	48.2	65.2
Husband in labor force, wife not in labor force	19.2	24.8	20.4	26.9	19.8	26.6
Wife in labor force, husband not in labor force	8.6	5.2	8.4	4.9	8.9	6.1
Both husband and wife not in labor force..........................	21.9	2.0	21.5	1.7	23.1	2.0
Other Families	240,781	123,308	241,299	127,663	247,420	127,703
Female householder, no spouse present	68.7	67.9	68.8	70.0	66.9	67.7
In labor force..........................	47.8	57.8	48.3	58.6	45.4	54.9
Not in labor force	20.9	10.1	20.5	11.4	21.4	12.9
Male householder, no spouse present..........................	31.3	32.1	31.2	30.0	33.1	32.3
In labor force..........................	25.5	29.5	24.7	27.4	26.5	29.2
Not in labor force	5.7	2.5	6.5	2.6	6.7	3.0

[1] 2020 ACS 5-Year estimates. 1-Year estimates were not released for 2020 due to the impact of COVID-19 on data collection that year. Data is not comparable to previous years, which are based on 1-year estimates.

Table OR-11. School Enrollment and Educational Attainment, 2021

(Number, percent.)

Item	State	U.S.
Enrollment		
Total population 3 years and over, enrolled in school	913,400	79,453,524
Enrolled in nursery school or preschool (percent)..........................	4.5	5.2
Enrolled in kindergarten (percent)..........................	4.8	5.0
Enrolled in elementary school, grades 1-8 (percent)..........................	42.0	41.3
Enrolled in high school, grades 9-12 (percent)..........................	22.1	21.8
Enrolled in college or graduate school (percent)..........................	26.7	26.7
Attainment		
Total population 25 years and over	3,030,635	228,193,464
Less than ninth grade (percent)..........................	3.3	4.8
9th to 12th grade, no diploma (percent)..........................	4.8	5.9
High school graduate, including equivalency (percent)..........................	21.9	26.3
Some college, no degree (percent)..........................	24.6	19.3
Associate's degree (percent)..........................	9.0	8.8
Bachelor's degree (percent)	22.4	21.2
Graduate or professional degree (percent)..........................	13.9	13.8
High school graduate or higher (percent)..........................	91.9	89.4
Bachelor's degree or higher (percent)..........................	36.3	35.0

Table OR-12. Public School Characteristics and Educational Indicators

(Number, percent; data derived from National Center of Education Statistics.)

Item	State	U.S.
Public Elementary and Secondary Schools		
Number of regular school districts, 2019-20	176	13,349
Number of operational schools, 2019-20..........................	1,255	98,469
Percent charter schools	10.6	7.7
Total public school enrollment, Fall 2021	576,201	49,433,092
Percent charter school enrollment	7.9	7.5
Student-teacher ratio, Fall 2019	20.2	15.9
Expenditures per student (unadjusted dollars), 2019-20	12,838	13,489
Four-year adjusted cohort graduation rate (ACGR), 2019-2020[1]..........................	82.6	86.5
Students eligible for free or reduced-price lunch (percent), 2019-20..........................	47.9	52.1
English language learners (percent), Fall 2020	9.3	10.3
Students age 3 to 21 served under IDEA, part B (percent), 2021-22	14.8	14.7

Public Schools by Type, 2019-20	Number	Percent of state public schools
Total number of schools..........................	1,255	100.0
Special education..........................	1	0.1
Vocational education..........................	-	-
Alternative education..........................	35	2.8

[1] Adjusted Cohort Graduation Rates (ACGR) differ from Averaged Freshmen Graduation Rates (AFGR).
- = Zero or rounds to zero.

Table OR-13. Reported Voting and Registration of the Voting-Age Population, November 2022

(Numbers in thousands, percent.)

Item	Total population	Total citizen population	Registered			Voted		
			Total registered	Percent registered (total population)	Percent registered (total citizen population)	Total voted	Percent voted (total population)	Percent voted (total citizen population)
U.S. Total	255,457	233,546	161,422	63.2	69.1	121,916	47.7	52.2
State Total	3,345	3,122	2,581	77.2	82.7	2,185	65.3	70.0
Sex								
Male	1,643	1,535	1,275	77.6	83.1	1,054	64.1	68.7
Female	1,702	1,587	1,306	76.8	82.3	1,131	66.5	71.3
Race								
White alone	2,961	2,788	2,321	78.4	83.3	1,983	67.0	71.1
White, non-Hispanic alone	2,598	2,570	2,204	84.8	85.8	1,906	73.4	74.2
Black alone	69	63	40	57.8	63.0	26	37.6	41.0
Asian alone	134	97	81	60.3	82.7	58	43.8	60.0
Hispanic (of any race)	421	262	145	34.5	55.6	100	23.9	38.4
White alone or in combination	3,098	2,917	2,426	78.3	83.2	2,076	67.0	71.2
Black alone or in combination	109	96	65	59.4	67.9	51	46.7	53.4
Asian alone or in combination	186	150	121	65.1	80.8	99	53.2	66.0
Age								
18 to 24 years	300	284	197	65.5	69.2	127	42.4	44.8
25 to 34 years	609	564	460	75.5	81.6	350	57.5	62.1
35 to 44 years	587	522	445	75.9	85.3	358	61.1	68.7
45 to 64 years	1,030	959	801	77.8	83.5	713	69.2	74.4
65 years and over	819	793	679	82.9	85.6	636	77.6	80.2

B = Base is less than 75,000 and therefore too small to show the derived measure.

Table OR-14. Health Indicators

(Number, rate as indicated in footnotes.)

Item	State	U.S.
Births		
Life Expectancy at Birth (years), 2020	78.8	77.0
Fertility Rate by State[1], 2021	48.9	56.3
Percent Home Births, 2021	2.6	1.4
Cesarean Delivery Rate[2], 2021	29.1	32.1
Preterm Birth Rate[3], 2021	8.9	10.5
Teen Birth Rate[4], 2021	9.5	13.9
Percentage of Babies Born Low Birthweight[5], 2021	6.9	8.5
Deaths[6]		
Heart Disease Mortality Rate, 2021	148.5	173.8
Cancer Mortality Rate, 2021	155.2	146.6
Stroke Mortality Rate, 2021	45.1	41.1
Diabetes Mortality Rate, 2021	25.9	25.4
Influenza/Pneumonia Mortality Rate, 2021	4.4	10.5
Suicide Mortality Rate, 2021	19.5	14.1
Drug Overdose Mortality Rate, 2021	26.8	33.6
Firearm Injury Mortality Rate, 2021	14.9	14.6
Homicide Mortality Rate, 2021	4.9	8.2
Disease and Illness		
Lifetime Asthma in Adults, 2020 (percent)	15.6	13.9
Lifetime Asthma in Children, 2020 (percent)[7]	NA	11.3
Diabetes in Adults, 2020 (percent)	8.4	8.2
Self-reported Obesity in Adults, 2021 (percent)	30.4	NA

SOURCE: National Center for Health Statistics, National Vital Statistics System 2020 data; https://wonder.cdc.gov.
[1] General fertility rate per 1,000 women aged 15–44.
[2] This represents the percentage of all live births that were cesarean deliveries.
[3] Babies born prior to 37 weeks of pregnancy (gestation).
[4] Number of births per 1,000 females aged 15–19
[5] Babies born weighing less than 2,500 grams or 5 lbs. 8oz.
[6] Death rates are the number of deaths per 100,000 total population.
[7] U.S. total includes data from 30 states and D.C.
NA = Not available.
- = Zero or rounds to zero.

Table OR-15. State Government Finances, 2021

(Dollar amounts in thousands, percent distribution.)

Item	Dollars	Percent distribution
Total Revenue	49,042,830	100.0
General revenue	41,602,320	84.8
Intergovernmental revenue	13,775,775	28.1
Taxes	17,799,808	36.3
General sales	-	-
Selective sales	2,386,620	4.9
License taxes	2,483,742	5.1
Individual income tax	11,256,904	23.0
Corporate income tax	1,223,523	2.5
Other taxes	449,019	0.9
Current charges	6,563,635	13.4
Miscellaneous general revenue	3,463,102	7.1
Utility revenue	86	-
Liquor stores revenue	792,060	1.6
Insurance trust revenue[1]	6,648,364	13.6
Total Expenditure	46,209,080	100.0
Intergovernmental expenditure	8,034,730	17.4
Direct expenditure	38,174,350	82.6
Current operation	31,232,117	67.6
Capital outlay	1,295,198	2.8
Insurance benefits and repayments	4,632,104	10.0
Assistance and subsidies	677,122	1.5
Interest on debt	337,809	0.7
Exhibit: Salaries and wages	5,693,286	12.3
Total Expenditure	46,209,080	100.0
General expenditure	41,027,360	88.8
Intergovernmental expenditure	8,034,730	17.4
Direct expenditure	32,992,630	71.4
General expenditure, by function:		
Education	12,102,796	26.2
Public welfare	14,469,993	31.3
Hospitals	2,834,995	6.1
Health	1,537,300	3.3
Highways	1,543,510	3.3
Police protection	300,408	0.7
Correction	1,141,634	2.5
Natural resources	585,929	1.3
Parks and recreation	106,858	0.2
Governmental administration	2,316,660	5.0
Interest on general debt	337,809	0.7
Other and unallocable	3,470,999	7.5
Utility expenditure	180,248	0.4
Liquor stores expenditure	525,069	1.1
Insurance trust expenditure	4,632,104	10.0
Debt at End of Fiscal Year	14,424,636	X
Cash and Security Holdings	133,485,698	X

X = Not applicable.
- = Zero or rounds to zero.
[1] Within insurance trust revenue, net earnings of state retirement systems is a calculated statistic (the item code in the data file is X08), and thus can be positive or negative. Net earnings is the sum of earnings on investments plus gains on investments minus losses on investments. The change made in 2002 for asset valuation from book to market value in accordance with Statement 34 of the Governmental Accounting Standards Board is reflected in the calculated statistics.

Table OR-16. State Government Tax Collections, 2022

(Dollars in thousands, percent.)

Item	Dollars	Percent distribution
Total Taxes	18,885,694	100.0
Property taxes	22,884	0.1
Sales and gross receipts	2,661,504	14.1
General sales and gross receipts	X	-
Selective sales and gross receipts	2,661,504	14.1
Alcoholic beverages	19,711	0.1
Amusements	12,427	0.1
Insurance premiums	85,403	0.5
Motor fuels	600,717	3.2
Pari-mutuels	3,156	-
Public utilities	22,101	0.1
Tobacco products	459,571	2.4
Other selective sales	1,458,418	7.7
Licenses	2,564,973	13.6
Alcoholic beverages	5,637	-
Amusements	1,448	-
Corporations in general	1,262,333	6.7
Hunting and fishing	59,255	0.3
Motor vehicle	895,677	4.7
Motor vehicle operators	58,248	0.3
Public utilities	13,899	0.1
Occupation and business, NEC	259,691	1.4
Other licenses	8,785	-
Income taxes	13,261,860	70.2
Individual income	11,772,886	62.3
Corporation net income	1,488,974	7.9
Other taxes	374,473	2.0
Death and gift	350,592	1.9
Documentary and stock transfer	3,859	-
Severance	16,484	0.1
Taxes, NEC	3,538	-

X = Not applicable.
- = Zero or rounds to zero.

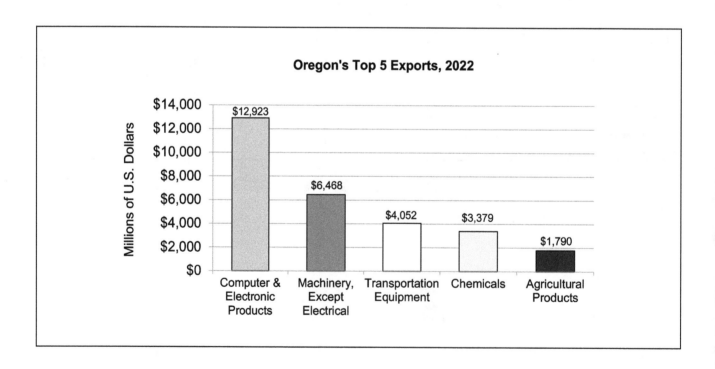

Oregon's Top 5 Exports, 2022

Export	Millions of U.S. Dollars
Computer & Electronic Products	$12,923
Machinery, Except Electrical	$6,468
Transportation Equipment	$4,052
Chemicals	$3,379
Agricultural Products	$1,790

PENNSYLVANIA

Facts and Figures

Location: Northeastern United States; bordered on the N by Lake Erie and New York, on the E by New York and New Jersey, on the S by Delaware, Maryland, and West Virginia, and on the W by West Virginia and Ohio

Area: 46,055 sq. mi. (119,283 sq. km.); rank—33rd

Population: 12,972,008 (2022 est.); rank—5th

Principal Cities: capital—Harrisburg; largest—Philadelphia

Statehood: December 12, 1787; 2nd state

U.S. Congress: 2 senators, 18 representatives

State Motto: Virtue, Liberty, and Independence

State Song: "Pennsylvania"

State Nicknames: The Keystone State; The Quaker State

Abbreviations: PA; Penn.

State Symbols: flower—mountain laurel; tree—Eastern hemlock; bird—ruffed grouse

At a Glance

- With an increase in population of 2.1 percent, Pennsylvania ranked 43rd among the states in growth from 2010 to 2022.

- Pennsylvania's median household income in 2021 was $68,957, and 12.1 percent of the population lived below the poverty level.

- Approximately 5.5 percent of Pennsylvanians did not have health insurance in 2021, compared to the national rate of 8.6 percent.

- Pennsylvania's real GDP of $726 billion ranked 6th in the country and comprised 3.6 percent of the U.S.'s total GDP in 2022.

- The unemployment rate in Pennsylvania was 4.4 percent in 2022, compared to the national unemployment rate of 3.6 percent.

Table PA-1. Population by Age, Sex, Race, and Hispanic Origin

(Number, percent, except where noted.)

Sex, age, race, and Hispanic origin	2010	2020	2022	Percent change, 2010–2022
Total Population.....................	12,702,379	13,002,689	12,972,008	2.1
Percent of total U.S. population	4.1	3.9	3.9	X
Sex				
Male...................	6,190,363	6,420,636	6,405,343	3.5
Female	6,512,016	6,582,053	6,566,665	0.8
Age				
Under 5 years...........	729,538	691,901	671,205	-8.0
Under 18 years...........	2,792,155	2,677,960	2,624,465	-6.0
18 to 64 years	7,950,917	7,896,010	7,805,617	-1.8
65 years and over	1,959,307	2,428,719	2,541,926	29.7
Median age (years)	40.1	40.8	40.9	2.0
Race and Hispanic Origin				
One race				
White	10,663,774	10,572,637	10,479,634	-1.7
Black	1,431,826	1,573,374	1,582,451	10.5
American Indian and Alaska Native	39,735	53,841	57,951	45.8
Asian...................	358,195	503,866	532,634	48.7
Native Hawaiian or Other Pacific Islander	7,115	11,206	12,056	69.4
Two or more races	201,734	287,765	307,282	52.3
Hispanic (of any race)	719,660	1,048,708	1,116,130	55.1

NOTE: Population figures for 2022 are July 1 estimates. The 2010 and 2020 estimates are taken from the respective censuses.
- = Zero or rounds to zero.
X = Not applicable.

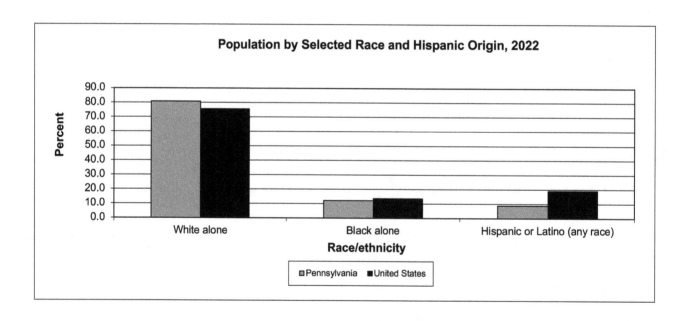

Population by Selected Race and Hispanic Origin, 2022

Table PA-2. Marital Status

(Number, percent distribution.)

Sex, age, race, and Hispanic origin	2000	2010	2021
Males, 15 Years and Over	4,686,277	5,031,761	5,275,218
Never married	30.1	35.9	37.3
Now married, except separated...................	57.4	50.6	49.8
Separated...................	1.9	2.0	1.5
Widowed...................	3.3	3.1	2.8
Divorced...................	7.3	8.5	8.5
Females, 15 Years and Over	5,175,436	5,406,494	5,491,436
Never married	24.6	29.8	31.6
Now married, except separated...................	51.5	46.2	46.5
Separated...................	2.4	2.7	1.9
Widowed...................	12.7	11.2	9.2
Divorced...................	8.8	10.2	10.8

Table PA-3. Households and Housing Characteristics

(Number, percent, dollars.)

Item	2000	2010	2021	Average annual percent change, 2010–2021
Total Households..	4,777,003	4,936,030	5,228,956	0.5
Family households	3,208,388	3,197,710	3,298,555	0.3
Married-couple family	2,467,673	2,381,094	2,449,955	0.3
Other family	740,715	816,616	848,600	0.4
Male householder, no wife present.....................	186,022	215,082	242,449	1.2
Female householder, no husband present.............	554,693	601,534	606,151	0.1
Nonfamily households	1,568,615	1,738,320	1,930,401	1.0
Householder living alone....................................	1,320,941	1,458,055	1,580,153	0.8
Householder not living alone..............................	247,674	280,265	350,248	2.3
Housing Characteristics				
Total housing units...	5,249,750	5,568,820	5,770,472	0.3
Occupied housing units	4,777,003	4,936,030	5,228,956	0.5
Owner occupied	3,406,337	3,461,678	3,657,478	0.5
Renter occupied	1,370,666	1,474,352	1,571,478	0.6
Average household size..	2.48	2.49	2.40	-0.3
Financial Characteristics				
Median gross rent of renter-occupied housing	531	763	1036	3.3
Median monthly owner costs for housing units with a mortgage	1,010	1,390	1,505	0.8
Median value of owner-occupied housing units...........	97,000	165,500	222,300	3.1

Table PA-4. Migration, Origin, and Language

(Number, percent.)

Characteristic	State 2021	U.S. 2021
Residence 1 Year Ago		
Population 1 year and over	12,842,522	328,464,538
Same house	89.2	87.2
Different house in the U.S...	10.4	12.3
Same county	5.7	6.7
Different county	4.8	5.7
Same state..	2.7	3.3
Different state	2.0	2.4
Abroad..	0.4	0.4
Place of Birth		
Native born	12,025,420	286,623,642
Male	49.4	49.7
Female	50.6	50.3
Foreign born	938,636	45,270,103
Male	48.8	48.7
Female	51.2	51.3
Foreign born; naturalized U.S. citizen...........................	519,531	24,044,083
Male	46.5	46.4
Female	53.5	53.6
Foreign born; not a U.S. citizen..................................	419,105	21,226,020
Male	51.5	51.2
Female	48.5	48.8
Entered 2010 or later	36.7	28.1
Entered 2000 to 2009	23.8	23.7
Entered before 2000..	39.5	48.2
World Region of Birth, Foreign		
Foreign-born population, excluding population born at sea	938,636	45,269,644
Europe..	17.2	10.7
Asia..	38.5	31.0
Africa...	9.3	5.7
Oceania...	0.3	0.6
Latin America..	32.8	50.1
North America...	1.8	1.7
Language Spoken at Home and Ability to Speak English		
Population 5 years and over..	12,285,978	313,232,500
English only	88.2	78.4
Language other than English.....................................	11.8	21.6
Speaks English less than "very well"...........................	4.7	8.3

Table PA-5. Median Income and Poverty Status, 2021

(Number, percent, except as noted.)

Characteristic	State		U.S.	
	Number	Percent	Number	Percent
Median Income				
Households (dollars)...............................	68,957	X	69,717	X
Families (dollars)	87,500	X	85,806	X
Below Poverty Level (All People)	1,519,032	12.1	41,393,176	12.8
Sex				
Male	662,566	10.7	18,518,155	11.6
Female	856,466	13.4	22,875,021	13.9
Age				
Under 18 years..	445,513	16.9	12,243,219	16.9
Related children under 18 years.............	435,928	16.6	11,985,424	16.6
18 to 64 years...	843,232	11.2	23,526,341	11.9
65 years and over..................................	230,287	9.6	5,623,616	10.3

X = Not applicable.

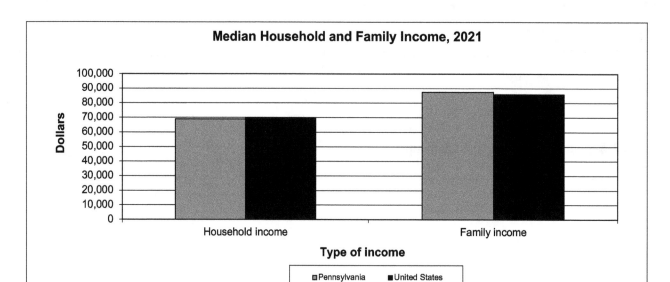

Median Household and Family Income, 2021

Table PA-6. Health Insurance Coverage Status for the Civilian Noninstitutionalized Population and Children Under 19 Years of Age

(Number, percent.)

Item	2011	2012	2013	2014	2015	2016	2017	2018	2019	2020 [2]	2021
Civilian Noninstitutionalized Population	12,539,757	12,559,315	12,569,375	12,582,815	12,599,417	12,579,422	12,602,472	12,604,311	12,593,136	12,590,644	12,767,386
Covered by Private or Public Insurance											
Number..	11,275,209	11,334,666	11,346,970	11,518,238	11,797,490	11,870,945	11,910,269	11,904,935	11,866,688	11,884,753	12,065,845
Percent..	89.9	90.2	90.3	91.5	93.6	94.4	94.5	94.5	94.2	94.4	94.5
Uninsured											
Number..	1,264,548	1,224,649	1,222,405	1,064,577	801,927	708,477	692,203	699,376	726,448	705,891	701,541
Percent..	10.1	9.8	9.7	8.5	6.4	5.6	5.5	5.5	5.8	5.6	5.5
Percent in the U.S. not covered...............	15.1	14.8	14.5	11.7	9.4	8.6	8.7	8.9	9.2	8.7	8.6
Children Under 19 Years of Age[1]	2,754,741	2,730,989	2,708,843	2,693,074	2,685,304	2,666,701	2,834,916	2,820,785	2,803,506	2,818,899	2,846,519
Covered by Private or Public Insurance											
Number..	2,605,514	2,592,035	2,561,540	2,553,957	2,573,940	2,550,327	2,709,999	2,697,004	2,675,599	2,690,074	2,720,352
Percent..	94.6	94.9	94.6	94.8	95.9	95.6	95.6	95.6	95.4	95.4	95.6
Uninsured											
Number..	149,227	138,954	147,303	139,117	111,364	116,374	124,917	123,781	127,907	128,825	126,167
Percent..	5.4	5.1	5.4	5.2	4.1	4.4	4.4	4.4	4.6	4.6	4.4
Percent in the U.S. not covered...............	7.5	7.2	7.1	6.0	4.8	4.5	5.0	5.2	5.7	5.2	5.4

[1] Data for years prior to 2017 are for individuals under 18 years of age.
[2] 2020 ACS 5-Year estimates. 1-Year estimates were not released for 2020 due to the impact of COVID-19 on data collection that year. Data is not comparable to previous years, which are based on 1-year estimates.

Table PA-7. Employment Status by Demographic Group, 2022

(Numbers in thousands, percent.)

Characteristic	Civilian noninstitutional population	Civilian labor force		Employed		Unemployed	
		Number	Percent of population	Number	Percent of population	Number	Percent of population
Total...	10,446	6,443	61.7	6,179	59.1	264	4.1
Sex							
Male..	5,087	3,385	66.5	3,242	63.7	143	4.2
Female..	5,359	3,058	57.1	2,937	54.8	121	4.0
Race, Sex, and Hispanic Origin							
White..	8,598	5,312	61.8	5,118	59.5	194	3.7
Male..	4,211	2,803	66.6	2,693	63.9	110	3.9
Female..	4,387	2,509	57.2	2,425	55.3	84	3.4
Black or African American..................	1,176	686	58.3	635	54.0	51	7.4
Male..	543	335	61.8	312	57.5	23	6.9
Female..	633	351	55.4	324	51.1	27	7.8
Hispanic or Latino ethnicity[1].............	697	443	63.5	412	59.1	30	6.9
Male..	354	256	72.3	239	67.6	17	6.6
Female..	343	186	54.3	173	50.4	14	7.3
Age							
16 to 19 years..................................	612	233	38.1	214	35.0	19	8.2
20 to 24 years..................................	851	616	72.4	572	67.1	45	7.3
25 to 34 years..................................	1,644	1,396	84.9	1,339	81.5	57	4.1
35 to 44 years..................................	1,583	1,342	84.8	1,287	81.3	55	4.1
45 to 54 years..................................	1,532	1,231	80.3	1,196	78.0	35	2.8
55 to 64 years..................................	1,767	1,164	65.9	1,127	63.8	37	3.2
65 years and over.............................	2,457	460	18.7	444	18.1	17	3.6

NOTE: Data in Table 7 are from the Current Population Survey (CPS) and do not match the estimates in Table 8. See notes and definitions for further information.
[1] May be of any race.

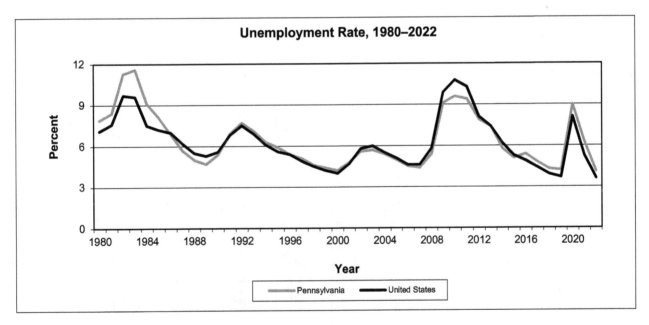

Unemployment Rate, 1980–2022

Table PA-8. Employment Status of the Civilian Noninstitutional Population Age 16 Years and Over

(Number, percent.)

Year	Civilian labor force	Civilian participation rate	Employed	Unemployed	Unemployment rate
2010..	6,360,605	63.3	5,838,498	522,107	8.2
2011..	6,381,749	63.1	5,886,748	495,001	7.8
2012..	6,449,023	63.5	5,955,409	493,614	7.7
2013..	6,419,837	63.1	5,962,130	457,707	7.1
2014..	6,389,059	62.6	6,010,075	378,984	5.9
2015..	6,423,155	62.9	6,076,402	346,753	5.4
2016..	6,458,891	63.1	6,114,644	344,247	5.3
2017..	6,485,250	62.6	6,161,013	323,340	5.0
2018..	6,500,149	62.6	6,210,098	290,051	4.5
2019..	6,560,773	63.0	6,266,508	294,265	4.5
2020..	6,482,770	62.2	5,893,583	589,187	9.1
2021..	6,406,185	61.5	5,999,442	406,743	6.3
2022..	6,479,077	61.8	6,196,385	282,692	4.4

Table PA-9. Employment and Average Wages by Industry

(Estimates are based on the 2012 North American Industry Classification System [NAICS].)

Industry	2014	2015	2016	2017	2018	2019	2020	2021
	Number of Jobs							
Wage and Salary Employment by Industry.............................	5,987,610	6,037,780	6,086,529	6,144,339	6,219,072	6,279,312	5,826,487	5,995,350
Farm Wage and Salary Employment......................................	21,096	23,223	28,025	27,002	22,230	20,404	17,198	21,285
Nonfarm Wage and Salary Employment.................................	5,966,514	6,014,557	6,058,504	6,117,337	6,196,842	6,258,908	5,809,289	5,974,065
Private wage and salary employment....................................	5,184,742	5,239,185	5,284,777	5,344,216	5,426,935	5,486,645	5,054,400	5,225,978
Forestry, fishing, and related activities............................	8,024	7,826	7,953	7,900	8,083	8,011	7,633	7,183
Mining..	36,747	32,872	24,196	25,676	27,834	27,956	22,390	21,044
Utilities..	21,466	24,200	23,961	23,749	23,728	23,171	22,662	22,361
Construction..	236,823	241,359	245,041	254,827	262,048	267,104	247,580	259,864
Manufacturing..	567,886	567,973	559,081	562,315	570,234	575,171	537,897	544,118
Durable goods manufacturing...	346,580	346,136	335,559	335,999	342,596	345,888	319,086	321,507
Nondurable goods manufacturing....................................	221,306	221,837	223,522	226,316	227,638	229,283	218,811	222,611
Wholesale trade...	226,870	225,646	220,519	219,699	217,966	218,073	205,029	205,227
Retail trade..	637,105	637,471	637,434	629,364	624,315	613,766	569,133	595,788
Transportation and warehousing.......................................	231,137	242,041	251,164	259,495	267,782	278,192	273,149	289,867
Information..	85,327	85,144	84,513	83,462	85,972	87,107	82,883	86,144
Finance and insurance...	266,776	266,531	264,978	270,081	272,992	278,992	279,488	277,785
Real estate and rental and leasing.....................................	61,758	63,333	63,907	64,526	66,433	67,085	63,662	65,693
Professional, scientific, and technical services	331,310	338,512	350,700	353,765	358,194	364,857	358,867	371,744
Management of companies and enterprises........................	132,872	132,518	135,026	136,171	136,949	136,177	126,850	137,933
Administrative and waste services.....................................	300,887	311,803	313,640	314,754	316,819	320,387	285,147	296,912
Educational services	249,647	252,468	259,240	263,081	270,238	272,155	256,903	272,448
Health care and social assistance......................................	952,147	964,511	988,061	1,011,187	1,040,734	1,062,802	1,023,383	1,017,223
Arts, entertainment, and recreation...................................	94,463	93,504	96,401	99,026	99,702	102,229	69,054	81,655
Accommodation and food services.....................................	447,976	455,122	464,703	471,716	476,066	479,595	358,747	399,256
Other services, except public administration......................	295,521	296,351	294,259	293,422	300,846	303,815	263,943	273,733
Government and government enterprises	781,772	775,372	773,727	773,121	769,907	772,263	754,889	748,087
	Dollars							
Average Wages and Salaries by Industry	49,495	51,062	51,337	52,865	54,542	56,347	60,612	63,202
Average Farm Wages and Salaries	26,710	21,053	20,021	18,858	23,838	19,945	23,546	19,113
Average Nonfarm Wages and Salaries	49,576	51,178	51,482	53,015	54,652	56,465	60,722	63,359
Average private wages and salaries....................................	49,789	51,351	51,616	53,193	54,802	56,684	61,187	63,997
Forestry, fishing, and related activities............................	29,173	30,631	32,097	32,815	34,011	34,998	37,413	40,298
Mining..	82,934	81,304	80,062	89,379	86,482	90,109	88,397	92,989
Utilities..	109,277	109,587	110,850	113,855	119,115	117,255	120,050	124,253
Construction..	58,765	60,153	61,596	64,759	66,844	68,602	70,615	73,503
Manufacturing..	58,546	59,552	59,789	61,084	62,570	64,234	66,934	69,374
Durable goods manufacturing...	59,320	60,099	60,042	62,072	63,762	65,026	66,906	69,722
Nondurable goods manufacturing....................................	57,335	58,698	59,408	59,618	60,775	63,040	66,974	68,872
Wholesale trade...	76,288	77,303	77,528	79,577	80,043	82,074	86,580	91,639
Retail trade..	26,242	27,322	27,810	28,281	29,150	30,260	33,175	35,178
Transportation and warehousing.......................................	44,447	45,863	45,493	47,070	48,311	49,221	51,448	53,233
Information..	70,632	73,526	75,193	78,915	87,093	94,858	107,322	114,876
Finance and insurance...	84,384	87,424	87,911	91,652	95,281	97,151	103,389	109,948
Real estate and rental and leasing.....................................	54,089	56,581	57,730	58,280	60,961	62,614	68,175	69,720
Professional, scientific, and technical services	84,902	87,760	89,048	92,312	94,902	99,357	103,941	109,324
Management of companies and enterprises........................	120,870	130,137	122,988	127,088	129,265	135,631	138,924	146,994
Administrative and waste services.....................................	32,854	33,735	34,241	35,472	36,796	38,413	42,079	45,900
Educational services	42,842	43,982	44,613	45,166	46,310	47,331	50,713	49,651
Health care and social assistance......................................	45,846	47,487	47,958	49,031	50,281	51,833	55,496	58,188
Arts, entertainment, and recreation...................................	33,314	34,629	34,798	34,043	35,377	37,123	42,479	43,089
Accommodation and food services.....................................	18,783	19,401	19,874	20,411	21,470	22,163	21,274	25,455
Other services, except public administration......................	31,094	32,331	32,977	34,013	35,318	36,429	40,409	41,716
Government and government enterprises.............................	48,162	50,006	50,568	51,783	53,597	54,910	57,609	58,899

Table PA-10. Employment Characteristics by Family Type

(Number, percent.)

Family type and labor force status	2019		2020 [1]		2021	
	Total	Families with own children under 18 years	Total	Families with own children under 18 years	Total	Families with own children under 18 years
All Families.........................	3,228,224	1,240,704	3,254,545	1,278,062	3,298,555	1,270,307
FAMILY TYPE AND LABOR FORCE STATUS						
Opposite-Sex Married-Couple Families............................	2,373,352	816,678	2,403,552	858,717	2,427,035	854,849
Both husband and wife in labor force........................	52.3	71.8	53.1	71.5	52.1	71.3
Husband in labor force, wife not in labor force	19.0	22.5	19.3	23.3	19.1	23.2
Wife in labor force, husband not in labor force	8.1	3.8	8.1	3.7	8.3	4.0
Both husband and wife not in labor force........................	19.9	1.4	19.5	1.4	20.5	1.5
Other Families	854,872	424,026	831,485	415,946	848,600	411,969
Female householder, no spouse present	70.9	72.7	72.0	73.6	71.4	73.0
In labor force........................	47.8	58.9	49.6	61.0	48.6	59.3
Not in labor force	23.1	13.8	22.5	12.6	22.8	13.7
Male householder, no spouse present........................	29.1	27.3	28.0	26.4	28.6	27.0
In labor force........................	22.6	24.5	21.4	23.6	21.7	24.1
Not in labor force	6.6	2.8	6.5	2.8	6.9	2.9

[1] 2020 ACS 5-Year estimates. 1-Year estimates were not released for 2020 due to the impact of COVID-19 on data collection that year. Data is not comparable to previous years, which are based on 1-year estimates.

Table PA-11. School Enrollment and Educational Attainment, 2021

(Number, percent.)

Item	State	U.S.
Enrollment		
Total population 3 years and over, enrolled in school	2,878,255	79,453,524
Enrolled in nursery school or preschool (percent)	5.1	5.2
Enrolled in kindergarten (percent)......................	4.8	5.0
Enrolled in elementary school, grades 1-8 (percent)......................	41.5	41.3
Enrolled in high school, grades 9-12 (percent)	21.8	21.8
Enrolled in college or graduate school (percent)......................	26.7	26.7
Attainment		
Total population 25 years and over	9,161,945	228,193,464
Less than ninth grade (percent)	2.9	4.8
9th to 12th grade, no diploma (percent)	5.2	5.9
High school graduate, including equivalency (percent)......................	33.3	26.3
Some college, no degree (percent)	15.2	19.3
Associate's degree (percent)......................	8.9	8.8
Bachelor's degree (percent)......................	20.6	21.2
Graduate or professional degree (percent)......................	13.9	13.8
High school graduate or higher (percent)	91.9	89.4
Bachelor's degree or higher (percent)	34.5	35.0

Table PA-12. Public School Characteristics and Educational Indicators

(Number, percent; data derived from National Center of Education Statistics.)

Item	State	U.S.
Public Elementary and Secondary Schools		
Number of regular school districts, 2019-20	500	13,349
Number of operational schools, 2019-20......................	2,958	98,469
Percent charter schools	6.1	7.7
Total public school enrollment, Fall 2021	1,695,092	49,433,092
Percent charter school enrollment	9.8	7.5
Student-teacher ratio, Fall 2019	13.9	15.9
Expenditures per student (unadjusted dollars), 2019-20	17,172	13,489
Four-year adjusted cohort graduation rate (ACGR), 2019-2020[1]	87.4	86.5
Students eligible for free or reduced-price lunch (percent), 2019-20......................	50.7	52.1
English language learners (percent), Fall 2020	4.2	10.3
Students age 3 to 21 served under IDEA, part B (percent), 2021-22	20.2	14.7

Public Schools by Type, 2019-20	Number	Percent of state public schools
Total number of schools........................	2,958	100.0
Special education........................	4	0.1
Vocational education........................	84	2.8
Alternative education........................	6	0.2

[1] Adjusted Cohort Graduation Rates (ACGR) differ from Averaged Freshmen Graduation Rates (AFGR).
- = Zero or rounds to zero.

Table PA-13. Reported Voting and Registration of the Voting-Age Population, November 2022

(Numbers in thousands, percent.)

Item	Total population	Total citizen population	Registered			Voted		
			Total registered	Percent registered (total population)	Percent registered (total citizen population)	Total voted	Percent voted (total population)	Percent voted (total citizen population)
U.S. Total	255,457	233,546	161,422	63.2	69.1	121,916	47.7	52.2
State Total......................................	10,124	9,741	7,009	69.2	72.0	5,843	57.7	60.0
Sex								
Male	4,929	4,739	3,389	68.7	71.5	2,838	57.6	59.9
Female	5,195	5,002	3,620	69.7	72.4	3,004	57.8	60.1
Race								
White alone....................................	8,345	8,221	6,007	72.0	73.1	5,029	60.3	61.2
White, non-Hispanic alone	7,878	7,851	5,824	73.9	74.2	4,896	62.2	62.4
Black alone....................................	1,141	1,048	732	64.2	69.9	624	54.7	59.5
Asian alone	369	216	134	36.2	61.8	104	28.3	48.2
Hispanic (of any race)......................	653	542	275	42.2	50.8	194	29.8	35.9
White alone or in combination	8,493	8,360	6,063	71.4	72.5	5,082	59.8	60.8
Black alone or in combination......................	1,217	1,116	760	62.5	68.1	643	52.9	57.6
Asian alone or in combination......................	398	245	149	37.4	60.7	119	30.0	48.7
Age								
18 to 24 years................................	1,145	1,093	610	53.3	55.8	437	38.2	40.0
25 to 34 years................................	1,680	1,611	1,041	62.0	64.6	776	46.2	48.2
35 to 44 years................................	1,531	1,397	1,007	65.8	72.1	784	51.2	56.1
45 to 64 years................................	3,139	3,043	2,328	74.2	76.5	1,995	63.6	65.5
65 years and over	2,630	2,597	2,024	77.0	77.9	1,851	70.4	71.3

Table PA-14. Health Indicators

(Number, rate as indicated in footnotes.)

Item	State	U.S.
Births		
Life Expectancy at Birth (years), 2020	76.8	77.0
Fertility Rate by State[1], 2021	54.7	56.3
Percent Home Births, 2021	2.5	1.4
Cesarean Delivery Rate[2], 2021	30.8	32.1
Preterm Birth Rate[3], 2021	9.8	10.5
Teen Birth Rate[4], 2021	11.5	13.9
Percentage of Babies Born Low Birthweight[5], 2021	8.3	8.5
Deaths[6]		
Heart Disease Mortality Rate, 2021	180.6	173.8
Cancer Mortality Rate, 2021	152.9	146.6
Stroke Mortality Rate, 2021	37.7	41.1
Diabetes Mortality Rate, 2021	23.5	25.4
Influenza/Pneumonia Mortality Rate, 2021	10.3	10.5
Suicide Mortality Rate, 2021	13.9	14.1
Drug Overdose Mortality Rate, 2021	43.2	33.6
Firearm Injury Mortality Rate, 2021	14.8	14.6
Homicide Mortality Rate, 2021	9.2	8.2
Disease and Illness		
Lifetime Asthma in Adults, 2020 (percent)..	15.3	13.9
Lifetime Asthma in Children, 2020 (percent)[7]	14.2	11.3
Diabetes in Adults, 2020 (percent)	9.8	8.2
Self-reported Obesity in Adults, 2021 (percent)..	33.3	NA

SOURCE: National Center for Health Statistics, National Vital Statistics System 2020 data; https://wonder.cdc.gov.
[1] General fertility rate per 1,000 women aged 15–44.
[2] This represents the percentage of all live births that were cesarean deliveries.
[3] Babies born prior to 37 weeks of pregnancy (gestation).
[4] Number of births per 1,000 females aged 15–19
[5] Babies born weighing less than 2,500 grams or 5 lbs. 8oz.
[6] Death rates are the number of deaths per 100,000 total population.
[7] U.S. total includes data from 30 states and D.C.
NA = Not available.
- = Zero or rounds to zero.

Table PA-15. State Government Finances, 2021

(Dollar amounts in thousands, percent distribution.)

Item	Dollars	Percent distribution
Total Revenue	136,016,605	100.0
General revenue	117,866,834	86.7
Intergovernmental revenue	46,255,973	34.0
Taxes	49,571,347	36.4
General sales	13,717,681	10.1
Selective sales	10,694,965	7.9
License taxes	2,955,413	2.2
Individual income tax	15,977,933	11.7
Corporate income tax	4,045,313	3.0
Other taxes	2,180,042	1.6
Current charges	13,524,124	9.9
Miscellaneous general revenue	8,515,390	6.3
Utility revenue	-	-
Liquor stores revenue	2,317,843	1.7
Insurance trust revenue[1]	15,831,928	11.6
Total Expenditure	126,801,633	100.0
Intergovernmental expenditure	25,631,968	20.2
Direct expenditure	101,169,665	79.8
Current operation	68,852,720	54.3
Capital outlay	9,366,806	7.4
Insurance benefits and repayments	19,606,100	15.5
Assistance and subsidies	1,703,761	1.3
Interest on debt	1,640,278	1.3
Exhibit: Salaries and wages	11,340,863	8.9
Total Expenditure	126,801,633	100.0
General expenditure	105,129,886	82.9
Intergovernmental expenditure	25,631,968	20.2
Direct expenditure	79,497,918	62.7
General expenditure, by function:		
Education	28,938,300	22.8
Public welfare	39,457,587	31.1
Hospitals	6,574,855	5.2
Health	4,144,165	3.3
Highways	9,122,738	7.2
Police protection	2,056,904	1.6
Correction	2,624,500	2.1
Natural resources	782,792	0.6
Parks and recreation	485,085	0.4
Governmental administration	3,785,517	3.0
Interest on general debt	1,640,278	1.3
Other and unallocable	3,916,173	3.1
Utility expenditure	1,567,003	1.2
Liquor stores expenditure	2,029,173	1.6
Insurance trust expenditure	19,606,100	15.5
Debt at End of Fiscal Year	53,216,521	X
Cash and Security Holdings	175,043,054	X

X = Not applicable.
- = Zero or rounds to zero.
[1] Within insurance trust revenue, net earnings of state retirement systems is a calculated statistic (the item code in the data file is X08), and thus can be positive or negative. Net earnings is the sum of earnings on investments plus gains on investments minus losses on investments. The change made in 2002 for asset valuation from book to market value in accordance with Statement 34 of the Governmental Accounting Standards Board is reflected in the calculated statistics.

Table PA-16. State Government Tax Collections, 2022

(Dollars in thousands, percent.)

Item	Dollars	Percent distribution
Total Taxes	53,679,801	100.0
Property taxes	39,729	0.1
Sales and gross receipts	25,762,609	48.0
General sales and gross receipts	14,760,853	27.5
Selective sales and gross receipts	11,001,756	20.5
Alcoholic beverages	458,047	0.9
Amusements	1,758,352	3.3
Insurance premiums	913,085	1.7
Motor fuels	3,180,204	5.9
Pari-mutuels	8,690	-
Public utilities	1,026,909	1.9
Tobacco products	1,223,160	2.3
Other selective sales	2,433,309	4.5
Licenses	2,914,911	5.4
Alcoholic beverages	30,134	-
Amusements	37,058	0.1
Corporations in general	2,984	-
Hunting and fishing	83,635	0.2
Motor vehicle	1,250,825	2.3
Motor vehicle operators	119,658	0.2
Public utilities	78,104	0.1
Occupation and business, NEC	1,291,254	2.4
Other licenses	21,259	-
Income taxes	22,389,126	41.7
Individual income	17,381,999	32.4
Corporation net income	5,007,127	9.3
Other taxes	2,573,426	4.8
Death and gift	1,502,404	2.8
Documentary and stock transfer	1,042,331	1.9
Severance	X	-
Taxes, NEC	28,691	0.1

X = Not applicable.
- = Zero or rounds to zero.

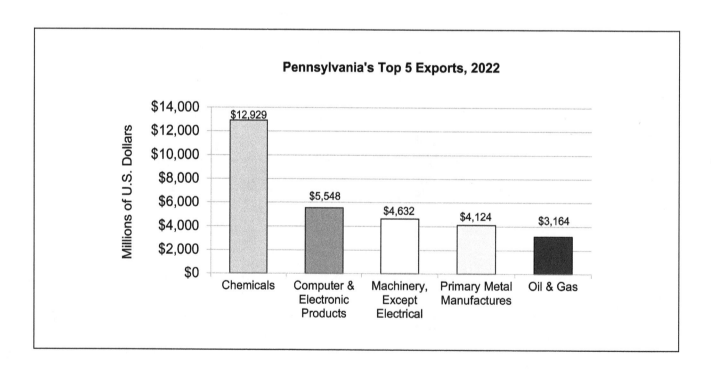

Pennsylvania's Top 5 Exports, 2022

Export	Millions of U.S. Dollars
Chemicals	$12,929
Computer & Electronic Products	$5,548
Machinery, Except Electrical	$4,632
Primary Metal Manufactures	$4,124
Oil & Gas	$3,164

RHODE ISLAND

Facts and Figures

Location: Eastern United States; bordered on the N by Massachusetts, on the E by Massachusetts and the Atlantic Ocean, on the S by Block Island Sound and the Atlantic Ocean, and on the W by Connecticut

Area: 1,545 sq. mi. (4,002 sq. km.); rank—50th

Population: 1,093,734 (2022 est.); rank—44th

Principal Cities: capital—Providence; largest—Providence

Statehood: May 29, 1790; 13th state

U.S. Congress: 2 senators, 2 representatives

State Motto: Hope

State Song: "Rhode Island"

State Nickname: The Ocean State

Abbreviations: RI; R.I.

State Symbols: flower—violet; tree—red maple; bird—Rhode Island red

At a Glance

- With an increase in population of 3.9 percent, Rhode Island ranked 35th among the states in growth from 2010 to 2022.

- In 2021, 4.3 percent of Rhode Islanders did not have health insurance, the 5th lowest percentage in the country.

- Rhode Island's drug overdose death rate in 2021 was 42.8 deaths per 100,000 population. The overall U.S. rate was 32.4 deaths per 100,000 population.

- The median income of Rhode Islanders in 2021 was $74,008, and 11.4 percent of its residents lived below the poverty level.

- In 2022, 18.6 percent of Rhode Island's population was under 18 years old, and 18.9 percent of its population was 65 years or older, compared to the national averages of 21.7 percent and 17.3 percent respectively.

Table RI-1. Population by Age, Sex, Race, and Hispanic Origin

(Number, percent, except where noted.)

Sex, age, race, and Hispanic origin	2010	2020	2022	Percent change, 2010–2022
Total Population.......................................	1,052,567	1,097,371	1,093,734	3.9
Percent of total U.S. population	0.3	0.3	0.3	X
Sex				
Male..	508,400	538,812	536,995	5.6
Female	544,167	558,559	556,739	2.3
Age				
Under 5 years..	57,448	54,863	52,700	-8.3
Under 18 years...	223,956	210,208	203,912	-8.9
18 to 64 years..	676,730	692,416	683,412	1.0
65 years and over	151,881	194,747	206,410	35.9
Median age (years)	39.4	40.2	40.6	3.0
Race and Hispanic Origin				
One race				
White	910,253	914,615	905,102	-0.6
Black	75,073	95,288	99,051	31.9
American Indian and Alaska Native	9,173	12,379	13,379	45.9
Asian..	31,768	40,335	40,312	26.9
Native Hawaiian or Other Pacific Islander	1,602	2,252	2,286	42.7
Two or more races	24,698	32,502	33,604	36.1
Hispanic (of any race)...	130,655	182,570	191,980	46.9

NOTE: Population figures for 2022 are July 1 estimates. The 2010 and 2020 estimates are taken from the respective censuses.
- = Zero or rounds to zero.
X = Not applicable.

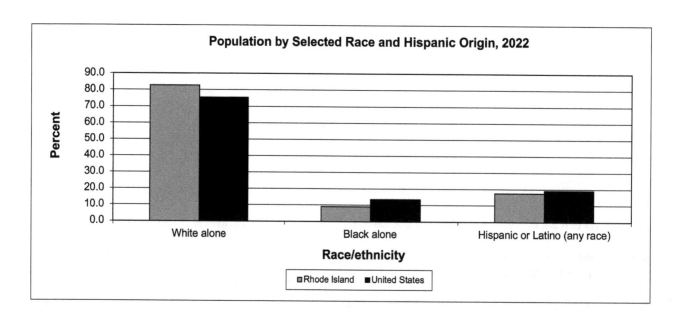

Table RI-2. Marital Status

(Number, percent distribution.)

Sex, age, race, and Hispanic origin	2000	2010	2021
Males, 15 Years and Over	396,396	414,628	449,258
Never married	32.5	39.8	40.2
Now married, except separated....................................	54.9	45.2	46.7
Separated...	1.5	1.6	1.3
Widowed...	3.0	3.1	2.6
Divorced...	8.0	10.3	9.2
Females, 15 Years and Over	445,107	456,425	476,300
Never married	27.1	32.4	34.8
Now married, except separated....................................	48.5	41.8	43.1
Separated...	2.3	2.4	1.7
Widowed...	11.5	10.4	8.3
Divorced...	10.7	13.0	12.2

Table RI-3. Households and Housing Characteristics

(Number, percent, dollars.)

Item	2000	2010	2021	Average annual percent change, 2010–2021
Total Households..	408,424	402,295	440,170	0.9
Family households	265,398	246,028	268,718	0.8
Married-couple family	196,757	173,848	194,722	1.1
Other family	68,641	72,180	73,996	0.2
Male householder, no wife present...	16,032	17,525	21,138	1.9
Female householder, no husband present.................................	52,609	54,655	52,858	-0.3
Nonfamily households	143,026	156,267	171,452	0.9
Householder living alone..	116,678	125,371	133,661	0.6
Householder not living alone..	26,348	30,896	37,791	2.0
Housing Characteristics				
Total housing units...	439,837	463,416	484,925	0.4
Occupied housing units	408,424	402,295	440,170	0.9
Owner occupied	245,156	244,516	278,449	1.3
Renter occupied	163,268	157,779	161,721	0.2
Average household size...	2.47	2.51	2.39	-0.4
Financial Characteristics				
Median gross rent of renter-occupied housing	553	868	1,142	2.9
Median monthly owner costs for housing units with a mortgage	1,205	1,837	1,932	0.5
Median value of owner-occupied housing units...........................	133,000	254,500	348,100	3.3

Table RI-4. Migration, Origin, and Language

(Number, percent.)

Characteristic	State 2021	U.S. 2021
Residence 1 Year Ago		
Population 1 year and over	1,085,539	328,464,538
Same house	88.4	87.2
Different house in the U.S..	11.1	12.3
Same county	5.4	6.7
Different county	5.7	5.7
Same state	1.7	3.3
Different state	4.0	2.4
Abroad	0.5	0.4
Place of Birth		
Native born	936,306	286,623,642
Male	49.1	49.7
Female	50.9	50.3
Foreign born	159,304	45,270,103
Male	48.5	48.7
Female	51.5	51.3
Foreign born; naturalized U.S. citizen.......................................	91,426	24,044,083
Male	47.9	46.4
Female	52.1	53.6
Foreign born; not a U.S. citizen...	67,878	21,226,020
Male	49.4	51.2
Female	50.6	48.8
Entered 2010 or later	28.7	28.1
Entered 2000 to 2009	18.9	23.7
Entered before 2000..	52.5	48.2
World Region of Birth, Foreign		
Foreign-born population, excluding population born at sea	159,304	45,269,644
Europe	20.3	10.7
Asia...	15.5	31.0
Africa	11.9	5.7
Oceania	0.4	0.6
Latin America	50.8	50.1
North America	1.2	1.7
Language Spoken at Home and Ability to Speak English		
Population 5 years and over	1,042,843	313,232,500
English only	70.1	70.4
Language other than English..	21.9	21.6
Speaks English less than "very well"..	8.6	8.3

Table RI-5. Median Income and Poverty Status, 2021

(Number, percent, except as noted.)

Characteristic	State		U.S.	
	Number	Percent	Number	Percent
Median Income				
Households (dollars)...	74,008	X	69,717	X
Families (dollars)	97,304	X	85,806	X
Below Poverty Level (All People)	120,055	11.4	41,393,176	12.8
Sex				
Male	51,194	9.9	18,518,155	11.6
Female	68,861	12.8	22,875,021	13.9
Age				
Under 18 years...	30,414	15.0	12,243,219	16.9
Related children under 18 years............................	29,733	14.7	11,985,424	16.6
18 to 64 years..	70,643	10.8	23,526,341	11.9
65 years and over	18,998	9.8	5,623,616	10.3

X = Not applicable.

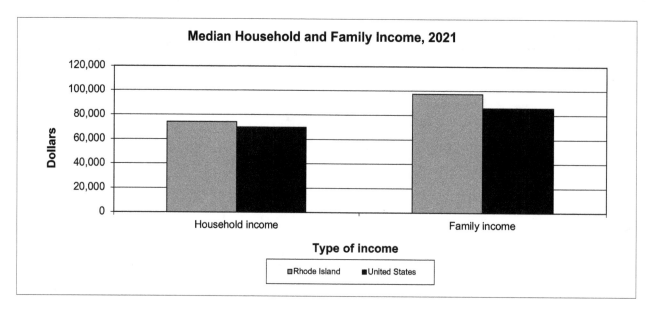

Median Household and Family Income, 2021

Legend: ▣ Rhode Island ■ United States

Table RI-6. Health Insurance Coverage Status for the Civilian Noninstitutionalized Population and Children Under 19 Years of Age

(Number, percent.)

Item	2011	2012	2013	2014	2015	2016	2017	2018	2019	2020[2]	2021
Civilian Noninstitutionalized Population	1,035,117	1,034,895	1,036,046	1,039,789	1,041,268	1,040,259	1,044,111	1,041,309	1,043,753	1,041,644	1,080,438
Covered by Private or Public Insurance											
Number..	923,283	920,030	915,586	962,670	981,858	995,293	995,921	998,828	1,001,033	997,069	1,033,493
Percent..	89.2	88.9	88.4	92.6	94.3	95.7	95.4	95.9	95.9	95.7	95.7
Uninsured											
Number..	111,834	114,865	120,460	77,119	59,410	44,966	48,190	42,481	42,720	44,575	46,945
Percent..	10.8	11.1	11.6	7.4	5.7	4.3	4.6	4.1	4.1	4.3	4.3
Percent in the U.S. not covered..........................	15.1	14.8	14.5	11.7	9.4	8.6	8.7	8.9	9.2	8.7	8.6
Children Under 19 Years of Age[1]	218,624	216,675	212,430	212,271	211,397	208,268	224,008	219,314	220,276	221,949	227,045
Covered by Private or Public Insurance											
Number..	209,952	206,885	200,866	205,164	204,137	204,269	219,375	214,529	216,095	216,529	221,348
Percent..	96.0	95.5	94.6	96.7	96.6	98.1	97.9	97.8	98.1	97.6	97.5
Uninsured											
Number..	8,672	9,790	11,564	7,107	7,260	3,999	4,633	4,785	4,181	5,420	5,697
Percent..	4.0	4.5	5.4	3.3	3.4	1.9	2.1	2.2	1.9	2.4	2.5
Percent in the U.S. not covered..........................	7.5	7.2	7.1	6.0	4.8	4.5	5.0	5.2	5.7	5.2	5.4

[1] Data for years prior to 2017 are for individuals under 18 years of age.
[2] 2020 ACS 5-Year estimates. 1-Year estimates were not released for 2020 due to the impact of COVID-19 on data collection that year. Data is not comparable to previous years, which are based on 1-year estimates.

Table RI-7. Employment Status by Demographic Group, 2022

(Numbers in thousands, percent.)

Characteristic	Civilian noninstitutional population	Civilian labor force		Employed		Unemployed	
		Number	Percent of population	Number	Percent of population	Number	Percent of population
Total..	902	577	64.0	557	61.8	20	3.5
Sex							
Male..	437	296	67.6	284	65.0	11	3.8
Female...	465	282	60.6	273	58.7	9	3.2
Race, Sex, and Hispanic Origin							
White	786	498	63.4	483	61.5	15	3.0
Male..	377	253	67.2	244	64.7	9	3.6
Female..	409	245	60.0	239	58.5	6	2.4
Black or African American...........................	71	45	63.8	43	60.6	2	5.0
Male..	NA	NA	NA	NA	NA	NA	NA
Female..	NA	NA	NA	NA	NA	NA	NA
Hispanic or Latino ethnicity[1]	99	64	64.3	60	60.5	4	6.0
Male..	NA	NA	NA	NA	NA	NA	NA
Female..	NA	NA	NA	NA	NA	NA	NA
Age							
16 to 19 years...	NA	NA	NA	NA	NA	NA	NA
20 to 24 years...	65	49	75.0	46	70.0	3	6.7
25 to 34 years...	160	136	85.2	132	82.5	4	3.2
35 to 44 years...	140	122	87.4	119	85.3	3	2.5
45 to 54 years...	125	107	85.8	104	83.3	3	3.0
55 to 64 years...	146	98	66.7	96	65.8	1	1.3
65 years and over	211	46	21.7	44	20.7	2	5.0

NOTE: Data in Table 7 are from the Current Population Survey (CPS) and do not match the estimates in Table 8. See notes and definitions for further information.
[1] May be of any race.

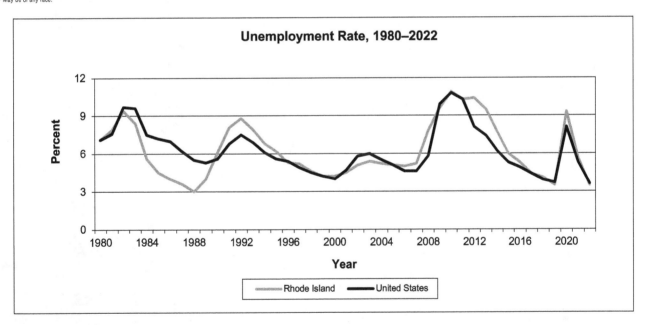

Unemployment Rate, 1980–2022

Table RI-8. Employment Status of the Civilian Noninstitutional Population Age 16 Years and Over

(Number, percent.)

Year	Civilian labor force	Civilian participation rate	Employed	Unemployed	Unemployment rate
2010..	571,505	67.8	504,957	66,548	11.6
2011..	562,061	66.6	500,109	61,952	11.0
2012..	560,204	66.1	502,897	57,307	10.2
2013..	558,747	65.7	505,776	52,971	9.5
2014..	556,635	65.2	513,406	43,229	7.8
2015..	555,272	64.9	521,767	33,505	6.0
2016..	553,231	64.5	524,438	28,793	5.2
2017..	568,144	64.4	542,552	25,592	4.5
2018..	571,152	64.3	547,994	23,158	4.1
2019..	572,382	64.2	552,057	20,325	3.6
2020..	567,055	63.3	514,911	52,144	9.2
2021..	571,034	63.6	538,969	32,065	5.6
2022..	569,455	63.3	551,220	18,235	3.2

Table RI-9. Employment and Average Wages by Industry

(Estimates are based on the 2012 North American Industry Classification System [NAICS].)

Industry	2014	2015	2016	2017	2018	2019	2020	2021
	\multicolumn{8}{c}{Number of Jobs}							
Wage and Salary Employment by Industry........................	491,596	499,350	502,469	506,216	512,429	516,468	475,325	494,738
Farm Wage and Salary Employment.................................	615	614	572	571	481	485	463	474
Nonfarm Wage and Salary Employment...........................	490,981	498,736	501,897	505,645	511,948	515,983	474,862	494,264
Private wage and salary employment.................................	419,162	426,862	429,804	433,213	439,088	441,727	401,416	420,768
Forestry, fishing, and related activities	(D)	(D)	(D)	(D)	(D)	(D)	(D)	548
Mining..	(D)	(D)	(D)	(D)	(D)	(D)	(D)	176
Utilities..	1,057	1,082	1,080	1,093	1,141	1,114	1,100	1,104
Construction	16,898	17,441	18,578	(D)	19,683	20,451	19,394	20,491
Manufacturing..	40,940	41,195	40,449	40,419	40,380	39,773	37,443	39,131
Durable goods manufacturing..	26,138	26,015	25,228	25,133	25,820	25,508	23,419	24,518
Nondurable goods manufacturing....................................	14,802	15,180	15,221	15,286	14,560	14,265	14,024	14,613
Wholesale trade	16,900	17,025	16,730	16,615	16,561	16,646	14,969	15,542
Retail trade..	47,480	48,376	48,511	48,852	49,014	48,370	44,402	46,881
Transportation and warehousing.......................................	9,934	10,255	10,350	10,587	10,908	11,300	11,086	11,858
Information	8,867	8,644	8,075	6,136	5,930	5,883	5,241	5,444
Finance and insurance	25,060	25,568	25,531	27,640	27,071	27,117	27,062	26,706
Real estate and rental and leasing..................................	6,024	6,129	6,219	6,309	6,527	6,610	5,859	6,071
Professional, scientific, and technical services	23,001	24,074	24,568	25,256	25,745	25,893	25,820	28,120
Management of companies and enterprises......................	12,013	12,572	13,394	13,509	13,330	13,236	12,634	12,323
Administrative and waste services...................................	26,262	27,347	28,055	28,980	29,803	29,538	27,200	28,423
Educational services	25,402	26,690	26,558	26,866	29,594	29,983	28,155	28,806
Health care and social assistance...................................	81,178	81,252	81,141	80,921	81,029	82,464	76,381	77,673
Arts, entertainment, and recreation.................................	9,098	9,040	9,463	9,557	9,233	8,013	5,784	6,707
Accommodation and food services	46,572	47,514	48,458	49,150	50,331	52,342	39,206	45,084
Other services, except public administration...................	21,718	21,838	21,839	21,739	22,069	22,219	18,894	19,680
Government and government enterprises	71,819	71,874	72,093	72,432	72,860	74,256	73,446	73,496
	\multicolumn{8}{c}{Dollars}							
Average Wages and Salaries by Industry	49,989	51,271	51,962	53,408	54,327	55,508	60,892	62,622
Average Farm Wages and Salaries	28,821	23,581	29,051	26,410	25,220	19,862	20,205	19,829
Average Nonfarm Wages and Salaries	50,016	51,306	51,989	53,438	54,354	55,542	60,932	62,663
Average private wages and salaries.................................	48,768	50,019	50,767	52,210	52,959	54,171	59,966	61,745
Forestry, fishing, and related activities	(D)	(D)	(D)	(D)	(D)	(D)	(D)	55,148
Mining..	(D)	(D)	(D)	(D)	(D)	(D)	(D)	66,000
Utilities..	97,868	98,678	104,545	109,432	118,575	116,879	118,731	121,415
Construction	56,100	57,771	59,346	(D)	62,694	64,476	68,168	70,366
Manufacturing..	56,772	57,995	58,276	59,848	60,788	62,668	66,118	66,658
Durable goods manufacturing..	58,117	59,026	59,576	61,935	62,737	64,761	68,426	69,419
Nondurable goods manufacturing....................................	54,397	56,228	56,122	56,416	57,330	58,927	62,425	62,027
Wholesale trade	70,479	70,989	72,725	76,171	76,911	79,311	87,883	92,591
Retail trade..	29,840	31,142	31,663	32,297	33,533	34,673	38,607	39,842
Transportation and warehousing.......................................	42,414	43,100	43,608	43,781	45,511	45,863	47,850	48,452
Information	70,540	71,966	74,904	73,152	76,855	78,913	90,462	94,658
Finance and insurance	93,725	93,749	96,726	101,774	100,390	104,088	112,374	112,038
Real estate and rental and leasing..................................	44,268	46,486	47,093	48,113	49,290	52,070	56,716	59,518
Professional, scientific, and technical services	72,371	74,492	75,048	77,387	79,616	83,182	87,977	92,517
Management of companies and enterprises......................	122,500	124,259	122,815	124,079	125,143	111,917	128,623	145,246
Administrative and waste services...................................	35,370	36,138	36,604	37,603	39,225	40,765	45,063	48,590
Educational services	42,729	42,446	41,207	42,624	40,920	41,726	45,692	44,936
Health care and social assistance...................................	45,198	46,935	47,374	48,182	49,341	51,188	55,702	57,271
Arts, entertainment, and recreation.................................	31,215	33,989	35,686	37,031	35,180	34,381	37,405	36,961
Accommodation and food services	20,673	21,570	22,672	23,529	25,146	26,497	26,310	31,006
Other services, except public administration...................	32,009	33,320	34,205	35,062	36,063	37,264	41,264	42,822
Government and government enterprises	57,301	58,947	59,271	60,785	62,767	63,699	66,213	67,919

D = Not shown to avoid disclosure of confidential information, but the estimates for this item are included in the total.

Table RI-10. Employment Characteristics by Family Type

(Number, percent.)

Family type and labor force status	2019 Total	2019 Families with own children under 18 years	2020 [1] Total	2020 [1] Families with own children under 18 years	2021 Total	2021 Families with own children under 18 years
All Families..	247,476	99,772	249,987	96,879	268,718	101,271
FAMILY TYPE AND LABOR FORCE STATUS						
Opposite-Sex Married-Couple Families...........................	174,713	63,545	179,776	61,595	191,659	65,796
Both husband and wife in labor force............................	55.6	74.6	56.5	77.2	55.7	76.7
Husband in labor force, wife not in labor force	18.5	20.5	16.7	17.6	17.6	16.4
Wife in labor force, husband not in labor force	6.6	2.3	8.0	3.9	8.7	5.0
Both husband and wife not in labor force.......................	18.1	1.7	18.1	1.1	18.1	1.9
Other Families	72,763	36,227	70,211	35,284	73,996	35,007
Female householder, no spouse present	72.9	76.0	68.9	71.0	71.4	79.8
In labor force	50.0	60.3	48.1	57.8	52.9	67.2
Not in labor force	22.9	15.7	20.8	13.2	18.6	12.7
Male householder, no spouse present............................	27.1	24.0	31.1	29.0	28.6	20.2
In labor force	19.7	20.2	25.0	26.5	21.1	17.0
Not in labor force	7.4	3.8	6.1	2.5	7.5	3.2

[1] 2020 ACS 5-Year estimates. 1-Year estimates were not released for 2020 due to the impact of COVID-19 on data collection that year. Data is not comparable to previous years, which are based on 1-year estimates.

Table RI-11. School Enrollment and Educational Attainment, 2021

(Number, percent.)

Item	State	U.S.
Enrollment		
Total population 3 years and over, enrolled in school	260,253	79,453,524
Enrolled in nursery school or preschool (percent)..	4.6	5.2
Enrolled in kindergarten (percent)...	3.4	5.0
Enrolled in elementary school, grades 1-8 (percent)...	37.3	41.3
Enrolled in high school, grades 9-12 (percent)	19.4	21.8
Enrolled in college or graduate school (percent)...	35.4	26.7
Attainment		
Total population 25 years and over	773,464	228,193,464
Less than ninth grade (percent)...	4.8	4.8
9th to 12th grade, no diploma (percent)...	6.1	5.9
High school graduate, including equivalency (percent)...	27.7	26.3
Some college, no degree (percent)	16.9	19.3
Associate's degree (percent)...	8.0	8.8
Bachelor's degree (percent)	20.9	21.2
Graduate or professional degree (percent)...	15.6	13.8
High school graduate or higher (percent)	89.1	89.4
Bachelor's degree or higher (percent)...	36.5	35.0

Table RI-12. Public School Characteristics and Educational Indicators

(Number, percent; data derived from National Center of Education Statistics.)

Item	State	U.S.
Public Elementary and Secondary Schools		
Number of regular school districts, 2019-20	36	13,349
Number of operational schools, 2019-20...	316	98,469
Percent charter schools	11.7	7.7
Total public school enrollment, Fall 2021..	138,566	49,433,092
Percent charter school enrollment	8.3	7.5
Student-teacher ratio, Fall 2019	13.4	15.9
Expenditures per student (unadjusted dollars), 2019-20	17,725	13,489
Four-year adjusted cohort graduation rate (ACGR), 2019-2020 [1]...................................	83.6	86.5
Students eligible for free or reduced-price lunch (percent), 2019-20.............................	47.7	52.1
English language learners (percent), Fall 2020	12.2	10.3
Students age 3 to 21 served under IDEA, part B (percent), 2021-22	17.2	14.7

Public Schools by Type, 2019-20	Number	Percent of state public schools
Total number of schools...	316	100.0
Special education...	1	0.3
Vocational education..	10	3.2
Alternative education...	3	0.9

[1] Adjusted Cohort Graduation Rates (ACGR) differ from Averaged Freshmen Graduation Rates (AFGR).

Table RI-13. Reported Voting and Registration of the Voting-Age Population, November 2022

(Numbers in thousands, percent.)

Item	Total population	Total citizen population	Registered			Voted		
			Total registered	Percent registered (total population)	Percent registered (total citizen population)	Total voted	Percent voted (total population)	Percent voted (total citizen population)
U.S. Total	255,457	233,546	161,422	63.2	69.1	121,916	47.7	52.2
State Total	880	843	626	71.2	74.3	458	52.1	54.4
Sex								
Male	431	407	307	71.1	75.4	211	49.0	52.0
Female	448	436	320	71.3	73.3	247	55.1	56.6
Race								
White alone	755	741	567	75.1	76.5	428	56.6	57.7
White, non-Hispanic alone	702	698	539	76.8	77.1	407	57.9	58.2
Black alone	74	59	27	36.9	45.8	15	20.4	25.3
Asian alone	37	29	23	61.5	79.6	8	22.2	28.8
Hispanic (of any race)	85	65	38	44.6	58.6	27	31.8	41.8
White alone or in combination	764	749	573	75.1	76.5	433	56.7	57.8
Black alone or in combination	79	65	32	40.3	49.1	19	23.7	28.9
Asian alone or in combination	37	29	23	61.5	79.6	8	22.2	28.8
Age								
18 to 24 years	94	93	57	60.7	61.2	25	27.1	27.3
25 to 34 years	163	152	95	58.2	62.5	47	29.1	31.2
35 to 44 years	140	133	101	72.0	75.8	77	55.0	57.9
45 to 64 years	276	262	201	72.7	76.7	159	57.7	60.9
65 years and over	206	203	173	83.9	85.2	148	72.1	73.3

B = Base is less than 75,000 and therefore too small to show the derived measure.

Table RI-14. Health Indicators

(Number, rate as indicated in footnotes.)

Item	State	U.S.
Births		
Life Expectancy at Birth (years), 2020	78.2	77.0
Fertility Rate by State[1], 2021	48.3	56.3
Percent Home Births, 2021	0.8	1.4
Cesarean Delivery Rate[2], 2021	33.6	32.1
Preterm Birth Rate[3], 2021	9.7	10.5
Teen Birth Rate[4], 2021	7.8	13.9
Percentage of Babies Born Low Birthweight[5], 2021	7.9	8.5
Deaths[6]		
Heart Disease Mortality Rate, 2021	158.7	173.8
Cancer Mortality Rate, 2021	142.0	146.6
Stroke Mortality Rate, 2021	28.8	41.1
Diabetes Mortality Rate, 2021	19.5	25.4
Influenza/Pneumonia Mortality Rate, 2021	7.4	10.5
Suicide Mortality Rate, 2021	10.3	14.1
Drug Overdose Mortality Rate, 2021	41.7	33.6
Firearm Injury Mortality Rate, 2021	5.6	14.6
Homicide Mortality Rate, 2021	3.6	8.2
Disease and Illness		
Lifetime Asthma in Adults, 2020 (percent)	15.8	13.9
Lifetime Asthma in Children, 2020 (percent)[7]	15.0	11.3
Diabetes in Adults, 2020 (percent)	9.0	8.2
Self-reported Obesity in Adults, 2021 (percent)	30.1	NA

SOURCE: National Center for Health Statistics, National Vital Statistics System 2020 data; https://wonder.cdc.gov.
[1] General fertility rate per 1,000 women aged 15–44.
[2] This represents the percentage of all live births that were cesarean deliveries.
[3] Babies born prior to 37 weeks of pregnancy (gestation).
[4] Number of births per 1,000 females aged 15–19
[5] Babies born weighing less than 2,500 grams or 5 lbs. 8oz.
[6] Death rates are the number of deaths per 100,000 total population.
[7] U.S. total includes data from 30 states and D.C.
NA = Not available.
- = Zero or rounds to zero.

Table RI-15. State Government Finances, 2021

(Dollar amounts in thousands, percent distribution.)

Item	Dollars	Percent distribution
Total Revenue	13,969,218	100.0
General revenue	12,681,272	90.8
Intergovernmental revenue	6,476,654	46.4
Taxes	4,344,340	31.1
General sales	1,334,931	9.6
Selective sales	797,057	5.7
License taxes	137,010	1.0
Individual income tax	1,757,678	12.6
Corporate income tax	257,943	1.8
Other taxes	59,721	0.4
Current charges	1,017,257	7.3
Miscellaneous general revenue	843,021	6.0
Utility revenue	18,334	0.1
Liquor stores revenue	-	-
Insurance trust revenue[1]	1,269,612	9.1
Total Expenditure	12,276,862	100.0
Intergovernmental expenditure	1,498,423	12.2
Direct expenditure	10,778,439	87.8
Current operation	7,778,403	63.4
Capital outlay	555,394	4.5
Insurance benefits and repayments	1,828,209	14.9
Assistance and subsidies	194,899	1.6
Interest on debt	421,534	3.4
Exhibit: Salaries and wages	1,567,108	12.8
Total Expenditure	12,276,862	100.0
General expenditure	10,323,946	84.1
Intergovernmental expenditure	1,498,423	12.2
Direct expenditure	8,825,523	71.9
General expenditure, by function:		
Education	2,513,054	20.5
Public welfare	3,573,322	29.1
Hospitals	194,668	1.6
Health	692,062	5.6
Highways	540,546	4.4
Police protection	125,848	1.0
Correction	264,226	2.2
Natural resources	85,425	0.7
Parks and recreation	16,567	0.1
Governmental administration	738,760	6.0
Interest on general debt	421,534	3.4
Other and unallocable	1,138,810	9.3
Utility expenditure	124,707	1.0
Liquor stores expenditure	-	-
Insurance trust expenditure	1,828,209	14.9
Debt at End of Fiscal Year	9,437,805	X
Cash and Security Holdings	21,300,544	X

X = Not applicable.
- = Zero or rounds to zero.
[1] Within insurance trust revenue, net earnings of state retirement systems is a calculated statistic (the item code in the data file is X08), and thus can be positive or negative. Net earnings is the sum of earnings on investments plus gains on investments minus losses on investments. The change made in 2002 for asset valuation from book to market value in accordance with Statement 34 of the Governmental Accounting Standards Board is reflected in the calculated statistics.

Table RI-16. State Government Tax Collections, 2022

(Dollars in thousands, percent.)

Item	Dollars	Percent distribution
Total Taxes	4,796,030	100.0
Property taxes	4,135	0.1
Sales and gross receipts	2,355,494	49.1
General sales and gross receipts	1,499,910	31.3
Selective sales and gross receipts	855,584	17.8
Alcoholic beverages	23,324	0.5
Amusements	20,385	0.4
Insurance premiums	159,612	3.3
Motor fuels	138,906	2.9
Pari-mutuels	515	-
Public utilities	89,400	1.9
Tobacco products	144,900	3.0
Other selective sales	278,542	5.8
Licenses	150,403	3.1
Alcoholic beverages	1,412	-
Amusements	265	-
Corporations in general	8,873	0.2
Hunting and fishing	2,176	0.0
Motor vehicle	32,582	0.7
Motor vehicle operators	8,554	0.2
Public utilities	2,809	0.1
Occupation and business, NEC	86,715	1.8
Other licenses	7,017	0.1
Income taxes	2,229,803	46.5
Individual income	1,939,003	40.4
Corporation net income	290,800	6.1
Other taxes	56,195	1.2
Death and gift	35,700	0.7
Documentary and stock transfer	20,495	0.4
Severance	X	-
Taxes, NEC	-	-

X = Not applicable.
- = Zero or rounds to zero.

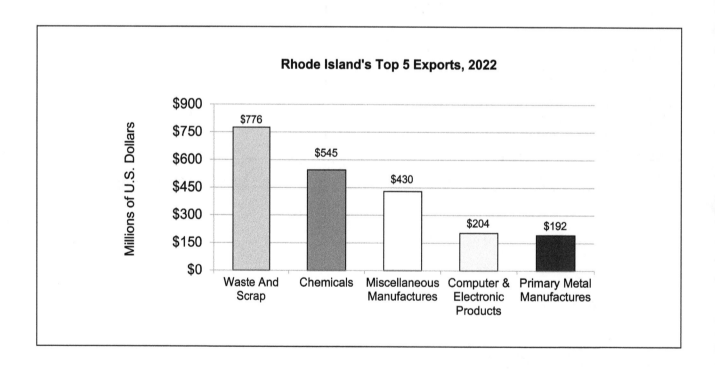

Rhode Island's Top 5 Exports, 2022

Export	Millions of U.S. Dollars
Waste And Scrap	$776
Chemicals	$545
Miscellaneous Manufactures	$430
Computer & Electronic Products	$204
Primary Metal Manufactures	$192

SOUTH CAROLINA

Facts and Figures

Location: Southeastern United States; bordered on the N by North Carolina, on the E by the Atlantic Ocean, on the S by the Atlantic Ocean and Georgia, and on the W by Georgia

Area: 32,020 sq. mi. (82,932 sq. km.); rank—40th

Population: 5,282,634 (2022 est.); rank—23rd

Principal Cities: capital—Columbia; largest—Columbia

Statehood: May 23, 1788; 8th state

U.S. Congress: 2 senators, 7 representatives

State Mottoes: *Animis opibusque parati* ("Prepared in mind and resources"); *Dum spiro, spero* ("While I breathe, I hope")

State Songs: "Carolina"; "South Carolina on My Mind"

State Nickname: The Palmetto State

Abbreviations: SC; S.C.

State Symbols: flower—yellow jessamine; tree—cabbage palmetto; bird—Carolina wren

At a Glance

- With an increase in population of 14.2 percent, South Carolina ranked 10th among the states in growth from 2010 to 2022.

- South Carolina's median household income in 2021 was $59,318, and 14.6 percent of the population lived below the poverty level.

- South Carolina had the 2nd highest rate of traffic fatalities in 2021, with 23.1 deaths per 100,000 population.

- In 2021, 10.0 percent of South Carolinians did not have health insurance, compared to 8.6 percent of the total U.S. population.

- South Carolina had the 3rd lowest drug overdose death rate in 2021, with 12.6 deaths per 100,000 population.

Table SC-1. Population by Age, Sex, Race, and Hispanic Origin

(Number, percent, except where noted.)

Sex, age, race, and Hispanic origin	2010	2020	2022	Percent change, 2010–2022
Total Population...	4,625,364	5,118,429	5,282,634	14.2
Percent of total U.S. population	1.5	1.5	1.6	X
Sex				
Male...	2,250,101	2,497,885	2,572,119	14.3
Female...	2,375,263	2,620,544	2,710,515	14.1
Age				
Under 5 years...	302,297	281,783	285,883	-5.4
Under 18 years..	1,080,474	1,100,944	1,117,872	3.5
18 to 64 years...	2,913,016	3,085,349	3,156,753	8.4
65 years and over...	631,874	932,136	1,008,009	59.5
Median age (years)	37.9	39.9	40.3	6.3
Race and Hispanic Origin				
One race				
White	3,164,143	3,509,784	3,637,779	15.0
Black...	1,302,865	1,372,920	1,386,941	6.5
American Indian and Alaska Native	24,665	28,713	30,137	22.2
Asian...	61,247	96,521	105,486	72.2
Native Hawaiian or Other Pacific Islander	3,957	5,196	5,666	43.2
Two or more races..	68,487	105,295	116,625	70.3
Hispanic (of any race)...	235,682	314,139	348,159	47.7

NOTE: Population figures for 2022 are July 1 estimates. The 2010 and 2020 estimates are taken from the respective censuses.
- = Zero or rounds to zero.
X = Not applicable.

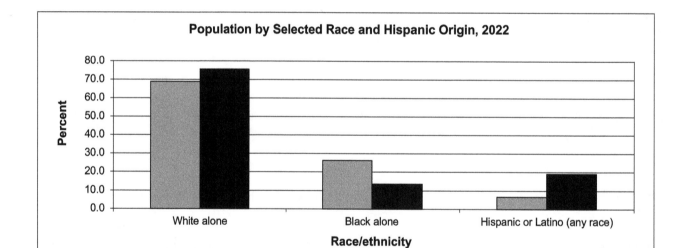

Table SC-2. Marital Status

(Number, percent distribution.)

Sex, age, race, and Hispanic origin	2000	2010	2021
Males, 15 Years and Over	1,516,125	1,797,441	2,056,575
Never married	28.8	35.2	35.2
Now married, except separated..	57.3	49.4	50.4
Separated...	2.8	3.0	2.0
Widowed...	2.7	2.8	3.1
Divorced...	8.3	9.5	9.3
Females, 15 Years and Over	1,652,793	1,939,054	2,220,138
Never married	23.4	29.1	30.6
Now married, except separated..	51.4	45.2	45.6
Separated...	3.8	3.9	2.3
Widowed...	11.5	10.6	9.9
Divorced...	9.9	11.2	11.5

Table SC-3. Households and Housing Characteristics

(Number, percent, dollars.)

Item	2000	2010	2021	Average annual percent change, 2010–2021
Total Households	1,533,854	1,761,393	2,049,972	1.5
Family households	1,072,822	1,180,687	1,337,289	1.2
Married-couple family	783,142	827,387	964,209	1.5
Other family	289,680	353,300	373,080	0.5
Male householder, no wife present	62,722	77,062	92,193	1.8
Female householder, no husband present	226,958	276,238	280,887	0.2
Nonfamily households	461,032	580,706	712,683	2.1
Householder living alone	383,142	489,995	595,718	2.0
Householder not living alone	77,890	90,711	116,965	2.6
Housing Characteristics				
Total housing units	1,753,670	2,140,337	2,395,957	1.1
Occupied housing units	1,533,854	1,761,393	2,049,972	1.5
Owner occupied	1,107,617	1,210,160	1,471,296	2.0
Renter occupied	426,237	551,233	578,676	0.5
Average household size	2.53	2.55	2.47	-0.3
Financial Characteristics				
Median gross rent of renter-occupied housing	510	728	976	3.1
Median monthly owner costs for housing units with a mortgage	894	1,177	1,289	0.9
Median value of owner-occupied housing units	94,900	138,100	213,500	5.0

Table SC-4. Migration, Origin, and Language

(Number, percent.)

Characteristic	State 2021	U.S. 2021
Residence 1 Year Ago		
Population 1 year and over	5,142,137	328,464,538
Same house	86.4	87.2
Different house in the U.S.	13.2	12.3
Same county	6.2	6.7
Different county	7.1	5.7
Same state	3.3	3.3
Different state	3.8	2.4
Abroad	0.3	0.4
Place of Birth		
Native born	4,919,425	286,623,642
Male	48.5	49.7
Female	51.5	50.3
Foreign born	271,280	45,270,103
Male	49.5	48.7
Female	50.5	51.3
Foreign born; naturalized U.S. citizen	122,751	24,044,083
Male	45.2	46.4
Female	54.8	53.6
Foreign born; not a U.S. citizen	148,529	21,226,020
Male	53.1	51.2
Female	46.9	48.8
Entered 2010 or later	34.1	28.1
Entered 2000 to 2009	24.7	23.7
Entered before 2000	41.2	48.2
World Region of Birth, Foreign		
Foreign-born population, excluding population born at sea	271,280	45,269,644
Europe	17.2	10.7
Asia	24.3	31.0
Africa	4.6	5.7
Oceania	0.2	0.6
Latin America	51.0	50.1
North America	2.6	1.7
Language Spoken at Home and Ability to Speak English		
Population 5 years and over	4,914,912	313,232,500
English only	92.4	70.4
Language other than English	7.6	21.6
Speaks English less than "very well"	2.8	8.3

Table SC-5. Median Income and Poverty Status, 2021

(Number, percent, except as noted.)

Characteristic	State Number	State Percent	U.S. Number	U.S. Percent
Median Income				
Households (dollars)..	59,318	X	69,717	X
Families (dollars)	73,901	X	85,806	X
Below Poverty Level (All People)	741,652	14.6	41,393,176	12.8
Sex				
Male	329,714	13.5	18,518,155	11.6
Female	411,938	15.7	22,875,021	13.9
Age				
Under 18 years...	220,768	20.1	12,243,219	16.9
Related children under 18 years....................................	218,026	19.9	11,985,424	16.6
18 to 64 years...	419,106	13.9	23,526,341	11.9
65 years and over	101,778	10.7	5,623,616	10.3

X = Not applicable.

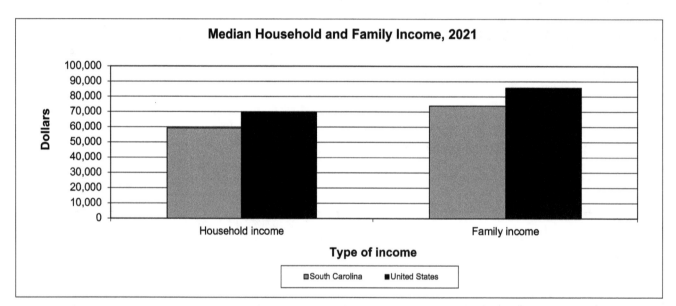

Table SC-6. Health Insurance Coverage Status for the Civilian Noninstitutionalized Population and Children Under 19 Years of Age

(Number, percent.)

Item	2011	2012	2013	2014	2015	2016	2017	2018	2019	2020 [2]	2021
Civilian Noninstitutionalized Population	4,579,231	4,623,171	4,678,122	4,733,742	4,801,301	4,861,188	4,928,260	4,990,240	5,048,513	4,990,992	5,099,812
Covered by Private or Public Insurance											
Number.....................................	3,812,927	3,844,990	3,939,270	4,092,185	4,278,073	4,375,282	4,386,727	4,467,781	4,500,847	4,472,269	4,587,877
Percent.....................................	83.3	83.2	84.2	86.4	89.1	90.0	89.0	89.5	89.2	89.6	90.0
Uninsured											
Number.....................................	766,304	778,181	738,852	641,557	523,228	485,906	541,533	522,459	547,666	518,723	511,935
Percent.....................................	16.7	16.8	15.8	13.6	10.9	10.0	11.0	10.5	10.8	10.4	10.0
Percent in the U.S. not covered..............	15.1	14.8	14.5	11.7	9.4	8.6	8.7	8.9	9.2	8.7	8.6
Children Under 19 Years of Age[1]	1,079,476	1,078,022	1,076,621	1,080,779	1,086,607	1,097,385	1,169,363	1,177,426	1,181,973	1,172,091	1,188,189
Covered by Private or Public Insurance											
Number.....................................	988,285	988,908	1,004,026	1,020,796	1,042,427	1,053,682	1,109,164	1,121,750	1,113,143	1,113,499	1,125,003
Percent.....................................	91.6	91.7	93.3	94.5	95.9	96.0	94.9	95.3	94.2	95.0	94.7
Uninsured											
Number.....................................	91,191	89,114	72,595	59,983	44,180	43,703	60,199	55,676	68,830	58,592	63,186
Percent.....................................	8.4	8.3	6.7	5.5	4.1	4.0	5.1	4.7	5.8	5.0	5.3
Percent in the U.S. not covered..............	7.5	7.2	7.1	6.0	4.8	4.5	5.0	5.2	5.7	5.2	5.4

[1] Data for years prior to 2017 are for individuals under 18 years of age.
[2] 2020 ACS 5-Year estimates. 1-Year estimates were not released for 2020 due to the impact of COVID-19 on data collection that year. Data is not comparable to previous years, which are based on 1-year estimates.

Table SC-7. Employment Status by Demographic Group, 2022

(Numbers in thousands, percent.)

Characteristic	Civilian noninstitutional population	Civilian labor force		Employed		Unemployed	
		Number	Percent of population	Number	Percent of population	Number	Percent of population
Total..	4,189	2,357	56.3	2,277	54.3	80	3.4
Sex							
Male..	1,988	1,210	60.9	1,165	58.6	45	3.7
Female	2,202	1,146	52.1	1,111	50.5	35	3.0
Race, Sex, and Hispanic Origin							
White	2,953	1,662	56.3	1,616	54.7	46	2.8
Male..	1,431	882	61.6	855	59.8	26	3.0
Female	1,523	780	51.2	761	50.0	20	2.5
Black or African American......................	1,066	600	56.2	568	53.3	31	5.2
Male..	477	275	57.8	258	54.2	17	6.3
Female	589	324	55.0	310	52.6	14	4.3
Hispanic or Latino ethnicity[1]	264	181	68.6	177	66.9	5	2.5
Male..	NA	NA	NA	NA	NA	NA	NA
Female	NA	NA	NA	NA	NA	NA	NA
Age							
16 to 19 years	NA	NA	NA	NA	NA	NA	NA
20 to 24 years	323	220	68.0	207	64.0	13	5.9
25 to 34 years	662	532	80.4	515	77.7	18	3.3
35 to 44 years	619	500	80.9	486	78.5	15	2.9
45 to 54 years	608	452	74.3	442	72.6	10	2.2
55 to 64 years	671	394	58.8	385	57.4	9	2.3
65 years and over	1,047	162	15.5	159	15.2	3	2.0

NOTE: Data in Table 7 are from the Current Population Survey (CPS) and do not match the estimates in Table 8. See notes and definitions for further information.
[1] May be of any race.

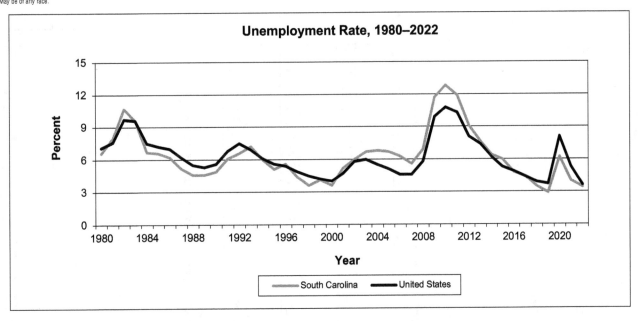

Unemployment Rate, 1980–2022

Table SC-8. Employment Status of the Civilian Noninstitutional Population Age 16 Years and Over

(Number, percent.)

Year	Civilian labor force	Civilian participation rate	Employed	Unemployed	Unemployment rate
2010..	2,174,535	61.0	1,928,442	246,093	11.3
2011..	2,185,171	60.5	1,957,493	227,678	10.4
2012..	2,190,203	59.9	1,992,957	197,246	9.0
2013..	2,197,876	59.3	2,034,404	163,472	7.4
2014..	2,222,426	59.1	2,082,941	139,485	6.3
2015..	2,267,837	59.3	2,134,087	133,750	5.9
2016..	2,286,054	58.8	2,174,301	111,753	4.9
2017..	2,261,766	58.0	2,166,708	95,058	4.2
2018..	2,279,431	57.7	2,202,377	77,054	3.4
2019..	2,321,189	58	2,256,313	64,876	2.8
2020..	2,330,863	57.4	2,191,331	139,532	6.0
2021..	2,364,366	57.4	2,269,813	94,553	4.0
2022..	2,374,975	56.5	2,297,927	77,048	3.2

Table SC-9. Employment and Average Wages by Industry

(Estimates are based on the 2012 North American Industry Classification System [NAICS].)

Industry	2014	2015	2016	2017	2018	2019	2020	2021
	Number of Jobs							
Wage and Salary Employment by Industry	2,032,855	2,090,400	2,133,752	2,173,815	2,231,951	2,268,283	2,164,308	2,222,660
Farm Wage and Salary Employment	6,085	7,511	7,270	9,290	6,389	6,340	5,854	5,617
Nonfarm Wage and Salary Employment	2,026,770	2,082,889	2,126,482	2,164,525	2,225,562	2,261,943	2,158,454	2,217,043
Private wage and salary employment	1,626,266	1,676,940	1,719,909	1,754,938	1,814,653	1,844,856	1,748,033	1,814,619
Forestry, fishing, and related activities	7,073	7,269	7,296	7,231	7,542	7,524	7,298	6,926
Mining	1,157	1,236	1,467	1,684	1,729	1,851	1,922	1,958
Utilities	12,349	12,347	12,370	12,356	12,003	11,494	11,241	10,918
Construction	84,712	89,164	96,912	103,350	106,822	109,211	106,162	106,880
Manufacturing	230,774	236,121	238,259	240,799	249,716	258,182	244,489	249,943
Durable goods manufacturing	133,704	137,653	139,580	139,909	146,201	152,566	145,156	148,906
Nondurable goods manufacturing	97,070	98,468	98,679	100,890	103,515	105,616	99,333	101,037
Wholesale trade	68,411	71,193	72,027	72,740	72,178	73,310	72,774	74,783
Retail trade	238,473	243,263	248,285	248,446	253,400	253,165	247,594	253,746
Transportation and warehousing	56,594	60,728	63,234	66,165	68,691	71,945	72,434	78,536
Information	26,472	27,057	27,045	27,471	28,050	26,886	24,725	27,425
Finance and insurance	70,386	70,804	72,039	73,543	74,454	75,343	77,356	79,245
Real estate and rental and leasing	27,629	28,691	29,800	30,250	31,799	32,478	30,992	32,169
Professional, scientific, and technical services	85,612	89,242	94,241	97,522	103,219	103,833	102,786	107,234
Management of companies and enterprises	17,039	16,699	17,946	20,250	21,416	25,019	24,297	24,548
Administrative and waste services	153,318	158,396	159,475	162,543	171,148	171,193	156,858	167,066
Educational services	32,184	33,170	33,487	33,254	33,508	33,750	31,332	33,064
Health care and social assistance	185,814	192,677	198,671	203,217	210,804	213,089	207,761	213,518
Arts, entertainment, and recreation	28,739	29,145	29,861	30,772	32,245	33,755	26,303	29,782
Accommodation and food services	201,982	210,983	218,999	224,939	233,147	238,032	202,512	217,970
Other services, except public administration	97,548	98,755	98,495	98,406	102,782	104,796	99,197	98,908
Government and government enterprises	400,504	405,949	406,573	409,587	410,909	417,087	410,421	402,424
	Dollars							
Average Wages and Salaries by Industry	42,033	43,277	44,189	45,499	46,285	47,880	50,819	53,868
Average Farm Wages and Salaries	23,408	22,974	19,459	14,836	19,581	14,572	14,509	20,222
Average Nonfarm Wages and Salaries	42,089	43,351	44,273	45,630	46,362	47,974	50,917	53,954
Average private wages and salaries	41,361	42,638	43,575	45,045	45,673	47,311	50,644	53,635
Forestry, fishing, and related activities	35,127	36,259	37,588	39,874	39,532	40,820	43,278	46,938
Mining	57,682	69,443	66,378	66,306	68,905	81,519	72,864	76,963
Utilities	87,453	92,420	95,116	97,384	94,413	102,768	104,378	103,441
Construction	47,210	48,886	51,066	54,422	53,649	56,280	59,044	62,083
Manufacturing	56,963	58,534	59,583	60,831	61,697	62,968	64,135	66,656
Durable goods manufacturing	59,814	60,997	62,306	63,452	64,161	64,986	65,546	68,218
Nondurable goods manufacturing	53,035	55,089	55,733	57,195	58,217	60,053	62,072	64,353
Wholesale trade	63,914	65,509	66,490	68,936	70,591	73,510	76,576	81,439
Retail trade	26,478	27,267	27,855	28,497	29,005	29,997	32,829	35,401
Transportation and warehousing	42,431	43,757	43,476	44,851	45,932	47,143	48,856	50,888
Information	57,901	59,157	60,341	63,639	64,358	68,503	76,438	86,964
Finance and insurance	61,840	65,044	66,814	69,284	71,940	74,777	82,019	86,136
Real estate and rental and leasing	40,796	42,450	43,302	45,502	46,953	49,630	53,752	57,652
Professional, scientific, and technical services	65,683	67,653	69,305	71,343	72,238	75,045	80,133	84,049
Management of companies and enterprises	71,921	74,614	77,309	81,919	85,116	87,997	92,932	97,172
Administrative and waste services	33,520	34,140	34,698	35,755	35,770	36,652	39,488	42,341
Educational services	30,636	31,100	32,161	32,303	33,831	33,647	37,487	37,082
Health care and social assistance	44,826	46,284	46,855	48,142	48,705	50,136	53,072	56,212
Arts, entertainment, and recreation	21,323	22,522	22,773	23,018	23,172	24,051	27,007	28,300
Accommodation and food services	18,572	19,138	19,794	20,350	20,894	21,735	21,472	26,068
Other services, except public administration	30,313	31,571	32,583	33,753	34,222	35,339	38,917	41,114
Government and government enterprises	45,041	46,296	47,227	48,139	49,403	50,907	52,084	55,390

Table SC-10. Employment Characteristics by Family Type

(Number, percent.)

Family type and labor force status	2019		2020 [1]		2021	
	Total	Families with own children under 18 years	Total	Families with own children under 18 years	Total	Families with own children under 18 years
All Families...................................	1,286,326	474,527	1,280,623	491,337	1,337,289	506,311
FAMILY TYPE AND LABOR FORCE STATUS						
Opposite-Sex Married-Couple Families.................	928,870	306,409	916,570	313,457	956,628	321,734
Both husband and wife in labor force................	47.0	69.4	47.0	67.5	45.5	66.3
Husband in labor force, wife not in labor force	20.8	25.0	21.4	27.1	21.6	27.8
Wife in labor force, husband not in labor force	8.3	4.1	8.6	3.8	8.6	4.5
Both husband and wife not in labor force............	23.4	1.1	23.0	1.6	24.3	1.5
Other Families	357,456	168,118	357,323	176,956	373,080	184,067
Female householder, no spouse present..............	75.6	79.2	76.3	78.7	75.3	78.6
In labor force........................	50.0	65.8	52.1	66.4	49.9	64.6
Not in labor force	25.6	13.5	24.3	12.3	25.4	14.0
Male householder, no spouse present................	24.4	20.8	23.7	21.3	24.7	21.4
In labor force........................	17.6	18.7	17.4	18.8	18.7	19.3
Not in labor force	6.7	2.1	6.3	2.5	6.0	2.1

[1] 2020 ACS 5-Year estimates. 1-Year estimates were not released for 2020 due to the impact of COVID-19 on data collection that year. Data is not comparable to previous years, which are based on 1-year estimates.

Table SC-11. School Enrollment and Educational Attainment, 2021

(Number, percent.)

Item	State	U.S.
Enrollment		
Total population 3 years and over, enrolled in school	1,175,906	79,453,524
Enrolled in nursery school or preschool (percent)................................	4.7	5.2
Enrolled in kindergarten (percent)................................	5.5	5.0
Enrolled in elementary school, grades 1-8 (percent)................................	42.8	41.3
Enrolled in high school, grades 9-12 (percent)................................	22.8	21.8
Enrolled in college or graduate school (percent)................................	24.2	26.7
Attainment		
Total population 25 years and over	3,598,398	228,193,464
Less than ninth grade (percent)................................	3.2	4.8
9th to 12th grade, no diploma (percent)................................	7.2	5.9
High school graduate, including equivalency (percent)................................	28.5	26.3
Some college, no degree (percent)................................	19.3	19.3
Associate's degree (percent)................................	10.3	8.8
Bachelor's degree (percent)................................	19.6	21.2
Graduate or professional degree (percent)................................	11.9	13.8
High school graduate or higher (percent)................................	89.6	89.4
Bachelor's degree or higher (percent)................................	31.5	35.0

Table SC-12. Public School Characteristics and Educational Indicators

(Number, percent; data derived from National Center of Education Statistics.)

Item	State	U.S.
Public Elementary and Secondary Schools		
Number of regular school districts, 2019-20	82	13,349
Number of operational schools, 2019-20................................	1,265	98,469
Percent charter schools	6.3	7.7
Total public school enrollment, Fall 2021................................	780,878	49,433,092
Percent charter school enrollment	6.3	7.5
Student-teacher ratio, Fall 2019	14.7	15.9
Expenditures per student (unadjusted dollars), 2019-20	11,286	13,489
Four-year adjusted cohort graduation rate (ACGR), 2019-2020[1]................................	82.2	86.5
Students eligible for free or reduced-price lunch (percent), 2019-20................................	63.2	52.1
English language learners (percent), Fall 2020	5.7	10.3
Students age 3 to 21 served under IDEA, part B (percent), 2021-22	14.0	14.7

Public Schools by Type, 2019-20	Number	Percent of state public schools
Total number of schools................................	1,265	100.0
Special education................................	8	0.6
Vocational education................................	44	3.5
Alternative education................................	15	1.2

[1] Adjusted Cohort Graduation Rates (ACGR) differ from Averaged Freshmen Graduation Rates (AFGR).

Table SC-13. Reported Voting and Registration of the Voting-Age Population, November 2022

(Numbers in thousands, percent.)

Item	Total population	Total citizen population	Registered			Voted		
			Total registered	Percent registered (total population)	Percent registered (total citizen population)	Total voted	Percent voted (total population)	Percent voted (total citizen population)
U.S. Total	255,457	233,546	161,422	63.2	69.1	121,916	47.7	52.2
State Total......................................	4,045	3,868	2,491	61.6	64.4	1,736	42.9	44.9
Sex								
Male	1,899	1,812	1,127	59.3	62.2	785	41.4	43.3
Female	2,147	2,056	1,364	63.6	66.3	951	44.3	46.3
Race								
White alone....................................	2,932	2,791	1,854	63.3	66.5	1,308	44.6	46.9
White, non-Hispanic alone	2,699	2,670	1,813	67.2	67.9	1,276	47.3	47.8
Black alone....................................	1,012	985	596	58.9	60.5	404	39.9	41.0
Asian alone....................................	49	46	21	41.9	45.3	10	20.3	21.9
Hispanic (of any race)	251	130	47	18.7	36.2	32	12.6	24.3
White alone or in combination	2,959	2,812	1,860	62.9	66.1	1,313	44.4	46.7
Black alone or in combination......................	1,032	1,004	599	58.0	59.6	407	39.4	40.5
Asian alone or in combination......................	52	48	23	45.0	48.5	13	24.6	26.5
Age								
18 to 24 years.................................	427	412	166	38.9	40.4	98	22.9	23.8
25 to 34 years.................................	618	588	393	63.6	66.8	216	34.9	36.7
35 to 44 years.................................	662	606	369	55.7	60.8	226	34.1	37.2
45 to 64 years.................................	1,255	1,192	779	62.1	65.4	572	45.6	48.0
65 years and over	1,083	1,070	784	72.4	73.3	625	57.7	58.4

B = Base is less than 75,000 and therefore too small to show the derived measure.

Table SC-14. Health Indicators

(Number, rate as indicated in footnotes.)

Item	State	U.S.
Births		
Life Expectancy at Birth (years), 2020	74.8	77.0
Fertility Rate by State[1], 2021..	57.5	56.3
Percent Home Births, 2021	1.3	1.4
Cesarean Delivery Rate[2], 2021...	33.5	32.1
Preterm Birth Rate[3], 2021..	12.1	10.5
Teen Birth Rate[4], 2021..	18.3	13.9
Percentage of Babies Born Low Birthweight[5], 2021	10.0	8.5
Deaths[6]		
Heart Disease Mortality Rate, 2021...	189.1	173.8
Cancer Mortality Rate, 2021..	155.2	146.6
Stroke Mortality Rate, 2021...	48.3	41.1
Diabetes Mortality Rate, 2021..	26.3	25.4
Influenza/Pneumonia Mortality Rate, 2021	9.4	10.5
Suicide Mortality Rate, 2021..	15.2	14.1
Drug Overdose Mortality Rate, 2021..	42.8	33.6
Firearm Injury Mortality Rate, 2021	22.4	14.6
Homicide Mortality Rate, 2021...	13.4	8.2
Disease and Illness		
Lifetime Asthma in Adults, 2020 (percent)..	14.0	13.9
Lifetime Asthma in Children, 2020 (percent)[7]	NA	11.3
Diabetes in Adults, 2020 (percent)..	11.9	8.2
Self-reported Obesity in Adults, 2021 (percent)...	36.1	NA

SOURCE: National Center for Health Statistics, National Vital Statistics System 2020 data; https://wonder.cdc.gov.
[1] General fertility rate per 1,000 women aged 15–44.
[2] This represents the percentage of all live births that were cesarean deliveries.
[3] Babies born prior to 37 weeks of pregnancy (gestation).
[4] Number of births per 1,000 females aged 15–19
[5] Babies born weighing less than 2,500 grams or 5 lbs. 8oz.
[6] Death rates are the number of deaths per 100,000 total population.
[7] U.S. total includes data from 30 states and D.C.
NA = Not available.
- = Zero or rounds to zero.

Table SC-15. State Government Finances, 2021

(Dollar amounts in thousands, percent distribution.)

Item	Dollars	Percent distribution
Total Revenue	40,393,477	100.0
General revenue	34,997,242	86.6
Intergovernmental revenue	13,037,780	32.3
Taxes	13,286,248	32.9
General sales	4,154,363	10.3
Selective sales	1,965,427	4.9
License taxes	707,027	1.8
Individual income tax	5,456,360	13.5
Corporate income tax	740,197	1.8
Other taxes	262,874	0.7
Current charges	6,098,447	15.1
Miscellaneous general revenue	2,574,767	6.4
Utility revenue	1,611,423	4.0
Liquor stores revenue	-	-
Insurance trust revenue[1]	3,784,812	9.4
Total Expenditure	40,269,096	100.0
Intergovernmental expenditure	7,269,642	18.1
Direct expenditure	32,999,454	81.9
Current operation	23,889,301	59.3
Capital outlay	1,961,452	4.9
Insurance benefits and repayments	5,090,219	12.6
Assistance and subsidies	1,483,339	3.7
Interest on debt	575,143	1.4
Exhibit: Salaries and wages	4,527,299	11.2
Total Expenditure	40,269,096	100.0
General expenditure	33,606,662	83.5
Intergovernmental expenditure	7,269,642	18.1
Direct expenditure	26,337,020	65.4
General expenditure, by function:		
Education	12,718,249	31.6
Public welfare	8,977,862	22.3
Hospitals	2,912,939	7.2
Health	1,698,875	4.2
Highways	1,831,596	4.5
Police protection	221,095	0.5
Correction	609,089	1.5
Natural resources	256,923	0.6
Parks and recreation	144,524	0.4
Governmental administration	962,724	2.4
Interest on general debt	246,166	0.6
Other and unallocable	2,996,957	7.4
Utility expenditure	1,572,215	3.9
Liquor stores expenditure	-	-
Insurance trust expenditure	5,090,219	12.6
Debt at End of Fiscal Year	12,856,658	X
Cash and Security Holdings	65,035,353	X

X = Not applicable.
- = Zero or rounds to zero.
[1] Within insurance trust revenue, net earnings of state retirement systems is a calculated statistic (the item code in the data file is X08), and thus can be positive or negative. Net earnings is the sum of earnings on investments plus gains on investments minus losses on investments. The change made in 2002 for asset valuation from book to market value in accordance with Statement 34 of the Governmental Accounting Standards Board is reflected in the calculated statistics.

Table SC-16. State Government Tax Collections, 2022

(Dollars in thousands, percent.)

Item	Dollars	Percent distribution
Total Taxes	16,051,549	100.0
Property taxes	86,957	0.5
Sales and gross receipts	6,988,768	43.5
General sales and gross receipts	4,876,547	30.4
Selective sales and gross receipts	2,112,221	13.2
Alcoholic beverages	222,505	1.4
Amusements	53,981	0.3
Insurance premiums	289,114	1.8
Motor fuels	944,249	5.9
Pari-mutuels	X	-
Public utilities	29,128	0.2
Tobacco products	27,914	0.2
Other selective sales	545,330	3.4
Licenses	678,982	4.2
Alcoholic beverages	13,717	0.1
Amusements	6,344	-
Corporations in general	163,072	1.0
Hunting and fishing	23,734	0.1
Motor vehicle	295,330	1.8
Motor vehicle operators	4,723	-
Public utilities	14,713	0.1
Occupation and business, NEC	140,838	0.9
Other licenses	16,511	0.1
Income taxes	8,059,011	50.2
Individual income	6,854,835	42.7
Corporation net income	1,204,176	7.5
Other taxes	237,831	1.5
Death and gift	X	-
Documentary and stock transfer	237,831	1.5
Severance	X	-
Taxes, NEC	-	-

X = Not applicable.
- = Zero or rounds to zero.

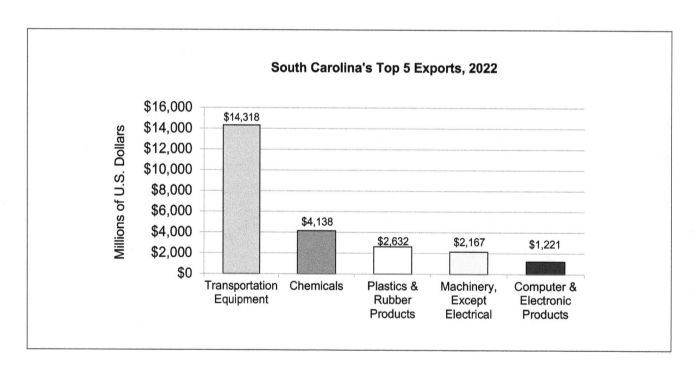

South Carolina's Top 5 Exports, 2022

SOUTH DAKOTA

Facts and Figures

Location: North central United States; bordered on the N by North Dakota, on the E by Minnesota and Iowa, on the S by Nebraska, and on the W by Wyoming and Montana

Area: 77,117 sq. mi. (199,731 sq. km.); rank—17th

Population: 909,824 (2022 est.); rank—46th

Principal Cities: capital—Pierre; largest—Sioux Falls

Statehood: November 2, 1889; 40th state

U.S. Congress: 2 senators, 1 representative

State Motto: Under God the People Rule

State Song: "Hail, South Dakota"

State Nickname: The Mount Rushmore State

Abbreviations: SD; S.D.; S. Dak.

State Symbols: flower—pasqueflower; tree—Black Hills spruce; bird—ring-necked pheasant

At a Glance

- With an increase in population of 11.7 percent, South Dakota ranked 15th among the states in growth from 2010 to 2022.

- In 2021, 9.5 percent of South Dakotans did not have health insurance, compared to 8.6 percent of the total U.S. population.

- South Dakota had the 2nd highest drug overdose death rate in the country in 2021, with 56.6 deaths per 100,000 population. The national drug overdose death rate was 32.4 deaths per 100,000 population.

- South Dakota's median household income in 2021 was $66,143, and 12.3 percent of its residents lived below the poverty level.

- In 2022, South Dakota's unemployment rate was 2.1 percent, which was the lowest unemployment rate in the country. The national unemployment rate was 3.6 percent.

Table SD-1. Population by Age, Sex, Race, and Hispanic Origin

(Number, percent, except where noted.)

Sex, age, race, and Hispanic origin	2010	2020	2022	Percent change, 2010–2022
Total Population...	814,180	886,677	909,824	11.7
Percent of total U.S. population	0.3	0.3	0.3	X
Sex				
Male..	407,381	450,952	462,723	13.6
Female	406,799	435,725	447,101	9.9
Age				
Under 5 years...	59,621	59,149	58,093	-2.6
Under 18 years...	202,797	59,149	219,165	8.1
18 to 64 years..	494,802	516,587	526,842	6.5
65 years and over	116,581	153,265	163,817	40.5
Median age (years)	36.9	37.6	37.9	2.7
Race and Hispanic Origin				
One race				
White	706,690	750,029	766,469	8.5
Black	10,533	21,341	23,377	121.9
American Indian and Alaska Native	72,782	76,623	77,481	6.5
Asian...	7,775	14,949	16,264	109.2
Native Hawaiian or Other Pacific Islander	517	874	1,170	126.3
Two or more races...	15,883	22,861	25,063	57.8
Hispanic (of any race)	22,119	39,475	44,508	101.2

NOTE: Population figures for 2022 are July 1 estimates. The 2010 and 2020 estimates are taken from the respective censuses.
- = Zero or rounds to zero.
X = Not applicable.

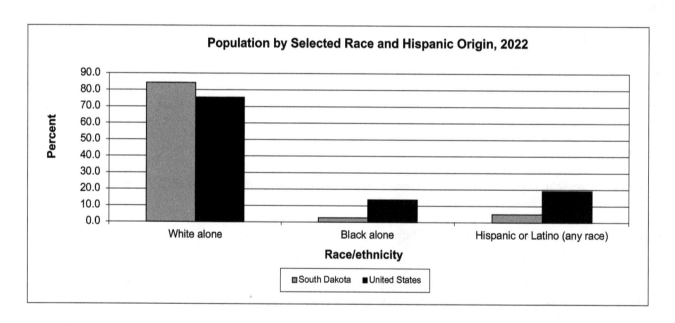

Table SD-2. Marital Status

(Number, percent distribution.)

Sex, age, race, and Hispanic origin	2000	2010	2021
Males, 15 Years and Over	289,858	322,689	358,839
Never married	29.8	33.5	35.7
Now married, except separated..	58.2	52.5	51.6
Separated...	1.0	0.9	1.3
Widowed..	2.4	2.8	2.3
Divorced..	8.5	10.3	9.1
Females, 15 Years and Over	299,754	325,640	353,086
Never married	22.5	26.0	28.1
Now married, except separated..	55.9	52.1	51.2
Separated...	1.1	1.0	1.0
Widowed..	11.4	9.5	8.8
Divorced..	9.0	11.4	10.8

Table SD-3. Households and Housing Characteristics

(Number, percent, dollars.)

Item	2000	2010	2021	Average annual percent change, 2010–2021
Total Households..	290,245	318,955	356,887	1.1
Family households	194,330	204,029	221,214	0.8
Married-couple family	157,391	161,534	175,003	0.8
Other family	36,939	42,495	46,211	0.8
Male householder, no wife present...	10,734	12,526	16,528	2.9
Female householder, no husband present...	26,205	29,969	29,683	-0.1
Nonfamily households	95,915	114,926	135,673	1.6
Householder living alone..	80,040	95,610	107,941	1.2
Householder not living alone...	15,875	19,316	27,732	4.0
Housing Characteristics				
Total housing units..	323,208	364,031	400,688	0.9
Occupied housing units	290,245	318,955	356,887	1.1
Owner occupied	197,940	216,821	247,630	1.3
Renter occupied	92,305	102,134	109,257	0.6
Average household size...	2.50	2.45	2.42	-0.1
Financial Characteristics				
Median gross rent of renter-occupied housing	426	591	830	3.7
Median monthly owner costs for housing units with a mortgage	828	1,151	1,415	2.1
Median value of owner-occupied housing units..	79,600	129,700	219,900	6.3

Table SD-4. Migration, Origin, and Language

(Number, percent.)

Characteristic	State 2021	U.S. 2021
Residence 1 Year Ago		
Population 1 year and over	884,616	328,464,538
Same house	85.9	87.2
Different house in the U.S...	13.9	12.3
Same county	6.7	6.7
Different county	7.2	5.7
Same state	4.1	3.3
Different state	3.1	2.4
Abroad	0.2	0.4
Place of Birth		
Native born	864,393	286,623,642
Male	50.7	49.7
Female	49.3	50.3
Foreign born	30,983	45,270,103
Male	43.6	48.7
Female	56.4	51.3
Foreign born; naturalized U.S. citizen...	14,552	24,044,083
Male	38.1	46.4
Female	61.9	53.6
Foreign born; not a U.S. citizen	16,431	21,226,020
Male	48.4	51.2
Female	51.6	48.8
Entered 2010 or later	48.9	28.1
Entered 2000 to 2009	24.6	23.7
Entered before 2000..	26.5	48.2
World Region of Birth, Foreign		
Foreign-born population, excluding population born at sea	30,983	45,269,644
Europe...	11.3	10.7
Asia..	41.6	31.0
Africa...	18.7	5.7
Oceania..	0.4	0.6
Latin America...	26.4	50.1
North America	1.7	1.7
Language Spoken at Home and Ability to Speak English		
Population 5 years and over...	837,297	313,232,500
English only	93.9	78.4
Language other than English...	6.1	21.6
Speaks English less than "very well"...	1.8	8.3

Table SD-5. Median Income and Poverty Status, 2021

(Number, percent, except as noted.)

Characteristic	State		U.S.	
	Number	Percent	Number	Percent
Median Income				
Households (dollars)..	66,143	X	69,717	X
Families (dollars)	82,562	X	85,806	X
Below Poverty Level (All People)	106,548	12.3	41,393,176	12.8
Sex				
Male	49,544	11.3	18,518,155	11.6
Female	57,004	13.3	22,875,021	13.9
Age				
Under 18 years...	31,413	14.6	12,243,219	16.9
Related children under 18 years..............................	30,723	14.3	11,985,424	16.6
18 to 64 years..	58,427	11.7	23,526,341	11.9
65 years and over	16,708	11.0	5,623,616	10.3

X = Not applicable.

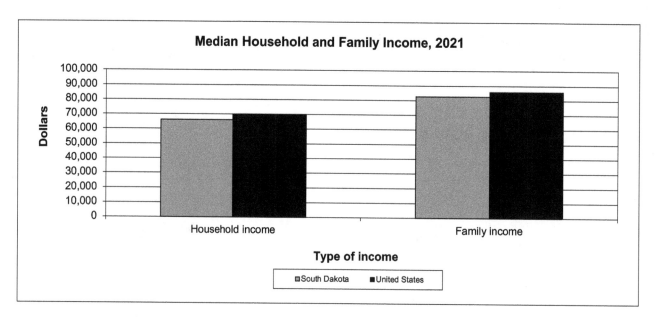

Median Household and Family Income, 2021

(Bar chart. Y-axis: Dollars, 0 to 100,000. X-axis: Type of income — Household income, Family income. Legend: South Dakota, United States.)

Table SD-6. Health Insurance Coverage Status for the Civilian Noninstitutionalized Population and Children Under 19 Years of Age

(Number, percent.)

Item	2011	2012	2013	2014	2015	2016	2017	2018	2019	2020 [2]	2021
Civilian Noninstitutionalized Population	805,505	816,425	827,039	835,403	841,363	848,774	851,826	864,598	867,305	861,933	877,855
Covered by Private or Public Insurance											
Number..	709,597	722,292	733,713	753,472	755,448	774,556	774,488	779,891	778,968	779,526	794,535
Percent..	88.1	88.5	88.7	90.2	89.8	91.3	90.9	90.2	89.8	90.4	90.5
Uninsured											
Number..	95,908	94,133	93,326	81,931	85,915	74,218	77,338	84,707	88,337	82,407	83,320
Percent..	11.9	11.5	11.3	9.8	10.2	8.7	9.1	9.8	10.2	9.6	9.5
Percent in the U.S. not covered.............................	15.1	14.8	14.5	11.7	9.4	8.6	8.7	8.9	9.2	8.7	8.6
Children Under 19 Years of Age[1]	200,704	203,033	207,264	209,586	208,580	212,981	224,414	225,191	226,171	226,065	231,767
Covered by Private or Public Insurance											
Number..	188,665	191,198	194,142	197,674	194,544	203,436	210,566	211,880	208,534	211,880	214,230
Percent..	94.0	94.2	93.7	94.3	93.3	95.5	93.8	94.1	92.2	93.7	92.4
Uninsured											
Number..	12,039	11,835	13,122	11,912	14,036	9,545	13,848	13,311	17,637	14,185	17,537
Percent..	6.0	5.8	6.3	5.7	6.7	4.5	6.2	5.9	7.8	6.3	7.6
Percent in the U.S. not covered.............................	7.5	7.2	7.1	6.0	4.8	4.5	5.0	5.2	5.7	5.2	5.4

[1] Data for years prior to 2017 are for individuals under 18 years of age.
[2] 2020 ACS 5-Year estimates. 1-Year estimates were not released for 2020 due to the impact of COVID-19 on data collection that year. Data is not comparable to previous years, which are based on 1-year estimates.

Table SD-7. Employment Status by Demographic Group, 2022

(Numbers in thousands, percent.)

Characteristic	Civilian noninstitutional population	Civilian labor force		Employed		Unemployed	
		Number	Percent of population	Number	Percent of population	Number	Percent of population
Total..	693	484	69.7	475	68.5	9	1.8
Sex							
Male...	349	264	75.8	259	74.3	5	2.0
Female..	345	219	63.6	216	62.6	4	1.6
Race, Sex, and Hispanic Origin							
White..	627	439	70.1	434	69.2	5	1.2
Male..	317	241	76.1	238	75.1	3	1.3
Female..	310	198	63.9	196	63.1	2	1.1
Black or African American....................	NA	NA	NA	NA	NA	NA	NA
Male..	NA	NA	NA	NA	NA	NA	NA
Female..	NA	NA	NA	NA	NA	NA	NA
Hispanic or Latino ethnicity[1]	NA	NA	NA	NA	NA	NA	NA
Male..	NA	NA	NA	NA	NA	NA	NA
Female..	NA	NA	NA	NA	NA	NA	NA
Age							
16 to 19 years...................................	NA	NA	NA	NA	NA	NA	NA
20 to 24 years...................................	NA	NA	NA	NA	NA	NA	NA
25 to 34 years...................................	115	102	88.9	100	87.2	2	2.0
35 to 44 years...................................	116	103	88.4	100	86.4	2	2.3
45 to 54 years...................................	96	87	90.6	86	89.8	1	0.8
55 to 64 years...................................	112	86	77.4	86	76.9	1	0.6
65 years and over	NA	NA	NA	NA	NA	NA	NA

NOTE: Data in Table 7 are from the Current Population Survey (CPS) and do not match the estimates in Table 8. See notes and definitions for further information.
[1] May be of any race.
NA = Not available.

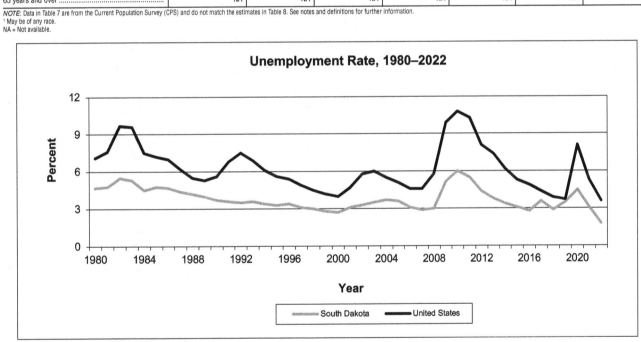

Table SD-8. Employment Status of the Civilian Noninstitutional Population Age 16 Years and Over

(Number, percent.)

Year	Civilian labor force	Civilian participation rate	Employed	Unemployed	Unemployment rate
2010..	443,618	71.6	421,815	21,803	4.9
2011..	445,866	71.5	425,367	20,499	4.6
2012..	447,056	70.8	428,943	18,113	4.1
2013..	447,479	70.1	430,834	16,645	3.7
2014..	450,769	70.0	435,733	15,036	3.3
2015..	453,091	69.9	439,293	13,798	3.0
2016..	455,133	69.5	441,418	13,715	3.0
2017..	455,339	69.2	441,450	13,889	3.1
2018..	457,328	68.9	444,569	12,759	2.8
2019..	461,610	68.9	448,619	12,991	2.8
2020..	461,624	68.4	441,550	20,074	4.3
2021..	468,015	68.5	453,511	14,504	3.1
2022..	475,065	68.2	465,250	9,815	2.1

Table SD-9. Employment and Average Wages by Industry

(Estimates are based on the 2012 North American Industry Classification System [NAICS].)

Industry	2014	2015	2016	2017	2018	2019	2020	2021
	Number of Jobs							
Wage and Salary Employment by Industry......................	444,468	447,390	450,749	453,399	458,271	461,941	448,972	462,954
Farm Wage and Salary Employment................................	6,366	4,908	4,622	4,979	5,611	5,625	6,899	6,697
Nonfarm Wage and Salary Employment...........................	438,102	442,482	446,127	448,420	452,660	456,316	442,073	456,257
Private wage and salary employment................................	353,666	358,339	361,171	362,636	366,517	369,233	357,645	369,562
Forestry, fishing, and related activities	2,426	2,442	2,463	2,458	2,501	2,585	2,514	2,300
Mining...	816	837	849	872	883	907	911	1,007
Utilities...	1,967	1,996	2,019	1,994	1,980	1,949	1,925	1,959
Construction	21,790	22,773	23,381	22,894	23,522	24,178	25,013	25,672
Manufacturing..	42,466	42,641	42,196	43,137	44,477	45,015	43,180	43,861
Durable goods manufacturing............................	28,506	28,528	27,569	27,597	28,676	28,735	26,970	27,296
Nondurable goods manufacturing......................	13,960	14,113	14,627	15,540	15,801	16,280	16,210	16,565
Wholesale trade	20,877	21,209	21,267	21,082	20,924	21,194	20,996	21,455
Retail trade..	52,151	53,247	54,108	53,333	52,654	51,584	50,039	52,011
Transportation and warehousing..........................	11,221	11,500	11,260	11,276	11,457	11,633	11,409	11,811
Information	6,063	5,895	5,771	5,724	5,585	5,501	5,071	5,055
Finance and insurance	27,131	26,920	26,482	26,582	26,488	26,252	25,766	25,213
Real estate and rental and leasing.......................	3,700	3,805	3,855	3,859	3,980	4,161	4,049	4,159
Professional, scientific, and technical services	12,477	12,623	13,001	13,454	14,187	14,672	14,994	16,137
Management of companies and enterprises..........	4,572	4,936	5,079	4,907	5,270	5,332	5,147	5,116
Administrative and waste services	13,371	13,330	13,378	13,107	13,124	13,333	12,855	13,543
Educational services	8,081	8,131	8,020	8,079	7,710	7,773	7,275	8,319
Health care and social assistance........................	60,004	60,849	62,349	63,848	64,973	65,984	66,345	67,107
Arts, entertainment, and recreation.....................	6,526	6,604	6,614	6,830	6,956	7,034	6,296	7,009
Accommodation and food services.......................	39,253	39,793	40,408	40,455	40,665	40,680	35,034	38,878
Other services, except public administration.........	18,774	18,808	18,671	18,745	19,181	19,466	18,826	18,950
Government and government enterprises	84,436	84,143	84,956	85,784	86,143	87,083	84,428	86,695
	Dollars							
Average Wages and Salaries by Industry	38,249	39,630	40,695	41,912	43,181	44,702	48,367	50,429
Average Farm Wages and Salaries	40,036	33,787	38,756	38,114	35,994	45,304	33,902	34,111
Average Nonfarm Wages and Salaries	38,223	39,695	40,715	41,954	43,270	44,695	48,592	50,668
Average private wages and salaries.....................	38,521	40,069	41,043	42,276	43,689	45,312	49,396	51,780
Forestry, fishing, and related activities	25,863	27,417	29,010	29,831	30,699	32,244	35,505	38,677
Mining...	58,757	60,718	58,178	60,280	63,360	63,972	67,336	81,213
Utilities...	74,705	76,281	78,359	80,303	84,378	87,278	91,066	93,539
Construction	42,883	44,987	47,666	47,374	48,975	50,981	54,008	55,853
Manufacturing..	44,506	45,447	45,993	47,888	49,333	50,220	53,293	56,078
Durable goods manufacturing............................	45,245	45,994	46,511	48,724	50,047	51,107	53,984	56,757
Nondurable goods manufacturing......................	42,997	44,343	45,018	46,402	48,037	48,654	52,145	54,959
Wholesale trade	54,998	56,251	57,027	58,393	60,773	62,146	66,279	71,035
Retail trade..	26,194	27,036	27,349	27,803	28,609	29,674	32,282	34,243
Transportation and warehousing..........................	43,893	44,983	45,476	46,137	47,301	48,033	50,629	51,841
Information	44,812	45,729	46,647	47,159	49,309	51,466	58,032	60,832
Finance and insurance	52,973	56,369	58,717	60,904	63,886	67,496	73,271	77,602
Real estate and rental and leasing.......................	32,335	34,794	33,888	35,580	36,636	39,225	42,639	46,774
Professional, scientific, and technical services	52,696	56,409	57,467	59,363	60,935	63,086	68,129	73,520
Management of companies and enterprises..........	92,717	93,532	96,695	102,847	99,656	104,001	112,108	119,034
Administrative and waste services	29,191	29,978	31,147	33,208	33,947	35,377	38,991	44,706
Educational services	25,068	25,598	26,422	25,859	27,382	26,658	31,656	29,315
Health care and social assistance........................	45,830	47,788	48,943	50,473	51,441	53,607	58,295	60,194
Arts, entertainment, and recreation.....................	18,802	19,711	19,414	19,851	20,391	20,875	22,736	24,226
Accommodation and food services.......................	16,083	17,171	17,874	18,341	19,209	19,782	20,032	23,653
Other services, except public administration.........	28,123	29,445	30,037	31,284	32,418	33,566	37,502	38,986
Government and government enterprises	36,973	38,099	39,319	40,593	41,490	42,076	45,190	45,931

Table SD-10. Employment Characteristics by Family Type

(Number, percent.)

Family type and labor force status	2019		2020 [1]		2021	
	Total	Families with own children under 18 years	Total	Families with own children under 18 years	Total	Families with own children under 18 years
All Families..	223,964	94,330	218,705	94,515	221,214	93,342
FAMILY TYPE AND LABOR FORCE STATUS						
Opposite-Sex Married-Couple Families..	177,534	67,439	171,022	66,190	173,924	66,353
Both husband and wife in labor force.............................	59.0	76.5	60.5	79.7	59.4	80.2
Husband in labor force, wife not in labor force	16.4	19.2	15.3	16.0	14.9	15.0
Wife in labor force, husband not in labor force	8.2	3.3	7.6	3.2	7.4	3.5
Both husband and wife not in labor force.............................	15.9	0.6	16.6	1.0	18.2	1.3
Other Families	46,430	26,891	46,787	28,146	46,211	26,735
Female householder, no spouse present.............................	66.4	70.0	66.6	68.9	64.2	66.9
In labor force..	48.7	61.3	49.6	58.7	48.3	56.8
Not in labor force	17.7	8.7	17.0	10.2	15.9	10.0
Male householder, no spouse present.............................	33.6	30.0	33.4	31.1	35.8	33.1
In labor force..	28.1	28.4	27.3	28.9	28.8	29.1
Not in labor force	5.5	1.6	6.1	2.2	7.0	4.0

[1] 2020 ACS 5-Year estimates. 1-Year estimates were not released for 2020 due to the impact of COVID-19 on data collection that year. Data is not comparable to previous years, which are based on 1-year estimates.

Table SD-11. School Enrollment and Educational Attainment, 2021

(Number, percent.)

Item	State	U.S.
Enrollment		
Total population 3 years and over, enrolled in school	217,810	79,453,524
Enrolled in nursery school or preschool (percent)	7.0	5.2
Enrolled in kindergarten (percent)	5.7	5.0
Enrolled in elementary school, grades 1-8 (percent)................................	44.2	41.3
Enrolled in high school, grades 9-12 (percent)................................	21.6	21.8
Enrolled in college or graduate school (percent)................................	21.4	26.7
Attainment		
Total population 25 years and over	590,377	228,193,464
Less than ninth grade (percent)................................	2.4	4.8
9th to 12th grade, no diploma (percent)	4.5	5.9
High school graduate, including equivalency (percent)................................	29.3	26.3
Some college, no degree (percent)	20.1	19.3
Associate's degree (percent)................................	12.0	8.8
Bachelor's degree (percent)................................	21.6	21.2
Graduate or professional degree (percent)................................	10.1	13.8
High school graduate or higher (percent)	93.1	89.4
Bachelor's degree or higher (percent)................................	31.7	35.0

Table SD-12. Public School Characteristics and Educational Indicators

(Number, percent; data derived from National Center of Education Statistics.)

Item	State	U.S.
Public Elementary and Secondary Schools		
Number of regular school districts, 2019-20	149	13,349
Number of operational schools, 2019-20................................	700	98,469
Percent charter schools	-	7.7
Total public school enrollment, Fall 2021	141,307	49,433,092
Percent charter school enrollment	NA	7.5
Student-teacher ratio, Fall 2019	14.1	15.9
Expenditures per student (unadjusted dollars), 2019-20	10,392	13,489
Four-year adjusted cohort graduation rate (ACGR), 2019-2020[1]................................	84.2	86.5
Students eligible for free or reduced-price lunch (percent), 2019-20................................	36.3	52.1
English language learners (percent), Fall 2020	4.8	10.3
Students age 3 to 21 served under IDEA, part B (percent), 2021-22	15.8	14.7

Public Schools by Type, 2019-20	Number	Percent of state public schools
Total number of schools................................	700	100.0
Special education................................	13	1.9
Vocational education................................	1	0.1
Alternative education................................	30	4.3

[1] Adjusted Cohort Graduation Rates (ACGR) differ from Averaged Freshmen Graduation Rates (AFGR).
NA = Not available.

Table SD-13. Reported Voting and Registration of the Voting-Age Population, November 2022

(Numbers in thousands, percent.)

Item	Total population	Total citizen population	Registered			Voted		
			Total registered	Percent registered (total population)	Percent registered (total citizen population)	Total voted	Percent voted (total population)	Percent voted (total citizen population)
U.S. Total	255,457	233,546	161,422	63.2	69.1	121,916	47.7	52.2
State Total	676	658	460	68.1	70.0	351	52.0	53.4
Sex								
Male	341	331	234	68.5	70.7	173	50.7	52.3
Female	334	327	226	67.7	69.2	178	53.3	54.5
Race								
White alone......................	588	578	425	72.2	73.4	332	56.4	57.3
White, non-Hispanic alone......................	573	569	421	73.5	74.1	330	57.6	58.0
Black alone......................	15	15	5	33.6	33.6	1	7.4	7.4
Asian alone......................	12	7	3	27.6	49.3	1	6.9	12.3
Hispanic (of any race)	19	14	5	24.6	33.8	3	14.4	19.8
White alone or in combination	593	583	427	71.9	73.1	334	56.2	57.2
Black alone or in combination......................	17	17	5	30.1	30.1	1	6.6	6.6
Asian alone or in combination......................	12	7	3	27.6	49.3	1	6.9	12.3
Age								
18 to 24 years......................	55	55	26	47.7	47.7	9	17.1	17.1
25 to 34 years......................	132	126	70	52.6	55.3	37	28.0	29.4
35 to 44 years......................	121	116	76	62.6	65.0	54	44.5	46.2
45 to 64 years......................	205	198	153	74.7	77.3	128	62.4	64.5
65 years and over......................	163	163	136	83.5	83.5	124	75.9	75.9

B = Base is less than 75,000 and therefore too small to show the derived measure.

Table SD-14. Health Indicators

(Number, rate as indicated in footnotes.)

Item	State	U.S.
Births		
Life Expectancy at Birth (years), 2020	76.7	77.0
Fertility Rate by State[1], 2021	68.6	56.3
Percent Home Births, 2021	1.3	1.4
Cesarean Delivery Rate[2], 2021	24.6	32.1
Preterm Birth Rate[3], 2021	10.5	10.5
Teen Birth Rate[4], 2021	17.0	13.9
Percentage of Babies Born Low Birthweight[5], 2021	7.1	8.5
Deaths[6]		
Heart Disease Mortality Rate, 2021......................	153.0	173.8
Cancer Mortality Rate, 2021......................	154.8	146.6
Stroke Mortality Rate, 2021......................	35.4	41.1
Diabetes Mortality Rate, 2021......................	28.9	25.4
Influenza/Pneumonia Mortality Rate, 2021	11.4	10.5
Suicide Mortality Rate, 2021......................	23.2	14.1
Drug Overdose Mortality Rate, 2021......................	12.6	33.6
Firearm Injury Mortality Rate, 2021......................	14.3	14.6
Homicide Mortality Rate, 2021......................	5.3	8.2
Disease and Illness		
Lifetime Asthma in Adults, 2020 (percent)......................	11.0	13.9
Lifetime Asthma in Children, 2020 (percent)[7]	NA	11.3
Diabetes in Adults, 2020 (percent)......................	7.0	8.2
Self-reported Obesity in Adults, 2021 (percent)......................	38.4	NA

SOURCE: National Center for Health Statistics, National Vital Statistics System 2020 data; https://wonder.cdc.gov.
[1] General fertility rate per 1,000 women aged 15–44.
[2] This represents the percentage of all live births that were cesarean deliveries.
[3] Babies born prior to 37 weeks of pregnancy (gestation).
[4] Number of births per 1,000 females aged 15–19
[5] Babies born weighing less than 2,500 grams or 5 lbs. 8oz.
[6] Death rates are the number of deaths per 100,000 total population.
[7] U.S. total includes data from 30 states and D.C.
NA = Not available.
- = Zero or rounds to zero.

Table SD-15. State Government Finances, 2021

(Dollar amounts in thousands, percent distribution.)

Item	Dollars	Percent distribution
Total Revenue	5,828,436	100.0
General revenue	5,205,080	89.3
Intergovernmental revenue	2,037,206	35.0
Taxes	2,149,543	36.9
General sales	1,273,575	21.9
Selective sales	510,407	8.8
License taxes	300,687	5.2
Individual income tax	-	-
Corporate income tax	53,960	0.9
Other taxes	10,914	0.2
Current charges	335,788	5.8
Miscellaneous general revenue	682,543	11.7
Utility revenue	1,977	-
Liquor stores revenue	-	-
Insurance trust revenue[1]	621,379	10.7
Total Expenditure	7,276,327	100.0
Intergovernmental expenditure	1,337,331	18.4
Direct expenditure	5,938,996	81.6
Current operation	3,777,308	51.9
Capital outlay	843,491	11.6
Insurance benefits and repayments	1,006,435	13.8
Assistance and subsidies	188,967	2.6
Interest on debt	122,795	1.7
Exhibit: Salaries and wages	823,828	11.3
Total Expenditure	7,276,327	100.0
General expenditure	6,250,843	85.9
Intergovernmental expenditure	1,337,331	18.4
Direct expenditure	4,913,512	67.5
General expenditure, by function:		
Education	1,741,171	23.9
Public welfare	1,737,683	23.9
Hospitals	41,406	0.6
Health	144,599	2.0
Highways	789,023	10.8
Police protection	61,392	0.8
Correction	146,314	2.0
Natural resources	172,338	2.4
Parks and recreation	42,298	0.6
Governmental administration	471,198	6.5
Interest on general debt	122,795	1.7
Other and unallocable	765,940	10.5
Utility expenditure	19,634	0.3
Liquor stores expenditure	-	-
Insurance trust expenditure	1,006,435	13.8
Debt at End of Fiscal Year	3,902,400	X
Cash and Security Holdings	21,698,019	X

X = Not applicable.
- = Zero or rounds to zero.
[1] Within insurance trust revenue, net earnings of state retirement systems is a calculated statistic (the item code in the data file is X08), and thus can be positive or negative. Net earnings is the sum of earnings on investments plus gains on investments minus losses on investments. The change made in 2002 for asset valuation from book to market value in accordance with Statement 34 of the Governmental Accounting Standards Board is reflected in the calculated statistics.

Table SD-16. State Government Tax Collections, 2022

(Dollars in thousands, percent.)

Item	Dollars	Percent distribution
Total Taxes	2,475,394	100.0
Property taxes	X	-
Sales and gross receipts	2,067,055	83.5
General sales and gross receipts	1,524,337	61.6
Selective sales and gross receipts	542,718	21.9
Alcoholic beverages	21,322	0.9
Amusements	12,323	0.5
Insurance premiums	97,571	3.9
Motor fuels	201,021	8.1
Pari-mutuels	113	-
Public utilities	4,024	0.2
Tobacco products	54,385	2.2
Other selective sales	151,959	6.1
Licenses	337,471	13.6
Alcoholic beverages	1,537	0.1
Amusements	5,473	0.2
Corporations in general	8,059	0.3
Hunting and fishing	37,940	1.5
Motor vehicle	93,882	3.8
Motor vehicle operators	6,145	0.2
Public utilities	X	-
Occupation and business, NEC	151,748	6.1
Other licenses	32,687	1.3
Income taxes	61,818	2.5
Individual income	X	-
Corporation net income	61,818	2.5
Other taxes	9,050	0.4
Death and gift	X	-
Documentary and stock transfer	195	-
Severance	8,035	0.3
Taxes, NEC	820	-

X = Not applicable.
- = Zero or rounds to zero.

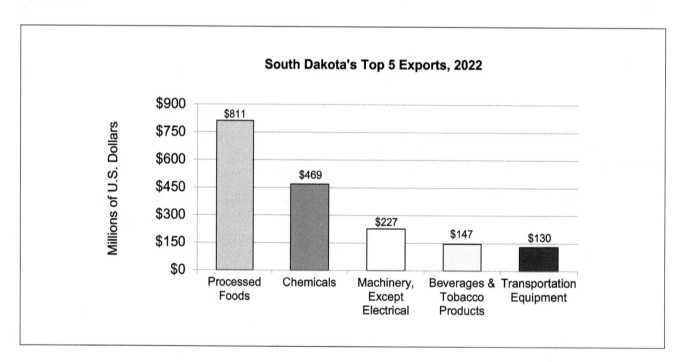

South Dakota's Top 5 Exports, 2022

TENNESSEE

Facts and Figures

Location: South central United States; bordered on the N by Kentucky and Virginia, on the E by North Carolina, on the S by Georgia, Alabama, and Mississippi, and on the W by Arkansas and Missouri

Area: 42,143 sq. mi. (109,151 sq. km.); rank—36th

Population: 7,051,339 (2022 est.); rank—15th

Principal Cities: capital—Nashville; largest—Nashville

Statehood: June 1, 1796; 16th state

U.S. Congress: 2 senators, 9 representatives

State Motto: Agriculture and Commerce

State Song: "The Tennessee Waltz"

State Nickname: The Volunteer State

Abbreviations: TN; Tenn.

State Symbols: flower—iris; tree—yellow poplar (tulip poplar); bird—mockingbird

At a Glance

- With an increase in population of 11.1 percent, Tennessee ranked 17th among the states in growth from 2010 to 2022.

- Tennessee's median household income in 2021 was $59,695, and 13.6 percent of the population lived below the poverty level.

- In 2021, 10.0 percent of Tennesseans did not have health insurance, compared to 8.6 percent of the total U.S. population.

- Tennessee's homicide rate was 12.2 deaths per 100,000 population, which ranked 9th in the country. The U.S. homicide rate was 8.2 deaths per 100,000 population.

- Tennessee's unemployment rate of 3.4 percent ranked 26th among the states in 2022 and was just below the national unemployment rate of 3.6 percent.

Table TN-1. Population by Age, Sex, Race, and Hispanic Origin

(Number, percent, except where noted.)

Sex, age, race, and Hispanic origin	2010	2020	2022	Percent change, 2010–2022
Total Population..	6,346,105	6,910,786	7,051,339	11.1
Percent of total U.S. population	2.1	2.1	2.1	X
Sex				
Male	3,093,504	3,398,764	3,462,358	11.9
Female	3,252,601	3,512,022	3,588,981	10.3
Age				
Under 5 years...	407,813	403,308	405,421	-0.6
Under 18 years..	1,496,001	1,526,613	1,538,137	2.8
18 to 64 years..	3,996,642	4,231,553	4,292,213	7.4
65 years and over	853,462	1,152,620	1,220,989	43.1
Median age (years)...	38.0	38.9	39.1	2.9
Race and Hispanic Origin				
One race				
White	5,056,311	5,410,392	5,521,401	9.2
Black	1,068,010	1,177,107	1,180,864	10.6
American Indian and Alaska Native	26,256	33,865	36,702	39.8
Asian	93,897	137,758	146,423	55.9
Native Hawaiian or Other Pacific Islander	5,426	7,208	7,744	42.7
Two or more races	96,205	144,456	158,205	64.4
Hispanic (of any race)..	290,059	407,370	449,510	55.0

NOTE: Population figures for 2022 are July 1 estimates. The 2010 and 2020 estimates are taken from the respective censuses.
- = Zero or rounds to zero.
X = Not applicable.

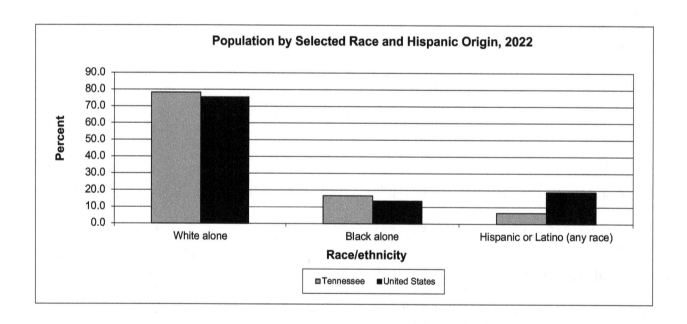

Table TN-2. Marital Status

(Number, percent distribution.)

Sex, age, race, and Hispanic origin	2000	2010	2021
Males, 15 Years and Over	2,169,327	2,461,573	2,766,108
Never married	26.6	31.4	33.9
Now married, except separated..	58.9	52.2	50.7
Separated...	1.7	2.1	1.7
Widowed...	2.5	2.7	3.1
Divorced...	10.4	11.7	10.7
Females, 15 Years and Over	2,353,303	2,652,823	2,941,324
Never married	20.7	25.3	28.5
Now married, except separated..	53.6	47.9	47.1
Separated...	2.3	2.7	2.1
Widowed...	11.2	10.3	9.3
Divorced...	12.2	13.7	13.0

Table TN-3. Households and Housing Characteristics

(Number, percent, dollars.)

Item	2000	2010	2021	Average annual percent change, 2010–2021
Total Households	2,232,905	2,440,663	2,770,395	1.2
Family households	1,547,835	1,644,896	1,782,813	0.8
Married-couple family	1,173,960	1,195,406	1,303,575	0.8
Other family	373,875	449,490	479,238	0.6
Male householder, no wife present	85,976	106,616	131,888	2.2
Female householder, no husband present	287,899	342,874	347,350	0.1
Nonfamily households	685,070	795,767	987,582	2.2
Householder living alone	576,401	675,565	807,862	1.8
Householder not living alone	108,669	120,202	179,720	4.5
Housing Characteristics				
Total housing units	2,439,443	2,815,087	3,087,992	0.9
Occupied housing units	2,232,905	2,440,663	2,770,395	1.2
Owner occupied	1,561,363	1,662,768	1,869,046	1.1
Renter occupied	671,542	777,895	901,349	1.4
Average household size	2.48	2.54	2.46	-0.3
Financial Characteristics				
Median gross rent of renter-occupied housing	505	697	981	3.7
Median monthly owner costs for housing units with a mortgage	882	1,161	1,333	1.3
Median value of owner-occupied housing units	93,000	139,000	235,200	6.3

Table TN-4. Migration, Origin, and Language

(Number, percent.)

Characteristic	State 2021	U.S. 2021
Residence 1 Year Ago		
Population 1 year and over	6,899,165	328,464,538
Same house	86.3	87.2
Different house in the U.S.	13.4	12.3
Same county	6.7	6.7
Different county	6.7	5.7
Same state	3.5	3.3
Different state	3.2	2.4
Abroad	0.3	0.4
Place of Birth		
Native born	6,604,453	286,623,642
Male	48.9	49.7
Female	51.1	50.3
Foreign born	370,765	45,270,103
Male	50.4	48.7
Female	49.6	51.3
Foreign born; naturalized U.S. citizen	151,036	24,044,083
Male	48.0	46.4
Female	52.0	53.6
Foreign born; not a U.S. citizen	219,729	21,226,020
Male	52.0	51.2
Female	48.0	48.8
Entered 2010 or later	39.1	28.1
Entered 2000 to 2009	26.5	23.7
Entered before 2000	34.4	48.2
World Region of Birth, Foreign		
Foreign-born population, excluding population born at sea	370,765	45,269,644
Europe	9.8	10.7
Asia	27.8	31.0
Africa	11.9	5.7
Oceania	0.6	0.6
Latin America	47.2	50.1
North America	2.8	1.7
Language Spoken at Home and Ability to Speak English		
Population 5 years and over	6,577,960	313,232,500
English only	92.5	78.4
Language other than English	7.5	21.6
Speaks English less than "very well"	3.2	0.0

Table TN-5. Median Income and Poverty Status, 2021

(Number, percent, except as noted.)

Characteristic	State		U.S.	
	Number	Percent	Number	Percent
Median Income				
Households (dollars)...	59,695	X	69,717	X
Families (dollars)	74,709	X	85,806	X
Below Poverty Level (All People)	927,587	13.6	41,393,176	12.8
Sex				
Male	407,132	12.3	18,518,155	11.6
Female	520,455	14.9	22,875,021	13.9
Age				
Under 18 years..	272,142	18.1	12,243,219	16.9
Related children under 18 years................................	266,785	17.8	11,985,424	16.6
18 to 64 years	537,029	13.0	23,526,341	11.9
65 years and over	118,416	10.2	5,623,616	10.3

X = Not applicable.

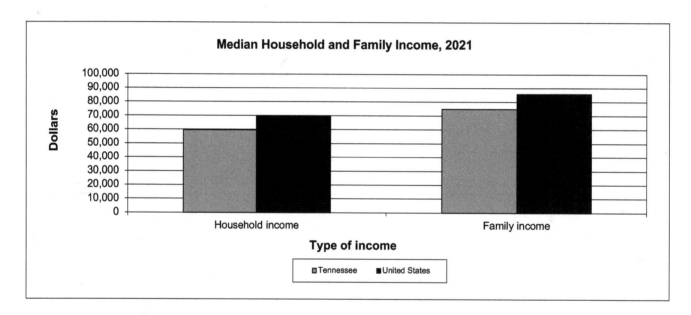

Table TN-6. Health Insurance Coverage Status for the Civilian Noninstitutionalized Population and Children Under 19 Years of Age

(Number, percent.)

Item	2011	2012	2013	2014	2015	2016	2017	2018	2019	2020 [2]	2021
Civilian Noninstitutionalized Population	6,302,351	6,354,629	6,394,644	6,448,737	6,496,300	6,546,914	6,612,552	6,667,784	6,719,315	6,664,134	6,872,677
Covered by Private or Public Insurance											
Number..	5,379,701	5,472,509	5,507,982	5,672,418	5,828,883	5,954,604	5,983,410	5,992,919	6,037,668	6,014,822	6,186,573
Percent..	85.4	86.1	86.1	88.0	89.7	91.0	90.5	89.9	89.9	90.3	90.0
Uninsured											
Number..	922,650	882,120	886,662	776,319	667,417	592,310	629,142	674,865	681,647	649,312	686,104
Percent..	14.6	13.9	13.9	12.0	10.3	9.0	9.5	10.1	10.1	9.7	10.0
Percent in the U.S. not covered....................	15.1	14.8	14.5	11.7	9.4	8.6	8.7	8.9	9.2	8.7	8.6
Children Under 19 Years of Age[1]	1,487,779	1,490,249	1,489,574	1,489,620	1,490,949	1,500,902	1,600,422	1,598,672	1,600,213	1,591,799	1,623,277
Covered by Private or Public Insurance											
Number..	1,402,852	1,405,719	1,404,287	1,412,007	1,428,845	1,447,865	1,529,643	1,515,748	1,519,741	1,513,221	1,543,151
Percent..	94.3	94.3	94.3	94.8	95.8	96.5	95.6	94.8	95.0	95.1	95.1
Uninsured											
Number..	84,927	84,530	85,287	77,613	62,104	53,037	70,779	82,924	80,472	78,578	80,126
Percent..	5.7	5.7	5.7	5.2	4.2	3.5	4.4	5.2	5.0	4.9	4.9
Percent in the U.S. not covered....................	7.5	7.2	7.1	6.0	4.8	4.5	5.0	5.2	5.7	5.2	5.4

[1] Data for years prior to 2017 are for individuals under 18 years of age.
[2] 2020 ACS 5-Year estimates. 1-Year estimates were not released for 2020 due to the impact of COVID-19 on data collection that year. Data is not comparable to previous years, which are based on 1-year estimates.

Table TN-7. Employment Status by Demographic Group, 2022

(Numbers in thousands, percent.)

Characteristic	Civilian noninstitutional population	Civilian labor force		Employed		Unemployed	
		Number	Percent of population	Number	Percent of population	Number	Percent of population
Total..	5,581	3,342	59.9	3,226	57.8	116	3.5
Sex							
Male..	2,683	1,773	66.1	1,723	64.2	49	2.8
Female.......................................	2,898	1,569	54.2	1,503	51.9	67	4.2
Race, Sex, and Hispanic Origin							
White...	4,515	2,700	59.8	2,619	58.0	81	3.0
Male..	2,190	1,460	66.7	1,426	65.1	34	2.3
Female.......................................	2,325	1,240	53.3	1,193	51.3	47	3.8
Black or African American.................	894	538	60.2	506	56.6	32	6.0
Male..	406	257	63.4	243	59.9	14	5.5
Female.......................................	489	281	57.5	263	53.8	18	6.4
Hispanic or Latino ethnicity[1]..............	324	236	73.1	227	70.2	9	3.9
Male..	175	148	84.8	145	82.7	4	2.5
Female.......................................	NA	NA	NA	NA	NA	NA	NA
Age							
16 to 19 years..............................	NA	NA	NA	NA	NA	NA	NA
20 to 24 years..............................	406	301	74.2	283	69.9	18	5.8
25 to 34 years..............................	947	786	83.0	753	79.5	33	4.2
35 to 44 years..............................	913	752	82.3	730	79.9	22	2.9
45 to 54 years..............................	857	675	78.8	664	77.5	11	1.6
55 to 64 years..............................	843	494	58.7	481	57.0	14	2.8
65 years and over..........................	1,279	211	16.5	205	16.0	5	2.5

NOTE: Data in Table 7 are from the Current Population Survey (CPS) and do not match the estimates in Table 8. See notes and definitions for further information.
[1] May be of any race.

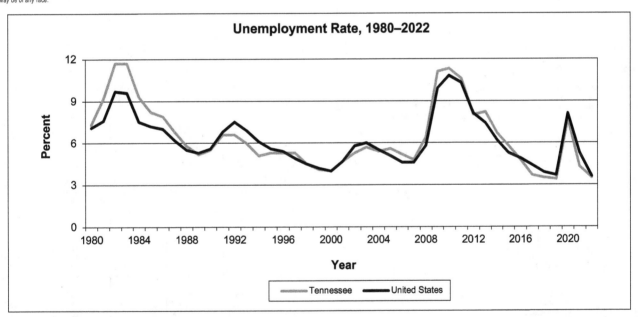

Unemployment Rate, 1980–2022

Legend: Tennessee — United States

Table TN-8. Employment Status of the Civilian Noninstitutional Population Age 16 Years and Over

(Number, percent.)

Year	Civilian labor force	Civilian participation rate	Employed	Unemployed	Unemployment rate
2010..	3,093,118	62.8	2,789,056	304,062	9.8
2011..	3,117,492	62.7	2,833,278	284,214	9.1
2012..	3,096,322	61.7	2,849,727	246,595	8.0
2013..	3,078,892	60.8	2,840,127	238,765	7.8
2014..	3,043,573	59.6	2,842,540	201,033	6.6
2015..	3,074,216	59.6	2,902,684	171,532	5.6
2016..	3,136,399	60.2	2,987,679	148,720	4.7
2017..	3,197,032	60.5	3,077,515	119,517	3.7
2018..	3,260,862	61	3,147,030	113,832	3.5
2019..	3,339,543	61.9	3,226,045	113,498	3.4
2020..	3,299,424	60.5	3,055,830	243,594	7.4
2021..	3,327,966	60.4	3,185,263	142,703	4.3
2022..	3,352,030	59.9	3,238,559	113,471	3.4

Table TN-9. Employment and Average Wages by Industry

(Estimates are based on the 2012 North American Industry Classification System [NAICS].)

Industry	2014	2015	2016	2017	2018	2019	2020	2021
	Number of Jobs							
Wage and Salary Employment by Industry........................	2,903,868	2,974,822	3,039,254	3,081,388	3,132,827	3,190,477	3,075,014	3,175,654
Farm Wage and Salary Employment................................	9,927	11,141	9,177	10,626	10,796	10,587	10,586	10,787
Nonfarm Wage and Salary Employment...........................	2,893,941	2,963,681	3,030,077	3,070,762	3,122,031	3,179,890	3,064,428	3,164,867
Private wage and salary employment.............................	2,448,513	2,521,355	2,585,872	2,624,991	2,670,469	2,725,842	2,612,998	2,716,377
Forestry, fishing, and related activities.......................	5,030	5,112	4,999	4,971	5,120	5,079	4,782	4,416
Mining..	3,430	3,457	3,061	3,276	3,511	3,631	3,378	3,467
Utilities...	3,380	3,366	3,395	3,577	3,546	3,633	3,652	3,869
Construction	109,155	115,688	117,844	123,092	127,456	133,276	133,248	139,505
Manufacturing..	325,377	332,659	343,890	348,777	351,241	355,242	335,227	349,775
Durable goods manufacturing.............................	205,524	210,630	219,138	221,877	224,894	227,581	211,076	221,537
Nondurable goods manufacturing........................	119,853	122,029	124,752	126,900	126,347	127,661	124,151	128,238
Wholesale trade	123,636	121,540	120,376	121,808	119,982	121,608	118,687	121,468
Retail trade..	322,890	327,928	335,900	337,984	339,531	336,320	327,044	336,313
Transportation and warehousing.............................	147,365	155,367	162,474	163,404	168,892	180,897	185,620	195,487
Information	43,349	43,622	44,961	45,507	44,859	45,120	42,967	46,625
Finance and insurance..	109,194	111,288	113,290	116,054	117,866	123,999	125,808	126,584
Real estate and rental and leasing...........................	34,943	37,129	38,776	40,319	41,606	43,175	40,889	42,637
Professional, scientific, and technical services	120,908	129,122	132,943	137,237	141,945	147,459	148,441	159,771
Management of companies and enterprises.................	37,306	41,468	44,066	44,796	50,104	50,955	49,338	51,504
Administrative and waste services...........................	216,801	224,740	229,108	226,877	227,724	230,050	219,143	229,108
Educational services	57,792	59,145	61,407	62,058	63,324	64,649	63,430	68,766
Health care and social assistance............................	350,288	360,644	367,745	372,876	377,007	382,003	377,570	380,245
Arts, entertainment, and recreation.........................	33,449	34,795	36,235	38,471	40,402	42,952	34,316	38,002
Accommodation and food services...........................	265,117	274,868	285,354	292,753	299,675	306,749	260,801	279,036
Other services, except public administration...............	139,103	139,417	140,048	141,154	146,678	149,045	138,657	139,799
Government and government enterprises......................	445,428	442,326	444,205	445,771	451,562	454,048	451,430	448,490
	Dollars							
Average Wages and Salaries by Industry	44,706	46,191	46,929	48,322	50,004	51,206	54,427	58,405
Average Farm Wages and Salaries	22,681	16,509	23,000	18,027	19,354	15,599	15,152	14,938
Average Nonfarm Wages and Salaries	44,782	46,303	47,002	48,427	50,110	51,324	54,563	58,553
Average private wages and salaries.............................	45,222	46,852	47,538	48,935	50,676	51,913	55,385	59,582
Forestry, fishing, and related activities.......................	25,861	26,648	28,616	29,113	30,341	32,161	34,130	36,457
Mining..	67,845	68,194	67,512	67,586	72,357	73,060	75,426	82,514
Utilities...	67,995	70,785	71,788	72,503	76,245	79,591	84,608	86,882
Construction	49,910	52,845	54,488	56,584	57,045	58,765	62,272	65,036
Manufacturing..	56,296	57,344	58,104	59,531	59,519	60,318	63,136	65,125
Durable goods manufacturing.............................	55,124	56,268	57,331	58,767	59,844	60,740	63,372	65,284
Nondurable goods manufacturing........................	58,307	59,201	59,463	60,865	58,941	59,566	62,735	64,849
Wholesale trade	64,271	67,297	70,120	70,828	72,531	74,262	77,953	84,672
Retail trade..	28,629	29,532	29,994	30,746	31,738	32,132	34,799	38,763
Transportation and warehousing.............................	51,231	52,646	53,035	54,950	56,894	56,903	59,572	65,231
Information	61,755	62,689	64,380	68,480	73,855	75,557	81,367	91,223
Finance and insurance..	74,945	75,997	77,912	79,722	86,608	86,270	93,946	103,703
Real estate and rental and leasing...........................	44,661	46,732	48,664	48,975	51,116	53,740	57,739	62,011
Professional, scientific, and technical services	72,042	75,858	75,701	75,515	80,010	82,949	87,427	92,129
Management of companies and enterprises.................	97,031	100,547	98,574	101,866	109,629	116,460	117,061	126,816
Administrative and waste services...........................	32,317	33,088	33,827	35,421	36,321	38,305	40,816	44,605
Educational services	36,349	36,903	37,476	38,365	39,020	40,339	43,198	41,669
Health care and social assistance............................	47,796	49,708	49,865	51,450	52,617	53,575	56,826	60,431
Arts, entertainment, and recreation.........................	47,047	53,613	50,397	53,822	55,741	52,504	51,110	55,404
Accommodation and food services...........................	18,869	19,417	20,214	20,947	22,396	23,046	22,103	27,057
Other services, except public administration...............	32,008	33,331	34,266	35,619	36,434	37,534	41,484	43,950
Government and government enterprises......................	42,358	43,173	43,882	45,437	46,764	47,791	49,806	52,321

Table TN-10. Employment Characteristics by Family Type

(Number, percent.)

Family type and labor force status	2019 Total	2019 Families with own children under 18 years	2020 [1] Total	2020 [1] Families with own children under 18 years	2021 Total	2021 Families with own children under 18 years
All Families.........................	1,727,895	678,657	1,726,939	694,368	1,782,813	692,832
FAMILY TYPE AND LABOR FORCE STATUS						
Opposite-Sex Married-Couple Families.....................	1,274,887	445,998	1,261,822	456,864	1,293,009	459,896
Both husband and wife in labor force..............	48.6	66.7	49.2	66.4	48.8	66.0
Husband in labor force, wife not in labor force	21.6	26.4	22.0	27.3	22.1	27.5
Wife in labor force, husband not in labor force	8.7	4.2	8.5	4.2	8.4	4.6
Both husband and wife not in labor force............	20.3	2.1	20.3	2.0	20.7	1.9
Other Families	453,008	232,659	455,977	235,461	479,238	230,432
Female householder, no spouse present	72.0	73.5	73.3	74.8	72.5	75.9
In labor force............	49.0	61.3	49.5	61.4	48.6	61.2
Not in labor force	23.0	12.2	23.9	13.4	23.8	14.7
Male householder, no spouse present............	28.0	26.5	26.7	25.2	27.5	24.1
In labor force............	21.6	24.4	19.9	22.7	20.7	22.1
Not in labor force............	6.5	2.1	6.8	2.5	6.8	2.0

[1] 2020 ACS 5-Year estimates. 1-Year estimates were not released for 2020 due to the impact of COVID-19 on data collection that year. Data is not comparable to previous years, which are based on 1-year estimates.

Table TN-11. School Enrollment and Educational Attainment, 2021

(Number, percent.)

Item	State	U.S.
Enrollment		
Total population 3 years and over, enrolled in school	1,571,789	79,453,524
Enrolled in nursery school or preschool (percent)	4.9	5.2
Enrolled in kindergarten (percent)........................	5.3	5.0
Enrolled in elementary school, grades 1-8 (percent)........................	43.0	41.3
Enrolled in high school, grades 9-12 (percent)........................	22.6	21.8
Enrolled in college or graduate school (percent)........................	24.2	26.7
Attainment		
Total population 25 years and over	4,814,533	228,193,464
Less than ninth grade (percent)........................	3.8	4.8
9th to 12th grade, no diploma (percent)	6.5	5.9
High school graduate, including equivalency (percent)........................	31.2	26.3
Some college, no degree (percent)........................	20.3	19.3
Associate's degree (percent)........................	7.8	8.8
Bachelor's degree (percent)........................	19.2	21.2
Graduate or professional degree (percent)........................	11.3	13.8
High school graduate or higher (percent)........................	89.7	89.4
Bachelor's degree or higher (percent)........................	30.5	35.0

Table TN-12. Public School Characteristics and Educational Indicators

(Number, percent; data derived from National Center of Education Statistics.)

Item	State	U.S.
Public Elementary and Secondary Schools		
Number of regular school districts, 2019-20	147	13,349
Number of operational schools, 2019-20........................	1,878	98,469
Percent charter schools	6.3	7.7
Total public school enrollment, Fall 2021	996,709	49,433,092
Percent charter school enrollment	4.4	7.5
Student-teacher ratio, Fall 2019	15.7	15.9
Expenditures per student (unadjusted dollars), 2019-20	9,974	13,489
Four-year adjusted cohort graduation rate (ACGR), 2019-2020[1]........................	90.4	86.5
Students eligible for free or reduced-price lunch (percent), 2019-20........................	58.8	52.1
English language learners (percent), Fall 2020	5.4	10.3
Students age 3 to 21 served under IDEA, part B (percent), 2021-22........................	12.8	14.7

Public Schools by Type, 2019-20	Number	Percent of state public schools
Total number of schools........................	1,878	100.0
Special education........................	16	0.9
Vocational education........................	11	0.6
Alternative education........................	21	1.1

[1] Adjusted Cohort Graduation Rates (ACGR) differ from Averaged Freshmen Graduation Rates (AFGR).

Table TN-13. Reported Voting and Registration of the Voting-Age Population, November 2022

(Numbers in thousands, percent.)

Item	Total population	Total citizen population	Registered			Voted		
			Total registered	Percent registered (total population)	Percent registered (total citizen population)	Total voted	Percent voted (total population)	Percent voted (total citizen population)
U.S. Total	255,457	233,546	161,422	63.2	69.1	121,916	47.7	52.2
State Total...........................	5,391	5,145	3,467	64.3	67.4	2,291	42.5	44.5
Sex								
Male	2,570	2,440	1,654	64.4	67.8	1,108	43.1	45.4
Female	2,821	2,705	1,812	64.2	67.0	1,183	41.9	43.7
Race								
White alone...........................	4,350	4,179	2,867	65.9	68.6	1,894	43.5	45.3
White, non-Hispanic alone	4,025	4,009	2,778	69.0	69.3	1,839	45.7	45.9
Black alone	843	804	527	62.5	65.5	338	40.1	42.0
Asian alone	118	81	24	20.4	29.7	18	15.4	22.4
Hispanic (of any race).................	325	171	89	27.4	52.2	55	17.0	32.3
White alone or in combination	4,403	4,232	2,896	65.8	68.4	1,915	43.5	45.3
Black alone or in combination...................	856	818	535	62.5	65.4	346	40.4	42.3
Asian alone or in combination..................	148	112	45	30.5	40.5	31	20.6	27.3
Age								
18 to 24 years........................	589	544	216	36.7	39.8	128	21.8	23.6
25 to 34 years........................	881	815	474	53.8	58.2	256	29.0	31.4
35 to 44 years........................	929	863	609	65.6	70.6	330	35.5	38.2
45 to 64 years........................	1,701	1,641	1,170	68.8	71.3	857	50.4	52.3
65 years and over	1,290	1,283	997	77.2	77.7	719	55.7	56.1

Table TN-14. Health Indicators

(Number, rate as indicated in footnotes.)

Item	State	U.S.
Births		
Life Expectancy at Birth (years), 2020	73.8	77.0
Fertility Rate by State[1], 2021	59.8	56.3
Percent Home Births, 2021	1.6	1.4
Cesarean Delivery Rate[2], 2021	32.4	32.1
Preterm Birth Rate[3], 2021	11.3	10.5
Teen Birth Rate[4], 2021	21.5	13.9
Percentage of Babies Born Low Birthweight[5], 2021	9.3	8.5
Deaths[6]		
Heart Disease Mortality Rate, 2021...	223.8	173.8
Cancer Mortality Rate, 2021..	166.3	146.6
Stroke Mortality Rate, 2021	46.2	41.1
Diabetes Mortality Rate, 2021..	31.4	25.4
Influenza/Pneumonia Mortality Rate, 2021	14.9	10.5
Suicide Mortality Rate, 2021..	17.0	14.1
Drug Overdose Mortality Rate, 2021..	56.6	33.6
Firearm Injury Mortality Rate, 2021	22.8	14.6
Homicide Mortality Rate, 2021..	12.2	8.2
Disease and Illness		
Lifetime Asthma in Adults, 2020 (percent)..	15.7	13.9
Lifetime Asthma in Children, 2020 (percent)[7]	NA	11.3
Diabetes in Adults, 2020 (percent)..	12.5	8.2
Self-reported Obesity in Adults, 2021 (percent)...	35.0	NA

SOURCE: National Center for Health Statistics, National Vital Statistics System 2020 data; https://wonder.cdc.gov.
[1] General fertility rate per 1,000 women aged 15–44.
[2] This represents the percentage of all live births that were cesarean deliveries.
[3] Babies born prior to 37 weeks of pregnancy (gestation).
[4] Number of births per 1,000 females aged 15–19
[5] Babies born weighing less than 2,500 grams or 5 lbs. 8oz.
[6] Death rates are the number of deaths per 100,000 total population.
[7] U.S. total includes data from 30 states and D.C.
NA = Not available.
- = Zero or rounds to zero.

Table TN-15. State Government Finances, 2021

(Dollar amounts in thousands, percent distribution.)

Item	Dollars	Percent distribution
Total Revenue	43,381,352	100.0
General revenue	41,714,603	96.2
Intergovernmental revenue	17,340,564	40.0
Taxes	19,977,968	46.1
General sales	11,060,457	25.5
Selective sales	3,432,404	7.9
License taxes	2,333,130	5.4
Individual income tax	179,379	0.4
Corporate income tax	2,564,458	5.9
Other taxes	408,140	0.9
Current charges	2,076,395	4.8
Miscellaneous general revenue	2,319,676	5.3
Utility revenue	-	-
Liquor stores revenue	-	-
Insurance trust revenue[1]	1,666,749	3.8
Total Expenditure	42,796,545	100.0
Intergovernmental expenditure	10,168,849	23.8
Direct expenditure	32,627,696	76.2
Current operation	24,083,812	56.3
Capital outlay	1,953,060	4.6
Insurance benefits and repayments	4,251,474	9.9
Assistance and subsidies	2,077,576	4.9
Interest on debt	261,774	0.6
Exhibit: Salaries and wages	4,532,019	10.6
Total Expenditure	42,796,545	100.0
General expenditure	38,544,422	90.1
Intergovernmental expenditure	10,168,849	23.8
Direct expenditure	28,375,573	66.3
General expenditure, by function:		
Education	12,013,449	28.1
Public welfare	14,218,433	33.2
Hospitals	433,043	1.0
Health	1,942,161	4.5
Highways	1,990,366	4.7
Police protection	276,704	0.6
Correction	1,015,067	2.4
Natural resources	539,136	1.3
Parks and recreation	109,654	0.3
Governmental administration	2,998,832	7.0
Interest on general debt	261,774	0.6
Other and unallocable	2,724,908	6.4
Utility expenditure	966	-
Liquor stores expenditure	-	
Insurance trust expenditure	4,251,474	9.9
Debt at End of Fiscal Year	6,919,362	X
Cash and Security Holdings	91,532,546	X

X = Not applicable.
- = Zero or rounds to zero.
[1] Within insurance trust revenue, net earnings of state retirement systems is a calculated statistic (the item code in the data file is X08), and thus can be positive or negative. Net earnings is the sum of earnings on investments plus gains on investments minus losses on investments. The change made in 2002 for asset valuation from book to market value in accordance with Statement 34 of the Governmental Accounting Standards Board is reflected in the calculated statistics.

Table TN-16. State Government Tax Collections, 2022

(Dollars in thousands, percent.)

Item	Dollars	Percent distribution
Total Taxes	22,650,165	100.0
Property taxes	X	-
Sales and gross receipts	16,585,002	73.2
General sales and gross receipts	12,887,107	56.9
Selective sales and gross receipts	3,697,895	16.3
Alcoholic beverages	292,498	1.3
Amusements	46,079	0.2
Insurance premiums	1,223,183	5.4
Motor fuels	1,274,055	5.6
Pari-mutuels	X	-
Public utilities	6,506	-
Tobacco products	228,231	1.0
Other selective sales	627,343	2.8
Licenses	2,517,390	11.1
Alcoholic beverages	1,842	-
Amusements	308	-
Corporations in general	1,535,207	6.8
Hunting and fishing	43,126	0.2
Motor vehicle	398,576	1.8
Motor vehicle operators	35,625	0.2
Public utilities	6,099	-
Occupation and business, NEC	486,472	2.1
Other licenses	10,135	-
Income taxes	3,008,777	13.3
Individual income	9,480	-
Corporation net income	2,999,297	13.2
Other taxes	538,996	2.4
Death and gift	640	-
Documentary and stock transfer	522,660	2.3
Severance	826	-
Taxes, NEC	14,870	0.1

X = Not applicable.
- = Zero or rounds to zero.

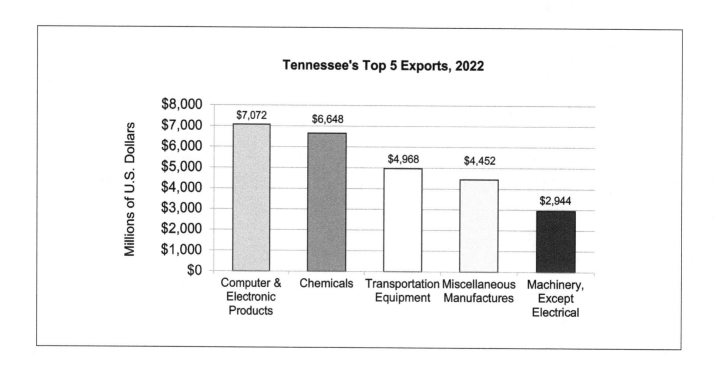

TEXAS

Facts and Figures

Location: West South Central United States; bordered on the N by Oklahoma, on the E by Arkansas and Louisiana, on the S by Mexico and the Gulf of Mexico, and on the W by Mexico and New Mexico

Area: 268,581 sq. mi. (695,621 sq. km.); rank—2nd

Population: 30,029,572 (2022 est.); rank—2nd

Principal Cities: capital—Austin; largest—Houston

Statehood: December 29, 1845; 28th state

U.S. Congress: 2 senators, 36 representatives

State Motto: Friendship

State Song: "Texas, Our Texas"

State Nickname: The Lone Star State

Abbreviations: TX; Tex.

State Symbols: flower—bluebonnet; tree—pecan; bird—mockingbird

At a Glance

- With an increase in population of 19.4 percent, Texas ranked 3rd among the states in growth from 2010 to 2022.

- In 2022, Texas ranked 2nd for the highest percent of its population under 18 years old (24.8 percent).

- Texas's median household income in 2021 was $66,963, and 14.2 percent of the population lived below the poverty level.

- Texas was the state with the highest percent of uninsured residents in 2021, with 18.0 percent of Texans not having health insurance.

- In 2021, Texas ranked 41st among states for its drug overdose death rate (21.1 deaths per 100,000 population). The U.S. rate was 32.4 deaths per 100,000 population.

Table TX-1. Population by Age, Sex, Race, and Hispanic Origin

(Number, percent, except where noted.)

Sex, age, race, and Hispanic origin	2010	2020	2022	Percent change, 2010–2022
Total Population..	25,145,561	29,145,428	30,029,572	19.4
Percent of total U.S. population	8.1	8.8	9.0	X
Sex				
Male..	12,472,280	14,587,661	15,019,450	20.4
Female	12,673,281	14,557,767	15,010,122	18.4
Age				
Under 5 years..	1,928,473	1,929,166	1,902,639	-1.3
Under 18 years..	6,865,824	7,408,775	7,456,338	8.6
18 to 64 years...	15,677,851	17,994,938	18,546,181	18.3
65 years and over	2,601,886	3,741,715	4,027,053	54.8
Median age (years)	33.6	35.1	35.5	5.7
Race and Hispanic Origin				
One race				
White	20,389,793	22,789,462	23,242,116	14.0
Black	3,070,440	3,817,370	4,020,772	31.0
American Indian and Alaska Native	251,209	304,937	322,443	28.4
Asian	1,000,473	1,569,704	1,716,675	71.6
Native Hawaiian or Other Pacific Islander	31,242	44,841	48,656	55.7
Two or more races	402,404	619,114	678,910	68.7
Hispanic (of any race)...	9,460,921	11,627,225	12,068,549	27.6

NOTE: Population figures for 2022 are July 1 estimates. The 2010 and 2020 estimates are taken from the respective censuses.
- = Zero or rounds to zero.
X = Not applicable.

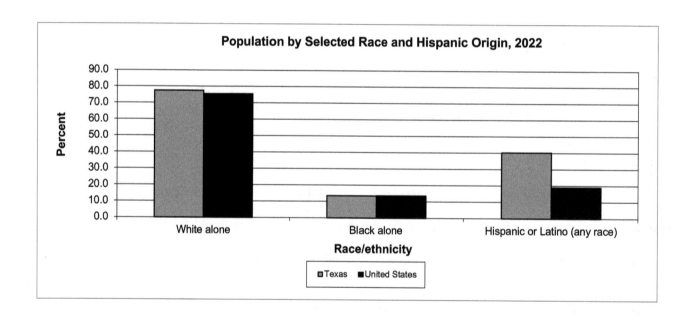

Table TX-2. Marital Status

(Number, percent distribution.)

Sex, age, race, and Hispanic origin	2000	2010	2021
Males, 15 Years and Over	7,820,248	9,587,343	11,592,742
Never married	28.6	34.6	36.2
Now married, except separated..	58.8	51.6	51.3
Separated...	2.0	2.3	1.8
Widowed..	2.1	2.2	2.3
Divorced..	8.5	9.4	8.6
Females, 15 Years and Over	8,117,395	9,903,147	11,781,239
Never married	22.6	27.6	30.8
Now married, except separated..	54.3	48.5	48.2
Separated...	2.9	3.3	2.4
Widowed..	9.1	8.1	7.3
Divorced..	11.0	12.5	11.3

Table TX-3. Households and Housing Characteristics

(Number, percent, dollars.)

Item	2000	2010	2021	Average annual percent change, 2010–2021
Total Households...	7,393,354	8,738,664	10,796,247	2.1
Family households	5,247,794	6,091,590	7,373,185	1.9
Married-couple family	3,989,741	4,386,996	5,341,490	2.0
Other family	1,258,053	1,704,594	2,031,695	1.7
Male householder, no wife present...............................	320,464	436,727	571,198	2.8
Female householder, no husband present.....................	937,489	1,267,867	1,460,497	1.4
Nonfamily households	2,145,560	2,647,074	3,423,062	2.7
Householder living alone...	1,752,141	2,166,469	2,768,892	2.5
Householder not living alone..	393,419	480,605	654,170	3.3
Housing Characteristics				
Total housing units	8,157,575	9,996,209	11,867,820	1.7
Occupied housing units	7,393,354	8,738,664	10,796,247	2.1
Owner occupied	4,716,959	5,555,903	6,761,002	2.0
Renter occupied	2,676,395	3,182,761	4,035,245	2.4
Average household size...	2.74	2.82	2.68	-0.5
Financial Characteristics				
Median gross rent of renter-occupied housing	574	801	1,167	4.2
Median monthly owner costs for housing units with a mortgage ...	986	1,402	1,765	2.4
Median value of owner-occupied housing units.................	82,500	128,100	237,400	7.8

Table TX-4. Migration, Origin, and Language

(Number, percent.)

Characteristic	State 2021	U.S. 2021
Residence 1 Year Ago		
Population 1 year and over	29,170,380	328,464,538
Same house	86.0	87.2
Different house in the U.S.	13.4	12.3
Same county	7.5	6.7
Different county	5.9	5.7
Same state	3.8	3.3
Different state	2.0	2.4
Abroad	0.6	0.4
Place of Birth		
Native born	24,435,809	286,623,642
Male	49.8	49.7
Female	50.2	50.3
Foreign born	5,092,132	45,270,103
Male	50.2	48.7
Female	49.8	51.3
Foreign born; naturalized U.S. citizen..	2,124,656	24,044,083
Male	48.5	46.4
Female	51.5	53.6
Foreign born; not a U.S. citizen..	2,967,476	21,226,020
Male	51.5	51.2
Female	48.5	48.8
Entered 2010 or later	31.3	28.1
Entered 2000 to 2009	24.2	23.7
Entered before 2000...	44.5	48.2
World Region of Birth, Foreign		
Foreign-born population, excluding population born at sea	5,092,132	45,269,644
Europe	4.5	10.7
Asia..	22.8	31.0
Africa	6.1	5.7
Oceania	0.3	0.6
Latin America	65.3	50.1
North America	1.1	1.7
Language Spoken at Home and Ability to Speak English		
Population 5 years and over..	27,636,314	313,232,500
English only	65.1	78.4
Language other than English..	34.9	21.6
Speaks English less than "very well"..	12.9	8.3

Table TX-5. Median Income and Poverty Status, 2021

(Number, percent, except as noted.)

Characteristic	State Number	State Percent	U.S. Number	U.S. Percent
Median Income				
Households (dollars)...	66,963	X	69,717	X
Families (dollars)	80,304	X	85,806	X
Below Poverty Level (All People)	4,122,538	14.2	41,393,176	12.8
Sex				
Male	1,860,589	13.0	18,518,155	11.6
Female	2,261,949	15.5	22,875,021	13.9
Age				
Under 18 years..	1,441,171	19.6	12,243,219	16.9
Related children under 18 years...........................	1,422,461	19.4	11,985,424	16.6
18 to 64 years...	2,228,596	12.6	23,526,341	11.9
65 years and over	452,771	11.8	5,623,616	10.3

X = Not applicable.

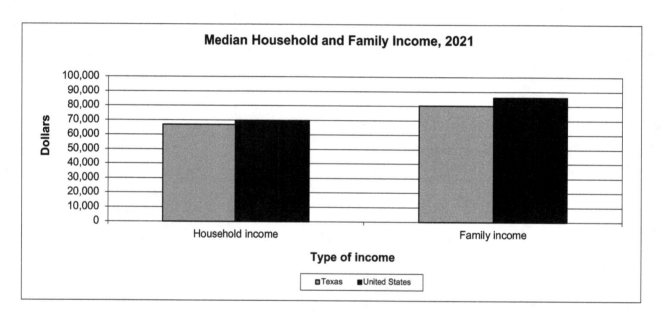

Median Household and Family Income, 2021

□ Texas   ■ United States

Table TX-6. Health Insurance Coverage Status for the Civilian Noninstitutionalized Population and Children Under 19 Years of Age

(Number, percent.)

Item	2011	2012	2013	2014	2015	2016	2017	2018	2019	2020 [2]	2021
Civilian Noninstitutionalized Population	25,197,453	25,584,499	25,976,562	26,485,838	26,990,435	27,386,023	27,836,924	28,243,191	28,514,428	28,169,961	29,066,872
Covered by Private or Public Insurance											
Number.....	19,407,607	19,822,141	20,228,395	21,438,361	22,375,210	22,840,643	23,019,956	23,240,298	23,280,468	23,292,892	23,842,828
Percent.....	77.0	77.5	77.9	80.9	82.9	83.4	82.7	82.3	81.6	82.7	82.0
Uninsured											
Number.....	5,789,846	5,762,358	5,748,167	5,047,477	4,615,225	4,545,380	4,816,968	5,002,893	5,233,960	4,877,069	5,224,044
Percent.....	23.0	22.5	22.1	19.1	17.1	16.6	17.3	17.7	18.4	17.3	18.0
Percent in the U.S. not covered..................	15.1	14.8	14.5	11.7	9.4	8.6	8.7	8.9	9.2	8.7	8.6
Children Under 19 Years of Age[1]	6,946,969	6,971,878	7,028,782	7,106,727	7,197,853	7,282,033	7,781,845	7,825,350	7,808,139	7,787,420	7,866,540
Covered by Private or Public Insurance											
Number.....	6,030,447	6,108,588	6,140,477	6,322,789	6,515,730	6,611,211	6,947,175	6,952,556	6,812,815	6,918,831	6,936,560
Percent.....	86.8	87.6	87.4	89.0	90.5	90.8	89.3	88.8	87.3	88.8	88.2
Uninsured											
Number.....	916,522	863,290	888,305	783,938	682,123	670,822	834,670	872,794	995,324	868,589	929,980
Percent.....	13.2	12.4	12.6	11.0	9.5	9.2	10.7	11.2	12.7	11.2	11.8
Percent in the U.S. not covered..................	7.5	7.2	7.1	6.0	4.8	4.5	5.0	5.2	5.7	5.2	5.4

[1] Data for years prior to 2017 are for individuals under 18 years of age.
[2] 2020 ACS 5-Year estimates. 1-Year estimates were not released for 2020 due to the impact of COVID-19 on data collection that year. Data is not comparable to previous years, which are based on 1-year estimates.

Table TX-7. Employment Status by Demographic Group, 2022

(Numbers in thousands, percent.)

Characteristic	Civilian noninstitutional population	Civilian labor force		Employed		Unemployed	
		Number	Percent of population	Number	Percent of population	Number	Percent of population
Total..	22,834	14,621	64.0	14,072	61.6	549	3.8
Sex							
Male..	11,187	8,007	71.6	7,703	68.9	304	3.8
Female...	11,647	6,614	56.8	6,368	54.7	245	3.7
Race, Sex, and Hispanic Origin							
White...	17,855	11,277	63.2	10,877	60.9	400	3.5
Male..	8,835	6,300	71.3	6,077	68.8	224	3.6
Female...	9,020	4,976	55.2	4,800	53.2	176	3.5
Black or African American...................	2,951	1,991	67.5	1,884	63.8	107	5.4
Male..	1,370	962	70.2	904	66.0	58	6.0
Female...	1,581	1,029	65.1	980	62.0	49	4.7
Hispanic or Latino ethnicity[1]...............	8,461	5,523	65.3	5,284	62.4	240	4.3
Male..	4,211	3,170	75.3	3,029	71.9	141	4.4
Female...	4,250	2,354	55.4	2,255	53.0	99	4.2
Age							
16 to 19 years.................................	1,745	562	32.2	497	28.5	65	11.6
20 to 24 years.................................	1,924	1,389	72.2	1,309	68.0	80	5.8
25 to 34 years.................................	4,125	3,404	82.5	3,284	79.6	119	3.5
35 to 44 years.................................	4,140	3,389	81.9	3,289	79.4	101	3.0
45 to 54 years.................................	3,640	2,970	81.6	2,889	79.4	81	2.7
55 to 64 years.................................	3,220	2,082	64.7	2,013	62.5	69	3.3
65 years and over.............................	4,041	826	20.4	791	19.6	34	4.2

NOTE: Data in Table 7 are from the Current Population Survey (CPS) and do not match the estimates in Table 8. See notes and definitions for further information.
[1] May be of any race.

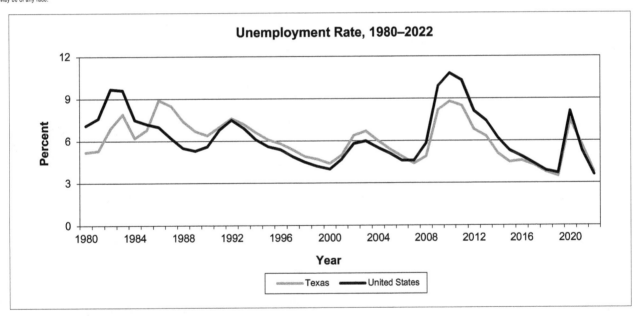

Table TX-8. Employment Status of the Civilian Noninstitutional Population Age 16 Years and Over

(Number, percent.)

Year	Civilian labor force	Civilian participation rate	Employed	Unemployed	Unemployment rate
2010..............................	12,260,100	66.0	11,255,444	1,004,656	8.2
2011..............................	12,499,595	65.9	11,498,869	1,000,726	8.0
2012..............................	12,639,465	65.4	11,794,975	844,490	6.7
2013..............................	12,832,035	65.2	12,022,272	809,763	6.3
2014..............................	13,006,202	64.8	12,333,076	673,126	5.2
2015..............................	13,090,961	63.8	12,503,464	587,497	4.5
2016..............................	13,346,836	63.8	12,728,898	617,938	4.6
2017..............................	13,473,991	63.8	12,888,025	585,966	4.3
2018..............................	13,684,009	63.8	13,149,672	534,337	3.9
2019..............................	13,871,780	63.7	13,381,020	490,760	3.5
2020..............................	13,870,874	62.7	12,808,616	1,062,258	7.7
2021..............................	14,220,446	63.3	13,413,036	807,410	5.7
2022..............................	14,662,558	63.9	14,092,833	569,725	3.9

Table TX-9. Employment and Average Wages by Industry

(Estimates are based on the 2012 North American Industry Classification System [NAICS].)

Industry	2014	2015	2016	2017	2018	2019	2020	2021
	Number of Jobs							
Wage and Salary Employment by Industry........................	12,019,579	12,306,014	12,448,418	12,644,682	12,973,344	13,269,719	12,730,770	13,173,522
Farm Wage and Salary Employment..............................	47,110	49,030	50,698	47,860	49,847	45,619	51,650	47,149
Nonfarm Wage and Salary Employment..........................	11,972,469	12,256,984	12,397,720	12,596,822	12,923,497	13,224,100	12,679,120	13,126,373
Private wage and salary employment............................	9,987,530	10,245,568	10,357,353	10,538,306	10,853,274	11,128,829	10,597,042	11,038,159
Forestry, fishing, and related activities	32,901	33,700	33,794	33,672	33,851	34,279	32,715	30,295
Mining..	307,690	271,697	218,710	219,594	243,205	246,894	189,282	177,941
Utilities...	49,026	49,508	49,806	50,333	51,769	52,660	51,586	52,838
Construction...	668,106	701,741	718,755	728,768	758,213	793,456	755,892	752,979
Manufacturing...	888,655	879,061	846,192	853,261	881,465	907,251	869,007	875,249
Durable goods manufacturing.................................	590,171	577,587	541,233	542,591	563,964	582,612	552,264	552,052
Nondurable goods manufacturing............................	298,484	301,474	304,959	310,670	317,501	324,639	316,743	323,197
Wholesale trade	576,387	590,924	583,155	590,939	598,175	611,387	592,505	595,834
Retail trade..	1,261,716	1,305,301	1,330,491	1,334,880	1,339,918	1,331,416	1,291,873	1,354,970
Transportation and warehousing................................	436,143	458,604	470,286	491,252	511,591	534,202	549,633	578,645
Information	203,226	201,364	202,421	202,359	204,029	208,816	198,516	207,595
Finance and insurance	517,251	534,354	545,239	561,632	572,251	591,172	605,903	626,546
Real estate and rental and leasing............................	199,652	205,198	208,164	217,434	226,935	235,548	225,746	232,242
Professional, scientific, and technical services	683,593	714,562	732,190	749,697	791,102	831,521	838,280	901,412
Management of companies and enterprises...................	111,922	116,858	119,357	128,420	142,215	147,831	141,058	151,538
Administrative and waste services.............................	760,783	775,344	786,004	800,972	817,985	826,963	792,744	860,272
Educational services	170,156	176,442	185,294	188,601	198,133	204,996	196,670	224,927
Health care and social assistance.............................	1,324,471	1,377,347	1,426,207	1,457,934	1,489,463	1,522,324	1,489,724	1,514,605
Arts, entertainment, and recreation...........................	128,047	131,235	137,691	142,018	147,298	152,313	117,934	133,397
Accommodation and food services.............................	1,069,189	1,117,193	1,159,908	1,185,162	1,217,465	1,251,745	1,070,846	1,169,800
Other services, except public administration.................	598,616	605,135	603,689	601,378	628,211	644,055	587,128	597,074
Government and government enterprises.....................	1,984,939	2,011,416	2,040,367	2,058,516	2,070,223	2,095,271	2,082,078	2,088,214
	Dollars							
Average Wages and Salaries by Industry	52,666	53,751	53,847	55,374	57,280	59,285	62,141	65,389
Average Farm Wages and Salaries	30,935	33,207	27,607	30,452	30,581	30,140	17,321	27,417
Average Nonfarm Wages and Salaries	52,751	53,833	53,955	55,468	57,383	59,386	62,324	65,526
Average private wages and salaries............................	53,784	54,792	54,750	56,314	58,324	60,409	63,421	66,806
Forestry, fishing, and related activities......................	27,553	28,642	30,331	31,860	33,052	34,455	36,596	39,465
Mining...	126,238	128,051	131,123	127,017	127,212	133,111	141,348	134,368
Utilities...	100,433	104,041	105,098	111,521	111,879	115,285	115,213	120,570
Construction	58,586	60,509	61,677	63,176	65,506	67,517	68,887	71,297
Manufacturing...	71,104	72,813	73,125	75,746	77,627	79,732	81,173	83,487
Durable goods manufacturing.................................	73,097	74,119	75,480	78,583	80,489	82,830	84,311	87,441
Nondurable goods manufacturing............................	67,163	70,312	68,945	70,791	72,544	74,173	75,703	76,734
Wholesale trade	75,833	77,269	78,022	79,901	83,355	86,418	89,715	95,900
Retail trade..	29,987	30,702	30,891	31,608	32,813	34,052	36,879	40,333
Transportation and warehousing................................	59,899	61,336	59,605	61,249	62,903	64,001	62,796	64,257
Information	76,634	79,628	81,189	84,286	87,060	90,847	102,848	112,431
Finance and insurance	79,588	82,456	83,654	87,273	90,549	94,088	100,669	106,176
Real estate and rental and leasing............................	57,272	58,248	58,868	61,355	64,060	66,762	68,567	73,965
Professional, scientific, and technical services	86,534	88,389	89,313	91,117	94,431	97,001	100,510	106,881
Management of companies and enterprises...................	123,337	123,876	123,032	131,917	132,870	136,130	139,218	149,083
Administrative and waste services.............................	40,649	41,809	42,169	43,380	44,822	46,673	50,136	54,711
Educational services	39,125	39,983	40,761	41,227	42,234	42,892	47,758	46,011
Health care and social assistance.............................	43,925	45,415	45,964	46,991	47,901	49,178	51,600	54,832
Arts, entertainment, and recreation...........................	33,555	35,508	36,479	37,484	37,622	39,671	42,752	44,366
Accommodation and food services.............................	20,546	21,055	21,497	22,115	23,284	24,021	22,736	27,193
Other services, except public administration.................	32,316	33,461	34,291	35,718	36,717	37,924	40,999	43,604
Government and government enterprises.....................	47,553	48,947	49,918	51,138	52,454	53,952	56,741	58,760

Table TX-10. Employment Characteristics by Family Type

(Number, percent.)

Family type and labor force status	2019 Total	2019 Families with own children under 18 years	2020[1] Total	2020[1] Families with own children under 18 years	2021 Total	2021 Families with own children under 18 years
All Families...	6,857,641	3,142,131	6,838,900	3,190,138	7,373,185	3,358,147
FAMILY TYPE AND LABOR FORCE STATUS						
Opposite-Sex Married-Couple Families...	4,954,566	2,153,548	4,932,575	2,199,935	5,277,980	2,312,990
Both husband and wife in labor force...	50.5	61.8	51.0	61.4	50.4	61.6
Husband in labor force, wife not in labor force	27.0	33.2	27.4	33.8	26.8	32.5
Wife in labor force, husband not in labor force	6.5	3.0	6.7	3.3	7.1	3.7
Both husband and wife not in labor force.................................	15.2	1.6	14.9	1.5	15.7	2.1
Other Families	1,903,075	988,583	1,864,312	980,993	2,031,695	1,032,105
Female householder, no spouse present	71.9	75.1	73.0	76.7	71.9	75.7
In labor force......................................	51.4	61.8	53.0	64.1	51.3	62.2
Not in labor force..................................	20.4	13.3	20.0	12.5	20.6	13.5
Male householder, no spouse present...................................	28.1	24.9	27.0	23.3	28.1	24.3
In labor force......................................	23.0	23.4	22.0	21.7	22.6	22.6
Not in labor force..................................	5.2	1.6	5.1	1.7	5.5	1.7

[1] 2020 ACS 5-Year estimates. 1-Year estimates were not released for 2020 due to the impact of COVID-19 on data collection that year. Data is not comparable to previous years, which are based on 1-year estimates.

Table TX-11. School Enrollment and Educational Attainment, 2021

(Number, percent.)

Item	State	U.S.
Enrollment		
Total population 3 years and over, enrolled in school	7,690,444	79,453,524
Enrolled in nursery school or preschool (percent)..	4.8	5.2
Enrolled in kindergarten (percent)...	5.4	5.0
Enrolled in elementary school, grades 1-8 (percent)..	43.7	41.3
Enrolled in high school, grades 9-12 (percent)...	22.7	21.8
Enrolled in college or graduate school (percent)..	23.5	26.7
Attainment		
Total population 25 years and over	19,224,688	228,193,464
Less than ninth grade (percent)...	7.6	4.8
9th to 12th grade, no diploma (percent)...	7.0	5.9
High school graduate, including equivalency (percent)......................................	24.6	26.3
Some college, no degree (percent)..	20.2	19.3
Associate's degree (percent)...	7.5	8.8
Bachelor's degree (percent)	21.2	21.2
Graduate or professional degree (percent)..	11.9	13.8
High school graduate or higher (percent)	85.4	89.4
Bachelor's degree or higher (percent)..	33.1	35.0

Table TX-12. Public School Characteristics and Educational Indicators

(Number, percent; data derived from National Center of Education Statistics.)

Item	State	U.S.
Public Elementary and Secondary Schools		
Number of regular school districts, 2019-20	1,024	13,349
Number of operational schools, 2019-20..	8,987	98,469
Percent charter schools	10.1	7.7
Total public school enrollment, Fall 2021	5,428,613	49,433,092
Percent charter school enrollment	8.2	7.5
Student-teacher ratio, Fall 2019	15.1	15.9
Expenditures per student (unadjusted dollars), 2019-20	10,394	13,489
Four-year adjusted cohort graduation rate (ACGR), 2019-2020[1]	NA	86.5
Students eligible for free or reduced-price lunch (percent), 2019-20....................	60.2	52.1
English language learners (percent), Fall 2020	20.1	10.3
Students age 3 to 21 served under IDEA, part B (percent), 2021-22	11.7	14.7

Public Schools by Type, 2019-20	Number	Percent of state public schools
Total number of schools..	8,987	100.0
Special education..	12	0.1
Vocational education	-	-
Alternative education...	866	9.6

[1] Adjusted Cohort Graduation Rates (ACGR) differ from Averaged Freshmen Graduation Rates (AFGR).
- = Zero or rounds to zero.
NA = Not available.

Table TX-13. Reported Voting and Registration of the Voting-Age Population, November 2022

(Numbers in thousands, percent.)

Item	Total population	Total citizen population	Registered			Voted		
			Total registered	Percent registered (total population)	Percent registered (total citizen population)	Total voted	Percent voted (total population)	Percent voted (total citizen population)
U.S. Total	255,457	233,546	161,422	63.2	69.1	121,916	47.7	52.2
State Total	22,057	19,029	12,416	56.3	65.2	8,935	40.5	47.0
Sex								
Male	10,811	9,223	5,931	54.9	64.3	4,239	39.2	46.0
Female	11,246	9,805	6,484	57.7	66.1	4,696	41.8	47.9
Race								
White alone..........................	17,444	15,006	9,921	56.9	66.1	7,189	41.2	47.9
White, non-Hispanic alone	9,950	9,689	6,886	69.2	71.1	5,307	53.3	54.8
Black alone...........................	2,871	2,715	1,605	55.9	59.1	1,125	39.2	41.5
Asian alone	1,188	802	550	46.3	68.6	338	28.5	42.2
Hispanic (of any race)	7,895	5,672	3,300	41.8	58.2	2,091	26.5	36.9
White alone or in combination...............	17,745	15,306	10,128	57.1	66.2	7,365	41.5	48.1
Black alone or in combination......................	2,966	2,811	1,661	56.0	59.1	1,182	39.8	42.0
Asian alone or in combination......................	1,248	861	560	44.9	65.0	348	27.9	40.4
Age								
18 to 24 years...........................	2,666	2,381	1,055	39.6	44.3	513	19.2	21.6
25 to 34 years...........................	4,190	3,469	1,967	47.0	56.7	1,152	27.5	33.2
35 to 44 years...........................	4,208	3,461	2,211	52.5	63.9	1,511	35.9	43.7
45 to 64 years...........................	6,932	5,923	4,357	62.9	73.6	3,329	48.0	56.2
65 years and over	4,062	3,796	2,826	69.6	74.4	2,430	59.8	64.0

Table TX-14. Health Indicators

(Number, rate as indicated in footnotes.)

Item	State	U.S.
Births		
Life Expectancy at Birth (years), 2020	76.5	77.0
Fertility Rate by State[1], 2021	60.7	56.3
Percent Home Births, 2021	1.0	1.4
Cesarean Delivery Rate[2], 2021	34.8	32.1
Preterm Birth Rate[3], 2021	11.4	10.5
Teen Birth Rate[4], 2021	20.3	13.9
Percentage of Babies Born Low Birthweight[5], 2021	8.7	8.5
Deaths[6]		
Heart Disease Mortality Rate, 2021.....................................	180.7	173.8
Cancer Mortality Rate, 2021..	143.3	146.6
Stroke Mortality Rate, 2021..	43.8	41.1
Diabetes Mortality Rate, 2021..	27.5	25.4
Influenza/Pneumonia Mortality Rate, 2021	10.5	10.5
Suicide Mortality Rate, 2021...	14.2	14.1
Drug Overdose Mortality Rate, 2021.....................................	16.8	33.6
Firearm Injury Mortality Rate, 2021....................................	15.6	14.6
Homicide Mortality Rate, 2021..	8.2	8.2
Disease and Illness		
Lifetime Asthma in Adults, 2020 (percent)...............................	12.3	13.9
Lifetime Asthma in Children, 2020 (percent)[7]	11.1	11.3
Diabetes in Adults, 2020 (percent).....................................	12.1	8.2
Self-reported Obesity in Adults, 2021 (percent)........................	36.1	NA

SOURCE: National Center for Health Statistics, National Vital Statistics System 2020 data; https://wonder.cdc.gov.
[1] General fertility rate per 1,000 women aged 15–44.
[2] This represents the percentage of all live births that were cesarean deliveries.
[3] Babies born prior to 37 weeks of pregnancy (gestation).
[4] Number of births per 1,000 females aged 15–19
[5] Babies born weighing less than 2,500 grams or 5 lbs. 8oz.
[6] Death rates are the number of deaths per 100,000 total population.
[7] U.S. total includes data from 30 states and D.C.
NA = Not available.
- = Zero or rounds to zero.

Table TX-15. State Government Finances, 2021

(Dollar amounts in thousands, percent distribution.)

Item	Dollars	Percent distribution
Total Revenue	214,868,203	100.0
General revenue	193,789,786	90.2
Intergovernmental revenue	88,753,054	41.3
Taxes	65,377,430	30.4
General sales	40,413,873	18.8
Selective sales	16,227,687	7.6
License taxes	3,646,437	1.7
Individual income tax	-	-
Corporate income tax	-	-
Other taxes	5,089,433	2.4
Current charges	18,645,318	8.7
Miscellaneous general revenue	21,013,984	9.8
Utility revenue	-	-
Liquor stores revenue	-	-
Insurance trust revenue[1]	21,078,417	9.8
Total Expenditure	201,786,634	100.0
Intergovernmental expenditure	37,203,862	18.4
Direct expenditure	164,582,772	81.6
Current operation	110,366,743	54.7
Capital outlay	13,221,320	6.6
Insurance benefits and repayments	34,484,570	17.1
Assistance and subsidies	4,717,288	2.3
Interest on debt	1,792,851	0.9
Exhibit: Salaries and wages	21,258,633	10.5
Total Expenditure	201,786,634	100.0
General expenditure	167,202,920	82.9
Intergovernmental expenditure	37,203,862	18.4
Direct expenditure	129,999,058	64.4
General expenditure, by function:		
Education	62,112,331	30.8
Public welfare	51,332,767	25.4
Hospitals	9,874,961	4.9
Health	9,597,879	4.8
Highways	13,091,488	6.5
Police protection	1,325,508	0.7
Correction	4,216,116	2.1
Natural resources	1,046,330	0.5
Parks and recreation	365,225	0.2
Governmental administration	3,818,906	1.9
Interest on general debt	1,792,851	0.9
Other and unallocable	8,445,228	4.2
Utility expenditure	161,385	0.1
Liquor stores expenditure	-	-
Insurance trust expenditure	34,484,570	17.1
Debt at End of Fiscal Year	52,664,275	X
Cash and Security Holdings	555,726,852	X

X = Not applicable.
- = Zero or rounds to zero.
[1] Within insurance trust revenue, net earnings of state retirement systems is a calculated statistic (the item code in the data file is X08), and thus can be positive or negative. Net earnings is the sum of earnings on investments plus gains on investments minus losses on investments. The change made in 2002 for asset valuation from book to market value in accordance with Statement 34 of the Governmental Accounting Standards Board is reflected in the calculated statistics.

Table TX-16. State Government Tax Collections, 2022

(Dollars in thousands, percent.)

Item	Dollars	Percent distribution
Total Taxes	82,259,732	100.0
Property taxes	X	-
Sales and gross receipts	66,917,512	81.3
General sales and gross receipts	48,866,003	59.4
Selective sales and gross receipts	18,051,509	21.9
Alcoholic beverages	1,655,325	2.0
Amusements	17,720	-
Insurance premiums	3,121,923	3.8
Motor fuels	3,783,904	4.6
Pari-mutuels	5,059	-
Public utilities	748,572	0.9
Tobacco products	1,210,716	1.5
Other selective sales	7,508,290	9.1
Licenses	4,396,703	5.3
Alcoholic beverages	104,801	0.1
Amusements	13,899	-
Corporations in general	276,856	0.3
Hunting and fishing	117,390	0.1
Motor vehicle	2,262,141	2.7
Motor vehicle operators	180,069	0.2
Public utilities	45,765	0.1
Occupation and business, NEC	1,209,890	1.5
Other licenses	185,892	0.2
Income taxes	X	-
Individual income	X	-
Corporation net income	X	-
Other taxes	10,945,517	13.3
Death and gift	X	-
Documentary and stock transfer	X	-
Severance	10,945,517	13.3
Taxes, NEC	X	-

X = Not applicable.
- = Zero or rounds to zero.

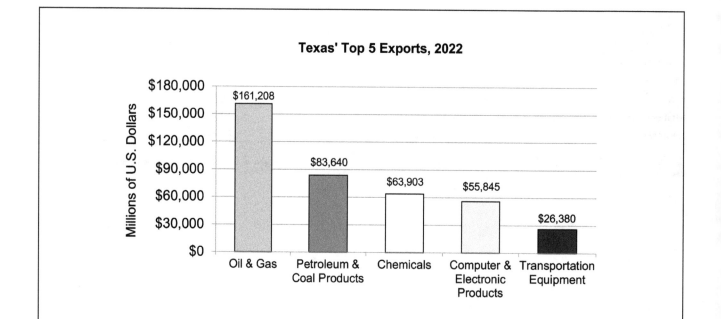

Texas' Top 5 Exports, 2022

Facts and Figures

Location: Western United States; bordered on the N by Idaho and Wyoming, on the E by Colorado, on the S by Arizona, and on the W by Nevada; Utah is one of the Four Corner states—at its SE corner it touches Arizona, Colorado, and New Mexico

Area: 84,899 sq. mi. (219,887 sq. km.); rank—13th

Population: 3,380,800 (2022 est.); rank—30th

Principal Cities: capital—Salt Lake City; largest—Salt Lake City

Statehood: January 4, 1896; 45th state

U.S. Congress: 2 senators, 4 representatives

State Motto: Industry

State Song: "Utah, We Love Thee"

State Nickname: The Beehive State

Abbreviations: UT

State Symbols: flower—sego lily; tree—blue spruce; bird—California seagull

At a Glance

- With an increase in population of 22.3 percent, Utah ranked 2nd among the states in growth from 2010 to 2022.

- Utah's homicide rate in 2021 of 2.7 deaths per 100,000 population was the 7th lowest in the country.

- Of all the states, Utah had the highest percent of children in 2022, with 27.6 percent of its population under age 18.

- Utah also has the highest birth rate among states in 2021, at a rate of 14.0 births per 1,000 population.

- In 2021, 9.0 percent of Utahns did not have health insurance, compared to 8.6 percent of the total U.S. population.

Table UT-1. Population by Age, Sex, Race, and Hispanic Origin

(Number, percent, except where noted.)

Sex, age, race, and Hispanic origin	2010	2020	2022	Percent change, 2010–2022
Total Population..	2,763,885	3,271,614	3,380,800	22.3
Percent of total U.S. population	0.9	1.0	1.0	X
Sex				
Male...	1,388,317	1,659,955	1,716,831	23.7
Female...	1,375,568	1,611,659	1,663,969	21.0
Age				
Under 5 years..	263,924	240,430	233,074	-11.7
Under 18 years...	871,027	938,825	931,608	7.0
18 to 64 years...	1,643,396	1,961,000	2,043,992	24.4
65 years and over..	249,462	371,789	405,200	62.4
Median age (years)	29.2	31.3	31.9	9.2
Race and Hispanic Origin				
One race				
White	2,547,329	2,958,989	3,043,600	19.5
Black	33,864	48,838	52,777	55.8
American Indian and Alaska Native	40,729	50,246	52,130	28.0
Asian..	57,800	87,961	94,519	63.5
Native Hawaiian or Other Pacific Islander	26,049	36,615	39,302	50.9
Two or more races	58,114	88,965	98,472	69.4
Hispanic (of any race).......................................	358,340	475,367	512,087	42.9

NOTE: Population figures for 2022 are July 1 estimates. The 2010 and 2020 estimates are taken from the respective censuses.
- = Zero or rounds to zero.
X = Not applicable.

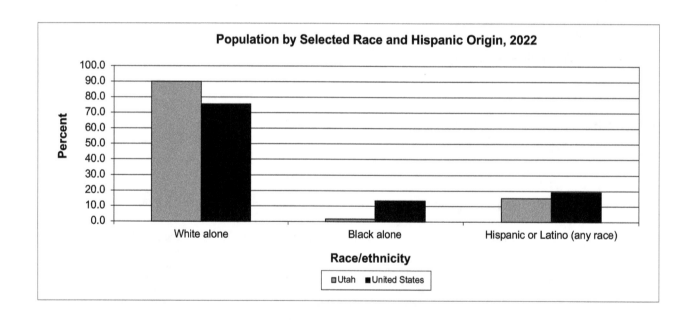

Table UT-2. Marital Status

(Number, percent distribution.)

Sex, age, race, and Hispanic origin	2000	2010	2021
Males, 15 Years and Over	813,693	1,014,706	1,293,128
Never married	30.6	31.3	34.6
Now married, except separated..............................	59.5	58.0	55.1
Separated..	1.1	1.3	1.1
Widowed..	1.6	1.8	1.7
Divorced..	7.3	7.6	7.5
Females, 15 Years and Over	852,995	1,019,010	1,268,428
Never married	25.2	25.8	28.3
Now married, except separated..............................	58.0	56.6	55.4
Separated..	1.4	1.6	1.2
Widowed..	6.6	5.8	5.3
Divorced..	8.8	10.1	9.8

Table UT-3. Households and Housing Characteristics

(Number, percent, dollars.)

Item	2000	2010	2021	Average annual percent change, 2010–2021
Total Households	701,281	880,025	1,101,499	2.3
Family households	535,294	665,964	798,045	1.8
Married-couple family	442,931	543,212	652,738	1.8
Other family	92,363	122,752	145,307	1.7
Male householder, no wife present	26,422	37,258	51,037	3.4
Female householder, no husband present	65,941	85,494	94,270	0.9
Nonfamily households	165,987	214,061	303,454	3.8
Householder living alone	124,756	164,863	226,995	3.4
Householder not living alone	41,231	49,198	76,459	5.0
Housing Characteristics				
Total housing units	768,594	981,821	1,190,154	1.9
Occupied housing units	701,281	880,025	1,101,499	2.3
Owner occupied	501,547	615,142	768,062	2.3
Renter occupied	188,734	264,883	333,437	2.4
Average household size	3.13	3.10	2.99	-0.3
Financial Characteristics				
Median gross rent of renter-occupied housing	597	796	1,208	4.7
Median monthly owner costs for housing units with a mortgage	1,102	1,433	1,671	1.5
Median value of owner-occupied housing units	146,100	217,200	421,700	8.6

Table UT-4. Migration, Origin, and Language

(Number, percent.)

Characteristic	State 2021	U.S. 2021
Residence 1 Year Ago		
Population 1 year and over	3,295,561	328,464,538
Same house	85.5	87.2
Different house in the U.S.	14.0	12.3
Same county	8.2	6.7
Different county	5.8	5.7
Same state	2.7	3.3
Different state	3.1	2.4
Abroad	0.5	0.4
Place of Birth		
Native born	3,059,639	286,623,642
Male	50.8	49.7
Female	49.2	50.3
Foreign born	278,336	45,270,103
Male	50.9	48.7
Female	49.1	51.3
Foreign born; naturalized U.S. citizen	124,162	24,044,083
Male	46.8	46.4
Female	53.2	53.6
Foreign born; not a U.S. citizen	154,174	21,226,020
Male	54.2	51.2
Female	45.8	48.8
Entered 2010 or later	32.1	28.1
Entered 2000 to 2009	25.3	23.7
Entered before 2000	42.7	48.2
World Region of Birth, Foreign		
Foreign-born population, excluding population born at sea	278,336	45,269,644
Europe	11.0	10.7
Asia	21.1	31.0
Africa	4.6	5.7
Oceania	3.7	0.6
Latin America	57.0	50.1
North America	2.6	1.7
Language Spoken at Home and Ability to Speak English		
Population 5 years and over	3,103,694	313,232,500
English only	84.7	78.4
Language other than English	15.3	21.6
Speaks English less than "very well"	4.8	8.3

Table UT-5. Median Income and Poverty Status, 2021

(Number, percent, except as noted.)

Characteristic	State Number	State Percent	U.S. Number	U.S. Percent
Median Income				
Households (dollars)..	79,449	X	69,717	X
Families (dollars)	92,192	X	85,806	X
Below Poverty Level (All People)	281,673	8.6	41,393,176	12.8
Sex				
Male	130,317	7.8	18,518,155	11.6
Female	151,356	9.3	22,875,021	13.9
Age				
Under 18 years..	76,102	8.1	12,243,219	16.9
Related children under 18 years................................	73,112	7.9	11,985,424	16.6
18 to 64 years...	176,152	8.9	23,526,341	11.9
65 years and over	29,419	7.7	5,623,616	10.3

X = Not applicable.

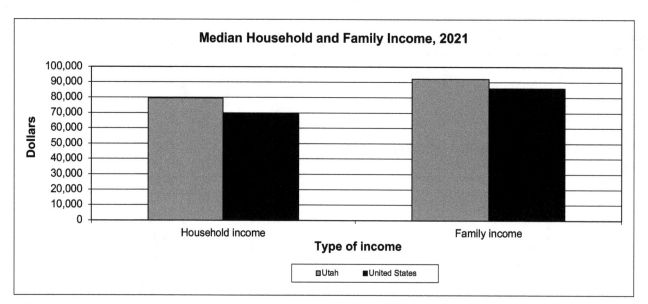

Table UT-6. Health Insurance Coverage Status for the Civilian Noninstitutionalized Population and Children Under 19 Years of Age

(Number, percent.)

Item	2011	2012	2013	2014	2015	2016	2017	2018	2019	2020 [2]	2021
Civilian Noninstitutionalized Population	2,789,648	2,829,001	2,874,213	2,916,303	2,971,003	3,024,767	3,076,318	3,135,573	3,178,394	3,124,563	3,309,594
Covered by Private or Public Insurance											
Number..	2,363,584	2,419,830	2,472,089	2,550,780	2,659,662	2,759,960	2,794,565	2,840,209	2,871,538	2,844,130	3,010,806
Percent..	84.7	85.5	86.0	87.5	89.5	91.2	90.8	90.6	90.3	91.0	91.0
Uninsured											
Number..	426,064	409,171	402,124	365,523	311,341	264,807	281,753	295,364	306,856	280,433	298,788
Percent..	15.3	14.5	14.0	12.5	10.5	8.8	9.2	9.4	9.7	9.0	9.0
Percent in the U.S. not covered................................	15.1	14.8	14.5	11.7	9.4	8.6	8.7	8.9	9.2	8.7	8.6
Children Under 19 Years of Age [1]	877,812	884,012	893,685	902,311	909,285	918,971	972,601	982,994	982,566	977,347	997,570
Covered by Private or Public Insurance											
Number..	780,570	794,321	808,794	817,543	844,090	865,371	901,414	910,736	900,949	909,622	918,533
Percent..	88.9	89.9	90.5	90.6	92.8	94.2	92.7	92.6	91.7	93.1	92.1
Uninsured											
Number..	97,242	89,691	84,891	84,768	65,195	53,600	71,187	72,258	81,617	67,725	79,037
Percent..	11.1	10.1	9.5	9.4	7.2	5.8	7.3	7.4	8.3	6.9	7.9
Percent in the U.S. not covered................................	7.5	7.2	7.1	6.0	4.8	4.5	5.0	5.2	5.7	5.2	5.4

[1] Data for years prior to 2017 are for individuals under 18 years of age.
[2] 2020 ACS 5-Year estimates. 1-Year estimates were not released for 2020 due to the impact of COVID-19 on data collection that year. Data is not comparable to previous years, which are based on 1-year estimates.

Table UT-7. Employment Status by Demographic Group, 2022

(Numbers in thousands, percent.)

Characteristic	Civilian noninstitutional population	Civilian labor force		Employed		Unemployed	
		Number	Percent of population	Number	Percent of population	Number	Percent of population
Total..	2,542	1,738	68.4	1,696	66.7	42	2.4
Sex							
Male..	1,274	978	76.8	955	74.9	23	2.4
Female	1,268	760	59.9	741	58.5	19	2.5
Race, Sex, and Hispanic Origin							
White..	2,335	1,596	68.3	1,559	66.8	37	2.3
Male...	1,175	903	76.9	882	75.1	21	2.3
Female	1,161	693	59.7	677	58.3	16	2.3
Black or African American................	NA	NA	NA	NA	NA	NA	NA
Male...	NA	NA	NA	NA	NA	NA	NA
Female	NA	NA	NA	NA	NA	NA	NA
Hispanic or Latino ethnicity[1]	324	237	73.1	229	70.7	8	3.3
Male...	160	135	84.1	132	82.4	3	2.1
Female	164	102	62.3	97	59.3	5	4.8
Age							
16 to 19 years	218	117	53.7	109	50.0	8	7.0
20 to 24 years	296	238	80.4	230	77.7	8	3.3
25 to 34 years	490	396	80.8	385	78.6	11	2.7
35 to 44 years	453	373	82.4	368	81.4	5	1.3
45 to 54 years	373	318	85.1	312	83.5	6	1.9
55 to 64 years	301	211	70.3	208	69.2	3	1.6
65 years and over	NA	NA	NA	NA	NA	NA	NA

NOTE: Data in Table 7 are from the Current Population Survey (CPS) and do not match the estimates in Table 8. See notes and definitions for further information.
[1] May be of any race.
NA = Not available.

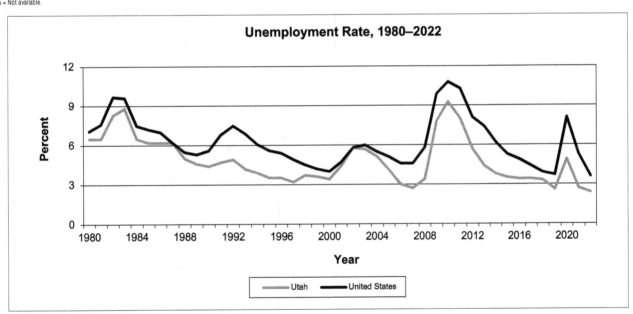

Unemployment Rate, 1980–2022

Table UT-8. Employment Status of the Civilian Noninstitutional Population Age 16 Years and Over

(Number, percent.)

Year	Civilian labor force	Civilian participation rate	Employed	Unemployed	Unemployment rate
2010..	1,350,173	68.5	1,242,907	107,266	7.9
2011..	1,341,427	67.4	1,246,797	94,630	7.1
2012..	1,348,557	66.6	1,284,149	64,408	4.8
2013..	1,385,908	67.2	1,327,560	58,348	4.2
2014..	1,415,779	67.4	1,364,353	51,426	3.6
2015..	1,453,457	67.9	1,401,945	51,512	3.5
2016..	1,500,137	68.4	1,449,981	50,156	3.3
2017..	1,554,352	68.8	1,505,413	48,939	3.1
2018..	1,583,703	68.5	1,537,389	46,314	2.9
2019..	1,618,055	68.4	1,576,421	41,634	2.6
2020..	1,640,426	67.9	1,562,799	77,627	4.7
2021..	1,681,494	67.9	1,636,150	45,344	2.7
2022..	1,743,054	68.7	1,702,674	40,380	2.3

Table UT-9. Employment and Average Wages by Industry

(Estimates are based on the 2012 North American Industry Classification System [NAICS].)

Industry	2014	2015	2016	2017	2018	2019	2020	2021
	Number of Jobs							
Wage and Salary Employment by Industry........................	1,381,561	1,428,802	1,480,533	1,524,228	1,577,719	1,622,060	1,605,868	1,688,168
Farm Wage and Salary Employment................................	4,501	4,373	4,619	5,557	4,963	4,975	5,257	4,786
Nonfarm Wage and Salary Employment..........................	1,377,060	1,424,429	1,475,914	1,518,671	1,572,756	1,617,085	1,600,611	1,683,382
Private wage and salary employment...........................	1,134,425	1,179,882	1,225,591	1,263,387	1,313,165	1,351,711	1,335,415	1,412,548
Forestry, fishing, and related activities.....................	1,513	1,573	1,621	1,582	1,619	1,667	1,680	1,624
Mining..	12,183	10,321	8,461	8,595	9,443	9,335	8,627	8,807
Utilities...	3,888	3,915	3,857	3,917	3,918	3,829	3,700	3,562
Construction...	80,601	86,833	93,815	99,788	106,791	112,064	118,253	125,003
Manufacturing..	120,068	122,991	125,143	128,499	132,253	136,238	135,724	145,028
Durable goods manufacturing...............................	79,085	81,595	82,418	84,489	86,919	89,340	88,178	93,565
Nondurable goods manufacturing...........................	40,983	41,396	42,725	44,010	45,334	46,898	47,546	51,463
Wholesale trade..	48,816	50,198	50,087	51,017	51,103	52,499	53,308	55,618
Retail trade..	152,529	159,094	165,764	169,104	173,800	174,665	171,513	183,202
Transportation and warehousing..............................	48,755	51,413	53,183	55,984	59,060	61,663	63,479	66,121
Information..	32,163	33,343	35,708	37,287	36,809	38,345	37,275	39,828
Finance and insurance..	59,435	63,203	65,413	67,606	70,142	71,980	76,044	78,862
Real estate and rental and leasing...........................	18,486	18,987	19,493	20,019	21,262	22,402	22,614	23,635
Professional, scientific, and technical services.............	83,585	88,787	92,619	96,767	105,595	110,379	113,883	120,349
Management of companies and enterprises.....................	18,134	18,334	18,469	18,192	17,970	18,546	19,042	18,820
Administrative and waste services...........................	82,572	86,584	90,535	91,474	93,592	94,522	91,985	94,555
Educational services	44,232	46,313	49,619	52,075	55,789	57,922	56,574	63,592
Health care and social assistance............................	132,587	138,703	145,168	149,665	154,147	159,165	159,197	165,270
Arts, entertainment, and recreation..........................	20,624	21,322	23,333	24,651	25,311	26,335	21,323	25,342
Accommodation and food services.............................	108,525	113,088	115,991	119,395	124,157	128,124	113,236	123,873
Other services, except public administration.................	65,729	64,880	67,312	67,770	70,404	72,031	67,958	69,457
Government and government enterprises	242,635	244,547	250,323	255,284	259,591	265,374	265,196	270,834
	Dollars							
Average Wages and Salaries by Industry	43,839	45,234	46,124	47,447	49,440	51,586	55,669	58,588
Average Farm Wages and Salaries	40,861	35,594	39,013	32,614	38,973	27,835	35,088	44,811
Average Nonfarm Wages and Salaries	43,849	45,263	46,146	47,502	49,473	51,659	55,736	58,627
Average private wages and salaries...........................	44,377	45,804	46,662	48,062	50,055	52,373	56,704	59,736
Forestry, fishing, and related activities.....................	31,914	31,907	33,722	35,690	38,056	39,197	42,226	42,286
Mining..	79,239	80,530	81,677	77,946	78,991	82,501	87,188	85,242
Utilities...	90,935	93,348	94,582	99,443	106,246	112,146	112,545	109,561
Construction...	45,693	47,341	48,319	49,962	51,976	54,318	58,445	61,370
Manufacturing..	54,549	56,323	56,929	58,471	59,930	61,302	63,840	67,357
Durable goods manufacturing...............................	57,764	59,238	59,770	62,236	63,563	65,207	67,355	72,004
Nondurable goods manufacturing...........................	48,344	50,576	51,450	51,242	52,965	53,863	57,321	58,908
Wholesale trade..	62,847	64,068	65,730	67,940	70,863	73,102	76,821	81,894
Retail trade..	29,770	31,252	32,223	33,030	34,614	35,872	39,916	41,892
Transportation and warehousing..............................	47,501	48,822	50,465	51,170	52,973	54,258	56,095	56,844
Information..	65,095	69,302	72,179	73,134	80,544	86,841	99,384	109,972
Finance and insurance..	66,148	69,967	70,161	71,762	75,725	79,298	88,946	96,271
Real estate and rental and leasing...........................	42,836	46,302	47,182	49,825	51,857	53,592	57,502	62,324
Professional, scientific, and technical services.............	66,889	67,988	68,578	71,711	75,332	82,554	86,211	90,623
Management of companies and enterprises.....................	84,988	86,742	90,523	93,593	98,537	98,924	101,935	108,670
Administrative and waste services...........................	32,155	33,000	34,958	36,761	37,645	40,433	43,127	46,658
Educational services	29,904	30,281	29,741	30,410	31,218	32,690	36,261	34,912
Health care and social assistance............................	41,403	42,042	43,537	44,204	45,462	46,565	49,245	51,346
Arts, entertainment, and recreation..........................	26,754	27,719	28,667	30,691	31,643	32,577	35,486	35,873
Accommodation and food services.............................	18,387	19,258	19,873	20,597	21,674	22,497	21,903	25,873
Other services, except public administration.................	43,432	45,644	45,436	47,132	48,231	49,806	55,659	59,229
Government and government enterprises	41,377	42,655	43,621	44,728	46,526	48,024	50,866	52,842

Table UT-10. Employment Characteristics by Family Type

(Number, percent.)

Family type and labor force status	2019		2020 [1]		2021	
	Total	Families with own children under 18 years	Total	Families with own children under 18 years	Total	Families with own children under 18 years
All Families..	760,968	368,068	746,286	368,294	798,045	383,565
FAMILY TYPE AND LABOR FORCE STATUS						
Opposite-Sex Married-Couple Families............................	619,250	297,203	606,066	296,795	645,997	311,172
Both husband and wife in labor force................................	52.9	60.5	52.8	59.4	52.3	59.5
Husband in labor force, wife not in labor force	26.9	35.3	27.9	37.0	27.3	36.8
Wife in labor force, husband not in labor force	5.5	2.6	5.3	2.4	5.1	2.6
Both husband and wife not in labor force....................	13.8	1.1	13.9	1.1	15.3	1.1
Other Families	141,718	70,865	134,916	70,166	145,307	70,647
Female householder, no spouse present	65.9	67.9	66.9	68.1	64.9	69.2
In labor force.......................................	49.5	58.5	50.0	58.8	48.1	61.0
Not in labor force	16.3	9.4	16.9	9.2	16.8	8.2
Male householder, no spouse present......................	34.1	32.1	33.1	31.9	35.1	30.8
In labor force.......................................	28.8	30.4	28.1	30.4	30.6	30.0
Not in labor force	5.4	1.7	5.1	1.6	4.5	0.8

[1] 2020 ACS 5-Year estimates. 1-Year estimates were not released for 2020 due to the impact of COVID-19 on data collection that year. Data is not comparable to previous years, which are based on 1-year estimates.

Table UT-11. School Enrollment and Educational Attainment, 2021

(Number, percent.)

Item	State	U.S.
Enrollment		
Total population 3 years and over, enrolled in school	1,022,486	79,453,524
Enrolled in nursery school or preschool (percent)..	5.1	5.2
Enrolled in kindergarten (percent)...	4.9	5.0
Enrolled in elementary school, grades 1-8 (percent)..	41.5	41.3
Enrolled in high school, grades 9-12 (percent)...	21.9	21.8
Enrolled in college or graduate school (percent)...	26.6	26.7
Attainment		
Total population 25 years and over	2,010,727	228,193,464
Less than ninth grade (percent)..	2.7	4.8
9th to 12th grade, no diploma (percent)...	4.1	5.9
High school graduate, including equivalency (percent)..	22.1	26.3
Some college, no degree (percent)..	24.7	19.3
Associate's degree (percent)...	9.5	8.8
Bachelor's degree (percent)..	24.1	21.2
Graduate or professional degree (percent)...	12.7	13.8
High school graduate or higher (percent)..	93.2	89.4
Bachelor's degree or higher (percent)...	36.8	35.0

Table UT-12. Public School Characteristics and Educational Indicators

(Number, percent; data derived from National Center of Education Statistics.)

Item	State	U.S.
Public Elementary and Secondary Schools		
Number of regular school districts, 2019-20	41	13,349
Number of operational schools, 2019-20...	1,071	98,469
Percent charter schools	12.3	7.7
Total public school enrollment, Fall 2021...	690,934	49,433,092
Percent charter school enrollment	11.3	7.5
Student-teacher ratio, Fall 2019..	22.6	15.9
Expenditures per student (unadjusted dollars), 2019-20	8,287	13,489
Four-year adjusted cohort graduation rate (ACGR), 2019-2020[1]..	88.2	86.5
Students eligible for free or reduced-price lunch (percent), 2019-20.......................................	32.7	52.1
English language learners (percent), Fall 2020...	8.1	10.3
Students age 3 to 21 served under IDEA, part B (percent), 2021-22	12.9	14.7

Public Schools by Type, 2019-20	Number	Percent of state public schools
Total number of schools..	1,071	100.0
Special education..	60	5.6
Vocational education...	7	0.7
Alternative education...	28	2.6

[1] Adjusted Cohort Graduation Rates (ACGR) differ from Averaged Freshmen Graduation Rates (AFGR).

Table UT-13. Reported Voting and Registration of the Voting-Age Population, November 2022

(Numbers in thousands, percent.)

Item	Total population	Total citizen population	Registered			Voted		
			Total registered	Percent registered (total population)	Percent registered (total citizen population)	Total voted	Percent voted (total population)	Percent voted (total citizen population)
U.S. Total	255,457	233,546	161,422	63.2	69.1	121,916	47.7	52.2
State Total....................................	2,455	2,278	1,536	62.6	67.4	1,204	49.0	52.8
Sex								
Male	1,231	1,134	781	63.4	68.9	589	47.9	52.0
Female	1,224	1,144	755	61.7	66.0	614	50.2	53.7
Race								
White alone..................................	2,264	2,119	1,463	64.6	69.0	1,163	51.4	54.9
White, non-Hispanic alone	1,933	1,907	1,381	71.4	72.4	1,113	57.6	58.4
Black alone..................................	31	31	12	36.9	36.9	10	30.6	30.6
Asian alone	60	37	24	39.6	64.7	16	26.5	43.2
Hispanic (of any race).................................	354	232	85	24.0	36.6	50	14.2	21.7
White alone or in combination	2,308	2,163	1,483	64.3	68.6	1,173	50.8	54.2
Black alone or in combination....................	43	43	14	31.6	31.6	10	22.1	22.1
Asian alone or in combination......................	81	58	38	46.4	65.2	21	25.9	36.3
Age								
18 to 24 years.............................	409	383	133	32.5	34.7	65	15.9	17.0
25 to 34 years.............................	476	416	281	59.1	67.5	179	37.6	43.0
35 to 44 years.............................	471	439	315	66.8	71.6	238	50.6	54.2
45 to 64 years.............................	668	614	449	67.2	73.1	387	57.9	63.0
65 years and over	431	425	359	83.3	84.3	335	77.7	78.8

B = Base is less than 75,000 and therefore too small to show the derived measure.

Table UT-14. Health Indicators

(Number, rate as indicated in footnotes.)

Item	State	U.S.
Births		
Life Expectancy at Birth (years), 2020	78.6	77.0
Fertility Rate by State[1], 2021...	63.6	56.3
Percent Home Births, 2021..	3.0	1.4
Cesarean Delivery Rate[2], 2021..	23.4	32.1
Preterm Birth Rate[3], 2021...	9.9	10.5
Teen Birth Rate[4], 2021..	9.7	13.9
Percentage of Babies Born Low Birthweight[5], 2021...	7.4	8.5
Deaths[6]		
Heart Disease Mortality Rate, 2021..	162.4	173.8
Cancer Mortality Rate, 2021..	121.0	146.6
Stroke Mortality Rate, 2021..	32.4	41.1
Diabetes Mortality Rate, 2021..	29.2	25.4
Influenza/Pneumonia Mortality Rate, 2021..	8.1	10.5
Suicide Mortality Rate, 2021...	20.1	14.1
Drug Overdose Mortality Rate, 2021..	21.1	33.6
Firearm Injury Mortality Rate, 2021..	13.9	14.6
Homicide Mortality Rate, 2021..	2.7	8.2
Disease and Illness		
Lifetime Asthma in Adults, 2020 (percent)...	16.3	13.9
Lifetime Asthma in Children, 2020 (percent)[7]..	8.7	11.3
Diabetes in Adults, 2020 (percent)...	8.5	8.2
Self-reported Obesity in Adults, 2021 (percent)...	30.9	NA

SOURCE: National Center for Health Statistics, National Vital Statistics System 2020 data; https://wonder.cdc.gov.
[1] General fertility rate per 1,000 women aged 15–44.
[2] This represents the percentage of all live births that were cesarean deliveries.
[3] Babies born prior to 37 weeks of pregnancy (gestation).
[4] Number of births per 1,000 females aged 15–19
[5] Babies born weighing less than 2,500 grams or 5 lbs. 8oz.
[6] Death rates are the number of deaths per 100,000 total population.
[7] U.S. total includes data from 30 states and D.C.
NA = Not available.
- = Zero or rounds to zero.

Table UT-15. State Government Finances, 2021

(Dollar amounts in thousands, percent distribution.)

Item	Dollars	Percent distribution
Total Revenue	29,984,752	100.0
General revenue	27,404,644	91.4
Intergovernmental revenue	7,403,999	24.7
Taxes	12,631,617	42.1
General sales	3,628,512	12.1
Selective sales	1,174,720	3.9
License taxes	371,684	1.2
Individual income tax	6,672,695	22.3
Corporate income tax	745,673	2.5
Other taxes	38,333	0.1
Current charges	5,780,881	19.3
Miscellaneous general revenue	1,588,147	5.3
Utility revenue	-	-
Liquor stores revenue	461147	1.5
Insurance trust revenue[1]	2,118,961	7.1
Total Expenditure	28,056,050	100.0
Intergovernmental expenditure	5,149,699	18.4
Direct expenditure	22,906,351	81.6
Current operation	16,747,813	59.7
Capital outlay	2,447,344	8.7
Insurance benefits and repayments	2,420,479	8.6
Assistance and subsidies	1,091,925	3.9
Interest on debt	198,790	0.7
Exhibit: Salaries and wages	4,458,161	15.9
Total Expenditure	28,056,050	100.0
General expenditure	25,301,054	90.2
Intergovernmental expenditure	5,149,699	18.4
Direct expenditure	20,151,355	71.8
General expenditure, by function:		
Education	10,911,619	38.9
Public welfare	5,322,287	19.0
Hospitals	2,631,944	9.4
Health	816,595	2.9
Highways	1,835,573	6.5
Police protection	179,021	0.6
Correction	439,790	1.6
Natural resources	334,404	1.2
Parks and recreation	93,958	0.3
Governmental administration	1,401,905	5.0
Interest on general debt	198,790	0.7
Other and unallocable	1,074,968	3.8
Utility expenditure	-	-
Liquor stores expenditure	334,517	1.2
Insurance trust expenditure	2,420,479	8.6
Debt at End of Fiscal Year	7,030,825	X
Cash and Security Holdings	47,800,441	X

X = Not applicable.
- = Zero or rounds to zero.
[1] Within insurance trust revenue, net earnings of state retirement systems is a calculated statistic (the item code in the data file is X08), and thus can be positive or negative. Net earnings is the sum of earnings on investments plus gains on investments minus losses on investments. The change made in 2002 for asset valuation from book to market value in accordance with Statement 34 of the Governmental Accounting Standards Board is reflected in the calculated statistics.

Table UT-16. State Government Tax Collections, 2022

(Dollars in thousands, percent.)

Item	Dollars	Percent distribution
Total Taxes	13,786,248	100.0
Property taxes	X	-
Sales and gross receipts	5,552,999	40.3
General sales and gross receipts	4,280,780	31.1
Selective sales and gross receipts	1,272,219	9.2
Alcoholic beverages	18,394	0.1
Amusements	X	-
Insurance premiums	189,609	1.4
Motor fuels	581,850	4.2
Pari-mutuels	X	-
Public utilities	61,486	0.4
Tobacco products	109,658	0.8
Other selective sales	311,222	2.3
Licenses	387,595	2.8
Alcoholic beverages	-	-
Amusements	X	-
Corporations in general	423	-
Hunting and fishing	33,955	0.2
Motor vehicle	254,894	1.8
Motor vehicle operators	30,838	0.2
Public utilities	X	-
Occupation and business, NEC	60,064	0.4
Other licenses	7,421	0.1
Income taxes	7,747,848	56.2
Individual income	6,812,367	49.4
Corporation net income	935,481	6.8
Other taxes	97,806	0.7
Death and gift	X	-
Documentary and stock transfer	X	-
Severance	97,393	0.7
Taxes, NEC	413	-

X = Not applicable.
- = Zero or rounds to zero.

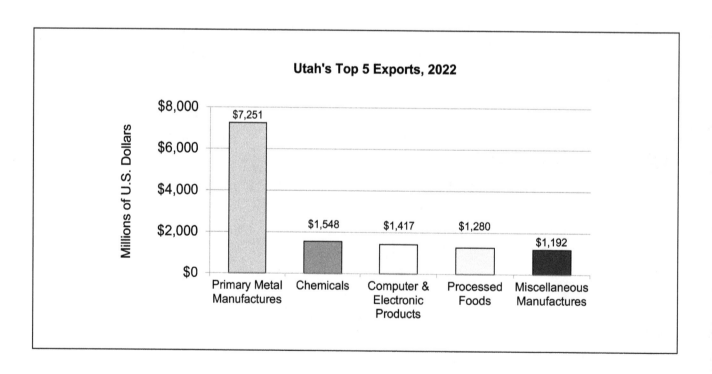

Utah's Top 5 Exports, 2022

(Bar chart, Millions of U.S. Dollars)

- Primary Metal Manufactures: $7,251
- Chemicals: $1,548
- Computer & Electronic Products: $1,417
- Processed Foods: $1,280
- Miscellaneous Manufactures: $1,192

VERMONT

Facts and Figures

Location: Northeastern United States; bordered on the N by Canada (Quebec), on the E by New Hampshire, on the S by Massachusetts, and on the W by New York

Area: 9,614 sq. mi. (24,901 sq. km.); rank—45th

Population: 647,064 (2022 est.); rank—50th

Principal Cities: capital—Montpelier; largest—Burlington

Statehood: March 4, 1791; the 14th state

U.S. Congress: 2 senators, 1 representative

State Motto: Freedom and Unity

State Song: "These Green Mountains"

State Nickname: The Green Mountain State

Abbreviations: VT; Vt.

State Symbols: flower—red clover; tree—sugar maple; bird—hermit thrush

At a Glance

- Vermont experienced an increase in population of 3.4 percent between 2010 and 2022, which ranked 37th in the country.

- Vermont's median household income in 2021 was $72,431, and 10.3 percent of the population lived below the poverty level.

- Vermont's homicide rate in 2021 was the 2nd lowest in the nation, with less than 0.45 homicide deaths per 100,000 population.

- In 2021, 3.7 percent of Vermonters did not have health insurance, which was the 2nd lowest percent in the country.

- Vermont had the lowest percent of its population under 18 years old in 2022, with

- 17.7 percent of its residents in this age group. It was also the state with the lowest birth rate in 2021, with 8.3 births per 1,000 population.

Table VT-1. Population by Age, Sex, Race, and Hispanic Origin

(Number, percent, except where noted.)

Sex, age, race, and Hispanic origin	2010	2020	2022	Percent change, 2010–2022
Total Population..	625,741	643,085	647,064	3.4
Percent of total U.S. population	0.2	0.2	0.2	X
Sex				
Male..	308,206	320,409	322,025	4.5
Female	317,535	322,676	325,039	2.4
Age				
Under 5 years..	31,952	28,823	27,594	-13.6
Under 18 years..	129,233	117,565	114,757	-11.2
18 to 64 years...	405,430	395,845	392,856	-3.1
65 years and over	91,078	129,675	139,451	53.1
Median age (years)	41.5	43.0	43.2	4.1
Race and Hispanic Origin				
One race				
White	598,592	605,498	607,189	1.4
Black	6,456	9,065	9,830	52.3
American Indian and Alaska Native	2,308	2,471	2,546	10.3
Asian...	8,069	12,921	13,354	65.5
Native Hawaiian or Other Pacific Islander	175	243	250	42.9
Two or more races	10,141	12,887	13,895	37.0
Hispanic (of any race)..	9,208	13,610	14,857	61.3

NOTE: Population figures for 2022 are July 1 estimates. The 2010 and 2020 estimates are taken from the respective censuses.
- = Zero or rounds to zero.
X = Not applicable.

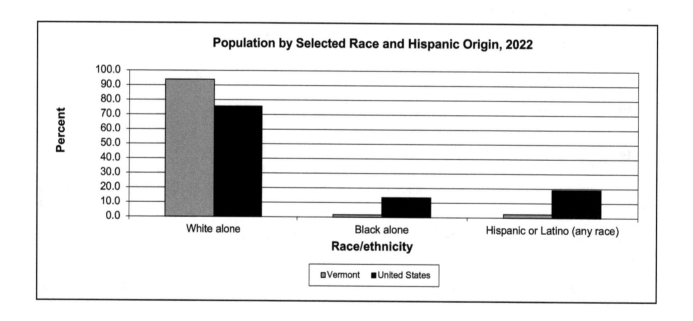

Population by Selected Race and Hispanic Origin, 2022

Legend: ▨ Vermont ■ United States

Table VT-2. Marital Status

(Number, percent distribution.)

Sex, age, race, and Hispanic origin	2000	2010	2021
Males, 15 Years and Over	236,517	254,288	271,002
Never married	29.7	34.2	35.6
Now married, except separated...	57.1	51.3	51.0
Separated...	1.2	1.3	0.8
Widowed...	2.4	2.5	2.1
Divorced...	9.6	10.7	10.5
Females, 15 Years and Over	251,764	266,860	279,274
Never married	23.9	27.7	30.3
Now married, except separated...	53.3	49.7	47.9
Separated...	1.4	1.4	1.1
Widowed...	10.0	8.2	8.4
Divorced...	11.5	13.0	12.3

Table VT-3. Households and Housing Characteristics

(Number, percent, dollars.)

Item	2000	2010	2021	Average annual percent change, 2010–2021
Total Households...	240,634	256,922	270,163	0.5
Family households	157,763	159,846	165,039	0.3
Married-couple family	126,413	125,678	130,749	0.4
Other family	31,350	34,168	34,290	-
Male householder, no wife present.................................	9,078	10,887	10,678	-0.2
Female householder, no husband present........................	22,272	23,281	23,612	0.1
Nonfamily households	82,871	97,076	105,124	0.8
Householder living alone...	63,112	75,243	75,327	-
Householder not living alone...	19,759	21,833	29,797	3.3
Housing Characteristics				
Total housing units..	294,382	322,698	336,747	0.4
Occupied housing units	240,634	256,922	270,163	0.5
Owner occupied	169,784	180,847	196,291	0.8
Renter occupied...	70,850	76,075	73,872	-0.3
Average household size...	2.44	2.34	2.29	-0.2
Financial Characteristics				
Median gross rent of renter-occupied housing	553	823	1,115	3.2
Median monthly owner costs for housing units with a mortgage ...	1,021	1,445	1,664	1.4
Median value of owner-occupied housing units................	111,500	216,800	271,500	2.3

- = Zero or rounds to zero.

Table VT-4. Migration, Origin, and Language

(Number, percent.)

Characteristic	State 2021	U.S. 2021
Residence 1 Year Ago		
Population 1 year and over	641,007	328,464,538
Same house	88.1	87.2
Different house in the U.S.	11.6	12.3
Same county	4.8	6.7
Different county	6.7	5.7
Same state	1.8	3.3
Different state	5.0	2.4
Abroad	0.3	0.4
Place of Birth		
Native born	618,367	286,623,642
Male	50.0	49.7
Female	50.0	50.3
Foreign born	27,203	45,270,103
Male	40.1	48.7
Female	59.9	51.3
Foreign born; naturalized U.S. citizen...............................	16,134	24,044,083
Male	38.2	46.4
Female	61.8	53.6
Foreign born; not a U.S. citizen..	11,069	21,226,020
Male	42.9	51.2
Female	57.1	48.8
Entered 2010 or later	33.0	28.1
Entered 2000 to 2009	18.7	23.7
Entered before 2000..	48.3	48.2
World Region of Birth, Foreign		
Foreign-born population, excluding population born at sea ...	27,203	45,269,644
Europe	24.3	10.7
Asia...	35.5	31.0
Africa...	3.6	5.7
Oceania	0.8	0.6
Latin America...	13.3	50.1
North America...	22.5	1.7
Language Spoken at Home and Ability to Speak English		
Population 5 years and over...	618,410	313,232,500
English only	94.4	78.4
Language other than English...	5.6	21.6
Speaks English less than "very well"..............................	1.1	8.3

Table VT-5. Median Income and Poverty Status, 2021

(Number, percent, except as noted.)

Characteristic	State		U.S.	
	Number	Percent	Number	Percent
Median Income				
Households (dollars)...	72,431	X	69,717	X
Families (dollars)	90,556	X	85,806	X
Below Poverty Level (All People)	63,720	10.3	41,393,176	12.8
Sex				
Male	29,567	9.6	18,518,155	11.6
Female	34,153	10.9	22,875,021	13.9
Age				
Under 18 years..	11,994	10.4	12,243,219	16.9
Related children under 18 years................................	11,739	10.2	11,985,424	16.6
18 to 64 years...	39,878	10.6	23,526,341	11.9
65 years and over	11,848	9.1	5,623,616	10.3

X = Not applicable.

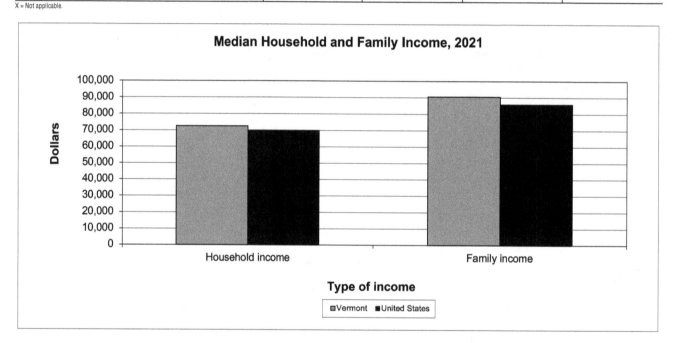

Median Household and Family Income, 2021

(Vertical axis: Dollars, 0 to 100,000; Horizontal axis: Type of income — Household income, Family income. Legend: Vermont, United States)

Table VT-6. Health Insurance Coverage Status for the Civilian Noninstitutionalized Population and Children Under 19 Years of Age

(Number, percent.)

Item	2011	2012	2013	2014	2015	2016	2017	2018	2019	2020 [2]	2021
Civilian Noninstitutionalized Population	620,159	619,928	620,896	620,453	620,107	618,622	617,556	620,066	618,064	618,184	639,228
Covered by Private or Public Insurance											
Number...	578,950	579,875	575,992	589,737	596,431	595,628	589,445	595,078	590,323	593,153	615,853
Percent..	93.4	93.5	92.8	95.0	96.2	96.3	95.4	96.0	95.5	96.0	96.3
Uninsured											
Number...	41,209	40,053	44,904	30,716	23,676	22,994	28,111	24,988	27,741	25,031	23,375
Percent..	6.6	6.5	7.2	5.0	3.8	3.7	4.6	4.0	4.5	4.0	3.7
Percent in the U.S. not covered...........................	15.1	14.8	14.5	11.7	9.4	8.6	8.7	8.9	9.2	8.7	8.6
Children Under 19 Years of Age[1]	125,599	123,563	123,812	121,472	119,828	118,351	127,105	124,839	124,542	125,558	126,087
Covered by Private or Public Insurance											
Number...	122,580	120,072	119,930	118,832	118,577	116,493	125,077	122,376	121,937	123,491	123,712
Percent..	97.6	97.2	96.9	97.8	99.0	98.4	98.4	98.0	97.9	98.4	98.1
Uninsured											
Number...	3,019	3,491	3,882	2,640	1,251	1,858	2,028	2,463	2,605	2,067	2,375
Percent..	2.4	2.8	3.1	2.2	1.0	1.6	1.6	2.0	2.1	1.6	1.9
Percent in the U.S. not covered...........................	7.5	7.2	7.1	6.0	4.8	4.5	5.0	5.2	5.7	5.2	5.4

[1] Data for years prior to 2017 are for individuals under 18 years of age.
[2] 2020 ACS 5-Year estimates. 1-Year estimates were not released for 2020 due to the impact of COVID-19 on data collection that year. Data is not comparable to previous years, which are based on 1-year estimates.

Table VT-7. Employment Status by Demographic Group, 2022

(Numbers in thousands, percent.)

Characteristic	Civilian noninstitutional population	Civilian labor force		Employed		Unemployed	
		Number	Percent of population	Number	Percent of population	Number	Percent of population
Total...	544	343	63.1	334	61.5	9	2.5
Sex							
Male...	268	174	64.9	169	63.0	5	3.0
Female.......................................	275	169	61.3	166	60.1	3	2.0
Race, Sex, and Hispanic Origin							
White...	513	324	63.2	316	61.7	8	2.4
Male..	253	165	65.1	160	63.2	5	2.8
Female.....................................	260	159	61.3	156	60.1	3	1.9
Black or African American.............	NA	NA	NA	NA	NA	NA	NA
Male..	NA	NA	NA	NA	NA	NA	NA
Female.....................................	NA	NA	NA	NA	NA	NA	NA
Hispanic or Latino ethnicity[1]........	NA	NA	NA	NA	NA	NA	NA
Male..	NA	NA	NA	NA	NA	NA	NA
Female.....................................	NA	NA	NA	NA	NA	NA	NA
Age							
16 to 19 years............................	NA	NA	NA	NA	NA	NA	NA
20 to 24 years............................	34	23	67.8	22	65.8	1	3.5
25 to 34 years............................	78	64	82.2	62	79.9	2	2.8
35 to 44 years............................	95	83	87.3	81	85.6	2	2.1
45 to 54 years............................	70	57	81.0	56	79.3	1	1.9
55 to 64 years............................	95	68	71.7	66	70.0	2	2.2
65 years and over........................	142	34	24.1	34	23.7	1	1.8

NOTE: Data in Table 7 are from the Current Population Survey (CPS) and do not match the estimates in Table 8. See notes and definitions for further information.
[1] May be of any race.
NA = Not available.

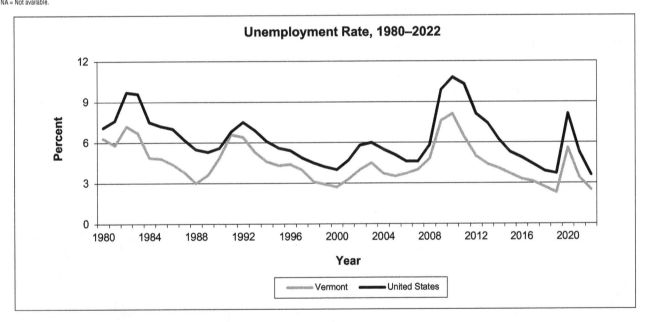

Unemployment Rate, 1980–2022

Legend: Vermont — United States

Table VT-8. Employment Status of the Civilian Noninstitutional Population Age 16 Years and Over

(Number, percent.)

Year	Civilian labor force	Civilian participation rate	Employed	Unemployed	Unemployment rate
2010.............................	359,692	70.8	336,920	22,772	6.3
2011.............................	357,676	70.1	337,779	19,897	5.6
2012.............................	353,947	69.2	336,899	17,048	4.8
2013.............................	350,175	68.3	334,684	15,491	4.4
2014.............................	348,697	67.9	334,742	13,955	4.0
2015.............................	346,512	67.3	334,262	12,250	3.5
2016.............................	345,851	67.1	335,043	10,808	3.1
2017.............................	355,385	67.3	344,698	10,687	3.0
2018.............................	350,450	67.2	347,125	9,331	2.6
2019.............................	355,950	66.9	347,600	8,350	2.3
2020.............................	341,137	63.8	322,078	19,059	5.6
2021.............................	328,216	61.0	316,941	11,275	3.4
2022.............................	342,119	63.2	333,081	9,038	2.6

Table VT-9. Employment and Average Wages by Industry

(Estimates are based on the 2012 North American Industry Classification System [NAICS].)

Industry	2014	2015	2016	2017	2018	2019	2020	2021
	Number of Jobs							
Wage and Salary Employment by Industry......................	323,339	325,842	326,845	327,624	329,216	329,628	300,757	308,827
Farm Wage and Salary Employment...............................	2,961	2,951	2,754	2,748	2,856	2,877	2,748	2,817
Nonfarm Wage and Salary Employment.........................	320,378	322,891	324,091	324,876	326,360	326,751	298,009	306,010
Private wage and salary employment.........................	261,972	264,746	266,002	266,990	268,458	268,689	242,569	251,274
Forestry, fishing, and related activities.....................	921	931	902	900	883	916	893	837
Mining..	600	646	639	616	612	623	601	605
Utilities...	1,727	1,548	1,342	1,261	1,254	1,237	1,198	1,212
Construction..	15,145	15,562	15,659	15,541	15,625	15,645	14,630	15,414
Manufacturing..	31,238	30,967	30,008	29,569	29,840	30,086	28,246	28,674
Durable goods manufacturing............................	20,392	19,699	18,771	18,294	18,413	18,660	17,270	17,408
Nondurable goods manufacturing......................	10,846	11,268	11,237	11,275	11,427	11,426	10,976	11,266
Wholesale trade..	9,279	9,339	9,518	9,336	9,066	9,111	8,752	8,661
Retail trade...	38,200	38,180	38,400	38,139	37,852	36,961	33,966	35,107
Transportation and warehousing............................	6,949	6,834	6,767	6,820	6,913	7,088	6,506	6,709
Information...	4,769	4,643	4,646	4,485	4,284	4,325	3,962	3,986
Finance and insurance	9,247	9,246	9,192	9,296	9,368	9,536	9,439	9,087
Real estate and rental and leasing........................	3,124	3,016	3,023	3,055	3,125	3,206	2,942	3,084
Professional, scientific, and technical services.........	13,965	14,334	14,438	14,626	14,781	15,136	15,166	16,144
Management of companies and enterprises............	2,081	2,219	2,086	2,026	2,018	2,025	2,060	2,052
Administrative and waste services........................	10,742	11,073	11,440	11,987	12,393	12,466	11,457	12,180
Educational services	14,571	14,980	15,819	15,811	15,910	15,763	14,245	15,113
Health care and social assistance..........................	49,980	50,794	51,663	52,564	53,093	52,984	49,870	50,056
Arts, entertainment, and recreation......................	4,341	4,181	4,325	4,483	4,554	4,595	3,259	3,760
Accommodation and food services.......................	31,060	32,087	32,126	33,007	32,849	32,807	22,913	25,901
Other services, except public administration............	14,033	14,166	14,009	13,468	14,038	14,179	12,464	12,692
Government and government enterprises	58,406	58,145	58,089	57,886	57,902	58,062	55,440	54,736
	Dollars							
Average Wages and Salaries by Industry	42,190	43,289	44,173	45,314	46,817	48,393	52,832	55,113
Average Farm Wages and Salaries	28,805	23,609	29,033	26,405	25,215	19,876	20,210	19,805
Average Nonfarm Wages and Salaries	42,314	43,469	44,302	45,474	47,006	48,644	53,133	55,438
Average private wages and salaries.........................	41,774	42,909	43,693	44,810	46,304	48,016	52,649	55,205
Forestry, fishing, and related activities............................	31,160	32,096	33,373	33,358	35,183	35,795	37,161	39,572
Mining...	55,833	57,243	59,197	59,641	61,928	62,490	63,158	64,853
Utilities..	104,380	123,169	105,244	103,795	109,886	103,793	110,937	108,329
Construction..	46,235	46,929	48,621	50,118	51,029	52,541	55,050	57,643
Manufacturing..	55,287	55,949	55,797	57,967	59,407	60,751	62,260	64,130
Durable goods manufacturing............................	59,214	59,890	59,465	62,039	64,453	65,972	66,146	68,565
Nondurable goods manufacturing......................	47,903	49,061	49,669	51,360	51,277	52,224	56,145	57,279
Wholesale trade..	56,473	59,043	62,971	61,460	64,990	65,610	70,561	75,022
Retail trade...	28,382	29,432	29,640	30,539	31,758	32,921	36,451	38,354
Transportation and warehousing............................	40,032	40,267	40,607	41,505	43,164	44,859	48,794	52,063
Information...	53,754	56,141	56,070	58,287	59,774	62,837	68,537	72,283
Finance and insurance	69,803	73,163	74,453	80,400	81,185	84,260	89,315	97,648
Real estate and rental and leasing........................	38,498	39,636	41,108	41,977	44,801	45,540	49,688	54,095
Professional, scientific, and technical services	70,921	73,622	75,514	77,731	80,189	83,984	90,701	99,095
Management of companies and enterprises............	87,230	86,148	92,751	92,827	92,388	108,487	105,731	117,190
Administrative and waste services........................	36,630	36,129	37,980	40,942	42,173	44,228	47,187	53,352
Educational services	33,323	32,994	36,115	37,356	38,384	38,853	40,927	37,911
Health care and social assistance..........................	42,055	43,519	44,286	44,433	46,321	48,219	53,118	54,937
Arts, entertainment, and recreation......................	25,641	25,125	26,246	26,449	27,855	26,934	31,945	32,680
Accommodation and food services.......................	22,636	23,629	24,190	25,142	26,200	27,236	27,959	32,031
Other services, except public administration............	28,376	29,506	30,551	31,493	32,470	33,208	36,783	38,390
Government and government enterprises.................	44,733	46,021	47,088	48,540	50,259	51,551	55,247	56,506

Table VT-10. Employment Characteristics by Family Type

(Number, percent.)

Family type and labor force status	2019		2020 [1]		2021	
	Total	Families with own children under 18 years	Total	Families with own children under 18 years	Total	Families with own children under 18 years
All Families.........	156,153	57,501	157,105	59,214	165,039	61,355
FAMILY TYPE AND LABOR FORCE STATUS						
Opposite-Sex Married-Couple Families............	121,034	37,866	122,168	40,229	128,814	41,680
Both husband and wife in labor force..........	56.8	81.5	56.8	77.4	57.0	79.4
Husband in labor force, wife not in labor force	14.2	13.6	15.2	16.7	14.0	14.6
Wife in labor force, husband not in labor force..........	8.7	3.5	9.4	4.5	8.8	3.5
Both husband and wife not in labor force........	19.2	0.9	18.6	1.5	20.2	2.4
Other Families	35,119	19,635	32,998	18,651	34,290	19,483
Female householder, no spouse present	65.5	67.3	68.4	70.4	68.9	70.0
In labor force.........	48.9	58.8	49.9	58.4	46.1	50.4
Not in labor force	16.6	8.4	18.5	11.9	22.7	19.6
Male householder, no spouse present.........	34.5	32.7	31.6	29.6	31.1	30.0
In labor force.........	26.7	30.8	25.6	26.3	25.4	27.1
Not in labor force.........	7.8	2.0	6.0	3.4	5.7	2.9

[1] 2020 ACS 5-Year estimates. 1-Year estimates were not released for 2020 due to the impact of COVID-19 on data collection that year. Data is not comparable to previous years, which are based on 1-year estimates.

Table VT-11. School Enrollment and Educational Attainment, 2021

(Number, percent.)

Item	State	U.S.
Enrollment		
Total population 3 years and over, enrolled in school	143,264	79,453,524
Enrolled in nursery school or preschool (percent).........	5.6	5.2
Enrolled in kindergarten (percent).........	4.7	5.0
Enrolled in elementary school, grades 1-8 (percent).........	37.1	41.3
Enrolled in high school, grades 9-12 (percent).........	18.7	21.8
Enrolled in college or graduate school (percent).........	33.8	26.7
Attainment		
Total population 25 years and over	462,705	228,193,464
Less than ninth grade (percent).........	1.7	4.8
9th to 12th grade, no diploma (percent).........	3.8	5.9
High school graduate, including equivalency (percent).........	26.2	26.3
Some college, no degree (percent)	15.8	19.3
Associate's degree (percent).........	8.2	8.8
Bachelor's degree (percent)	26.0	21.2
Graduate or professional degree (percent).........	18.4	13.8
High school graduate or higher (percent).........	94.5	89.4
Bachelor's degree or higher (percent).........	44.4	35.0

Table VT-12. Public School Characteristics and Educational Indicators

(Number, percent; data derived from National Center of Education Statistics.)

Item	State	U.S.
Public Elementary and Secondary Schools		
Number of regular school districts, 2019-20	128	13,349
Number of operational schools, 2019-20.........	308	98,469
Percent charter schools	-	7.7
Total public school enrollment, Fall 2021.........	83,975	49,433,092
Percent charter school enrollment	NA	7.5
Student-teacher ratio, Fall 2019	10.8	15.9
Expenditures per student (unadjusted dollars), 2019-20	22,124	13,489
Four-year adjusted cohort graduation rate (ACGR), 2019-2020[1].........	83.1	86.5
Students eligible for free or reduced-price lunch (percent), 2019-20.........	35.1	52.1
English language learners (percent), Fall 2020	2.3	10.3
Students age 3 to 21 served under IDEA, part B (percent), 2021-22	18.2	14.7

Public Schools by Type, 2019-20	Number	Percent of state public schools
Total number of schools.........	308	100.0
Special education.........	-	-
Vocational education.........	15	4.9
Alternative education.........	1	0.3

[1] Adjusted Cohort Graduation Rates (ACGR) differ from Averaged Freshmen Graduation Rates (AFGR).
NA = Not available.
- = Zero or rounds to zero.

Table VT-13. Reported Voting and Registration of the Voting-Age Population, November 2022

(Numbers in thousands, percent.)

Item	Total population	Total citizen population	Registered			Voted		
			Total registered	Percent registered (total population)	Percent registered (total citizen population)	Total voted	Percent voted (total population)	Percent voted (total citizen population)
U.S. Total	255,457	233,546	161,422	63.2	69.1	121,916	47.7	52.2
State Total	528	521	393	74.5	75.4	324	61.4	62.2
Sex								
Male	259	256	192	74.3	75.2	157	60.7	61.5
Female	269	265	200	74.6	75.6	167	62.2	62.9
Race								
White alone.......................................	497	494	380	76.6	77.0	314	63.3	63.6
White, non-Hispanic alone	491	489	377	76.7	77.1	311	63.3	63.7
Black alone.......................................	5	3	1	28.0	42.2	1	20.1	30.3
Asian alone	12	10	5	41.3	50.1	4	36.7	44.4
Hispanic (of any race)	8	7	4	53.0	58.8	3	40.0	44.3
White alone or in combination	507	504	385	75.9	76.3	318	62.7	63.1
Black alone or in combination	8	7	3	34.1	42.6	2	29.4	36.7
Asian alone or in combination	14	12	6	42.1	49.2	5	38.2	44.6
Age								
18 to 24 years	47	46	27	58.0	59.8	19	39.7	41.0
25 to 34 years	77	76	51	66.3	67.2	33	43.0	43.6
35 to 44 years	96	96	71	74.1	74.6	54	56.6	57.0
45 to 64 years	164	162	124	75.4	76.2	107	65.3	66.0
65 years and over	144	142	120	83.4	84.3	111	77.2	78.0

B = Base is less than 75,000 and therefore too small to show the derived measure.

Table VT-14. Health Indicators

(Number, rate as indicated in footnotes.)

Item	State	U.S.
Births		
Life Expectancy at Birth (years), 2020	78.8	77.0
Fertility Rate by State[1], 2021	44.9	56.3
Percent Home Births, 2021	3.0	1.4
Cesarean Delivery Rate[2], 2021	27.2	32.1
Preterm Birth Rate[3], 2021	8.0	10.5
Teen Birth Rate[4], 2021	6.4	13.9
Percentage of Babies Born Low Birthweight[5], 2021	7.0	8.5
Deaths[6]		
Heart Disease Mortality Rate, 2021	175.7	173.8
Cancer Mortality Rate, 2021	154.0	146.6
Stroke Mortality Rate, 2021	31.9	41.1
Diabetes Mortality Rate, 2021	17.9	25.4
Influenza/Pneumonia Mortality Rate, 2021	4.5	10.5
Suicide Mortality Rate, 2021	20.3	14.1
Drug Overdose Mortality Rate, 2021	42.3	33.6
Firearm Injury Mortality Rate, 2021	11.9	14.6
Homicide Mortality Rate, 2021	0.0	8.2
Disease and Illness		
Lifetime Asthma in Adults, 2020 (percent)	15.1	13.9
Lifetime Asthma in Children, 2020 (percent)[7]	11.3	11.3
Diabetes in Adults, 2020 (percent)	6.7	8.2
Self-reported Obesity in Adults, 2021 (percent)	29.0	NA

SOURCE: National Center for Health Statistics, National Vital Statistics System 2020 data; https://wonder.cdc.gov.
[1] General fertility rate per 1,000 women aged 15–44.
[2] This represents the percentage of all live births that were cesarean deliveries.
[3] Babies born prior to 37 weeks of pregnancy (gestation).
[4] Number of births per 1,000 females aged 15–19
[5] Babies born weighing less than 2,500 grams or 5 lbs. 8oz.
[6] Death rates are the number of deaths per 100,000 total population.
[7] U.S. total includes data from 30 states and D.C.
NA = Not available.
- = Zero or rounds to zero.

Table VT-15. State Government Finances, 2021

(Dollar amounts in thousands, percent distribution.)

Item	Dollars	Percent distribution
Total Revenue	8,419,220	100.0
General revenue	7,838,219	93.1
Intergovernmental revenue	2,694,118	32.0
Taxes	4,102,929	48.7
General sales	507,259	6.0
Selective sales	740,358	8.8
License taxes	143,501	1.7
Individual income tax	1,233,157	14.6
Corporate income tax	166,841	2.0
Other taxes	1,311,813	15.6
Current charges	598,310	7.1
Miscellaneous general revenue	442,862	5.3
Utility revenue	-	-
Liquor stores revenue	108155	1.3
Insurance trust revenue[1]	472,846	5.6
Total Expenditure	10,455,844	100.0
Intergovernmental expenditure	2,101,753	20.1
Direct expenditure	8,354,091	79.9
Current operation	5,455,844	52.2
Capital outlay	328,336	3.1
Insurance benefits and repayments	2,249,803	21.5
Assistance and subsidies	214,236	2.0
Interest on debt	105,872	1.0
Exhibit: Salaries and wages	1,022,446	9.8
Total Expenditure	10,455,844	100.0
General expenditure	8,120,254	77.7
Intergovernmental expenditure	2,101,753	20.1
Direct expenditure	6,018,501	57.6
General expenditure, by function:		
Education	3,191,172	30.5
Public welfare	2,090,413	20.0
Hospitals	25,600	0.2
Health	441,341	4.2
Highways	486,990	4.7
Police protection	178,490	1.7
Correction	165,157	1.6
Natural resources	146,406	1.4
Parks and recreation	41,375	0.4
Governmental administration	261,109	2.5
Interest on general debt	105,872	1.0
Other and unallocable	939,949	9.0
Utility expenditure	42,553	0.4
Liquor stores expenditure	76,318	0.7
Insurance trust expenditure	2,249,803	21.5
Debt at End of Fiscal Year	3,426,102	X
Cash and Security Holdings	10,322,241	X

X = Not applicable.
- = Zero or rounds to zero.
[1] Within insurance trust revenue, net earnings of state retirement systems is a calculated statistic (the item code in the data file is X08), and thus can be positive or negative. Net earnings is the sum of earnings on investments plus gains on investments minus losses on investments. The change made in 2002 for asset valuation from book to market value in accordance with Statement 34 of the Governmental Accounting Standards Board is reflected in the calculated statistics.

Table VT-16. State Government Tax Collections, 2022

(Dollars in thousands, percent.)

Item	Dollars	Percent distribution
Total Taxes	4,415,490	100.0
Property taxes	1,235,599	28.0
Sales and gross receipts	1,391,177	31.5
General sales and gross receipts	545,564	12.4
Selective sales and gross receipts	845,613	19.2
Alcoholic beverages	12,064	0.3
Amusements	X	-
Insurance premiums	68,799	1.6
Motor fuels	121,774	2.8
Pari-mutuels	X	-
Public utilities	9,705	0.2
Tobacco products	75,991	1.7
Other selective sales	557,280	12.6
Licenses	143,122	3.2
Alcoholic beverages	491	-
Amusements	21	-
Corporations in general	3,292	0.1
Hunting and fishing	8,061	0.2
Motor vehicle	74,974	1.7
Motor vehicle operators	13,796	0.3
Public utilities	X	-
Occupation and business, NEC	32,384	0.7
Other licenses	10,103	0.2
Income taxes	1,508,701	34.2
Individual income	1,268,299	28.7
Corporation net income	240,402	5.4
Other taxes	136,891	3.1
Death and gift	13,997	0.3
Documentary and stock transfer	113,493	2.6
Severance	X	-
Taxes, NEC	9,401	0.2

X = Not applicable.
- = Zero or rounds to zero.

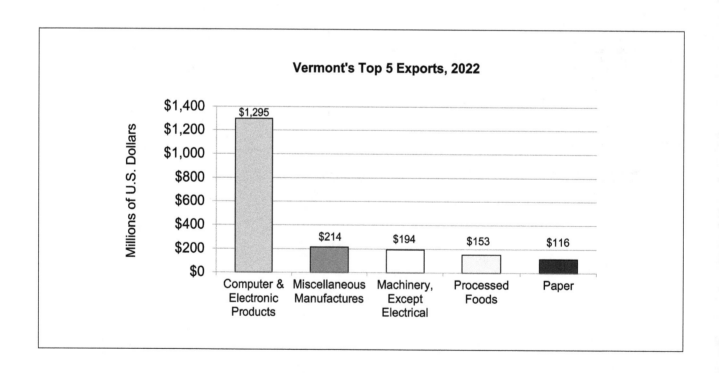

Vermont's Top 5 Exports, 2022

Export	Millions of U.S. Dollars
Computer & Electronic Products	$1,295
Miscellaneous Manufactures	$214
Machinery, Except Electrical	$194
Processed Foods	$153
Paper	$116

VIRGINIA

Facts and Figures

Location: Eastern United States; bordered on the N and NE by Maryland and the District of Columbia, on the E by the Atlantic Ocean, on the S by North Carolina and Tennessee, and on the W by Kentucky and West Virginia

Area: 42,774 sq. mi. (110,785 sq. km.); rank—35th

Population: 8,683,619 (2022 est.); rank—12th

Principal Cities: capital—Richmond; largest—Virginia Beach

Statehood: June 25, 1788; 10th state

U.S. Congress: 2 senators, 11 representatives

State Motto: *Sic semper tyrannis* ("Thus always to tyrants")

State Song: "Our Great Virginia" and "Sweet Virginia Breeze"

State Nickname: The Old Dominion State

Abbreviations: VA; Va.

State Symbols: flower—flowering dogwood; tree—flowering dogwood; bird—cardinal

At a Glance

- With an increase in population of 8.5 percent, Virginia ranked 19th among the states in growth from 2010 to 2022.

- The life expectancy at birth in Virginia in 2020 was 77.6 years, compared to the national life expectancy of 77.0 years.

- In 2022, 2.9 percent of Virginians were unemployed, compared to 3.6 percent of the total U.S. population.

- Virginia's median household income in 2021 was $80,963, which ranked 11th in the country. Virginia's poverty rate was 10.2 percent, which ranked 44th among all states.

- Virginia's voter turnout for the November 2022 election ranked 28th in the nation, with 48.8 percent of the population casting votes.

Table VA-1. Population by Age, Sex, Race, and Hispanic Origin

(Number, percent, except where noted.)

Sex, age, race, and Hispanic origin	2010	2020	2022	Percent change, 2010–2022
Total Population..	8,001,024	8,631,384	8,683,619	8.5
Percent of total U.S. population	2.6	2.6	2.6	X
Sex				
Male..	3,925,983	4,275,544	4,299,114	9.5
Female...	4,075,041	4,355,840	4,384,505	7.6
Age				
Under 5 years..	509,625	499,920	487,493	-4.3
Under 18 years..	1,853,677	1,886,455	1,866,910	0.7
18 to 64 years	5,170,410	5,369,900	5,351,721	3.5
65 years and over	976,937	1,375,029	1,464,988	50.0
Median age (years)	37.5	38.6	39.0	4.0
Race and Hispanic Origin				
One race				
White	5,725,432	5,955,055	5,947,332	3.9
Black	1,579,414	1,722,299	1,737,910	10.0
American Indian and Alaska Native	41,525	48,144	50,576	21.8
Asian...	449,149	613,366	637,656	42.0
Native Hawaiian or Other Pacific Islander	8,201	10,439	10,996	34.1
Two or more races	197,303	282,081	299,149	51.6
Hispanic (of any race)...	631,825	862,480	911,003	44.2

NOTE: Population figures for 2022 are July 1 estimates. The 2010 and 2020 estimates are taken from the respective censuses.
- = Zero or rounds to zero.
X = Not applicable.

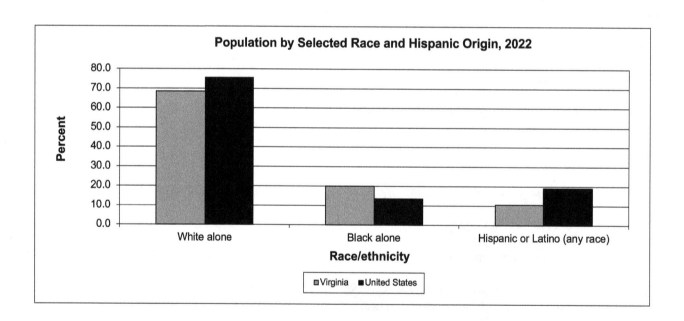

Table VA-2. Marital Status

(Number, percent distribution.)

Sex, age, race, and Hispanic origin	2000	2010	2021
Males, 15 Years and Over	2,724,334	3,156,115	3,473,594
Never married	29.1	34.2	36.0
Now married, except separated...............................	58.2	52.6	51.4
Separated..	2.6	2.3	1.7
Widowed..	2.3	2.3	2.5
Divorced..	7.9	8.5	8.4
Females, 15 Years and Over	2,899,294	3,331,264	3,614,449
Never married	23.5	28.0	30.7
Now married, except separated...............................	53.4	49.0	47.7
Separated..	3.2	2.9	2.1
Widowed..	9.9	8.7	8.0
Divorced..	10.0	11.4	11.5

Table VA-3. Households and Housing Characteristics

(Number, percent, dollars.)

Item	2000	2010	2021	Average annual percent change, 2010–2021
Total Households............	2,699,173	2,992,732	3,331,461	1.0
Family households	1,847,796	2,013,520	2,164,944	0.7
Married-couple family	1,426,044	1,517,627	1,629,590	0.7
Other family	421,752	495,893	535,354	0.7
Male householder, no wife present............	101,462	124,273	153,061	2.1
Female householder, no husband present............	320,290	371,620	382,293	0.3
Nonfamily households	851,377	979,212	1,166,517	1.7
Householder living alone............	676,907	794,535	942,665	1.7
Householder not living alone............	174,470	184,677	223,852	1.9
Housing Characteristics				
Total housing units	2,904,192	3,368,674	3,652,329	0.8
Occupied housing units	2,699,173	2,992,732	3,331,461	1.0
Owner occupied	1,837,939	2,025,240	2,252,170	1.0
Renter occupied	861,234	967,492	1,079,291	1.1
Average household size............	2.54	2.6	2.52	-0.3
Financial Characteristics				
Median gross rent of renter-occupied housing	650	1,019	1,331	2.8
Median monthly owner costs for housing units with a mortgage	1,144	1,728	1,818	0.5
Median value of owner-occupied housing units............	125,400	249,100	330,600	3.0

- = Zero or rounds to zero

Table VA-4. Migration, Origin, and Language

(Number, percent.)

Characteristic	State 2021	U.S. 2021
Residence 1 Year Ago		
Population 1 year and over	8,557,020	328,464,538
Same house	86.3	87.2
Different house in the U.S.	13.2	12.3
Same county	4.9	6.7
Different county	8.2	5.7
Same state	5.1	3.3
Different state	3.2	2.4
Abroad	0.5	0.4
Place of Birth		
Native born	7,571,927	286,623,642
Male	49.6	49.7
Female	50.4	50.3
Foreign born	1,070,347	45,270,103
Male	48.6	48.7
Female	51.4	51.3
Foreign born; naturalized U.S. citizen............	611,644	24,044,083
Male	47.2	46.4
Female	52.8	53.6
Foreign born; not a U.S. citizen	458,703	21,226,020
Male	50.4	51.2
Female	49.6	48.8
Entered 2010 or later	31.5	28.1
Entered 2000 to 2009	27.1	23.7
Entered before 2000............	41.4	48.2
World Region of Birth, Foreign		
Foreign-born population, excluding population born at sea	1,070,347	45,269,644
Europe	9.4	10.7
Asia	42.9	31.0
Africa	11.0	5.7
Oceania	0.2	0.6
Latin America	35.1	50.1
North America	1.3	1.7
Language Spoken at Home and Ability to Speak English		
Population 5 years and over............	8,161,282	313,232,500
English only	00.5	78.4
Language other than English............	16.5	21.6
Speaks English less than "very well"............	5.8	8.3

Table VA-5. Median Income and Poverty Status, 2021

(Number, percent, except as noted.)

Characteristic	State Number	State Percent	U.S. Number	U.S. Percent
Median Income				
Households (dollars)...	80,963	X	69,717	X
Families (dollars)	100,763	X	85,806	X
Below Poverty Level (All People)	854,145	10.2	41,393,176	12.8
Sex				
Male	379,401	9.2	18,518,155	11.6
Female	474,744	11.1	22,875,021	13.9
Age				
Under 18 years...	242,656	13.1	12,243,219	16.9
Related children under 18 years...............................	237,715	12.8	11,985,424	16.6
18 to 64 years...	500,608	9.7	23,526,341	11.9
65 years and over	110,881	8.0	5,623,616	10.3

X = Not applicable.

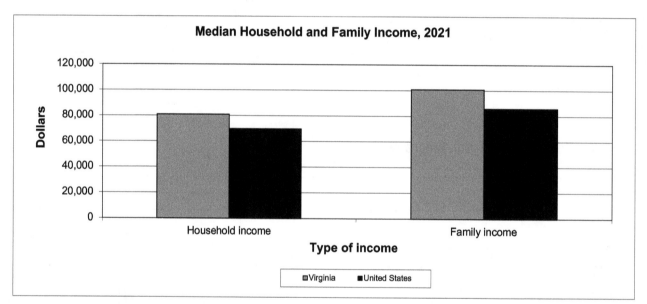

Median Household and Family Income, 2021

Table VA-6. Health Insurance Coverage Status for the Civilian Noninstitutionalized Population and Children Under 19 Years of Age

(Number, percent.)

Item	2011	2012	2013	2014	2015	2016	2017	2018	2019	2020 [2]	2021
Civilian Noninstitutionalized Population	7,887,164	7,973,466	8,054,191	8,114,884	8,162,517	8,199,576	8,256,810	8,301,038	8,303,671	8,282,997	8,412,758
Covered by Private or Public Insurance											
Number..	6,904,303	6,973,731	7,063,565	7,231,248	7,416,224	7,484,692	7,527,631	7,569,569	7,645,385	7,601,635	7,838,580
Percent..	87.5	87.5	87.7	89.1	90.9	91.3	91.2	91.2	92.1	91.8	93.2
Uninsured											
Number..	982,861	999,735	990,626	883,636	746,293	714,884	729,179	731,469	658,286	681,362	574,178
Percent..	12.5	12.5	12.3	10.9	9.1	8.7	8.8	8.8	7.9	8.2	6.8
Percent in the U.S. not covered...............	15.1	14.8	14.5	11.7	9.4	8.6	8.7	8.9	9.2	8.7	8.6
Children Under 19 Years of Age[1]	1,849,081	1,851,845	1,861,658	1,864,738	1,867,092	1,864,852	1,983,006	1,992,518	1,975,387	1,987,112	2,000,106
Covered by Private or Public Insurance											
Number..	1,740,598	1,747,907	1,760,407	1,757,636	1,776,406	1,775,840	1,881,588	1,890,950	1,878,818	1,887,993	1,911,928
Percent..	94.1	94.4	94.6	94.3	95.1	95.2	94.9	94.9	95.1	95.0	95.6
Uninsured											
Number..	108,483	103,938	101,251	107,102	90,686	89,012	101,418	101,568	96,569	99,119	88,178
Percent..	5.9	5.6	5.4	5.7	4.9	4.8	5.1	5.1	4.9	5.0	4.4
Percent in the U.S. not covered...............	7.5	7.2	7.1	6.0	4.8	4.5	5.0	5.2	5.7	5.2	5.4

[1] Data for years prior to 2017 are for individuals under 18 years of age.
[2] 2020 ACS 5-Year estimates. 1-Year estimates were not released for 2020 due to the impact of COVID-19 on data collection that year. Data is not comparable to previous years, which are based on 1-year estimates.

Table VA-7. Employment Status by Demographic Group, 2022

(Numbers in thousands, percent.)

Characteristic	Civilian noninstitutional population	Civilian labor force		Employed		Unemployed	
		Number	Percent of population	Number	Percent of population	Number	Percent of population
Total...	6,824	4,399	64.5	4,275	62.6	124	2.8
Sex							
Male...	3,299	2,262	68.6	2,202	66.8	60	2.7
Female	3,526	2,136	60.6	2,073	58.8	64	3.0
Race, Sex, and Hispanic Origin							
White	4,810	3,075	63.9	3,000	62.4	75	2.4
Male	2,368	1,632	68.9	1,595	67.3	37	2.3
Female	2,442	1,443	59.1	1,406	57.6	38	2.6
Black or African American...................	1,323	862	65.2	822	62.2	40	4.6
Male	609	399	65.4	379	62.2	20	4.9
Female	714	464	65.0	443	62.1	20	4.4
Hispanic or Latino ethnicity[1]	683	512	75.0	494	72.3	18	3.6
Male	340	279	82.1	274	80.6	5	1.9
Female	343	233	67.9	220	64.1	13	5.6
Age							
16 to 19 years	NA	NA	NA	NA	NA	NA	NA
20 to 24 years	564	405	71.8	383	67.9	22	5.5
25 to 34 years	1,098	943	85.8	915	83.3	28	3.0
35 to 44 years	1,096	910	83.0	885	80.7	26	2.8
45 to 54 years	1,072	913	85.1	897	83.7	15	1.7
55 to 64 years	1,144	779	68.1	764	66.8	14	1.8
65 years and over	1,382	281	20.3	276	20.0	5	1.7

NOTE: Data in Table 7 are from the Current Population Survey (CPS) and do not match the estimates in Table 8. See notes and definitions for further information.
[1] May be of any race.

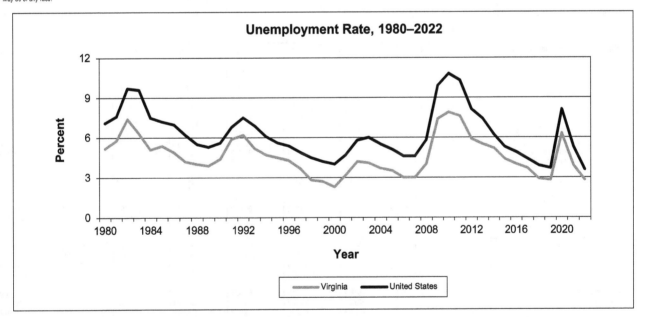

Unemployment Rate, 1980–2022

Table VA-8. Employment Status of the Civilian Noninstitutional Population Age 16 Years and Over

(Number, percent.)

Year	Civilian labor force	Civilian participation rate	Employed	Unemployed	Unemployment rate
2010.................................	4,163,293	67.8	3,858,466	304,827	7.3
2011.................................	4,205,184	67.4	3,929,008	276,176	6.6
2012.................................	4,217,529	66.7	3,967,151	250,378	5.9
2013.................................	4,238,377	66.4	4,002,057	236,320	5.6
2014.................................	4,258,856	66.1	4,040,908	217,948	5.1
2015.................................	4,233,981	65.2	4,048,081	185,900	4.4
2016.................................	4,254,348	65.0	4,084,822	169,526	4.0
2017.................................	4,352,977	65.7	4,193,290	159,687	3.7
2018.................................	4,384,657	65.7	4,255,213	129,444	3.0
2019.................................	4,455,015	66.0	4,332,617	123,168	2.8
2020.................................	4,368,772	64.6	4,097,860	270,912	6.2
2021.................................	4,267,656	62.9	4,100,803	166,853	3.9
2022.................................	4,435,858	64.9	4,308,805	127,053	2.9

Table VA-9. Employment and Average Wages by Industry

(Estimates are based on the 2012 North American Industry Classification System [NAICS].)

Industry	2014	2015	2016	2017	2018	2019	2020	2021
	Number of Jobs							
Wage and Salary Employment by Industry	3,972,994	4,049,013	4,100,137	4,138,213	4,199,504	4,257,748	4,036,637	4,128,556
Farm Wage and Salary Employment	14,301	12,948	11,967	9,671	12,389	13,428	8,195	8,530
Nonfarm Wage and Salary Employment	3,958,693	4,036,065	4,088,170	4,128,542	4,187,115	4,244,320	4,028,442	4,120,026
Private wage and salary employment	3,088,877	3,162,460	3,210,985	3,249,618	3,303,338	3,351,424	3,168,846	3,262,909
Forestry, fishing, and related activities	6,073	6,797	7,001	7,063	6,994	6,544	6,232	5,909
Mining	7,465	6,840	5,771	5,976	5,939	5,956	5,116	5,145
Utilities	10,646	10,784	10,857	10,761	10,837	10,804	10,850	10,650
Construction	182,886	189,681	193,073	198,104	203,098	208,202	207,581	210,928
Manufacturing	232,106	233,595	232,335	234,535	240,029	243,881	234,337	237,496
Durable goods manufacturing	137,574	138,392	135,300	136,353	140,360	143,751	138,549	140,326
Nondurable goods manufacturing	94,532	95,203	97,035	98,182	99,669	100,130	95,788	97,170
Wholesale trade	111,311	111,346	111,529	111,738	110,590	110,666	106,664	108,642
Retail trade	416,581	421,521	422,544	420,641	416,882	409,960	389,967	403,268
Transportation and warehousing	108,481	115,418	119,078	121,844	124,274	131,341	133,104	136,955
Information	71,686	69,890	68,241	67,993	67,336	68,125	65,352	66,252
Finance and insurance	135,832	139,224	141,973	146,413	148,506	152,061	153,180	151,637
Real estate and rental and leasing	52,364	53,838	53,873	55,121	56,752	58,513	55,726	56,916
Professional, scientific, and technical services	392,536	403,041	413,335	421,166	433,074	440,561	444,933	454,369
Management of companies and enterprises	73,973	74,196	73,355	73,939	76,294	81,020	80,653	80,213
Administrative and waste services	216,546	227,201	232,924	238,538	245,910	249,987	236,585	247,228
Educational services	72,542	73,979	75,481	76,626	79,334	80,028	73,036	81,110
Health care and social assistance	410,403	423,026	434,626	439,581	448,220	459,176	441,832	448,256
Arts, entertainment, and recreation	51,158	53,503	55,948	55,943	56,635	58,401	44,877	52,459
Accommodation and food services	323,323	334,632	345,633	351,255	354,533	354,833	282,512	305,958
Other services, except public administration	212,965	213,948	213,408	212,381	218,101	221,365	196,309	199,518
Government and government enterprises	869,816	873,605	877,185	878,924	883,777	892,896	859,596	857,117
	Dollars							
Average Wages and Salaries by Industry	54,334	55,696	56,253	58,022	59,879	61,653	66,523	69,508
Average Farm Wages and Salaries	22,123	19,960	24,784	27,832	22,674	16,611	26,435	25,513
Average Nonfarm Wages and Salaries	54,451	55,810	56,345	58,093	59,989	61,795	66,605	69,599
Average private wages and salaries	53,784	55,172	55,613	57,458	59,456	61,441	66,758	69,695
Forestry, fishing, and related activities	31,634	33,137	34,691	35,588	38,219	40,312	42,347	45,500
Mining	71,032	69,121	68,091	70,475	75,390	76,406	75,395	78,865
Utilities	105,902	105,707	105,738	109,278	119,944	120,902	122,048	125,161
Construction	51,003	52,584	54,339	57,182	59,120	61,612	64,678	67,233
Manufacturing	58,535	59,981	58,740	60,126	62,332	63,701	66,460	67,527
Durable goods manufacturing	61,942	63,605	61,914	64,098	66,273	67,671	69,962	71,008
Nondurable goods manufacturing	53,578	54,712	54,313	54,609	56,782	58,001	61,395	62,500
Wholesale trade	75,536	78,168	78,724	81,411	84,546	87,660	91,801	98,504
Retail trade	28,233	29,041	29,466	30,127	31,060	32,419	35,298	37,536
Transportation and warehousing	52,041	52,004	51,807	53,341	54,992	55,081	56,216	57,974
Information	92,735	97,572	99,388	100,649	103,275	110,493	120,718	132,139
Finance and insurance	86,107	89,737	90,627	95,093	99,594	101,838	111,814	117,485
Real estate and rental and leasing	51,425	53,944	54,540	56,639	58,319	60,768	65,180	69,452
Professional, scientific, and technical services	99,143	100,973	102,208	104,474	107,163	110,615	115,777	120,727
Management of companies and enterprises	114,626	121,816	118,025	125,683	130,230	130,072	136,328	142,915
Administrative and waste services	39,273	40,563	41,355	43,100	45,093	46,952	51,309	55,029
Educational services	39,260	39,432	40,035	40,317	40,756	41,260	47,490	45,508
Health care and social assistance	48,040	48,964	49,618	51,001	52,194	53,285	56,591	59,769
Arts, entertainment, and recreation	28,178	28,877	28,592	29,859	30,520	31,442	36,675	36,610
Accommodation and food services	20,292	20,889	21,384	22,008	23,141	24,053	23,504	27,949
Other services, except public administration	37,793	39,155	40,056	41,424	42,367	43,290	48,286	50,142
Government and government enterprises	56,820	58,119	59,023	60,441	61,980	63,126	66,039	69,232

Table VA-10. Employment Characteristics by Family Type

(Number, percent.)

Family type and labor force status	2019		2020 [1]		2021	
	Total	Families with own children under 18 years	Total	Families with own children under 18 years	Total	Families with own children under 18 years
All Families..	2,094,763	865,993	2,103,100	888,138	2,164,944	900,244
FAMILY TYPE AND LABOR FORCE STATUS						
Opposite-Sex Married-Couple Families...	1,590,659	617,211	1,585,566	635,037	1,612,562	635,026
Both husband and wife in labor force..........................	53.8	70.9	54.6	69.7	53.9	70.0
Husband in labor force, wife not in labor force	20.4	24.4	21.3	25.5	20.9	25.6
Wife in labor force, husband not in labor force	7.7	3.0	7.5	3.4	7.9	3.5
Both husband and wife not in labor force........................	17.2	1.3	16.6	1.3	17.2	1.0
Other Families	504,104	248,782	504,155	250,319	535,354	261,749
Female householder, no spouse present	72.3	75.0	72.8	75.2	71.4	72.9
In labor force..	52.0	65.4	52.3	64.0	50.6	61.5
Not in labor force	20.3	9.6	20.5	11.2	20.8	11.5
Male householder, no spouse present............................	27.7	25.0	27.2	24.8	28.6	27.1
In labor force..	21.7	23.4	21.6	23.2	22.8	24.9
Not in labor force	5.9	1.6	5.6	1.6	5.8	2.2

[1] 2020 ACS 5-Year estimates. 1-Year estimates were not released for 2020 due to the impact of COVID-19 on data collection that year. Data is not comparable to previous years, which are based on 1-year estimates.

Table VA-11. School Enrollment and Educational Attainment, 2021

(Number, percent.)

Item	State	U.S.
Enrollment		
Total population 3 years and over, enrolled in school	2,087,185	79,453,524
Enrolled in nursery school or preschool (percent)................................	4.8	5.2
Enrolled in kindergarten (percent).............................	4.8	5.0
Enrolled in elementary school, grades 1-8 (percent)............................	40.0	41.3
Enrolled in high school, grades 9-12 (percent).............................	21.4	21.8
Enrolled in college or graduate school (percent)..........................	29.1	26.7
Attainment		
Total population 25 years and over	5,942,672	228,193,464
Less than ninth grade (percent).............................	3.5	4.8
9th to 12th grade, no diploma (percent)	5.1	5.9
High school graduate, including equivalency (percent)............................	23.9	26.3
Some college, no degree (percent)	18	19.3
Associate's degree (percent)............................	7.7	8.8
Bachelor's degree (percent).............................	23.5	21.2
Graduate or professional degree (percent)............................	18.3	13.8
High school graduate or higher (percent).............................	91.4	89.4
Bachelor's degree or higher (percent)..............................	41.8	35.0

Table VA-12. Public School Characteristics and Educational Indicators

(Number, percent; data derived from National Center of Education Statistics.)

Item	State	U.S.
Public Elementary and Secondary Schools		
Number of regular school districts, 2019-20	132	13,349
Number of operational schools, 2019-20..	2,122	98,469
Percent charter schools	0.4	7.7
Total public school enrollment, Fall 2021..	1,249,815	49,433,092
Percent charter school enrollment	0.1	7.5
Student-teacher ratio, Fall 2019	14.9	15.9
Expenditures per student (unadjusted dollars), 2019-20	12,941	13,489
Four-year adjusted cohort graduation rate (ACGR), 2019-2020[1]..	88.8	86.5
Students eligible for free or reduced-price lunch (percent), 2019-20................................	45.1	52.1
English language learners (percent), Fall 2020	9.6	10.3
Students age 3 to 21 served under IDEA, part B (percent), 2021-22	13.8	14.7

Public Schools by Type, 2019-20	Number	Percent of state public schools
Total number of schools..	2,122	100.0
Special education..	40	1.9
Vocational education..	89	4.2
Alternative education..	122	5.7

[1] Adjusted Cohort Graduation Rates (ACGR) differ from Averaged Freshmen Graduation Rates (AFGR).

Table VA-13. Reported Voting and Registration of the Voting-Age Population, November 2022

(Numbers in thousands, percent.)

Item	Total population	Total citizen population	Registered			Voted		
			Total registered	Percent registered (total population)	Percent registered (total citizen population)	Total voted	Percent voted (total population)	Percent voted (total citizen population)
U.S. Total	255,457	233,546	161,422	63.2	69.1	121,916	47.7	52.2
State Total..........................	6,583	6,043	4,487	68.2	74.3	3,216	48.8	53.2
Sex								
Male	3,176	2,928	2,118	66.7	72.3	1,567	49.3	53.5
Female	3,407	3,115	2,369	69.5	76.1	1,649	48.4	52.9
Race								
White alone..........................	4,601	4,336	3,244	70.5	74.8	2,446	53.2	56.4
White, non-Hispanic alone	4,062	4,000	3,035	74.7	75.9	2,308	56.8	57.7
Black alone..........................	1,274	1,194	868	68.1	72.7	524	41.1	43.9
Asian alone	557	374	276	49.5	73.8	157	28.2	42.0
Hispanic (of any race)	648	394	236	36.3	59.7	138	21.3	35.1
White alone or in combination	4,715	4,443	3,317	70.3	74.6	2,508	53.2	56.5
Black alone or in combination....................	1,334	1,247	899	67.4	72.1	550	41.2	44.1
Asian alone or in combination....................	583	399	301	51.7	75.4	177	30.4	44.3
Age								
18 to 24 years	786	729	383	48.8	52.6	198	25.2	27.1
25 to 34 years	1,100	953	747	67.9	78.4	451	41.0	47.3
35 to 44 years	1,082	965	691	63.9	71.6	458	42.4	47.5
45 to 64 years	2,035	1,910	1,486	73.0	77.8	1,140	56.0	59.7
65 years and over	1,579	1,485	1,180	74.7	79.5	969	61.4	65.3

Table VA-14. Health Indicators

(Number, rate as indicated in footnotes.)

Item	State	U.S.
Births		
Life Expectancy at Birth (years), 2020	77.6	77.0
Fertility Rate by State[1], 2021	56.1	56.3
Percent Home Births, 2021	1.3	1.4
Cesarean Delivery Rate[2], 2021	32.5	32.1
Preterm Birth Rate[3], 2021	9.9	10.5
Teen Birth Rate[4], 2021	11.7	13.9
Percentage of Babies Born Low Birthweight[5], 2021	8.3	8.5
Deaths[6]		
Heart Disease Mortality Rate, 2021	167.2	173.8
Cancer Mortality Rate, 2021	150.5	146.6
Stroke Mortality Rate, 2021	42.1	41.1
Diabetes Mortality Rate, 2021	25.8	25.4
Influenza/Pneumonia Mortality Rate, 2021	9.7	10.5
Suicide Mortality Rate, 2021	13.2	14.1
Drug Overdose Mortality Rate, 2021	30.5	33.6
Firearm Injury Mortality Rate, 2021	14.3	14.6
Homicide Mortality Rate, 2021	7.2	8.2
Disease and Illness		
Lifetime Asthma in Adults, 2020 (percent)..........................	13.5	13.9
Lifetime Asthma in Children, 2020 (percent)[7]	NA	11.3
Diabetes in Adults, 2020 (percent)..........................	9.8	8.2
Self-reported Obesity in Adults, 2021 (percent)..........................	34.2	NA

SOURCE: National Center for Health Statistics, National Vital Statistics System 2020 data; https://wonder.cdc.gov.
[1] General fertility rate per 1,000 women aged 15–44.
[2] This represents the percentage of all live births that were cesarean deliveries.
[3] Babies born prior to 37 weeks of pregnancy (gestation).
[4] Number of births per 1,000 females aged 15–19
[5] Babies born weighing less than 2,500 grams or 5 lbs. 8oz.
[6] Death rates are the number of deaths per 100,000 total population.
[7] U.S. total includes data from 30 states and D.C.
NA = Not available.
- = Zero or rounds to zero.

Table VA-15. State Government Finances, 2021

(Dollar amounts in thousands, percent distribution.)

Item	Dollars	Percent distribution
Total Revenue	77,518,291	100.0
General revenue	72,187,671	93.1
Intergovernmental revenue	24,111,868	31.1
Taxes	32,328,105	41.7
General sales	6,527,477	8.4
Selective sales	5,191,915	6.7
License taxes	995,094	1.3
Individual income tax	17,066,596	22.0
Corporate income tax	1,579,303	2.0
Other taxes	967,720	1.2
Current charges	10,116,177	13.1
Miscellaneous general revenue	5,631,521	7.3
Utility revenue	-	-
Liquor stores revenue	1091350	1.4
Insurance trust revenue[1]	4,239,270	5.5
Total Expenditure	70,951,130	100.0
Intergovernmental expenditure	14,452,229	20.4
Direct expenditure	56,498,901	79.6
Current operation	40,925,493	57.7
Capital outlay	5,015,900	7.1
Insurance benefits and repayments	7,858,768	11.1
Assistance and subsidies	1,598,049	2.3
Interest on debt	1,100,691	1.6
Exhibit: Salaries and wages	8,797,857	12.4
Total Expenditure	70,951,130	100.0
General expenditure	61,709,108	87.0
Intergovernmental expenditure	14,452,229	20.4
Direct expenditure	47,256,879	66.6
General expenditure, by function:		
Education	19,638,816	27.7
Public welfare	18,568,263	26.2
Hospitals	4,819,030	6.8
Health	1,963,248	2.8
Highways	6,038,592	8.5
Police protection	808,015	1.1
Correction	1,702,936	2.4
Natural resources	371,609	0.5
Parks and recreation	182,108	0.3
Governmental administration	2,274,347	3.2
Interest on general debt	1,100,691	1.6
Other and unallocable	3,486,739	4.9
Utility expenditure	1,073,287	1.4
Liquor stores expenditure	898,696	1.3
Insurance trust expenditure	7,858,768	11.1
Debt at End of Fiscal Year	31,041,855	X
Cash and Security Holdings	153,697,997	X

X = Not applicable.
- = Zero or rounds to zero.
[1] Within insurance trust revenue, net earnings of state retirement systems is a calculated statistic (the item code in the data file is X08), and thus can be positive or negative. Net earnings is the sum of earnings on investments plus gains on investments minus losses on investments. The change made in 2002 for asset valuation from book to market value in accordance with Statement 34 of the Governmental Accounting Standards Board is reflected in the calculated statistics.

Table VA-16. State Government Tax Collections, 2022

(Dollars in thousands, percent.)

Item	Dollars	Percent distribution
Total Taxes	36,754,617	100.0
Property taxes	54,712	0.1
Sales and gross receipts	12,931,327	35.2
General sales and gross receipts	7,097,323	19.3
Selective sales and gross receipts	5,834,004	15.9
Alcoholic beverages	274,380	0.7
Amusements	37,153	0.1
Insurance premiums	683,923	1.9
Motor fuels	1,596,148	4.3
Pari-mutuels	1,543	-
Public utilities	491,211	1.3
Tobacco products	278,758	0.8
Other selective sales	2,470,888	6.7
Licenses	1,090,979	3.0
Alcoholic beverages	16,474	-
Amusements	37,206	0.1
Corporations in general	78,259	0.2
Hunting and fishing	26,942	0.1
Motor vehicle	471,211	1.3
Motor vehicle operators	78,868	0.2
Public utilities	716	-
Occupation and business, NEC	313,906	0.9
Other licenses	67,397	0.2
Income taxes	21,711,446	59.1
Individual income	19,732,749	53.7
Corporation net income	1,978,697	5.4
Other taxes	966,153	2.6
Death and gift	29	-
Documentary and stock transfer	853,896	2.3
Severance	3,831	-
Taxes, NEC	108,397	0.3

- = Zero or rounds to zero.

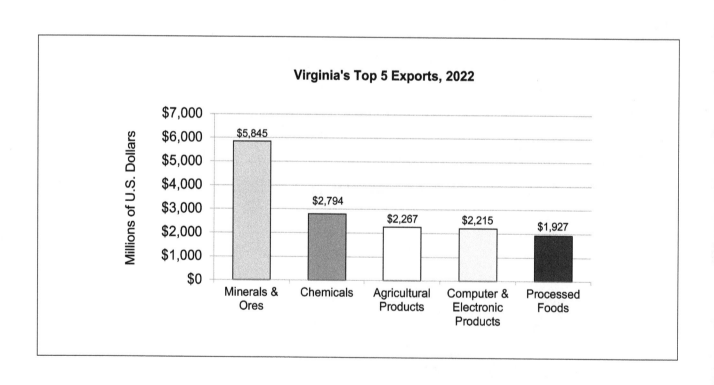

Virginia's Top 5 Exports, 2022

Minerals & Ores: $5,845
Chemicals: $2,794
Agricultural Products: $2,267
Computer & Electronic Products: $2,215
Processed Foods: $1,927

(Millions of U.S. Dollars)

Facts and Figures

Location: Northwestern United States; bordered on the N by Canada (British Columbia), on the E by Idaho, on the S by Oregon, and on the W by the Pacific Ocean

Area: 71,300 sq. mi. (184,665 sq. km.); rank—18th

Population: 7,785,786 (2022 est.); rank—13th

Principal Cities: capital—Olympia; largest—Seattle

Statehood: November 11, 1889; 42nd state

U.S. Congress: 2 senators, 10 representatives

State Motto: *Alki* ("By and by")

State Song: "Washington, My Home"

State Nickname: The Evergreen State

Abbreviations: WA; Wash.

State Symbols: flower—coast rhododendron; tree—Western hemlock; bird—willow goldfinch

At a Glance

- With an increase in population of 15.8 percent, Washington ranked 8th among the states in growth from 2010 to 2022.

- Washington's median household income in 2021 was $84,247, and 9.9 percent of the population lived below the poverty level.

- In 2021, 6.4 percent of Washingtonians did not have health insurance, compared to 8.6 percent of the total U.S. population.

- Washington had the highest drug overdose death rate in the country in 2021, with 90.9 overdose deaths per 100,000 population. The national rate was 32.4 drug overdose deaths per 100,000 population.

- Washington had the 2nd highest life expectancy at birth in 2020, with a life expectancy of 79.2 years. The national life expectancy at birth in 2020 was 77.0 years.

Table WA-1. Population by Age, Sex, Race, and Hispanic Origin

(Number, percent, except where noted.)

Sex, age, race, and Hispanic origin	2010	2020	2022	Percent change, 2010–2022
Total population	6,724,540	7,705,247	7,785,786	15.8
Percent of total U.S. population	2.2	2.3	2.3	X
Sex				
Male	3,349,707	3,889,157	3,928,342	17.3
Female	3,374,833	3,816,090	3,857,444	14.3
Age				
Under 5 years	439,657	445,246	425,829	-3.1
Under 18 years	1,581,354	1,675,933	1,646,573	4.1
18 to 64 years	4,315,509	4,809,287	4,830,653	11.9
65 years and over	827,677	1,220,027	1,308,560	58.1
Median age (years)	37.3	37.8	38.3	2.7
Race and Hispanic origin				
One race				
White	5,535,262	6,009,520	5,982,306	8.1
Black	252,333	340,173	357,430	41.7
American Indian and Alaska Native	122,649	149,650	154,178	25.7
Asian	491,685	752,062	814,238	65.6
Native Hawaiian or Other Pacific Islander	43,505	61,364	65,973	51.6
Two or more races	279,106	392,478	411,661	47.5
Hispanic (of any race)	755,790	1,032,618	1,093,313	44.7

NOTE: Population figures for 2022 are July 1 estimates. The 2010 and 2020 estimates are taken from the respective censuses.
- = Zero or rounds to zero.
X = Not applicable.

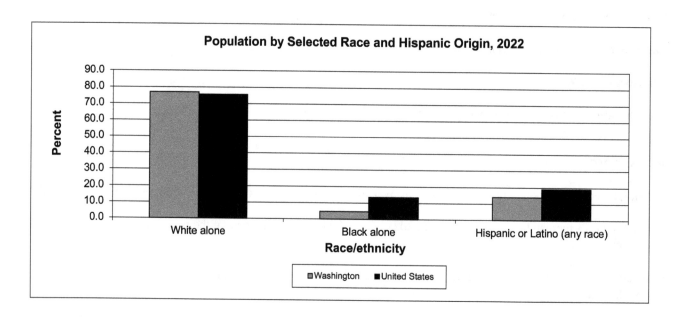

Table WA-2. Marital Status

(Number, percent distribution.)

Sex, age, race, and Hispanic origin	2000	2010	2021
Males, 15 Years and Over	2,287,431	2,686,801	3,183,142
Never married	29.8	33.8	35.7
Now married, except separated	56.6	52.0	51.6
Separated	1.4	1.6	1.1
Widowed	2.1	2.1	2.1
Divorced	10.1	10.5	9.5
Females, 15 Years and Over	2,352,091	2,746,158	3,163,061
Never married	22.8	26.4	28.5
Now married, except separated	54.1	50.6	49.8
Separated	1.8	2.1	1.6
Widowed	8.6	7.8	6.8
Divorced	12.7	13.2	13.2

Table WA-3. Households and Housing Characteristics

(Number, percent, dollars.)

Item	2000	2010	2021	Average annual percent change, 2010–2021
Total Households...	2,271,398	2,606,863	3,022,255	1.4
Family households	1,499,127	1,681,386	1,937,081	1.4
Married-couple family	1,181,995	1,297,240	1,503,723	1.4
Other family	317,132	384,146	433,358	1.2
Male householder, no wife present................................	92,514	114,187	139,845	2.0
Female householder, no husband present........................	224,618	269,959	293,513	0.8
Nonfamily households	772,271	925,477	1,085,174	1.6
Householder living alone..	594,325	731,452	819,693	1.1
Householder not living alone..	117,946	194,025	265,481	3.3
Housing Characteristics				
Total housing units..	2,451,075	2,888,594	3,257,140	1.2
Occupied housing units	2,271,398	2,606,863	3,022,255	1.4
Owner occupied	1,467,009	1,644,939	1,933,901	1.6
Renter occupied	804,389	961,924	1,088,354	1.2
Average household size..	2.53	2.53	2.51	-0.1
Financial Characteristics				
Median gross rent of renter-occupied housing	663	908	1,484	5.8
Median monthly owner costs for housing units with a mortgage	1,268	1,736	2,110	2.0
Median value of owner-occupied housing units.....................	168,300	271,800	485,700	7.2

Table WA-4. Migration, Origin, and Language

(Number, percent.)

Characteristic	State 2021	U.S. 2021
Residence 1 Year Ago		
Population 1 year and over	7,657,350	328,464,538
Same house	84.6	87.2
Different house in the U.S.	14.8	12.3
Same county	8.8	6.7
Different county	6.0	5.7
Same state	3.1	3.3
Different state	2.9	2.4
Abroad	0.6	0.4
Place of Birth		
Native born	6,595,381	286,623,642
Male	50.7	49.7
Female	49.3	50.3
Foreign born	1,143,311	45,270,103
Male	48.5	48.7
Female	51.5	51.3
Foreign born; naturalized U.S. citizen...	560,282	24,044,083
Male	45.8	46.4
Female	54.2	53.6
Foreign born; not a U.S. citizen...	583,029	21,226,020
Male	51.1	51.2
Female	48.9	48.8
Entered 2010 or later	33.0	28.1
Entered 2000 to 2009	24.8	23.7
Entered before 2000..	42.2	48.2
World Region of Birth, Foreign		
Foreign-born population, excluding population born at sea	1,143,311	45,269,644
Europe	15.1	10.7
Asia...	45.3	31.0
Africa	6.3	5.7
Oceania	2.1	0.6
Latin America..	26.9	50.1
North America	4.3	1.7
Language Spoken at Home and Ability to Speak English		
Population 5 years and over...	7,306,168	313,232,500
English only	79.2	78.4
Language other than English..	20.8	21.6
Speaks English less than "very well"...	7.9	8.3

Table WA-5. Median Income and Poverty Status, 2021

(Number, percent, except as noted.)

Characteristic	State Number	State Percent	U.S. Number	U.S. Percent
Median Income				
Households (dollars)...	84,247	X	69,717	X
Families (dollars)	102,178	X	85,806	X
Below Poverty Level (All People)	754,315	9.9	41,393,176	12.8
Sex				
Male	339,987	8.9	18,518,155	11.6
Female	414,328	10.9	22,875,021	13.9
Age				
Under 18 years..	198,149	12.0	12,243,219	16.9
Related children under 18 years.................................	191,871	11.7	11,985,424	16.6
18 to 64 years	455,274	9.6	23,526,341	11.9
65 years and over	100,892	8.2	5,623,616	10.3

X = Not applicable.

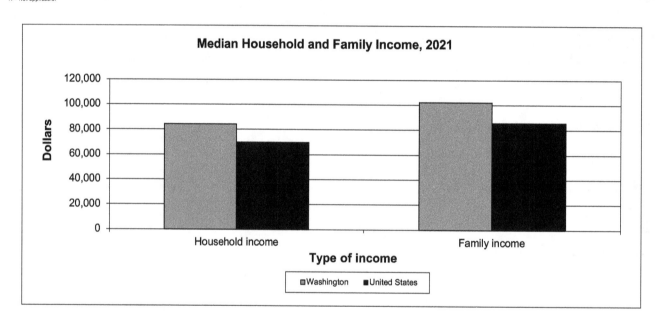

Table WA-6. Health Insurance Coverage Status for the Civilian Noninstitutionalized Population and Children Under 19 Years of Age

(Number, percent.)

Item	2011	2012	2013	2014	2015	2016	2017	2018	2019	2020 [2]	2021
Civilian Noninstitutionalized Population	6,716,822	6,793,078	6,864,149	6,954,806	7,066,812	7,184,110	7,299,812	7,427,599	7,497,453	7,397,932	7,618,375
Covered by Private or Public Insurance											
Number...	5,764,192	5,848,307	5,904,158	6,312,152	6,598,845	6,756,018	6,853,706	6,950,315	7,001,406	6,939,704	7,130,322
Percent..	85.8	86.1	86.0	90.8	93.4	94.0	93.9	93.6	93.4	93.8	93.6
Uninsured											
Number...	952,630	944,771	959,991	642,654	467,967	428,092	446,106	477,284	496,047	458,228	488,053
Percent..	14.2	13.9	14.0	9.2	6.6	6.0	6.1	6.4	6.6	6.2	6.4
Percent in the U.S. not covered....................	15.1	14.8	14.5	11.7	9.4	8.6	8.7	8.9	9.2	8.7	8.6
Children Under 19 Years of Age[1]	1,578,179	1,583,595	1,594,503	1,601,029	1,610,562	1,627,304	1,739,832	1,755,094	1,757,459	1,745,214	1,765,688
Covered by Private or Public Insurance											
Number...	1,480,971	1,492,516	1,499,708	1,526,102	1,568,043	1,585,868	1,693,734	1,707,612	1,703,314	1,695,768	1,711,069
Percent..	93.8	94.2	94.1	95.3	97.4	97.5	97.4	97.3	96.9	97.2	96.9
Uninsured											
Number...	97,208	91,079	94,795	74,927	42,519	41,436	46,098	47,482	54,145	49,446	54,619
Percent..	6.2	5.8	5.9	4.7	2.6	2.5	2.6	2.7	3.1	2.8	3.1
Percent in the U.S. not covered....................	7.5	7.2	7.1	6.0	4.8	4.5	5.0	5.2	5.7	5.2	5.4

[1] Data for years prior to 2017 are for individuals under 18 years of age.
[2] 2020 ACS 5-Year estimates. 1-Year estimates were not released for 2020 due to the impact of COVID-19 on data collection that year. Data is not comparable to previous years, which are based on 1-year estimates.

Table WA-7. Employment Status by Demographic Group, 2022

(Numbers in thousands, percent.)

Characteristic	Civilian noninstitutional population	Civilian labor force		Employed		Unemployed	
		Number	Percent of population	Number	Percent of population	Number	Percent of population
Total..	6,195	3,984	64.3	3,810	61.5	174	4.4
Sex							
Male..	3,084	2,162	70.1	2,065	67.0	97	4.5
Female...	3,111	1,822	58.6	1,745	56.1	77	4.2
Race, Sex, and Hispanic Origin							
White...	4,882	3,109	63.7	2,974	60.9	134	4.3
Male..	2,446	1,695	69.3	1,621	66.3	74	4.4
Female...	2,437	1,413	58.0	1,353	55.5	60	4.3
Black or African American...................	267	188	70.4	174	65.0	14	7.7
Male..	140	97	69.4	88	62.5	10	9.9
Female...	NA	NA	NA	NA	NA	NA	NA
Hispanic or Latino ethnicity[1]...............	779	563	72.2	529	68.0	33	5.9
Male..	412	333	80.8	314	76.1	19	5.8
Female...	367	230	62.6	216	58.8	14	6.1
Age							
16 to 19 years....................................	385	145	37.7	123	32.0	22	15.1
20 to 24 years....................................	440	317	72.1	288	65.5	29	9.2
25 to 34 years....................................	1,147	956	83.3	908	79.2	47	4.9
35 to 44 years....................................	1,082	899	83.1	862	79.7	37	4.1
45 to 54 years....................................	1,015	822	81.0	804	79.3	18	2.2
55 to 64 years....................................	941	620	65.9	606	64.5	13	2.1
65 years and over	1,186	226	19.1	218	18.4	9	3.8

NOTE: Data in Table 7 are from the Current Population Survey (CPS) and do not match the estimates in Table 8. See notes and definitions for further information.
[1] May be of any race.

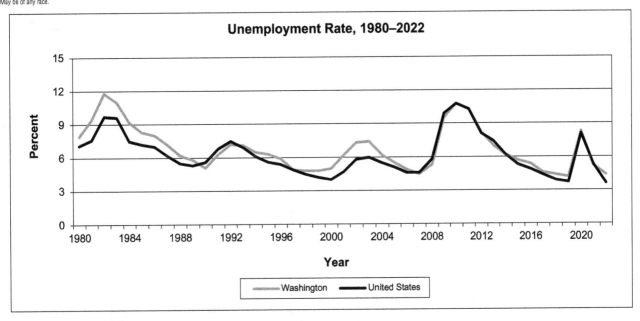

Unemployment Rate, 1980–2022

Table WA-8. Employment Status of the Civilian Noninstitutional Population Age 16 Years and Over

(Number, percent.)

Year	Civilian labor force	Civilian participation rate	Employed	Unemployed	Unemployment rate
2010..	3,458,451	65.9	3,142,109	316,342	9.1
2011..	3,437,871	64.7	3,144,459	293,412	8.5
2012..	3,468,738	64.5	3,203,294	265,444	7.7
2013..	3,460,772	63.6	3,230,947	229,825	6.6
2014..	3,495,153	63.3	3,287,904	207,249	5.9
2015..	3,554,826	63.3	3,361,249	193,577	5.4
2016..	3,648,558	63.7	3,459,527	189,031	5.2
2017..	3,727,683	63.7	3,554,754	172,929	4.6
2018..	3,813,320	64.1	3,644,274	169,046	4.4
2019..	3,933,774	65.2	3,764,634	169,140	4.3
2020..	3,929,477	64.4	3,596,814	332,663	8.5
2021..	3,913,513	63.7	3,708,738	204,775	5.2
2022..	3,990,343	64.1	3,822,319	168,024	4.2

Table WA-9. Employment and Average Wages by Industry

(Estimates are based on the 2012 North American Industry Classification System [NAICS].)

Industry	2014	2015	2016	2017	2018	2019	2020	2021
	Number of Jobs							
Wage and Salary Employment by Industry.........................	3,281,417	3,361,935	3,448,656	3,523,477	3,613,897	3,686,545	3,496,277	3,589,012
Farm Wage and Salary Employment...............................	53,511	51,723	52,493	53,491	53,523	53,994	58,976	59,217
Nonfarm Wage and Salary Employment...........................	3,227,906	3,310,212	3,396,163	3,469,986	3,560,374	3,632,551	3,437,301	3,529,795
Private wage and salary employment...............................	2,606,842	2,680,960	2,756,713	2,821,787	2,901,659	2,967,431	2,796,919	2,886,428
Forestry, fishing, and related activities	31,300	32,341	31,742	31,891	32,607	33,541	32,172	30,959
Mining..	2,245	2,400	2,435	2,562	2,634	2,306	2,116	2,169
Utilities..	4,838	4,943	4,646	4,823	5,120	5,246	5,290	5,400
Construction	164,788	179,299	191,759	204,557	218,279	224,317	217,926	227,970
Manufacturing...	288,634	291,161	289,695	283,889	287,353	293,480	271,618	259,335
Durable goods manufacturing..................................	209,565	211,198	207,338	200,185	201,881	206,681	189,644	175,405
Nondurable goods manufacturing.............................	79,069	79,963	82,357	83,704	85,472	86,799	81,974	83,930
Wholesale trade	130,909	133,520	133,481	134,739	136,337	136,615	131,356	131,496
Retail trade...	345,122	358,633	372,116	387,173	388,696	393,493	388,464	406,342
Transportation and warehousing..................................	94,264	98,304	100,601	103,145	110,166	111,937	107,731	114,775
Information	109,682	114,614	120,859	126,574	133,778	144,742	149,223	157,391
Finance and insurance	98,130	99,063	99,959	102,082	103,017	104,325	104,814	105,660
Real estate and rental and leasing...............................	48,215	50,404	51,412	53,315	56,606	58,914	56,130	57,439
Professional, scientific, and technical services	184,546	190,534	197,459	202,313	209,391	216,253	217,570	232,087
Management of companies and enterprises....................	39,992	41,939	43,177	44,300	44,657	45,083	43,517	43,283
Administrative and waste services	152,139	160,239	164,876	170,082	172,893	176,055	164,982	175,175
Educational services	55,123	55,986	55,722	56,724	56,160	57,220	51,727	56,047
Health care and social assistance................................	402,147	398,408	411,309	419,621	433,020	444,671	438,872	446,544
Arts, entertainment, and recreation.............................	48,749	48,645	51,180	52,754	54,298	55,262	36,067	41,105
Accommodation and food services...............................	252,062	264,141	274,954	280,824	289,663	294,519	227,081	243,822
Other services, except public administration..................	153,957	156,386	159,331	160,419	166,984	169,452	150,263	149,429
Government and government enterprises......................	621,064	629,252	639,450	648,199	658,715	665,120	640,382	643,367
	Dollars							
Average Wages and Salaries by Industry	55,329	56,997	58,950	61,893	65,694	68,927	75,550	81,245
Average Farm Wages and Salaries	27,985	29,479	32,384	27,430	27,192	28,673	30,965	29,543
Average Nonfarm Wages and Salaries	55,783	57,427	59,361	62,424	66,273	69,526	76,315	82,113
Average private wages and salaries................................	56,229	57,892	59,906	63,159	67,388	70,728	78,140	84,629
Forestry, fishing, and related activities.........................	35,368	35,427	37,589	38,643	40,194	40,053	42,732	44,947
Mining..	63,998	68,064	67,940	71,680	71,478	75,360	74,123	76,371
Utilities..	87,775	93,335	91,146	94,130	101,022	107,824	116,383	114,244
Construction	55,717	57,726	59,871	62,232	65,288	68,543	70,617	74,558
Manufacturing...	75,435	74,874	75,007	76,408	79,422	81,330	82,066	83,273
Durable goods manufacturing..................................	84,307	83,290	83,516	85,322	89,017	90,934	90,823	92,509
Nondurable goods manufacturing.............................	51,921	52,645	53,584	55,091	56,759	58,461	61,809	63,972
Wholesale trade	71,040	73,204	74,439	77,499	80,617	82,899	87,638	95,522
Retail trade...	38,844	42,090	46,320	52,829	59,036	62,382	71,536	76,445
Transportation and warehousing..................................	55,148	56,551	58,115	60,274	62,303	66,650	67,553	71,178
Information	150,237	150,574	159,038	172,239	194,375	206,778	241,810	268,490
Finance and insurance	81,936	85,411	87,599	90,555	94,281	100,066	111,979	123,982
Real estate and rental and leasing...............................	46,141	48,009	50,193	52,468	55,806	59,011	63,985	71,042
Professional, scientific, and technical services	85,691	86,061	89,155	92,941	101,271	103,986	112,359	125,999
Management of companies and enterprises....................	109,039	108,964	109,700	112,746	118,246	123,439	127,267	135,446
Administrative and waste services	44,639	46,249	47,357	48,797	50,588	53,304	57,224	61,739
Educational services	30,918	31,780	31,883	32,222	33,869	34,473	39,082	38,689
Health care and social assistance................................	44,888	48,251	49,419	51,378	52,947	54,839	56,725	60,312
Arts, entertainment, and recreation.............................	32,607	33,513	33,826	35,023	35,965	36,484	41,358	44,829
Accommodation and food services...............................	23,035	23,739	24,570	26,874	28,498	29,658	27,349	33,430
Other services, except public administration..................	33,679	34,756	36,634	38,004	38,948	40,309	44,513	48,609
Government and government enterprises......................	53,909	55,447	57,010	59,222	61,357	64,161	68,348	70,822

Table WA-10. Employment Characteristics by Family Type

(Number, percent.)

Family type and labor force status	2019 Total	2019 Families with own children under 18 years	2020 [1] Total	2020 [1] Families with own children under 18 years	2021 Total	2021 Families with own children under 18 years
All Families	1,882,896	792,196	1,874,376	801,815	1,937,081	801,250
FAMILY TYPE AND LABOR FORCE STATUS						
Opposite-Sex Married-Couple Families	1,448,372	565,882	1,436,613	577,662	1,482,222	572,481
Both husband and wife in labor force	51.1	65.3	51.2	64.1	50.1	63.9
Husband in labor force, wife not in labor force	22.2	29.1	22.7	30.4	21.8	29.6
Wife in labor force, husband not in labor force	7.4	3.7	7.6	4.0	8.2	5.0
Both husband and wife not in labor force	17.9	1.1	18.4	1.6	19.8	1.5
Other Families	434,524	226,314	418,134	220,662	433,358	224,821
Female householder, no spouse present	66.8	68.3	67.2	68.8	67.7	68.4
In labor force	47.4	56.5	48.5	57.7	46.8	53.4
Not in labor force	19.4	11.8	18.8	11.1	20.9	15.0
Male householder, no spouse present	33.2	31.7	32.8	31.2	32.3	31.6
In labor force	27.2	28.9	26.5	28.6	25.8	28.6
Not in labor force	6.1	2.8	6.2	2.6	6.5	3.1

[1] 2020 ACS 5-Year estimates. 1-Year estimates were not released for 2020 due to the impact of COVID-19 on data collection that year. Data is not comparable to previous years, which are based on 1-year estimates.

Table WA-11. School Enrollment and Educational Attainment, 2021

(Number, percent.)

Item	State	U.S.
Enrollment		
Total population 3 years and over, enrolled in school	1,761,985	79,453,524
Enrolled in nursery school or preschool (percent)	5.1	5.2
Enrolled in kindergarten (percent)	4.9	5.0
Enrolled in elementary school, grades 1-8 (percent)	43.1	41.3
Enrolled in high school, grades 9-12 (percent)	21.4	21.8
Enrolled in college or graduate school (percent)	25.5	26.7
Attainment		
Total population 25 years and over	5,401,149	228,193,464
Less than ninth grade (percent)	3.6	4.8
9th to 12th grade, no diploma (percent)	4.1	5.9
High school graduate, including equivalency (percent)	21.6	26.3
Some college, no degree (percent)	21.7	19.3
Associate's degree (percent)	10.1	8.8
Bachelor's degree (percent)	23.8	21.2
Graduate or professional degree (percent)	15.1	13.8
High school graduate or higher (percent)	92.3	89.4
Bachelor's degree or higher (percent)	39	35.0

Table WA-12. Public School Characteristics and Educational Indicators

(Number, percent; data derived from National Center of Education Statistics.)

Item	State	U.S.
Public Elementary and Secondary Schools		
Number of regular school districts, 2019-20	298	13,349
Number of operational schools, 2019-20	2,473	98,469
Percent charter schools	0.4	7.7
Total public school enrollment, Fall 2021	1,081,835	49,433,092
Percent charter school enrollment	0.4	7.5
Student-teacher ratio, Fall 2019	18.4	15.9
Expenditures per student (unadjusted dollars), 2019-20	14,542	13,489
Four-year adjusted cohort graduation rate (ACGR), 2019-2020 [1]	83.0	86.5
Students eligible for free or reduced-price lunch (percent), 2019-20	43.9	52.1
English language learners (percent), Fall 2020	11.8	10.3
Students age 3 to 21 served under IDEA, part B (percent), 2021-22	13.6	14.7

Public Schools by Type, 2019-20	Number	Percent of state public schools
Total number of schools	2,473	100.0
Special education	89	3.6
Vocational education	20	0.8
Alternative education	319	12.9

[1] Adjusted Cohort Graduation Rates (ACGR) differ from Averaged Freshmen Graduation Rates (AFGR).

Table WA-13. Reported Voting and Registration of the Voting-Age Population, November 2022

(Numbers in thousands, percent.)

Item	Total population	Total citizen population	Registered			Voted		
			Total registered	Percent registered (total population)	Percent registered (total citizen population)	Total voted	Percent voted (total population)	Percent voted (total citizen population)
U.S. Total	255,457	233,546	161,422	63.2	69.1	121,916	47.7	52.2
State Total...............................	6,016	5,511	4,140	68.8	75.1	3,292	54.7	59.7
Sex								
Male	3,021	2,747	2,068	68.5	75.3	1,632	54.0	59.4
Female	2,996	2,764	2,072	69.2	75.0	1,660	55.4	60.1
Race								
White alone.............................	4,701	4,372	3,427	72.9	78.4	2,875	61.1	65.8
White, non-Hispanic alone	4,017	3,954	3,164	78.8	80.0	2,696	67.1	68.2
Black alone.............................	245	222	135	55.1	60.9	76	31.0	34.2
Asian alone	561	422	275	49.1	65.2	166	29.5	39.2
Hispanic (of any race)	771	499	320	41.5	64.1	231	30.0	46.3
White alone or in combination	4,953	4,615	3,599	72.7	78.0	2,972	60.0	64.4
Black alone or in combination	353	330	209	59.1	63.3	105	29.8	32.0
Asian alone or in combination......................	657	509	347	52.8	68.1	191	29.2	37.6
Age								
18 to 24 years	635	591	279	44.0	47.3	164	25.9	27.8
25 to 34 years	1,170	1,047	727	62.2	69.5	492	42.1	47.0
35 to 44 years	1,050	915	695	66.2	76.0	504	48.0	55.1
45 to 64 years	1,908	1,738	1,405	73.6	80.8	1,175	61.6	67.6
65 years and over	1,254	1,220	1,033	82.4	84.7	956	76.2	78.4

Table WA-14. Health Indicators

(Number, rate as indicated in footnotes.)

Item	State	U.S.
Births		
Life Expectancy at Birth (years), 2020	79.2	77.0
Fertility Rate by State[1], 2021	54.2	56.3
Percent Home Births, 2021	2.5	1.4
Cesarean Delivery Rate[2], 2021	29.0	32.1
Preterm Birth Rate[3], 2021	8.9	10.5
Teen Birth Rate[4], 2021	10.1	13.9
Percentage of Babies Born Low Birthweight[5], 2021	7.0	8.5
Deaths[6]		
Heart Disease Mortality Rate, 2021	147.7	173.8
Cancer Mortality Rate, 2021	149.3	146.6
Stroke Mortality Rate, 2021	37.7	41.1
Diabetes Mortality Rate, 2021	24.8	25.4
Influenza/Pneumonia Mortality Rate, 2021	5.9	10.5
Suicide Mortality Rate, 2021	15.3	14.1
Drug Overdose Mortality Rate, 2021	28.1	33.6
Firearm Injury Mortality Rate, 2021	11.2	14.6
Homicide Mortality Rate, 2021...	4.5	8.2
Disease and Illness		
Lifetime Asthma in Adults, 2020 (percent)...	15.0	13.9
Lifetime Asthma in Children, 2020 (percent)[7]	NA	11.3
Diabetes in Adults, 2020 (percent)..	7.9	8.2
Self-reported Obesity in Adults, 2021 (percent)..................................	28.8	NA

SOURCE: National Center for Health Statistics, National Vital Statistics System 2020 data; https://wonder.cdc.gov.
[1] General fertility rate per 1,000 women aged 15–44.
[2] This represents the percentage of all live births that were cesarean deliveries.
[3] Babies born prior to 37 weeks of pregnancy (gestation).
[4] Number of births per 1,000 females aged 15–19
[5] Babies born weighing less than 2,500 grams or 5 lbs. 8oz.
[6] Death rates are the number of deaths per 100,000 total population.
[7] U.S. total includes data from 30 states and D.C.
NA = Not available.
- = Zero or rounds to zero.

Table WA-15. State Government Finances, 2021

(Dollar amounts in thousands, percent distribution.)

Item	Dollars	Percent distribution
Total Revenue	74,134,158	100.0
General revenue	63,376,345	85.5
Intergovernmental revenue	21,113,014	28.5
Taxes	32,614,091	44.0
General sales	19,056,609	25.7
Selective sales	4,956,647	6.7
License taxes	2,072,634	2.8
Individual income tax	-	-
Corporate income tax	-	-
Other taxes	6,528,201	8.8
Current charges	6,346,369	8.6
Miscellaneous general revenue	3,302,871	4.5
Utility revenue	-	-
Liquor stores revenue	-	-
Insurance trust revenue[1]	10,757,813	14.5
Total Expenditure	76,187,889	100.0
Intergovernmental expenditure	20,881,933	27.4
Direct expenditure	55,305,956	72.6
Current operation	37,660,934	49.4
Capital outlay	2,399,480	3.1
Insurance benefits and repayments	12,127,397	15.9
Assistance and subsidies	1,687,228	2.2
Interest on debt	1,430,917	1.9
Exhibit: Salaries and wages	10,336,618	13.6
Total Expenditure	76,187,889	100.0
General expenditure	64,021,974	84.0
Intergovernmental expenditure	20,881,933	27.4
Direct expenditure	43,140,041	56.6
General expenditure, by function:		
Education	25,392,734	33.3
Public welfare	15,468,194	20.3
Hospitals	4,240,018	5.6
Health	4,606,821	6.0
Highways	3,258,372	4.3
Police protection	557,278	0.7
Correction	1,359,420	1.8
Natural resources	1,076,106	1.4
Parks and recreation	359,831	0.5
Governmental administration	1,350,557	1.8
Interest on general debt	1,430,917	1.9
Other and unallocable	4,294,428	5.6
Utility expenditure	145,342	0.2
Liquor stores expenditure	-	-
Insurance trust expenditure	12,127,397	15.9
Debt at End of Fiscal Year	30,206,602	X
Cash and Security Holdings	189,065,160	X

X = Not applicable.
- = Zero or rounds to zero.
[1] Within insurance trust revenue, net earnings of state retirement systems is a calculated statistic (the item code in the data file is X08), and thus can be positive or negative. Net earnings is the sum of earnings on investments plus gains on investments minus losses on investments. The change made in 2002 for asset valuation from book to market value in accordance with Statement 34 of the Governmental Accounting Standards Board is reflected in the calculated statistics.

Table WA-16. State Government Tax Collections, 2022

(Dollars in thousands, percent.)

Item	Dollars	Percent distribution
Total Taxes	36,071,826	100.0
Property taxes	4,399,803	12.2
Sales and gross receipts	26,739,775	74.1
General sales and gross receipts	21,477,182	59.5
Selective sales and gross receipts	5,262,593	14.6
Alcoholic beverages	481,287	1.3
Amusements	4,432	-
Insurance premiums	823,878	2.3
Motor fuels	1,598,550	4.4
Pari-mutuels	1,285	-
Public utilities	725,502	2.0
Tobacco products	353,075	1.0
Other selective sales	1,274,584	3.5
Licenses	1,909,969	5.3
Alcoholic beverages	203,169	0.6
Amusements	20,573	0.1
Corporations in general	54,390	0.2
Hunting and fishing	43,606	0.1
Motor vehicle	834,226	2.3
Motor vehicle operators	128,448	0.4
Public utilities	23,093	0.1
Occupation and business, NEC	426,738	1.2
Other licenses	175,726	0.5
Income taxes	X	-
Individual income	X	-
Corporation net income	X	-
Other taxes	3,022,279	8.4
Death and gift	371,246	1.0
Documentary and stock transfer	2,468,426	6.8
Severance	41,103	0.1
Taxes, NEC	141,504	-

X = Not applicable.
- = Zero or rounds to zero.

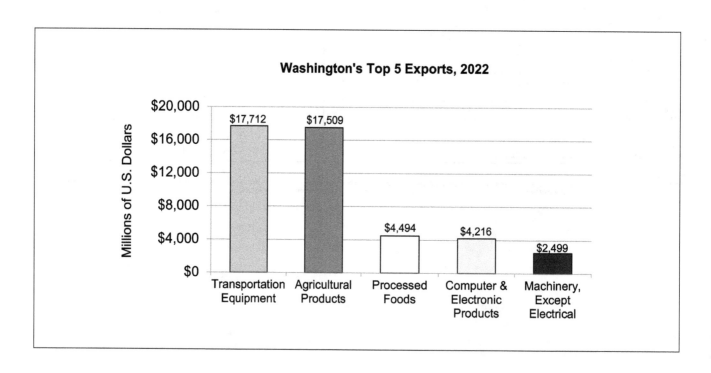

Washington's Top 5 Exports, 2022

- Transportation Equipment: $17,712
- Agricultural Products: $17,509
- Processed Foods: $4,494
- Computer & Electronic Products: $4,216
- Machinery, Except Electrical: $2,499

WEST VIRGINIA

Facts and Figures

Location: East central United States; bordered on the N by Ohio and Pennsylvania, on the E by Pennsylvania, Maryland, and Virginia, on the S by Virginia and Kentucky, and on the W by Kentucky and Ohio

Area: 24,230 sq. mi. (62,755 sq. km.); rank—41st

Population: 1,775,156 (2022 est.); rank—39th

Principal Cities: capital—Charleston; largest—Charleston

Statehood: June 20, 1863; 35th state

U.S. Congress: 2 senators, 3 representatives

State Motto: *Montani semper liberi* (Mountaineers are always free)

State Songs: "West Virginia Hills"; "This Is My West Virginia"; "West Virginia, My Home Sweet Home"

State Nickname: The Mountain State

Abbreviations: WV; W. Va.

State Symbols: flower—rhododendron (great laurel); tree—sugar maple; bird—cardinal

At a Glance

- West Virginia experienced the largest population decline among the states from 2010 to 2022, with its population decreasing 4.2 percent.

- West Virginia's median household income was $51,248 in 2021, the 2nd lowest among the states, and 16.8 percent of the state's population lived below the poverty level.

- With 38.2 percent of the voting-age population casting votes, West Virginia had the lowest voter turnout among the states in the November 2022 midterm election.

- West Virginia had the smallest percent of residents that self-identified as "Hispanic or Latino" in 2022, with 1.9 percent of its population in this demographic.

- West Virginia had the highest homeownership rate of all the states in 2022, with 78.6 percent of homes being owner-occupied.

Table WV-1. Population by Age, Sex, Race, and Hispanic Origin

(Number, percent, except where noted.)

Sex, age, race, and Hispanic origin	2010	2020	2022	Percent change, 2010–2022
Total Population...	1,852,994	1,793,755	1,775,156	-4.2
Percent of total U.S. population	0.6	0.5	0.5	X
Sex				
Male...	913,586	896,545	886,306	-3.0
Female..	939,408	897,210	888,850	-5.4
Age				
Under 5 years...	104,060	90,477	87,997	-15.4
Under 18 years..	387,418	359,498	351,922	-9.2
18 to 64 years...	1,168,172	1,068,284	1,047,135	-10.4
65 years and over..	297,404	365,973	376,099	26.5
Median age (years)	41.3	42.7	42.8	3.6
Race and Hispanic Origin				
One race				
White..	1,746,513	1,671,351	1,648,034	-5.6
Black..	63,885	65,488	66,210	3.6
American Indian and Alaska Native	3,975	4,668	4,888	23.0
Asian..	12,637	15,477	16,291	28.9
Native Hawaiian or Other Pacific Islander	485	621	617	27.2
Two or more races	25,499	36,150	39,116	53.4
Hispanic (of any race)..	22,268	33,379	36,790	65.2

NOTE: Population figures for 2022 are July 1 estimates. The 2010 and 2020 estimates are taken from the respective censuses.
- = Zero or rounds to zero.
X = Not applicable.

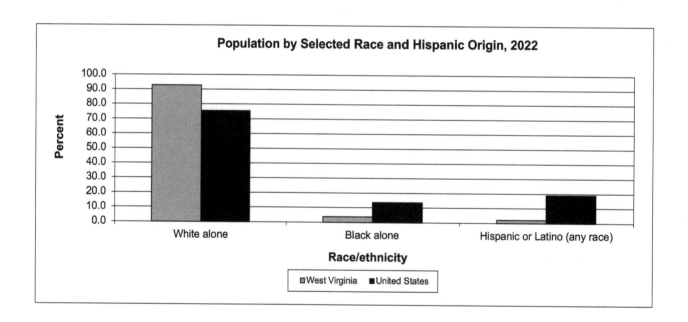

Population by Selected Race and Hispanic Origin, 2022

Table WV-2. Marital Status

(Number, percent distribution.)

Sex, age, race, and Hispanic origin	2000	2010	2021
Males, 15 Years and Over	710,443	750,542	734,595
Never married	25.4	30.3	32.1
Now married, except separated..	59.9	52.1	50.8
Separated...	1.3	1.6	1.1
Widowed..	3.2	3.4	3.6
Divorced...	10.1	12.6	12.4
Females, 15 Years and Over	768,858	785,182	751,596
Never married	19.1	22.6	25.3
Now married, except separated..	54.7	49.7	47.9
Separated...	1.6	1.7	1.6
Widowed..	13.9	12.8	11.0
Divorced...	10.8	13.2	14.3

Table WV-3. Households and Housing Characteristics

(Number, percent, dollars.)

Item	2000	2010	2021	Average annual percent change, 2010–2021
Total Households..	736,481	741,940	722,201	-0.2
Family households	504,055	485,652	462,328	-0.4
Married-couple family	397,499	372,301	345,572	-0.7
Other family	106,556	113,351	116,756	0.3
Male householder, no wife present..................................	27,436	28,515	35,843	2.3
Female householder, no husband present........................	79,120	84,836	80,913	-0.4
Nonfamily households	232,426	256,288	259,873	0.1
Householder living alone..	199,587	219,848	215,639	-0.2
Householder not living alone..	32,839	36,440	44,234	1.9
Housing Characteristics				
Total housing units..	844,623	882,213	858,462	-0.2
Occupied housing units	736,481	741,940	722,201	-0.2
Owner occupied	553,699	553,429	542,805	-0.2
Renter occupied	182,782	188,511	179,396	-0.4
Average household size...	2.40	2.43	2.41	-0.1
Financial Characteristics				
Median gross rent of renter-occupied housing	401	571	767	3.1
Median monthly owner costs for housing units with a mortgage	713	918	1,071	1.5
Median value of owner-occupied housing units.....................	72,800	95,100	143,200	4.6

Table WV-4. Migration, Origin, and Language

(Number, percent.)

Characteristic	State	U.S.
	2021	2021
Residence 1 Year Ago		
Population 1 year and over	1,767,792	328,464,538
Same house	89.6	87.2
Different house in the U.S.	10.3	12.3
Same county	4.9	6.7
Different county	5.3	5.7
Same state	2.9	3.3
Different state	2.5	2.4
Abroad	0.1	0.4
Place of Birth		
Native born	1,755,098	286,623,642
Male	49.8	49.7
Female	50.2	50.3
Foreign born	27,861	45,270,103
Male	48.5	48.7
Female	51.5	51.3
Foreign born; naturalized U.S. citizen...............................	13,819	24,044,083
Male	43.0	46.4
Female	57.0	53.6
Foreign born; not a U.S. citizen..	14,042	21,226,020
Male	53.9	51.2
Female	46.1	48.8
Entered 2010 or later	35.4	28.1
Entered 2000 to 2009	17.1	23.7
Entered before 2000..	47.4	48.2
World Region of Birth, Foreign		
Foreign-born population, excluding population born at sea	27,861	45,269,644
Europe	23.1	10.7
Asia	43.2	31.0
Africa	7.9	5.7
Oceania	0.7	0.6
Latin America	23.0	50.1
North America	2.2	1.7
Language Spoken at Home and Ability to Speak English		
Population 5 years and over...	1,694,175	313,232,500
English only	97.7	70.4
Language other than English..	2.3	21.6
Speaks English less than "very well"................................	0.5	8.3

Table WV-5. Median Income and Poverty Status, 2021

(Number, percent, except as noted.)

Characteristic	State Number	State Percent	U.S. Number	U.S. Percent
Median Income				
Households (dollars)..	51,248	X	69,717	X
Families (dollars)	66,669	X	85,806	X
Below Poverty Level (All People)	291,930	16.8	41,393,176	12.8
Sex				
Male	127,898	14.9	18,518,155	11.6
Female	164,032	18.7	22,875,021	13.9
Age				
Under 18 years...	73,022	20.7	12,243,219	16.9
Related children under 18 years..	71,961	20.5	11,985,424	16.6
18 to 64 years..	177,303	17.4	23,526,341	11.9
65 years and over	41,605	11.5	5,623,616	10.3

X = Not applicable.

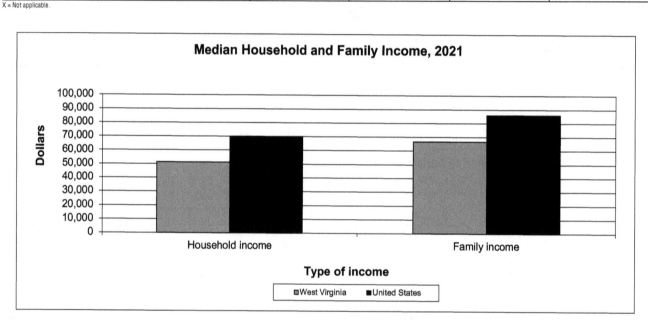

Table WV-6. Health Insurance Coverage Status for the Civilian Noninstitutionalized Population and Children Under 19 Years of Age

(Number, percent.)

Item	2011	2012	2013	2014	2015	2016	2017	2018	2019	2020 [2]	2021
Civilian Noninstitutionalized Population	1,826,485	1,826,512	1,824,821	1,820,836	1,815,505	1,802,572	1,787,126	1,776,965	1,762,052	1,778,080	1,755,887
Covered by Private or Public Insurance											
Number...	1,554,198	1,562,703	1,569,752	1,664,746	1,707,423	1,706,690	1,678,237	1,662,859	1,644,408	1,668,236	1,649,070
Percent..	85.1	85.6	86.0	91.4	94.0	94.7	93.9	93.6	93.3	93.8	93.9
Uninsured											
Number...	272,287	263,809	255,069	156,090	108,082	95,882	108,889	114,106	117,644	109,844	106,817
Percent..	14.9	14.4	14.0	8.6	6.0	5.3	6.1	6.4	6.7	6.2	6.1
Percent in the U.S. not covered.............................	15.1	14.8	14.5	11.7	9.4	8.6	8.7	8.9	9.2	8.7	8.6
Children Under 19 Years of Age[1]	385,302	382,980	381,156	382,225	378,396	375,790	399,352	388,032	380,871	387,727	380,836
Covered by Private or Public Insurance											
Number...	368,308	367,957	360,851	370,788	367,613	368,007	388,819	374,932	367,446	376,610	368,220
Percent..	95.6	96.1	94.7	97.0	97.2	97.9	97.4	96.6	96.5	97.1	96.7
Uninsured											
Number...	16,994	15,023	20,305	11,437	10,783	7,783	10,533	13,100	13,425	11,117	12,616
Percent..	4.4	3.9	5.3	3.0	2.8	2.1	2.6	3.4	3.5	2.9	3.3
Percent in the U.S. not covered.............................	7.5	7.2	7.1	6.0	4.8	4.5	5.0	5.2	5.7	5.2	5.4

[1] Data for years prior to 2017 are for individuals under 18 years of age.
[2] 2020 ACS 5-Year estimates. 1-Year estimates were not released for 2020 due to the impact of COVID-19 on data collection that year. Data is not comparable to previous years, which are based on 1-year estimates.

Table WV-7. Employment Status by Demographic Group, 2022

(Numbers in thousands, percent.)

Characteristic	Civilian noninstitutional population	Civilian labor force		Employed		Unemployed	
		Number	Percent of population	Number	Percent of population	Number	Percent of population
Total..	1,444	778	53.9	749	51.9	29	3.8
Sex							
Male..	712	416	58.4	399	56.1	17	4.0
Female.....................................	732	362	49.5	350	47.8	12	3.4
Race, Sex, and Hispanic Origin							
White......................................	1,358	722	53.2	697	51.3	25	3.5
Male.....................................	667	385	57.7	371	55.5	14	3.7
Female..................................	691	337	48.8	326	47.2	11	3.3
Black or African American.................	NA	NA	NA	NA	NA	NA	NA
Male.....................................	NA	NA	NA	NA	NA	NA	NA
Female..................................	NA	NA	NA	NA	NA	NA	NA
Hispanic or Latino ethnicity[1].............	NA	NA	NA	NA	NA	NA	NA
Male.....................................	NA	NA	NA	NA	NA	NA	NA
Female..................................	NA	NA	NA	NA	NA	NA	NA
Age							
16 to 19 years............................	NA	NA	NA	NA	NA	NA	NA
20 to 24 years............................	101	71	70.1	68	67.0	3	4.5
25 to 34 years............................	200	159	79.5	150	75.3	8	5.2
35 to 44 years............................	225	182	80.9	175	78.0	7	3.6
45 to 54 years............................	206	151	73.4	147	71.1	5	3.0
55 to 64 years............................	251	132	52.7	129	51.5	3	2.5
65 years and over.........................	377	55	14.5	54	14.3	1	1.3

NOTE: Data in Table 7 are from the Current Population Survey (CPS) and do not match the estimates in Table 8. See notes and definitions for further information.
[1] May be of any race.
NA = Not available.

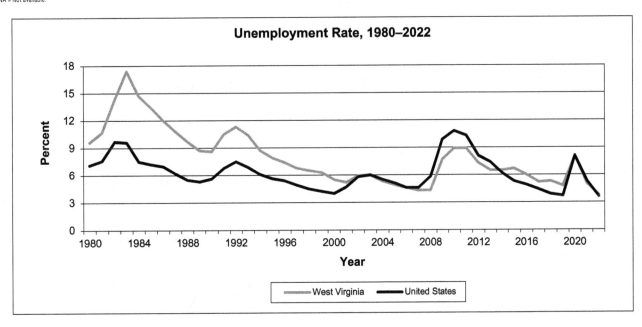

Table WV-8. Employment Status of the Civilian Noninstitutional Population Age 16 Years and Over

(Number, percent.)

Year	Civilian labor force	Civilian participation rate	Employed	Unemployed	Unemployment rate
2010..	810,101	54.9	739,891	70,210	8.7
2011..	806,568	54.3	743,346	63,222	7.8
2012..	808,022	54.3	749,587	58,435	7.2
2013..	799,481	53.8	745,849	53,632	6.7
2014..	795,733	53.6	743,955	51,778	6.5
2015..	791,526	53.5	739,455	52,071	6.6
2016..	785,104	53.3	737,205	47,899	6.1
2017..	784,744	53.5	743,786	40,958	5.2
2018..	793,715	54.4	752,726	40,989	5.2
2019..	796,776	54.8	757,484	39,292	4.9
2020..	783,027	54.1	719,175	63,852	8.2
2021..	788,826	54.7	749,132	39,694	5.0
2022..	785,115	54.7	754,453	30,662	3.9

Table WV-9. Employment and Average Wages by Industry

(Estimates are based on the 2012 North American Industry Classification System [NAICS].)

Industry	2014	2015	2016	2017	2018	2019	2020	2021
	Number of Jobs							
Wage and Salary Employment by Industry........................	740,039	733,992	721,162	720,173	730,807	725,804	679,085	692,643
Farm Wage and Salary Employment................................	1,703	1,912	1,575	1,823	1,577	1,546	1,546	1,576
Nonfarm Wage and Salary Employment...........................	738,336	732,080	719,587	718,350	729,230	724,258	677,539	691,067
Private wage and salary employment................................	581,584	576,322	563,322	563,483	576,464	570,751	527,138	541,222
Forestry, fishing, and related activities...........................	1,412	1,481	1,512	1,486	1,439	1,488	1,268	1,300
Mining..	29,202	25,012	19,344	20,909	21,677	21,516	16,676	16,958
Utilities..	5,204	5,051	5,167	5,299	5,334	5,275	5,033	5,073
Construction..	34,632	33,267	30,806	32,334	41,151	36,306	30,333	31,477
Manufacturing...	47,885	47,756	46,878	46,603	46,967	47,001	44,454	45,369
Durable goods manufacturing....................................	28,942	28,696	28,067	27,999	28,526	28,328	25,945	26,379
Nondurable goods manufacturing..............................	18,943	19,060	18,811	18,604	18,441	18,673	18,509	18,990
Wholesale trade..	22,721	22,356	21,225	20,803	20,462	20,288	19,191	18,823
Retail trade...	87,324	87,340	87,425	85,311	83,611	80,944	76,961	79,287
Transportation and warehousing..................................	20,862	21,468	20,253	20,602	21,574	21,601	19,815	20,223
Information..	9,591	9,646	9,667	8,619	8,278	8,074	7,204	7,234
Finance and insurance...	19,646	19,304	19,083	18,974	19,312	19,451	19,511	19,480
Real estate and rental and leasing..............................	6,924	6,951	6,749	6,573	6,722	6,826	6,527	6,618
Professional, scientific, and technical services.............	26,359	26,116	25,174	25,625	27,124	26,992	25,625	26,957
Management of companies and enterprises....................	6,381	6,406	6,247	6,469	6,930	7,086	7,656	7,589
Administrative and waste services...............................	34,625	35,067	34,578	34,688	35,437	35,428	32,916	34,178
Educational services	8,912	8,962	9,491	9,461	9,606	9,766	8,158	8,490
Health care and social assistance................................	113,942	114,846	115,653	115,937	116,875	117,770	117,631	118,285
Arts, entertainment, and recreation..............................	7,919	7,673	7,659	7,933	7,977	8,308	6,783	8,088
Accommodation and food services...............................	66,900	67,331	66,974	66,908	66,615	67,158	54,938	59,008
Other services, except public administration..................	31,143	30,289	29,437	28,949	29,373	29,473	26,458	26,785
Government and government enterprises	156,752	155,758	156,265	154,867	152,766	153,507	150,401	149,845
	Dollars							
Average Wages and Salaries by Industry	40,634	41,195	41,158	42,871	45,537	46,022	47,885	49,812
Average Farm Wages and Salaries	22,682	16,503	22,992	18,027	19,261	15,602	15,152	14,933
Average Nonfarm Wages and Salaries	40,676	41,260	41,198	42,934	45,594	46,087	47,960	49,891
Average private wages and salaries...............................	40,594	41,134	40,952	43,012	45,967	46,207	47,737	49,913
Forestry, fishing, and related activities..........................	28,929	29,738	30,026	30,334	30,896	33,495	35,227	37,465
Mining...	80,803	78,790	75,296	80,779	84,040	84,438	82,501	87,852
Utilities..	85,132	88,951	89,160	91,707	93,303	97,407	101,597	101,587
Construction..	53,522	53,331	52,550	57,999	72,158	64,460	60,426	60,880
Manufacturing...	55,058	55,910	56,523	58,657	60,501	61,092	62,378	65,156
Durable goods manufacturing....................................	51,405	51,693	52,289	54,373	56,835	57,839	58,445	61,178
Nondurable goods manufacturing..............................	60,638	62,259	62,840	65,106	66,172	66,027	67,892	70,682
Wholesale trade..	54,980	55,982	56,166	58,694	60,945	63,421	65,822	68,748
Retail trade...	24,633	25,612	26,022	26,583	27,545	28,454	30,322	32,059
Transportation and warehousing..................................	50,045	50,354	49,873	51,742	51,562	52,504	53,708	56,764
Information..	48,738	51,247	50,706	50,441	52,553	53,247	58,121	63,788
Finance and insurance...	49,393	50,858	52,058	54,909	57,317	58,923	61,782	65,568
Real estate and rental and leasing..............................	37,839	37,967	37,454	38,818	42,801	42,996	43,010	44,041
Professional, scientific, and technical services	55,173	56,153	56,925	59,814	63,564	61,997	63,765	65,214
Management of companies and enterprises....................	72,396	73,968	72,210	77,409	82,066	85,345	80,638	85,032
Administrative and waste services...............................	31,294	31,921	32,173	34,222	36,761	37,973	39,253	42,811
Educational services	24,749	25,205	24,596	25,505	25,266	26,391	30,671	29,976
Health care and social assistance................................	41,005	42,735	43,911	45,604	47,101	48,823	51,477	53,997
Arts, entertainment, and recreation..............................	19,271	19,999	19,987	19,793	20,573	20,612	22,102	23,046
Accommodation and food services...............................	18,047	18,729	19,151	19,582	20,546	20,878	20,371	23,512
Other services, except public administration..................	28,221	29,082	29,892	31,243	32,518	33,338	35,620	37,035
Government and government enterprises.............................	40,978	41,723	42,086	42,653	44,189	45,642	48,742	49,812

Table WV-10. Employment Characteristics by Family Type

(Number, percent.)

Family type and labor force status	2019 Total	2019 Families with own children under 18 years	2020 [1] Total	2020 [1] Families with own children under 18 years	2021 Total	2021 Families with own children under 18 years
All Families..	470,472	166,204	470,391	169,583	462,328	160,920
FAMILY TYPE AND LABOR FORCE STATUS						
Opposite-Sex Married-Couple Families...............................	352,587	109,336	353,287	113,390	343,639	105,844
Both husband and wife in labor force...............................	41.2	61.8	41.6	63.5	40.1	62.3
Husband in labor force, wife not in labor force	20.3	26.4	20.2	25.8	20.8	26.6
Wife in labor force, husband not in labor force	12.0	7.6	10.6	6.5	10.2	7.3
Both husband and wife not in labor force...........................	26.2	3.5	27.6	4.2	29.0	3.8
Other Families	117,885	56,868	114,711	55,676	116,756	54,586
Female householder, no spouse present............................	67.3	69.2	69.2	70.1	69.3	73.6
In labor force...	37.4	50.3	39.7	52.8	41.6	58.2
Not in labor force	29.9	18.8	29.5	17.4	27.7	15.4
Male householder, no spouse present..............................	32.7	30.8	30.8	29.9	30.7	26.4
In labor force...	20.3	25.1	19.6	24.6	18.7	21.5
Not in labor force	12.4	5.7	11.3	5.2	12.0	4.9

[1] 2020 ACS 5-Year estimates. 1-Year estimates were not released for 2020 due to the impact of COVID-19 on data collection that year. Data is not comparable to previous years, which are based on 1-year estimates.

Table WV-11. School Enrollment and Educational Attainment, 2021

(Number, percent.)

Item	State	U.S.
Enrollment		
Total population 3 years and over, enrolled in school	356,283	79,453,524
Enrolled in nursery school or preschool (percent)...	4.2	5.2
Enrolled in kindergarten (percent)..	5.4	5.0
Enrolled in elementary school, grades 1-8 (percent)..	44.0	41.3
Enrolled in high school, grades 9-12 (percent)..	22.9	21.8
Enrolled in college or graduate school (percent)..	23.6	26.7
Attainment		
Total population 25 years and over	1,265,439	228,193,464
Less than ninth grade (percent)..	3.2	4.8
9th to 12th grade, no diploma (percent)...	7.9	5.9
High school graduate, including equivalency (percent)...	39.1	26.3
Some college, no degree (percent)..	17.6	19.3
Associate's degree (percent)...	8.0	8.8
Bachelor's degree (percent)..	14.2	21.2
Graduate or professional degree (percent)..	9.9	13.8
High school graduate or higher (percent)...	88.8	89.4
Bachelor's degree or higher (percent)..	24.1	35.0

Table WV-12. Public School Characteristics and Educational Indicators

(Number, percent; data derived from National Center of Education Statistics.)

Item	State	U.S.
Public Elementary and Secondary Schools		
Number of regular school districts, 2019-20	55	13,349
Number of operational schools, 2019-20...	725	98,469
Percent charter schools	-	7.7
Total public school enrollment, Fall 2021	252,720	49,433,092
Percent charter school enrollment	NA	7.5
Student-teacher ratio, Fall 2019...	14.0	15.9
Expenditures per student (unadjusted dollars), 2019-20	12,647	13,489
Four-year adjusted cohort graduation rate (ACGR), 2019-2020[1]...................................	92.1	86.5
Students eligible for free or reduced-price lunch (percent), 2019-20...............................	51.2	52.1
English language learners (percent), Fall 2020	0.7	10.3
Students age 3 to 21 served under IDEA, part B (percent), 2021-22	18.5	14.7

Public Schools by Type, 2019-20	Number	Percent of state public schools
Total number of schools..	725	100.0
Special education..	2	0.3
Vocational education...	34	4.7
Alternative education..	34	4.7

[1] Adjusted Cohort Graduation Rates (ACGR) differ from Averaged Freshmen Graduation Rates (AFGR).
NA = Not available.

Table WV-13. Reported Voting and Registration of the Voting-Age Population, November 2022

(Numbers in thousands, percent.)

Item	Total population	Total citizen population	Registered			Voted		
			Total registered	Percent registered (total population)	Percent registered (total citizen population)	Total voted	Percent voted (total population)	Percent voted (total citizen population)
U.S. Total	255,457	233,546	161,422	63.2	69.1	121,916	47.7	52.2
State Total....................................	1,406	1,400	877	62.3	62.6	538	38.2	38.4
Sex								
Male	689	687	424	61.6	61.7	263	38.1	38.2
Female	717	713	452	63.1	63.5	275	38.3	38.6
Race								
White alone..................................	1,310	1,305	831	63.4	63.7	516	39.4	39.5
White, non-Hispanic alone	1,292	1,290	819	63.4	63.5	511	39.6	39.6
Black alone...................................	43	43	20	47.4	47.4	9	22.3	22.3
Asian alone	13	11	3	22.2	26.1	-	-	-
Hispanic (of any race)	29	27	16	54.7	59.2	6	22.0	23.8
White alone or in combination	1,343	1,339	852	63.4	63.6	528	39.3	39.5
Black alone or in combination	59	59	29	49.3	49.3	11	19.6	19.6
Asian alone or in combination	18	16	6	32.0	36.1	1	6.4	7.2
Age								
18 to 24 years	146	146	62	42.6	42.6	21	14.2	14.2
25 to 34 years	201	198	118	58.5	59.6	48	24.0	24.5
35 to 44 years	224	223	138	61.5	61.9	80	35.5	35.8
45 to 64 years	429	429	275	64.1	64.1	181	42.3	42.3
65 years and over	406	405	284	69.9	70.1	208	51.2	51.3

B = Base is less than 75,000 and therefore too small to show the derived measure.
- = Zero or rounds to zero.

Table WV-14. Health Indicators

(Number, rate as indicated in footnotes.)

Item	State	U.S.
Births		
Life Expectancy at Birth (years), 2020	72.8	77.0
Fertility Rate by State[1], 2021..	54.7	56.3
Percent Home Births, 2021	1.2	1.4
Cesarean Delivery Rate[2], 2021	34.0	32.1
Preterm Birth Rate[3], 2021	12.8	10.5
Teen Birth Rate[4], 2021	20.9	13.9
Percentage of Babies Born Low Birthweight[5], 2021	9.8	8.5
Deaths[6]		
Heart Disease Mortality Rate, 2021...	223.0	173.8
Cancer Mortality Rate, 2021...	184.7	146.6
Stroke Mortality Rate, 2021	41.2	41.1
Diabetes Mortality Rate, 2021	47.6	25.4
Influenza/Pneumonia Mortality Rate, 2021	16.5	10.5
Suicide Mortality Rate, 2021	20.6	14.1
Drug Overdose Mortality Rate, 2021	90.9	33.6
Firearm Injury Mortality Rate, 2021	17.3	14.6
Homicide Mortality Rate, 2021...	6.9	8.2
Disease and Illness		
Lifetime Asthma in Adults, 2020 (percent)....................................	16.9	13.9
Lifetime Asthma in Children, 2020 (percent)[7]	NA	11.3
Diabetes in Adults, 2020 (percent)..	13.1	8.2
Self-reported Obesity in Adults, 2021 (percent)...............................	40.6	NA

SOURCE: National Center for Health Statistics, National Vital Statistics System 2020 data; https://wonder.cdc.gov.
[1] General fertility rate per 1,000 women aged 15–44.
[2] This represents the percentage of all live births that were cesarean deliveries.
[3] Babies born prior to 37 weeks of pregnancy (gestation).
[4] Number of births per 1,000 females aged 15–19
[5] Babies born weighing less than 2,500 grams or 5 lbs. 8oz.
[6] Death rates are the number of deaths per 100,000 total population.
[7] U.S. total includes data from 30 states and D.C.
NA = Not available.
- = Zero or rounds to zero.

Table WV-15. State Government Finances, 2021

(Dollar amounts in thousands, percent distribution.)

Item	Dollars	Percent distribution
Total Revenue	17,735,301	100.0
General revenue	16,194,098	91.3
Intergovernmental revenue	6,899,273	38.9
Taxes	6,046,197	34.1
General sales	1,537,245	8.7
Selective sales	1,431,309	8.1
License taxes	196,902	1.1
Individual income tax	2,253,788	12.7
Corporate income tax	320,487	1.8
Other taxes	306,466	1.7
Current charges	1,607,894	9.1
Miscellaneous general revenue	1,640,734	9.3
Utility revenue	3,760	-
Liquor stores revenue	127,796	0.7
Insurance trust revenue[1]	1,409,647	7.9
Total Expenditure	18,546,551	100.0
Intergovernmental expenditure	3,505,147	18.9
Direct expenditure	15,041,404	81.1
Current operation	11,084,505	59.8
Capital outlay	1,320,382	7.1
Insurance benefits and repayments	1,955,815	10.5
Assistance and subsidies	372,321	2.0
Interest on debt	308,381	1.7
Exhibit: Salaries and wages	2,143,294	11.6
Total Expenditure	18,546,551	100.0
General expenditure	16,476,067	88.8
Intergovernmental expenditure	3,505,147	18.9
Direct expenditure	12,970,920	69.9
General expenditure, by function:		
Education	5,064,953	27.3
Public welfare	5,492,543	29.6
Hospitals	200,868	1.1
Health	423,401	2.3
Highways	1,694,635	9.1
Police protection	145,886	0.8
Correction	436,879	2.4
Natural resources	265,320	1.4
Parks and recreation	58,278	0.3
Governmental administration	702,473	3.8
Interest on general debt	308,381	1.7
Other and unallocable	1,666,801	9.0
Utility expenditure	28,172	0.2
Liquor stores expenditure	102,146	0.6
Insurance trust expenditure	1,955,815	10.5
Debt at End of Fiscal Year	13,368,743	X
Cash and Security Holdings	29,514,837	X

X = Not applicable.
- = Zero or rounds to zero.
[1] Within insurance trust revenue, net earnings of state retirement systems is a calculated statistic (the item code in the data file is X08), and thus can be positive or negative. Net earnings is the sum of earnings on investments plus gains on investments minus losses on investments. The change made in 2002 for asset valuation from book to market value in accordance with Statement 34 of the Governmental Accounting Standards Board is reflected in the calculated statistics.

Table WV-16. State Government Tax Collections, 2022

(Dollars in thousands, percent.)

Item	Dollars	Percent distribution
Total Taxes	7,064,214	100.0
Property taxes	7,908	0.1
Sales and gross receipts	3,200,985	45.3
General sales and gross receipts	1,655,483	23.4
Selective sales and gross receipts	1,545,502	21.9
Alcoholic beverages	20,775	0.3
Amusements	39,214	0.6
Insurance premiums	135,847	1.9
Motor fuels	419,593	5.9
Pari-mutuels	2,937	-
Public utilities	111,101	1.6
Tobacco products	165,066	2.3
Other selective sales	650,969	9.2
Licenses	191,808	2.7
Alcoholic beverages	1,763	-
Amusements	3,215	-
Corporations in general	1,079	-
Hunting and fishing	15,301	0.2
Motor vehicle	5,059	0.1
Motor vehicle operators	146,854	2.1
Public utilities	391	-
Occupation and business, NEC	13,630	0.2
Other licenses	4,516	0.1
Income taxes	2,869,144	40.6
Individual income	2,502,828	35.4
Corporation net income	366,316	5.2
Other taxes	794,369	11.2
Death and gift	X	X
Documentary and stock transfer	17,856	0.3
Severance	768,794	10.9
Taxes, NEC	7,719	0.1

- = Zero or rounds to zero.
X = Not applicable.

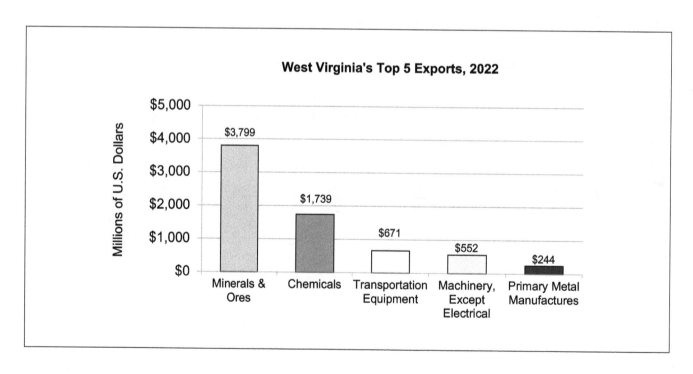

West Virginia's Top 5 Exports, 2022

Export	Millions of U.S. Dollars
Minerals & Ores	$3,799
Chemicals	$1,739
Transportation Equipment	$671
Machinery, Except Electrical	$552
Primary Metal Manufactures	$244

WISCONSIN

Facts and Figures

Location: North central United States; bordered on the N by Michigan and Lake Superior, on the E by Lake Michigan, on the S by Illinois, and on the W by Iowa and Minnesota

Area: 65,498 sq. mi. (169,639 sq. km.); rank—23rd

Population: 5,892,539 (2022 est.); rank—20th

Principal Cities: capital—Madison; largest—Milwaukee

Statehood: May 29, 1848; 30th state

U.S. Congress: 2 senators, 8 representatives

State Motto: Forward

State Song: "On, Wisconsin!"

State Nickname: The Badger State

Abbreviations: WI; Wis.; Wisc.

State Symbols: flower—wood violet; tree—sugar maple; bird—robin

At a Glance

- With an increase in population of 3.6 percent, Wisconsin ranked 36th among the states in growth from 2010 to 2022.

- Wisconsin's drug overdose death rate of 18.9 deaths per 100,000 population ranked 44th in the country in 2021. The national rate was 32.4 drug overdose deaths per 100,000 population.

- Wisconsin's median household income in 2021 was $67,125, and 12.8 percent of the population lived below the poverty level.

- In the November 2022 midterm election, 59.1 percent of Wisconsin's eligible voters cast ballots, ranking it 6th in the nation for voter turnout.

- The unemployment rate in Wisconsin in 2022 was 2.9 percent, compared to the national rate of 3.6 percent.

Table WI-1. Population by Age, Sex, Race, and Hispanic Origin

(Number, percent, except where noted.)

Sex, age, race, and Hispanic origin	2010	2020	2022	Percent change, 2010–2022
Total Population...	5,686,986	5,893,725	5,892,539	3.6
Percent of total U.S. population	1.8	1.8	1.8	X
Sex				
Male..	2,822,400	2,956,490	2,955,306	4.7
Female..	2,864,586	2,937,235	2,937,233	2.5
Age				
Under 5 years...	358,443	324,518	312,622	-12.8
Under 18 years..	1,339,492	1,276,351	1,245,629	-7.0
18 to 64 years...	3,570,180	3,582,304	3,544,791	-0.7
65 years and over..	777,314	1,035,070	1,102,119	41.8
Median age (years)	38.5	39.8	40.4	4.9
Race and Hispanic Origin				
One race				
White	5,036,923	5,119,188	5,103,755	1.3
Black..	367,021	391,490	390,428	6.4
American Indian and Alaska Native...........................	60,100	70,491	71,555	19.1
Asian..	131,828	184,083	190,698	44.7
Native Hawaiian or Other Pacific Islander	2,505	3,534	3,612	44.2
Two or more races..	88,609	124,939	132,491	49.5
Hispanic (of any race)...	336,056	428,882	448,151	33.4

NOTE: Population figures for 2022 are July 1 estimates. The 2010 and 2020 estimates are taken from the respective censuses.
- = Zero or rounds to zero.
X = Not applicable.

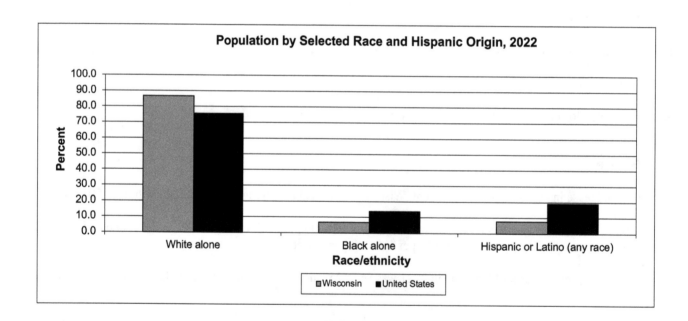

Table WI-2. Marital Status

(Number, percent distribution.)

Sex, age, race, and Hispanic origin	2000	2010	2021
Males, 15 Years and Over	2,072,397	2,261,022	2,417,315
Never married...	30.2	34.1	36.4
Now married, except separated..	57.9	52.1	50.6
Separated..	1.1	1.0	0.8
Widowed..	2.4	2.6	2.5
Divorced..	8.4	10.2	9.8
Females, 15 Years and Over	2,167,164	2,328,733	2,435,101
Never married...	24.3	28.1	30.0
Now married, except separated..	54.6	50.1	49.2
Separated..	1.3	1.2	1.0
Widowed..	10.2	9.2	7.9
Divorced..	9.7	11.4	11.8

Table WI-3. Households and Housing Characteristics

(Number, percent, dollars.)

Item	2000	2010	2021	Average annual percent change, 2010–2021
Total Households..	2,084,544	2,279,532	2,449,970	0.7
Family households	1,386,815	1,453,332	1,514,656	0.4
Married-couple family	1,108,597	1,125,314	1,162,694	0.3
Other family	278,218	328,018	351,962	0.7
Male householder, no wife present............................	77,918	96,237	114,292	1.7
Female householder, no husband present...................	200,300	231,781	237,670	0.2
Nonfamily households	697,729	826,200	935,314	1.2
Householder living alone..	557,875	669,106	742,202	1.0
Householder not living alone......................................	139,854	157,094	193,112	2.1
Housing Characteristics				
Total housing units...	2,321,144	2,625,477	2,748,274	0.4
Occupied housing units	2,084,544	2,279,532	2,449,970	0.7
Owner occupied	1,426,361	1,566,039	1,668,575	0.6
Renter occupied	658,183	713,493	781,395	0.9
Average household size..	2.50	2.43	2.35	-0.3
Financial Characteristics				
Median gross rent of renter-occupied housing	540	715	921	2.6
Median monthly owner costs for housing units with a mortgage ...	1,024	1,404	1,464	0.4
Median value of owner-occupied housing units.............	112,200	169,400	230,700	3.3

Table WI-4. Migration, Origin, and Language

(Number, percent.)

Characteristic	State 2021	U.S. 2021
Residence 1 Year Ago		
Population 1 year and over	5,838,954	328,464,538
Same house	87.7	87.2
Different house in the U.S.	12.0	12.3
Same county	6.5	6.7
Different county	5.5	5.7
Same state	3.4	3.3
Different state	2.1	2.4
Abroad	0.2	0.4
Place of Birth		
Native born	5,595,148	286,623,642
Male	50.1	49.7
Female	49.9	50.3
Foreign born	300,760	45,270,103
Male	49.8	48.7
Female	50.2	51.3
Foreign born; naturalized U.S. citizen..	147,691	24,044,083
Male	47.7	46.4
Female	52.3	53.6
Foreign born; not a U.S. citizen..	153,069	21,226,020
Male	51.8	51.2
Female	48.2	48.8
Entered 2010 or later	29.7	28.1
Entered 2000 to 2009	27.7	23.7
Entered before 2000..	42.6	48.2
World Region of Birth, Foreign		
Foreign-born population, excluding population born at sea	300,760	45,269,644
Europe	15.1	10.7
Asia..	35.4	31.0
Africa..	7.1	5.7
Oceania..	0.5	0.6
Latin America..	39.7	50.1
North America	2.3	1.7
Language Spoken at Home and Ability to Speak English		
Population 5 years and over..	5,580,644	313,232,500
English only	91.3	78.4
Language other than English...	8.7	21.6
Speaks English less than "very well"....................................	3.0	8.3

Table WI-5. Median Income and Poverty Status, 2021

(Number, percent, except as noted.)

Characteristic	State		U.S.	
	Number	Percent	Number	Percent
Median Income				
Households (dollars)...	67,125	X	69,717	X
Families (dollars)	85,810	X	85,806	X
Below Poverty Level (All People)	621,125	10.8	41,393,176	12.8
Sex				
Male	280,493	9.8	18,518,155	11.6
Female	340,632	11.8	22,875,021	13.9
Age				
Under 18 years..	167,864	13.4	12,243,219	16.9
Related children under 18 years........................	163,160	13.1	11,985,424	16.6
18 to 64 years...	363,431	10.5	23,526,341	11.9
65 years and over	89,830	8.7	5,623,616	10.3

X = Not applicable.

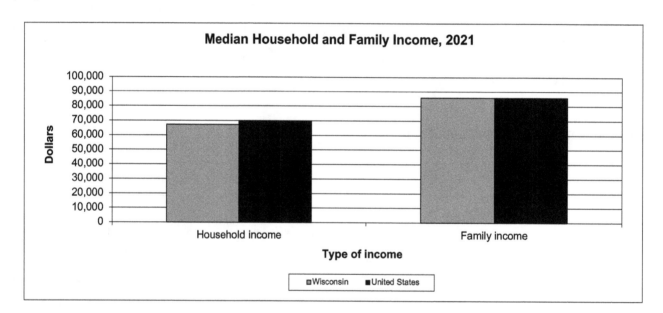

Median Household and Family Income, 2021

□ Wisconsin   ■ United States

Table WI-6. Health Insurance Coverage Status for the Civilian Noninstitutionalized Population and Children Under 19 Years of Age

(Number, percent.)

Item	2011	2012	2013	2014	2015	2016	2017	2018	2019	2020 [2]	2021
Civilian Noninstitutionalized Population	5,634,063	5,652,085	5,669,266	5,684,725	5,698,995	5,706,681	5,723,963	5,740,669	5,751,404	5,735,703	5,828,354
Covered by Private or Public Insurance											
Number..	5,127,389	5,146,087	5,151,470	5,267,002	5,376,379	5,406,475	5,414,559	5,427,511	5,422,750	5,422,999	5,516,183
Percent..	91.0	91.0	90.9	92.7	94.3	94.7	94.6	94.5	94.3	94.5	94.6
Uninsured											
Number..	506,674	505,998	517,796	417,723	322,616	300,206	309,404	313,158	328,654	312,704	312,171
Percent..	9.0	9.0	9.1	7.3	5.7	5.3	5.4	5.5	5.7	5.5	5.4
Percent in the U.S. not covered...........................	15.1	14.8	14.5	11.7	9.4	8.6	8.7	8.9	9.2	8.7	8.6
Children Under 19 Years of Age[1]	1,322,921	1,315,276	1,304,781	1,297,792	1,290,350	1,283,539	1,361,508	1,350,222	1,344,601	1,354,142	1,351,732
Covered by Private or Public Insurance											
Number..	1,264,685	1,253,719	1,243,493	1,240,181	1,244,122	1,238,131	1,308,778	1,299,125	1,293,888	1,301,866	1,297,308
Percent..	95.6	95.3	95.3	95.6	96.4	96.5	96.1	96.2	96.2	96.1	96.0
Uninsured											
Number..	58,236	61,557	61,288	57,611	46,228	45,408	52,730	51,097	50,713	52,276	54,424
Percent..	4.4	4.7	4.7	4.4	3.6	3.5	3.9	3.8	3.8	3.9	4.0
Percent in the U.S. not covered...........................	7.5	7.2	7.1	6.0	4.8	4.5	5.0	5.2	5.7	5.2	5.4

[1] Data for years prior to 2017 are for individuals under 18 years of age.
[2] 2020 ACS 5-Year estimates. 1-Year estimates were not released for 2020 due to the impact of COVID-19 on data collection that year. Data is not comparable to previous years, which are based on 1-year estimates.

Table WI-7. Employment Status by Demographic Group, 2022

(Numbers in thousands, percent.)

Characteristic	Civilian noninstitutional population	Civilian labor force		Employed		Unemployed	
		Number	Percent of population	Number	Percent of population	Number	Percent of population
Total..	4,738	3,054	64.5	2,955	62.4	99	3.2
Sex							
Male..	2,348	1,638	69.8	1,578	67.2	59	3.6
Female	2,390	1,416	59.3	1,377	57.6	40	2.8
Race, Sex, and Hispanic Origin							
White	4,245	2,721	64.1	2,642	62.2	79	2.9
Male..	2,117	1,461	69.0	1,413	66.8	48	3.3
Female	2,128	1,260	59.2	1,228	57.7	31	2.5
Black or African American......................	274	174	63.6	160	58.6	14	8.0
Male..	NA	NA	NA	NA	NA	NA	NA
Female	NA	NA	NA	NA	NA	NA	NA
Hispanic or Latino ethnicity[1]	308	197	64.0	188	61.1	9	4.6
Male..	NA	NA	NA	NA	NA	NA	NA
Female	NA	NA	NA	NA	NA	NA	NA
Age							
16 to 19 years..................................	288	163	56.5	151	52.5	11	7.0
20 to 24 years..................................	394	325	82.5	308	78.3	17	5.1
25 to 34 years..................................	746	638	85.5	612	82.1	25	4.0
35 to 44 years..................................	730	616	84.5	597	81.9	19	3.0
45 to 54 years..................................	674	566	84.0	557	82.6	9	1.6
55 to 64 years..................................	831	562	67.6	549	66.1	13	2.3
65 years and over	1,076	184	17.1	180	16.7	5	2.6

NOTE: Data in Table 7 are from the Current Population Survey (CPS) and do not match the estimates in Table 8. See notes and definitions for further information.
[1] May be of any race.
NA = Not available.

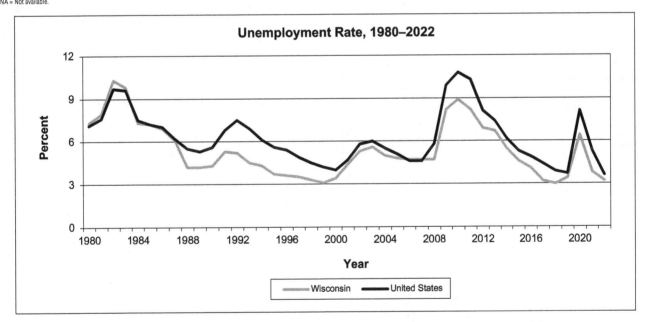

Unemployment Rate, 1980–2022

Table WI-8. Employment Status of the Civilian Noninstitutional Population Age 16 Years and Over

(Number, percent.)

Year	Civilian labor force	Civilian participation rate	Employed	Unemployed	Unemployment rate
2010..	3,082,935	69.5	2,820,620	262,315	8.5
2011..	3,072,157	68.9	2,839,987	232,170	7.6
2012..	3,070,033	68.5	2,857,150	212,883	6.9
2013..	3,077,801	68.3	2,871,988	205,813	6.7
2014..	3,077,981	68.0	2,913,764	164,217	5.3
2015..	3,084,207	67.9	2,947,048	137,159	4.4
2016..	3,110,466	68.1	2,988,744	121,722	3.9
2017..	3,141,757	68.0	3,039,348	102,409	3.3
2018..	3,120,386	67.4	3,036,071	93,315	3.0
2019..	3,120,590	66.8	3,021,491	99,099	3.2
2020..	3,105,882	66.2	2,909,004	196,878	6.3
2021..	3,134,439	66.5	3,016,039	118,400	3.8
2022..	3,082,128	65.0	2,992,049	90,079	2.9

Table WI-9. Employment and Average Wages by Industry

(Estimates are based on the 2012 North American Industry Classification System [NAICS].)

Industry	2014	2015	2016	2017	2018	2019	2020	2021
	Number of Jobs							
Wage and Salary Employment by Industry.........................	2,912,213	2,945,464	2,980,084	3,000,006	3,032,198	3,044,352	2,879,827	2,949,218
Farm Wage and Salary Employment................................	24,495	22,635	22,731	21,672	24,974	26,984	23,015	25,307
Nonfarm Wage and Salary Employment...........................	2,887,718	2,922,829	2,957,353	2,978,334	3,007,224	3,017,368	2,856,812	2,923,911
Private wage and salary employment...............................	2,451,523	2,488,641	2,518,437	2,542,669	2,570,541	2,581,648	2,436,393	2,501,529
Forestry, fishing, and related activities	5,890	6,209	6,560	6,568	6,534	6,788	(D)	6,458
Mining...	3,407	3,448	2,999	3,623	3,968	3,474	(D)	2,832
Utilities..	10,418	10,536	9,701	9,549	9,210	8,864	8,499	8,305
Construction..	106,118	112,456	115,418	120,186	125,393	127,430	126,964	129,608
Manufacturing...	465,362	467,976	464,773	467,973	476,008	483,852	459,098	468,021
Durable goods manufacturing..................................	283,764	284,907	280,088	281,024	287,308	289,260	269,312	274,990
Nondurable goods manufacturing.............................	181,598	183,069	184,685	186,949	188,700	194,592	189,786	193,031
Wholesale trade...	120,908	122,828	124,192	126,488	127,994	124,024	120,059	122,076
Retail trade..	304,680	307,242	311,206	310,405	307,967	300,773	290,329	297,325
Transportation and warehousing..................................	93,660	96,967	99,425	101,178	103,980	106,899	106,371	112,739
Information..	48,073	49,100	49,077	47,808	47,200	47,049	44,916	44,993
Finance and insurance..	126,681	127,472	127,522	128,684	128,244	130,120	130,342	131,101
Real estate and rental and leasing...............................	24,852	25,478	25,964	26,831	27,326	27,794	26,713	27,434
Professional, scientific, and technical services	102,141	105,705	108,325	109,993	113,266	116,321	114,968	120,011
Management of companies and enterprises.....................	59,397	62,454	68,686	69,129	68,034	66,289	64,630	64,217
Administrative and waste services................................	147,916	147,260	147,568	147,343	148,790	145,739	132,340	136,061
Educational services	56,059	55,936	55,958	56,554	55,721	56,676	52,824	57,478
Health care and social assistance................................	379,312	384,882	393,796	398,377	403,853	408,952	398,015	400,598
Arts, entertainment, and recreation..............................	37,833	38,317	40,351	41,393	43,044	44,523	32,610	37,637
Accommodation and food services...............................	228,394	234,048	237,281	240,818	241,407	242,793	196,992	213,714
Other services, except public administration..................	130,422	130,327	129,635	129,769	132,602	133,288	121,321	120,921
Government and government enterprises	436,195	434,188	438,916	435,665	436,683	435,720	420,419	422,382
	Dollars							
Average Wages and Salaries by Industry	44,431	45,878	46,532	47,804	49,544	51,052	54,407	57,041
Average Farm Wages and Salaries	35,368	32,312	39,052	38,048	36,250	33,163	30,390	32,900
Average Nonfarm Wages and Salaries	44,507	45,983	46,589	47,875	49,654	51,212	54,600	57,250
Average private wages and salaries...............................	44,972	46,501	47,200	48,534	50,438	51,991	55,481	58,352
Forestry, fishing, and related activities	34,352	36,377	37,456	38,835	40,490	42,177	(D)	48,665
Mining...	67,095	63,674	63,308	64,713	67,271	68,439	(D)	76,815
Utilities..	101,383	103,025	100,327	105,613	108,672	109,682	115,298	116,139
Construction..	56,152	58,031	59,588	60,990	62,983	64,778	67,428	70,416
Manufacturing...	56,035	57,114	57,030	58,779	59,987	60,987	63,135	66,516
Durable goods manufacturing..................................	57,766	58,403	58,418	60,534	61,552	62,509	64,265	68,102
Nondurable goods manufacturing.............................	53,330	55,107	54,925	56,141	57,603	58,726	61,533	64,256
Wholesale trade	61,723	63,602	64,908	67,229	70,258	72,651	76,461	82,308
Retail trade..	25,527	26,651	26,985	27,754	28,871	29,817	31,942	34,035
Transportation and warehousing..................................	44,622	45,017	44,439	45,565	46,959	47,502	49,681	51,982
Information..	65,528	69,571	71,176	73,947	77,557	84,649	90,787	95,592
Finance and insurance..	69,262	72,880	74,665	76,788	79,956	82,535	89,069	92,484
Real estate and rental and leasing...............................	37,087	39,293	41,301	42,187	44,770	46,693	50,479	53,369
Professional, scientific, and technical services	67,288	69,966	71,179	72,513	75,365	78,108	81,720	86,747
Management of companies and enterprises.....................	93,747	96,956	98,489	96,710	104,451	107,535	111,183	116,870
Administrative and waste services................................	28,566	29,805	30,724	32,067	33,423	34,909	37,588	41,089
Educational services	36,096	37,047	38,952	39,066	41,282	42,327	45,913	44,779
Health care and social assistance................................	45,290	46,685	47,161	48,602	50,251	51,993	54,183	57,219
Arts, entertainment, and recreation..............................	30,649	29,953	30,155	31,408	34,954	34,237	37,465	38,619
Accommodation and food services...............................	15,750	16,416	17,004	17,687	18,697	19,285	19,108	22,551
Other services, except public administration..................	29,402	30,664	31,647	32,956	34,202	35,380	39,838	41,535
Government and government enterprises	41,899	43,011	43,081	44,029	45,041	46,596	49,494	50,726

Table WI-10. Employment Characteristics by Family Type

(Number, percent.)

Family type and labor force status	2019		2020 [1]		2021	
	Total	Families with own children under 18 years	Total	Families with own children under 18 years	Total	Families with own children under 18 years
All Families......	1,470,116	593,666	1,479,364	614,156	1,514,656	618,391
FAMILY TYPE AND LABOR FORCE STATUS						
Opposite-Sex Married-Couple Families......	1,140,000	406,282	1,140,756	414,953	1,152,647	410,140
Both husband and wife in labor force......	56.2	77.0	56.4	76.8	54.2	75.7
Husband in labor force, wife not in labor force	15.5	17.9	16.0	18.7	16.2	19.6
Wife in labor force, husband not in labor force	7.9	3.8	7.9	3.5	7.9	3.4
Both husband and wife not in labor force......	19.7	0.9	19.7	1.0	21.8	1.2
Other Families	330,116	187,384	330,765	197,859	351,962	205,916
Female householder, no spouse present......	67.6	69.4	67.9	69.4	67.5	68.8
In labor force......	49.7	59.6	51.4	59.8	49.8	58.9
Not in labor force	17.9	9.8	16.5	9.6	17.8	9.9
Male householder, no spouse present......	32.4	30.6	32.1	30.6	32.5	31.2
In labor force......	26.3	28.4	26.6	28.4	26.1	28.4
Not in labor force	6.1	2.3	5.6	2.2	6.4	2.8

[1] 2020 ACS 5-Year estimates. 1-Year estimates were not released for 2020 due to the impact of COVID-19 on data collection that year. Data is not comparable to previous years, which are based on 1-year estimates.

Table WI-11. School Enrollment and Educational Attainment, 2021

(Number, percent.)

Item	State	U.S.
Enrollment		
Total population 3 years and over, enrolled in school	1,365,700	79,453,524
Enrolled in nursery school or preschool (percent)	4.7	5.2
Enrolled in kindergarten (percent)......	5.7	5.0
Enrolled in elementary school, grades 1-8 (percent)......	42.3	41.3
Enrolled in high school, grades 9-12 (percent)	22.1	21.8
Enrolled in college or graduate school (percent)......	25.3	26.7
Attainment		
Total population 25 years and over	4,076,339	228,193,464
Less than ninth grade (percent)	2.4	4.8
9th to 12th grade, no diploma (percent)	4.3	5.9
High school graduate, including equivalency (percent)......	30	26.3
Some college, no degree (percent)	19.5	19.3
Associate's degree (percent)......	11.3	8.8
Bachelor's degree (percent)......	21.5	21.2
Graduate or professional degree (percent)......	11.0	13.8
High school graduate or higher (percent)	93.3	89.4
Bachelor's degree or higher (percent)......	32.5	35.0

Table WI-12. Public School Characteristics and Educational Indicators

(Number, percent; data derived from National Center of Education Statistics.)

Item	State	U.S.
Public Elementary and Secondary Schools		
Number of regular school districts, 2019-20	420	13,349
Number of operational schools, 2019-20......	2,255	98,469
Percent charter schools	10.5	7.7
Total public school enrollment, Fall 2021	829,359	49,433,092
Percent charter school enrollment	6.0	7.5
Student-teacher ratio, Fall 2019	14.3	15.9
Expenditures per student (unadjusted dollars), 2019-20	12,794	13,489
Four-year adjusted cohort graduation rate (ACGR), 2019-2020[1]......	90.4	86.5
Students eligible for free or reduced-price lunch (percent), 2019-20......	39.7	52.1
English language learners (percent), Fall 2020	5.5	10.3
Students age 3 to 21 served under IDEA, part B (percent), 2021-22	14.8	14.7

Public Schools by Type, 2019-20	Number	Percent of state public schools
Total number of schools......	2,255	100.0
Special education......	13	0.6
Vocational education......	5	0.2
Alternative education......	97	4.3

[1] Adjusted Cohort Graduation Rates (ACGR) differ from Averaged Freshmen Graduation Rates (AFGR).
NA = Not available.

Table WI-13. Reported Voting and Registration of the Voting-Age Population, November 2022

(Numbers in thousands, percent.)

Item	Total population	Total citizen population	Registered			Voted		
			Total registered	Percent registered (total population)	Percent registered (total citizen population)	Total voted	Percent voted (total population)	Percent voted (total citizen population)
U.S. Total	255,457	233,546	161,422	63.2	69.1	121,916	47.7	52.2
State Total............................	4,591	4,461	3,225	70.2	72.3	2,715	59.1	60.9
Sex								
Male	2,258	2,202	1,545	68.5	70.2	1,287	57.0	58.4
Female	2,334	2,259	1,679	72.0	74.3	1,428	61.2	63.2
Race								
White alone............................	4,169	4,095	3,010	72.2	73.5	2,553	61.2	62.4
White, non-Hispanic alone	3,918	3,895	2,904	74.1	74.6	2,486	63.5	63.8
Black alone............................	277	253	149	53.8	58.8	96	34.8	38.0
Asian alone	90	57	40	44.4	69.5	40	44.4	69.5
Hispanic (of any race)	265	214	113	42.6	52.8	74	27.8	34.5
White alone or in combination	4,202	4,128	3,031	72.1	73.4	2,574	61.3	62.4
Black alone or in combination	299	276	164	54.8	59.4	111	37.2	40.3
Asian alone or in combination..........	90	57	40	44.4	69.5	40	44.4	69.5
Age								
18 to 24 years............................	588	579	341	58.0	58.8	286	48.7	49.4
25 to 34 years............................	724	679	474	65.5	69.9	371	51.2	54.7
35 to 44 years............................	693	669	447	64.5	66.8	373	53.8	55.8
45 to 64 years............................	1,473	1,440	1,107	75.1	76.9	908	61.6	63.0
65 years and over	1,113	1,095	856	76.9	78.2	777	69.8	71.0

Table WI-14. Health Indicators

(Number, rate as indicated in footnotes.)

Item	State	U.S.
Births		
Life Expectancy at Birth (years), 2020	77.7	77.0
Fertility Rate by State[1], 2021	55.7	56.3
Percent Home Births, 2021	3.1	1.4
Cesarean Delivery Rate[2], 2021	27.3	32.1
Preterm Birth Rate[3], 2021	10.0	10.5
Teen Birth Rate[4], 2021	10.1	13.9
Percentage of Babies Born Low Birthweight[5], 2021	7.7	8.5
Deaths[6]		
Heart Disease Mortality Rate, 2021............................	171.7	173.8
Cancer Mortality Rate, 2021............................	147.2	146.6
Stroke Mortality Rate, 2021............................	35.9	41.1
Diabetes Mortality Rate, 2021............................	22.6	25.4
Influenza/Pneumonia Mortality Rate, 2021........................	7.5	10.5
Suicide Mortality Rate, 2021............................	15.1	14.1
Drug Overdose Mortality Rate, 2021............................	31.6	33.6
Firearm Injury Mortality Rate, 2021............................	13.5	14.6
Homicide Mortality Rate, 2021............................	6.4	8.2
Disease and Illness		
Lifetime Asthma in Adults, 2020 (percent)........................	13.8	13.9
Lifetime Asthma in Children, 2020 (percent)[7]	10.0	11.3
Diabetes in Adults, 2020 (percent)............................	7.6	8.2
Self-reported Obesity in Adults, 2021 (percent).................	33.9	NA

SOURCE: National Center for Health Statistics, National Vital Statistics System 2020 data; https://wonder.cdc.gov.
[1] General fertility rate per 1,000 women aged 15–44.
[2] This represents the percentage of all live births that were cesarean deliveries.
[3] Babies born prior to 37 weeks of pregnancy (gestation).
[4] Number of births per 1,000 females aged 15–19
[5] Babies born weighing less than 2,500 grams or 5 lbs. 8oz.
[6] Death rates are the number of deaths per 100,000 total population.
[7] U.S. total includes data from 30 states and D.C.
NA = Not available.
- = Zero or rounds to zero.

Table WI-15. State Government Finances, 2021

(Dollar amounts in thousands, percent distribution.)

Item	Dollars	Percent distribution
Total Revenue	50,260,813	100.0
General revenue	45,328,576	90.2
Intergovernmental revenue	14,225,073	28.3
Taxes	22,300,918	44.4
General sales	6,373,483	12.7
Selective sales	2,811,139	5.6
License taxes	1,340,711	2.7
Individual income tax	9,035,988	18.0
Corporate income tax	2,517,169	5.0
Other taxes	222,428	0.4
Current charges	4,987,692	9.9
Miscellaneous general revenue	3,814,893	7.6
Utility revenue	-	-
Liquor stores revenue	-	-
Insurance trust revenue[1]	4,932,237	9.8
Total Expenditure	50,903,217	100.0
Intergovernmental expenditure	12,535,007	24.6
Direct expenditure	38,368,210	75.4
Current operation	26,526,587	52.1
Capital outlay	2,415,623	4.7
Insurance benefits and repayments	7,641,188	15.0
Assistance and subsidies	1,221,750	2.4
Interest on debt	563,062	1.1
Exhibit: Salaries and wages	4,871,088	9.6
Total Expenditure	50,903,217	100.0
General expenditure	43,243,049	85.0
Intergovernmental expenditure	12,535,007	24.6
Direct expenditure	30,708,042	60.3
General expenditure, by function:		
Education	13,378,261	26.3
Public welfare	13,958,757	27.4
Hospitals	2,649,369	5.2
Health	1,205,877	2.4
Highways	2,901,041	5.7
Police protection	53,644	0.1
Correction	1,222,869	2.4
Natural resources	641,934	1.3
Parks and recreation	30,053	0.1
Governmental administration	1,306,976	2.6
Interest on general debt	563,062	1.1
Other and unallocable	5,317,353	10.4
Utility expenditure	21,425	-
Liquor stores expenditure	-	-
Insurance trust expenditure	7,641,188	15.0
Debt at End of Fiscal Year	21,978,336	X
Cash and Security Holdings	174,138,464	X

X = Not applicable.
- = Zero or rounds to zero.
[1] Within insurance trust revenue, net earnings of state retirement systems is a calculated statistic (the item code in the data file is X08), and thus can be positive or negative. Net earnings is the sum of earnings on investments plus gains on investments minus losses on investments. The change made in 2002 for asset valuation from book to market value in accordance with Statement 34 of the Governmental Accounting Standards Board is reflected in the calculated statistics.

Table WI-16. State Government Tax Collections, 2022

(Dollars in thousands, percent.)

Item	Dollars	Percent distribution
Total Taxes	23,363,814	100.0
Property taxes	88,838	0.4
Sales and gross receipts	9,877,449	42.3
General sales and gross receipts	6,978,336	29.9
Selective sales and gross receipts	2,899,113	12.4
Alcoholic beverages	73,769	0.3
Amusements	108	-
Insurance premiums	247,174	1.1
Motor fuels	1,179,935	5.1
Pari-mutuels	0	-
Public utilities	384,026	1.6
Tobacco products	580,949	2.5
Other selective sales	433,152	1.9
Licenses	1,336,599	5.7
Alcoholic beverages	2,352	-
Amusements	68	-
Corporations in general	29,726	0.1
Hunting and fishing	64,890	0.3
Motor vehicle	715,639	3.1
Motor vehicle operators	39,527	0.2
Public utilities	68,200	0.3
Occupation and business, NEC	355,818	1.5
Other licenses	60,379	0.3
Income taxes	11,922,098	51.0
Individual income	8,994,997	38.5
Corporation net income	2,927,101	12.5
Other taxes	138,830	0.6
Death and gift	3	-
Documentary and stock transfer	121,382	0.5
Severance	1,793	-
Taxes, NEC	15,652	0.1

- = Zero or rounds to zero.

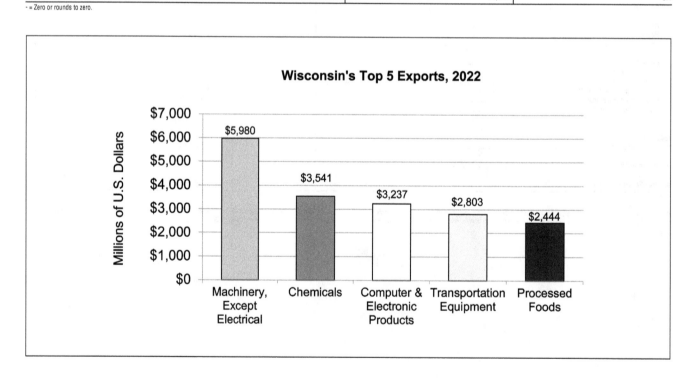

Wisconsin's Top 5 Exports, 2022

WYOMING

Facts and Figures

Location: Western United States; bordered on the N by Montana, on the E by South Dakota and Nebraska, on the S by Colorado and Utah, and on the W by Utah and Idaho

Area: 97,814 sq. mi. (253,336 sq. km.); rank—10th

Population: 581,381 (2022 est.); rank—51st

Principal Cities: capital—Cheyenne; largest—Cheyenne

Statehood: July 10, 1890; 44th state

U.S. Congress: 2 senators, 1 representative

State Motto: Equal Rights

State Song: "Wyoming"

State Nicknames: The Equality State; The Cowboy State

Abbreviations: WY; Wyo.

State Symbols: flower—Indian paintbrush; tree—cottonwood; bird—Western meadowlark

At a Glance

- With an increase in population of 3.2 percent, Wyoming ranked 39th among the states in growth from 2010 to 2022.

- Wyoming had the lowest drug overdose death rate in the country in 2021 (8.1 deaths per 100,000 population). The national drug overdose death rate was 32.4 deaths per 100,000 population.

- Wyoming's median household income in 2021 was $65,204, which ranked 32nd in the nation.

- In 2021, 11.4 percent of Wyoming residents and 13.4 percent of Wyoming's children lived below the poverty level, compared to the national poverty rates of 12.8 percent and 16.9 percent respectively.

- In 2021, 12.2 percent of Wyoming residents did not have health insurance, compared to 8.6 percent of total U.S. residents.

Table WY-1. Population by Age, Sex, Race, and Hispanic Origin

(Number, percent, except where noted.)

Sex, age, race, and Hispanic origin	2010	2020	2022	Percent change, 2010–2022
Total Population..	563,626	576,837	581,381	3.2
Percent of total U.S. population	0.2	0.2	0.2	X
Sex				
Male...	287,437	296,048	297,954	3.7
Female	276,189	280,789	283,427	2.6
Age				
Under 5 years...	40,203	33,268	31,340	-22.0
Under 18 years...	135,402	132,787	130,114	-3.9
18 to 64 years..	358,134	344,056	343,208	-4.2
65 years and over	70,090	99,994	108,059	54.2
Median age (years)	36.8	38.5	39.2	6.5
Race and Hispanic Origin				
One race				
White	529,110	533,338	536,573	1.4
Black...	5,135	7,021	7,162	39.5
American Indian and Alaska Native	14,457	16,188	16,273	12.6
Asian..	4,649	6,316	6,506	39.9
Native Hawaiian or Other Pacific Islander	521	617	627	20.3
Two or more races	9,754	13,357	14,240	46.0
Hispanic (of any race)..	50,231	60,059	62,808	25.0

NOTE: Population figures for 2022 are July 1 estimates. The 2010 and 2020 estimates are taken from the respective censuses.
- = Zero or rounds to zero.
X = Not applicable.

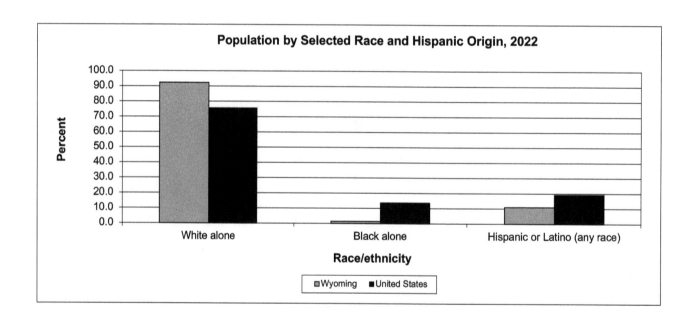

Table WY-2. Marital Status

(Number, percent distribution.)

Sex, age, race, and Hispanic origin	2000	2010	2021
Males, 15 Years and Over	195,412	228,725	240,718
Never married	26.6	29.0	31.2
Now married, except separated..	58.8	56.2	52.9
Separated..	1.0	1.3	1.4
Widowed	2.3	2.4	2.9
Divorced..	11.3	11.2	11.5
Females, 15 Years and Over	195,433	220,169	230,508
Never married	20.0	20.7	23.6
Now married, except separated..	57.5	55.1	54.8
Separated..	1.3	2.0	1.3
Widowed	9.2	8.6	7.2
Divorced..	12.0	13.6	13.1

Table WY-3. Households and Housing Characteristics

(Number, percent, dollars.)

Item	2000	2010	2021	Average annual percent change, 2010–2021
Total Households..	193,608	222,803	242,763	0.8
Family households..	130,497	147,394	150,833	0.2
Married-couple family...	106,179	119,756	120,894	0.1
Other family..	24,318	27,638	29,939	0.8
Male householder, no wife present................................	7,481	7,804	11,264	4.0
Female householder, no husband present......................	16,837	19,834	18,675	-0.5
Nonfamily households...	63,111	75,409	91,930	2.0
Householder living alone...	50,980	61,775	75,088	2.0
Householder not living alone..	12,131	13,634	16,842	2.1
Housing Characteristics				
Total housing units..	223,854	262,286	274,373	0.4
Occupied housing units	193,608	222,803	242,763	0.8
Owner occupied..	135,514	155,278	173,247	1.1
Renter occupied..	58,094	67,525	69,516	0.3
Average household size..	2.48	2.47	2.33	-0.5
Financial Characteristics				
Median gross rent of renter-occupied housing	437	693	889	2.6
Median monthly owner costs for housing units with a mortgage ...	825	1,300	1,490	1.3
Median value of owner-occupied housing units...................	96,600	180,100	266,400	4.4

Table WY-4. Migration, Origin, and Language

(Number, percent.)

Characteristic	State 2021	U.S. 2021
Residence 1 Year Ago		
Population 1 year and over	573,476	328,464,538
Same house	83.9	87.2
Different house in the U.S.	15.8	12.3
Same county	8.6	6.7
Different county	7.2	5.7
Same state	2.4	3.3
Different state	4.8	2.4
Abroad	0.4	0.4
Place of Birth		
Native born	558,905	286,623,642
Male	51.3	49.7
Female	48.7	50.3
Foreign born	19,898	45,270,103
Male	48.0	48.7
Female	52.0	51.3
Foreign born; naturalized U.S. citizen..	8,178	24,044,083
Male	39.8	46.4
Female	60.2	53.6
Foreign born; not a U.S. citizen...	11,720	21,226,020
Male	53.7	51.2
Female	46.3	48.8
Entered 2010 or later	25.7	28.1
Entered 2000 to 2009	34.6	23.7
Entered before 2000...	39.7	48.2
World Region of Birth, Foreign		
Foreign-born population, excluding population born at sea	19,898	45,269,644
Europe	22.1	10.7
Asia	19.9	31.0
Africa	4.2	5.7
Oceania	0.2	0.6
Latin America...	45.5	50.1
North America..	8.1	1.7
Language Spoken at Home and Ability to Speak English		
Population 5 years and over...	548,570	313,232,500
English only	93.0	78.4
Language other than English...	7.0	21.6
Speaks English less than "very well"...	1.7	8.3

Table WY-5. Median Income and Poverty Status, 2021

(Number, percent, except as noted.)

Characteristic	State		U.S.	
	Number	Percent	Number	Percent
Median Income				
Households (dollars)...	65,204	X	69,717	X
Families (dollars)	83,789	X	85,806	X
Below Poverty Level (All People)	64,224	11.4	41,393,176	12.8
Sex				
Male	29,151	10.1	18,518,155	11.6
Female	35,073	12.7	22,875,021	13.9
Age				
Under 18 years...	17,330	13.4	12,243,219	16.9
Related children under 18 years.........................	16,878	13.1	11,985,424	16.6
18 to 64 years..	40,086	12.0	23,526,341	11.9
65 years and over	6,808	6.7	5,623,616	10.3

X = Not applicable.

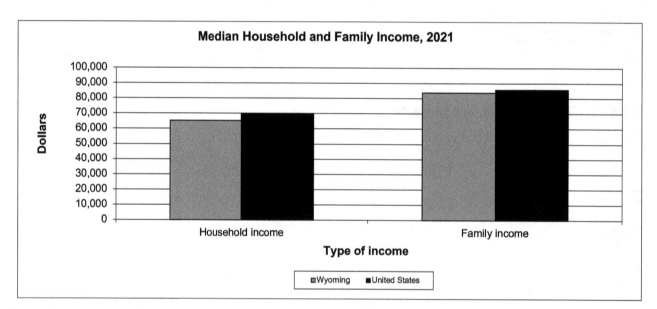

Table WY-6. Health Insurance Coverage Status for the Civilian Noninstitutionalized Population and Children Under 19 Years of Age

(Number, percent.)

Item	2011	2012	2013	2014	2015	2016	2017	2018	2019	2020 [2]	2021
Civilian Noninstitutionalized Population	558,832	567,082	573,210	574,798	576,557	576,027	568,891	567,008	568,859	571,005	570,046
Covered by Private or Public Insurance											
Number..	473,001	479,998	496,182	506,050	510,063	509,514	499,176	507,671	498,806	505,708	500,738
Percent..	84.6	84.6	86.6	88.0	88.5	88.5	87.7	89.5	87.7	88.6	87.8
Uninsured											
Number..	85,831	87,084	77,028	68,748	66,494	66,513	69,715	59,337	70,053	65,297	69,308
Percent..	15.4	15.4	13.4	12.0	11.5	11.5	12.3	10.5	12.3	11.4	12.2
Percent in the U.S. not covered...............................	15.1	14.8	14.5	11.7	9.4	8.6	8.7	8.9	9.2	8.7	8.6
Children Under 19 Years of Age[1]	134,594	136,132	139,291	137,296	138,953	140,464	145,904	142,042	143,312	141,959	139,940
Covered by Private or Public Insurance											
Number..	122,956	123,417	131,357	129,159	128,097	128,136	131,974	131,918	128,067	129,376	124,037
Percent..	91.4	90.7	94.3	94.1	92.2	91.2	90.5	92.9	89.4	91.1	88.6
Uninsured											
Number..	11,638	12,715	7,934	8,137	10,856	12,328	13,930	10,124	15,245	12,583	15,903
Percent..	8.6	9.3	5.7	5.9	7.8	8.8	9.5	7.1	10.6	8.9	11.4
Percent in the U.S. not covered...............................	7.5	7.2	7.1	6.0	4.8	4.5	5.0	5.2	5.7	5.2	5.4

[1] Data for years prior to 2017 are for individuals under 18 years of age.
[2] 2020 ACS 5-Year estimates. 1-Year estimates were not released for 2020 due to the impact of COVID-19 on data collection that year. Data is not comparable to previous years, which are based on 1-year estimates.

Table WY-7. Employment Status by Demographic Group, 2022

(Numbers in thousands, percent.)

Characteristic	Civilian noninstitutional population	Civilian labor force		Employed		Unemployed	
		Number	Percent of population	Number	Percent of population	Number	Percent of population
Total...	458	290	63.3	279	61.1	10	3.5
Sex							
Male..	232	159	68.5	154	66.3	5	3.2
Female...	226	131	58.0	126	55.7	5	3.9
Race, Sex, and Hispanic Origin							
White...	427	269	62.9	260	60.9	9	3.2
Male..	215	146	68.0	142	65.9	5	3.1
Female...	212	122	57.7	118	55.8	4	3.3
Black or African American......................	NA	NA	NA	NA	NA	NA	NA
Male..	NA	NA	NA	NA	NA	NA	NA
Female...	NA	NA	NA	NA	NA	NA	NA
Hispanic or Latino ethnicity[1]	39	25	64.2	24	61.5	1	4.3
Male..	NA	NA	NA	NA	NA	NA	NA
Female...	NA	NA	NA	NA	NA	NA	NA
Age							
16 to 19 years...................................	32	15	45.7	13	39.3	2	13.9
20 to 24 years...................................	31	24	76.4	22	71.5	2	6.4
25 to 34 years...................................	70	57	82.1	55	79.5	2	3.1
35 to 44 years...................................	81	69	85.8	67	83.1	2	3.2
45 to 54 years...................................	57	50	86.2	49	84.7	1	2.0
55 to 64 years...................................	77	52	67.7	51	66.1	1	2.5
65 years and over...............................	110	23	21.1	23	20.6	1	2.2

NOTE: Data in Table 7 are from the Current Population Survey (CPS) and do not match the estimates in Table 8. See notes and definitions for further information.
[1] May be of any race.
NA = Not available.

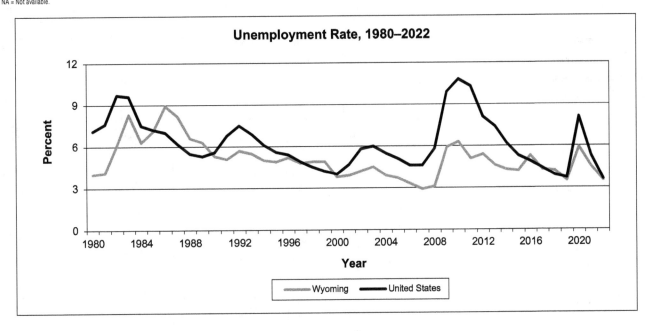

Unemployment Rate, 1980–2022

Table WY-8. Employment Status of the Civilian Noninstitutional Population Age 16 Years and Over

(Number, percent.)

Year	Civilian labor force	Civilian participation rate	Employed	Unemployed	Unemployment rate
2010...	301,893	70.1	280,953	20,940	6.9
2011...	302,932	69.3	284,273	18,659	6.2
2012...	303,748	68.4	287,110	16,638	5.5
2013...	302,201	67.4	287,792	14,409	4.8
2014...	302,865	67.3	289,694	13,171	4.3
2015...	301,608	66.8	288,894	12,714	4.2
2016...	300,546	66.6	284,439	16,107	5.4
2017...	293,802	65.0	281,164	12,638	4.3
2018...	292,781	65.7	280,909	11,872	4.1
2019...	294,380	65.8	283,377	11,003	3.7
2020...	293,722	65.3	276,739	16,983	5.8
2021...	290,404	64.1	277,372	13,032	4.5
2022...	291,756	63.7	281,343	10,413	3.6

Table WY-9. Employment and Average Wages by Industry

(Estimates are based on the 2012 North American Industry Classification System [NAICS].)

Industry	2014	2015	2016	2017	2018	2019	2020	2021
	Number of Jobs							
Wage and Salary Employment by Industry	303,951	302,522	291,463	289,601	291,670	297,577	279,934	284,326
Farm Wage and Salary Employment	3,566	3,822	3,871	4,480	3,906	4,112	3,835	3,430
Nonfarm Wage and Salary Employment	300,385	298,700	287,592	285,121	287,764	293,465	276,099	280,896
Private wage and salary employment	225,017	222,859	211,367	209,803	213,713	218,157	202,878	206,985
Forestry, fishing, and related activities	1,168	1,170	1,171	(D)	1,200	1,228	(D)	1,037
Mining	27,130	23,740	18,703	19,566	20,614	20,638	16,265	14,738
Utilities	2,489	2,535	2,541	2,476	2,510	2,432	(D)	2,347
Construction	24,377	23,865	21,649	20,056	20,749	23,402	21,769	21,494
Manufacturing	9,819	9,767	9,229	(D)	9,729	10,055	9,590	9,779
Durable goods manufacturing	4,875	4,713	4,145	(D)	4,638	5,109	4,794	4,937
Nondurable goods manufacturing	4,944	5,054	5,084	(D)	5,091	4,946	4,796	4,842
Wholesale trade	9,532	9,541	8,532	8,156	8,224	8,420	7,685	7,354
Retail trade	29,979	30,979	30,858	29,871	29,501	29,087	28,900	29,873
Transportation and warehousing	13,238	13,158	11,749	11,648	12,015	12,285	11,641	11,706
Information	3,780	3,782	3,747	3,687	3,552	3,435	3,001	2,962
Finance and insurance	7,195	7,240	7,240	7,306	7,370	7,437	7,559	7,705
Real estate and rental and leasing	4,505	4,366	4,066	4,160	4,311	4,374	4,032	4,070
Professional, scientific, and technical services	9,600	9,465	8,935	8,996	9,387	9,911	9,502	9,978
Management of companies and enterprises	1,014	1,025	901	868	865	857	736	852
Administrative and waste services	7,948	8,158	8,090	8,301	8,637	8,549	8,278	8,963
Educational services	2,139	2,208	2,274	2,263	2,146	2,250	2,134	2,424
Health care and social assistance	24,436	24,617	25,161	25,093	25,742	26,007	25,682	25,762
Arts, entertainment, and recreation	3,092	3,174	3,341	3,694	3,673	3,664	3,321	3,753
Accommodation and food services	32,458	33,145	32,703	32,808	32,922	33,556	29,192	32,257
Other services, except public administration	11,118	10,924	10,477	10,320	10,566	10,570	10,024	9,931
Government and government enterprises	75,368	75,841	76,225	75,318	74,051	75,308	73,221	73,911
	Dollars							
Average Wages and Salaries by Industry	47,400	47,182	46,006	47,285	49,252	50,678	52,051	54,256
Average Farm Wages and Salaries	38,757	30,603	34,981	30,400	36,432	24,776	35,386	46,001
Average Nonfarm Wages and Salaries	47,503	47,394	46,154	47,551	49,426	51,041	52,282	54,357
Average private wages and salaries	48,043	47,558	45,696	47,307	49,447	51,509	52,278	54,746
Forestry, fishing, and related activities	25,927	26,729	28,324	(D)	29,803	31,093	(D)	35,926
Mining	88,868	88,770	85,792	89,302	91,876	94,939	93,192	96,206
Utilities	88,876	92,338	92,152	94,797	99,113	102,331	(D)	104,600
Construction	52,318	51,927	51,253	51,753	54,454	58,064	57,629	59,343
Manufacturing	62,391	64,758	66,016	(D)	69,021	70,646	72,406	71,657
Durable goods manufacturing	53,721	54,105	53,216	(D)	58,971	59,180	59,357	60,496
Nondurable goods manufacturing	70,939	74,692	76,452	(D)	78,177	82,489	85,449	83,036
Wholesale trade	64,232	61,196	59,071	62,818	65,749	67,783	67,085	69,760
Retail trade	28,581	29,011	28,766	29,651	30,206	31,251	32,958	34,776
Transportation and warehousing	59,073	58,805	56,770	59,921	61,741	63,880	64,089	64,429
Information	45,939	47,473	47,614	48,615	49,534	51,151	57,009	63,922
Finance and insurance	57,977	60,080	60,113	62,237	64,764	68,997	74,166	88,051
Real estate and rental and leasing	49,020	47,499	44,354	47,083	50,201	51,918	51,212	54,162
Professional, scientific, and technical services	62,523	61,921	60,076	62,164	65,188	69,422	74,910	78,643
Management of companies and enterprises	100,183	103,816	102,041	101,373	106,654	104,286	145,262	209,574
Administrative and waste services	32,613	33,508	33,041	35,175	37,104	39,265	39,234	52,666
Educational services	29,832	28,337	28,521	29,093	33,115	33,667	40,629	38,301
Health care and social assistance	42,603	43,820	43,511	44,141	44,931	46,130	48,204	49,578
Arts, entertainment, and recreation	23,780	23,962	24,498	24,767	26,520	27,441	29,192	30,930
Accommodation and food services	21,224	21,735	22,220	22,844	24,747	25,503	25,525	28,790
Other services, except public administration	33,198	34,095	33,509	34,397	35,953	37,485	39,263	41,318
Government and government enterprises	45,890	46,913	47,426	48,231	49,363	49,684	52,294	53,267

(D) = Not shown to avoid disclosure of confidential information; estimates are included in higher-level totals.

Table WY-10. Employment Characteristics by Family Type

(Number, percent.)

Family type and labor force status	2019 Total	2019 Families with own children under 18 years	2020 [1] Total	2020 [1] Families with own children under 18 years	2021 Total	2021 Families with own children under 18 years
All Families...	152,859	61,466	149,353	62,804	150,833	65,260
FAMILY TYPE AND LABOR FORCE STATUS						
Opposite-Sex Married-Couple Families..	123,545	44,726	120,294	45,360	119,848	47,016
Both husband and wife in labor force..	52.7	70.8	53.1	70.1	51.1	71.2
Husband in labor force, wife not in labor force	20.4	26.3	21.3	26.6	20.7	23.5
Wife in labor force, husband not in labor force	7.6	2.1	7.8	2.5	7.4	3.5
Both husband and wife not in labor force	19.0	0.7	17.8	0.8	20.7	1.8
Other Families	29,314	16,740	28,187	17,327	29,939	18,231
Female householder, no spouse present	64.3	64.7	65.5	68.2	62.4	64.7
In labor force..	47.7	57.2	48.3	58.5	50.1	59.8
Not in labor force	16.5	7.5	17.2	9.7	12.3	4.8
Male householder, no spouse present..	35.7	35.3	34.5	31.8	37.6	35.3
In labor force..	28.7	33.7	28.6	30.5	28.9	32.3
Not in labor force	7.0	1.5	6.0	1.3	8.7	3.1

[1] 2020 ACS 5-Year estimates. 1-Year estimates were not released for 2020 due to the impact of COVID-19 on data collection that year. Data is not comparable to previous years, which are based on 1-year estimates.

Table WY-11. School Enrollment and Educational Attainment, 2021

(Number, percent.)

Item	State	U.S.
Enrollment		
Total population 3 years and over, enrolled in school	140,986	79,453,524
Enrolled in nursery school or preschool (percent)..	5.6	5.2
Enrolled in kindergarten (percent)...	5.1	5.0
Enrolled in elementary school, grades 1-8 (percent)...	43.8	41.3
Enrolled in high school, grades 9-12 (percent)..	22.9	21.8
Enrolled in college or graduate school (percent)...	22.5	26.7
Attainment		
Total population 25 years and over	395,348	228,193,464
Less than ninth grade (percent)...	1.8	4.8
9th to 12th grade, no diploma (percent)...	4.6	5.9
High school graduate, including equivalency (percent)..	27.3	26.3
Some college, no degree (percent)...	24.7	19.3
Associate's degree (percent)..	12.4	8.8
Bachelor's degree (percent)..	18.5	21.2
Graduate or professional degree (percent)...	10.7	13.8
High school graduate or higher (percent)	93.6	89.4
Bachelor's degree or higher (percent)...	29.2	35.0

Table WY-12. Public School Characteristics and Educational Indicators

(Number, percent; data derived from National Center of Education Statistics.)

Item	State	U.S.
Public Elementary and Secondary Schools		
Number of regular school districts, 2019-20	48	13,349
Number of operational schools, 2019-20...	360	98,469
Percent charter schools	1.4	7.7
Total public school enrollment, Fall 2021..	93,093	49,433,092
Percent charter school enrollment	0.7	7.5
Student-teacher ratio, Fall 2019...	12.8	15.9
Expenditures per student (unadjusted dollars), 2019-20	16,665	13,489
Four-year adjusted cohort graduation rate (ACGR), 2019-2020[1].....................................	82.3	86.5
Students eligible for free or reduced-price lunch (percent), 2019-20..............................	34.6	52.1
English language learners (percent), Fall 2020	2.7	10.3
Students age 3 to 21 served under IDEA, part B (percent), 2021-22................................	17.1	14.7

Public Schools by Type, 2019-20	Number	Percent of state public schools
Total number of schools...	360	100.0
Special education	3	0.8
Vocational education	-	-
Alternative education..	9	2.5

[1] Adjusted Cohort Graduation Rates (ACGR) differ from Averaged Freshmen Graduation Rates (AFGR).
- = Zero or rounds to zero.

Table WY-13. Reported Voting and Registration of the Voting-Age Population, November 2022

(Numbers in thousands, percent.)

Item	Total population	Total citizen population	Registered			Voted		
			Total registered	Percent registered (total population)	Percent registered (total citizen population)	Total voted	Percent voted (total population)	Percent voted (total citizen population)
U.S. Total	255,457	233,546	161,422	63.2	69.1	121,916	47.7	52.2
State Total.................................	440	437	274	62.3	62.8	214	48.6	49.0
Sex								
Male	222	220	135	60.7	61.3	108	48.6	49.0
Female	218	216	139	63.8	64.2	106	48.6	48.9
Race								
White alone................................	413	411	264	63.8	64.2	207	50.1	50.4
White, non-Hispanic alone	387	386	253	65.3	65.4	199	51.5	51.6
Black alone...............................	3	3	1	22.2	22.2	-	-	-
Asian alone	2	2	1	43.3	43.3	1	43.3	43.3
Hispanic (of any race)	33	31	13	40.3	43.9	10	29.4	32.0
White alone or in combination	425	423	269	63.2	63.6	211	49.6	49.9
Black alone or in combination	3	3	1	22.2	22.2	-	-	-
Asian alone or in combination........	3	3	1	28.4	28.4	1	28.4	28.4
Age								
18 to 24 years............................	49	49	21	42.5	43.0	10	20.8	21.0
25 to 34 years............................	70	70	32	45.3	45.6	19	26.7	26.9
35 to 44 years............................	75	74	45	59.3	60.7	32	42.8	43.8
45 to 64 years............................	136	135	92	67.5	67.7	76	55.8	56.0
65 years and over	110	109	85	77.5	77.8	77	70.1	70.3

- = Zero or rounds to zero.
B = Base is less than 75,000 and therefore too small to show the derived measure.

Table WY-14. Health Indicators

(Number, rate as indicated in footnotes.)

Item	State	U.S.
Births		
Life Expectancy at Birth (years), 2020	76.3	77.0
Fertility Rate by State[1], 2021	57.5	56.3
Percent Home Births, 2021	2.3	1.4
Cesarean Delivery Rate[2], 2021	26.7	32.1
Preterm Birth Rate[3], 2021	10.8	10.5
Teen Birth Rate[4], 2021	16.0	13.9
Percentage of Babies Born Low Birthweight[5], 2021	9.4	8.5
Deaths[6]		
Heart Disease Mortality Rate, 2021	159.4	173.8
Cancer Mortality Rate, 2021	156.7	146.6
Stroke Mortality Rate, 2021	31.5	41.1
Diabetes Mortality Rate, 2021	23.9	25.4
Influenza/Pneumonia Mortality Rate, 2021	11.9	10.5
Suicide Mortality Rate, 2021	32.3	14.1
Drug Overdose Mortality Rate, 2021	18.9	33.6
Firearm Injury Mortality Rate, 2021	26.1	14.6
Homicide Mortality Rate, 2021...	0.0	8.2
Disease and Illness		
Lifetime Asthma in Adults, 2020 (percent)...	15.0	13.9
Lifetime Asthma in Children, 2020 (percent)[7]	NA	11.3
Diabetes in Adults, 2020 (percent)..	7.5	8.2
Self-reported Obesity in Adults, 2021 (percent)..	32.0	NA

SOURCE: National Center for Health Statistics, National Vital Statistics System 2020 data; https://wonder.cdc.gov.
[1] General fertility rate per 1,000 women aged 15–44.
[2] This represents the percentage of all live births that were cesarean deliveries.
[3] Babies born prior to 37 weeks of pregnancy (gestation).
[4] Number of births per 1,000 females aged 15–19
[5] Babies born weighing less than 2,500 grams or 5 lbs. 8oz.
[6] Death rates are the number of deaths per 100,000 total population.
[7] U.S. total includes data from 30 states and D.C.
NA = Not available.
- = Zero or rounds to zero.

Table WY-15. State Government Finances, 2021

(Dollar amounts in thousands, percent distribution.)

Item	Dollars	Percent distribution
Total Revenue	7,505,301	100.0
General revenue	6,375,373	84.9
Intergovernmental revenue	3,103,070	41.3
Taxes	1,874,876	25.0
General sales	734,785	9.8
Selective sales	192,304	2.6
License taxes	212,497	2.8
Individual income tax	-	-
Corporate income tax	-	-
Other taxes	735,290	9.8
Current charges	248,934	3.3
Miscellaneous general revenue	1,148,493	15.3
Utility revenue	422	-
Liquor stores revenue	152139	2.0
Insurance trust revenue[1]	977,367	13.0
Total Expenditure	7,555,184	100.0
Intergovernmental expenditure	1,505,148	19.9
Direct expenditure	6,050,036	80.1
Current operation	4,390,561	58.1
Capital outlay	494,644	6.5
Insurance benefits and repayments	1,054,912	14.0
Assistance and subsidies	84,681	1.1
Interest on debt	25,238	0.3
Exhibit: Salaries and wages	753,257	10.0
Total Expenditure	7,555,184	100.0
General expenditure	6,370,921	84.3
Intergovernmental expenditure	1,505,148	19.9
Direct expenditure	4,865,773	64.4
General expenditure, by function:		
Education	2,205,802	29.2
Public welfare	893,307	11.8
Hospitals	2,937	0.0
Health	481,135	6.4
Highways	555,757	7.4
Police protection	47,337	0.6
Correction	143,804	1.9
Natural resources	398,859	5.3
Parks and recreation	25,323	0.3
Governmental administration	329,776	4.4
Interest on general debt	25,238	0.3
Other and unallocable	1,139,260	15.1
Utility expenditure	23,319	0.3
Liquor stores expenditure	129,351	1.7
Insurance trust expenditure	1,054,912	14.0
Debt at End of Fiscal Year	924,246	X
Cash and Security Holdings	39,877,167	X

X = Not applicable.
- = Zero or rounds to zero.
[1] Within insurance trust revenue, net earnings of state retirement systems is a calculated statistic (the item code in the data file is X08), and thus can be positive or negative. Net earnings is the sum of earnings on investments plus gains on investments minus losses on investments. The change made in 2002 for asset valuation from book to market value in accordance with Statement 34 of the Governmental Accounting Standards Board is reflected in the calculated statistics.

Table WY-16. State Government Tax Collections, 2022

(Dollars in thousands, percent.)

Item	Dollars	Percent distribution
Total Taxes	2,441,007	100.0
Property taxes	268,292	11.0
Sales and gross receipts	1,177,747	48.2
General sales and gross receipts	978,080	40.1
Selective sales and gross receipts	199,667	8.2
Alcoholic beverages	2,204	0.1
Amusements	5,402	0.2
Insurance premiums	33,611	1.4
Motor fuels	119,353	4.9
Pari-mutuels	9,436	0.4
Public utilities	4,984	0.2
Tobacco products	21,569	0.9
Other selective sales	3,108	0.1
Licenses	216,748	8.9
Alcoholic beverages	X	-
Amusements	1,132	-
Corporations in general	21,559	0.9
Hunting and fishing	42,311	1.7
Motor vehicle	101,003	4.1
Motor vehicle operators	5,238	0.2
Public utilities	X	-
Occupation and business, NEC	45,505	1.9
Other licenses	-	-
Income taxes	X	-
Individual income	X	-
Corporation net income	X	-
Other taxes	778,220	31.9
Death and gift	-	-
Documentary and stock transfer	X	-
Severance	770,487	31.6
Taxes, NEC	7,733	0.3

X = Not applicable.
- = Zero or rounds to zero.

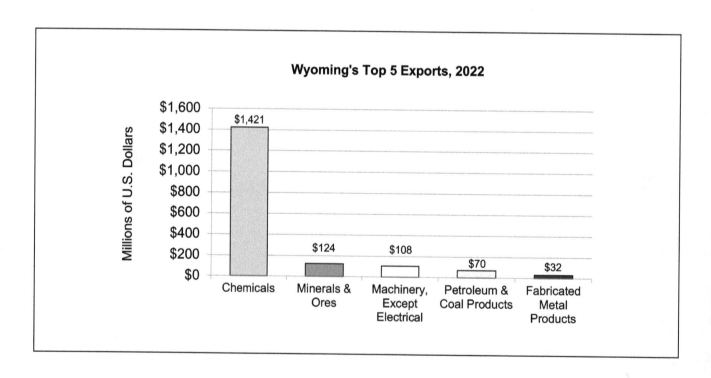

Wyoming's Top 5 Exports, 2022

NOTES AND DEFINITIONS

The state chapters in this book follow a standard plan of organization, and the same data sources are used for the tables and figures found in each chapter. These notes describe the standard data sources, which are presented by topic in the order in which they appear in each chapter. Definitions, brief descriptions of methodology, and sources of additional information are also provided.

Symbols used are included in the footnotes of the tables.

Table 1.
Source: U.S. Department of Commerce. U.S. Census Bureau. 2010 and 2020 Decennial Census. Population Estimates Program, Vintage 2022 Estimates.
<https://www.census.gov/programs-surveys/popest.html>

Population estimates data are accessed from the U.S. Census Bureau's website. The data for percent change, 2010–2022, were calculated by the editor.

Population estimates and the decennial census. Population data are estimates produced by the Census Bureau. The Bureau's Population Estimates Program (PEP) produces estimates of the population as of July 1 for each year following the most recently published decennial census (the actual physical count of the population made every ten years, which is described below). Existing data on births, deaths, and domestic and international immigration are used to update the decennial census base. PEP estimates are used to set federal funding allocations, update national surveys, and monitor recent demographic changes.

Noncitizens residing in the United States are included, regardless of their immigration status.

Persons temporarily away from their usual residence on Census Day (April 1), for reasons such as vacation or business trips, were counted as being at their usual residence. People who live at more than one residence during the week, month, or year were counted as being at the place in which they lived most of the year. However, people without a usual residence were counted as being where they were staying on Census Day.

Age, sex, race, and ethnicity. While estimates of the age and sex of the population are straightforward, estimates of race and ethnicity are not. Decennial census data on race and ethnicity are based on self-identification by the respondent, and the same respondent may answer differently on separate occasions. On the 2000 decennial census, respondents could report more than one race; in previous censuses, respondents had to identify themselves as belonging to only one race.

The Census Bureau treats Hispanic or Latino origin as a separate and distinct concept from race. Beginning with the 2000 census, a separate self-identification question was asked regarding Hispanic or Latino origin. Persons of Hispanic or Latino origin are those who classified themselves as belonging to one of the specific categories listed on the questionnaire—Mexican, Puerto Rican, Cuban, or Other Spanish/Hispanic origin (including those whose origins are from Spain, the Spanish-speaking countries of Central and South America, or the Dominican Republic). People who are Hispanic may be of any race, and people in each race group may be Hispanic. The overlap of race and Hispanic origin is a major comparability issue because Hispanic individuals may be of any race. For a further discussion of this issue, see: U.S. Census Bureau. *U.S. Census Bureau Guidance on the Presentation and Comparison of Race and Hispanic Origin Data.* (June 12, 2003.) <https://www.census.gov/topics/population/hispanic-origin/about/comparing-race-and-hispanic-origin.html>.

Table 2.
Source: U.S. Department of Commerce. U.S. Census Bureau. 2000 and 2010 Decennial Census. American Community Survey, 2000, 2010, and 2021 (ACS 1-Year Estimates).
<https://data.census.gov>

Data on marital status were tabulated for persons 15 years and over. Marital status was reported for each person as either "now married," "widowed," "divorced," "separated," or "never married." Individuals who were living together (unmarried people, people in commonlaw marriages) reported the marital status they considered most appropriate.

Now Married, Except Separated. Includes people whose current marriage has not ended through widowhood, divorce, or separation (regardless of previous marital history). The category may also include couples who live together or people in common-law marriages if they consider this category the most appropriate. In certain tabulations, currently married people are further classified as "spouse present" or "spouse absent."

Separated. Refers to people who were not living with their spouse due to marital discord.

Divorced. Indicates people who reported being divorced and had not remarried.

Widowed. Refers to people whose last marriage ended with the death of their spouse and who had not remarried.

Never married. The term applies to those who had never been legally married or people whose only marriage ended in an annulment.

Table 3.
Source: U.S. Department of Commerce. U.S. Census Bureau. 2000 and 2010 Decennial Census. American Community Survey, 2000, 2010, and 2021 (ACS 1-Year Estimates).
<https://data.census.gov>

The annual data were obtained from the Census Bureau. The data for average annual percent change, 2010–2021, were calculated by the editor.

Households. A household comprises one or more persons occupying a single housing unit, such as a house, apartment, or a room occupied as separate living quarters. A household may consist of a person living alone, a single family, two or more families living together, or any other group of unrelated individuals sharing a housing unit.

Householder. The person, or one of the people, in whose name the home is owned, being bought, or rented. If there is no such person present, any household member 15 years old and over can serve as the householder for the purposes of the census. Two types of householders are distinguished: a family householder and a nonfamily householder. A family householder is a householder living with one or more people related to him or her by birth, marriage, or adoption. The householder and all people in the household related to him are family members. A nonfamily householder is a householder living alone or with nonrelatives only.

Housing unit. A house, an apartment, a mobile home or trailer, a group of rooms, or a single room occupied as separate living quarters, or if vacant, intended for occupancy as separate living quarters.

Median gross rent. The monthly amount of contract rent plus the estimated average monthly cost of utilities (electricity, gas, water, and sewer) and fuels (oil, coal, kerosene, wood, etc.).

Median monthly owner costs for housing units with a mortgage. The sum of payments for mortgages, deeds of trust, contracts to purchase, or similar debts on the property (including payments for the first mortgage, second mortgages, home equity loans, and other junior mortgages); real estate taxes; fire, hazard, and flood insurance on the property; utilities (electricity, gas, water, and sewer); and fuels (oil, coal, kerosene, wood, etc.). It also includes, where appropriate, the monthly condominium fee for condominiums and mobile home costs (installment loan payments, personal property taxes, site rent, registration fees, and license fees). Selected monthly owner costs were tabulated for all owner-occupied units, and usually are shown separately for units "with a mortgage" and for units "not mortgaged."

Median value of owner-occupied housing units. Data for the median value of owner-occupied housing units are respondents' estimates of how much their property would sell for if it was currently on the market.

Table 4.
Source: U.S. Department of Commerce. U.S. Census Bureau. American Community Survey, 2021 (ACS 1-Year Estimates).
<https://data.census.gov>

The annual data derives from Census estimates. The data for percent change were calculated by the editor.

Residence 1 year ago. The data on residence 1 year ago were derived from answers to Question 15, which were asked of the population 1 year and older. For the American Community Survey, people who had moved from another residence in the United States or Puerto Rico 1 year earlier were asked to report the exact address (number and street name); the name of the city, town, or post office; the name of the U.S. county; and the ZIP Code where they lived 1 year ago. People living outside the United States and Puerto Rico were asked to report the name of the foreign country or U.S. Island Area where they were living 1 year ago.

Native born. The native population includes anyone who was a U.S. citizen or a U.S. national at birth. This includes respondents who indicated they were born in the United States, Puerto Rico, a U.S. Island Area (such as Guam), or abroad of an American (U.S. citizen) parent or parents.

Foreign born. The foreign-born population includes anyone who was not a U.S. citizen or a U.S. national at birth. This includes respondents who indicated they were a U.S. citizen by naturalization or not a U.S. citizen.

Respondent's ability to speak English. Respondents who reported speaking a language other than English were asked to indicate their English-speaking ability based on one of the following categories: "Very well," "Well," "Not well," or "Not at all." Those who answered "Well," "Not well," or "Not at all" are sometimes referred as "Less than 'very well.'" Respondents were not instructed on how to interpret the response categories in this question. Households in which no one 14 and over speaks English only or speaks a language other than English at home and speaks English "very well" identifies households that may need English language assistance. This arises when no one 14 and over meets either of two conditions: (1) they speak English at home or (2) even though they speak another language, they also report that they speak English "very well".

Table 5.
Source: U.S. Department of Commerce. U.S. Census Bureau. American Community Survey, 2021 (ACS 1-Year Estimates).
<https://data.census.gov>

Median household income. Includes the income of the householder and all other individuals 15 years old and over in the household, whether they are related to the householder or not. Because many households consist of only one person, average household income is usually less than average family income. Total income is the sum of the amounts reported separately for wage or salary income; net self-employment income; interest, dividends, or net rental or royalty income or income from estates and trusts; Social Security or railroad retirement income; Supplemental Security Income (SSI); public assistance or welfare payments; retirement, survivor, or disability pensions; and all other income. Receipts from the following sources are not included as income: capital gains, money received from the sale of property (unless the recipient was engaged in the business of selling such property); the value of income "in kind" from food stamps, public housing subsidies, medical care, employer contributions for individuals, etc.; withdrawal of bank deposits; money borrowed; tax refunds; exchange of money between relatives living in the same household; gifts; and lump-sum inheritances, insurance payments, and other types of lump-sum receipts.

Median family income. The incomes of all members 15 years old and over related to the householder are summed and treated as a single amount.

Poverty. Following the Office of Management and Budget standards that have been in use since the late 1960s, the Census Bureau uses a set of money income thresholds that vary by family size and composition to determine the proportion of Americans in poverty. If a household's total income is less than the threshold for the applicable family size, age of householder, and number of children present in the family under 18 years of age, every individual in that household is considered to be living in poverty.

Table 6.
Source: U.S. Department of Commerce. U.S. Census Bureau. American Community Survey, 2011-2021 (ACS 5-Year Estimates for 2020).
<https://data.census.gov>

The data on health insurance coverage were derived from answers to Question 16 in the American Community Survey (ACS), which was asked of all respondents. Respondents were instructed to report their current coverage and to mark "yes" or "no" for each of the eight types of private and public insurance listed. Health insurance coverage in the ACS and other Census Bureau surveys define coverage to include plans and programs that provide comprehensive health coverage. Plans that provide insurance for specific conditions or situations such as cancer and long-term care policies are not considered coverage. Likewise, other types of insurance like dental, vision, life, and disability insurance are not considered health insurance coverage.

Private health insurance. Coverage through an employer or union, a plan purchased by an individual from a private company, or TRICARE or other military health care.

Public health insurance. Coverage includes the federal programs Medicare, Medicaid, and VA Health Care (provided through the Department of Veterans Affairs); the Children's Health Insurance Program (CHIP); and individual state health plans.

Table 7.
Source: U.S. Department of Labor. Bureau of Labor Statistics. Current Population Survey.
<https://www.bls.gov/cps>

Annual data on the labor force, employment, and unemployment for state and local areas are available from two major sources: the Current Population Survey (CPS) and the Local Area Unemployment Statistics (LAUS) program. In Table 7, the data are obtained from the CPS. The CPS is a monthly survey of approximately 60,000 households conducted by the Census Bureau for the Bureau of Labor Statistics. It provides comprehensive data on topics such as the labor force, employment, unemployment, and persons not in the labor force. The data for 2021 in Table 7 are preliminary, so the data may differ slightly from the final table when it is released.

Civilian noninstitutional population included are persons 16 years of age and older residing in the 50 States and the District of Columbia who are not inmates of institutions (for example, penal and mental facilities, homes for the aged), and who are not on active duty in the Armed Forces.

Civilian labor force includes all persons classified as employed or unemployed who are not inmates of institutions (for example, penal and mental facilities, homes for the aged), and who are not on active duty in the Armed Forces. Civilians 16 years of age and over in the noninstitutional population who are not classified as employed or unemployed are defined as not in the labor force.

Employment includes persons 16 years and over in the civilian noninstitutional population who, during the reference week, (a) did any work at all (at least 1 hour) as paid employees; worked in their own business, profession, or on their own farm, or worked 15 hours or more as unpaid workers in an enterprise operated by a member of the family; and (b) all those who were not working but who had jobs or businesses from which they were temporarily absent because of vacation, illness, bad weather, childcare problems, maternity or paternity leave, labor-management dispute, job training, or other family or personal reasons, whether or not they were paid for the time off or were seeking other jobs.

Unemployed persons. All civilians who were not employed (according to the above definition) during the reference week, but who were available for work—except for temporary illness—and who had made specific efforts to find employment sometime during the previous four weeks. Persons who did not look for work because they were on layoff are also counted as unemployed.

Unemployment rate. The number of unemployed as a percentage of the civilian labor force.

NOTE: Data in Table 7 are from the Current Population Survey (CPS) and do not match the data in Table 8, which are derived from the Local Area Unemployment Statistics (LAUS).

Table 8.
Source: U.S. Department of Labor. Bureau of Labor Statistics. Local Area Unemployment Statistics.
<https://www.bls.gov/lau/home.htm>

The Local Area Unemployment Statistics (LAUS) program is a Federal-State cooperative effort in which monthly estimates of total employment and unemployment are prepared for approximately 7,300 areas.

The concepts and definitions underlying LAUS data come from the Current Population Survey (CPS), the household survey that is the official measure of the labor force for the nation. State monthly model estimates are controlled in "real time" to sum to national monthly labor force estimates from the CPS. These models combine current and historical data from the CPS, the Current Employment Statistics (CES) program, and State unemployment insurance (UI) systems. Estimates for seven large areas and their respective balances of State are also model-based. Estimates for the remainder of the substate labor market areas are produced through a building-block approach known as the "Handbook method." This procedure also uses data from several sources, including the CPS, the CES program, State UI systems, and the decennial census, to create estimates that are adjusted to the statewide measures of employment and unemployment. Below the labor market area level, estimates are prepared using disaggregation techniques based on inputs from the decennial census, annual population estimates, and current UI data.

Table 9.
Source: U.S. Department of Commerce. Bureau of Economic Analysis.
<https://www.bea.gov/regional>.

In this table, the data by industry reflect the North American Industry Classification System (NAICS), a supply- or production-based system that replaced the Standard Industrial Classification (SIC) system in January 2003. Estimates of state employment and earnings by industry use NAICS. NAICS was adopted to more fully reflect the current composition of U.S. businesses and to establish a standard measure of industry classification throughout the United States, Canada, and Mexico, in accordance with the North American Free Trade Agreement, to enhance cross-border comparisons among these trading partners.

Wage and salary employment, also referred to as wage and salary jobs, measures the average annual number of full-time and part-time jobs in each area by place-of-work. All jobs for which wages and salaries are paid are counted. Full-time and part-time jobs are counted with equal weight. Jury and witness service, as well as paid employment of prisoners, are not counted as wage and salary employment; the payments for these activities are classified as "other labor income" in the personal income measure. Corporate directorships are counted as self-employment. This concept of employment differs from that in the Current Population Survey (CPS), which is the source of the employment data in the table on population and labor force. The CPS is a household survey. It counts each individual only once, no matter how many jobs the person holds, and it includes only civilian employment.

Wages and salaries consist of the monetary remuneration of employees, including corporate officer salaries and bonuses, commissions, pay-in-kind, incentive payments, and tips. It reflects the amount of payments disbursed, but not necessarily earned during the year. Wage and salary disbursements are measured before deductions, such as social security contributions and union dues. In recent years, stock options have become a point of discussion. Wage and salary disbursements include stock options of nonqualified plans at the time that they have been exercised by the individual. Stock options are reported in wage and salary disbursements. The value that is included in wages is the difference between the exercise price and the price that the stock options were granted. Average annual wages and salaries were calculated by the editor by dividing total wages and salaries paid during the year in each sector by total wage and salary employment in that sector.

Table 10.
Source: U.S. Department of Commerce. U.S. Census Bureau. American Community Survey, 2019-2021. (ACS 5-Years Estimates used for 2020)
<https://data.census.gov>.

Civilian labor force. (See definition under Table 7.)

Employment. (See definition under Table 7.)

Family. A family consists of a householder and one or more other people living in the same household who are related to the householder by birth, marriage, or adoption. All people in a household who are related to the householder are regarded as members of his or her family. A family household may contain people not related to the householder, but those people are not included as part of the householder's family in tabulations. Thus, the number of family households is equal to the number of families, but family households may include more members than do families. A household can contain only one family for purposes of tabulations. Not all households contain families since a household may be comprised of a group of unrelated people or of one person living alone – these are called nonfamily households. Families are classified by type as either a "married-couple family" or "other family" according to the sex of the householder and the presence of relatives. The data on family type are based on answers to questions on sex and relationship that were asked of all people.

Married-couple family. A family in which the householder and his or her spouse are listed as members of the same household.

Other family:

Male householder, no wife present. A family with a male householder and no spouse of householder present.

Female householder, no husband present. A family with a female householder and no spouse of householder present.

Table 11.
Source: U.S. Department of Commerce. U.S. Census Bureau. American Community Survey, 2021.
<https://www.census.gov/programs-surveys/acs.html>.

Data on school enrollment and educational attainment were derived from a sample of the population. Persons were classified as enrolled in school if they reported attending a "regular" public or private school (or college) during the year. The instructions were to "include only nursery school, kindergarten, elementary school, and schooling which would lead to a high school diploma or a college degree" as regular school. The Census Bureau defines a public school as "any school or college controlled and supported by a local, county, state, or federal government." Schools primarily supported and controlled by religious organizations or other private groups are defined as private schools.

Data on educational attainment are tabulated for the population 25 years old and over. The data were derived from a question that asked respondents for the highest level of school completed or the highest degree received. Persons who had passed a high school equivalency examination were considered high school graduates. Schooling received in foreign schools was to be reported as the equivalent grade or years in the regular American school system.

Vocational and technical training, such as barber school training; business, trade, technical, and vocational schools; or other training for a specific trade are specifically excluded.

High school graduate or more. This category includes persons whose highest degree was a high school diploma or its equivalent, and those who reported any level higher than a high school diploma.

Bachelor's degree or more. This category includes persons who have received bachelor's degrees, master's degrees, professional school degrees (such as law school or medical school degrees), and doctoral degrees.

Graduate degree or more. This category includes persons who have a master's degree, including the traditional MA and MS degrees and field-specific degrees, such as MSW, MEd, MBA, MLS, and MEng., or a professional school degree: medicine, dentistry, chiropractic, optometry, osteopathic medicine, pharmacy, podiatry, veterinary medicine, law, and theology.

Table 12.
Source: U.S. Department of Education, National Center for Education Statistics. *Common Core of Data.* <https://nces.ed.gov/ccd>.

The data are from the Common Core of Data (CCD), which is made up of a set of five surveys sent to state education departments. Most of the data are obtained from administrative records maintained by the state education agencies (SEAs). Statistical information is collected annually from approximately 100,000 public elementary and secondary schools and approximately 18,000 public school districts (including supervisory unions and regional education service agencies) in the 50 states, the District of Columbia, Department of Defense Schools, and the outlying areas. The SEAs compile CCD requested data into prescribed formats and transmit the information to NCES.

A **school district** or Local Education Agency (LEA) is the agency at the local level whose primary responsibility is to operate public schools or to contract for public school services.

The primary grades include pre-kindergarten through grade 4. Middle school grades included grades 5 through 8. High school grades include grades 9 through 12. Ungraded students are included in the total but are not separately listed. Some states have no ungraded students.

The student-teacher ratio is calculated by dividing the number of students in all schools by the number of full-time equivalent teachers employed by all schools and agencies.

Current expenditures per student are derived by dividing total current expenditures by the fall student membership count from the CCD. Current expenditures are comprised of expenditures for the day-to-day operation of schools and school districts for public elementary and secondary education, including expenditures for staff salaries and benefits, supplies, and purchased services. They exclude expenditures for construction, equipment, property, debt services, and programs outside of public elementary and secondary education, such as adult education and community services. Student membership consists of the count of students enrolled on or about October 1 and is comparable across all states. Please see the NCES website for the exact beginning and ending dates of fiscal years for each state.

The 4-year adjusted cohort graduation rate (ACGR) is the number of students who graduate in 4 years with a regular high school diploma divided by the number of students who form the adjusted cohort for the graduating class. From the beginning of 9th grade (or the earliest high school grade), students who are entering that grade for the first time form a cohort that is "adjusted" by adding any students who subsequently transfer into the cohort and subtracting any students who subsequently transfer out, emigrate to another country, or die.

Students are eligible for **free and reduced-price lunch** under the National School Lunch Program, which was established by President Truman in 1946. The program is a federally assisted meal program operated in public and private nonprofit schools and residential childcare centers and provides cash subsidies for free or reduced-price meals to students based on family size and income criteria. Participation in the National School Lunch Program depends on income, and eligibility is often used to estimate student needs.

An **English language learner** is an individual who, due to any of the reasons listed below, has enough difficulty speaking, reading, writing, or understanding the English language that it affects their ability to learn in an English-speaking classroom. Such an individual (1) was not born in the United States or has a native language other than English; (2) comes from environments where a language other than English is dominant; or (3) is an American Indian or Alaska Native and comes from environments where a language other than English has had a significant impact on the individual's level of English language proficiency.

Individuals with Disabilities Education Act (IDEA) is a federal law requiring services to children with disabilities throughout the nation. IDEA governs how states and public agencies provide early intervention, special education, and related services to eligible infants, toddlers, children, and youth with disabilities. Infants and toddlers with disabilities (birth–age 2) and their families receive early intervention services under IDEA, Part C. Children and youth (ages 3–21) receive special education and related services under IDEA, Part B.

Public School Types

A **special education school** focuses primarily on special education—including instruction for students with any of the following conditions: autism, deaf-blindness, developmental delay, hearing impairment, mental retardation, multiple disabilities, orthopedic impairment, serious emotional disturbance, specific learning disability, speech or language impairment, traumatic brain injury, visual impairment, and other health impairments—and that adapts curriculum, materials, or instruction for students served.

A **vocational education school** focuses primarily on providing formal preparation for semiskilled, skilled, technical, or professional occupations for high school-age students who have opted to develop or expand their employment opportunities, often in lieu of preparing for college entry.

An **alternative education school** is an elementary/secondary school that (1) addresses needs of students that typically cannot be met in a regular school, (2) provides nontraditional education, (3) serves as an adjunct to a regular school, or (4) falls outside the categories of regular, special education, or vocational education.

Table 13.
Source: U.S. Department of Commerce. U.S. Census Bureau. November Supplement to the Current Population Survey (CPS). *Voting and Registration in the Election of November 2022.*
<https://www.census.gov/topics/public-sector/voting/data/tables.html>

Voter participation data are obtained from additional questions regarding voting and voter registration, which are added to the Current Population Survey each November.

Because these data are from a sample of the noninstitutional population, they differ from the "official" tally of voter participation reported by the Clerk of the U.S. House of Representatives.

Voting, people eligible to register. The population of voting age includes a considerable number of people who meet the age requirement but cannot register and vote. People who are not citizens are not eligible to vote. Among citizens of voting age, some people are not permitted to vote because they have been committed to penal institutions, mental hospitals, or other institutions, or because they fail to meet state and local resident requirements for various reasons. The eligibility to register is governed by state laws, which differ in many respects.

Registration is the act of qualifying to vote by formally enrolling on a list of voters. People who have moved to another election district must take steps to have their names placed on the voting rolls in their new place of residence.

In a few states or parts of states, no formal registration is required. Voters merely present themselves at the polling place on Election Day with proof that they are of age and have met the appropriate residence requirements. Therefore, in these areas people who are citizens and of voting age, and who meet the residence requirement, would be considered as being registered.

Voter, reported participation. Voter participation data are derived from replies to the following question asked of people (excluding noncitizens) of voting age: "In any election some people are not able to vote because they are sick or busy, or have some other reason, and others do not want to vote. Did (this person) vote in the election held on November (date varies)?"

Those of voting age were classified as "voted" or "did not vote." In most tables, this "did not vote" class includes those reported as "did not vote," "do not know," noncitizens, and nonrespondents. Nonrespondents and people who reported that they did not know if they voted were included in the "did not vote" class because of the general over-reporting by respondents in the sample.

Voter, reported registration. The data on registration were obtained by tabulating replies to the following question for those people included in the category "did not vote." "Was (this person) registered to vote in the November (date varies) election?"

All people reported as having voted were assumed to have been registered. Therefore, the total registered population is obtained by combining the number of people who voted and people included in the category "did not vote," but who had registered.

Table 14.
Source: U.S. Centers for Disease Control and Prevention. National Center for Health Statistics.
<https://www.cdc.gov> **AND** <https://wonder.cdc.gov>.

Birth Data Overview

Vital statistics natality data are a fundamental source of demographic, geographic, and medical and health information on all births occurring in the United States. This is one of the few sources of comparable health-related data for small geographic areas over an extended time period. The data are used to present the characteristics of babies and their mothers, track trends such as birth rates for teenagers, and compare natality trends with those in other countries.

The birth file includes characteristics of the baby, such as sex, birthweight, and weeks of gestation; demographic information about the parents, such as age, race, Hispanic origin, parity, educational attainment, marital status, and state of residence; medical and health information, such as prenatal care based on hospital records; and behavioral risk factors for the birth, such as mother's tobacco use during pregnancy.

Coverage

Birth data presented in *Health, United States* are based on reporting from all 50 states and D.C. Data for Alaska have been included starting in 1959, and data for Hawaii starting in 1960, after each gained statehood. Beginning with 1970, births to nonresidents of the United States are excluded.

Methodology

In the United States, state laws require birth certificates to be completed for all births. The registration of births is the responsibility of the professional attendant at birth, generally a physician or midwife. The birth certificate must be filed with the local registrar of the district in which the birth occurs. Each birth must be reported promptly; the reporting requirements vary from state to state, ranging from 24 hours to 10 days after the birth.

Federal law mandates national collection and publication of birth and other vital statistics data (Pub. L. 93-353). NVSS is the result of cooperation between NCHS and the states to provide access to statistical information from birth certificates. Standard forms for the collection of the data, and model procedures for uniform registration of the events, are developed and recommended for state use through cooperative activities of the states and NCHS. NCHS shares the costs incurred by the states in providing vital statistics data for national use.

Life expectancy at birth reflects the average number of years that a person could expect to live, if he or she were to pass through life exposed to the sex- and age-specific death rates prevailing at the time of his or her birth in the U.S.

The **fertility rate** is the total number of live births, regardless of the age of the mother, per 1,000 women of reproductive age (aged 15–44). Beginning in 1997, the birth rate for the maternal age group 45–49 includes data for mothers aged 45 and over in the numerator and is based on the population of women aged 45–49 in the denominator.

Home birth is defined as a birth occurring at a private residence. It includes both planned and unplanned home births.

Cesarean delivery rate is the percentage of all live births that were cesarean deliveries.

Preterm birth rate is the percent of babies born prior to 37 weeks of pregnancy (gestation).

The **teen birth rate** is the number of births per 1,000 teenagers ages 15-19.

The **percentage born low birthweight** is the percentage of babies born weighing less than 2,500 grams or 5 lbs. 8oz.

Mortality Data

The National Vital Statistics System analyzes ~2.8 million records each year to produce timely and accurate information on death and its causes in the United States.

Death rates are calculated by dividing the number of deaths in a population in a year by the midyear resident population. The rate may be restricted to deaths in specific age, race, sex, or geographic groups or from specific causes of death (specific rate), or it may be related to the entire population (crude rate).

Age Adjustment

Age-adjusted mortality rates are used to compare risks for two or more populations with different age distributions. Age-adjusted rates are computed using the direct method by applying age-specific rates in a population of interest to a standardized age distribution. This eliminates differences in observed rates that result from age differences in population composition. Age-adjusted rates should be viewed as relative indexes rather than actual measures of risk.

Death rates are age adjusted to the projected year 2000 U.S. standard population. Before 2001 data, age-adjusted rates were calculated using standard million proportions based on rounded population numbers. Starting with 2001 data, unrounded population numbers are used to adjust age.

Drug overdose mortality rate is the age-adjusted death rate for drug overdoses. Includes deaths due to intentional drug poisonings (homicide and self-harm) and unintentional drug poisonings. Does not include other drug-induced causes of death.

Firearm injury mortality rate is the age-adjusted death rate for firearm-related fatalities. Includes homicide, intentional self-harm, and accidental discharge of firearms.

Homicide mortality rate is the age-adjusted death rate for injuries inflicted by another person with intent to injure or kill.

Disease and Illness Data

Lifetime asthma in adults and children estimates were derived from the National Health Interview Survey (NHIS), a multistage probability sample survey conducted annually by the National Center for Health Statistics (NCHS), Centers for Disease Control and Prevention (CDC). The NHIS administers face-to-face interviews in a nationally representative sample of households. The U.S. total for lifetime asthma in children in Table 14 includes data from 30 states and D.C.

Diabetes in adults estimates (unless otherwise noted) were derived from various data systems of CDC, Indian Health Service (IHS), Agency for Healthcare Research and Quality (AHRQ), and US Census Bureau, and from published research studies. Estimated percentages and total number of people with diabetes and prediabetes were derived from the National Health and Nutrition Examination Survey (NHANES), National Health Interview Survey (NHIS),

IHS National Data Warehouse (NDW), Behavioral Risk Factor Surveillance System (BRFSS), United States Diabetes Surveillance System (USDSS), and US resident population estimates.

Obesity in adults estimates are self-reported data from the Behavioral Risk Factor Surveillance System, an on-going state-based, telephone interview survey conducted by CDC and state health departments. Weight that is higher than what is considered healthy for a given height is described as overweight or obesity. Body Mass Index (BMI) is a screening tool for overweight and obesity. BMI is a person's weight in kilograms divided by the square of height in meters. A high BMI can indicate high body fatness. A BMI of 30.0 or higher is considered obese.

Table 15.
Source: U.S. Department of Commerce. U.S. Census Bureau.
<https://www.census.gov/topics/public-sector/government-finances.html>

The Census Bureau conducts an annual survey covering a range of government finance activities carried out by all state and local governments in the United States, including revenue, expenditures, debt, and assets. The data in this volume relate to state revenues and expenditures only, with the exception of the District of Columbia, for which local government data was used. General revenue comprises all revenue except utilities, liquor store, and insurance trust revenue. Intergovernmental revenue is funds from other governments (mainly the federal government), including general support, grants, shared taxes, and loans or advances. Other data on government finance by state, not shown in this volume, include federal government expenditures, obligations, contract awards, and insurance programs. The data are shown in this volume are for each state and the District of Columbia for fiscal year 2021.

Table 16.
Source: U.S. Department of Commerce. U.S. Census Bureau.
<https://www.census.gov/topics/public-sector/government-finances.html>.

State tax data include all required taxes taken by government for public purposes, except for employer and employee assessments for Social Security and unemployment compensation. The data are shown in this volume are for each state and the District of Columbia for fiscal year 2022.

INDEX

HIGH SCHOOL GRADUATES

HISPANIC OR LATINO ORIGIN, POPULATION BY

HOMEOWNERSHIP RATES

HOMICIDE MORTALITY RATE

HOUSEHOLDS AND HOUSING CHARACTERISTICS

WAGES BY INDUSTRY

WASHINGTON

Printed in the USA
CPSIA information can be obtained
at www.ICGtesting.com
LVHW011344081123
762709LV00001B/1

9 781636 714127